A DIRECTORY OF AMERICAN POETS AND FICTION WRITERS

1999–2000 Edition

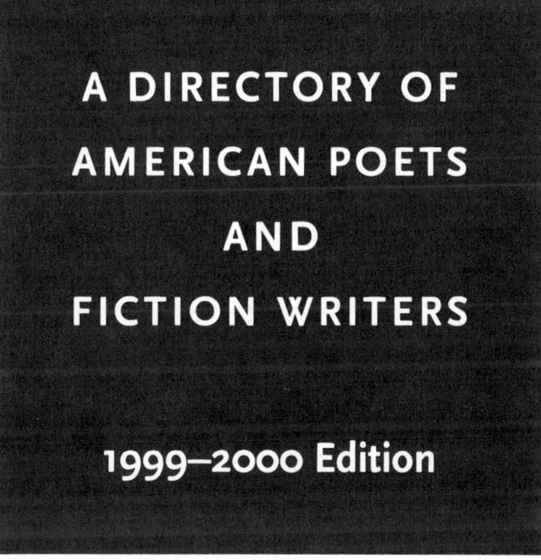

A DIRECTORY OF AMERICAN POETS AND FICTION WRITERS

1999–2000 Edition

Names and addresses of over 7,400 contemporary poets,
fiction writers and performance writers.

PUBLISHED BY POETS & WRITERS, INC.

Acknowledgments

A Directory of American Poets and Fiction Writers is compiled and edited by the Literary Horizons program at Poets & Writers, Inc., Heather Shayne Blakeslee, Associate Director, and Amy Holman, Director.

We would like to express our gratitude to the poets, fiction writers and performance writers who responded on time to the *Directory* update mailing, and who, between editions, keep their address and publication listings up to date.

We thank the writers listed in the *Directory* who granted us permission to put their faces on the cover of the 1999-2000 edition, the publicity department of Penguin Putnam, the Carol Mann Agency, Georges Borchardt Literary Agency, Boston University, and the photographers who granted us permission to use their photographs.

We are also grateful to Shoshanna Wingate and Miki Meese for their data entry from 3000 update forms; and to Travis O'Donnell, who helped us alphabetize all the forms for proofing, turning the office floor into The Thousand Islands for a week. Thanks also to our troubleshooter, Poets & Writers MIS Administrator Jason Chapman. Special thanks go to our highly focused and loyal proofreader, Anna Cerami; and to Dika Lam for speedy and expert entry of all the changes.

This year's edition of *A Directory of American Poets and Fiction Writers* changed dramatically in just a few months and we are deeply grateful both to our typesetter, Frank Caputo, at AGC/Sedgwick, and to our printer, Ray Freiman, of Ray Freiman & Company for their flexibility producing this detailed book in its new format. Leah S. Kalotay of H Plus, Inc. designed the attractive new book cover and we are grateful to her for working swiftly and amiably with us.

Cover Photographs, left to right: Top row: Sekou Sundiata, Paul Auster, and Robert Pinsky. Middle row: Philip Levine and Maxine Kumin. Bottom row: T. Coraghessan Boyle (Pablo Campos, photo), Dorothy Allison (Jill Posener, photo), and Joy Harjo.

Book design by Leah S. Kalotay, H Plus, Inc., New York, NY. Original edition produced by Stanley Barkan, Cross-Cultural Communications.

Typeset by AGC/Sedgwick, Princeton, NJ.

Manufactured in the United States of America by Ray Freiman and Company.

ISSN 0734-0605
ISBN 0-913734-61-6
Price: $29.95; $34.95 for institutions.

Contents

Preface

It looks kind of plain, just page after page of names and addresses, but *A Directory of American Poets and Fiction Writers*, first published in 1973, has long been considered a vital link between writers and the publishing world. It is a biennial publication of living poets, fiction writers, and performance writers who've published or performed their written work. Think of what these 7,414 names represent—the community of our peers and both the audience we are to each other and the one we attract through our work. As the novelist and Chenango Valley Writers Conference Director, Frederick Busch' puts it, "The work is by definition lonely and, to boot, I live in the middle of a hundred or so wild acres pretty far from anything resembling the literary community. The *Directory* keeps me as in touch as I can be, and I'm grateful to use it to reach my colleagues and to be reached by them." All the writers who are listed with Poets & Writers, Inc., are available for readings and teaching jobs, or want to contribute their opinion or their manuscripts.

Suppose you run an independent reading series at a library in Kentucky and just received funding to allow you to pay poets and short story writers to give readings. You don't have a budget for travel and you want to support new Appalachian writing. You can use the *Directory* to contact writers of the mid-south region. Or, you've started a literary magazine and want to solicit established writers for stories and poems. Use the *Directory* to look up your favorites.

Suppose you have a new novel coming out with a publisher that doesn't have the budget to promote the book the way you'd dreamed. Terry McMillan used the *Directory* to find the addresses of writers she admired who reviewed books and sent letters that introduced them to her first book, *Mama*. It was reviewed in more than 30 periodicals. Maybe you've lost touch with writers you've met through the years at conferences and workshops and want to invite them to your book party. The *Directory* has an alphabetical index of all writers, so you won't have to guess in which state they may live.

Suppose you have a yen to attend a writers conference, but are not really familiar with the names in the brochure. The *Directory* lists books, anthologies, and magazines. If you see a certain collection of publishers represented under a name, you can get a sense of that writer's work—maybe she/he is an environmental poet, or an experimental novelist. It can also help you with low residency MFA programs, whose faculty live and work in different parts of the country. It's good to know ahead of time how far your correspondence will have to travel.

But what of the hidden uses of this great *Directory*? In the Literary Horizons program at Poets & Writers, we advocate detective work. Emerging writers can use the community of the printed page to find out where to publish their own work. Writers who read continue to discover new voices in literary journals and anthologies. If you use the *Directory* to look up contemporary writers who have an aesthetic similar to your own, their publication credits may list literary journals whose editors would be interested in your poems or stories, or cause you to discover the names of unfamiliar book publishers who may like your novel or collection.

Just don't do what Bech did in John Updike's short story, "Bech Noir", recently published in the *New Yorker*. Criminally insulted by old, bad reviews, Bech sets about eliminating his critics and when he can't find one of them, he looks her up in "P&W's Directory."

Amy Holman
Director, Literary Horizons

General Information about the *Directory*:

The 1999–2000 edition of the *Directory* contains information about 4,096 poets, 1,911 fiction writers and 1,254 poets and fiction writers. Some additional poets and fiction writers are also listed as performance poets. The three largest numbers of listed writers are in New York, California and Massachusetts.

As of December 3, 1998, the *Directory* is as complete and accurate as possible. Additions and changes are received frequently. A portion of the *Directory* is also online at our web site, http://www.pw.org/directry. (No misprint—leave out the 'o'). Only those who gave permission to have their listing online will be found in this searchable web version, which is updated monthly. Newly listed writers who give permission for an online listing will also be accessible here. No telephone numbers are included.

As a supplement to *A Directory of American Poets and Fiction Writers*, specialized up-to-date computer mailing labels are available on magnetic tape, pressure-sensitive, and Cheshire formats. These mailing labels are a resource for individuals and organizations that wish to do targeted mailings to specific groups of writers, for example, all poets living in New York, New Jersey, and Connecticut; fiction writers in Massachusetts, New Hampshire and Vermont; performance poets in New York and California; etc. Call Direct Communications in Vermont at (802) 747-3322 for details on mailing lists.

How to Use *A Directory of American Poets and Fiction Writers*

A Directory of American Poets and Fiction Writers is organized geographically by state, and alphabetically within state or country. New York is divided into two sections: writers listed in the five boroughs of New York City and writers listed elsewhere in the state. District of Columbia and Puerto Rico are included in the state listings. Writers who live outside the United States can be found following the Wyoming section. If you are looking up a particular writer, check the complete alphabetical index of all writers in the back of the book.

Each entry includes the name of the writer, genre identity, contact information, and publications.

Name: This is the name under which the writer writes, not necessarily the legal/full name. Pseudonyms are cross-referenced in the index.

Genre identity: Letter symbols to the right of entry indicate the type(s) of writing for which the writer is listed.

P	=	poet
W	=	fiction writer
PP	=	performance poet/writer (Those who create works intended for performance or multimedia presentation.)
P&W	=	poet and fiction writer
PP&P	=	performance poet and poet
PP&W	=	performance poet and fiction writer
PP&P&W	=	performance poet, poet and fiction writer.

Contact information: Every entry has a mailing address for the writer—home or business address, post office box, agent or publisher. Telephone numbers and, e-mail or Internet addresses are optional.

Publications (Pubs): Every poet or fiction writer listed in the Directory has had work published. The order of listing is 1. Books; 2. Anthologies; and 3. Magazines. Books and anthologies are listed with book titles followed by the publisher and date. Only magazine titles are listed, not the titles of the works published in them.

All information is provided by the listed writers, who are given an opportunity to change or amend their listing with an update mailing every two years, and who must send changes of address at any other time of the year. Space is increased with this edition, but is still limited in some cases to the most recent publications. Performance poets may list performance pieces and venues where their work has been performed, as well as audiotape/CD recordings.

The following are examples of listings in this Directory:

Wendy Brenner   W
150 Capon Rd, Brockport, NY 14420
    Pubs: Large Animals In Everday Life (U Georgia Pr, 1996), New Stories From The South: Anth (Algonquin, 1995), Ploughshares, Southern Exposure, Puerto del Sol

In this example, the writer has a book, published by the University of Georgia Press, work in an anthology, published by Algonquin Books, and several magazines.

Pamela Malone   P&W
169 Prospect St, Leonia, NJ 07605, 201-944-7104
    Pubs: Cat's Meow: Anth (Maine Rhode Pub, 1995), Hungry Poets Cookbook: Anth (Applezaba Pr, 1987), The Sun, Chelsea, Belletrist Rev, Bellowing Ark, West Branch, Blue Unicorn

In this example, the poet and fiction writer has had work in two anthologies and several magazines. We know from the title of second anthology that her poetry was published, but the first title could be poetry or fiction.

A list of Frequently Used Abbreviations precedes the listings in this *Directory*.

Please note that all writers listed in this *Directory* must meet the publication requirements. We screen applications on a quarterly basis, and once a writer is accepted, their listing continues for life. Check your eligibility for listing in the next section. Listing as a poet or fiction writer has different requirements than listing as a performance writer. If a writer does not update the listing, the entry from the last edition of the *Directory* is retained, unless we know the address to be incorrect. Then, the listing is exempted from that edition.

Abbreviations Frequently Used

Space limitations have made it necessary to use abbreviations in listing author addresses and publication credits. Because some of these abbreviations may seem cryptic, the following list has been created to serve as a general guide.

Acad	Academy		Jrnl	Journal
ACM	Another Chicago Magazine		Knopf	Alfred A. Knopf
ALR	American Literary Review		LIQ	Long Island Quarterly
Amer	American		Lit	Literary *or* Literature
Anth	Anthology		Little, Brown	Little, Brown & Company
APR	American Poetry Review		LSU	Louisiana State University
Apt	Apartment		Ltd	Limited
Assn	Association		Mag	Magazine
Assoc	Associates		Morrow	William Morrow & Company
Ave	Avenue		MPR	Manhattan Poetry Review
Bk	Book		Mtn	Mountain
BkMk	Bookmark		MWPA	Maine Writers & Publishers Alliance
Bldg	Building		NAL	New American Library
BLQ	Bread Loaf Quarterly		NAR	North American Review
BOMC	Book of the Month Club		Natl	National
BPJ	Beloit Poetry Journal		NAW	New American Writing
c/o	care of		NER	New England Review
CCC	Cross-Cultural Communications		Norton	W. W. Norton & Co.
Cir	Circle		NW	Northwest
Ctr	Center		NYQ	New York Quarterly
Cnty	County		Pitt	Pittsburgh
Co	Company		Pl	Place
CQ	California State Poetry Quarterly		Pr	Press
CSM	Christian Science Monitor		Pub	Publications
Ct	Court		Pubs	Publishers
Dr	Drive		QRL	Quarterly Review of Literature
Edtn	Edition		Qtly	Quarterly
Fdn	Foundation		Rev	Review
FSG	Farrar, Straus & Giroux		Rm	Room
H Holt	Henry Holt & Co		S&S	Simon & Schuster
H&R	Harper & Row		SPR	Southern Poetry Review
HB	Harcourt Brace & Co		St	Street
HBJ	Harcourt, Brace, Jovanovich		Sta	Station
HC	HarperCollins Publishers		Ste	Suite
HM	Houghton Mifflin		SW	Southwest
HR&W	Holt, Rinehart & Winston		TLS	Times Literary Supplement
Hse	House		TriQtly	TriQuarterly
Hwy	Highway		U/Univ	University
Inc	Incorporated		Unltd	Unlimited
Inst	Institute		VLS	Voice Literary Supplement
Intl	International			

How to Apply for Listing with Poets & Writers, Inc.

Writers interested in being listed should request an application by calling the Literary Horizons program at Poets & Writers, (212) 226-3586. All applications must be accompanied by a one-time screening fee, so don't be surprised by the $7 requirement.

In order to be eligible for listing as a poet or fiction writer, you must be a U.S. citizen or permanent resident and satisfy at least 12 points in credits as established in the point system below. If you are applying as both a poet and fiction writer, you will need only 12 points combined, instead of in each genre. Note a change from previous editions each poem and story is now 2 and 3 points, respectively.

Points for Eligibility:

2 pts	Each poem published in a literary periodical*, anthology, or book.
3 pts	Each story or chapter published in a literary periodical, anthology, or book.
12 pts	Each standard length book of poetry or chapbook of ten pages or more.
12 pts	Each published collection of stories or novel or chapbook of four stories.
4 pts	Each 1st, 2nd, or 3rd place in an established national or state arts council literary award or magazine contest open to all state or U.S. citizens.

Forthcoming works counts for up to one third of publishing credits. Collaborations for two or more writers count for half the credits for each writer.

*A literary periodical is defined as a distributed magazine that regularly publishes poetry or fiction.

The following **do not count** as points for listing:

1. Self published works
2. Translations
3. Plays or dramatic treatments
4. Works you have edited
5. Teaching positions
6. Credits with publications that do not regularly publish poetry or fiction
7. Writing for children under 12
8. High School/College/University/Membership Society publications if more than 50% of work is from faculty, students, or members.
9. Any work of nonfiction, including creative nonfiction, essays, journalism, and critical works.
10. Awards for which you received "Honorable Mention"
11. Publications and awards from vanity/subsidy presses*

   *Vanity/subsidy presses unfairly portray themselves as standard publishers but do not pay the writer, nor distribute the printed texts.

To be eligible for listing as a performance poet/writer, you must be a U.S. citizen or permanent resident and provide the necessary information detailed below. If you are applying as a poet or fiction writer, you must complete that separate application.

Requirements:

1. Provide a list of at least five performances/non-print media shows in at least three different venues open to the public. Include performance title, sponsoring venue, city, state, and date of performance.

2. Documentation of such list in the form of photos, slides, reviews, videos, posters, flyers, or press releases. Provide an SASE for the return of videos, photos, or slides. Photocopies of printed materials are best.

3. Personal statement of artistic purpose or aesthetics that describes your work or particular performance. It must differentiate your performance from the traditional poetry or fiction reading and explain why it is necessary to perform the work instead of simply reading it off the printed page.

4. A descriptive letter from the sponsor of your most recent performance. This does not have to include a review and cannot be an account of the audience's reaction.

Collaborative work for two or more performance poets counts for half the credits for each writer. Work for children under the age of 12 does not count.

Poets & Writers: The Organization

Since 1970 Poets & Writers, Inc., a nonprofit service organization for writers, has provided support, information, and publications to help writers in their professional lives.

Literary Horizons is a new program for the professional development of writers. Responsible for the content, production, and marketing of *A Directory of American Poets and Fiction Writers* and *Rising Voices: A Guide To Young Writers Resources,* Literary Horizons also offers seminars on how to publish, panel discussions, lectures, online services, helpful products, and free information packets. Writers who have attended the publishing seminars have gone on to publish their work in *Poetry, Virginia Quarterly Review, New Novel Review* and *Crescent Review.*

Poets & Writers Magazine keeps writers appraised of what they need to know. Six times a year, *Poets & Writers Magazine* reports on grants and awards for writers, including deadlines for applications; publishes manuscript requests from editors and publishers; covers topics such as book contracts, taxes, writers' colonies, and publishing trends; and features essays by and interviews with poets and fiction writers, both emerging and established.

From research compiled for *Poets & Writers Magazine* and from the knowledge of what concerns writers most come Poets & Writers books: *Into Print: Guides to the Writing Life, Literary Agents: A Writer's Guide, A Writer's Guide to Copyright*, and *Rising Voices: A Guide to Young Writers' Resources* in addition to Poets & Writers' major reference publication: *A Directory of American Poets and Fiction Writers.*

Poets & Writers Online makes Poets & Writers' resources available on the World Wide Web and uses the unprecedented potential of the Internet to provide a central meeting place, community center, information bank and ongoing forum for the literary community. P&W Online gives writers, readers, librarians, editors, students and teachers 24-hour-a-day, 7-day-a-week access to a wealth of valuable information. http://www.pw.org

Poets & Writers, Inc., helps writers with more than information. The Readings/Workshops Program provides matching fee money to pay poets, fiction writers, essayists, and literary performance artists to give readings and writing workshops. Workshops and readings not only supplement writers' incomes but also reach new audiences and develop more discriminating readers. In 1970, with major funding from the New York State Council on the Arts, Poets & Writers pioneered in supporting public literary programs in New York State.

Today, thanks to major grants from the James Irvine Foundation, the Lannan Foundation, and the Lila Wallace-Reader's Digest Fund, Poets & Writers Readings/Workshops support is also available in California, as well as Detroit and Chicago. As in New York, community-based organizations are eligible to apply for funding, and writers and performance artists are welcome to initiate programs with sponsors.

The Writers Exchange is a national program designed to introduce emerging writers to literary communities outside their home states. Writers are selected on a competitive basis. They meet with a variety of editors, publishers, and well-known authors, and share their work through public readings. Only writers from selected states are eligible for the exchange. States that have participated in the Writers Exchange include California, Illinois, Indiana, Massachusetts, Minnesota, Mississippi, Montana, New Mexico, New York, North Carolina, Ohio, Oregon, Pennsylvania, South Carolina, Texas, Utah, Virginia, Washington, and Wyoming. Future states will be announced as they are selected.

Writers On Site, funded in part by the James Irvine Foundation, offers multi-disciplinary residencies for writers in visual arts sites in California. In addition to creating new work, participating writers develop community activities using the resources of partnered visual arts and literary organizations; these include leading workshops, organizing readings and panel discussions, and other activities that involve the intersection of the visual and literary arts.

The services and publications of Poet & Writers, Inc. are made possible, in part, by the National Endowment for the Arts, the New York State Council on the Arts, and the New York City Department of Cultural Affairs. Our programs require additional funds, however, and contributions from foundations, corporations, and individuals provide essential support.

For more detailed information, please write or call
Poets & Writers, Inc., 72 Spring Street, New York, NY 10012.
Telephone (212) 226-3586, Fax (212) 226-3963.
http://www.pw.org

ALABAMA

Robin Behn   P
2916 Woodland Hills Dr, Tuscaloosa, AL 35405-5425,
205-562-8035
Internet: rbehn@english.as.ua.edu
    Pubs: *The Red Hour* (HC, 1993), *Paper Bird* (Texas Tech
U, 1988), *Iowa Rev, Field, Missouri Rev, Crazyhorse,*
Denver Qtly, Indiana Rev.

Richard G. Beyer   P
1131 Hermitage Dr, Florence, AL 35630, 205-764-6312
    Pubs: *Alabama Poets: Anth* (Livingston U Pr, 1990),
Negative Capability, Panhandler, Potato Eyes.

Margaret Key Biggs   P
Country Rd Box 852, Heflin, AL 36264, 205-748-3203
    Pubs: *Parnassus of India: Anth* (Parnassus of India, 1995),
Pen Woman, Pelican Tracks, Earthwise, Negative
Capability.

William Cobb   W
200 Shady Hill Dr, Montevallo, AL 35115, 205-665-7959
    Pubs: *Somewhere In All This Green, Harry Reunited* (Black
Belt Pr, 1998, 1995), *A Walk Through Fire* (Morrow, 1993),
Amaryllis, Orpheus, Story, Southern Living, Arete.

Robert Collins   P
205 Humanities Building, English Dept UAB, Birmingham, AL
35294, 205-934-4250
Internet: collinsr@uab.edu
    Pubs: *Lives We Have Chosen* (Middle Tennessee State U
Pr, 1998), *The Glass Blower* (Pudding House, 1997), *The*
Inventor (Glass Blower Pr, 1981), *Prairie Schooner,*
Southern Poetry Rev, Portland Rev, Connecticut Rev.

Michael Driver   W
PO Box 6406, Montgomery, AL 36106-0406, 205-271-6384
    Pubs: *Infinity Ltd, Pearl, Road King Mag, Rockford Rev,*
Nihilistic Rev, NOMOS.

Charles Ghigna   P
204 W Linwood Dr, Homewood, AL 352093926,
205-870-4261
Internet: www.inkspot.com/author/ghigna
    Pubs: *Mice Are Nice* (Random Hse, 1999), *Plastic Soup:*
Dream Poems (Black Belt Pr, 1998), *Speaking in Tongues*
(Livingston U Pr, 1994), *Tickle Day: Poems from Father*
Goose (Disney/Hyperion, 1994), *Harper's, Playboy,*
McCall's, Highlights For Children.

Virginia Gilbert   P
Alabama A&M Univ, Box 453, English Dept, Normal, AL
35762, 205-464-9130
    Pubs: *That Other Brightness* (Black Star Pub, 1996), *The*
Earth Above (Catamount Pr, 1993), *Prairie Schooner, Mss.,*
PSA Poetry Rev, NAR.

Ralph Hammond   P
Box 486, Arab, AL 35016, 205-586-4151
    Pubs: *Vincent Van Gogh: A Narrative Journey* (Livingston
Pr, 1997), *Crossing Many Rivers: Poems Along The Way,*
Upper Alabama: Poems of Light (Clemmons Creek Pr,
1995, 1993), *Wolfe Rev, Amaryllis, Harp-String.*

Peter Huggins   P
Auburn Univ, 9030 Haley, Auburn Univ, AL 36849-5203,
334-844-4620
    Pubs: *Hard Facts* (Livingston Pr, 1997), *Colorado Rev,*
Cumberland Poetry Rev, Negative Capability, New Virginia
Rev, Southern Poetry Rev, Zone 3.

Sandy Huss   W
Univ Alabama, English Dept, Box 870244, Tuscaloosa, AL
35487, 205-348-5065
Internet: shuss@english.as.ua.edu
    Pubs: *Labor For Love: Stories* (U Missouri Pr, 1992),
Georgia Rev, TriQuarterly, Crazyhorse, River Styx, 2 Girls
Rev, Spelunker Flophouse.

Tim Jones   W
Box 1644, Valdez, AL 99686, 907-835-4125
Internet: tjones@alaska.net
    Pubs: *Keep the Round Side Down* (McRoy & Blackburn,
1996), *Soundings.*

Hank Lazer   P
Univ Alabama, Box 870268, Tuscaloosa, AL 35487,
205-345-1543
Internet: hlazer@as.ua.edu
    Pubs: *3 of 10* (Chax Pr, 1996), *Doublespace: Poems*
1971-1989 (Segue Bks, 1992), *INTER(IR)RUPTIONS*
(Generator Pr, 1992), *Central Park, Temblor, Virginia*
Quarterly Rev, River City, Hambone, New Orleans Rev,
Experioddicist, Mythosphere.

Susan Militzer Luther   P
2115 Buckingham Dr SW, Huntsville, AL 35803,
256-881-2245
    Pubs: *Impact: Tenth Anniversary Anth* (Act 1 Creativity Ctr,
1994), *Alabama Poets: Anth* (Livingston U Pr, 1990),
Astarte, Centennial Rev, Birmingham Rev, Sycamore Rev,
Noccalula, Blood and Fire Rev.

Fred A. Marchman   P
1803 Clearmont St, Mobile, AL 36606, 205-473-5237
    Pubs: *Dox Dixie Duograms* (Mail Pr, 1993), *Mobile Bay*
Monthly, For the Love of Life, Downtown.

Michael Martone   W
PO Box 21179, Tuscaloosa, AL 35402, 205-344-5059
Internet: mmartone@english.as.ua.edu
    Pubs: *Seeing Eye* (Zoland Bks, 1996), *Pensees: The*
Thoughts of Dan Quayle (Broadripple Pr, 1995), *Flyway,*
Epoch, Iowa Rev, Story, Harper's.

Marianne Merrill Moates   W
640 Peckerwood Creek Trail, Sylacuaga, AL 35151,
205-249-4225
Internet: marimoates@aol.com
    Pubs: *Writer's Digest, Seventeen, Birmingham, Sewanee News.*

Georgette Perry   P
2519 Roland Rd SW, Huntsville, AL 35805, 256-536-9801
    Pubs: *The Flutes of Power* (Great Elm Pr, 1995), *The Unitarian Universalist Poets: Anth* (Pudding Hse Pubs, 1996), *Lilliput Rev, Cedar Hill Rev, Green Fuse, Phase and Cycle.*

Carol J. Pierman   P
1508 13 St, Tuscaloosa, AL 35401, 205-758-2358
Internet: cpierman@woodsquad.as.ua.edu
    Pubs: *The Age of Krypton* (Carnegie Mellon U Pr, 1989), *Naturalized Citizen* (New Rivers, 1981), *Iowa Rev, Carolina Qtly, Black Warrior Rev.*

Thomas Rabbitt   P
Star Rte, Box 58, Elrod, AL 35458, 205-339-3548
    Pubs: *The Abandoned Country* (Carnegie Mellon, 1988), *The Booth Interstate* (Knopf, 1981), *Poetry.*

Charles Bernard Rodning   P
Univ South Alabama Med Center, 2451 Fillingim St, Mobile, AL 366172293, 334-471-7034
    Pubs: *Tradition of Excellence, Love Knot* (American Literary Pr, 1994), *Swaying Grass, Papering Dreams* (Scots Plaid Pr, 1998, 1994), *Negative Capability, Ko, Mayfly, Modern Haiku, New Cicada, Brussels Sprout.*

Sue Scalf   P
152 Lawrence St, Prattville, AL 36067, 205-365-9661
    Pubs: *Ceremony of Names* (Druid Pr, 1990), *Devil's Wine* (Troy State U Pr, 1978), *Southern Rev, America, Elk River Rev, Carolina Qtly, English Jrnl, Poem.*

Carolynne Scott   W
5305 9th Ave S, Birmingham, AL 35212, 205-595-3228
    Pubs: *The Green and the Burning Alike, Country Roads* (Portals Pr, 1994, 1979), *Outerbridge, Short Story Intl, Flannery O'Connor Bulletin, Aura, The Distillery, Noccalula.*

Anne Nall Stallworth   P&W
4316 Wilderness Rd, Birmingham, AL 35213, 205-871-0140
    Pubs: *Go, Go, Said the Bird, This Time Next Year* (Vanguard Pr, 1984, 1972), *McCall's, Birmingham Mag, This Week.*

Lorraine Standish   P&W
10478 County Rd 99, Lillian, AL 365490657, 334-961-3259
    Pubs: *Life's Seasons: Anth* (Southern Poetry Association, 1994), *The Lillian News, Onlooker, The Legend, Southern Poetry Rev, Best Poetry of 1997.*

Joe Taylor   W
R.R. 2, Box 90-D, Coatopa, AL 35470, 205-652-3470
Internet: jwt@uwamail.westal.edu
    Pubs: *Oldcat & Ms. Puss: A Book of Days* (Black Belt Pr, 1997), *TriQuarterly, Montana Rev, Cimarron Rev, Florida Rev, Virginia Qtly Rev.*

Jeanie Thompson   P
568 Forest Park Cir, Auburn, AL 36830-3827
    Pubs: *How To Enter The River* (Holy Cow! Pr, 1985), *The Best of Crazyhorse: Anth* (U Arkansas Pr, 1990), *NAR, Poem, Missouri Rev, Ploughshares, Black Warrior Rev.*

Sandra S. Thompson   P
316 Woodland Dr, Birmingham, AL 35209, 205-879-3800

Sue Walker   P
Univ South Alabama, Humanities/English Dept, Mobile, AL 36688, 205-460-6146
    Pubs: *Baker's Dozen* (Druid Pr, 1988), *Traveling My Shadow* (Negative Capability Pr, 1982), *Kentucky Rev.*

Wallace Whatley   P&W
826 Tullahoma, Auburn, AL 36830, 205-821-1399
    Pubs: *New Stories From the South: Best of 1986 Anth* (Algonquin Pr, 1986), *Minnesota Rev, Outerbridge, Virginia Qtly Rev, Southern Poetry Rev, Kansas Qtly, Greensboro Rev.*

James P. White   P&W
PO Box 428, Montrose, AL 36559, 334-928-3711
    Pubs: *Where Joy Resides* (FSG, 1993), *Clara's Call* (Texas Ctr for Writers Pr, 1991), *The Persian Oven & California Exit* (Methuen, 1989).

Lex Williford   W
Univ Alabama, PO Box 870244, Tuscaloosa, AL 35487-0244, 205-348-5605
Internet: lwillifo@english.as.ua.edu
    Pubs: *Macauley's Thumb* (U Iowa Pr, 1994), *Scribner's Anth of Contemporary Short Fiction* (S&S, 1999), *Glimmer Train, Sou'wester, Fiction, Quarterly West, New Texas, Laurel Rev, Virginia Qtly Rev, Story Qtly, Southern Rev, Shenandoah.*

William J. Wilson   P&W
1239 Blevins Gap Rd SE, Huntsville, AL 35802, 205-881-8002
    Pubs: *Horror Story: Anth* (Underwood-Miller, 1990), *Poem, Haunts, Old Hickory Rev, The Scribbler, Black Lotus.*

A. J. Wright   P
119 Pintail Dr, Pelham, AL 35124-2121, 205-663-3403
Internet: meds002@uabdpo.dpo.uab.edu
    Pubs: *Right Now I Feel Like Robert Johnson* (Timberline Pr, 1981), *Alabama Poets: A Contemporary Anth* (Livingston U, 1990), *Aura, Morpo Rev, Semiotext(e).*

ALASKA

Jean Anderson W
509 Aquila St, Fairbanks, AK 99712, 907-457-7692
Pubs: *In Extremis* (Plover Pr, 1989), *Inroads: Anth* (ASCA, 1988), *Northern Rev, Polyarnya Izvezda, Alaska Qtly Rev, Chariton Rev, Stories, Connotations.*

Ann Fox Chandonnet P
6552 Lakeway Dr, Anchorage, AK 99502-1949, 907-243-9172
Internet: afchan@alaska.net
Pubs: *Alaska's Arts, Crafts and Collectibles, Whispered Secrets* (Sedna Pr, 1998, 1991), *Last New Land* (Alaska Northwest Bks, 1996), *Canoeing in the Rain: Poems for my Aleut-Athabascan Son* (Mr. Cogito Pr, 1990), *Alaska, Lands' End Catalog.*

Richard Dauenhauer P
3740 N Douglas Hwy, Juneau, AK 99801, 907-586-4708
Pubs: *Phenologies* (Thorp Springs Pr, 1988), *Frames of Reference* (Black Current Pr, 1987), *Haa Tuwunaagu Yis, For Healing Our Spirit: Anth* (U Washington Pr, 1990).

John Haines P
1300 W 7 Ave, #113, Anchorage, AK 99501-3266, 907-272-3055
Pubs: *A Guide To The Four-Chambered Heart* (Larkspur Pr, 1996), *Where The Twilight Never Ends* (Limberlost Pr, 1991), *Ohio Rev, Sewanee Rev, Manoa, ELF, Nimrod.*

Sharon Ann Jaeger P
2633 E 17th Ave, Anchorage, AK 995083207
Internet: sajaeger@ciue.edu.ee
Pubs: *The Chain of Dead Desire, Filaments of Affinity* (Park Slope Edtns, 1990, 1989), *X-Connect.*

Nancy Lord W
PO Box 558, Homer, AK 99603
Internet: nlord@xyz.net
Pubs: *Survival* (Coffee Hse Pr, 1991), *The Compass Inside Ourselves* (Fireweed Pr, 1984), *NAR, Ploughshares, High Plains Literary Rev, Passages North, Other Voices.*

Donna Mack W
5000 Vi St, Anchorage, AK 99507, 907-349-2680
Pubs: *The Whole Apple, Essence, Raven.*

Linda McCarriston P
1746 Alder Dr, Anchorage, AK 99508, 907-786-4378
Pubs: *Eva-Mary* (TriQuarterly Bks, 1991), *Talking Soft Dutch* (Texas Tech U Pr, 1984), *Atlantic, Sojourner, TriQuarterly, Poetry, Georgia Rev, Seneca Rev.*

John Morgan P
3240 Rosie Creek Rd, Fairbanks, AK 99709, 907-479-4936
Internet: ffjwm@aurora.alaska.edu
Pubs: *Walking Past Midnight, The Arctic Herd* (U Alabama Pr, 1989, 1984), *New Yorker, APR, Poetry, Paris Rev, New Republic, Kenyon Rev.*

Sheila Nickerson P&W
540 W 10 St, Juneau, AK 99801, 907-586-6553
Pubs: *In An August Garden* (Black Spruce Pr, 1997), *Feast of the Animals* (Old Harbor Pr, 1991), *In the Compass of Unrest* (Trout Creek Pr, 1988).

Lori Jo Oswald P&W
3015 Emory St, Anchorage, AK 99508-4467
Pubs: *Poetry North Rev, Day Tonight/Night Today, Alura, Negative Capability, Nettles & Nutmeg.*

James Ruppert P
3266 Bluebird Ave, Fairbanks, AK 99709, 907-479-3132
Internet: ffjkr@alaska.aurora.edu
Pubs: *Natural Formations* (Blue Cloud Qtly Pr, 1981), *Contact II, New Mexico Humanities Rev, Blue Mesa.*

Tom Sexton P
1972 Wildwood Ln, Anchorage, AK 99517, 907-272-1060
Pubs: *Leaving For A Year* (Adastra Pr, 1998), *The Bend Toward Asia* (Salmon Run, 1993), *Late August on the Kenai River* (Limner Pr, 1992), *Terra Incognita* (Solo Pr, 1974), *Hayden's Ferry Rev, Paris Rev, Zone 3, Zyzzyva, Chariton Rev.*

Peggy Shumaker P
Univ Alaska, English Dept, Fairbanks, AK 99775, 907-479-7048
Internet: peggyzoe@sprynet.com
Pubs: *Wings Moist From the Other World, The Circle of Totems* (U Pitt Pr, 1994, 1988), *Braided River* (Limner Pr, 1993), *APR, NAR, Alaska Qtly Rev.*

John E. Smelcer P
4101 University Dr, #328, Anchorage, AK 99508
Pubs: *Changing Seasons* (South Head Pr, 1995), *Kesugi Ridge* (Aureole Pr, 1995), *Native American Poetry: Anth* (Dover, 1996), *Durable Breath: Contemporary Native American Poetry: Anth* (Salmon Run, 1994), *Atlantic, CSM, American Voice, Kenyon Rev.*

Ronald Spatz W
Univ Alaska Anchorage, Anchorage, AK 99508, 907-786-4361
Pubs: *Fiction, Transatlantic Rev, New Letters, Panache, Telescope, The Wayne Rev, Third Coast, In the Dreamlight, Inroads.*

Ken Waldman P&W
Box 22498, Juneau, AK 99802
Pubs: *The MacGuffin, High Plains Literary Rev, Yankee, Exquisite Corpse, Manoa, Beloit Poetry Jrnl.*

Mark Arvid White   P&W
PO Box 1771, Palmer, AK 99645, 907-746-2566
Internet: www.geocities.com/athens/acropolis/5766/erala.html
    Pubs: *Readers Break Vol III: Anth* (Pine Grove Pr, 1996),
    Haiku Moment: Anth (C. Tuttle Co., 1993), *Windows of the
    Soul: Anth* (Natl Arts Society, 1990), *Webster Rev, Modern
    Haiku, Candelabrum, Riverrun, Woodnotes, Arnazella,
    Minas Tirith Evening-Star.*

ARIZONA

Ai   P
6125 E Indian School Rd, #108, Scottsdale, AZ 85251,
602-423-8590
    Pubs: *Vice: New & Selected, Greed* (Norton, 1999, 1993),
    Fate, Sin, Killing Floor, Cruelty (HM, 1991, 1986, 1979,
    1973), *APR, Iowa Rev, Caprice, Poetry Int'l, Agni,
    Onthebus.*

Pamela Alexander   P
7273 E Caminito, Contento, AZ 85710
Internet: pamela@o-farrell.com
    Pubs: *Commonwealth of Wings* (Wesleyan, 1991),
    Navigable Waterways (Yale U Pr, 1985), *Atlantic, New
    Yorker, Michigan Qtly Rev, Shankpainter, Field, Margin.*

Jon Anderson   P
633 N Stewart, Tucson, AZ 85716, 602-323-9255
    Pubs: *The Milky Way: Poems 1968-1983* (Ecco, 1985),
    Cypresses (Graywolf, 1981).

Dick Bakken   P
3 Old Douglas Rd, Bisbee, AZ 85603, 520-432-2771
    Pubs: *Feet with the Jesus* (Lynx Hse, 1989), *The Other
    Side* (Brushfire, 1986), *Ironwood, Ploughshares, Yellow
    Silk, Poetry Northwest, Poetry Flash, Willow Springs.*

Diane Beeson   P
685 S. La Posada Cir, #1701, Green Valley, AZ 85614,
520-625-4541
    Pubs: *Tiny Tales, Vols 6, 4-5, 1-3* (Co-author; Mangold
    Santillana, 1991, 1990, 1989).

Beth R. Blakeman   P
1625 S Augusta Pl, Tucson, AZ 85710, 602-296-1294
    Pubs: *The Animal's Agenda.*

Jay Boyer   P&W
Arizona State Univ, Tempe, AZ 85287-0302, 602-965-7644
Internet: jmboyer@asu.edu
    Pubs: *As Far Away As China* (Pratt, 1990), *Newsweek,
    Paris Rev, The Nation.*

Charles Brownson   W
Arizona State Univ Library, Tempe, AZ 85287, 602-965-5250
    Pubs: *In Uz* (Noumenon Pr, 1985), *Ancestors* (Jump River
    Pr, 1984).

Ron Carlson   W
Arizona State Univ, 8839 East Thoroughbred Trail,
Scottsdale, AZ 85258-1335, 602-596-8376
Internet: ron.carlson@asu.edu
    Pubs: *The Hotel Eden, Plan B for the Middle Class, The News
    of the World, Truants, The Norton Anth of Contemporary
    Fiction: Anth,* (Norton, 1997, 1992, 1987, 1981, 1997), *GQ,
    Harper's, Story, Esquire, New Yorker, Carolina Qtly.*

Jefferson Carter   P
Pima Community College, 1255 N Stone, Box 5027, Tucson,
AZ 85709-3000, 520-884-6135
    Pubs: *Tough Love* (Riverstone Pr, 1993), *None of This Will
    Kill Me* (Moon Pony Pr, 1987), *Gentling the Horses*
    (Maguey, 1979), *Metro, Carolina Qtly.*

Emily Pritchard Cary   W
27653 N 72nd Way, Scottsdale, AZ 85255-1105,
602-502-0528
Internet: 110221.2534@compuserve.com
    Pubs: *The Ghost of Whitaker Mountain, My High Love
    Calling* (Bouregy, 1979, 1977), *Roeper Rev, British
    Heritage, Pennsylvania Mag, Chesapeake Bay Mag, Phi
    Delta Kappan, Dog Fancy, Pittsburgh Pr Sunday Mag.*

James V. Cervantes   P
Univ of Arizona Press, 1230 N. Park Ave, #102, Tucson, AZ
857194140
    Pubs: *The Headlong Future* (New Rivers, 1990), *Pacific
    Rev, Altadena Rev, Northern Arizona Rev.*

Virgil Chabre   P
7166 E Lindner Ave, Mesa, AZ 85208-4986
    Pubs: *San Fernando Poetry Jrnl, The Archer, Prophetic
    Voices, Deros, Poetica, Pub 9, Manna.*

David Chorlton   P
118 W Palm Ln, Phoenix, AZ 85003, 602-253-5055
    Pubs: *Fever Dreams* (U of Arizona Pr, 1997), *Outposts
    (Taxus Pr, 1994), Forget the Country You Came From
    (Singular Street, 1992), Devil's Millhopper, Green Fuse,
    Heaven Bone, Poet Lore, Webster Rev, Lucid Stone,
    Parting Gifts, Pembroke Mag, Eratica.*

Neil Claremon   P
1444 N Duncan Rd, Nogales, AZ 85621, 602-287-5554

Joel Climenhaga P&W
115 San Jose Dr, Bisbee, AZ 85603-3009, 520-432-3410
Internet: joelrayc@hotmail.com
   Pubs: *Exploration of the Great Northwest While Traveling
   With the Fat Man* (Transient Pr, 1997), *Moan of Raping
   Bees, Bottom of the Spittoon, The Treachery of Innocence*
   (Shadow Pr, 1996, 1995, 1994), *Ascending Shadows,
   Mirage, Lucid Stone.*

Paul Cook P
1108 W Cornell, Tempe, AZ 85283, 602-831-7062
   Pubs: *Fortress on the Sun* (Penguin, 1997), *On the Rim of
   the Mandala, Halo, Duende Meadow* (Bantam Bks, 1987,
   1986, 1985), *Amazing Stories, Mag of Sci-Fi, New Letters.*

David Coy P
Arizona Western College, PO Box 929, Yuma, AZ
85364-0929, 602-344-7577
Internet: aw_coy@awc.cc.az.us
   Pubs: *Lean Creatures* (Church of the Head Pr, 1994), *Rural
   Views* (Mother of Ashes Pr, 1991), *Antioch Rev, Widener
   Rev, Colorado North Rev, Slant.*

Linda Lee Curtis P
1919 W Adams, Phoenix, AZ 85009, 602-254-2876
   Pubs: *Head Shots* (Winter Wheat Pr, 1993), *Harriet E. P.
   Spofford: Anth* (Bristol Banner Books, 1996), *Arizona
   Journal: Anth* (High Desert Pub, 1995), *Voices, True
   Liberty, Muse of Fire, It's Not Qtly, Quickenings,
   Roadrunner, Life Scribes.*

Alison Hawthorne Deming P
Univ Arizona Poetry Ctr, 1216 N Cherry Ave, Tucson, AZ
85719, 602-321-7760
Internet: aldeming@aol.com
   Pubs: *The Monarchs: A Poem Sequence, Science & Other
   Poems* (Louisiana State U Pr, 1997, 1994), *Georgia Rev,
   Sonora Rev, Hayden's Ferry Rev, Crazyhorse, Denver Qtly,
   Rio Grande Rev.*

Laura Deming W
2929 N 70 St, #3025, Scottsdale, AZ 85251-6301,
602-423-1109
   Pubs: *Descant, Cimarron Rev, Crosscurrents, San Jose
   Studies.*

Wally Depew P&W
PO Box 215, Patagonia, AZ 856240215, 520-394-2779
Internet: wdepew@dakotacom.net
   Pubs: *Girltalk, Pure Flip, Quatrains, Fortune, Book of the
   Dead, Dead Birds, Toxic* (Bright Moments, 1996, 1996,
   1991, 1991, 1991, 1991, 1991).

Marvin Diogenes W
Univ Arizona, Modern Languages 445, Tucson, AZ 85721,
520-621-5976
Internet: diogenes@u_arizona.edu
   Pubs: *O. Henry Festival Stories 1993: Anth* (Trans-Verse
   Pr, 1993), *American Fiction 91: Anth* (Birch Lane, 1991),
   Other Voices, Cimarron Rev, Beloit Fiction.

Norman Dubie P
700 W Brown #6, Tempe, AZ 85281, 603-965-3168
   Pubs: *Selected & New Poems* (Norton, 1983), *The City of
   Olesha Fruit* (Doubleday, 1979).

Sally Ehrman P
PO Box 777, Bisbee, AZ 85603, 602-432-3995
   Pubs: *Fennel Stalk, Clarion, Z Misc, Piedmont Literary Rev,
   San Fernando Poetry Journal, Archer.*

Elizabeth Evans W
Univ Arizona, Modern Language Bldg, Tucson, AZ 85721,
520-621-1836
   Pubs: *Carter Clay* (HC, 1999), *The Blue Hour* (Algonquin,
   1994), *Locomotion* (New Rivers, 1986), *The Quarterly, Prairie
   Schooner, Crazyhorse, American Fiction, Sonora Rev.*

Anne U. Forer W
4765 E Baker St, Tucson, AZ 85711-2116, 602-795-6245
   Pubs: *Hot Type: Anth* (Collier Bks, 1988), *Heresies, Green
   Mountains Rev, Exquisite Corpse, Minotaur.*

Rita Garitano P
3109 E Circulo Del Tenis, Tucson, AZ 85716-1074,
520-319-0877
   Pubs: *Rainy Day Man* (Norton, 1985), *Feeding the Hungry
   Heart* (Bobbs-Merrlll, 1982), *Walking the Twilight: Anth*
   (Northland Pr, 1994), *Tucson Guide Qtly.*

Michael Gessner P&W
Central Arizona College, 8470 N Overfield Rd, Coolidge, AZ
85228, 520-836-1274
   Pubs: *American Literary Rev, Wallace Stevens Jrnl,
   Sycamore Rev, Pacific Rev, Poem, Wisconsin Rev.*

Drummond Hadley P
Guadalupe Ranch, Box 1093, Douglas, AZ 85607
   Pubs: *Tierra: Contemporary Short Fiction of New Mexico:
   Anth* (Cinco Puntos Pr, 1989).

Catherine Hammond P&W
4676 W Ivanhoe, Chandler, AZ 85226, 602-961-3337
Internet: cathmorrow@aol.com
   Pubs: *Contemporary Arizona Poets: Anth* (U Arizona,
   1997), *Chicago Rev, Mississippi Rev, NAR, Puerto del Sol,
   Laurel Rev, Passages North.*

Alan Harrington W
2831 N Orlando Ave, Tucson, AZ 85712, 602-326-4559
   Pubs: *The White Rainbow, Paradise I* (Little, Brown, 1981,
   1977), *Harper's, Atlantic, Chicago Rev.*

Mark Harris   W
2014 E Balboa Dr, Tempe, AZ 85282
> Pubs: *The Tale Maker, The Diamond: Baseball Writings, Speed* (Donald I. Fine, 1994, 1994, 1990), *Arizona Qtly, Denver Qtly, Virginia Qtly Rev, Sequoia, Esquire.*

Simon Hawke   W
HCR-1, Box 466, Tuscon, AZ 85736
> Pubs: *War, The Seeker* (TSR, Inc., 1996, 1994), *Whims of Creation* (Warner Bks, 1994).

Robert Haynes   P
6117 East Nisbet Rd, Scottsdale, AZ 85254, 602-368-9812
Internet: bhaynes@inficad.com
> Pubs: *Poetry Northwest, Poet Lore, New Letters, Zone 3, Kentucky Poetry Rev, Cape Rock, Cimarron Rev, Atom Mind.*

Robert Houston   W
Univ Arizona, English Dept, Tucson, AZ 85721
> Pubs: *The Fourth Codex* (Houghton Mifflin, 1988), *The Line* (Ballantine, 1986), *NER/BLQ, New York Times.*

Richard Hughes   W
Silver Mountain Press, PO Box 12994, Tucson, AZ 85732, 520-790-1561
> Pubs: *Isla Grande* (Silver Mountain Pr, 1994).

Jeremy Ingalls   P
6269 E Rosewood, Tucson, AZ 85711
> Pubs: *Summer Liturgy, This Stubborn Quantum* (Capstone Edtns, 1985, 1983), *Tahl* (Knopf, 1945).

Will Inman   P&W
2551 W Mossman Rd, Tucson, AZ 85746-5102, 520-883-3419
> Pubs: *Surfing the Dark Sound* (Pudding Hse Pr, 1998), *Blackbird: Anth* (Phoenix Pr, 1998), *Lucid Stone, Home Planet News, One Trick Pony, Waterways, Atom Mind, Rain City Rev.*

Nadine Kachur   P
PO Box 663, Scottsdale, AZ 85252, 602-389-9444
Internet: lynn9@imap3.asu.edu
> Pubs: *South Ash Pr, Ingis Fatuus Rev, Twisted Nipples, Damaged Wine, Mirage.*

Barbara Kingsolver   P&W
PO Box 31870, Tucson, AZ 85751
> Pubs: *The Poisonwood Bible, High Tide in Tucson, Pigs in Heaven, Animal Dreams* (HarperCollins, 1998, 1995, 1993, 1990), *Another America* (Seal Pr, 1992).

John Levy   P
8987 E Tanque Verde Rd, Box 11, Tucson, AZ 85749-9399, 520-749-4188
> Pubs: *Scribble and Expanse* (Tel-Let, 1995), *We Don't Kill Snakes Where We Come From* (Querencia Pr, 1994), *Origin, Shearsman, Longhouse.*

Jonathan F. Lowe   P&W
PO Box 26073, Tucson, AZ 85726, 520-326-3007
Internet: jonflowe@aol.com
> Pubs: *Dark Fire, Postmarked for Death* (www.e-pulp.com, 1998, 1998), *Snapshots* (Atlantic Disk Pub, 1996), *Ghost Rider* (Spectravision Electronic Pub, 1994), *Arizona Highways, Rider, Porthole.*

Delma Luben   P
906 Forest Hylands Dr, Prescott, AZ 86303, 602-778-7860
> Pubs: *Ghost Writers In the Sky* (Vision Pr, 1990), *Parnassus, Heartland Jrnl, New Jersey Rev of Literature.*

Nancy Mairs   P&W
1527 E Mabel St, Tucson, AZ 85719, 602-623-2388
Internet: nmairs@earthlink.net
> Pubs: *Waist-High In The World, Voice Lessons, Ordinary Time* (Beacon, 1997, 1994, 1993), *Glamour, American Voice, TriQuarterly, Mss..*

Robert Matte, Jr.   P
5741 E Waverly St, Tucson, AZ 85712, 602-721-4445
> Pubs: *Asylum Picnic* (Duck Down Pr, 1979), *Star Kissing* (Vagabond Pr, 1975), *Bellingham Rev.*

Patricia McConnel   W
Bldg 300-417, 2700 Woodlands Village Blvd, Dead Cat, AZ 86001, 520-525-1225
Internet: mcconnel@wordsculptors.com
> Pubs: *Eye of the Beholder* (Logoria, 1998), *Sing Soft, Sing Loud* (Atheneum, 1989), *Neon, Catalyst, Crosscurrents, Passages North, 13th Moon.*

Judith McDaniel   P
1412 S Moonflower Ln, Tucson, AZ 85748-7431, 520-721-8915
Internet: jandj1412@aol.com
> Pubs: *Yes I Said Yes I Will* (Naiad Pr, 1996), *Just Say Yes, Metamorphosis: Reflections on Recovery, Sanctuary: A Journey* (Firebrand, 1991, 1989, 1987).

Gregory McNamee   P&W
1128 E 10 St, Tucson, AZ 85719, 520-882-4340
> Pubs: *Christ on the Mount of Olives, Inconstant History* (Broken Moon Pr, 1991, 1990).

Jane Miller   P
4990 N Acacia Ln, Tucson, AZ 85745-9262, 520-743-7474
> Pubs: *Wherever You Lay Your Head, Memory At These Speeds: Selected Poems, American Odalisque* (Copper Canyon Pr, 1999, 1996, 1987), *American Voice, Kenyon Rev, Ploughshares, APR.*

N. Scott Momaday   P&W
5675 Camino Esplendora #2211, Tucson, AZ 85718-4583

Sheila E. Murphy   P
3701 E Monterosa St, #3, Phoenix, AZ 85018-4848
Internet: shemurph@aol.com
    Pubs: *Fallin In Love Falling In Love With You Syntax: Selected and New Poems* (Potes & Poets Pr, 1997), *A Clove of Gender* (U.K.; Stride, 1995), *Pure Mental Breath* (Canada; Gesture, 1994), *New York Qtly, Avec, Abacus, Experioddicist, Lost & Found, Antenym.*

Tenney Nathanson   P
Univ Arizona, 445 Modern Language Bldg, Tucson, AZ 85721, 520-621-1836
Internet: nathanso@ccit.arizona.edu
    Pubs: *Rif/t, Social Text, Ironwood, Tamarisk, Caterpillar, Massachusetts Rev.*

Rodney Nelson   P&W
PO Box 22271, Flagstaff, AZ 860022271, 520-774-2829
    Pubs: *Villy Sadness* (New Rivers Pr, 1987), *Thor's Home* (Holmganger's Pr, 1984), *American Letters & Comments.*

Steve Orlen   P
Univ Arizona, English Dept, Tucson, AZ 85721, 520-621-7405
Internet: sorlen@u.arizona.edu
    Pubs: *Kisses, The Bridge of Sighs,* (Miami U Pr, 1997, 1992), *A Place at the Table* (HR&W, 1982), *Permission to Speak* (Wesleyan, 1978), *Atlantic, Agni, Yale Rev, Ploughshares, Gettysburg Rev.*

Simon J. Ortiz   P&W
3535 N 1st Ave #R-10, Tucson, AZ 85719-1725
    Pubs: *A Good Journey* (Sun Tracks/U Arizona Pr, 1984), *Fightin'* (Thunder's Mouth Pr, 1983).

Diane Payne   W
PO Box 52, Tumacacori, AZ 85640-0052
Internet: jlw@ccit.arizona.edu
    Pubs: *Contemporary American Satire: Anth* (Exile Pr, 1992), *Common Journeys, Hanson's Mag, Stet Mag, Walden Rev, The Bridge, In These Times.*

Jonathan Penner   W
2232 E Seneca St, Tucson, AZ 85719-3834, 520-327-6961
Internet: pennerj@u.arizona.edu
    Pubs: *Natural Order* (Poseidon, 1990), *Private Parties* (U Pitt Pr, 1983), *Harper's, Commentary, Paris Rev, Antaeus, Grand Street, Ploughshares.*

Michael Rattee   P
2833 E Kaibab Vista, Tucson, AZ 85713, 520-884-9392
    Pubs: *Calling Yourself Home* (Cleveland State U, 1986), *Men of Our Time: Anth* (U Georgia Pr, 1992), *Laurel Rev, Poet Lore, Santa Clara Rev, The Signal.*

David Ray   P&W
2033 E 10 St, Tucson, AZ 857195925, 520-622-6332
Internet: djray@gci-net.com
    Pubs: *Kangaroo Paws* (Thomas Jefferson U Pr, 1995), *Wool Highways* (Helicon Nine Edtns, 1993), *New Yorker, Chicago Rev, Paris Rev, Atlantic, Westerly, Georgia Rev, Nation, Grand Street.*

Judy Ray   P&W
2033 E 10 St, Tucson, AZ 85719-5925, 520-622-6332
Internet: djray@gci-net.com
    Pubs: *Pigeons in the Chandeliers* (Timberline Pr, 1993), *The Jaipur Sketchbook* (Chariton Rev Pr, 1991), *Fathers: A Collection of Poems: Anth* (St. Martin's Pr, 1997), *Stiletto, American Voice, Westerly, Helicon Nine, New Millennium.*

A. E. Reiff   P&W
2532 N Foote Dr, Phoenix, AZ 85008-1920
    Pubs: *Nineteen Women Without A Husband* (Papago Pr, 1997), *Living Jewels: A Treasury of Lyric Poetry* (Fine Arts Pr, 1993), *Planet 3: Help Send This Book Into Space* (Newfoundland Bks, 1986), *Broken Streets IV.*

Del Reitz   P
PO Box 26244, Tucson, AZ 85726-6244, 520-294-7031
    Pubs: *Little Lieu and Other Waifs, Second Inago Anth of Poetry, First Inago Anth of Poetry* (Inago Pr, 1996, 1995, 1985), *Various Artists, Mendocino Rev, South Ash Pr, Blue Unicorn.*

Jewell Parker Rhodes   W
Arizona State Univ, English Dept, Box 870302, Tempe, AZ 85287-0302, 602-965-6856
Internet: jewell.rhodes@asu.edu
    Pubs: *Magic City* (HarperCollins, 1997), *Voodoo Dreams* (St. Martin's Pr, 1993), *Seattle Rev, Callaloo, Feminist Studies, Calyx.*

Alberto Alvaro Rios   P
Arizona State Univ, Tempe, AZ 85287, 602-965-3168
    Pubs: *Teodoro Luna's Two Kisses* (Norton, 1990), *The Lime Orchard Woman, Five Indiscretions* (Sheep Meadow Pr, 1988, 1985), *New Yorker, Story, APR, Paris Rev.*

William Pitt Root   P
2022 E 5 St, Tucson, AZ 85719-5203, 602-791-2816
    Pubs: *Trace Elements From A Recurring Kingdom* (Confluence Pr, 1994), *Faultdancing* (U Pitt Pr, 1986), *Manoa, Commonweal, Switched-On Guttenberg.*

Yvette A. Schnoeker-Shorb   P
PO Box 12226, Prescott, AZ 86304
    Pubs: *Midwest Qtly, New Thought Jrnl, Green Hills Literary Lantern, Slant, Sulphur River Rev, Eureka Literary Mag, Blueline, Puerto del Sol, Concho River Rev, Pleiades, Pendragon, Sucarnochee Rev, Widener Rev.*

Susanne Shaphren W
823 E Brook Hollow Dr, Phoenix, AZ 85022
    Pubs: *Authorship, Crosscurrents, Hibiscus, The Writer.*

Richard Shelton P
Univ Arizona, English Dept, Tucson, AZ 85721,
602-743-7864
    Pubs: *Going Back to Bisbee* (U Arizona Pr, 1992), *The Other Side of the Story* (Confluence Pr, 1987), *Hohokam* (Sun/Gemini Pr, 1986).

Shirley Sikes W
PO Box 65496, Tucson, AZ 857285496, 520-299-5733
    Pubs: *O. Henry Prize Stories: Anth* (Doubleday, 1973), *Sonora Rev, Denver Qtly, Remark, Kansas Qtly, Calyx, Travelin Woman.*

Leslie Marmon Silko P&W
8000 W Camino del Cerro, Tucson, AZ 85745
    Pubs: *Almanac of the Dead* (S&S, 1991), *Storyteller* (Seaver Bks, 1981), *Ceremony* (Viking, 1977).

Beverly Silva P&W
624 S Crows Nest Dr, Gilbert, AZ 85233-7129, 602-545-5842
Internet: silva_b@mc.maricopa.edu
    Pubs: *The Cat, The Second Street Poems* (Bilingual Pr, 1986, 1983), *Infinite Divisions: An Anth of Chicana Literature* (U Arizona Pr, 1992).

Jim Simmerman P
Northern Arizona Univ, Box 6032, English Dept, Flagstaff, AZ 86011, 520-523-6269
    Pubs: *Kingdom Come, Moon Go Away, I Don't Love You No More* (Miami U Pr, 1999, 1994), *Dog Music: Poetry About Dogs: Anth* (St. Martin's Pr, 1996), *Antaeus, Antioch Rev, Iowa Rev, Laurel Rev, New Letters, Poetry, Prairie Schooner.*

Linda Smukler P&W
544 S 5th Ave, Apt E, Tucson, AZ 85701
    Pubs: *Normal Sex* (Firebrand Bks, 1994), *Love's Shadow: Anth* (Crossing Pr, 1993), *Ploughshares, American Voice, Prose Poem: Intl Jrnl, Kenyon Rev.*

John Spaulding P
4140 W Lane Ave, Phoenix, AZ 85051
    Pubs: *Walking in Stone* (Wesleyan, 1989), *The Roses of Starvation* (Riverstone Pr, 1987), *APR, Poetry, Iowa Rev, Prairie Schooner.*

Laurel Speer P&W
PO Box 12220, Tucson, AZ 85732, 520-747-2047
    Pubs: *Descant, Hollins Critic, Southern Humanities Rev, Massachusetts Rev, Prairie Schooner, Santa Barbara Rev.*

Lawrence Sturhahn W
PO Box 50704, Tucson, AZ 85703, 520-887-8878
    Pubs: *NAR.*

Virginia Chase Sutton P
1709 W Rovey Ave, Phoenix, AZ 85015, 602-433-2684
Internet: sutton@pc.maricopa.edu
    Pubs: *Fever Dreams: Contemporary Arizona Poets: Anth* (U Arizona Pr, 1997), *Boulevard, Poet Lore, Quarterly West, Puerto del Sol, Illinois Rev, Interim, Beloit Poetry Jrnl, Spoon River Poetry Rev, Antioch Rev.*

Rhoda S. Tagliacozzo W
4748 E Quail Creek Dr, Tucson, AZ 85718
    Pubs: *Saving Graces* (St. Martin's, 1979), *New York Woman, New York Times Sunday Mag, McCall's, Cosmopolitan.*

Tobi Taylor P&W
6022 E Redbird Rd, Cave Creek, AZ 85331
Internet: tobi.taylor@asu.edu
    Pubs: *Layers of History* (Northland Research, 1995), *In My Life: Encounters with the Beatles: Anth* (Fromm Intl, 1998), *Rockford Rev, Oregon Rev, South Ash Pr, Gryphon, Colorado North Rev, Ripples.*

Pamela Uschuk P
2022 E 5 St, Tucson, AZ 85719-5203, 520-791-2816
Internet: marchu@ibm.net
    Pubs: *Without Birds, Without Flowers, Without Trees* (Flume, 1991), *Light From Dead Stars* (Full Count, 1981), *American Voice, Parnassus Rev, Agni, Poetry, Nimrod, Parabola.*

Anna Lee Walters P&W
PO Box 276, Tsaile, AZ 86556, 602-724-3311
    Pubs: *Ghost Singer* (U New Mexico Pr, 1995), *Talking Indian* (Firebrand Bks, 1992), *The Spirit Seekers* (Chronicle Bks, 1989).

Frank Waters W
5630 N Blue Bonnet Rd, Tucson, AZ 85743, 602-743-7097
    Pubs: *The Man Who Killed The Deer* (U Ohio Pr, 1992), *Book of the Hopi* (Viking, 1992).

Ramona Martinez Weeks P
326 W Dobbins Rd, Phoenix, AZ 85041, 602-268-9169
    Pubs: *Her Work* (Shearer Pub, 1982), *Lincoln County Poems* (Konocti Pr, 1973), *Virginia Qtly Rev, Forum.*

Dana Weimer P
324 E 14 St, Tempe, AZ 85281, 602-966-2852
    Pubs: *Moving Bodies* (Sun/Gemini Pr, 1992), *Gargoyle Mag, Onthebus, Hayden's Ferry Rev, New Laurel Rev, Zone Mag.*

Wendy White-Ring W
6224 E Calle Rosa, Scottsdale, AZ 85251, 602-946-0236
    Pubs: *Micro Fiction: Anth* (Norton, 1996), *Breaking Up is Hard to Do: Anth* (Crossing Pr, 1994), *NAR, American Literary Rev, Sun Dog: Southeast Rev, Great Stream Rev.*

Peter Wild P
Univ Arizona, English Dept, Modern Languages, Tucson, AZ
85721, 602-621-1836
   Pubs: *The Desert Reader* (U Utah Pr, 1991), *The Brides of
   Christ* (Mosaic, 1991), *APR, Iowa Rev.*

George T. Wright P
2617 W Crown King Dr, Tucson, AZ 85741-2569
   Pubs: *New Yorker Book of Poetry: Anth* (Viking, 1969),
   *New Yorker, American Rev, Sewanee Rev, Poetry
   Northwest, Esquire, Counter/Measures, Nation, Dacotah
   Territory.*

Leilani Wright P
448 N. Matlock, Mesa, AZ 85203, 602-461-0425
Internet: laniw@aztec.asu.edu
   Pubs: *A Natural Good Shot* (White Eagle Coffee Store Pr,
   1994), *Contemporary Arizona Poets Anth* (U Arizona Pr,
   1997), *Hawaii Rev, Hayden's Ferry Rev, South Carolina
   Rev, Blue Mesa Rev, CSM.*

ARKANSAS

Lee Barwood P&W
PO Box 519, Salem, AR 72576, 501-895-3182
   Pubs: *Sisters in Fantasy II: Anth* (NAL, 1992),
   Horsefantastic: Anth (DAW Bks, 1991), *Weirdbook,
   Fantasy, Ellery Queen's Mag, Paradox, Haunts.*

Mark Blaeuer P
414 Veranda Trail, Pearcy, AR 71964, 501-525-4798
   Pubs: *The Small Pond, Lilliput Rev, Mockingbird, Tapjoe,
   Rag Shock, The Plastic Tower, Slant, Wind, Hiram Poetry
   Rev, Poetry Motel.*

Sue Abbott Boyd P
2301 Quarry Dr, Van Buren, AR 72956-6440, 501-782-7642

Besmilr Brigham P&W
Rt 1, Box 292, Horatio, AR 71842
   Pubs: *Cries of the Spirit: Anth* (Beacon, 1990), *Cradle & All:
   Anth* (Faber & Faber, 1989), *Mississippi Writers III and I:
   Anths* (U Mississippi Pr, 1988, 1985).

Andrea Hollander Budy P
PO Box 1107, Mountain View, AR 725601107, 870-269-4586
Internet: ahbudy@mvtel.net
   Pubs: *House Without A Dreamer* (Story Line Pr, 1993),
   What The Other Eye Sees (Wayland Pr, 1991), *NER,
   Poetry, Georgia Rev, Kenyon Rev, Southern Poetry Rev.*

Ralph Burns P
Univ Arkansas, English Dept, Little Rock, AR 72204,
501-569-3160
   Pubs: *Mozart's Starling* (Ohio Rev Bks, 1990), *Any Given
   Day* (U of Alabama, 1985), *Poetry, The Atlantic.*

Crescent Dragonwagon W
Rte 4, Box 7, 1 Frisco St, Eureka Springs, AR 72632-9401
Internet: 76500.3276@compuserve.com
   Pubs: *Dairy Hollow House Soup & Bread* (Workman, 1992),
   Home Place, The Year It Rained (Macmillan, 1991, 1984),
   Lear's, New York Times Book Rev, Ms., Mode.

Ellen Gilchrist P&W
834 Easwood Dr, Fayetteville, AR 72701
   Pubs: *Light Can Be Both Wave and Particle, The Anna
   Papers* (Little, Brown, 1989, 1988).

Michael Heffernan P
Univ Arkansas, Fayetteville, AR 72701, 501-575-5990
   Pubs: *The Man At Home* (U Arkansas Pr, 1988), *To The
   Wreakers Of Havoc* (U Georgia Pr, 1984), *Iowa Rev, The
   Quarterly, Shenandoah.*

David Jauss P&W
Univ Arkansas, 2801 S University, Little Rock, AR 72204,
501-569-8316
Internet: drjauss@ualr.edu
   Pubs: *Black Maps* (U Massachusetts Pr, 1996), *Improvising
   Rivers* (Cleveland State U Pr, 1995), *The Nation, Missouri
   Rev, Iowa Rev, Paris Rev, Poetry, Georgia Rev, NER.*

Linda Kay P
PO Box 553, Jacksonville, AR 72078, 501-988-1317
Internet: ridgewritr@aol.com
   Pubs: *Only Morning in Her Shoes: Anth* (Utah State U Pr,
   1990), *Prairie Schooner, Slant, Jacaranda, Voices Intl,
   ByLine.*

Paul Lake P&W
400 S Commerce Ave, Russellville, AR 72801, 501-967-2174
   Pubs: *Among the Immortals* (Story Line Pr, 1994), *Another
   Kind of Travel* (U Chicago Pr, 1988), *Paris Rev, Yale Rev,
   New Republic.*

Norman Lavers W
3068 CR 901, Jonesboro, AR 72401-0754, 980-935-8543
   Pubs: *Growing Up In Berkeley With the Bomb* (Summer
   Hse, 1998), *The Northwest Passage* (Fiction Collective,
   1984), *APR, NAR, Short Story Intl, Missouri Rev.*

Anna Mahanaim P
PO Box 155, Marshall, AR 72650
   Pubs: *Just This Side of Madness* (U California Pr/U
   Pennsylvania Pr, 1990), *Along the River: Anth*
   (Mockingbird, 1987).

Jo McDougall P
6 Perdido Cir, Little Rock, AR 722112142, 501-223-3540
   Pubs: *From Darkening Porches, Towns Facing Railroads, A
   New Geography of Poets: Anth* (U Arkansas Pr, 1996,
   1991, 1993), *Earth Poems: Anth* (HC, 1996), *Kenyon Rev,
   The Quarterly, Controlled Burn, Poetry East, Louisiana
   Literature.*

Phillip H. McMath W
711 W 3 St, Little Rock, AR 72201, 501-664-8990
> Pubs: *Arrival Point* (M&M Pr, 1991), *Native Ground* (August Hse, 1984).

Rebecca Newth P&W
611 Oliver Ave, Fayetteville, AR 72701
Internet: rharriso@comp.uark.edu
> Pubs: *Great North Woods* (Will Hall Bks, 1994), *19 Poems* (Picadilly Pr, 1993), *Cries of the Spirit: Anth* (Beacon Pr, 1991), *Iris, Lamia Ink, Quarterly West.*

Carter Patteson W
2700 Harrisburg Rd, Jonesboro, AR 72401, 501-932-8453
> Pubs: *Texas Qtly, Wind, Mississippi Valley Rev, Roanoke Rev.*

Kenneth Salzmann P
1933 Broken Arrow Dr, North Little Rock, AR 721183724, 501-771-4636
Internet: kensalzmann@compuserve.com
> Pubs: *Poetry Motel, CQ: California State Poetry Qtly, SYZYGY, Medicinal Purposes, Musing Mag, Rattle, Afterthoughts, Sheila-na-gig.*

James Whitehead P&W
517 E Lafayette, Fayetteville, AR 72707, 501-575-4301

Miller Williams P
1111 Valley View Dr, Fayetteville, AR 72701, 501-521-2934
Internet: mwms1000@aol.com
> Pubs: *The Ways We Touch, Points of Departure* (U Illinois Pr, 1997, 1995), *Adjusting to the Light* (U Missouri Pr, 1992), *Living on the Surface: New and Selected Poems* (Louisiana State U, 1989), *Patterns of Poetry.*

Allen Woodman W
PO Box 23310, Flagstaff, AR 860022310, 520-523-5651
Internet: allen.woodman@nau.edu
> Pubs: *Saved By F. Scott Fitzgerald* (Livingston Pr 1997), *All-You-Can-Eat, Alabama* (Apalachee Pr, 1994), *The Bear Who Came To Stay* (Bradbury Pr, 1994), *Cows Are Going To Paris* (Boyd Mills Pr, 1991), *Story, Mirabella, Flash Fiction, Sudden Fiction Continued.*

Terry Wright P
Univ Central Arkansas, English Dept, Conway, AR 72035, 501-450-5108
Internet: terryw@cc1.uca.edu
> Pubs: *No More Nature* (Kairos Edtns Pr, 1993), *Pig Iron, Rolling Stone, Urbanus, Puerto del Sol, Sequoia, Plastic Tower.*

CALIFORNIA

William H. Abbott W
5000 Coldwater Canyon #4, Sherman Oaks, CA 91423, 818-761-3630
> Pubs: *Cat's Eye, Seems, Trace, Sunset Palms Hotel, Citadel.*

Steve Abee P&W
1614 Lucretia Ave, Los Angeles, CA 90026, 213-481-2677
Internet: abeecat@earthlink.net
> Pubs: *King Planet* (Bork Press/Incommunicado, 1997), *Revival: Anth* (Manic D Press, 1994), *Quarry West, Poet's Fest, Spillway.*

Elmaz Abinader P
4200 Park Blvd 138, Oakland, CA 94602, 510-444-4389
Internet: elmaza@california.com
> Pubs: *Children of the Roojne* (U Wisconsin Pr, 1997), *Grape Leaves: A Century of Arab-American Poetry: Anth* (U Utah Pr, 1988).

SDiane Adamz-Bogus P&W
PO Box 2087, Cupertino, CA 95015-2087, 408-279-6626
Internet: womaninmoon@earthlink.net
> Pubs: *The New Age Reader: Anth* (S&S, 1998), *Buddhism in the Classroom, The Chant of the Woman of Magdalena, Dykehands* (Woman in the Moon Pubs, 1996, 1994, 1994), *MLA Newsletter, Connexions, Spirit, Sinister Wisdom, Common Lives, Black Scholar.*

Kim Addonizio P&W
1725 Quintara St, San Francisco, CA 94116-1234
Internet: blue728@aol.com
> Pubs: *Jimmy & Rita, The Philosopher's Club* (BOA Edtns, 1997, 1994), *A New Geography of Poets: Anth* (U Arkansas, 1992), *Threepenny Rev.*

Opal Palmer Adisa P&W
PO Box 10625, Oakland, CA 94610, 510-268-0704
Internet: www.geocites.com/Athens/Aegean/7854
> Pubs: *It Begins with Tears* (Heinemann, 1997), *Tamarind and Mango Women* (Sister Vision Pr, 1992), *Bake-Face and Other Guava Stories* (Kelsey Street Pr, 1986), *Traveling Woman* (Jukebox Pr, 1979), *Zyzzyva, Obsidian II, Frontiers, Sage, Black Elegance.*

Frances Payne Adler P
CA State Univ, Monterey Bay, 100 Campus Ctr, Seaside, CA 93955-8001, 408-582-3982
Internet: frances_payne_adler@csumb.edu
> Pubs: *Raising the Tents* (Calyx, 1993), *When the Bough Breaks* (Newsage Pr, 1993), *Progressive, Women's Rev of Bks, Prism Intl, Ms., Exquisite Corpse.*

Mandy Aftel   W
1518 Walnut, Berkeley, CA 94709, 510-841-2111
    Pubs: *Out of Step and Out of Detroit* (Inkblot, 1986).

Pancho Aguila   P
3341 18 St, San Francisco, CA 94110

Ellery Akers   P&W
1592 Union, #211, San Francisco, CA 94123
    Pubs: *Knocking on the Earth* (Wesleyan, 1989), *Sierra,
    APR, Ploughshares, Intro 6.*

Askia Akhnaton   P
6432 Fulton St, San Francisco, CA 94121, 415-386-5831
    Pubs: *The Last Black Man* (Soul Visions, 1994),
    Indianapolis U Mag.

Mimi Albert   W
Napa Valley College, 2100 Napa Vallejo Hwy, Napa, CA
94558, 510-918-5510
Internet: abriel@well.com
    Pubs: *A Different Beat: Early Works of Beat Women: Anth*
    (Serpent's Tail Pr, 1997), *Skirts* (Baskerville, 1994), *The
    House on Via Gambito: Anth* (Two Rivers Pr, 1991),
    *Crazyquilt, Metro Mag, San Francisco Chronicle, Poetry
    Flash, Caprice, Southern Lights.*

Adele Aldridge   P
6363 Christie Ave, #2106, Emeryville, CA 94608-1945
    Pubs: *Once I Was A Square, Notpoems* (Magic Circle Pr,
    1974, 1972).

Jean Aldriedge   P
1020 Bay St, Apt C, Santa Monica, CA 90405, 213-396-0825
    Pubs: *Circus Maximus, Interstate, Encore, Village Idiot,
    Dekalb Literary Arts Journal, Pig Iron.*

Karl Alexander   W
c/o Polly Fox, 1380 Manzanita Ave, Palm Springs, CA 92264,
760-327-2988
Internet: katkarl@pacbell.net
    Pubs: *Papa & Fidel* (Tor/St. Martin's Pr, 1989), *Curse of the
    Vampire* (Pinnacle, 1982), *Time After Time* (Delacorte/Dell,
    1979).

T. Diener Allen   W
PO Box 2775, Carmel-By-The-Sea, CA 93921, 408-624-6121
    Pubs: *The Color-Coded Allergy Cookbook* (Bobbs-Merrill,
    1983).

Dorothy Allison   P&W
PO Box 460908, San Francisco, CA 941460908,
415-641-5606
Internet: rhydab@aol.com
    Pubs: *Cavedweller, Two or Three Things I Know For Sure,
    Bastard Out of Carolina* (Dutton, 1998, 1995, 1992), *Trash*
    (Firebrand, 1988).

David Alpaugh   P
Small Poetry Press, PO Box 5342, Concord, CA 94524,
510-798-1411
Internet: davalpaugh@aol.com
    Pubs: *Counterpoint* (Story Line Pr, 1994), *The Literature of
    Work: Anth* (U Phoenix Pr, 1991), *Asylum, BPR, Exquisite
    Corpse, Poets On, Poet & Critic, Wisconsin Rev.*

Cathryn Alpert   W
Box 624, Aptos, CA 95001
Internet: cathryn@alpert.com
    Pubs: *Making the Twilight I and II* (Northland Pub, 1996),
    Rocket City (Vintage, 1996), *Sudden Fiction (Continued):
    Anth, Best of the West: Anth* (Norton, 1996, 1992), *Puerto
    del Sol, Zyzzyva.*

Alta   P&W
PO Box 5540, Berkeley, CA 94705, 510-547-7544
    Pubs: *Traveling Tales* (Acapella, 1990), *Deluged With
    Dudes* (Shameless Hussy Pr, 1989).

Alurista   P
California Polytechnic State, Foreign Language Dept, San
Luis Obispo, CA 93407, 805-546-2992
    Pubs: *Return* (Bilingual Pr, 1982), *Spik in glyph?* (Arte
    Publico Pr, 1981), *Calafia, Caracol.*

Jorge Alvarez   P
1004 S Ferris Ave, Los Angeles, CA 90022, 213-262-7120
    Pubs: *Homenaje a la Ciudad de Los Angeles: Anth*
    (Xismearte Pr, 1982), *El Espejo: Selected Chicano
    Literature* (Quinto Sol Pubs, 1972).

Ameen Alwan   P
992 N Madison Ave, Pasadena, CA 91104, 213-684-4002
    Pubs: *Nation, Kenyon Rev, New Republic, Michigan Qtly
    Rev, TriQuarterly, Chelsea, Epoch, Kayak.*

Georgia Alwan   P
992 N Madison Ave, Pasadena, CA 91104
    Pubs: *Paris Rev, Boundary 2, Canto.*

Karla M. Andersdatter   P
PO Box 790, Sausalito, CA 94966, 415-383-8447
    Pubs: *Wild Onions* (In Between Bks, 1997), *The Broken
    String, The Doorway* (Plain View Pr, 1994, 1990), *Butterfly
    Chronicles Vol 2.*

Douglas Anderson   P
Pitzer College, 1050 N Mills Ave, Claremont, CA 91711-6110,
909-621-8000
    Pubs: *The Moon Reflected Fire* (Alice James Bks, 1994),
    The Four Way Reader: Anth (Four Way Bks, 1996), *Virginia
    Qtly Rev, Ploughshares, Southern Rev, Massachusetts
    Rev.*

Susan D. Noyes Anderson   P
PO Box 2250, Saratoga, CA 95070-0250
   Pubs: *At the End of Your Rope, There's Hope* (Deseret
   Bks, 1997), *Age Happens: Anth, For Better and for Worse:
   Anth, The Funny Side of Parenthood: Anth* (Meadowbrook
   Pr, 1996, 1995, 1994), *Lyric, Poetpourri, Perceptions,
   Comstock Rev, Mobius, Ensign.*

Michael Andrews   P&W
1092 Loma Dr, Hermosa Beach, CA 90254, 310-374-7672
   Pubs: *In Country, The Poet From The City of the Angels*
   (Bombshelter Pr, 1994, 1991), *Arizona Qtly, Onthebus,
   Exquisite Corpse, Wormwood Rev.*

Ralph Angel   P
838 Bank St, South Pasadena, CA 91030, 213-259-9049
   Pubs: *Neither World* (Miami U Pr, 1995), *Anxious Latitudes*
   (Wesleyan U Pr, 1986), *APR, Antioch Rev, New Yorker,
   Partisan Rev, Poetry.*

Roger R. Angle   P&W
2225 Pacific Ave, Apt D, Costa Mesa, CA 92627,
949-642-9523
   Pubs: *Caprice, California State Poetry Qtly, Kryptogame,
   StarWeb Paper, Italia America, Los Angeles Rev, Center,
   Fiction West, Coldspring Jrnl, El Corno Emplumado.*

David Antin   P&W
Univ California/San Diego, La Jolla, CA 92093, 619-534-6552
   Pubs: *What It Means To Be Avant Garde* (New Directions,
   1993), *Selected Poems 1963-1973* (Sun & Moon Pr, 1991),
   Conjunctions, Critical Inquiry, Genre.

Eleanor Antin   PP&P
Univ California/San Diego, La Jolla, CA 92093, 619-755-4619
   Pubs: *Eleanora Antinova Plays* (Sun & Moon Pr, 1994),
   Being Antinova (Astro Artz Pr, 1984).

Gloria E. Anzaldua   P&W
126 Centennial St, Santa Cruz, CA 95060, 408-429-6041
   Pubs: *Borderlands/La Frontera: The New Mestiza*
   (Spinsters/Aunt Lute, 1987), *Sinister Wisdom.*

Roger Aplon   P
16776 Bernardo Ctr Dr, Ste 110, San Diego, CA 92128,
619-746-5250
Internet: 72172.1742@compuserve.com
   Pubs: *It's Mother's Day* (Barracuda Pr, 1996), *By Dawn's
   Early Light at 120 MPH, Stiletto* (Dryad Pr, 1983, 1976).

Samuel Appelbaum   P
3949 N Poppyseed Pl, Calabasas, CA 913022947,
818-880-0183
Internet: appelsam@pacbell.net
   Pubs: *Chtcheglov, Judea Capta* (Asylum Arts, 1998, 1995),
   Saturn (Quixote Pr, 1978).

Jacki Apple   PP
3532 Jasmine Ave #2, Los Angeles, CA 900344947,
310-836-2771
Internet: jaworks@sprintmail.com or www.somewhere.org
   Pubs: *Errant Bodies: Anth* (Brandon LaBelle, 1996),
   *Ghost.Dances/On the Event Horizon, Thank You For Flying
   American* (CDs; Cactus, 1996, 1995), *Public Art Rev,
   Performing Arts Jrnl, Revista de arte sonora.*

Helen Arana   P
405 King Dr, S San Francisco, CA 94080, 415-877-8046

Ivan Arguelles   P
1740 Walnut St, #4, Berkeley, CA 94709, 510-848-6846
Internet: iarguell@library.berkeley.edu
   Pubs: *Enigma & Variations* (Pantograph Pr, 1996), *Primary
   Trouble: Anth* (Talisman Hse Pubs, 1996), *Caliban, Poetry
   USA, Lost & Found Times.*

Rae Armantrout   P
4774 E Mountain View Dr, San Diego, CA 92116,
619-563-3598
Internet: raea100900@aol.com
   Pubs: *Made To Seem, Necromance* (Sun & Moon, 1995,
   1990), *Poems For the Millennium, Vol. 2: Anth* (U
   California, 1998), *Postmodern American Poetry: Anth*
   (Norton, 1994), *NAR, Iowa Rev, River City, Salt, Boxkite,
   Conjunctions, Grand Street, Zyzzyva.*

Linda "Gene" Armstrong   P
5243 Lincoln Ave, Los Angeles, CA 90042, 213-257-4016
   Pubs: *Early Tigers* (Bellowing Ark Pr, 1995), *Birmingham
   Poetry Rev, Rockford Rev, Bitterroot, Earth's Daughters,
   Slant, Spirit That Moves Us.*

Mary Armstrong   P
PO Box 571, Woodland Hills, CA 91365, 818-348-9668
Internet: mwa302@aol.com
   Pubs: *Grand Passion: Anth* (Red Wind Bks, 1995),
   Harbinger: Anth (L.A. Festival, 1990), *Spoon River Poetry
   Rev, Kalliope, Zone 3, Birmingham Rev, Cream City Rev.*

Alfred Arteaga   P
346 Spring St, Santa Cruz, CA 95060, 510-642-3467
Internet: arteaga@altavista.net
   Pubs: *House With the Blue Bed* (Mercury Hse, 1997),
   Chicano Poetics (Cambridge U Pr, 1997), *Cantos* (Chusma
   Hse Pub, 1991), *New Chicano Writing: Anth* (U Arizona Pr,
   1992), *Chispa, 9 Items or Less, Berkeley Poetry Rev, Blue
   Mesa Rev, Mandorla, River Styx.*

Kenneth John Atchity   P
435 S Curson, #8E, Los Angeles, CA 90036
Internet: aeikja@lainet.com
   Pubs: *A Writer's Time* (Norton, 1988), *Sleeping with an
   Elephant* (Valkyrie Pr, 1978), *Poetry/L.A., Southern Poetry,
   Huron Rev, Kansas Qtly, Ball State Forum.*

Hope Athearn   P
32 Bretano Way, Greenbrae, CA 94904, 415-461-0621
    Pubs: *Asimov's, Amazing, Star*Line, Ploughshares, Blue
    Unicorn, Gaia.*

Charles O. Atkinson   P
142 Hagar Ct, Santa Cruz, CA 95064
Internet: charles_atkinson@macmail.ucsc.edu
    Pubs: *The Best of Us on Fire* (Wayland, 1992), *The Only Cure
    I Know* (San Diego Poets Pr, 1991), *Nimrod, Pennsylvania
    Rev, Southern Poetry Rev, River Styx, Poet Lore.*

Mark Axelrod   P&W
Dept of English & Comparative, Chapman University, Orange,
CA 92866, 714-997-6586
Internet: axelrod@chapman.edu
    Pubs: *Cardboard Castles, Bombay California or Hollywood,
    Somewhere West of Vine* (Pacific Writers Pr, 1996, 1994),
    *Exquisite Corpse, Thanatos, Americas Rev, La Fusta, Iowa
    Rev, Splash, New Novel Rev, Pannus Index, Rev of
    Contemporary Fiction.*

Hillary Ayer   P
944 Fletcher Ln, #9, Hayward, CA 94544, 415-841-9032

Dale Alan Bailes   P
5318 Breakers Way, Oxnard, CA 93035-1009, 805-984-1573
Internet: dab2001@aol.com
    Pubs: *Recycling in L.A.* (Select Poets Series, 1996), *Ashes
    in the Grate* (South Carolina Arts Commission, 1983),
    *Southern Poetry Rev, River Talk, Permafrost, Jrnl of
    Quantum Pataphysis.*

Jane Bailey   P
24 Kempton Ave, San Francisco, CA 94132
    Pubs: *Tuning* (Slow Loris, 1978), *Pomegranate* (Black
    Stone, 1976), *Calyx, Columbia.*

Eric Baizer   P
PO Box 23042, Santa Barbara, CA 93121, 805-687-4067
    Pubs: *Woodstock Poetry Rev, Coldspring Jrnl, Northern
    Pleasure, Cumberland Jrnl.*

Laura Baker   W
79 Roble Rd, Berkeley, CA 94705-2826
    Pubs: *New Letters, San Francisco Focus, West Branch,
    Poetry East.*

Charlene Baldridge   P
4435 Hamilton St, #5, San Diego, CA 92116, 619-296-8044
Internet: charb8@aol.com
    Pubs: *Winter Roses* (Wordsperson Pr, 1990), *Poetry
    Conspiracy, Thirteen, Broomstick, Time of Singing, Sunrust,
    Song, Christianity Today.*

Sheila Ballantyne   W
Mills College, English Dept, 5000 MacArthur, Oakland, CA
94613, 510-430-2217
    Pubs: *Life On Earth* (Linden Pr, 1988), *Imaginary Crimes,
    Norma Jean the Termite Queen* (Penguin, 1983, 1983).

Baloian   P
PO Box 429, Half Moon Bay, CA 94019-0429
    Pubs: *Eclipses* (Dark Sky Pr, 1995), *Ararat Papers* (Ararat
    Pr, 1979), *Anth of Mag Verse & Yrbk of American Poetry*
    (Monitor Bks, 1997), *Antioch Rev, Whole Notes, Poets On,
    Green Fuse, Ararat, Sensations, The Midwest Qtly,
    Midwest Poetry Rev, Rain City Rev.*

George Bamber   W
2057 Willow Glen Rd, Fallbrook, CA 92028, 760-728-6786
    Pubs: *The Sea Is Boiling Hot* (Ace Bks, 1971), *Rogue Mag.*

Joan Baranow   P
73 Hillside Ave, Mill Valley, CA 94941
    Pubs: *Morning: Three Poems* (Radiolarian Pr, 1997),
    *Western Humanities Rev, Antioch Rev, Spoon River Poetry
    Rev, Cream City Rev, U.S. 1 Worksheets.*

Ramon Sender Barayon   W
3922 23rd St, San Francisco, CA 94114, 415-821-2090
Internet: rabar@well.com
    Pubs: *A Death in Zamora* (U New Mexico Pr, 1989), *Zero
    Weather* (Family Pub Co., 1981).

John Barbato   P
20391 New Rome Rd, Nevada City, CA 95959, 916-265-8757
    Pubs: *Wild Duck Rev, Northern Contours, Tule Rev, Glyphs,
    Community Endeavor, Deepest Valley Rev, Zyzzyva.*

George Barlow   P
DeAnza College, 21250 Stevens Creek Blvd, Cupertino, CA
95014, 408-996-4547
    Pubs: *Gumbo* (Doubleday, 1981), *Gabriel* (Broadside Pr,
    1974), *Iowa Rev, River Styx, Antaeus, APR.*

Dick Barnes   P
Pomona College, 140 W 6 St, Claremont, CA 91711-6335,
909-621-8873
Internet: rbarnes@pomona.edu
    Pubs: *Few and Far Between* (Ahsahta Pr, 1995), *A Lake on
    the Earth* (Momentum Pr, 1982), *Poetry, Paris Rev, Santa
    Monica Rev, Antioch, APR, Harvard.*

Dorothy Barresi   P
California State Univ, Northridge, CA 91330-8248,
818-885-3431
    Pubs: *The Post-Rapture Diner* (U Pittsburgh Pr, 1996), *All
    of the Above* (Beacon Pr, 1991), *Antioch, Agni, Gettysburg
    Rev, Parnassus, Michigan Qtly Rev, Harvard Rev.*

Anita Barrows P
546 The Alameda, Berkeley, CA 94707, 510-525-4899
Pubs: *The Road Past the View* (QRL, 1992), *No More Masks* (Doubleday, 1973), *Nation, Revision, Bridges, Metis, Wild Duck Rev, Sonoma Mandala, Blind Donkey, Montemora, Aphra.*

Ellen Bass P
PO Box 5296, Santa Cruz, CA 950605296, 781-631-6722
Internet: kelallyn@aol.com
Pubs: *Our Stunning Harvest* (New Society, 1985), *No More Masks!: Anth* (HarperCollins, 1993), *Ms., Atlantic, Greensboro Rev, Calyx, Ploughshares.*

Peter S. Beagle W
2135 Humboldt Ave, Davis, CA 95616-3084, 916-753-8538
Pubs: *Giant Bones* (Dutton/Signet, 1997), *The Rhinoceros Who Quoted Nietzche* (Tachyon Pub, 1997), *The Unicorn Sonata* (Turner Pub, 1996), *In the Presence of Elephants* (Capra Pr, 1995), *Harper's, Saturday Evening Post, Atlantic, Holiday, Ladies Home Jrnl.*

Beau Beausoleil P
719 Lisbon St, San Francisco, CA 94112-3523
Pubs: *Has That Carrying* (Jungle Garden Pr, 1985), *Aleppo* (Sombre Reptiles Pr, 1984).

Richard Beban P
Box 676, Santa Monica, CA 904060676, 310-535-2559
Internet: beban@mediaone.net
Pubs: *Beside Prayers: Anth* (HarperCollins, 1997), *Soul Moments: Anth* (Conari Pr, 1997), *Caffeine, Rattle, Spillway, Sabado Gigante, Neon Qtly, Blue Satellite, 51%.*

Art Beck P
2528 25th Ave, San Francisco, CA 94116, 415-661-8502
Internet: artbeck@aol.com
Pubs: *Simply to See* (Poltroon Pr, 1990), *Literature of Work: Anth* (U Phoenix Pr, 1992), *Once More With Feeling: Anth* (Vagabond, 1990), *Rilke* (Elysian Pr, 1983), *Alaska Qtly, Artful Dodge, Painted Bride Qtly, Passages North, Invisible City, Sequoia.*

Merle Ray Beckwith P
3732 Monterey Pine, #A109, Santa Barbara, CA 93105, 805-687-0310
Pubs: *Abingdon Speeches and Recitations: Anth* (Abingdon, 1994).

Robin Beeman W
PO Box 963, Occidental, CA 954650963, 707-874-2091
Internet: robinbee@wclynx.com
Pubs: *A Minus Tide, A Parallel Life and Other Stories* (Chronicle Bks, 1995, 1992), *NAR, Crazyhorse, Ascent, Cutbank, Fiction Network, Other Voices, PEN Syndicated Fiction.*

James Scott Bell P
22136 Clarendon St, Woodland Hills, CA 91367, 818-703-7875
Pubs: *The Night Carl Sagan Stepped On My Cat* (Compendium Pr, 1988), *Broken Streets II.*

Molly Bendall P
Univ of Southern California, Los Angeles, CA 90089-0354, 213-740-3748
Pubs: *Dark Summer* (Miami U Pr, 1999), *After Estrangement* (Peregrine Smith Bks, 1992), *Paris Rev, Poetry, Colorado Rev, APR.*

Joyce Lorentzson Benson P
1220 Hampel St, Oakland, CA 94602-1112
Pubs: *Lift, Io, Caterpillar, Redhandbook II, Boundary II, Rolling Stock, Exquisite Corpse.*

Rachelle Benveniste P
5215 Sepulveda Blvd, #8-D, Culver City, CA 90230, 310-398-9316
Pubs: *Rapunzel, Rapunzel* (McBooks Pr, 1980), *Gridlock: An Anth About Southern California* (Applezaba Pr, 1990), *13th Moon, Sing Heavenly Muse, Mindscapes, Playgirl.*

Marsha Lee Berkman W
1600 Hopkins Ave, Redwood City, CA 94062, 415-368-6516
Pubs: *Mothers: Anth* (Northpoint Pr, 1996), *The Schocken Book of Contemporary Jewish Fiction: Anth* (Schocken Pr, 1992), *Other Voices, Sifrut Rev.*

Bill Berkson P
25 Grand View Ave, San Francisco, CA 94114, 415-826-2947
Internet: berkson@sirius.com
Pubs: *Lush Life* (Z Pr, 1984), *Red Devil* (Smithereens, 1983), *Start Over* (Tombouctou, 1983), *o.blek, The World, Mudfish, Intent.*

Christopher Bernard P&W
400 Hyde St, #606, San Francisco, CA 94109-7445
Pubs: *The Dilettante of Cruelty: Deserts* (Meridien Pressworks, 1996), *Gilded Abattoir: Wreckage from a Journey* (Small Poetry Pr, 1986), *ACM, Caesura, Ampersand, Caveat Lector, The Drummer, Metier, Haight-Ashbury Jrnl.*

Mira-Lani Bernard W
Art Options, PO Box 29476, Los Angeles, CA 900290476, 213-655-8433
Internet: miralani@pacbell.net
Pubs: *Athena Louise Replies* (Coffee Hse Pr, 1990), *Word of Mouth: Anth* (Crossing Pr, 1990), *Exquisite Corpse, Fiction Intl, Los Angeles 1956, Fizz.*

Jeff Berner P
PO Box 244, Dillon Beach, CA 94929-0244
Internet: jeffberner@jeffberner.com
   Pubs: *The Joy of Working From Home* (Berret-Koehler,
   1994), *The Photographic Experience* (Doubleday/Anchor,
   1975), *Kayak, Stolen Paper Rev, Antioch Rev, Liberation.*

Alan Bernheimer P
1613 Virginia St, Berkeley, CA 94703, 415-843-7460
   Pubs: *State Lounge* (Tuumba, 1981), *Up Late: Anth* (4
   Walls 8 Windows, 1987).

Lisa Bernstein P
PO Box 20663, Oakland, CA 94620, 510-261-6054
   Pubs: *Free Me for the Joy* (Piece of Pie Records, 1998),
   The Transparent Body (Wesleyan, 1989), *Anorexia* (Five
   Fingers, 1985), *Brilliant Corners, Poetry Intl, Liberty Hill,
   Psychic Reader, Bastard Rev, Zyzzyva, Calyx, Tikkun,
   Ploughshares, Kenyon Rev.*

John Berry P&W
579 Crane Blvd, Los Angeles, CA 90065
   Pubs: *Flight of White Crows, Krishna Fluting* (Macmillan,
   1960, 1959), *Chelsea, Manhattan Poetry Rev.*

Maur Bettman W
Sonoma Mountain Rd, Petaluma, CA 94952, 707-763-3341
   Pubs: *Chicago Rev, Confrontation, Ascent, Virginia Qtly
   Rev, Kansas Qtly, Apalachee Qtly.*

Michael F. Biehl P
615 Central Ave, #301, Alameda, CA 94501-3875,
510-521-4063
   Pubs: *Graham House Rev, Concho River Rev, Great River
   Rev, Plains Poetry Jrnl, Creeping Bent, Bitterroot, Interim,
   Image: A Jrnl of Arts & Religion, Callaloo.*

Duane Big Eagle P&W
210 Cleveland Ave, Petaluma, CA 94952-1775,
707-778-3107
   Pubs: *America Street: Anth* (Persea Bks, 1993), *Zyzzyva,
   Mattoid, Headlands Jrnl, Inside Osage.*

Judith Bishop P
240 Fulton St, Palo Alto, CA 94301, 650-324-1379
   Pubs: *The Burning Place* (Fithian Pr, 1994), *The Longest
   Light* (Five Fingers Rev Pr, 1991), *The Muse Strikes Back:
   Anth* (Story Line Pr, 1997), *Coastlight: Anth* (Coastlight Pr,
   1981), *Kalliope, Taos Rev, Small Garlic Pr, Fresh Hot
   Bread, Montserrat Rev.*

Bette-Jean Black P&W
3747-105 Vista Campana S, Oceanside, CA 92057,
619-754-6832
   Pubs: *Hawaii Rev, Tide Pools, Green's Mag, Pig Iron,
   Mississippi Valley Rev, Northwoods Jrnl, Dekalb Literary
   Arts Jrnl, Family Living.*

David Black W
ICM, 8942 Wilshire Blvd, Beverly Hills, CA 90211,
310-550-4000
   Pubs: *Peep Show* (Doubleday, 1986), *The Plague Years*
   (S&S, 1985), *Murder at the Met* (Dial, 1983), *Smart, Rolling
   Stone, Harper's.*

Clark Blaise W
130 Rivoli St, San Francisco, CA 94117
Internet: clarquito@aol.com
   Pubs: *If I Were Me, Man And His World, Lunar Attractions*
   (Porcupine's Quill, 1997, 1992, 1990), *I Had A Father*
   (Addison-Wesley, 1993), *Resident Alien* (Penguin, 1986),
   Mother Jones, Bomb, Descant.

Ella Blanche P
6817 Adolphia Dr, Carlsbad, CA 92009
   Pubs: *Whispering to God, Searching the Shadows*
   (Realities Library, 1986, 1984), *Maize, Poetry View,
   Impetus, Realities, Poetic Justice.*

Douglas Blazek P
2751 Castro Way, Sacramento, CA 95818, 916-456-5734
   Pubs: *We Sleep As the Dream Weaves Outside Our Minds*
   (Alantansi Pr, 1994), *The Party Train: Anth* (New Rivers Pr,
   1996), *Zyzzyva, APR, Poetry, Nation.*

Lucy Jane Bledsoe W
1226 Cedar St, Berkeley, CA 94702, 510-526-7771
Internet: lucyjane1@msn.com
   Pubs: *Working Parts, Sweat: Stories and a Novella* (Seal
   Pr, 1997, 1995), *Newsday, Fiction Intl, Northwest Literary
   Forum, Wig, Lambda Book Report, The Writer.*

Chana Bloch P
12 Menlo Pl, Berkeley, CA 94707, 510-524-8459
Internet: chana@mills.edu
   Pubs: *Mrs. Dumpty* (U Wisconsin Pr, 1998), *The Song of
   Songs* (U California, 1998), *The Past Keeps Changing*
   (Sheep Meadow, 1992), *Poetry, Field, Iowa Rev,
   Ploughshares, Poetry Northwest, Atlantic, Nation, New
   Yorker, Marlboro Rev, Salmagundi.*

Robert Bloch W
4450 Placidia Ave, #2, Toluca Lake, CA 91602-2434

Layeh Bock Pallant P
642 Alcatraz Ave #106, Oakland, CA 94609, 510-547-5360
   Pubs: *Through the Hill Anthology, Poetry Flash, Yellow Silk,
   Haight-Ashbury Literary Jrnl, Beatitude.*

Maclin Bocock W
635 Gerona Road, Stanford, CA 94305, 415-327-6687
   Pubs: *New Directions 51 & 46: Anths* (New Directions,
   1987, 1983), *Southern Rev, Sequoia, Fiction.*

Deborah Boe P
PO Box 2521, Santa Barbara, CA 93120
  Pubs: *Mojave* (Hanging Loose Pr, 1987), *Poetry, Poetry Northwest, Hanging Loose, Ohio Rev.*

Laurel Ann Bogen P
836 North La Cienega Blvd, #21, West Hollywood, CA 90069, 310-288-7118
Internet: labogen@mindspring.com
  Pubs: *Fission* (Red Dancefloor Pr, 1998), *The Last Girl In the Land Of The Butterflies, The Burning* (Red Wind Bks, 1996, 1991), *The Stand-Up Poetry Anth* (California State U Pr, 1994), *Bakunin, Los Angeles Times, Yellow Silk, Milkweed Chronicle.*

Lucile Bogue W
2611 Brooks Ave, El Cerrito, CA 945301416, 510-232-0346
  Pubs: *One Woman, One Ranch, One Summer* (Strawberry Hill Pr, 1997), *I Dare You! How to Stay Young Forever* (Bristol Pub, 1990), *Pegasus Anth Series* (Kendall Hunt Pub, 1992), *Pen Woman, Blue Unicorn, Galley Sail Rev.*

Margot Bollock P
2015 Belle Monte Ave, Belmont, CA 94002, 415-593-7753

Maryetta Kelsick Boose P
1537 W 20 St, San Bernardino, CA 92411, 714-887-6170
  Pubs: *Fragrant African Flowers* (Guild Pr, 1988), *Mosaic, Essence, Black American Lit Forum.*

David Borofka W
Reedley College, 995 N Reed Ave, Reedley, CA 936542099, 209-638-3641
Internet: dborofka@ix.netcom.com
  Pubs: *The Island* (MacMurray & Beck, 1997), *Hints of His Mortality* (U Iowa Pr, 1996), *Black Warrior Rev, Santa Monica Rev, West Branch, South Dakota Rev, Carolina Qtly, Greensboro Rev, Crosscurrents, Missouri Rev, Southern Rev, Gettysburg Rev, Witness.*

Terry Borst P
23515 Lyons Ave, #280, Santa Clarita, CA 91355
  Pubs: *Gargoyle, Asylum, American Classic Anth, Nebo, Blue Unicorn, Oyez Rev, Tequila Poetry Rev.*

Greg Boyd P&W
c/o Asylum Arts Publishing, 5847 Sawmill Rd, Paradise, CA 95969, 530-876-1454
Internet: asyarts@sunset.net
  Pubs: *Sacred Hearts* (Hi Jinx Pr, 1996), *Water & Power* (Asylum Arts, 1991), *Puppet Theatre, The Masked Ball* (Unicorn Pr, 1989, 1987), *Florida Rev, Fiction Intl, Central Park, Caliban, Bakunin, Asylum, Poet Lore.*

Ray Bradbury W
10265 Cheviot Dr, Los Angeles, CA 90064

Cecilia Manguerra Brainard W
PO Box 5099, Santa Monica, CA 90409, 310-392-7562
Internet: cbrainard@aol.com
  Pubs: *Acapulco at Sunset and Other Stories, Contemporary Fiction by Filipinos in America: Anth* (Anvil, 1995, 1998), *When the Rainbow Goddess Wept* (Dutton, 1995), *Filipinas Mag, Sunstar, Mirror Weekly, West/Word Jrnl, Philippine Graphic.*

John Brander P
Small Poetry Press, 362 Odin Pl, Pleasant Hill, CA 94523
  Pubs: *Trail of the Moon* (Inevitable Pr, 1992), *Drawing Dreams* (Sunlight Pub, 1991), *Nexus, Hermosa Rev, San Miguel Writer, Poetry/L.A., Galley Sail Rev.*

Donn Brannon P
Box 105, Castella, CA 96017, 916-235-2303
  Pubs: *Bread Journal.*

Charles Brashear W
5614 Dorothy Dr, San Diego, CA 92115, 619-287-0850
  Pubs: *Contemporary Insanities* (MacDonald & Reinecke, 1990), *Aniyunwiya: Contemporary Cherokee Prose: Anth* (Greenfield Rev Pr, 1995), *Vignette, Callaloo.*

Luke Breit P
2119 7th Ave, Sacramento, CA 95818, 916-446-7638
Internet: http://www.tomatoweb.com/lukesac/
  Pubs: *Unintended Lessons, Messages—New And Selected Poems* (QED Pr, 1998, 1989), *Words The Air Speaks* (Wilderness Poetry Pr, 1978), *New Yorker, Pacific Coast Literary Rev, Talkhard!, Haight Ashbury Literary Rev, Poetry Now, One Dog Press, Oro Madre.*

Summer Brenner W
1727 Addison St, Berkeley, CA 94703, 510-644-3099
  Pubs: *One Minute Movies* (Thumbscrew Pr, 1996), *Dancers & the Dance* (Coffee Hse Pr, 1990).

David Breskin P&W
1061 Francisco St, San Francisco, CA 94109-1126, 415-921-3354
  Pubs: *Fresh Kills* (Cleveland State U, 1997), *The Real Life Diary of a Boomtown Girl* (Viking Penguin, 1989), *New Yorker, TriQuarterly, Paris Rev, Boulevard, Nimrod, Salmagundi, NAW.*

Peter Brett P
PO Box 1771, Ross, CA 949571771, 415-459-2566
  Pubs: *Borrowing The Sky* (Kastle, 1979), *Seneca Rev, Kansas Qtly, Zyzzyva, Olympia Rev, Florida Rev, Wisconsin Rev, Rain City, Acorn, Red Owl, Silver Black Qtly, Lactuca.*

Herb Brin P
1101 E Loma Alta Dr, Altadena, CA 91001, 213-737-2122
  Pubs: *Where Are the Children, My Spanish Years And Other Poems* (Jonathan David Pubs, 1991, 1985).

Armand Brint   P
215 Thompson St, Ukiah, CA 95482, 707-468-8906
    Pubs: *Plowman, Five Fingers Poetry, Lactuca, Pearl,*
Poetry Flash, North Atlantic Rev.

Mae Briskin   W
3604 Arbutus Dr, Palo Alto, CA 94303, 415-493-4639
    Pubs: *The Tree Still Stands, A Boy Like Astrid's Mother*
(Norton, 1991, 1988), *Ascent, Chicago Tribune Mag, San*
Francisco Chronicle Mag, St. Anthony Messenger, Western
Humanities Rev, Mid-American Rev.

Bill Broder   W
68 Central Ave, Sausalito, CA 94965, 415-332-4364
    Pubs: *Remember This Time* (w/G.K. Broder; Newmarket
Bks, 1983).

Leslie Brody   P&W
238 San Jose Ave, San Francisco, CA 94110, 415-641-1795
    Pubs: *Monsieur Dada, Boxcar, Isthmus.*

David Bromige   P&W
461 High St, Sebastopol, CA 95472
    Pubs: *A Cast of Tens* (Avec Bks, 1994), *From The Other*
Side of the Century (Sun & Moon Bks, 1994), *Avec, Object*
Permanence, River City, Sulfur, Fragmente.

Lynne Bronstein   P
215 Bay St, #1, Santa Monica, CA 90405, 310-392-2728
    Pubs: *Thirsty in the Ocean* (Graceful Dancer Pr, 1980),
Gridlock: Anth (Applezaba Pr, 1990), *Caffeine, California*
Poetry Calendar.

Beverly J. Brown   W
121 Sierra St, Escondido, CA 92025, 714-745-9454
    Pubs: *True Story, True Love, True Confessions, True Life*
Secrets, Intimate Story.

Cecil Brown   W
38 Panoramic Way, Berkeley, CA 94704

Diana Brown   W
PO Box 2846, Carmel, CA 93921-2846
    Pubs: *The Blue Dragon, The Hand of a Woman, The*
Sandalwood Fan (St. Martin's, 1988, 1984, 1983).

James Brown   W
California State Univ, 5500 University Pkwy, San Bernardino,
CA 92407, 909-880-5894
    Pubs: *Lucky Town* (HB, 1994), *Second Story Theatre &*
Two Encores (Story Line Pr, 1993), *Final Performance*
(Morrow, 1988), *Chicago Tribune, L.A. Times Mag.*

Linda A. Brown   P
1006 Hermes Ave, Leucadia, CA 92024
    Pubs: *Contemporary Women Poets* (Merlin, 1977), *Canta*
Una Mujer (Athena, 1973), *Ms., Malahat Rev.*

Lennart Bruce   P
31 Los Cerros Pl, Walnut Creek, CA 94598, 925-932-8234
    Pubs: *The Coffee Break, The Ways of a Carpetbagger*
(Symposion, 1995, 1993), *Speak To Me* (The Spirit That
Moves Us Pr, 1990).

Bruce-Novoa   P&W
Univ California, Irvine, CA 92717, 714-856-7265
    Pubs: *RetroSpace* (Arte Publico, 1990), *Inocencia Perversa*
(Baleen, 1976), *Periodico de Poesia, Confluencia, Plural,*
Quimera, Hispania.

John J. Brugaletta   P
California State Univ, 800 N State College Blvd, Fullerton, CA
92634, 714-773-2723
    Pubs: *The Tongue Angles* (Negative Capability Pr, 1990),
Random House Treasury of Light Verse: Anth (Random
Hse, 1995), *Formalist, Hellas Rev.*

Christopher Buckley   P
Univ California Riverside, Creative Writing Department,
Riverside, CA 925210118, 909-787-2414
Internet: cbuckley@mail.ucr.edu
    Pubs: *Fall From Grace* (BkMk Pr, 1998), *Camino Cielo*
(Orchises Pr, 1997), *Dark Matter* (Copper Beech Pr, 1993),
APR, Poetry, Iowa Rev, Quarterly West, Hudson Rev,
Crazyhorse, Kenyon Rev.

Y. Stephan Bulbulian   P
113 Carter Way, Fowler, CA 93625-2000
    Pubs: *Saroyan's World* (William Saroyan Society, 1998),
Poets of the Vineyard: Anths (Vintage, 1997, 1996, 1995),
Ararat, Armenian Weekly, Hye Sharzoom, Asbarez, Poets
of the Vineyard, Nor Hayastan.

Richard Alan Bunch   P
248 Sandpiper Dr, Davis, CA 95616
    Pubs: *South By Southwest* (Cedar Bay Pr, 1997), *Black*
Moon (Dream Tyger Prod, 1996), *The Foggy Morning*
(Mandrake Pr, 1996), *Wading the Russian River* (Norton
Coker Pr, 1993), *Hawaii Rev, Coe Rev, Brownstone Rev,*
Poetry Nottingham, Black Mountain Rev.

Claire Burch   P&W
Regent Press, 6020A Adeline, Oakland, CA 94608,
510-547-7602
    Pubs: *Homeless In The 90's, You Be The Mother Follies*
(Regent Pr, 1994, 1994), *Life, McCall's, Good*
Housekeeping, Redbook, Southwest Rev.

Jean Burden   P
1129 Beverly Way, Altadena, CA 91001
    Pubs: *Taking Light From Each Other* (U Pr Florida, 1992),
American Scholar, Georgia Rev, Poetry.

Brio Burgess PP&P
c/o Gail Tolley, 5 Cuyler St, Albany, CA 12202, 518-447-7448
Internet: streetkids@worldnet.att.net
> Pubs: *Street Kids & Other Plays: Anth* (Angel Enterprises, 1995), *Outlaw Blues: Anth* (Tawanna L. Brace Knowles, 1992), *Bay Area Poets Anth, Poetalk, Open Mic, Bay Area Poets Coalition.*

William Burns P
200 E Florence Ave, #A, La Habra, CA 90631-4781
> Pubs: *Crack Pressures Recalled* (Ali Baba Pr, 1984), *Texas Rev, Yankee, Kenyon Rev, Sewanee Rev.*

Robert A. Burton W
1 Daniel Burnham Ct, #335-C, San Francisco, CA 94109, 415-922-0605
Internet: raburton@ix.netcom.com
> Pubs: *Cellmates* (Russian Hill Pr, 1997), *Final Therapy* (Berkley, 1994), *Doc-in-a-Box* (Soho Pr, 1991).

Mary Bucci Bush W
1007 Palm Terr, Pasadena, CA 91104, 818-797-6642
Internet: mbush@calstatela.edu
> Pubs: *A Place of Light* (Morrow, 1990), *The Voices We Carry: Anth* (Guernica Edtns, 1994), *Ploughshares, Missouri Rev, Black Warrior Rev.*

Emilya Cachapero P
1101 Plymouth Ave, San Francisco, CA 94112

Michael Cadnum P
555 Pierce St #143, Albany, CA 94706
Internet: 72142,1434@compuserve.com
> Pubs: *Heat, Taking It* (Viking, 1998, 1995), *In A Dark Wood* (Orchard Bks, 1998), *The Judas Glass* (Carroll & Graf, 1996), *America, Commonweal, SPR, Poetry Northwest, Writers' Forum, Willow Springs, Literary Rev, West Branch, Poem.*

Stratton F. Caldwell P
80 N Kanan Rd, Agoura, CA 913011105, 818-991-3746
> Pubs: *Somatics, Quest, Fat Tuesday, Parnassus Literary Jrnl, Yellow Butterfly, Pinchpenny, Arete, Mendocino Rev.*

Pat Califia W
2215R Market St, #261, San Francisco, CA 94114
> Pubs: *Doc and Fluff* (Alyson, 1990), *Macho Sluts* (Alyson, 1988), *The Advocate, On Our Backs.*

Jamie Callan W
5328 Hermitage Ave, #216, North Hollywood, CA 91607, 818-506-1210
> Pubs: *Just Too Cool, The Young & The Soapy* (NAL, 1987, 1984), *Turnstile, Gypsy, Verve.*

Camincha P
723 Moana Way, Pacifica, CA 94044, 415-359-0890
> Pubs: *Hard Love: Anth* (Queen of Swords Pr, 1997), *Apocalypse 4: Anth* (Northeastern Illinois U Pr, 1997), *Four By Four: Anth* (Amaranth Edtns, 1993), *Cups, Passager.*

Janine Canan P
772 Earnest Dr, Sonoma, CA 95476, 707-939-2771
Internet: jancanan@vom.com
> Pubs: *Her Magnificent Body: New and Selected Poems* (Manroot, 1986), *She Rises Like the Sun: Anth* (Crossing Pr, 1989), *Color Wheel, Crone Chronicles, Open Bone Rev, Poetalk, Potato Eyes, California Qtly, Conditions, Kalliope.*

Patricia E. Canterbury P
PO Box 160127, Sacramento, CA 95816, 916-483-1046
Internet: patmyst@aol.com
> Pubs: *The Secret of St. Gabriel's Tower* (Regeje Pr, 1998), *Dreams Of 21st Century — Rivers V* (Sacramento Poetry Ctr, 1993), *Shadowdrifters... Images of China* (Georgia State Poetry Society, 1990).

Jo-Anne Cappeluti P&W
1100 N Lemon, #H-4, Fullerton, CA 92832
> Pubs: *Short Story, Literary Rev, Negative Capability, The Journal, Lyric, New York Qtly, South Coast Poetry Jrnl, Mosaic, Plains Poetry Rev, Bluegrass Literary Rev.*

Eve La Salle Caram P&W
UCLA Extension, Dept of Arts, 10995 Le Conte Ave, Los Angeles, CA 90024, 213-663-1095
> Pubs: *Wintershine, Dear Corpus Christi* (Plain View Pr, 1994, 1991), *Snowy Egret, Mindscapes, Greenfield Rev, Sou'wester, Wisconsin Rev, Cottonwood, Buffalo Pr.*

Henry Carlisle W
1100 Union St, #301, San Francisco, CA 94109
> Pubs: *The Jonah Man* (Knopf, 1984).

R. S. Carlson P
Azusa Pacific Univ, 901 E Alosta Ave, Azusa, CA 91702, 818-815-6000
Internet: rcarlson@apu.edu
> Pubs: *Pacific Rev, Viet Nam Generation, Poet Lore, Hawaii Rev, Cape Rock, Hollins Critic.*

Josephine Carson W
PO Box 210240, San Francisco, CA 94121
> Pubs: *Listening to Ourselves: Anth* (Anchor Bks, 1994), *American Short Fiction, Poetry USA, auto/bio.*

Marie Cartier P
974 Haverford Ave, #4, Pacific Palisades, CA 90272, 310-459-7601
Internet: ezmerelda@earthlink.net
> Pubs: *Freeze Count, Come Out, Come Out, Wherever You Are Stumbling Into Light* (Dialogos Pr, 1995 1995), *I Am Your Daughter, Not Your Lover* (Clothespin Fever Pr, 1995), *Sinister Wisdom, Heresies, Colorado Rev.*

Xam Cartier W
PO Box 10732, Oakland, CA 94610
> Pubs: *Muse-Echo Blues, Be-Bop, Re-Bop* (Ballantine, 1992, 1990).

Peter Cashorali   P
857 1/2 N Hayworth, Los Angeles, CA 90046
    Pubs: *Bachy, Rara Avis, Poetry/L.A., Barney, Magazine,
    Beyond Baroque, Mouth of the Dragon.*

Marsh G. Cassady   P&W
MCD R-03, PO Box 439016, San Diego, CA 92143
    Pubs: *The Times of the Double Star, Perverted Proverbs
    and Sudden Drama* (Spectrum Pr, 1994, 1994), *Brussels
    Sprout, Chiron Rev.*

Cyrus Cassells   P
2190 Belden Pl, Escondido, CA 92029, 619-745-9156
    Pubs: *The Mud Actor* (Henry Holt, 1982), *Under 35: The
    New Generation of American Poets: Anth* (Doubleday,
    1989), *Kenyon Rev, Ploughshares, Callaloo, Agni.*

Irene Chadwick   P
4336 Copper Cliff Ln, Modesto, CA 953558967,
209-524-3066
Internet: irenekooi@aol.com
    Pubs: *Dawn Pearl* (Ietje Kooi Pr, 1994), *Mindprint Rev,
    Napa Rev, INA Coolbrith Circle, Images of Oracle.*

Pamela Herbert Chais   W
611 N Oakhurst Dr, Beverly Hills, CA 90210, 213-276-6215

Jeffrey Paul Chan   W
San Francisco State Univ, 1600 Holloway, San Francisco, CA
94132, 415-338-1796
Internet: jefchan@sfsu.edu
    Pubs: *The Big Aiiieeeee!: An Anth of Chinese-American
    and Japanese-American Literature* (NAL, 1990).

Janet Carncross Chandler   P
436 Old Wagon Rd, Trinidad, CA 95570, 916-448-6248
    Pubs: *Why Flowers Bloom, Flight of the Wild Goose*
    (Papier-Mache Pr, 1994, 1989), *Significant Relationships*
    (Chandler, 1988).

Joyce A. Chandler   P
5310 S Marina Pacifica, Key 20, Long Beach, CA 90803,
213-594-4131
    Pubs: *Haiku Headlines, Z Misc, Muses Mill, Red Pagoda,
    Thirteen, Poetry Unlimited, Windows, With.*

Kay Chang   P
60 Taylor Dr, Fairfax, CA 94930, 415-453-2765
    Pubs: *Elephant Rocks* (Grove Pr, 1996), *Flamingo
    Watching* (Copper Beech Pr, 1994), *New Yorker, Atlantic,
    New Republic, Paris Rev, Georgia Rev, Yale Rev.*

Kosrof Chantikian   P
20 Millard Rd, Larkspur, CA 94939
    Pubs: *Prophecies & Transformations, Imaginations &
    Self-Discoveries* (KOSMOS, 1978, 1974).

Elizabeth Biller Chapman   P
121 Fulton St, Palo Alto, CA 94301-1320, 650-323-9331
    Pubs: *Backbone of Night, Creekwalker* (Mother Tongue Pr,
    1997, 1995), *Blueline, CQ, Chaplaincy Notes, CPU Rev,
    Green Hills Literary Lantern, Poet Lore, Prairie Schooner,
    Small Pond, Yankee, Blue Unicorn, Bellowing Ark, Sow's
    Ear Poetry Rev.*

Maxine Chernoff   P&W
369 Molino Ave, Mill Valley, CA 94941, 415-389-1877
Internet: maxpaul@sfsu.edu
    Pubs: *American Heaven* (Coffee Hse Pr, 1996), *Signs of
    Devotion, Plain Grief* (S&S, 1993, 1991), *North American
    Rev, Sulfur, Chicago Rev, TriQuarterly.*

Marilyn Chin   P
San Diego State Univ, San Diego, CA 921828140,
619-697-1941
Internet: chin2@mail.sdsu.edu
    Pubs: *The Phoenix Gone, The Terrace Empty* (Milkweed,
    1994), *Dwarf Bamboo* (Greenfield Rev Pr, 1987), *Best
    American Poetry: Anth* (S&S, 1996), *Pushcart Prize XX:
    Anth* (Pushcart Pr, 1996), *Kenyon Rev, Parnassus, Iowa
    Rev, Ploughshares, Zyzzyva.*

John Christgau   W
2704 Comstock, Belmont, CA 94002, 415-591-4045
    Pubs: *The Origins of the Jump Shot* (U of Nebraska Pr,
    1999), *Mower County Poems, Sierra Sue II* (Great Plains
    Pr, 1998, 1994), *Spoon* (Viking, 1978), *Amelia, Window,
    Rainbow City Express, Camellia, Cream City Rev, Great
    River Rev.*

Leonard J. Cirino   P
2434 C St, Eureka, CA 955014111, 707-268-1274
    Pubs: *71 Sonnets Facing Conviction, The Terrible
    Wilderness of Self* (Cedar Hill Pub, 1990, 1998), *You Must
    Be Present To Win* (Gorda Plate Pr, 1996), *Henry's Will: A
    Tribute to John Berryman* (Mandrake Pr, 1995), *Lungfish,
    Dog River Rev, Exquisite Corpse.*

Ralph Cissne   W
409 N Pacific Coast Hwy, #465, Redondo Beach, CA 90277,
310-281-7341
Internet: cissne@earthlink.net
    Pubs: *American Way, Playboy, Writing on the Wall, Info.*

Tom Clark   P&W
1740 Marin Ave, Berkeley, CA 94707, 415-524-6550
    Pubs: *Junkets on a Sad Planet: Scenes From The Life of
    John Keats* (Black Sparrow Pr, 1994), *The Exile of Celine*
    (Random Hse, 1987).

Killarney Clary   P
2517 Kenilworth Ave, Los Angeles, CA 90039, 213-913-3710
    Pubs: *By Common Salt* (Oberlin College Pr, 1996), *Who
    Whispered Near Me* (FSG, 1989), *Ploughshares, APR,
    Yale Rev, Colorado Rev, Paris Rev, Partisan.*

Karen Claussen   P
PO Box 248, Crescent City, CA 95531-0248, 707-465-3228
Internet: kkc@gte.net
    Pubs: *R. C. Lion, Primer, Poetry &, Altadena Rev, Janus/Seth.*

Richard Cloke   P&W
San Fernando Poetry Journal, 18301 Halsted St, Northridge,
CA 91325, 213-349-2080
    Pubs: *Earth Ovum* (Cerulean Pr, 1982), *Yvar* (Kent Pub,
1981), *San Fernando Poetry Jrnl, Quindaro, Abraxas,
Ptolomy.*

Peter Clothier   P
2341 Ronda Vista Dr, Los Angeles, CA 90027, 213-661-6349
    Pubs: *David Hockney* (Abbeville Pr, 1995), *Dirty-Down*
(Atheneum, 1987), *Chiaroscuro* (St. Martin's Pr, 1985), *Art
News, Artspace.*

Cathy Cockrell   W
3917 Elston Ave, Oakland, CA 94602-1620, 510-336-0484
Internet: cac@pa.urel.berkeley.edu
    Pubs: *A Simple Fact, Undershirts and Other Stories* (Hanging
Loose Pr, 1987, 1982), *Croton Rev, Hanging Loose Mag.*

Judith Cody   P
Box 1107, Los Altos, CA 94023, 415-941-3120
    Pubs: *Sequoia, Foreground, Poetry Project Four,
Stonecloud, Androgyne, Amphichoria.*

Tony Cohan   W
1842 Union St, San Francisco, CA 94173, 415-921-2910
Internet: tobo@compuserve.com
    Pubs: *On Mexican Time* (Broadway Bks, 1999), *Mexicolor*
(Chronicle Bks, 1998), *Secret Angel* (Acrobat, 1995),
Opium (S&S, 1984), *Canary* (Doubleday, 1981).

Wanda Coleman   P
Black Sparrow Press, 24 10th St, Santa Rosa, CA 95401
    Pubs: *Bathwater Wine, Hand Dance, African Sleeping
Sickness* (Black Sparrow, 1998, 1993, 1990), *Postmodern
American Poetry: Anth* (Norton, 1994), *Best American
Poetry 1996, Critical Condition, ACM.*

Michael R. Collings   P&W
Pepperdine Univ, Malibu, CA 90263, 805-469-3032
    Pubs: *Matrix* (White Crow, 1995), *Dark Transformation*
(Starmont, 1990), *In The Image of God* (Greenwood, 1990),
*Georgetown Rev, Poet, Dialogue, Star*Line.*

Julia Connor   P
2265 2nd Ave, Sacramento, CA 95818, 916-737-2736
    Pubs: *A Canto for the Birds* (Tule Pr, 1995), *Making the
Good* (Tooth of Time, 1988), *New American Writing, First
Intensity, Tyuonyi.*

Andree Connors   W
PO Box 273, Mendocino, CA 95410
    Pubs: *Amateur People* (Fiction Collective, 1977).

Gillian Conoley   P
Sonoma State Univ, Nichols Hall, Rm 362, Rohnert Park, CA
94928, 707-664-2140
    Pubs: *Tall Stranger, Some Gangster Pain* (Carnegie Mellon
U Pr, 1991, 1987), *APR, New American Writing, Poetry,
Denver Qtly, Kenyon Rev.*

Edith Cook   P&W
5609 Huasna Rd, Arroyo Grande, CA 93420, 805-489-0908
    Pubs: *An Anth of the Tuesday Poets* (Tabula Rasa Pr,
1984), *Sing Heavenly Muse!, Encodings, CQ, Women's Pr.*

Geoffrey Cook   P
PO Box 4233, Berkeley, CA 94704-0233, 510-654-9251
Internet: gcook69833@aol.com
    Pubs: *The Heart of the Beast* (Hiram Poetry Rev, 1995),
Azrael (Androgyne Pr, 1992), *Nation, Tropos, Poetpourri,
Tight, Volume Number, Studia Mystica.*

Carolyn Cooke   W
25524 Ten Mile Cutoff, PO Box 462, Point Arena, CA 95468,
707-882-2106
Internet: redtag@mcn.org
    Pubs: *Prize Stories 1998: The O. Henry Awards: Anth*
(Anchor, 1998), *The Best American Short Stories: Anth*
(HM, 1997), *Breaking Up is Hard to Do: Anth* (Crossing Pr,
1994), *Paris Rev, NER.*

Ellen Cooney   P
919 Sutter, #9, San Francisco, CA 94109
    Pubs: *Within the Labyrinth All, House Holding, The Quest
for the Holy Grail, The Silver Rose* (Duir Pr, 1992, 1984,
1981, 1979).

M. Truman Cooper   P
6575 Camino Caseta, Goleta, CA 93117-1533, 805-683-2340
    Pubs: *Substantial Holdings* (Pudding Hse, 1987), *Poetry
Northwest, New Letters, Prairie Schooner, South Dakota
Rev, Tar River Poetry.*

Lise King Couchot   P&W
808 Mission St, San Luis Obispo, CA 93405-2343,
805-969-4479
    Pubs: *Thin Scars/Purple Leaves* (Mudborn Pr, 1981),
Crosscurrents, Amelia, Connexions.

Michael Covino   P&W
2525 Ashby Ave #4, Berkeley, CA 94705-2218
    Pubs: *The Off-Season* (Persea Bks, 1985), *Unfree
Associations* (Berkeley Poets Pr, 1982).

Robert Crosson   P
2060 Escarpa Dr, Los Angeles, CA 90041
    Pubs: *The Blue Soprano* (Lomardelli Pr, 1994), *The
Gertrude Stein Awards in Innovative North American
Poetry: Anth* (Sun & Moon Pr, 1994).

Irene Culver P
2858 Westwood Ln #6, Carmichael, CA 95608, 916-486-9507
Pubs: *Word Weavers Seven, Bellowing Ark, Sulphur River, The Plastic Tower, Poems for Nobody, Black Buzzard Rev.*

Barney Currer W
10280 Brooks Rd, Windsor, CA 95492-9464
Internet: barney45@aol.com
Pubs: *Free Fire Zone Anth* (McGraw-Hill, 1973), *Hawaii Rev, Aboriginal Sci Fi, Antioch Rev, Thema.*

Daniel Curzon W
City College San Francisco, L 196, San Francisco, CA 94112, 415-585-3410
Internet: curzon@pacbell.net
Pubs: *Superfag* (Igna Bks, 1996), *Queer View Mirror* (Arsenal Pump Pr, 1996), *Curzon in Love* (Knights Pr, 1988), *Kenyon Rev.*

Bruce Cutler P
260 High St #110, Santa Cruz, CA 95060, 408-420-1443
Pubs: *Seeing the Darkness* (BkMk Pr, 1998), *Afterlife* (Juniper Pr, 1997), *The Massacre at Sand Creek* (U Oklahoma Pr, 1995), *Poetry, Shenandoah, New Letters.*

Jane Cutler W
352 27th St, San Francisco, CA 94131, 415-550-7288
Pubs: *FM Five, Medical Heritage, Wind, CP West, Epoch, NAR, Ascent, Plainswoman.*

Beverly Dahlen P
15 Mirabel Ave, San Francisco, CA 94110, 415-824-6649
Pubs: *A Reading 8-10* (Chax Press, 1992), *Moving Borders: Anth* (Talisman House, 1998), *The Art of Practice: 45 Contemporary Poets: Anth* (Potes & Poets, 1994), *River City, Bombay Gin, Iowa Rev, Temblor, Camerawork, Poetics Jrnl, Fourteen Hills, Mirage.*

Ruth Daigon P
86 Sandpiper Cir, Corte Madera, CA 94925, 415-924-0568
Internet: ruthart@aol.com
Pubs: *Electronic Chapbook* (Web Del Sol, 1998), *Between One Future And The Next* (Papier-Mache Pr, 1995), *Southern California Anth* (U Southern California Pr, 1996), *Contemporary Authors Autobiography Series: Anth* (Gale Pub, 1996).

Catherine Daly P
533 South Alandele, Los Angeles, CA 900363250, 213-933-3880
Pubs: *Mudfish, Lightning & Ash, Pivot, Graffiti Rag, Gulf Coast, Hubbub, Limestone, Ascent, Lullwater Rev, Paper Salad, Lucid Stone, Small Pond.*

Saralyn R. Daly W
6211 Gyral Dr, Tujunga, CA 91042-2533, 818-353-7382
Internet: sbssett@linkonline.net
Pubs: *Love's Joy, Love's Pain* (Fawcett, 1983), *Book of True Love* (Pennsylvania State U Pr, 1978), *A Shout in the Street, Western Humanities Rev, Beyond Baroque, Epos, Descant, Bywords.*

John M. Daniel W
PO Box 21922, Santa Barbara, CA 93121, 805-962-1780
Internet: dandd@danielpublishing.com
Pubs: *The Woman by the Bridge* (Dolphin-Moon Pr, 1991), *Play Melancholy Baby* (Perseverance Pr, 1986), *Fish Stories, Quarterly West, Zyzzyva, Amelia, Ambergris, Crosscurrents, Sequoia, Aberrations, Vignette.*

Karen M. Daniels P&W
46040 Paseo Gallante, Temecula, CA 92592
Internet: redwolfess@aol.com
Pubs: *Tenacity.*

Keith Allen Daniels P&W
PO Box 51115, Palo Alto, CA 94303, 415-255-8366
Internet: kdaniels@ix.netcom.com
Pubs: *Satan Is A Mathematician, Notes from the Antipodes, Dyscrasias, What Rough Book* (Anamnesis Pr, 1998, 1997, 1997, 1992), *Loopy Is the Inner Ear* (Quick Glimpse Pr, 1993), *Asimov's SF, Recursive Angel, Alphadrive, Weird Tales, Hadrosaur Tales.*

Jonathan Daunt P
609 D St, Davis, CA 95616
Pubs: *Stone Age Robin Hood* (Allegany Mtn Pr, 1979), *Coyote's Jrnl: Anth* (Wingbow Pr, 1982), *Beloit Poetry Jrnl, Denver Qtly, Mississippi Rev, Prairie Schooner.*

Michael Davidson P
Univ California, San Diego, 9500 Gilman Dr, Dept 0410, La Jolla, CA 92093-0410, 619-534-2101
Internet: rdavidson@uscd.edu
Pubs: *The Arcades* (O Books, 1999), *Post Hoc* (Avenue B Pr, 1990), *Analogy of the Ion* (The Figures, 1988).

Angela J. Davis P
505 S Beverly, #488, Beverly Hills, CA 90212, 310-277-3976
Pubs: *Eureka Anth* (U Iowa Pr, 1995), *Art/Life, Onthebus, Permafrost, Yellow Silk, Sequoia, Cream City Rev.*

Lucille Lang Day P
1057 Walker Ave, Oakland, CA 94610, 510-763-3874
Internet: lucyday@autobahn.org
Pubs: *Fire in the Garden* (Mother's Hen, 1997), *Self-Portrait with Hand Microscope* (Berkley Pr, 1982), *Mother Songs: Anth* (Norton, 1995), *Blue Unicorn, Hudson Rev, Threepenny Rev, Portland Rev, Chattahoochee Rev, Hawaii Pacific Rev, Poet Lore.*

Richard Cortez Day   W
PO Box 947, Arcata, CA 95518-0947, 707-822-8877
Internet: rcd1@axe.humboldt.edu
    Pubs: *When In Florence* (Doubleday, 1986), *Imagining
    Worlds: Anth* (McGraw-Hill, 1995), *Kenyon Rev, Quarterly
    West, Redbook, Carolina Qtly, NER, Witness.*

Jacqueline De Angelis   P&W
3244 Madera Ave, Los Angeles, CA 90039, 213-663-8354
Internet: jdeangelis@yahoo.com
    Pubs: *The Main Gate* (Paradise, 1984), *Hers: Anth* (Faber &
    Faber, 1996), *In a Different Light: Anth* (Clothespin Fever Pr,
    1988), *Agni, International Qtly, Rara Avis, Momentum Mag.*

Viviana Chamberlin De Aparicio   P&W
1769 Las Lunas St, Pasadena, CA 91106, 213-793-8379

Terri de la Pena   W
Univ California, 405 Hilgard Ave, Los Angeles, CA 90024,
310-206-1853
Internet: terrid@college.ucla.edu
    Pubs: *Latin Satins, Margins* (Seal Pr, 1994, 1992), *Chicana
    Lesbians: Anth* (Third Woman Pr, 1992), *Lesbian Rev of
    Bks, Conmocion, Matrix.*

Ruth de Menezes   P
2821 Arizona Ave, Santa Monica, CA 90404, 510-828-2868
Internet: e-mail 310-453-8448
    Pubs: *The Heart's Far Cry* (Small Poetry Pr, 1996), *Love
    Ascending* (Trinity Comm, 1987), *Woman Songs*
    (Claremont Pr, 1982), *Poetic Voices Of America: Anth*
    (Sparrowgrass Poetic Forum, 1998), *America, Catholic
    World, Magnificat, St. Anthony Messenger, Visions.*

Richard De Mille   W
960 Lilac Dr, Santa Barbara, CA 93108, 805-969-4887
    Pubs: *Two Qualms & A Quirk* (Capra Pr, 1973), *Antioch
    Rev.*

John Deming   W
16634 McCormick, Encino, CA 91436, 818-501-5059
    Pubs: *Descant, Crosscurrents, Chariton Rev, Richmond
    Qtly, Uncommon Reader, Missouri Rev, Other Voices.*

Diane di Prima   P&W
PO Box 410990 Suite 346, San Francisco, CA 94141,
415-841-0717
    Pubs: *Loba: Books 1 & 2* (Peguin, 1998), *Pieces of a Song*
    (City Lights, 1990), *Unsettling America: Anth* (Viking, 1994),
    *L.A. Times Book Rev, Disclosure, Paterson Lit Rev, Yoga
    Jrnl, Heaven Bone, First Intensity, Mother Jones, Long
    News in a Short Century.*

N. A. Diaman   W
Box 14022, San Francisco, CA 941140022, 415-775-6143
Internet: personapro@aol.com
    Pubs: *Private Nation, Castro Street Memories, Reunion, Ed
    Dean Is Queer* (Persona Pr, 1997, 1988, 1983, 1978).

Ray Clark Dickson   P&W
Kerouac Connection/Beloit Poet, 1978 Oceanaire Dr, San
Luis Obispo, CA 93405-6829, 805-773-6530
    Pubs: *Saturday Evening Post, Wormwood Rev,
    HaightAshbury Literary Jrnl, Coffeehouse Poets' Qtly, Beloit
    Poetry Jrnl.*

Gavin Geoffrey Dillard   P
Star Rte, 5 Cherry, Bolinas, CA 94924-9705, 415-868-0650
    Pubs: *Between the Cracks* (Daedalus, 1996), *Yellow Snow,
    The Naked Poet, Pagan Love Songs* (Bhakti, 1994, 1992,
    1989), *In the Flesh* (Penguin, 1993).

Millicent G. Dillon   W
83 6th Ave, San Francisco, CA 94118-1323
    Pubs: *Dance of the Mothers, After Egypt* (Dutton, 1991,
    1990), *The One in the Back Is Medea* (Viking, 1973),
    Southwest Rev, Ascent, Threepenny Rev.

Chitra Banerjee Divakaruni   P&W
Foothill College, English Dept, Los Altos, CA 94022,
415-949-7250
    Pubs: *Black Candle* (Calyx Bks, 1991), *The Reason for
    Nasturtiums* (Berkeley Poets Pr, 1990), *Ms., Beloit Poetry
    Jrnl, Chicago Rev, Zyzzyva, Chelsea.*

Mario Divok   P
5 Misty Meadow, Irvine, CA 92715, 714-854-1322
    Pubs: *Forbidden Island—Complete Works Two, The
    Birthday* (Triton, 1986, 1984), *Poetalk, California: A Qtly
    Mag, American Poetry.*

Carl Djerassi   P&W
Stanford Univ, Stanford, CA 94305-5080, 650-723-2783
Internet: djerassi@stanford.edu
    Pubs: *Menachem's Seed, The Bourbaki Gambit* (Penguin,
    1998, 1996), *No, Marx, Deceased* (U Georgia Pr, 1998,
    1996), *The Clock Runs Backwards* (Story Line Pr, 1991),
    *Hudson Rev, Southern Rev, New Letters, Grand Street,
    Kenyon Rev, Midwest Rev.*

Harriet Doerr   W
494 Bradford St, Pasadena, CA 91105
    Pubs: *The Tiger in the Grass, Stones for Ibarra* (Viking,
    1995, 1984), *Consider This, Senora* (HB, 1993), *Under an
    Aztec Sun* (Yolla Bolly Pr, 1990).

Richard Dokey   W
4471 W Kingdon Rd, Lodi, CA 95242, 209-463-8314
    Pubs: *Late Harvest* (Paragon Hse, 1992), *Intro to Literature:
    Anth, Intro to Fiction: Anth* (Norton, 1995, 1995),
    TriQuarterly, Missouri Rev, Southwest Rev, New Letters.

Diane C. Donovan   P
12424 Mill St, Petaluma, CA 94952-9728
    Pubs: *General Store, Tightrope, Owlflight, Night Voyages,
    The Bookwatch, Kliatt Book Guide.*

Carol Dorf   P&W
1400 Delaware St, Berkeley, CA 94702, 510-848-4701
    Pubs: *A Breath Would Destroy That Symmetry* (E.G. San
    Francisco, 1989), *Feminist Studies, Five Fingers Rev,
    Liberty Hill, Heresies, Caprice, Metaphors.*

Philip Dow   P
2193 Ethel Porter Dr, Napa, CA 94558, 707-224-9463
    Pubs: *19 New American Poets of the Golden Gate: Anth*
    (HBJ, 1985), *Boundary 2.*

Frank Dwyer   P
2345 Merton Ave #118, Eagle Rock, CA 90041,
213-258-6173
    Pubs: *John Adams, King James I, King Henry VIII, Danton*
    (Chelsea House, 1989, 1988, 1988, 1987).

Kathryn Eberly   P&W
301 Precita Ave, #2, San Francisco, CA 94110,
415-824-5809
Internet: keberly164@aol.com
    Pubs: *Women and Death* (Ground Torpedo Pr, 1996), *It's
    All The Rage: Anth* (Andrew Mountain Pr, 1997), *If I Had A
    Hammer: Women's Work in Poetry & Fiction: Anth*
    (Papier-Mache Pr, 1990), *Rhino, Evergreen Chronicles,
    Ruah.*

Bart Edelman   P
394 Elmwood Dr, Pasadena, CA 91105, 213-340-8121
Internet: bedelman@glendale.cc.ca.us
    Pubs: *Under Damaris' Dress* (Lightning Pub, 1996),
    Crossing the Hackensack (Prometheus Pr, 1993).

Nancy Edwards   P
Bakersfield College, 1801 Panorama Dr, Bakersfield, CA
93305, 805-831-1067
    Pubs: *The Woman Within* (Bakersfield College, 1994),
    *Network Africa, Orpheus, Amelia, Roadrunner, The Plastic
    Tower, CQ, Little Balkans Rev, The Forum.*

Susan Efros   P
41 Pine Dr, Fairfax, CA 94930
    Pubs: *Two Way Streets* (Jungle Garden Pr, 1976), *This Is
    Women's Work: Anth* (Panjandrum Pr, 1974), *Amelia,
    Footwork, Lowell Pearl, Ascent, Paris Transcontinental,
    Christopher Street.*

Terry Ehret   P
924 Sunnyslope Rd, Petaluma, CA 94952, 707-762-2698
    Pubs: *Lost Body* (Copper Canyon Pr, 1993), *Suspensions*
    (White Mountain Pr, 1990), *How We Go On Living: Anth*
    (Protean Pr, 1995), *Nimrod.*

Samuel A. Eisenstein   P&W
1015 Prospect Blvd, Pasadena, CA 91103
    Pubs: *Price of Admission, The Inner Garden* (Sun & Moon
    Pr, 1992, 1986).

el rivera   PP
1036 S Bonson, #4, Los Angeles, CA 90019-3216
    Pubs: *A Woman's Reading: Blues at Midnight Special,
    Black Gold at The World Stage, Autumn Leaves at The
    Black Gallery, Summation at Highways Performance
    Space.*

Gary Elder   P&W
95 Carson Ct, Shelter Cove, Whitethorn, CA 95589,
707-986-7700
    Pubs: *Arnulfsaga* (Dustbooks, 1979), *The Far Side of the
    Storm: Anth* (San Marcos, 1975).

Sergio D. Elizondo   P
627 Lilac Ln, Imperial, CA 92251, 619-353-8233
    Pubs: *Suruma* (Dos Pasos, 1990), *Muerte en una Estrella*
    (Sainz-Luiselli, 1984).

Ellen   P
6353 Malibu Park Ln, Malibu, CA 90265, 310-457-3585
    Pubs: *In the Garden: Anth* (International Forum, 1996),
    Women of the 14th Moon: Anth (Crossing Pr, 1991), *ACM,
    Slant, COE Rev, Coastal Forest Rev, Prime Time, Blue
    Unicorn.*

Ella Thorp Ellis   W
1438 Grizzly Peak, Berkeley, CA 94708, 510-549-9871
Internet: ehellis@ieee.org
    Pubs: *Swimming With The Whales* (Holt, 1995), *Hugo &
    The Princess Nina, Sleepwalkers Moon* (Atheneum, 1983,
    1980), *Mademoiselle.*

Kenneth Ellsworth   P&W
6055 Calmfleld Ave, Agoura Hills, CA 91301, 818-991-4757
    Pubs: *Christian Blues: Anth* (Amador Pub, 1995), *Black
    Buzzard Rev, Rivertalk, Toast, Illya's Honey, California
    Qtly, Farmer's Market, Atom Mind, Sell Outs, Gargoyle,
    Iconoclast, Bohemian Chronicle, Verve, Buffalo Bones,
    Etcetera, Knocked.*

Alan C. Engebretsen   P
8220 Rayford Dr, Los Angeles, CA 90045, 310-649-1645
    Pubs: *A Rage of Blue* (Poetic Justice, 1985), *California
    State Poetry Qtly, Wind, Pudding Mag, Prophetic Voices,
    Orphic Lute, Proof Rock, Amelia.*

Charles Entrekin   P&W
10736 Indian Shack Rd, Nevada City, CA 95959
    Pubs: *In This Hour, Casting for the Cutthroat* (Berkeley
    Poets, 1988, 1980), *Madison Rev, Passager, Xanadu,
    Literature of Work, Birmingham Poetry Rev.*

Catherine Henley Erickson   P
764 Valparaiso, Claremont, CA 91711, 9095933511x435
Internet: henleyer@ulv.edu
    Pubs: *Contemporary Women Poets: Anth* (Merlin Pr, 1977),
    Rara Avis, Beyond Baroque, Poetry/L.A..

John Espey W
Univ California, 405 Hilgard Ave, Los Angeles, CA 90024,
213-825-4173
    Pubs: *Winter Return, Two Schools of Thought* (w/C. See),
Strong Drink, Strong Language (Daniel, 1992, 1991, 1990),
The Nine Lives of Algernon (Capra Pr, 1988).

Maria Espinosa W
3396 Orchard Valley Ln, Lafayette, CA 94549, 510-283-4314
Internet: paulamar@aol.com
    Pubs: *Dark Plums, Longing, Three Day Flight: Anth* (Arte
Publico Pr, 1995, 1995, 1994).

Rudy Espinosa W
250 Drake St, San Francisco, CA 94112, 415-585-0395

David Evanier W
2213 Glendon Ave, Los Angeles, CA 90064-2008,
310-470-9525
    Pubs: *Red Love* (Scribner, 1991), *Congregation* (HBJ,
1988), *The One-Star Jew* (North Point, 1983), *New
Republic, Paris Rev, Antioch Rev, NAW.*

George Evans P
1590 21st Ave, San Francisco, CA 94122
    Pubs: *Sudden Dreams: New & Selected Poems* (Coffee
Hse Pr, 1991), *Conjunctions, New Directions, Sulfur.*

Martha Evans P
1022 57th St, Oakland, CA 94608, 415-653-5566
    Pubs: *New Letters, Chelsea, New York Qtly, Chicago Rev,
CutBank, Synapse, Ironwood.*

Mary Fabilli P
2445 Ashby Ave, Berkeley, CA 94705, 510-841-6300
    Pubs: *Winter Poems* (Inverno Pr, 1983), *Aurora Bligh &
Early Poems* (Oyez, 1968), *Talisman, To, Sierra Jrnl,
Banner Bks.*

Marcia Falk P
2905 Benvenue Ave, Berkeley, CA 94705, 510-548-8018
Internet: marciafalk@aol.com
    Pubs: *Book of Blessings, Song of Songs* (Harper, 1996,
1990), *This Year in Jerusalem* (State Street, 1986), *Nice
Jewish Girls: Anth* (Plume, 1996), *APR, Women's Rev of
Bks, Tikkun, PSA Bulletin, Anth of Mag Verse and
Yearbook of American Poetry.*

Thomas Farber W
Box 2, 1678 Shattuck Ave, Berkeley, CA 94709,
510-644-4193
    Pubs: *The Face of the Deep* (Mercury Hse, 1998), *Through
A Liquid Mirror* (Editions Limited, 1997), *On Water* (Ecco Pr,
1994), *Learning to Love It* (Capra Pr, 1993).

Dion N. Farquhar P&W
249 Dickens Way, Santa Cruz, CA 95064, 408-425-8680
Internet: hml@cats.ucsc.edu
    Pubs: *Sulfur, Crazyquilt, Poet Lore, Visions, And Then,
Hawaii Rev, Red Bass, Painted Bride Qtly, Alea, Asylum,
Boundary 2, Burning Cloud Rev, Vowel Movement, Juxta.*

Curtis Faville P
34 Franciscan Way, Kensington, CA 94707, 415-526-3412

Jean Femling W
2384 Cornell Dr, Costa Mesa, CA 92626, 714-549-2493
Internet: jfemling@aol.com
    Pubs: *Getting Mine, Hush, Money* (St. Martin's, 1991,
1989), *Interfaces: Anth* (Ace, 1980), *Backyard* (H&R, 1975),
Descant.

Paul Fericano P&W
PO Box 236, Millbrae, CA 94030
    Pubs: *The One-Minute President* (w/Ligi), *Sinatra, Sinatra*
(Poor Souls Pr, 1987, 1982), *Stoogism Anth* (Scarecrow
Bks, 1977), *Wormwood Rev, Realist, Krokodil, Second
Coming, Free Lunch, Wine Rings.*

Lawrence Ferlinghetti P&W
City Lights Books, 261 Columbus Ave, San Francisco, CA
94133, 415-362-1901
    Pubs: *These Are My Rivers: New and Selected Poems
1955-1993* (New Directions, 1993), *Love in the Days of
Rage* (Dutton/Penguin, 1989).

Anne Finger W
5809 Fremont, Oakland, CA 94608, 570-658-7513
    Pubs: *Bone Truth* (Coffee Hse Pr, 1994), *Past Due* (Seal
Pr, 1990), *Kenyon Rev, Southern Rev, Antioch Rev, 13th
Moon, Feminist Studies, Kaleidoscope.*

Molly Fisk P
PO Box 592, Stinson Beach, CA 94970, 415-868-1248
    Pubs: *Salt Water Poems* (Jungle Garden Pr, 1994), *Love's
Shadow: Anth* (Crossing Pr, 1993), *Harvard Rev, Manoa,
Zyzzyva, Poetry East, Passages North, Calyx.*

Lawrence Fixel P&W
1496 Willard St, San Francisco, CA 94117, 415-661-3870
    Pubs: *Unlawful Assembly: Poems 1940-1992* (Cloud
Forms, 1994), *Truth, War, And The Dream-Game: Selected
Prose Poems And Parables* (Coffee Hse Pr, 1992).

Ted Fleischman P
13 El Camino Moraga, Orinda, CA 94563, 510-376-3431
    Pubs: *Half a Bottle of Catsup, Berkeley Poets Cooperative
Anth* (Berkeley Poets Pr, 1978, 1980), *Berkeley Poets
Co-op, Outerbridge, In a Nutshell.*

Gerald Fleming   P
PO Box 529, Lagunitas, CA 949380529, 415-488-4226
Internet: uncleennui@aol.com
    Pubs: *Seeds Flying in a Fresh Light* (Allyn & Bacon, 1990),
    *New Letters, Volt, Five Fingers Rev, Puerto del Sol,
    Americas Rev, Pequod.*

Stewart Florsheim   P
170 Sandringham Rd, Piedmont, CA 94611, 510-530-7773
Internet: stew@sirius.com
    Pubs: *Unsettling America: Anth* (Viking Penguin, 1994),
    Ghosts of the Holocaust: Anth (Wayne State U Pr, 1989),
    *DoubleTake, Karamu, Dimension, Round Table, Blue
    Unicorn, Berkeley Poets Cooperative.*

Jack Foley   P&W
2569 Maxwell Ave, Oakland, CA 94601-5521, 510-532-3737
Internet: jasfoley@aol.com
    Pubs: *Advice to the Lovelorn* (Texture Pr, 1998), *New
    Poetry from California: Dead/Requiem* (w/Ivan Arquelles),
    Exiles, Adrift (Pantograph Pr, 1998, 1996, 1993), *O Her
    Blackness Sparkles* (3300 Club Pr, 1995), *Gershwin*
    (Norton Coker Pr, 1991), *Juxta.*

CB Follett   P
PO Box 401, Sausalito, CA 949660401, 415-331-2503
Internet: runes@aol.com
    Pubs: *Visible Bones* (Plain View Pr, 1998), *Gathering the
    Mountains, The Latitude of Their Going* (Hot Pepper Pr,
    1995, 1993), *The MacGuffin, Cumberland Rev, The Bridge,
    Confluence, Calyx, Heaven Bone, New Letters,
    Birmingham Poetry Rev.*

Elizabeth Foote-Smith   P&W
2635 Regent St, Berkeley, CA 94704, 510-849-0800
    Pubs: *Never Say Die, Gentle Albatross* (Putnam, 1980,
    1978), *Michigan Qtly Rev.*

Jeanne Foster   P
St. Mary's College, PO Box 4700, Moraga, CA 945754700,
925-631-4511
Internet: jfoster@stmarys-ca.edu
    Pubs: *A Blessing of Safe Travel* (QRL, 1980), *Great Horned
    Owl* (White Pine, 1980), *Ploughshares, Hudson Rev,
    TriQuarterly, North American Rev, APR, Paris Rev.*

William L. Fox   P
503 S Fuller Ave, Los Angeles, CA 90036, 213-692-0889
    Pubs: *One Wave Standing* (La Alameda Pr, 1998), *Silence
    and License* (Light & Dust, 1994), *Geograph* (Black Rock
    Pr, 1994), *TumbleWords: Anth* (U Nevada Pr, 1995),
    Caliban, Chain.

Peter Frank   P
PO Box 24 A36, Los Angeles, CA 90024-1036, 310-271-9740
Internet: pfrank@scf.usc.edu
    Pubs: *New, Used & Improved* (Abbeville Pr, 1987),
    Travelogues (Sun & Moon Pr, 1982).

Thaisa Frank   W
459 66thSt, Oakland, CA 94609, 510-658-1225
    Pubs: *Enchanted Men, A Brief History of Camouflage*
    (Black Sparrow Pr, 1994, 1991), *Whole Earth Rev, City
    Lights Rev, Forehead.*

Kathleen Fraser   P
1936 Leavenworth St, San Francisco, CA 94133,
415-474-8911
Internet: kfraser@sfsu.edu
    Pubs: *il cuore: the heart, Selected Poems 1970-1997*
    (Wesleyan U Pr, 1997), *When New Time Folds Up* (Chax,
    1993), *Chicago Rev, Conjunctions, Talisman.*

Devery Freeman   W
9481 Cherokee Ln, Beverly Hills, CA 90210, 213-274-3606
    Pubs: *Father Sky* (Morrow, 1979), *American Mag, Liberty.*

Melvyn Freilicher   PP&P
3945 Normal St, #5, San Diego, CA 92103, 619-299-4859
    Pubs: *River Styx, New Novel Rev, Fiction Intl, Frame-Work:
    Jrnl of Images & Culture, EL-E-PHANT: Language Arts
    Rev, Central Park, Crawl Out Your Window.*

Elliot Fried   P
Cal State Univ, Long Beach, English Dept, Long Beach, CA
90840, 310-433-1998
    Pubs: *Marvel Mystery Oil* (Red Wind Pr, 1991), *New
    Geography of Poets: Anth* (U Arkansas Pr, 1993), *Anth of
    Movie Poetry* (Faber & Faber, 1993), *Green Mtns Rev.*

S. L. Friedman   P
732 N June St, Los Angeles, CA 90038, 213-464-5802
Internet: carolineshona@sprynet.com
    Pubs: *Hanging by Our Teeth & Rising by Our Bootstraps,
    Some Light Through the Blindfold* (Friedman, 1991, 1988),
    *Wordworths Socks, Plains Poetry Jrnl, California Poetry
    Jrnl, Quartet, Epos.*

Gloria Frym   P&W
2119 Eunice St, Berkeley, CA 94709, 510-524-6069
    Pubs: *How I Learned* (Coffee Hse Pr, 1992), *By Ear* (Sun &
    Moon Pr, 1991), *The World, Before Columbus, Exquisite
    Corpse, Zyzzyva.*

Daniel Fuchs   W
430 S Fuller Ave, #9C, Los Angeles, CA 90036,
213-935-9090

Blair Fuller   W
565 Connecticut St, San Francisco, CA 94107, 415-824-8132
    Pubs: *A Butterfly Net and A Kingdom* (Creative Arts Bk Co.,
    1989), *Birth of A Fan: Anth* (Macmillan, 1993).

Len Fulton   W
Box 100, Paradise, CA 95967-0100, 916-877-6110
    Pubs: *Dark Other Adam Dreaming* (Dustbooks, 1976), *The
    Grassman* (Penguin, 1975).

Robert Funge   P
PO Box 1225, San Carlos, CA 94070, 650-592-7720
    Pubs: *Daughter* (Small Poetry Pr, 1996), *Literary Rev,
    Hiram Poetry Rev, Hayden's Ferry Rev, Seattle Rev,
    Cumberland Poetry Rev, Midwest Qtly, The Literary Rev,
    Chariton Rev, Libido, Hawaii Rev.*

Gary G. Gach   P
1243 Broadway, #4, San Francisco, CA 94109-2771,
415-771-7793
Internet: ggg@well.com
    Pubs: *What Book!?* (Parallax, 1998), *Two Lines, APR,
    Zyzzyva, Heaven Bone, American Cinematographer, Exiled
    in the World.*

Susan M. Gaines   W
4085 Westside Rd, Healdsburg, CA 95448, 707-431-0714
    Pubs: *Sacred Ground: Writings About Home: Anth*
    (Milkweed Edtns, 1996), *Best of the West: Anth* (Norton,
    1992), *Cream City Rev, NAR, Missouri Rev.*

Kate Gale   P&W
Red Hen Press, PO Box 902582, Palmdale, CA 93590-2582,
818-831-0649
Internet: kgale@bigfoot.com
    Pubs: *Where Crows and Men Collide, Blue Air* (Red Hen
    Pr, 1995, 1995), *Water Moccasins* (Tidal Wave Pr, 1994).

Sally M. Gall   P
5820 Folsom Dr, La Jolla, CA 92037-7323
Internet: librettist@aol.com
    Pubs: *Eleanor Roosevelt* (Oxford U Pr, 1996), *Kill Bear
    Comes Home* (VM Music, 1994), *Southern Rev,
    Ploughshares, Confrontation, Present Tense, Missouri Rev,
    The Humanist, Footwork.*

Dick Gallup   P
1450 Castro St, #17, San Francisco, CA 94114,
415-550-0638
Internet: ice@tlcs.com
    Pubs: *Plumbing the Depths of Folly* (Smithereens Pr,
    1983), *Where I Hang My Hat* (H&R, 1967).

Reymundo Gamboa   P&W
408 Chaparral, Santa Maria, CA 93454, 805-922-1339
    Pubs: *Cenzotle: Chicano Literary Prize* (U California Irvine,
    1988), *The Baby Chook And Other Remnants* (Other
    Voices, 1976), *Chicanos: Antologia Historica de Literatura*
    (Fondo de Cultura Economica, 1980), *Denver Qtly, Morning
    of '56, El Oficio, Script.*

evvy garrett   P
PO Box 7155, San Diego, CA 921677155, 619-226-7310
Internet: egarrett@ix.netcom.com
    Pubs: *New York Qtly, AKA, Pearl, Capper's, Arizona
    Unconservative, Rant, Alura, December Rose, Copper Hill
    Qtly, Poetic Space, Radient Woman.*

Phyllis Gebauer   W
515 W Scenic Dr, Monrovia, CA 91016, 626-303-4154
    Pubs: *The Pagan Blessing* (Viking, 1979), *Iowa English
    Bulletin, Modern Maturity, Sight Lines.*

Merrill Joan Gerber   W
542 Santa Anita Ct, Sierra Madre, CA 910242623,
626-355-0384
Internet: www.cco.caltech.edu/ mjgerber
    Pubs: *Anna In Chains* (Syracuse U Pr, 1998), *Old Mother,
    Little Cat, The Kingdom of Brooklyn* (Longstreet Pr, 1995,
    1992), *New Yorker, Atlantic, Redbook, Sewanee Rev,
    Shenandoah, Commentary.*

Amy Gerstler   P&W
4430 Palo Verde Terr, San Diego, CA 92115
    Pubs: *Crown of Weeds, Nerve Storm* (Viking Penguin,
    1997, 1993), *Bitter Angel* (North Point Pr, 1990).

Art Gibney   W
PO Box 711, Fairfax, CA 949780771
    Pubs: *Story Qtly, Zyzzyva, Estero, Clockwatch Rev,
    Tennessee Qtly, International Qtly, South Dakota Rev.*

Barry Gifford   P&W
833 Bancroft Way, Berkeley, CA 94710, 510-848-4956
    Pubs: *The Sinaloa Sotry, The Phantom Father: A Memoir,
    Baby Cat-Face* (HB, 1998, 1997, 1995), *Hotel Room Trilogy*
    (U Pr Mississippi, 1995), *First Intensity, Esquire, Rolling
    Stone, Hot Wired, Speak, Shenandoah, Projections, Buzz,
    Panta, Exquisite Corpse.*

D.H.L. Gilbert   W
514 Lighthouse Ave, Santa Cruz, CA 95060, 408-458-1454
    Pubs: *Iowa Rev, Northwest Rev, NAR, Antioch Rev, Quarry
    West.*

Dorothy Gilbert   P
784 Baylor Ave, Claremont, CA 91711, 415-848-4881
    Pubs: *Iowa Rev, Epoch, Nation, New Yorker, The
    Spectator, CQ.*

Jack Gilbert   P
136 Montana St, San Francisco, CA 94112, 415-585-6055
    Pubs: *Kochan* (Tamarack Pr, 1984), *Monolithos* (Knopf,
    1983), *Views of Jeopardy* (Yale U Pr, 1962).

Sandra M. Gilbert   P&W
Univ California, English Dept, Davis, CA 95616,
916-752-2257
Internet: sgilbert@ucdavis.edu
    Pubs: *Wrongful Death: A Medical Tragedy, Ghost Volcano:
    Poems* (Norton, 1995, 1995), *Poetry, Ontario Rev, Kenyon
    Rev, Poetry Northwest, Field, APR.*

Anna-Carolyn Stirewa Gilbo   P
17th ASG CM, Box 3623, Unit 45013 APO AP, CA 96338
    Pubs: *Weymouth* (St. Andrews Pr, 1987), *I Hate You! Love,
    Don* (Lexis Pr, 1985), *Black Sun.*

Elizabeth Gilchrist W
1915 El Camino de la Luz, Santa Barbara, CA 93109,
805-963-3108
Pubs: *Second Chances* (Dell, 1986), *Your Cheatin' Heart*
(Macmillan, 1979).

Molly Giles W
PO Box 137, Woodacre, CA 94973
Pubs: *Rough Translations* (U Georgia Pr, 1985), *Caprice,
San Jose Studies, Real Fiction, Manoa, Greensboro Rev,
McCall's, Sundog, Shenandoah.*

S. E. Gilman P&W
1725 Lehigh Dr, Davis, CA 95616, 916-757-1920
Pubs: *Letters to our Children* (Franklin Watts, 1997),
Anyone Can Be A Target, Even Margaret (Consummated
Productions, 1978), *Americas Rev, Modern Words.*

Dana Gioia P
7190 Faught Rd, Santa Rosa, CA 95403, 707-836-0354
Pubs: *The Gods of Winter, Daily Horoscope* (Graywolf Pr,
1991, 1986), *Hudson Rev, Poetry, New Yorker.*

Robert Franklin Gish W
PO Box 947, San Luis Obispo, CA 93406, 805-756-2304
Internet: www.lavaland.com
Pubs: *Dreams of Quivira* (Clear Light Pub, 1998), *Bad Boys
and Black Sheep, First Horses* (U Nevada Pr, 1993), *North
Dakota Qtly, New Mexico Mag, Mirage, Urbanus.*

David Gitin P
PO Box 1792, Monterey, CA 93942, 408-646-9181
Pubs: *Fire Dance, This Once* (Blue Wind, 1989, 1979),
Vacuum Tapestries (BB Bks, 1981), *Intent, Paideuma,
Poetry Flash.*

Maria Gitin P
287 La Vida Rd, Aptos, CA 95003, 408-722-8535
Internet: msgitin@got.net
Pubs: *Night Shift* (Blue Wind Pr, 1978), *The Melting Pot*
(Crossing Pr, 1977), *Little Movies* (Ithaca Hse, 1976), *In
Celebration of the Muse: Anth* (Quarry West/UC Santa
Cruz, 1997), *Poetry Flash, Alternative Press, Telephone,
Sun & Moon, Hanging Loose.*

Jan Glading P
1536 9th St #D, Alameda, CA 94501, 510-521-7366
Pubs: *Gridlock: Anth* (Applezaba Pr, 1990), *Peace or
Perish: Anth* (Poets for Peace, 1983), *Napa Rev,
Kaleidoscope, Disability.*

David Glotzer P
1648 Waller, San Francisco, CA 94117, 415-752-1278
Pubs: *Occasions Of Grace* (Heron Pr, 1979), *Mulch, River
Styx, Lillabulero, Works, B'way Boogie.*

Robert Gluck P&W
4303 20th St, San Francisco, CA 94114, 415-821-3004
Internet: chrisko@sirius.com
Pubs: *Jack the Modernist, Margery Kempe* (Serpent's Tail
Bks/High Risk, 1995, 1994), *Reader* (Lapis Pr, 1989).

Dale Going P
541 Ethel Ave, Mill Valley, CA 94941, 415-381-1243
Internet: dalegoing@aol.com
Pubs: *The View They Arrange* (Kelsey Street Pr, 1994),
She Pushes With Her Hands, Or Less (Em Pr, 1992, 1991).

Herbert Gold W
1051-A Broadway, San Francisco, CA 94133, 415-673-1761
Pubs: *Bohemia: Digging the Roots of Cool, Best Nightmare
on Earth: A Life in Haiti* (S&S, 1993, 1991), *Travel &
Leisure, New York Times Mag, Islands.*

Reuven Goldfarb P
2020 Essex St, Berkeley, CA 94703, 510-848-0965
Pubs: *To Be a Jew...* (Inter-oco Pr, 1977), *New Menorah,
Exquisite Corpse, Oxygen, Voice of the Trees, Agada,
Robert Frost Rev.*

Stephen Goldin W
2709 Bettancourt Ln, #36, Rancho Cordova, CA 95670
Pubs: *The Eternity Brigade* (Fawcett, 1980).

Juan Gomez-Quinones P
507 Grande Vista Ave, Los Angeles, CA 90063
Pubs: *5th And Grande Vista* (Editorial Mensaje, 1974),
Revista Chicano-Riquena.

Jorge R. Gonzalez P
1615 San Leandro Ln, Santa Barbara, CA 93108

N. V. M. Gonzalez W
California State Univ, English Dept, Hayward, CA 94542
Pubs: *The Bread of Salt & Other Stories* (Washington U Pr,
1993), *Mindoro And Beyond* (Hawaii U Pr, 1991), *A Season
Of Grace* (BkMk Pr, 1975).

Rafael Jesus Gonzalez P&W
2514 Woolsey St, Berkeley, CA 94705, 510-841-5903
Internet: rjgonzal@sirius.com
Pubs: *El Hacedor De Juegos/The Maker Of Games* (Casa
Editorial, 1978), *West Coast Rev, Contact II.*

Cesar A. Gonzalez-T. P&W
San Diego Mesa College, 7250 Mesa College Dr, San Diego,
CA 92111, 619-627-2751
Pubs: *Unwinding the Silence* (Lalo-Bilingual Pr, 1987),
Paper Dance: Anth (Persea Bks, 1995), *San Diego Writers
Monthly, Prairie Schooner, Bilingual Rev.*

Mary Lee Gowland P
49386 Cavin Ln, Coarsegold, CA 93614, 209-683-6876
Pubs: *Remembering August* (Mountain Arts Council, 1994), *Fresno Bee, Onthebus, Z Miscellaneous, Rag Mag, Poetry/L.A. Sculpture Gardens Rev, Fat Tuesday*.

Taylor Graham P
PO Box 39, Somerset, CA 95684, 530-621-1833
Internet: jalapep@innercite.com
Pubs: *Casualties* (Coal City, 1995), *Looking For Lost* (Hot Pepper Pr, 1991), *Ascent, The MacGuffin, Maryland Poetry Rev, Santa Clara Rev, Willow Springs, America, Iowa Rev, Passages North, Southern Humanities Rev, 1997 Anth of Mag Verse*.

Toni Graham W
345 Prospect Ave, San Francisco, CA 94110, 415-641-7858
Pubs: *The Daiquiri Girls* (U Massachussetts Pr, 1998), *Mississippi Rev, American Fiction, Ascent, Clockwatch Rev, Worcester Rev, Green Mountains Rev, Writers' Forum, Mississippi Mud, The Bridge*.

Judy Grahn P&W
4221 Terrace St, Oakland, CA 94611-5127
Pubs: *Mundane's World* (Crossing Pr, 1988), *The Queen of Swords, Another Mother Tongue* (Beacon Pr, 1987, 1984).

Cynthia D. Grant W
Box 95, Cloverdale, CA 954250095, 707-894-3420
Pubs: *The White Horse, Mary Wolf, Uncle Vampire, Shadow Man, Keep Laughing* (Atheneum, 1998, 1995, 1993, 1993, 1991).

Jack Grapes P
6684 Colgate Ave, Los Angeles, CA 90048, 213-651-5488
Pubs: *Trees, Coffee, And the Eyes of Deer* (Bombshelter Pr, 1987), *Men of Our Time: Anth* (U Georgia Pr, 1992), *The Maverick Poets: Anth* (Gorilla Pr, 1988).

Wallace Graves W
California State Univ, Northridge, CA 91330, 818-885-3431

Alice Wirth Gray P&W
1001 Merced St, Berkeley, CA 94707, 510-524-8958
Internet: awgray@aol.com
Pubs: *What the Poor Eat* (Cleveland State U Poetry Ctr, 1993), *American Scholar, Atlantic, Poetry*.

Benjamin Green P&W
3415 Patricks Point Dr #3, Trinidad, CA 95570, 707-677-3084
Pubs: *Beyond Roses are Red...* (Cottonwood Pr, 1996), *The Sound of Fish Dreaming* (Bellowing Ark, 1996), *Green Grace* (Punla Pub, 1993), *Monologs from the Realm of Silence* (Ransom Note Pub, 1990).

Geoffrey Green W
San Francisco State Univ, 1600 Holloway Ave, San Francisco, CA 94132, 415-338-7414
Internet: ggreen@sfsu.edu
Pubs: *Freud and Nabokov, Literary Criticism & the Structures of History* (U Nebraska Pr, 1988, 1983), *Fiction*.

Suzanne Greenberg W
257 1/2 Park Ave, Long Beach, CA 90803
Pubs: *New Virginia Rev, Indiana Rev, Turnstile, Mississippi Rev, The Washington Rev, Florida Rev*.

Linda Gregg P
PO Box 475, Forest Knolls, CA 949330475, 415-488-9587
Pubs: *Chosen by the Lion, The Sacraments of Desire* (Graywolf, 1994, 1991), *Paris Rev, Atlantic, The Quarterly, TriQuarterly, Columbia Rev, Partisan Rev, Ploughshares*.

Arpine Konyalian Grenier P
990 S Marengo Ave, Pasadena, CA 91106, 626-441-3249
Pubs: *Whores From Samarkand* (Florida Literary Foundation Pr, 1993), *St. Gregory's Daughter* (U La Verne Pr, 1991), *Columbia Poetry Rev, Iowa Rev, Tinfish, Sulfur, CQ, Kiosk*.

Susan Griffin P&W
904 Keeler Ave, Berkeley, CA 94708-1420
Pubs: *Bending Home Poems Selected and New, Unremembered Country* (Copper Canyon, 1998, 1988), *A Chorus of Stones: The Private Life of War* (Doubleday, 1992), *Utne Reader, L.A. Times, City Lights Rev, Mother Jones, APR*.

Morton Grinker P
1367 Noe St, San Francisco, CA 94131, 415-648-0272
Pubs: *The Gran Phenician Rover: Book 5, Books 1-4, To the Straying Aramaean* (Thorp Springs, 1994, 1992, 1972).

Hugh Gross W
880 N Hilldale Ave #16, West Hollywood, CA 90069, 310-652-5844
Pubs: *16 Bananas, Same Bed, Different Dreams* (Mid-List Pr, 1995, 1991).

Richard Grossinger W
258 Yale Ave, Kensington, CA 94708
Internet: chard@lanminds.com
Pubs: *Out of Babylon, New Moon* (Frog Ltd, 1997, 1996), *The Night Sky* (J.P. Tarcher, 1988), *Embryogenesis* (North Atlantic Bks, 1986).

Richard Grossman P
2050 Cummings Dr, Los Angeles, CA 90027, 213-665-2116
Internet: museumpoet@aol.com
Pubs: *The Alphabet Man* (Fiction Collective, 1993), *The Animals* (Graywolf, 1990), *Tycoon Boy* (Kayak, 1977).

Mark Grover   P&W
PO Box 2369, Del Mar, CA 92014, 619-755-0544
    Pubs: *What Touched His Life* (Noble Crown, 1995), *Words & Poets* (Revorg, 1994).

Albert J. Guerard   W
Stanford Univ, Stanford, CA 94305, 415-327-6687
    Pubs: *The Hotel in the Jungle* (Baskerville Pub, 1996), *Gabrielle* (Donald I. Fine, 1992), *Christine/Annette* (Dutton, 1985), *Fiction.*

Judith Guest   W
Patricia Karlan Agency, 3575 Cahvenga Blvd Suite 210, Los Angeles, CA 90068, 818-752-4800
    Pubs: *Errands* (Ballantine Bks, 1997), *The Mythic Family* (Milkweed Edtns, 1988), *Ordinary People* (Viking-Penguin Pr, 1976).

Thom Gunn   P
1216 Cole St, San Francisco, CA 94117
    Pubs: *Collected Poems, The Man With Night Sweats* (FSG, 1994, 1992), *Threepenny Rev, New Yorker, Times Literary Supplement.*

Carol L. Gunther   P
PO Box 876, Sutter Creek, CA 95685, 209-267-0332
    Pubs: *The Return of Mr. Trespass* (Black Tape Pr, 1990), *Cincinnati Poetry Rev, Boston Literary Rev.*

Katharine Haake   W
California State Univ, Northridge, CA 91330
    Pubs: *No Reason on Earth* (Dragon Gate, 1986), *Iowa Rev, Mississippi Rev, Minnesota Rev, Michigan Qtly Rev, Quarterly West, Witness, NER/BLQ.*

Philip Hackett   P
PO Box 330168, San Francisco, CA 94133
    Pubs: *Selected Poems* (Madras, India, 1998), *Two American Poets* (Little City Pr, 1997), *Iraq, Jordan, and Egypt Poems, Poems To My Son Dylan* (Pegasus, 1994, 1992), *Boston Mag, Electrum, Stone Country, Deep Valley, A Publications, Haight Ashbury.*

D. R. Hakim   P
Prometheus Press, PO Box 1569, Glendale, CA 91209
    Pubs: *Posed Perfectly in Dreams, Smoke of Signal Dreams* (Prometheus Pr, 1992, 1989), *Verve, L.A. Driver, The Moment, Counterfeit Monday, Red Dance Floor.*

Jane Hall   P&W
1516 Euclid Ave, Berkeley, CA 94708, 510-849-2540
    Pubs: *Anth of New England Writers* (New England Writers, 1997), *Fourteen Hills, Berkeley Poetry Rev, Ruah, Sonoma Literary Rev, Americas Rev.*

Judith Hall   P
3544 Ocean Dr, Oxnard, CA 93035
    Pubs: *Anatomy, Errata* (Ohio State, 1998), *To Put The Mouth To* (Morrow, 1992).

Irving Halperin   W
San Francisco State Univ, 1600 Holloway Ave, San Francisco, CA 94132, 415-338-2578
    Pubs: *Here I Am: A Jew in Today's Germany* (Westminster Pr, 1971), *Prairie Schooner, Massachusetts Rev, New England Rev.*

James A. Hamby   P
Drawer 1124, Arcata, CA 95521, 707-826-4189
    Pubs: *New Mexico Mag, Idaho Heritage, Pandora, Western Rev, South Dakota Rev.*

Forrest Hamer   P
5275 Miles Ave, Oakland, CA 94618, 510-601-6334
Internet: FHamer8580@aol.com
    Pubs: *Call and Response* (Alice James Bks, 1995), *Best American Poetry: Anth* (Scribner, 1994).

Rose Hamilton-Gottlieb   W
2997 Lakeview Way, Fullerton, CA 92835, 714-526-6395
Internet: rjhg@aol.com
    Pubs: *At Our Core: Women Writing About Power: Anth, Grow Old Along With Me: Anth, The Best is Yet to Be: Anth* (Papier-Mache Pr, 1998, 1997, 1996), *Farm Wives & Other Iowa Stories: Anth* (Mid-Prairie Bks, 1995), *The Ear, Room of One's Own.*

Sam Hamod   P
PO Box 927554, San Diego, CA 92192, 619-457-0218
Internet: hhamod1@san.rr.com
    Pubs: *The Arab Poems: New & Selected Poems* (Cedar Creek,1998), *Unsettling America: Anth* (Viking/Penguin, 1994), *Konch, Paterson Rev, Stand.*

Joseph Hansen   P&W
2638 Cullen St, Los Angeles, CA 90034, 213-870-2604
    Pubs: *Living Upstairs* (Dutton, 1993), *Bohannon's Country* (Viking, 1993), *Ellery Queen's Mystery, Alfred Hitchcock's Mystery, South Dakota Rev.*

C. G. Hanzlicek   P
738 E Lansing Way, Fresno, CA 93704, 209-226-1528
Internet: charles_hanzlicek@csufresno.edu
    Pubs: *Against Dreaming* (U Missouri Pr, 1994), *When There Are No Secrets, Calling the Dead* (Carnegie Mellon U Pr, 1986, 1982).

Joy Harjo   P
PO Box 3277, Hollywood, CA 90078, 213-650-0873
Internet: katcvpoet@aol.com
    Pubs: *Reinventing the Enemy's Language, The Woman Who Fell From The Sky* (Norton, 1997, 1994), *The Spiral of Memory* (U Michigan Pr, 1996), *In Mad Love & War* (Wesleyan, 1990).

Alfred Harris   W
29377 Quail Run Dr, Agoura, CA 91301, 818-889-8238
Internet: 102533.3316@compuserve.com
    Pubs: *Bullseye* (Bks in Motion, 1997), *Baroni, The Joseph
    File* (Putnam, 1975, 1974).

Mark Jonathan Harris   W
Univ Southern California, Los Angeles, CA 90089,
213-740-3317
    Pubs: *Solay, Come The Morning* (Bradbury Pr, 1993,
    1989), *Buffalo Mag, New Mexico Humanities Rev.*

William Harrison   W
William Morris Agency, 151 El Camino Dr, Beverly Hills, CA
90212, 310-274-7451
    Pubs: *Three Hunters* (Random Hse, 1989), *Burton and
    Speke* (St. Martin's Pr, 1982).

John Hart   P
PO Box 4262, San Rafael, CA 94913-4166, 415-507-9230
Internet: johnhart@crl.com
    Pubs: *The Climbers* (U Pitt Pr, 1978), *Ascent, Aethlon, Blue
    Unicorn, Interim, Southern Poetry Rev.*

William Hart   P&W
2721 Piedmont #3, Montrose, CA 91020, 818-249-6704
    Pubs: *Paris, Monsoon* (Timberline Pr, 1996, 1991),
    *Commonweal, Black Bear Rev, Florida Rev, Ko, Lilliput
    Rev, Brussels Sprout, Poetry Nippon.*

Suzanne Hartman   W
17290 Redwood Springs Dr, Fort Bragg, CA 95437
Internet: suzanne_byerle@redwoodfn.org
    Pubs: *Kansas Qtly, Mississippi Valley Rev, Ladies Home
    Jrnl, Confrontation, Woman's Day, Gamut.*

Gerald Haslam   W
PO Box 969, Penngrove, CA 949510969, 707-792-2944
Internet: ghaslam@sonic.net
    Pubs: *The Great Tejon Club Jubilee* (Devil Mountain Bks,
    1996), *Condor Dreams and Other Fictions* (U Nevada,
    1994), *The Great Central Valley* (U California, 1993), *Los
    Angeles Times Mag, Nation, Sierra, This World, Sky.*

Robert Hass   P
Box 807, Inverness, CA 94937
    Pubs: *Human Wishes, Twentieth Century Pleasures, Praise*
    (Ecco Pr, 1988, 1984, 1979).

Barbara Hauk   P
10181 Beverly Dr, Huntington Beach, CA 92646-5426,
714-968-7530
    Pubs: *Confetti* (Event Horizon Pr, 1993), *Pearl, Chiron Rev,
    Onthebus, Cape Rock, Genre, Beloit Poetry Jrnl.*

Marjorie Hawksworth   P
2516 Selrose Ln, Santa Barbara, CA 93109, 805-965-8380
    Pubs: *Silent Voices* (Ally Pr, 1978), *Connecticut Poetry
    Rev, Centennial Rev, Pulpsmith, Spectrum, New York Qtly.*

Mary Haynes   P
PO Box 292, Dillon Beach, CA 94929, 707-878-2396
    Pubs: *Temblor, Momentum, Bachy, Chelsea, New Yorker,
    Massachusetts Rev, Canadian Forum, Exile, Boxcar.*

Gwen Head   P
72 Eucalyptus Rd, Berkeley, CA 94705, 510-654-4270
Internet: gth58435@aol.com
    Pubs: *Frequencies: A Gamut of Poems* (U Utah Pr, 1992),
    The Ten Thousandth Night (U Pitt Pr, 1979), *Southern Rev,
    APR, NAR.*

Eloise Klein Healy   P
Antioch Univ Los Angeles, 13274 Fiji Way, Marina Del Rey,
CA 90292, 310-578-1080
Internet: eloise_klein_healy@elmer.antiochla.edu
    Pubs: *Artemis in Echo Park/The Women's Studies
    Chronicle* (CD), *Artemis in Echo Park* (Firebrand, 1994),
    The Arch of Love: Anth (Scribner, 1996), *Solo, High Plains
    Literary Rev, Caffeine, 51%, Poetry L.A..*

Kevin Hearle   P
102 Hobart Ave, San Mateo, CA 94402, 650-571-6390
Internet: kevinhearle@earthlink.net
    Pubs: *Each Thing We Know Is Changed Because We
    Know It and Other Poems* (Ahsahta Pr, 1994), *Georgia
    Rev, Yale Rev, Quarterly West, Windsor Rev, Poetry
    Flash.*

Mary Hedin   P&W
182 Oak Ave, San Anselmo, CA 94960, 415-454-4422
    Pubs: *Direction* (West Country, 1982), *Fly Away Home* (U
    Iowa, 1980).

Anne Hedley   P
5870 Birch Ct, Oakland, CA 94618, 510-655-1430

Leslie Woolf Hedley   P&W
Exile Press, 241 S Temelec Cir, Sonoma, CA 95476
    Pubs: *& Other Stories* (Exile Pr, 1992), *Blood To
    Remember: Poems* (U Texas Tech Pr, 1991), *Baseball:
    The Game of Life* (Birchbook Pr, 1990).

Lyn Hejinian   P
2639 Russell St, Berkeley, CA 94705, 510-548-1817
    Pubs: *The Cold of Poetry, My Life* (Sun & Moon Pr, 1994,
    1987), *Oxota* (The Figures, 1991), *Avec, Grand Street,
    Temblor, Bomb, o.blek, Lingo.*

Padma Hejmadi   W
2135 Humboldt Ave, Davis, CA 95616, 530-753-8538
    Pubs: *Birthday Deathday* (Penguin Bks India, 1992), *Dr.
    Salaam & Other Stories* (Capra Pr, 1978), *Mirrorwork: Anth*
    (Owl Pr, 1997), *New Yorker, Parabola, American Book Rev,
    Southern Rev.*

Carol Henrie   P
24929 Minnie Ct, Hayward, CA 94541, 510-886-1018
    Pubs: *Ironwood, Poetry, Poetry Northwest, New Republic,
    Prairie Schooner, Poetry Flash, Five Fingers Rev.*

Barbara Hernandez   P
1432 Celis St, San Fernando, CA 91340

Elizabeth Carothers Herron   P&W
PO Box 41, Bodega, CA 94922, 707-823-4622
    Pubs: *The Stones The Dark Earth* (Harlequin Ink, 1995),
    While the Distance Widens (Floating Island, 1994), *Desire
    Being Full of Distances* (Calliopea, 1983).

John Herschel   P
Univ California, Q-022, La Jolla, CA 92093, 619-534-3068
    Pubs: *The Floating World* (New Rivers Pr, 1979),
    Minnesota Rev, Invisible City, Seattle Rev, APR.

Donna Hilbert   P&W
5615 Seaside Walk, Long Beach, CA 90803, 562-434-4172
Internet: donnahilbert@earthlink.net
    Pubs: *Deep Red, Mansions* (Event Horizon Pr, 1993,
    1990), *Rosebud, Pearl, Chiron Rev, Staple, Slow Dancer,
    Tears in the Fence.*

Nellie Hill   P&W
1178 Euclid Ave #3, Berkeley, CA 94708, 415-526-5365
    Pubs: *Having Come This Far* (Keeler, 1978), *Sideshow,
    Aikido Today, Harvard Mag, Studia Mystica, Margin,
    American Writing.*

Brenda Hillman   P
St. Mary's College, Moraga, CA 94575, 925-631-4472
    Pubs: *Loose Sugar, Bright Existence, Death Tractates,
    Fortress* (Wesleyan, 1997, 1993, 1992, 1989), *APR.*

Mimi Walter Hinman   P
1085 Normington Way, San Jose, CA 95136, 408-723-0522
Internet: DeskAnt@aol.com
    Pubs: *Autumn Sun* (Zapizdat Pubs, 1995), *Wind
    Five-Folded* (AHA Bks, 1994), *Marilyn, My Marilyn: Anth*
    (Pennywhistle Pr, 1998), *Poetpourri, Japanophile, Poet,
    Pearl, Cicada, Thema.*

Jack Hirschman   P
1314 Kearny St, San Francisco, CA 94133, 415-398-1953
    Pubs: *The David Arcane, The Donmeh* (Amerus Pr, 1982,
    1980).

Jane Hirshfield   P
367 Molino Ave, Mill Valley, CA 94941, 415-381-2319
Internet: jh@well.com
    Pubs: *The Lives of the Heart, Nine Gates: Essays on
    Poetry, The October Palace* (HarperCollins, 1997, 1997,
    1994), *Of Gravity & Angels* (Wesleyan, 1988), *Atlantic, New
    Yorker, Nation, APR, Paris Rev, Poetry.*

Sandra Hoben   P
129 Sunnyside, Mill Valley, CA 94941, 415-388-7641
    Pubs: *Snow Flowers* (Westigan Rev Pr, 1979), *Partisan
    Rev, Ironwood, Quarterly West, Mickle Street Rev.*

Marilyn Hochheiser   P
5406 E Los Angeles Ave, #93, Simi Valley, CA 93063,
805-527-5534
    Pubs: *A View Through the Thicket* (Outpost Pubs, 1977),
    *California Confederation of the Arts, Daybreak, Art/Life,
    Verve, Crosscurrents.*

Cecelia Holland   W
520 Palmer Blvd, Fortuna, CA 95540

Scott C. Holstad   P
PO Box 10608, Glendale, CA 91209-3608
Internet: sch@well.com
    Pubs: *Places* (Sterling Hse, 1995), *Distant Visions, Again
    and Again* (Poet Tree, 1994), *Poetry Ireland Rev, Textual
    Studies in Canada, Arkansas Rev, Minnesota Rev,
    Wisconsin Rev, Southern Rev.*

Paul Hoover   P&W
369 Molino Ave, Mill Valley, CA 94941, 415-389-1877
Internet: maxpaul@sfsu.edu
    Pubs: *Viridian* (U Georgia Pr, 1997), *Postmodern American
    Poetry: Anth* (Norton, 1994).

Toke Hoppenbrouwers   W
California State Univ, Northri, 1811 Nordhoff St, Northridge,
CA 91330-8255, 818-667-2827
    Pubs: *Autumn Sea* (Astarte Shell Pr, 1996).

Bill Hotchkiss   P&W
Sierra College, 5000 Rocklin Rd, Rocklin, CA 95677,
916-624-3333
Internet: 75213.20@compuserve.com
    Pubs: *Yosemite, Sierra Santa Cruz, To Fell the Giants*
    (Bantam, 1995, 1992, 1991).

Lindy Hough   P
258 Yale Ave, Kensington, CA 947081048
    Pubs: *Outlands And Inlands* (Truck Pr, 1984), *Nuclear
    Strategy and the Code of the Warrior: Anth* (North Atlantic
    Bks, 1984).

Sevrin Housen   P
3408 L St, Sacramento, CA 95816-5334, 916-451-7659
    Pubs: *Feathers & Bones* (Halcyon Pr, 1981), *Bellingham
    Rev, Quercus, Suttertown News.*

James D. Houston   W
2-1130 E Cliff Dr, Santa Cruz, CA 95062
Internet: jhouston@cruzio.com
    Pubs: *The Last Paradise* (U Oklahoma Pr, 1998), *In the Ring of Fire* (Mercury Hse, 1997), *Continental Drift* (U California Pr, 1996), *The Men In My Life* (Graywolf Pr, 1994), *Utne Reader, Manoa, Ploughshares, San Francisco Rev, Common Boundary, Faultline.*

Clark Howard   W
PO Box 8145, Palm Springs, CA 92263
    Pubs: *The Wardens* (Putnam, 1978), *Six Against The Rock, The Hunters* (Dial, 1977, 1976).

Noni Howard   P
New World Press, 744 Stoneyford Dr, Daly City, CA 94015-3642, 650-758-1437
    Pubs: *Tiger Balm, The Politics of Love* (New World Pr, 1997, 1996), *Share My Fantasies* (Beatitude, 1996), *Bloodjet Literary Mag, Haight Ashbury Literary Jrnl.*

Fanny Howe   P
Univ California, La Jolla, CA 92093
    Pubs: *De Ultima Die* (O Bks, 1992), *Saving History, The Deep North* (Sun & Moon Pr, 1992, 1988), *Grand Street, Ploughshares.*

George F. Howell   P&W
3342 Hamilton Way, Los Angeles, CA 90026
    Pubs: *The Sartre Situation* (Howell, 1984), *Working Book* (Periplus Pr, 1978), *Angle of Repose.*

Mary Hower   P
1831 Castro St, San Francisco, CA 94131
Internet: maryhower@aol.com
    Pubs: *The World Between Women: Anth* (Her Bks, 1987), *Virginia Qtly Rev, Threepenny Rev, Pacific Intl, California Qtly, Iowa Rev, Hubbub, Bellingham Rev.*

Andrew Hoyem   P
460 Bryant St, San Francisco, CA 94107, 415-777-9651
    Pubs: *What If: Poems 1969-87, Picture/Poems* (Arion Pr, 1987, 1975).

Elias N. Hruska   P
PO Box 2157, Los Gatos, CA 95031-2157, 408-866-2229
    Pubs: *Perceptions Volume III: Anth* (The Wright Experience, 1992), *Many Voices/Many Lands: Anth* (Poetry Ctr, 1989), *Cafe Solo Anth* (Solo Pr, 1974), *Poetry Mag.*

Jim Hubert   P
PO Box 3791, Napa, CA 94558, 707-224-9277
    Pubs: *Between Gray Stones & Freezing Stars* (Ancient Mariner Pr, 1988), *Permafrost, Tempest, Envee, Redstart.*

Richard G. Hubler   W
PO Box 793, Ojai, CA 93023, 805-646-3200
    Pubs: *Inside Ojai, Wheeler* (Creek Hse, 1976, 1970), *Soldier & Sage* (Crown Pub, 1966).

Barbara Hull   P
9449 Manzanita Ave, Ben Lomond, CA 95005-9422, 408-336-4240
Internet: barbh@cruzio.com
    Pubs: *This House She Dreams In* (Kuhn Spit Pr, 1990), *California Qtly, Seattle Rev, Interim, Poet Lore, Poetry Seattle, Footwork.*

Nan Hunt   P&W
23301 Clarendon St, Woodland Hills, CA 91367-4162, 818-887-0031
    Pubs: *If I Had My Life To Live Over: Anth* (Papier-Mache Pr, 1992), *To Be A Woman: Anth* (J.P. Tarcher/St. Martin's Pr, 1991), *Ms., Americas Rev, Beloit Poetry Jrnl, Borderlands, Crosscurrents, Barnabe Mountain Rev.*

Terryl Hunter   P
415 15th St, #12, Huntington Beach, CA 92648, 213-255-3730
    Pubs: *Poetry Loves Poetry: Anth* (Momentum Pr, 1985), *Rara Avis, Magazine, Gramercy Rev, OntheBus.*

Maureen Hurley   P
7491 Mirabel Rd, #5, Forestville, CA 95436, 707-887-2046
    Pubs: *Atomic Ghost: Poets Respond to the Nuclear Age: Anth* (Coffee Hse Pr, 1995), *Poems on the Korean War Conflict: Anth* (Ctr for Korean Studies, 1995), *House on Via Gambito: Women Writers Abroad: Anth* (New Rivers Pr, 1991).

Paula Huston   W
California Poly, San Luis Obis, English Dept, San Luis Obispo, CA 93407, 805-756-2596
    Pubs: *A Land Divided By Rivers, Daughters of Song* (Random Hse, 1997, 1995), *Story, American Short Fiction, NAR, Missouri Rev, Mss., Massachusetts Rev.*

Kathleen Iddings   P
PO Box 8638, La Jolla, CA 92038, 619-457-1399
    Pubs: *Rings of Saturn: Selected and New Poems, 1980-90* (West Anglia, 1999), *The Muse Strikes Back* (Story Line Pr, 1997) *A New Geography of Poets* (U of Arkansas Pr, 1992) *L.A. Times, Writer's Digest, English Jrnl, Crosscurrents, Poets On, Ohioana Qtly.*

Momoko Iko   W
PO Box 172, Hollywood, CA 90028

Ruth G. Iodice   P
22 Avon Rd, Kensington, CA 94707, 415-526-8439
    Pubs: *South Coast Poetry Jrnl, Blue Unicorn, Poet Lore, Long Pond Rev, Negative Capability.*

Susan K. Ito P&W
6034 Valley View Rd, Oakland, CA 94611, 510-339-0622
Internet: itoroark@sprintmail.com
   Pubs: *Making More Waves: Anth* (Beacon Pr, 1997),
Growing Up Asian American: Anth (Morrow, 1993), *Two
Worlds Walking: Anth* (New Rivers, 1992), *Side Show Anth*
(Somersault Pr, 1992), *Hip Mama, Santa Barbara Rev.*

Spoon Jackson P
B-92377, #2184, CMC-East Box 8101, San Luis Obispo, CA
934098101
   Pubs: *No Distance Between Two Points* (Month of
Mondays Pr, 1987), *Brother's Keeper: Anth* (M. Datcher,
1992), *Exquisite Corpse, Community Endeavor.*

Harold Jaffe P&W
3551 Granada Ave, San Diego, CA 92104, 619-294-4924
Internet: hjaffe@mail.sdsu.edu
   Pubs: *Straight Razor* (Black Ice Bks, 1995), *Eros Anti-Eros*
(City Lights, 1990), *Fiction Intl, Chicago Rev, New
Directions Annual, City Lights Rev.*

Maggie Jaffe P
3551 Granada Ave, San Diego, CA 92104-4144,
619-294-4924
Internet: mjaffe@mail.sdsu.edu
   Pubs: *7th Circle* (Cedar Hill Pub, 1998), *How The West
Was One, Continuous Performance* (Burning Cities Pr,
1996, 1992), *Getting By: Anth* (Bottom Dog Pr, 1996),
*Cedar Hill Rev, Rattle, Pemmican Pr, Viet Nam Generation,
Green Fuse, International Qtly.*

Frances Jaffer P
801 27th St, San Francisco, CA 94131, 415-695-0174
   Pubs: *Alternate Endings* (How/Ever, 1985), *She Talks To
Herself in the Language of an Educated Woman* (Kelsey
Street Pr, 1980).

T. R. Jahns P
21141 Canada Rd, #1D, Lake Forest, CA 92630-7703
   Pubs: *Poetry Northwest, Denver Qtly, Southwest Rev, Ohio
Rev.*

Marnell Jameson W
3957 Pacheco Dr, Sherman Oaks, CA 91403, 818-784-2204
   Pubs: *The Book of Blessings, The Song of Songs*
(Harper, 1995, 1990), *California Palms* (Sunstone Pr,
1990), *L.A. Times, Valley Mag, Cimarron Rev, APR,
Tikkun.*

Barbara Jamison P&W
2841 23rd St, San Francisco, CA 94110, 415-285-9597
   Pubs: *The Visitor's Seduction* (Futhave Pr, 1994), *Marylin,
My Marylin: Anth* (Pennywhistle Pr, 1994), *Nation.*

Jean Janzen P
5508 East Ln, Fresno, CA 93727, 209-251-9006
Internet: jjanzen@qnis.net
   Pubs: *Snake In the Parsonage* (Good Bks, 1995), *The
Upside Down Tree* (Windflower Comm, 1992), *Piecework:
19 Fresno Poets: Anth* (Silver Snakes Pr, 1987), *Poetry,
Gettysburg Rev, Antioch Rev.*

Joyce Jenkins P
1450 4th St #4, Berkeley, CA 94710, 510-525-5476
   Pubs: *Prayers at 3 A.M.: Anth* (HarperCollins, 1995), *Portal*
(Pennywhistle Pr, 1993), *Berkeley Poetry Rev, Zyzzyva.*

Francisco Jimenez W
Modern Languages Dept, 204 Walsh, Santa Clara, CA
95053, 408-554-4533
Internet: fjimenez@mailer.scu.edu
   Pubs: *The Circuit: Stories From The Life of a Migrant Child*
(U New Mexico Pr, 1997), *Mosaico de la Vida* (HBJ, 1984),
Fearon's American Literature: Anth (S&S, 1996), *Points of
View: Anth* (Mentor, 1995), *California History, Riversedge,
L.A. Times Bk Rev.*

Donas John P&W
1629 Cimarron St, Los Angeles, CA 90019, 213-732-3359
   Pubs: *Peace is Our Profession* (East River Pr, 1981), *Now
Times, Rainbow City Pr, Gypsy, Connecticut Fireside, Poet
Lore, Archer.*

Diane Johnson W
24 Edith, San Francisco, CA 94133, 415-981-5334
   Pubs: *Natural Opium, Health and Happiness, Persian
Nights* (Knopf, 1993, 1990, 1987).

Robin Johnson P
Wide Awake Ranch, Rd 208, Madera, CA 93638,
209-822-2528
   Pubs: *Denver Qtly, Massachusetts Rev, Poetry Northwest,
Antioch Rev, Southwest Rev, Outerbridge.*

Sheila Goldburgh Johnson P&W
1498 Tunnel Rd, Santa Barbara, CA 93105, 805-682-4618
Internet: chtodel@humanitas.ucsb.edu
   Pubs: *Walking the Twilight II: Women Writers: Anth*
(Northland Pub, 1996), *Shared Sightings: Anth* (J. Daniel &
Co., 1996), *We Speak for Peace: Anth* (KIT Inc., 1993),
*Atlanta Rev, Puerto Del Sol, Negative Capability,
Soundings East, Karamu, Crosscurrents.*

Alice Jones P
6239 College Ave, #304, Oakland, CA 94618, 510-420-8803
Internet: ajones@idiom.com
   Pubs: *The Knot* (Alice James Bks, 1992), *Best American
Poetry 1994: Anth* (Macmillan, 1994), *Poetry, NER,
Pequod, Kenyon Rev, Zyzzyva, Denver Qtly, Ploughshares.*

Patricia Thuner Jones P&W
4831 8th St #2, Carpinteria, CA 93013-1959, 805-684-1113
Pubs: *Science of Mind, Unity, Perspectives, Science of Thought Rev, Listen, Santa Barbara Mag, Life/Times.*

Silas Jones W
7818 S Hobart Blvd, Los Angeles, CA 90047, 213-971-8443
Pubs: *Children Of All* (Funkshunal Features, 1978), *The Price Of Dirt* (Accent, 1974), *Black World.*

June Jordan P
Univ California-Berkeley, Berkeley, CA 94720, 510-642-2743
Pubs: *Living Room* (Thunder's Mouth Pr, 1985), *Civil Wars* (Beacon Pr, 1981).

Jorg P
125 Beach, #44, Santa Cruz, CA 95060
Pubs: *Revolution Fruit Pie, Honking Geese* (Stone Pr, 1978, 1978), *Sitting Frog.*

Andrew Joron P
2009 Cedar St, Berkeley, CA 94709, 510-843-7853
Internet: andrew_joron@sfbayguardian.com
Pubs: *The Removes* (Hard Pr, 1998), *Primary Trouble* (Talisman Hse, 1996), *Science Fiction* (Pantograph Pr, 1992), *Force Fields* (Starmont Hse, 1987), *Sulfur, New American Writing.*

Natasha Josefowitz P
2235 Calle Guaymas, La Jolla, CA 92037, 619-456-2366
Internet: natashaj@mail.sdsu.edu
Pubs: *Too Wise To Want To Be Young Again* (Blue Mountain Pr, 1995).

David Joseph P&W
298 9th Ave, San Francisco, CA 94118, 415-387-3412
Pubs: *Homeless But Not Helpless: Anth* (Harvest, 1988), *Central Park, Rolling Stone.*

William Jovanovich W
Harcourt Brace Jovanovich, 1250 Sixth Ave, San Diego, CA 92101, 619-699-6263
Pubs: *The Money Trail* (HBJ, 1990), *Madmen Must, Now: Barabbus* (H&R, 1978, 1964), *Harper's.*

Gerald Kaminski P&W
2165 Carlmont Dr, #205, Belmont, CA 94002, 415-595-3500
Internet: www.datatamers.com/ romusa
Pubs: *Circumstantial Evidence, Writing is a Social Disease* (Cove View Pr, 1993, 1986), *Xanadu, University Rev.*

Howard Kaplan W
2242 Guthrie Dr, Los Angeles, CA 90034-1030
Pubs: *Passage To Baalbek* (Atheneum, 1979), *The Damascus Cover* (Dutton, 1977).

Pamala Karol P
1608 N Cahuenga Blvd, Ste 562, Hollywood, CA 90028-6202, 213-482-4822
Internet: adobesmog@aol.com
Pubs: *Adventures on the Isle of Adolescence* (City Lights Bks, 1989), *Scars: Anth* (U Alabama Pr, 1996), *AMC, Threepenny Rev, City Lights Rev, Jacaranda Rev.*

Pearl L. Karrer P
570 Kingsley Ave, Palo Alto, CA 94301
Pubs: *Weathering, River Poems: Anth* (Slapering Hol Pr, 1993, 1992), *Whetstone, Visions Intl, Poets On, CQ, Berkeley Poetry Rev, Devil's Millhopper.*

Hiroshi Kashiwagi P&W
4314 Pacheco St, San Francisco, CA 94116
Pubs: *The Big Aiiieeeee: Anth* (Meridian-Penguin Bks, 1991), *On a Bed of Rice: Anth* (Anchor Bks, 1995), *Ayumi: Anth* (Japanese American Anth Committee, 1979).

Michael J. Katz W
1631 Barry Ave #6, Los Angeles, CA 90025, 213-826-9475
Pubs: *The Big Freeze, Last Dance in Redondo Beach* (Putnam, 1990, 1989).

Sam Keen W
16321 Norrbom Rd, Sonoma, CA 95476, 707-996-9010
Pubs: *Faces of the Enemy* (H&R, 1987).

George Keithley P&W
1302 Sunset Ave, Chico, CA 95926, 530-345-0865
Pubs: *Earth's Eye* (Story Line Pr, 1994), *The Burning Bear* (Heatherstone Pr, 1991), *The Donner Party* (Braziller, 1987), *Harper's, Agni, New Letters, Yale Rev, TriQuarterly, North American Rev.*

Robert Kelsey W
650 N McPherson St, Fort Bragg, CA 95437, 707-964-7649
Pubs: *Virginia Qtly Rev, Massachusetts Rev, The Sun, New Press, Snake Nation Rev.*

Troxey Kemper P&W
3108 W Bellevue Ave, Los Angeles, CA 90026, 213-413-0789
Pubs: *Texas for the Duration* (Derivations, 1998), *Lean into the Wind* (Morris Pub, 1997), *Mood Swings* (Small Poetry Pr, 1996), *Under a Sky of Azure* (Bear Hse Pubs, 1993), *Part Comanche* (Bennet & Kitchel, 1991), *Roswell Literary Rev, Tucumcari Literary Rev.*

Robert Kendall P
1800 White Oak Dr, Menlo Park, CA 94025
Internet: http://www.wenet.net/ rkendall
Pubs: *A Life Set For Two* (Eastgate Systems, 1996), *A Wandering City* (Cleveland State U Poetry Ctr, 1992), *The WPWF Poetry Anth* (Bunny & Crocodile Pr, 1992), *Contact II, River Styx, New York Qlly, Indiana Rev, Raccoon, Literary Rev.*

Susan Kennedy   P
PO Box 421, Cazadero, CA 95421, 707-632-5818
  Pubs: *Cazadero Poems* (Floating Island Pr, 1994), *A New
  Geography of Poets: Anth* (U Arkansas Pr, 1992), *The
  Temple, White Heron Poetry Rev, Ruah, The Tomcat,
  Haight Ashbury Literary Jrnl, Zyzzyva.*

Joseph Kent   P
1372 Pine St, San Francisco, CA 94109
  Pubs: *Streams, White Wind* (Sunlight Pub, 1996, 1989),
  The Irreversible Man: Anth (Ars Poetica Pr, 1991), *In The
  Company of Poets, CQ.*

Rolly Kent   P
10520 Wilshire Blvd #1503, Los Angeles, CA 90024,
310-441-9105
  Pubs: *Queen of Dreams* (S&S, 1991), *Spirit, Hurry*
  (Confluence Pr, 1985), *The Wreck in the Post Office
  Canyon* (Maguey Pr, 1977).

Roger Lee Kenvin   W
575 Fairview Ave, Arcadia, CA 91007, 626-445-4420
  Pubs: *The Cantabrigian Rowing Society's Saturday Night
  Bash, Harpo's Garden* (July Blue Pr, 1998, 1997), *South
  Carolina Rev, Garm Lu, Spindrift, Roanoke Rev, Oasis, The
  Distillery, ELF, Crescent Rev, Other Voices, New Letters,
  Connexions, River Oak Rev.*

Karen Kenyon   P
PO Box 12604, La Jolla, CA 92039, 619-587-9027
  Pubs: *Writing By Heart* (Sunshower, 1989), *Sunshower*
  (Putnam/Marek, 1981), *Redbook, Ladies Home Jrnl, CSM,
  British Heritage, Westways, Writer's Digest.*

T. S. Kerrigan   P
13122 Weddington St, Sherman Oaks, CA 91401-6033
  Pubs: *Branches Among The Stars* (Aran Pr, 1988), *Drastic
  Measures, Kansas Qtly, The Epigrammatist, Pacific Rev,
  Southern Rev, Tennessee Qtly.*

Jascha Kessler   P&W
218 16th St, Santa Monica, CA 90402-2216
Internet: jkessler@ucla.edu
  Pubs: *Siren Songs: 50 Stories* (McPherson & Co., 1992),
  Catullan Games: Poems (Marlboro Pr, 1989), *Hellas,
  Bookpress, Kenyon Rev, Black Ace 5, Grist On-Line,
  Venice West Rev, Galley Sail Rev.*

David Kherdian   P
284 Hutchins Ave, Sebastopol, CA 95472, 707-823-6671
Internet: gatehouse@earthlink.net
  Pubs: *I Called It Home, My Racine* (Forkroads Pr, 1997,
  1994), *Friends: A Memoir* (Globe Press Bks, 1993), *Asking
  the River* (Orchard Bks, 1993).

Daphne Rose Kingma   P
PO Box 5244, Santa Barbara, CA 93150-5244, 805-969-4171
  Pubs: *Kansas Qtly, Spectrum, Circus Maximus.*

Maxine Hong Kingston   W
Univ California, English Dept, Berkeley, CA 94720,
510-643-5127
  Pubs: *China Men, Tripmaster Monkey* (Knopf, 1990, 1989),
  Hawaii One Summer (Meadow Pr, 1987).

Diane Kirsten-Martin   P
68 Ashton Ave, San Francisco, CA 94112-2206,
415-337-7408
Internet: dkmartin@well.com
  Pubs: *Zyzzyva, Yellow Silk, Hayden's Ferry, Blue Mesa,
  Onthebus, Bellingham Rev.*

Ed Kissam   P
Box 2041, Sebastopol, CA 95473, 707-829-5696
  Pubs: *Poems Of The Aztec Peoples* (Bilingual Rev Pr,
  1983), *Jerusalem & The People* (Anvil, 1975).

Pat Kite   W
5318 Stirling Ct, Newark, CA 94560-1352
  Pubs: *Highlights, Prime Monthly, Botanical Garden.*

Carolyn Kizer   P
19772 8th St E, Sonoma, CA 95476
  Pubs: *Harping on Poems: 1985-1995, The Nearness of
  You, Mermaids in the Basement* (Copper Canyon Pr, 1996,
  1986, 1984), *The Essential John Clare, 100 Great Poems
  By Women: Anth* (Ecco Pr, 1993, 1995), *Antaeus, Paris
  Rev, Michigan Qtly Rev.*

Sheila Solomon Klass   W
Ruth Cohen, Inc., PO Box 7626, Menlo Park, CA 94025
  Pubs: *In a Cold Open Field* (Black Heron Pr, 1997), *The
  Uncivil War* (Holiday Hse, 1997), *Next Stop: Nowhere,
  Rhino, Kool Ada* (Scholastic, 1995, 1993, 1991),
  Credit-Card Carole, Page Four (Scribner, 1987, 1986).

Edward Kleinschmidt   P
2022 Broderick St, San Francisco, CA 94115, 415-922-3904
  Pubs: *To Remain* (Heyeck Pr, 1990), *First Languages* (U
  Massachusetts Pr, 1990), *New Yorker, APR, Poetry, New
  England Rev, Massachusetts Rev, Volt.*

Mary Julia Klimenko   P
1392 West K St, Benicia, CA 94510, 707-746-1645
Internet: vescamaria@aol.com
  Pubs: *Territory* (Brighton Pr, 1993), *New Letters, Transfer
  Magazine, Suisun Valley Rev, Transfer 45, Berkeley Poetry
  Rev, Art Well, Psychopoetica.*

Arthur Winfield Knight   P&W
PO Box 2580, Petaluma, CA 94953, 707-769-1828
Internet: www.geocities.com/Athens/Forum/2188
  Pubs: *Johnnie D.* (Tor Bks, 1999), *The Darkness Starts Up
  Where You Stand* (Depth Charge, 1996), *The Secret Life of
  Jesse James* (Burnhillwolf, 1996), *Outlaws, Lawmen & Bad
  Women* (Potpourri Pub, 1993), *New York Qtly, Poet Lore,
  Windsor Rev, Atom Mind.*

Kit Knight　　P
PO Box 2580, Petaluma, CA 94953-2580, 707-769-1828
　　Pubs: *Women of Wanted Men* (Potpourri Pr, 1994),
　　Redneck Rev of Literature, Caprice, Pittsburgh Qtly,
　　Waterways, Green's Mag.

Chris Kobayashi　　P
298 Coleridge St, San Francisco, CA 94110, 415-821-3012
　　Pubs: *Networks* (Vortex Edtns, 1979), *Azumi* (Japanese
　　American Anth Committee, 1979).

Michael Koepf　　W
Box 1055, Elk, CA 95432, 707-877-3518
　　Pubs: *Icarus* (w/Mat Crawford; Atheneum, 1987), *Save the*
　　Whale (McGraw-Hill, 1978).

Phyllis Koestenbaum　　P
982-E La Mesa Terr, Sunnyvale, CA 94086, 408-732-2756
　　Pubs: *Criminal Sonnets* (Jacaranda/Writer's Center Edtns,
　　1998), *Best American Poetry: Anths* (Macmillan, 1993,
　　1992), *Michigan Qtly Rev, Epoch, American Letters &*
　　Commentary, Brooklyn Rev, Poet Lore, Poetry New York,
　　Prairie Schooner, Verse, First Intensity.

Ken Kolb　　W
PO Box 30022, Cromberg, CA 96103, 530-836-2332
　　Pubs: *Night Crossing* (Playboy, 1974), *Couch Trip*
　　(Random Hse, 1970), *Redbook, Esquire, Playboy.*

Susan Kolodny　　P
6239 College Ave Ste 304, Oakland, CA 94618,
510-339-2877
Internet: slk1012@aol.com
　　Pubs: *Verse and Universe: Poems About Science and Math:*
　　Anth (Milkweed Edtns, 1998), *Anthology of Magazine Verse:*
　　Anth (Yearbook of American Poetry, 1997), *New England*
　　Rev, Bellingham Rev, New England Rev, River Styx, Black
　　Warrior Rev.

Lynda Koolish　　P
1020 Grizzly Peak Blvd, Berkeley, CA 94708, 510-524-4994
　　Pubs: *Journeys on the Living* (Ariel, 1973), *Mosaic,*
　　Networks, Yellow Silk, Berkeley Poets Co-op.

Stephen Kopel　　P
187 Beaver St, San Francisco, CA 941141516, 415-626-1395
　　Pubs: *Troubadour, The Acorn, Naples Review, Villager,*
　　Silver Quill, Oatmeal & Poetry, Buffalo Bones, Anthology
　　Magazine, Improvijazzation Nation, Lone Stars, Writer's
　　Gazette, Snake River Reflections.

Steve Koppman　　W
1960 Magellan Dr, Oakland, CA 94611, 510-339-6339
　　Pubs: *The Literature of Work: Anth* (U Phoenix Pr, 1991),
　　Zyzzyva, Berkeley Monthly, Jewish Currents, Agada, Sifrut,
　　Wind.

Dennis Koran　　P
6156 Wilkinson Ave, North Hollywood, CA 91606
　　Pubs: *After All* (Norton Coker Pr, 1992), *Vacancies* (Mother
　　Hen, 1975), *Poetry Now, Beatitudes, Abraxas, Panjandrum.*

Steve Kowit　　P
PO Box 184, Potrero, CA 91963-0184, 619-478-2129
　　Pubs: *Pranks* (Bloody Twin Pr, 1990), *Lurid Confessions*
　　(Carpenter Pr, 1983), *The Maverick Poets: Anth* (Gorilla Pr,
　　1988).

Michael H. Krekorian　　W
San Diego State Univ, Eng Dept/Comparative Literatur, San
Diego, CA 921828140, 619-594-5443
Internet: mkrekorian@juno.com
　　Pubs: *Channel Zero* (Plover Pr, 1996), *Corridor* (Ashod Pr,
　　1989), *New Novel Rev, Fiction Intl, AM Lit, Bateria, Central*
　　Park, Mississippi Mud.

Ian Krieger　　P
216 Westminster Ave, Venice, CA 90291, 310-215-0071
　　Pubs: *An Unnamed Aesthetic* (Stolen Images, 1987),
　　Pavans (Ommation Pr, 1985).

S. Allyx Kronenberg　　PP&P&W
2215A Ocean Ave, Santa Monica, CA 90405, 310-399-4245
　　Pubs: *Incantations of the Grinning Dream Woman*
　　(Sagittarius Pr, 1990), *Always I Was Getting Ready To Go*
　　(Black Heron Pr, 1989), *California Qtly, MPR.*

Judy Kronenfeld　　P
3314 Celeste Dr, Riverside, CA 92507, 909-682-5096
Internet: jkronen@citrus.ucr.edu
　　Pubs: *Shadow of Wings* (Bellflower Pr, 1991), *Poets On,*
　　Lilliput Rev, Light, Cape Rock, Verse, Kansas Qtly,
　　Passages North, Chariton Rev, NAR, MPR, Poetry Intl,
　　Free Lunch, Blue Unicorn, Under The Sun, Crazyquilt.

Lewis Kruglick　　P
118 Calera Canyon Rd, Salinas, CA 93908, 408-484-9623
　　Pubs: *Spring Bandits* (Leviathan Pr, 1981), *The Unknown*
　　Angel (Tree Bks, 1971).

James Krusoe　　P
504 Pier Ave, Santa Monica, CA 90405, 818-901-7858
　　Pubs: *Hotel de Dream,*
　　ABCDEFGHIJKLMNOPQRSTUVWXYZ (Illuminati, 1991,
　　1984), *Jungle Girl* (Little Caesar, 1982), *APR, Field,*
　　Denver Qtly.

Geraldine Kudaka　　P
4470-107 Sunset Blvd, Ste 331, Los Angeles, CA 90027
Internet: 103070.266@compuserve.com
　　Pubs: *Persona* (Street Agency Pub, 1988), *Numerous*
　　Avalanches At The Point of Intersection (Greenfield Rev Pr,
　　1979), *Y'Bird.*

Joanne Kyger P
PO Box 688, Bolinas, CA 94924, 415-868-0272
Pubs: *Just Space* (Black Sparrow, 1991), *Phenomological* (Further Studies, 1989), *Going On* (Dutton, 1983).

Joan La Bombard P
814 Teakwood Rd, Los Angeles, CA 90049, 310-476-5437
Pubs: *The Winter Watch of the Leaves, The Counting of Grains* (San Diego Poets Pr, 1993, 1990), *Wherever Home Begins: Anth* (Orchard Bks, 1995), *Poetry Northwest, Tar River Poetry, Colorado Rev, Nation, Virginia Qtly, Prairie Schooner.*

Joyce La Mers P
2514 Greencastle Ct, Oxnard, CA 93035, 805-985-6336
Internet: joylam@aol.com
Pubs: *Grandma Rationalizes An Enthusiasm For Skydiving* (Mille Grazie Pr, 1996), *The Muse Strikes Back: Anth* (Story Line Pr, 1997), *Sometime the Cow Kick Your Head: Anth* (Bits Pr, 1988), *Plains Poetry Jrnl, Piedmont Literary Rev, Saturday Evening Post.*

Salvatore La Puma W
PO Box 20147, Santa Barbara, CA 93210-0147, 805-569-1633
Pubs: *A Time for Wedding Cake* (Norton, 1991), *The Boys of Bensonhurst* (U Georgia, 1987).

Jennifer Lagier P&W
165 Dolphin Cir, Marina, CA 939332220, 408-883-9587
Internet: pcmc@igc.apc.org
Pubs: *Coyote Dream Cantos* (Iota Pr, 1992), *New to North America: Anth* (Burning Bush Pub, 1998), *At Our Core: Women Writing About Power: Anth, If I Had My Life to Live Over: Anth* (Papier-Mache Pr, 1998, 1992), *Poetrymagazine.com, Poets Edge.*

Michael Lally P&W
2102 Neilson Way, Santa Monica, CA 90405
Pubs: *Can't Be Wrong* (Coffee Hse Pr, 1996), *Catch My Breath* (Salt Lick Pr, 1995), *Attitude* (Hanging Loose Pr, 1982), *Forkroads, XY, Rain City Rev.*

Philip Lamantia P
261 Columbus Ave, San Francisco, CA 94113, 415-362-8193
Pubs: *Meadowlark West, Becoming Visible* (City Lights Bks, 1986, 1981), *Sulfur, City Lights Rev, Arsenal, Exquisite Corpse, Caliban.*

Jeanne Lance P
218 Appleton Dr, Aptos, CA 95003, 408-685-9518
Pubs: *Water Burial* (e.g. Pr, 1985), *Mass Psychosis* (Jungle Garden Pr, 1983), *6ix, Switched-On Gutenberg, Santa Cruz County Sentinel, North Beach Now.*

Mervin Lane P
258 E Mountain Dr, Santa Barbara, CA 93108, 805-969-2990
Pubs: *Going to Town* (Sadhe Pr, 1987), *Black Mountain College: Sprouted Seeds: Anth* (U Tennessee, 1990).

A. J. Langguth W
Univ Southern California, ASC102, Los Angeles, CA 900890281, 213-740-3919
Internet: langguth@usc.edu
Pubs: *Saki: Life of Hector Munro* (S&S, 1981).

Daniel J. Langton P
1673 Oak St, San Francisco, CA 94117-2013, 415-552-2994
Pubs: *Life Forms, The Inheritance* (Cheltenham, 1995, 1989).

Marina deBellagente LaPalma PP&P
491 Jersey St, San Francisco, CA 94114-3632, 415-824-6187
Internet: lapalma@well.com
Pubs: *Half-Life* (The Present Pr, 1990), *Persistence: Anth* (Diderot Pr, 1994), *Rooms, Antigones, Afterimage, Resolutions.*

John Laue P
8 Morehouse Dr, La Selva Beach, CA 95076, 408-684-0854
Pubs: *Paradise Lost* (North Star Pr, 1997), *Ribet: A Celebration of Frogs and Toads* (Jill Carpenter, 1996), *Grow Old Along with Me: Anth* (Papier-Mache Pr, 1996), *English Jrnl, Chiron Rev, Santa Barbara Rev, New Press Qtly, Modern Poetry, Chaminade Rev.*

Steven Paul LaVoie P
3717 Magee Ave, Oakland, CA 94619, 510-531-4694
Pubs: *Original Panorama* (Poltroon Pr, 1995), *Up Late: American Poetry Since 1970: Anth* (Doors & Windows, 1986), *Future Sex, Philippine News.*

J. T. Ledbetter P
California Lutheran Univ, Thousand Oaks, CA 91360, 805-492-2411
Pubs: *Crosscurrents, Puerto del Sol, The Formalist, Kansas Qtly, Southern Poetry Rev, Poetry.*

Stellasue Lee P
4872 Topanga Canyon Blvd #262, Woodland Hills, CA 91364, 818-999-5080
Internet: stellasuel@aol.com
Pubs: *Over to You, After I Fall: Anth* (Bombshelter Pr, 1991, 1991), *Onthebus, Herman Rev, On Target, Voices, Bloodpudding, Inky Blue, Rattle, Spillway.*

Diane Lefer W
7955 Blackburn Ave, Los Angeles, CA 900484461
Pubs: *The Circles I Move In* (Zoland Bks, 1994), *Breaking Up Is Hard To Do: Anth* (Crossing Pr, 1994), *Kenyon Rev, Manoa, Western Humanities Rev, Boulevard.*

John Leggett P&W
1781 Partrick Rd, Napa, CA 94558
Pubs: *Making Believe, Gulliver House* (Houghton Mifflin, 1986, 1979), *Ross & Tom* (S&S, 1974).

Carolyn Lei-lanilau P
6167 Harwood Ave, Oakland, CA 94618, 510-658-5378
Pubs: *Ono Ono Girl's Hula* (U Wisconsin, 1997), *Best American Poetry: Anth* (Scribner, 1996), *Chicago Rev, Blue Mesa, Manoa, Raven Chronicles, American Voice, Occident, NAW.*

Emily Wortis Leider P
PO Box 210105, San Francisco, CA 94121
Pubs: *WPFW 89.3 FM Anth, Rapid Eye Movement: Anth* (Bunny & Crocodile Pr, 1992, 1976), *Chicago Rev, Poets On, Mockingbird, Berkeley Poetry Rev, Hurricane Alice.*

Cornel Adam Lengyel P&W
El Dorado National Forest, 7700 Wentworth Springs Rd, Georgetown, CA 95634, 916-333-4224
Pubs: *Late News From Adam's Acres* (Dragon's Teeth, 1985), *Blood To Remember: Anth* (Texas Tech U Pr, 1991), *Old Crow, Confrontation, CQ, Dusty Dog, Mandrake, Poetry Rev.*

George H. Leong P
1819 25th Ave, San Francisco, CA 94122, 415-441-2458
Pubs: *A Lone Bamboo Doesn't Come From Jackson Street* (Isthmus, 1977), *Califia, Time To Greez.*

Russell C. Leong P&W
3924 Tracy St, Los Angeles, CA 90027, 310-825-2974
Internet: rleong@ucla.edu
Pubs: *The Country of Dreams and Dust* (West End Pr, 1993), *Strange Attraction: Anth* (U Nevada, 1995), *The Open Boat: Anth* (Doubleday, 1993), *Charlie Chan is Dead: Anth* (Penguin, 1993), *Nebraska Rev, Tricycle Buddhist Rev, Phatitudes.*

Arthur Lerner P
520 S Burnside Ave, #11C, Los Angeles, CA 90036, 213-936-4992
Pubs: *Words For All Seasons* (Being Bks, 1983), *Spring, Literary Rev, Poet & Critic, Poet, Orbis.*

Eugene Lesser P
Box 656, Woodacre, CA 94973, 415-488-4760

Ken Letko P
College of the Redwoods, 883 W Washington Blvd, Crescent City, CA 95531, 707-464-7457
Internet: kletko@telis.org
Pubs: *All This Tangling* (Mardi Gras Pr, 1995), *Shelter for Those Who Need It* (O2 Pr, 1985), *Greenfield Rev, Cottonwood, Permafrost, World Order.*

Bob Levin W
2039 Shattuck, #201, Berkeley, CA 94704, 510-848-3868
Pubs: *Fully Armed* (Baskerville, 1995), *The Best Ride To New York* (H&R, 1978), *Karamu, Comics Jrnl, Massachusetts Rev, Berkeley Insider, Cavalier, Carolina Qtly.*

Philip Levine P
4549 N Van Ness Blvd, Fresno, CA 93704, 209-226-3361
Pubs: *The Simple Truth, What Work Is* (Knopf, 1994, 1991), *New Yorker, Atlantic, Poetry, Paris Rev, Nation, Hudson Rev.*

Aurora Levins-Morales W
1678 Shattuck Ave, Box 133, Berkeley, CA 94709, 510-524-0617
Pubs: *Getting Home Alive* (Co-author; Firebrand, 1986), *In Other Words: Anth* (Arte Publico, 1994), *Ms., American Voice, Bridges, Callaloo.*

Frieda L. Levinsky P&W
1697 Calle Leticia, La Jolla, CA 92037
Pubs: *Poetic Liberty, Tucumcari Rev, San Fernando Poetry Jrnl, Dog River, Parnassus, Atticus, Hob-Nob, Omnific, Poetpourri.*

James Heller Levinson P&W
21727 Tuba St, Chatsworth, CA 91311, 818-882-9331
Pubs: *Another Line* (Watermark Pr, 1990), *Bad Boy Poems* (Bombshelter Pr, 1993), *Pulled Apart* (Third Lung Pr, 1989), *Hawaii Rev, Dog River Rev, Spoon River Poetry Rev, Center, Bakunin, Nexus.*

Peter Levitt P
PO Box 1601, Topanga, CA 902901601, 310-455-9404
Internet: levgram@aol.com
Pubs: *One Hundred Butterflies, Bright Root, Dark Root* (Broken Moon Pr, 1992, 1991), *A Book of Light* (Amargi Pr, 1982), *Poetry/L.A..*

Janet Lewis P&W
143 W Portola Ave, Los Altos, CA 94022
Pubs: *The Legend, Libretto* (John Daniel, 1987), *Numbers, Ohio Rev, Pennsylvania Rev, Southern Rev.*

John L'Heureux P&W
Stanford Univ, Stanford, CA 94305-2087, 415-725-1209
Internet: jex@leland.stanford.edu
Pubs: *The Handmaid of Desire* (Soho Pr, 1996), *The Shrine At Altamira* (Penguin, 1995), *An Honorable Profession* (Viking, 1991), *Atlantic, New Yorker.*

Genny Lim P
New College of California, 766 Valencia St, San Francisco, CA 94110
Internet: meehdj516@aol.com
Pubs: *The Politics of Experience* (Temple U, 1993), *Two Plays: Paper Angels and Bitter Cane* (Kalamaku, 1991), *Winter Place* (Kearney Street Wkshp, 1991), *Wings for Lai Ho* (East/West, 1982), *Oxford Book of Women's Writing: Anth* (Oxford U, 1995).

Jim Lindsey P
PO Box 1470, Ukiah, CA 95482, 704-849-1822
Pubs: *The Difficult Days* (Princeton U Pr, 1984), *In Lieu of Mecca* (U Pittsburgh Pr, 1976).

Shelley List W
2919 Grand Canal, Venice, CA 90291

Leo Litwak W
246 Chattanooga St, San Francisco, CA 94114

Myra Cohn Livingston P
9308 Readcrest Dr, Beverly Hills, CA 90210, 310-273-2909
    Pubs: *Flights of Fancy & Other Poems, I Never Told & Other Poems* (Macmillan, 1994, 1992).

D. H. Lloyd W
Applezaba Press, PO Box 4134, Long Beach, CA 90804
    Pubs: *Bible Bob Responds to a Jesus Honker* (Applezaba Pr, 1986), *Wormwood Rev, AKA Mag, Pearl.*

Mona Locke P
PO Box 1800, Paradise, CA 95969-2926, 530-872-4934
    Pubs: *Coffeehouse Poetry: Anth* (Bottom Dog Pr, 1996), *Sculpture Gardens Rev III: Anth* (Pacific Voices Pr, 1991), *The New Los Angeles Poets: Anth* (Bombshelter Pr, 1990), *South Dakota Rev, Onthebus, Negative Capability, CQ, Poets On, Blue Unicorn.*

Gerald Locklin P&W
California State Univ, Long Beach, CA 90840, 310-985-5285
Internet: glocklin@csulb.edu
    Pubs: *Go West, Young Toad, Charles Bukowski: A Sure Bet* (Water Row Pr, 1998, 1992), *The Firebird Poems* (Event Horizon Pr, 1992), *Gold Rush and Other Stories* (Applezaba Pr, 1989), *Pearl, Chiron Rev.*

Rachel Loden P
3072 Stelling Dr, Palo Alto, CA 94303-3968, 650-493-4799
Internet: rloden@concentric.net
    Pubs: *American Poets Say Goodbye to the 20th Century: Anth* (Four Walls Eight Windows, 1996), *Best American Poetry: Anth* (Scribner, 1995), *Paris Rev, Chelsea, Witness, Boulevard, NAW, Antioch Rev, No Roses Rev, Prose Poem, Seneca Rev.*

Jonathan London P
PO Box 537, Graton, CA 95444, 707-823-4003
    Pubs: *The Candystore Man* (Morrow, 1998), *Hip Cat* (Chronicle Bks, 1993), *The Owl Who Became the Moon* (Dutton, 1993), *All My Roads* (Beehive Pr, 1981), *Gargoyle.*

Cathleen Long P
Santa Monica College, 1900 Pico Blvd, Santa Monica, CA 90405, 310-452-9242
    Pubs: *Truth & Lies That Press For Life: Anth* (Artifact Pr, 1991), *The New Los Angeles Poets: Anth* (Bombshelter Pr, 1989), *Sculpture Gardens Rev.*

Perie J. Longo P
9 East Mission, Santa Barbara, CA 93101, 805-687-9535
    Pubs: *The Privacy of Wind, Milking the Earth* (John Daniel & Co, 1997, 1986), *Prairie Schooner, Lucid Stone, California State Poetry Qtly, Pudding, Prattle, Embers.*

David Wong Louie W
3155 S Barrington Ave #B, Los Angeles, CA 90066-1133
    Pubs: *Pangs of Love* (Knopf, 1991), *Best American Short Stories: Anth* (HM, 1989), *Chicago Rev, Ploughshares, Fiction Intl.*

Iven Lourie P
PO Box 2119, Nevada City, CA 95959, 530-272-0180
Internet: ilourie@oro.net
    Pubs: *Miro's Dream* (Gateways Bks, 1988), *Alternatives, Poetry, Hanging Loose, Midstream.*

B. D. Love P&W
3740 Valleybrink Rd, Los Angeles, CA 90039, 213-669-1332
Internet: bdlove@earthlink.net
    Pubs: *Cut Salt Fire Grace: Sonnets Love & Other* (Rhythm Dog Edtns, 1995), *Sweet Nothings: Rock & Roll in Poetry* (Indiana U, 1994), *New Orleans Rev, Tennessee Qtly, Many Mountains Moving, The Literary Rev, Writers' Forum, Pacific Coast Jrnl.*

Bia Lowe P&W
2252 Bronson Hill Dr, Los Angeles, CA 90068, 213-463-3377
Internet: bialowe@aol.com
    Pubs: *Wild Ride* (HarperCollins, 1995), *Helter Skelter: Anth* (Los Angeles Museum of Contemporary Art, 1993), *Kenyon Rev, Witness, Harper's, Salmagundi.*

Suzanne Lummis P
PO Box 27924, Los Angeles, CA 90027, 213-660-4306
    Pubs: *Stand Up Poetry: Anth* (California State U Pr, 1994), *Blood Whispers II: Anth* (Silverton Pr, 1994), *Southern Poetry Rev, Bakunin.*

Kirk Lumpkin P
1133-B Filbert St, San Francisco, CA 94109, 415-474-6159
    Pubs: *Earth First! Campfire Poems* (Feral Pr, 1998), *Co-Hearing* (Zyga Multimedia Research, 1983), *Peace Or Perish: A Crisis Anth* (Poets For Peace, 1983), *Earth First Jrnl, Tenderloin Times, Am Here Forum, Terrain.*

Rick Lupert P
5336 Kester Ave #103, Sherman Oaks, CA 91411, 818-995-4457
Internet: rick@poetrysuperhighway.com
    Pubs: *Beyond the Valley of the Contemporary Poets, You'll Wonder How You Ever Got Along Without It, 51%, Blue Satellite, Caffeine.*

Toby Lurie P
150 Seal Rock Dr, San Francisco, CA 94121, 415-221-2446

Glenna Luschei   P
Box 2814, Atascadero, CA 93422, 805-543-1058
> Pubs: *Matriarch* (The Smith, 1992), *Bare Roots Seasons* (Oblong, 1990), *Farewell to Winter* (Daedalus, 1988), *Blue Mesa Rev, Calapooya Collage.*

Celia S. Lustgarten   P&W
317 3rd Ave, San Francisco, CA 94118, 415-386-3592
Internet: csli@pge.com
> Pubs: *Apocalypse 3: Anth* (Apocalypse Literary Arts Coalition, 1997), *Shock Treatment* (Peak Output Unltd, 1988), *For Poets Only, Perceptions, Chanticleer, New Canadian Rev, Z Misc, Grasslands Rev.*

William Luvaas   W
664 Kaylyn Way, San Marcos, CA 92069, 619-739-1817
> Pubs: *Going Under* (Putnam, 1994), *The Seductions of Natalie Bach* (Little, Brown, 1986), *Glimmer Train, Village Voice, American Literary Rev, Confrontation.*

Annette Peters Lynch   P
833 Garfield Ave, South Pasadena, CA 91030-1928, 818-799-7836
> Pubs: *Christmas Blues: Anth* (Amador Pub, 1995), *Blue Unicorn, Pointed Circle, Poem, Maryland Poetry Rev.*

Susan Macdonald   P
Printers Inc. Bookstore, 310 California Ave, Palo Alto, CA 94025, 415-323-7342
> Pubs: *A Smart Dithyramb* (Heyeck Pr, 1979), *Dangerous As Daughters* (Five Trees Pr, 1976).

Clarence Major   P&W
Univ California, English Dept, Davis, CA 95616-7532, 916-752-5677
> Pubs: *Dirty Bird Blues, Such Was the Season* (Mercury Hse, 1996, 1989), *Painted Turtle: Woman with Guitar* (Sun & Moon, 1988).

devorah major   P
PO Box 423634, San Francisco, CA 94102, 415-621-1664
Internet: dmajor1@ix.netcom.com
> Pubs: *Street Smarts* (Curbstone, 1996), *An Open Weave* (Seal Pr, 1995), *Zyzzyva, Onthebus, Black Scholar, Shooting Star, Caprice, Callaloo.*

Gerard Malanga   P
Black Sparrow Press, 24 Tenth St, Santa Rosa, CA 95401, 707-579-4011
> Pubs: *Uma Thurman's Breasts* (Edtns Objets Trouves, 1994), *Three Diamonds, Mythologies of the Heart: Anth* (Black Sparrow, 1991, 1996).

River Malcolm   W
625 Serpentine Dr, Del Mar, CA 92014, 619-755-7845
> Pubs: *Womanspirit, Sinister Wisdom, Thursday's Child.*

Lee Mallory   P
Santa Ana College, 17th at Bristol, Santa Ana, CA 92706, 714-564-6526
> Pubs: *Holiday Sheer* (Inevitable Pr, 1997), *Full Moon, Empty Hands* (Lightning Pubs, 1994), *Invisible City, Mojo Navigator, Hyperion, The Smith, Forum, Riverside Qtly.*

Eileen Malone   P&W
1544 Sweetwood Dr, Colma, CA 94015-2029, 650-756-5279
Internet: wrigrps@aol.com
> Pubs: *Half Tones to Jubilee, Louisville Rev, A Gathering of the Tribes, Americas Rev, Lucid Stone, Fugue, Sun Dog, West Wind Rev, Santa Clara Rev.*

Marvin Malone   P
722 Bedford Rd, Stockton, CA 95204-5214, 209-466-8231
> Pubs: *Bucolics And Cheromanics* (Callahan, 1963), *TriQuarterly, Vagabond, Wormwood, December, Nihilistic Rev, Stovepiper.*

Oscar Mandel   W
California Inst Technology, Pasadena, CA 91125, 626-395-4078
> Pubs: *Blossoms and Incantations, Prince Poupon Needs A Wife,* (www.onlineoriginals.com, 1997, 1997), *Sigismund, Prince of Poland: A Baroque Entertainment* (U Pr America, 1988), *Kenyon Rev, Prairie Schooner.*

Angela Consolo Mankiewicz   P
752 N Mansfield Ave, Los Angeles, CA 90038
> Pubs: *Cancer Poems* (UBP-Los Angeles, 1995), *Chiron Rev, Poetpourri, Comstock Rev, Slipstream, Hawaii Rev, Amelia, Phase and Cycle, Karamu, The Lyric.*

Victoria Lena Manyarrows   P
2440 16th St, #146, San Francisco, CA 94103, 415-824-1170
Internet: earrows@itsa.ucsf.edu
> Pubs: *Songs from the Native Lands* (Nopal Pr, 1995), *The Arc of Love: Anth* (Scribner, 1996), *Catalyst, Evergreen Chronicles, Indigenous Woman, Callaloo, XCP: Cross Cultural Poetics, ELF.*

Adrianne Marcus   P
79 Twin Oaks, San Rafael, CA 94901, 415-454-6062
Internet: medea999@aol.com
> Pubs: *Carrion House World Of Gifts* (St. Martin's Pr, 1993), *Confrontation, Ladies Home Journal, Solo, Cosmopolitan, Descant, Barnabe Mountain Rev.*

Morton Marcus   P
1325 Laurel St, Santa Cruz, CA 95060, 408-429-9085
> Pubs: *When People Could Fly: Prose Poems* (Hanging Loose Pr, 1997), *Pages From A Scrapbook of Immigrants* (Coffee Hse Pr, 1988), *TriQuarterly, Red Dirt, Zyzzyva, Ploughshares, The Prose Poem: Intl Jrnl, Denver Qtly, Hanging Loose, Fiction.*

William J. Margolis   P
1507 Cabrillo Ave, Venice, CA 902913709, 310-399-0040
    Pubs: *A Book of Touch & Other Poems* (Mendicant Edtns,
    1988), *Beat Voices: Anth* (Henry Holt, 1995), *Black Ace 5,
    Grist On-Line, Venice West Rev, Galley Sail.*

Stefanie Marlis   P
36 Madrone Ave, San Anselmo, CA 94960, 415-459-2920
Internet: marlis@well.com
    Pubs: *Rife* (Sarabande Bks, 1998), *Sheet of Glass*
    (Floating Island Pr, 1994), *Slow Joy* (U Wisconsin Pr,
    1989), *APR, Manoa, Plum Rev, Poetry, Poetry East,
    Zyzzyva, Arshile, Five Fingers Rev, Gettysburg Rev,
    Ploughshares, Volt.*

Jack Marshall   P
4248 Moraga St, San Francisco, CA 94122
    Pubs: *Sesame, Arabian Nights* (Coffee Hse Pr, 1993,
    1987), *APR, Talisman, Zyzzyva, Exquisite Corpse, Caliban,
    Sifrut.*

Sally Marshall   P
167 Lowell Ave, Glendora, CA 91740, 818-335-8945
    Pubs: *Gridlock: Anth* (Applezaba, 1990), *Wellspring, CQ,
    Nostalgia, Manna, Starline, Pudding.*

Jim Martin   P
303 Estrella Dr, Scotts Valley, CA 95066
Internet: bjxmsc@tevm2.nsc.com
    Pubs: *Shadows of My World* (Rush-Franklin Pub, 1993).

Joan M. Martin   P
670 Walton Dr, Red Bluff, CA 06080, 530-529-3033
Internet: diakeuast@aol.com
    Pubs: *Z Miscellaneous, The Courier, Times-Argus,
    Prophetic Voices, Yellow Butterfly, Deros.*

Jack Matcha   W
7716 Teesdale Ave, North Hollywood, CA 91605
    Pubs: *No Trumpets, No Drums* (Powell, 1970), *Prowler In
    The Night* (Fawcett, 1959), *Gamma.*

David Matlin   P&W
4635 56th Street, San Diego, CA 92115, 619-583-7572
Internet: dmatlin@mail.sdsu.edu
    Pubs: *How the Night is Divided* (McPherson & Co., 1993),
    Dressed in Protective Fashion (Other Wind, 1990), *Avant-Pop:
    Fiction Anth* (Black Ice Bks, 1993), *Apex of the M.*

Clive Matson   P
472 44th St, Oakland, CA 94609, 415-654-6495
Internet: clive@matson.ford.com
    Pubs: *Hourglass* (Seagull Pr, 1988), *Equal in Desire*
    (Manroot, 1983), *Exquisite Corpse, Nimrod, Visions Intl,
    Fine Madness, Centennial Rev, Hanging Loose.*

George Mattingly   P
820 Miramar Ave, Berkeley, CA 947071807, 510-525-2098
Internet: gmd@dnai.com
    Pubs: *A Guide To "Ready, Set, Go"* (S. Foresman, 1989),
    Breathing Space (Blue Wind Pr, 1975), *None of the Above:
    Anth* (Crossing Pr, 1977).

Frances Mayes   P&W
San Francisco State University, San Francisco, CA 94132
    Pubs: *Under the Tuscan Sun* (Broadway Bks, 1997), *Ex
    Voto, Hours* (Lost Roads, 1995, 1984), *Atlantic, Virginia
    Qtly, Southern Rev, Iowa Rev, Gettysburg Rev.*

Marysia Maziarz   W
321 Wawona Ave, Shell Beach, CA 93449, 805-773-6530
    Pubs: *Here's The Story: Anth* (Spirit That Moves Us, 1985),
    Short Story Intl, Round Table, Slipstream.

Sara McAulay   W
California State Univ, English Dept, Hayward, CA 94542
Internet: www.tinamou2.com
    Pubs: *Chance, Catch Rides* (Knopf, 1982, 1975), *Hot
    Flashes: Anth* (Faber & Faber, 1996), *Zyzzyva, Third
    Coast, Chili Verde Rev, Southern Ocean Rev, Black
    Warrior Rev, Real Fiction, California Qtly.*

Kate McCarthy   W
14854 Sutton St, Sherman Oaks, CA 91403, 818-784-0711
    Pubs: *Calliope, Exquisite Corpse, Sewanee Rev.*

Lee McCarthy   P&W
8200 Kroll Way, #174, Bakersfield, CA 93311
    Pubs: *Combing Hair with a Seashell* (Ion Bks, 1992),
    Desire's Door (Story Line Pr, 1991), *Intro 8: Anth* (Anchor
    Bks, 1977), *Raccoon 24/25, Solo, Daybreak.*

Michael McClintock   P
560 Meridian Terr, Los Angeles, CA 90042, 213-255-0074

Frances Ruhlen Mcconnel   P
Scripps College, Claremont, CA 91711, 714-621-8000
    Pubs: *Gathering Light, One Step Closer* (Pygmalion Pr,
    1979, 1975), *Iowa Rev, Seattle Rev, The Nation.*

Brian McCormick   P&W
Creative Artists Agency, 9830 Wilshire Blvd, Beverly Hills, CA
90212
    Pubs: *The Immortality Project* (Word Made Flesh/Printed
    Matter Bks, 1991), *Atlantic, Permafrost, Blueline,
    Zyzzyva, Fine Madness, Harper's, Santa Monica Rev.*

Jennifer McDowell   P
PO Box 5602, San Jose, CA 95150
    Pubs: *Ronnie Goose Rhymes for Grownups, Contemporary
    Women Poets: Anth* (Merlin Pr, 1984, 1977), *Chock, Snowy
    Egret, X, Tigris & Euphrates, Open Cell.*

Whitman McGowan   P
PO Box 471493, San Francisco, CA 94147-1493,
415-441-0846
Internet: margwhit@ix.netcom.com
    Pubs: *Contents May Have Shifted* (Viridiana, 1994), *No, I Am Not Walt Whitman's Great Grandson* (Mel Thompson Pub, 1993), *Daedalus Anthology of Kinky Verse* (Daedalus, 1996), *Nebo, Lynx Eye, Green Egg, Margin, Fan, Yggdrasil, Tomorrow, Paris/Atlantic, Cups.*

Michael McLaughlin   P&W
c/o Don't Trip Press, PO Box 14244, San Luis Obispo, CA 93401
    Pubs: *Southern California Anthology* (MPW, 1988, 1984), *Crack, Coffeehouse Poet's Qtly, convolvus, Asylum Annual, Frank.*

Elnora McNaughton   P
PO Box 7054, Oxnard, CA 93031, 805-485-5425
    Pubs: *Rivertalk: Anths* (The Little Horse Pr, 1997, 1996, 1995, 1994), *Verve, Embers, Art/Life, Wind, CQ, Daybreak.*

Sandra McPherson   P
2052 Calaveras Ave, Davis, CA 95616-3021, 530-753-9672
Internet: sjmcpherson@ucdavis.edu
    Pubs: *The Spaces Between Birds, Edge Effect: Trails and Portrayals* (Wesleyan/UPNE, 1996, 1996), *The God of Indeterminacy* (U Illinois Pr, 1993), *New Yorker.*

Kat Meads   P&W
144 Walti St, Santa Cruz, CA 95060
    Pubs: *Born Southern And Restless* (Duquesne U Pr, 1996), *Wayward Women* (Illinois Writers Inc., 1995), *Women and Death: Anth* (Ground Torpedo Pr, 1994).

Maude Meehan   P
2150 Portola Dr, Santa Cruz, CA 95062, 408-476-6164
    Pubs: *Washing The Stones: A Collection 1975-1995* (Papier-Mache Pr, 1996), *Before the Snow* (Moving Parts, 1991), *Chipping Bone* (Embers Pr, 1988).

Ib J. Melchior   W
8228 Marmont Ln, Los Angeles, CA 90069, 213-654-6679
    Pubs: *Quest* (Presidio Pr, 1990), *Steps & Stairways* (Co-author; Rizzoli, 1989).

David Meltzer   P&W
New College of California, 776 Valencia St, San Francisco, CA 94110, 415-626-1694
Internet: dmelt@ccnet.com
    Pubs: *Under* (Rhinoceros, 1995), *Arrows: Selected Poems, 1984-91* (Black Sparrow Pr, 1993), *Reading Jazz: Anth* (Mercury Hse, 1994), *Washington Post, Davka.*

Roger Ladd Memmott   P&W
512 S Crawford Ave, Willows, CA 95988, 530-934-7062
Internet: rlmstory@aol.com
    Pubs: *Catharsis* (Millennium Pr, 1980), *Blue Unicorn, Colorado Qtly, Confrontation, Sou'wester, Bachy, Cumberland Poetry Rev, Cincinnati Poetry Rev.*

Ann Menebroker   P
2738 4th Ave, Sacramento, CA 95818
    Pubs: *Mailbox Boogie* (w/Robertson; Zerx Pr, 1991), *Time Capsule: Anth* (Creative Time, 1995), *Caprice, Atom Mind, Pearl, Painted Bride Qtly, Bogg, Smell Feast.*

Sarah Menefee   P
1655 Sacramento #1, San Francisco, CA 94109, 415-885-6344
    Pubs: *This Perishable Hand* (Multimedia Edizioni, 1995), *Please Keep My Word* (Worm in the Rain Pub, 1991), *The Blood About the Heart, I'm Not Thousandfurs, Poetry Like Bread: Anth* (Curbstone Press, 1992, 1986, 1994).

Don Meredith   W
PO Box 2674, Guerneville, CA 95446-2674
    Pubs: *Home Movies, Morning Line* (Avon, 1982, 1980), *Folio, Kingfisher, Greensboro Rev, Texas Rev.*

Douglas Messerli   P
Sun & Moon Press, 6026 Wilshire Blvd, Los Angeles, CA 90036, 213-857-1115
    Pubs: *The Walls Come True: An Opera For Spoken Voices, Along Without: A Film For Fiction in Poetry* (Littoral, 1994, 1993).

Deena Metzger   P&W
PO Box 186, Topanga, CA 90290, 213-455-1089
    Pubs: *Tree: Essays and Pieces* (North Atlantic Bks, 1997), *A Sabbath Among the Ruins* (Parallax Pr, 1992), *What Dinah Thought* (Viking, 1989), *Intimate Nature: Anth* (Ballantine, 1998), *Anima, Turning Wheel, Poetry Flash, Creation, Jacaranda Rev, Lilith.*

Robert Mezey   P
Pomona College, 140 W 6 St, Claremont, CA 91711-6335, 909-607-2809
Internet: rmezey@pomona.edu
    Pubs: *Evening Wind* (Wesleyan, 1987), *New Criterion, Raritan, Paris Rev, New Yorker, Hudson Rev, New York Rev of Bks.*

Leonard Michaels   W
Univ California, Berkeley, CA 94720, 415-642-2764
    Pubs: *I Would Have Saved Them If I Could* (FSG, 1975).

Jack Micheline   P&W
41 Sutter St, Box 1269, San Francisco, CA 94104
    Pubs: *The Last Round Up, Poems of Fire and Light* (Midnight Special Edtns, 1992, 1990), *Letter to Kerouac in Heaven* (Zeitgeist Pr, 1991).

Rondo Mieczkowski P&W
PO Box 29478, Los Angeles, CA 90029, 213-661-5449
Pubs: *Sundays at Seven: Anth* (Alamo Square Pr, 1996), *Sonora Rev, James White Rev, Wisconsin Rev, Modern Words, Poetry/L.A.*.

Kattie M. Miles-Cumbo P
1006 1/2 Central Ave, Priv Hse, Alameda, CA 94501, 510-522-1514
Pubs: *Black Sister* (Indiana U Pr, 1982), *Poets, Poems & Poetic Comments* (Guyana National Pr, 1976).

Sara Miles P
824 Shotwell St, San Francisco, CA 94110-3213
Internet: smiles@igc.org
Pubs: *Native Dancer* (Curbstone Pr, 1986), *Ordinary Women* (Ow Bks, 1984), *Opposite Sex: Anth* (NYU Pr, 1998), *Iowa Rev, Essence, Ms., XXXFruit, Nation, New Yorker, Wired, Essence*.

Adam David Miller P
PO Box 162, Berkeley, CA 947010162, 510-845-8098
Internet: eliseadm@sirius.com
Pubs: *Apocalypse Is My Garden* (Eshu Hse Pub, 1997), *Forever Afternoon* (Michigan State U Pr, 1994), *Neighborhood and Other Poems* (Mina Pr, 1993), *Dices or Black Bones* (HM, 1973).

Brown Miller P
City College of San Francisco, 50 Phelan Ave, San Francisco, CA 94112, 415-239-4793
Pubs: *Hiroshima Flows Through Us* (Cherry Valley Edtns, 1977), *New Letters, Xanadu, Ohio Rev*.

Lorraine Millings P
PO Box 2291, Lancaster, CA 93539-2291, 805-949-8687
Internet: PoetRaini@aol.com
Pubs: *Report to Hell, Verve, Plaza, Pirate Writings, Poetic Eloquence, Friendship Rose*.

Paul L. Mills PP
3426 Keystone Ave #4, Los Angeles, CA 90034-4731
Pubs: *The Co-op Songbook* (New York Musicians Co-op, 1983), *Think & Do* (Co-op Records, 1983), *Boston Phoenix, Creem, Fusion, Outpost, Stroker*.

Stephen Minot W
2225 Mt Vernon Ave, Riverside, CA 92507, 909-369-3938
Pubs: *Surviving The Flood* (Second Chance Pr, 1986), *Ghost Images* (H&R, 1979), *Virginia Qtly Rev, Sewanee Rev, Harper's, Agni, Paris Rev, Atlantic*.

Janice Mirikitani P
Glide Foundation, 330 Ellis St, San Francisco, CA 94102, 415-771-6300
Pubs: *We The Dangerous, Shedding Silence: Anth* (Celestial Arts Pub, 1995, 1990), *Awake in the River* (Isthmus Pr, 1982).

Hayley R. Mitchell P
23106 Kent Ave, Torrance, CA 90505, 760-734-1216
Internet: grimmgirl@aol.com
Pubs: *Bite to Eat: Anth* (Redwood Coast Pr, 1995), *Southern Poetry Rev, Pudding Mag, New Delta Rev, Poetry Northwest, Rattle, Wordwrights*.

Peter Money P
1412 Martin Luther King Jr. Wa, Berkeley, CA 94709, 510-558-1476
Internet: ruralwanab@aol.com
Pubs: *Between Ourselves* (Backwoods Broadsides Series, 1997), *A Big Yellow* (Cloud, 1996), *APR, North Dakota Qtly, Hawaii Rev, Wallace Stevens Jrnl, Writer's Almanac*.

R. Bruce Moody W
PO Box 9555, Berkeley, CA 94709, 415-787-2706
Pubs: *The Decline And Fall Of Daphne Finn* (Coward, 1966), *New Yorker, Bottege Oscure, Michigan Qtly*.

Brian Moore W
33958 Pacific Coast Hwy, Malibu, CA 90265, 213-457-7940
Pubs: *The Silence of Lies* (Doubleday, 1990), *The Color of Blood, Black Robe* (Dutton, 1987, 1985).

Raylyn Moore W
302 Park St, Pacific Grove, CA 93950, 408-372-0113
Pubs: *What Happened To Emily Goode After The Great Exhibition* (Donning, 1978).

Rosalie Moore P
1130 7th St, #B-26, Novato, CA 94945, 415-892-3073
Pubs: *Learned And Leaved* (Marin Poetry Center, 1909), *Of Singles & Doubles* (Woolmer/Brotherson, 1979).

Cherrie Moraga P&W
1042 Mississippi St, San Francisco, CA 94107
Pubs: *Loving In The War Years* (South End Pr, 1983).

Dorinda Moreno P
5505 Esplanada, Orcutt, CA 93455, 805-937-3067

Richard W. Morris P
2421 Buchanan St, San Francisco, CA 94115-1927
Internet: rwmorris@ix.netcom.com
Pubs: *Adventures of God* (Ghost Dance Pr, 1994), *Assyrians* (The Smith, 1991).

Henry J. Morro P
2209 Dufour St, #A, Redondo Beach, CA 90278-1414, 310-370-9659
Internet: hjmorro@aol.com
Pubs: *Corpses of Angels* (Bombshelter Pr, 1998), *Marilyn, My Marilyn: Anth* (Pennywhistle Pr, 1994), *Invocation L.A.: Anth* (West End Pr, 1989), *Seneca Rev, Black Warrior Rev, Jacaranda Rev, Pacific Rev*.

Carlos Morton P&W
San Francisco Mime Troupe, 855 Treat St, San Francisco, CA 94110
Pubs: *White Heroin Winter* (One Eye Pr, 1971).

Lois Moyles P
4243 Norton Ave, Oakland, CA 94602, 510-531-1375
Pubs: *Alleluia Chorus* (Woolmer/Brotherson, 1979), *Partisan Rev, Shenandoah, Delos, Hawaii Pacific Rev, New Yorker, Manhattan Rev.*

Frederick Mugler, Jr. W
580 St. Francis Pl, Menlo Park, CA 94025, 650-322-9650
Internet: fredmugler@aol.com
Pubs: *The Madrona Murders* (Xlibris Pr, 1998), *Pavilion* (Putnam, 1982), *Emergency Room* (Delacorte 1975).

Harryette Mullen P
UCLA English Dept, 405 Hilgard Ave, Los Angeles, CA 90095, 310-825-7553
Pubs: *Muse & Drudge* (Singing Horse Pr, 1995), *Trimmings* (Tender Buttons Bks, 1991), *Callaloo, Agni, Chain, Antioch, World, Bombay Gin.*

Alejandro Murguia W
1799 Revere Ave, San Francisco, CA 94124-2345, 415-822-2543
Pubs: *Southern Front* (Bilingual Rev Pr, 1988), *Farewell to the Coast* (Heirs Pr, 1980).

Merilene M. Murphy P
Telepoetics, Inc, 1939 1/4 W Washington Blvd, Los Angeles, CA 90018, 213-766-1266
Internet: http://this.is/telepoetics
Pubs: *under peace rising* (Woman In The Moon Pubs, 1994), *Trouble: Naropa Summer Writing Anth* (Kavayantra Pr, 1995), *Coffee House Poets Qtly, L.A. Mag.*

Pat Murphy W
3601 Lyon St, San Francisco, CA 94123, 415-561-0336
Pubs: *Points of Departure, The Shadow Hunter, The City, Not Long After* (Bantam, 1990, 1990, 1989).

William K. Murphy P
6635 Sepulveda Blvd, Van Nuys, CA 91411-1204, 818-787-2764
Internet: uxorcist@pacbell.net
Pubs: *Nightland, Walk Along the Seashore* (Solo Pr, 1988, 1987), *Redstart, Cafe Solo, Kite.*

Carol Muske-Dukes P&W
Univ Southern California, University Park Campus, Los Angeles, CA 900890354, 213-740-2808
Internet: carolmd@usc.edu
Pubs: *An Octave Above Thunder: New & Selected* (Penguin, 1997), *Women & Poetry* (U Michigan Pr, 1997), *Red Trousseau, Saving St. Germ* (Viking, 1993, 1993), *Dear Digby* (Washington Square Pr, 1991), *Paris Rev, APR, New Yorker, Field, Poetry, Nation.*

Edward Mycue P
PO Box 640543, San Francisco, CA 94164-0543, 415-922-0395
Pubs: *Rainbow Behind Irene* (Panjandrum Pr/Nuomenal Edtns, 2000), *Night Boats, Split-Life Is Built From the Inside Out* (w/Jim Grove) (Norton Coker Pr, 1999, 1994), *Because We Speak The Same Language* (Spectacular Diseases Pr, 1994).

Majid Naficy P
1144 12th St #103, Santa Monica, CA 90403, 310-395-6993
Pubs: *In A Tiger's Skin* (Amir Kabir, 1969), *The Literary Rev.*

Peter Najarian W
1521 Stuart St, Berkeley, CA 94703, 415-548-1407
Pubs: *Daughters of Memory* (City Miner, 1986), *Voyages* (Ararat, 1980), *Wash Me On Home, Mama.*

Martin Nakell P&W
3787 Maplewood Ave, Los Angeles, CA 90066
Internet: mnakell@chapman.edu
Pubs: *The Library of Thomas Rivka* (Sun & Moon Pr, 1996), *The Myth of Creation* (Parenthesis Writing Series, 1993), *Literal Latte, Hanging Loose, Hyper Age.*

Rochelle Nameroff P
1102 Neilson St, Albany, CA 94706-2400
Pubs: *Body Prints* (Ithaca Hse, 1972), *Tendril, Antioch Rev, Poetry Northwest, Malahat Rev.*

Brenda Nasio P
216 Fair Oaks St, San Francisco, CA 94110
Pubs: *Paris Rev, Open Places, Amelia, Negative Capability, CutBank, Crab Creek Rev, Pudding.*

Leonard Nathan P
40 Beverly Rd, Kensington, CA 94707, 510-527-0362
Pubs: *The Potato Eaters* (Orchises Pr, 1997), *Diary of a Left-Handed Birdwatcher* (Graywolf Pr, 1996), *Carrying On: New & Selected Poems* (U Pitt Pr, 1985), *Manoa, Poet Lore, Salmagundi, Atlantic, Southwestern Rev, New Yorker, Wilderness.*

Opal Louis Nations P
1939 M. L. King Jr. Way, Berkeley, CA 94704, 510-530-5785
Pubs: *Neo-Absurdities* (Changed Species Pr, 1988), *Coach House Poets Collection: Anth* (Norton, 1988), *Rampike.*

Louise Nayer P
1165 Bosworth St, San Francisco, CA 94131-2801
Pubs: *The Houses Are Covered in Sound* (Blue Light Pr, 1990), *Keeping Watch* (Birthstone Pr, 1981).

Crawdad Nelson P&W
P.O. Box 219, Bayside, CA 955240219, 707-268-1274
Internet: mrsteelie@aol.com
    Pubs: *The Bull of the Woods, When the Eagle Shits* (Gorda
    Plate Pr, 1997, 1996), *Truth Rides to Work* (Poetic Space
    Bks, 1993), *Rosebud, The Sun, Poetry Flash, Mockingbird,
    Cedar Hills Rev, Rain City Rev, American Voice, Oxygen.*

Mildred Nelson P&W
3448 Amber Ln, Oceanside, CA 92056-4841
    Pubs: *The Island* (Pocket Bks, 1973), *Light Year: Anth* (Bits
    Pr, 1986), *Mediphors, Georgia Rev, McCall's, San
    Fernando Poetry Jrnl, Writers Jrnl, Crosscurrents.*

Peter E. Nelson P
1303 Allesandro St, Los Angeles, CA 90026
    Pubs: *Spring Into Light* (Green Tree Pr, 1978), *Between
    Lives* (Ironwood Pr, 1974), *Choice, Poetry.*

Ray Faraday Nelson W
333 Ramona Ave, El Cerrito, CA 94530, 415-526-8356
    Pubs: *Dog Headed Death* (Strawberry Hill, 1988),
    Timequest (Tor, 1985).

David Nemec W
1517 Irving St, San Francisco, CA 94122-1908,
415-564-6506
    Pubs: *Stonesifer* (Monterey Pacific, 1998), *Early Poems*
    (Beisbol Pr, 1998), *The Beer and Whiskey League* (Lyons
    & Burford, 1994), *The Systems of M.R. Shurnas* (John
    Calder, 1986), *Transatlantic Rev, Playgirl, Twilight Zone.*

Peter Neumeyer P&W
45 Marguerita Rd, Kennsington, CA 947071019,
619-463-2229
    Pubs: *The Phantom of the Opera, Homage to John Clare*
    (Peregrine Smith, 1988, 1980), *Donald and The...*
    (Addison-Wesley, 1969), *New Mexico Qtly.*

Joel Newman W
PO Box 2611, Los Angeles, CA 90028
    Pubs: *Dead Man's Tears* (Beaufort Bks, 1981).

Rebecca Newman W
20 Bali Ln, Pacific Palisades, CA 90272, 310-573-2028
    Pubs: *Ely and the Komodo Dragon* (Ancient Mariners Pr,
    1991), *Adam the Detective* (Midwest Express, 1991), *The
    Divorce of Mrs. Dracula* (Redstart, 1988).

Kristy Nielsen P&W
2529 Betlo Ave, Mountain View, CA 94043, 415-988-8971
Internet: nielsen@cris.com
    Pubs: *The Party Train: North American Prose Poetry Anth*
    (New Rivers, 1996), *Sarajevo: For Bosnian Relief: Anth* (Elgin
    Community College, 1993), *Spoon River Poetry Rev, ACM.*

Ann Nietzke W
466 N Hobart Blvd, #12, Los Angeles, CA 90004-1851,
213-660-5983
    Pubs: *Solo Spinout: Stories and a Novella, Windowlight*
    (Soho Pr, 1996, 1996), *Shenandoah, Other Voices,
    Massachusetts Rev.*

Nona Nimnicht P
303 Adams, #210, Oakland, CA 94610
    Pubs: *In The Museum Naked* (Second Coming Pr, 1978),
    *Ploughshares, Poetry Northwest, Quarterly West,
    Crosscurrents, Prairie Schooner, Nimrod.*

Larry Niven W
3961 Vanalden Ave, Tarzana, CA 91356

Harold Norse P&W
537 Jones St, Box 263, San Francisco, CA 94102,
415-863-7208
    Pubs: *Memoirs of a Bastard Angel* (Morrow, 1989), *The
    Love Poems: 1940-85* (Crossing Pr, 1986).

John Norton P&W
444A 14th St, San Francisco, CA 94103, 415-558-9066
Internet: jnorton@us.oracle.com
    Pubs: *The Light at the End of the Bog* (Black Star Series,
    1989), *Posthum(or)ous* (e.g. Pr, 1986), *Before Columbus
    Fdn Anth* (Norton, 1991), *Kayak.*

John Noto P&W
PO Box 420803, San Francisco, CA 941420803,
415-921-6829
Internet: john_r._noto@sfbayguardian.com
    Pubs: *Psycho-Motor Breathscapes* (Vatic Hum Pr, 1997),
    Crash Worship: Runaway (Juxta/3300 Pr, 1997), *Talisman,
    Caliban, Central Park, Fiction Intl, Mandorla, First Intensity,
    NAW, CTheory.*

Susan Nunes W
1 Tamalpais Rd, Berkeley, CA 94708
Internet: charlesfad@aol.com
    Pubs: *The Last Dragon* (Clarion, 1995), *A Small Obligation
    & Other Stories of Hilo* (Bamboo Ridge, 1982), *Graywolf
    Annual: Anth* (Graywolf, 1991), *Home to Stay: Anth*
    (Greenfield Rev, 1990).

Heidi Nye P
2273 Euclid Ave, Long Beach, CA 90815-2518
    Pubs: *Water From the Moon* (Forever a Foreigner Pr,
    1992), *Australian Wellbeing, California Poetry Qtly, L.A.
    View, Pearl, Natural Health, Bad Haircut.*

Mark O'Brien   P
c/o Helen McGrath, 1406 Idaho Ct, Concord, CA 94521,
510-672-6211
Internet: hmcg@ix.netcom.com
    Pubs: *Staring Back* (Dutton, 1997), *Breathing* (LittleDog Pr,
    1990), *Our Mothers' Spirits: Anth* (HarperCollins, 1997),
    *Whole Earth Rev, Tight, Expressions, The Sun, St.
    Andrews Rev.*

Raymond Obstfeld   W
2936 Ballesteros Ln, Tustin, CA 92680, 714-730-9074
    Pubs: *The Remington Contract* (Worldwide, 1988), *The
    Reincarnation of Reece Erikson* (Tor, 1988).

Philip F. O'Connor   W
821 Gonzalez Dr, San Francisco, CA 94123-2235
    Pubs: *Martin's World* (Bottom Dog Pr, 1993), *Finding
    Brendan* (S&S, 1991), *Defending Civilization* (Weidenfeld &
    Nicolson, 1988).

Joyce Odam   P
2432 48th Ave, Sacramento, CA 95822, 916-421-4597
    Pubs: *Lemon Center For Hot Buttered Roll* (Hibiscus Pr,
    1975), *Blue Unicorn, Impulse.*

Ron Offen   P
28182 Via Chocano, Mission Viejo, CA 92692, 949-770-2239
Internet: afreelunch@aol.com
    Pubs: *Answers/Questions* (Inevitable Pr, 1996), *Instead of
    Gifts* (Pudding Hse, 1995), *Poet As Bad Guy* (Cyfoeth
    Pubs, 1963), *Interim, Pearl, Mockingbird, Pacific Coast Jrnl,
    Zyzzyva, Cedar Hill Rev, Interim, Lightning and Ash,
    Parting Gifts, Whole Notes.*

Jamie O'Halloran   P
8446 Fenwick St, Sunland, CA 91040, 818-353-7203
Internet: ohalloran@mindspring.com
    Pubs: *The Landscape From Behind* (V.C. Pr, 1997),
    Grand Passion: Poets of Los Angeles: Anth (Red Wind
    Bks, 1995), *Cream City Rev, Southern California Anth,
    Blue Satellite, Seattle Rev, Blue Moon Rev, 51%,
    Snakeskin.*

Diana O'Hehir   P
2855 Jackson St, #301, San Francisco, CA 94115,
415-928-1261
    Pubs: *Spells For Not Dying Again* (Eastern Washington U
    Pr, 1997), *Home Free, The Bride Who Ran Away, I Wish
    This War Were Over* (Atheneum, 1988, 1988, 1984),
    *Poetry, Kenyon Rev, American Voice, Poetry Northwest,
    Shenandoah.*

Jennifer Olds   P
1403 W Locust St, Ontario, CA 91762-5327, 714-988-3237
    Pubs: *Rodeo and the Mimosa Tree* (Event Horizon Pr,
    1991), *Gypsy, Tsunami, Pearl, Slipstream, Staple,
    Onthebus, Envoi, New Spokes.*

Carole Simmons Oles   P
California State Univ, Chico, CA 959290830, 530-898-6151
Internet: carole_oles@macgate.csuchico.edu
    Pubs: *Stunts* (GreenTower, 1992), *The Deed* (LSU Pr,
    1991), *American Poetry Rev, Field, Georgia Rev, Kenyon
    Rev, Poetry, NER, Prairie Schooner, APR.*

Beverly Olevin   W
2252 Beverly Glen Pl, Los Angeles, CA 90077-2506,
310-474-0959
Internet: 74634.1153@compuserve.com
    Pubs: *The Breath of Juno* (Elk Horn Pr, 1996), *Sweet Peas*
    (Juno Pr, 1991), *Ms., America West, Sun Dog: Southeast
    Rev, Oxford Mag, Portland Rev, MacGuffin.*

Robert Oliphant   W
California State Univ, Northridge, CA 91330
    Pubs: *A Trumpet for Jackie, A Piano for Mrs. Cimino*
    (Prentice-Hall, 1983, 1980).

David Oliveira   P
820A W Victoria St, Santa Barbara, CA 93101, 805-963-8408
    Pubs: *Rivertalk: Anth* (Little Horse Pr, 1995), *Ten California
    Poets: Anth* (North/South Pr, 1990), *Cafe Solo, Americas
    Rev, Evergreen Chronicles.*

Tillie Olsen   W
1435 Laguna, #6, San Francisco, CA 94115-3742,
415-346-1137
    Pubs: *Mother to Daughter, Daughter to Mother* (Feminist
    Pr, 1986), *Silences* (Delacorte, 1978).

Sharon Olson   P
Palo Alto Main Library, 1213 Newell Rd, Palo Alto, CA 94303,
650-329-2438
Internet: slopoet@well.com
    Pubs: *Fire In The Hills* (Adler, 1992), *Clouds Brushed in
    Later* (San Jose Poetry Ctr Pr, 1987), *Kalliope, Santa Clara
    Rev, Palo Alto Rev, Kansas Qtly, Seattle Rev, American
    Literary Rev, Worcester Rev.*

Regina O'Melveny   P
3071 Crest Rd, Rancho Palos Verde, CA 90275,
310-833-6580
    Pubs: *Blue Wolves* (Bright Hill Pr, 1997), *Cathedrals of the
    Spirit: Anth* (Harperperennial, 1996), *Spreading the
    Word/L.A. Poetry Contest Winners: Anth* (Red Wind Bks,
    1993), *Yellow Silk Anth* (Crown Pubs, 1990), *The Sun,
    Jacaranda Rev, Poetry/L.A..*

Philip D. Ortego   P&W
San Jose State Univ, San Jose, CA 95912, 408-277-2242

Antonio G. Ortiz   P
2006 S Genesee Ave, Los Angeles, CA 90016, 213-935-3313
    Pubs: *Flor y Canto II and I* (U Southern California Pr, 1978,
    1976), *Urbis Mag, New Mexico Mag.*

Mark Osaki　　P
Rand Corporation, 1700 Main St, PO Box 2138, Santa
Monica, CA 90407
　　Pubs: *Carrying the Darkness: Poetry of the Viet Nam War:
　　Anth* (Texas Tech U, 1989), *Hawaii Rev, Berkeley Poetry
　　Rev, South Carolina Rev, Georgia Rev.*

John Jay Osborn　　W
14 Fair Oaks St, San Francisco, CA 94110, 415-282-1629
　　Pubs: *The Associates, The Man Who Owned New York*
　　(Houghton Mifflin, 1982, 1981).

Ernest John Oswald　　P
Thumb Tree Poetry Service, 128 Laguna St, San Francisco,
CA 94102, 415-431-8791
　　Pubs: *Apricot Two Step* (E. Oswald, 1976), *New York Qtly,
　　Small Pond, Cincinnati Rev, Offerta Speciale.*

Mary Overton　　W
La Questa Press, 211 La Questa Way, Woodslde, CA 94062
Internet: http://home.att.net/ mob
　　Pubs: *The Wine of Astonishment* (La Questa Pr, 1997),
　　*Glimmer Train, Potomac Rev, Wordwrights!, Belletrist Rev,
　　Spelunker Flophouse, Southern Anth.*

Ellis Ovesen　　P
Box 482, Los Altos, CA 94023, 415-941-3552
　　Pubs: *The Year of the Horse* (Golden Quill, 1991), *Beloved
　　II* (Chitana Literary Society, 1990), *The Year of the Snake*
　　(Wyndham Hall, 1989).

Rosella Pace　　P
2750 Hilltop Ct, Arcata, CA 95521-5221
　　Pubs: *Portugal: The Villages, Anth of Los Angeles Poets*
　　(Red Hill Pr, 1977, 1972), *Cafe Solo, Bachy, Beyond
　　Baroque, San Marcos Rev.*

Javier Pacheco　　PP&P
5162 Berryman Ave, Culver City, CA 90230, 213-390-2579
　　Pubs: *Canciones De La Raza* (Fuego De Aztlan, 1978),
　　Chismearte, Rayas, Electrum, Maize.

Barbara Gordon Paine　　P
Chaspaine, 803 15th Ave, Menlo Park, CA 94025,
650-326-2212
Internet: chaspaine@aol.com
　　Pubs: *Eidolon* (Ligda, 1962), *Prairie Schooner, New York Qtly.*

Charlotte Painter　　W
6450 Mystic St, Oakland, CA 94618, 408-423-9129
　　Pubs: *Conjuring Tibet* (Mercury Hse, 1997), *Who Made The
　　Lamb* (Creative Arts Bks, 1988), *Gifts of Age* (Chronicle
　　Bks, 1986).

Michael Palmer　　P
265 Jersey St, San Francisco, CA 94114, 415-282-8522
　　Pubs: *The Lion Bridge, At Passages* (New Directions, 1998,
　　1995), *Sun* (North Point Pr, 1985), *Grand Street, Sulfur,
　　Chicago Rev, NAW, Chain, Avec, Common Knowledge.*

Nicole Panter　　W
PO Box 862, Venice, CA 90294, 310-396-5937
Internet: nicolep7@aol.com
　　Pubs: *Mr. Right On & Other Stories, Unnatural Disasters:
　　Recent Writings from the Golden State: Anth*
　　(Incommunicado Pr, 1994, 1996).

Richard Parque　　P&W
200 Main St, Lakewood, CA 90712
　　Pubs: *A Distant Thunder, Flight of the Phantom, Firefight*
　　(Zebra Books, 1988, 1987, 1986).

John B. Passerello　　P
6825 Ashfield Way, Fair Oaks, CA 95628-4207
Internet: passerellojandb@worldnet.att.net
　　Pubs: *Homeless Not Helpless: Anth* (Fox Sparrow, 1989),
　　We Speak For Peace: Anth (KIT, 1993), *Tapjoe, Peace &
　　Freedom, Pudding, Feelings, Aristos, CQ.*

Louis Patler　　P
36 Shell Rd, Mill Valley, CA 94941, 415-388-8344
Internet: bit@nbn.com
　　Pubs: *An American Ensemble* (Poltroon Pr, 1980), *Acts,
　　Intent, Rootdrinker, Convivid, Mill Valley Mag, Pacific
　　Poetry & Fiction Rev.*

Jim Paul　　P&W
1170 Guerrero St, Loft, San Francisco, CA 94110,
415-641-5308
Internet: jimpaul@sirius.com
　　Pubs: *Medieval In L.A.* (Counterpoint, 1996), *Catapult:
　　Harry and I Build a Siege Weapon* (Villard Bks, 1991),
　　Antioch Rev, Paris Rev, Mss..

Walter Pavlich　　P
2052 Calaveras Ave, Davis, CA 95616, 916-753-9672
Internet: wpavlich@davis.com
　　Pubs: *Running Near The End of the World* (U Iowa Pr,
　　1992), *Atlantic, APR, Yale Rev, Poetry, Manoa, Iowa Rev,
　　Antioch Rev.*

Paul J. J. Payack　　P&W
234 Remington Loop, Danville, CA 94526, 510-855-9418
Internet: payack@post.harvard.edu
　　Pubs: *New Letters, Paris Rev, Boulevard, Creative
　　Computing, New Infinity Rev.*

Gerrye Payne　　P
10582 Barnett Valley Rd, Sebastopol, CA 95472,
707-829-4705
　　Pubs: *The Year-God* (Ahsahta Pr, 1992), *An Amateur Plays
　　Satie* (Loon Pr, 1984), *Dog River Rev, Kansas Qtly,
　　Kalliope, Creeping Bent, Loon, Primavera, Fish Drum,
　　Karamu, Hayden's Ferry Rev.*

Victor Pearn   P
215 1/2 Hollister Ave., Santa Monica, CA 90405,
310-450-4156
  Pubs: *Pyromaniac* (The Plowman, 1995), *Swans Pausing*
  (Foothills Pub, 1994), *Negative Capability, Long Islander,
  Midwest Qtly, Mind Matters Rev, Sulphur River Literary
  Rev, Whole Notes.*

Oscar Penaranda   P&W
Logan High School, 1800 H St, Union City, CA 94587,
510-471-2520
  Pubs: *Fiction By Filipinos in America: Anth* (New Day Pubs,
  1993), *Filipinas Mag, Bay-Loot.*

James Pendergast   P
685 Fano Ln, Sonoma, CA 95476, 707-996-7743
  Pubs: *Anth of Mag Verse* (Monitor Book Co., 1981), *The
  New Mag, Ruhtra, Hyperion.*

Sam Pereira   7/24/9
1548 Canal Farm Ln #1C, Los Banos, CA 936354425,
209-826-2072
Internet: litsam@telis.org
  Pubs: *Brittle Water* (Penumbra Pr, 1987), *The Marriage of
  the Portuguese* (L'Epervier Pr, 1978) *Piecework: Anth*
  (Silver Skates Publishing, 1987), *APR, Poetry, Antioch Rev.*

Anne S. Perlman   P
41 Fifth Ave, San Francisco, CA 94118, 415-752-2517
  Pubs: *Sorting It Out* (Carnegie Mellon, 1984), *Songs From
  Unsung Worlds: Anth* (Aviva, 1987).

Robert Peters   P
9431 Krepp Dr, Huntington Beach, CA 92646, 714-968-7546
  Pubs: *Feather: A Child's Death and Life* (U Wisconsin Pr,
  1997), *Selected Poems 1967-1994* (Asylum Arts Pr, 1994),
  *American Bk Rev, James White Rev, Chiron Rev, Bakunin,
  Small Press Rev, Chicago Rev.*

Geoff Peterson   P
25 San Juan Ave, San Francisco, CA 94112, 415-585-4808
  Pubs: *Medicine Dog* (St. Martin's Pr, 1989), *Letter From
  Wyoming: Anth* (Wyoming Council on the Arts, 1991),
  Peregrine, Z Miscellaneous, Aileron, New York Qtly.

Robert Peterson   P
PO Box 417, Fairfax, CA 94978-0417, 415-455-8209
  Pubs: *All the Time in the World* (Hanging Loose Pr, 1996),
  The Only Piano Player in La Paz (Black Dog, 1985).

Steve D. Petterson   W
8190E Mira Mesa Blvd, Ste 323, San Diego, CA 92126,
619-695-3091
  Pubs: *Lost in the Material World* (Excalibur Pub Co., 1992),
  Positive Living News.

Dennis Phillips   P
Sun & Moon Press, 6026 Wilshire Blvd, Los Angeles, CA
90036, 213-857-1115
  Pubs: *20 Questions* (Jahbone, 1992), *Arena, A World* (Sun
  & Moon Pr, 1992, 1989), *The Hero is Nothing* (Kajun Pr,
  1985), *o.blek, Tyuonyi, Hambone.*

Frances Phillips   P
194 Onondaga Ave, San Francisco, CA 94112, 415-626-2787
  Pubs: *Up at Two, For A Living* (Hanging Loose Pr, 1991,
  1981), *Hanging Loose, Five Fingers Rev, Volt, New York
  Qtly, Zyzzyva, Feminist Studies, Hungry Mind Rev.*

Felice Picano   P&W
386 S Burnside Ave 9L, Los Angeles, CA 90036
Internet: felicepic@aol.com
  Pubs: *A House On The Ocean, A House On The Bay*
  (Faber & Faber, 1997), *Like People In History* (Viking,
  1995), *Window Elegies* (Close Grip Pr, 1985),
  Ambidextrous (Gay Press of New York, 1985), *No
  Apologies, San Francisco Examiner, Harvard Gay Rev.*

Susan Lewis Policoff   P&W
2807 Milvia St, Berkeley, CA 94703
  Pubs: *Love's Shadow* (Crossing Pr, 1993), *Life on the Line*
  (Negative Capability, 1993), *Folio, Reed, Sequoia, Oxygen,
  Other Voices, First/For Women.*

James Polster   W
3311 Mandeville Canyon Rd, Los Angeles, CA 90049,
310-471-1805
  Pubs: *Brown* (Longstreet Pr, 1995), *A Guest in the Jungle*
  (Mercury Hse, 1987), *Smoke, New Orleans Rev.*

Edward Pomerantz   W
The Artists Agency, 10000 Santa Monica Blvd #305, Los
Angeles, CA 90067, 310-277-7779
  Pubs: *Brisburial Play* (Magic Circle Pr, 1981), *Into It A
  Novel* (Dial Pr, 1972), *Tyuonyi.*

Melinda Popham   W
12179 Greenock Ln, Los Angeles, CA 90049, 310-471-4336
  Pubs: *Skywater* (Graywolf, 1990), *A Blank Book*
  (Bobbs-Merrill, 1974).

Michael Porges   P
850 Tucson Ct, San Dimas, CA 91773-1852
  Pubs: *Songs, Portraits, Poems, Songs Out Of Season*
  (Landor Pr, 1981, 1979), *Verve.*

Paul C. Portuges   P
3888 Fairfax Rd, Santa Barbara, CA 93110, 805-682-2060
  Pubs: *Paper Song* (Ross-Erikson, 1984), *The Turquoise
  Mockingbird of Light* (Mudborn, 1979), *Eye.*

Evelyn Posamentier   P
210 Hoffman Ave, San Francisco, CA 94114, 415-285-0477
  Pubs: *Ghosts of the Holocaust: Anth* (Wayne State U Pr,
  1989), *Processed World, APR, Chrysalis.*

Jonathan V. Post P&W
3225 N Marengo Ave, Altadena, CA 91001, 818-398-1673
Pubs: *Project Solar Sail* (NAL, 1990), *Nebula Awards Anth 23* (HBJ, 1989), *Amazing Stories, Analog, Fantasy Book, Omni, Quantum, Science.*

Holly Prado P&W
1256 N. Mariposa Ave, Los Angeles, CA 900291416, 213-664-3640
Pubs: *Esperanza: Poems for Orpheus, Specific Mysteries* (Cahuenga Pr, 1998, 1990), *Gardens* (HBJ, 1985), *Grand Passion: Poets of Los Angeles: Anth* (Red Wind Bks, 1995), *Exquisite Corpse, Denver Qtly, Kenyon Rev, Colorado Rev, Poetry Intl, The Tule Rev.*

Skip Press W
710 E Palm Ave, Burbank, CA 90274-9150, 818-954-8900
Internet: spress@aol.com
Pubs: *Star Families* (Crestwood Hse, 1995), *Cliffhanger* (Saddleback Pub, 1992), *Disney Adventures, Reader's Digest, Writer's Digest, Grit.*

Jonathan Price P
1127 Fresno St, Berkeley, CA 94707

Jean Pumphrey P
650 Main St, Sausalito, CA 94965-2338, 415-332-5436
Internet: jean@sirius.com
Pubs: *Sheltered At The Edge* (Solo Pr, 1982), *Poetry: The Way Through Language* (H&R, 1975), *Beside the Sleeping Maiden: Anth* (Arctos Pr, 1997), *Stones & Amulets: Anth* (Wordsworth, 1996).

Barbara Quick P&W
17 Edgecroft Rd, Kensington, CA 947071412, 510-528-1228
Internet: bqwriter@aol.com
Pubs: *Northern Edge: A Novel of Survival in Alaska's Arctic* (HarperCollins West, 1994), *New York Times Bk Rev, Ms., Newsweek.*

Leroy V. Quintana P
9230-C Lake Murray, San Diego, CA 92119
Pubs: *The History of Home* (Bilingual Pr, 1993), *Interrogations* (Viet Nam Generation, 1992), *Colorado Rev, Prairie Schooner, Puerto del Sol, Zyzzyva.*

Frederick A. Raborg, Jr. P&W
329 E St, Bakersfield, CA 93304, 805-323-4064
Pubs: *Posing Nude, Hakata, Tule* (Amelia Pr, 1989, 1988, 1986), *Westways, Cimarron Rev, Tendril, Crazyquilt, Prairie Schooner.*

Rebecca Radner P
3025 Steiner, #12, San Francisco, CA 94123-3911, 415-563-8746
Internet: rebecca.r@sirius.com
Pubs: *What Book!?: Anth* (Parallax Pr, 1998), *Harvard Mag, NER/BLQ, Berkeley Poets' Co-op, Iowa Rev, Minnesota Rev, California Qtly, Central Park, Caliban.*

James Ragan P
1516 Beverwil Dr, Los Angeles, CA 90035, 310-277-1914
Pubs: *Lusions, The Hunger Wall* (Grove Pr, 1996, 1995), *Womb Weary* (Carol Pub, 1990), *Ohio Rev, Antioch Rev, NAR, Poetry, The Nation, Southern California Anth.*

Carl Rakosi P
1456 17th Ave, San Francisco, CA 94122-3403, 415-566-3425
Pubs: *The Earth Suite* (England; Etruscan Bks, 1997), *Poems, 1923-1941* (Sun & Moon Pr, 1995), *Collected Poems, Collected Prose* (Natl Poetry Fdn, 1986, 1983), *Talisman, Conjunctions, NAW, Sulfur, Zyzzyva, APR, Arshile.*

Karen Randlev P
20 Sunnyside Ave, #A153, Mill Valley, CA 94941, 415-389-1534
Internet: readk@earthlink.net
Pubs: *Light Runner* (Fireweed Pr, 1987), *The Last New Land: Anth* (Alaska Northwest Bks, 1996), *A New Geography of Poets: Anth* (U Arkansas Pr, 1992), *Exquisite Corpse, CSM.*

Jan Theodora Randolph P
635 Alhambra Ln, Martinez, CA 94553
Pubs: *Onion Snow* (Latitudes, 1988).

Jerry Ratch P
4333 Holden St, Studio #54, Emeryville, CA 94608, 510-428-2660
Pubs: *Light* (O Bks, 1990), *How the Net Is Gripped: Anth* (Stride, 1992), *Avec, Tight, Sonoma Mandala, Carolina Qtly, Contact II, Seems.*

Stephen Ratcliffe P
Mills College, 5000 MacArthur Blvd, Oakland, CA 94613, 510-430-2245
Internet: sratcliff@mills.edu
Pubs: *Sculpture* (Littoral Bks, 1996), *Present Tense* (The Figures, 1995), *Conjunctions, Talisman, Chain, New American Writing, o.blek, Avec.*

Susan Rawlins P
1517 Ada St, Berkeley, CA 94703, 510-527-1244
Pubs: *Grand Street, Shenandoah, Zyzzyva, Feminist Studies, The Quarterly, Poet & Critic.*

Dennis J. Reader P
2045 Green Valley Rd, Watsonville, CA 95076, 408-728-1988
Pubs: *Coming Back Alive* (Avon, 1983), *Virginia Qtly Rev.*

Ishmael Reed P&W
PO Box 3288, Berkeley, CA 94703
Pubs: *The Terrible Threes, The Terrible Twos* (St. Martin's Pr, 1989, 1982), *God Made Alaska For The Indians* (Garland, 1982), *Yardbird Reader.*

Diane Reichick   P
2058 Ardenwood Ave, Simi Valley, CA 93063
  Pubs: *Color Wheel, Vol No, Verve, Orphic Lute, CQ, Red Dancefloor.*

Gay Beste Reineck   P
1425 Cole St, San Francisco, CA 94117

Ingrid Reti   P
1650 Descanso St, San Luis Obispo, CA 93405,
805-544-3605
  Pubs: *Each In Her Own Way: Anth* (Queen of Swords Pr, 1994), *We Speak for Peace: Anth* (KIT, 1993), *Iowa Woman, Portlandia, San Luis Obispo Mag.*

Tim Reynolds   P
327 1/2 E 1st St, #4, Los Angeles, CA 90012
  Pubs: *Dawn Chorus* (Ithaca Hse, 1980), *The Women Poem* (Phoenix, 1973).

Marilee Richards   P
1725 San Jose Ave, Alameda, CA 94501, 510-865-2533
  Pubs: *Poetry Northwest, National Forum, The Journal, Literary Rev, Sou'wester, Cimarron Rev, Poet Lore.*

Cena Golder Richeson   W
PO Box 268, Knightsen, CA 94548, 510-672-5229
  Pubs: *Horse Tales: Anth* (Wordware, 1994), *The West That Was: Anth* (Random Hse, 1993), *Daughters of Our Land: Anth* (Maverick Pub, 1988).

Steve Richmond   P
137 Hollister Ave, Santa Monica, CA 90405, 213-396-1996

John M. Ridland   P
1725 Hillcrest Rd, Santa Barbara, CA 93103, 805-965-9613
Internet: jridland@silcom.com
  Pubs: *Palms* (Buckner Pr, 1993), *Hudson Rev, Sticks, Light, Robert Frost Rev, Snakeskin, Independent, Overland, Quadrant, Antithesis, Epigrammatist.*

Agnes Riedmann   W
777 Rand Ave, Oakland, CA 94610-2236
  Pubs: *The Story of Adamsville* (Wadsworth Publishing Co, 1977), *Dismal River Rev, Intro.*

Tom Riley   P
1441 Brown St, Napa, CA 94559, 707-253-9675
  Pubs: *Writing Poems: Anth* (Little, Brown, 1987), *Byline, Art Times, Dialogue, The Lyric, The Formalist, Blue Unicorn.*

Stuart Robbins   P&W
660 Santa Ray Ave, Oakland, CA 94610, 510-208-3389
  Pubs: *Poetry Now, Berkeley Poet's Co-op, Paragraph, Amazing Stories, Berkeley Poetry Rev, Ararat.*

Gillian Roberts   W
PO Box 423, Tiburon, CA 94920, 415-435-5889
Internet: judygilly@aol.com
  Pubs: *Time and Trouble* (St. Martin's Pr, 1998), *The Bluest Blood, The Mummers' Curse, In The Dead Of Summer* (Ballantine Bks, 1998, 1996, 1995).

Lillian S. Robinson   P
1520 O'Farrell St, San Francisco, CA 94115, 415-567-4195
  Pubs: *The Old Life* (SUNY Buffalo, 1977).

Shelba Cole Robison   W
PO Box 6359, Los Osos, CA 93412, 805-528-4182
Internet: dwcs90a@prodigy.com
  Pubs: *Appalachian Heritage, Pembroke Mag, Poughkeepsie.*

Alfred A. Robles   P
520 6th Ave, San Francisco, CA 94118, 415-387-5783
  Pubs: *Rappin' With Ten Thousand Carabaos* (U California Pr, 1996), *Looking for Ifugao Mountain* (Children's Pr, 1976), *Amerasia Jrnl, Bridge.*

Aleida Rodriguez   P
1811 Baxter St, Los Angeles, CA 90026-1935, 213-660-1546
Internet: arodedit@aol.com
  Pubs: *In Short: Anth* (Norton, 1996), *Grand Passion: Anth* (Red Wind Bks, 1995), *Ploughshares, Prairie Schooner, Progressive, Kenyon Rev, Phoebe, Rattle.*

Zack Rogow   P
358 27th St, San Francisco, CA 94131
Internet: zrogow@uclink2.berkeley.edu
  Pubs: *The Epistolary Form & The Letter as Artifact* (Pig Iron Pr, 1991), *Left-Hand Maps: San Francisco Bay Area Poets: Anth* (A Small Garlic Pr, 1998), *Time Is the Longest Distance: Anth* (HarperCollins, 1991), *Rhino, Calliope, APR, Switched-On Gutenberg.*

Richard Ronan   P
4845 17th St, San Francisco, CA 94117, 415-566-1922
  Pubs: *A Radiance Like Wind or Water, Narratives from America* (Dragon Gate Bks, 1984, 1982), *APR.*

Judith Rose   P&W
752 Sunnyside Rd, St Helena, CA 94574, 707-963-1449
Internet: jmrose@fcs.net
  Pubs: *Prairie Schooner, Indiana Rev, Iowa Rev, Virginia Qtly Rev, Equinox, Carbuncle.*

Wendy Rose   P
41070 Lilley Mountain Dr, Coarsegold, CA 93614-9622,
209-658-8018
Internet: lostcopper@aol.com
  Pubs: *Bone Dance: New & Selected Poems* (U Arizona Pr, 1994), *Now Poof She Is Gone* (Firebrand Pr, 1994), *Going to War With All My Relations* (Northland Pr, 1993).

Gerald Rosen   W
320 Winfield St., San Francisco, CA 94110, 415-648-2140
Internet: jerrydutch@aol.com
   Pubs: *Mahatma Gandhi in a Cadillac* (North Atlantic Bks,
   1995), *Carmen Miranda Memorial Flagpole* (Avon, 1978).

Marion Rosen   P
5041 Fulton Ave, Sherman Oaks, CA 91423
   Pubs: *Death By Education, Don't Speak To Strangers* (St.
   Martin's Pr, 1993, 1993).

Sylvia Rosen   P
42127 67th St W, #5A, Quartz Hill, CA 93536-3830
   Pubs: *Dreaming the Poems, A Dream Journal* (Red Wind
   Bks, 1994), *Stand-Up Poetry: Anth* (USCLB Pr, 1994),
   Onthebus, Pegasus.

Elizabeth Rosner   P&W
468 Vincente Ave, Berkeley, CA 94707, 510-526-4644
Internet: erosner900@aol.com
   Pubs: *Psychological Perspectives, Southern Poetry Rev,
   Faultline, Blue Mesa Rev, Poetry East, ACM, Cream City
   Rev, Green Hills Literary Lantern, Many Mountains Moving.*

Lee Rossi   P
1341 Centinela Ave, #103, Santa Monica, CA 90404,
213-453-6303
   Pubs: *Grand Passion: Anth* (Red Wind Bks, 1995), *Beyond
   Rescue* (Bombshelter Pr, 1991), *Apalachee Qtly, Chelsea,
   Bakunin, Faultline, Poetry East, L.A. Times.*

Alexis Rotella   P
16651 Marchmont Dr, Los Gatos, CA 95032-5608
   Pubs: *Looking For A Prince* (Jade Mountain Pr, 1991),
   Haiku Moment: Anth (Tuttle, 1993), *Blue Mesa Rev, New
   Letters, Median Literary Rev.*

Jerome Rothenberg   PP&P
1026 San Abella, Encinitas, CA 92024, 619-436-9923
Internet: jrothenb@carla.ucsd.edu
   Pubs: *Seedings & Other Poems* (New Directions, 1996),
   Poems For the New Millennium: Anths (U California Pr,
   1998, 1995), *Sulfur, Conjunctions, Apex of the M, Poetry
   USA, Po&sie, Gare Du Nord.*

Eugene Ruggles   P
106 Washington St, #326, Petaluma, CA 949522308
   Pubs: *The Lifeguard In The Snow* (U Pittsburgh, 1977),
   Passages North: Anth (Milkweed Edtns, 1990), *Poetry Now,
   New Yorker, Poetry, Nation, Manoa, Poetry Northwest, Field.*

Beverly A. Russell   P
10836 Kling St #201, Toluca Lake, CA 91602, 818-980-6759
   Pubs: *Murmurs of the Past, Full Circle 14, 12: Anths* (Guild
   Pr, 1988, 1991, 1990).

Ray Russell   P&W
8523 Sunset Blvd, Los Angeles, CA 90069
   Pubs: *Dirty Money* (St. Martin's Pr, 1988), *The Night Sound*
   (Dream House, 1987).

Michael Ryan   P
Univ California, English Dept, Irvine, CA 92697,
949-824-8773
Internet: mryan@uci.edu
   Pubs: *Secret Life* (Vintage, 1995), *God Hunger* (Viking, 1989),
   In Winter (HRW, 1981), *Threats Instead of Trees* (Yale, 1974).

Floyd Salas   P&W
1206 Delaware St, Berkeley, CA 94702, 510-527-2594
   Pubs: *Color of My Living Heart, State of Emergency, What
   Now My Love* (Arte Publico Pr, 1996, 1996, 1994), *Tattoo
   the Wicked Cross* (Second Chance Pr, 1982), *Lay My Body
   On the Line* (Y Bird Pr, 1978).

Dixie Salazar   P&W
704 E Brown, Fresno, CA 93704, 209-227-6914
   Pubs: *Limbo* (White Pine Pr, 1995), *Hotel Fresno* (Blue
   Moon, 1988), *Unsettling America: Anth* (Viking, 1994),
   Ploughshares, Santa Barbara Rev, Oregon Rev.

Rachel Salazar   W
PO Box 6173, Albany, CA 94706-6173
   Pubs: *Spectator: A Novel* (Fiction Collective, 1986),
   Chick-Lit 2: Anth (FC2, 1996), *Mondo Elvis: Anth* (St.
   Martin's Pr, 1994), *American Letters and Commentary.*

Dennis Saleh   P
1996 Grandview, Seaside, CA 93955, 408-394-4288
   Pubs: *Rhymses' Book* (Quicksilver, 1999), *This Is Not
   Surrealism* (Willamette River Bks, 1993), *First Z Poems*
   (Bieler Pr, 1980), *Poetry, Paris Rev, The Quarterly, Santa
   Barbara Rev, Art/Life, Pannus Index, Happy, Artword Qtly.*

Mark Salerno   P
PO Box 3749, Los Angeles, CA 90078-3749
   Pubs: *Hate* (96 Tears Pr, 1995), *Exquisite Corpse, Ribot,
   Arshile, Oxygen, Galley Sail Rev, First Intensity, Apex of The
   M, Explosive, Membrane, Mike and Dale's Younger Poets.*

Louis Omar Salinas   P
2009 9th St, Sanger, CA 93657, 209-875-4747
   Pubs: *Follower of Dusk* (Flume Pr, 1991), *Sadness of Days*
   (Arte Publico Pr, 1989).

Benjamin Saltman   P
California State Univ, Northridge, CA 91330, 818-885-3431
   Pubs: *Deck* (Ithaca Hse, 1980), *The Leaves The People*
   (Red Hill Pr, 1974), *Event, Hudson Rev.*

Steve Sanfield   P
22000 Lost River Rd, Nevada City, CA 95959, 530-292-3353
   Pubs: *The Great Turtle Drive* (Knopf, 1996), *American Zen
   By A Guy Who Tried It* (Larkspur Pr, 1994), *Poetry Flash,
   Shambala Sun, Tree Rings, Storytelling.*

Sally Love Saunders P
2030 Vallejo St, #501, San Francisco, CA 94123,
215-356-0849
Pubs: *Manna, New York Times, Times Intl, London Times.*

Minas Savvas P
San Diego State Univ, English & Comparative Literatu, San
Diego, CA 92182, 619-582-5873
Pubs: *The House Vacated* (Parentheses Series, 1989),
TriQuarterly, Seneca Rev, Antioch Rev, APR.

Martin Schechter W
Linda Chester Literary Agency, 1678 Shattuck Ave, Ste 331,
Berkeley, CA 94709, 510-704-0971
Pubs: *Two Halves of New Haven* (Crown, 1992), *Other
Voices.*

Gilbert Schedler P
Univ of the Pacific, Stockton, CA 95211, 209-946-2161
Pubs: *Starting Over* (Pisces Pr, 1992), *Waking Before
Dawn* (Wampeter Pr, 1978), *CQ, Blue Unicorn, Christian
Century, California English, Minotaur, The Windless
Orchard.*

James Schevill P&W
1309 Oxford St, Berkeley, CA 94709, 510-845-2802
Pubs: *The Complete American Fantasies, 5 Plays 5*
(Swallow/Ohio U Pr, 1996, 1993).

Tom Schmidt P
8036 California Ave, Fair Oaks, CA 95628
Pubs: *Watching From the Sky: Anth* (Pinyon Pine Pr, 1989),
The Salmon, Pinchpenny, Poet News.

Dennis Schmitz P
1348 57th St, Sacramento, CA 95819, 916-456-6641
Pubs: *About Night: Selected & New Poems* (Field Edtns,
1993), *Eden* (U Illinois Pr, 1989), *Singing, String* (Ecco Pr,
1985, 1980).

Roy Schneider W
PO Box 151388, San Diego, CA 92175, 619-589-0644
Pubs: *I Know What You Look Like Naked* (Graffiti Comix,
1987), *Suburban Graffiti* (Second Coming Pr, 1986), *City
Lights Rev, Fiction Intl.*

P. Schneidre P
PO Box 67E07, Los Angeles, CA 90067, 310-398-8005
Pubs: *Zyzzyva, Rolling Stone, Paris Rev, Exquisite Corpse,
Antioch Rev.*

Darrell g. h. Schramm P&W
473 28th Ave, San Francisco, CA 94121, 415-221-8779
Internet: schrammd@usfca.edu
Pubs: *A Member of the Family: Anth* (Dutton, 1992),
Silences, Bones & Angled Rain (Bogota, 1974), *Alaska Qtly
Rev, Pittsburgh Qtly, Carolina Qtly, Illinois Rev, North
Dakota Qtly.*

Ruth Wildes Schuler P&W
94 Santa Maria Dr, Novato, CA 949473737, 415-897-5679
Pubs: *Mistress of the Darkened Rooms & Other Short
Stories, Shades of Salem* (Heritage Trails, 1988, 1988),
*Greens Mag, Kavita India, Potpourri, Tears in the Fence,
Yomimono, Timber Creek Rev.*

Carol Schwalberg P&W
629 Palisades Ave, Santa Monica, CA 90402, 310-451-0098
Pubs: *Sailing On Land: Anth* (New Voices, 1993), *If I Had My
Life To Live Over I Would Pick More Daisies: Anth*
(Papier-Mache Pr, 1992), *Palo Alto Rev, West, Wordplay,
Black River Rev, Black Buzzard Rev, Yet Another Small Mag.*

Ruth L. Schwartz P
6035 Majestic Ave, Oakland, CA 94605, 510-638-2956
Internet: ruthpoet@aol.com
Pubs: *Accordion Breathing and Dancing* (U Pitt Pr, 1996),
*Outlook, Nimrod, Yellow Silk, Zone Three, Sow's Ear,
Confrontation, Evergreen Chronicles, Prairie Schooner,
Chelsea, The Sun, Marlboro Rev, New Letters.*

Leah Schweitzer P&W
171 North Church Ln, Unit 606, Los Angeles, CA 90049,
310-471-3817
Internet: leyeleh@aol.com
Pubs: *Without a Single Answer* (Judah L. Magnes Museum,
1990), *Only Morning in Her Shoes* (Utah State U Pr, 1990),
*Literary Monitor, Apalachee Qtly, Shirim, Confrontation,
Slipstream, California State Poetry Qtly.*

James Scully P
2865 Bryant St, San Francisco, CA 94110
Pubs: *Raging Beauty* (Azul Edtns, 1994), *Line Break:
Poetry as Social Practice* (Bay Pr, 1988).

Anna Sears W
1440 Guerrero St, San Francisco, CA 94110, 415-285-3136
Pubs: *Exile* (Goddesses We Ain't Pr, 1996), *Caveat Lector,
Furious Fictions, Alchemy, Other Voices, Volition One.*

Carolyn See W
17339 Tramonto #303, Pacific Palisades, CA 90272
Pubs: *Making History* (HM, 1991), *Golden Days, 110
Shanghai Road* (McGraw-Hill, 1986, 1986).

Hubert Selby, Jr. W
550 North Orlando, #102, West Hollywood, CA 90048
Pubs: *The Willow Tree, Song of the Silent Snow* (Marion
Boyars, 1998, 1988), *Requiem For A Dream, The Demon*
(Playboy, 1979, 1976), *Last Exit to Brooklyn* (Grove, 1964).

Barbara Selfridge W
476 43rd St, Oakland, CA 94609, 510-658-8351
Internet: banterw8@aol.com
Pubs: *Pushcart Prize XVIII: Anth* (Pushcart Pr, 1994),
*Witness, American Voice, Global City Rev, The Sun,
Caribbean Writer, Other Voices.*

Peter Serchuk P
1762 Midvale Ave, Los Angeles, CA 90024, 213-477-3947
　　Pubs: *Waiting for Poppa at the Smithtown Diner* (U Illinois
　　Pr, 1990), *Manhattan Poetry Rev, Indiana Rev, Poetry.*

Judith Serin P
259 Staples Ave, San Francisco, CA 94112
　　Pubs: *Hiding In the World* (Eidolon Edtns, 1998), *Breaking
　　Up is Hard to Do: Anth, What's A Nice Girl Like You Doing
　　in a Relationship Like This?: Anth* (Crossing Pr, 1994,
　　1992), *Barnabe Mountain Rev.*

Nina Serrano P
551 Radnor Rd, Oakland, CA 94606, 415-832-6603
　　Pubs: *Madison: The Adventure of Exile* (Temple U Pr,
　　1989), *Heart Songs* (Poncho Che, 1980).

Bruce W. Severy P
827 Oxford Ave, Marina Del Rey, CA 90292-5431,
213-820-4111
　　Pubs: *The Woman's Lib* (Plirto Pr, 1979).

Shaka Aku Shango P&W
6551 Warner Ave #35, Huntington Beach, CA 92647,
714-841-1293
　　Pubs: *Incoming* (Island Pubs, 1994), *Between A Rock & A
　　Hard Place* (BkMk Pr, 1978), *Catalyst, Sacrifice The
　　Common Sense, New Letters, Iowa Rev, Poets On.*

Helen Shanley P&W
6601 Eucalyptus Dr, #97, Bakersfield, CA 93306,
805-366-8693
　　Pubs: *Poetry, Cream City Rev, CQ, Ecphorizer, Bohemian
　　Chronicle, Reach, Arts Connection.*

Karl Shapiro P&W
904 Radcliffe Dr, Davis, CA 95616, 916-753-0988
　　Pubs: *The Younger Son* (Algonquin, 1988), *New &
　　Selected Poems: 1940-1986* (U Chicago Pr, 1987).

Deirdre Sharett P
106 Candlewood Dr, Petaluma, CA 94954, 707-763-3850
　　Pubs: *Language of a Small Space* (Hartmus Pr, 1980),
　　*Poetry Now, Footwork, Eleventh Muse, Telephone, Sheaf,
　　Star Route Jrnl.*

Saundra Sharp P
Poets Pay Rent, Too, PO Box 75796, Sanford Sta, Los
Angeles, CA 90075, 213-993-6006
　　Pubs: *On The Sharp Side* (Poets Pay Rent, Too, 1993),
　　Black Women For Beginners (Writers & Readers, 1993), *I
　　Hear A Symphony: Anth* (Anchor Bks, 1994), *Healthquest,
　　Black Film Rev, Essence, Crisis.*

Robin Shectman P
1863 N Craig Ave, Altadena, CA 91001, 626-797-1926
Internet: robin@shadow.ociw.edu
　　Pubs: *Poetry, American Scholar, Kenyon Rev, Beloit Poetry
　　Jrnl, Cumberland Poetry Rev, Literary Rev, Blue Unicorn,
　　Seneca Rev, Embers, Yankee, Kansas Qtly.*

Martha A. Shelley P
705 Shrader St, San Francisco, CA 94117, 510-601-0353
　　Pubs: *Haggadah: A Celebration of Freedom* (Aunt Lute
　　Bks, 1997), *Lovers and Mothers* (Sefir Pub, 1981),
　　Crossing the DMZ (Women's Pr Collective, 1974), *On The
　　Issues, Common Lives/Lesbian Lives, Amazon Qtly.*

Jack Shields PP
PO Box 36, Railroad Flat, CA 95248, 209-293-4437
　　Pubs: *Heritage Festival, Arnold Crafts Fair, Borders Books
　　& Music, Fair Oak Coffeehouse, Lord Buckley Festival of
　　Poetry & Music, Sonora Arts Council Poetry Reading,
　　KDVS Radio, Maxwells Bookmark, Whole Earth Fair, Avery
　　Ranch.*

Ruth Shigezawa W
34 Cresthaven, Irvine, CA 92604, 714-786-6722
　　Pubs: *Celeste* (Candlelight Pr, 1993), *The Women Who
　　Walked Through Fire: Anth* (Crossing Pr, 1990), *Amelia,
　　Cicada, Outerbridge, Pulpsmith.*

Max Shulman W
1100 Alta Loma Rd, #1505, Los Angeles, CA 90069

Al Shultz P
1422 Selborn Pl, San Jose, CA 95126, 408-289-8489
Internet: alshultz@earthlink.net
　　Pubs: *Phantasm, New Laurel Rev, California Oranges,
　　Sheaf, Dacotah Territory, Mango, Transfer.*

Aaron Shurin P
1661 Oak St, San Francisco, CA 94117, 415-552-0991
　　Pubs: *Unbound: A Book Of AIDS, Into Distances* (Sun &
　　Moon Pr, 1997, 1993), *A's Dream* (O Bks, 1989), *Grand
　　Street, Sulfur, Talisman, Hambone.*

Noelle Sickels P&W
3424 Larissa Dr, Los Angeles, CA 90026
　　Pubs: *Walking West* (St. Martin's, 1995), *American Fiction:
　　Anth* (Birch Lane Pr, 1991), *Mediphors, Wordplay,
　　Raconteur, Fathoms, Ignis Fatuus Rev.*

Alan Siegler W
581 Baughman, Claremont, CA 91811
　　Pubs: *Icarus, Midstream.*

Richard Silberg P&W
2140 Haste St, Berkeley, CA 94704, 510-848-5156
　　Pubs: *Totem Pole* (3300 Rev Pr, 1996), *The Fields*
　　(Pennywhistle Pr, 1989), *APR, Denver Qtly, Zyzzyva.*

John Oliver Simon P
2209 California, Berkeley, CA 94703, 510-549-2456
Internet: josimon@lanminds.com
    Pubs: *Son Caminos* (Hotel Ambosmundos, 1997), *Lord of the House of Dawn* (Bombshelter, 1991), *Zyzzyva, Elysian Fields Qtly, The Temple, Two Lines, Poetry Flash, Onthebus, Artful Dodge, Caliban, APR.*

Maurya Simon P
Univ California, Riverside, Riverside, CA 925210318, 909-787-5312
Internet: maurya.simon@ucr.edu
    Pubs: *The Golden Labyrinth* (U Missouri Pr, 1995), *Days of Awe, The Enchanted Room* (Copper Canyon, 1989, 1986), *Gettysburg Rev, Prairie Schooner, Poetry.*

Willie Sims PP
11369 Gladstone Ave, Lake View Terrace, CA 91342, 818-899-7209
Internet: gagsaguy@pipeline.com
    Pubs: *Beyond The Valley of Contemporary Poets: Anth* (Sacred Beverage Pr, 1996), *Grand Passion: Poets of Los Angeles: Anth* (Red Wind Bks, 1995), *Beyond Baroque, McGroarty Arts Ctr, UCLA Wight Art Gallery, Fullerton Art Museum, Los Angeles Cty Art Museum.*

Jean Sirius P
PO Box 9665, Oakland, CA 94613
Internet: www.bayscenes.com/ac/sirius/
    Pubs: *And Every One of Us a Witch* (Sirius Bks, 1982), *Poetry of Sex: Anth* (Banned Bks, 1992), *Wanting Women: Anth* (Sidewalk Revolution Pr, 1992).

Jack Skelley P
1140 1/2 Nowita Pl, Venice, CA 90291
    Pubs: *Under 35: The New Generation of American Poets: Anth* (Anchor/Doubleday, 1989), *Brooklyn Rev, Amnesia, Poetry in Motion.*

Don Skiles P&W
172 Palm Ave, #1, San Francisco, CA 94118, 415-386-5390
    Pubs: *Miss America* (Marion Boyars, 1982), *Between C & D, Short Story Rev, Real Fiction, Chelsea.*

G. P. Skratz P&W
5524 Vicente Way, Oakland, CA 94609, 510-428-2915
    Pubs: *Sundae Missile* (Generator Pr, 1992), *The Gates of Disappearance* (Konglomerati Pr, 1982), *Exquisite Corpse, High Performance, Score, Paragraph.*

Richard Slota P
1058 Century Dr, Napa, CA 94558, 707-258-0108
Internet: rlslota@aol.com
    Pubs: *Famous Michael* (Samisdat Pr, 1989), *Abraxas, Blue Buildings, Plainswoman, Deros, Quercus, Yellow Silk.*

Edward Smallfield P&W
1009 Peralta Ave, Albany, CA 94706, 510-524-1308
Internet: esmallf@aol.com
    Pubs: *Trio* (Specter Pr, 1995), *Seven Hundred Kisses: Anth* (Harper San Francisco, 1997), *Fourteen Hills, Santa Clara Rev, Sarasota Poetry Rev, Barnabe Mountain Rev, Yellow Silk, Fiction, Ironwood, Zyzzyva, Margin, Five Fingers Rev, Caliban, Manoa.*

D. James Smith P
62 E Fedora, Fresno, CA 93704
    Pubs: *Prayers for the Dead Ventriloquist, Poetry of the American West: Anth* (Ahsahta Pr, 1995, 1996), *The Quarterly, Quarterly West, Southern Poetry Rev, Willow Springs, Carolina Qtly, Green Mountains Rev, Laurel Rev, New Virginia Rev, Stand.*

Lawrence R. Smith P&W
374 N Cypress Dr, #5, Laguna Beach, CA 92651, 714-497-7437
    Pubs: *The Map of Who We Are* (U Oklahoma Pr, 1997), *The Plain Talk of the Dead* (Montparnasse Edtns, 1988), *River Styx, Paris Rev, Iowa Rev, Pacific Rev.*

Rick Smith P
8591 Hamilton St, Alta Loma, CA 91701
    Pubs: *Hand To Mouth* (Deep Dish, 1981), *Exhibition Game* (G Sack Pr, 1973), *Poetry/L.A..*

Steven Phillip Smith W
1847 S Sherbourne Dr, Los Angeles, CA 90035, 213-559-9370
    Pubs: *American Flyers* (Bantam, 1985), *First Born* (Pocket Bks, 1984), *American Boys* (Avon, 1984).

Virginia E. Smith P
2286-Q Via Puerta, Laguna Hills, CA 92653, 714-830-1688
    Pubs: *A Changeling Eye* (Royal Literary Productions, 1996), *Future Tense* (Tiger Moon, 1992), *Now, San Fernando Jrnl, Poet Mag.*

Clifton Snider P
2719 Eucalyptus Ave, Long Beach, CA 90806-2515, 310-426-3669
    Pubs: *The Age of the Mother* (Laughing Coyote, 1992), *Impervious to Piranhas* (Academic & Arts Pr, 1989), *Sundays at Seven: Anth* (Alamo Square Pr, 1996).

Gary Snyder P
Univ California, Davis, CA 95616
    Pubs: *No Nature* (Pantheon, 1992), *The Practice of the Wild, Left Out in the Rain* (North Point Pr, 1990, 1986), *Yale Rev, Grand Street.*

Margery Snyder   P
PO Box 471493, San Francisco, CA 94147-1493,
415-441-0846
Internet: poetry.guide@miningco.com
  Pubs: *The Gods, Their Feathers* (Blue Beetle Pr, 1992),
  Loving Argument (Viridiana, 1991), *Wise Woman's Garden,
  Coracle, Lynx Eye, Liberty Hill Rev, Talking Raven,
  Onthebus.*

Mary Ellen Solt   P
25520 Wilde Ave, Stevenson Ranch, CA 91381,
805-287-0089
  Pubs: *The People Mover 1968: A Demonstration Poem*
  (West Coast Poetry Rev, 1978), *A Book of Women Poets
  From Antiquity to Now: Anth* (Schocken Bks, 1980), *Poor
  Old Tired Horse, Poetry, 13th Moon, Redstart, Beloit
  Poetry Jrnl.*

Scott Alejandro Sonders   PP&P&W
Apex Media Group, 15445 Ventura Blvd, Ste 279, Sherman
Oaks, CA 91403-3005, 818-754-4410
Internet: news7@letterbox.com
  Pubs: *Orange Messiahs* (Yale Pr, 1999), *Prisoners Rules*
  (Mangrove, 1998), *Litany* (Caravan Pr, 1987), *Meet the
  People* (Perf; PBS Special, 1995), *Write On! Best Short
  Stories Anth* (Center Pr, 1995), *Parnassus, Chiron Rev.*

R. Soos, Jr.   P
2745 Monterey Rd #76, San Jose, CA 95111, 408-578-3546
Internet: soos@soos.com
  Pubs: *Garden Songs, The Son is Breaking Through, His
  Power* (Carpenter's Creative Rev, 1995, 1992, 1988).

Gary Soto   P&W
43 The Crescent, Berkeley, CA 94708, 510-845-4718
  Pubs: *Junior College, New & Selected Poems* (Chronicle
  Bks, 1997, 1995), *Buried Onions, Jesse* (HB, 1997, 1994).

Lily Iona Soucie   P
619 39th St, Richmond, CA 94805, 510-237-7991
  Pubs: *Ink Mag, Berkeley Poetry Rev, Lip Service Mag,
  Green's Mag, Crazyquilt Qtly, Earth's Daughters, San
  Francisco Qtly.*

Barry Spacks   P&W
1111 Bath St, Santa Barbara, CA 93101
Internet: snospx@silcom.com
  Pubs: *Brief Sparrow* (Illuminati, 1988), *Spacks Street*
  (Johns Hopkins, 1982).

Roswell Spafford   P
Univ California, Santa Cruz, CA 95064, 408-927-2688
  Pubs: *Networks, Mississippi Rev, Room, Berkeley Poets
  Co-op Mag, Umbral, Sunbury.*

Rona Spalten   W
6815 Paso Robles, Oakland, CA 94611, 415-339-2978
  Pubs: *New Worlds* (Avon, 1975), *City Miner, Fiction.*

Roberta L. Spear   P
3712 E Balch St, Fresno, CA 93702, 209-233-1483
  Pubs: *The Pilgrim Among Us* (Wesleyan, 1991), *Talking To
  Water* (HRW, 1985), *Ploughshares, Field.*

Carol Speed   W
375 S 3 St, #511, San Jose, CA 95112-3649
  Pubs: *Inside Black Hollywood* (Holloway Hse, 1980),
  Buffalo Soldier Mag.

James Spencer   P&W
155 Lake Rd, Portola Valley, CA 940288116, 650-851-2775
  Pubs: *Playwrights For Tomorrow: Anth* (U Minnesota Pr,
  1975), *The Girl in the Black Raincoat: Anth* (Duell, Sloan,
  Pearce, 1966), *Perspective, Blue Mesa Rev, Santa Barbara
  Rev, Gettysburg Rev, American Literary Rev, Manhattan
  Rev, Ontario Rev, Kayak.*

Lawrence P. Spingarn   P&W
Perivale Press & Agency, 13830 Erwin St, Van Nuys, CA
914012914
  Pubs: *Elegy for Amelia* (Typographeum Bks, 1994),
  Journey to the Interior, Going Like Seventy (Perivale Pr,
  1992, 1988), *Sephardic American Voices: Anth* (Brandeis U
  Pr, 1997), *Critical Qtly, Harper's, New Yorker, The
  European, Transatlantic Rev.*

Susan St. Aubin   P&W
5 Pastori Ave, San Anselmo, CA 94960, 415-459-2100
  Pubs: *Herotica 5: Anth, Herotica 4: Anth* (Penguin/Plume,
  1998, 1996), *Best American Erotica: Anth* (S&S, 1995),
  Yellow Silk, Libido.

David St. John   P
Univ Southern California, University Park, English Dept, Los
Angeles, CA 90089-0354, 213-740-3748
  Pubs: *Where The Angels Come Toward Us* (White Pine Pr,
  1995), *Study For The World's Body* (HC, 1994), *Terrace of
  Rain* (Recursos Bks, 1991).

Jayne Lyn Stahl   P
1441 S. Beverly Glen, #302, Los Angeles, CA 90024
  Pubs: *The Stiffest of the Corpse: Anth* (City Lights Bks,
  1989), *Jacaranda Rev, City Lights Rev, Pulpsmith.*

Hans Jorg Stahlschmidt   P&W
1446 Scenic Ave, Berkeley, CA 94708, 510-848-4040
Internet: hanss49@idt.net
  Pubs: *The Practice of Peace: Anth, XY Files: The Truth
  About Men: Anth* (Sherman Asher Publishing, 1998, 1997),
  *Anthology of Mag Verse, Yearbook of American Verse:
  Anths* (Monitor Bk Co, 1997, 1997), *Atlanta Rev,
  Cumberland Poetry Rev, Nightsun.*

Albert Stainton   P
478 Bartlett St, San Francisco, CA 94110
  Pubs: *The Crossing* (Puckerbrush Pr, 1974), *Paris Rev,
  Poetry, Chelsea, Poetry Now, Wormwood Rev.*

Domenic Stansberry W
4104 24th St, #355, San Francisco, CA 94114, 415-821-7879
Pubs: *Exit Paradise* (Lynx Hse Pr, 1991), *The Spoiler* (Atlantic Monthly Pr, 1987), *Ploughshares, Colorado State Rev, Mississippi Mud.*

Elaine Starkman P&W
PO Box 4071, Walnut Creek, CA 94596, 510-932-1144
Pubs: *Learning to Sit in the Silence* (Papier-Mache Pr, 1993), *Vital Lines* (St. Martin's Pr, 1990), *Shaking Eve's Tree: Anth* (Jewish Pub Soc, 1991).

Marian Steele P
1371 Marinette Rd, Pacific Palisades, CA 90272-2627, 310-454-1887
Internet: cmszego@ucla.edu
Pubs: *The American Dream: Anth* (Pig Iron Pr, 1994), *Life on the Line: Anth* (Negative Capability Pr, 1992), *Ellipsis, South Dakota Rev, Black Buzzard Rev, Press Ltd, New Renaissance, Connecticut River Rev, Poets On.*

Timothy Steele P
1801 Preuss Rd, Los Angeles, CA 90035, 310-837-8675
Pubs: *All The Fun's In How You Say A Thing* (Ohio U Pr/Swallow, 1999), *Sapphics and Uncertainties: Poems 1970-86, Missing Measures* (U Arkansas Pr, 1995, 1990), *The Color Wheel* (Johns Hopkins U Pr, 1994).

Dona Luongo Stein P
318 Cliff Dr, Aptos, CA 95003
Pubs: *Heavenly Bodies* (Jacaranda Pr, 1995), *Women of the 14th Moon* (Crossing Pr, 1994), *Children Of The Mafiosi* (West End Pr, 1977), *Prairie Schooner.*

Hannah Stein P
1118 Bucknell Dr, Davis, CA 95616, 530-753-5382
Internet: skstein@ucdavis.edu
Pubs: *Schools of Flying Fish* (State Street Pr, 1990), *American Literary Rev, Solo, Poetry Now, Beloit Poetry Jrnl, American Voice, Prairie Schooner, Kansas Qtly, Kalliope.*

Julia Stein P
1233 1/2 N Genesse Ave, Los Angeles, CA 90046
Internet: jstein@laedu.lalc.k12.ca.us
Pubs: *Desert Soldiers* (California Classics, 1992), *Under the Ladder to Heaven* (West End, 1984), *Calling Home: Anth* (Rutgers, 1990), *Ikon, Onthebus, Women's Studies Qtly, Pearl, American Book Rev.*

Gary C. Sterling P&W
Marshall Secondary School, 990 N Allen Ave, Pasadena, CA 91104, 818-798-0713
Pubs: *Puerto del Sol, The Clearing House, Oyez Rev, Palo Alto Rev, Reading Improvement, Habersham Rev.*

Janet Sternburg P
16065 Royal Oak Rd, Encino, CA 91436
Pubs: *The Writer On Her Work: Volume II, Volume I* (Norton, 1991, 1981), *Between Women, Tangled Vines.*

Ben Stoltzfus W
Univ California, Literatures & Languages Dept, Riverside, CA 92521, 714-787-5610
Pubs: *Red White And Blue* (York Pr, 1989), *The Eye of the Needle* (Viking, 1967), *Fiction Intl, New Novel Rev, Alaluz, Chelsea, Mosaic.*

Earle Joshua Stone P
72-685 Haystack Rd, Palm Desert, CA 92260
Pubs: *Song of the Toad* (Paige Pub, 1989), *Pub Mirrors, Pine Needles, Arts of Asia Mag, Haiku Headlines, Poetry Nippon, Intl Art Collectors Mag.*

Jennifer Stone P&W
KPFA Pacifica Public Radio, 2207 Shattuck Ave, Berkeley, CA 94704, 415-848-6767
Pubs: *Stone's Throw* (North Atlantic, 1989), *Mind Over Media* (Cayuse, 1988), *Mother Jones, Realist.*

Robert Joe Stout P&W
PO Box 5074, Chico, CA 95927, 916-894-7024
Pubs: *They Still Play Baseball The Old Way* (White Eagle Coffee Store Pr, 1994), *City Lights* (Stout, 1992), *Notre Dame Mag, Penthouse, Christian Century.*

Phyllis Stowell P
St. Mary's College, Moraga, CA 94575, 501-631-4473
Internet: pstowell@galileo.stmarys-ca.edu
Pubs: *Who Is Alice?* (Pennywhistle, 1989), *Columbia, International Qtly, Five Fingers Rev, New Orleans Rev, 13th Moon, Epoch.*

Austin Straus P
PO Box 29154, Los Angeles, CA 90029
Pubs: *Laureate Without A Country: Poems 1976-89* (Ambrosia Pr, 1992), *Hollywood Rev, Slipstream.*

Jane Strong P&W
50 Sunset Ln, Berkeley, CA 94708, 510-527-0569
Pubs: *Blue Unicorn, Primavera, Crosscurrents.*

Dorothy Stroup W
10 Claremont Cres, Berkeley, CA 94705, 510-841-9758
Internet: dstroup@uclink3.berkeley.edu
Pubs: *In the Autumn Wind* (Scribner, 1987).

Denver Stull P&W
318 Cliff Dr, Aptos, CA 95003, 408-662-0197
Pubs: *It Only Hurts When I Smile* (Modern Images, 1988), *Women of the 14th Moon: Anth* (Crossing Pr, 1991), *Looking For Home: Anth* (Milkweed Pr, 1990).

Evelin Sullivan   W
4050 Farm Hill Blvd, #8, Redwood City, CA 94061,
415-367-7770
    Pubs: *Four of Fools, Games of the Blind* (Fromm Intl Pub
    Corp, 1995, 1994), *The Dead Magician* (Dalkey Archive Pr,
    1989).

Amber Coverdale Sumrall   P&W
434 Pennsylvania Ave, Santa Cruz, CA 95062, 408-459-9377
Internet: ambers@sasquatch.com
    Pubs: *Litany of Wings* (Many Names Pr, 1998), *Atomic
    Ghost* (Coffee Hse Pr, 1995), *Bless Me Father* (NAL,
    1994), *Storming Heaven's Gate: Anth* (Plume, 1997), *I
    Am Becoming the Woman I've Wanted: Anth*
    (Papier-Mache, 1994).

Terese Svoboda   P
335 Concord Ave, Menlo Park, CA 94025, 650-324-0743
Internet: sbull@el.net
    Pubs: *Mere Mortals, All Aberration* (U Georgia Pr, 1995,
    1985), *Cannibal* (NYU Pr, 1994), *Laughing Africa* (U Iowa
    Pr, 1990), *Paris Rev, New York Bk Rev, New Republic,
    APR, Nation.*

David Swanger   P
Univ California—Santa Cruz, 301 Dickens Way, Santa Cruz,
CA 95064, 408-426-1292
Internet: dswanger@cats.ucsc.edu
    Pubs: *This Waking Unafraid* (U Missouri Pr, 1995), *Family*
    (Small Poets Pr, 1994), *Georgia Rev, Poetry Northwest,
    Chariton Rev, Kansas Qtly, Poet and Critic.*

Robert Sward   P&W
PO Box 7062, Santa Cruz, CA 95061-7062, 408-426-5247
Internet: http://www.cruzio.com/ scva/rsward.html
    Pubs: *A Much Married Man* (Ekstasis Edtns, 1996), *Four
    Incarnations: New & Selected Poems* (Coffee Hse Pr,
    1991), *New Yorker, Paris Rev, Poetry Chicago.*

Robert Burdette Sweet   W
1761 Edgewood Rd, Redwood City, CA 94062
    Pubs: *Writing Towards Wisdom: The Writer as Shaman*
    (Helios Hse, 1990).

Cole Swensen   P
PO Box 927, Fairfax, CA 94978, 415-453-3331
Internet: 102573.414@compuserve.com
    Pubs: *Noon* (Sun & Moon Pr, 1996), *Numen* (Burning Deck,
    1995), *Conjunctions, Zyzzyva, Five Fingers Rev, Common
    Knowledge, Avec, o.blek.*

Ruth Swensen   P&W
2587 Daisy Ln, Fallbrook, CA 92028, 760-728-8183
Internet: rswen2@juno.com
    Pubs: *McGee Park Poets Anth* (Carlsbad Library, 1993),
    Tide Pools Anth (Mira Costa College, 1993).

Rob Swigart   P&W
2995 Woodside Rd, Ste 400, Woodside, CA 94062,
415-851-5490
    Pubs: *Venom, Toxin, Portal* (St. Martin's Pr, 1991, 1989,
    1988), *New England Rev, Poetry Northwest.*

Michael Sykes   P
PO Box 296, Cedarville, CA 961040296, 530-279-2337
    Pubs: *From An Island In Time* (Jungle Garden Pr, 1984),
    *Neon, Northern Contours, Barnabe Mountain Rev, Floating
    Island, Fallow Deer, Estero.*

Luis Salvador Syquia   P
574 8th Ave, San Francisco, CA 94118

Barbara Szerlip   P
532-B Lombard St, San Francisco, CA 94133, 415-398-3112
    Pubs: *The Ugliest Woman In The World & Other Histories*
    (Gallimaufry, 1978), *The Party Train: A Collection of North
    American Prose Poetry: Anth* (New Rivers Pr, 1996),
    National Geographic, Elle.

Ross Talarico   P
National Univ, 4025 Camino del Rio S, San Diego, CA 92108,
619-563-2572
    Pubs: *All Things As They Are* (David Lang, 1988), *Atlantic,
    Poetry, NAR, Nation, Iowa Rev, APR.*

William Talcott   P
1331 26th Ave, San Francisco, CA 94122, 415-566-3367
Internet: 104174.426@compuserve.com
    Pubs: *Benita's Book* (Thumbscrew Pr, 1997), *Kidstuff*
    (Norton Coker Pr, 1992), *Calling in Sick* (End of the Century
    Bks, 1989), *Exquisite Corpse, NAW, 33 Rev.*

Elizabeth Tallent   W
Univ California, English Dept, Davis, CA 95616,
916-752-6388
    Pubs: *Time with Children, Museum Pieces, In Constant
    Flight* (Knopf, 1987, 1985, 1983), *New Yorker.*

Judith Tannenbaum   P
3120 Yosemite Ave, El Cerrito, CA 94530
    Pubs: *In the Crook of Grief's Arm, Songs in the Night*
    (Nehama Pr, 1993, 1988), *Poetry Flash, Tule Rev, Rain
    City Rev, Steelhead Special, Ink, Sequoia.*

Carol Tarlen   P&W
1001 Bridgeway #729, Sausalito, CA 94965, 415-332-0305
    Pubs: *Homeless Not Helpless: Anth* (Canterbury Pr, 1991),
    Calling Home: Anth (Rutgers U Pr, 1990), *Exquisite
    Corpse, Rain City Rev, Hurricane Alice.*

Roger Taus   P
1418 Stanford St, #7, Santa Monica, CA 90404-3147
    Pubs: *If You Ask Me Where I've Been* (Igneus Pr, 1998),
    Poems From The Combat Zone (Tao Anarchy Bks, 1984),
    Going For Coffee: Anth (Canada; Harbour Pub, 1981),
    Neologisms, Left Curve, Third Rail.

Judith Taylor P
3252 Mandeville Canyon Rd, Los Angeles, CA 90049,
310-472-2752
Internet: judithtay@aol.com
   Pubs: *American Poetry Rev, Antioch Rev, Third Coast,
   American Voice, Crab Orchard Rev, Marlboro Rev, Nimrod,
   Plum Rev, Sonora Rev, Poetry, Spoon River Rev, Nimrod.*

Kent Taylor P
1450 10th Ave, San Francisco, CA 94122, 415-665-8073
   Pubs: *Rabbits Have Fled, Late Show At The Starlight
   Laundry* (Black Rabbit, 1991, 1989), *The Quarterly,
   Abraxas, Onthebus, Rain City Rev.*

Susan Terence P
2153 Hayes St, San Francisco, CA 94117-1010,
415-995-2659
   Pubs: *Nebraska Rev, San Francisco Bay Guardian,
   Halftones to Jubilee, Southern Poetry Rev, Negative
   Capability, Lake Effect.*

Susan Terris P&W
11 Jordan Ave, San Francisco, CA 94118, 415-386-7333
Internet: sdt11@aol.com
   Pubs: *Curved Space* (La Jolla Poets Pr, 1998), *Nell's Quilt,
   Author! Author!* (FSG, 1996, 1990), *Killing in the Comfort
   Zone* (Pudding Hse Pubs, 1995), *Antioch Rev, Spoon River
   Poetry Rev, Southern Poetry Rev.*

Roland Tharp P
307 Dickens Way, Santa Cruz, CA 95064
   Pubs: *Highland Station* (Poetry Texas Pr, 1977), *Prairie
   Schooner, Hawaii Rev, Southwest Rev.*

Raul Thomas W
116 San Jose, #2, San Francisco, CA 94110, 415-641-8766
   Pubs: *Las Caras de la Luna, dicen que soy. . . , y aseguran
   que estoy* (Spain; Betania, 1996, 1993).

Gary Thompson P
California State Univ, English Dept, Chico, CA 95929,
530-898-5125
Internet: gthompson@oavax.csuchico.edu
   Pubs: *As For Living* (Red Wing Pr, 1995), *Hold Fast*
   (Confluence Pr, 1984), *Colorado Rev, Laurel Rev, Nebraska
   Rev, Writers' Forum, Hayden's Ferry Rev, Chariton Rev.*

Joanna Thompson P
1515 Umeo Rd, Pacific Palisades, CA 90272, 213-454-1696
   Pubs: *American Scholar, California Qtly, Southwest Rev,
   New Orleans Rev, Phantasm, America.*

Sabina Thorne W
PO Box 1413, Bethel Island, CA 94511-2413
   Pubs: *Of Gravity and Grace* (Janus Pr, 1982), *Reruns*
   (Viking Pr, 1981).

Terry Tierney P
1185 Glencourt Dr, Oakland, CA 94611, 510-339-0704
Internet: ttierney@geoworks.com
   Pubs: *Abraxas, Blue Buildings, California Qtly,
   Centennial Rev, Chattahoochee Rev, Concerning Poetry,
   Contact II, Cottonwood Rev, Great River Rev, Kalliope,
   Kansas Qtly, Milkweed Chronicle, Poetry at 33, Poetry
   Northwest, Puerto del Sol, South Dakota Rev.*

Gioia Timpanelli PP
Katherine Boyle Veritas Litera, 1157 Valencia, Ste 4, San
Francisco, CA 94110, 415-647-6964
   Pubs: *Sometimes the Soul: 2 Novellas of Sicily* (Norton,
   1998), *Travelling Images & Observations* (Italy; Grafiche
   AZ, 1987).

JoAnn Byrne Todd P
21627 Ocean Vista Dr, South Laguna, CA 92677,
714-499-2112
   Pubs: *Voices Intl, Wind Chimes, Modern Haiku, Pulp, Blue
   Grass, Literary Rev.*

Sotere Torregian P
1010 Tamarack Ave, San Carlos, CA 94070-3746,
415-592-6079
   Pubs: *The Young Englishwoman* (Printmasters, 1989), *The
   Age of Gold* (Kulchur, 1976), *Paris Rev.*

Paul Trachtenberg P
9431 Krepp Dr, Huntington Beach, CA 92646, 714-968-7546
   Pubs: *Alphabet Soup: A Laconic Lexicon* (Wordworks,
   1997), *Ben's Exit, Making Waves* (Cherry Valley Edtns,
   1994, 1990).

Truong Tran P
337 10th Ave, #5, San Francisco, CA 94118, 415-387-1121
Internet: celan@primenet.com
   Pubs: *Zyzzyva, ACM, American Voice, Crazyhorse,
   Poetry East, Onthebus, Prairie Schooner, Berkeley
   Poetry Rev, Blue Mesa Rev, Fourteen Hills, North
   Dakota Qtly, Reed.*

Laurel Trivelpiece P&W
23 Rocklyn Ct, Corte Madera, CA 94925, 415-924-9130
   Pubs: *Just A Little Bit Lost* (Scholastic, 1988), *Blue Holes*
   (Alice James Bks, 1987), *Poetry.*

Quincy Troupe P
1655 Nautilus St, La Jolla, CA 92037
   Pubs: *Avalanche: New Poems* (Coffee Hse Pr, 1996),
   Weather Reports: New & Selected Poems (Harlem River
   Pr, 1991), *Kenyon Rev, Ploughshares, Pequod.*

Kitty Tsui P
1010 Church St, San Francisco, CA 94114, 415-824-8460
Internet: baisve888@aol.com
   Pubs: *Breathless* (Firebrand, 1996).

Mike Tuggle P
PO Box 421, Cazadero, CA 95421, 707-632-5818
Pubs: *Cazadero Poems* (Floating Island Pub, 1994), *White Heron Rev, Temple, Poetry Flash, Zyzzyva, Manoa, Americas Rev, CPITS Anth, Psychological Perspectives, Floating Island, Slant.*

David L. Ulin P&W
8126 Blackburn Ave, Los Angeles, CA 90048
Pubs: *Cape Cod Blues* (Red Dust, 1992), *Unbearables: Anth* (Autonomedia, 1995), *Exquisite Corpse, Rampike, Vignette, Brooklyn Rev, B City, Sensitive Skin.*

Charles Upton P
245 Nova Albion Way, San Rafael, CA 94903-3529, 415-454-2343
Pubs: *Snake of Mute River* (Artaud's Elbow, 1979), *Panic Grass* (City Lights Bks, 1968), *Longhouse.*

Amy Uyematsu P
13000 Oxnard Ave, Van Nuys, CA 91401, 818-781-1400
Internet: uyematsua@aol.com
Pubs: *Nights of Fire, Nights of Rain, 30 Miles from J-Town* (Story Line Pr, 1998, 1992), *Blue Mesa Rev, Solo, Asian Pacific American Jrnl, Crab Orchard Rev, Zyzzyva, Daybreak.*

Lequita Vance-Watkins P
PO Box 221847, Carmel, CA 93922, 408-624-5068
Pubs: *White Flash/Black Rain* (Milkweed Edtns, 1995), *Dark With Stars* (High Coo Pr, 1984), *Out of the Dark: Anth* (Queen of Swords Pr, 1995).

Paul Vangelisti P
2060 Escarpa Dr, Los Angeles, CA 90041
Pubs: *Nemo* (Sun & Moon Pr, 1995), *Villa* (Littoral Bks, 1991), *Another You* (Red Hill, 1981).

Richard Vasquez W
3345 Marengo, Altadena, CA 91001, 213-794-9825

Bob Vickery W
769 Cole St #2, San Francisco, CA 94117, 415-386-3088
Internet: cseiter@concentric.net
Pubs: *Cock Tales* (Leyland Pub, 1997), *Up All Hours* (Alyson Bks, 1997), *Butch Boys, Skin Deep* (Masquerade Bks, 1997, 1994), *Advocate Men.*

Alma Luz Villanueva P
4135 Gladys Ave, Santa Cruz, CA 95062
Internet: almaluz@aol.com
Pubs: *Desire, Weeping Woman: La Llorona and Other Stories, Naked Ladies, Planet* (Bilingual Pr, 1998, 1994, 1993, 1993), *The Ultraviolet Sky* (Doubleday, 1993).

Marianne Villanueva W
2431 Hopkins Ave, Redwood City, CA 94062
Internet: hf.mrv@forsythe.stanford.edu
Pubs: *Ginseng and Other Tales From Manila* (Calyx Bks, 1991), *The Nuyorasian Anth, Flippin: Filipinos in America* (Asian American Writers Workshop, 1998, 1996), *Into the Fire: Anth* (Greenfield Rev, 1996), *Charlie Chan is Dead: Anth* (Viking, 1993).

Victor Edmundo Villasenor W
Rancho Villasenor, 1302 Stewart St, Oceanside, CA 92054, 619-454-1550
Pubs: *Walking Star* (Arte Publico Pr, 1994), *Rain of Gold* (Dell, 1992), *Jury* (Little, Brown, 1978), *Macho* (Bantam, 1973).

Stephen Vincent P
3514 21st St, San Francisco, CA 94114, 415-641-0739
Internet: steph484@aol.com
Pubs: *Walking* (Junction Bks, 1993).

Gerald Robert Vizenor P
Univ California, 301 Campbell Hall, Berkeley, CA 94720, 510-642-6593
Internet: vizenor@uclink4.berkeley.edu
Pubs: *Fugitive Poses* (U Nebraska Pr, 1998), *Hotline Healers* (Wesleyan U Pr, 1997).

Eric B. Vogel P
29190 Verdi Rd, Hayward, CA 94544, 510-538-1638
Internet: erichv@tdl.com
Pubs: *Antigonish Rev, Stand, Envoi, Poetry Motel, Encodings, Sublime Odyssey, Raindog Rev, Mobius, Parting Gifts.*

Arthur Vogelsang P
1730 N Vista St, Los Angeles, CA 90046, 213-874-2220
Pubs: *Cities and Towns* (U Massachusetts Pr, 1996), *Twentieth Century Women* (U Georgia Pr, 1988).

Susan Vreeland W
6246 Caminito Araya, San Diego, CA 92122, 619-587-9351
Internet: svreeland@abac.com
Pubs: *What Love Sees* (Thorndike/S&S, 1996), *Family: A Celebration: Anth* (Peterson's Guides, 1995), *New Millennium, Dominion Rev, Crosscurrents, Ambergris, Missouri Rev, Confrontation, Manoa, Alaska Qtly Rev, Crescent Rev.*

Christy Wagner W
PO Box 1628, Mendocino, CA 95460, 707-937-2410
Internet: cwagner@mcn.org
Pubs: *Mustang Je T'aime* (Gorde Plata Pr, 1996).

Jeanne Wagner P
23 Edgecroft Rd, Kensington, CA 94707, 510-526-4190
Pubs: *Denny Poems, Ekphrasis, Poet's Guild, Blue Unicorn, Lucid Stone, Silver Quill, Spoon River.*

John Walke W
5671 E Waverly Ln, Fresno, CA 93727-5437, 209-456-9255
Pubs: *Nethula Jrnl, Pulp, Apalachee Qtly, Bachy, Bridge, Backwash, Second Coming, Tandava.*

Mary Alexander Walker W
PO Box 151615, San Rafael, CA 94915, 415-461-1025
Pubs: *Scathach and Maeve's Daughters, Brad's Box, Maggot, To Catch A Zombie* (Atheneum, 1990, 1988, 1980, 1979).

David Foster Wallace W
Frederick Hill Associates, 1842 Union St, San Francisco, CA 94123
Pubs: *Girl With Curious Hair* (Norton, 1989), *Broom of the System* (Viking, 1987), *Harper's.*

William Wallis P
Los Angeles Valley College, 5800 Fulton Ave, Van Nuys, CA 91401, 818-781-1200
Internet: walliswg@laccd.cc.ca.us
Pubs: *Dutton's Books, Eros* (Stone and Scott Pubs, 1995, 1994), *Biographer's Notes* (Yellow Barn Pr, 1984).

Diane Ward P
1023 Centinela Ave, Santa Monica, CA 90403, 310-828-1060
Pubs: *Human Ceiling* (Roof Bks, 1996), *Imaginary Movie* (Potes & Poets, 1992), *Out of Everywhere: Anth* (Reality Street Edtns, 1996), *Raddle Moon, Ribot.*

Lynn Watson P&W
PO Box 1253, Occidental, CA 95465
Pubs: *Catching the Devil* (Keegan Pr, 1994), *Amateur Blues* (Taurean Horn Pr, 1990), *Oxygen.*

Charles Harper Webb P&W
California State Univ, 1250 Bellflower Blvd, Long Beach, CA 90840, 562-985-4244
Internet: cwebb@csulb.edu
Pubs: *Reading the Water* (Northeastern U Pr, 1998), *Best American Poetry 1995: Anth* (S&S, 1995), *Stand Up Poetry: Anth* (University Pr, 1994), *Iowa Rev, Paris Rev, Michigan Qtly Rev, Ploughshares, APR, Gettysburg Rev.*

Brenda Webster W
2671 Shasta Rd, Berkeley, CA 94708, 510-548-2618
Internet: brenda1@well.com
Pubs: *Tattoo Bird* (Fiction Net, 1996), *Sins of the Mothers* (Baskerville Pr, 1993), *Chariton Rev, Women's Studies, Crazyquilt.*

Richard J. Weekley P
24721 Newhall Ave, Newhall, CA 91321, 805-254-0851
Pubs: *Small Diligences* (L.A. Poets Pr, 1988), *Mayan Night* (Domina Bks, 1981), *These Things Happen: Anth* (Inevitable Pr, 1997), *Blue Buildings, Crosscurrents, Gryphon, Kansas Qtly, Poetry/L.A., Literary Rev.*

Florence Weinberger P
17143 Albers St, Encino, CA 91316, 818-789-3786
Pubs: *The Invisible Telling Its Shape* (Fithian Pr, 1997), *Breathing Like A Jew* (Chicory Blue Pr, 1997), *Truth And Lies That Press for Life* (Artifact Pr, 1991), *Grand Passion: Anth* (Red Wind Bks, 1995), *Tikkun, ACM, Calyx, Daybreak, Rohwedder, Pacific Rev.*

Kenneth Weisner P
528 Windham St, Santa Cruz, CA 95062, 408-426-5172
Internet: gyre@cats.ucsc.edu
Pubs: *Porter Gulch Rev, Oyez, Berkeley Poetry Rev, Brooklyn Rev, Antioch Rev, Lighthouse Point, Eye Prayers, New Honolulu Rev.*

Jason Lee Weiss P
1101 Spruce St, Berkeley, CA 94707, 415-655-9694

Mark Weiss P
Box 40537, San Diego, CA 92164-0537, 619-282-0371
Internet: junction@earthlink.net
Pubs: *Fieldnotes* (Junction Pr, 1995), *A Blockprint by Kuniyoshi* (Four Zoas/Night Hse, 1994).

ruth weiss P
PO Box 509, Albion, CA 95410, 707-937-5619
Internet: http://shell3.ba.best.com/ lcamag/cover.html
Pubs: *For These Women of the Beat* (3300 Pr, 1997), *Women of the Beat Generation: Anth* (Conari Pr, 1996), *Poetry at the 33, Bombay Gin, Discourse, Beatitude, Poetry Now, Kerouac Connection, Typewriter, Mendonesian.*

David Weissmann P
Stanford Univ, Stanford, CA 94305, 415-497-1700
Pubs: *Poetry, Southern Rev, Poetry Northwest, Antioch Rev, Shenandoah, Epoch, Stand.*

Michael Dylan Welch P
248 Beach Park Blvd, Foster City, CA 94404, 650-571-9428
Internet: welchm@aol.com
Pubs: *Red Moon Anthology 1997* (Red Moon, 1998), *Haiku World: Anth* (Kodansha, 1996), *Haiku Moment: Anth* (Charles E. Tuttle Co., 1993), *Spring: E. E. Cummings Society Jrnl, Woodnotes, Modern Haiku, Black Bough, Tundra.*

Marion deBooy Wentzien W
19801 Merribrook Ct, Saratoga, CA 95070, 408-867-0306
Pubs: *Desert Shadows* (Avalon Bks, 1988), *Seventeen, New Letters, This World, Fact & Fiction.*

Michael West P
323 Martin, Rio del Mar, CA 95003, 408-688-6253
Pubs: *Odes and Other Modes, Eye Quilt* (Wire Wind Ink, 1984, 1971), *Street, Lost & Found Times, Paper Radio, Swift Kick, Bird Effort, Abbey.*

David Westheimer W
11722 Darlington Ave, #2, Los Angeles, CA 90049
Pubs: *Death Is Lighter Than A Feather* (U North Texas Pr, 1995), *Sitting It Out* (Rice U Pr, 1992), *My Sweet Charlie* (Doubleday, 1965).

Philip Whalen P&W
Hartford Street Zen Center, 57 Hartford St, San Francisco, CA 94114
Pubs: *You Didn't Even Try & Imaginary Speeches for a Brazen Head* (Zephyr, 1985).

Jackson Wheeler P
PO Box 954, Ventura, CA 93002-0954, 805-483-1905
Internet: tc2lz@tri-counties.org
Pubs: *How Good Fortune Surprises Us* (Solo Pr, 1998), *Swimming Past Iceland* (Mille Grazie Pr, 1993), *Beyond the Valley of the Contemporary Poets: Anth* (Sacred Beverage Pr, 1997), *Daybreak, Rivertalk, Artlife.*

Betty Coon Wheelwright P
PO Box 1359, Pt Reyes Station, CA 94956
Pubs: *Seaward* (Berkeley Poets Co-op, 1978), *Calyx, Southern Poetry Rev, Psych Perspectives, Women's Qtly Rev, Wooster Rev.*

Robin White W
California State Polytechnic, 3801 W Temple Ave, Pomona, CA 91768, 714-869-3940
Pubs: *Moses the Man* (Monograph, 1981), *San Francisco, Focus, Spring Harvest, Pulpsmith, Hard Copies, Portfolio, Arizona Qtly.*

Theresa Whitchill P
1751 Cameron Rd, Elk, CA 95432, 707-877-1816
Internet: writing@coloredhorse.com
Pubs: *A Natural History of Mill Towns* (Pygmy Forest Pr, 1993), *Montserrat Rev, Semi-Dwarf Rev, Mendonesian, Steelhead Special, Art/Life, MidAir, Yellow Silk, Mendocino Rev, Oxygen.*

William Wiegand W
San Francisco State Univ, 1600 Holloway Ave, San Francisco, CA 94132, 415-469-1021
Pubs: *The Chester A. Arthur Conspiracy* (Dial Pr, 1983), *School of Soft Knocks* (Lippincott, 1968).

Rosemary C. Wilkinson P
3146 Buckeye Ct, Placerville, CA 95667, 916-626-4166
Pubs: *Poetry: Nature, Collected Poems* (E.J. Co., 1996, 1994), *Cambrian Zephyr* (Amarin Printing Group, 1994).

Sylvia Wilkinson W
514 Arena St, El Segundo, CA 90245-3016, 310-322-2814
Pubs: *On the 7th Day God Created the Chevrolet, Cale* (Algonquin Bks, 1993, 1986).

Daniel Williams P
General Delivery, Yosemite, CA 953899999, 209-375-6721
Pubs: *XY Files: Poems on the Male Experience: Anth* (Sherman Asher Pub, 1997), *North Dakota Qtly, Midwest Qtly, Moody Street Rev, Men As We Are, Seattle Rev, Manzanita, Kerf, The Acorn, Z Miscellaneous, Sunrust.*

Paul Osborne Williams P
2718 Monserat Ave, Belmont, CA 94002, 415-591-2733
Internet: powms@aol.com
Pubs: *Footsteps in the Fog, Fig Newtons: Anth* (Press Here, 1994, 1993), *Modern Haiku, Frog Pond, Woodnotes.*

Sherley Anne Williams P
Univ California, La Jolla, CA 92093, 619-534-3210
Pubs: *Working Cotton* (HBJ, 1992), *Dessa Rose, Some One Sweet Angel Chile* (Morrow, 1986, 1982).

Robin Williamson P&W
PO Box 27522, Los Angeles, CA 90027
Pubs: *Selected Writings 1980-83, Five Denials on Merlin's Grave* (Pigs Whisker Music, 1984, 1979).

Paul Willis P&W
Westmont College, Santa Barbara, CA 93108-1099, 805-565-7174
Internet: willis@westmont.edu
Pubs: *No Clock In the Forest* (Avon Bks, 1993), *Best American Poetry: Anth* (Scribner, 1996), *Poets On, Green Fuse, Weber Studies, Christian Century, Image, Slant, Poetry, Petroglyph.*

Eric Wilson W
1319 Pearl St, Santa Monica, CA 90405, 213-452-3452
Pubs: *Prize Stories 1985: The O. Henry Awards: Anth* (Doubleday, 1985), *Witness, Massachusetts Rev, Epoch.*

Dick Wimmer W
11845 Olympic Blvd, Ste 645, Los Angeles, CA 90064, 310-312-8660
Pubs: *Boyne's Lassie* (Zoland, 1998), *Irish Wine* (Mercury Hse, 1989), *Baseball Fathers, Baseball Sons* (Morrow, 1988), *Tales of the Heart, Nassau Rev, Flash-Bopp.*

A. D. Winans P&W
P.O. Box 31249, San Francisco, CA 94131, 415-826-1768
Pubs: *America* (Black Bear Pr, 1998), *San Francisco Streets* (Ye Olde Font Shoppe, 1997), *In Memoriam* (Alpha Beat, 1990), *New York Qtly, Kansas Qtly, Confrontation, Karamu, Atom Mind, Longshot, Nexus, Split Shift, Beat Scene.*

Mary Wings W
168 1/2 Precita Ave, San Francisco, CA 94110
Internet: wingsm@sirius.com
Pubs: *She Came by the Book* (Berkley Prime Crime, 1996), *Divine Victim, She Came in a Flash* (NAL, 1993, 1989), *She Came Too Late* (Crossing Pr, 1987).

Bayla Winters P
2700 Scott Rd, Burbank, CA 91504-2314, 818-846-1879
Internet: wb6osc@aol.com
Pubs: *Seeing Eye Wife, Shooting from the Lip* (Gideon Pr, 1997, 1995), *Sacred and Propane* (Croton Rev, 1989), *Life on the Line: Anth* (Negative Capability Pr, 1992), *Graffiti Rag, Convolvulus, Maverick Pr, El Locofoco, Iconoclast, Phoenix, Fuel.*

Anne F. Wittels P
2116 Via Alamitos, Palos Verdes Estat, CA 90274, 213-378-5812
Pubs: *Lost & Found* (Coco Palm Tree Pr, 1982), *Bitterroot, Palos Verdes Rev, Women.*

Maia Wojciechowska W
Pebble Beach Press, PO Box 1171, Pebble Beach, CA 07430
Pubs: *Dreams of World Cup, Dreams of Wimbledon, Dreams of Golf* (Pebble Beach Pr, 1994, 1994, 1993).

Tad Wojnicki P&W
PO Box 3198, Carmel, CA 93921, 408-770-0107
Internet: wojnicki@aol.com
Pubs: *Lie Under the Fig Trees* (Angels by the Sea Pr, 1998), *Scrawls on a Crate of Oranges* (Pomost Pubs, 1987), *Mosaic, Leviathan, Coffeehouse, Poets' Paper, The Literary Jrnl.*

Murray E. Wolfe P
PO Box 280550, Northridge, CA 913280550, 818-885-0101
Internet: banker@pacificnet.net
Pubs: *Blessed Be the Beast* (Ambrosia Pr, 1981).

Geoffrey Wolff W
202 South Orange Dr, Los Angeles, CA 90036, 949-824-3745
Internet: gwolff@uci.edu
Pubs: *Providence, The Duke of Deception* (Vintage, 1991, 1990), *Granta, Esquire, Paris Rev, TriQuarterly, Atlantic.*

Jean Walton Wolff P&W
PO Box 275, Aptos, CA 95001, 408-688-9425
Pubs: *Sleeping With Dionysis: Anth* (Crossing Pr, 1992), *Porter Gulch Rev, Milvia Street, Bakunin.*

Joel M. Y. Wolk PP
1343 Oak St, San Francisco, CA 94117, 415-552-3883
Internet: globalpoet@aol.com
Pubs: *The Jazz Poetry Anthology* (Indiana U Pr, 1991), *Tree 3, Sou'wester, Monument, Poetry Bag, Off the Wall, Sala De Puerto Rico at MIT, Hayden Gallery at MIT, Writers' Forum, Old Red Kimono, Focus Midwest.*

Cecilia Woloch P
5921 Whitworth Dr #201, Los Angeles, CA 90019, 213-933-8718
Internet: ceciwo@aol.com
Pubs: *Sacrifice* (Cahuenga Pr, 1997), *Grand Passion: Anth* (Red Wing Bks, 1995), *Breaking Up Is Hard To Do: Anth* (Crossing Pr, 1994), *Catholic Girls: Anth* (Penguin/Plume, 1992), *Prose Poem, Antioch Rev, Zyzzyva, Literal Latte, Chelsea Hotel.*

Ko Won P
11754 Castillo Ln, Northridge, CA 91326, 818-363-5325
Pubs: *Some Other Time* (Bombshelter Pr, 1990), *The Turn of Zero* (Cross-Cultural Communications, 1974), *Amerasia, Chicago Rev, The Literary Realm, Bitter Oleander.*

Nanying Stella Wong P
1537 Comstock Ct, Berkeley, CA 947031030, 510-524-2229
Pubs: *Bearing Dreams, Shaping Visions: Anth* (Washington State U Pr, 1993), *Peace & Pieces: Contemporary American Poetry: Anth* (Peace & Pieces Pr, 1973), *Sunset Mag, California Living.*

Nellie Wong P
549 Chenery St, San Francisco, CA 94131-3031, 415-584-7097
Pubs: *Stolen Moments* (Chicory Blue Pr, 1997), *The Death of Long Steam Lady* (West End Pr, 1986), *Dreams In Harrison Railroad Park* (Kelsey Street Pr, 1977), *Forkroads, Open Boat, Dissident Song, Long Shot, Lente Case Del Tempo.*

Stella Worley P
708 Inglewood Dr, Broderick, CA 95605, 916-372-0250
Pubs: *Three Panels For December* (Hearthstone, 1979), *Blue Unicorn, Dekalb Literary Arts Jrnl, CPU Rev.*

Alice F. Worsley P
California State College, English/Foreign Languages Dept, Turlock, CA 95380, 209-633-2361

Elizabeth Wray P
834 Elizabeth St, San Francisco, CA 94114, 415-863-1289
Pubs: *Partisan Rev, Kayak, Epoch, Denver Qtly, Pacific Sun Literary Qtly, Berkeley Poets Co-op.*

Kirby Wright P&W
3259 Alma St, Palo Alto, CA 94306, 650-856-8141
Pubs: *Artful Dodge, Blue Mesa Rev, Santa Clara Rev, Hawaii Rev, Welter Mag, West Mag.*

Mark Wunderlich P
3164 22nd St #19, San Francisco, CA 94110, 415-824-0941
Internet: vonwunder@aol.com
Pubs: *Things Shaped in Passing: Anth* (Persea Bks, 1997), *Night Out: Anth* (Milkweed Edtns, 1997), *Paris Rev, Boston Rev, Yale Rev, Poetry, Agni, Chelsea, Southwest Rev, Harvard Rev, Graham Hse Rev, Sonora Rev.*

Robert Wynne P
10041 Benares Pl, Sun Valley, CA 913524207, 818-545-9846
Pubs: *Northridge Rev, Caffeine, Verve, Sheila-Na-Gig, Red Dancefloor, Convergence, Paper Radio.*

Mitsuye Yamada P&W
6151 Sierra Bravo Rd, Irvine, CA 92715, 714-854-8699
Pubs: *Camp Notes and Other Poems, Desert Run: Poems & Stories* (Kitchen Table Pr, 1992, 1988), *Sowing Ti Leaves: Anth* (Multicultural Women Writers, 1991).

Hisaye Yamamoto DeSoto W
4558 Mont Eagle Pl, Los Angeles, CA 90041
Pubs: *Seventeen Syllables and Other Stories* (Rutgers U Pr, 1998), *Charlie Chan Is Dead: Anth* (Penguin, 1993), *The Big Aiiieeeee!: Anth* (Meridian, 1991), *Rafu.*

Stephen Yenser P
10322 Tennessee Ave, Los Angeles, CA 90064, 310-203-9833
Internet: yenser@humnet.ucla.edu
Pubs: *The Fire in All Things* (LSU Pr, 1993), *Best American Poetry: Anths* (Scribner, 1995, 1992), *Paris Rev.*

Al Young P&W
514 Bryant St, Palo Alto, CA 94301, 415-329-1189
Pubs: *Heaven: Collected Poems, 1956-1990* (Creative Arts Bk Co., 1992), *Seduction By Light* (Delacorte, 1988).

C. Dale Young P
4210 Judah St, #303, San Francisco, CA 941221016
Internet: cdaleyoung@rocketmail.com
Pubs: *The Best American Poetry 1996: Anth* (Scribner, 1996), *The Writing Path 1: Anth* (U Iowa Pr, 1995), *Antioch Rev, New Criterion, NAR, Partisan Rev, Southern Rev, Southwest Rev, Salmagundi, Yale Rev.*

Gary Young P
3965 Bonny Doon Rd, Santa Cruz, CA 95060, 408-426-4355
Pubs: *Days* (Silverfish Rev Pr, 1997), *The Dream of a Moral Life* (Copper Beech Pr, 1990), *Antaeus, APR, Kenyon Rev.*

John A. Youril P
8420 Olivine Ave, Citrus Heights, CA 95610, 916-729-7072
Pubs: *Realm of the Vampire, Mixed Bag, Haunted Jrnl, Bitterroot, Stone Country, Metrosphere, Poetry & Fiction, Lapis, Poetry Today, The Archer.*

Rich Yurman P
2514 24th Ave, San Francisco, CA 94116, 415-665-8649
Pubs: *A Perfect Pair: he whispered/she shouted* (Secon Avenyuh Pr, 1989), *Liberty Hill, Slipstream, New York Qtly, Small Pond, Mudfish, Amelia.*

Jeffrey A. Z. Zable P&W
50 Parnassus Ave, San Francisco, CA 94117, 415-731-5250
Pubs: *Zable's Fables* (Androgyne Pr, 1990), *Wormwood Rev, Writ, Long Shot, Central Park, Caliban, New York Qtly.*

Stella Zamvil P&W
821 Thornwood Dr, Palo Alto, CA 943034437, 650-494-7791
Pubs: *In the Time of the Russias* (John Daniel, 1985), *Harpoon, Greensboro Rev, Palo Alto Rev, Canadian Jewish Outlook, Louisville Rev.*

Franklin Zawacki W
2156 Irvin Way, Sacramento, CA 95822, 916-457-1123
Pubs: *Hell Coal Annual, Cowhunting.*

Paul Zelevansky PP&P
5625 Valley Oak Dr, Los Angeles, CA 90068-2556
Pubs: *The Shadow Architecture At the Crossroads Annual 19__* (CNC, 1988).

Merla Zellerbach W
Fred Hill Literary Agency, 1842 Union St, San Francisco, CA 94123, 415-751-4535
Pubs: *The Allergy Sourcebook* (Lowell Hse, 1996), *Rittenhouse Square* (Random Hse, 1991), *Sugar, Cavett Manor* (Ballantine, 1989, 1987), *Town & Country, Travel & Leisure, Reader's Digest, Prevention, Cosmopolitan.*

Rafael Zepeda P&W
California State Univ LB, Long Beach, CA 90840, 562-985-4243
Pubs: *The Witchita Poems* (Pearl Pr, 1997), *Horse Medicine* (Applezaba Pr, 1993), *The Yellow Ford of Texas* (Vergin Pr, 1993), *Higher Elevations: Anth* (Swallow Pr, 1993), *A New Geography of Poets: Anth* (U Arkansas Pr, 1993), *The Wormwood Rev, Pearl Mag.*

Paul Edwin Zimmer P&W
Greyhaven, 90 El Camino Real, Berkeley, CA 94705, 510-658-6033
Pubs: *La Chramata Degli Eroi* (Casa Editrice Nord, 1993), *Return to Avalon: Anth* (Daw Bks, 1996), *Mythic Circle, Berserkrgangr.*

Harriet Ziskin W
187 Ney St, San Francisco, CA 94112
Pubs: *The Adventures of Mona Pinsky* (Calyx Bks, 1995), *Broomstick, Jacob's Letter, Ceilidh, Outerbridge.*

Bonnie ZoBell W
Mesa College, 7250 Mesa College Dr, San Diego, CA 92111, 619-627-2912
Internet: bzobell@cts.com
Pubs: *American Fiction: Anth* (New Rivers, 1997), *Greensboro Rev, San Diego Writers Monthly, PEN Syndicated Project, Cimarron Rev, Bellingham Rev, Gulf Stream Mag.*

Al Zolynas P
2380 Viewridge Pl, Escondido, CA 92026, 760-740-9098
Internet: azolynas@usiu.edu
Pubs: *Under Ideal Conditions* (Laterthanever Pr, 1994),
A Book of Luminous Things: Anth (HB, 1996), *A New
Geography of Poets: Anth* (U Arkansas Pr, 1992).

COLORADO

Keith Abbott P&W
Naropa Writing Dept, 2130 Arapahoe, Boulder, CO 80302,
303-682-9664
Pubs: *Downstream from Trout Fishing in America* (Capra
Pr, 1989), *The First Thing Coming* (Coffee Hse, 1987).

Mark Amerika W
PO Box 241, Boulder, CO 80306, 303-499-9331
Internet: http://www.altx.com
Pubs: *Sexual Blood, The Kafka Chronicles* (Fiction
Collective Two, 1995, 1993), *Lettre Intl, Fiction Intl,
Witness, Central Park, American Book Rev.*

Nancy Andrews P
1942 Mt. Zion Dr, Golden, CO 80401, 303-279-1277
Pubs: *Kansas Qtly.*

Dana W. Atchley P
Box 183, Crested Butte, CO 81224, 303-349-6506

Geoffrey Becker W
30 Boulder Cr #500, Colorado Springs, CO 80903
Pubs: *Bluestown* (St. Martin's Pr, 1996), *Dangerous Men* (U
Pitt Pr, 1995).

Leslee Becker W
Colorado State Univ, 359 Eddy, Fort Collins, CO 80523,
970-491-7374
Internet: lbecker@vines.colostate.edu
Pubs: *The Sincere Cafe* (Mid-List Pr, 1996), *Contemporary
West Coast Fiction: Anth* (Globe Pequot Pr, 1993),
American Fiction: Anth (Wesley Pr, 1988), *Sonora, Atlantic
Monthly, Ploughshares, Iowa Rev, Gettysburg Rev.*

Don Bendell P&W
PO Box 276, Canon City, CO 81215, 719-275-4158
Pubs: *The B-52 Overture, Valley of Tears* (Dell, 1992,
1992), *Crossbow* (Berkley Pub Group, 1990), *Pembroke
Mag, Bowhunter.*

Bruce Berger P
Box 482, Aspen, CO 816120482, 970-925-1647
Internet: bberger@rof.net
Pubs: *Almost An Island* (U Arizona Pr, 1998), *The Telling
Distance* (Anchor/Doubleday, 1991), *Poetry, Negative
Capability, Poetry Northwest, New Letters, Sierra, Orion.*

Edward Bryant W
PO Box 18349, Denver, CO 80218-0349, 303-480-5363
Internet: ebryant666@aol.com
Pubs: *Flirting With Death* (Deadline Bks, 1996),
Strangeness & Charm (Voyager Bks, 1996), *Evening's
Empires* (Nemo Pr, 1989), *Omni, Penthouse.*

Reed Bye P
2227 W Nicholl St, Boulder, CO 80304, 303-440-4091
Pubs: *Nice To See You: Homage to Ted Berrigan* (Coffee
Hse, 1990), *Out of This World: Anth* (Crown, 1991), *Up
Late: Anth* (4 Walls 8 Windows, 1989).

Lorna Dee Cervantes P
820 33rd St, Boulder, CO 80303-2410, 303-938-9176
Pubs: *From the Cables of Genocide: Poems on Love &
Hunger* (Arte Publico Pr, 1990), *Red Dirt.*

Jack Collom P
1838 Pine St, Boulder, CO 80302, 303-444-1886
Pubs: *Entering the City* (The Backwaters Pr, 1997),
Calluses of Poetry (CD; Treehouse Pr, 1996), *Arguing With
Something Plato Said* (Rocky Ledge, 1990), *The Fox*
(United Artists, 1981).

Robert Cooperman P
2061 S Humboldt St, Denver, CO 80210, 303-722-2107
Pubs: *In the Household of Percy Bysshe Shelley* (U Pr
Florida, 1993), *The Trial of Mary McCormick* (Slipstream,
1990), *Caseworker Days: Anth* (Pudding Hse Pub, 1997),
*APR, Centennial Rev, Literary Rev, Poetry East, Santa
Clara Rev, Comstock Rev.*

Michele Corriel P
807 Foxtail St, Fort Collins, CO 80524, 303-221-2925
Pubs: *ABC No Rio: Anth* (1986), *Natl Poetry Mag of the
Lower East Side, Che.*

Mary Crow P
Colorado State Univ, Fort Collins, CO 80523, 970-491-6428
Internet: mcrow@vines.colostate.edu
Pubs: *I Have Tasted The Apple, Borders* (BOA Edtns,
1996, 1987), *APR, Ploughshares, NAR, New Letters,
Graham House Rev, Prairie Schooner.*

Robert Dassanowsky PP&P
Univ Colorado, Colorado Springs, CO 80933-7150,
719-262-3562
Internet: rvondass@mail.uccs.edu
Pubs: *Phantom Empires* (Ariadne, 1996), *Verses of a
Marriage* (Event Horizon, 1996), *Abraxas, Osiris, Poesie
Europe, High Performance, Le Guepard.*

Andrew J. Dephtereos W
Teikyo Loretto Heights Univ, 3001 S Federal Blvd, Denver,
CO 80236, 303-937-4260
Pubs: *Literary Rev, Chattahoochee Rev, Blueline, Dry
Creek Rev, Short Story Intl.*

Edward Dorn P
Univ Colorado, Boulder, CO 80309, 303-442-7631

James Doyle P
PO Box 271156, Fort Collins, CO 80527
Pubs: *The Sixth Day* (Pygmy Forest, 1988), *The Governor's Office* (Black Bear, 1986), *Literature: An Intro to Critical Reading: Anth* (Prentice Hall, 1996), *Ohio Rev, Poetry, Carolina Qtly, Literary Rev, Midwest Qtly, Willow Springs*.

Jean Dubois P
PO Box 1430, Golden, CO 80402
Internet: sweetyellow@juno. com
Pubs: *The Same Sweet Yellow, Silent Stones, Empty Passageways* (San Miguel Pr, 1994, 1992, 1992), *Wind Five-Folded: Anth* (AHA Bks, 1994), *Cicada, Mayfly, Modern Haiku, Passager, Poets On, Sijo West, Still, Frogpond, Lynx, Black Bough*.

Rikki Ducornet W
Denver Univ, University Park, Denver, CO 80208-0001, 303-871-2890
Internet: rducorne@du.edu
Pubs: *The Word "Desire"* (Henry Holt, 1997), *Phospor In Dreamland, The Stain, The Complete Butcher's Tales, The Jade Cabinet* (Dalkey Archive, 1995, 1995, 1994, 1993), *Conjunctions, Parnassus, Sulphur*.

Lawrence Dunning W
1655 Leyden, Denver, CO 80220, 303-321-2658
Pubs: *Taking Liberty* (Avon, 1981), *Stories from Virginia Qtly Review: Anth* (U Pr Virginia, 1990), *Virginia Qtly Rev, Colorado Qtly, Aspen Anth, Carolina Qtly, Descant, Rio Grande Rev*.

Jacqui Earley P
Metamorphosis Arts, 1331 Marshall St, Boulder, CO 80302-5803
Pubs: *Love For The Journey, Earthwoman, Healer Of The Mind* (Earley, 1978, 1978, 1975).

Jacqueline Eis W
1006 Hinsdale Dr, Fort Collins, CO 80526-3902, 970-229-9790
Pubs: *Imaginary Lives: Anth* (Mica Pr, 1996), *CSM, The MacGuffin, Crescent Rev, Crosscurrents, Prairie Schooner, Writers' Forum, Happy, 13th Moon, Minimus*.

Larry Fagin P
Naropa Institute, 2130 Arapahoe Ave, Boulder, CO 80302, 303-444-0202
Pubs: *Complete Fragments* (Z Pr, 1983), *I'll Be Seeing You* (Fullcourt Pr, 1978).

Ida Fasel P
165 Ivy St, Denver, CO 80220, 303-377-4498
Pubs: *Where Is the Center of the World* (Small Poetry Pr, 1998), *On the Meaning of the Cleave* (Eakin Pubs, 1979), *Clap Hands And Sing: Anth* (Nimrod, 1991), *Lyric, Blue Unicorn, Lucid Stone, Skylark, Slant*.

Fred Ferraris P
PO Box 65, Lyons, CO 80540-0065, 303-823-9362
Pubs: *Older Than Rain* (Selva Ed, 1997), *Marpa Point* (Blackberry Bks, 1976), *Measure, Kuksu, Glassworks, Rocky Mountain Rev, Boulder Planet, Phase & Cycle*.

Rick Fields P
1345 Spruce St, Boulder, CO 80302, 303-444-0190

Merrill Gilfillan P&W
PO Box 18194, Boulder, CO 80308
Pubs: *Sworn Before Cranes* (Orion Bks, 1994), *Magpie Rising: Sketches from the Great Plains* (Vintage, 1991), *River Through Rivertown* (The Figures, 1983).

Sidney Goldfarb P
Univ Colorado, Boulder, CO 80302, 303-443-2211

Art Goodtimes P
Cloud Acre, Box 160, Norwood, CO 81423, 970-327-4767
Internet: goodtimes@infozone.org
Pubs: *Que Linda!* (No Fat Mama & A/C Dick Pr, 1993), *Mushroom Cloud Redeye* (Western Eye Pr, 1990), *Slow Rising Smoke* (Blackberry Bks, 1987), *Upriver Downriver, Word, The Sun, Petroglyph, Poiesis, Wild Earth*.

Robert O. Greer, Jr. W
180 Adams St, Ste 250, Denver, CO 80206, 303-320-6827
Pubs: *The Devil's Red Nickel, The Devil's Hatband* (Warner/Mysterious Pr, 1997, 1996), *Higher Elevations* (Swallow Pr, 1993), *Agni, South Dakota Rev*.

Aimee Grunberger P
2100 Mesa Dr, Boulder, CO 80304
Pubs: *Ten Degrees Cooler Inside* (Dead Metaphor Pr, 1992), *American Poets Say Goodbye to the 20th Century: Anth* (Four Walls Eight Windows, 1995).

David Hall P
2206 Hiawatha Ct, Ft Collins, CO 80525, 303-224-2773
Pubs: *Werewolf & Other Poems* (Bald Mountain Pr, 1981), *Pawn Rev, Southwest Rev*.

Danielle D'Ottavio Harned W
27657 Timber Trail, Conifer, CO 80433
Pubs: *The Perimeter of Light* (New Rivers Pr, 1992), *Sing Heavenly Muse, Kansas Qtly, Permafrost*.

Joan Harvey W
1100 Stage Rd, Aspen, CO 81611, 970-925-9332
Internet: jmharvey@sopris.net
    Pubs: *Between C&D: Anth* (Penguin, 1988), *Another Chicago Mag, To: A Jrnl of Poetry, Prose & Visual Arts, Global City Rev, Mississippi Mud, Bomb, Osiris, Tampa Rev.*

Bobbie Louise Hawkins P&W
2515 Bluff St, Boulder, CO 80304
    Pubs: *My Own Alphabet, One Small Saga* (Coffee Hse Pr, 1988, 1984).

Jana Hayes P
c/o Janice Hays, 4835 St. Anton Road, Colorado Springs, CO 80918, 719-599-9633
    Pubs: *Wingbone* (Sudden Jungle Pr, 1986), *New House, A Book of Women* (San Marcos Pr, 1972), *Beloit Poetry Jrnl, Writers' Forum, Ithaca Women's Anth, South Dakota Rev, Eleventh Muse, Hamline Jrnl, Frontiers, Ekphrasis.*

Lois Beebe Hayna P
403 Locust Dr, Colorado Springs, CO 80907, 719-599-0502
Internet: lhayna@kktv.com
    Pubs: *Northern Gothic* (Morgan Pr, 1992), *Never Trust a Crow* (James Andrews Pub, 1990), *The Bridge, Nimrod.*

James B. Hemesath W
117 Poncha Ave, Alamosa, CO 81101-2166, 719-589-9374
    Pubs: *Where Past Meets Present: Anth* (U Colorado Pr, 1994), *Best of Wind: Anth* (Wind Pub, 1994), *Redneck Rev of Literature, New Mexico Humanities Rev, Wind.*

Jane Hilberry P
Colorado College, English Dept, 14 E Cache la Po, Colorado Springs, CO 80903, 719-389-6501
    Pubs: *The Girl With The Pearl Earring* (Jones Alley Pr, 1995), *Virginia Qtly Rev, Flyway, High Plains Literary Rev, Michigan Qtly Rev.*

Anselm Hollo P
Naropa Institute, 2130 Arapahoe Ave, Boulder, CO 80302, 303-449-0691
Internet: jdhollo@aol.com
    Pubs: *AHOE: And How On Earth* (Smokeproof Pr, 1997), *Corvus* (Coffee Hse Pr, 1995), *Postmodern American Poetry: Anth* (Norton, 1994), *Exquisite Corpse, Lingo, NAW, Puerto del Sol, Talisman, World, Conjuctions, Sulphur, Gare Du Nord, Arshile, Gas.*

Joseph Hutchison P
City Limits Books, Inc, PO Box 266, Indian Hills, CO 804540266, 303-697-3344
Internet: jgh@citylim.com
    Pubs: *Bed of Coals* (U Colorado Pr, 1996), *House of Mirrors* (J. Andrews & Co., 1992), *Sweet Nothing Noise* (Wayland Pr, 1992), *Poetry, Hudson Rev, Mississippi Rev, Tar River Poetry, Northeast.*

Mark Irwin P
3875 S Cherokee St, Englewood, CO 801103511, 303-762-6336
    Pubs: *Quick, Now, Always* (BOA Edtns, 1996), *Against the Meanwhile* (Wesleyan U Pr, 1988), *Antaeus, Kenyon Rev, Atlantic, Nation, APR.*

David James P
PO Box 1156, Denver, CO 80201-1156
    Pubs: *A Heart Out of This World* (Carnegie Mellon, 1984), *Iowa Rev, Poem, Caliban, Kansas Qtly.*

Don Jones P
2221 S Prairie Ave, Lot 84, Pueblo, CO 81005-2800, 719-561-0676
    Pubs: *Medical Aid* (Samisdat, 1978), *Miss Liberty, Meet Crazy Horse* (Swallow, 1972), *Massachusetts Rev, SPR, Prairie Schooner, Poet & Critic.*

Suzanne Juhasz P
Univ Colorado, Boulder, CO 80309, 303-492-8948
    Pubs: *Benita To Reginald: A Romance* (Out of Sight Pr, 1978), *Conditions, San Jose Studies.*

Steve Katz P
669 Washington St #602, Denver, CO 80203-3837, 303-832-2534
Internet: elbonoz@cu.campus.mci.net
    Pubs: *Swanny's Ways, 43 Fiction* (Sun & Moon Pr, 1995, 1992).

Jessica Kawasuna Saiki W
1901 E 13 Ave, #9-C, Denver, CO 802062041, 303-333-1087
    Pubs: *From The Lanai and Other Hawaii Stories, Once, A Lotus Garden, The Talking of Hands: Anth* (New Rivers Pr, 1991, 1987, 1998).

Bruce F. Kawin P
Univ Colorado, Boulder, CO 80309-0226, 303-449-4845
Internet: bkawin@aol.com
    Pubs: *How Movies Work* (U California Pr, 1992), *The Mind of the Novel* (Princeton U Pr, 1982), *Film Qtly, Rolling Stock.*

Eleanor Keats PP&P
9261 E Berry Ave, Greenwood Village, CO 80111, 303-779-1297
Internet: dkeats@du.edu
    Pubs: *A Water Cycle, Touching This Earth: Anth* (Dawn Valley Pr, 1986, 1977), *Antioch Rev, Sojourner, Denver Qtly, Bloomsbury Rev, Sunrust, St. Andrews Rev.*

Baine Kerr W
411 Spruce, Boulder, CO 80302
    Pubs: *Jumping-Off Place* (U of Missouri Pr, 1981), *Best American Short Stories: Anth* (HM, 1977), *Missouri Rev, Shenandoah, Denver Qtly, Place, Hawaii Rev.*

Patricia Dubrava Keuning   P
2732 Williams St, Denver, CO 80205
    Pubs: *Holding the Light* (James Andrews & Co., 1994),
These Are Not Sweet Girls: Anth (White Pine Pr, 1994),
International Qtly, Sulphur River Literary Rev.

Rita Kiefer   P
Univ Northern Colorado, Greeley, CO 80634, 303-351-2787
    Pubs: *Trying On Faces* (Monkshood Pr, 1995), *Unveiling*
(Chicory Blue Pr, 1993), *Ploughshares, Intl Poetry
Forum, Kansas Qtly, Southwest Rev, Bloomsbury Rev.*

Karl Kopp   P
1517 S Dexter Way, Denver, CO 80222, 303-759-5985
    Pubs: *Crossing the River: Anth* (Permanent Pr, 1987), *City
Kite on a Wire: Anth* (Mesilla, 1986), *Chiron Rev,
Bloomsbury Rev, Chariton Rev.*

Leota Korns   P&W
PO Box 1617, Durango, CO 81302, 970-247-4468
    Pubs: *Kansas Mag, Women: A Jrnl of Liberation, San Juan
Voices, Matrix, Raindrops of Spring.*

Marilyn Krysl   P&W
Univ Colorado, English Dept, Boulder, CO 80309,
303-492-8944
    Pubs: *How to Accommodate Men* (Coffee Hse Pr, 1998),
Warscape With Lovers (Cleveland State Poetry Ctr, 1997),
Soulskin (NLN Pr, 1996), *What We Have To Live With* (Teal
Pr, 1989), *Atlantic, Nation, New Republic, Antaeus, NAR,
Iowa Rev, Prairie Schooner.*

Daniela Kuper   W
656 Pleasant St, Boulder, CO 80302, 303-440-5303
Internet: dfkuper@earthlink.net
    Pubs: *Cherries In the Snow* (Picador USA, 1999), *Storming
Heaven's Gate: Anth* (Penguin, 1996), *Many Mountains
Moving, The Sun, Cream City Rev, Coe Rev, Amaranth
Rev, Mobius, Lilith, Poetry Forum.*

R. D. Lakin   P
405 Scott, Ft Collins, CO 80521, 303-221-5661
    Pubs: *American Passport, The MacDowell Poems*
(Typographeum Pr, 1992, 1977), *Kansas Qtly, West
Coast Rev, Antioch Rev, Nation, Cottonwood Rev,
Michigan Qtly.*

Marcela Lucero   P
8614 Princeton St, Westminster, CO 80030, 303-589-5970
    Pubs: *The Third Woman* (Houghton Mifflin, 1979).

Russell Martin   W
15201 County Rd 25, Dolores, CO 81323, 970-882-4775
Internet: russellmartin@compuserve.com
    Pubs: *Beautiful Islands* (S&S, 1988), *New Writers of the
Purple Sage: Anth* (Penguin, 1992).

David Mason   P&W
Colorado College, 14 East Cache La Poudre, Colorado
Springs, CO 809033298, 719-389-6853
    Pubs: *The Country I Remember, The Buried Houses* (Story
Line Pr, 1996, 1991), *Small Elegies* (Dacotah Territory,
1990), *Hudson Rev, Georgia Rev, Poetry, New Criterion,
Harvard Rev, American Scholar.*

Katherine "Kaki" May   P
111 Emerson St, #1423, Denver, CO 80218-3791
    Pubs: *Some Inhuman Familiars* (Cabbage Head Pr, 1983),
Brandings (Cummington, 1968), *New York Times.*

Mary McArthur   P
622 W Pine St, Louisville, CO 80027, 303-665-7605
Internet: mary.mcarthur@colorado.edu
    Pubs: *Nation, Luminaria, Maryland Poetry Rev, Light Year,
Portland, Feminist Renaissance.*

Peter Michelson   P
Univ Colorado, Box 226, English Dept, Boulder, CO 80309,
303-492-7381
    Pubs: *Speaking the Unspeakable* (SUNY Pr, 1993), *Pacific
Plainsong* (Another Chicago Pr, 1987), *Rolling Stock,
Boundary 2, ACM, Notre Dame Rev, Exquisite Corpse,
Cincinnati Poetry Rev, Spoon River Rev, Many Mountains
Moving.*

Tony Moffeit   P
1501 E 7th, Pueblo, CO 81001, 719-549-2751
Internet: moffeit@uscolo.edu
    Pubs: *Poetry is Dangerous, The Poet is an Outlaw* (Floating
Island Pubs, 1995), *Neon Peppers* (Cherry Valley Edtns,
1992), *Amelia, Taos Rev, Chiron Rev.*

Laura Mullen   P
Colorado State Univ, 359 Eddy Building, Ft Collins, CO
80523, 303-419-6845
    Pubs: *The Surface* (U Illinois Pr, 1991), *American Letters &
Commentary, Agni, Denver Qtly, Antaeus, Volt.*

David J. Nelson   PP
PO Box 2993, Denver, CO 80201, 302-294-0653
    Pubs: *Cracking the Pavement* (Baculite Pub Co, 1990),
Rocky Mountain Arsenal.

Kent Nelson   W
PO Box 40, Ouray, CO 81427, 970-325-4791
    Pubs: *Discoveries* (Western Reflections, 1998), *Toward the
Sun* (Breakaway Bks, 1998), *Language in the Blood, The
Middle of Nowhere* (Gibbs Smith, 1992, 1992), *Virginia Qtly
Rev, Sewanee Rev, Gettysburg Rev, Glimmer Train,
Southern Rev, Shenandoah.*

Dianemarie O'Malley   P
PO Box 2745, Estes Park, CO 80517
    Pubs: *Echos, Arulo, Driftwood East, Gusto, Authors Of The
World.*

Tom Parson   P
157 S Logan, Denver, CO 80209, 303-777-8951
Pubs: *Some Trouble* (Now It's Up To You Pr, 1980), *City Kite on a Wire: Anth* (Mesilla Pr, 1986).

Veronica Patterson   P
11 Gregg Dr, Loveland, CO 80538, 303-669-7010
Internet: rpatterson@duke.com
Pubs: *The Bones Remember* (Stone Graphics, 1992), *How to Make a Terrarium* (Cleveland State U Poetry Ctr, 1987), *Many Mountains Moving, Willow Springs, Georgia Rev, Louisville Rev, Caliban, Malahat Rev.*

Naomi Rachel   P&W
954 Arroyo Chico, Boulder, CO 80302, 303-449-4031
Internet: milopapers@juno.com
Pubs: *The Temptation of Extinction* (Senex Pr, 1993), *Yale Rev, Nimrod, NAR, Hampden-Sydney Poetry Anth, Canadian Literature, Hawaii Rev.*

Bin Ramke   P
Univ Denver, English Dept, Denver, CO 80208, 303-871-2889
Internet: bramke@du.edu
Pubs: *Massacre of the Innocents* (U Iowa Pr, 1995), *The Erotic Light of Gardens* (Wesleyan, 1989), *The Language Student* (LSU Pr, 1986).

Deborah Robson   W
P.O. Box 484, Fort Collins, CO 80522, 970-226-3590
Internet: 75120.3701@compuserve.com
Pubs: *Spin-Off, Shuttle, Spindle & Dyepot, Country Jrnl, Nantucket Rev, Frets, Seattle Post, Intelligencer, Writers' Forum, Twigs, Dogsoldier, Port Townsend Jrnl.*

Pattiann Rogers   P
7412 Berkeley Cir, Castle Rock, CO 80104, 303-660-0851
Internet: www.mindspring.com/ pattiann_rogers
Pubs: *Eating Bread and Honey, Firekeeper: New and Selected Poems* (Milkweed Edtns, 1997, 1994), *Geocentric* (Gibbs Smith, 1993), *Hudson Rev, Paris Rev, Poetry, Georgia Rev, Gettysburg Rev, Prairie Schooner.*

Reg Saner   P
Univ Colorado, English Dept, Box 226, Boulder, CO 80309, 303-494-8951
Pubs: *The Four-Cornered Falcon* (Johns Hopkins U Pr, 1993), *Red Letters* (Qtly Rev of Literature, 1989), *Essay on Air* (Ohio Rev Bks, 1984).

Bienvenido N. Santos   W
2524 W 13 St, Greeley, CO 80631, 303-356-1121
Pubs: *What The Hell For You Left Your Heart in San Francisco* (New Day, 1987).

Andrew Schelling   P
Naropa Institute, 2130 Arapahoe Ave, Boulder, CO 80302, 303-543-1166
Pubs: *The Road To Ocosigno* (Smokeproof Pr, 1998), *The Cane Groves of Narmada River* (City Lights, 1998), *Old Growth: Poems & Notebooks 1986-1994* (Rodent Pr, 1995), *Moon is a Piece of Tea* (Last Generation, 1993), *Sulfur, Terra Nova, NAW, Grand Street.*

Joel Scherzer   P
PO Box 222, Pueblo, CO 81002, 719-543-6858
Pubs: *More Bronx Zen* (Baculite Pub, 1992), *Bronx Zen* (Academic & Arts Pr, 1989), *Rocky Mountain Arsenal of the Arts, Blue Light Rev, Apalachee Qtly.*

Jay Schneiders   P
3955 E Exposition Ave #316, Denver, CO 80209-5032, 303-649-6651
Internet: jaysch@concentric.net
Pubs: *Georgia Rev, Quarterly West, Manoa, The Journal, Tampa Rev, Prism Intl.*

Gary Schroeder   P
1429 N Castlewood Dr, Franktown, CO 80116-9015, 303-470-9952
Pubs: *Adjacent Solitudes* (Wayland Pr, 1991), *Only Morning In Her Shoes: Anth* (Utah State U Pr, 1990), *Eleventh Muse, Environment Essence & Issue, JAMA.*

Steven Schwartz   W
2943 Skimmerhorn St, Fort Collins, CO 80526-6288, 970-282-8755
Internet: sschwartz@vines.colostate.edu
Pubs: *A Good Doctor's Son* (Morrow, 1998), *Therapy: A Novel* (Penguin/Plume, 1995), *Lives of the Fathers* (U Illinois Pr, 1991), *Ploughshares, Tikkun, Redbook, Virginia Qtly, Antioch Rev, Epoch, Missouri Rev.*

Sandra Shwayder   P&W
1955 Holly, Denver, CO 80220, 303-399-5927
Pubs: *The Nun* (Plainview Pr, 1992), *Connections, The Long Story, The Dream, COE Rev.*

Charles Squier   P
Univ Colorado, Campus Box 226, Boulder, CO 80309, 303-492-7381
Pubs: *Mrs. Beaton's Tea Party* (Reading Dog Pr, 1996), *Sniper Logic, Ohio Rev, Open Places, Midwest Qtly, Midwest Rev, Rolling Stock, Light Year, Chinook.*

Stephanie Stearns   P&W
3980 W Radcliff, Denver, CO 80236, 303-798-0229
Pubs: *The Saga Of The Sword That Sings & Other Realities* (Dubless Pr, 1981), *Eldritch Tales.*

Roger Steigmeier   P
2770 Moorhead Ave, #204, Boulder, CO 80303
Pubs: *Light Traveling Dark Traveling Light* (First East Coast Theater & Pub Co., 1984), *Poet.*

Constance E. Studer   P&W
1617 Parkside Cir, Lafayette, CO 80026-1967, 303-665-3818
Internet: wrqu20a@prodigy.com
    Pubs: *The Age of Koestler: Anth* (Practices of the Wind,
    1994), *Birmingham Poetry Rev, Earth's Daughters, Zone 3.*

Ronald Sukenick   W
Univ Colorado, English Dept, Box 226, Boulder, CO 80309,
303-492-7381
Internet: sukenick@spot.colorado.edu
    Pubs: *Up, 98.6* (FC 2, 1998, 1994), *Doggy Bag* (FC2/Black
    Ice Bks, 1994), *Blown Away* (Sun & Moon Pr, 1986).

Steve Rasnic Tem   P&W
2500 Irving St, Denver, CO 80211, 303-477-0235
    Pubs: *Excavation* (Avon, 1987), *The Umbral Anth of
    Science Fiction Poetry* (Umbral Pr, 1982).

James Tipton   P&W
1742 DS Rd, Glade Park, CO 81523, 970-245-5760
    Pubs: *The Wizard of Is* (Bread & Butter Pr, 1995), *The Third
    Coast Anth, Cimarron Rev, Greensboro Rev, High Plains
    Literary Rev, American Literary Rev, Writers' Forum,
    Pinyon Poetry, Woodnotes, South Dakota Rev, The Nation,
    Esquire, APR.*

Rawdon Tomlinson   P
2020 S Grant, Denver, CO 80210, 303-733-6736
    Pubs: *Deep Red* (U Pr Florida, 1995), *Spreading the Word:
    Anth* (Bench Pr, 1990), *Sewanee Rev, Commonweal,
    Kansas Qtly, Poetry Northwest, Southern Poetry Rev, Ohio
    Rev, Midwest Qtly.*

Bill Tremblay   P
3412 Lancaster Dr, Fort Collins, CO 80525 2817,
970-226-0311
Internet: watremblay@aol.com
    Pubs: *The June Rise* (Utah State U Pr, 1994), *A Gathering
    of Poets: Anth* (Kent State U Pr, 1993), *Jazz Poetry Anth*
    (Indiana U Pr, 1993), *High Plains Literary Rev, Midwest
    Qtly, Massachusetts Rev, Willow Springs, Dry Creek Rev.*

Anne Waldman   PP&P
375 S 45 St, Boulder, CO 80303, 303-444-0202
Internet: a.waldman@mindspring.com
    Pubs: *Fast Speaking Woman* (City Lights, 1997), *Iovis: All is
    Full of Jove: Bks II and I, A Poem* (Coffee Hse Pr, 1997,
    1993), *Kill Or Cure* (Penguin, 1996), *Conjunctions, Sulfur, City
    Lights Jrnl, Apex of the M, Poetry Project Newsletter, APR.*

David L. Wann   P&W
PO Box 714, Indian Hills, CO 80454, 303-679-8089
    Pubs: *Log Rhythms* (North Atlantic Bks, 1983), *New York
    Qtly, Lake Superior Rev, Samisdat.*

Marc Weber   P
2 N 24 St, Colorado Springs, CO 80904, 719-634-8010
    Pubs: *Quest* (Lion's Roar, 1989), *Circle of Light* (San
    Marcos, 1976).

Robert Lewis Weeks   P
6767 E Dartmouth Ave, Denver, CO 80224, 303-756-4274
    Pubs: *As A Master of Clouds* (Juniper Pr, 1971), *APR,
    Sewanee Rev, Prairie Schooner, West Branch, Georgia
    Rev, The Quarterly, Shenandoah, Beloit Poetry Jrnl.*

Thomas A. West, Jr.   P&W
6282 Chimney Rock Trail, Morrison, CO 80465-2151,
303-697-4772
    Pubs: *Writing Under Fire: Anth* (Dell, 1978), *Panhandler,
    New Mexico Qtly Rev, Touchstone, Oxford Mag, Short
    Story Intl, Shorelines, Nebraska Mag, New Renaissance.*

Richard Wilmarth   P
PO Box 2076, Boulder, CO 80306, 303-417-9398
Internet: wilmartr@colorado.edu
    Pubs: *Voices in the Room* (Dead Metaphor Pr, 1993),
    More! Henry Miller Acrostics: Anth (Standish Bks, 1996),
    *Iconoclast, Tangents, Lucid Moon, Blind Man's Rainbow,
    Fan, Bombay Gin, Third Lung Rev, Fell Swoop.*

Renate Wood   P
1900 King Ave, Boulder, CO 80302, 303-447-2796
Internet: rwood38@juno.com
    Pubs: *Raised Underground, Carnegie Mellon Anth of
    Poetry* (Carnegie Mellon U Pr, 1991, 1993), *APR,
    TriQuarterly, Virginia Qtly Rev, Ploughshares, NER,
    Massachusetts Rev.*

James Yaffe   W
1215 N Cascade, Colorado Springs, CO 80903
    Pubs: *Mom Among The Liars, Mom Doth Murder Sleep,
    Mom Meets Her Maker* (St. Martin's Pr, 1992, 1991, 1990).

William Zaranka   P&W
Univ Denver, Denver, CO 80110, 303-871-2966
    Pubs: *Blessing* (Wayland Pr, 1988), *Brand-X Anth of
    Fiction, Brand-X Anth of Poetry* (Apple-wood Pr, 1984,
    1983), *Poetry, TriQuarterly, Prairie Schooner.*

CONNECTICUT

Dick Allen   P
74 Fern Cir, Trumbull, CT 06611, 203-375-1927
    Pubs: *Ode to the Cold War: New & Selected* (Sarabande
    Bks, 1997), *The Best American Poetry: Anths*
    (Scribner,1998, 1994), *Gettysburg Rev, Boulevard, Poetry,
    Hudson Rev, Image, American Arts Qtly, Urbanus.*

Dennis Barone   P&W
Saint Joseph College, English & American Studies, West
Hartford, CT 06117, 860-232-4571
    Pubs: *Echoes, Forms/Forms* (Potes and Poets, 1997,
    1988), *The Returns* (Sun & Moon, 1996), *Waves of Ice,
    Waves of Rumor* (Zasterle Pr, 1993).

Wendy Battin   P
15 Rogers Dr, Mystic, CT 06355, 860-572-9323
Internet: wjbat@conncoll.edu
> Pubs: *Little Apocalypse* (Ashland Poetry Pr, 1997), *In the
> Solar Wind* (Doubleday, 1984), *The Sacred Place: Anth* (U
> Utah Pr, 1996), *Yale Rev, Nation, Gettysburg Rev,
> Threepenny Rev, Poetry, NER.*

Tricia Bauer   P&W
PO Box 34, West Redding, CT 06896-0034
> Pubs: *Boondocking, Working Women And Other Stories*
> (Bridge Works Pub, 1997, 1995), *The Next Parish Over*
> (New Rivers Pr, 1993), *Eating Our Hearts Out* (Crossing Pr,
> 1993), *Western Humanities, Indiana Rev, Massachusetts
> Rev, American Literary Rev.*

Paul Beckman   W
PO Box 609, Madison, CT 06443, 203-245-0835
Internet: pb1@aol.com
> Pubs: *Come! Meet My Family and Other Stories* (Weighted
> Anchor Pr, 1995), *Cat's Meow! An Anth of Cat Tales* (Maine
> Rhode Pubs, 1996), *The Artful Mind, Verve, Maverick Pr,
> Other Voices, Parting Gifts, Northeast Mag.*

Ted Bent   W
60 Hinkle Rd, Washington, CT 067931001, 860-868-0590
Internet: tedbent@snet.net
> Pubs: *The Girl In The Black Raincoat* (Duell, Sloan &
> Pearce, 1966), *Massachusetts Rev.*

Elaine Bissell   W
10-B Heritage Village, Southbury, CT 06488
> Pubs: *Empire* (Worldwide Library, 1990), *Family Fortunes*
> (St. Martin's Pr, 1986), *Let's Keep In Touch* (Pocket Bks,
> 1983), *Women Who Wait* (Popular Library, 1979).

Blanche McCrary Boyd   W
Connecticut College, Box 5421, 270 Mohegan Ave, New
London, CT 06320
> Pubs: *The Revolution of Little Girls, The Redneck Way of
> Knowledge* (Knopf, 1991, 1981), *VLS, New York Times
> Sunday Mag, Vanity Fair, Esquire, Premiere.*

George Bradley   P
82 W Main St, Chester, CT 06412, 203-526-3900
> Pubs: *The Fire Fetched Down, Of the Knowledge of Good
> and Evil* (Knopf, 1996, 1991), *Terms to Be Met* (Yale U Pr,
> 1986), *New Yorker, Paris Rev.*

Brian Butterick   P
31 Friendship St, Willimantic, CT 06226

Michael Casey   P
Yale University Press, 92A Yale Sta, New Haven, CT 06520
> Pubs: *Millrat* (Adastra, 1996), *Obscenities* (Yale U Pr,
> 1972), *College English, TriQuarterly, Michigan Qtly Rev,
> Rolling Stone, Panhandler, America.*

Ina B. Chadwick   P
2 Redcoat Rd, Westport, CT 06880, 203-221-0655
> Pubs: *Considerate Gestures Of Love* (Greens Farms Pr,
> 1979), *New York Times, Antioch Rev.*

David Chura   P
477 Newtown Turnpike, Redding, CT 06875
Internet: dchura@i84.net
> Pubs: *Queer Dharma: Anth* (Gay Sunshine Pr, 1998), *Anth
> of New England Writers, Adirondack, Turning Wheel,
> English Jrnl, Blueline, Evergreen Chronicles, Connecticut
> River Rev, Embers, Earth's Daughters.*

Gene Coggshall   W
The Perkin-Elmer Corp M/S 887, 100 Wooster Heights Rd,
Danbury, CT 06810, 203-744-4000

Stanley I. Cohen   W
322 Pine Tree Dr, Orange, CT 06477, 203-795-4058
> Pubs: *Angel Face* (St. Martin's Pr, 1982), *330 Park*
> (Putnam, 1977), *Year's Best Mystery & Suspense Stories:
> Anth* (Walker, 1991), *Best Detective Stories of the Year:
> Anth* (Dutton, 1975), *Alfred Hitchcock's Mystery, Ellery
> Queen's Mystery.*

James Coleman   W
Three Rivers C-T College, 7 Mahan Dr, English Dept,
Norwich, CT 06360, 860-823-2896
> Pubs: *South Dakota Rev, Elkhorn Rev, December,
> Centennial Rev, St. Andrews Rev, Red Fox Rev,
> Information.*

Leo Connellan   P
PO Box 224, Hanover, CT 06350, 860-822-6884
> Pubs: *Provincetown and Other Poems* (Curbstone Pr,
> 1995), *The Clear Blue Lobster — Water Country* (HBJ,
> 1985), *Harper's, Georgia Rev, New England Rev, Chelsea,
> Nation.*

Tony Connor   W
44 Brainerd Ave, Middletown, CT 06457, 860-344-0815
Internet: jconnor@wesleyan.edu
> Pubs: *Metamorphic Adventures, Spirits of the Place* (Anvil
> Poetry Pr, 1996, 1986), *Best American Short Plays 1992-93*
> (Applause Theatre Bks, 1993).

Charlotte Garrett Currier   P
12 Long Hill Farm, Guilford, CT 06437, 203-453-5472
> Pubs: *Not to Look Back* (CD; w/D. Currier), *Poem Box*
> (Trefoil Arts, 1998, 1993), *Presences* (The Pr of Night
> Owl, 1977), *Southern Rev, Southern Humanities Rev,
> Embers.*

David Curtis   P
126 Ardmore Rd, Milford, CT 06460, 203-874-5102
Internet: dcurtis@sacredheart.edu
> Pubs: *Update From Pahrump* (Wyndam Hall, 1992), *Four
> Quarters, Dalhousie Rev, Descant, Writer's Digest, The
> Writer, Poem, Pegasus Rev, Potato Eyes, Inlet.*

Cortney Davis   P
PO Box 678, West Redding, CT 06896, 203-938-2697
    Pubs: *Details of Flesh* (Calyx Bks, 1997), *The Body Flute*
    (Adastra Pr, 1994), *Between the Heartbeats: Anth* (U Iowa
    Pr, 1995), *Hudson Rev, Crazyhorse, Poetry East, Ms.,
    Pivot, Literature & Medicine, Witness, Prairie Schooner,
    Hanging Loose.*

Ellen Kitzes Delfiner   P
1 Strawberry Hill Ct #6J, Stamford, CT 06902
Internet: eskd@juno.com
    Pubs: *Response, Art Times, New Authors Jrnl, Jam Today,
    Treasure House, Aura, Slant.*

Theodore Deppe   P
107 Water St, Stonington, CT 06378, 860-535-4112
Internet: wmassdeppe@aol.com
    Pubs: *The Wanderer King, Children of the Air* (Alice James
    Bks, 1996, 1990), *Kenyon, Harper's, Poetry, Boulevard,
    Poetry Northwest, Crazyhorse.*

Concetta Ciccozzi Doucette   P&W
2799 Ellington Rd, South Windsor, CT 06074, 860-644-2352
    Pubs: *Connecticut Poets V: Anth* (Fairfield U, 1996),
    Footwork: Paterson Literary Rev: Anth (Passaic County
    Community College, 1995), *Italian Americana,
    Beanfeast, Mediphors, Apostrophe, Women's Words.*

Franz Douskey   P
50 Ives St, Mount Carmel, CT 06518, 203-248-4615
    Pubs: *Archaeological Nights* (Pharos Books, 1982), *Yellow
    Silk, Colorado Qtly, New York Qtly, New Yorker, Georgia
    Rev, Rolling Stone, Minnesota Rev.*

Russell Edson   P&W
29 Ridgeley St, Darien, CT 06820, 203-655-1575
    Pubs: *The Tunnel: Selected Poems* (Oberlin College Pr,
    1994), *The Song of Percival Peacock* (Coffee Hse Pr,
    1992).

James Finnegan   P
18 Woodrow St, West Hartford, CT 06107, 860-521-0358
Internet: jforjames@aol.com
    Pubs: *Poetry Northwest, Shenandoah, Tar River Poetry,
    Southern Rev, Chelsea, Ploughshares, Poetry East,
    Virginia Qtly Rev, Willow Springs.*

Henry George Fischer   P
29 Mauweehoo Hill, Sherman, CT 06784, 860-354-2719
    Pubs: *More Than Timely Rhymes, Timely Rhymes from
    The Sherman Sentinel* (Singular Speech Pr, 1996, 1993),
    Random House Treasury of Light Verse: Anth (Random
    Hse, 1995), *Lyric, Sparrow, Candelabrum, ELF, American
    Poets and Poetry.*

Eleni Fourtouni   P
1218 Forest Rd, New Haven, CT 06515, 203-397-3902
    Pubs: *Greek Women in Resistance, Watch the Flame*
    (Thelphini Pr, 1985, 1983).

Vernon Frazer   PP&P&W
132 Woodycrest Dr, East Hartford, CT 06118, 860-569-3101
Internet: www.tiac.net/users/vfrazer
    Pubs: *Sing Me One Song of Evolution* (Echolalia Pr, 1998),
    Demon Dance (Woodcrest, 1995), *Massacre, Plain Brown
    Wrapper, Magic Realism, Nude Beach, Shockbox, Atom
    Mind, Knot Room/Knitting Factory, Mind in Motion, Nerve
    Cowboy.*

William T. Freeman   P
205 Orange St, Waterbury, CT 06704, 203-753-7743
    Pubs: *Obsidian, Greenfield Rev, Pudding, Parnassus,
    Laurels.*

Margaret Gibson   P
152 Watson Rd, Preston, CT 063658837, 860-886-1777
Internet: mckaingibson@juno.com
    Pubs: *Earth Elegy: New & Selected Poems, The Vigil, Out
    in the Open, Memories of the Future, Long Walks in the
    Afternoon* (LSU Pr, 1997,1993, 1989, 1986, 1982),
    *Southern Rev, Georgia Rev, Indiana Rev, Shenandoah,
    Iowa Rev, Gettysburg Rev.*

John Gilmore   P
11 Oakwood Dr, Weston, CT 06883, 203-227-3684

Jody Gladding   P
Yale University Pr, PO Box 209040, New Haven, CT
06520-9040, 203-432-0960
    Pubs: *Stone Crop* (Yale U Pr, 1995), *Best American Poetry:
    Anth* (Simon & Schuster, 1995), *Paris Rev, Wilderness,
    Agni, Poetry Northwest, Yale Rev.*

Ruth Good   P
119 Old Rd, Westport, CT 06880, 203-255-4231
    Pubs: *Southern Poetry Rev, Literary Rev, Carleton
    Miscellany, Prairie Schooner, Chariton Rev.*

Jeffrey Greene   P
254 Bradley St, New Haven, CT 065101103, 203-772-0266
Internet: jgreene@pasteur.fr
    Pubs: *American Spirituals* (Northeastern U Pr, 1998), *To
    the Left of the Worshiper* (Alice James Books, 1991),
    Glimpses of the Invisible World in New Haven (Coreopsis
    Books, 1995), *Parnassus, The New Yorker, Ploughshares,
    Boulevard, Poetry.*

Antoni Gronowicz   P&W
128 Brookmoor Rd, Avon, CT 06001, 203-673-9291
    Pubs: *God's Broker* (Richardson & Snyder, 1984), *An
    Orange Full Of Dreams* (Dodd, Mead, 1973).

Jayseth Guberman   P
294 S Quaker Ln, West Hartford, CT 06119-2119,
203-233-8722
    Pubs: *Voices Israel, Martyrdom & Resistance, European
    Judaism, Rashi, Prophetic Voices, Poet, Black Buzzard
    Rev, Jewish Spectator.*

Joan Joffe Hall P&W
64 Birchwood Heights, Storrs, CT 06268, 203-429-6580
Pubs: *Summer Heat: Three Stories* (Kutenai Pr, 1991),
Romance & Capitalism At The Movies (Alice James,
1985), *Kansas Qtly, Alaska Qtly, North Dakota Qtly,
Fiction Intl.*

Jay Halpern W
58 Jackson Cove Rd, Oxford, CT 06478, 203-888-4976
Internet: alicorn@wtco.net
Pubs: *The Jade Unicorn* (Macmillan, 1979), *Icarus, Hobo
Jungle, Noiseless Spider, Tapestry, Enigma.*

Richard F. Harteis P&W
337 Kitemaug Rd, Uncasville, CT 06382, 860-848-8486
Internet: rfhar@conncoll.edu
Pubs: *Keeping Heart* (Orpheus Hse, 1996), *Marathon*
(Norton, 1989), *Internal Geography, Window on the Black
Sea: Anth* (Carnegie Mellon U Pr, 1987, 1992), *Virginia
Rev, Ploughshares, Seneca Rev, New Letters.*

Dolores Hayden P
125 Prospect Ave, Guilford, CT 06437-3114
Internet: dolores.hayden@yale.edu
Pubs: *Playing House* (Robert Barth, 1998), *City A/Z: Anth*
(Wiley, 1998), *Hellas, Witness, Poetry Northwest, Radcliffe
Qtly, Formalist, Landscape Jrnl.*

Hank Heifetz W
548 Orange St #406, New Haven, CT 06511, 203-865-8801
Pubs: *The Origin of the Young God, For The Lord of the
Animals* (U California Pr, 1990, 1987), *Where Are the
Stars In New York?* (Dutton, 1973), *Evergreen Rev, VLS.*

Peggy Heinrich P
625 Gilman St, Bridgeport, CT 06605, 203-333-3938
Pubs: *Sharing The Woods* (Old Sandal Pr, 1992), *A Patch
of Grass* (High/Coo Pr, 1984), *Negative Capability, Texas
Rev, Blue Unicorn, Rio Grande Rev, Passager.*

Madeleine Hennessy P
70 Puritan Rd, Trumbull, CT 06611, 203-377-3971
Pubs: *Pavor Nocturnus* (Washout Pub Co., 1979), *Yankee,
Connecticut River Rev, Greenfield Rev, New York Qtly,
Groundswell.*

E. Ward Herlands P
179 Fox Ridge Rd, Stamford, CT 06903, 203-322-3811
Pubs: *Literature: Reading Fiction, Poetry, Drama and the
Essay: Anth* (McGraw-Hill, 1998), *Prairie Schooner, The
Prose Poem: An Intl Jrnl, New York Times, Pittsburgh Qtly.*

Pati Hill P&W
20 Grand St, Stonington, CT 06378, 203-535-1747

Barbara Holder P
55 Gallow Hill Rd, Redding, CT 06896, 203-938-4043
Pubs: *Literature 4th Ed.: Anth, Modern American Poets:
Voices and Visions: Anth* (McGraw-Hill 1998, 1993), *Writing
Through Literature: Anth* (Prentice Hall Bks, 1995), *Slow
Dancer, Wind, Earth's Daughters, Footwork, Poetic Justice,
Kentucky Poetry Rev.*

David Holdt P
Watkinson School, 180 Bloomfield Ave, Hartford, CT
06105-1096, 860-236-5618
Internet: dmholdt@connix.com
Pubs: *In the Place of the Long River: Anth* (Blue Moon Pr,
1996), *River of Dreams: Anth* (Glover, 1990), *Northeast,
Spitball, Stone Country, Amelia.*

John Hollander P
Yale Univ, PO Box 208302, New Haven, CT 06520-8302,
203-432-2231
Pubs: *Selected Poetry, Tesserae, Harp Lake* (Knopf, 1993,
1993, 1988), *Melodious Guile* (Yale U Pr, 1988), *Blue Wine*
(Hopkins, 1979).

Donald Honig W
2322 Cromwell Gdns, Cromwell, CT 06416

Paul Horgan W
Wesleyan University, Box 2600, Middletown, CT 06457

Peyton Houston P
11 Indian Chase Dr, Greenwich, CT 06830, 203-869-7672
Pubs: *The Changes/Orders/Becomings* (Jargon Society,
1990), *Paris Rev, Open Places, Hudson Rev.*

Susan Howe P
115 New Quarry Rd, Guilford, CT 06437
Pubs: *The Nonconformist's Memorial* (New Directions,
1993), *Singularities* (Wesleyan, 1990), *American Poetry
Since 1950: Anth* (Marsilio, 1993).

Gray Jacobik P
Eastern Connecticut State Univ, English Dept, Willimantic, CT
06226, 860-963-0440
Internet: grayj@snet.net
Pubs: *The Double Task* (U Massachusetts Pr, 1998), *The
Best American Poetry: Anth* (Scribner, 1997), *The Writing
Path: Anth* (U Iowa Pr, 1996), *Prairie Schooner,
Ploughshares, Georgia Rev, NAR, Alaska Qtly Rev, Prose
Poem, Tar River Poetry, Alkali Flats.*

Leland Jamieson, Jr. P
86 Ledgewood Rd, West Hartford, CT 06107, 860-521-6359
Internet: jamassoc@erols.com
Pubs: *American Poets & Poetry, Astrophysicist's Tango
Partner Speaks, Aurorean, Avocet, California Qtly, Coffee &
Chicory, Connecticut Writer, Inlet, Laughing Boy Rev, Folio,
Pivot, Alura, Yet Another Small Mag, Fire, Poetic Justice,
Kansas.*

John Jurkowski   W
6 Walnut Ridge Rd, New Fairfield, CT 06812-0214,
203-746-7673
Pubs: *New Yorker, Redbook, Shenandoah, Quarterly Review of Literature, NAR.*

Susan A. Katz   P
121 Painter Ridge Rd, Washington Depot, CT 06793,
860-868-3549
Internet: skatz203.com
Pubs: *Teaching Creatively By Working the Word* (Allyn and Bacon, 1996), *An Eye For Resemblances* (Aegina, 1991), *Life on The Line: Anth* (Negative Capability Pr, 1992), *When I Am An Old Woman I Shall Wear Purple: Anth* (Papier-Mache Pr, 1991).

Susan Baumann Kinsolving   P
PO Box 175, Bridgewater, CT 06752-0175
Pubs: *House Lights* (Grove Pr, 1999), *Among Flowers* (Clarkson Potter/Random Hse, 1993), *Mixed Bouquet* (Panache Pr/Random Hse, 1993), *Grand Street, Kansas Qtly, Western Humanities Rev, New Republic, Nation, Harvard Mag, Beloit Poetry Jrnl, Antioch Rev.*

Binnie Klein   P
142 East Rock Rd, New Haven, CT 06511, 203-781-8161
Internet: binnie@ct1.nai.net
Pubs: *Twilight Zones* (Co-author; U California Pr, 1997), *Sequoia, Dreamworks, Stone Country, Panache, Minnesota Rev, Confrontation, Center, Etcetera.*

Kenneth M. Koprowski   P
340 Bayberrie Dr, Stamford, CT 06902

Eileen Kostiner   P
19 Thompson Rd, Storrs, CT 06268, 203-429-6983
Internet: ekostiner@sprynet.com
Pubs: *Love's Other Face, Poetry Like Bread: Anth* (Curbstone Pr, 1994, 1982), *MacGuffin, Nostalgia, Mediphors, Labyris, Creative Woman.*

Norman Kraeft   P
86 Bellamy Ln, Bethlehem, CT 06751-1203, 203-266-5113
Pubs: *The Lyric, Sparrow, Orbis, Prairie Schooner, Connecticut River Rev, Bogg: An Anglo-American Jrnl, Pivot, Blue Unicorn.*

Janet Krauss   P
585 Gilman St, Bridgeport, CT 06605, 203-333-7779
Pubs: *A Pamphlet of Poems* (Palanquin Pr, 1995), *American Goat, Painted Hills, Green Hills Literary Lantern, Blue Buildings, Amaranth, California State Poetry Soc, MacGuffin, Jabberwok, Rockhurst Rev, Dickinson Rev.*

Philip Watson Kuepper   P&W
233 Bouton St W, Stamford, CT 06807, 203-968-0165
Pubs: *American Poetry Annual: Anths* (Amherst Soc, 1997, 1996, 1995), *Connecticut Poets on AIDS: A Cross Culture Collection: Anth* (Andrew Mountain Pr, 1996), *Currents.*

Helen Lawson   P&W
56 Old Mill Ln, West Hartford, CT 06107
Pubs: *Live Me A River, Women As I Know Them* (Blue Spruce Pr, 1981, 1978), *Bronte Street, Caprice, Dan River Rev.*

Rena Lee   P
179 Ledge Dr, Torrington, CT 06790
Pubs: *Present Tense, Pulp, Bitterroot, Poet Lore, Shofar.*

Ann Z. Leventhal   P&W
19 Woodside Cir, Hartford, CT 06105-1120
Internet: azlhdl@ct2.nai.net
Pubs: *Life-Lines* (Magic Circle Pr, 1986), *Publishers Weekly, Passages North, Cottonwood, Remark, Pacific Rev, Lake Effect, New York Times Book Rev, Georgia Rev, Other Voices, South Dakota Rev, Mississippi Rev.*

Leonard C. Lewin   W
6 Long Hill Farm, Guilford, CT 06437
Pubs: *Triage, Report From Iron Mountain* (Dial, 1972, 1967), *Harper's, Nation, New York Times.*

Pam Lewis   W
128 Courtyard Ln, Storrs Mansfield, CT 06250
Pubs: *Wee Girls* (Spinifex, 1997), *New Yorker, Puerto del Sol, Intro 14.*

Rick Lyon   P
29 Pratt St, Essex, CT 06426, 860-767-0628
Pubs: *Bell 8* (BOA Edtns, 1994), *Missouri Rev, Partisan Rev, Kansas Qtly, Agni, Massachusetts Rev, Nation, Tar River Poetry, APR, Ironwood, Colorado Rev.*

Chopeta C. Lyons   W
198 Jared Sparks Rd, West Willington, CT 06279
Pubs: *Discover Writing* (Prentice-Hall, 1984), *Northeast, Primavera, Negative Capability, Aura.*

Paula Maclan   P
220 Day Rd, Pomfret Center, CT 06259, 203-963-7774
Pubs: *It Was The Year of the Scalping* (Still Waters Pr, 1991), *Samisdat, Up Against the Wall Mother, Slant.*

Robin Magowan   P
PO Box 511, Salisbury, CT 06068, 203-435-4876
Pubs: *Lilac Cigarette In a Wish Cathedral* (U South Carolina Pr, 1998), *New Wine* (Pasdeloup, 1994), *Fabled Cities of Central Asia* (Abbeville, 1990), *Margin, New Republic, Paris Rev, Yale Rev.*

Saul Maloff W
659-B Heritage Village, Southbury, CT 06488, 203-264-4885
Pubs: *Heartland, Happy Families* (Scribner, 1973, 1969), *New York Times Book Rev, Nation.*

Alice Mattison P&W
15 Anderson St, New Haven, CT 06511, 203-624-0332
Pubs: *Men Giving Money, Women Yelling, Hilda and Pearl, The Flight of Andy Burns* (Morrow, 1997, 1995, 1993), *New Yorker, New England Rev, NAR, Boston Rev, Shenandoah, Grand Street, Glimmer Train, Boulevard, Southern Humanities Rev.*

Carole Spearin McCauley P&W
23 Buena Vista Dr, Greenwich, CT 06831, 203-531-6192
Internet: mcaulea@concentric.net
Pubs: *Cold Steal, Happenthing In Travel On* (Women's Pr, 1991, 1990), *Nightshade Reader: Anth* (Nightshade Pr, 1995), *Baba Yaga: Anth* (Woman of Wands, 1995), *Natural Way, Science of Mind, Berkshire Rev, Unity.*

J. D. McClatchy P
The Yale Review, Box 208243, New Haven, CT 065208243, 203-432-0499
Pubs: *Ten Commandments, The Rest of the Way* (Knopf, 1998, 1990), *Stars Principal* (Macmillan, 1986), *Scenes From Another Life* (Braziller, 1981), *Vintage Book of Contemporary American Poetry: Anth* (Vintage, 1990).

Rennie McQuilkin P
21 Goodrich Rd, Simsbury, CT 06070, 203-658-1728
Pubs: *We All Fall Down* (Swallow's Tale, 1988), *Poetry, Yale Rev, Southern Rev, Poetry Northwest, Hudson Rev, Atlantic.*

Christopher Merrill P&W
PO Box 172, East Woodstock, CT 06244, 860-963-2399
Internet: cmerrill@holycross.edu
Pubs: *Watch Fire* (White Pine Pr, 1994), *The Grass of Another Country* (Henry Holt, 1993), *Prairie Schooner, Paris Rev, New Virginia Rev, Nation, Sierra, Sports Illustrated, APR.*

David L. Meth P
Writers' Productions, PO Box 630, Westport, CT 06881, 203-227-8199
Pubs: *American Pen, Confrontation, Poet Lore, Valley Views, Lake Superior Rev, Jeopardy.*

Barbara Milton W
32 Elm St, Milford, CT 06460, 203-877-0668
Pubs: *A Small Cartoon* (Wordbeat Pr, 1983), *Paris Rev, NAR, Apalachee Qtly.*

Honor Moore P
PO Box 305, Kent, CT 067570305, 860-927-3418
Internet: honorm@aol.com
Pubs: *The White Blackbird* (Penguin, 1997), *Memoir* (Chicory Blue, 1988), *A Formal Feeling Comes: Anth* (Story Line Pr, 1994), *New Yorker, Seneca Rev, Paris Rev, American Poetry Rev.*

H. L. Mountzoures W
29 Old Black Point Rd, Niantic, CT 06357
Pubs: *The Bridge, The Empire of Things* (Scribner, 1972, 1968), *New Yorker, Yankee, Redbook, Atlantic.*

Bryanne Nanfito P
4 S Broad St, Unit One, Meriden, CT 06450, 203-634-6675
Pubs: *Greenfield Rev, New York Qtly, Kansas Qtly.*

Peter Neill W
PO Box 3131, Stony Creek, CT 06405, 203-488-3424
Pubs: *Acoma, A Novel* (Leete's Island Bks, 1978).

Sol Newman P
116 Putnam Ave, Hamden, CT 06517, 203-288-4836
Pubs: *New Black Mask* (HBJ, 1986).

Gunilla B. Norris P
PO Box 337, Mystic, CT 06355-0337, 203-264-6043
Pubs: *Journeying in Place, Sharing Silence, Becoming Bread, Being Home* (Bell Tower Bks, 1994, 1994, 1992, 1991), *Learning from the Angel* (Lotus, 1985).

Hugh Ogden P
331 Chestnut Hill Rd, Glastonbury, CT 06033, 203-657-3293
Internet: hugh.ogden@trincoll.edu
Pubs: *Windfalls* (Andrew Mountain Pr, 1996), *Two Roads and This Spring* (CRS Outloud Bks, 1993), *New Letters, Poetry Northwest, North Dakota Qtly, Malahat Rev.*

Jo Anna O'Keefe P
Knight St, Norwalk, CT 06856, 203-847-4543
Pubs: *Come to the Garden* (C. R. Gibson Co., 1992), *Christian Living.*

Maureen A. Owen P
109 Dunk Rock Rd, Guilford, CT 06437, 203-453-1921
Pubs: *American Rush: Selected Poems, Moving Borders: Anth* (Talisman Hse Pub, 1998, 1998), *Untapped Maps* (Potes & Poets Pr, 1993), *Imaginary Income* (Hanging Loose Pr, 1992), *Five Fingers Rev, o.blek, Long News in the Short Century, NAW, 6ix, Hanging Loose.*

Joan Pond W
277 Long Mtn, New Milford, CT 06776
Pubs: *Reflections, Rose Garden* (Life-Link Bks, 1990, 1989).

C. E. Poverman W
67 Trumbull St, New Haven, CT 06510, 203-562-0570

Joseph Raffa P
Box 414, Glastonbury, CT 06033, 203-659-3424
> Pubs: *No Archaeologist, Death Depends On Our Dark Silence* (John Brown Pr, 1987, 1986), *New York Qtly, Crosscurrents, Samisdat, Wisconsin Rev, Windless Orchard.*

Kit Reed W
45 Lawn Ave, Middletown, CT 06457, 212-265-7330
Internet: http://www.focus-consulting.co.uk/kreed/reed.html
> Pubs: *Weird Women, Wired Women* (Wesleyan U Pr, 1998), *J. Eden* (U Pr New England, 1996), *Twice Burned, Gone* (Little, Brown, 1993, 1992), *Thief of Lives and Other Stories* (U Missouri Pr, 1992).

Nicholas M. Rinaldi P&W
32 Indian Rd, Trumbull, CT 06611, 203-452-5266
> Pubs: *Bridge Fall Down* (St. Martin's, 1985), *The Luftwaffe In Chaos* (Negative Capability, 1985).

Becky Rodia P
PO Box 184, Trumbull, CT 06611, 203-452-9652
Internet: brodyjean@aol.com
> Pubs: *Another Fire* (Adastra Pr, 1997), *Weber Studies, Laurel Rev, Cream City Rev, Poet Lore, Georgetown Rev.*

Lawrence Russ P
33 Westford Dr, Southport, CT 06490-1444, 860-808-5090
Internet: lruss@snet.net
> Pubs: *The Burning-Ground* (Owl Creek Pr, 1981), *Nation, Image, Virginia Qtly Rev, Iowa Rev, Parabola, Chelsea.*

Maria Sassi P
11 Paxton Rd, West Hartford, CT 06107, 860-521-2095
> Pubs: *Hooted In Stars* (Singular Speech Pr, 1998), *What I See* (Hanover Pr, 1997), *American Anth of Contemporary Poetry* (Great Lakes Poetry Pr, 1988), *Connecticut River Rev, Padre, Italian-Americana, Blue Unicorn.*

Leslie Scalapino P
Wesleyan Univ Press, 110 Mt. Vernon St, Middleton, CT 064590433
> Pubs: *The Return of Painting* (Talisman Hse Pub, 1997), *The Front Matter Dead Souls* (Wesleyan U Pr, 1996), *Crowd And Not Evening Or Light, What Is The Inside What Is Outside?: Anth* (O Bks, 1992, 1991), *How Phenomena Appear to Unfold* (Potes & Poets, 1990).

Jeffrey Schwartz P
289 Woodridge Ave, Fairfield, CT 06430
> Pubs: *Contending with the Dark* (Alice James Bks, 1978), *Pennsylvania Rev, Yankee, Connecticut Poetry Rev.*

James R. Scrimgeour P
36 Caldwell Dr, New Milford, CT 06776
> Pubs: *Dikel, Your Hands* (Spoon River, 1979), *Margins, Wormwood Rev, Oyez, Cave, Aspect, Zahir.*

Thalia Selz W
52 Coolidge St, Hartford, CT 06106-3720, 860-527-4141
> Pubs: *American Fiction 3: Anth* (Birch Lane, 1992), *Oktoberfest V: Anth* (Druid Pr, 1990), *Antaeus, Partisan Rev, Missouri Rev, New Letters, Chicago, Kansas Qtly.*

Joan Shapiro P
17 Fairview Dr/Box 752, South Windsor, CT 06074, 203-644-2311
> Pubs: *The Puppet Lady: Poems, Coloring Book: Poems* (Blue Spruce, 1982, 1978).

Vivian Shipley P
Southern Connecticut Univ, 501 Crescent St, New Haven, CT 06473, 203-288-5718
> Pubs: *Devil's Lane* (Negative Capability, 1996), *Poems Out of Harlan County* (Ithaca Hse, 1989), *American Scholar, New Letters, Indiana Rev, Michigan Qtly Rev, Texas Rev.*

Joan Seliger Sidney P
74 Lynwood Rd, Storrs, CT 06268-2012, 860-429-7271
Internet: jsidney@juno.com
> Pubs: *The Way The Past Comes Back* (Kutenai Pr, 1991), *Her Face in the Mirror: Anth* (Beacon Pr, 1994), *Israel Horizons, Massachusetts Rev, Michigan Qtly Rev, New York Qtly.*

Sharyn Jeanne Skeeter P&W
PO Box 16819, Stamford, CT 06905
Internet: sjskeeter1@aol.com
> Pubs: *In Search of Color Everywhere: Anth* (Stewart, Tabori & Chang, 1994), *Connecticut River Rev, Cafe Rev, Obsidian, Callaloo, Greenfield Rev, Fiction.*

Paul Smyth P&W
PO Box 2964, New Haven, CT 06515-0064
> Pubs: *Conversions* (U Georgia Pr, 1974), *Poetry, Kenyon Rev, Sewanee Rev, Beloit Poetry Jrnl.*

Rod Steier P
39 Pheasant Hill Dr, West Hartford, CT 06107
> Pubs: *28 Days To Satori, Kevin* (Bartholomew's Cobble, 1976, 1975).

William Styron W
Rucum Rd, Roxbury, CT 06783
> Pubs: *This Quiet Dust, Sophie's Choice* (Random Hse, 1982, 1979).

William Swarts P
27 Wright St, Westport, CT 06880-9113, 203-259-7566
> Pubs: *Treehouse Of The Mind* (Andrew Mountain Pr, 1981), *Small Pond, Embers, Outerbridge, Poets On.*

Lisa C. Taylor   P
PO Box 484, Mansfield Center, CT 06250, 860-429-8274
Internet: taylor@neca.com
    Pubs: *Falling Open* (Alpha Beat Pr, 1994), *Written with a Spoon: Anth* (Sherman Asher Publishing, 1995), *Pudding Magazine, Xanadu, Poetry Digest, Free Focus.*

Randeane Tetu   W
41 Old Turnpike Rd, Haddam, CT 06438, 860-345-4226
    Pubs: *Flying Horses, Secret Souls, Merle's & Marilyn's Mink Ranch, When I Am An Old Woman I Shall Wear Purple: Anth* (Papier-Mache Pr, 1997, 1991, 1987), *Massachusetts Rev, Minnesota Rev.*

Sue Ellen Thompson   P
PO Box 326, Mystic, CT 063550326, 860-536-0215
Internet: iambic@aol.com
    Pubs: *The Wedding Boat* (Owl Creek Pr, 1995), *This Body of Silk* (Northeastern U Pr, 1986), *Georgia Rev, Louisville Rev, New Virginia Rev, Laurel Rev.*

Edwina Trentham   P
364 Central Ave, New Haven, CT 06515
    Pubs: *Atomic Ghost: Anth* (Coffee Hse Pr, 1995), *Pivot, Yankee Mag, Massachusetts Rev, Sun, Embers, Dickinson Rev, Harvard Mag, American Voice, New Virginia Rev.*

Peter J. Ulisse   P
65 Rivercliff Dr, Devon, CT 06460-5025, 203-874-0618
Internet: ho_ulisse@commnet.edu
    Pubs: *Wings and Roots* (Icarus Pr, 1985), *Poet, Poets On, Poetry South, Wayfarers, Connecticut River Rev.*

Katrina Van Tassel   P
6 Broad St, Guilford, CT 06437, 203-453-2328
    Pubs: *Trundlewheel* (Andrew Mountain Pr, 1981), *Yankee, Embers, Red Fox Rev, Stone Country, Footworks.*

Theresa C. Vara   P
56 Shane Dr, Southbury, CT 06488
    Pubs: *Poeti Italo-Americani/Italian-American Poets: Anth* (Italbooks, 1992), *Reflections of a County: Anth* (White Pond Center, 1982), *Earthwise, Beanfeast.*

Patricia Volk   W
Box 295, Sharon, CT 06069
    Pubs: *All It Takes* (Atheneum, 1990), *The Yellow Banana* (Word Beat, 1984), *New York Times Mag, Redbook, Playboy, New Yorker, Atlantic, Mirabella.*

Marilyn Nelson Waniek   P
Univ Connecticut, Storrs, CT 06268, 203-486-2141
Internet: http://www.ucc.uconn.edu/ waniek/
    Pubs: *In Search of Color Everywhere* (Stewart, Tabori & Chang, 1994), *Every Shut Eye Ain't Asleep: Anth* (Little, Brown, 1994), *Southern Rev, Kenyon, APR.*

Susan Watson   P
200 Bedford Rd, Greenwich, CT 06830, 203-869-1133
    Pubs: *Birds That Stay* (Arrow Graphics, 1983), *Alaska Qtly, Scratch Gravel Hills.*

Katharine Weber   W
108 Beacon Rd, Bethany, CT 06524, 203-782-1956
    Pubs: *The Music Lesson* (Crown, 1999), *Objects In Mirror Are Closer Than They Appear* (Picador, 1996), *New Yorker, Story, Redbook.*

Max Wilk   W
29 Surf Rd, Westport, CT 06880, 203-226-7669
    Pubs: *They're Playing Our Song* (Da Capo, 1996), *OK! The Story of Oklahoma* (Grove-Atlantic, 1993).

J. Barrett Wolf   P
190 Henry St, 6th Fl, Stamford, CT 06902-5829, 203-357-9761
    Pubs: *Old North Field and Other Poems* (Bear Pause Pubs, 1993), *Enchante Mag, Black Bear Rev, Fireheart.*

Adrienne Wolfert   P
89 Skytop Dr, Fairfield, CT 064321216, 203-372-3802
Internet: wolfrite@aol.com
    Pubs: *Peeling Tomatoes* (Mother Daughter Pr, 1995), *Morning Star* (Hazelnut Pubs, 1993), *Songs of the Dybbuk, Discovery of a Human Fossil* (Lintel, 1990, 1985), *Natal Fire* (Branden Pr, 1975), *Galaxy of Verse: Anth* (M. Evans, 1980), *NAR, Poet Lore.*

Ann Yarmal   P
Yuganta Press, 6 Rushmore Cir, Stamford, CT 06905, 203-322-5638
    Pubs: *The North Star and the Southern Cross, On This Crust of Earth: Anth of Fairfield County Poets* (Yuganta Pr, 1989, 1987), *Black Bear Rev.*

Virginia Brady Young   P
44 Currier Pl, Cheshire, CT 06410, 203-272-2434
    Pubs: *The Way A Live Thing Moves* (Croton Rev Pr, 1989), *Wind in the Long Grass: Anth* (S&S, 1993), *Frogpond Mag, Haiku Intl, Modern Haiku, Woodnotes Haiku Mag.*

Sondra Zeidenstein   P
795 East St N, Goshen, CT 06756, 860-491-2271
Internet: 103310,732@compuserve.com
    Pubs: *A Detail in that Story, Late Afternoon Woman* (Chicory Blue Pr, 1998, 1992), *Passionate Lives: Anth* (Queen of Swords Pr, 1998), *Calliope, Ledge, Mudfish, Lungfull, Lilith, Earth's Daughters, Black Buzzard Rev, Embers, Poet Lore, Rhino.*

Feenie Ziner   W
182 Shore Dr, Branford, CT 06405, 203-481-9095
    Pubs: *Squanto* (Shoe String Pr, 1988), *Within This Wilderness* (Norton, 1978), *I Always Meant To Tell You: Anth* (Pocket Bks, 1997), *Na'amat Woman, Northeast.*

DELAWARE

Jocelyn Hollis   P
304 Mederia Cir, Newark, DE 19702-1562, 302-454-7205
    Pubs: *Persian Gulf Poems, Selected Poems of Jocelyn Hollis* (American Poetry & Literature Pr, 1992, 1991), *Burning Light Jrnl, Bookman's, Dreamstreets, Fiddlehead.*

Fleda Brown Jackson   P
195 Starr Road, Newark, DE 19711, 302-369-8181
Internet: fleda@udel.edu
    Pubs: *Do Not Feel The Birches, Fishing With Blood* (Purdue U Pr, 1993, 1988), *Poetry, Georgia Rev, Ariel, Midwest Qtly, Indiana Rev, Iowa Rev, Southern Poetry Rev.*

Bernard Kaplan   W
Univ Delaware, English Dept, Newark, DE 19711, 302-831-2361
    Pubs: *Obituaries, Prisoners Of This World* (Grossman, 1976, 1970).

Devon Miller-Duggan   P
213 Sypherd Dr, Newark, DE 19711-3626, 302-453-0564

Francis Poole   P
335 Paper Mill Rd, Newark, DE 19711-2254
    Pubs: *Gestures* (Anhinga, 1979), *Zero Zero* (Broken Arrow Pr, 1972), *Lost & Found Times, Poetry East, Pearl, Blades, Exquisite Corpse, Poem.*

Cruce Stark   W
1316 N Clayton St, Wilmington, DE 19806, 302-658-9440
    Pubs: *Chasing Uncle Charley* (SMU Pr, 1992).

Z. Vance Wilson   W
8 Phelps Ln, Newark, DE 19711-3512, 302-738-8755
    Pubs: *The Quick and the Dead* (Arbor Hse, 1986), *Jrnl of Short Story in English, Missouri Rev.*

DISTRICT OF COLUMBIA

Jonetta Rose Barras   P
PO Box 21232, Washington, DC 20009, 202-882-2838
Internet: jrbarras@aol.com
    Pubs: *The Corner Is No Place for Hiding* (Bunny & The Crocodile Pr, 1996), *In Search of Color Everywhere* (Tabori & Chang, 1995), *New Republic.*

Edward L. Beach   W
1622 29th St NW, Washington, DC 20007-2901, 202-337-7359
    Pubs: *Keepers of the Sea* (USNI, 1983), *Cold is the Sea* (HRW, 1978), *Proceedings, Naval History Mag, American Heritage, Reader's Digest, Bluebook.*

Wayne Biddle   W
2032 Belmont Rd NW, #210, Washington, DC 20009, 202-234-2868
    Pubs: *Barons of the Sky* (Simon & Schuster, 1991), *Coming to Terms* (Viking, 1980), *The Nation.*

Rick Cannon   P
19 Eye St NW, Washington, DC 20001, 202-336-7159
    Pubs: *Xanadu, Sidewalks, Cumberland Poetry Rev, Slant, America, Iowa Rev, Verve, Whetstone, Midwest Qtly, Antietam Rev, Cimarron Rev, Folio, Mudfish.*

Emily Blair Chewning   P
3901 Hillandale Ct, Washington, DC 20007, 202-944-9644
Internet: twobi@aol.com
    Pubs: *Anatomy Illustrated* (S&S, 1980), *The Illustrated Flower* (Crown, 1979), *Family Life, Art & Antiques.*

Eric Cheyfitz   P
Georgetown Univ, Washington, DC 20057, 202-625-4949
    Pubs: *Bones & Ash* (Cymric Press, 1977), *Esquire, The New Review, Times Literary Supplement.*

Maxine Clair   P&W
George Washington Univ, Washington, DC 20052, 202-994-6180
    Pubs: *Rattlebone* (FSG, 1994), *October Brown* (Time Printers, 1992), *Coping With Gravity* (Washington Writers' Pub Hse, 1988).

William Claire   P
Washington Resources, Inc., 1250 24th St NW, Ste 300, Washington, DC 20037, 202-463-0388
    Pubs: *Literature & Medicine: The Physician as Writer* (Johns Hopkins U Pr, 1985), *Delos, Horizon, American Scholar, Carleton Miscellany, Chelsea, Nation, Washingtonian.*

Shirley Graves Cochrane   P&W
127 7th St SE, Washington, DC 20003, 202-546-1020
    Pubs: *Letters to the Quick/Letters to the Dead, Everything That's All* (Signal Bks, 1998, 1991), *The Fair-haired Boy* (Word Works/Mica Pr, 1997), *Truths & Half Truths* (Washington Expatriates Pr, 1996), *Family & Other Strangers* (Word Works, 1986).

Maxine Combs   P&W
2216 King Pl NW, Washington, DC 20007
    Pubs: *Handbook of the Strange* (Signal Bks, 1996), *The Foam of Perilous Seas* (Slough Pr, 1990), *Swimming Out of the Collective Unconscious* (The Wineberry Pr, 1989), *Habersham Rev, Kalliope, Iris.*

Noemi Escandell   P&W
1525 Q St NW, #11, Washington, DC 20009-7802, 202-328-7197
    Pubs: *Palabras/Words, Cuadros* (SLUSA, 1986, 1982), *CPU Rev, Third Woman, Letras Femeninas, Plaza, Stone Country, Peregrine.*

Laura Fargas P
621 Lexington Pl NE, Washington, DC 20002, 202-546-2347
Pubs: *Strange Luck* (U California Pr, 1994), *Reflecting What Light We Can't Absorb* (Riverstone Pr, 1993), *Georgia Rev, Paris Rev, Atlantic, Poetry.*

Julia Fields P
3636 16 St NW #B-647, Washington, DC 20010
Pubs: *A Summoning, A Shining* (Red Clay Pr, 1976), *East Of Moonlight* (Poets' Pr, 1973).

Candida Fraze P&W
3722 Harrison St NW, Washington, DC 20015
Pubs: *Renifleur's Daughter* (Henry Holt, 1987), *Poet Lore.*

Edward Gold P
3702 Jenifer St NW, Washington, DC 20015, 202-966-5724
Pubs: *Owl* (Scop Pub, 1983), *New York Qtly, Crab Creek Rev, Red Cedar Rev, Gargoyle, Poet Lore, Kansas Qtly.*

Pat Gray P&W
Library of Congress, Poetry at Noon, Washington, DC
205414912, 202-707-1308
Internet: pgray@ loc.gov
Pubs: *The Denny Poems* (Lincoln U Pr, 1996), *Old Wounds, New Words: Anth* (Jesse Stuart Foundation, 1994), *The MacGuffin, Poetry East, Shenandoah, Poet Lore.*

Ron Green P
American Univ, Washington, DC 20016, 202-687-2450

Patricia Browning Griffith W
1215 Geranium St, NW, Washington, DC 20012,
202-829-7780
Pubs: *Supporting the Sky, The World Around Midnight* (Putnam, 1996, 1991), *Tennessee Blue* (Clarkson Potter, 1981), *Harper's.*

Anthony Hecht P
4256 Nebraska Ave NW, Washington, DC 20016
Pubs: *The Venetian Vespers, The Hard Hours* (Atheneum, 1979, 1967).

Anne Sue Hirshorn PP
2039 37th St NW, Washington, DC 20007

David E. Hubler W
Jenny Bent Graybill & English, 1920 N St NW #660,
Washington, DC 20036, 202-861-0106
Pubs: *Politicians' Health, Diet and Sex Guide* (Tribeca, 1984), *You Gotta Believe* (NAL/Signet, 1983), *McCall's, American Way, Islands, Lifestyles.*

Mark C. Huey P
1515 Caroline St NW, Washington, DC 20009
Pubs: *The Persistence Of Red Dreams* (Alderman Pr, 1980), *Shenandoah, Virginia Literary Rev.*

Gretchen Johnsen P
3038 N St NW, Washington, DC 20007, 202-333-1544
Pubs: *Journal: August 1978-August 1981* (Cumberland Jrnl, 1981), *Paper Air, Aerial, Frank, Bogg.*

Dan Johnson P
1328 E Capitol St NE, Washington, DC 20003, 202-546-9865
Internet: johnsond@wfs.org
Pubs: *Come Looking* (Washington Writer's Pub Hse, 1995), *Suggestions From The Border* (State Street Pr, 1983), *Lullwater Rev, Dickinson Rev, Lip Service, Virginia Mag.*

Beth Baruch Joselow P
2927 Tilden St, NW, Washington, DC 20008, 202-966-5998
Internet: bjoselow@cais.com
Pubs: *Excontemporary, Broad Daylight* (Story Line Pr, 1989, 1989), *Mississippi Rev, APR.*

William Joyce P&W
2200 40 St NW #3, Washington, DC 20007, 202-338-3365
Pubs: *The Recorder of Births and Deaths, First Born of an Ass* (Water Mark Pr, 1990, 1989).

Yala Korwin P
U.S. Holocaust Memorial Museum, Washington, DC 20024
Pubs: *To Tell The Story, Poems of The Holocaust* (Holocaust Pubs, 1987), *The Muse Strikes Back: Anth* (Story Line Pr, 1997), *Anth of Mag Verse* (Monitor, 1997), *Blood to Remember: Anth* (Texas Tech, 1990), *Poetry Digest, Blue Unicorn, Midstream.*

David Kresh P
601 N Carolina SE, Washington, DC 20003, 202-547-6197
Internet: dakr@loc.gov
Pubs: *Sketches After "Pete's Beer"* (Stone Man, 1986), *Bloody Joy: Love Poems* (Slow Dancer, 1981).

Kwelismith PP
1820 Valley Terr SE, Washington, DC 20032, 202-889-2674
Pubs: *Brown Girl in the Ring* (Washington Writer's Publishing Hse, 1992), *Slavesong: The Art of Singing* (Anacostia Repertory Co., 1989).

Kala Ladenheim P
1707 Columbia Rd NW, #419, Washington, DC 20009
Internet: kalae@gwis2.circ.gwu.edu
Pubs: *Not Far From The Mountains Of The Moon* (Dog Ear Pr, 1982), *Kennebec, Maze, 4 Zoas, Glitch, Cafe Rev, Frontiers, Maine Times.*

Mary Ann Larkin P
221 Channing St NE, Washington, DC 20002, 202-832-3978
Internet: pepperlarkin@juno.com
Pubs: *White Clapboard* (Carol Allen, 1988), *The Coil of the Skin* (WWPH, 1982), *Ireland in Poetry: Anth, America in Poetry: Anth* (Abrams, 1990, 1988), *Poetry Ireland, New Letters, Potato Eyes, Potomac Rev.*

Joyce E. Latham   P
3001 Veazy NW, Washington, DC 20008, 202-966-2494
Internet: jlcomm@erols.com
    Pubs: *Beached: Anth* (Pittenbruach Pr, 1997), *Poetry Motel,
    Sliver Quill, Allusive Images, Art Inspires Writing, Poet
    Magazine, Federal Poet, Journal of Graduate Liberal
    Studies, Poetry Day.*

Joanne Leedom-Ackerman   P&W
3229 R St NW, Washington, DC 20007
    Pubs: *The Dark Path to the River, No Marble Angels*
    (Saybrook Pub, 1988, 1987).

Kate Lehrer   W
Ronald Goldfarb & Assoc., 918 16th St, NW, Washington, DC
20006, 202-466-3030
    Pubs: *Out of Eden, When They Took Away The Man In The
    Moon* (Harmony Bks, 1996, 1993), *Best Intentions* (Little,
    Brown & Co., 1987).

Sharon Lerch   W
1733 Riggs Pl NW, Washington, DC 20009-6114,
202-462-2511
Internet: 71674,3440@compuserve.com
    Pubs: *Virginia Qlty Rev, Kansas Qtly, Literary Rev, Black
    Warrior Rev.*

Vladimir Levchev   P
221 42 St NW #1, Washington, DC 20007, 202-337-0373
Internet: vlevchev@aol.com
    Pubs: *Leaves from the Dry Tree* (Cross-Cultural
    Communications, 1996), *Anthology of Magazine Verse:
    Anth, Yearbook of American Poetry: Anth* (Monitor Bk Co,
    1997), *Clay and Stars: Contemporary Bulgarian Poets:
    Anth* (Milkweek Edtns, 1992).

Gregory Luce   P
1421 Massachusetts Ave NW #408, Washington, DC 20005,
202-483-2949
Internet: gluce@erols.com
    Pubs: *Kansas Qtly, Iron, Cimarron Rev, Rikka, Dancing
    Shadow Rev, Shades of Gray.*

Richard McCann   P
American Univ, Literature Dept, 4400 Massachusetts Ave
NW, Washington, DC 20009, 202-885-2978
Internet: rmccann@american.edu
    Pubs: *Things Shaped in Passing* (Persea Bks, 1996),
    Ghost Letters (Alice James Bks, 1994), *Atlantic, Esquire,
    Ploughshares, American Short Fiction.*

Terry McMillan   W
5301 Wisconsin Ave NW Ste 330, Washington, DC 20015,
202-686-3221
Internet: spkrsww@aol.com
    Pubs: *How Stella Got Her Groove Back, Waiting To Exhale,
    Disappearing Acts, Breaking Ice: Anth* (Viking, 1996, 1992,
    1989, 1990), *Mama* (HM, 1987), *Essence, Esquire, Elle.*

Larry McMurtry   W
1209 31st St, Washington, DC 20007, 202-338-0366
    Pubs: *Buffalo Girls, All My Friends Are Going To Be
    Strangers, Anything For Billy* (Pocket Bks, 1995, 1992,
    1989), *Cadillac Jack* (Simon & Schuster, 1982).

E. Ethelbert Miller   P
Howard Univ, PO Box 441, Washington, DC 20059,
202-291-1560
Internet: emiller698@aol.com
    Pubs: *Whispers, Secrets and Promises, First Light: New
    and Selected Poems* (Black Classic Pr, 1998, 1994), *In
    Search of Color Everywhere: Anth* (Stewart, Tabori &
    Chang, 1994).

Faye Moskowitz   P&W
3306 Highland Pl NW, Washington, DC 20008, 202-363-8628
Internet: faymos@gwu.edu
    Pubs: *And The Bridge Is Love, Her Face in the Mirror: Anth*
    (Beacon Pr, 1991, 1994), *Calyx, Prairie Schooner, 13th
    Moon, Woman's Day, Victoria Mag, Feminist Studies.*

Jean Nordhaus   P
623 E Capitol St SE, Washington, DC 20003, 202-543-1905
Internet: jean_nordhaus@worldnet.att.net
    Pubs: *A Purchase of Porcelain* (Kinloch Rivers Chapbooks,
    1998), *My Life in Hiding* (QRL, 1991), *A Bracelet of Lies*
    (Washington Writers Pub Hse, 1987), *Poetry, APR, Prairie
    Schooner, Hudson Rev, West Branch, Washington Rev.*

Michael Novak   W
American Enterprise Institute, 1150 17th St NW, Rm 1200,
Washington, DC 20036, 202-862-5838
    Pubs: *This Hemisphere of Liberty* (AEI, 1990).

Andrew Oerke   P
2949 Macomb St NW, Washington, DC 20008, 202-966-8819

Alicia Partnoy   W
PO Box 21425, Washington, DC 20009, 202-483-5549
    Pubs: *Revenge of the Apple: Poems, The Little School*
    (Cleis Pr, 1992, 1986).

Fred Rachford   P
609 12th St NE, Washington, DC 20002

Elisavietta Ritchie   P&W
3207 Macomb St NW, Washington, DC 10008, 202-363-8036
Internet: ehfarnsworth@compuserve.com
    Pubs: *Elegy For The Other Woman, The Arc of the Storm,
    Flying Time* (Signal Bks, 1995, 1995, 1992), *Poetry,
    American Scholar, New York Qtly, Press, Confrontation.*

Robert Sargent   P
815 A St NE, #2, Washington, DC 20002, 202-543-1868
    Pubs: *Fish Galore* (Bunny & Crocodile Pr, 1989), *A Woman
    From Memphis, Aspects of a Southern Story* (Word Works,
    1987, 1983), *Poetry, Kansas Qtly.*

Mary McGowan Slappey   P
National Writers Association, 4500 Chesapeake St NW,
Washington, DC 20016, 202-363-9082
> Pubs: *Swiss Songs & Other Selected Poetry, Lafayette and
> Harriet, Glory of Wooden Walls* (Interspace Bks, 1995,
> 1989, 1986).

Laurie Stroblas   P
2500 Wisconsin Ave NW, #549, Washington, DC 20007,
202-333-1026
> Pubs: *The First Yes: Poems About Communicating: Anth*
> (Dryad Pr, 1997),*Hungry As We Are:* Anth (Washington
> Writers Pub Hse, 1995), *George Washington Rev, Poet
> Lore, Gargoyle, Calyx, Asha Jrnl, Outerbridge.*

Mary Swope   P
3927 Idaho Ave NW, Washington, DC 20008, 212-363-1394
> Pubs: *The Book of Falmouth: Anth* (Falmouth Historical
> Commission, 1986), *Radcliffe Qtly.*

Joseph Thackery   P&W
4201 Harrison St, NW, Washington, DC 20015,
202-363-7675
> Pubs: *The Dark Above Mad River* (Washington Writers'
> Pub Hse, 1992), *Evidence of Community* (Center for
> Washington Area Studies, 1984).

Rebecca Thompson   P
The Lansburgh, 425 8th St NW, 244, Washington, DC
200042111, 202-737-4545
> Pubs: *New Virginia Rev, Feelings, New York Qtly, Midwest
> Poetry Rev, Aireings, Primitive Bikini, Midwest Qtly.*

Roberto H. Vargas   P
1627 New Hampshire NW, Washington, DC 20009,
202-387-4371
> Pubs: *Nicaragua, I Sing You Kisses, Bullets, Visions Of
> Liberty* (Pocho Che, 1979).

David Veronese   W
4200 Cathedral Ave NW, #907, Washington, DC 20016,
202-234-0047
Internet: dveronese@aol.com
> Pubs: *JANA* (Serpent's Tail, 1993), *Prism Intl, Club,
> Mystery Scene, Blue Zebra.*

Hugh Walthall   P
1603 Kearny St NE, Washington, DC 20018, 202-232-1876
> Pubs: *Ladidah* (Ithaca Hse, 1978).

Edward Weismiller   P&W
2400 Virginia Ave NW, #C1119, Washington, DC
20037-2664, 202-223-0333
> Pubs: *The Branch of Fire* (Word Works, 1980), *The Serpent
> Sleeping* (Putnam, 1962).

Faith Williams   P
3768 McKinley St NW, Washington, DC 20015,
202-362-0189
Internet: fmwill@aol.com
> Pubs: *Woman the Gatherer: Anth* (Yale U Pr, 1981), *Bogg,
> Poet Lore, Earth's Daughters, The Bridge, Nimrod, Kansas
> Qtly, Kalliope, Boston Literary Rev.*

Joyce Winslow   W
2800 Wisconsin Ave NW, #403, Washington, DC 20007,
202-686-1747
> Pubs: *Best American Short Stories: Anth* (HM, 1969), *New
> Virginia Rev, River City, Yankee, The Washington Post,
> Redbook, Town & Country, Mademoiselle.*

Mary Kay Zuravleff   W
3730 Jocelyn St NW, Washington, DC 20015-1808,
202-966-9535
> Pubs: *The Frequency of Souls* (FSG, 1996), *Women's
> Glibber: Anth* (Crossing Pr, 1993), *Gila Rev, Gargoyle,
> Appearances, New Mexico Humanities Rev.*

FLORIDA

Dame Marnie Adler   P
266 W Casurina Pl, Beverly Hills, FL 34465, 352-746-0998
> Pubs: *Anths of Florida State Poetry Society* (Florida State
> Poetry Soc, 1995, 1994), *Bitterroot, Harpstrings, Voices
> Israel, Poets Forum.*

Eileen Annie   P&W
PO Box 485, Eastpoint, FL 32328, 904-670-8518
> Pubs: *Half The Bran Muffin Is Gone, Life On A Beanstalk*
> (Bench Pr, 1991, 1986), *Long Island Qtly, Confrontation.*

Mark Ari   P&W
943 Seashell Ln, Ponte Vedra Beach, FL 32082,
904-285-9477
Internet: markari@aol.com
> Pubs: *The Shoemaker's Tale* (Zephyr Pr, 1994), *The
> Stroker Anthology* (Stroker, Papandrea, Schumann, 1995),
> *Lost Creek Letters, Home Planet News.*

Mary Alice Ayers   W
Univ Miami, 327 Ashe Bldg, English Dept, Coral Gables, FL
33124, 305-284-3090
> Pubs: *Partisan Rev, Village Advocate, Newsday Mag,
> Florida Mag, Impact.*

John Balaban   P&W
Univ Miami, PO Box 248145, Coral Gables, FL 331248145,
305-284-2182
> Pubs: *Locusts At the Edge of Summer, Words for My
> Daughter* (Copper Canyon Pr, 1997, 1991), *Coming Down
> Again* (S&S, 1989), *Blue Mountain* (Unicorn, 1982),
> *Harper's, TriQuarterly, Ploughshares.*

Mary Baron   P
Univ North Florida, 4567 St. Johns Bluff Rd S, Jacksonville,
FL 32216, 904-646-2580
    Pubs: *Wheat Among Bones* (Sheep Meadow Pr, 1990),
Letters For The New England Dead (Godine, 1974),
Southern Rev, Northward Jrnl.

Lynne Barrett   W
Florida International Univ, N Miami Campus, North Miami, FL
33181, 305-919-5506
    Pubs: *The Secret Names of Women, The Land of Go*
(Carnegie Mellon U Pr, 1998, 1988), *Mondo Barbie: Anth*
(St. Martin's Pr, 1993), *Tampa Rev, Other Voices,*
Redbook, Ellery Queen's Mystery Mag.

Dina D. Ben-Lev   P
c/o Rhoden, 2626 Danielle Dr, Oveido, FL 32765,
407-366-1616
    Pubs: *Broken Helix* (Mid-List Pr, 1997), *Sober on a Small*
Plane (Wind Publications, 1995), *Note for a Missing Friend*
(Slapering Hol Pr, 1991).

Judith A. Berke   P
5600 Collins Ave, #11P, Miami Beach, FL 33140-2411,
305-868-3302
    Pubs: *Acting Problems* (Silverfish Rev Pr, 1993), *White*
Morning (Wesleyan U Pr, 1989), *APR, Atlantic, Poetry,*
Field, Massachusetts Rev, Ohio Rev, Iowa Rev.

Wendy Bishop   P
Florida State Univ, English Dept, Tallahassee, FL 32306,
850-893-1381
Internet: wbishop@english.fsu.edu
    Pubs: *Working Words: The Process of Creative Writing*
(Mayfield Pub, 1992), *Colors of a Different Horse: Anth*
(Natl Council of Teachers of English, 1994).

Margaret Blaker   P
210 Lake Howard Dr NW, Winter Haven, FL 33880,
941-294-2226
    Pubs: *Light Year: Anth* (Bits Pr, 1989), *Norton Book of Light*
Verse: Anth (Norton, 1986), *Amelia, Fiction Qtly, Pig Iron.*

Bocaccio   PP
1700 Glenhouse Dr, #406, Sarasota, FL 34241-6766

Barbara Boncek   P
5220 Sydney St, Port Orange, FL 32127
    Pubs: *Sunrust, Resoundings, Wide Open Mag, Stone*
Ridge Poetry, Oxalis, Outloud, Echoes, Almanac.

Van K. Brock   P
Florida State Univ, Tallahassee, FL 32306, 904-644-4230
    Pubs: *The Window* (Chase Avenue Pr, 1981), *American*
Voice, National Forum, Southern Poetry Rev.

Harry Brody   P
3033 Pinecrest St, Sarasota, FL 34239-7037, 941-923-5098
    Pubs: *For We Are Constructing the Dwelling of Feeling*
(Bluestone Pr, 1992), *Fields* (Ion Bks, 1987), *Chariton Rev,*
Carolina Qtly, Spirit That Moves Us.

Rick Bundy   P
RR1, Box 209D, Quincy, FL 32351, 904-442-4146
Internet: mattyalou@aol.com
    Pubs: *The Breathers at St. Marks* (Wellberry Pr, 1994),
Prairie Schooner, Southern Poetry Rev, Missouri Rev,
Georgia Rev, Puerto del Sol.

Janet Burroway   P&W
Florida State Univ, Tallahassee, FL 32306, 904-222-8272
    Pubs: *Cutting Stone* (HM, 1992), *Opening Nights*
(Atheneum, 1986), *Prairie Schooner, New Letters, New*
Virginia Rev.

R. F. Caldwell   P
Griffwood Mobile Home Park, 03896-132 Picciola Rd,
Fruitland Park, FL 34731-6371, 904-728-8898
    Pubs: *Healthbeat, Golden Life Styles, Florida Gardener,*
Azalea Rev.

Howard Camner   P
10440 SW 76 St, Miami, FL 33173, 305-274-1871
    Pubs: *Brutal Delicacies, Bed of Nails, Jammed Zipper,*
Banned in Babylon, Stray Dog Wail (Camelot Pub Co.,
1996, 1995, 1994, 1993, 1992), *Florida in Poetry: Anth*
(Pineapple Pr, 1995), *Reporting to Hell, Without Halos,*
Security Blanket.

Eli Cantor   P&W
384 N Washington Dr, Sarasota, FL 34236
    Pubs: *Love Letters, Enemy in the Mirror* (Crown, 1979,
1977), *Esquire, Story, Accent, Poetry Mag, Coronet,*
Saturday Rev.

Ella Cavis   P
1408 56th St W, Bradenton, FL 34209
    Pubs: *Florida Qtly, Sarasota Qtly, Mobius, Voices Intl,*
Tucumcari, Prophetic Voices, MPR, Slant, Orphic Lute, Old
Hickory Rev, Parnassus.

Joanne Childers   P
3504 NW 7th Pl, Gainesville, FL 32607, 904-376-9773
    Pubs: *Moving Mother Out* (Florida Literary Fdn, 1992),
Aisles of Flowers: Anth (Anhinga Pr, 1995), *Massachusetts*
Rev, Poet & Critic, Chattahoochee Rev, Kalliope, Kentucky
Rev.

Elsa Colligan   P
3 Portside Dr, Ft Lauderdale, FL 33316, 305-462-0809
    Pubs: *The Aerialist* (Barlenmir House, 1979), *Harper's, New*
York Qtly, Chicago Rev, Poets On, Beloit Poetry Jrnl,
Footwork.

Kirby Congdon P
715 Baker's Ln, Key West, FL 33040, 305-294-6979
Pubs: *Party Train: North American Prose Poetry: Anth* (New Rivers Pr, 1996), *Gay Roots: Anth* (Gay Sunshine Pr, 1991), *Small Press Rev, Caprice, Cayo, Pivot.*

John Charles Cooper P&W
70 East Cahill Ct, Big Pine Key, FL 33043
Internet: v-cooper@juno.com
Pubs: *Cast A Single Shadow* (Northwest Pub Co., 1996), *Vicki's Lake* (Harrodsburg Herald, 1989), *Christianity Today, Scripset, Time of Singing, Rant, Wind.*

Patricia Corbus P
PO Box 5601, Sarasota, FL 342775601, 941-349-0325
Pubs: *Folio, Antigonish Rev, Wallace Stevens Jrnl, Windsor Rev, Greensboro Rev, South Carolina Rev, Cream City Rev, Paris Rev, Antioch Rev, Georgia Rev, Iconoclast, Cincinnati Poetry Rev, Kestrel.*

Harry Crews W
Univ Florida, Gainesville, FL 32601, 904-392-0777

Edwin Crusoe P
2222 Middle Torch Rd, Summerland Key, FL 33042, 305-872-9073
Pubs: *Wanderings* (Rip Off Pr, 1971), *Key West Poetry Guild Anth* (Key West Poetry Guild, 1989), *Hidden Path, Florida Keys Maritime Historical Jrnl, Key West Rev.*

Ron De Maris P
9621 SW 103 Pl, Miami, FL 33176, 305-271-9455
Pubs: *APR, Nation, Sewanee Rev, Poetry Northwest, New Letters, New Orleans Rev, Carolina Qtly, Southern Rev, New England Rev, Ploughshares, Gettysburg Rev, Atlanta Rev, New Republic.*

Donna Decker P
74 Westview, Panacea, FL 32346, 850-984-0151
Pubs: *Three Thirds* (Word Banks Pr, 1984), *North of Wakulla: Anth* (Anhinga Pr, 1989), *American Voice, New Collage, Snake Nation Rev, Gulf Stream.*

Barbara Dunning Deffner P
1480 Masters Cir, #171, Delray Beach, FL 33445, 407-495-5606
Pubs: *Sandscript.*

Lenny DellaRocca P
2800 Fiore Way #107, Delray Beach, FL 33445, 561-278-4072
Internet: dellarocca@earthlink.net
Pubs: *Wisconsin Rev, Nimrod, Poet Lore, Apalachee Qtly, Negative Capability, Sun Dog, Seattle Rev.*

Matthew Diomede P
125 10th St E, Tierra Verde, FL 33715-2206
Pubs: *Apalachee Qtly, Riverside Qtly, Rolling Coulter, Wisconsin Rev, Centennial Rev, Oyez Rev, Christianity & Literature, The Viet Nam Generation, Big Book, Black Buzzard Rev, Western Ohio Jrnl.*

Frances Driscoll P
56 Seaplace, 901 Ocean Blvd, Atlantic Beach, FL 32233, 904-241-5075
Internet: pbstudio@pbstudio.com
Pubs: *The Rape Poems* (Pleasure Boat Studio, 1997), *Talk To Me* (Black River, 1987), *Pushcart Prize Anth XIX* (Pushcart Pr, 1994), *Mudlark, Ploughshares.*

Didi S. Dubelyew P
PO Box 1330, Anthony, FL 32617-1330, 352-622-5802
Internet: ddsw@earthling.net
Pubs: *Just Remember, I Told You So...* (Whird Whirrx, 1985), *Monkey Part I: Liner Note* (Koch Jazz, 1996), *Rapscallion's Dream, Telephone.*

John Dufresne P&W
Florida International Univ, N Miami Campus, North Miami, FL 33181, 305-919-4568
Internet: borzilleri@aol.com
Pubs: *Love Warps The Mind A Little, Louisiana Power & Light, The Way That Water Enters Stone* (Norton, 1997, 1994, 1991), *Mississippi Rev, Missouri Rev, Greensboro Rev.*

Juni Dunklin P&W
617 Peachtree Dr, Sandersville, FL 31082

Page Edwards, Jr. W
PO Box 1117, St Augustine, FL 32085-1117, 904-829-9341
Internet: oldhouse@aug.com
Pubs: *The Search for Kate DuVal, American Girl, The Lake* (Marion Boyars Pub, 1996, 1990, 1986).

Sheila Natasha Simro Friedman PP
15451 SW 67 Ct, Miami, FL 33157, 305-233-4280

Sue Gambill W
509 Curtis Rd, Tallahassee, FL 32311, 904-942-6597
Pubs: *Heartscape* (Naiad Pr, 1989), *Word of Mouth: Anth* (Crossing Pr, 1990), *Moonseed.*

Nola Garrett P
2228 Orchard Park Dr, Spring Hill, FL 34608, 352-666-5867
Internet: ngarrett@atlantic.net
Pubs: *The Pastor's Wife Considers Pinball* (Wordart, 1998), *The Muse Strikes Back: Anth* (Story Line, 1997), *Odd Angles of Heaven: Anth* (Harold Shaw, 1994), *Formalist, Georgia Rev, Cimarron Rev, Christian Century, Poet Lore, Crab Orchard Rev, Yellow Silk.*

Jim Gerard P
1227 West Orange, Lake City, FL 32055, 904-752-6325

Stephen M. Gibson   P
119 Royal Pine Cir North, Royal Palm Beach, FL 33411,
407-793-6552
> Pubs: *Bodies in the Bog* (Texas Rev Pr, 1984), *Paris Rev,
> New England Rev, Poetry, Chelsea, Texas Rev, Boulevard.*

Andrew Glaze   P
825 NW 14 Ct, Miami, FL 33125, 305-649-6944
Internet: andrewglaze@juno.com
> Pubs: *Someone Will Go On Owing: Selected Poems, Fall
> Gallop: New & Selected* (Black Belt Pr, 1998, 1997), *Reality
> Street* (St. Andrews Pr, 1991), *Atlantic, Negative Capability,
> Pivot, New York Qtly, New Yorker.*

Herman Gold   P
9420 W Bay Harbor Dr, Bay Harbor Island, FL 33154,
305-868-1039
> Pubs: *New York Qtly, Poetry Now, Confrontation, Tropic,
> Wormwood Rev, Contact II, Samisdat.*

Bonnie Gordon   W
2464 SW 19 Terr, Miami, FL 33145, 305-856-2776
> Pubs: *Childhood In Reno* (Street New York, 1982), *Songs
> From Unsung Worlds: Anth* (Birkhauser, 1986).

Deborah Eve Grayson   P
The Center for Natural Health, 4227 W Commercial Blvd,
Tamarac, FL 33319, 305-739-5751
> Pubs: *Breath Marks in the Wind* (Breath Marks/IDF, 1988),
> *Journal of Poetry Therapy, Pudding Mag.*

Daniel Green   P
1248 Belleflower St, Sarasota, FL 34232-1107, 941-366-6573
Internet: d9green@aol.com
> Pubs: *All Told, Better Late, On Second Thought* (Fithian Pr,
> 1997, 1994, 1992).

Debora Greger   P
Univ Florida, English Dept, PO Box 117310, Gainesville, FL
32611-7310, 352-392-0777
> Pubs: *Desert Fathers, Uranium Daughters* (Penguin, 1996),
> *Norton Anthology of Poetry* (Norton, 1996), *New Yorker,
> New York Times, New Republic, Nation, Yale Rev.*

J. Warren Gresham   P
5385 SW 83 Pl, Ocala, FL 344763799, 352-873-3976
> Pubs: *The Red Candle Treasury: Anth* (Red Candle Pr,
> 1999), *American Poets & Poetry, El Dorado Poetry Rev,
> Mobius, The Neovictorian/Cochlea, Satire, Tucumcari
> Literary Rev.*

Bob Grumman   P
1708 Hayworth Rd, Port Charlotte, FL 33952-4529,
813-629-8045
Internet: bobgrumman@nut-n-but.net
> Pubs: *Mathemaku 1-5* (Tel-Let, 1992), *The World of Zines:
> Anth* (Penguin, 1992), *Score, Lost & Found Times,
> Windless Orchard, Kaldron, The Experioddicist.*

Jim Hall   P
Florida International Univ, Miami, FL 33199
> Pubs: *False Statements, The Mating Reflex* (Carnegie
> Mellon, 1985, 1980).

Peter Hargitai   P&W
Florida International Univ, Miami, FL 33199, 305-348-3405
> Pubs: *Magyar Tales* (U Massachusetts Intl Studies
> Program, 1989), *Budapest to Bellevue, The Art of
> Taxidermy* (Palmetto Pr, 1988, 1988).

Anne Haskins   P
4714 NW 57 Dr, Gainesville, FL 32606-4369
> Pubs: *Overtures, Mati, Ommation, The Earthquake On Ada
> Street Anth.*

Lola Haskins   P
PO Box 18, LaCrosse, FL 326580018, 904-462-3117
Internet: lola@cise.ufl.edu
> Pubs: *Extranjera* (Story Line Pr, 1997), *Hunger* (U Iowa
> Pr/Story Line, 1996), *Beloit Poetry Jrnl, Southern Rev,
> Georgia Rev, Crazyhorse, Missouri Rev.*

Gerald Hausman   P&W
12699 Cristi Way, Bokeelia, FL 33922-3321
Internet: ghausman@compuserve.com
> Pubs: *The Kebra Nagast: The Lost Bible of Rastafarian
> Wisdom, The Mythology of Cats, Wilderness* (w/R.
> Zelazny), *Tunkashila: From the Birth of Turtle Island to the
> Blood of Wounded Knee* (St. Martin's, 1998, 1998, 1994,
> 1993).

Hunt Hawkins   P
Florida State Univ, Tallahassee, FL 32306, 904-644-0238
Internet: hhawkins@garnet.acns.fsu.edu
> Pubs: *The Domestic Life* (U Pitt Pr, 1994), *A New
> Geography of Poetry: Anth* (U Arkansas Pr, 1992),
> *TriQuarterly, Southern Rev, Georgia Rev, Apalachee Qtly,
> Poetry, Minnesota Rev.*

Jonellen Heckler   W
5745 SW 75 #322, Gainesville, FL 32608, 352-332-1005
Internet: jonellenh@aol.com
> Pubs: *Final Tour, Circumstances Unknown* (Pocket Bks,
> 1994, 1993), *White Lies, A Fragile Peace, Safekeeping*
> (Putnam, 1989, 1986, 1983).

Judith Hemschemeyer   P&W
436 Knowles Ave #2, Winter Park, FL 327893232,
407-644-9116
> Pubs: *Certain Animals* (Snake Nation Pr, 1998), *The
> Harvest* (Pig Iron Pr, 1998), *The Ride Home* (Texas Tech U
> Pr, 1987), *Very Close and Very Slow* (Wesleyan U Pr,
> 1975), *Hudson Rev, Colorado Rev, Tampa Rev, Dickinson
> Rev, Florida Rev.*

Michael Hettich   P
561 NE 95 St, Miami Shores, FL 33138-2731, 305-757-5907
    Pubs: *Having A Wonderful Time* (S&S, 1997), *Many Simple Things, Immaculate Bright Rooms* (March Street Pr, 1997, 1994), *The Party Train: American Prose Poems: Anth* (Three Rivers Pr, 1995), *Literary Rev, Poetry East, Abiko Qtly.*

Patricia Higginbotham   P
3211 Swann Ave, Apt 310, Tampa, FL 33109, 813-874-3498
Internet: higginp2@mail.firn.edu
    Pubs: *Orbis, Tower Poetry, ELF, Poetpourri, Lyric, The Formalist, Staple.*

Richard F. Hill   W
226 Gunlock Ave, Tampa, FL 33609-1430, 813-879-7400
    Pubs: *Shoot the Piper* (St. Martin's Pr, 1994), *Riding Solo with the Golden Horde* (U Georgia Pr, 1994), *Pig Iron, Kenyon Rev, American Rev, Witness, Esquire.*

Rochelle Lynn Holt   P&W
15223 Coral Isle Ct, Ft Myers, FL 33919, 941-454-6546
    Pubs: *Scars: A Novel, Bolts: Fractured Sonnets* (Kindred Spirit Pr, 1998, 1998), *Riverwoman on Fire* (Cassette; Neworld Pubs, 1997), *360 Degrees, Mentor, Pilot, Gulf Coast Woman, Kalliope, Synesthesia, Chiron Rev, River King, The Pilot, Kalliope.*

Susan Hubbard   P&W
Shell Cove Ln, Orlando, FL 328171657, 407-823-2212
Internet: shubbard@pegasus.cc.ucf.edu
    Pubs: *Walking On Ice and Other Stories* (U Missouri Pr, 1990), *NAR, Ploughshares, Passages North, Wooster Rev, Dickinson, Green Mountains Rev.*

John Kapsalis   P
5776 Deauville Lake Cir, #308, Naples, FL 34112, 941-793-4530
Internet: johnathy@aol.com
    Pubs: *The Saga of Chrysodontis Pappas, Tales of Pergamos* (Aegina Pr, 1994, 1988), *Bitterroot, Dark Horse, Indigo, Joycean Lively Arts Guild Rev, Northeastern Jrnl, Nebraska Rev.*

David A. Kaufelt   W
PO Box 182, Key West, FL 33041, 305-292-1288
    Pubs: *The Winter Women Murders, The Fat Boy Murders* (Pocket Bks, 1994, 1993), *American Tropic* (Poseidon, 1987), *Cosmopolitan.*

Marcia Gale Kester-Doyle   P
516 NE 6 St, Pompano Beach, FL 33060, 954-943-0685
    Pubs: *Driving Through Nebraska* (Cooper Hse, 1991), *The Healing Stone: Anth* (Golden Apple Pr, 1998), *Baby's World, Green Hills Literary Lantern, Southern Poetry Rev, Twinsworld, Bereavement, The Poet, Echoes.*

Daniel Keyes   W
7491 N Federal Hwy, Ste C5-110, Boca Raton, FL 33487
    Pubs: *Unveiling Claudia* (Bantam Bks, 1986), *The Minds of Billy Milligan* (Random Hse, 1981), *Flowers for Algernon* (Harcourt Brace, 1966).

David Kirby   P
1168 Seminole Dr, Tallahassee, FL 32301, 850-877-7411
Internet: dkirby@english.fsu.edu
    Pubs: *Big-Leg Music* (Orchises, 1995), *Saving the Young Men of Vienna* (U Wisconsin Pr, 1987), *Parnassus, Chicago Rev, New Orleans Rev, Kenyon Rev, Southern Rev, Ploughshares, Northwest Rev, Denver Qtly.*

Smith Kirkpatrick   W
Univ Florida, Gainesville, FL 32601, 904-392-0777
    Pubs: *The Sun's Gold* (Houghton Mifflin, 1974).

Jeffrey Knapp   P
3457 Sheridan Ave, Miami Beach, FL 33140, 305-531-4309
    Pubs: *The Acupuncture of Heaven* (Do Something Pr, 1989), *Palmetto Rev, Free Lunch, La Bete.*

Nancy Roxbury Knutson   P
9791 NW 10 St, Plantation, FL 33322-4880
Internet: knutson@bcfreenet.seflin.lib.fl.us
    Pubs: *Nothing Shall Fall To Waste* (Arts Wayland Fdn, 1983), *If I Had a Hammer: Anth* (Papier-Mache Pr, 1990), *APR, Calyx, Iowa Rev, Nimrod, New Virginia Rev.*

Alison Kolodinsky   P
26 Twelve Oaks Trail, Ormond Beach, FL 32174-8519, 904-677-8227
    Pubs: *Isle of Flowers: Anth* (Anhinga Pr, 1995), *Florida In Poetry: Anth* (Pineapple Pr, 1995), *Poetry, Jama, Cream City Rev, Whetstone, Florida Rev, Kalliope.*

Sam Koperwas   W
2701 NE 35 Dr, Ft Lauderdale, FL 33308, 305-561-5937
    Pubs: *Easy Money* (Morrow, 1983), *Hot Stuff* (Dutton, 1978).

Steve Kronen   P
6871 SW 76 Terr, S Miami, FL 33143, 305-662-1614
    Pubs: *Empirical Evidence* (U Georgia Pr, 1992), *Isle of Flowers: Anth* (Anhinga Pr, 1995), *Poetry, Paris Rev, Southern Rev, Georgia Rev, Agni, Virginia Qtly Rev, New Republic.*

Elsie Bowman Kurz   P
Isle of Capri B50, Kings Point, Delray Beach, FL 33484, 407-498-2733
    Pubs: *Rhyming the Bible: Songs Your Mother Never Taught You, Endangered Species* (PPB Pr, 1996, 1996), *We Speak For Peace: Anth* (KIT, 1993), *Passager, Harp Strings, Poets Forum.*

P. V. LeForge   P&W
2037 W Pensacola St, Tallahassee, FL 32304, 904-576-7369
Pubs: *The Secret Life of Moles* (Anhinga Pr, 1992), *The Principle of Interchange* (Paperback Rack Bks, 1990), *Q Mag, Nightstallion, Mid-American Rev.*

Edith Mize Lewis   P
8919 Old Pine Rd, Boca Raton, FL 33433-3152, 561-487-4508
Pubs: *Haiku is...A Feeling* (Pippin Bks, 1990).

Duane Locke   P
2716 Jefferson St, Tampa, FL 33602, 813-223-5174
Pubs: *Watching Wisteria* (Vida Pr, 1995), *Ghost Dance: Anth* (Whitston, 1994), *Black Moon, Bitter Oleander, Glass Cherry, APR, American Literary Rev, Nation.*

William Logan   P
210 NE 7 St, Gainesville, FL 32601, 352-371-7780
Internet: wlogan@english.ufl.edu
Pubs: *Vain Empires, Sullen Weedy Lakes* (Godine, 1996, 1988).

Jo Ann Lordahl   P
PO Box 6165, Bradenton, FL 34281, 941-752-0016
Internet: http://www.afn.org/ jlordahl

Carol Mahler   P
6269 NW Oak Hill Ave, Arcadia, FL 34266, 813-494-5034
Pubs: *When Life Mates Die: Stories of Love Loss and Healing: Anth* (Fairview Pr, 1997), *Passages North, Beloit Poetry Jrnl, Poets On, New Collage Mag, Negative Capability, Fan Mag, Red Brick Rev, Stone Country.*

Michael Margolin   P
1801 S Ocean Dr, #837, Hallandale, FL 33009-4947
Pubs: *NAR, Shenandoah, Carleton Miscellany, Southern Poetry Rev, Smith, Epoch.*

Dionisio D. Martinez   P
4509 N Lincoln Ave, Tampa, FL 33614-6631, 813-874-6747
Internet: ddmartinez@aol.com
Pubs: *Bad Alchemy* (Norton, 1995), *History as a Second Language* (Ohio State U Pr, 1993), *New Republic, Colorado Rev, APR, Iowa Rev, Prairie Schooner, Virginia Qtly Rev, Georgia Rev, Denver Qtly, Kenyon Rev.*

Richard Mathews   P
Univ of Tampa, PO Box 19-F, Tampa, FL 33606, 813-253-3333
Internet: rmathews@alpha.utampa.edu
Pubs: *Numbery* (Borgo Pr, 1995), *A Mummery* (Konglomerati, 1975), *Southern Poetry Rev, Louisville Rev, Berkeley Rev.*

Irma McClaurin   P
5128 NW 16 Pl, Gainesville, FL 32605-3302, 352-336-2154
Internet: mcclauri@anthro.ufl.edu
Pubs: *Pearl's Song* (Lotus Pr, 1988), *A Rock Against the Wind: Anth* (Perigee, 1996), *Slant, Essence, Sage, Drum Rev, Obsidian II.*

Jane McClellan   P
2838 NE 14 Ave, Ocala, FL 34470-3700, 352-622-6145
Internet: doctorjmcc@aol.com
Pubs: *Centennial Rev, Wayne Literary Rev, Cape Rock, Midwest Qtly, Northeast, Whiskey Island, Wisconsin Rev, West Wind Rev, Webster Rev, Blue Unicorn, Greensboro Rev, Southern Poetry Rev, Commonweal.*

Tom McDaniel   P
249 Lake Ave E, Longwood, FL 32750-5442
Pubs: *Pulpsmith, Wind, Plains Poetry Jrnl, Blue Unicorn, Florida Rev, Kansas Qtly.*

Campbell McGrath   P
Florida International Univ, N Miami Campus, North Miami, FL 33181, 305-919-5954
Pubs: *Spring Comes to Chicago, American Noise* (Ecco Pr, 1996, 1994), *New Yorker, Antaeus, Paris Rev, Ploughshares, TriQuarterly, Ohio Rev.*

Pablo Medina   P&W
14862 SW 69 St, Miami, FL 33193, 305-380-6867
Pubs: *The Marks of Birth* (FS&G, 1994), *Arching Into The Afterlife* (Bilingual Pr, 1991), *APR, Antioch Rev, Poetry, Pivot.*

Peter Meinke   P&W
147 Wildwood Ln SE, St Petersburg, FL 33705, 813-896-1862
Internet: meinkep@acasun.eckerd.edu
Pubs: *Scars, Liquid Paper: New & Selected Poems* (U Pitt Pr, 1996, 1991), *Atlantic, New Yorker, Gettysburg Rev, Georgia Rev, Poetry, New Republic.*

A. McA Miller   P
New Collage Magazine, 5700 North Tamiami Trail, Sarasota, FL 342432197, 813-359-5605
Pubs: *Beloit Poetry Journal, Epos, Gryphon, Negative Capability, Spirit That Moves Us, Tendril.*

Karl F. Miller   P&W
1999 NW 83 Dr, Coral Springs, FL 33071, 305-341-8672
Pubs: *A Warning* (Merging Media, 1990), *Galley Sail Rev, Black Buzzard Rev, Bassettown Rev, Portland Rev, Mudfish, Bad Haircut, Riverrun, Impetus, RE:AL, Glass Cherry.*

Michael G. Minassian   P
1921 NW 93 Ave, Pembroke Pines, FL 33024, 305-431-2229
Pubs: *Ararat, Wind, Western Poetry, Passaic Rev, Pegasus Rev, San Fernando Poetry Jrnl.*

Susan Mitchell   P
9287-C Boca Gardens Circle S, Boca Raton, FL 33496,
407-451-4326
Internet: sunmil1@aol.com
    Pubs: *The Water Inside the Water, Rapture* (HarperCollins,
    1994, 1992), *Atlantic, Ploughshares, APR, New Yorker,*
    New Republic, Paris Rev.

Harry Morris   P
3940 W Kelly Rd, Tallahassee, FL 32301, 904-877-4307

Bridget Balthrop Morton   P
736 Espanola Way, Melbourne, FL 32901, 407-724-9636
Internet: bridgetbal@aol.com
    Pubs: *Song for Occupations: Anth* (Wayland Pr, 1991),
    Good Housekeeping, America, Visions Intl, U.S. Air,
    Commonweal, Gulf Stream.

William Moseley   W
102 Highview Dr, Cocoa, FL 32922, 407-639-1538
    Pubs: *Earth Tones* (Vergin Pr, 1994), *People Around You:*
    Anth (Germany; Schoningh, 1997), *Polyphany: Anth of*
    Florida Poets (Panther Pr, 1989), *Kansas Rev, Scripsit,*
    Virginia Qtly Rev.

Joseph M. Moxley   P&W
Univ South Florida, Tampa, FL 33620, 813-974-2421
    Pubs: *Paragraph.*

George E. Murphy, Jr.   P
PO Box 2626, Key West, FL 33045
    Pubs: *The Key West Reader* (Tortugas, 1990), *Rounding*
    Ballast Key (Ampersand Pr, 1987).

Patrick J. Murphy   W
3612 Monmouth Ct, Tallahassee, FL 32308, 850-386-8698
Internet: pjmurph@aol.com
    Pubs: *Way Below E* (White Pine Pr, 1994), *Tampa Rev,*
    New Orleans Rev, Nexus, Gamut, Cream City Rev, Kiosk,
    Descant, The Quarterly, Buffalo Spree, Sequoia.

Patricia Muse   W
2118 Cochise Trail, Casselberry, FL 32707, 305-339-6999
    Pubs: *Eight Candles Glowing* (Ballantine Bks, 1976), *The*
    Belle Claudine (Avalon Bks, 1971).

Norman Nathan   P&W
Stratford Ct #219, 6343 Via de Sonrisa del Sur, Boca Raton,
FL 33433, 407-391-2716
    Pubs: *Prince William B* (Mouton, 1975), *Contemporary*
    American Satire: Anth (Exile Pr, 1988), *Poetry Event,*
    Wisconsin Rev, Chaminade, Fiction, Z Miscellaneous,
    Poem.

Barbra Nightingale   P
2231 N 52 Ave, Hollywood, FL 330213310, 954-961-7126
Internet: bnighting@aol.com
    Pubs: *Lunar Equations* (East Coast Edtns, 1993), *Lovers*
    Never Die (Pteranodon Pr, 1981), *Having A Wonderful*
    Time: Anth (Harcourt Brace, 1997), *Florida in Poetry: Anth*
    (Pineapple Pr, 1996), *Chattahoochee Rev, Birmingham*
    Rev, Many Mountains Moving.

Richard O'Connell   P
1147 Hillsboro Mile #907, Hillsboro Beach, FL 33062,
954-428-0419
    Pubs: *The Bright Tower, Voyages, Retro Worlds: Selected*
    Poems (U Salzburg, 1997, 1995, 1993), *The Caliban*
    Poems (Atlantis Edtns, 1992), *New Yorker, Paris Rev, The*
    Atlantic.

Sheila Ortiz-Taylor   P&W
Florida State Univ, English Dept, Tallahassee, FL
323061580, 850-644-5776
Internet: sotaylor@english.fsu.edu
    Pubs: *Imaginary Parents, Coachella* (U New Mexico Pr,
    1998, 1996), *Faultline* (Naiad Pr, 1982), *Americas Rev,*
    Sinister Wisdom, Common Lives/Lesbian Lives, Innisfree,
    Apalachee.

Joseph Papaleo   W
150 Cypress Pl, Oldsmar, FL 34677, 813-781-4605
    Pubs: *Picasso at Ninety One* (Seaport Bks, 1988),
    Unsettling America: Anth (Viking Penguin, 1994), *Paterson*
    Literary Rev, Paris Rev.

Ricardo Pau-Llosa   P
Miami-Dade Community College, 11011 SW 104 St, Miami,
FL 33176, 305-237-2510
    Pubs: *Cuba* (Carnegie Mellon Pr, 1993), *Bread of the*
    Imagined (Bilingual Pr, 1992), *Kenyon Rev, TriQuarterly,*
    APR, Denver Qtly, Missouri Rev, NER.

Robin Perry   W
541 Nightingale Dr, Indialantic, FL 32903, 407-777-3310
    Pubs: *Videography, Shadows Of The Mind* (Writer's Digest
    Bks, 1985, 1981).

Mario A. Petaccia   P
4110-B Brewster Rd, Tallahassee, FL 32308, 904-942-8686
    Pubs: *Walking On Water* (CCC, 1986), *Florida in Poetry:*
    Anth (Pineapple Pr, 1995), *Yankee, Poet, Southern Poetry*
    Rev, Apalachee Qtly, New York Qtly, Greenfield Rev.

Emmett Peter, Jr.   W
813 Rosemere Cir, Orlando, FL 32835-4474
    Pubs: *Florida Rev, Sunrust, Other Voices, Exile, Oasis,*
    Carolina Qtly.

Allan Peterson P
5397 Soundside Dr, Gulf Breeze, FL 32561, 904-932-3077
Internet: aandf@gulf.net
Pubs: *Small Charities* (Panhandler Pr, 1995), *Stars on a Wire* (Parallel Edtns, 1989), *Agni, Gettysburg Rev, Willow Springs, River Styx, Epoch, Green Mountains Rev.*

Geoffrey Philp P&W
18558 NE 18 Ave, #103, North Miami Shores, FL 33179, 305-949-1708
Internet: d000094c@dcfreenet.seflin.lib.fl.us
Pubs: *Hurricane Center, Uncle Obadiah and the Alien, Florida Bound* (Peepal Tree Pr, 1998, 1997, 1994), *Florida In Poetry: Anth* (Pineapple Pr, 1994), *Mississippi Rev, Compost, Caribbean Writer, Michigan Rev, Gulf Stream, International Qtly.*

Padgett Powell P&W
Univ Florida, Gainesville, FL 32611, 904-392-0777
Pubs: *A Woman Named Drown, Edisto* (FSG, 1987, 1984).

Ilmars Purens P
1244 Bel Aire Dr, Daytona Beach, FL 32118, 904-255-6644
Pubs: *The New Time, Kayak, Wisconsin Rev, Epoch, Poetry Now, The Nation, The Little Rev.*

Anne Giles Rimbey P
6119 E 112 Ave, Tampa, FL 33617-3131, 813-989-1430
Internet: arimbey@ij.net
Pubs: *Dusty Sandals* (Skin Drum Pr, 1992), *I Am Becoming the Woman I've Wanted: Anth* (Papier-Mache Pr, 1994), *Tampa Rev, Birmingham Poetry Rev, Kalliope, Press, Crosscurrents, The Alembic.*

Andres Rivero W
CSP Publications, PO Box 650909, Miami, FL 33265, 305-380-6833
Internet: andres.rivero@gte.net
Pubs: *Cuentos Torvos, Nina Melancolia, Somos Como Somos, Recuerdos* (CSP Pub, 1998, 1993, 1982, 1980), *El Nuevo Herald, Diario Las Americas, Spanish Today Mag.*

Marcia J. Roessler P&W
966 Red Bay Terr NW, Murdock, FL 33948
Internet: mroess7170@aol.com
Pubs: *Traveled Paths* (Haworth Society, 1998), *Wordspinners: Anth* (Burlington County, 1994), *Wide Open Magazine, Feelings.*

David Rosenberg P
11121 SW 62 Ave, Miami, FL 33156-4003
Internet: fieldbridg@aol.com
Pubs: *The Book of David* (Harmony Bks, 1997), *The Lost Book of Paradise, A Poet's Bible* (Hyperion, 1993, 1991), *Five Fingers Rev, Harper's, APR, The Nation.*

Sandra Russell P&W
508 Simonton, #3, Key West, FL 33040
Pubs: *Solares Hill, Ball State U Pr, Croton Rev, Forum, Aspen Anth, Amelia, Sunrust, Toad Highway.*

Verna Safran P
833 S Bahama Dr, Tallahassee, FL 32311, 904-877-0840
Internet: verna325@aol.com
Pubs: *Stepping Stones* (Fruittree Pr, 1996), *Womanstages* (Her Pr, 1980), *Cosmopolitan, Sun, Home Planet News, Kentucky Poetry Jrnl, Penumbra.*

Brian Salchert P
3530 SW 24 Ave, Lot 41, Gainesville, FL 32608, 904-338-0902
Pubs: *Teasings, First Pick* (Thinking Lizard, 1986, 1982), *Rooted Sky* (Monday Morning Pr, 1972), *Wisconsin Rev, Sou'wester, Saltillo, Studia Mystica.*

Nicholas Samaras P
1874 Kinsmere Dr, New Port Richey, FL 34655
Internet: saddlema@gte.net
Pubs: *Survivors of the Moving Earth* (U Salzburg Pr, 1998), *Hands of the Saddlemaker* (Yale U Pr, 1992), *Paris Rev, Poetry, American Scholar, New Yorker, New Criterion, Poetry, Kenyon Rev.*

Bonny Barry Sanders P
1411 E Blackhawk Trail, Jacksonville, FL 32225, 904-744-3511
Pubs: *New Voices: Anth* (Colorado State U, 1994), *Environment: Essence & Issue: Anth* (Pig Iron Pr, 1992), *Hayden's Ferry Rev, Kennebec, Plainsongs, Puckerbrush Rev, CSM, Phase and Cycle, George Washington Rev, South Dakota Rev, Kalliope, Negative Capability.*

Christy Sheffield Sanford P&W
714 Northeast Blvd, Gainesville, FL 32601-4375, 352-375-7565
Internet: http://gnv.fdt.net/ christys/index.html
Pubs: *Sur Les Pointes* (White Eagle Coffee Store, 1995), *The H's: The Spasms Of A Requiem* (Bloody Twin, 1994), *Coffeehouse: Writings From the Web: Anth* (Manning, 1997), *American Poets Say Goodbye to the 20th Century: Anth* (4 Walls, 8 Windows, 1996).

Jack Saunders W
231 N Lakewood Dr, Panama City, FL 32404, 904-763-1429
Pubs: *Forty* (Popular Reality, 1988), *Evil Genius, Open Book* (Mixed Breed, 1986), *Black Messiah.*

Lin Schlossman P
4480 Deer Trail Blvd, Sarasota, FL 34238-5606
Pubs: *Panhandler, Treasure House, Crazyquilt, Poem, Maryland Poetry Rev, Poetpourri, Birmingham Poetry Rev, Cincinnati Judaica Rev, Owen Wister Rev.*

Peter Schmitt   P
Box 248145, Coral Gables, FL 33124, 305-284-4074
> Pubs: *Hazard Duty, Country Airport* (Copper Beech Pr, 1995, 1989), *Nation, Paris Rev, Ploughshares, Poetry, Southern Rev, Hudson Rev.*

Edmund Skellings   P
600 NE 2nd Pl, Dania, FL 33004, 954-929-3595
Internet: poet1@laureate.cec.fau.edu
> Pubs: *Collected Poems 1958-1998, Selected Poems* (CD), *Living Proof, Showing My Age, Face Value* (U Pr Florida, 1998, 1997, 1987, 1978, 1977).

Elaine Campbell Smith   W
5587 W Kelly Rd, Tallahassee, FL 32311, 850-878-9788
Internet: kamilane@yahoo.com
> Pubs: *A Wish Too Soon* (Silhouette, 1986), *Fantasy Lover* (Harlequin, 1984), *Southern Rev, Snap, Whispering Palms, Ellery Queen's Mystery Mag.*

Patrick D. Smith   W
1370 Island Dr, Merritt Island, FL 32952, 407-452-6590
> Pubs: *Angel City* (Valkyrie, 1991), *Forever Island* (Dell, 1990), *A Land Remembered* (Pineapple Pr/Signet, 1986).

Jim Sorcic   P
2348 NW 98 Way, Coral Springs, FL 33065, 305-345-3662
> Pubs: *This Could Lead To Dancing, The Cost of Living, The Secret Oral Teachings of Jim The House* (Morgan Pr, 1991, 1980, 1971).

Les Standiford   W
Florida International Univ, N Miami Campus, North Miami, FL 33181, 305-253-7053
Internet: standifo@fiu.edu
> Pubs: *Black Mountain* (Putnam, 1999), *Presidential Deal, Done Deal* (HarperCollins, 1998, 1993), *Spill* (Atlantic Monthly Pr, 1991), *Confrontation, Kansas Qtly, Beloit Poetry Jrnl, Image, Travel Holiday, Writer's Digest.*

Thomas Starling   W
PO Box 2222, Cocoa, FL 329232222, 407-639-3162
Internet: dicki4@juno.com
> Pubs: *Peter Paladine of the Great Heart, Jethrow's Cabin* (Spindrift Pr, 1995, 1982).

Millie Taylor   P&W
PO Box 5001, Jacksonville, FL 32247-5001
> Pubs: *Thema, Kalliope, South Dakota Rev, Passager.*

Sandra Thompson   W
3020 W Harbor View Ave, Tampa, FL 33611, 813-831-3311
Internet: thomsher@gte.net
> Pubs: *Wild Bananas* (Atlantic Monthly Pr, 1985), *Close-Ups* (U Georgia Pr, 1984).

Dorothy Twiss   P
5125 Soundside Dr, Gulf Breeze, FL 32561-8923, 904-932-5619
> Pubs: *Mississippi Writers: Reflections of Childhood & Youth: Anth* (U Pr Mississippi, 1988).

Kathryn Van Spanckeren   P
Univ Tampa, English Dept, Tampa, FL 33606, 813-253-6229
Internet: vspanckeren@alpha.utampa.edu
> Pubs: *Salt and Sweet Water, Mountains Hidden in Mountains* (Empty Window, 1993, 1992), *APR, Ploughshares, 13th Moon, Carolina Qtly, Contact II, Boundary 2.*

Fanny Ventadour   P&W
PO Box 547067, Orlando, FL 32854-7067, 407-647-0418
> Pubs: *The Centre Holds, Blue Is Recessive As In Irises* (Two Cities Edtns, 1977, 1966), *Gryphon.*

Bruce Wallace   P
PO Box 6614, Key West, FL 33041
> Pubs: *Poet Lore, Z Miscellaneous, Zone 3, Plainsongs, Rambunctious Rev, Poetpourri, Columbia.*

Sterling Watson   W
Eckerd College, PO Box 12560/Letters Collegium, St Petersburg, FL 33733, 813-864-8281
> Pubs: *Deadly Sweet* (S&S, 1994), *The Calling* (Dell, 1989), *Blind Tongues* (Delacorte, 1989).

Craig Weeden   P
95 Sandy Hood Rd S, Sarasota, FL 34242-1681
> Pubs: *American Sports Poems: Anth* (Orchard, 1988), *Poetry Now, New Orleans Rev, Chowder Rev, Southern Poetry Rev, Cimarron Rev, Calliope.*

Jean West   P
Box 2710, Rollins College, Winter Park, FL 32789-4499, 407-646-2666
> Pubs: *Holding The Chariot* (Open Hse, 1976), *Florida In Poetry: Anth* (Pineapple Pr, 1995), *Lullwater Rev, Kalliope, Confrontation, CSM.*

William M. White   P&W
721 Navigator's Way, Edgewater, FL 32141, 904-423-8633
> Pubs: *Where I Stand* (Tudor Pubs, 1992).

Millie Mae Wicklund   P
3623 N Long Pine Point, Beverly Hills, FL 34465, 352-527-9729
> Pubs: *Wallorvisions, Moving Paper, The History of My Parachute* (Ghost Dance, 1995, 1990, 1986), *Altered State, Art/Life.*

Lois Wickstrom   W
10612 Altman St, Tampa, FL 33612, 813-971-3742
> Pubs: *The Clarion Awards: Anth* (Doubleday, 1985), *American Way, Fantasy, Owlflight, Jack and Jill, St. Petersburg Times, Tampa Tribune.*

Joy Williams   W
8128 Midnight Pass Rd, Siesta Key, FL 33581
    Pubs: *Escapes* (Atlantic Monthly Pr, 1990), *Breaking and
    Entering* (Random Hse, 1988), *Granta.*

Nancy Leffel Wilson   P&W
4000 Old Settlement Rd, Merritt Island, FL 32952,
407-453-5224
    Pubs: *Pilgrimage, Onionhead, Saturday Evening Post, The
    Panhandler.*

Robley Wilson   P&W
PO Box 4009, Winter Park, FL 32793
Internet: robley.wilson@uni.edu
    Pubs: *The Victim's Daughter, Terrible Kisses* (S&S, 1991,
    1989), *A Pleasure Tree* (U Pitt Pr, 1990), *Iowa Rev, Prairie
    Schooner, Epoch, Southern California Anth.*

Norma Woodbridge   P
2606 Zoysia Ln, North Fort Myers, FL 33917, 941-731-6564
    Pubs: *Poetry Norma Woodbridge* (International Poets,
    1995), *Graces* (Harper, 1994), *When God Speaks, Joy in
    the Morning, Meditations of a Modern Pilgrim, Resting
    Places* (Star Books, 1991, 1990, 1989, 1988), *Woman's
    World, Broken Streets.*

Fred W. Wright, Jr.   P
PO Box 86158, St Petersburg, FL 33738, 813-595-5004
    Pubs: *Fiddler Crab, Pegasus, Reiki Jrnl, Gryphon,
    Chattahoochee Rev, Sharing, Pudding.*

Stephen Caldwell Wright   P
Seminole Community College, 100 Weldon Blvd, Sanford, FL
32773-6199, 407-328-2063
    Pubs: *With Fortitude, The Chicago Collective,
    Circumference, Talking To the Mountains*
    (Christopherr-Burghardt, 1991, 1990, 1989, 1988).

Wyatt Wyatt   W
Univ Central Florida, English Dept, Orlando, FL 32816,
305-275-2212
    Pubs: *Deep In The Heart* (Atheneum, 1981), *Catching Fire*
    (Random Hse, 1977).

Jim Young   P
4811 NW 17 Pl, Gainesville, FL 32605, 904-378-4208
    Pubs: *Plains Poetry Jrnl, Light Year, Lyric, Wind, Stone
    Country, Sunrust, Negative Capability.*

Iris M. Zavala   P
100 Kings Point Dr, #1707, Miami, FL 33160-4731
    Pubs: *Kiliagonia* (Mexico, 1980), *Que-Nadiemuera Sin
    Amar El Mar* (Spain, 1982), *Third Woman.*

GEORGIA

Ken Anderson   P
Floyd College, 5198 Ross Road, Acworth, GA 30102,
770-975-4150
Internet: kanderso@mail.FC.peachnet.edu
    Pubs: *Smooth 'N' Sassy, The Intense Lover: A Suite of
    Poems,* (Star Bks, 1998, 1995), *Chattahoochee Rev,
    Lullwater Rev, Connecticut Poetry Rev, James White Rev,
    Bay Windows, Beloit Poetry Rev.*

Joan Anson-Weber   P
Cherokee Publishing Co., 4331 Lake Chimney Ct, Roswell,
GA 30075, 770-587-3077
    Pubs: *Snuffles* (Cherokee Pub Co., 1995), *The Gate of the
    Year* (Kingham Pr, 1993), *Before the Trees Turn Gray*
    (Wings Pr, 1981), *Poets At Work, Creative Arts and
    Science, Nashville Newsletter, Poets of Now, Ultimate
    Writer, Small Pond.*

Rebecca Baggett   P
330 College Cir, Athens, GA 30605, 706-548-0029
Internet: rbaggett@franklin.uga.edu
    Pubs: *Still Life with Children* (Pudding Hse Pub, 1996), *A
    More Perfect Union: Anth* (St. Martin's Pr, 1998), *For She is
    the Tree of Life: Anth* (Conari Pr, 1994), *Cries of the Spirit:
    Anth* (Beacon, 1990), *Southern Poetry Rev, New England
    Rev, Ms., The Sun.*

Coleman Barks   P
196 Westview Dr, Athens, GA 30606, 706-543-2148
    Pubs: *The Essential Rumi* (Harper SF, 1995), *Gourd Seed*
    (Maypop, 1992), *Georgia Rev, Kenyon Rev, New England
    Rev.*

Dianna Eden Bergis   W
3833 Peachtree Rd NE, #916, Atlanta, GA 30319,
404-266-1157
    Pubs: *Family Life Today, The Haunted Sun, Twisted.*

Ka Bowles   P
358 Oakland Ave, SE, Alpharetta, GA 30312
    Pubs: *Poem, Lullwater Rev, Panhandler, Bellingham Rev,
    Voices Intl, Cape Rock.*

Gloria G. Brame   P&W
PO Box 18552, Atlanta, GA 31126, 404-364-9968
Internet: http://gloria-brame.com/
    Pubs: *Elf, Thermopylae.*

Roy Bush   W
Box 6, Colquitt, GA 31737, 912-758-3524

Lucas Carpenter P
Oxford College of Emory Univ, English Dept, Oxford, GA
30267, 404-784-8301
Internet: lcarpen@emory.edu
  Pubs: *John Gould Fletcher & Southern Modernism* (U
  Arkansas Pr, 1990), *Carolina Qtly, Minnesota Rev,
  Crescent Rev, Kansas Rev, College English, The Journal,
  Southern Humanities Rev, South Carolina Rev.*

Turner Cassity P
510 E Ponce De Leon Ave, Apt J, Decatur, GA 30030,
404-373-3514
  Pubs: *The Destructive Element* (Ohio U Pr, 1998), *Between
  the Chains, Hurricane Lamp* (U Chicago Pr, 1991, 1986),
  Poetry.

Mary Ann Coleman P
205 Sherwood Dr, Athens, GA 30606, 404-548-2666
  Pubs: *Disappearances* (Anhinga Pr, 1978), *Kansas Qtly,
  National Forum, Negative Capability, Literary Rev.*

Stephen Corey P&W
357 Parkway Dr, Athens, GA 30606-4951, 706-542-3481
Internet: scorey@arches.uga.edu
  Pubs: *All These Lands You Call One Country* (U Missouri
  Pr, 1992), *Isle of Flowers: Anth* (Anhinga Pr, 1995), *Kenyon
  Rev, Poetry, Yellow Silk.*

Gary Corseri P&W
2455 Kingsland Dr, Atlanta, GA 30360, 404-396-8377
  Pubs: *Random Descent, North of Wakulla: Anth* (Anhinga
  Pr, 1989, 1989), *City Lights Rev, Redbook, Georgia Rev,
  Poetry Northwest, Florida Rev.*

Doris Davenport P&W
PO Box 135, Cornelia, GA 30531-0135, 704-535-3121
  Pubs: *Voodoo Chile/Slight Return* (Soque Street Pr, 1991),
  Eat Thunder & Drink Rain (Self, 1982), *Melus,
  Mid-American Rev, Women's Rev of Bks, Lesbian Studies.*

Cynde Gregory De Acevedo Jerez P
2615 Ridge Brook Trail, Duluth, GA 30096, 770-797-9099
Internet: nordgirl@earthlink.net
  Pubs: *Satori, Black Ice, Instructor Mag, Beloit Poetry Jrnl,
  North Country Anth, Calyx.*

John Ehrlichman W
795 Hammond Dr #1607, Atlanta, GA 30328
  Pubs: *The China Card, Witness to Power* (S&S, 1986,
  1983), *Parade Mag, Texas Monthly, New York Mag.*

Gene Ellis P
1086 Burton Dr NE, Atlanta, GA 30329, 404-636-1932
  Pubs: *Winter in the Tropics* (Poetry Atlanta Pr, 1988), *Arvon
  Intl Poetry Anth* (Arvon Foundation, 1987).

Nadine Estroff P
3134 Edinburgh Dr, Augusta, GA 30909-3316
  Pubs: *Hollins Critic, New York Qtly, Southern Rev,
  Southwest Rev, Carleton Miscellany, Texas Qtly, Kansas
  Qtly, Lyrical Voices.*

Blanche Farley P&W
1501 N Decatur Rd NE, #3, Atlanta, GA 303071042,
404-264-9811
  Pubs: *The Bedford Introduction to Literature: Anth* (St.
  Martin's Pr, 1990), *Southern Humanities Rev, Pilgrimage,
  Catalyst.*

Richard Flynn P
310 Savannah Ave, Statesboro, GA 304585259,
912-681-5471
Internet: rflynn@gsvms2.cc.gasou.edu
  Pubs: *The Age of Reason* (Hawkhead Pr, 1993), *Reaper,
  Washington Rev, lower limit speech.*

Starkey Flythe, Jr. W
403 Telfair St, Augusta, GA 30901, 404-722-9067
  Pubs: *The American Story* (Curtis Pub, 1977), *Georgia
  Rev, Greensboro Rev, Ploughshares, Wind.*

H. E. Francis W
Frederic C. Beil, Publisher, 609 Whitaker St, Savannah, GA
31401
  Pubs: *Sudden Fictions* (Peregrine Smith, 1986), *A
  Disturbance of Gulls* (Braziller, 1983), *Itinerary of Beggars*
  (Iowa, 1973), *Kenyon Rev, Alaska Qtly, Ontario Rev, Beloit
  Fiction, Literary Rev, Missouri Rev.*

James Gallant W
642 Atlanta Ave SE, Atlanta, GA 30312-3640
  Pubs: *Press, Exquisite Corpse, Raritan, Rhino, Georgia
  Rev, Epoch, Kansas Qtly, Mississippi Rev, NAR, Catalyst,
  Massachusetts Rev, StoryQtly.*

Walter Griffin P
2518 Maple St, East Point, GA 30344, 404-762-9196
  Pubs: *Western Flyers* (U West Florida, 1990), *Atlantic,
  Evergreen, Paris Rev, Literary Rev, Southern Rev, New
  Criterion, Poetry, Harper's.*

Gary D. Grossman P
237 Highland Ave, Athens, GA 30606, 706-549-5897
Internet: http://www.arches.uga.edu/ grossman
  Pubs: *Mobius, Old Red Kimono, Brussels Sprout, In Your
  Face, Midwest Poetry Rev, Opus Literary Rev, Poetry
  Motel, Feh, The Acorn, Cotton Gin, Pearl, Lilliput Rev,
  Blood and Fire Rev.*

Linda Lee Harper P
3693 Inverness Way, Augusta, GA 30907, 706-860-1876
Internet: lleeharper@aol.com
>Pubs: *Blue Flute* (Adastra Pr, 1998), *Toward Desire* (Word Works, 1996), *A Failure of Loveliness* (Nightshade Pr, 1994), *Anth of South Carolina Poets* (Ninety-Six Pr, 1994), *Georgia Rev, Massachusetts Rev, Illinois Rev, Kansas Qtly, Laurel Rev, Passages North.*

Robert Hays P
3360 Trickum Rd, Marietta, GA 30066, 770-924-9228
Internet: haysr@aol.com
>Pubs: *Parnassus Literary Jrnl, Dekalb Literary Arts Jrnl, Reach of Song, Alura.*

Robert W. Hill P
Kennesaw State College, 1000 Chastain Rd, Kennesaw, GA 30144-5591, 404-423-6297
>Pubs: *Human Factors* (Poetry Atlanta Pr, 1989), *James Dickey* (G.K. Hall, 1983), *Southern Rev.*

Robert Holland P
140 Ridley Cir, Decatur, GA 30030, 404-378-2103
>Pubs: *Norton Introduction To Literature: Anth* (Norton, 1978), *Georgia Rev, Midwest Qtly.*

Emmett Jarrett P
Episcopal Church, 6740 Memorial Dr, Stone Mountain, GA 30083-2235
>Pubs: *To Heal the Sin-Sick Soul* (Episcopal Urban Caucus, 1996), *God's Body* (Hanging Loose Pr, 1975), *Hanging Loose, Fellowship Papers, Jubilee Pubs.*

Greg Johnson W
808 Amsterdam Ave, Atlanta, GA 30306, 770-423-6491
Internet: rjohn713@aol.com
>Pubs: *I Am Dangerous and Other Stories, A Friendly Deceit* Johns Hopkins Pr, 1996, 1992), *Pagan Babies* (Dutton, 1993), *Distant Friends* (Ontario Rev Pr, 1990), *Southern Rev,* Shenandoah.

Seaborn Jones P
PO Box 469, Lizella, GA 31052, 912-935-3659
>Pubs: *X-Ray Movies* (Georgia Arts Council, 1988), *Drowning From the Inside Out* (Cherry Valley, 1983).

Anthony Kellman P&W
796 Palatine Ave S.E., Atlanta, GA 30316-2490, 404-622-7017
>Pubs: *The Long Gap, The Coral Rooms, Watercourse* (Peepal Tree Pr, 1996, 1994, 1990), *Chelsea, Callaloo.*

Gary Kerley P
4720 Creek Wood Dr, Gainesville, GA 30507, 770-532-3430
>Pubs: *From the Green Horseshoe: Poems by James Dickey's Students: Anth* (U South Carolina, 1987), *Southern Poetry Rev, Yankee.*

Robert S. King P
RR 1 Box 222, Carlton, GA 30627-9620, 706-743-3098
Internet: rskgaia@uga.cc.uga.edu
>Pubs: *Immortelles: Anth* (Xavier Rev Pr, 1995), *Kenyon Rev, Spoon River Poetry Rev, Visions Intl, California Qtly, Negative Capability, Southern Poetry Rev.*

Diane Kistner P
738 Ormewood Ave SE, Atlanta, GA 30312
>Pubs: *Falling In Caves* (Bootlaig Pr, 1982), *Poem, Aura, Literary Arts Rev, North Carolina Sun.*

Martin Lammon P
Georgia College and State Univ, Campus Box 44, Milledgeville, GA 31061, 912-455-3176
Internet: mlannon@gcsu.edu
>Pubs: *News From Where I Live* (U Arkansas Pr, 1998), *Nimrod, Gettysburg Rev, Midwest Qtly Rev, Ploughshares.*

M. Rosser Lunsford P
456 Rockville Springs Dr, Eatonton, GA 31024, 404-485-3449
>Pubs: *Thoughts About Life* (Rainbow Bks, 1988), *Sparrowgrass Anth* (Washington U, 1998), *Reach of Song Anth* (Georgia Poetry Society, 1997), *Arizona Highways,* Jean's Jrnl, Rhyme Time.

Marion Montgomery P&W
Box 115, Crawford, GA 30630, 706-743-5359
>Pubs: *The Men I Have Chosen for Fathers* (U Missouri Pr, 1990), *The Trouble With You Innerleckchuls* (Christendom College Pr, 1988).

Janice Townley Moore P
Young Harris College, Young Harris, GA 30582, 828-389-6394
>Pubs: *The Bedford Intro to Literature: Anth* (St. Martin's Pr, 1996), *When I Am An Old Woman I Shall Wear Purple: Anth* (Papier-Mache Pr, 1987), *Southern Poetry Rev, Georgia Rev, Atlanta Rev.*

Cynthia A. Mortus P
509 Cross Creek, Stone Mountain, GA 300875328, 770-879-9704
Internet: ca425010@aol.com
>Pubs: *Connecticut River Rev, Black Bear Rev, Poem, Cotton Boll, Spoon River Qtly, Encore, Earth's Daughters, Virginia Country.*

Chuck Oliveros P
1206 Lyndale Dr SE, Atlanta, GA 30316, 404-624-1524
>Pubs: *Bleeding From the Mouth, The Pterodactyl In The Wilderness* (Dead Angel, 1992, 1982), *Caliban.*

Lee Passarella P
1384 Township Dr, Lawrenceville, GA 30243, 404-995-9475
>Pubs: *Out of A/Maze: Anth* (Chiron Review Pr, 1996), *Sun, JAMA, Chelsea, Literary Rev, Formalist, Cream City Rev.*

Phyllis E. Price P
509 Cross Creek Pt, Stone Mountain, GA 30087,
404-841-5515
Pubs: *Cotton Boll, Connecticut River Rev, Virginia Country Mag, Embers, Oxford, Appalachian Heritage, Poem.*

Rosetta Radtke P&W
PO Box 2123, Savannah, GA 31402-2123
Pubs: *Staten Island, Passages North, Blue Pitcher, Off Main Street, Wind, Pembroke, Poetry Now.*

Helon Raines W
Armstrong Atlantic Univ, 11935 Abercorn St, Savannah, GA 31419-1997, 912-921-5621
Internet: helon_raines@mailgate.armstrong.edu
Pubs: *Denver Qtly, Mississippi Rev, Outerbridge, Earth's Daughters, Worksheet, Wind Singers.*

Paul Rice P
Brunswick College, Altama at Fourth, Brunswick, GA 31523, 912-264-7357
Pubs: *Georgia Rev, Chattahoochee Rev, Tar River Rev, Blue Unicorn, Barataria Rev, Mountain Rev.*

William P. Robertson P
PO Box 14532, Savannah, GA 31416
Pubs: *Life After Sex Life* (Four Winds Pr, 1983).

Jalane Rogers P
4461 Florence St, Tucker, GA 30084
Pubs: *Broken Streets, Living Streams, Silver Wings, Parnassus, The Red Pagoda, Archer Mag.*

Larry Rubin P
Box 15014, Druid Hills Branch, Atlanta, GA 30333, 404-636-4548
Pubs: *All My Mirrors Lie* (Godine, 1975), *Lanced in Light* (HBJ, 1967), *Unanswered Calls: Anth* (Kendall/Hunt, 1997), *New Yorker, Harper's, Poetry, Yale Rev, Sewanee Rev, Kenyon Rev.*

Esta Seaton P
1200 Beech Valley Rd NE, Atlanta, GA 30306, 404-874-0147

Bettie M. Sellers P
PO Box 274, Young Harris, GA 30582
Pubs: *Wild Ginger* (Imagery, 1988), *Liza's Monday & Other Poems* (Appalachian Consortium, 1986).

Lladoow S. Shevshenko P&W
4008 Kemper Ave, Macon, GA 31206, 912-784-8260
Internet: shevshenko@mailexcite.com
Pubs: *Rob Amsterdam, Ice House* (Moon Dog Pr, 1996, 1996), *The Paper Moon* (Moon Calf Pr, 1995), *In the Wind, Expresso Poetry, Sounds of Poetry, Dream Intl Qtly, Deathrealm Magazine, Poet's Review, Nightshade.*

Kristina Simms P
710 Mason Terr, #40, Perry, GA 31069, 912-988-8560
Pubs: *Zone 3, Habersham Rev, Poem, Aura, Snake Nation Rev, Chattahoochee Rev.*

Alan Sondheim P&W
878 Briarcliff Rd NE, #A-2, Atlanta, GA 30306, 404-892-3500
Pubs: *ETR* (Mike Metz, 1988), *Disorders of the Real* (Station Hill, 1988), *Blatant Artifice.*

Terrill Shepard Soules P
1616 Piedmont Ave NE, #S-3, Atlanta, GA 30324, 404-881-1988
Pubs: *Vacations, The Selectric Poems* (Pynyon Pr, 1986, 1983), *Esquire, Kayak, San Jose Studies.*

George E. Statham P
699 McRidge Rd, Hiawassee, GA 30546, 706-896-5431
Pubs: *Gunny's Rhymes, Poetic Injustice* (Fireside Pub, 1996, 1996), *Writers Exchange, Parnassus Literary Jrnl, Laureate Letter Newsletter, Leatherneck Mag, Lines and Rhymes, Poetic Eloquence, Blind Man's Rainbow, Ultraflight Mag, Apostrophe.*

Leon Stokesbury P
Georgia State Univ, Atlanta, GA 30303, 404-651-2900
Pubs: *Autumn Rhythm, The Made Thing, The Drifting Away* (U Arkansas Pr, 1996, 1987, 1986), *New Yorker, Georgia Rev, Kenyon Rev.*

John Stone P
Emory Univ/School Of Medicine, WHSCAB-1440 Clifton Rd NE, Atlanta, GA 30322, 404-727-4335
Pubs: *In the Country of Hearts* (Delacorte, 1992), *The Smell of Matches, In All This Rain* (LSU, 1988, 1980).

Eileen H. Stratidakis P
PO Box 941954, Atlanta, GA 31141, 770-270-9392
Pubs: *Partisan Rev, Sycamore Rev, Cape Rock, Florida Qtly, Cottonwood, Lullwater Rev.*

Heather Tosteson P&W
P.O. Box 2359, Decatur, GA 30031
Internet: htosteson@mindspring.com
Pubs: *The Nation, Pequod, Calyx, Southern Poetry Rev, New Virginia Rev, Cottonwood Rev, Southern Rev, Northwest Rev.*

Memye Curtis Tucker P
184 Rhodes Dr, Marietta, GA 30068-3672, 770-971-1834
Internet: mctucker@avana.net
Pubs: *The Watchers* (Ohio U Pr, 1998), *Admit One* (State Street Pr, 1998), *Holding Patterns* (Poetry Atlanta Pr, 1988), *Georgia Rev, Colorado Rev, Prairie Schooner, Southern Rev, Denver Qtly, CSM.*

James E. Warren, Jr.   P
St. Anne's Terrace, 3100 Northside Pkwy NW, #309, Atlanta, GA 30327, 404-233-0712
Pubs: *All Years Be Praised* (microPRINT, 1989), *Poems of Lovett* (The Lovett School, 1986), *Intl Poetry Rev, Lullwater Rev, Blue Unicorn.*

Sharon Webb   W
Rt 2, Box 2600, Blairsville, GA 30512, 404-745-4454
Pubs: *Pestis 18* (Tor/St. Martin's Pr, 1987), *Ram Song* (Bantam, 1985).

Janet Wondra   P
The Georgia Review, Univ Georgia, Athens, GA 306020047, 706-542-3481
Internet: jwondra@arches.uga.edu
Pubs: *Long Division* (Holocene Pub, 1998), *The Wandering Mother, Emerging Island Cultures: Anth* (Emerging Island Cultures Pr, 1989, 1984), *Southern Rev, Michigan Qtly Rev, Denver Qtly, Witness, New Orleans Rev, Berkeley Poetry Rev.*

Carolyne Wright   P&W
551 Clairmont Cir, #6, Decatur, GA 300335344, 404-633-3339
Internet: clwrigh@emory.edu
Pubs: *A Choice of Fidelities* (Ashland U Pr, 1994), *A Map of Hope: Women and Human Rights: Anth* (Rutgers U Pr, 1999), *Walk on the Wild Side: Urban American Poetry: Anth* (Scribner, 1994), *American Scholar, TriQuarterly, Agni, New Yorker, Grand Street.*

HAWAII

Nell Altizer   P
Univ Hawaii, 1733 Donaghho Rd, Honolulu, HI 96822, 808-948-7619
Pubs: *The Man Who Died En Route* (U Massachusetts Pr, 1989), *Hawaii Rev, Ploughshares, Chaminade Rev, Massachusetts Rev.*

Laureen Ching   P
2930 Varsity Cir, #4, Honolulu, HI 96826, 808-955-7982
Pubs: *Rosalind, Thea* (Fawcett, 1985, 1985), *Hawaii Rev, Mississippi Valley Rev, Dacotah Territory.*

Eric E. Chock   P
95-1053 Kopalani St, Mililani, HI 96789
Pubs: *Last Days Here* (Bamboo Ridge Pr, 1990), *The Open Boat, Poems of Asian America: Anth* (Anchor, 1993), *Seattle Rev, Zyzzyva, Jrnl of Ethnic Studies.*

Kermit Coad   P
1802 Mokehana Pl, Kihei, HI 967537920, 808-879-1782
Pubs: *Stoogism Anthology* (Scarecrow Bks, 1977), *Poetry Hawaii: A Contemporary Anth* (U Hawaii Pr, 1979), *The Spirit that Moves Us, Makali'i, Bamboo Ridge.*

Tony D'Arpino   P
PO Box 6776, Captain Cook, HI 96704, 808-327-7512
Pubs: *The Shape of the Stone* (Deep Forest, 1990), *The Tree Worshipper* (Imagine Pr, 1983), *Bloomsbury Rev, Intl Qtly, Psychopoetica, Vol No Mag.*

Reuel Denney   P
2957 Kalakaua Ave, #315, Honolulu, HI 96815, 808-923-9618
Pubs: *Feast of Strangers* (Greenwood Pr, 1996), *In Praise of Adam* (U Chicago Pr, 1961), *New Directions, Kaimana, Poetry, Chelsea, Kenyon Rev, Hudson Rev.*

Ray Freed   P
PO Box 2883, Kailua-Kona, HI 967452883, 808-326-1138
Internet: www.tropweb.com/indigo/poets.htm
Pubs: *All Horses are Flowers, Much Cry Little Wool* (Street Pr, 1998, 1990), *The Juggler's Ball* (Hualalai Pr, 1996).

Norman Hindley   P
46-049 Aliianela Pl, #1721, Kaneohe, HI 96744-3703, 808-236-2229
Internet: dlanska@lava.net
Pubs: *A Good Man* (Fawcett, 1993), *Winter Eel* (Petronium Pr, 1984), *Chaminade Literary Rev, Hawaii Rev, Hawaii Literary Arts, Poetry.*

Faye Kicknosway   P
Univ Hawaii at Manoa, 412 Kuykendall, Honolulu, HI 96822, 808-956-7619
Pubs: *Listen to Me, The Violence of Potatoes* (Ridgeway Pr, 1992, 1990), *All These Voices* (Coffee Hse Pr, 1986).

Irina Kirk   W
475 Front St, #323, Lahaina, HI 96761, 808-661-4835
Pubs: *Chekhov* (Twayne, 1980), *Profile in Russian Resistance* (Quadrangle, 1975).

Jim Kraus   P
Chaminade Univ, 3140 Waialae Ave, Honolulu, HI 96816, 808-735-4863
Internet: jkraus@chaminade.edu
Pubs: *Poetry Hawaii* (U Hawaii Pr, 1979), *Virginia Qtly Rev, San Marcos Rev, Pequod, Hawaii Rev, Ramrod, Kentucky Poetry Rev, Chaminade Literary Rev.*

Patrick Leahy   W
3651 Ahukini Rd, Lihue, HI 96766-9713
Pubs: *Bachy, Rocky Mountain Rev, Pulp.*

Darrell H. Y. Lum W
990 Hahaione St, Honolulu, HI 96825, 808-626-1481
Internet: darrel@hawaii.edu
 Pubs: *Pass On, No Pass Back!, The Best of Bamboo Ridge: Anth* (Bamboo Ridge Pr, 1990, 1986), *Into the Fire: Asian American Prose: Anth* (Greenfield Rev Pr, 1996), *Seattle Rev, Manoa, Chaminade Rev.*

Wing Tek Lum P
80 N King St, Honolulu, HI 96817, 808-531-5200
 Pubs: *Expounding the Doubtful Points* (Bamboo Ridge, 1987).

Alan Decker McNarie P&W
PO Box 10247, Hilo, HI 96721, 808-935-7210
 Pubs: *Yeshua: The Gospel of St. Thomas* (Pushcart Pr, 1993), *Chaminade Literary Mag, Hawaii Pacific Rev, Kaimana, Bamboo Ridge, Cape Rock, Poultry, Wind.*

Adele NeJame P
Hawaii Pacific Univ, 1188 Fort St, Honolulu, HI 96813
 Pubs: *Field Work* (Petronium Pr, 1996), *Inheritance* (Ridgeway Pr, 1989), *American Nature Writing, Ploughshares, Poetry Kanto, Nimrod, Manoa.*

William J. Puette P
3363-A Keanu St, Honolulu, HI 96816, 808-735-3661
 Pubs: *The Hilo Massacre* (U Hawaii Pr, 1988), *Guide to the Tale of Genji* (Tuttle, 1983).

Tony Quagliano P
509 University Ave #902, Honolulu, HI 96826
 Pubs: *Poetry of Solitude: Anth* (Rizzoli, 1995), *Rolling Stone, New Directions, New York Qtly, Harvard Rev, Exquisite Corpse, Yankee, JAMA, Kaimana.*

Robert Shapard W
Univ Hawaii-Manoa, 1733 Donaghho Rd, Honolulu, HI 96822, 808-456-3070
 Pubs: *Sudden Fiction Continued: Anth, Sudden Fiction Intl: Anth* (Norton, 1996, 1989), *NER, Kenyon Rev, Literary Rev, Prism Intl, Mid-American Rev, Cimarron Rev.*

Stephen Shrader P
41-945b Laumilo St, Waimanalo, HI 96795, 808-259-5692

Cathy Song P
PO Box 27262, Honolulu, HI 96827, 808-599-4823
 Pubs: *School Figures* (U Pitt Pr, 1994), *Frameless Windows, Squares of Light* (Norton, 1988), *Picture Bride* (Yale U Pr, 1983), *Poetry, Shenandoah, Southern Rev, Kenyon Rev, Michigan Qtly Rev, Carolina Qtly Rev, Poetry Ireland, New England Rev.*

Joseph Stanton P
Box 27270, Honolulu, HI 96827, 808-956-4050
Internet: jstanton@hawaii.edu
 Pubs: *Imaginary Museum* (Time Being Bks, 1999), *What the Kite Thinks* (U Hawaii, 1994), *Poetry, Poetry East, Harvard Rev, New York Qtly, Yankee, Southern Poetry Rev, Chaminade Literary Rev, Ramrod, Image.*

Frank Stewart P
Univ Hawaii, English Dept, Honolulu, HI 96822, 808-956-3064
 Pubs: *Flying the Red Eye, The Open Water* (Floating Island, 1986, 1982), *Ploughshares, Zyzzyva, Ironwood, Orion.*

Jean Yamasaki Toyama P
Univ Hawaii, 1890 East-West Rd, Moore 485, Honolulu, HI 96822, 808-956-4185
Internet: toyama@hawaii.edu
 Pubs: *What The Kite Thinks: A Linked Poem* (U Hawaii Pr, 1994), *The Forbidden Stitch: Anth* (Calyx, 1989), *Illuminations, Kaimana, Caprice, Redneck Rev, Michigan Qtly Rev.*

Dorothy Winslow Wright P&W
2119 Ahapii Pl, Honolulu, HI 96821, 808-734-0846
 Pubs: *Computer Legends, Lies, and Lore* (Ageless Pr, 1994), *The Book Group Book: Anth* (Chicago Rev Pr, 1993), *Poet, Mature Living, Blue Unicorn.*

IDAHO

William C. Anderson W
4857 Lake Shore Pl, Boise, ID 83703, 208-853-4812
 Pubs: *Please Don't Tailgate The Real Estate* (Trailer Life Bks, 1997), *Lady Bluebeard, Taming Mighty Alaska: An RV Odyssey* (Fred Pruett Pub, 1994, 1990), *Motorhome Mag, Reader's Digest, Good Housekeeping.*

Gary L. Bennett W
1107 N 16 St, Boise, ID 83702-3411
 Pubs: *The Star Sailors* (St. Martin's Pr, 1980), *Popular Science, Astronomy, Technology Rev.*

Mark Geston W
1829 Edgecliff Terr, Boise, ID 83702, 208-344-8535
 Pubs: *Mirror to the Sky* (Morrow, 1992), *Lords of the Starship* (Ace, 1967), *Amazing Stories, Fantasy and Science Fiction.*

Gary Gildner   P&W
RR 2, Box 219, Grangeville, ID 835309615, 208-983-1663
> Pubs: *The Bunker in the Parsley Fields, The Warsaw Sparks* (U Iowa Pr, 1997, 1990), *Clackamas* (Carnegie Mellon, 1991), *A Week in South Dakota* (Algonquin, 1987), *Poetry, Georgia Rev, New Letters, Shenandoah, NAR, Poetry Northwest, Witness.*

Janet Campbell Hale   P&W
799 Wildshoe Dr, Desmet, ID 83824, 208-274-2034
> Pubs: *The Owl's Song And Other Stories* (HarperCollins, 1995), *Bloodlines* (Random Hse, 1993).

Miriam Halliday-Borkowski   P
Nagy/Draznin Property, PO Box 1330, Challis, ID 83226, 208-224-6965
> Pubs: *For the Beloved* (Handbuilt Bks/San Raphael, 1996), *In Memoriam Jo Ann Yellow Bird* (Colouredpoetry/Handbuilt Bks, 1988), *Columbia, Beatitude, Kansas Qtly.*

Daryl Jones   P
Boise State Univ, 1910 University Dr, Boise, ID 83725, 208-385-1202
Internet: aprjones@bsu.idbsu.edu
> Pubs: *Someone Going Home Late* (Texas Tech U Pr, 1990), *Sewanee Rev, TriQuarterly, New Orleans Rev.*

Ron McFarland   P&W
857 E 8 St, Moscow, ID 83843, 208-882-0849
Internet: ronmcf@uidaho.edu
> Pubs: *The Haunting Familiarity of Things* (Singular Speech Pr, 1993), *Tumblewords: Writers Reading the West* (U Nevada Pr, 1995), *Poetry Northwest, American Literary Rev, Midwest Qtly, Willow Springs, Talking River Rev, Urbanus Mag.*

Lance Olsen   W
Bear Creek Cabin, 1490 Ailor Rd, Deary, ID 83823, 208-877-1422
Internet: lolsen@uidaho.edu
> Pubs: *Time Famine, Tonguing the Zeitgeist* (Permeable Pr, 1996, 1994), *Scherzi, I Believe* (Wordcraft, 1994), *Fiction Intl, Mondo 2000, VLS, Black Ice, ACM, Gargoyle, Iowa Rev, Hudson Rev.*

Joan Silva   P
PO Box 67, Emmett, ID 83617, 208-365-5812
> Pubs: *Attila* (Black Scarab Pr, 1976), *Slipstream, Tandava, Pteranadon, Contact II, Exquisite Corpse, Gryphon, Prickly Pear.*

William Studebaker   P
2616 E 4000 N, Twin Falls, ID 83301, 208-733-8584
> Pubs: *Travelers in an Antique Land* (U Idaho Pr, 1997), *River Religion, The Rat Lady at the Company Dump* (Limberlost, 1997, 1990), *Dickinson Rev, Ohio Rev, High Country News, George Washington Rev, Mid-American Rev, Tar River Poetry.*

Eberle Umbach   W
Box 172, McCall, ID 83638
> Pubs: *Northwest Rev, Timbuktu, Oh Idaho Mag, Whole Earth Rev.*

Norman Weinstein   P
730 E Bannock St, Boise, ID 83712, 208-345-8516
Internet: nweinste@micron.net
> Pubs: *A Night in Tunisia: Imaginings of Africa in Jazz* (Scarecrow Pr, 1992), *Village Voice, Sulfur, Io, Tree.*

Robert Wrigley   P
RR 1, Box 98W4, Lenore, ID 83541, 208-836-5691
> Pubs: *In The Bank of Beautiful Sins* (Penguin, 1995), *What My Father Believed, Moon In A Mason Jar* (U Illinois Pr, 1991, 1986).

Harald Wyndham   P
243 S 8th Avenue, Pocatello, ID 83201, 208-232-5118
> Pubs: *The Christmas Sonnets, Heavenly Rhythm & Blues: Poems 1982-1993* (Blue Scarab Pr, 1996, 1993).

ILLINOIS

Carol M. Adorjan   W
1667 Winnetka Rd, Glenview, IL 60025, 847-657-8502
Internet: writenow4@aol.com
> Pubs: *I Can! Can You?, WKID: Easy Radio Plays* (Albert Whitman, 1990, 1988), *NAR, Redbook, Denver Qtly, Woman's Day, Natl Radio Theatre.*

Michael A. Anania   P&W
5755 Sunset Ave, La Grange, IL 60525, 312-996-3260
> Pubs: *Selected Poems* (Moyer Bell, 1994).

Arnold Aprill   PP
2850 N Seminary, Chicago, IL 60657, 312-281-0927

Asa Baber   W
247 E Chestnut, Chicago, IL 60611

Mary Shen Barnidge   P
1030 W Dakin St, Chicago, IL 60613, 312-871-3904
> Pubs: *Detours* (Lonesome Traveler Pub, 1997), *Piano Player at the Dionysia* (Thompson Hill, 1984), *Whetstone, Overtures, Leatherneck, Howling Dog, Kaleidoscope, DEROS.*

Jill Barrie   P
10S 272 Alma Ln, Naperville, IL 60564
Internet: jbarrie104@aol.com
> Pubs: *Calapooya Collage, Gulf Stream, American Literary Rev, Cimarron, New Virginia Rev, Calliope, Black River Rev, Southern Poetry Rev, American Literary Rev.*

Saul Bellow   W
1126 E 59 St, Chicago, IL 60637
    Pubs: *The Dean's December* (H&R, 1982), *Herzog* (Viking,
    1964).

Ronald Belluomini   P
1721 Juliet Ln, Libertyville, IL 60048, 708-367-4218
    Pubs: *The Thirteenth Labor* (Dragon's Teeth Pr, 1985),
    Rhino, FOC Rev, Menagerie.

Brooke Bergan   P
1150 N Lake Shore Dr #19F, Chicago, IL 60611-1025
    Pubs: *Storyville* (Moyer Bell, 1993), *Distant Topologies,
    Windowpane* (Wine Pr, 1976, 1974), *ACM, Oyez, Wire.*

Susan Bergman   P&W
21693 Hanover Hill, Barrington, IL 60010, 847-381-0004
Internet: scbergman@aol.com
    Pubs: *Buried Life, Anonymity* (FS&G, 1999, 1994), *Martyrs:
    Contemporary Writers on Modern Lives of Faith: Anth* (HC,
    1996), *Prairie Schooner, Chelsea, Indiana Rev.*

Leslie Bertagnolli   P
2800 Prudential Plaza, Chicago, IL 60601, 312-861-8617
    Pubs: *Family Photographs* (Red Herring Pr, 1979).

Leigh Buchanan Bienen   W
639 Central St, Evanston, IL 60201-1732
    Pubs: *The Ways We Live Now: Anth* (Ontario Rev Pr,
    1986), *O. Henry Prize Stories 1983: Anth* (Doubleday,
    1983), *Descant, Ontario Rev.*

James Bonk   P
400 N Main St, Mt Prospect, IL 60056, 312-253-7673
    Pubs: *Poetry Connection — Dial A Poem Chicago Anth*
    (City of Chicago, 1991), *America, Minnesota Rev,
    Commonweal.*

Catherine Bowman   P
Indiana University, 442 Ballantine Hall English De,
Bloomington, IL 47401, 812-855-1834
Internet: cabowman@indiana.edu
    Pubs: *Rock Farm, 1-800-HOT-RIBS* (Gibbs Smith, 1997,
    1993), *Best American Poetry: Anths* (Scribner, 1995, 1994),
    TriQuarterly, River Styx, Paris Rev.

Walter L. Bradford   P
932 E 50 St, Chicago, IL 60615, 312-373-2957

Ardyth Bradley   P
514 Broadway, Libertyville, IL 60048, 708-362-4635
    Pubs: *Inside the Bones is Flesh* (Ithaca House, 1978),
    Benchmark Anth of Contemporary Illinois Poetry (Stormline
    Pr, 1988), *Three Winter Poems: Anth* (Penumbra Pr, 1986),
    *Poetry, Parting Gifts, Shenandoah, Cutbank, Ironwood,
    Tendril.*

John M. Bradley   P
504 Sycamore Rd, DeKalb, IL 60115, 815-756-1533
    Pubs: *To Dance With Uranium* (Lake Effect Pr, 1995),
    Atomic Ghost (Coffee Hse, 1995), *Prose Poem, Poetry
    East, Another Chicago Mag, Sonora.*

Becky Bradway   W
204 William Dr, Normal, IL 61761, 309-454-7175
Internet: bbradway@mail.millikin.edu
    Pubs: *Green Mountains Rev, Beloit Fiction Jrnl,
    Greensboro Rev, Ascent, Other Voices, Cream City Rev,
    River Styx, Laurel Rev, Third Coast, Writing on the Edge,
    American Fiction.*

Sandra Braman   P
803 S Coler, Urbana, IL 61801, 217-337-1506
    Pubs: *A True Story* (Tansy/Zelot, 1985), *Spokeheards*
    (Longspoon, 1983), *Exquisite Corpse, Island.*

June Rachuy Brindel   P&W
2740 Lincoln Ln, Wilmette, IL 60091, 847-251-9228
    Pubs: *Phaedra* (St. Martin's Pr, 1985), *Nobody Is Ever
    Missing* (Story Pr, 1984), *Sound of Writing, Other Voices,
    Mss., Iowa Rev, Story Qtly, Cimarron Rev.*

Gwendolyn Brooks   P
Third World Press, 7822 S Dobson, Chicago, IL 60619
    Pubs: *Children Coming Home* (David Co., 1991), *Blacks,
    The Near-Johannesburg Boy* (Third World Pr, 1991, 1991).

Glen Brown   P
100 S Brainard Ave, La Grange, IL 60525-2100,
708-579-6300
Internet: ghbrown@kiwi.dep.anl.gov
    Pubs: *Yes, No, Maybe* (Lake Shore Pub, 1995), *Don't Ask
    Why* (Thorntree Pr, 1994), *Poetry, Poet & Critic, Negative
    Capability, Spoon River Poetry Rev.*

Rosellen Brown   P&W
5421 S Cornell, #16, Chicago, IL 60615, 773-288-3349
Internet: hoff@consortium-chicago.org
    Pubs: *Cora Fry's Pillow Book, Before and After* (FSG, 1994,
    1992), *Rosellen Brown Reader* (U Pr New England, 1992),
    Street Games (Milkweed, 1991).

Michael H. Brownstein   P
PO Box 268805, Chicago, IL 606268805, 312-409-6762
    Pubs: *The Principle of the Thing* (Tight Pr, 1994), *Poems
    from the Body Bag* (Ommation Pr, 1989), *Samisdat, Cafe
    Rev, Rosewell Literary Rev, Artisan, Wordwrights,
    Potpourri, Beyond Baroque, Melting Tree Rev, Planet
    Chaos, Indelible Ink.*

Debra M. Bruce   P
Northeastern Illinois Univ, 5500 N St. Louis Ave, Chicago, IL 60625
Internet: D-Bruce-kinnebrew@neiu.edu
    Pubs: *What Wind Will Do* (Miami U Pr, 1997), *Sudden Hunger, Pure Daughter* (U Arkansas Pr, 1987, 1984), *APR, Kenyon Rev, Michigan Qtly Rev, Poetry, Virginia Qtly Rev, Atlantic Monthly.*

Rex Burwell   P
417 May St, Elgin, IL 60120
    Pubs: *Anti-History* (Smokeroot Pr, 1977), *Chicago Rev, Shenandoah, Big Scream.*

Anne Calcagno   W
DePaul Univ, 802 W Belden, Chicago, IL 60614-3214, 312-325-7000
Internet: acalcagn@wppost.depaul.edu
    Pubs: *Pray For Yourself, Fiction of the Eighties: Anth* (TriQuarterly Bks, 1993, 1990), *American Fiction: Anth* (Birch Lane Pr, 1991), *NAR, TriQuarterly, Epoch, Denver Qtly.*

Paul Carroll   P
Univ Illinois, PO Box 4348, English Dept, Chicago, IL 60680, 312-996-3260
    Pubs: *Poems* (Spoon River Poetry, 1988), *The Garden of Earthly Delights* (Chicago Public Library, 1986).

Ana Castillo   P&W
3036 N Sawyer, Chicago, IL 60618, 312-327-0447
    Pubs: *The Mixquiahuala Letters* (Bilingual Rev Pr, 1985), *Spoon River Qtly, River Styx, Maize.*

George Chambers   P&W
318 Sarah Barnewolt Dr, Peoria, IL 61604, 309-637-0454
    Pubs: *The Great Blue Sea* (Snowberries Pr, 1994), *The Last Man Standing* (Fiction Collective Two, 1990), *Caprice, Situation, Iowa Rev, Prose Poem.*

Joan Colby   P
10N226 Muirhead Rd, Elgin, IL 60123, 847-464-5250
Internet: joanmc@aol.com
    Pubs: *The Atrocity Book* (Lynx Hse, 1987), *The Lonely Hearts Killers* (Spoon River, 1986), *Poetry, Illinois Rev, New Renaissance, Cream City Rev, Grand Street.*

Judith Cooper   W
6620 N Glenwood, Chicago, IL 60626, 773-338-4807
Internet: dialexltd@aol.com
    Pubs: *Southern Rev, ACM, Whetstone, Black Warrior Rev, Louisville Rev, Nebraska Rev, MacGuffin, Permafrost.*

Mark Costello   W
Univ Illinois, Urbana, IL 61801

Carlos Cumpian   P
March, Inc., PO Box 2890, Chicago, IL 60690, 312-935-6188
    Pubs: *Coyote Sun, Emergency Tacos* (March/Abrazo Pr, 1990, 1989), *3rd World: Anth* (Pig Iron, 1989).

David Curry   P&W
2045 N Dayton, Chicago, IL 60614, 312-528-4120
    Pubs: *Contending To Be The Dream, Here* (New Rivers Pr, 1979, 1970), *Karamu.*

Molly Daniels   W
Creative Writing School, 410 S. Michigan Ave #720, Chicago, IL 60605, 773-684-5985
Internet: mollydan@aol.com
    Pubs: *Father Gander Rhymes and Other Poems: Anth, The Clothesline Rev, No 4: Anth* (The Clothesline Rev Pr, 1996, 1989), *Chicago Rev.*

Nat David   P
1718 Sherman Ave #203, Evanston, IL 60201
    Pubs: *Heartdance* (Doublestar Pr, 1989), *Primal Voices, Strong Coffee, Hammers, Chaminade Literary Rev, Footwork: The Paterson Literary Rev.*

Ronda Marie Davis   P
10454 S Calumet, Chicago, IL 60628, 312-955-2971

Connie Deanovich   P
c/o A. Denoyer, 5534 N Parkside, Chicago, IL 60630
    Pubs: *Watusi Titanic* (Timken, 1996), *Walk on the Wild Side: Contemporary Urban Poetry Anth* (Scribner, 1994), *Parnassus, Sulfur, Gertrude Stein Awards, New American Writing, Grand Street, Bomb, See.*

Helen Degen Cohen   P
1166 Osterman, Deerfield, IL 60015, 847-945-0487
    Pubs: *Sarajevo Anth, Blood To Remember: Poets on the Holocaust: Anth* (Texas Tech U Pr, 1993, 1991), *Partisan Rev, ACM, Stand, Outerbridge.*

John J. Desjarlais   W
934 Crest Ct, Byron, IL 61010, 815-234-4833
Internet: jdesjar@kougars.kish.cc.il.us
    Pubs: *Relics* (Thomas Nelson, 1993), *The Throne of Tara* (Crossway Bks, 1990).

John Dickson   P
2249 Sherman Ave, Evanston, IL 60201, 708-864-4793
    Pubs: *Waving At Trains* (Thorntree, 1986), *Victoria Hotel* (Chicago Rev Pr, 1979), *Poetry, TriQuarterly, American Scholar, Willow Rev, Wire, Whetstone.*

George Drury   P
2674 N Burling St, Chicago, IL 60614-1514, 773-244-0095
    Pubs: *Strong Coffee, Big Scream, Blind Alleys, Action, An Evening Without Lawrence Welk.*

Elizabeth Eddy   P
1050 W Jeffrey, Kankakee, IL 60901, 708-946-3167
    Pubs: *The Tie That Binds* (Papier-Mache Pr, 1988), *Spoon River Qtly, Whetstone, Korone, New Poetry Jrnl.*

Cassie Edwards   P&W
RR #3, Box 60, Mattoon, IL 61938
    Pubs: *Savage Thunder, Savage Sunrise, Savage Winds* (Leisure Bks, 1994, 1993, 1993), *Wild Splendor, Wild Embrace, Wild Desire* (NAL, 1994, 1993, 1993).

Jim Elledge   P&W
Illinois State Univ, English Dept/4240, Normal, IL 61790-4240, 309-438-7705
Internet: jmelled@ilstu.edu
    Pubs: *Earth as It Is* (Ashland Poetry Pr, 1995), *Into the Arms of the Universe* (Stonewall Series, 1995), *Fiction Intl, James White Rev, Paris Rev.*

Charles Elwert   P
681-A Katherine Ln, Addison, IL 60101, 630-916-4876
Internet: 85corvette@compuserve.com
    Pubs: *Poetry Connection 1981-1991* (Hydra, 1991), *Paris Rev, Spoon River Qtly.*

Pamela Erbe   W
3608 N Pine Grove Ave, #B7, Chicago, IL 60613-4556
    Pubs: *American Fiction: Anth* (New Rivers Pr, 1995), *New Stories from the South: Anth* (Algonquin Bks, 1994), *River Oak Rev, Antioch Rev, Columbia, NAR, Ms..*

Dave Etter   P
628 E Locust St, Lanark, IL 61046, 815-493-6778
    Pubs: *How High the Moon, Sunflower County* (Spoon River, 1996, 1994), *I Want to Talk About You* (Crossroads Pr, 1995).

Ronald Fair   W
201 W 92 St, Chicago, IL 60620

H. R. Felgenhauer   P&W
PO Box 146486, Chicago, IL 60614, 312-772-8686
    Pubs: *IAPT3, Insects Are People Two* (Puffn' Stuff Productions, 1998, 1996), *Bouillabaisse, Gotta Write, Mind in Motion, Fantasy Commentator.*

Peter Fellowes   P
3225 W Foster, Chicago, IL 60625, 312-583-2700
    Pubs: *Yale Rev, APR, Commonweal, Shenandoah, Ontario Rev, Epoch, Poetry Now, TriQuarterly.*

Calvin Forbes   P
School of the Art Institute, 37 S Wabash Ave, Chicago, IL 60603, 312-899-5187
    Pubs: *From the Book of Shine* (Burning Deck, 1979), *Blue Monday* (Wesleyan U Pr, 1974).

Phyllis Ford-Choyke   P
29 E Division St, Chicago, IL 60610, 312-337-1482
    Pubs: *Apertures to Anywhere* (Harper Square Pr, 1979), *Poetry Northwest, Voices Israel, Rhino.*

Rich Foss   P&W
RR 2, Box 2A, Tiskilwa, IL 61368, 815-646-4264
    Pubs: *Jonas and Sally* (Good Bks, 1994), *Poet's Page, North Country, Christian Poetry Jrnl, Christianity & Literature.*

Alan Friedman   W
Univ Illinois, Chicago, IL 60680, 312-413-2200
    Pubs: *Hermaphrodeity* (Knopf, 1972), *The Turn of the Novel* (Oxford U, 1966), *Raritan, Partisan Rev, Paris Rev.*

Paul Friedman   W
310 W Illinois St, Urbana, IL 61801, 217-328-3247
    Pubs: *Serious Trouble, And If Defeated Allege Fraud* (U Illinois Pr, 1986, 1971), *Mid-American Rev, Boulevard, Cimarron Rev.*

Richard Friedman   P
5819 N Sacramento, Chicago, IL 60659, 312-275-7154
    Pubs: *Physical Culture* (Yellow Pr, 1979).

Paul Friedrich   P
1130 East 59th St, Chicago, IL 60637, 773-702-7004
    Pubs: *Music in Russian Poetry* (Peter Lang, 1998), *The Language Parallax* (U Texas Pr, 1987), *Speaking in Tongues: Anth* (Black Buzzard Pr, 1994), *Mississippi Valley Rev, Blue Unicorn, Flutter By Pr, Kansas Qtly.*

Robert Fromberg   W
734 N La Salle Dr, #1114, Chicago, IL 60610-3530, 312-440-9129
Internet: rmf880@nwu.edu
    Pubs: *Blue Skies* (Floating Island Pubs, 1992), *Indiana Rev, Bellingham Rev, Tennessee Qtly, Salmon, Colorado Rev, Northeast.*

Al Gabor   P&W
1630 Mulford, Evanston, IL 60202, 847-475-2483
Internet: a-gabor@nwu.edu
    Pubs: *XY Files: Anth* (Sherman Asher, 1997), *ACM, Cream City Rev, Ascent, Puerto del Sol, Great River Rev, Mississippi Valley Rev, Chattahoochee Rev, Plainsongs.*

Cynthia Gallaher   P
PO Box A3604, Chicago, IL 60690, 773-539-9638
Internet: gallaher@trustmarkins.com
    Pubs: *Swimmer's Prayer* (Missing Spoke Pr, 1999), *Private, On Purpose* (Mulberry Pr, 1993), *Night Ribbons* (Polar Bear Pr, 1990), *Bloomsbury Rev, Sing Heavenly Muse, Green Fuse Poetry, Riversedge, Eureka Literary Mag, Slipstream, Heartlands Today.*

Bruce M. Gans W
5324 Hyde Park Blvd #1, Chicago, IL 60615, 312-643-8888
Internet: bmg1030@tezcat.com
Pubs: *Here's the Story: Fiction With Heart: Anth* (Spirit That Moves Us Pr, 1986), *American Scholar, Hawaii Rev, Playboy, Mademoiselle, Kansas Qtly, Memphis State Rev.*

David C. D. Gansz P
310 Busse Hwy, #227, Park Ridge, IL 60068, 847-384-0501
Internet: dgansz@umi.com
Pubs: *Co-Relation, Lett*(er)*ings, Re-Collection: Anth, The Enduring: Anth* (Logres, 1998, 1997, 1996, 1995), *Sulfur, o.blek, Temblor, Ashen Meal.*

Bill Garson P&W
PO Box 3126, Rockford, IL 61106-0126, 815-398-5414
Pubs: *Where Are You Now, Boy Billie?* (Fithian Pr, 1992), *Brother Earth* (Imagination Plus), *Hardboiled Detective, Grit, Sunshine.*

Lucia C. Getsi P
Illinois State Univ, Normal, IL 61790-4240, 309-438-7906
Internet: lcgetsi@rs6000.cmp.ilstu.edu
Pubs: *Intensive Care* (New Rivers, 1995), *No One Taught This Filly to Dance* (Pikestaff Pr, 1989), *Many Mountains Moving, Women's Rev of Bks, Willow Rev.*

Reginald Gibbons P&W
Northwestern Univ, 215 University Hall, Evanston, IL 602082240
Internet: rgibbons@nwu.edu
Pubs: *Sparrow: New and Selected Poems* (Louisiana State U Pr, 1997), *Sweetbitter* (Penguin, 1996), *Maybe It Was So* (U Chicago, 1991), *APR, Harper's, Southern Rev, QRL, Atlantic.*

Netta Gillespie P
211 East Sherwin Dr, Urbana, IL 618027129, 217-328-7268
Internet: gillesp1.uiuc.edu
Pubs: *Circus* (Red Herring Pr, 1980), *Matrix, South Dakota Rev, Spoon River Qtly, Mati, Karamu, Apocalypse, Mississippi Valley Rev, Banyan Anth.*

Philip Graham P&W
605 W Vermont St, Urbana, IL 61801-4824, 217-337-6898
Internet: p-graham@uiuc.edu
Pubs: *Interior Design, How To Read An Unwritten Language* (Scribner, 1996, 1995), *New Yorker, NAR, Paris Rev, Fiction, Missouri Rev, Washington Post.*

Cindy Guentherman P
7721 Venus St, Loves Park, IL 61111, 815-654-8491
Internet: haikupup@aol.com
Pubs: *Midwest Poetry Rev, Rockford Rev, Dragonfly, Without Halos, Heart & Soul, Kumquat Meringue, Modern Haiku, Parnassus, Riverrun, Lynx, Impetus, American Poets & Poetry.*

Mary Hanford P
RR 2, Box 78, Aledo, IL 61231
Pubs: *Spoon River Qtly, Another Place to Publish, Brushfire, Spectrum, The Carillion.*

Barbara Harr P
20 S Fremont St, Naperville, IL 60540-4329, 708-778-9528
Pubs: *The Mortgaged Wife* (Swallow, 1970), *Nation, Rough Edges, Choice, Womanspirit, Shenandoah.*

Kent Haruf W
Southern Illinois Univ, English Dept, Carbondale, IL 62901, 618-453-6867
Pubs: *Where You Once Belonged* (S&S, 1990), *Where Past Meets Present: Anth* (U Colorado Pr, 1994), *Best American Short Stories: Anth* (HM, 1987), *Grand Street.*

M. M. M. Hayes W
431 Sheridan Rd, Kenilworth, IL 60043, 847-256-6998
Internet: hayesbox@interaccess.com
Pubs: *New Stories from the South: Anth* (Algonquin Bks, 1995), *Awards XVI: Katherine Anne Porter Award: Anth* (Nimrod, 1996), *NAR, Redbook, High Plains Literary Rev.*

Robert R. Hellenga W
Knox College, English Dept, Galesburg, IL 61401, 3093430112x359
Internet: rhelleng@knox.knox.edu
Pubs: *The Sixteen Pleasures* (Dell, 1995), *Mississippi Valley Rev, Chicago Rev, Iowa Rev, California Qtly, Columbia, Ascent, Crazyhorse, TriQuarterly.*

Greg Herriges W
c/o William Rainey, Harper Col, 1200 Algonquin Rd, Palatine, IL 60047
Internet: herriges3@aol.com
Pubs: *The Winter Dance Party Murders* (Wordcraft, 1998), *Secondary Attachment* (William Morrow, 1986), *Some Place Safe* (Avon, 1985).

Richard Holinger P&W
335 Colonial Cir, Geneva, IL 60134-3640, 630-232-9996
Internet: www.rholinger.hotmail.com
Pubs: *Iowa Rev, Witness, Boulevard, Southern Rev, Chelsea, Ohio Rev, ACM, Hampden-Sydney Poetry Rev, Cream City Rev, New Renaissance, Writers' Bar-B-Q, Zone 3, Other Voices.*

Barbara Savadge Horton P
5423 S Hyde Park Blvd, Chicago, IL 60615, 773-667-8170
Pubs: *The Verb To Love* (Silver Apples Pr, 1989), *Anth of Magazine Verse* (Monitor Bk Co, 1997), *Passages North, Poetry Northwest, Kansas Qtly, New Letters, Southern Poetry Rev, ACM.*

Jean Howard   PP&P
3404 N Troy, Chicago, IL 60618, 312-539-9744
Internet: jeanhoward@aol.com
   Pubs: *Dancing in Your Mother's Skin* (Tia Chucha Pr,
   1991), *Banyon Anth* (Banyon Pr, 1982), *Harper's, Spoon
   River Rev, ACM, Hammers, Harley & The Hill.*

Dan Howell   P
738 W Aldine Ave, #1W, Chicago, IL 60657, 312-935-9244
   Pubs: *Lost Country* (U Massachusetts Pr, 1993).

Bette Howland   W
5020 S Lake Shore Dr #2601, Chicago, IL 60615-3247

Mary Gray Hughes   W
2610 Central Park Ave, #2, Evanston, IL 60201,
708-864-6082
   Pubs: *The Empty Lot* (Another Chicago Pr, 1992), *The
   Calling* (U Illinois, 1980), *Virginia Qtly Rev, Poetry,
   Sou'wester, Southern Rev, Descant, Puckerbrush Rev,
   American Literary Rev.*

John Jacob   P&W
417 South Taylor Apt 3B, Oak Park, IL 603024300,
708-383-3167
   Pubs: *Hungers* (Lake Shore Pub, 1995), *Long Ride Back*
   (Thunder's Mouth, 1988), *TriQuarterly, Partisan Rev,
   Poetry, Mississippi Rev, Chicago Mag.*

Phyllis Janik   P
805 W Chicago Ave, Hinsdale, IL 60521, 708-887-1674
   Pubs: *Fuse* (ACP Books, 1989), *No Dancing/No Acts of
   Dancing* (BkMk Pr, 1982), *New Renaissance.*

Curt Johnson   W
PO Box 302, Highland Park, IL 60035, 847-940-4122
   Pubs: *Thanksgiving in Vegas* (Bottlehouse Pr, 1995), *The
   Mafia Manager* (St. Martin's Pr, 1995), *Song for Three
   Voices* (Carpenter Pr, 1984).

Joyce Sandeen Johnson   P
6532 Spring Brook Rd #212, Rockford, IL 611148136,
815-654-0502
   Pubs: *Impressions Chapbook* (River City Pr, 1994),
   *Pegasus, Midwestern Poetry Rev, Oatmeal and Poetry,
   Rockford Rev, Quarter Moon, Jean's Jrnl, Lynx, Parnassus,
   Mobius, The Poet's Pen.*

Richard Jones   P
DePaul University, 802 W Belden Ave, Chicago, IL 60614,
312-362-5115
   Pubs: *A Perfect Time, At Last We Enter Paradise* (Copper
   Canyon Pr, 1994, 1991), *APR, Poetry, TriQuarterly.*

Allison Joseph   P
Southern Illinois Univ, English Dept, Faner Hall, Carbondale,
IL 62901, 618-453-5321
Internet: aljoseph@aol.com
   Pubs: *In Every Seam* (U Pitt 1997), *Soul Train* (Carnegie
   Mellon U Pr, 1997), *What Keeps Us Here* (Ampersand Pr
   1992), *Callaloo, American Voice, Tamaqua.*

Henry Kanabus   P
2925 N Kenneth Ave, Apt 1, Chicago, IL 60641,
312-725-3973
   Pubs: *Night Ministry and Other Stories* (Brigham Hse,
   1990), *Capillary Sun* (Lebensraum Pr, 1989).

David Michael Kaplan   P&W
4100 N Springfield, Chicago, IL 60618, 312-509-0760
   Pubs: *Skating in the Dark* (Pantheon, 1991), *Comfort*
   (Viking, 1987), *Mississippi Rev, Ohio Rev, Atlantic, Fiction,
   Story, Playboy, Redbook, TriQuarterly, Mirabella.*

Brigit Pegeen Kelly   P
506 W Main St, Urbana, IL 61801-2504, 217-384-6933
   Pubs: *Song* (BOA Limited Edtns, 1994), *In the Place of
   Trumpets* (Yale U Pr, 1988), *New England Rev, Antioch
   Rev, Southern Rev, Yale Rev, Massachusetts Rev.*

Kathryn Kerr   P
11947 Deer Run Road, Marion, IL 62959, 618-964-1917
Internet: kkerr@siu.edu
   Pubs: *I Feel A Little Jumpy Around You* (S&S, 1996), *First
   Frost, Benchmark Anth* (Stormline Pr, 1985, 1987), *ACM,
   Ascent, Thema, River Styx, Spoon River, Tamaqua,
   Karamu.*

William Kir-Stimon   P
729 Emerson St, Evanston, IL 60201, 708-475-5548
   Pubs: *Inside the Open Cage* (Cooperfield, 1984), *Voices,
   Pilgrimage, NU ILR Jrnl, Jrnl of Poetry Therapy, CPU Rev,
   Midwest Rev.*

Elizabeth Klein   P&W
610 S Chicago Ave, Champaign, IL 61821, 217-356-2683
Internet: EKleinS@aol.com
   Pubs: *Reconciliations* (Berkley Bks, 1984), *Approaches*
   (Red Herring Pr, 1980), *ACM, Farmer's Market, Jewish
   Spectator, Shofar, Prairie Schooner.*

John Knoepfle   P
1008 W Adams, Auburn, IL 62615, 217-438-6079
   Pubs: *The Chinkapin Oak* (Rosehill Pr, 1966), *Begging An
   Amnesty* (Druid Pr, 1965), *Centennial Rev, International
   Qtly, Private Arts, New Letters, Crosscurrents.*

Art Lange   P
6553 N Artesian, Chicago, IL 60645
   Pubs: *Needles at Midnight* (Z Pr, 1986), *Evidence* (Yellow
   Pr, 1981), *New American Writing, Transfer, Partisan Rev,
   Washington Rev.*

William Leahy W
1929 W Waveland Ave, #2, Chicago, IL 60613, 312-871-3402
Pubs: *Verb, Cyphurs, Nit & Wit Mag, Northwest Challenge, City, North Dakota Qtly.*

Li-Young Lee P
853 W Lawrence Ave, Chicago, IL 60640, 312-275-3054
Pubs: *The City In Which I Love You, Rose* (BOA Edtns, 1990, 1986), *Grand Street, TriQuarterly.*

Lynn Leone P
328 W Mulberry St, Kankakee, IL 60901, 815-932-5130
Pubs: *Tangents* (Tangents Pr, 1985).

Laurence Lieberman P
Univ Illinois, 608 S Wright, 208 English Bldg, Urbana, IL 61801, 217-367-7186
Pubs: *The Regatta in the Skies: Long Poems* (U Georgia Pr, 1998), *Compass of the Dying, Dark Songs: Slave House and Synagogue* (U Arkansas Pr, 1998, 1996), *New and Selected Poems: 1962-1992* (U Illinois Pr, 1993), *APR, Sewanee Rev, Nation, Boulevard.*

C. A. Lofton P
Olive Harvey College, 10001 S Woodlawn Ave, Chicago, IL 60628, 312-568-3700
Pubs: *Friends Journal, Audio Pubs.*

Beth Lordan W
Southern Illinois Univ, English Dept, Carbondale, IL 62901, 618-453-6849
Internet: lordcurt@siu.edu
Pubs: *And Both Shall Row* (Picador USA, 1998), *August Heat* (Harper & Row, 1989), *Atlantic, Sycamore Rev, Farmer's Market, Gettysburg Rev.*

William F. Love W
940 Cleveland Rd, Hinsdale, IL 60521, 708-325-9097
Pubs: *Bloody Ten, The Fundamentals of Murder, The Chartreuse Clue* (Donald I. Fine, 1992, 1991, 1990).

James M. Loverde P
3719 N Southport Ave #219, Chicago, IL 60613-3756, 312-477-8217
Pubs: *Mutated Viruses, FEH!, Haunted Jrnl, 'scapes, Wolf's Season, Silver Apple Branch, Art/Life.*

Haki R. Madhubuti P
PO Box 730, Chicago, IL 60619, 312-651-0700
Pubs: *Black Men: Obsolete, Single, Dangerous?* (Third World Pr, 1990).

Florence Szerlag Maerz P
830 69th St, Darien, IL 60561, 708-969-9429
Pubs: *Clothes Don't Warm the Heart* (New Horizons Poetry Club, 1983), *Bronte Street, Amelia.*

Michael Patrick Malone W
Northern Illinois Univ, Dekalb, IL 60115, 815-753-6065
Pubs: *PEN Short Story Collection: Anth* (Ballantine, 1986), *Kansas Qtly, New Letters, Ascent, Chicago Reader, U.S. Catholic, Mississippi Rev.*

Norma Marder W
1009 W Church St, Champaign, IL 61821, 217-352-1824
Pubs: *An Eye For Dark Places* (Little, Brown, 1993), *Georgia Rev, Gettysburg Rev.*

Marion M. Markham W
2415 Newport Rd, Northbrook, IL 60062
Internet: mmrbm@juno.com
Pubs: *The St. Patrick's Day Shamrock Mystery, The April Fool's Day Mystery* (HM, 1995, 1991), *McCall's, House Beautiful, Alfred Hitchcock's Mystery, London Mystery, American Way, Buffalo Spree.*

Cris Mazza W
Univ of Illinois at Chicago, Chicago, IL 60607, 312-413-2200
Internet: cmazza@uic.edu
Pubs: *Former Virgin, Revelation Countdown* (FC2, 1997, 1993), *Dog People, Your Name Here:___, Exposed, How to Leave a Country* (Coffee Hse Pr, 1997, 1995, 1994, 1992), *Fiction Intl, High Plains Literary Rev.*

James McGowan P
410 E Walnut St, Bloomington, IL 61701, 309-828-0807
Internet: jmcgowan@titan.iwu.edu

James McManus P&W
School of the Art Institute, 37 S. Wabash, Chicago, IL 606033017, 847-256-4109
Pubs: *Going To The Sun, Great America* (HarperCollins, 1996, 1993), *Out of the Blue, Ghost Waves, Chin Music* (Grove Pr, 1989, 1988, 1987), *Best American Poetry 1994: Anth* (S&S, 1994), *Atlantic Monthly, American Poetry Rev, DoubleTake, Paris Rev, Poetry.*

Florri McMillan W
232 E Walton Pl, #3W, Chicago, IL 60611, 312-642-4735
Internet: fabflo@aol.com
Pubs: *Redbook, Chicago, Savvy, American Fiction Anth, Quarterly West, Greensboro Rev, Family Circle.*

Erica Helm Meade PP
Open Court Publishing Co., 332 S Michigan Ave, Ste #2000, Chicago, IL 60604
Pubs: *Tell It By Heart, Crossroads: Anth* (Open Court Pub, 1995, 1996), *Walking Swiftly: Anth* (Ally Pr, 1992), *Common Ground, The Sun.*

Orlando Ricardo Menes P
4947 N Harlem Ave Apt 1, Chicago, IL 60656, 773-763-5892
Pubs: *Borderlands with Angels* (Bacchae Pr, 1995), *Indiana Rev, Negative Capability, Ploughshares, Antioch Rev, Callaloo, Chelsea.*

Michael Mesic   P
2112 Orrington Ave, Evanston, IL 60201, 312-328-9147

Robin Metz   P&W
695 N Broad St, Galesburg, IL 61401, 309-343-6746
   Pubs: *National Poetry Competition Anthology* (Chester H.
Jones, 1996), *Paris Rev, Epoch, Other Voices, Writers'
Forum, Visions Intl, Intl Poetry Rev, Storytellers, December
Mag.*

Effie Mihopoulos   P
5548 N Sawyer, Chicago, IL 60625, 773-539-5745
   Pubs: *Languid Love Lyrics, The Moon Cycle* (Ommation Pr,
1993, 1991), *Tomorrow, Volume No, Lost & Found Times,
Hammers, Perceptions, Hob-Nob.*

Jordan Miller   P
334 Hawthorn Ave, Glencoe, IL 60022, 312-751-7302
   Pubs: *Bequest: Poems 1959-1979* (Academy Chicago Ltd,
1980), *Gallery Poets, Choice, Midwest.*

Pamela Miller   P
7538 N Bell, #3A, Chicago, IL 60645, 773-973-6690
Internet: pchwedyk@irem.org
   Pubs: *Mysterious Coleslaw* (Ridgeway, 1993), *Fast Little
Shoes* (Erie Street Pr, 1986), *Tomorrow Mag, Zuzu's Petals
Qtly, Seven-Oh-Eight, Free Lunch, Clutch, Poetry Motel,
Krax, Moon Jrnl.*

Patricia Monaghan   P
De Paul University, 243 S Wabash, Chicago, IL 606042302,
708-633-9094
Internet: pmonagha@wppost.depaul.edu
   Pubs: *Seasons of the Witch* (Delphi Pr, 1992), *The Next
Parish Over: Anth* (New Rivers Pr, 1994), *Creation
Spirituality, Sou'wester, River Oak Rev, NAR.*

Lisel Mueller   P
27240 N Longwood Rd, Lake Forest, IL 60045, 847-362-7722
   Pubs: *Alive Together, Waving from Shore, Second
Language* (LSU Pr, 1996, 1989, 1986), *Learning to Play By
Ear* (Juniper Pr, 1990), *Paris Rev, Poetry.*

G. E. Murray   P
1401 Jackson, River Forest, IL 60305, 312-366-4144
   Pubs: *Oils of Evening* (Lake Shore Pr, 1996), *Walking the
Blind Dog* (U Illinois Pr, 1992), *Repairs* (U Missouri Pr,
1979), *Poetry, Hudson Rev, Georgia Rev, TriQuarterly.*

George Nelson   P
2304 Hastings Ave, Evanston, IL 60201, 847-475-7006
Internet: gnelson262@aol.com
   Pubs: *NAW, Wire, ACM, Private, The Critic.*

Richard L. Newby   P
1007 Porter Ln, Normal, IL 61761, 309-452-1726
   Pubs: *Ball State University Forum, Mississippi Rev,
Gryphon, Descant, Small Pond.*

John Frederick Nims   P
3920 Lake Shore Dr, Chicago, IL 60613
   Pubs: *The Six-Cornered Snowflake* (New Directions, 1990),
Zany in Denim (U Arkansas Pr, 1990).

Dwight Okita   P
426 W Surf, #111, Chicago, IL 60657, 312-883-5219
   Pubs: *Crossing With The Light* (Tia Chucha Pr, 1992),
Unsettling America: Anth (Penguin, 1994), *ACM, Hyphen
Mag, Asian Pacific American Jrnl, New City.*

Elaine Fowler Palencia   W
1608 W Healey, Champaign, IL 61821, 217-356-3893
Internet: epalenci@uiuc.edu
   Pubs: *Taking the Train* (Grex Pr, 1997), *Small Caucasian
Woman* (U Missouri Pr, 1993), *Virginia Qtly Rev, Byline,
Pegasus, Other Voices, Sow's Ear Poetry Rev, Iowa
Woman, Willow Rev, Chattahoochee Rev, Appalachian
Heritage.*

Elise Paschen   P
Poetry Society of America, 612 West Deming Pl, Chicago, IL
60614, 773-871-6339
Internet: elisep@poetrysociety.org
   Pubs: *Infidelities* (Story Line Pr, 1996), *New Yorker, Poetry,
New Republic, Nation.*

Rob Patton   P
1142 S Euclid Ave, Oak Park, IL 60304, 312-848-3824
   Pubs: *Dare, Thirty-Seven Poems* (Ithaca Hse, 1977, 1971),
Greenfield Rev.

Lucia Maria Perillo   P
Southern Illinois Univ, Carbondale, IL 62901
   Pubs: *The Body Mutinies* (Purdue U Pr, 1996), *Dangerous
Life* (Northeastern U Pr, 1989), *Ploughshares, Atlantic,
Kenyon Rev, Poetry East, Pushcart Anth.*

Mark Perlberg   P
612 Stratford Pl, Chicago, IL 60657-2632, 312-477-3287
   Pubs: *The Feel Of The Sun* (Ohio U/Swallow, 1982), *The
Burning Field* (Morrow, 1970), *New Yorker, Illinois Rev,
Poetry East, Poetry, Hudson Rev, Prairie Schooner.*

Bob Perlongo   P&W
820 Reba Pl, Evanston, IL 602022691, 847-475-6645
Internet: bokkmann@megsinet.net
   Pubs: *All Hours of the Night* (Writers Workshop Calcutta,
1998), *Boulevard, Reed, The Little Mag, Massachusetts
Rev, Playboy, New York Times, Village Voice.*

Karen Peterson   P&W
633 S Lombard, Oak Park, IL 60304, 708-848-8498
   Pubs: *American Fiction 2: Anth* (Birch Lane Pr, 1991),
*Poetry, Quarterly West, Other Voices, West Branch, Spoon
River Qtly, Karamu.*

Irene Pilibosian P&W
107 Cedar Ave, Morton, IL 61550
Internet: isedeora@aol.com
Pubs: *Bay Area Poets Coalition: Anth* (Panther Lake Pr,
1998), *Skylark, Downstate Story, Reflections, Second
Glance, Poetry Motel, Alley Cat Productions, Parting Gifts,
The Artful Mind, The Catbird Seat, Verse Unto Us, The
Poets' Edge Mag.*

Deborah Rebollar Pintonelli P&W
77 W Wacker Dr, Chicago, IL 60601-1696, 312-326-8803
Pubs: *Ego Monkey* (Another Chicago Pr, 1991),
Unbearables: Anth (Autonomedia, 1995), *Jungles
D'Amerique: Anth* (Arbres a Cames, 1993).

James Plath P&W
Illinois Wesleyan Univ, English Dept, Bloomington, IL
61702-2900, 309-556-3352
Pubs: *Courbet, On the Rocks* (White Eagle Coffee Store Pr,
1994), *Men of Our Time: Anth* (U Georgia Pr, 1992), *Gulf
Stream, Apalachee Qtly, Mississippi Valley Rev.*

Frederik Pohl W
855 S Harvard Dr, Palatine, IL 60067, 708-991-6009
Pubs: *O Pioneer* (Tor, 1998), *Stopping at Slowyear*
(Bantam Bks, 1992), *Mining the Oort* (Ballantine/Del Rey,
1992), *The World at the End of Time* (Ballantine, 1990).

Enid Levinger Powell W
1300 Lake Shore Dr, #21B, Chicago, IL 60610, 312-787-7451
Internet: enidbertpowell@prodigy.com
Pubs: *The Divorce Handbook* (Random Hse, 1984),
McCall's, Mississippi Valley Rev, Yankee.

David Radavich P
1832 Ashby Dr, Charleston, IL 61920-3217, 217-345-9280
Internet: cfdar@eiu.edu
Pubs: *By the Way* (Buttonwood, 1998), *Slain Species*
(Court Poetry, 1980), *Die Weiten Horizonte: Anth* (Pressler
Verlag, 1985), *International Qtly, Kansas Qtly, Louisville
Rev, Northwoods Jrnl.*

Eugene B. Redmond P
Southern Illinois Univ, Box 1431, Edwardsville, IL
62026-1431, 618-692-2060
Pubs: *The Eye in the Ceiling* (Writers & Readers/Harlem
River Pr, 1991), *Drumvoices Revue: Anth* (Southern Illinois
U Pr, 1993), *Eyeball Mag, World Blues Digest.*

Rosemary Roberts P
RR 1, Box 89, Broughton, IL 62817
Pubs: *Let His Light Shine* (American Arts Assn, 1989),
Voices in Poetics: Anth (Yes Pr, 1986).

Carolyn M. Rodgers P
PO Box 804271, Chicago, IL 60680, 312-409-6124
Pubs: *A Train Called Judah, Chosen to Believe* (Eden Pr,
1996, 1996), *Daughters of Africa* (Pantheon, 1993),
Essence, Nation, Black Scholar, Caprice, Nommo.

Paulette Roeske P&W
1200 Harvard Terr, Evanston, IL 60202, 708-475-5228
Internet: com426@clc.cc.il.us
Pubs: *Divine Attention* (Louisiana State U, 1995), *The Body
Can Ascend No Higher* (Illinois Writers, 1992), *Poetry East,
Willow Springs, Virginia Qtly Rev, Kansas Qtly, Georgia
Rev, Glimmer Train, Poetry, Poetry Northwest, The Journal.*

Alane Rollings P
5455 S Ridgewood Ct, Chicago, IL 60615, 773-947-0759
Pubs: *The Logic of Opposites* (TriQuarterly Bks, 1998), *The
Struggle To Adore* (Story Line Pr, 1993), *In Your Own
Sweet Time* (Wesleyan, 1989), *Transparent Landscapes*
(Raccoon Bks, 1984).

Charles Rossiter PP&P
3 Guys From Albany, 705 S Gunderson Ave, Oak Park, IL
60304, 708-660-9376
Internet: posey@juno.com
Pubs: *No, I Didn't Steal This Baby, I'm the Dad* (APD,
1995), *Passionate Hearts: Anth* (New World Library, 1996),
A Gathering of Poets: Anth (Kent State U Pr, 1992),
*Nuyorican Poets Cafe, Green Fuse, Paterson Poetry Rev,
Lips.*

Linda Roth P
6207 Blomberg Rd, Cherry Valley, IL 61016, 815-874-7131
Pubs: *Southern Rev, Massachusetts Rev, Midwest Qtly,
Trestle Creek Rev, Rockford Rev.*

Biff Russ P
913 Elmwood Ave, #A1, Evanston, IL 60202, 847-869-4959
Internet: bruss@interaccess.com
Pubs: *Black Method* (Helicon Nine Edtns, 1991), *Fathers:
Anth* (St. Martin's Pr, 1997), *Prairie Schooner, Cream City
Rev, Poetry East, Indiana Rev, Berkeley Poetry Rev,
Passages North, Boulevard.*

Alice J. Ryerson Hayes P
5550 S Shore Dr #615, Chicago, IL 60037, 773-753-4395
Pubs: *Journal of the Lake* (Open Bks, 1997), *Water
Sheba's Story* (Bookwrights Pr, 1997), *New & Selected
Poems* (Spoon River, 1987), *Do Not Disturb: Anth* (Writer's
Digest Bks, 1989), *Spoon River Qtly, Prairie Schooner,
Whetstone, Women's Rev of Bks.*

Thomas Sanfilip P
PO Box 34807, Chicago, IL 60634
Pubs: *Myth/A Poem* (Iliad Pr, 1994), *Shore Poetry Anth*
(Shore Pub, 1972), *Towers, Thalassa, Nit & Wit, Ivory
Tower, Tomorrow.*

R. Craig Sautter P
DePaul Univ, 243 S Wabash Ave, Chicago, IL 60604,
312-262-5806
Pubs: *Wicked City Chicago* (w/C. Johnson), *Express Lane
Through the Inevitable City* (December Pr, 1994, 1990),
Central Park, Assembling.

John Schultz   W
Columbia College, 600 S Michigan, Chicago, IL 60605,
312-281-7642
> Pubs: *The Chicago Conspiracy Trial* (Da Capo, 1993),
> *Writing from Start to Finish* (Heinemann, 1990), *Georgia
> Rev, Reader, f2.*

Paul C. Schuytema   W
602 N 11th St, Monmouth, IL 61462, 309-734-3225
> Pubs: *Forbidden Lines, Argonaut, Aboriginal SF.*

Whitney Scott   PP&P&W
Outrider Press, 1004 E Steger Rd #C-3, Crete, IL 60417,
708-672-6630
Internet: outriderpr@aol.com
> Pubs: *Scratching It Out, Dancing to the End of the Shining
> Bar, Freedom's Just Another Word: Anth, Prairie Hearts:
> Anth* (Outrider Pr, 1998, 1994, 1998, 1996), *Howling Dog,
> Art & Understanding, Potomac Rev, Amethyst, Pearl,
> Kaleidoscope, Jane's Stories, CQ.*

Maureen Seaton   P
2309 W Wilson Ave #109, Chicago, IL 60625-2150,
312-989-8479
> Pubs: *Furious Cooking* (U Iowa, 1996), *Fear of Subways*
> (Eighth Mountain, 1991), *Missouri Rev, Atlantic, Kenyon
> Rev, New England Rev, Iowa Rev.*

Lynette Seator   P
1609 Mound Ave, Jacksonville, IL 62650, 217-245-6427
Internet: lseator@csj.net
> Pubs: *After The Light* (North Woods Pr, 1992), *Mississippi
> Valley Rev, Praxis, Pulpsmith, Melus, Lodestar, Open
> Places, Kalliope.*

John Sennett   P
237 Park Trail Ct, Schaumburg, IL 60173, 847-517-1690
> Pubs: *Magic Changes, Mississippi Valley Rev, Washout
> Rev, Derby City News, Bloodroot.*

Gregg Shapiro   P&W
5209 N Ashland, Chicago, IL 60640-2001, 773-784-8258
Internet: gregg1959@aol.com
> Pubs: *Reclaiming the Heartland: Anth* (U Minnesota, 1996),
> *Unsettling America: Anth* (Viking, 1994), *Mondo Barbie: Anth*
> (St. Martin's Pr, 1993), *Christopher Street, Columbia Poetry
> Rev, Modern Words, Faultline, Gargoyle, Illinois Rev.*

Harry B. Sheftel   P
900 Coach Rd, Homewood, IL 60430-4143
> Pubs: *Quotations From My Questing, Of Truths and
> Wonderments, From Alpha To Omega* (Jesse Poet Pubs,
> 1991, 1991, 1991), *CSM, Now Mag, Modern Maturity.*

Reginald Shepherd   P
737 W Cornelia Ave, #2A, Chicago, IL 60657, 773-404-5826
Internet: rshepherd@worldnet.att.net
> Pubs: *Angel, Interrupted, Some Are Drowning* (U Pitt Pr,
> 1996, 1994), *Best American Poetry: Anths* (S&S, 1996,
> 1995), *Nation, Poetry, Paris Rev.*

Randy Michael Signor   W
1756 W Belle Plaine, 1st Fl, Chicago, IL 60613,
312-883-9798
> Pubs: *Cottonwood, L.A. Reader, NRG, Fell Swoop, Howling
> Dog, Carolina Qtly.*

Barry Silesky   P&W
3709 N Kenmore, Chicago, IL 60613, 773-248-7665
Internet: btsds@aol.com
> Pubs: *One Thing That Can Save Us* (Coffee Hse Pr, 1994),
> *The New Tenants* (Eye of the Comet Pr, 1991), *Boulevard,
> Witness, NAW, Fiction, Exquisite Corpse, Poetry East,
> Poetry, The Prose Poem, Witness, Fiction Intl.*

Brian Skinner   W
4044 N. Avers, Chicago, IL 60618, 773-866-2610
Internet: gileac@earthling.net
> Pubs: *Liars, Tattlers & Weavers* (Monadnock Group Pubs,
> 1992), *Christmas Blues: Anth* (Amador Pubs, 1995), *Other
> Voices, Magic Realism, Karamu, Atom Mind.*

James Park Sloan   W
Univ Illinois, English Dept, Box 4348, Chicago, IL 60680,
312-996-3282
> Pubs: *The Last Cold-War Cowboy* (Morrow, 1987), *The
> Case History of Comrade U* (Avon, 1972).

Jared Smith   P
409 N Vine St, Hinsdale, IL 60521, 312-887-7338
> Pubs: *Keeping the Outlaw Alive* (Erie Street Pr, 1988), *Dark
> Wing* (Norton, 1984), *New York Qtly.*

Michael S. Smith   P
Rte 13, Box 219, Bloomington, IL 61704-8935, 309-828-0703
> Pubs: *XY Files: Poems on the Male Experience: Anth*
> (Sherman Asher Pub, 1997), *Passionate Hearts: Anth* (New
> World Library, 1996), *Writers' Forum, ELF, Hellas,
> Plainsongs, Thema, Roanoke Rev, Cathartic, Artworld Qtly,
> Comstock Rev, Spoon River.*

Paul Andrew E. Smith   P&W
McHenry Cty Creative Comm, PO Box 354, Cary, IL 60013,
708-639-9200
> Pubs: *Scenes from The Postmodern Butler* (White Eagle
> Coffee Store Pr, 1992), *Willow Rev, Hawaii Rev, Fly Rod &
> Reel, Whetstone, Alaska Qtly Rev, Carolina Qtly.*

Sharon Solwitz   W
3709 N Kenmore, Chicago, IL 60613, 312-248-7665
> Pubs: *Blood and Milk* (Sarabande, 1997), *TriQuarterly,
> Ploughshares, American Short Fiction, Boulevard, Tikkun,
> Mademoiselle, Sassy.*

Sheryl St. Germain　　　　　　　　　　　P
Knox College, English Dept, Box 66, Galesburg, IL
61407-4999, 309-343-3568
Internet: sgermain@knox.knox.edu
　　Pubs: *The Journals of Scheherazade, How Heavy the
　　Breath of God* (U North Texas Pr, 1996, 1994), *Making
　　Bread at Midnight* (Slough Pr, 1992), *TriQuarterly, 5 A.M.,
　　Calyx.*

Scott Starbuck　　　　　　　　　　　　P
955 4th St, Apt 7, Charleston, IL 61920, 217-345-4430
Internet: cwaterstone@hotmail.com
　　Pubs: *Atom Mind, High Country News, Kerf, Awareness
　　Jrnl, Going Down Swinging, Wild Earth, The Climbing Art,
　　Calapooya Collage, Green Fuse, Moksha Jrnl, Dry Heat,
　　Mandrake Poetry Rev.*

Kevin Stein　　　　　　　　　　　　　P
Bradley Univ, Peoria, IL 61625, 309-677-2480
Internet: kstein@bradley.edu
　　Pubs: *Bruised Paradise* (U Illinois Pr, 1996), *A Circus of
　　Want* (U of Missouri Pr, 1992), *The Figures Our Bodies
　　Make* (St. Louis Poetry Ctr, 1988), *Poetry, NAR.*

Richard Stern　　　　　　　　　　　　W
Univ Chicago, English Dept, 1050 E 59 St, Chicago, IL
60637, 773-702-8536
Internet: rstern@midway.uchicago.edu
　　Pubs: *A Sistermony* (Donald I. Fine, 1995), *One Person
　　and Another* (Baskerville, 1993), *Shares and Other Fictions*
　　(Delphinium, 1992), *Noble Rot: Stories* (ACP, 1991), *A
　　Father's Words* (Phoenix, 1990), *TriQuarterly, Paris Rev,
　　Antioch Rev, Iowa Rev.*

Anthony E. Stockanes　　　　　　　　W
2201 E Vermont Ave, Urbana, IL 61801
　　Pubs: *Ladies Who Knit For A Living* (U Illinois Pr, 1981),
　　Sewanee Rev, Ascent, Chicago Magazine.

Lucien Stryk　　　　　　　　　　　　P
342 Delcy Dr, Dekalb, IL 60115, 815-756-8817
　　Pubs: *And Still Birds Sing: New & Collected Poems, Of Pen
　　and Ink and Paper Scraps* (Swallow/Ohio U Pr, 1998,
　　1989), *Where We Are: Selected Poems & Zen Translations*
　　(England; Skoob Bks Ltd, 1997).

Walter Sublette　　　　　　　　　　P&W
Aurora Univ, 347 S Gladstone, Aurora, IL 60506,
708-844-5407
　　Pubs: *The Resurrection On Friday Night* (U Ohio Pr, 1981),
　　Go Now in Darkness (Baker Pr, 1965).

Jean Thompson　　　　　　　　　　　W
Univ Illinois, 608 S Wright St, English Dept, Urbana, IL
61801, 217-333-2391
　　Pubs: *The Woman Driver, Little Face, My Wisdom* (Watts,
　　1985, 1984, 1982), *Mademoiselle, American Short Fiction,
　　New England Rev, Ploughshares, New Yorker.*

Phyllis Alexander Tickle　　　　　　　P
5114 1/2 Main St, Downers Grove, IL 60515, 630-852-5298
Internet: jdurepos@aol.com
　　Pubs: *God-Talk In America, Re-Discovering the Sacred*
　　(Crossroad Pub, 1997, 1996), *My Father's Prayer: A
　　Remembrance* (Upper Room Bks, 1996).

Martha M. Vertreace　　　　　　　　P
Illinois Wesleyan Univ, PO Box 2900, Bloomington, IL
61702-2900, 312-363-0766
　　Pubs: *Light Caught Bending* (Diehard Pr, 1994), *Under A
　　Cat's-Eye Moon* (Clockwatch Rev Pr, 1991), *Dominion Rev,
　　Tamaqua, Spoon River Qtly, Bluff City.*

Doris Vidaver　　　　　　　　　　　P&W
Rush Univ, 600 S Paulina St, Chicago, IL 60612,
312-942-2063
　　Pubs: *Arch of a Circle* (Swallow, 1981), *Articulations: Anth*
　　(U Iowa Pr, 1994), *Literary Rev, Illinois Rev, ACM, Prairie
　　Schooner, Poetry, American Scholar, Chelsea.*

J. Weintraub　　　　　　　　　　　P&W
5442 E View Pk, #3, Chicago, IL 60615
　　Pubs: *Bite to Eat Place: Anth* (Redwood Coast Pr, 1995),
　　Movieworks: Anth (Little Theatre Pr, 1990), *New Criterion,
　　Formalist, Kansas Qtly, Chicago Reader.*

David Buffington Wham　　　　　　　W
860 Hinman Ave, #724, Evanston, IL 60202, 708-733-8015
　　Pubs: *CPU Rev, Pilgrimage, Maelstrom, The Fair, Means,
　　Charlatan, December, Woodwind.*

Eugene Wildman　　　　　　　　　　W
2705 N Mildred, Chicago, IL 60614, 312-281-7167

Michael Wilkerson　　　　　　　　　W
1260 N Green Bay, Lake Forest, IL 60045, 708-234-1063
　　Pubs: *Mondo Elvis: Anth* (St. Martin's Pr, 1994), *Townships:
　　Anth* (U Iowa Pr, 1990), *Where We Live: Anth, New
　　Territory: Anth* (Indiana U Pr, 1990, 1990).

Anne Winters　　　　　　　　　　　P
Northwestern Univ, Evanston, IL 60201, 708-491-7294
　　Pubs: *The Key to the City* (U Chicago Pr, 1986),
　　Salamander (Princeton U Pr, 1979), *Paris Rev, Yale Rev,
　　Threepenny Rev.*

S. L. Wisenberg　　　　　　　　　　W
1209 W Waveland Ave, #3W, Chicago, IL 60613-3803,
312-871-5361
Internet: slw644@nwu.edu
　　Pubs: *Nice Jewish Girls: Anth* (Plume-Penguin, 1996),
　　Feminism 3: Anth (Westview Pr, 1996), *Tikkun, New
　　Yorker, NAR, Kenyon Rev, Wigwag, ACM, Calyx.*

David Wojahn P
1542 W Norwood, Chicago, IL 60660, 812-855-7967
Internet: wojahn@ucs.indiana.edu
Pubs: *The Falling Hour, Late Empire, Mystery Train* (U Pitt Pr, 1997, 1994, 1990), *Poetry, New Yorker, APR, TriQuarterly, Ploughshares, Southern Rev.*

Gene Wolfe W
PO Box 69, Barrington, IL 60011, 312-381-1840
Pubs: *Castleview, Soldier of Arete, There Are Doors* (Tor, 1990, 1989, 1988).

Etta L. Worthington P&W
233 N Taylor, Oak Park, IL 60302, 708-848-2184
Internet: etta@compuserve.com
Pubs: *Emergence III: Anth* (Emergence Pr, 1996), *Farm Wives & Other Iowa Stories: Anth* (MidPrairie Pr, 1995), *Jane's Stories: Anth* (Wild Dove Pr, 1994), *Christian Century, Slipstream, Verve, Secret Alameda, Ariel.*

Joanne Zimmerman W
18255 Perth Ave, Homewood, IL 60430, 708-798-8136
Pubs: *An Intricate Weave: Anth* (Iris Edtns, 1997), *Family: The Possibility of Tradition: Anth* (Pig Iron Pr, 1996), *Shenandoah, Antioch Rev, Descant.*

Yvonne Zipter P
4710 W Hutchinson, Chicago, IL 60641-1607
Internet: yzipter@journals.uchicago.edu
Pubs: *Contemporary Lesbian Love Poems: Anth* (Ballantine Bks, 1996), *The Poetry of Sex: Anth* (Banned Bks, 1992), *Modern Words, Columbia Poetry Rev, Ikon.*

INDIANA

Deborah Bacharach P
1585 N Oakhill Dr, South Bend, IN 46637, 219-243-9853
Internet: bacharach@aol.com
Pubs: *Kalliope, Bellowing Ark, College English, Atom Mind, Stuff, Slipstream, South Coast Poetry Jnrl, Wellspring, Bridges, Soundings East, Paramour, Poet Lore.*

B. E. Balog P
264 N Lake St, Gary, IN 46403
Pubs: *Loaves & Fishes Anth* (Free Writer's Pr, 1982), *Alternatives, Indiannual, Skylark.*

Willis Barnstone P
Indiana Univ, Bloomington, IN 47405, 812-855-9780
Internet: barnston@indiana.edu
Pubs: *Selected Poems* (Sheep Meadow Pr, 1997), *The Secret Reader: 501 Sonnets* (U Pr New England, 1996), *Partisan Rev, New Yorker.*

Marianne Boruch P
415 Maple St, West Lafayette, IN 47906, 765-743-1420
Pubs: *A Stick That Breaks and Breaks, Moss Burning* (Oberlin College Pr, 1997, 1993), *Descendant* (Wesleyan, 1989), *New Yorker, APR, Iowa Rev, Field, Georgia Rev, Denver Qtly.*

James H. Bowden P&W
2078 Ball Diamond Hill Rd, Lanesville, IN 47136
Pubs: *Peter De Vries* (G. K. Hall, 1983), *Shenandoah, College English, Negative Capability.*

Matthew Brennan P
Indiana State Univ, English Dept, Terre Haute, IN 47809, 812-237-3277
Internet: ejmcb@root.indstate.edu
Pubs: *The Music of Exile* (Cloverdale Bks, 1994), *Seeing in the Dark* (Hawkhead Pr, 1993), *Poem, Footwork, Classical Outlook, Poetry Ireland Rev, Poet Lore, Descant.*

Edward Byrne P
Valparaiso Univ, English Dept, Valparaiso, IN 46383, 219-464-5278
Internet: ebyrne@exodus.valpo.edu
Pubs: *East of Omaha* (Pecan Grove Pr, 1996), *Words Spoken, Words Unspoken* (Chimney Hill Pr, 1995), *Along the Dark Shore* (BOA Edtns, 1977), *APR, Porch.*

Jared Carter P
1220 N State Ave, Indianapolis, IN 46201-1162, 317-638-8136
Pubs: *Les Barricades Mysterieuses, Work, For the Night is Coming, After the Rain* (Cleveland State U Poetry Ctr, 1999, 1995, 1993), *Smarty Pants, Peepers, Playboy, Advocate, Bitterroot, Harpstrings, Voices of Israel, Redbook, Ms..*

Richard Cecil P
Indiana Univ, Ballantine Hall 442, English D, Bloomington, IN 47405, 812-855-8224
Pubs: *In Search Of The Great Dead* (Southern Illinois U Pr, 1999), *Alcatraz* (Purdue U Pr, 1992), *Einstein's Brain* (Utah U Pr, 1986), APR, *Poetry, Crazyhorse, New England Rev, Ploughshares, American Scholar, Virginia Qtly, Georgia Rev.*

Elizabeth Christman W
Univ Notre Dame, Notre Dame, IN 46556, 219-239-7316
Pubs: *Ruined for Life* (Paulist Pr, 1987), *A Broken Family* (Morrow, 1981), *The Critic.*

Stephen R. Clark P&W
36 Walnut St, Indianapolis, IN 46227-5187
Pubs: *The Godtouch: Poems* (Northwoods Pr, 1985), *Christianity & Literature, Christian Herald, Encore, Face-to-Face, Alive Now!, Wellspring.*

Ruth Allison Coates　　　　　　　　　P&W
8140 Township Line Rd, Indianapolis, IN 46260,
317-824-9548
　　Pubs: *Waiting for the Westbound* (Ocean Tree Bks, 1992),
　　Great American Naturalists (Lerner Pubs, 1974), *Minnesota
　　Rev, Boys' Life, Byline.*

Marilyn Durham　　　　　　　　　　　W
1508 Howard St, Evansville, IN 47713, 812-423-3342
　　Pubs: *Flambard's Confession, Dutch Uncle, The Man Who
　　Loved Cat Dancing* (HBJ, 1982, 1973, 1972).

Darlene M. Eddy　　　　　　　　　　P
1409 W Cardinal St, Muncie, IN 47303, 317-285-8584
　　Pubs: *Leaf Threads, Wind Rhymes* (Barnwood Pr, 1986),
　　Alternatives: An American Poetry Anth (Best Cellar, 1987),
　　Blue Unicorn, Pebble, Cottonwood, Calyx.

Leslie Harold Edgerton　　　　　　　W
4941 Maple Ridge Dr, Fort Wayne, IN 46835-3930,
219-485-9207
Internet: ledger7633@aol.com
　　Pubs: *Over Easy* (Random Hse, 1998), *Monday's Meal,
　　The Death of Tarpons* (U North Texas Pr, 1997, 1996),
　　*South Carolina Rev, Arkansas Qtly/Kansas Rev, Hopewell
　　Rev, NAR, Breeze, Flyway Literary Rev.*

Douglas Eichhorn　　　　　　　　　P
208 W Main, Centerville, IN 47330, 317-855-3398
　　Pubs: *Rituals: A Book Of Poems* (Salt Mound Pr, 1968).

William C. Elkington　　　　　　　　P
10433 Haverford Pl, Fort Wayne, IN 46845-6504
　　Pubs: *Snowy Egret, Laurel Rev, Karamu, North Country,
　　Denver Qtly, Aldebaran, Third Eye, Gravida.*

Lenny Emmanuel　　　　　　　　　　P
Indiana Univ Medical Center, 930 W Michigan St,
Indianapolis, IN 46223, 317-274-1744
　　Pubs: *The Ice Cream Lady* (Ramparts, 1996), *The
　　Cathartic, Descant, Poetry Rev, Outposts, Imago, Jrnl of
　　Teaching Writing, Exquisite Corpse, Windless Orchard.*

Mari Evans　　　　　　　　　　　　P
PO Box 483, Indianapolis, IN 46206, 317-926-5229

Christine Farris　　　　　　　　　　P
Indiana Univ, Bloomington, IN 47405
　　Pubs: *Mining The Beaches For Watches And Small
　　Change* (Konglomerati Pr, 1981), *Some, Kairos.*

Stephen Fredman　　　　　　　　　P
Univ Notre Dame, Notre Dame, IN 46556, 219-631-7555
　　Pubs: *Sagetrieb, Talisman, Boundary 2, o.ars, North
　　Dakota Qtly, 20th Century Literature.*

Alice Friman　　　　　　　　　　　P
6312 Central Ave, Indianapolis, IN 462201738, 317-257-2105
Internet: bgentry@uindy.edu
　　Pubs: *Inverted Fire* (BkMk Pr, 1997), *Driving for Jimmy
　　Wonderland* (Barnwood Pr, 1992), *Insomniac Heart* (Years
　　Pr, 1990), *Poetry, Georgia Rev, Shenandoah, Ohio Rev,
　　Gettysburg Rev, Prairie Schooner, Poetry Rev* (UK).

Helen Frost　　　　　　　　　　　　P
6108 Old Brook Dr, Fort Wayne, IN 46835, 219-485-1785
Internet: frost-thompson@worldnet.att.net
　　Pubs: *Skin of a Fish, Bones of a Bird* (Ampersand Pr, 1993),
　　Season of Dead Water: Anth (Breitenbush, 1990), *Ms., Chile
　　Verde, Antioch Rev, Calyx, Calliope, Malahat Rev.*

Sonia Gernes　　　　　　　　　　　P
Univ Notre Dame, 210 Decio Hall, Notre Dame, IN 46556,
219-631-5218
Internet: sonia.g.gernes.1@nd.edu
　　Pubs: *A Breeze Called The Fremantle Doctor, Women at
　　Forty* (U Notre Dame Pr, 1997, 1990), *Southern Rev,
　　Poetry Northwest, Sewanee Rev, American Short Fiction,
　　Georgia Rev, New Letters.*

Elaine Gottlieb　　　　　　　　　　W
PO Box 1312, South Bend, IN 46624
　　Pubs: *Indiannual 6: Anth* (Indianapolis Writers Ctr, 1992),
　　Selected Stories from the Southern Rev: Anth (LSU Pr,
　　1988), *Kenyon Rev, Southern Rev.*

Paul E. Grabill　　　　　　　　　　W
905 S Spring St, Evansville, IN 47714, 812-477-2584
　　Pubs: *Youth's A Stuff Will Not Endure* (Avon, 1977),
　　Bitterroot.

Matthew Graham　　　　　　　　　P
Univ Southern Indiana, 8600 University Blvd, Evansville, IN
47712, 812-464-1953
　　Pubs: *1946, New World Architecture* (Galileo, 1991, 1985),
　　Indiana Rev, Harvard Rev.

Anne Haines　　　　　　　　　　　P
PO Box 2501, Bloomington, IN 47402-2501
Internet: http://php.indiana.edu/ ahaines
　　Pubs: *Northwest Rev, Kansas Qtly, Sojourner, Prairie
　　Schooner, Sidewalks, Common Lives/Lesbian Lives, New
　　Zoo Poetry Rev, Sinister Wisdom.*

Ruth Hammond　　　　　　　　　　W
730 1/2 Columbia Ave, Fort Wayne, IN 46805-4304
　　Pubs: *Lake Street Rev, Northeast Mag, Newsday, Portland
　　Oregonian, Minneapolis Tribune, Kansas Qtly.*

Patricia Henley　　　　　　　　　P&W
PO Box 259, Battle Ground, IN 47920, 765-567-2058
Internet: phenley@omni.cc.purdue.edu
　　Pubs: *The Secret of Cartwheels, Friday Night at Silver Star
　　(Graywolf, 1992, 1986), Learning to Die* (Three Rivers,
　　1979), *Atlantic, Ploughshares.*

Joe L. Hensley										W
2315 Blackmore, Madison, IN 47250, 812-273-1683
Pubs: *Grim City* (St. Martin's Pr, 1994).

Marc Hudson										P
Wabash College, Crawfordsville, IN 47933, 317-364-4232
Pubs: *Journal for an Injured Son* (Lockhart Pr, 1991),
*Kenyon Rev, Massachusetts Rev, Prairie Schooner, Poetry
East, Fine Madness.*

Karen I. Jaquish									P
4817 W Arlington Park Blvd, Fort Wayne, IN 46835
Internet: kijaquish@prodigy.net
Pubs: *Southern Poetry Rev, Plainsongs, Connecticut
Poetry Rev, 11th Muse, Poet Lore, South Carolina Rev,
Nation, Hopewell Rev, Free Songs, Flying Island, Denver
Qtly.*

George Kalamaras									P
1202 Illsley Pl, Fort Wayne, IN 46807, 219-456-3151
Internet: kalamara@ipfw.edu
Pubs: *Beneath the Breath* (Tilton Hse Pr, 1988), *Heart
Without End* (Leaping Mountain Pr, 1986), *Best American
Poetry: Anth* (S&S, 1997), *Chariton Rev, Epoch, Sulfur,
New Letters, Iowa Rev.*

Margaret Kingery									W
4103 N Redding Rd, Muncie, IN 47304-1338, 317-289-5022
Pubs: *Dark Horse* (Ball State U, 1997), *The Whirlwind*
(Samisdat Pr, 1979), *South Dakota Rev, Hopewell Rev,
Texas Rev, Confrontation, Kansas Qtly, Prairie Schooner,
Earth's Daughters, Thema, Emrys Jrnl.*

Haven Koontz										P
2700 S Whitney Rd, Selma, IN 47383, 317-288-0145
Pubs: *Hopewell Rev, Flying Island, Sycamore Rev, Arts
Indiana, Indiannual.*

Tom Koontz										P
Ball State Univ, Muncie, IN 47306-8584, 317-285-8584
Internet: 00twkoontz@wp.bsu.edu
Pubs: *In Such a Light* (Mississinewa Pr, 1996), *Charms*
(Barnwood Pr, 1983), *Black Fly Rev, Hopewell Rev,
Birmingham Poetry Rev, Flying Island, PBQ.*

Karen Kovacik										P
1325 North Central, #6, Indianapolis, IN 46202
Pubs: *Return of the Prodigal* (Poetry Atlanta Pr, 1991), *A
Gathering of Poets: Anth* (Kent State U Pr, 1992),
Salmagundi, Beloit Poetry Jrnl, Confrontation.

Marcia H. Kruchten									W
442 S Maple St, Orleans, IN 47452, 812-865-2663
Pubs: *Too Many Parents, The Ghost In The Mirror*
(Willowisp Pr, 1996, 1996), *Indianapolis Woman, Writer's
Digest, Prim-Aid.*

D. E. Laczi										P
805 S 9th St, Lafayette, IN 47905, 317-742-2539
Internet: midwayog@wcic.cioe.com
Pubs: *Tears in the Fence, New Stone Circle, Black Buzzard
Rev, Oyez Rev, Maverick Pr, Phoebe, Metis, Pacific Coast
Jrnl, Sistersong, Kentucky Writing, Piedmont Literary Rev,
Onion River Rev.*

Roslyn Rosen Lund									W
9220 East Prairie Rd, Apt #410, Evanston, IN 602031644
Pubs: *Her Face in the Mirror: Anth* (Beacon Pr, 1995), *Loss
of the Ground-Note: Anth* (Clothespin Fever Pr, 1992),
Prism Intl, Crosscurrents, Ascent, Descant, Other Voices.

John Matthias										P
Univ Notre Dame, Notre Dame, IN 46556, 219-239-7226
Internet: john.e.matthias.1@nd.edu
Pubs: *Swimming at Midnight, Beltane at Aphelion* (Swallow
Pr, 1995, 1995), *TriQuarterly, Salmagundi, ACM, Southern
Rev, Stand.*

John A. McCluskey, Jr.								W
Indiana Univ, Memorial Hall, #31, Bloomington, IN 47401
Pubs: *Mr. America's Last Season Blues* (LSU, 1983), *Black
American Literary Forum, Southern Rev, Callaloo.*

Joan McIntosh										P
213 Wakewa Ave, South Bend, IN 46617, 219-232-4502
Pubs: *Lake Michigan Shore, Branch & Shadow Branch*
(Writer's Center of Indianapolis, 1997, 1982), *Cumberland
Poetry Rev, Connecticut River Rev, Shenandoah.*

Howard McMillen									W
Indiana State Univ, Terre Haute, IN 47809, 812-237-3168
Pubs: *The Many Mansions of Sam Peeples* (Viking, 1972),
Literary Mag Rev, Gambling Times, Win Magazine.

Brent Michael									P&W
1513 East Market St Apt 3, New Albany, IN 47150,
812-949-1963
Internet: bsm@aye.net
Pubs: *Chance Mag, Struggle, Twisted Savage, Mount Olive
Rev, Atom Mind, Curmudgeon, Jefferson Rev, Appalachian
Heritage.*

Roger Mitchell									P
1010 E 1st St, Bloomington, IN 47401, 812-332-1045
Pubs: *Braid* (The Figures, 1997), *The Word For Everything,
Adirondack* (BkMk Pr, 1996, 1988), *Clearpond* (Syracuse
U, 1991), *A Clear Space on a Cold Day* (Cleveland State U
Pr, 1986), *New England Rev, NAW, Ohio Rev, Crazyhorse,
Denver Qtly, Farmer's Market.*

Neil Myers										P
901 N Chauncey, West Lafayette, IN 47906, 317-743-9806
Pubs: *The Blade of Manjusri* (Sun Moon Bear, 1989), *All
That, So Simple* (Purdue U Pr, 1980).

Susan Neville W
Butler Univ, 4600 Sunset Ave, Box 135, Indianapolis, IN
46208, 317-940-9676
Internet: sneville@thomas.butler.edu
　　Pubs: *Indiana Winter* (Indiana U Pr, 1999), *In The House of
　　Blue Lights* (Notre Dame Pr, 1998), *Invention of Flight* (U
　　Georgia Pr, 1984), *NAR, Boulevard, Georgia Rev,
　　Sycamore Rev, Crazyhorse, Mid-American Rev.*

William O'Rourke W
Univ Notre Dame, Notre Dame, IN 46556, 219-631-7377
Internet: william.a.o'rourke.1@nd.edu
　　Pubs: *Campaign America '96: The View From the Couch,
　　Notts* (Marlowe & Co., 1997, 1996), *Signs of the Literary
　　Times* (SUNY, 1993), *Nation, ACM, Hopewell Rev.*

Harry Mark Petrakis W
80 E Rd, Dune Acres, Chesterton, IN 46304, 219-787-8283
　　Pubs: *Empirical Evidence* (U Georgia Pr, 1992), *Paris Rev,
　　APR, Poetry, Georgia Rev, Threepenny Rev, Virginia Qtly
　　Rev.*

Roger Pfingston P
4020 Stoutes Creek Rd, Bloomington, IN 47404,
812-339-2482
Internet: snapshot@bluemarble.net
　　Pubs: *Something Iridescent* (Barnwood Pr, 1987), *The
　　Party Train: Anth* (New Rivers Pr, 1996), *Inheriting the
　　Land: Anth* (U Minnesota Pr, 1993), *Yankee.*

Richard Pflum P
1473 Shannon Ave, Indianapolis, IN 46201-1758,
317-356-2048
Internet: drahcir@indy.net
　　Pubs: *A Strange Juxtaposition of Parts* (Writers' Ctr Pr of
　　Indianapolis, 1995), *A New Geography of Poets: Anth* (U
　　Arkansas Pr, 1992), *Flying Island, Hopewell Rev.*

Michael Joseph Phillips P
238 N Smith Rd #25, Bloomington, IN 47408-3188,
812-336-2530
　　Pubs: *Dreamgirls* (Cambric, 1989), *Selected Love Poems*
　　(Wm. Hackett, 1980), *Massachusetts Rev, Nation.*

Fran Quinn P
599 W Westfield Blvd #38, Indianapolis, IN 46208,
317-259-9096
　　Pubs: *The Goblet Crying For Wine* (Ally Pr, 1995), *At The
　　Edge of The Worlds* (Presada Pr, 1994).

Ernest Sandeen P
17831 Ponsha St, South Bend, IN 46635, 219-272-7728
　　Pubs: *A Later Day, Another Year, Selected Poems* (Notre
　　Dame, 1989, 1977).

Scott Russell Sanders W
1113 E Wylie St, Bloomington, IN 47401
Internet: sanders1@indiana.edu
　　Pubs: *Writing From The Center* (Indiana U Pr, 1995),
　　Staying Put, Secrets of the Universe (Beacon Pr, 1993,
　　1991), *Harper's, Omni, Georgia Rev, NAR.*

Valerie Sayers W
Univ Notre Dame, Notre Dame, IN 46617, 219-631-7160
　　Pubs: *Brain Fever, The Distance Between Us, Who Do You
　　Love* (Doubleday, 1996, 1996, 1991).

John Sherman P
4175 Central Ave, Indianapolis, IN 46205, 317-923-6775
Internet: shermco@compuserve.com
　　Pubs: *America Is A Negro Child: Race Poems* (Mesa Verde
　　Pr, 1981), *Dying: A Book of Comfort: Anth* (Doubleday,
　　1996), *Xavier Rev, Indiannual, Arts Indiana.*

Dennis Sipe P
4897 W Watertower Rd, Austin, IN 47401, 812-794-2201
　　Pubs: *My Days Are Stray Dogs That Won't Come When I
　　Call* (LongRod Pr, 1993), *Black Fly Rev, Louisville Rev,
　　American Writing, Wind, Permafrost.*

R. E. Smith W
520 Terry Ln, West Lafayette, IN 47906, 317-743-1074
　　Pubs: *Unknown Texas: Anth* (Macmillan, 1988), *South By
　　Southwest: Anth* (U Texas Pr, 1986), *Concho River Rev,
　　Chariton Rev, Descant, Texas Rev.*

Maura Stanton P&W
Indiana Univ, Ballantine Hall 442, English D, Bloomington, IN
47405, 812-855-1296
Internet: stanton@indiana.edu
　　Pubs: *Life Among the Trolls* (Carnegie Mellon, 1998), *Tales
　　of the Supernatural* (Godine, 1988), *The Country I Come
　　From* (Milkweed Edtns, 1988), *Ploughshares, Crazyhorse,
　　APR, Southern Rev, Paris Rev, Crab Orchard Rev.*

Felix Stefanile P
103 Waldron St, West Lafayette, IN 47906, 765-743-0530
　　Pubs: *The Dance At St. Gabriel's* (Story Line Pr, 1995), *The
　　Unsettling of America: Anth* (Penguin, 1994), *Sewanee
　　Rev, Hudson Rev, Formalist, Dark Horse, Poetry, Sparrow.*

Bronislava Volkova P
926 Commons Dr, Bloomington, IN 47401, 812-339-3618
Internet: volkova@indiana.edu
　　Pubs: *Shattered Worlds* (Votobia, 1995), *Courage of the
　　Rainbow* (Sheep Meadow, 1993), *The Deaf & Dumb Hand*
　　(Pm D, 1993), *Metamorphoses, Visions, Poetry East,
　　Nimrod, Midwest Poetry Rev, Witness.*

Elizabeth Weber P
4771 Stansbury Ln, Indianapolis, IN 46254
　　Pubs: *Small Mercies* (Owl Creek, 1984), *Puerto del Sol,
　　Florida Rev, 6ix.*

Henry Weinfield P
1113 N St. Joseph, South Bend, IN 46617, 219-288-7648
Pubs: *Sonnets Elegiac And Satirical, In The Sweetness Of New Time* (House of Keys, 1982, 1980), *Best American Poetry, Pequod, Denver Qtly, Talisman.*

Joanna H. Wos W
8148 Lieber Rd, Indianapolis, IN 46260, 317-255-6086
Internet: jhwriter@indy.net
Pubs: *A House of Butter* (Writers Center Pr, 1998), *Loss of the Groundnote* (Clothespin Fever Pr, 1992), *Flash Fiction: Anth* (Norton, 1992), *Malahat Rev, Kalliope, Permafrost, Webster Rev, MacGuffin, Quarterly West.*

Marguerite Young P&W
2506 Knollwood Dr, Indianapolis, IN 46208-2188

IOWA

Nina Barragan W
3880 Owl Song Ln SE, Iowa City, IA 52240-9044, 319-351-4700
Pubs: *The House on Via Gambito, No Peace at Versailles* (New Rivers Pr, 1991, 1991), *B'nai B'rith Intl Jewish Monthly.*

Marvin Bell P
1416 E College St, Iowa City, IA 52245, 319-337-5217
Internet: marvin-bell@uiowa.edu
Pubs: *Wednesday: Selected Poems 1966-1997* (Ireland; Salmon Pub, 1998), *Ardor: The Book of the Dead Man, Vol 2, The Book of the Dead Man* (Copper Canyon, 1997, 1994), *A Marvin Bell Reader* (Middlebury/U Pr of New England, 1994), *Poetry, New Yorker, APR.*

Virginia Bensheimer P
Route 1, Box 68, Macedonia, IA 51549
Pubs: *Visions, Green's Mag, The Little Mag, Urthkin, Long Pond Rev, Truely Fine.*

Frederick Bock P
Embassy Manor Care Center, 200 S 8th Ave E, Newton, IA 50208
Pubs: *The Fountains Of Regardlessness* (Macmillan, 1961), *Ascent, Poetry, Antaeus, Iowa Rev.*

Michael Borich P
1308 Vermont St, Waterloo, IA 50702, 319-232-0275
Pubs: *Nana's Ark* (Thomas Nelson, 1984), *A Different Kind of Love* (HR&W, 1984).

Jerry Bumpus W
619 Church St Suite 127, Ottumwa, IA 52501
Pubs: *The Civilized Tribes* (U Akron Pr, 1995), *Dawn of the Flying Pigs* (Carpenter Pr, 1992), *Esquire, Paris Rev, Partisan Rev, Yellow Silk, December Mag.*

Daniel Campion P
1700 E Rochester Ave, Iowa City, IA 52245, 319-337-2067
Pubs: *Calypso* (Syncline, 1981), *Ascent, Borderlands, Light, Poetry, Slant, Poet Lore.*

Rick Christman W
6601 Lincoln Ave, Des Moines, IA 50322, 515-276-9317
Pubs: *Falling in Love at the End of the World, The Party Train: Anth* (New Rivers Pr, 1998, 1996), *Descant, River Oak Rev, Indiana Rev, River City, Red Rock Rev, Permafrost, The Alembic.*

Robert Dana P
1466 Westview Dr, Coralville, IA 52241, 319-354-2171
Internet: robertdana@aol.com
Pubs: *What I Think I Know: New & Selected Poems, Yes, Everything* (Another Chicago Pr, 1994, 1994), *Georgia Rev, High Plains Literary Rev.*

Irma Dovey P
1224 13th St NW #321, Cedar Rapids, IA 524052404, 319-363-1966
Pubs: *Long About Tuesday* (Dovey, 1989), *Lyrical Iowa: Anths* (Iowa Poetry Association, 1995, 1994, 1990), *Midwest Chaparral, Thirteen, Quickenings, Story Friends.*

Jim Dunlap P
2830 Brattleboro #2, Des Moines, IA 503114008, 515-279-3540
Internet: writer23@juno.com
Pubs: *Entwined in Wonder* (Cedar Bay Pr, 1996), *Mindful Of Poetry* (Jelling Pr, 1996), *Word Magic* (Fine Arts Pr, 1991), *Mobius, Dream Intl Qtly, Infinity Limited, Mind In Motion, Prophetic Voices, Candelabrum, Plainsongs, Stand Alone, Lyrical Iowa, Potpourri.*

Gary Eller W
1243 24th St, Ames, IA 50010, 515-232-4654
Internet: gbe4@aol.com
Pubs: *Thin Ice and Other Risks* (New Rivers, 1994), *Flyaway, Other Voices, Crescent Rev, River City, Sidewalks, The New Press.*

Jocelyn Emerson P
Univ of Iowa, 308 EPB, Iowa City, IA 52242
Pubs: *Carolina Qtly, Colorado Rev, Common Lives/Lesbian Lives, Cosmos, Denver Qtly, The Journal, Seneca Rev, Sojourner, NAW.*

William Ford P
1808 Morningside Dr, Iowa City, IA 52245
Pubs: *Poetry, Pennsylvania Rev, Three Rivers Poetry Jrnl.*

Jorie Graham P
Univ Iowa, Iowa City, IA 52240, 319-353-4986
Pubs: *Erosion, Hybrids Of Plants And Of Ghosts* (Princeton, 1983, 1980), *APR, Antaeus.*

Phillip H. Hey   P
2750 Malloy Rd, Sioux City, IA 51103, 712-277-2811
Internet: hey@briar-cliff.edu
   Pubs: *A Change of Clothes* (Celestial Light, 1989), *Voices
   on the Landscape: Anth* (Loess Hills Pr, 1996), *Zone 3,
   Art/Life, Briar Cliff Rev.*

Jan D. Hodge   P
Morningside College, Sioux City, IA 51106, 712-274-5265
Internet: jdhoo5@alpha.morningside.edu
   Pubs: *Poems to Be Traded for Baklava* (Onionhead, 1997),
   Things Taking Shape (Harold's Pr, 1992), *Voices On the
   Landscape: Anth* (Loess Hills Pr, 1996), *South Coast
   Poetry Rev, Black Bear Rev, Beloit, ELF.*

Carole Johnston   P&W
Box 55, Onawa, IA 51040, 712-423-3982
   Pubs: *Early Iowa Schoolhouses* (Quixote Pr, 1993), *Cat of
   Many Colors* (Tiger Moon Pr, 1992), *English Jrnl, Decision,
   Ideals, New Writer, Alive Now!.*

Donald Justice   P
338 Rocky Shore Dr, Iowa City, IA 52246
   Pubs: *Orpheus Hesitated Beside the Black River* (Anvil Pr,
   1998), *New and Selected Poems* (Knopf, 1995).

Juliet Yli-Mattila Kaufmann   P
428 Clark St, Iowa City, IA 52240, 319-351-0969
   Pubs: *Cold Pastoral* (Virgil Burnett & Robert Williams,
   1974), *Lake Effect, Chicago Rev, Rochester Rev.*

Theodore Krieger   P
403 8th Ave, Charles City, IA 506162309, 515-228-2270
   Pubs: *Novitiate* (Unified Pub, 1987), *Bearing It Alone*
   (Ansuda, 1980), *Spoon River Qtly, Poetry Now, Sou'wester,
   Pteranodon, Pawn Rev.*

Rustin Larson   P
501 North C St, Fairfield, IA 52556, 515-472-1370
Internet: rlarson@lisco.com
   Pubs: *Voices on the Landscape: Anth* (Loess Hill Pr, 1996),
   *Iowa Rev, Cimarron Rev, William & Mary Rev, Passages
   North, The New Yorker, Boundary 2, Poetry East, Indiana
   Rev, America.*

Todd Lieber   W
789 Jesup St, Indianola, IA 50125, 515-961-7691
   Pubs: *Crazyhorse, Sycamore Rev, Nimrod, Mss., Missouri
   Rev, Yale Rev.*

Lucille Gripp Maharry   P
300 N Sumner Ave, Creston, IA 50801
   Pubs: *Decision, Sunday Digest, Secret Place, Delta Kappa
   Gamma Bulletin, Bible Advocate, Evangel, Green's Mag,
   One Hundred Words, Minnesota Monthly, Poetpourri,
   Buffalo Spree.*

Julie McDonald   W
2802 E Locust St, Davenport, IA 52803, 319-355-7246
   Pubs: *My Brother, Grant Wood* (State Historical Society of
   Iowa, 1993), *Young Rakes* (East Hall Pr, 1991), *Nils
   Discovers America* (Penfield, 1990).

James McKean   P
1164 E Court St, Iowa City, IA 52240, 509-586-8977
   Pubs: *Headlong* (U Utah Pr, 1987), *Ironwood, Poetry
   Northwest, Seneca Rev, California Qtly, Iowa Rev.*

Gordon W. Mennenga   W
1805 Windsor Ct, Iowa City, IA 52245, 319-338-7255
   Pubs: *Oxford Mag, Folio, NAR, Foothills Qtly, Seems, Seven.*

Chuck Miller   P
PO Box 2814, Iowa City, IA 52244, 319-335-9223
   Pubs: *How in the Morning* (Spirit That Moves Us Pr, 1989),
   From Oslo (Friends Pr, 1988), *Harvestors* (Coffee Hse Pr,
   1984).

Eleanora Miller   P
208 SW Church St, Leon, IA 50144, 515-446-4401
   Pubs: *Lyrical Iowa: Anth* (Iowa Poetry Assn, 1992), *A Song of
   Myself: Anth* (CSS Pub, 1987), *Polestar, Sandcutters, Cats.*

Nancy Price   P&W
Univ Northern Iowa, Cedar Falls, IA 50614, 319-273-2821
   Pubs: *Night Woman* (Pocket Bks, 1992), *Sleeping With The
   Enemy* (S&S, 1987), *An Accomplished Woman* (Coward
   McCann Geoghegan, 1979).

John Quinn   P
PO Box 847, Cedar Falls, IA 50613-0847
   Pubs: *The Wolf Last Seen* (Pacific House Bks, 1987), *Easy
   Pie* (Buttonmaker, 1986), *Interim, College English, Laurel
   Rev, Hudson Rev, Puerto del Sol.*

James Calvin Schaap   W
Dordt College, English Dept, Sioux Center, IA 51250,
712-722-6250
Internet: jschaap@dordt.edu
   Pubs: *The Secrets of Barneveld Calvary, In the Silence
   There Are Ghosts* (Baker Bks, 1997, 1995), *Called to Die*
   (Eerdmans, 1994), *Prairie Schooner, Other Side, Image,
   Wind, Poet & Critic.*

Ann Struthers   P&W
503 Forest Dr SE, Cedar Rapids, IA 52403, 319-362-3764
   Pubs: *The Alcott Family Arrives* (Coe Rev Pr, 1993),
   Stoneboat & Other Poems (Pterodactyl Pr, 1988), *Poetry,
   Hudson Rev, American Scholar, Iowa Woman.*

Adrienne Su P
PO Box 630, Iowa City, IA 522440630, 207-778-7071
Internet: ajsu@aol.com
> Pubs: *Middle Kingdom* (Alice James Bks, 1997), *Aloud: Anth* (Holt, 1994), *Massachusetts Rev, Prairie Schooner, Epoch, Greensboro Rev, A Gathering of the Tribes, Interim, Mid-American Rev.*

James Sutton P
4324 Kingman Blvd, Des Moines, IA 50311-3418, 515-255-7031
Internet: jamessutton@juno.com
> Pubs: *Minnesota Rev, Phi Delta Kappan, College English, Teacher, Stand Alone.*

Jody Swilky P
Drake Univ, 2707 University Ave, Des Moines, IA 50312, 515-271-2853
> Pubs: *A City Of Fences* (La Huerta Pr, 1977), *NAR, Mid-American Rev, Chelsea, New Boston Rev, Yale Rev, Raccoon, Ohio Rev, Missouri Rev, Georgia Rev.*

Thomas Swiss P
Drake Univ, English Dept, Des Moines, IA 50311, 515-271-3777
> Pubs: *Measure* (U Alabama, 1986), *Ploughshares, American Scholar, Sewanee Rev.*

Fred Truck P
4225 University, Des Moines, IA 50311, 515-255-3552
> Pubs: *Art Engine Texts* (Electric Bank, 1989), *Simulation Stimulation* (Art Com Electronic, 1986).

Melvin Wilk P
3013 Terrace Dr, Des Moines, IA 50312, 515-255-3346
> Pubs: *In Exile* (BkMk Pr, 1979), *Mss., New Yorker, Poetry, Massachusetts Rev.*

Frederic Will P
617 7th St N, Mt Vernon, IA 52314

Valorie Broadhurst Woerdehoff P
3246 St. Anne Dr, Dubuque, IA 52001, 319-556-3534
Internet: vwoerde@loras.edu
> Pubs: *Haiku World: An Intl Anth* (Kodansha America Inc, 1996), *Haiku Moment: Anth* (C.E. Tuttle Co., 1993), *Midwest Haiku: Anth* (High/Coo Pr, 1992), *Modern Haiku, Frogpond, Cottonwood Rev, Spoon River, Iowa Woman, 100 Words, Cicada.*

Sarah Wormhoudt P
10 Arbor Hill Cir, #33, Iowa City, IA 52245-3829, 319-351-5062
> Pubs: *Angels, Words and Wayward Beasts* (Pine Glen Pr, 1982), *Embers, Poem.*

Ray A. Young Bear P
751 Meskwaki Rd, Tama, IA 52339
Internet: blkeagle@pcpartner.net
> Pubs: *Black Eagle Child, Remnants of the First Earth* (Grove, 1997, 1996), *The Invisible Musician* (Holy Cow! Pr, 1990), *Winter of the Salamander* (H&R, 1980), *The Best American Poetry: Anth* (Scribner, 1996), *Ploughshares, Akwekon.*

KANSAS

Marie A. Asner P
9000 W 82 Pl, Overland Park, KS 66204
> Pubs: *Angels* (Maka, 1998), *The Tree of Life* (Kindred Spirit Pr, 1996), *Man of Miracles II: The Followers* (New Spirit Pr, 1994), *An Inquiring Mind* (Green Meadow Pr, 1993), *Prairie Woman, Rockford Rev, Clavier, Poet, Poetpourri, Domestique, Metro Voice.*

Thomas Fox Averill W
Washburn Univ, 1700 College, Topeka, KS 66621, 913-231-1010
Internet: zzaver@washburn.edu
> Pubs: *Seeing Mona Naked* (Watermark, 1989), *Prize Stories 1991: O. Henry Award: Anth* (Doubleday, 1991), *The Best of The West #4: Anth* (Norton, 1991), *Cimarron Rev, Cottonwood, DoubleTake, Greensboro Rev.*

Gar Bethel P
212 N Iowa, Winfield, KS 67156, 316-221-0939
> Pubs: *Small Wonder, Dust, Rivers and Stars* (Point Riders Pr, 1996, 1992), *Fresh Eggs* (Wythe Hse Pr, 1992).

Donald Caswell P
421 N 19 St, Kansas City, KS 66102-4101, 913-341-4633
> Pubs: *The Boy That Was Made Out of Wood* (Wellberry Bks, 1991).

G. W. Clift W
Kansas State Univ, Manhattan, KS 66506, 913-532-6716
> Pubs: *Bill Made Up A Point of History* (BkMk Pr, 1994), *Illinois Rev, Borderlands, Wind, Uncle, Vanderbilt Rev, Union Street Rev, Salad, Kansas Qtly, Fiction Rev, Bakunin.*

Kay L. Closson P
2033 S Dellrose St, Wichita, KS 67218-5107, 316-681-3248
> Pubs: *Smith, Pulpsmith, Newsart, Taurus, Occasional Rev, Dog River Rev, Ms., Ghost Dance.*

Marilyn Coffey P&W
305 W 15 St, Hays, KS 67601-3719, 913-628-5376
> Pubs: *Great Plains Patchwork* (Iowa State U, 1989), *Marcella* (Quartet, 1976), *Atlantic, Natural History, Ms..*

Victor Contoski   P
4110 W 12 St, Lawrence, KS 66049, 913-842-5303
Pubs: *A Kansas Sequence* (Cottonwood-Tellus, 1983),
Names (New Rivers, 1979).

Marjorie Culver   P
8027 W 113 St, Overland Park, KS 66210, 913-362-2912
Pubs: *Turn West at Jefferson* (Potpourri Pub Co., 1993), *A
Garden of Cucumbers* (Mid-America Pr, 1977), *Passager,
Missouri Poets, DeKalb Literary Arts.*

Celia A. Daniels   P
1521 SW College Ave, Topeka, KS 66604
Pubs: *Fissures* (Singular Speech Pr, 1993), *Midwest Qtly,
Cottonwood Rev, English Jrnl, Kansas Qtly, Spoon River
Qtly, Inscape, Z-Misc.*

A. A. Dewey   P
PO Box 154, Eudora, KS 66025-0154, 913-842-1782
Pubs: *Heartland II: Poets Of The Midwest: Anth* (Northern
Illinois U Pr, 1975), *Hanging Loose.*

Fred Dings   P
1817 N Doreen, Wichita, KS 67206, 316-691-1202
Pubs: *Roses, Coals* (U South Carolina Pr, 1997), *After the
Solstice: Anth* (Orchises Pr, 1993), *Poetry, Paris Rev, New
Republic, New Yorker, Western Humanities Rev.*

Elizabeth Dodd   P
Kansas State Univ, Manhattan, KS 66506, 913-532-6716
Pubs: *Like Memory, Caverns* (NYU Pr, 1992), *Tar River
Poetry, Seneca Rev, Ascent, Crab Orchard Rev,
Crazyhorse, High Plains Literary Rev.*

Carolyn Doty   W
Univ Kansas, 1630 Barker, English Dept, Lawrence, KS
660443765, 785-843-6254
Internet: cdoty@kuhub.cc.ukans.edu
Pubs: *Whisper* (Scribner, 1992), *What She Told Him, Fly
Away Home, A Day Late* (Viking, 1985, 1982, 1980).

Harley Elliott   P
328 E Beloit, Salina, KS 67401, 913-827-2807
Pubs: *The Monkey of Mulberry Pass* (Woodley Pr, 1991),
The Citizen Game (Basilisk Pr, 1988), *Darkness at Each
Elbow* (Hanging Loose Pr, 1981).

James P. Girard   W
11 Circle Dr, Newton, KS 67114, 316-283-1798
Pubs: *The Late Man* (Atheneum, 1993), *A Killing in Kansas*
(Fawcett, 1991), *Snake Nation Rev, Black Warrior Rev,
Virginia Qtly Rev, Penthouse.*

Albert Goldbarth   P
Wichita State Univ, Wichita, KS 67208, 316-683-6191
Pubs: *Marriage, And Other Science Fiction* (Ohio State U Pr
1994), *Across The Layers: Poems Old And New* (U Georgia
Pr, 1993), *New Yorker, Poetry, Paris Rev, Georgia Rev.*

James Gunn   W
2215 Orchard Ln, Lawrence, KS 66049, 913-864-3380
Internet: jgunn@falcon.cc.ukans.edu
Pubs: *The Joy Machine* (Pocket Bks, 1996), *Inside Science
Fiction* (Borgo, 1992), *The Road to Science Fiction #5: Anth*
(White Wolf Pub, 1998), *Analog, Sci Fi Age.*

Jeanine Hathaway   P&W
Wichita State Univ, Box 14, Wichita, KS 67260-0014,
316-978-3130
Pubs: *Motherhouse* (Hyperion, 1993), *Georgia Rev, Ohio
Rev, New Orleans Rev, Poetry Northwest, Kansas Qtly.*

Michael Hathaway   P
702 N Prairie, St John, KS 675761516, 316-549-6156
Pubs: *Between the Cracks* (Daedalus Publishing Co, 1997),
Ratboy, Etc., Joyful Noise: Anth (Kings Estate Pr, 1994, 1996),
Excerpt (Mutated Viruses Pr, 1989), *Pearl, Nerve Cowboy,
Cripes!, Hodge Podge, Medicinal Purposes, Minotaur.*

Stephen Hathaway   W
Wichita State Univ, Wichita, KS 67208, 316-689-3130
Pubs: *A Kind of Redemption* (Louisiana State U, 1990),
Accent On Fiction, Itinerary Four, Kansas Qtly.

Steve F. Heller   W
Kansas State Univ, Manhattan, KS 66506, 913-532-6716
Pubs: *The Automotive History of Lucky Kellerman*
(Doubleday, 1989), *Chariton Rev.*

Steven Hind   P
Washburn Univ, 1700 SW College, Topeka, KS 66621
Pubs: *In a Place with No Map* (Woodley Pr, 1997), *That Trick
of Silence* (Ctr for Kansas Studies, 1990), *Anth of Magazine
Verse & Yearbook of American Poetry* (Monitor, 1997).

Jonathan Holden   P
Kansas State Univ, Denison Hall, English Dept, Manhattan,
KS 66506, 785-532-0388
Internet: jonhold@ksu.edu
Pubs: *The Sublime* (U Texas Pr, 1996), *American Gothic* (U
Georgia Pr, 1992), *Against Paradise* (U Utah, 1990), *The
Name of the Rapids* (U Massachusetts, 1985).

Robert B. Hutchinson   P&W
Regency Health Care Center, 915 McNair, Halstead, KS
67056, 316-835-2276
Pubs: *Standing Still* (Eakins, 1971), *Poetry, Harper's, Atlantic.*

Kenneth Irby   P
Univ of Kansas, Lawrence, KS 66045, 913-864-3118
Pubs: *Call Steps* (Station Hill/Tansy, 1992), *A Set, Catalpa*
(Tansy, 1983, 1977), *Orexis* (Station Hill, 1981).

Dan Jaffe   P
10315 W 119 Terr, Overland Park, KS 66213, 816-444-2152
Pubs: *Saturday Rev, Chouteau Rev, Mademoiselle, Prairie
Schooner, New Letters, Focus Midwest.*

Michael L. Johnson									P
1621 N 1st St, Baldwin City, KS 660066901, 785-594-4823
	Pubs: *XY Files: Poems on the Male Experience: Anth*
	(Sherman Asher, 1997), *Violence and Grace* (Cottonwood
	Pr, 1993), *Owen Wister Rev, Rhino, Oregon Rev, Chouteau
	Rev, Midwest Qtly, Sequoia, Roanoke Rev, The Literary
	Rev.*

Ronald Johnson									P
3901 SW Drury Ln, Topeka, KS 66604-2413, 913-272-2035
	Pubs: *Ark* (drive he said pr, 1996), *Eyes & Objects* (Jargon
	Pr, 1976), *Conjunctions, Sulfur, Chicago Rev, Sagetrieb,
	Parnassus, Occident.*

Denise Low									P
1916 Stratford Rd, Lawrence, KS 66044, 913-841-5757
Internet: dlowweso@ross1.cc.haskell.edu
	Pubs: *Touching the Sky, Tulip Elegies* (Penthe, 1994,
	1993), *Vanishing Point* (Mulberry Pr, 1991), *Starwater*
	(Cottonwood Pr, 1988), *Kestrel, Controlled Burn, Sycamore
	Roots, Midwest Qtly, Chariton Rev, Stiletto.*

Jim McCrary									P
1041 Kentucky, Lawrence, KS 66044, 913-841-8370
	Pubs: *West of Mass* (Tansy Bks, 1992), *And/Or* (e.g. Pr,
	1991).

Stephen Meats									P&W
2310 E 8 St, Pittsburg, KS 66762, 316-231-2998
Internet: smeats@pittstate.edu
	Pubs: *Looking For The Pale Eagle: Poems, Kansas Stories:
	Anth* (Woodley, 1994, 1989), *Leftbank Rev, The Quarterly,
	Blue Unicorn, Poetry East, Tampa Rev.*

W. R. Moses									P
314 Denison Ave, Manhattan, KS 66502, 913-537-1954
	Pubs: *Edges, Memoir, Double View* (Juniper Pr, 1994,
	1992, 1984).

Michael Paul Novak									P
Saint Mary College, Leavenworth, KS 66048, 913-682-5151
	Pubs: *Whatever Flames Upon The Night* (Potpourri, 1994),
	A Story to Tell (BkMk Pr, 1990), *Kenyon Rev,
	Confrontation, Hudson Rev, New Letters, Kansas Qtly.*

David Ohle									W
911 Hilltop Dr, Lawrence, KS 66044, 913-842-3310
	Pubs: *Motorman* (Knopf, 1972), *Paris Rev, Esquire,
	Harper's, Caliban, Missouri Rev.*

Emanuela O'Malley									P
Box 279 Nazareth, Concordia, KS 66901, 913-243-2113
	Pubs: *Cloud of Darkness: The Pain of Apartheid*
	(Winston-Derek, 1990).

Tom Page									P
PO Box 4446, Wichita, KS 67204-0446, 316-775-5287
Internet: thomas.page@twsubbs.twsu.edu
	Pubs: *Going Places With the Kids, The Fort Scott Poems*
	(Free Soil Pr, 1997, 1994), *The Name of the Place* (John
	Brown Pr, 1989), *Minnesota Rev, Phoenix, Caprice, Viet
	Nam Generation, Blue Light, Pemmican, Galley Sail.*

Cynthia S. Pederson									P
1521 College Ave, Topeka, KS 66604, 913-232-0332
	Pubs: *Fissures* (Singular Speech Pr, 1993), *Roll Along:
	Poems on Wheels Anth* (Margaret A. McElderry Bks, 1993),
	Great River Rev, Kansas Qtly, River Styx.

Antonia Quintana Pigno									P
Kansas State Univ, Eisenhower Hall, Manhattan, KS 66506,
785-532-1924
Internet: apigno@ksu.edu
	Pubs: *Old Town Bridge, La Jornada* (Zauberberg Pr, 1987,
	1987), *Kenyon Rev, Kansas Qtly, Puerto del Sol, Cyphens,
	Writers' Forum, Ploughshares.*

Trish Reeves									P
5307 W 51 St, Roeland Park, KS 66205-1242
	Pubs: *Returning the Question* (Cleveland State U Pr, 1988),
	Ploughshares, Ironwood, Passages North.

R. Stephen Russell									P
Wichita State Univ, Wichita, KS 67208, 316-689-3130
	Pubs: *Paris Rev, Carleton Miscellany, Denver Qtly, Kansas
	Qtly, Midwest Qtly, Impact.*

Mark Scheel									P&W
5738 Maple Dr, Shawnee Mission, KS 66202, 913-262-4281
	Pubs: *Poet, Nostalgia, Kansas Qtly, Cincinnati Poetry Rev,
	Facet, Telescope.*

G. S. Sharat Chandra									P&W
9916 Juniper, Overland Park, KS 66207
	Pubs: *Sari of the Gods* (Coffee Hse Pr, 1998), *Family of
	Mirrors* (BkMk Pr, 1993), *Poetry, London Mag, Poetry Rev,
	Partisan Rev, New Criterion, Missouri Rev.*

Ann Slegman									P&W
6531 Overbrook, Shawnee Mission, KS 66208, 913-362-7885
Internet: slegdog@aol.com
	Pubs: *Return to Sender* (Helicon Nine Edtns, 1995), *Coal
	City Rev, New Letters, Helicon Nine.*

Roderick Townley									P&W
PO Box 13302, Shawnee Mission, KS 66282, 913-381-1984
	Pubs: *Final Approach* (Countryman Pr, 1986), *Minor Gods*
	(St. Martin's Pr, 1977), *Paris Rev, NAR, New Letters,
	Western Humanities Rev.*

Wyatt Townley P
PO Box 13302, Shawnee Mission, KS 66282, 913-381-1984
Pubs: *Perfectly Normal* (The Smith, 1990), *JM: A
Remembrance: Anth* (Academy of American Poets, 1996),
Paris Rev, Western Humanities Rev, New Letters.

Patricia Traxler P&W
PO Box 1216, Salina, KS 67402-1216, 785-827-3954
Pubs: *Forbidden Words* (U Missouri Pr, 1994), *Best
American Poetry: Anth* (Scribner, 1994), *Kenyon Rev,
Ploughshares, Nation, Glimmer Train, Ms., Agni.*

Donna Trussell P&W
7520 Briar, Prairie Village, KS 662084325, 913-648-1632
Internet: touche@aol.com
Pubs: *Texas Bound Book II: Anth* (Southern Methodist U,
1998), *Growing Up Female: Anth* (Mentor/Penguin, 1993),
New Stories From the South: Anth (Algonquin Bks, 1990),
*TriQuarterly, Poetry, Chicago Rev, Poetry Northwest, New
Letters, Massachusetts Rev.*

KENTUCKY

Rebecca Bailey P&W
2465 Rock Fork Rd, Morehead, KY 40351, 606-783-1811
Pubs: *How They Met Themselves, Three Women Alone in
the Woods* (Trillium, 1992, 1992), *Jrnl of Kentucky Studies,
Asheville Poetry Rev, Emrys Jrnl, Now & Then.*

Barbara Banks P&W
Boone's Creek Rd, Lancaster, KY 40444, 606-792-4692
Pubs: *Home Girls: Anth* (Kitchen Table, 1982), *Keeping
The Faith: Anth* (Fawcett, 1974).

Garry Barker P&W
269 Gravel Lick Branch Rd, Dreyfus, KY 40385-9526,
606-986-0597
Internet: garry_barker@berea.edu
Pubs: *Notes From A Native Son, Appalachia Inside Out:
Anth* (U Tennessee Pr, 1995, 1995), *Groundwater: Anth*
(Lexington Pr, 1992), *Appalachian Heritage.*

Joy Bale Boone P
PO Box 188, Elkton, KY 42220-0188

Pat Carr W
Western Kentucky Univ, English Dept, Bowling Green, KY
42101, 502-745-5998
Pubs: *Sonahchi* (Cinco Puntos Pr, 1994), *Our Brother's
War* (Sulgrave Pr, 1993), *Southern Rev, Southern Mag,
Texas Monthly, Kansas Qtly, Arizona Qtly.*

Rick Clewett P
Eastern Kentucky Univ, Lexington, KY 40475, 606-272-4247
Pubs: *Salome, Encore, Bitterroot, Confrontation, Poetry
Mag, Pudding, Samisdat, Microcosm.*

Jenny Galloway Collins P&W
HC 87, Box 1400, Thornton, KY 41858, 606-633-0952
Pubs: *A Cave And A Cracker* (Elkhorn Pub, 1996),
Blackberry Tea (Appalapple Productions, 1988),
Appalachian Heritage, Back Home in Kentucky.

Guy Davenport P&W
621 Sayre Ave, Lexington, KY 40508, 606-257-6972
Pubs: *Charles Burchfield's Seasons* (Pomegranate Bks,
1994), *A Table of Green Fields* (New Directions, 1993),
Antaeus, New Criterion, Yale Rev.

Judith DeGroote P
Box 72, 2nd St, Corydon, KY 42406, 502-533-6753
Pubs: *Visions Intl, Blue Unicorn, Phoenix, Birmingham
Poetry Rev, South Florida Poetry Rev, Thema, Another
Small Mag.*

Kim Edwards W
126 Arcadia Pk, Lexington, KY 40503

Normandi Ellis W
2369 Sullivan Ln, Frankfort, KY 40601, 502-223-0402
Internet: normandi@aol.com
Pubs: *Voice Forms* (Watersign Pr, 1998), *Sorrowful
Mysteries* (Arrowood Bks, 1991), *Agni Rev, Appalachian
Heritage, Southern Humanities Rev, Between C & D, New
Blood, Mediphors, Wind.*

John D. Engle, Jr. P
6395 Old Highway 519, West Liberty, KY 41472-8906,
606-743-7576
Pubs: *Tree People, Laugh Lightly II* (Engle's Angle, 1990,
1989), *Writer's Digest, Lake Effect, Poetpourri, Byline,
Science of Mind, Unity.*

Jane Gentry P
340 Morgan St, Versailles, KY 40383, 606-873-5700
Internet: jgvanc00@ukcc.uky.edu
Pubs: *A Garden In Kentucky* (LSU Pr, 1995), *Cries of the
Spirit* (Beacon Pr, 1990), *Elvis in Oz: Hollins Writing
Program Anth* (U Pr Virginia, 1992), *American Voice.*

Sarah Gorham P
Sarabande Books, 2234 Dundee Rd, Ste 200, Louisville, KY
40205, 502-458-4028
Internet: sarabandes@aol.com
Pubs: *The Tension Zone* (Four Way Bks, 1996), *Don't Go
Back to Sleep* (Galileo Pr, 1989), *Paris Rev, Antaeus,
Nation, Poetry, Georgia Rev, Ohio Rev, Grand Street.*

Jonathan Greene P
PO Box 475, Frankfort, KY 40602-0475, 502-223-1858
Internet: jgnomon@aol.com
Pubs: *Of Moment, Inventions of Necessity* (Gnomon, 1998),
The Man Came to Haul Stone (Dim Gray Bar Pr, 1995), *Les
Chambres des Poetes* (French Broad, 1990), *Idylls* (North
Carolina Wesleyan, 1990), *Longhouse, Hummingbird.*

Robert Gregory   P
404 Harrodswood Rd Apt 15, Frankfort, KY 40601,
502-227-5779
Internet: rdgreg0@pop.uky.edu
    Pubs: *Boy Picked Up The Wind* (Bluestem Pr, 1992),
    Interferences (Poltroon Pr, 1988), *Caliban, Oasis, Central
    Park, Exquisite Corpse, River Styx, ACM, Mississippi Mud,
    Willow Springs, Painted Bride, Poetry Flash, American
    Letters.*

James Baker Hall   P&W
617 Dividing Ridge Rd S, Sadieville, KY 40370,
606-234-6481
    Pubs: *Fast Signing Mute* (Larkspur Pr, 1993), *Stopping on
    the Edge to Wave* (Wesleyan, 1988), *New Yorker, Poetry,
    Ploughshares, Hudson Rev, Paris Rev.*

Wade Hall   P
1568 Cherokee Rd, Louisville, KY 40205, 502-451-5516
Internet: adeway@aol.com
    Pubs: *Hell-Bent For Music: The Life of Pee Wee King, The
    Rest Of The Dream: Black Odyssey of Lyman Johnson* (U
    Pr Kentucky, 1996, 1988), *Jefferson Rev.*

Marcia L. Hurlow   P
Asbury College, Wilmore, KY 403901198, 606-858-3511
Internet: marcia.hurlow@asbury.edu
    Pubs: *Dangers of Travel* (Riverstone, 1994), *Aliens Are
    Intercepting My Brain Waves* (State Street Pr, 1991),
    *Nimrod, Nebraska Rev, Poetry, Poetry Northwest, Poetry
    East, Poetry Wales, Chicago Rev, Another Chicago
    Magazine, Crab Creek Rev, Malahat Rev.*

Ann Jonas   P
2425 Ashwood Dr, Louisville, KY 40205, 502-459-0701
    Pubs: *a MERTON concelebration* (Ave Maria Pr, 1981),
    Ipso Facto: an Intl Poetry Anth (Hub Pub, 1975), *American
    Voice, Poetry Rev, Orbis, Kentucky Poetry Rev, Prism Intl,
    The Quest, Southern Rev, Southern Humanities Rev,
    Colorado Qtly, Carolina Qtly.*

Jane Wilson Joyce   P
Centre College, Danville, KY 40422, 606-236-5211
    Pubs: *Appalachian Heritage, Sing Heavenly Muse!, Laurel
    Rev, Appalachian Jrnl, Poet Lore.*

Tamara Kennelly   W
Rt 3, Owenton, KY 40359, 502-484-5215

Kenneth King   P
PO Box 720, Somerset, KY 42502, 606-423-3553
    Pubs: *Poetry Northwest, College English, Northwest Rev,
    Kansas Qtly, Appalachian Jrnl.*

Wallace E. Knight   W
819 16th St, Ashland, KY 41101, 606-324-0867
    Pubs: *Lightstruck* (Little, Brown, 1979), *The Literature Of
    The South* (Scribner, 1979), *Atlantic.*

Karen S. Lee   P
12892 Hwy 42, Walton, KY 41094
    Pubs: *SPA's Finest: Anth* (Southern Poetry Assoc, 1992),
    Riding on Golden Wings: Anth (Geryon Pr, 1989), *Feelings,
    Kentucky Explorer, The Journal, Tucumcari Literary Rev,
    Instructor Mag, Southern Poetry Assoc, Rio Grande Pr,
    Poetry Only, Poetry Pr.*

George Ella Lyon   P&W
913 Maywick Dr, Lexington, KY 40504, 606-278-3956
Internet: sglyon@lex.infi.net
    Pubs: *Counting on the Woods, With a Hammer For My
    Heart* (DK Ink, 1998, 1997), *Here and Then* (Orchard,
    1994), *Catalpa* (Wind Pubs, 1993), *The United States of
    Poetry: Anth* (Harry N. Abrams, 1996), *Mossy Creek
    Reader, Booklinks, Louisville Mag.*

Leah Maines   P
PO Box 76181, Highland Heights, KY 410760181,
606-441-0043
Internet: lmaines@aol.com
    Pubs: *Looking to the East with Western Eyes* (Finishing
    Line Pr, 1998), *California Qtly, Flyaway, Nebo, This: A
    Serial Rev, A New Song, Sunday Suitor, Upsouth, Licking
    River Rev, Owen Wister Rev.*

Kristina McGrath   P&W
1214 Cherokee Rd, Louisville, KY 40204
    Pubs: *House Work* (Bridge Works, 1994), *Pushcart Prize
    XIV: Anth* (Pushcart Pr, 1989), *Iowa Rev, Paris Rev,
    Kenyon Rev, American Voice, Yale Rev, Harper's.*

Jim Wayne Miller   P&W
1512 Eastland Dr, Bowling Green, KY 42104-3314,
502-842-0049
    Pubs: *His First, Best Country* (Gnoman Pr, 1993),
    Newfound (Orchard Bks, 1989), *Appalachian Jrnl,
    Appalachian Heritage, Southern Folklore, ACE Mag.*

R. Meir Morton   P
3923 Central Ave, Louisville, KY 40218, 502-458-7396
    Pubs: *Pegasus, Reaching, Brentwood Bee.*

Joseph Napora   P
2205 Moore St, Ashland, KY 41101, 606-324-1953
Internet: napora@ramlink.net
    Pubs: *The Walam Olum* (Greenfield Rev Pr, 1990), *Bloom
    Blood* (Bottom Dogs Pr, 1988), *Texture, First Intensity,
    Asheville Poetry Rev, Small Press Rev.*

Sena Jeter Naslund   W
Univ Louisville, Louisville, KY 40208, 502-588-6801
    Pubs: *Ice Skating at the North Pole* (Ampersand, 1989),
    Michigan Qtly Rev, Georgia Rev, American Voice.

Gurney Norman   W
43 1/2 Richmond Ave, Lexington, KY 40502, 606-269-9594
    Pubs: *Divine Rights Trip, Kinfolks* (Gnoman Pr, 1990,
    1990), *Crazy Quilt* (Larkspur, 1990).

Rose Orlich   P
1345 Knapp Ave, Morehead, KY 40351, 606-784-6384
   Pubs: *The Rosewood Poems* (Small Poetry Pr, 1996),
   Rose-Bloom At My Fingertips (Adams Pr, 1981), *Wind,
   Catholic School Jrnl, Poet.*

Phil Paradis   P
Northern Kentucky Univ, Literature & Language Dept,
Highland Heights, KY 41076, 606-572-6636
   Pubs: *Along the Path* (White Fields, 1996), *Something of
   Ourselves* (Cedar Creek Pr, 1994), *Poetry, Cimarron Rev,
   American Scholar, Poet & Critic, Tar River Poetry.*

Lee Pennington   P&W
Univ Kentucky, PO Box 1036, Louisville, KY 40202,
502-584-0181
   Pubs: *Appalachian Quartet, The Scotian Women* (Arion Pr,
   1984, 1984), *Writer's Digest, Wind.*

Nolan Porterfield   W
564 Boyce Fairview Hd, Alvaton, KY 42122-9648
   Pubs: *Country: The Music & the Musicians* (Abbeville Pr,
   1988), *Sewanee Rev, NAR, Harper's.*

Bruce Rogers   P
5615 Ridgecrest Rd, Louisville, KY 40218
   Pubs: *Starships* (Whippoorwill Pr, 1973), *Minnesota Rev,
   New Salt Creek Reader, Handsel, Dust.*

Daryl Rogers   P
PO Box 24198, Lexington, KY 40524, 606-277-8601
   Pubs: *Wormwood Rev, Slipstream, Clutch, Sepia, Blank
   Gun Silencer, Caprice, New York Qtly, Berkeley Rev of
   Bks, Atom Mind, Parting Gifts, Poetry Motel.*

Jeffrey Skinner   P&W
Univ Louisville, College of Arts & Sciences, Louisville, KY
40292, 502-588-5920
   Pubs: *The Company of Heaven* (U Pitt Pr, 1992), *Real
   Toads In Imaginary Gardens* (Chicago Rev Pr, 1991), *Last
   Call: Anth* (Sarabande Bks, 1997), *Atlantic.*

Frederick Smock   P&W
Bellarmine College, 2001 Newburg Rd, Louisville, KY 40205,
502-452-8000
   Pubs: *Gardencourt: Poems* (Larkspur Pr, 1997), *Iowa Rev,
   Poetry, International Qtly, Poet & Critic.*

Philip St. Clair   P
P.O. Box 189, Rush, KY 411680189, 606-474-0219
Internet: pstclair@unix.ashcc.uky.edu
   Pubs: *Acid Creek* (Bottom Dog Pr, 1997),
   Little-Dog-Of-Iron, At The Tent Of Heaven (Ahsahta Pr,
   1985, 1984), *Harper's, Cincinnati Poetry Rev, Gettysburg
   Rev, Greensboro Rev, Minnesota Rev, Ploughshares,
   Black Warrior Rev, Chattahoochee Rev, Shenandoah.*

Alex Stiber   P
9504 Tiverton Way, Louisville, KY 40222, 502-339-0730
   Pubs: *The American Voice, Stone Country, Long Pond
   Rev, The Fiddlehead, Event, Louisville Rev.*

Martha Bennett Stiles   W
861 Hume-Bedford Rd, Paris, KY 40361, 606-987-4158
   Pubs: *Lonesome Road* (Gnomon Pr, 1998), *Kate of Still
   Waters, Sarah The Dragon Lady* (Macmillan, 1990, 1986),
   *Esquire, TriQuarterly, Georgia Rev, Virginia Qtly Rev,
   Missouri Rev, New Orleans Rev, Horsemen's Jrnl.*

James Still   P&W
Univ Press Kentucky, PO Box 865, Hindman, KY 41822,
606-785-0721
   Pubs: *An Appalachian Mother Goose, Sporty Creek, Jack
   and the Wonder Beans, The Wolfpen Notebooks, The
   Wolfpen Poems, Pattern of a Man, The Run for the Elbertas*
   (U Pr Kentucky Pr, 1998, 1998, 1996, 1991, 1986, 1976,
   1953), *American Voice.*

George Strange   W
347 Wolf Gap Rd, Berea, KY 40403, 606-986-1257
   Pubs: *Lullwater Rev, Descant, Appalachian Heritage,
   Habersham Rev.*

Jane Stuart   P&W
1000 W-Hollow, Greenup, KY 41144, 606-473-7294
   Pubs: *Journeys* (Summit Poetry Pr, 1998), *Moon Over
   Miami* (Poetry Forum Pr, 1995), *Passage Into Time* (Big
   Easy Pr, 1994), *Bloodroot: Anth* (U Kentucky Pr, 1998),
   *Byron Poetry Works, White River Qtly, Afterthoughts, Poet's
   Challenge, American Voice.*

Joe Survant   P
Western Kentucky Univ, Bowling Green, KY 42101,
502-842-4511
Internet: joe.survant@wku.edu
   Pubs: *Anne & Alpheus, 1842-1882* (U Arkansas Pr, 1996),
   We Will All Be Changed (State Street Pr, 1995), *American
   Voice, Nimrod, Cincinnati Poetry Rev.*

Dorothy Sutton   P&W
115 Southland Dr, Richmond, KY 40475, 606-623-6071
Internet: d.sutton@acs.eku.edu
   Pubs: *Grolier Prize Poems: Anth* (Grolier Bks, 1991),
   Chester H. Jones Natl Poetry Competition Winners: Anth
   (Chester H. Jones Fdn, 1991), *Poetry Ireland Rev,
   Southern Rev, Virginia Qtly Rev, Antioch Rev, American
   Voice, Prairie Schooner.*

Lynne Taetzsch   W
105 Country East, Morehead, KY 40351, 606-784-6905
Internet: l.taetzsch@morehead-st.edu
   Pubs: *Hippo, Eotu, Pacific Rev, Asylum, Atticus Rev, Potato
   Eyes.*

Richard Taylor   P&W
335 Holt Ln, Frankfort, KY 40601, 502-223-5775
    Pubs: *Earth Bones* (Gnomon Pr, 1979), *Girty* (Turtle Island
Foundation, 1977).

Jeff Worley   P
136 Shawnee Pl, Lexington, KY 40503, 606-277-0257
    Pubs: *Natural Selections* (w/Lance Olsen; Still Waters Pr,
1993), *Other Heart* (Devil's Millhopper, 1991), *NER, New
Virginia Rev, Missouri Rev, Boulevard, Yankee.*

LOUISIANA

Thomas Atkins   W
Univ New Orleans, Drama & Communications Dept, New
Orleans, LA 70148, 504-286-6345
    Pubs: *The Blue Man, The Fire Came By* (Doubleday, 1978,
1976).

Fredrick Barton   W
63 Versailles Blvd, New Orleans, LA 70125, 504-861-1668
    Pubs: *With Extreme Prejudice* (Villard/Random Hse, 1993),
The El Cholo Feeling Passes (Dell, 1988), *Xavier Rev,
Louisiana Literature99, Cresset.*

John Biguenet   P&W
Loyola Univ, Box 50, English Dept, New Orleans, LA 70118,
504-865-2474
Internet: biguenet@loyno.edu
    Pubs: *Foreign Fictions* (Vintage, 1978), *NAR, Witness,
Ploughshares, Boulevard, Threepenny Rev, Georgia Rev,
Granta, Story.*

Thomas Bonner, Jr.   P&W
25 West Park Pl, New Orleans, LA 70124, 504-488-9014
    Pubs: *Poiesis, Potpourri, Maple Leaf Rag, New Laurel Rev,
White Jade, Negative Capability, Old Hickory Rev,
Bluegrass Literary Rev, Louisiana English Jrnl.*

Vance Bourjaily   W
Louisiana State Univ, Baton Rouge, LA 70803, 504-388-2862
    Pubs: *Old Soldier* (Donald I. Fine, 1990), *The Great Fake
Book* (Wiedenfeld & Nicolson, 1987), *A Game Men Play*
(Dial, 1980).

Catharine Savage Brosman   P
1550 2nd St #7-I, New Orleans, LA 70130, 504-899-6016
    Pubs: *Passages, Journeying From Canyon de Chelly*
(Louisiana State U, 1996, 1990), *Abiding Winter* (R. L.
Barth, 1983), *Sewanee Rev, Southern Rev, American
Scholar, New England Rev, Southwest Rev.*

Robert Olen Butler   W
McNeese State Univ, Box 92012, Lake Charles, LA 70609
Internet: www.webdelsol.com/butler
    Pubs: *The Deep Green Sea, They Whisper, A Good Scent
From A Strange Mountain* (Henry Holt, 1998, 1994, 1992),
*Esquire, New Yorker, GQ, Paris Rev, Harper's, Sewanee
Rev, Hudson Rev, Virginia Qtly Rev.*

Maxine Cassin   P
2131 General Pershing St, New Orleans, LA 70115,
504-891-3458
    Pubs: *The Other Side of Sleep* (Portals Pr, 1995), *Turnip's
Blood* (Sisters Grim Pr, 1985), *Chicago Rev, New Republic,
New Orleans Rev, New York Times.*

Andrei Codrescu   P&W
Louisiana State Univ, Baton Rouge, LA 70803
    Pubs: *Messiah* (S&S, 1999), *Ay, Cuba!* (St. Martin's Pr,
1999), *Alien Candor: Collected Poems* (Black Sparrow,
1998), *Road Scholar* (Hyperion, 1993), *The Muse Is Always
Half-Dressed In New Orleans.*

Carlos Colon   P
185 Lynn Ave, Shreveport, LA 71105, 318-868-8932
Internet: ccolon@smlnet.sml.lib.la.us
    Pubs: *Nothing Inside* (Proof Pr, 1996), *Haiku Compass*
(Haiku Intl Society, 1994), *Red Moon Anth 1997* (Red Moon
Pr, 1998), *Haiku World: Anth* (Kodansha Intl, 1996),
*Modern Haiku, Writer's Digest, Frogpond, Golf Digest,
Piedmont Literary Rev, Reader's Digest.*

Peter Cooley   P
Tulane Univ, New Orleans, LA 70118, 504-862-8174
Internet: pjcooley@msn.com
    Pubs: *Sacred Conversations, The Astonished Hours, The
Van Gogh Notebook* (Carnegie Mellon, 1998, 1992, 1987),
*New Yorker, Atlantic, Poetry, Esquire, Nation, New
Republic.*

Moira Crone   W
Louisiana State Univ, Baton Rouge, LA 70808, 504-388-2987
    Pubs: *New Stories by Southern Women: Anth* (U South
Carolina Pr, 1989), *Boston Sunday Globe Mag, Southern
Rev.*

Joel Dailey   P
3003 Ponce De Leon St, New Orleans, LA 70119,
504-943-5198
    Pubs: *Release Window* (Semiquasi Pr, 1998), *Audience,
Ambience, Ambulance* (Blank Gun Silencer Pr, 1993),
Doppler Effects (Shockbox Pr, 1993), *American Poets Say
Goodbye to 20th Century: Anth* (Four Walls Eight Windows,
1996), *Exquisite Corpse.*

Tom Dent   P
Box 50584, New Orleans, LA 70150, 504-944-2412
    Pubs: *Blue Lights & River Songs* (Lotus Pr, 1982),
Magnolia Street (Edwards Publishing Co., 1976).

Jim Donahoe P
1380 Sigur Ave, Metairie, LA 70005, 504-833-3893

Don Keck DuPree P&W
PO Box 41188, Shreveport, LA 71134-1188
Pubs: *Chattahoochee Rev, Missouri Rev, Ploughshares, Southern Rev.*

Charles East W
1455 Knollwood Dr, Baton Rouge, LA 70808, 504-926-3304
Pubs: *Distant Friends And Intimate Strangers* (U Illinois Pr, 1996), *Where the Music Was* (HBJ, 1965), *Sewanee Rev, Mademoiselle, Yale Rev, Southern Rev.*

Daniel Mark Fogel P
Louisiana State Univ, Allen Hall, Baton Rouge, LA 70810, 504-388-3161
Pubs: *A Trick Of Resilience* (Ithaca, 1975), *Southern Rev, National Forum, Western Humanities.*

Ernest J. Gaines W
Univ Southwestern Louisiana, PO Box 44691, Lafayette, LA 70503, 318-232-2034
Pubs: *A Lesson Before Dying, A Gathering of Old Men* (Knopf, 1993, 1984).

Timothy Martin Gautreaux P&W
Southeastern Louisiana Univ, PO Box 889, Hammond, LA 70402, 504-549-5022
Internet: runner@i-ss.com
Pubs: *The Next Step In The Dance, Same Place, Same Things* (Picador/St. Martin's, 1998, 1996), *New Stories From The South: Anth* (Algonquin Pr, 1996), Harper's, Atlantic, GQ, Story, Massachusetts Rev, Virginia Qtly Rev.

Andrea Saunders Gereighty P
257 Bonnabel Blvd, Metairie, LA 70005-3738, 504-833-0641
Internet: ager80@worldnet.att.net
Pubs: *The Season of the Crane* (Gris Gris Pubs Pr, 1998), *Illusions and Other Realities* (Medusa Pr, 1974), *New Laurel Rev, Dalliance.*

Norman German P&W
108 McVay St, Lake Charles, LA 70605, 318-478-1285
Pubs: *No Other World* (Blue Heron Pr, 1992), *The Liberation of Bonner Child* (Aegina, 1992), *Hawaii Rev, Beloit Poetry Jrnl, Worcester Rev, Wisconsin Rev.*

John Gery P
Univ New Orleans, New Orleans, LA 701482315, 504-280-6133
Internet: jogeg@uno.edu
Pubs: *The Enemies of Leisure* (Story Line Pr, 1995), *Three Poems* (Lestat Pr, 1989), *The Burning of New Orleans* (Amelia Pr, 1988), *Iowa Rev, Kenyon Rev, Louisiana Literature, Paris Rev, Sparrow, West Branch, War Literature & the Arts, Southern Anth.*

Hedwig Irene Gorski PP
327 Clinton St, Lafayette, LA 70501-8101, 318-261-0239
Internet: hxg6638@usl.edu
Pubs: *Slow Paradise, Polish Gypsy with Ghost* (Shinebone Pr, 1998, 1998).

Lee Meitzen Grue P
New Laurel Review, 828 Lesseps St, New Orleans, LA 70117, 504-947-6001
Pubs: *Good Bye Silver, Silver Cloud* (Plain View Pr, 1994), *Inheritance of Light: Anth* (U North Texas Pr, 1996), *Ploughshares, Xavier Rev, Louisiana Literature, Quimera.*

Nancy C. Harris P
8418 Freret St, New Orleans, LA 70118, 504-861-7162
Internet: apewoman@poetic.com
Pubs: *The Ape Woman Story* (Pirogue, 1989), *From A Bend In the River: Anth* (Runagate Pr, 1998), *Maple Leaf Rag II: Anth* (Portals Pr, 1994), *Hawaii Rev, New Orleans Rev, Ellipsis, Negative Capability, Black Warrior Rev, Nightsun.*

Ava Leavell Haymon P
672 Nelson Dr, Baton Rouge, LA 70808, 504-766-4739
Pubs: *Why the Groundhog Fears Her Shadow* (March Street Pr, 1995), *Staving Off Rapture* (Flume Pr, 1994), *Built In Fear of Heat* (Nightshade Pr, 1994).

Don A. Hoyt P
RR 2 Box 107, Downsville, LA 71234, 318-644-2012
Pubs: *A New Kerygma* (Bootleg Pr, 1993), *Crossroads, Redneck Rev, Avra, Florida Rev, Whiskey Island, Oxford Mag, Pacific Rev, Pannus Index, MacGuffin.*

Joe C. Ireland P
410 Huntlee Dr, Algiers, LA 70131, 504-394-8003
Pubs: *Short Order* (New Orleans Poetry Forum, 1974), *The Smith, Dust, Bouillabaisse, Kumquat Meringue, Oxy.*

Rodger Kamenetz P
1209 Pine St, New Orleans, LA 70118-5218
Pubs: *The Jew in the Lotus* (Harper SF, 1994), *The Missing Jew: New & Selected Poems* (Time Being Bks, 1992), *New Republic, Grand Street, Prairie Schooner, Ploughshares.*

Julie Kane P
955 Laurie Ln, #1, St Gabriel, LA 70776, 504-642-5743
Internet: jebkane@aol.com
Pubs: *The Bartender Poems* (Greville Pr, 1991), *Body And Soul* (Pirogue Pub, 1987), *London Mag, Feminist Studies, Epoch, Mademoiselle, Negative Capability, Thema.*

Pinkie Gordon Lane P
2738 77 Ave, Baton Rouge, LA 70807, 504-356-3450
Pubs: *Girl at the Window* (LSU Pr, 1991), *Double Stitch: Black Women Write About Mothers and Daughters: Anth* (Beacon Pr, 1991).

David Madden   PP&P&W
LSU, Baton Rouge, LA 70803, 504-344-3630
Internet: madden@www.cwc.lsu.edu
  Pubs: *Sharpshooter* (U Tennessee Pr, 1996), *Revising
  Fiction* (NAL, 1988), *Southern Rev, New Letters,
  Gettysburg Rev, Kenyon Rev, Playboy.*

Carolyn Maisel   P
Univ New Orleans/Lakefront, New Orleans, LA 70148
  Pubs: *Witnessing* (L'Epervier Pr, 1978), *NAR, New Yorker,
  Choice.*

Leo Luke Marcello   P&W
PO Box 5508, Lake Charles, LA 70606
  Pubs: *Nothing Grows in One Place Forever* (Time Being
  Bks, 1998), *The Secret Proximity of Everywhere* (Blue
  Heron Pr, 1994), *Blackrobe's Love Letters* (Xavier Rev Pr,
  1994), *Uncommon Places: Anth* (Louisiana State U Pr,
  1998), *North Stone, Commonweal.*

Martha McFerren   P
2679 Verbena St, New Orleans, LA 70122, 504-944-2707
  Pubs: *Women in Cars* (Helicon Nine Edtns, 1992),
  Contours for Ritual (Louisiana State U Pr, 1988), *Georgia
  Rev, Southern Rev, Shenandoah, New Laurel Rev,
  Louisiana Literature, Poetry Northwest.*

Bryan T. McMahon   P
PO Box 743, Ponchatoula, LA 70454, 504-386-2877
  Pubs: *Kree* (New Voices Pr, 1971), *The Ponchatoula
  Times.*

Harold B. McSween   P&W
PO Box 12907, Alexandria, LA 71315, 318-442-3215
  Pubs: *Hampden-Sydney Poetry Rev, South Carolina Rev,
  Virginia Qtly Rev, Poet & Critic, Sewanee Rev, Southern
  Rev.*

Kay A. Murphy   P&W
"F" St. John Ct, New Orleans, LA 70119, 504-488-5552
  Pubs: *The Autopsy* (Spoon River Poetry Pr, 1985), *Fiction
  Intl, St. Andrews Rev, Poetry.*

James Nolan   P
925 Dauphine St, New Orleans, LA 70116, 504-522-5934
  Pubs: *What Moves Is Not The Wind, Why I Live In The
  Forest* (Wesleyan, 1980, 1974), *Georgia Rev, City Lights
  Rev, Southern Rev, Exquisite Corpse, Poetry, New Letters.*

Brenda Marie Osbey   P
c/o LSU Press, The French House, Baton Rouge, LA 70122
Internet: osbey@bellsouth.net
  Pubs: *All Saints: New and Selected Poems* (LSU Pr, 1997),
  Desperate Circumstance, Dangerous Woman (Story Line,
  1990), *In These Houses* (Wesleyan, 1988), *American
  Poetry Rev, Callaloo, American Voice, Georgia Rev,
  Southern Rev.*

Sue Owen   P
2015 General Cleburne Ave, Baton Rouge, LA 70810,
504-769-3449
  Pubs: *My Doomsday Sampler* (Louisiana State U Pr, 1999),
  The Book of Winter (Ohio State U Pr, 1988), *Harvard Mag,
  Iowa Rev, Massachusetts Rev, The Nation, Poetry,
  Southern Rev.*

Burton Raffel   P&W
203 Mannering Ave S, Lafayette, LA 70508, 318-232-4112
Internet: bnraffel@net-connect.net
  Pubs: *Founders Fury* (Pocket Bks, 1988), *Paris Rev,
  Michigan Qtly Rev, Literary Rev, Denver Qtly, Western
  Humanities Rev, North Atlantic Rev.*

Stan Rice   P
1239 1st St, New Orleans, LA 70130, 504-566-1544
  Pubs: *The Radiance of Pigs, Fear Itself, Singing Yet: New
  and Selected Poems* (Knopf, 1998, 1995, 1992), *Body of
  Work* (Lost Roads, 1983), *Some Lamb* (Figures, 1976),
  Whiteboy (Mudra, 1975).

Kalamu ya Salaam   P&W
Box 52723, New Orleans, LA 70152, 504-523-4443
  Pubs: *What is Life?* (Third World Pr, 1994), *Word Up: Black
  Poetry of the 80's From the Deep South: Anth* (Beans and
  Brown Rice, 1990), *African American Rev.*

Dave Smith   P&W
1430 Knollwood Dr, Baton Rouge, LA 70808, 504-923-0388
  Pubs: *Fate's Kite* (Louisiana State U Pr, 1996), *Night
  Pleasures* (Bloodaxe Bks, 1992), *Cuba Night* (Morrow,
  1992), *New Yorker, Atlantic, Yale Rev, Poetry, Georgia
  Rev.*

Don Ray Thornton   P
Thornton Publishing, 1504 Howard St, New Iberia, LA 70560,
318-364-2752
  Pubs: *Ascending, Mentor* (Thornton Pub, 1993, 1993), *A
  Walk on Water* (Cajun Pub, 1985), *Catalyst, Slipstream,
  Muse.*

Keith Veizer   W
825 Gallier St, New Orleans, LA 70117, 504-944-4649
  Pubs: *Intro, NAR, Sou'wester, Exquisite Corpse, Fell
  Swoop, Story Qtly, Pulpsmith.*

Jan Villarrubia   P
38 Crane, New Orleans, LA 70124, 504-288-0153
  Pubs: *Odd Fellows Rest* (Xavier Rev Pr, 1996), *Miz Lena's
  Backyard* (Dramatic Pub Co., 1994), *Mississippi Valley
  Rev, Third Wind, Literary Rev, Negative Capability.*

Bernice Webb   W
159 Whittington Dr, Lafayette, LA 70503, 318-234-5397
  Pubs: *Mating Dance, Spider Web* (Spider Pr, 1996, 1993),
  Born To Be A Loser (w/Johnnie Allan; Jadfel Pub Co.,
  1993), *Voices Intl.*

Leilah Wendell   P
5219 Magazine St, New Orleans, LA 70115-1858
   Pubs: *The Necromantic Ritual Book, The Complete Books
   of Azrael, Shadows in the Half-Light* (Westgate Pr, 1994,
   1992, 1989), *Carpe Noctem, Esoterra, Elegia.*

Tom Whalen   W
6109 Magazine St, New Orleans, LA 70118, 504-895-5619
   Pubs: *Elongated Figures* (Red Dust, 1991), *Northwest Rev,
   Fiction Intl, The Quarterly, NAR.*

Gail White   P
1017 Spanish Moss Ln, Breaux Bridge, LA 70517
   Pubs: *Landscape With Women* (Singular Speech Pr, 1998),
   All Night in the Churchyard (Proof-Rock, 1986), *A Formal
   Feeling Comes: Anth* (Story Line Pr, 1994), *The Formalist,
   Cape Rock, Cream City Rev, Hellas, Light, Midwest Qtly,
   Tennessee Qtly, The Lyric.*

Angus Woodward   W
1045 East River Oaks, Baton Rouge, LA 70815,
504-926-5213
Internet: awoodw@mailcity.com
   Pubs: *Dominion Rev, Laurel Rev, Innisfree, Soundings
   East, Habersham Rev, Gulf Stream, Louisiana Literature.*

Yictove   P
2832 St. Bernard Ave, New Orleans, LA 70119-2120
   Pubs: *D. J. Soliloquy* (Thrown Stone Pr, 1988).

Ahmos Zu-Bolton, II   P
1616 Marigny St, New Orleans, LA 70117, 504-949-1648
   Pubs: *The Widow Paris: A Folklore of Marie Laveau*
   (Copastetic, 1986), *Marquee, Black Voices.*

MAINE

Jonathan Aldrich   P
41 Oakhurst Rd, Cape Elizabeth, ME 04107, 207-799-6028
   Pubs: *The Death of Michelangelo* (Puckerbrush Pr, 1985).

Kate Barnes   P
432 Appleton Ridge Rd, Appleton, ME 04862
   Pubs: *Where the Deer Were* (Godine, 1994), *Crossing the
   Field* (Blackberry Bks, 1992), *Beloit Poetry Jrnl, Harper's,
   New England Rev, Kenyon Rev, New Yorker.*

Ingrid Bengis   W
Box 421, Stonington, ME 04681
   Pubs: *The Writer & Her Work* (Norton, 1980), *I Have Come
   Here To Be Alone* (S&S, 1977).

Steve Benson   P
RR 1, Box 614, Surry, ME 046845709
   Pubs: *Roaring Spring* (Zasterle Pr, 1998), *Reverse Order*
   (Potes & Poets, 1991), *Blue Book* (The Figures, 1988),
   *Poetics Jrnl, Language, Aerial, Zyzzyva, o.blek, Avec,
   Crayon, This, Writing, Raddle Moon.*

Jim Bishop   P
PO Box 1448, Bucksport, ME 04416
   Pubs: *Mother Tongue* (Contraband Pr, 1976).

Alice Bolstridge   P&W
Maine School of Science & Math, 77 High St, Limestone, ME
04750, 207-325-3303
Internet: bolstridgea@mssm.org
   Pubs: *Sleeping With Dionysus: Anth* (Crossing Pr, 1998),
   An Intricate Weave: Anth (Iris Edtns, 1997), *Cimarron,
   Cincinnati Poetry Rev, Slant, Kalliope, Passager, Magic
   Realism.*

Philip Booth   P
PO Box 330, Castine, ME 04421, 207-326-4644
   Pubs: *Lifelines, Pairs, Selves, Relations: Poems 1950-1985*
   (Penguin, 1999, 1994, 1990, 1986), *Trying to Say It* (U
   Michigan, 1996), *Georgia Rev, APR, DoubleTake, Poetry,
   Yale Rev, Beloit Poetry Jrnl.*

Myrna Bouchey   P
RR 1, Box 2285, Jonesport, ME 04649-9717
   Pubs: *Malahat, Niagara, Beloit, Hard Pressed, Heirs, Maine
   Times, Kennebec, Lakes & Prairies.*

Henry Braun   P
Box 84, Weld, ME 04285, 207-585-2218
   Pubs: *The Vergil Woods* (Atheneum, 1968), *Maine Speaks:
   Anth* (Maine Writers & Publishers, 1989), *Painted Bride
   Qtly, APR, Poetry, Massachusetts Rev.*

William Carpenter   P&W
Box 1297, Stockton Springs, ME 04981, 207-567-4172
Internet: carpenter@acadia.net
   Pubs: *A Keeper of Sheep* (Milkweed Edtns, 1994),
   Speaking Fire at Stones (Tilbury Hse, 1992), *Rain*
   (Northeastern U Pr, 1985).

Erleen J. Christensen   P&W
Rte 1, Box 2315, Unity, ME 04988
   Pubs: *Kennebec, Amelia, Wind, Prairie Schooner, Kansas
   Qtly, Cottonwood, Memphis State Rev.*

Robert M. Chute   P
85 Echo Cove Ln, Poland, ME 04274
   Pubs: *Androscoggin Too, Woodshed on the Moon*
   (Nightshade Pr, 1997, 1991), *Barely Time To Study Jesus*
   (Cider Pr, 1996), *Samuel Sewall Sails For Home* (Coyote
   Love Pr, 1986), *Beloit Poetry Jrnl, Literary Rev, Texas Rev,
   Cape Rock, Ascent, Cafe Rev.*

Roger L. Conover   P
55 Lambert Rd, Freeport, ME 04032
Pubs: *The Last Lunar Baedeker* (Jargon Pr, 1982), *Shenandoah, Ironwood, Montemora, Epoch.*

Paul G. Corrigan, Jr.   P
146 Denbow Rd, St Albans, ME 04971, 207-438-4651
Pubs: *At the Grave of the Unknown Riverdriver* (North Country Pr, 1992).

H. R. Coursen   P&W
Frog Prince Manor, 21 Toad's Landing, Brunswick, ME 04011, 207-725-2130
Pubs: *History Lessons, The Green of Spring* (Mad River 1998, 1997), *The Search for Archerland, Graves of the Poets* (EM Pr, 1994, 1993), *Tar River, Small Pond, Literary Rev, Hollins Critic, South Carolina Rev, Iconoclast.*

Louis Coxe   P
Box 5478, RD 5, Adams Rd, Brunswick, ME 04011

Alfred DePew   W
31 Pine St, Portland, ME 04102-3807
Pubs: *The Melancholy of Departure* (U Georgia Pr, 1991).

Kathleen Lignell Ellis   P
9 Harris Rd, Orono, ME 04473-1522, 207-581-3825
Internet: kathleen_ellis@umit.maine.edu
Pubs: *Red Horses* (Northern Lights, 1991), *The Eloquent Edge* (Acadia, 1989), *NER, Columbia, Antioch, NAR, Southwest Rev, New Letters, Beloit Poetry Jrnl.*

Theodore Enslin   P
RFD Box 289, Kansas Rd, Milbridge, ME 04658, 207-546-7636
Pubs: *Then, and Now: Selected Poems: 1943-1993* (National Poetry Foundation, 1998), *Skeins* (Origin-Longhouse, 1998), *The House of the Golden Windows, Love and Science* (Light and Dust Bks, 1993, 1990), *Conjunctions, Talisman, Furnitures.*

Welch D. Everman   W
123 Forest Ave, Orono, ME 04473, 207-866-7450
Pubs: *Who Says This* (U Southern Illinois Pr, 1988), *The Harry & Sylvia Stories* (Sun & Moon Pr, 1988).

Christopher Fahy   P&W
6 Mechanic St, Thomaston, ME 04861, 207-354-8191
Pubs: *The Fly Must Die* (Washington Inst for Creative Activity, 1993), *The King Is Dead, Tales of Elvis: Anth* (Delta, 1994).

Tom Fallon   P&W
226 Linden St, Rumford, ME 04276, 207-364-7237
Internet: http://www.exploremaine.com/ aopoetry/fallon/
Pubs: *The Man on the Moon* (Small-Small Pr, 1988), *Maine Speaks: Anth* (MWPA, 1991), *Panhandler, Black Fly Rev, Kennebec, Cafe Rev, Puckerbrush Rev.*

Rod Farmer   P
10 Anson St, Farmington, ME 04938, 207-778-9298
Internet: farmer@maine.maine.edu
Pubs: *Universal Essence* (Brunswick Pub Co., 1986), *ELF, Phase & Cycle, Riverrun, Webster Rev, Thorny Locust, Without Halos.*

Robert Farnsworth   P
19 Ware St, Lewiston, ME 04240, 207-784-0416
Internet: rfarnswo@bates.edu
Pubs: *Honest Water, Three Or Four Hills And A Cloud* (Wesleyan, 1989, 1982), *Southern Rev, New England Rev, Beloit Poetry Jrnl, Hudson Rev, Seneca Rev.*

Richard Flanagan   W
179 Covell Rd, Fairfield, ME 04937, 617-239-4256
Internet: flanagan@babson.edu
Pubs: *Last of the Hippies* (Paycock, 1984), *San Jose Studies, Earth's Daughters.*

Richard Foerster   P
PO Box 1040, York Beach, ME 03910-1040, 207-363-8220
Internet: rafoerster@aol.com
Pubs: *Trillium* (BOA Edtns, 1998), *Patterns of Descent, Sudden Harbor* (Orchises Pr, 1993, 1992), *Kenyon Rev, Southern Rev, Poetry, Gettysburg.*

Elaine Ford   W
Univ Maine, 304 Neville, Orono, ME 04469, 207-581-3834
Internet: elfin@nemaine.com
Pubs: *Life Designs* (Zoland, 1997), *Monkey Bay, Ivory Bright* (Viking, 1989, 1986), *Missed Connections* (Random Hse, 1983).

M. Ekola Gerberick   P
999 High St, Bath, ME 04530
Pubs: *Siirtolaisuus, Kansas Qtly, Passages North, Finnish Americana, Beloit Poetry Jrnl, Gravida.*

Richard Gillman   P&W
19 Federal St #1B, Brunswick, ME 04011, 207-725-9874
Pubs: *The Quotable Moose: A Contemporary Maine Reader Anth* (U Pr New England, 1994), *Sewanee Rev, New England Rev.*

Mitchell Goodman   P&W
RD 17, Temple, ME 04984, 207-778-3717
Pubs: *The End of It* (FSG, 1990), *More Light, A Life in Common* (Dog Ear Pr, 1989, 1984).

Paul Guernsey   W
1247 Middle Rd, Warren, ME 04864, 207-623-1940
Pubs: *Angel Falls* (S&S, 1990), *Unhallowed Ground* (Morrow, 1986).

Gunnar Hansen   P
PO Box 268, Northeast Harbor, ME 04662
Pubs: *True Coast* (Harpswell, 1991), *Mt. Desert: An Informal History* (Mt. Desert, 1989).

Anne Hazlewood-Brady   P
Box 534, Kennebunkport, ME 04046
    Pubs: *One To The Many* (Puckerbrush Pr, 1979), *The Cross, The Anchor & The Heart* (Victoria, 1976).

Nancy Heiser   W
25 Hemlock Rd, Brunswick, ME 04011, 207-725-4253
Internet: heiscoh@pwi.net
    Pubs: *Nightshade Nighstand Reader: Anth* (Nightshade Pr, 1995), *Seattle Rev, Potpourri, Footwork, Out of the Cradle.*

Lucille Iverson   P&W
133 North Main St, Morrill, ME 04952-9750, 207-342-5792
Internet: lucylake@hotmail.com
    Pubs: *We Become New* (Bantam, 1975), *Outrage Poems* (Know Inc., 1974), *Soho Weekly News, Connections, Sunbury.*

James Koller   P&W
PO Box 629, Brunswick, ME 04011, 207-371-2247
Internet: jindcjinak@aol.com
    Pubs: *Et Nous Les Os* (La Main Courante, 1996), *Dans La Gueule Du Loup* (AIOU, 1995), *AIOU, Gate, Active In Airtime, Copice Biancaneve, Doc*(k)s.

Sharon Kraus   P
c/o Alice James Books, 98 Maine St, Farmington, ME 04938, 207-778-7071
    Pubs: *Generation* (Alice James Bks, 1997), *Agni, TriQuarterly, Prairie Schooner, Mississippi Rev, Columbia: A Jrnl of Literature and Art.*

Diane Kruchkow   P
RR #1, Box 780, New Sharon, ME 04955
    Pubs: *Green Isle In The Sea* (December, 1986), *Stony Hills, Small Press News.*

Kris Larson   P
PO Box 189, East Machias, ME 04630, 207-255-6525
    Pubs: *Second Thoughts, Groundwork* (Salt-Works Pr, 1976, 1974), *The Egg, Opinion, Downeast Coastal Press.*

Gary Lawless   P
617 E Neck Rd, Nobleboro, ME 04555, 207-729-5083
    Pubs: *Caribouddhism, First Sight of Land* (Blackberry Bks, 1998, 1990), *Somewhere Inside The Shell Mound* (Bull Head, 1995), *Earth Prayers* (H&R, 1991), *Green Fuse, Wild Earth, Raise the Stakes, Beloit, Napalm Health Spa, Northern Forest Forum.*

Denis Ledoux   W
Soleil Press, 95 Gould Rd, Lisbon Falls, ME 042529707, 207-353-5454
Internet: memoirs@ime.net
    Pubs: *What Became of Them & Other Stories from Franco-America, Lives In Translation: Anth* (Soleil Pr, 1988, 1991), *Mountain Dance and Other Stories* (Coastwise Pr, 1990).

James Lewisohn   P
108 West St, #5, Bar Harbor, ME 04609, 207-288-4078
    Pubs: *Finkel, New & Selected Poems* (Horizon Pr, 1990), *New Yorker, New York Qtly, Sojourner.*

Carl Little   P
PO Box 273, Mount Desert, ME 04660, 207-288-5015
Internet: ckl@ecology.coa.edu
    Pubs: *13,000 Dreams Explained* (Nightshade Pr, 1992), *The Portable Moose: Anth* (U Pr New England, 1995), *Portland, Down East, Town & Country.*

Leni Mancuso   P
Box 303, Castine, ME 04421-0303, 207-326-9381
    Pubs: *Portfolio #6: "Rothko's Cave" & Others* (Puckerbrush Rev, 1998), *Trenton Rev, Beloit Poetry Jrnl, Puckerbrush Rev, CSM, Potato Eyes, Paideuma.*

Katherine McAlpine   P
11 Mitchell St, Eastport, ME 04631
    Pubs: *The Muse Strikes Back: Anth* (Story Line Pr, 1997), *Literature: The Human Experience: Anth* (St. Martin's Pr, 1997), *The Best Contemporary Women's Humor: Anth* (Crossing Pr, 1994), *Nation, Formalist, Sparrow, Dark Horse, Light, Hellas.*

James McKenna   P
5 Summer St, Augusta, ME 04330, 207-289-3661
    Pubs: *Zone 3, Potato Eyes, Negative Capability, The Ledge, Kennebec, Slant, WordWrights.*

Wesley McNair   P
1 Chicken St, Mercer, ME 04957, 207-587-4681
    Pubs: *Talking in the Dark, The Town of No & My Brother Running* (Godine, 1998, 1997), *Atlantic, Poetry, Iowa Rev, Sewanee Rev, Ploughshares, Gettysburg Rev.*

Mark Melnicove   P
132 Water St, Gardiner, ME 04345, 207-737-8116
Internet: thpub@aol.com
    Pubs: *Uncensored Guide to Maine* (Lance Tapley, 1984), *Advanced Memories* (Bern Porter, 1983), *Kennebec, Cold-Drill, Puckerbrush Rev.*

Robin Morgan   P
Edite Kroll Literary Agency, 12 Grayhurst Park, Portland, ME 04102
    Pubs: *Upstairs in the Garden: Selected Poems* (Norton, 1991).

Paul Nelson   P
HC 70, Box 1085, Machiasport, ME 04655
    Pubs: *The Hard Shapes of Paradise* (U of Alabama Pr, 1988), *Days Off* (U Pr of Virginia, 1982).

Edward Nobles   P
7 Orchard Hill Pkwy, Bangor, ME 04401, 207-973-3331
Internet: enobles@maine.edu
> Pubs: *Through One Tear* (Persea, 1997), *Boulevard,
> Denver Qtly, Gettysburg Rev, Paris Rev, Volt, Witness,
> Kenyon Rev.*

Katharine O'Brien   P
130 Hartley St, Portland, ME 04103
> Pubs: *Excavation & Other Verse* (Anthoensen Pr, 1967),
> *Sequences* (Houghton Mifflin, 1966).

Patricia O'Donnell   W
Univ Maine, Roberts Learning Center, Farmington, ME
04938, 207-645-4872
Internet: podonnell@maine.maine.edu
> Pubs: *The Quotable Moose: Anth* (New England Pr, 1994),
> *New Yorker, NAR, Agni, Short Story.*

Carolyn Page   P
PO Box 76, Troy, ME 04987, 207-948-3427
> Pubs: *Troy Corner Poems* (Nightshade Pr, 1994), *Barn
> Flight, Life on the Line: Anth* (Negative Capability, 1995,
> 1992), *Parnassus, Comstock Rev, Now and Then,
> Pembroke, One Trick Pony, Fiddlehead, Zone3.*

Arnold Perrin   P
PO Box 809, Union, ME 04862, 207-785-4355
> Pubs: *Noah* (East Coast Edtns, 1993), *View from Hill Cabin*
> (Northwoods Pr, 1979), *Puckerbrush Rev, Kennebec,
> Potato Eyes, Maine Life, CSM, The Sun.*

Mary Peterson   W
148 Pepperrell Rd, Kittery Point, ME 03905, 207-439-1640
> Pubs: *Mercy Flights* (U Missouri Pr, 1985), *StoryQtly, South
> Dakota Rev, NAR, Ms..*

Judith Rachel Platz   P
5 Atwood Ln, Brunswick, ME 04011, 207-725-0018
Internet: moosepnd@javanet.com
> Pubs: *A Gathering of Poets: Anth* (Kent State U Pr, 1992),
> *Cafe Rev, SlugFest, Maine Poets & Writers, Haight
> Ashbury Literary Jrnl, Milkweed Chronicle, Long Shot.*

J. A. Pollard   P&W
RFD #2, Eames Rd, Box 5115, Winslow, ME 04902,
207-873-6443
> Pubs: *The Ice Ladder* (Windswept Hse, 1987), *Haunted
> New England: Anth* (Yankee Bks, 1989), *Karamu, Amelia,
> Pozitzia, Amazing Stories, Pinehurst Jrnl.*

Sylvester Pollet   P
RR5, Box 3630, Winkumpaugh Rd, Ellsworth, ME
04605-9529, 207-667-2255
Internet: pollet@maine.maine.edu
> Pubs: *The Dandelion Sutras* (Backwoods Broadsides
> Chaplets, 1994), *Maine Speaks: Anth* (MWPA, 1989),
> *Exquisite Corpse, Poetry New York, New York Qtly,
> Bullhead.*

Bern Porter   P&W
22 Salmond St, Belfast, ME 04915
> Pubs: *Symbols* (Spoon Pr, 1994), *Less Than Overweight*
> (Plaster Cramp, 1993), *Sounds That Arouse Me* (Tilbury,
> 1992), *The Formalist.*

Patricia Smith Ranzoni   P
HCR 78, Box 173, Bucksport, ME 04416
Internet: pranzoni@aol.com
> Pubs: *Claiming* (Puckerbrush Pr, 1995), *Prayers to Protest:
> Anth* (Pudding Hse, 1998), *Starving Poets' Cookbook: Anth*
> (Free Lunch Arts Alliance, 1994), *Cafe Rev, Blueline, River
> Rev, Island Jrnl, Talus & Scree, Green Fuse, Poets On,
> Jeopardy.*

Kenneth Rosen   P
Univ Southern Maine, Portland, ME 04103, 207-780-4296
> Pubs: *Reptile Mind, Longfellow Square* (Ascenius Pr, 1993,
> 1993), *Paris Rev, Ploughshares, Western Humanities Rev,
> Massachusetts Rev, Poetry.*

John Rosenwald   P
Box 389, South Andover, ME 04216-0389, 207-392-1872
Internet: rosey@beloit.edu
> Pubs: *Descant, Wisconsin Poets Calendar, Beloit Poetry
> Jrnl, Kennebec, Kansas Qtly, Literary Rev.*

Ira Sadoff   P&W
53 Middle St, Hallowell, ME 04347, 207-872-3297
Internet: i_sadoff@colby.edu
> Pubs: *Grazing* (U Illinois Pr, 1998), *An Ira Sadoff Reader* (U
> New England Pr, 1992), *Emotional Traffic* (Godine, 1990),
> *APR, New Yorker, Antaeus, Paris Rev.*

Lee Sharkey   P&W
RR 2, Box 4122, Farmington, ME 04938-9501, 207-293-2390
Internet: sharkey@maine.maine.edu
> Pubs: *To a Vanished World, First Moments* (Puckerbrush
> Pr, 1995, 1987), *The Eloquent Edge: 15 Maine Women:
> Anth* (Acadia Pr, 1990), *Cream City Rev.*

Betsy Sholl   P
24 Brentwood St, Portland, ME 04103, 207-774-9414
> Pubs: *The Red Line* (U Pitt Pr, 1992), *Pick a Card*
> (Coyote/Bark Pub, 1991), *Rooms Overhead* (Alice James
> Bks, 1986).

Alix Kates Shulman   W
Long Island, ME 04050
> Pubs: *In Every Woman's Life, On the Stroll, Burning
> Questions* (Knopf, 1987, 1981, 1978).

Pam Burr Smith   P&W
Star Rte 3, Box 365, Bath, ME 04530, 207-443-9390
> Pubs: *Air Fish* (Omega Cat Pr, 1993), *Black Fly Rev, Kansas
> Qtly, Kennebec, Cafe Rev, Slow Dancer, Coyote's Jrnl.*

Karen South P

PO Box 235, Matinicus Island, ME 04851, 207-366-3425
Pubs: *National Forum, Abraxas, Hampden-Sydney Poetry Rev, Ploughshares, MPR.*

Debra Spark W

Colby College, 5284 Mayflower Hill Dr, Waterville, ME 04901-8852, 207-872-3257
Internet: daspark@colby.edu
Pubs: *Coconuts for the Saint* (Faber & Faber, 1996), *On the Tail of the Dog Star* (Chikuma Shobo, 1990), *Twenty Under Thirty: Anth* (Scribner, 1996), *Passages North, Boston Globe Mag, Epoch, Agni, NAR, Ploughshares, Esquire, New York Times Travel Mag, Yankee.*

Martin Steingesser PP&P

28 Taylor St, Portland, ME 04102-3718, 207-828-9937
Internet: ngouffa1@maine.pp.com
Pubs: *The Wildman, Speaking of New England* (North Country Pr, 1998, 1993), *This Sporting Life: Anth* (Milkweed Edtns, 1996), *Wherever Home Begins: 100 Contemporary Poems: Anth* (Orchard Bks, 1995), *APR, American Voice, Puerto del Sol, Beloit Poetry Jrnl.*

Linda Tatelbaum P&W

About Time Press, 1050 Guinea Ridge Rd, Appleton, ME 048627032, 207-785-4634
Internet: http://www.colby.edu/l_tatelb/personal
Pubs: *Carrying Water As A Way of Life* (About Time Pr, 1997), *Jewish Women's Literary Annual: Anth* (National Council for Jewish Women, 1996), *Maine Times, Maine in Print.*

Lewis Turco P&W

Mathom Bookstore, 38 Blinn Hill Rd, P.O. Box 161, Dresden Mills, ME 04342-0161, 207-737-4512
Internet: mathom@agate.net
Pubs: *A Book of Fears* (Bordighera, 1998), *Bordello* (Grey Heron Pr, 1996), *World Treasury of Poetry: Anth* (Norton, 1998), *Edge City Rev, ELF, The Formalist, New Orleans Rev, Hampden-Sydney Poetry Rev, Voices in Italian Americana.*

John Stevens Wade P

PO Box 5, Weld, ME 04285, 207-293-3531
Pubs: *Homecoming* (Icarus Pr, 1978), *Some Of My Best Friends Are Trees* (Sparrow Pr, 1977).

Carol Wainright P

RR 1, Box 449, Deer Isle, ME 04627, 207-348-2580
Pubs: *Distant Mountain* (Wind Chimes Pr, 1985), *Christian Science Monitor.*

David C. Walker P

Box 82, Freedom, ME 04941, 207-382-6267
Internet: dwalker@portland.maine.edu
Pubs: *Voiceprints* (Romulus Edtns, 1989), *The Maine Reader: Anth* (HM, 1991), *Poetry, Northwest Rev, New Yorker, Georgia Rev, Antioch Rev.*

Douglas "Woody" Woodsum P

PO Box 265, Scarborough, ME 04070, 207-799-3425
Pubs: *Antioch Rev, Southern Rev, Massachusetts Rev, Prairie Schooner, Denver Qtly, Yankee, Webster Rev, Exquisite Corpse, Sun Dog, Albany Rev.*

Baron Wormser P

19 1/2 Pleasant St Place, Hallowell, ME 04347, 207-622-7052
Internet: baron@mint.net
Pubs: *When* (Sarabande Bks, 1997), *Atoms, Soul Music and Other Poems* (Paris Rev Edtns, 1989), *Harper's, New Republic, Paris Rev.*

Helen Yglesias W

Bay Rd, North Brooklin, ME 04616, 207-359-8584
Pubs: *How She Died, Isabel Bishop, The Saviors* (HM, 1992, 1989, 1987), *Sweetsir* (S&S, 1981).

Leroy Zarucchi P

PO Box 76, Troy, ME 04987, 207-948-3427
Internet: potatoeyes@uninet.net
Pubs: *Gunner's Moon* (Cider Pr, 1996), *Sparse Rain* (Pygmy Forest Pr, 1996), *Spirit That Moves Us: Anth* (Spirit That Move Us, 1993), *Onthebus, Pembroke Mag, The Fiddlehead.*

MARYLAND

Karren LaLonde Alenier P&W

4601 North Ave, #301, Chevy Chase, MD 20815, 301-652-7638
Internet: karren77@aol.com
Pubs: *Bumper Cars* (MICA Pr, 1996), *Her Face In The Mirror: Anth* (Beacon Pr, 1994), *Whose Woods These Are: Anth* (WordWorks, 1983), *MacGuffin, Crescent Rev, Jrnl of Poetry Therapy, Poet Lore, Negative Capability, Mississippi Rev, Jewish Currents.*

Indran Amirthanayagam P

4810 Mercury Dr, Rockville, MD 20853, 301-946-8085
Internet: iamirthanayagam@hotmail.com
Pubs: *The Elephants of Reckoning* (Hanging Loose Pr, 1993), *Four Way Reader: Anth* (Four Way Bks, 1996), *United States of Poetry: Anth* (Abrams, 1996).

Ellen Argo W

63 Conduit St, Annapolis, MD 21401, 301-268-3151
Pubs: *Yankee Girl, Crystal Star, Jewel of the Seas* (Putnam, 1981, 1979, 1977).

Barri Armitage P
13904 N Gate Dr, Silver Spring, MD 20906-2217,
301-871-6656
    Pubs: *Double Helix* (Washington Writers Pub Hse, 1993),
*Prairie Schooner, Poet Lore, Bridge, Poetry, Georgia Rev,
Ohio Rev.*

Ed Baker P
8215 Flower Ave, Takoma Park, MD 20912-6858,
301-587-1875
    Pubs: *Okeanos Rhos, The City, Hexapoem I, II, & III, This
Wood* (Red Ochre Pr, 1995, 1994, 1982), *Odysseus,
Athanor, Calvert Rev, Cold Spring Jrnl.*

Diane DeMichele Barkett P
5394 Annapolis Dr, Mount Airy, MD 21771-5709
    Pubs: *Tempest, Archer, Up Against the Wall Mother, San
Fernando Poetry Journal, Piedmont Literary Rev.*

John Barth W
Johns Hopkins Univ, Baltimore, MD 21218, 410-516-7562
    Pubs: *On With The Story, The Last Voyage of Somebody
the Sailor* (Little, Brown, 1996, 1991).

Robin Bayne P&W
215 Treherne Rd, Lutherville, MD 21093-1244
Internet: rlbayne@juno.com
    Pubs: *Words of Wonder: Anth* (Anderie Poetry Pr, 1995),
Joy of the Journey: Anth (Golden Apple Pr, 1995),
*Thresholds Qtly, Potomac Rev, Tucumcari Literary Rev,
Writer's Jrnl, Black Moon, Dogwood Tales, Sensations,
Artisan.*

Mary Beach W
Cherry Valley Editions, 3510 Olympic St, Silver Spring, MD
20906, 301-946-0947

David Beaudouin P
2840 St. Paul St, Baltimore, MD 21218-4311, 410-467-6292
    Pubs: *The American Night* (Blue Nude, 1992),
Catenae—Set 1 (Apathy Pr, 1988), *Open 24 Hours, Stony
Run.*

Madison Smartt Bell W
Goucher College, English Dept, Towson, MD 21204,
410-337-6282
Internet: mbell@goucher.edu
    Pubs: *Ten Indians, All Soul's Rising* (Pantheon, 1996,
1995), *Doctor Sleep* (HBJ, 1991), *Barking Man* (Ticknor &
Fields, 1990), *Harper's, Hudson Rev.*

Donald Berger P
105 Hodges Ln, Takoma Park, MD 20912-4229
    Pubs: *Quality Hill* (Lost Roads, 1993).

David Bergman P
3024 N Calvert St, #C5, Baltimore, MD 21218, 410-467-8070
Internet: dbergman@towson.edu
    Pubs: *Heroic Measures, Cracking the Code* (Ohio State,
1998, 1985), *Gaiety Transfigured* (U Wisconsin, 1991),
*Poetry, New Republic, Raritan, Paris Rev, Kenyon Rev,
New Criterion.*

Cathy Drinkwater Better P
119 Caraway Rd Apt B1, Reisterstown, MD 21136,
410-833-1537
Internet: cbetter@juno.com
    Pubs: *The Moon Tonight* (Los Hombres Pr, 1996), *Don't Hit
Your Brother With Your Mouth Full* (Acme Pr, 1995),
*Writer's Digest, St. Anthony Messenger, Modern Haiku,
American Cowboy Poet Mag, Silver Web, Humpty Dumpty
Mag, Psychopoetica, Raw Nervz.*

Harold Black P
7537 Spring Lake Dr, #C-1, Bethesda, MD 20817,
301-469-0865
    Pubs: *My Father Abraham* (Spring Lake Pr, 1989), *Heritage*
(Black Buzzard Pr, 1982), *Virginia, Visions, Jewish
Spectator, Slant, Orphic Lute.*

Jody Bolz P
4004 Maryland Ave, Brookmont, MD 20816, 301-229-6578
    Pubs: *Her Face in the Mirror: Anth* (Beacon Pr, 1994),
*Indiana Rev, Southern Poetry Rev, River Styx, Women's
Rev of Bks, Ascent, Poet Lore, Ploughshares.*

Betty Booker P
27826 Island Dr, Salisbury, MD 21801, 410-546-1712
    Pubs: *Plainsong, Croton Rev, Stone Country, Artemis,
Christian Century, America, Poetry Now.*

Dennis Braden P
212 Croyden Ave, Rockville, MD 20850, 301-279-8684
    Pubs: *In Things Completed* (Konglomerati, 1986),
Wingbone: Poetry from Colorado (Sudden Jungle, 1986).

Alan Britt P
233 Northway Rd, Reisterstown, MD 21136, 410-833-9424
    Pubs: *Bodies of Lightning* (Cypress Bks, 1995), *Fathers: A
Collection of Poems: Anth* (St. Martin's Pr, 1997), *Rising
Waters: Anth* (Pekitanoui Pub, 1995), *Black Moon, Bitter
Oleander, Chariton Rev, Exquisite Corpse, Borderlands:
Texas Rev, New Letters.*

Melvin Edward Brown P
1311 Kitmore Rd, Baltimore, MD 21239, 410-323-3708

Barbara Browne P
6120 Edmondson Ave, Catonsville, MD 21228, 301-747-1090
    Pubs: *Studia Mystica, Wind, Anima, Poet's Pride.*

Marion Buchman   P
11 Slade Ave, #315, Baltimore, MD 21208, 410-764-3327
 Pubs: *In His Pavilion* (Haskell Hse Pub, 1986), *America*
 (Thornhill Pr, 1976), *Redbook, Stanza.*

Lynn Buck   P
13801 York Rd, Apt K-10, Cockeysville, MD 21030-1899,
410-771-0916
 Pubs: *Two Minus One* (Birnham Wood, 1994), *Autumn
 Fires* (Red Creek Pr, 1989), *Crazyquilt, Live Poets, Long
 Pond Rev, Long Island Qtly, Heartland.*

Michael Scott Cain   P&W
19 N Symington Ave, Catonsville, MD 21228, 301-788-6208
 Pubs: *Seven Questions for Phil Ochs* (Placebo Pr, 1984).

Roser Caminals-Heath   W
Hood College, 401 Rosemont Ave, Frederick, MD 21701,
301-696-3474
Internet: rheath@nimue.hood.edu
 Pubs: *Un Scglc De Prodigis* (Spain; Columbia, 1995), *Once
 Remembered, Twice Lived* (Peter Lang Pub, 1993),
 Georgia Rev, American Book Rev.

Grant Carrington   W
Box 1120, Laurel, MD 20725, 301-490-6142
 Pubs: *Time's Fool* (Doubleday, 1981), *Amazing, Fantastic,
 Cavalier, Canadian Forum, Eternity, Asimov's SF Mag.*

John Carter   P
332 Lincoln Ave, Takoma Park, MD 20912
 Pubs: *Impetus, Poetry USA, Poetry SF, The Pearl,
 Prisoners of the Night, Gargoyle, Lactuca.*

Lucille Clifton   P
St. Mary's College, St Mary's City, MD 20686
 Pubs: *Terrible Stories, Quilting* (BOA Edtns, 1996, 1991),
 The Book of Light (Copper Canyon Pr, 1994), *Ten
 Oxherding Poems* (Moving Parts Pr, 1988).

Michael Collier   P
111 Smithwood Ave, Catonsville, MD 21228, 410-719-7312
Internet: mc33@umail.umd.edu
 Pubs: *The Neighbor* (U Chicago, 1995), *The Folded Heart,*
 (Wesleyan, 1989), *Atlantic, New Yorker.*

Geraldine Connolly   P
8706 Fallen Oak Dr, Bethesda, MD 20817, 301-365-1359
 Pubs: *Province of Fire* (Iris Press, 1998), *Food For The
 Winter* (Purdue U Pr, 1990), *The Red Room* (Heatherstone
 Pr, 1988), *Antioch Rev, Poetry, Shenandoah, Cream City
 Rev, Hayden's Ferry Rev.*

Sarah Cotterill   P
9624 Evergreen St, Silver Spring, MD 20901, 301-588-8983
 Pubs: *In the Nocturnal Animal House* (Purdue U Pr, 1991),
 The Hive Burning (Sleeping Bird Pr, 1983), *APR, Poetry
 Northwest, Ploughshares, Nimrod, Kansas Qtly.*

Judith Speizer Crandell   W
12 Hilltop Rd, Silver Spring, MD 20910, 301-431-1462
Internet: crandellink@juno.com
 Pubs: *Hudson River Anthology, Cleveland Magazine, Allied
 Pub, Laughing Bear, Whiskey Island.*

James Cross   W
4814 Falstone Ave, Chevy Chase, MD 20815, 301-652-5665
 Pubs: *To Hell For Half A Crown* (Random House, 1968),
 Maryland Poetry Rev.

Bruce V. J. Curley   P&W
11404 Brundidge Terr, Germantown, MD 20876-5578,
301-540-8323
Internet: eamon@erols.com
 Pubs: *Under A Gull's Wing: Anth* (Down the Shore Pr,
 1996), *Baltimore Rev, Pannus Index, Lynx Eye, Mad Poets
 Rev, Voices Israel, Potomac Rev.*

Ann Darr   P
4902 Falstone Ave, Chevy Chase, MD 20815, 301-652-4292
Internet: anndarr@aol.com
 Pubs: *Flying the Zuni Mountains* (Forest Woods Media
 Productions, 1994), *Hungry As We Are: Anth* (Washington
 Writers Pub Hse, 1995).

Robert Day   W
Washington College, 300 Washington Ave, Chestertown, MD
21620, 410-778-2800
 Pubs: *Speaking French in Kansas* (Cottonwood, 1989), *The
 Four Wheel Drive Quartet* (Galileo, 1986), *TriQuarterly.*

Enoch Dillon   P
6310 Hollins Dr, Bethesda, MD 20817, 301-530-7795
Internet: enochdillon@email.msn.com
 Pubs: *Love, From the Ends of the Earth, The Bicentennial
 Blues* (Fithian Pr, 1990, 1988), *Poet Lore, Visions, Light,
 Friends Jrnl, Heaven Bone, Deus Ex Machina, Mediphors.*

Margaret Diorio   P
1015 Kenilworth Dr, Towson, MD 21204, 410-821-7807
 Pubs: *End of Summer, Bringing in the Plants* (Icarus Bks,
 1993, 1980), *Yankee, Commonweal, Centennial Rev,
 Maryland Poetry Rev, U Windsor Rev, CSM.*

Stephen Dixon   W
Johns Hopkins Univ, Writing Seminars Gilman 135,
Baltimore, MD 21218, 410-825-8038
 Pubs: *Gould* (Henry Holt, 1997), *Interstate* (Owl Bks, 1997),
 *TriQuarterly, Boulevard, Harper's, Virginia Qtly Rev,
 DoubleTake, American Short Fiction.*

Thomas A. Dorsett   P
4408 Wickford Rd, Baltimore, MD 21210, 410-467-4316
 Pubs: *Dance Fire Dance* (Icarus Pr, 1992), *Confrontation,
 Descant, Verse, Paintbrush, America, Slant, Intl Poetry
 Rev.*

Maura Eichner   P
College of Notre Dame, Baltimore, MD 21210
  Pubs: *Hope Is A Blind Bard* (Harold Shaw Pub, 1989),
  What We Women Know (Sparrow, 1980).

Daniel Mark Epstein   P
843 W University Pkwy, Baltimore, MD 21210-2911
  Pubs: *The Boy In The Well, Sprits* (The Overlook Pr/Viking,
  1995, 1987), *Sister Aimee* (HB, 1993), *Love's Compass*
  (Addison-Wesley, 1990), *New Yorker, Atlantic, New
  Republic, Paris Rev, Nation, New Criterion.*

Michael Fallon   P
3041 St. Paul St, Baltimore, MD 21218-3943, 410-366-6850
  Pubs: *A History of the Color Black* (Dolphin Moon Pr, 1989),
  *The Salmon, Puerto del Sol, Poets On, Maryland Poetry
  Rev, Potomac Rev.*

Diana J. Felts   P
113 Byway Rd, Owings Mills, MD 21117, 301-356-6984
  Pubs: *Impetus, Up Against The Wall Mother, Piedmont
  Literary Mag, The Mountain Laurel, Proof Rock.*

Roland Flint   P
8605 Milford Ave, Silver Spring, MD 20910, 301-585-7685
Internet: rhflint@aol.com
  Pubs: *Pigeon in the Night* (Fakel Pr, 1994), *Stubborn* (U
  Illinois Pr, 1991), *Pigeon* (North Carolina Wesleyan College
  Pr, 1990).

Elizabeth Follin-Jones   P&W
4896 Chevy Chase Blvd, Chevy Chase, MD 20815,
301-652-4346
  Pubs: *Bite to Eat Place* (Redwood Coast Pr, 1995), *One
  Flight from the Bottom* (Artscape, 1990), *Poet Lore,
  Maryland Poetry Rev, Embers, Free State.*

Martin Galvin   P
Walt Whitman School, 7100 Whittier Blvd, Bethesda, MD
20817, 301-320-6600
  Pubs: *Wild Card* (Washington Writer's Pub Hse, 1989),
  Making Beds (Sedwick Hse, 1989), *Descant.*

CJeanean Gibbs   P
Palm Tree Enterprises, Inc., 1514 Roosevelt Ave, Landover,
MD 20785, 301-322-5510
  Pubs: *Spirits of the Ancestors, Gurus and Griots* (Palm Tree
  Enterprises, 1993, 1987).

Michael S. Glaser   P
PO Box 1, Saint Mary's City, MD 20686, 301-862-9676
Internet: msglaser@osprey.smcm.edu
  Pubs: *In the Men's Room & Other Poems* (Painted Bride
  Qtly, 1996), *A Lover's Eye* (Bunny & Crocodile Pr, 1989),
  CSM, New Letters, Sun, Midstream, Poet Lore.

Barbara Goldberg   P
6623 Fairfax Rd, Chevy Chase, MD 20815, 301-907-7994
Internet: bgoldberg@asha.org
  Pubs: *Marvelous Pursuits* (Snake Nation Pr, 1995),
  Cautionary Tales (Dryad Pr, 1990), *Paris Rev, Poetry,
  NER, American Scholar, Poet Lore.*

Ivy Goodman   W
3204 Crest Ave, Cheverly, MD 20785
  Pubs: *Heart Failure* (U Iowa Pr, 1983), *Gettysburg Rev,
  Confrontation, Epoch, DoubleTake, Witness, Michigan Qtly
  Rev, Ploughshares.*

Jennifer Gostin   W
1 S Rolling Rd, Baltimore, MD 21228
Internet: gostinj@aol.com
  Pubs: *Peregrine's Rest* (Permanent Pr, 1996), *The Mage,
  North Shore Life, The Gamut, Whiskey Island, Byline,
  Monocacy Valley Rev.*

Beatrice Greene   W
6418 Bannockburn Dr, Bethesda, MD 20817, 301-229-6355
  Pubs: *New Orleans Rev, Mississippi Rev, Panache, The
  Fiddlehead, Style, Calvert Rev.*

Allen R. Grossman   P
Johns Hopkins Univ, Baltimore, MD 21218
  Pubs: *The Ether Dome and Other Poems New and
  Selected 1979-1991, The Bright Nails Scattered on the
  Ground* (New Directions, 1991, 1986).

Greg Hannan   P
207 Hodge St, Takoma Park, MD 20912
  Pubs: *A Shout In The Street, The Poet Upstairs, Gargoyle,
  Cycloflame.*

Jean Harmon   P&W
12813 Falmouth Dr, Silver Spring, MD 20904, 301-622-0442
  Pubs: *Thirteen, Z Misc, Popular Reality, Renegade,
  American Organist, Anathema Rev, 'Scapes, New Voices,
  Metropolitan, Opera Monthly, Neologisms, Verse Unto Us,
  Sacred Music News, Church Musician, Christianity & the
  Arts.*

Clarinda Harriss   P
Towson Univ, Towson, MD 21252, 401-830-2869
Internet: charriss@towson.edu or www.towson.edu
  Pubs: *Minarets of Vienna* (Chestnut Hills Pr, 1996), *Lesbian
  Speakers Bureau* (Stonewall, 1996), *License Renewal For
  the Blind* (Cooper House, 1994), Epoch, California Qtly,
  Maryland Poetry Rev, South Coast Poetry Rev, The Sun,
  Spoon River Anth, Genre.*

John Hayes   P&W
1409 Kirkwood Rd, Baltimore, MD 21207, 410-719-7541
Internet: johnhayesaw@worldnet.att.net
  Pubs: *Fire On the Hills: Anth* (Highlights for Children, 1995),
  *Lynx Eye, Bogg, Alabama Literary Rev, Thema, Rockford
  Rev, Onionhead, Fresh Ground, Implosion, Baltimore Rev.*

William Heath   P
Mount St. Mary's College, Emmitsburg, MD 21727,
301-694-5365
Internet: heath@msmary.edu
    Pubs: *The Children Bob Moses Led* (Milkweed, 1997), *The
    Walking Man* (Icarus, 1994), *Kenyon Rev, Southern Rev,
    Massachusetts Rev, South Carolina Rev, Texas Rev,
    Monocacy Valley Rev.*

David Hilton   P
413 Grinstead Rd, Severna Park, MD 21146, 410-544-6318
    Pubs: *No Relation to the Hotel* (Coffee Hse Pr, 1989),
    Huladance (Crossing Pr, 1976), *Poetry Northwest, Beloit
    Poetry Jrnl, Exquisite Corpse, Poetry, Iowa Rev.*

Geoffrey Himes   P
8 E 39 St, Baltimore, MD 21218-1801, 410-235-6627
Internet: geoffhimes@aol.com
    Pubs: *City Paper, Salt Lick, Columbia Flier, Maryland
    English Jrnl, Baltimore Sun, December.*

Carol F. Hoover   W
4817 Tallahassee Ave, Rockville, MD 20853, 301-949-2514
    Pubs: *Story, Denver Qtly, Texas Qtly, Potomac Rev,
    Crescent Rev.*

Josephine Jacobsen   P&W
13801 York Rd T-366, Cockeysville, MD 21030,
301-889-0152
    Pubs: *What Goes Without Saying, In the Crevice of Time*
    (Johns Hopkins Pr, 1996, 1995), *Distances* (Bucknell U
    Fine Edtns, 1992), *On the Island* (Ontario Rev Pr, 1988),
    Best American Poetry: Anth (Scribner, 1993), *Poetry, New
    Letters, New Yorker.*

Judy B. Jason   P&W
12105 Merricks Ct, Monrovia, MD 21770
    Pubs: *Collage: Feminae Vitae* (Sideling Pr, 1984), *George
    Washington Rev, Up Against The Wall Mother.*

Philip K. Jason   P
11500 Patriot Ln, Potomac, MD 20854, 301-299-4190
Internet: pjason@aol.com
    Pubs: *The Separation* (Viet Nam Generation, 1995),
    Creative Writer's Handbook (Prentice-Hall, 1990), *Near the
    Fire* (Dryad, 1983).

Eugene L. Jeffers   W
13412 Oriental Ct, Rockville, MD 20853, 301-460-0265
    Pubs: *A Rumor of Distant Tribes* (Ariadne Pr, 1994),
    *Pulpsmith, Crosscurrents, Orbis, Format: Art & The World,
    Virginia Country.*

Pam Jekel   P&W
6123 Orient Ln, Columbia, MD 21045-4315, 301-531-6737
    Pubs: *Third Jungle Book* (Bookmakers, 1990), *Last of the
    California Girls* (Zebra, 1988).

Rod Jellema   P
4526 Avondale St, #4, Bethesda, MD 20814, 301-907-8824
Internet: rjellema@wam.umd.edu
    Pubs: *The Sound that Remains* (Eerdmans, 1990), *The
    Eighth Day* (Dryad Pr, 1985), *Field, Plum Rev.*

Lane Jennings   P
6373 Barefoot Boy, Columbia, MD 21045, 301-596-2943
Internet: lanejen@aol.com
    Pubs: *Open Secrets, White Lies* (Black Buzzard Pr, 1998,
    1984), *Virtual Futures* (Other Worlds Pr, 1996), *White Lies,
    Visions, Amelia, Catalyst, Gargoyle, Starline, Treasure
    House.*

Halvard Johnson   P
118 S Collington Ave, Baltimore, MD 21231, 410-327-7980
Internet: hjohnson@umbc.edu
    Pubs: *Mixed Voices, This Sporting Life* (Milkweed Edtns,
    1991, 1987), *Synaesthetic, Ironwood, Puerto del Sol,
    Mudfish, St. Andrews Rev, Gulf Stream.*

Lynn Kanter   W
3312 Camalier, Chevy Chase, MD 20815
    Pubs: *The Mayor of Heaven, On Lill Street* (Third Side Pr,
    1997, 1992), *Breaking Up Is Hard To Do: Anth, The Time of
    Our Lives: Anth* (Crossing Pr, 1994, 1993).

Wayne Karlin   W
PO Box 239, St Mary's City, MD 20686, 301-862-9871
Internet: waynek@charles.cc.md.us
    Pubs: *Prisoners, Rumors And Stones, The Other Side of
    Heaven: Anth* (Curbstone Pr, 1998, 1996, 1995), *Us, Lost
    Armies* (Holt, 1993, 1988), *New Stories from the South,
    Prairie Schooner, Indiana Rev, Glimmer Train, Crab
    Orchard Rev.*

Madeleine Keller   P
4613 Wilmslow Rd, Baltimore, MD 21210
    Pubs: *Pearl, Stony Run, Tamarind, Telephone, Niagara,
    The Spirit That Moves Us, Knock-Knock.*

Marta Knobloch   P
PO Box 48, Galena, MD 21635, 410-648-5080
    Pubs: *The Room of Months/La Stanza dei Mesi* (Book
    Editore, 1995), *Sky Pond* (SCOP Pub, 1992), *Amelia,
    Leggere Donna, Maryland Poetry Rev, Lyric, Visions Intl,
    Delos, Poesie, Poetry Australia.*

Ann B. Knox   P&W
PO Box 65, Hancock, MD 21750-0065, 202-244-2198
Internet: tinkerword@aol.com
    Pubs: *Staying Is Nowhere* (SCOP Pubs, 1996), *Late
    Summer Break* (Papier-Mache, 1995), *Poetry, Atlanta Rev,
    Plum Rev, Poets On, The MacGuffin.*

Susan Land   W
7004 Exsair Rd, Bethesda, MD 20814, 301-652-4982
    Pubs: *Confrontation, Quarry West, West Branch, Other Voices, Wind, Kansas Qtly, Mississippi Rev, Alaska Qtly Rev.*

Charles R. Larson   W
3600 Underwood St, Chevy Chase, MD 20815, 301-656-9370
    Pubs: *Arthur Dimmesdale* (Avon, 1984), *The Insect Colony* (HRW, 1978).

Kevin J. Lavey   W
PO Box 1583, Baltimore, MD 21203, 410-752-4708
    Pubs: *It's On My Wall: Anth* (Northwoods Pr, 1989), *Dan River Anth* (Dan River Pr, 1988), *Licking River Rev.*

Barbara F. Lefcowitz   P&W
4989 Battery Ln, Bethesda, MD 20814, 301-652-0835
Internet: blefcowitz@aol.com
    Pubs: *The Minarets of Vienna* (Chestnut Hills, 1996), *Red Lies & White Lies* (East Coast Bks, 1994), *Shadows & Goatbones* (SCOP Pubs, 1992), *Other Voices, Minnesota Rev.*

Kathy Pearce Lewis   P
10501 Montrose Ave #102, Bethesda, MD 20814-4141, 301-530-4692
Internet: klew@erols.com
    Pubs: *Free State, The Cooke Book: A Seasoning of Poets: Anth* (SCOP Pub, 1989, 1987), *Taurus, Visions, Yet Another Small Mag, Bogg, Potomac Rev.*

Harrison Edward Livingstone   W
PO Box 7149, Baltimore, MD 21218
    Pubs: *Baltimore, Harvard, John* (Conservatory Pr, 1988, 1987), *The Wild Rose: A Novel of the Sea* (Word of Mouth Pr, 1980), *David Johnson Passed Through Here* (Little, Brown, 1971).

Jose H. Llubien   P
8907 Heathermore Blvd, #201, Upper Marlboro, MD 20772-5175

Kathy Auchincloss Lorr   P
302 Windsor St, Silver Spring, MD 20910, 301-585-7667
    Pubs: *Science 82, Poet Lore, Poets On, Dark Horse, Vision, Womanspirit, Gargoyle.*

Kathy Mangan   P
3003 St. Paul St, Baltimore, MD 21218, 410-243-0242
Internet: kmangan@wmdc.edu
    Pubs: *Above the Tree Line* (Carnegie Mellon U Pr, 1995), *Pushcart Prize XV: Anth* (Pushcart Pr, 1991), *Georgia Rev, Gettysburg Rev, Shenandoah, Southern Rev.*

Sharon Bell Mathis   P&W
PO Box 44714, Fort Washington, MD 20744-7119
    Pubs: *Running Girl: The Diary of Ebonee Rose* (HB/Browndeer Pr, 1997), *Red Dog, Blue Fly: Football Poems* (Viking Penguin, 1991).

Lena Dale Matthews   P
4014 Roland Ave, Baltimore, MD 21211, 301-235-6769

John Mazur   P
247 S Ellwood Ave, Baltimore, MD 21224, 410-342-6843
    Pubs: *Lover's Lane: Anth, Ever Green and Sunsets Red: Anth, Little Verse, Big Thought: Anth* (Golden Apple Pr, 1998, 1997, 1995), *Images of the Mind: Anth* (Modern Poetry Society, 1996), *eNteLechY.*

Phillip McCaffrey   P
4121 Westview Rd, Baltimore, MD 21218
    Pubs: *Freud & Dora* (Rutgers U Pr, 1984), *Teaching the Door to Close* (Lame Johnny, 1983), *Poetry.*

Jean McGarry   W
Johns Hopkins Univ, The Writing Seminars, Baltimore, MD 21218
    Pubs: *Gallagher's Travels, Home At Last, The Very Rich Hours* (Johns Hopkins U Pr, 1997, 1994, 1987), *The Courage of Girls* (Rutgers U Pr, 1992), *New Yorker, Southwest Rev, Boulevard, Yale Rev.*

Ann Landis McLaughlin   W
6702 Maple Ave, Chevy Chase, MD 20815, 301-654-6877
    Pubs: *Sunset at Rosalie, The Balancing Pole* (John Daniel & Co., 1996, 1991).

Margaret Meacham   W
Box 402, Brooklandville, MD 21002, 410-337-0736
Internet: mmeac@aol.com
    Pubs: *Oyster Moon* (Tidewater, 1997), *Call Me Cathy* (Archway Pocket, 1995), *Vacation Blues, Love in Focus* (Berkley Pubs, 1985, 1983).

Carol A. Michalski   P
8601 Richmond Cir, Ste 204, Baltimore, MD 21234, 410-882-0834
    Pubs: *Through the Years With Feelings: Anth* (Andrea Poetry Pr, 1996), *Don't Blame God: Making Sense Out of T&S* (Impact Christian Bks, 1995), *Fauquier Poetry Jrnl, Perceptions, Feelings Poetry, Versus, The Brobdingnagian Times.*

Elizabeth J. Morris   W
8708 Ewing Dr, Bethesda, MD 20817, 301-530-3267
    Pubs: *Metropolitan, The Writing On the Wall, Gyst 6, Short Story, Crazyquilt.*

Phyllis Reynolds Naylor   W
9910 Holmhurst Rd, Bethesda, MD 20817, 301-530-2340
Pubs: *Achingly Alice, Sang Spell, The Fear Place, All But Alice, Shiloh, Send No Blessings* (Atheneum, 1998, 1998, 1994, 1992, 1991, 1990).

Gloria Oden   P
Univ Maryland, Baltimore County, Catonsville, MD 21228, 301-455-2384
Pubs: *The Tie that Binds, Resurrections* (Olivant Pr, 1980, 1978), *Ms., Saturday Rev, Nimrod.*

Irene Orgel   W
6042 Green Meadow Pkwy, Baltimore, MD 21209
Pubs: *The Odd Tales Of Irene Orgel* (New York Eakins Pr, 1967), *Harper's, Mademoiselle.*

Betty Parry   P
4814 Falstone Ave, Chevy Chase, MD 20815, 301-652-5665
Pubs: *Shake the Parrot Cage* (New Poets Series, 1994), *Free State, A Harvest of Maryland Poets: Anth* (SCOP Prod, 1992), *Maryland Poetry Rev.*

Linda Pastan   P
11710 Beall Mountain Rd, Potomac, MD 20854, 301-299-2362
Pubs: *Carnival Evening: New and Selected Poems, An Early Afterlife, Heroes in Disguise, The Imperfect Paradise* (Norton, 1998, 1995, 1991, 1988), *Paris Rev, Kenyon Rev, Ohio Rev, Poetry, Gettysburg Rev, Georgia Rev.*

John Retallack   P&W
4419 Ridge St, Chevy Chase, MD 20815, 301-656-8156
Pubs: *Circumstantial Evidence* (SOS, 1987), *The Best American Poetry: Anth* (Macmillan, 1990).

Marijane G. Ricketts   P
10203 Clearbrook Pl, Kensington, MD 208954121, 301-564-0852
Pubs: *The Child Without, The Child Within: Anth* (Earth's Daughters, 1994), *A Diamond Anthology of Prose and Poetry* (The Writers League of Washington, 1992), *Free State: Anth* (SCOP Pubs, 1989), *Poet Lore, Potomac Rev, Poet, Potato Eyes, Public Voices.*

Doris Rochlin   W
10100 Baldwin Ct, Bethesda, MD 20817, 301-581-0051
Pubs: *In the Spanish Ballroom* (Doubleday, 1991), *Frobisch's Angel* (Taplinger Pub Co., 1987).

Jean Rubin   P
1227 Park Ave, #10, Baltimore, MD 21217-4135, 410-669-0344
Pubs: *Combinazioni III* (Theodore Presser, 1983), *The Ear's Chamber: Anth* (Metro, 1981), *le bayou, College Music Symposium, Notre Dame English Jrnl.*

Peter Sacks   P
Johns Hopkins Univ, 34th & N Charles St, Baltimore, MD 21218, 301-338-7564
Pubs: *Promised Lands* (Viking, 1990), *In These Mountains* (Macmillan, 1986).

Karen Sagstetter   P
6004 Madawaska Rd, Bethesda, MD 20816, 301-229-2370
Pubs: *Ceremony* (State Street Pr, 1981), *Half The Story* (Charles Street Pr, 1981), *Washington Rev, Shenandoah.*

Diane Scharper   P
Towson Univ, 8000 York Rd-Linthicum 219K, Towson, MD 212040001, 410-830-2868
Internet: dscharpe@towson.edu
Pubs: *Radiant* (Cathedral Fdn Pr, 1996), *The Laughing Ladies* (Dolphin Moon Pr, 1993), *Maryland Rev, City Paper, Saltimbanquers.*

Steven Schutzman   P&W
2903 Ailsa Ave, Baltimore, MD 21214-2524, 410-254-7870
Pubs: *Smoke the Burning Body Makes* (Panjandrum, 1978), *The History of Sleep* (Gallimaufry, 1976), *Sudden Fiction: Anth* (Gibbs Smith, 1986), *TriQuarterly.*

Myra Sklarew   P&W
6521 Marywood Rd, Bethesda, MD 20817, 202-885-2811
Internet: msklarew@erols.com
Pubs: *Lithuania: New & Selected Poems* (Azul Edtns, 1995), *Eating the White Earth* (Israel; Tag Pub, 1994), *Poetry, JAMA, Jerusalem Report.*

Susan Sonde   P
2011 St Stephens Woods Dr, Crownsville, MD 21032-2200, 301-858-1528
Pubs: *In The Longboats With Others* (New Rivers, 1988), *Quarterly West, Carolina Qtly, Cimarron, Conjunctions, Northwest Rev, Chelsea.*

Elizabeth Spires   P
6208 Pinehurst Rd, Baltimore, MD 21212, 410-532-9752
Pubs: *Worldling* (Norton, 1995), *Annonciade* (Viking Penguin, 1989), *Swan's Island* (Holt, 1985), *New Yorker.*

Margaret Stavely   P
26096 Lambs Meadow Rd P.O. Box, Worton, MD 216780008, 410-348-2320
Pubs: *Stopping the Sun* (Kent County Arts Council, 1982), *The Poets Domain: A Little Nonsense Vol 14: Anth, The Poets Domain: Straightaway Dangerous: Anth* (Road Pub, 1997, 1996), *Sun Mag, Little Balkans Rev, Tapestry of the Mind, Maryland Poetry Rev.*

Adele Steiner   P
6211 Wagner Ln, Bethesda, MD 20816
Pubs: *Fat Mega Book, Refracted Love* (Bootleg Pr, 1994, 1993), *Black Buzzard Rev, M Mag, So To Speak, Maryland Rev, Schmooze.*

Elisabeth Stevens   P&W
6604 Walnutwood Cir, Baltimore, MD 21212, 410-377-8338
Pubs: *In Foreign Parts: Nine Stories, The Night Lover: Art & Poetry* (Birch Brook, 1997, 1995), *Horse & Cart: Stories from the Country* (Wineberry, 1990), *Crosscurrents, Wind, Farmer's Market, Maryland Poetry Rev, Potomac Rev, Baltimore Rev.*

Joseph McNair Stover   P&W
20854 Sandstone St, Lexington Park, MD 206532439
Pubs: *Commander Coatrack Returns* (HM, 1989), *South Florida Poetry Rev, Florida Rev, The Cathartic, Potomac Rev, Connections.*

John Strausbaugh   P&W
3603 Elkader Rd, Baltimore, MD 21218
Pubs: *Red Zone, Flying Fish* (Dolphin-Moon, 1988, 1986), *High Performance, Bartleby.*

Ron Tanner   W
Writing & Media Dept, 4501 N Charles St, Baltimore, MD 21210-2699, 410-617-2434
Pubs: *Best of the West: Anth* (Norton, 1991), *The Pushcart Prize XIV: Anth* (Pushcart Pr, 1990), *20 Under 30: Anth* (Scribner, 1986), *Michigan Qtly Rev.*

James Taylor   P
Dolphin-Moon Press, PO Box 22262, Baltimore, MD 21203, 410-444-7758
Pubs: *Shocked and Amazed! On & Off the Midway, Artifacture* (Dolphin-Moon Pr, 1995, 1989), *Puerto del Sol, Lips.*

Michelle M. Tokarczyk   P
Goucher College, English Dept, Baltimore, MD 21204, 410-337-6165
Pubs: *The House I'm Running From* (West End Pr, 1989), *For A Living: Poetry of Work: Anth* (U Illinois Pr, 1995), *College English, Minnesota Rev, Pearl, Poetry New York.*

Margot Treitel   P
5508 Mystic Ct, Columbia, MD 21044, 410-730-8575
Pubs: *The Inside Story* (Tropos Pr, 1987), *Chicago Rev, Prairie Schooner, Literary Rev, NER, Carolina Qtly.*

Mary M. Truitt   W
418 Duvall Ln, Annapolis, MD 21403, 410-268-8526
Pubs: *1990 PEN Syndicated Fiction Project, Louisville Rev, Gargoyle, Mississippi Mud.*

Stacy Tuthill   P&W
713 Maiden Choice Ln, #5303, Catonsville, MD 21228, 410-536-1877
Internet: 102047.3727@compuserve.com
Pubs: *House of Change* (Forest Woods Media, 1996), *Taste of Smoke* (East Coast Bks, 1995), *Wisconsin Rev, Hawaii Pacific Rev, Poet Lore, Emrys Jrnl, Poets On.*

Anne Tyler   W
222 Tunbridge Rd, Baltimore, MD 21212
Pubs: *A Patchwork Planet, Ladder of Years, Saint Maybe, Breathing Lessons, The Accidental Tourist* (Knopf, 1998, 1995, 1991, 1988, 1985).

Kevin Urick   W
114 Hutchins Ct, Havre de Grace, MD 21078, 410-939-7062
Pubs: *Snow World, The Death of Colonel Jones* (White Ewe, 1983, 1980).

Patricia Valdata   P&W
36 Gina Ct, Elkton, MD 21921
Internet: pvaldata@dol.net
Pubs: *Crosswind* (Wind Canyon Pub, 1996), *Grasslands Rev, Phoebe, Onion River Rev, Icarus, So To Speak.*

Michael Waters   P
Salisbury State Univ, 1101 Camden Ave, Salisbury, MD 21801, 410-742-2559
Internet: mgwaters@ssu.edu
Pubs: *Green Ash, Red Maple, Black Gum* (BOA Edtns, 1997), *Bountiful, The Burden Lifters, Anniversary of the Air* (Carnegie Mellon, 1992, 1989, 1985).

Tara Waters   P&W
2050 Geist Rd, Glyndon, MD 21071, 301-584-2867
Pubs: *Buffalo Spree, Earth's Daughters, Color Wheel, Context South, Zeitgeist.*

Debra Riggin Waugh   P&W
PO Box 5243, Takoma Park, MD 20913, 301-891-3953
Internet: debradyke@aol.com
Pubs: *Women's Glib: Anth, Word of Mouth: Short Short Writings By Women: Anth* (Crossing Pr, 1991, 1991).

Irving Weiss   P&W
319 Rosin Dr, Chestertown, MD 21620-2823, 410-778-2951
Internet: www.geocities.com/soho/cafe/1493/index.html
Pubs: *Visual Voices, Number Poems: Anth* (Runaway Spoon Pr, 1994, 1997), *Reflections on Childhood* (ABC-Clio, 1991), *Score, Caliban, Context, Wordimage, Lazy Bones Rev, Montserrat Rev, Synaesthetic, Ubu, Rio Mag, Spilled Ink Forum, Abraxas.*

Julia Wendell   P
3637 Blackrock Rd, Upperco, MD 21155, 410-239-4662
Pubs: *Wheeler Lane* (Igneous Pr, 1998), *An Otherwise Perfect History* (Ithaca Hse, 1988), *Missouri Rev, Prairie Schooner, Crazyhorse, The Journal.*

John Milton Wesley   P
3942 Reisterstown Rd, Baltimore, MD 21215, 410-578-8226
Pubs: *The Soybean Field* (Wesley, 1985), *Black Southern Voices: Anth* (NAL, 1985), *Metropolitan.*

Philip Wexler   P
9208 Chanute Dr, Bethesda, MD 20814, 301-897-8367
Internet: philip_wexler@nlm.nih.gov
    Pubs: *Slow Dancer, Kansas Qtly, Z Miscellaneous, Painted
    Hills Rev, Mudfish, Jacaranda Rev, Monocacy Valley Rev.*

Reed Whittemore   P
4526 Albion Rd, College Park, MD 20740, 301-779-0194
    Pubs: *Six Literary Lives* (U Missouri Pr, 1993), *The Past,
    The Future, The Present* (U Arkansas Pr, 1990).

Gary D. Wilson   W
5009 Falls Rd Terr, Baltimore, MD 21210, 410-323-9356
    Pubs: *Street Songs: New Voices in Fiction Anth* (Longstreet
    Pr, 1990), *Glimmer Train, Quarterly West, City Paper of
    Baltimore, Witness, Amelia.*

Terence Winch   P
10113 Greeley Ave, Silver Spring, MD 20902, 301-681-8956
    Pubs: *Best American Poetry 1997: Anth* (Scribner, 1998),
    The Great Indoors, Contenders (Story Line Pr, 1995, 1989),
    NAW, APR, New Republic, Western Humanities Rev.

Phyllis Winston   P&W
2306 Tucker Ln, Baltimore, MD 21207, 410-448-2740
    Pubs: *Nerval's Magic Alphabet* (Peter Lang Pub, 1989),
    *Catonsville Times, Arbutus Times, Baltimore Sun,
    Sub-Stance, Modern Language Notes, Minnesota Rev.*

Marly Youmans   P&W
The Potomac Literary Agency, 19062 Mills Choice Rd, Ste
#5, Gaithersburg, MD 20879, 301-208-0674
    Pubs: *Catherwood* (FSG, 1996), *Little Jordan* (David R.
    Godine, 1995), *Carolina Qtly, South Carolina Rev,
    Southern Humanities.*

Winnie Zerne   P
731 Old Herald Harbor Rd, Crownsville, MD 21032-1524
    Pubs: *Maria, Daughter Of Shadow* (Pacific Pr, 1976).

Maree Zukor-Cohen   P
4708 Roland Ave, #4, Baltimore, MD 21210, 410-243-8852
    Pubs: *New Oregon Rev, Hampden-Sydney Rev, Sojourner,
    Sheba Rev, Vanderbilt Rev, Touchstone.*

MASSACHUSETTS

Janet E. Aalfs   P&W
29 Fort St, Northampton, MA 01060, 413-586-6831
    Pubs: *Sister/Stranger* (Sidewalk Evolution Pr, 1993),
    Outrage (Women's Pr, 1993), *And A Deer's Ear* (Cleis Pr,
    1990), *This Wood Sang Out: Anth* (Literary Project, 1995),
    *Onion River Rev, California State Poetry Qtly, Peregrine,
    Evergreen Chronicles.*

Jonathan Aaron   P
100 Larch Rd, Cambridge, MA 02138
    Pubs: *Corridor* (Wesleyan-New England, 1992), *Second
    Sight* (Harper & Row, 1982), *The Best American Poetry:
    Anths* (Scribner, 1992, 1991), *Partisan Rev.*

Robert H. Abel   W
27 Stockwell Rd, North Hadley, MA 01035, 413-584-6257
    Pubs: *Riding A Tiger* (Asia 2000, 1997), *Ghost Traps* (U of
    Georgia Pr, 1991), *Glimmer Train, Manoa, Writer's Forum,
    Colorado Rev.*

Kathleen Aguero   P
3 Gladstone St, Cambridge, MA 02140
    Pubs: *The Real Weather* (Hanging Loose Pr, 1987), *An Ear
    to the Ground: Anth* (U Georgia Pr, 1989), *Poetry,
    Sojourner.*

Alan Albert   P
63 Indian Meadow Dr, Northboro, MA 01532-2437,
508-393-9014
Internet: aa1000@aol.com
    Pubs: *Worcester Rev, California Qtly, Mississippi Rev,
    Wisconsin Rev, APR, Madrona, Southwest Rev, Kansas
    Qtly, Obras Mag, New Infinity Rev.*

Samuel Albert   P
1550 Worcester Rd, #102W, Framingham, MA 01701,
508-879-5113
    Pubs: *This Sporting Life: Anth* (Milkweed, 1987), *As Is*
    (Wampeter, 1983), *Hozannah The Home Run* (Little,
    Brown, 1972), *Atlantic, Hudson Rev, Beloit Poetry Jrnl,
    Harvard Mag, Agni.*

Samuel W. Allen   P
145 Cliff Ave, Winthrop, MA 02152, 617-846-1996
    Pubs: *Every Round & Other Poems* (Lotus Pr, 1987), *Paul
    Vesey's Ledger* (Paul Breman Pr, 1975).

Keith Althaus   P
PO Box 163, North Truro, MA 026520163, 508-487-2557
    Pubs: *Rival Heavens* (Provincetown Arts Pr, 1993), *APR,
    Agni, Virginia Qtly Rev, Seneca Rev, Provincetown Arts,
    Grand Street.*

Peter Anastas   W
PO Box 211, Gloucester, MA 01931-0211, 978-283-4582
Internet: panastas@shore.net
    Pubs: *Maximus to Gloucester* (Ten Pound Island Bk Co.,
    1992), *Mostly Maine, Split Shift, The Cafe Rev, Sulfur,
    Pollis.*

Sarah Appleton   P
16 Fairfield St, Cambridge, MA 02140-1911
    Pubs: *Ladder Of The World's Joy, The Plentitude We Cry
    For* (Doubleday, 1976, 1972).

Tony Ardizzone   P&W
Christina Ward Literary Agency, PO Box 515, North Scituate,
MA 02060, 781-545-1375
Internet: ardizzon@indiana.edu
   Pubs: *In the Garden of Papa Santuzzu* (Picadora USA,
   1999), *Taking it Home* (U Illinois Pr, 1996), *Larabi's Ox:
   Stories of Morocco* (Milkweed Edtns, 1992), *Georgia Rev,
   Prairie Schooner, Gettysburg Rev, TriQuarterly, Witness.*

Frieda Arkin   W
6 Manning St, Ipswich, MA 01938, 508-768-7587
   Pubs: *The Essential Kitchen Gardener* (Henry Holt, 1990),
   The Dorp (Dial, 1969), *McCall's, Georgia Rev, Yale Rev,
   Transatlantic Rev, California Qtly, Kenyon Rev.*

Jeannine Atkins   W
PO Box 226, Whately, MA 01093
   Pubs: *Fiction Network, NAR, Pacific Rev, PEN Syndicated
   Fiction, Jam To-Day.*

Robert Bagg   P
1862 Howe Rd, Great Barrington, MA 01230
   Pubs: *Body Blows: Poems New and Selected* (U
   Massachusetts, 1988), *The Scrawny Sonnets and Other
   Narratives* (Illinois U Pr, 1973), *Atlantic, Poetry, Boston Rev.*

Carol Baker   P
2 Main St, PO Box 307, Montague, MA 01351-0307,
413-367-0367
   Pubs: *Sojourner, Ploughshares, New York Qtly, Mississippi
   Rev, Stand, Women's Rev of Bks, Massachusetts Rev,
   Nation.*

Donald W. Baker   P&W
61 Seaway, East Brewster, MA 02631, 508-896-7963
   Pubs: *Search Patterns, The Readiness* (Sugar
   Creek/Steppingstone, 1996, 1995), *The Day Before,
   Unposted Letters, Formal Application* (Barnwood Pr, 1988,
   1985, 1982).

Stanislaw Baranczak   P
Harvard Univ, 313 Boylston Hall, Cambridge, MA 02138
   Pubs: *Breathing Under Water, A Fugitive from Utopia*
   (Harvard U Pr, 1991, 1987), *Selected Poems: The Weight
   of the Body* (Another Chicago Pr, 1989).

Jane Barnes   P&W
119 Fayerweather St, #1, Cambridge, MA 02138
   Pubs: *Gay & Lesbian Poetry in Our Time: Anth* (St. Martin's
   Pr, 1989), *Chapel Hill Advocate.*

R. Bartkowech   W
54 Beach St, Woburn, MA 01801, 781-937-0389
Internet: rayb@ziplink.net or www.ziplink.net/ rayb
   Pubs: *Fiction Intl, Mississippi Rev, Southern Poetry Rev,
   ACM, Greenfield Rev, APR.*

Milton Bass   W
View Dr, Rte 49, Pittsfield, MA 01201, 413-698-2271
   Pubs: *The Broken-Hearted Detective, The Half-Hearted
   Detective* (Pocket Bks, 1994, 1993).

June Beisch   P
19 Brown St, Cambridge, MA 02138, 617-497-2241
   Pubs: *Take Notes* (Epiphany Pubs, 1992), *Radcliffe Qtly,
   Epiphany, North Essex Rev, Dialogue, Northland Qtly,
   Literary Rev, Tendril.*

Suzanne E. Berger   P
23 Billingham St, Somerville, MA 02144, 617-625-3041
   Pubs: *Legacies* (Alice James Pr, 1984), *These Rooms*
   (Penmaen Pr, 1979), *Harvard Rev, New York Times, We
   Animals, Texas Qtly Anth, Ploughshares, Sojourner.*

Denise Bergman   P
82 Elm St, Cambridge, MA 02139
   Pubs: *City River of Voices: Anth* (West End Pr, 1992),
   *Mudfish, Frontiers, Kalliope, Moving Out, 5 A.M., Sojourner,
   South Florida Poetry Rev, Sing Heavenly Muse, Pig Iron,
   Nimrod, Oxford Rev.*

Sylvia Berkman   W
330 Broadway, Cambridge, MA 02139-1894, 617-876-1323
   Pubs: *Blackberry Wilderness* (Doubleday, 1959), *Southern
   Rev, Harper's Bazaar, Botteghe Obscure.*

Anne Bernays   W
16 Francis Ave, Cambridge, MA 02138, 617-354-2577
   Pubs: *Professor Romeo* (Weidenfeld & Nicolson, 1989),
   Growing Up Rich (Little, Brown, 1975), *Sports Illustrated,
   New Woman, American Heritage, New Republic,
   Sophisticated Traveler, The Nation, Town and Country.*

MaryEllen Beveridge   W
40 Linnaean St, #11, Cambridge, MA 02138-1566
   Pubs: *New Orleans Rev, new renaissance, Georgia Rev.*

Frank Bidart   P
63 Sparks St #3, Cambridge, MA 02138, 617-497-1226
   Pubs: *Desire, In The Western Night: Collected Poems
   1965-90* (FSG, 1997, 1990).

Barbara A. Blatner   P
69 Oxford St, #1, Somerville, MA 02143, 617-629-2070
   Pubs: *No Star Shines Sharper* (Baker's Plays, 1990), *The
   Pope In Space* (Intertext Pr, 1986), *13th Moon, Lift,
   Fireheart, New York Qtly, Mildred, Groundswell.*

F. C. Blessington   P
Northeastern Univ, Boston, MA 02115, 617-437-2512
   Pubs: *Lorenzo de Medici* (U Pr America, 1992), *Lantskip*
   (Wm. L. Bauhan, 1987), *Wind, Southern Rev, Piedmont
   Literary Rev, Cumberland Poetry Rev, Harvard Mag.*

Corinne Demas Bliss   W
Mount Holyoke College, South Hadley, MA 01075,
413-538-2146
    Pubs: *What We Save For Last* (Milkweed Edtns, 1992),
    Matthew's Meadow (HBJ, 1992), *Daffodils or the Death of
    Love* (Missouri U Pr, 1983).

Mark Bogen   P
8 Cherry St, Newburyport, MA 01950, 508-462-9737
    Pubs: *A Christmas Fable* (Atheneum, 1990), *Narrative of
    the Broken Winter* (North Atlantic Bks, 1988), *Origin, Sulfur.*

Harold Bond   P
11 Chestnut St, Melrose, MA 02176-5306, 781-662-7806
    Pubs: *Articulations: The Body In Poetry: Anth* (U Iowa Pr,
    1994), *The Magical Pine Ring: Anth* (Wayne State U Pr,
    1992), *Ararat, Kaleidoscope, Raft.*

Paula Bonnell   P
44 Codman Hill Ave, Boston, MA 02124, 617-367-5990
    Pubs: *Poet Lore, Blue Buildings, Southern Poetry Rev,
    Manhattan Poetry Rev, Blue Unicorn, Pulpsmith, Floating
    Island, Invisible City.*

Lisa Borders   W
47 Avon St, Somerville, MA 02143, 617-489-7203
Internet: borderslk@aol.com
    Pubs: *Iowa Woman, Painted Bride Qtly, Agassiz Rev,
    Snake Nation Rev, Black Warrior Rev, Bananafish,
    Washington Square.*

Daniel Bosch   P
Expository Writing, 8 Prescott St, Cambridge, MA 021383929,
617-496-8472
Internet: bosch@fas.harvard.edu
    Pubs: *Agni, New Republic, Harvard Rev, Western
    Humanities Rev, Denver Qtly, Beloit Poetry Jrnl.*

Laure-Anne Bosselaar   P
21 Follen St, Cambridge, MA 02138, 617-576-2887
Internet: 103325,2023@compuserve.com
    Pubs: *The Hour Between Dog and Wolf* (BOA Edtns, 1997),
    Night Out: Anth, Drive They Said: Anth (Milkweed Editions,
    1997, 1995), *Ploughshares, Harvard Rev, Marlboro Rev,
    Massachusetts Rev, Crazyhorse.*

Marguerite Guzman Bouvard   P
6 Brookfield Cir, Wellesley, MA 02181, 781-237-1340
Internet: marguerite.bouvard@worldnet.att.net
    Pubs: *The Body's Burning Fields* (Wind Pub, 1997), *Of
    Light and Silence* (Zoland Bks, 1990), *With the Mothers of
    the Plaza de Mayo* (Igneus Pr, 1993), *Journeys Over
    Water, 50th Anniversary Anth* (QRL, 1980, 1994).

John Bovey   W
19 Chauncy St, #2A, Cambridge, MA 02138
    Pubs: *The Silent Meteor* (Bovey, 1988), *Desirable Aliens* (U
    Illinois Pr, 1980), *Virginia Qtly Rev, Canto, Literary Rev,
    NER, Confrontation, New Renaissance, Ploughshares.*

Sally Ryder Brady   W
Brady Literary Management, 267 Dudley Rd, Bedford, MA
01730, 617-275-1842
    Pubs: *Yankee Christmas* (Yankee Bks/Rodale Pr, 1993),
    Instar (Doubleday, 1976), *Good Housekeeping, Woman's
    Day, Catholic Digest.*

Jeanne Braham   P
239 River Rd, Sunderland, MA 01375, 413-665-7857
    Pubs: *Starry, Starry Night* (Brookline Bks/Lumen Ed, 1998),
    Crucial Conversations (Teachers College Pr/Columbia,
    1995), *A Sort Of Columbus* (U Georgia Pr, 1984), *One
    Means Of Telling Time* (Geryon Pr, 1981).

Melanie Braverman   P&W
PO Box 1404, Provincetown, MA 02657, 508-487-6576
Internet: mrb@mail1.wn.net
    Pubs: *Welcome to Your Life: Anth* (Milkweed Edtns, 1998),
    East Justice (Permanent Pr, 1996), *American Voice,
    Carolina Qtly, Provincetown Arts, APR.*

Lucie Brock-Broido   P
Harvard Univ, 34 Kirkland St, Cambridge, MA 02138
    Pubs: *A Hunger* (Knopf, 1988), *American Voice, Paris Rev,
    APR, New Republic, Southwest Rev, Ploughshares,
    Virginia Qtly, Mississippi Rev, Ironwood, Kenyon Rev.*

Martin Broekhuysen   P
22 Traymore St, Cambridge, MA 02140, 617-492-4510
    Pubs: *Nation, Southern Poetry Rev, Niagara Mag, Nimrod,
    Miscellany.*

Ben Brooks   W
PO Box 440387, West Somerville, MA 02144-0387,
617-623-3719
Internet: bbrooks@mos.org
    Pubs: *The Icebox* (Amelia Pr, 1987), *Sewanee Rev,
    Mississippi Rev, O. Henry Prize Stories, American Short
    Fiction, Alaska Qtly Rev, Confrontation.*

Olga Broumas   P
162 Mill Pond Dr, Brewster, MA 02631, 508-896-6001
    Pubs: *Sappho's Gymnasium* (w/T. Begley), *Perpetua*
    (Copper Canyon Pr, 1994, 1989), *APR, American Voice,
    Sonora Rev, Zyzzyva.*

Kurt Brown   P
21 Follen St, Cambridge, MA 02138, 617-576-2887
Internet: kurt_brown@compuserve.com
    Pubs: *Return of the Prodigals* (Four Way Bks, 1999), *Drive,
    They Said: Anth* (Milkweed Edtns, 1994), *Harvard Rev,
    Crazyhorse, Indiana Rev, Ploughshares, Southern Poetry
    Rev, Massachusetts Rev.*

Robert Edward Brown   P
PO Box 442, Brimfield, MA 01010-0442
    Pubs: *Gathering The Light* (Red Hill Pr, 1976), *Altadena
    Rev, Bachy, Coast, Sunset Palms Hotel.*

Steven Ford Brown P
PO Box 2764, Boston, MA 02208
Pubs: *Astonishing World* (Milkweed Edtns, 1993), *The Sky Is Guilty of An Oblique, Considered Music* (Harrington-Black, 1989), *Harvard Rev, Seneca Rev.*

Jane Brox P
1334 Broadway, Dracut, MA 01826
Pubs: *Here and Nowhere Else* (Beacon Pr, 1995), *In Short: Anth* (Norton, 1996), *Georgia Rev, Gettysburg Rev, Salamander, NER, Hudson Rev.*

Roy Bryan P
Cross Place Rd, Washington, MA 01235, 413-623-6446
Pubs: *Winter Lightning* (Wild Thistle Pr, 1979), *Poetry East, Home Planet News.*

Ruth Buchman P
5 Mountain Ave, Somerville, MA 02143, 617-623-3874
Pubs: *Sou'wester, Harvard Rev, Antioch Rev, Embers, Birmingham Poetry Rev, Cricket, Sojourner, Sing Heavenly Muse.*

Claudia Buckholts P&W
15 Clarendon Ave, Somerville, MA 02144-1704, 617-666-9040
Internet: lanbuck@ix.netcom.com
Pubs: *Prairie Schooner, Harvard Mag, Connecticut Poetry Rev, Minnesota Rev, Midwest Qtly, Kansas Qtly.*

Julia Budenz P
1616 Massachusetts Ave, #5, Cambridge, MA 02138, 617-868-4769
Pubs: *From The Gardens Of Flora Baum* (Wesleyan, 1984), *A Formal Feeling Comes: Anth* (Storyline, 1994), *Notre Dame Rev, Vergilius, The American Voice, The Tennessee Rev, Italian American, Sparrow.*

Carol Burnes P
Box 364, Weston, MA 02193, 781-899-7518
Internet: jburnes@earthwatch.org
Pubs: *An Episode of Buttons* (Flarestack Pub UK, 1998), *Fine Lines* (Headland Pubs, 1992), *Roots & Wings* (Emerald Pr, 1986), *13th Moon, The Little Mag, Pipe Works UK, Rhino, Sail, CSM, Connections, Connecticut Mag.*

Gray Burr P
7 Snows Rd, Box 575, Truro, MA 02666, 508-349-7327
Pubs: *Afterlives* (Singular Speech Pr, 1996), *Sparrow, Northeast.*

Teresa Cader P
20 Clarke St, Lexington, MA 02173, 617-863-0166
Pubs: *Guests* (Ohio State U Pr, 1991), *Touchstones: Anth* (U Pr of New England, 1996), *TriQuarterly, Harvard Mag, Ploughshares, Agni, Parnassus: Poetry in Rev.*

Jeffrey A. Carver W
102 Melrose St, Arlington, MA 02174, 781-646-1375
Internet: http://starrigger.net/ or jeff@starrigger.net
Pubs: *The Infinite Sea, Strange Attractors, Neptune Crossing* (Tor, 1996, 1995, 1994), *Science Fiction Age, Galaxy, Galileo, Fiction, Fantasy & Science Fiction.*

John Case P&W
37A Prentiss St, Cambridge, MA 02140

Elena Castedo P&W
Accent Media, 36 Lancaster St, Cambridge, MA 02140-2840, 617-492-6026
Pubs: *Paradise* (Grove Pr, 1995), *El Paraiso* (Ediciones B, 1994), *Prairie Schooner, New Letters, Phoebe, Afro-Hispanic Rev, Listening to Ourselves, Iguana Dreams, Mirrored Garden.*

Ed Cates P
72 Moreland St, 1st Fl, Somerville, MA 02145, 617-625-1945
Pubs: *Remember Your Dreams* (Olympic Music Pub, 1981), *Geopolitics* (Arm-in-Arm, 1979), *Imagine, Z Misc, Moody Street Rev, Noctaluca, Boston Literary Rev, Door #3.*

Karen Chase P&W
Box 634, Lenox, MA 01240, 413-637-0505
Pubs: *Norton Introduction to Literature: Anth, Norton Introduction to Poetry: Anth* (Norton, 1998, 1998), *Under One Roof: Anth* (Mad River Pr, 1992), *Yellow Silk Erotic Arts and Letters: Anth* (Crown, 1990), *New Yorker, Gettysburg Rev, Shenandoah, Seattle Rev.*

Naomi Feigelson Chase P
PO Box 1231, 66 Depot Rd, Truro, MA 02666-1231, 508-349-1991
Pubs: *Stacked, Waiting for the Messiah in Somerville, MA* (Garden Street Pr, 1998, 1993), *Listening for Water* (Archival Pr, 1987), *Harvard Rev, South Coast Poetry Jrnl, Yankee, American Literary Rev, Prairie Schooner, Amaranth, ELF, Lowell Rev.*

Polly Chase P
17 Lovers Ln, Groton, MA 01450, 508-448-5093
Pubs: *Cancelled Reservations* (Poet Pr, 1986), *Poet Lore, Driftwood East, Jean's Jrnl.*

Helen Chasin P
9 South St Ct, Rockport, MA 01966, 508-546-2937
Pubs: *Casting Stones* (Little, Brown, 1975), *Coming Close* (Yale Univ Pr, 1968).

Laura Chester P&W
25 Rose Hill, Alford, MA 01230, 413-528-0458
Pubs: *The Story of the Lake* (Faber & Faber, 1995), *Bitches Ride Alone* (Black Sparrow, 1991), *The Unmade Bed: Anth* (HarperCollins, 1992).

James William Chichetto   P
PO Box 136, South Easton, MA 023750136
Internet: chichetto@stonehill.edu
Pubs: *Homage To Father Sorin* (Connecticut Poetry Rev
Pr, 1993), *Blood To Remember: American Poets on the
Holocaust: Anth* (Texas Tech U, 1991), *Poem, Colorado
Rev, Boston Globe.*

John J. Clayton   W
Univ Massachusetts, Amherst, MA 01003, 413-548-9645
Internet: jclayton@english.umass.edu
Pubs: *Bodies Of The Rich* (U Illinois, 1984), *What Are
Friends For?* (Little, Brown, 1979), *Esquire, Agni, Playboy,
TriQuarterly, Georgia Rev, Virginia Qtly Rev.*

Bradley Clompus   P
75 Brookings St, Medford, MA 02155
Pubs: *Backwash, Outerbridge, Scape, Soundings/East,
Cream City Rev, Police Beat, Pavement, Passages North,
West Branch, Poet Lore, Amelia.*

Richard Cluster   W
33 Jackson St, Cambridge, MA 02140, 617-876-8464
Pubs: *Obligations of the Bone* (St. Martin's Pr, 1992),
Return to Sender (Dutton, 1988).

Andrew Coburn   W
3 Farrwood Dr, Andover, MA 01810, 508-475-8701
Pubs: *Birthright* (S&S, 1997), *Voices in the Dark, No Way
Home* (Dutton, 1994, 1992), *Goldilocks* (Scribner, 1989),
Love Nest, Sweetheart (Macmillan, 1987, 1985), *A Woolf in
Vita's Clothing, Lilacs, Charley Judd, Transatlantic Rev,
Ellery Queen.*

Judith Beth Cohen   W
Lesley College Graduate School, 29 Everett St, Cambridge,
MA 02138
Pubs: *Seasons* (Permanent Pr, 1984), *High Plains Literary
Rev, Rosebud, Rockford Rev, American Rev, New Letters.*

Martha Collins   P&W
66 Martin St, #3, Cambridge, MA 02138, 617-661-0785
Internet: mcollins@umbsky.cc.umb.edu
Pubs: *A History of Small Life On A Windy Planet* (U
Georgia Pr, 1993), *The Arrangement of Space* (Peregrine
Smith, 1991).

Pat Lowery Collins   P&W
3 Wauketa Rd, Gloucester, MA 01930-1423, 978-283-2749
Internet: patlc19@mail.idt.net
Pubs: *The Quiet Woman Wakes Up Shouting* (Folly Cove
Bks, 1998), *Parting Gifts: Anth* (March Street Pr, 1994), *I
Am An Artist* (Millbrook Pr, 1992), *U.S. 1 Worksheets,
Visions Intl, Wind, Small Pond, Before the Rapture,
Primavera.*

William Conelly   P&W
131 Montague Rd, Leverett, MA 01054, 413-548-9430
Pubs: *Foothills, Nine Years After: Anth* (R. L. Barth, 1987,
1989), *Tennessee Qtly, Dark Horse, Poets On, Pleiades,
Epigrammatist, Sticks.*

D. L. Cooke   P
131 Old State Rd, Berkshire, MA 01224, 413-499-9877
Pubs: *Civil Rites, Cowboy Amok* (Black Scholar Pr, 1996,
1987), *Black Scholar, Open Places, Minnesota Rev, New
Collage.*

William Corbett   P
9 Columbus Sq, Boston, MA 02116, 617-266-5466
Pubs: *City Nature III, On Blue Note* (Zoland Bks, 1991,
1989), *o.blek, Lift, NAW, Talisman, Notus.*

Christopher Jane Corkery   P
20 Kenwood St, Dorchester, MA 02124, 617-288-8512
Pubs: *Blessing* (Princeton, 1985), *Boston Rev, Poetry,
Ironwood, New England Rev.*

Bill Costley   P
One Sunset Rd, Wellesley, MA 021814615, 781-431-1314
Internet: sunset@gis.net
Pubs: *Siciliconia* (Beehive Pr, 1995), *Terrazzo* (Malfunction
Pr, 1993), *A*(y)s(h)a, *Rag*(a)s (Ghost Dance, 1988, 1978),
Ploughshares.

Dean Crawford   W
800 Northwest Hill Rd, Williamstown, MA 01267
Pubs: *Lay of the Land* (Viking, 1987), *Epoch, New England
Rev.*

George Cuomo   P&W
276 Pelham Rd, Amherst, MA 01002, 413-253-0636
Internet: cuomo@english.umass.edu
Pubs: *A Couple of Cops, Trial by Water* (Random Hse,
1995, 1993).

Siouxie D   P
12 Wendell St #3, Cambridge, MA 02138, 617-491-8973
Internet: recept4@harvard.edu
Pubs: *After Gary, It's Only Life* (Self/Aardvark Enterprises,
1996, 1992), *Quest, Heartlight Jrnl, Poet's Pen Qtly, Pagan
America, Vision Seeker.*

Ellen Darion   W
335A Harvard St, Apt 12, Cambridge, MA 02139,
617-492-2793
Pubs: *Gettysburg Rev, Special Report: Fiction, Epoch.*

Helene Davis   P
76 Kinnaird St, Cambridge, MA 02139, 617-864-1315

Hope Hale Davis   W
1600 Massachusetts Ave, #704, Cambridge, MA 02138,
617-497-5988
    Pubs: *Great Day Coming* (Steerforth Pr, 1994), *The Dark
    Way to the Plaza* (Doubleday, 1968), *New Leader, New
    Yorker, Radcliffe Qtly.*

Peter Davison   P
70 River St, Boston, MA 02108-1125, 617-742-0342
Internet: davispoe@aol.com
    Pubs: *The Fading Smile: Poets in Boston 1955-1960*
    (Norton, 1996), *The Poems of Peter Davison 1957-1995,
    The Great Ledge* (Knopf, 1995, 1989), *Atlantic, Yale Rev,
    Frank, Nation, Poetry, APR.*

Benjamin Demott   W
Amherst College, Amherst, MA 01002

Diana Der-Hovanessian   P
2 Farrar St, Cambridge, MA 02138, 617-864-2224
    Pubs: *Any Day Now, Circle Dancers, Selected Poems*
    (Sheep Meadow Pr, 1999, 1997, 1994), *American Scholar,
    Agni, Graham Hse, Partisan Rev, CSM, Nation, Prairie
    Schooner, Yankee.*

William Devoti   P
Foley Rd, Sheffield, MA 01257, 413-229-8461
Internet: dotbill@bcn.net
    Pubs: *October Mountain* (Mountain Pr, 1991), *Coming Out
    of It* (Hollow Springs, 1981), *Third Berkshire Anth*
    (Berkshire Writers, 1982).

Richard Dey   P
178 Gardner St, Hingham, MA 02043, 617-740-2920
    Pubs: *New Bequia Poems* (Offshore Pr, 1996), *The Bequia
    Poems* (Caribbean; Macmillan, 1989), *Sail, Poetry, Harvard
    Mag, Light, Caribbean Writer, Caribbean Compass.*

Carol Dine   P
7 Lynn Shore Dr, Lynn, MA 01902-4905
    Pubs: *Trying to Understand the Lunar Eclipse* (Erie Street
    Pr, 1992), *Naming the Sky* (Golden Quill, 1989), *Speaking
    of New England: Anth* (North Country Pr, 1993), *Out of
    Season: Anth* (Amagansett Pr, 1993), *Women's Rev of
    Books,* Prairie Schooner.

Gerard Dombrowski   P
PO Box C, Somerville, MA 02143, 617-623-8017

David F. Donavel   P
54 Pearl St, Amesbury, MA 01913, 508-388-2337
    Pubs: *Cape Rock, Windless Orchard, Tendril, Snowy Egret,
    Wind, Fireland Arts Rev, Kansas Qtly.*

Susan Donnelly   P
32 Shepard St, #21, Cambridge, MA 02138, 617-491-4559
Internet: sedonne@aol.com
    Pubs: *Tenderly Pressed* (Every Other Thursday Pr, 1993),
    Eve Names The Animals (Northeastern U Pr, 1985), *The
    Norton Introduction To Poetry: Anth* (Norton, 1995),
    Ploughshares, Southern Poetry Rev.

Susan Donovan   P
Box 2662, Amherst, MA 010042662, 413-545-3897
    Pubs: *White Lobster* (Blue Willow Inn, 1980), *Georgia Rev,
    Massachusetts Rev, New Letters.*

Mary Harris Driscoll   P
206 W Main St, Milbury, MA 01527, 508-865-4242
    Pubs: *Soundings East: Anth* (Salem State College, 1985),
    *Skylark, Pegasus, Night Sun, Sounds of Poetry, Manhattan
    Poetry Rev, Embers, Riverwind, Potpourri, Prairie Dog,
    Green Mountains Rev, Black Fly Rev.*

Andre Dubus   W
753 E Broadway, Haverhill, MA 01830
    Pubs: *Broken Vessels, Selected Stories* (Godine, 1991,
    1988).

Andre Dubus, III   W
24 Allen St, Newburyport, MA 01950-3002, 508-462-1010
    Pubs: *Bluesman* (Faber & Faber, 1993), *The Cage Keeper
    & Other Stories* (Dutton, 1989), *Playboy, Yankee,
    Crazyhorse, Epoch, Crescent Rev, Image.*

Ann duCille   P
Bridgewater State College, English Dept, Bridgewater, MA
02324, 617-697-1258
    Pubs: *For Neruda/For Chile: Anth* (Beacon Pr, 1975), *APR,
    Bridgewater Rev, Iowa Rev, New Letters.*

Alan Dugan   P
Box 97, Truro, MA 02666
    Pubs: *New & Collected Poems: 1961-1983* (Ecco Pr, 1983).

Susan Eisenberg   P
9 Rockview St, Jamaica Plain, MA 02130
Internet: ssneisnbrg@aol.com
    Pubs: *Pioneering* (Cornell U Pr, 1998), *It's A Good Thing
    I'm Not Macho* (Whetstone, 1984), *If I Had My Life To Live
    Over: Anth* (Papier-Mache, 1992), *Prairie Schooner, Willow
    Springs, Mothering, Seattle Rev, Many Mountains Moving.*

Craig Ellis   P
40 Potter St, Concord, MA 01742, 978-369-5592
    Pubs: *Sparrow in the Supermarket* (Beehive Pr, 1997),
    *Aspect, Assembling, Gallimaufry, Intrepid, Nostoc,
    Wormwood Rev.*

David Ely W
PO Box 1387, East Dennis, MA 02641
    Pubs: *A Journal of the Flood Year, Always Home and Other Stories* (Donald I. Fine, 1992, 1991), *Atlantic, Redbook, Playboy, Kenyon Rev.*

Leslie Epstein W
23 Parkman St, Brookline, MA 02146, 617-734-3896
    Pubs: *King of the Jews* (Norton, 1992), *Pinto & Sons* (HM, 1990), *Goldkorn Tales* (Dutton, 1985), *Pandemonium: Anth* (St. Martin's, 1997), *Playboy, Georgia Rev, Harper's, Atlantic, TriQuarterly, Yale Rev, Nation.*

Martin Espada P
Univ Massachusetts, English Dept, Bartlett Hall, Amherst, MA 01003, 413-545-6594
    Pubs: *Imagine the Angels of Bread, City of Coughing and Dead Radiators* (Norton, 1996, 1993), *Rebellion is the Circle of a Lover's Hands* (Curbstone, 1990).

Rhina P. Espaillat P
12 Charron Dr, Newburyport, MA 01950-3705, 508-462-9144
Internet: espmosk@juno.com
    Pubs: *Where Horizons Go* (New Odyssey Pr, 1998), *Lapsing to Grace* (Bennett & Kitchel, 1992), *A Formal Feeling Comes: Anth* (Story Line Pr, 1994), *In Other Words: Anth* (Arte Publico Pr, 1994), Poetry, *Formalist, Pivot, American Scholar, Sparrow, Hellas.*

Nancy Esposito P
34 Trowbridge St, Belmont, MA 02478, 617-484-7479
Internet: nesposito@bentley.edu
    Pubs: *Changing Hands, Quarterly Rev of Literature 50th Anniversary Anth* (QRL, 1984, 1993), *Prairie Schooner, Southwest Rev, Indiana Rev, Nation, APR, Seattle Rev.*

Howard Faerstein P
123 West St, Sandisfield, MA 01255
    Pubs: *Play A Song On The Drums He Said* (Owl's Head Pr, 1977), *Airplane, Tuatara, Confrontation, Painted Bride Qtly, Touchstone, Berkshire Rev.*

Richard J. Fein P
46 Irving St, Cambridge, MA 02138, 617-354-2785
    Pubs: *At The Turkish Bath* (Chestnut Hills Pr, 1994), *Kafka's Ear* (The New Poets Series, 1990).

Alan Feldman P&W
399 Belknap Rd, Framingham, MA 01701, 508-877-4370
    Pubs: *Anniversary* (Chekhov & Co., 1992), *Lucy Mastermind* (Dutton, 1985), *Iowa Rev, Denver Qtly, Mississippi Rev.*

Jyl Lynn Felman W
8 High Meadow Rd, Northampton, MA 01060-2625, 413-586-8080
    Pubs: *Hot Chicken Wings* (Aunt Lute Bks, 1992), *Her Face In The Mirror: Anth, The Tribe of Dina: Anth* (Beacon, 1994, 1989).

William Ferguson P&W
1 Tahanto Rd, Worcester, MA 01602, 508-757-1683
    Pubs: *Freedom And Other Fictions* (Knopf, 1984), *Mississippi Rev, Fiction, Harper's, Paris Rev.*

Vincent Ferrini P
126 E Main St, Gloucester, MA 01930, 508-283-5640
    Pubs: *Deluxe Daring* (Atelier, 1994), *Magdalene Silences, A Tale of Psyche* (Igneus, 1992, 1991), *Why, Atelier, First Intensity, House Organ, Left Curve.*

David Ferry P
8 Ellery St, Cambridge, MA 02138, 617-354-7327
Internet: dferry@wellesley.edu
    Pubs: *Dwelling Places: Poems & Translations* (Chicago U Pr, 1993), *The Odes of Horace, Gilgamesh: A New Rendering in English Verse* (FSG, 1997, 1992), *Raritan, Partisan Rev, Threepenny Rev, TriQuarterly, Arion, Agni.*

Andrew Fetler W
125 Amity St, Amherst, MA 01002-2202, 413-549-5056
    Pubs: *Norton Anth of Short Fiction* (Norton, 1994), *Prize Stories: The O. Henry Awards Anth* (Doubleday, 1984), *Atlantic, TriQuarterly, New American Rev.*

Thomas Filbin W
104 Clear Pond Dr, Walpole, MA 02801
    Pubs: *William and Mary Rev, Cache Rev, Proof Rock, Mississippi Valley Rev, Boston Rev, the new renaissance.*

Brent Filson W
RFD White Oaks Rd, Williamstown, MA 01267, 413-458-5285
    Pubs: *Exploring With Lasers* (S&S, 1984), *The Puma* (Doubleday, 1984), *Yankee, Vermont Life.*

Jack Flavin P
634 Armory St, Springfield, MA 01104, 413-732-0435
    Pubs: *Atlantic, Massachusetts Rev, Epoch, Poetry Northwest, Plains Poetry Rev, Galley Sail Rev, Sonoma Mandala, Apalachee Qtly, Spoon River Poetry Rev, Midwest Qtly.*

Ann Fletcher P
PO Box 147, West Stockbridge, MA 012660147
    Pubs: *Quarterly West, South Florida State Rev, Cimarron Rev, Prairie Schooner, Sing Heavenly Muse.*

Marjorie Fletcher P
36 Moon Hill Rd, Lexington, MA 02173, 617-861-9659
    Pubs: *33, Us: Women* (Alice James Bks, 1976, 1974).

Maria Flook P&W
PO Box 2022, Truro, MA 02666, 508-487-7918
    Pubs: *My Sister Life: The Story of My Sister's Disappearance, You Have The Wrong Man, Open Water, Family Night* (Pantheon, 1998, 1996, 1995, 1993), *New Yorker, New Criterion, Ploughshares, Bomb.*

Aaron Fogel   P
Boston Univ, 236 Bay State Rd, Boston, MA 02215
Internet: amfogel@acs.bu.edu
   Pubs: *Best American Poetry: Anths* (Scribner, 1995, 1990),
The Stud Duck, Agni, Boulevard.

Jack Ford   P&W
Box 6098, Newburyport, MA 01950, 617-462-8985
   Pubs: *12 Surrealist Fairy Tales* (Alphaville Bks, 1975),
Chicago Rev, Small Press Rev, Aiieee Mag.

Jan Frazier   P
183 Mt Hermon Rd, Northfield, MA 01360, 413-498-2952
Internet: janf@javanet.com
   Pubs: *Our Mothers, Our Selves: Anth* (Bergin & Garvey,
1996), *Yankee Mag, Passages North, Plum Rev, High
Plains Literary Rev, Artful Dodge, Kalliope, Calyx.*

K. C. Frederick   W
68 Chestnut St, #1, West Newton, MA 02165-2549
Internet: frederick@umbsky.cc.umb.edu
   Pubs: *Country of Memory* (Permanent Pr, 1998), *Sacred
Ground* (Milkweed Edtns, 1996), *Epoch, Shenandoah,
Kansas Qtly, Fiction Intl, Ascent, Quarterly West, Beloit
Fiction Jrnl.*

Jan Freeman   P
PO Box 487, Ashfield, MA 01330, 413-628-0051
Internet: parispr@crocker.com
   Pubs: *Hyena* (Cleveland State U Poetry Ctr, 1993), *Autumn
Sequence* (Paris Pr, 1993), *Oxford Book of Women's
Writing in the U.S.: Anth* (Oxford U Pr, 1995), *Chelsea,
Massachusetts Rev, APR, American Voice.*

Margaret Howe Freydberg   W
RR Box 21 Stonewall Pond, Chilmark, MA 02535,
508-645-2518
   Pubs: *Growing Up in Old Age* (Parnassus, 1998), *Winter
Concert* (Countryman, 1985).

B. H. Friedman   W
Box 276, Becket, MA 01223, 413-623-5170
   Pubs: *Between the Flags* (Fiction Collective, 1990), *The
Polygamist* (Atlantic, 1981), *Epoch.*

D. Dina Friedman   P
PO Box 1164, Northampton, MA 01061, 413-586-2388
Internet: dina@frugal.fun.com
   Pubs: *Calyx, The Sun, Hurricane Alice, Paragraph, Black
Bear Rev, Amelia, Oxalis, Worcester Rev, Permafrost,
Pacific Poetry & Fiction Rev.*

Barbara Friend   P
Amherst College, Amherst, MA 01002, 413-542-2328
   Pubs: *Thirtieth Year To Heaven* (Jackpine Pr, 1980),
Virginia Qtly Rev, Ms., Yankee.

Kenny Fries   P
42 Day Ave, Northampton, MA 01060
   Pubs: *The Healing Notebooks* (Open Bks, 1990), *Body,
Remember: Anth* (Dutton, 1997), *Anesthesia: Anth*
(Avacado Pr, 1996), *Kenyon Rev, American Voice,
Ploughshares, The Progressive.*

Rocco Fumento   W
1100 Main St, Dalton, MA 01226, 413-684-4006
   Pubs: *The Sea Wolf* (SLU Pr, 1998), *42nd Street* (U
Wisconsin Pr, 1980), *Tree of Dark Reflection* (Knopf, 1963),
Devil by the Tail (McGraw-Hill, 1954), *Chicago, Ramparts.*

Erica Funkhouser   P
179 Southern Ave, Essex, MA 01929
   Pubs: *Sure Shot* (HM, 1992), *Natural Affinities* (Alice James
Bks, 1983), *Poetry, Ploughshares, Paris Rev, New Yorker,
Atlantic.*

Brendan Galvin   P
PO Box 383, Truro, MA 026660383, 508-349-6077
   Pubs: *Hotel Malabar* (U Iowa Pr, 1998), *Sky and Island
Light, Saints in their Ox-Hide Boat, Wampanoag Traveler*
(LSU Pr, 1997, 1992, 1989), *Great Blue: New & Selected
Poems* (U Illinois Pr, 1990).

Kinereth Gensler   P
221 Mt Auburn St, #404, Cambridge, MA 02138,
617-576-7243
Internet: kgens@worldnet.att.net
   Pubs: *Journey Fruit: Poems & a Memoir, Without Roof*
(Alice James Bks, 1997, 1981), *Connection* (Teachers &
Writers, 1978), *American Voice, The Bridge, Poetry,
Ploughshares, Sou'wester, Massachusetts Rev.*

David Giannini   P
PO Box 630, Otis, MA 01253-0630
   Pubs: *Keys* (Leave Bks, 1993), *Antonio & Clara* (Adastra
Pr, 1992), *The Unmade Bed: Anth* (HarperCollins, 1992),
Shadowplay, Sonora Rev, Tel-Let, Talisman.

Celia Gilbert   P
15 Gray Gardens W, Cambridge, MA 02138, 617-864-8778
Internet: cgilbert@nucleus.harvard.edu
   Pubs: *An Ark of Sorts, Bonfire* (Alice James Bks, 1998,
1983), *Queen Of Darkness* (Viking, 1977), *Poetry, New
Yorker, Grand Street.*

Michael Gizzi   P
36 Cliffwood St, Lenox, MA 01240, 413-637-4215
   Pubs: *Continental Harmony* (Roof Bks, 1991), *Vers
d'Aigrefin* (Les Cahiers de Royaumont, 1991), *TXT, Shiny,
Talisman, Tyuonyi, Sulfur, Temblor.*

Perry Glasser   W
Box 1913, Haverhill, MA 01831, 508-373-2687
   Pubs: *Singing On The Titanic* (U Illinois Pr, 1987),
Suspicious Origins (New Rivers Pr, 1983), *Ms., NAW,
TriQuarterly, Confrontation, Special Reports: Fiction.*

James Glickman W
51 McGilpin Rd, Sturbridge, MA 01566-1230
Internet: jaglickman@aol.com
Pubs: *Sounding the Waters* (Crown, 1996), *Kansas Qtly, Redbook, Ladies Home Journal.*

Georgia Gojmerac-Leiner P
9 Union St, Natick, MA 01760-4709, 508-655-8073
Internet: gojmerac@bcvms.bc.edu
Pubs: *Whose Woods These Are: Anth* (Word Works, 1983), *96 Inc., Vermont Times, Onion River Rev, Embers, Green Mountains.*

E. S. Goldman P&W
PO Box 561, South Orleans, MA 02662, 508-255-2312
Pubs: *The Palmer Method, Big Chocolate Cookies* (John Daniel Co., 1995, 1988), *Earthly Justice* (TriQuarterly, 1990), *Atlantic, Missouri Rev, Cimarron.*

Elizabeth Goldring P
383 Old Ayes Rd, Groton, MA 01450, 978-448-5240
Internet: goldring@mit.edu
Pubs: *Laser Treatment* (Blue Giant Pr, 1983), *Without Warning* (Helicon Nine Edtns, 1995), *Asylum, Helicon Nine.*

Susan Goldwitz P
9 Mendum St, Roslindale, MA 02131
Pubs: *Dreams Of The Hand* (Empty Bowl Pr, 1984), *Bellingham Rev, Eleven, Gargoyle, Dalmona.*

Deborah Gorlin P
20 Maplewood Dr, Amherst, MA 01002, 413-549-4146
Internet: dgorlin@hampshire.edu
Pubs: *Bodily Course* (White Pine Pr, 1997), *Connecticut Qtly, Massachusetts Rev, Poetry, Prairie Schooner, Crazy Horse, New England Rev.*

Tzivia Gover P&W
74 Ranney Corner Rd, Ashfield, MA 01330
Internet: tz11@aol.com
Pubs: *My Lover Is A Woman: Anth* (Ballantine Bks, 1996), *Peregrine, Malachite & Agate, Evergreen Chronicles, Sinister Wisdom, Japanophile, Sojourner, Amelia, Lesbian Short Fiction.*

E. J. Graff W
197 Westminster Ave, Watertown, MA 02172, 617-924-5172
Internet: ejgraff@aol.com
Pubs: *What Is Marriage For?* (Beacon Pr, 1999), *Tasting Life Twice: Anth* (Avon Morrow, 1995), *Voices of the X-iled: Anth* (Doubleday, 1994), *Iowa Rev, Kenyon Rev, Nation, Out.*

Maria Grande-Conley P
724 Plymouth St, Holbrook, MA 02343
Pubs: *The Rolling Coulter* (Missouri Western State College, 1990), *Anth of Italian American Poets* (Malefemmina Pr, 1993), *la bella figura.*

Christina J. Green P
40 Ocean Ave, Salem, MA 019705406, 978-745-8720
Internet: c1phd@aol.com
Pubs: *Up Against the Wall Mother, Poetalk, Wide Open Mag, Poetry Peddler, Free Focus, Jrnl of Poetry Therapy, The Pen, Poems of the World, Not Your Average Zine, Event.*

Barbara L. Greenberg P&W
770 Boylston St, Apt 6-1, Boston, MA 02199-7705
Pubs: *What Nell Knows* (Summer Hse/Snowberries Pr, 1997), *The Never-Not Sonnets* (U Pr Florida, 1989), *Fire Drills* (U Missouri Pr, 1982).

Bette Greene W
338 Clinton Rd, Brookline, MA 02146, 617-232-9855
Pubs: *Them That Glitter* (Knopf, 1983), *Philip Hall Likes Me* (Dial, 1974).

Carolyn Gregory P
50 Green St, #106, Brookline, MA 02146
Pubs: *Playing By Ear* (Green Street Pr, 1994), *Tour of Light: Anth* (Pressford, 1996), *Artword Qtly, Yankee, The MacGuffin, Seattle Rev, Georgetown Rev.*

Joe Haldeman W
MIT, Writing Program, 14E-303, Cambridge, MA 02139
Pubs: *Worlds Enough and Time, The Hemingway Hoax, Buying Time* (Morrow, 1992, 1990, 1989), *Tool of the Trade* (Avon, 1988).

Anne Halley P&W
244 Amity St, Amherst, MA 01002, 413-549-5083
Pubs: *Rumors of the Turning Wheel* (Aife Pr, 1986), *The Bearded Mother* (U Massachusetts Pr, 1979).

Paul Hannigan W
22 Fayette St, #2, Cambridge, MA 02139-1112
Pubs: *Bringing Back Slavery* (Dolphin Edtns, 1976).

Jeffrey Harrison P
59 Highland Rd, Andover, MA 01810
Pubs: *Signs of Arrival* (Copper Beech Pr, 1996), *The Singing Underneath* (Dutton, 1988), *Nation, Paris Rev, New Yorker, New Republic, Poetry.*

James Haug P
15 Washington Ave, Northampton, MA 01060
Pubs: *Fox Luck* (Center for Book Arts, 1998), *The Stolen Car* (U Massachusetts Pr, 1989), *DoubleTake, Green Mountains Rev, American Literary Rev, Gettysburg Rev, Witness, Quarterly West, Ploughshares, Massachusetts Rev, Crazyhorse, Poetry East.*

Stratis Haviaras P&W
Harvard Univ, Cambridge, MA 02138, 617-495-2454
Pubs: *The Heroic Age, When the Tree Sings* (S&S, 1984, 1979), *Crossing the River Twice* (Cleveland State U Pr, 1976), *Harvard Rev, Iowa Rev, Columbia Rev.*

Juanita Havill   P
Houghton Mifflin Co, 222 Berkeley St, Boston, MA
02116-3764
> Pubs: *Jamaica's Blue Marker, Jamaica and Brianna* (HM,
> 1995, 1993), *Saving Owen's Toad* (Hyperion, 1994), *The
> Most Wonderful Books: Anth* (Milkweed Edtns, 1997),
> *Ladybug, Cricket, Five Owls, Us Kids.*

Mary Hazzard   W
452 Woodward St, Waban, MA 02168, 617-332-6009
Internet: 102153,2370@compuserve.com
> Pubs: *Sheltered Lives* (Pinnacle, 1981), *Idle And Disorderly
> Persons* (Madrona, 1981), *Northern Rev, New England
> Writers Network, 96 Inc..*

Judy Page Heitzman   P
746 Forest St, Marshfield, MA 02050
> Pubs: *Maybe Grace* (Sandstone Pub, 1994), *Bedford
> Introduction to Literature: Anth* (Bedford Bks of St. Martin's
> Pr, 1993), *New Yorker, Sojourner, Three Rivers Poetry Jrnl,
> Yankee.*

DeWitt Henry   W
33 Buick St, Watertown, MA 02172, 617-924-0012
Internet: bakofpak@aol.com
> Pubs: *Fathering Daughters: Anth* (Beacon, 1998), *The
> Pushcart Prize XIV: Anth* (Pushcart Pr, 1989), *Boulevard,
> Texas Rev, Agni, Antioch Rev, Missouri Rev, Iowa Rev,
> Nebraska Rev, Colorado Rev, American Voice, Nerve.*

Marcie Hershman   W
46 Stanton Rd, Brookline, MA 02246, 617-566-0035
Internet: mhershma@emerald.tufts.edu
> Pubs: *Safe In America, Tales of the Master Race*
> (HarperCollins, 1995, 1991), *New York Times Mag, The
> Writer, Ms., Tikkun, Ploughshares, Agni.*

Alan V. Hewat   W
Thomas Hart Literary Agency, 20 Kenwood St, Dorchester,
MA 02124, 617-288-8512
> Pubs: *Lady's Time* (H&R, 1985), *Esquire, Ascent, Iowa
> Rev, New Boston Rev of the Arts, Massachusetts Rev.*

Emily Hiestand   P
Palmer & Dodge Agency, 1 Beacon St, Boston, MA 02108,
617-573-0468
Internet: collard@delphi.com
> Pubs: *Angela The Upside-Down Girl, The Very Rich Hours*
> (Beacon Pr, 1998, 1992), *Green The Witch-Hazel Wood*
> (Graywolf Pr, 1989), *New Yorker, Atlantic, Partisan Rev,
> Georgia Rev, Michigan Qtly Rev, Nation, Orion, Southeast
> Rev.*

George V. Higgins   W
50 Staniford St, Boston, MA 02114

John Hildebidle   P&W
MIT, 14N-434, Cambridge, MA 02139, 617-253-4452
Internet: jjhildeb@mit.edu
> Pubs: *Defining Absence* (Ireland; Salmon Pub, 1999), *One
> Sleep, One Waking* (Wyndham Hall Pr, 1994), *The Errand
> of Keeping Alive: Anth* (Harvard U Pr, 1989), *Yankee,
> Ploughshares, Poetry, Thema.*

Hollis Hodges   W
PO Box 436, Stockbridge, MA 01262, 413-298-4980
> Pubs: *Norman Rockwell's Greatest Painting* (Paul S.
> Eriksson, 1988).

Richard Hoffman   P
3 Gladstone St, Cambridge, MA 02140, 617-661-8043
> Pubs: *Half the House* (HB, 1995), *An Ear to the Ground:
> Anth* (U Georgia Pr, 1990), *Hudson Rev, Shenandoah, The
> Sun, American Rev.*

William Holinger   W
20 Chapel St, #511-B, Brookline, MA 02146-5458
> Pubs: *The Football Wars, 21st Century Fox* (Scholastic,
> 1992, 1989), *Fence-Walker* (SUNY Pr, 1985), *Iowa Rev,
> Texas Rev, New Directions, Agni.*

Lucy Honig   W
111 Dorchester St, Squantum, MA 02171
> Pubs: *Prize Stories: O. Henry Awards: Anths* (Doubleday,
> 1996, 1992), *Best American Short Stories: Anth* (HM,
> 1988), *Gettysburg Rev, Witness, Georgia Rev, Fiction,
> Agni, DoubleTake, Ploughshares, Glimmer Train Stories.*

Shel Horowitz   P
PO Box 1164, Northampton, MA 01061, 413-586-2388
Internet: www.frugalfun.com or shel@frugalfun.com
> Pubs: *XY Files: Anth* (Sherman-Asher, 1997), *Breathe!*
> (Warthog Pr, 1980), *Against The Wall, Riverrun, Pudding,
> Home Planet News, North Country, Anvil.*

Frances Minturn Howard   P&W
46 Mt Vernon St, Boston, MA 02108
> Pubs: *Poetry, New Yorker, Atlantic, Poetry Now, Virginia
> Qtly Rev.*

William Hunt   P
125 Christian Hill Rd, Great Barrington, MA 01230,
413-528-1639
> Pubs: *Oceans And Corridors Of Orpheus* (Elpenor Pr,
> 1979), *Of The Map That Changes* (Swallow Pr, 1974),
> *APR, Paris Rev, TriQuarterly, Formations.*

Thomas G. Hurley   P
4 Longfellow Pl, #1904, Boston, MA 02114
> Pubs: *Louisville Rev, Altadena Rev, Earthwise, Beacon
> Rev, Crazyquilt, Stone Country, Slant, Grolier Annual.*

Barbara Helfgott Hyett   P
71 Mason Terr, Brookline, MA 02146
Internet: 73563.2004@compuserve.com
    Pubs: *The Tracks We Leave, The Double Reckoning of
    Christopher Columbus* (U Illinois, 1996, 1992), *Hudson
    Rev, New Republic, Partisan Rev, Nation, Prairie
    Schooner, Agni.*

Ruth Ice   W
204 Aspinwall Ave, Brookline, MA 02146
    Pubs: *Epoch, Literary Rev, Kansas Qtly, Catholic Worker.*

Henry Gray James   P
68 Lafayette St, Fairhaven, MA 02719, 508-996-4982
    Pubs: *Limericks, Fables and Poems* (Universal Research,
    1988).

Mildred M. Jeffrey   P&W
Charles River Park, 9 Hawthorne Pl, Apt 5M, Boston, MA
02114
    Pubs: *Detours & Intersections* (Pleasure Dome Pr, 1987),
    In Autumn: Anth (Birnham Wood Graphics, 1994),
    American Land Forum, NAR, Live Poets, Xanadu.

Paul Jenkins   P
40 Manning Rd, Conway, MA 01341
    Pubs: *Radio Tooth* (Four Way Bks, 1997), *Forget The Sky*
    (L'Epervier Pr, 1979), *New Yorker, Gettysburg Rev, Paris
    Rev, Kenyon, Prairie Schooner, Chelsea, Poetry Northwest,
    Malahat Rev.*

Donald Junkins   P
63 Hawks Rd, Deerfield, MA 01342, 413-774-3475
    Pubs: *Playing For Keeps* (Lynx Hse, 1991), *Crossing By
    Ferry* (U Massachusetts Pr, 1978), *APR, New Yorker,
    Atlantic, Sewanee Rev, Antioch Rev, Poetry.*

Roberta Kalechofsky   W
Micah Publications, 255 Humphrey St, Marblehead, MA
01945, 617-631-7601
Internet: rkalechofsky@mecn.mass.edu
    Pubs: *A Boy, A Chicken, And the Lion of Judah, K'tia; A
    Savior of the Jewish People* (Micah Pubs, 1996, 1995),
    Between the Species, On the Issues.

Judy Katz-Levine   P
10 Hillshire Ln, Norwood, MA 02062-3009, 617-769-5931
    Pubs: *A Curious Architecture: Anth* (Stride Pr, 1996),
    Diamonds Are A Girl's Best Friend: Anth (Faber & Faber,
    1994), *Salamander, Shadowplay, Hummingbird.*

William Kemmett   P
PO Box 777, Bryantville, MA 02327-0777, 617-293-9915
    Pubs: *The Bradford Poems, Flesh of a New Moon* (Igneus
    Pr, 1995, 1991), *Faith of Stone* (Wampeter Pr, 1983),
    Poetry East, Seattle Rev, Atelier.

X. J. Kennedy   P
22 Revere St, Lexington, MA 024204424
    Pubs: *Uncle Switch* (S&S, 1997), *Dark Horses: New Poems*
    (Johns Hopkins U Pr, 1992).

Rod Kessler   W
Salem State College, Salem, MA 01970, 978-542-6378
Internet: rod.kessler@salem.mass.edu
    Pubs: *Off in Zimbabwe* (U Missouri Pr, 1985), *Flash Fiction:
    Anth* (Norton, 1992), *North Shore Mag, Dudley Rev,
    Chariton Rev, Calliope, Harvard Rev, Radcliffe Qtly.*

Claire Keyes   P
12 Higgins Rd, Marblehead, MA 01945-2122, 781-631-9454
Internet: ckeyes@salem.mass.edu
    Pubs: *Onset Rev, Fresh Ground, Vermont Literary Rev,
    Spoon River Poetry Rev, Earth's Daughters, Zone 3,
    Crania@digitaldaze.com, The Eleventh Muse, Sojourner.*

Robert Lord Keyes   P
40 S Valley Rd, Amherst, MA 01002, 413-253-2739
    Pubs: *Green Age, Spitball, Westwind Rev, Green
    Mountains Rev, Critical Times, Embers, The Fan, Wind,
    Beloit Poetry Jrnl, Black Buzzard Rev, The Eleventh Muse.*

Rudy John Kikel   P
154 West Newton St, Boston, MA 02118, 617-421-6987
Internet: rudyk@aol.com
    Pubs: *Period Pieces* (Pride Imprints, 1997), *Long Division*
    (Writers Block Pub, 1993), *Lasting Relations* (Sea Horse,
    1984), *Gents, Bad Boys and Barbarians: Anth* (Alyson Pub,
    1995), *Kenyon Rev, Massachusetts Rev, Shenandoah.*

Richard E. Kim   W
59 Leverett Rd, Shutesbury, MA 01072
    Pubs: *In Search of Lost Years* (Korea; Suh Moon Pub,
    1985).

Norman Andrew Kirk   P
14 Bayfield Rd, Wayland, MA 01778
    Pubs: *Panda Zoo* (West of Boston, 1983), *Some Poems My
    Friends* (Four Zoas/Night Hse, 1981), *Atlantic, Bitterroot,
    Poet Lore, Poem, Negative Capability.*

Michael Klein   P&W
PO Box 381414, Cambridge, MA 02238, 617-576-9466
    Pubs: *1990* (Provincetown Arts Pr, 1993), *In the Company
    of My Solitude: AIDS Prose Anth* (Persea Bks, 1994), *New
    England Rev, Columbia, Kenyon Rev.*

Stanley Koehler   P
54 Hills Rd, Amherst, MA 01002, 413-549-1505
    Pubs: *The Perfect Destroyers: Poems of WWII* (Stinehour
    Pr, 1995), *The Fact of Fall* (U Massachusetts Pr, 1969),
    Sewanee Rev, Poetry, Yale Rev, Massachusetts Rev.

Norman Kotker W
45 Lyman Rd, Northampton, MA 01060, 413-586-5207
Pubs: *Billy in Love* (Zoland, 1996), *Learning About God* (Holt, 1988), *Miss Rhode Island* (FSG, 1978).

Zane Kotker W
160 Main St, Northampton, MA 010603134, 413-584-4597
Internet: zane@crocker.com
Pubs: *Try to Remember* (Random Hse, 1997), *White Rising, A Certain Man, Bodies in Motion* (Knopf, 1981, 1976, 1972), *Mademoiselle.*

Herbert Krohn P
53 Centre St, Brookline, MA 02146, 617-232-6904
Pubs: *Partisan Rev, Nation, New Yorker, Evergreen Rev, Boston Phoenix, Chelsea, Village Voice.*

Joseph Langland P
16 Morgan Cir, Amherst, MA 01002-1131, 413-549-6517
Pubs: *Selected Poems* (APR, 1992), *Twelve Poems* (Adastra Pr, 1991), *A Dream of Love* (Pleiades Pr, 1986), *New Yorker, Paris Rev, Massachusetts Rev, Nation.*

Thelma Lantz P
60 Brook Haven Dr, #5, Attleboro, MA 02703, 617-222-6653
Pubs: *The Archer, Joycean Lively Arts Guild Rev, Gusto, Poets Monthly, Driftwood East.*

Jacqueline Lapidus P
PO Box 902, Provincetown, MA 02657
Pubs: *Ultimate Conspiracy* (Lynx Pubs, 1987), *Starting Over* (Out & Out, 1977), *Conditions, Sinister Wisdom, Hanging Loose, Women's Rev of Bks.*

Joseph Lease P
25 Story St #1, Boston, MA 02127, 617-268-6211
Pubs: *Human Rights* (Zoland Bks, 1998), *Grand Street, Talisman, Paris Rev, Lingo, Colorado Rev, Denver Qtly, Pequod, Agni, NAW, Boston Rev.*

Anne D. LeClaire W
PO Box 656, South Chatham, MA 02659, 508-432-6395
Pubs: *Sideshow* (Viking, 1994), *Grace Point* (Signet, 1993), *Every Mother's Son, Land's End* (Bantam, 1987, 1985).

Jane LeCompte W
PO Box 1393, Boston, MA 02117-1393
Pubs: *Moon Passage* (Harper & Row, 1989).

Jacob Leed P
111 Gore St, Cambridge, MA 02141
Pubs: *3x3* (Toucan Pr, 1986), *You Reading, Looking At Chinese Pictures* (Shelley's Pr, 1983, 1981).

Judith Leet P
16 Gate House Rd, Chestnut Hill, MA 02167, 617-277-3857
Pubs: *Flowering Trees And Shrubs: The Botanical Painting of Esther Heins* (H. Abrams, 1987), *Agni.*

Ruth Lepson P
49 Phillips St, Watertown, MA 02172-3917, 617-926-6990
Internet: rlepson@lynx.neu.edu
Pubs: *Dreaming in Color* (Alice James Bks, 1980), *Women's Rev of Bks, Ploughshares, Helicon Nine, Sojourner, Contact II, Harbor Rev, Poet Lore.*

Kathleen Leverich W
40 Rogers Ave, Somerville, MA 02144
Pubs: *The New You, Best Enemies Forever* (Greenwillow Bks, 1998, 1995), *Brigid the Bad, Brigid the Bewitched* (Random Hse, 1995, 1994), *Ascent, Yankee, Mademoiselle, Cosmopolitan.*

Ruth Levin P
221 Mt Auburn St, #307, Cambridge, MA 02138-4847, 617-491-7229
Pubs: *Birthmark* (CCC, 1992), *To Whom it May Concern* (William L. Bouhan, 1986), *Southern Rev, Sewanee Rev, new renaissance, Prairie Schooner, Nation.*

Miriam Levine P
26-A Academy St, Arlington, MA 02174, 617-646-2618
Internet: mlevine@ma.ultranet.com
Pubs: *Devotion: A Memoir* (U Georgia Pr, 1993), *APR, Paris Rev, Kenyon Rev, Ploughshares, Boston Phoenix, Women's Rev of Books, American Voice.*

Sharon Libera P
139 Taylor St, Granby, MA 01033
Pubs: *The First Anth of Missouri Women Writers* (Sheba Rev, 1987), *Ploughshares, Poetry.*

Karen Lindsey P
33 Jefferson St, Cambridge, MA 02141
Pubs: *A Company Of Queens* (Bloody Mary Pr, 1977), *Falling Off The Roof* (Alice James Bks, 1975).

Margaret Lloyd P
17 Lilly St, Florence, MA 01062, 413-584-2752
Internet: Margaret_Lloyd@scns.spfldcol.edu
Pubs: *This Particular Earthly Scene* (Alice James Bks, 1993), *Poetry East, NER, The Journal, Willow Springs, Gettysburg Rev, American Voice, Planet.*

Edward Locke P
12 Flagstaff Hill Terr, Canton, MA 02021, 781-828-3978
Internet: http://users.aol.com/jlocke6/harlequinade.html
Pubs: *What Time is It?, Names for the Self, Green Bank, Advancing Back* (Harlequinade Pr, 1998, 1997, 1995, 1994), *Yale Rev, Poetry, Georgia Rev, Dalhousie Rev, Saturday Rev, Beloit Poetry Jrnl, Nation.*

Edward Lodi W
41 Walnut St, Middleboro, MA 02346, 508-946-4738
Pubs: *Northcote Anth of Short Stories* (Harold Shaw Pub, 1992), *Abortion Stories: Fiction on Fire Anth* (MinRef Pr, 1992), *Snowy Egret, Space and Time, Mediphors, New England Writers Network, Terminal Fright.*

Gian S. Lombardo P
781 E Guinea Rd, Williamsburg, MA 01096, 413-268-7012
Internet: lombardo@quale.com
  Pubs: *Sky Open Again, Standing Room, Between Islands,*
  (Dolphin-Moon, 1997, 1989, 1984), *Lift, Denver Qtly,*
  Talisman, Prose Poem, Iowa Rev, Colorado North Rev,
  Agni, Quarter After Eight, Third Coast, Quarterly West.

Dick Lourie P
16 Alder-Sea, Prospect Hill, Somerville, MA 02143
  Pubs: *Anima* (Hanging Loose, 1977), *Stumbling* (Crossing,
  1973), *Sun, Cottonwood Rev, Nation.*

Steve Lowe W
2 Laurie Ln, Natick, MA 01760, 508-655-8701
  Pubs: *Aurora* (Dodd, Mead, 1985).

Michael Lowenthal W
11 Seaverns Ave #3F, Jamaica Plain, MA 02130,
617-983-8772
Internet: maxfranz@aol.com
  Pubs: *The Same Embrace* (Dutton, 1998), *Best American*
  Gay Fiction: Anth (Litttle, Brown, 1996), *Men on Men 5:*
  Anth (Penguin/Plume, 1994), *Best American Erotica: Anth*
  (Touchstone, 1994), *Kenyon Rev, Crescent Rev, Other*
  Voices, Yellow Silk.

Betty Lowry P
79 Moore Rd, Wayland, MA 01778, 508-358-4098
Internet: bettylowry@aol.com
  Pubs: *Yankee, Earthwise, Midwest Poetry Rev, Orpheus,*
  Bittersweet, Widener Rev, America.

Jean Lunn P
25 Harvard St, Hyannis, MA 02601
  Pubs: *Yankee, Manhattan Poetry Rev, Sow's Ear,*
  Hampden-Sydney Rev, Devil's Millhopper, Webster Rev.

Thomas Lux P
52 Chester Ave, Waltham, MA 02154
  Pubs: *The Drowned River, Half Promised Land, Sunday*
  (HM, 1990, 1986, 1979), *Antaeus, Ploughshares.*

David Lyon P
6 Crawford St, #11, Cambridge, MA 02139, 617-864-0361
  Pubs: *The Sound of Horns* (L'Epervier Pr, 1984),
  Massachusetts Rev, NAR, Beloit Poetry Jrnl.

Jeanette C. Maes P
64 Harrison Ave, Lynn, MA 01905, 781-599-1349
  Pubs: *The Way of Ignorance, Fantastic Confusions* (Sunlit
  Waters Pr, 1994, 1990).

Carol Magun W
90 Marion Rd, Watertown, MA 02172, 617-924-8874
  Pubs: *Circling Eden* (Academy Chicago Publishers, 1995),
  American Fiction, Artful Dodge, Jewish Women's Literary
  Annual.

Elissa Malcohn P&W
PO Box 1764, Cambridge, MA 02238, 617-547-6533
  Pubs: *Full Spectrum: Anth* (Bantam, 1988), *Tales of the*
  Unanticipated, Ice River, Diarist's Journal.

Karen A. Malley W
North Village, #F23, Amherst, MA 01002, 413-546-4112
  Pubs: *Iowa Rev, Bottomfish, Sonora Rev, Kansas Qtly.*

John Maloney P
Allen Farm Rd, Chilmark, MA 02535, 508-645-9688
  Pubs: *Proposal* (Zoland Bks, 1999), *Poetry, Poetry*
  Northwest, Ploughshares, Southern Poetry Rev, New York
  Times, North Atlantic.

Marvin Mandell W
102 Anawan Ave, West Roxbury, MA 02132
  Pubs: *Best American Short Stories* (HM, 1972), *Cape Cod*
  Compass, English Jrnl, Offshore.

Laura Marello W
216 Bradford, Provincetown, MA 02657
  Pubs: *The Voices We Carry: Italian-American Women's*
  Fiction Anth (Guernica Pr, 1994), *The Quarterly, Mississippi*
  Rev, New Directions, Sonora Rev, Shankpainter, Colorado
  North Rev.

Paul Mariani P
PO Box M, Montague, MA 01351, 413-367-2820
Internet: pmariani@english.umass.edu
  Pubs: *The Great Wheel, Salvage Operations: New and*
  Selected Poems (Norton, 1996, 1990), *Image, America,*
  Poetry.

Paul Marion P
44 Highland St, Lowell, MA 01852, 978-454-4883
Internet: marlonpf@aol.com
  Pubs: *The First Yes: Anth* (Dryad Pr, 1997), *For a Living:*
  Anth (U Illinois, 1995), *Yankee, Salamander, Fan, Christian*
  Science Monitor, River Rev, Bridge Rev.

Ralph G. Martell P
Westfield State College, Westfield, MA 01086
  Pubs: *Palabras/Words, Cuadros, Ciclos* (Slusa, 1986,
  1982, 1982), *Peregrine, Stone Country.*

Richard J. Martin P
40 Searle Rd, West Roxbury, MA 02132-3014, 617-323-2547
  Pubs: *White Man Appears on Southern California Beach*
  (Bottom Fish Pr, 1991), *Fell Swoop, ACM, Exquisite*
  Corpse, Asylum Annual, Bellingham Rev.

Valerie M. Martin W
Houghton Mifflin Co., 222 Berkeley St, Boston, MA
02116-3764, 617-725-5000
  Pubs: *Alexandra, Set In Motion* (FSG, 1979, 1978).

Suzanne Matson P&W
Boston College, Chestnut Hill, MA 02167, 617-552-3716
Internet: suzanne.matson@bc.edu
Pubs: *The Hunger Moon* (Norton, 1997), *Durable Goods, Sea Level* (Alice James Bks, 1993, 1990), *Harvard Rev, APR, Poetry, Indiana Rev, Shenandoah, Poetry Northwest, New York Times Mag.*

Mary Mattfield P
1 Emerson Pl, #5-Q, Boston, MA 02114
Pubs: *Paintbrush, Poetry Now, Tendril, Descant, Panache, Southern Poetry Rev, Harbinger, Folio, Graham Hse Rev, Webster Rev, Seattle Rev, Poetry East, Nimrod.*

Mary Maxwell P
PO Box 1120, Truro, MA 02666, 508-349-7395
Pubs: *New Republic, Nation, Western Humanities Rev, Paris Rev, Salmagundi, Southern Rev, Pequod.*

Ben Mazer P
c/o Barbara Matteau Editions, PO Box 381280, Cambridge, MA 022381280, 617-547-5122
Pubs: *White Cities* (Barbara Matteau Edtns, 1995), *Verse, Harvard Mag, Lift, Atelier, Boston Phoenix, Poetry East, Dark Horse, Englynion, Stand, Compost.*

Gail Mazur P
5 Walnut Ave, Cambridge, MA 02140, 617-868-5753
Pubs: *The Common* (U Chicago Pr, 1995), *The Pose of Happiness* (David Godine, 1986), *Atlantic, New Republic, Partisan Rev, Boulevard, Agni, Slate, Ploughshares, Poetry.*

Grace Dane Mazur W
35 Arlington St, Cambridge, MA 02140, 617-547-3895
Internet: gdm@math.harvard.edu
Pubs: *Silk* (Brookline Bks, 1996), *Southern Rev, Harvard Rev, NER/BLQ, Story.*

David R. McCann P
Harvard Univ, EALC 2 Divinity Ave, Cambridge, MA 02138, 617-495-8378
Internet: dmccann@fas.harvard.edu
Pubs: *Form and Freedom in Korean Poetry* (E.J. Brill, 1988), *Winter Sky* (Qtly Rev of Literature, 1981).

Elizabeth McKim P
108 Winthrop Rd, Brookline, MA 02146
Pubs: *Boat of the Dream* (Troubadour, 1988), *Burning Through, Family Salt* (Wampeter, 1987, 1981), *To Stay Alive* (Audiotape; Talking Stone Pr, 1992).

Reginald McKnight W
Christina Ward, P.O. Box 515, N Scituate, MA 02060, 781-545-1375
Pubs: *White Boys* (Holt, 1998), *The Kind of Light That Shines On Texas* (SMU Pr, 1996), *O'Henry Awards 1990: Anth* (Doubleday, 1990), *New Stories From the South: Anth* (Algonquin, 1990), *Kenyon Rev, Callaloo, Black American Literary Forum.*

Anthony McNeill P
Univ Massachusetts, Amherst, MA 01002, 413-545-0031

Michael McWey W
34 Sparks St, Cambridge, MA 02138, 617-876-1784
Pubs: *Redbook, Seventeen, Special Report, YM, 'Teen, Apalachee Qtly, Crescent Rev, Sou'wester, Woman, Faith 'N Stuff, Rosebud, Satire, Guideposts for Kids.*

Mameve S. Medwed W
58 Washington Ave, Cambridge, MA 02140, 617-868-8805
Pubs: *Mail* (Warner Bks, 1997), *Ascent, Yankee, Redbook, Playgirl, Boston Globe, Missouri Rev.*

Mark Mendel PP&P
Box 343, Monterey, MA 01245, 413-528-4136

Ifeanyi Menkiti P
8 Malvern Ave, Somerville, MA 02144, 617-666-2855
Pubs: *The Jubilation Of Falling Bodies* (Pomegranate, 1978), *Affirmations* (Third World, 1971).

Paul Metcalf P&W
509 Quarry Rd, Chester, MA 010110386
Pubs: *Collected Works Vols. 3, 2, 1* (Coffee Hse Pr, 1997, 1997, 1997), *Genoa* (U New Mexico Pr, 1991), *Araminta and the Coyotes* (Jargon Society, 1991), *Conjunctions, Ironwood, Sulfur, To.*

Gary Metras P
16 Reservation Rd, Easthampton, MA 01027, 413-527-3324
Pubs: *Today's Lesson* (Bull Thistle Pr, 1997), *Seagull Beach* (Adastra Pr, 1995), *Atomic Ghost* (Coffee Hse, 1995), *American Voice, Poetry East, Potlatcxh, North Dakota Qtly.*

Richard Michelson P
PO Box 657, Amherst, MA 01004, 413-586-3964
Pubs: *Animals That Ought To Be* (S&S, 1996), *Tap Dancing for the Relatives* (U Central Florida Pr, 1985), *Poetry Northwest, Madison Rev.*

Paul Milenski W
PO Box 592, Dalton, MA 01227-0592, 413-684-2066
Pubs: *Power Play: Individuals in Conflict: Anth* (Prentice Hall Regents, 1996), *Sudden Fiction Intl: Anth* (Norton, 1989), *Witness, Wind Literary Jrnl, World of English, Berkshire Rev, Quarterly West, Great River Rev.*

Christopher Millis　　　　　　　　P
290 Massachusetts Ave, Cambridge, MA 02139,
617-225-9608
Internet: ninadm@mit.edu
　　Pubs: *Impossible Mirrors* (Singular Speech Pr, 1995), *On The Verge, Emerging Poets and Artists: Anth* (Agni Pr, 1993), *The Quarterly, International Qtly, Harvard Rev, Seneca Rev.*

Joan Millman　　　　　　　　W
30 Ackers Ave, #1, Brookline, MA 02146
Internet: joanmillman@aol.com
　　Pubs: *The Effigy & Other Stories* (U Missouri Pr, 1990), *Carolina Qtly, Virginia Qtly Rev, Ascent, Cimarron, Moment Mag.*

Helena Minton　　　　　　　　P
5 Random Ln, Andover, MA 01810, 508-475-6345
Internet: minton@noble.mass.edu
　　Pubs: *The Canal Bed, Personal Effects* (Alice James Bks, 1985, 1976), *Poet & Critic, 5 A.M., Soundings East.*

Wendy M. Mnookin　　　　　　　　P
40 Woodchester Dr, Chestnut Hill, MA 02167, 617-964-7759
Internet: jwmnookin@mediaone.net
　　Pubs: *Guenever Speaks* (Round Table, 1991), *Modern Arthurian Literature: Anth* (Garland Pub, 1992), *Beloit Poetry Jrnl, Cimarron Rev, Kansas Qtly, Passages North, Radcliffe Qtly, Wisconsin Rev.*

Jean Monahan　　　　　　　　P
121 Thorndike St, Cambridge, MA 02141, 617-661-9560
Internet: jehane@world.std.com
　　Pubs: *Believe It Or Not* (Orchises Pr, 1999), *Hands* (Anhinga, 1992), *Shenandoah, Seneca, New Republic, Graham Hse, Chelsea, Webster Rev, Columbia, Nimrod.*

Christine Palamidess Moore　　　　　　　　W
35 Buena Vista, Cambridge, MA 02140, 617-491-6542
Internet: palami@aol.com
　　Pubs: *The Virgin Knows* (St. Martin's Pr, 1995).

Richard Moore　　　　　　　　P&W
81 Clark St, Belmont, MA 02478, 617-489-0519
　　Pubs: *Pygmies and Pyramids, No More Bottom* (Orchises Pr, 1998, 1991), *The Mouse Whole* (Negative Capability, 1996), *The Investigator* (Story Line Pr, 1991), *The Education of a Mouse* (Countryman, 1983), *Poetry, Hudson Rev, APR, The New Yorker, Harper's.*

Andrea Moorhead　　　　　　　　P
PO Box 297, Deerfield, MA 01342
Internet: moorhead@k125.phast.umass.edu
　　Pubs: *From A Grove of Aspen* (U Salzburg Pr, 1997), *La Blancheur Absolue, le silence nous entoure* (Les Ecrits des Forges, 1995, 1992), *Winter Light* (Oasis, 1994), American Writing, Illinois Rev, Abraxas, Beacons, Spoon River Poetry Rev, Oasis.

Emma Morgan　　　　　　　　P
491 Bridge Rd, #613, Northampton, MA 01060
Internet: elmf85@hamp.hampshire.edu
　　Pubs: *A Stillness Built of Motion* (Hummingwoman Pr, 1995), *Gooseflesh* (Clothespin Fever Pr, 1993), *A Bird in the Heart: Anth* (Zamora, 1993), *Lucid Stone.*

Rose Moss　　　　　　　　W
PO Box 515, North Scituate, MA 02060
　　Pubs: *Agni, Other Voices, Crosscurrents, Confrontation, Colorado Qtly, Cimarron Rev, New Voices, Little Mag, Shenandoah, Antioch Rev, Massachusetts Rev, Echad, Twigs.*

Rich Murphy　　　　　　　　P
Bradford College, 320 Main St, Bradford, MA 01835, 508-372-7161
　　Pubs: *Grand Street, Slant, Seattle Rev, Blue Unicorn, International Poetry Rev, Sulphur River Rev.*

Liza Ketchum Murrow　　　　　　　　W
PO Box 120, Lincoln, MA 01773
　　Pubs: *Twelve Days In August, Fire In The Heart, West Against the Wind* (Holiday Hse, 1993, 1989, 1987).

Dennis Must　　　　　　　　W
32 Estabrook Rd, Swampscott, MA 01907, 781-581-0173
Internet: must19@idt.net
　　Pubs: *Fiction 2000: Anth* (Red Hen Pr, 1998), *Salt Hill Jrnl, Writers' Forum, Crossconnect, Blue Moon Rev, Atom Mind, Porcupine Literary Arts Mag, Southeast Rev, Java Snob Rev, The Oval, Fly by Night Mag, Foibler.*

Mildred J. Nash　　　　　　　　P
39 Sunset Dr, Burlington, MA 01803, 617-272-0206
　　Pubs: *Beyond Their Dreams* (Pocahontas Pr, 1989), *Lyric, Formalist, Piedmont Literary Rev, Polyphon.*

Valery Nash　　　　　　　　P
7 Linwood Ave, Rockport, MA 01966, 978-546-2900
　　Pubs: *October Swimmer* (Folly Cove Bks, 1996), *The Narrows* (Cleveland State U, 1980), *Field, Poetry Northwest, Yankee, Southern Poetry Rev, New Virginia Rev, The Bridge.*

Tema Nason　　　　　　　　W
93 Longwood Ave, #4, Brookline, MA 02146
　　Pubs: *Ethel: Fictional Autobiography of Ethel Rosenberg* (Delacorte, 1990), *Crimson Tide: Anth* (Chicory Blue Pr, 1996), *Puckerbrush Rev, Brooklyn Literary Rev.*

John L. Natkie　　　　　　　　P
69 Circuit St, Hanover, MA 02339
　　Pubs: *Screams! From An Unpadded Cell* (Cosmep Prison Project, 1979), *Greenfield Rev.*

Judith Neeld   P
PO Box 132, Menemsha, MA 02552
 Pubs: *Naming the Island* (Thorntree Pr, 1988), *Sea Fire*
 (Adastra Pr, 1987), *Oxford Mag, Texas Rev, Yarrow, Rhino,
 Massachusetts Rev, Xanadu.*

Jay Neugeboren   W
35 Harrison Ave, Northampton, MA 01060, 413-586-3732
Internet: neug@english.umass.edu
 Pubs: *Imagining Robert* (Morrow, 1997), *Don't Worry About
 the Kids* (U Massachusetts, 1997), *Poli: A Mexican Boy in
 Early Texas* (Corona, 1989), *Before My Life Began* (S&S,
 1985).

Leslea Newman   P&W
PO Box 815, Northampton, MA 010610815, 413-584-3865
Internet: lezel@aol.com
 Pubs: *Still Life With Buddy* (Pride Pubs, 1997), *Too Far
 Away To Touch* (Clarion, 1995), *Fat Chance* (Putnam,
 1994), *Every Woman's Dream* (New Victoria, 1994).

Philip Nikolayev   P
334 Harvard St Apt D-2, Cambridge, MA 02139,
617-864-7874
Internet: nikolay@fas.harvard.edu
 Pubs: *Artery Lumen* (Barbara Matteau Edtns, 1996), *Verse,
 Grand Street, Culture Front, Exquisite Corpse.*

Joan Norris   P
1126 Broadway, Hanover, MA 02339, 781-826-8931
 Pubs: *Banquet* (Penmaen Pr, 1978), *Prairie Schooner, The
 Nation, Ploughshares.*

Marian Novick   W
313 Brookline St, Needham, MA 02192
 Pubs: *At Her Age* (Scribner, 1985), *Prize Stories: O. Henry
 Awards: Anth* (Doubleday, 1981), *Massachusetts Rev.*

Nina Nyhart   P
185 Warren St, Brookline, MA 02146, 617-734-2698
Internet: nnyhart@aol.com
 Pubs: *Green Ruins* (Prose Poems Pr, 1998), *French for
 Soldiers, Openers* (Alice James Bks, 1987, 1979), *The
 Poetry Connection* (T&W, 1978).

Mary Oliver   P
Molly Malone Cook Agency, Box 338, Provincetown, MA
02657, 508-487-1931
 Pubs: *New & Selected Poems, House of Light* (Beacon,
 1992, 1990), *Dream Work* (Atlantic Monthly Pr, 1986), *Paris
 Rev, Sierra, Southern Rev, Poetry.*

David Olsen   P
14 Vine Brook Rd, Westford, MA 01886-4212, 978-392-8617
Internet: olsendavid@aol.com
 Pubs: *The Gulf War: Many Perspectives: Anth* (Vergin Pr,
 1992), *Homeless Not Helpless: Anth* (Canterbury Pr, 1991),
 *Poetry S.F., Sunrust, Bad Haircut Qtly, Black Bear, Amelia,
 Poetry Connoisseur, Cicada, Bogg, Tomcat, Rockford Rev,
 Snakeskin, Common Touch.*

Dzvinia Orlowsky   P
Four Way Books, PO Box 607, Marshfield, MA 02050,
781-837-4887
 Pubs: *Edge of House, A Handful of Bees* (Carnegie Mellon
 U Pr, 1999, 1994).

Rosalind Pace   P
Box 687, Truro, MA 02666, 508-349-2487
 Pubs: *Carnegie Mellon Anth of Poetry* (Carnegie Mellon U
 Pr, 1993), *APR, Ploughshares, Ontario Rev, Denver Qtly.*

Pamela Painter   W
65 Marlborough St, Boston, MA 02116, 617-267-6799
 Pubs: *Getting to Know the Weather* (U Illinois Pr, 1985),
 Atlantic, Harper's, Story, Ploughshares, NAR, Harvard Rev.

Carol Ann Parikh   W
54 Babcock St, #5, Brookline, MA 02146-3026, 617-731-2175
 Pubs: *Side Show: Anths* (Somersault Pr, 1996, 1995),
 *Canto, Confrontation, Indiana Rev, The Journal, Literary
 Rev.*

Ruth M. Parks   P
1550 Beacon St, #11A, Brookline, MA 02146
 Pubs: *Treacle on the Tongue* (Penrose Pub Co., 1994),
 *Candlelight, Castalian Springs, Poetry Digest, SPSM&H,
 The Lyric, Byline, Time of Singing, Coastal Forest Rev.*

Marian Parry   P
60 Martin St, Cambridge, MA 02138, 617-876-0407
 Pubs: *Margin, Shenandoah, Grand Street, 2+2, Negative
 Capability, Antioch Rev, Carleton Miscellany.*

Mark Pawlak   P
44 Thingvalla Ave, Cambridge, MA 02138, 617-491-6416
Internet: pawlak@umbsky.cc.umb.edu
 Pubs: *Special Handling: Newspaper Poems New &
 Selected, All the News* (Hanging Loose, 1993, 1985),
 *Abraxas, 5 A.M., Pig Iron, Transfer, Exquisite Corpse,
 Imagine, Bogg, Hanging Loose, Synaesthetic.*

Peter Payack   P
64 Highland Ave, Cambridge, MA 02139-1054, 617-492-2913
 Pubs: *The Zen of America* (The Idea Works, 1992), *No
 Free Will in Tomatoes* (Zoland Bks, 1989), *Paris Review
 Anth* (Norton, 1990), *Asimov's Sci-Fi Mag.*

Edith Pearlman — W
21 Elba St, Brookline, MA 02146, 617-731-1387
Pubs: *Fiddlehead, Iowa Qtly, Alaska Qtly, New England Rev, Other Voices, Boston Rev, Response, Tikkun.*

Roland F. Pease, Jr. — P
Zoland Books, Inc, 384 Huron Ave, Cambridge, MA 02138, 617-864-6252
Pubs: *Held Up For Answers* (Imaginary Pr, 1980), *Dreamworks, New York Times, Paris Rev.*

Jean Pedrick — P
48 Mt Vernon St, Boston, MA 02108, 617-227-9731
Pubs: *Mitteleuropa* (Small Poetry Pr, 1992), *An Ear to the Ground: Anth* (U Georgia Pr, 1989), *Yankee, Granite Rev, Compost, Antioch Rev, Southern Rev, Light, Press, Passager.*

Joyce Peseroff — P
24 Balfour St, Lexington, MA 02421, 781-862-9333
Internet: jpeseroff@aol.com
Pubs: *A Dog in the Lifeboat* (Carnegie Mellon U, 1991), *Ploughshares, New Republic, New Letters, Agni, Kenyon Rev, Massachusetts Rev.*

Stuart Peterfreund — P
Northeastern Univ, 360 Huntington Ave, Boston, MA 02115-5096, 617-373-2512
Internet: speterfr@lynx.neu.edu
Pubs: *Interstatements* (Curbstone, 1986), *Harder Than Rain* (Ithaca Hse, 1977), *Sow's Ear, New Rev, The Bridge, Wallace Stevens Jrnl, Abiko Qtly, Compost.*

Michael Pettit — P
217 W Pelham Rd, Shutesbury, MA 01072, 413-259-1602
Internet: mpettit@alumni.princeton.edu
Pubs: *Cardinal Points* (U Iowa Pr, 1988), *American Light* (U Georgia Pr, 1984), *Kenyon Rev, Gettysburg Rev, Southern Rev, Atlantic.*

Steven J. Peyster — P
66 West St, New Salem, MA 01355, 508-544-3887
Pubs: *Alphabet For Zina* (Window Edtns, 1981), *City Lights Jrnl, River Styx, Telephone, Poets On, Home Planet News, Natl Poetry Mag of the Lower East Side.*

Stephen Philbrick — P
34 Shaw Rd, Windsor, MA 01270-9573
Pubs: *Smith, Poetry Now, Chouteau Rev, Anyart Journal, Grub Street, Greensboro Rev.*

Marge Piercy — P&W
Box 1473, Wellfleet, MA 026671473, 508-349-3163
Internet: www.capecod.net/ tmpiercy
Pubs: *Storm Tide* (w/Ira Wood), *City of Darkness, City Of Light, The Longings of Women* (Fawcett, 1998, 1996, 1994), *What Are Big Girls Made Of, Mars And Her Children, He, She, And It* (Knopf, 1997, 1994, 1991).

Ronald William Pies — P&W
297 Bedford St, Lexington, MA 02173-3340, 781-862-8124
Internet: rpies@compuserve.com
Pubs: *Riding Down Dark* (Nightshade Pr, 1992), *Blood To Remember: Anth* (Texas Tech U Pr, 1991), *Vital Signs: Anth* (UCLA Med School, 1990), *Literary Rev, Oasis.*

Helene Pilibosian — P
171 Maplewood St, Watertown, MA 02172-1324, 617-926-2602
Internet: rsarkiss@ultranet.com
Pubs: *At Quarter Past Reality, They Called Me Mustafa, Carvings from an Heirloom* (Ohan Pr, 1998, 1992, 1983), *Half Tones to Jubilee, New Mexico Humanities Rev, Pacific Rev, Hawaii Rev, Cape Rock, Interim, Potpourri, Panhandler.*

Robert Pinsky — P
Boston Univ, 236 Bay State Rd, Boston, MA 02215, 617-353-2821
Internet: rpinsky@acs.bu.edu
Pubs: *The Figured Wheel, The Inferno of Dante* (Farrar, Straus & Giroux, 1996, 1994), *The Want Bone* (Ecco Pr, 1990), *Agni, New Yorker, Threepenny Rev.*

Susan Lyon Pope — W
PO Box 82, Monument Beach, MA 02553
Pubs: *Catching the Light* (Viking, 1990), *Best of Wind: Anth* (Wind Pubs, 1994), *Northern New England Rev, Calliope, The Writing Self.*

Linda Portnay — P
21 Robbins Rd, Lexington, MA 02173, 617-862-6004
Pubs: *Wishing for the Worst* (Warthog Pr, 1993), *Radcliffe Qtly, Northern Rev, Gulfstream, Thema, Kalliope, Sandscript, Slant, Worcester Rev, Wisconsin Rev.*

Carol Potter — P
120A Poole Rd, Belchertown, MA 01007-9480
Pubs: *Before We Were Born* (Alice James, 1990), *Blueline, Massachusetts Rev, Sojourner, Iowa Rev, Out/Look, Field, APR, High Plains, Women's Rev of Bks, New Letters.*

Stan Proper — P
Wentworth Institute, 550 Huntington Ave, #8-408, Boston, MA 02115, 617-442-9010
Pubs: *Portraits: Kith, Kin & Neighbors, Love Lyrics* (Poets' Pr, 1998, 1996), *Laurels: Anth* (E. Blanche, 1994), *We Speak for Peace: Anth* (KIT, 1993).

Sarah Provost — P
86 Longmeadow Dr, Amherst, MA 01002
Pubs: *Inland, Thinking of Waves* (Cleveland State U, 1991), *APR, Southern Poetry Rev, Poetry.*

Lawrence Raab P
139 Bulkley St, Williamstown, MA 01267, 413-458-3870
Internet: lawrence.e.raab@williams.edu
Pubs: *What We Don't Know About Each Other* (Penguin, 1993), *Other Children* (Carnegie Mellon, 1987).

Pat Rabby P
23 Meriam St, Lexington, MA 02173, 617-861-0692
Pubs: *Connecticut Poetry Rev, Lynx, Boston Today, Glassworks, Women/Poems, The Bridge, Antigones.*

Richard F. Radford W
8 Juniper St, #29, Brookline, MA 02146, 617-734-9893
Pubs: *Drug Agent USA* (St. Martin's, 1991), *Trooper* (Quinlan, 1987), *New England Sampler, Alcoholism, American Man, Pegasus, New Earth Rev, The Word.*

David Raffeld P
54 Henderson Rd, Williamstown, MA 01267, 413-458-4815
Pubs: *The Ballad of Harmonica George & Other Poems* (Adastra Pr, 1989), *Poetry East, Phoebe, October Mountain, Longhouse.*

Louise Rafkin W
PO Box 1604, Provincetown, MA 02657, 508-487-4514
Pubs: *Other People's Dirt* (Algonquin Bks, 1998), *Queer and Pleasant Danger: Writing Out My Life, Different Mothers: Anth* (Cleis Pr, 1992, 1991).

Edward Rayher P
323 Pelham Rd, Amherst, MA 01002-1654, 413-256-8531
Pubs: *Buffalo Spree, Antigonish Rev, Washout Rev, Colorado Qtly.*

Monica E. Raymond P
57 Brookline, Cambridge, MA 02139
Pubs: *Sinister Wisdom, Iowa Rev, Heresies, Sojourner, Village Voice, Light.*

Liam Rector P
183 Willow Ave, Somerville, MA 02144-2316, 617-623-2211
Pubs: *American Prodigal* (Story Line, 1994), *The Sorrow of Architecture* (Dragon Gate, 1984), *Paris Rev, New Republic, APR, Boston Phoenix, Boulevard, Agni.*

Jennifer Regan P
992 Memorial Dr, #206, Cambridge, MA 02138-4872
Pubs: *Cries of the Spirit: Anth* (Beacon Pr, 1991), *Black Mountain Rev, Prairie Schooner, The Reaper, Ohio Rev, Confrontation, Hudson Rev, Chelsea.*

James S. Reinbold W
44 School St, Rehoboth, MA 02769-2204

Steven Riel P
PO Box 679, Natick, MA 01760
Pubs: *How To Dream* (Amherst Writers & Artists, 1992), *Badboy Book of Erotic Poetry: Anth* (Masquerade Bks, 1995), *Minnesota Rev, Christopher Street, Peregrine.*

David Rivard P
72 Inman St, Apt A, Cambridge, MA 02139, 617-661-6388
Internet: drivard@channel1.com
Pubs: *Wise Poison* (Graywolf, 1996), *Torque* (U Pitt Pr, 1988), *Poetry, Ploughshares, TriQuarterly, NAR, NER.*

Laura Rodley P
PO Box 63, Shelburne Falls, MA 01370
Pubs: *Massachusetts Rev, Prose Poem, Cathartic, Valley Women's Voice, Peregrine, Connecticut River Rev, Manna, Paragraph, Blueline.*

Tony Rogers W
58 Larchmont Ave, Waban, MA 02168, 617-965-5125
Internet: roge@med.mit.edu
Pubs: *Painted Hills Rev, Outerbridge, Alabama Fiction Rev, Half Tones to Jubilee, Wooster Rev, Four Quarters, Boston Monthly, Oak Square, Wind, Thema.*

John J. Ronan P
Box 5524, Gloucester, MA 01930, 978-525-2022
Internet: jronan@nscc.mass.edu
Pubs: *The Catching Self* (Folly Cove Bks, 1996), *Baseball I Gave You the Best Years of My Life: Anth* (North Atlantic Pr, 1977), *Threepenny Rev, Southern Poetry Rev, Folio, Greensboro Rev, NER, Yankee.*

Daniel Asa Rose W
138 Bay State Rd, Rehoboth, MA 02769, 508-252-6315
Pubs: *Small Family With Rooster, Flipping For It* (St. Martin's Pr, 1988, 1987), *Esquire, Playboy, Vanity Fair, New Yorker, GQ, New York Times Mag, Partisan Rev.*

George H. Rosen W
2 Barberry Heights Rd, Gloucester, MA 019301202, 978-281-3561
Internet: georosen@tiac.net
Pubs: *Black Money* (Scarborough Hse, 1990), *Descant, NAR, Yale Rev, Harper's, A Matter of Crime, Ascent.*

Karen Rosenberg W
Harvard Univ, 78 Mount Auburn St, Cambridge, MA 02138, 617-495-2485
Pubs: *Water Baby: Anth* (John Murray, 1995), *The Year's Best: Anth* (Tickled by Thunder, 1996), *Orbis, Metropolitan, Vigil, Potato Eyes, Oasis, Swansea Rev, Response, Prop.*

Sarah Rossiter W
72 Church St, Weston, MA 02193, 617-894-6184
Pubs: *Beyond This Bitter Air* (U Illinois Pr, 1987), *The Human Season* (Little, Brown, 1987).

Eleanor Roth   W
131 Clarendon St, North Dartmouth, MA 02747,
508-993-3328
    Pubs: *Female, Living, Herworld, The Humanist, Asia Mag,
    Asian Wall Street Jrnl, Green's Fiction Mag.*

Lee Rudolph   P
Clark Univ, 950 Main St, Worcester, MA 01610
    Pubs: *Contemporary New England Poetry: Anth* (Texas
    Rev Pr, 1987), *New Yorker, Clark Now.*

Marieve Rugo   P
31 Fayerweather St, Cambridge, MA 02138-3329,
617-969-6667
    Pubs: *Fields Of Vision* (U Alabama Pr, 1983), *Kenyon Rev,
    Chelsea, Black Warrior, New Letters, Southern Poetry Rev,
    North Dakota Qtly.*

Hilary Russell   P
PO Box 578, Sheffield, MA 01257, 413-229-2549
    Pubs: *Beloit Poetry Jrnl, Ploughshares, Carolina Qtly,
    Country Jrnl, Boulevard.*

Catherine Sasanov   P
50 Follen St, Apt 101, Cambridge, MA 021383506,
617-661-7256
    Pubs: *Traditions of Bread and Violence* (Four Way Bks,
    1996), *Agni, Caliban, Virginia Qtly Rev, Mid-American Rev,
    Graham House Rev, Marlboro Rev.*

Peter Saunders   P
Steppingstone, Box 327, Chatham, MA 02633, 508-945-5283
    Pubs: *Steppingstone, Saltwind, Longfellow, Aurorean,
    Cape Codder, Cape Cod Chronicle.*

Cheryl Savageau   P&W
19 Walnut Hill Dr, Worcester, MA 01602, 508-752-3953
    Pubs: *Dirt Road Home, Poetry Like Bread: Anth* (Curbstone
    Pr, 1995, 1994), *Massachusetts Rev, Agni, River Styx,
    Indiana Rev, Nebraska English Jrnl, Boston Rev.*

Mark Schafron   W
100 Brookhaven Dr, Attleboro, MA 02703-5174,
508-226-3519
Internet: writecraft@aol.com
    Pubs: *Raconteur, Atom Mind, Fresh! Mag, American
    Epitaph, Fiction Forum.*

Randi Schalet   W
157 DeForest St, Boston, MA 02131, 617-323-8481
    Pubs: *Lunch* (Clothespin Fever Pr, 1994).

Ada Jill Schneider   P
120 Friends Cove, Somerset, MA 02726, 508-672-5989
Internet: schneidr@massmed.org
    Pubs: *The Museum of My Mother, Fine Lines and Other
    Wrinkles* (Gratlau Pr, 1996, 1993), *Her Face in the Mirror:
    Anth* (Beacon Pr, 1994), *Synaesthetic, Newport Rev,
    Crone's Nest, Mediphors, Everyday Epiphanies, Muddy
    River Poetry Rev.*

Nina Schneider   W
Music St, West Tisbury, MA 02575, 508-693-5746
    Pubs: *The Woman Who Lived In A Prologue* (Houghton
    Mifflin, 1980), *Paris Rev.*

Pat Schneider   P&W
PO Box 1076, Amherst, MA 01004, 413-253-3307
Internet: awapress@javanet.com
    Pubs: *Wake Up Laughing* (Negative Capability Pr, 1998),
    The Writer as an Artist (Lowell House, 1995), *Long Way
    Home* (Amherst Writers & Artists, 1993), *Ms., Sewanee
    Rev, Minnesota Rev, Exquisite Corpse, Earth's Daughters,
    Negative Capability.*

Ron Schreiber   P
9 Reed St, Cambridge, MA 02140
    Pubs: *John* (Hanging Loose Pr/Calamus Bks, 1988),
    Tomorrow Will Really Be Sunday (Calamus, 1985).

Lloyd Schwartz   P
27 Pennsylvania Ave, Somerville, MA 02145, 617-666-3233
Internet: schwartzll@umbsky.cc.umb.edu
    Pubs: *Goodnight, Gracie* (U Chicago Pr, 1992), *Best
    American Poetry 1994: Anth* (Scribner/Macmillan, 1994),
    *New Yorker, Paris Rev, Boulevard, Harvard Mag, Poetry,
    New Republic.*

Elizabeth Searle   W
18 College Ave, Arlington, MA 02174, 781-641-2906
Internet: jhodgkinson@mediaone.net
    Pubs: *A Four-Sided Bed* (Graywolf Pr, 1998), *My Body to
    You* (U Iowa Pr, 1993), *Lovers: Anth* (Crossing Pr, 1992),
    *Ploughshares, Redbook, Kenyon Rev, Boulevard, Epoch,
    California Qtly, Agni.*

Richard Seltzer   W
PO Box 161, West Roxbury, MA 02132
Internet: www.samizdat.com
    Pubs: *The Lizard of Oz* (B&R Samizdat Express, 1994),
    The Name Of The Hero (J. P. Tarcher/Houghton Mifflin,
    1981), *Antic, Analog.*

Richard C. Shaner   P
701 Nantascot Pl, 155 George Washington Blvd, Hull, MA
02045, 617-925-2654
Internet: shaner@umbsky.cc.umb.edu
    Pubs: *A Nantucket Bestiary* (Poets Corner Pr, 1980),
    *College English, American Land Forum, Passages North,
    Waves, Hanging Loose.*

Roger W. Shattuck P
Boston Univ, 745 Commonwealth Ave, Boston, MA 02215
Pubs: *Half Tame* (U Texas, 1964), *Harper's, New Republic,
New Yorker, Poetry, Virginia Qtly.*

Beverly Shaw-Johnson P
217 Scudder Ave, Hyannis, MA 02601, 508-771-3471
Pubs: *Massachusetts State Poetry Society Anth*
(Massachusetts State Poetry Soc, 1980), *Arizona
Highways, Back Bay View, Worcester Rev, Itsblotto
Karmics, Jlag Rev, Gargoyle.*

Robert B. Shaw P
Mount Holyoke College, South Hadley, MA 01075,
413-538-2444
Internet: rshaw@mtholyoke.edu
Pubs: *The Post Office Murals Restored* (Copper Beech Pr,
1994), *The Wonder of Seeing Double* (U Massachusetts Pr,
1988), *Comforting the Wilderness* (Wesleyan, 1977).

Tom F. Sheehan P
217 Central St, Saugus, MA 01906, 617-233-5041
Pubs: *Hummers, Knucklers and Slow Curves* (U Illinois,
1991), *The Best of Spitball: Anth* (Pocket Bks, 1989), *Hiram
Poetry Rev, Puerto del Sol, Cape Rock.*

Nancy Sherman P
2 Brenda Ln, Belchertown, MA 01007-9758, 413-586-6151
Internet: nsherman@hampshire.edu
Pubs: *Ploughshares, Grolier Annual, Massachusetts Rev,
Seneca Rev, Cream City Rev, AWP Chronicle.*

Nina Silver P&W
734 Huntington Rd, Worthington, MA 01098, 413-238-7769
Pubs: *Birthing* (Woman In The Moon Pubs, 1996),
Women's Glib: Anth (Crossing Pr, 1991), *Off Our Backs,
New Internationalist, New Press, Jewish Currents.*

Lazare Seymore Simckes W
Williams College, 301 Stetson, Williamstown, MA 01267
Pubs: *The Comatose Kids* (Fiction Collective, 1976), *Seven
Days of Morning* (Random Hse, 1963).

Louise Simons P
44 Arrowhead Rd, Weston, MA 02193, 781-891-1246
Pubs: *Three Rivers Poetry Jrnl, 13th Moon, Caprice,
Minnesota Rev, Painted Bride Qtly, Exquisite Corpse.*

Jonathan Sisson P
19 Barna Road, Boston, MA 021244713, 617-825-5430
Pubs: *Where Silkwood Walks* (Lake Street Rev Pr, 1981),
Poetry, Paris Rev, Antaeus.

R. D. Skillings W
730 Commercial St, Provincetown, MA 026572018,
508-487-3768
Pubs: *In a Murderous Time, P-Town Stories* (Applewood
Bks, 1984, 1980).

John Skoyles P
PO Box 2022, Truro, MA 02666, 508-487-7918
Internet: jskoyles@emerson.edu
Pubs: *Definition of the Soul, Permanent Change, A Little
Faith* (Carnegie Mellon, 1998, 1990, 1981), *The Smoky
Mountain Cage Bird Society* (Kodansha America, 1997).

Tom Sleigh P
1 Stinson Ct #3, Cambridge, MA 02139, 617-876-9002
Pubs: *The Chain, Waking* (U Chicago Pr, 1996, 1990), *After
One* (HM, 1983), *New Yorker, Poetry, Threepenny Rev,
Partisan Rev, New Republic, Grand Street, Slate,
TriQuarterly, Paris Rev.*

Joel Sloman P
82 Harvard Ave, Medford, MA 02155, 781-488-3788
Internet: sloman@wind.mit.edu
Pubs: *Stops* (Zoland Bks, 1997), *Virgil's Machines* (Norton,
1966).

Jacques Sollov P
White Eagle Pub, PO Box 1332/Dept S-0111, Lowell, MA
01853, 603-881-5392
Pubs: *Gold of the Stars, Reborn Again In The Kingdom*
(White Eagle Pub, 1983, 1982).

Paul B. Solyn P
35 Mt Hood Rd, #2, Brighton, MA 021461340
Pubs: *Mistress Quickly's Garden* (Raintree Pr, 1978), *New
Letters, Minnesota Rev, Northeast.*

William Sonzski W
PO Box 722, Boston, MA 02117-0722
Pubs: *Punch Goes The Judy* (Delacorte Pr, 1971),
TriQuarterly.

Stephen Sossaman P
Westfield State College, Westfield, MA 01086, 413-572-5335
Internet: ssossaman@wisdom.wsc.mass.edu
Pubs: *Viet Nam Anth* (Bowling Green U Pr, 1987), *Paris
Rev, The Formalist, Dalhousie Rev, Centennial Rev, South
Carolina Rev, Kentucky Poetry Rev.*

Kathleen Spivack P
53 Spruce St, Watertown, MA 02172, 617-926-1637
Pubs: *The Beds We Lie In* (Scarecrow, 1986), *The
Honeymoon* (Graywolf, 1986), *Kansas Qtly, New Yorker,
Atlantic, Ploughshares.*

Sue Standing P
1 Stinson Ct, Cambridge, MA 02139-4415
Internet: sstandin@wheatonma.edu
Pubs: *Gravida* (Four Way Bks, 1995), *Deception Pass*
(Alice James Bks, 1984), *APR, Iowa Rev, Nation, Partisan
Rev, Poetry Northwest, Southwest Rev.*

Judith W. Steinbergh   P
99 Evans Rd, Brookline, MA 02146, 617-734-1416
Internet: judithst@aol.com
>   Pubs: *A Living Anytime* (Talking Stone Pr, 1988),
>   *Motherwriter* (Wampeter Pr, 1983), *Sojourner, Calyx.*

Robert Steinem   P
40 Stranahan, Colrain, MA 01340, 413-624-3709
Internet: robstei@aol.com
>   Pubs: *This Wood Sang Out: Anth* (Literacy Project, 1995),
>   *Optimist, Poetry Motel, Sanctuary, ELF, Poems for a
>   Livable Planet, Written Arts, Peregrine, Folio.*

Harry Stessel   P
Westfield State College, Westfield, MA 01086, 413-568-3311
>   Pubs: *American Studies* (Raindust Pr, 1975), *Connecticut
>   River Rev, Southern Poetry Rev, Xanadu, Mss.,
>   Cottonwood Rev, Commonwealth Rev, Kansas Qtly.*

Jadene Felina Stevens   P
Salt Wind Poets, 12 Olde Homestead Way, East Harwich, MA
02645, 508-432-6661
>   Pubs: *The Original Trinity* (Stepping Stone Pr, 1994), *Salt
>   Wind Poets Anth* (Blue Moon Pr, 1991), *Quilt, Proof Rock,
>   Transnational Perspectives, Sunrust.*

Susan Stinson   P&W
PO Box 433, Northampton, MA 01060, 413-584-2736
Internet: sestinson@aol.com
>   Pubs: *Martha Moody, Fat Girl Dances With Rocks*
>   (Spinsters Ink, 1995, 1994), *Kenyon, Sinister Wisdom,
>   Heresies, Yellow Silk, Bay Windows.*

Lewis Hammond Stone   P
PO Box 545, Mattapoisett, MA 02739
>   Pubs: *The Nutritive & Therapeutic Uses of the Banana:
>   Anth* (Church Hse, 1990), *Northeast Jrnl, Ararat, Green
>   Fuse, The Lowell Pearl, Temper, Chelsea.*

Jane Strete   P
106 Pleasant St, #2, Cambridge, MA 02139, 617-354-9487
>   Pubs: *City River Voices* (West End Pr, 1992), *Ourselves,
>   Growing Older: Anth* (S&S, 1987), *South Coast Poetry Intl,
>   Timbrel, Maine Times.*

Jonathan Strong   W
Tufts University, Medford, MA 02155
>   Pubs: *The Old World, Offspring, An Untold Tale,
>   Companion Pieces, Secret Words* (Zoland, 1997, 1995,
>   1993, 1993, 1992), *Elsewhere* (Ballantine, 1985).

Jack Sughrue   P
13 Martin Rd, Box 459, East Douglas, MA 01516
>   Pubs: *The Book of Books, The Link* (Pakka Pr, 1993,
>   1978), *JLAG Rev, Poets, Little Apple, The Lobe, Gargoyle.*

James Sullivan   P
590A Sunrise Ave, P.O. Box 451, Barre, MA 01005-0451,
978-355-4389
>   Pubs: *In Order of Appearance: 400 Poems* (Adams Printing
>   Co., 1988), *America, Commonweal, Worcester Rev.*

Stanley Sultan   W
138 Brown Ave, Boston, MA 02131, 617-325-1482
>   Pubs: *Eliot, Joyce and Company* (Oxford U Pr, 1990),
>   *Writing the Culture: American Sephardic Authors: Anth* (U
>   Pr New England, 1996), *Offshore.*

Iris Summers   W
92 Brayton Rd, #2, Boston, MA 02135-3042
>   Pubs: *Whitefire* (Ballantine, 1978).

Wally Swist   P
PO Box 2574, Amherst, MA 01004-2574
>   Pubs: *The Mown Meadow* (Los Hombres Pr, 1994), *For the
>   Dance* (Adastra Pr, 1991), *Frogpond, Modern Haiku,
>   Outerbridge, Rag Mag, Snowy Egret, Yankee.*

John T.   P
7 Silverwood Terr, South Hadley, MA 01075

Cecilia M. Tan   W
Circlet Press Inc, 1770 Massachusetts Ave, #278,
Cambridge, MA 02140, 617-864-0492
Internet: ctan@circlet.com
>   Pubs: *Black Feathers* (HarperCollins, 1998), *The Velderet*
>   (Circlet Pr, 1998), *Herotica, Penthouse, S&M Utopia
>   Guardian, Paramour, Looking for Mr. Preston, On a Bed of
>   Rice, By Her Subdued, No Other Tribute, Dark Angels,
>   Taste of Latex, Ms., Sojourner.*

Stephen J. Tapscott   P
66 Martin St, #2, Cambridge, MA 02138, 617-876-6121
>   Pubs: *From The Book of Changes* (Carcanet, 1996),
>   *Another Body* (Cleveland State U Poetry Ctr, 1989),
>   *Mesopotamia* (Wesleyan, 1975).

James Tate   P
16 Jones Rd, Amherst, MA 01002
>   Pubs: *Distance From Loved Ones, Reckoner* (Wesleyan U,
>   1990, 1986), *APR, Poetry, Massachusetts Rev.*

Jill Teitelman   W
33 Lakeville Rd, #3, Jamaica Plain, MA 02130, 617-522-8593
>   Pubs: *Transatlantic Rev, Chicago Rev, Story Qtly, World
>   34.*

Janice Thaddeus   P
58 Garfield St, Cambridge, MA 02138, 617-547-7806
>   Pubs: *Lot's Wife* (Saturday Pr, 1986), *Mountain Rev,
>   Louisville Rev, Shenandoah, Cold.*

Alexander Louis Theroux   W
Willow St, West Barnstable, MA 02668

Jack Thibeau   P
11 Royce Rd, Newton Centre, MA 02159, 617-969-6952

Jessica Treadway   W
17 Old Colony Ln, Arlington, MA 021743205, 781-646-2748
    Pubs: *Absent Without Leave and Other Stories* (Delphinium
    Bks, 1993), *Ploughshares, Agni, Atlantic, Hudson Rev.*

Florence Trefethen   P
23 Barberry Rd, Lexington, MA 02173, 617-862-0644
    Pubs: *The Little, Brown Reader: Anth* (HarperCollins,
    1993), *Fairbank Remembered: Anth* (Harvard U Pr, 1992),
    Bellingham Rev, Connecticut Rev, Negative Capability.

Jean Lorraine Tupper   P
165 Tilting Rock Rd, Wrentham, MA 02093
    Pubs: *Castings: Anth* (Aubade Pr, 1991), *Worcester Rev,*
    Blue Unicorn, Southern Poetry Rev, Connecticut River Rev,
    Piedmont Literary Rev, Voices Intl.

Gregoire Turgeon   P
5 Sherlock Ln, Westford, MA 01886
    Pubs: *Painted Bride Qtly, Poetry, Poetry Northwest,*
    Southern Poetry Rev, Louisville Rev.

Sondra Upham   P
37 Manters Pt., Plymouth, MA 02360, 781-871-0000
    Pubs: *Out of Season: Anth* (Amagansett Pr, 1993), *We*
    Speak For Peace: Anth (KIT, 1993), *Prairie Schooner,*
    Phoebe, New Virginia Rev, Sojourner, Eclectic Literary
    Forum.

Cornelia Veenendaal   P
14 Wellesley Pk, Dorchester, MA 02124, 617-825-7262
    Pubs: *What Seas What Shores* (Rowan Tree Pr, 1984),
    Arvon Fdn, Prairie Schooner, Sojourner, Soundings East,
    Ploughshares, Hanging Loose, Commonweal.

Peter Viereck   P
12 Silver St, South Hadley, MA 01075-1616, 413-534-5504
    Pubs: *Tide & Continuities* (U Arkansas Pr, 1995), *The*
    Unadjusted Man (Greenwood Pr, 1973), *New Yorker, Paris*
    Rev, Parnassus, APR, New Republic.

Tino Villanueva   P
89 Massachusetts Ave, Ste 270, Boston, MA 02115,
617-267-2592
    Pubs: *Chronicle of My Worst Years* (Northwestern U Pr,
    1994), *Scene from the Movie "Giant"* (Curbstone Pr, 1993),
    Bloomsbury Rev, Agni.

Arturo Vivante   W
Box 3005, Wellfleet, MA 02667-3005, 508-349-6619
    Pubs: *The Tales of Arturo Vivante* (Sheep Meadow Pr,
    1990), *Leopardi Poems, Italian Poetry: Anth* (Delphinium
    Pr, 1988, 1996), *New Yorker, Bostonia, Yankee, Italian*
    Qtly.

Diane Wald   P
52 Paine St, Boston, MA 02131, 617-524-0072
    Pubs: *Double Mirror* (Runaway Spoon Pr, 1996), *My Hat*
    That Was Dreaming (Literary Renaissance, 1994), *Boston*
    Literary Rev, APR, New Rev, Kayak, Missouri Rev.

William J. Walsh   P
298 Main St, Charlestown, MA 02129-2955
    Pubs: *Upsouth, Poetry Only, Amaranth Rev, Rainbow's*
    End, Poetry Co-op, Perceptions, Manna.

Victor Walter   W
204 Aspinwall Ave, Brookline, MA 02146, 617-566-2158
    Pubs: *The Voice of Manush* (White Pine Pr, 1996), *Boston*
    Globe Mag, Ellipsis, Short Story, Cimarron Rev, New
    England Rev, Chaminade Rev, Magic Realism.

Richard Waring   P
33 Chandler St, Belmont, MA 02178, 617-489-1630
Internet: rbw_elpr_1440@elpr.nejm.org
    Pubs: *The Unitarian Universalist Poets: Anth* (Pudding Hse
    Pr, 1996), *Pine River Papers, Noctiluca, Dark Horse, O.ars,*
    Polis, Dragonfly, Contact II, Zone.

Rosanna Warren   P
11 Robinwood Ave, Needham, MA 02192
    Pubs: *Stained Glass, Each Leaf Shines Separate* (Norton,
    1993, 1984).

Ellen Dori Watson   P
Manning Rd, Conway, MA 01341, 413-369-4414
Internet: ewatson@external.umass.edu
    Pubs: *We Live in Bodies* (Alice James Bks, 1997), *Broken*
    Railings (Owl Creek Pr, 1997), *Night Out: Anth* (Milkweed
    Edtns, 1997), *The New Yorker, Boulevard, APR,*
    Ploughshares, Prairie Schooner.

Nancy Dingman Watson   W
Box 32, Truro, MA 02666, 508-349-2324
    Pubs: *Tommy's Mommy's Fish* (Viking, 1996), *Blueberries*
    Lavender (Addison Wesley, 1977).

Afaa Michael Weaver   P&W
Simmons College, 300 The Fenway, Boston, MA 021155898,
617-521-2175
Internet: afaa@mindspring.com
    Pubs: *Talisman* (Tia Chucha Pr, 1998), *Timber and Prayer*
    (U Pitt Pr, 1995), *Stations in a Dream* (Dolphin-Moon Pr,
    1993), Cream City Rev, Long Shot, One Trick Pony, Plum
    Rev, Solo, Kenyon Rev, Obsidian II, African-American Rev,
    Calliope, Pequod.

Howard L. Weiner   W
114 Somerset Rd, Brookline, MA 02146, 617-738-5343
    Pubs: *The Children's Ward* (Putnam, 1980).

Chester Weinerman   P
20 Payson Rd, Brookline, MA 02167, 617-566-1611
   Pubs: *Poets For Life: Anth* (Crown, 1989), *Partisan Rev,*
Bitterroot, Southern Poetry Rev, Lips.

Ron Welburn   P&W
PO Box 420, Hadley, MA 01035, 413-584-0419
Internet: rwelburn@english.umass.edu
   Pubs: *Council Decisions* (American Native Pr Archives,
1991), *Returning the Gift: Anth* (U Arizona Pr, 1995),
Durable Breath: Anth (Salmon Run, 1994), *Red Owl,*
Cimarron Rev, Callaloo.

Susan B. Weston   P&W
80 Park St #55, Brookline, MA 02146, 617-566-8672
   Pubs: *Children of the Light* (St. Martin's Pr, 1985), *Other*
Voices, Kansas Qtly, Fiction Rev, Croton Rev, Literal Latte,
Press, Potpourri, Changes.

Dara Wier   P
504 Montague Rd, Amherst, MA 01002
   Pubs: *Our Master Plan, Blue for the Plough, The Book of*
Knowledge, All You Have In Common (Carnegie Mellon,
1999, 1992, 1988, 1984), *APR, NAR, Gettysburg Rev,*
Boulevard, Seattle Rev, Hollins Critic, Conduit.

Richard Wilbur   P&W
87 Dodwells Rd, Cummington, MA 01026
   Pubs: *More Opposites, New and Collected Poems* (HBJ,
1991, 1988).

Bosley Wilder   P
121 Cold Hill, Granby, MA 01033, 413-467-3191
   Pubs: *You Once Had Wings* (China; Heilongjiang People's
Pub Hse, 1991), *The Wind Is Mine* (Academic Bks, 1985),
Zuzu's Petals Qtly.

Mame Willey   W
33 Bay State Ave, Somerville, MA 02144-2132,
617-623-3611
   Pubs: *Anthology of New England Writers* (New England
Writers, 1998), *New Press Literary Qtly, Albany Rev,*
Hudson Rev, Colorado Qtly, Mississippi Rev, Hanging
Loose, Blueline, U.S.1 Worksheets.

Emmett Williams   P
Harvard Univ, Cambridge, MA 02138

Jane Williams   W
19 Cottage St, Cambridge, MA 02139, 617-547-3737
   Pubs: *Family Affairs* (H&R, 1977), *Harvard Mag, Boston*
Globe.

Irene Willis   P
2 Cornwall Dr, Great Barrington, MA 01230, 413-528-1924
   Pubs: *They Tell Me You Danced* (U Pr Florida, 1995),
Crazyhorse, Laurel Rev, New York Qtly, Kansas Qtly,
Yankee, Florida Rev.

Irene K. Wilson   P
9 Foster Rd, Lexington, MA 02173-5505, 781-861-1044
   Pubs: *The Cat's Meow!: Anth* (Maine Rhode Pubs, 1996),
Rosebud, Tucumcari Literary Rev, Redbook, Piedmont
Literary Rev, Calapooya Collage, Poetry Nippon, Pegasus.

Joseph Wilson   P
RFD #1, Irish Ln, Rutland, MA 01543, 617-886-6786

Barbara Winder   P
81 Old Mystic St, Arlington, MA 02174-1005, 413-548-9646
   Pubs: *Pinochle Under the Stars* (Andrew Mountain Pr,
1988), *Sundog, New Letters, Thema, Kansas Qtly.*

Ellen Wittlinger   P
47 Beach Ave, Swampscott, MA 01907, 617-599-6951
Internet: pritchwitt@aol.com
   Pubs: *Hard Love* (S&S, 1999), *Noticing Paradise,*
Lombardo's Law (HM, 1995, 1993), *Breakers* (Sheep
Meadow Pr, 1979), *Iowa Rev, American Voice, Midwest*
Qtly, Ploughshares.

Ira Wood   W
Box 1473, Wellfleet, MA 02667, 508-349-1925
Internet: leapfrog@capecod.net
   Pubs: *Storm Tide* (Fawcett-Columbine, 1998), *Going*
Public, The Kitchen Man (Ballantine, 1992, 1987).

Douglas Worth   P
31 Maple Ave, #1, Cambridge, MA 02139, 617-244-5671
   Pubs: *Once Around Bullough's Pond* (William Bauhan,
1987), *From Dream, From Circumstance: New & Selected*
Poems 1963-1983 (Apple-Wood Bks, 1984).

Gene Zeiger   P
RFD 1, #274 Patten Hill Rd, Shelburne, MA 01370,
413-625-6113
   Pubs: *Leaving Egypt* (White Pine Pr, 1994), *Sudden*
Dancing (Amherst Writers & Artists Pr, 1988), *Georgia Rev,*
Tar River Poetry, Prose Poem, The Sun.

Tony Zizza   P
13 Butterworth Rd, Beverly, MA 01915, 508-922-5704
   Pubs: *The Magic of an Open Mind* (Readable Heart Pub,
1987).

Marilyn Zuckerman   P
153 Medford St, Arlington, MA 02174, 617-643-8483
Internet: marizuck@aol.com
   Pubs: *Poems of the Sixth Decade* (Garden Street Pr,
1993), *Claiming the Spirit Within: Anth* (Beacon Pr, 1996),
City River of Voices: Anth (West End Pr, 1992), *Pig Iron,*
Rethinking Marxism, Karamu, Nimrod, The Little Mag.

MICHIGAN

Betsy Adams   P
Chelsea Cats, Inc., PO Box 296, Dexter, MI 48130
    Pubs: *The Dead Birth, Itself* (Paul Green/Spectacular
Diseases, 1990).

Debra Allbery   P
640 Hidden Valley Dr, #301, Ann Arbor, MI 48104
    Pubs: *Walking Distance, The Pittsburgh Book of
Contemporary American Poetry: Anth* (U Pitt Pr, 1991,
1993), *Poetry, Iowa Rev.*

Carroll Arnett   P
5586 Ten-Mile Rd, Mecosta, MI 49332, 616-972-7396
    Pubs: *Spells* (Bloody Twin Pr, 1995), *Night Perimeter: New
& Selected Poems 1958-1990* (Greenfield Rev Pr, 1991).

Alvin Aubert   P
18234 Parkside Ave, Detroit, MI 48221, 313-345-4790
Internet: bernieaub@aol.com
    Pubs: *Harlem Wrestler* (Michigan State U Pr, 1995), *If
Winter Come* (Carnegie Mellon U Pr, 1994), *African
American Rev, Callaloo, Drumvoices.*

Sue A. Austin   P
2211 Eastlawn Dr #7, Midland, MI 48642-5042
    Pubs: *The Three Moons of Earth, Not Your Usual Hearts
And Flowers* (Curtis, 1991, 1990), *Lucidity, Bone and Flesh,
Howling Dog, Cokefish, Color Wheel.*

Axtatl   P&W
468 Prentis, #2, Detroit, MI 482011210, 313-832-2841
    Pubs: *Todo Nada* (Red Age Unlimited Pr, 1998), *Masks,
Folk Dances & A Whole Bunch More* (Ridgeway Pr, 1989),
Callaloo: Anth (Hopkins U Pr, 1994), *California Qtly, Black
Bear Rev, Poetry East, Gatherings.*

Leon Baker   P&W
Macomb Correctional Facility, 26 Mile Rd, New Haven, MI
48048-9999
    Pubs: *Justice & Democracy, In & Out of Doors, Forest of
Algae* (Ivy Pr, 1990, 1985, 1984), *Redbook.*

Carolyn Balducci   W
Univ Michigan, Residential College, Ann Arbor, MI
481091245, 734-647-4388
    Pubs: *Earwax* (Houghton Mifflin, 1972), *Alternative Rev,
Sipario Intl, Antologia Nuova.*

Ann Bardens   P
Central Michigan Univ, Mt Pleasant, MI 48859, 517-774-3101
Internet: 3yun66c@cmich.edu
    Pubs: *Stone and Water* (Canoe Pr, 1992), *The MacGuffin,
Mobius, Plainsongs, Kansas Qtly.*

Jackie Bartley   P
646 Pinecrest Dr, Holland, MI 49424, 616-392-6556
Internet: bartley@hope.edu
    Pubs: *The Terrible Boundaries of the Body* (White Eagle
Coffee Store Pr, 1997), *When Prayer Is Far From Our Lips*
(Franciscan U Pr, 1994), *For A Living: Anth* (U Illinois Pr,
1995), West Branch, Calliope, Cincinnati Poetry Rev,
Aileron, Blue Mesa Rev.

Charles Baxter   P
1585 Woodland Dr, Ann Arbor, MI 48103, 313-769-0059
Internet: cbaxter@umich.edu
    Pubs: *Believers* (Pantheon, 1997), *Burning Down the
House* (Graywolf, 1997), *Shadow Play, A Relative Stranger*
(Norton, 1993, 1990).

Therese Becker   P&W
2401 Eaton Gate Rd, Lake Orion, MI 48360, 248-391-1093
Internet: rbecker115@aol.com
    Pubs: *Contemporary Michigan Poetry: Anth* (Wayne State
U Pr, 1988), *Woman Poet — The Midwest: Anth* (Women In
Literature, 1985), *Poetry East, Witness, New York Qtly.*

Elinor Benedict   P&W
8627 S Lakeside Dr, Rapid River, MI 49878, 906-474-9273
    Pubs: *The Tree Between Us, Chinavision* (March Street Pr,
1997, 1995), *The Green Heart* (Illinois State U, 1994),
*Americas Rev, Borderlands: Texas Poetry, Sow's Ear
Poetry Rev.*

Norma Blair   P
2025 McCann Rd, Hastings, MI 49058, 616-795-7503
    Pubs: *What's A Nice Girl Like You Doing in a Relationship
Like This?: Anth* (Crossing Pr, 1992), *CityBook V:
Sideshow Anth* (Flying Buffalo, 1991).

Beth Brant   P&W
18890 Reed, Melvindale, MI 48122, 313-381-3550
    Pubs: *Food & Spirits* (Firebrand Bks, 1991), *Kenyon Rev,
American Voice, Turtle Qtly, Forum, Tiger Lily, Woman of
Power.*

Alfred J. Bruey   P
201 S Grinnell St, Jackson, MI 49203, 517-784-1411
Internet: ajbruey@aol.com
    Pubs: *Practising Insanity* (Pudding Hse Pub, 1987),
Wherever You Go, There You Are (Suburban Wilderness
Pr, 1985), *Pudding, Poetry Motel, Amelia, Attention Please.*

Gary Bundy   P
172 Jacaranda, Battle Creek, MI 49015, 616-962-8236
Internet: gbundy2034@aol.com
    Pubs: *CQ, Poetry Motel, Sell Outs Literary Mag, Without
Halos, Chiron Rev, Spitball, Blue Light Rev, Birmingham
Poetry Rev, Westering, Boar's Tusk.*

Martin Burwell   P
1394 Roslyn Rd, Grosse Pointe, MI 48236, 313-884-4625
 Pubs: *Cranbrook Rev, Riverrun, Bad Haircut, Wind, Huron
 Rev, Big Two-Hearted, Poetry Detroit.*

Elizabeth Kane Buzzelli   W
60185 Lamplight Ct, Washington, MI 48094
 Pubs: *Gift of Evil* (Bantam, 1983).

Carol Carpenter   P&W
10005 Berwick, Livonia, MI 48150, 734-525-6586
 Pubs: *Resourceful Woman* (Visible Ink Pr, 1994),
 Generation to Generation: Anth (Papier-Mache Pr, 1998),
 *Hawaii Rev, Wisconsin Rev, Quarterly West, Cape Rock,
 Writers' Forum, Nit & Wit, Indiana Rev, Confrontation, Iowa
 Woman, Colorado Woman.*

John Carpenter   P
1606 Granger Ave, Ann Arbor, MI 48104, 313-996-4351
Internet: jcarpen172@aol.com
 Pubs: *Slant, Embers, New Yorker, New York Rev of Bks,
 The Kenyon Rev, Grand Street, Michigan Qtly,
 Crosscurrents.*

Andrew G. Carrigan   P
212 W Henry St, Saline, MI 48176, 313-429-5868
 Pubs: *To Read, To Read, The King, You Poems* (Crowfoot
 Pr, 1981, 1981, 1979).

Christina-Marie   P
149 Washington St, Petoskey, MI 49770, 616-347-1775
Internet: christin@freeway.net
 Pubs: *Images and Language* (Writers North, 1987), *Hiram
 Poetry Rev, MacGuffin, Caliban, Chicago Rev, Poetry Rev,
 Negative Capability.*

Patricia Clark   P
Grand Valley State Univ, English Dept, Allendale, MI 49401,
616-895-3199
Internet: clarkp@gvsu.edu
 Pubs: *North of Wondering* (Women-In-Literature, 1998),
 Worlds in Our Words: Anth (Blair/Prentice Hall, 1997),
 *Seattle Rev, Mississippi Rev, New Criterion, CutBank, New
 England Rev, NAR, Nebraska Rev, Poetry.*

Charles Cline   P
9866 S Westnedge, Portage, MI 49024, 616-327-7135
 Pubs: *Ultima Thule* (Tagore Inst of Creative Writing, 1984),
 Riverrun, Poet, Auraq, Sou'wester.

Margaret Jean Condon   P
400 Maynard St, Ste 506, Ann Arbor, MI 48104,
313-995-8627
 Pubs: *Topographics* (Lame Johnny Pr, 1977).

Nicholas Delbanco   W
Univ Michigan, Hopwood Room, 1006 Angell Hall, Ann Arbor,
MI 48109, 734-662-7963
 Pubs: *Old Scores, In The Name of Mercy* (Warner Bks,
 1997, 1995), *Running In Place* (Atlantic Monthly Pr, 1989),
 *Shenandoah, Salmagundi, Southern Rev, New York Times,
 Atlantic.*

Michael Delp   P
Interlochen Arts Academy, PO Box 199, Interlochen, MI
49643, 616-276-9747
 Pubs: *Under the Influence of Water, Over the Graves of
 Horses* (Wayne State U Pr, 1992, 1988), *Playboy, Poetry
 Northwest, Memphis State Rev.*

Patricia Demetri   P
11313 Rockland Ave, Redford, MI 48239, 313-937-1827
 Pubs: *Manna, Alura, Iadr, Buselinesii, Jean's Journal,
 Canadian Contingent Pr, Still Night Writings.*

Pamela Ditchoff   P&W
605 Butterfield, East Lansing, MI 48823
Internet: pamela@voyager.net
 Pubs: *The Mirror of the Monsters and Prodigies* (Coffee
 House Pr, 1995), *Lexigram Learns* (Interact Pr, 1994),
 Whose Woods These Are: Anth (Ecco Pr, 1993), *Home For
 The Holidays: Anth* (Papier-Mache Pr, 1997), *West.*

Stephen Dunning   P&W
517 Oswego St, Ann Arbor, MI 48104, 734-668-7723
Internet: dunnings@umich.edu
 Pubs: *Hunter's Park: 13 Stories, To the Beautiful Women:
 Stories* (S. Russell, 1996, 1990), *Good Words* (March
 Street Pr, 1991), *New Letters, Crescent Rev, Synaesthesia.*

Stuart Dybek   P&W
320 Monroe, Kalamazoo, MI 49006, 616-344-5590
 Pubs: *The Coast of Chicago* (Knopf, 1990), *Childhood &
 Other Neighborhoods* (Ecco, 1987), *Harper's, New Yorker,
 Atlantic, DoubleTake, Poetry, Paris Rev.*

Ed Engle, Jr.   P
1 Birnwick, Adrian, MI 49221, 517-265-2035
 Pubs: *Baking Catholic* (Summer Stream Pr, 1985), *Blue
 Horse, Crab Creek Rev, New Collage Mag.*

Clayton Eshleman   P
210 Washtenaw Ave, Ypsilanti, MI 48197, 313-483-9787
 Pubs: *From Scratch, Under World Arrest* (Black Sparrow
 Pr, 1998, 1994), *Antiphonal Swing: Selected Prose 1962-87*
 (McPherson, 1988), *Terra Nova, Lusitania, Poesie* (Paris),
 Hambone, Grand Street, Paris Rev.

Leslie D. Foster   P
Box 357, Marquette, MI 49855, 906-228-5131
 Pubs: *Myths for Dorothy* (Foster, 1992), *Northeast, Georgia
 Rev, Christian Century, Sisters Today, Interim, Anglican
 Theological Rev, Ariel.*

Linda Nemec Foster   P
2024 Wilshire Dr SE, Grand Rapids, MI 49506, 616-452-7204
Internet: mfapwgrr9@aol.com
   Pubs: *Living in the Fire Nest* (Ridgeway Pr, 1996), *Trying to Balance the Heart* (Sun Dog Pr, 1993), *New Poems From the Third Coast: Anth* (Wayne State U Pr, 1999), *Georgia Rev, Indiana Rev, River Styx, Nimrod, Quarterly West, DoubleTake.*

Connie Fox   P&W
526 Forest, East Lansing, MI 48823, 515-351-5977
   Pubs: *Entre Nous* (Trout Creek Pr, 1992), *Our Lady of Laussel* (Spectacular Diseases, 1991).

Lucia Fox   P&W
Michigan State Univ, 546 Wells Hall, East Lansing, MI 48823, 517-332-5622
   Pubs: *Tales Of An Indian Princess, Un Cierto Lugar* (Shambhala, 1979, 1978).

Berrien Fragos   PP
PO Box 455, Suttons Bay, MI 49682, 616-271-4089
   Pubs: *10 Field Notes by Berrien* (New York Jrnl of Folklore, 1987).

Randall R. Freisinger   P
Michigan Technological Univ, Humanities Dept, Houghton, MI 49931, 906-487-3229
Internet: rfreisi@mtu.edu
   Pubs: *Plato's Breath* (Utah State U Pr, 1997), *Hand Shadows* (Green Tower, 1988), *Runnin Patterns* (Flume, 1985), *Tar River Poetry, Cream City Rev, Zone 3, New Letters, Tendril, Centennial Rev, Atlanta Rev.*

Sonya Friedman   W
111 S Woodward, Ste 212B, Birmingham, MI 48009, 313-644-4794
   Pubs: *A Hero Is More Than Just A Sandwich* (Putnam, 1986).

Alice Fulton   P&W
2370 LeForge Rd, RR #13, Ypsilanti, MI 48198-9638, 313-482-7197
Internet: www.umich.edu/ slippage/afhome.html
   Pubs: *Sensual Math* (Norton, 1995), *Powers of Congress* (Godine, 1990), *Palladium* (U Illinois, 1986), *New Yorker, Parnassus, TriQuarterly, Pequod, American Voice.*

Ken Gaertner   P&W
11447 Weiman Dr, Pinckney, MI 48169, 313-878-3711
   Pubs: *Koan Bread* (Survivor's Manual, 1977), *Christian Century, New Oxford Rev, America, Poem.*

Dan Gerber   P&W
PO Box 39, Fremont, MI 49412, 616-924-3464
   Pubs: *A Last Bridge Home, A Voice From The River, Grass Fires* (Clark City, 1992, 1990, 1989), *New Yorker, Nation, Georgia Rev.*

Laurence Goldstein   P
408 2nd St, Ann Arbor, MI 48103, 313-769-9899
   Pubs: *Cold Reading, The Three Gardens* (Copper Beech, 1995, 1987), *The Faber Book of Movie Verse: Anth* (F&F, 1994), *Iowa Rev, Ontario Rev, Poetry, Salmagundi, TriQuarterly.*

Jaimy Gordon   P&W
Western Michigan Univ, Kalamazoo, MI 49008, 616-387-2631
Internet: gordonj@wmich.edu
   Pubs: *She Drove Without Stopping* (Algonquin, 1990), *Best American Short Stories: Anth* (HM, 1995), *Michigan Qtly Rev, Ploughshares, Missouri Rev, Gargoyle, Shankpainter.*

Judith Goren   P
21525 W 13 Mile Rd, Beverly Hills, MI 48025, 248-644-7149
Internet: jagoren@mich.com
   Pubs: *Traveling Toward the Heart* (Ridgeway Pr, 1994), *Contemporary Michigan Poetry: Anth* (Wayne State U Pr, 1988), *Centennial Rev, Moving Out, Green River Rev, The Bridge.*

Delcie Southall Gourdine   W
325 Yellow Creek Dr, St Joseph, MI 49085, 616-983-7328
   Pubs: *Redbook, Obsidian, Green's Mag.*

Linda Gregerson   P
4881 Hidden Brook Ln, Ann Arbor, MI 48105, 313-996-2702
Internet: gregerso@umich.edu
   Pubs: *The Woman Who Died In Her Sleep: Anth* (HM, 1996), *Fire In The Conservatory: Anth* (Dragon Gate, 1982), *Atlantic, Poetry, TriQuarterly, Yale Rev.*

Jim Gustafson   P
411 Pleasant, Birmingham, MI 48009, 313-642-1542
   Pubs: *Aloha Street* (Avatar Edtns, 1989), *Virtue and Annihilation* (The Alternative Pr, 1988).

Robert Haight   P
PO Box 744, Marcellus, MI 49067-0744, 616-372-5452
   Pubs: *Water Music* (Ridgeway Pr, 1993), *Passages North Anth* (Milkweed Edtns, 1990), *Contemporary Michigan Poetry: Anth* (Wayne State U Pr, 1989), *Northeast, South Florida Poetry Rev, Oxford Mag, South Coast Poetry Jrnl, Reed Mag, Onion River Rev.*

Charles Hanson   P
449 Moran Rd, Grosse Pointe Farm, MI 48236, 313-882-3627
   Pubs: *Poetry Ohio, Ego Flights, Anth of Mag Verse, White Rock Rev, Yellow Butterfly, Beloit Poetry Jrnl, Stone Country, Crab Creek Rev.*

Jim Harrison   P&W
PO Box 135, Lake Leelanau, MI 49653-0135
   Pubs: *Sundog* (Dutton, 1984), *Warlock, Legends* (Delacorte, 1981, 1979), *Farmer* (Viking, 1976).

Janet Ruth Heller   P
2719 Pfitzer Ave, Portage, MI 49024, 616-323-2014
Internet: jheller@albion.edu
Pubs: *Modern Poems on the Bible: Anth* (Jewish Pub Society, 1994), *Women's Glib: A Collection of Women's Humor: Anth* (Crossing Pr, 1991), *Anima.*

Conrad Hilberry   P
1601 Grand Ave, Kalamazoo, MI 49006, 616-337-7043
Internet: hilberry@kzoo.edu
Pubs: *Sorting the Smoke* (U Iowa, 1990), *Luke Karamazov* (Wayne State U, 1987), *Tamaqua, Gettysburg Rev, Shenandoah, Virginia Qtly, Poetry.*

J. Kline Hobbs   P
657 E Michigan Ave, Battle Creek, MI 49017, 616-962-2453
Pubs: *Arrivals and Departures, Diary of the Ultimate One Night Stand—and that Other Quest* (Expedition Pr, 1981, 1979), *Green River Rev.*

Patricia Hooper   P
616 Yarmouth Rd, Bloomfield Townshi, MI 48301
Pubs: *The Flowering Trees* (State Street Pr, 1995), *Other Lives* (Elizabeth Street Pr, 1984), *Atlantic, New Criterion, Poetry, Hudson Rev, American Scholar.*

Daniel Hughes   P
17524 3rd Ave, #104, Detroit, MI 48203, 313-345-5834
Pubs: *You Are Not Stendhal* (Wayne State U Pr, 1992), *Spirit Traps, Falling* (Copper Beech Pr, 1988, 1979).

Deborah L. Hunt   W
PO Box 85960, Westland, MI 48185
Internet: dlhunt1052@aol.com
Pubs: *Mystic Fiction, Mythic Circle, New Authors Jrnl, Space & Time, Aberrations, Heliocentric Net, Mobius, New Altars, Outer Darkness, Perceptions.*

Arnold Johnston   P&W
471 West South St #102, Kalamazoo, MI 49008, 616-381-6316
Internet: arnie.johnston@wmich.edu
Pubs: *What the Earth Taught Us* (March Street Pr, 1996), *Embers, Rockford Rev, ELF, Malahat Rev, Colorado Qtly, Alabama Literary Rev, Indiana Rev, Cumberland Poetry Rev, Passages North, Hiram Poetry Rev, Tar River Poetry.*

Laura Kasischke   P
2997 S Fletcher Rd, Chelsea, MI 48118, 313-475-7485
Pubs: *Suspicious River* (Houghton Mifflin, 1996), *Housekeeping in a Dream* (Carnegie Mellon, 1995), *Wild Brides* (NYU Pr, 1991), *Poetry.*

Janet Kauffman   P&W
14671 W Cadmus Rd, Rte 1, Hudson, MI 49247, 517-448-4973
Pubs: *The Body in Four Parts* (Graywolf, 1993), *Obscene Gestures for Women* (Knopf, 1989).

Elizabeth Kerlikowske   P
2423 Russet Dr, Kalamazoo, MI 49008, 616-343-4003
Internet: mme642@aol.com
Pubs: *The Seven, Her Bodies, Postcard* (March Street Pr, 1997, 1995, 1990), *Stand-Up Poetry: Anth* (U California Pr, 1993), *Parting Gifts, Visions Intl, Blue Violin, Mobius, Poetry Motel, Renegade, Iris, Creative Woman, Perhaps, Mediphors.*

Judith Kerman   P
Saginaw Valley State Univ, 7400 Bay Rd, University Center, MI 48710, 517-790-4063
Internet: kerman@tardis.svsu.edu
Pubs: *Mothering & Dream of Rain* (Ridgeway, 1997), *Driving for Yellow Cab* (Tout Pr, 1985), *Mothering* (Uroboros/Allegheny Mtn Pr, 1978), *Chelsea, Michigan Qtly Rev, Eastgate Qtly Rev, Controlled Burn, House Organ, Snowy Egret, Hiram Poetry Rev, Oxalis.*

John Ketzer   W
Jayell Enterprises, Inc., PO Box 2616, Ft Dearborn Sta, Dearborn, MI 48123
Pubs: *My First Year Out* (Jayell Enterprises, 1984).

Lionel Bruce Kingery   P
947 Francis, Rochester Hills, MI 48307
Pubs: *The Popular Songs of Bruce Kingery* (North American Mentor, 1980), *Arcadia Poetry Anth* (Arcadia Poetry Pr, 1992), *Verses, Voices Intl, Second Coming.*

Ray Kytle   W
Central Michigan Univ, Mount Pleasant, MI 48858, 517-774-3275
Pubs: *Last Voyage* (Dell, 1979), *Meltdown, Fire And Ice* (David McKay, 1976, 1975).

Margo LaGattuta   P
2134 W Gunn Rd, Rochester, MI 48306, 810-693-7227
Internet: lagapvp@aol.com
Pubs: *Embracing the Fall* (Plain View Pr, 1994), *The Dream Givers* (Lake Shore Pub, 1990), *Sun, Yankee, Bridge, Passages North, Calliope, Woman Poet.*

Christine Lahey   P
1540 Boulan Rd, Troy, MI 48084, 810-643-6525
Pubs: *Blood To Remember: American Poets on the Holocaust Anth* (Texas Tech U Pr, 1991), *All's Normal Here: Anth* (Ruddy Duck Pr, 1985), *Planet Detroit, Michigan Qtly Rev.*

Betty Rita Gomez Lance   P&W
1562 Spruce Dr, Kalamazoo, MI 49008-2227, 616-345-0649
Pubs: *Siete Cuerdas* (Ediciones Cardenoso, 1996), *Alas en el Alba* (Compotex, 1987), *Hoy Hacen Corro las Ardillas* (Editorial Papiro, 1985).

Douglas W. Lawder   P
Michigan State Univ, Morrill Hall, East Lansing, MI 48824
    Pubs: *Trolling* (Little, Brown, 1977), *Nation, Poetry, Virginia
    Qtly Rev, The Seventies.*

Stephen Leggett   P
PO Box 4551, Ann Arbor, MI 48106, 313-461-1574
    Pubs: *The Form It Takes* (Ridgeway Pr, 1988), *The
    All-Forest* (Waves, 1980).

Christopher Towne Leland   W
Wayne State Univ, 51 W Warren, Detroit, MI 48202,
313-577-2450
Internet: ctllnd@aol.com
    Pubs: *The Professor of Aesthetics, Letting Loose: Anth*
    (Zoland, 1994, 1996), *The Book of Marvels* (Scribner,
    1990), *Mrs. Randall* (HM, 1987).

Kathleen Ripley Leo   P
42185 Baintree Cir, Northville, MI 48167-3447, 810-349-4827
    Pubs: *The Circle is Assembled: Glass Poems, The Old
    Ways* (Sun Dog Pr, 1994, 1991), *Town One South,
    Northville Poems* (Northville Arts, 1988).

M. L. Liebler   P&W
31725 Courtland, St Clair Shores, MI 48082, 810-294-7378
    Pubs: *Stripping the Adult Century Bare* (Viet Nam
    Generation Pr, 1994), *Breaking the Voodoo* (Parkville Pub,
    1990), *Onthebus, Rolling Stock.*

Judith Wood Lindenau   P
7707 Fouch Rd, Traverse City, MI 49684-9513,
616-947-9803

Thomas Lynch   P&W
328 E Liberty, Milford, MI 48381, 810-684-6645
Internet: thoslynch@aol.com
    Pubs: *Still Life in Milford, The Undertaking* (Norton 1998,
    1997), *Grimalkin and Other Poems* (Cape/Random Hse,
    1994), *New Yorker, Harper's, Poetry, London Rev of Bks,
    Paris Rev, New York Times Mag.*

Daniel Lyons   W
501 W Hoover Ave, Ann Arbor, MI 48103-4864
    Pubs: *The Last Good Man* (U Massachusetts Pr, 1992).

Naomi Long Madgett   P
18080 Santa Barbara Dr, Detroit, MI 48221, 313-342-9174
Internet: nlmadgett@aol.com
    Pubs: *Remembrances of Spring* (Michigan State U Pr, 1993),
    Pink Ladies In The Afternoon (Lotus Pr, 1990), *Octavia And
    Other Poems* (Third World Pr, 1988), *Witness, Essence,
    Obsidian, Michigan Qtly Rev, Sage, Black Scholar.*

Denise Martinson   P&W
Poetic Page, PO Box 71192, Madison Heights, MI
48071-0192
    Pubs: *Pieces of Eight: Anth* (Wordsmith Pub, 1992), *Canto,
    Elk River Rev, Mobius, Metro Singles Lifestyle.*

Beverly Matherne   P
Northern Michigan Univ, 1401 Presque Isle, Marquette, MI
49855-1556, 906-227-1386
Internet: fabe@nmu.edu
    Pubs: *La Grande Pointe* (Cross-Cultural Communications,
    1995), *Two Worlds Walking: Anth* (New Rivers Pr, 1994),
    Great River Rev, Kansas Qtly, Metamorphoses.

Claire McAllister   P
PO Box 6616, Grand Rapids, MI 49516-6616, 616-458-2922
    Pubs: *Arms Of Light* (Knopf, 1964), *New York Qtly, Poetry
    London.*

Richard E. McMullen   P
128 Marvin St, Milan, MI 48160, 313-439-7112
    Pubs: *Like Heaven* (Limited Mailing Pr, 1993), *Trying to Get
    Out* (Crowfoot Pr, 1981), *I Feel A Little Jumpy Around You:
    Anth* (S&S, 1996), *CSM, Commonweal, Epoch, Hanging
    Loose, Massachusetts Rev, New York Times, Southern
    Poetry Rev, Wisconsin Rev.*

Ken Mikolowski   P
1207 Henry St, Ann Arbor, MI 48104-4340, 313-662-1286
    Pubs: *Big Enigmas* (Past Tents Pr, 1991), *Little Mysteries*
    (Toothpaste Pr, 1979), *Re:view, Rolling Stock, Exquisite
    Corpse, Notus.*

Sam Mills   P
116 W Maple St, Lansing, MI 48906, 517-482-4037
    Pubs: *Burning the Stratocaster* (Sleeping Buddha Pr,
    1992), *A Long Drink* (Poetry Centre, 1975), *In This Corner,
    Red Cedar Rev, Triage.*

Ronald Milner   P
15865 Montevista, Detroit, MI 48238

Judith Minty   P
7113 S Scenic Dr, New Era, MI 49446, 616-894-2121
Internet: judminty@aol.com
    Pubs: *Dancing the Fault* (U Central Florida Pr, 1991), *Yellow
    Dog Journal* (Parallax Pr, 1991), *Mad Painter Poems, Poetry,
    Caliban, New Yorker, Iowa Rev, Hawaii Rev.*

Edward Morin   P
2112 Brockman Rd, Ann Arbor, MI 48104-4530,
313-668-7523
    Pubs: *Labor Day at Walden Pond* (Ridgeway Pr, 1996),
    The Dust of Our City (Clover Pr, 1978), *Hudson Rev,
    Ploughshares, TriQuarterly, Iowa Rev, River Styx.*

Carol Morris   P
912 Rose Ave, Ann Arbor, MI 48104-4349, 313-761-5616
Internet: silkrhino@aol.com
    Pubs: *Atomic Picnic* (Stellar Productions, 1995), *Sweet
    Uprisings* (Years Pr, 1990), *Slipstream, MacGuffin,
    Psychopoetica.*

Calvin Murry   P&W
11714 Dyar St, Hamtramck, MI 48212
   Pubs: *My Brother's Keeper* (M. Datcher, 1992), *Prisoner
   Aboard S.S. Beagle, Light From Another Country*
   (Greenfield Rev Pr, 1983, 1982), *Poetry, Art/Life.*

Duane Niatum   P&W
Univ Michigan, 410 Mason Hall, Ann Arbor, MI 48109,
313-763-1460
   Pubs: *Drawings of The Song Animals: New And Selected
   Poems* (Holy Cow! Pr, 1991), *North Dakota Qtly, Archae
   Mag, Seattle Rev, Michigan Qtly Rev, Chariton Rev.*

William P. Osborn   W
145 Crestwood NW, Grand Rapids, MI 49504, 616-791-0049
Internet: osbornb@gvsu.edu
   Pubs: *Gettysburg Rev, ACM, Western Humanities Rev,
   Texas Rev, Carolina Qtly, Mississippi Rev.*

Charlene Noel Palmer   P
2310 Calumet St, Flint, MI 485032811, 810-238-5919
   Pubs: *Anti-War Poem, Vol. II: Anth* (Stephen Gill, 1986),
   Voices For Peace: Anth (Disarmament and Peace Task
   Force, 1983), *Peace or Perish: A Crisis Anth* (Poets For
   Peace, 1983), *Odyssey, Axios, Christian Century,
   Mediphors, December, Handmaiden.*

David Palmer   P
2310 Calumet St, Flint, MI 485032811, 810-238-5919
   Pubs: *Quickly, Over the Wall* (Wake-Brook, 1966), *Songs
   From Unsung Worlds: Anth* (AAAS, 1985), *Peace or Perish:
   A Crisis Anth* (Poets For Peace, 1983), *Beloit, Kayak,
   Passages North, Poets On, Immobius, Slipstream.*

Miriam Pederson   P
Aquinas College/English Dept, 1607 Robinson Rd, SE, Grand
Rapids, MI 49506, 616-459-8281
Internet: pedermir@aquinas.edu
   Pubs: *New Poems from the Third Coast: Anth, The Third
   Coast, Contemporary Michigan Poets: Anth* (Wayne State
   U Pr, 1999, 1990), *The Book of Birth Poetry: Anth* (Bantam
   Bks, 1995), *Passages North, MacGuffin, Sing Heavenly
   Muse.*

William S. Penn   W
963 Lantern Hill Dr, East Lansing, MI 48823-2831,
517-337-0694
Internet: penn@pilot.msu.edu
   Pubs: *The Absence of Angels* (Permanent Pr, 1994), *All My
   Sins Are Relative* (U Nebraska Pr, 1994), *Antaeus, Stand,
   Grain, Quarterly West, Missouri Rev, Bananas.*

Rosalie Sanara Petrouske   P
262 Whetstone Rd, Marquette, MI 49855, 906-225-8085
   Pubs: *The Geisha Box* (March Street Pr, 1996), *It's All the
   Rage: Anth* (Andrew Mountain Pr, 1997), *Poets On,
   Paintbrush, The MacGuffin, Passages North, Southern
   Poetry Rev, Seattle Rev, Parting Gifts, Rhino, Windless
   Orchard, Antigonish Rev.*

Simone Juda Press   P
2215 Chaucer Ct, Ann Arbor, MI 48103, 313-665-2164
   Pubs: *The Secret Garden* (Lydia Mendelssohn Theater,
   1987), *Riding On Stars* (Trueblood Theater, 1987), *Lifting
   Water* (Crowfoot Pr, 1979), *Village Voice.*

Patricia Rachal   P
2133 Ridge Rd, Kalamazoo, MI 49008, 616-345-3682

Dudley Randall   P
12651 Old Mill Pl, Detroit, MI 48238, 313-935-1188
   Pubs: *Litany Of Friends* (Lotus, 1981), *Black Poets: Anth*
   (Bantam, 1971).

John R. Reed   P
Wayne State Univ, 51 W Warren, Detroit, MI 48202,
313-861-4298
Internet: jreed@cms.cc.wayne.edu
   Pubs: *Life Sentences* (Wayne State U Pr, 1996), *Great Lake*
   (Ridgeway Pr, 1995), *Poetry, American Scholar, Michigan Qtly
   Rev, Ontario Rev, Southwest Rev, Partisan Rev.*

Danny Rendleman   P
Univ Michigan, 326 Crob, Flint, MI 48502, 810-762-3388
   Pubs: *The Middle West, Victrola* (Ridgeway Pr, 1995,
   1994), *APR, Field, o.blek, Epoch, Passages North,
   Antigonish Rev.*

Jack Ridl   P
2309 Auburn Ave, Holland, MI 49424, 616-399-5925
Internet: ridl@hope.edu
   Pubs: *Approaching Poetry* (St. Martin's Pr, 1997), *Poems
   from The Same Ghost and Between* (Dawn Valley Pr,
   1993), *For A Living: Poems of Work: Anth* (U Illinois, 1995),
   *Georgia Rev, The Journal, Artful Dodge, Poetry East,
   Ploughshares, Denver Qtly.*

Daniel Rosochacki   P
2223 Fremont, Grand Rapids, MI 49504

Gil Saenz   P
19211 Wall St, Melvindale, MI 48122
   Pubs: *Graffiti Rag* (Charara & Fahrenkopf, 1995), *Colorful
   Impressions* (Casa de Unidad, 1994).

William Schoenl   P
2643 Roseland, East Lansing, MI 48823, 517-351-0456
   Pubs: *Big Two-Hearted, Alura Qtly, Riverrun, Parnassus
   Literary Jrnl.*

Herbert Scott   P
PO Box 2615, Kalamazoo, MI 49003, 616-342-5715
Internet: herbert.scott@wmich.edu
   Pubs: *The Wishing Heart* (Sutton Hoo Pr, 1999), *Durations*
   (LSU, 1984), *Groceries* (U Pittsburgh Pr, 1976), *Poetry
   Northwest, Michigan Qtly Rev, Black Warrior Rev,
   Shenandoah, Kenyon Rev.*

Heather Laurie Sellers   P&W
Hope College, 126 E 10 St, Holland, MI 494239000,
616-395-7116
Internet: sellers@hope.edu
    Pubs: *Your Whole Life: Poems* (Panhandler, 1994), *Sun,
William & Mary Rev, Sonora Rev, The Sun, Five Points,
New Virginia Rev, Indiana Rev, Alaska Qtly Rev.*

Maryl Shackett   P
323 Jefferson, Marine City, MI 48039, 810-765-4383
    Pubs: *This is My Beloved* (Anderie Poetry Pr, 1997),
Lucidity (Bear Hse Pr, 1997), *Changes in the Heart* (Lyre
Loon, 1996), *The Seasons of Us, Lovesounds*
(Riverside-Popular, 1980, 1979), Southill Gazette.

Marc Sheehan   P
15795 Peacock Rd, Haslett, MI 48840, 517-339-5985
Internet: marcsheehan@worldnet.att.net
    Pubs: *Greatest Hits* (New Isues Pr, 1999), *Third Coast,
Sky, Controlled Burn, Burning World, Pannus Index,
Gulfstream, Parting Gifts.*

Anita Skeen   P
Michigan State Univ, 201 Morrill Hall, English Dept, East
Lansing, MI 48824, 517-355-7570
Internet: skeen@pilot.msu.edu
    Pubs: *Portraits* (Kida Pr, 1993), *Each Hand A Map* (Naiad
Pr, 1986), *Ploughshares, New Letters, Kansas Qtly, Prairie
Schooner, Ms., Nimrod, Atlanta Rev.*

Elizabeth Anne Socolow   P
University Ligget School, 1045 Cook Rd, Grosse Pte Woods,
MI 48236, 313-884-4444
    Pubs: *Laughing at Gravity, Conversations with Isaac
Newton* (Beacon, 1988), *Bluestones and Salthay: Anth*
(Rutgers U Pr, 1990), *Michigan Qtly Rev.*

Julie L. Stone   P
1890 Carriage Rd #215, Muskegon, MI 49442, 616-773-0885
    Pubs: *Playgirl, Berkeley Monthly, The Poet, The Hunter,
Scene, Vega, Hoosier Challenger.*

Diane Suess-Brakeman   P
English Dept, Kalamazoo Colleg, 1200 Academy St,
Kalamazoo, MI 49006, 616-337-7043
Internet: kylsb@aol.com
    Pubs: *It Blows You Hollow* (New Issues Pr, 1998), *Poetry
Northwest, Alaska Qtly, Third Coast, Primavera, Indiana
Rev, Tamaqua, Northwest Rev, Cumberland Poetry Rev.*

Keith Taylor   P&W
1715 Dexter Ave, Ann Arbor, MI 48103, 734-665-5341
Internet: cgolus@aol.com
    Pubs: *Everything I Need* (March Street Pr, 1996), *Life
Science & Other Stories* (Hanging Loose Pr, 1995), *Detail
from the Garden of Delights* (Limited Mailing Pr, 1993),
*Witness, Hanging Loose, Story, Pivot, Caliban, Michigan
Qtly Rev.*

F. Richard Thomas   P
Michigan State Univ, East Lansing, MI 48824-1033,
517-355-2400
Internet: thomasff@pilot.msu.edu
    Pubs: *Miracles* (Canoe Pr, 1996), *Frog Praises Night*
(Southern Illinois U Pr, 1980), *The Bridge, Beloit Poetry
Jrnl, New York Qtly, Sou'wester, English Jrnl, Images.*

Vonnie Thomas   P
8757 Berridge Rd, Greenville, MI 48838, 616-754-8698
    Pubs: *Gift of Time, Changing View* (Belding, 1992, 1990),
The View Beyond the Tree (Greenville, 1981).

Ben Tibbs   P
2127 Audley Dr NE, Grand Rapids, MI 49505, 616-349-2763
    Pubs: *Graffiti Book, Italics Mine, Approaches* (Stovepipe Pr,
1984, 1983, 1982), *Celery.*

Richard Tillinghast   P&W
1317 Granger Ave, Ann Arbor, MI 48104-4480, 313-930-0532
Internet: rwtill@umich.edu
    Pubs: *Today in the Cafe Trieste* (Salmon/Dufour, 1997),
The Stonecutter's Hand (David R. Godine, 1997), *Our Flag
Was Still There* (Wesleyan, 1984), *Paris Rev, New Yorker,
Nation, Atlantic, New Criterion.*

Eric Torgersen   P&W
8475 Chippewa Trail, Mount Pleasant, MI 48858,
517-773-4559
Internet: eric.torgersen@cmich.edu
    Pubs: *Dear Friend: Rilke & P. Modersohn-Becker*
(Northwestern U Pr, 1998), *Good True Stories* (Lynx Hse,
1994), *The Door to the Moon* (March Street Pr, 1993),
Hudson Rev, APR, Literary Rev, Gettysburg Rev, River
Styx.

Stephen H. Tudor   P
14447 Harbor Island, Detroit, MI 48215, 313-822-4895
Internet: http://www.quicklink.com/ monella/haul.html
    Pubs: *Haul-Out: New and Selected Poems, Hangdog Reef:
Poems Sailing the Great Lakes* (Wayne State U, 1996,
1989), *Michigan Qtly Rev, Bridge.*

Robert Vandermolen   P
2771 Glencairin Dr NW, Grand Rapids, MI 49504,
616-453-7056
    Pubs: *Peaches* (Sky Pr, 1998), *Night Weather* (Northern
Lights Pr, 1991), *Of Pines* (Paradigm Pr, 1989), *Mudfish,
NAW, Artful Dodge, Exquisite Corpse, Caliban, Sulfur,
Grand Street, House Organ, Epoch.*

Diane Wakoski   P
607 Division St, East Lansing, MI 48823, 517-332-3385
Internet: dwakoski@aol.com
    Pubs: *Argonaut Rose, The Emerald City of Las Vegas,
Jason The Sailor, Medea The Sorceress* (Black Sparrow
Pr, 1998, 1995, 1993, 1990).

Sylvia Watanabe W
145 Crestwood NW, Grand Rapids, MI 49504, 616-791-0049
Pubs: *Talking to the Dead and Other Stories* (Doubleday, 1992).

Barrett Watten P
English Dept, Wayne State University, Detroit, MI 48202, 313-577-3067
Internet: b.watten@wayne.edu
Pubs: *Bad History* (Atelos Pr, 1998), *Frame, 1971-1990* (Sun & Moon Pr, 1997), *Under Erasure* (Zasterle Pr, 1991), *Leningrad: American Writers in the Soviet Union: Anth* (Mercury Hse, 1991), *Conduit* (Gaz, 1986), *The World, Common Knowledge, Poetics Jrnl.*

Ron Weber P
2160 N. County Line Rd, Watervliet, MI 490989535, 616-463-4049
Pubs: *Bluff View From the Twin Cities: Poems from the West Bank* (Harbor Hse 1993), *Voices Intl, Tempo, Catalyst, Peninsula Poets, Poet, Analecta.*

Robert E. Wegner W
Alma College, Alma, MI 48801, 517-463-7270
Pubs: *The Third Coast: Anth* (Wayne State, 1982), *Short Story Intl, Karamu, Southwest Rev.*

Patricia Jabbeh Wesley P&W
Western Michigan University, Spau Tower, Kalamazoo, MI 490085092, 616-387-2572
Internet: nyemadi@juno.com
Pubs: *Before the Palm Could Bloom* (New Issues Pr, 1998), *Michigan College English Association Jrnl, Institute for Liberian Studies Jrnl.*

Gloria Whelan W
9797 N Twin Lake Rd NE, Mancelona, MI 49659, 616-587-9501
Pubs: *Farewell to the Island* (HC, 1998), *Forgive the River, Forgive the Sky, That Wild Berries Should Grow* (Eerdmans, 1998, 1994), *Night of the Full Moon* (Knopf, 1993), *Bringing the Farmhouse Home* (S&S, 1992).

Carolyn White P&W
1661 Mt Vernon Ave, East Lansing, MI 48823, 517-351-5866
Pubs: *Whuppity Stoorie* (Putnam, 1997), *The Tree House Children* (S&S, 1994), *Parabola, Magical Blend, Book of Contemporary Myth, Michigan Qtly Rev, Studia Mystica.*

Laurie Anne Whitt P
PO Box 195, Chassell, MI 49916, 906-523-4566
Internet: lawhitt@mtu.edu
Pubs: *Icarus 95: Anth* (Kenan Pr, 1995), *New Voices: Anth* (Mosaic Pr, 1984), *Spoon River Poetry Rev, Puerto del Sol, Wisconsin Rev, Cottonwood, Hawaii Rev, Malahat Rev, Prism Intl.*

Margaret Willey P&W
431 Grant St, Grand Haven, MI 494171834, 616-846-1759
Internet: joannisr@river.it.gvsu.edu
Pubs: *Facing the Music, The Melinda Zone, Saving Lenny* (Bantam, 1996, 1993, 1990), *If Not For You, Finding David Dolores* (H&R, 1988, 1986), *Hungry Mind Rev, New Moon Network, Calyx, Passages North, Redbook, Quarterly West.*

Thomas Wiloch P&W
43672 Emrick Dr, Canton, MI 48187
Internet: twiloch@gale.com
Pubs: *Neon Trance, Decoded Factories of the Heart* (Runaway Spoon Pr, 1997, 1994), *Mr. Templeton's Toyshop* (Wordcraft, 1995), *Publishers Weekly, Carpe Noctem, Bloomsbury Rev, Urbanite, Recursive Angel, Epitaph.*

Melinda Wolf P
1761 Oxford Rd SE, Grand Rapids, MI 49506, 616-956-9105
Pubs: *Anth of Mag Verse & Yearbook of American Poetry, New York Qlly, Mudfish, American Literary Rev, Cape Rock, Kalliope, Outerbridge, Intro, Pig Iron, South Coast Poetry Rev.*

Anne Ohman Youngs P
5171 Hwy M35, Escanaba, MI 49829, 906-789-1934
Pubs: *A Bracelet of Mouse Hands* (Frank Cat Pr, 1995), *Markers* (Andrew Mountain Pr, 1988), *Prose Poem, Cream City Rev, Mid-American Rev, Midwest Qtly, Tar River.*

Janice Zerfas P
Lake Michigan College, 2755 E Napier Ave, Benton Harbor, MI 49022, 616-927-3571
Pubs: *Sky, Footwork: The Paterson Literary Rev, Blossom Rev, Shoreline Voices, Red Cedar Rev, Graffitti Rag.*

Jack Zucker P
14050 Vernon St, Oak Park, MI 48237
Pubs: *From Manhattan* (Pointe Pr, 1989), *Beginnings* (Katydid Pr, 1982), *The Bridge, Poetry Northwest, Esquire, Literary Rev.*

MINNESOTA

C. Abartis W
St. Cloud State Univ, St Cloud, MN 56301, 612-255-3061
Pubs: *Twilight Zone Mag, Lady's Circle, The Quarterly, Beloit Fiction Jrnl.*

Harold Adams W
12916 Greenwood Rd, Minnetonka, MN 55343, 612-938-6426
Pubs: *The Ditched Blonde, A Way With Widows, A Prfctly Prpr Mrdr, The Mn Who Was Tllr Thn God* (Walker, 1995, 1994, 1993, 1992).

Jonis Agee   P&W
College of St Catherine, 2004 Randolph, St Paul, MN 55105
Internet: jagee@umich.edu
  Pubs: *South of Resurrection* (Viking, 1997), *Strange
  Angels, Sweet Eyes* (HC, 1994, 1992), *38 Special and a
  Broken Heart, Bend This Heart* (Coffee Hse Pr, 1995,
  1989).

Paulette Bates Alden   W
4900 Washburn Ave S, Minneapolis, MN 55410,
612-920-1896
  Pubs: *Crossing the Moon* (Hungry Mind Pr, 1996), *Feeding
  the Eagles* (Graywolf Pr, 1988), *Ploughshares, Mississippi
  Rev, Antioch Rev, New York Times Mag, First.*

Floyce Alexander   P&W
1211 Beltrami Ave NW, Bemidji, MN 56601-2826,
218-751-7382
Internet: fmklalex@mail.paulbunyan.net
  Pubs: *Memory of the Future* (Red Dragonfly Pr, 1998), *Red
  Deer* (L'Epervier, 1982), *Bottom Falling Out of The Dream*
  (Lynx Hse Pr, 1976), *Nation, TriQuarterly, Greenfield Rev,
  Contact II, Colorado Rev.*

Patricia Axxinn   P
286 Laurel Ave, St Paul, MN 55102
Internet: hampl001@maroon.tc.umn.edu
  Pubs: *A Romantic Education* (HM, 1992), *Virgin Time*
  (FSG, 1992), *Spillville* (Milkweed Edtns, 1987), *New Yorker,
  Antaeus, Paris Rev.*

Daniel Bachhuber   P
1312 Osceola Ave, St Paul, MN 55105, 612-699-1560
  Pubs: *Mixed Voices: Anth, Minnesota Writes: Poetry Anth*
  (Milkweed Edtns, 1991, 1987), *Iowa Rev, Great River Rev,
  Lake Street Rev.*

Patricia Barone   P
686 Kimball St, NE, Fridley, MN 55432, 612-784-3386
Internet: baronel@juno.com
  Pubs: *Handmade Paper, The Wind* (New Rivers Pr, 1994,
  1987), *Visions Intl, And Rev, West Wind Rev, Widener Rev,
  Pleiades, Permafrost, Sidewalks, American Writing, Seattle
  Rev.*

David Bengtson   P
626 Oak Ct S, Long Prairie, MN 56347, 320-732-6297
Internet: david_bengtson@mail.lpge.k12.mn.us
  Pubs: *Open Windows* (Juniper Pr, 1990), *26 Minnesota
  Writers: Anth* (Nodin Pr, 1995), *Biggy's Candy Store: Anth*
  (The Loft, 1992), *Ascent, New Letters, New England Rev,
  Northeast, Sidewalks, Lake County Jrnl.*

Sigrid Bergie   P
1912 Hennepin S #4, Minneapolis, MN 55403, 612-879-0683
  Pubs: *Turning Out the Lights* (New Rivers Pr, 1988).

Candace Black   P
824 Baker Ave, Mankato, MN 56001, 507-625-6104
  Pubs: *The Decade Dance: Anth* (Sandhills Pr, 1991),
  *Conscience, Milkweed Chronicle, Iowa Woman,
  Pennsylvania Rev, Seattle Rev, Gulf Stream Mag.*

Carol Bly   W
1668 Juno Ave, St Paul, MN 551161415, 612-699-5427
Internet: carolmbly@aol.com
  Pubs: *Changing the Bully Who Rules the World: Anth*
  (Milkweed Edtns, 1996), *New Yorker, TriQuarterly, Laurel
  Review, Iowa Rev.*

Robert Bly   P
1904 Girard Ave S, Minneapolis, MN 55403-2945,
612-377-9817
  Pubs: *Meditations on the Insatiable Soul, What Have I Ever
  Lost by Dying?* (HarperCollins, 1994, 1993), *The Nation,
  The Sun, Kenyon Rev, Common Boundary.*

William Borden   P&W
Route 6, Box 284, Bemidji, MN 56601, 218-586-2765
Internet: wborden@paulbunyan.net
  Pubs: *Superstoe* (Orloff, 1996), *Slow Step and Dance*
  (Loonfeather Pr, 1991), *North Coast Rev, City Legacy,
  Prague Rev, Poets On, South Dakota Rev, Milkweed
  Chronicle, New Orleans Rev.*

John Brandi   P&W
Holy Cow! Press, PO Box 3170, Mt. Royal Sta, Duluth, MN
55803
  Pubs: *In the Desert We Do Not Count The Days, Hymn For
  A Night Feast* (Holy Cow! Pr, 1990, 1988).

Jonathan Brannen   P&W
7 Circle Pines St, Morris, MN 56267-2103
  Pubs: *Thing Is The Anagram of Night* (Texture Pr, 1996),
  Nothing Doing Never Again (Score Pr, 1995), *Black Ice,
  Situation, Fiction Intl, Asylum Annual, 6ix.*

Jill Breckenridge   P
708 N 1st St, #534, Minneapolis, MN 55401-1152
  Pubs: *How To Be Lucky* (Blue Stem Pr, 1990), *Civil Blood*
  (Milkweed Edtns, 1986), *Noeva: 3 Women Poets: Anth*
  (Dakota Pr, 1975).

Kerri R. Brostrom   P
2512 E 125 St, Burnsville, MN 55337, 612-728-0053
  Pubs: *Byline Mag, Portable Wall, Green's Mag, Alura,
  Hudson Valley Echoes, Negative Capability, Cape Rock,
  Maryland Poetry Rev, Black River Rev, Rattle, Madison
  Rev.*

Michael Dennis Browne   P
Univ Minnesota, Lind Hall, 207 Church St, Minneapolis, MN
55455, 612-626-9555
Internet: mdb@tc.umn.edu
    Pubs: *Selected Poems 1965-1995, You Won't Remember
    This, Smoke from the Fires, The Sun Fetcher* (Carnegie
    Mellon, 1997, 1992, 1985, 1978), *APR, TriQuarterly.*

Emilie Buchwald   P&W
Milkweed Editions, 430 First Ave N, Ste 400, Minneapolis,
MN 55406, 612-332-3192
    Pubs: *The Sporting Life: Anth, The Poet Dreaming in the
    Artist's House: Anth, Transforming A Rape Culture: Anth*
    (Milkweed Edtns, 1987, 1984, 1993).

Alan Burns   W
Univ Minnesota, 207 Church St SE, Minneapolis, MN 55455,
612-625-3363
    Pubs: *Revolutions of the Night* (Schocken, 1987), *The Day
    Daddy Died* (Allison & Busby, 1981).

John Caddy   P
8870 202nd St N, Forest Lake, MN 55025, 612-464-6684
    Pubs: *The Color of Mesabi Bones, Eating the Sting*
    (Milkweed Edtns, 1989, 1986), *Dacotah Territory.*

Katherine Carlson   W
2912 34th Ave S, #2, Minneapolis, MN 55406, 612-296-6605
    Pubs: *Casualties* (New Rivers, 1982), *Minneapolis/St. Paul
    Mag, New Directions for Women, In These Times, VIA,
    Minnesota Women's Pr, Spirit.*

Barry Casselman   P
1414 S 3rd St, #102, Minneapolis, MN 55454-1172,
612-321-9044
    Pubs: *Among Dreams* (Kraken Pr, 1985), *Language is Not
    Words* (Lingua Pr, 1980), *APR, Another Chicago Mag,
    Calcutta 2000, Kansas Qtly, North Stone Rev.*

Nadia Christensen   P
1545 Fulham St, St Paul, MN 55108, 612-644-4057
    Pubs: *Turkestan* (France; w/Kling; Chene, 1991), *Action,
    Reflection, Celebration* (ARC, 1988).

Kathleen Coskran   W
152 Bank St SE, Minneapolis, MN 55414-1009,
612-822-8847
    Pubs: *The High Price of Everything, The House on Via
    Gambito: Anth* (New Rivers Pr, 1988, 1991), *Going Up
    Country: Anth* (Scribner, 1994).

Jeanette M. Cox   P&W
Rte 4, Box 4, McGregor, MN 55760, 218-768-3851
    Pubs: *Variations in Time and Tempo* (Zigzag Pr, 1993),
    Dust & Fire: An Anth of Women's Writing (Bemidji State U,
    1994), *Minnesota Women's Pr, North Woods Patchwork.*

Florence Chard Dacey   P
Box 31, Cottonwood, MN 56229, 507-423-6652
    Pubs: *The Necklace* (Midwest Villages & Voices, 1988),
    The Swoon (Minnesota Writers Pub Hse, 1979).

Philip Dacey   P
Southwest State Univ, Marshall, MN 56258, 507-537-7155
Internet: dacey@ssu.southwest.msus.edu
    Pubs: *The Deathbed Playboy* (Eastern Washington U Pr,
    1999), *What's Empty Weighs The Most* (Black Dirt Pr,
    1997), *Night Shift at the Crucifix Factory* (U Iowa Pr, 1991),
    *Nation, Hudson Rev, Poetry, Georgia Rev, Paris Rev,
    Partisan Rev.*

Alan Davis   P&W
Moorhead State Univ, PO Box 229, Moorhead, MN 56563,
218-236-4681
Internet: davisa@mhdl.moorhead.msus.edu
    Pubs: *American Fiction, Rumors From the Lost World* (New
    Rivers, 1996, 1995), *The Quarterly, Hudson Rev, North
    Dakota Qtly, South Dakota Rev, Chattahoochee Rev,
    Image.*

Emilio DeGrazia   W
211 W 7 St, Winona, MN 55987, 507-454-6564
    Pubs: *Seventeen Grams Worth of Soul* (Lone Oak Pr,
    1994), *Billy Brazil* (New Rivers Pr, 1992).

James M. Dochniak   P&W
PO Box 8803, Minneapolis, MN 55408, 612-593-1221
    Pubs: *Friends, Pause & Look This Way* (Blue Cloud Qtly
    Pr, 1985), *Subversive Agent, The Alley, Pemmican.*

Leigh Donaldson   P&W
c/o North East Arts, PO Box 94, Kittery, MN 03904,
207-439-8465
    Pubs: *City River of Voices, Cafe Rev, Shooting Star Rev,
    atelier, Art & Understanding, World Poetry 1998, Catalyst
    Magazine, Intntl Poetry Rev, Potato Eyes, Manhattan
    Poetry Rev, Portfolio Mag, Hawaii Rev, Obsidian II, AIM
    Qrtly, Art Times, Minnesota Ink.*

Scott Edelstein   W
3800 Aldrich Ave S, #1, Minneapolis, MN 55409-1027,
612-823-5838
Internet: comconse@aol.com
    Pubs: *Ellery Queen's Mystery Mag, Artist's Mag, Writer's
    Yearbook, Artlines, New Worlds, City Miner.*

John Engman   P
1916 Colfax Ave S, Minneapolis, MN 55403, 612-874-9097
    Pubs: *Keeping Still, Mountain* (Galileo Pr, 1983), *New
    American Poets of the Nineties: Anth* (Godine, 1992),
    *Prairie Schooner, Virginia Qtly Rev, Iowa Rev, Poetry
    Northwest.*

Barbara Juster Esbensen P
5602 Dalrymple Rd, Edina, MN 55424, 612-929-2065
Internet: esbensen@sprynet.com
Pubs: *Echoes For The Eye, Dance With Me, Who Shrank My Grandmother's House?* (HarperCollins, 1996, 1995, 1992).

Michael Finley P
2096 Dayton Ave, St Paul, MN 55104, 612-644-4540
Pubs: *Looking for China* (Kraken Pr, 1994), *Pushcart Prize XI: Anth* (Pushcart Pr, 1986), *Paris Rev, New American & Canadian Poetry, Great River Rev.*

Kevin FitzPatrick P
3740 48th Ave S, Minneapolis, MN 55406, 612-721-1499
Pubs: *Rush Hour, Down on the Corner* (Midwest Villages & Voices, 1997, 1987).

Dee Fonville P
2636 Freemont Ave S, #106, Minneapolis, MN 55408, 612-374-4160
Pubs: *Iris: A Jrnl About Women, Caprice, New Letters, Poetry Northwest, Intro, Carolina Qtly, Memphis State Rev, Squeezebox Mag.*

David J. Fraher P
Hennepin Center for the Arts, 528 Hennepin Ave, Ste 310, Minneapolis, MN 55403
Pubs: *Western Humanities Rev, American Poetry Rev, New Letters, Slackwater Rev.*

Terry A. Garey P
3149 Park Ave S, Minneapolis, MN 55407, 612-824-5157
Pubs: *Time Frames: Anth of Speculative Poetry* (Rune Pr, 1991), *Raw Sacks: Anth* (Bag Person Pr, 1991), *Hurricane Alice, Weird Tales, Star*Line, AntiDog.*

Diane Glancy P
Macalester College, 1600 Grand, St Paul, MN 55105, 612-696-6516
Internet: glancy@macalester.edu
Pubs: *Flutie* (Moyer Bell, 1998), *The West Pole* (U Minnesota Pr, 1997), *Pushing the Bear* (HB, 1996), *Monkey Secret* (TriQuarterly/Northwestern U, 1995), *American Voice, Prairie Schooner, Ploughshares, The Journal, Agni, Carolina Qtly.*

Kate Green P&W
430 1st Ave N, Ste 416, Minneapolis, MN 55401, 612-332-8640
Pubs: *Shooting Star* (HarperCollins, 1992), *The Fossil Family Tales* (Creative Education, 1992), *Night Angel* (Delacorte, 1989), *APR, Hungry Mind Rev.*

Alvin Greenberg P&W
1113 Lincoln Ave, St Paul, MN 55105, 612-290-9732
Internet: greenberg@macalester.edu
Pubs: *How the Dead Live* (Graywolf Pr, 1998), *Why We Live With Animals, The Man in the Cardboard Mask* (Coffee Hse, 1990, 1985), *Heavy Wings* (Ohio Rev Pr, 1988), *NAR, Gettysburg Rev, Georgia Rev, Chelsea, American Literary Rev.*

Keith Gunderson P
1212 Lakeview Ave S, Minneapolis, MN 55416, 612-374-4339
Pubs: *A Continual Interest In The Sun And Sea & Inland Missing The Sea* (Nodin, 1977), *Milkweed, North Stone Rev, Baja Jrnl.*

Joanne Hart P
Box 356, Grand Portage, MN 55605
Pubs: *Minnesota Poetry Calendar: Anth* (Black Hat Pr, 1998), *The Women's Great Lakes Reader: Anth* (Holy Cow! Pr, 1998), *Inheriting the Land: Anth* (U Minnesota Pr, 1993), *Mixed Voices: Anth* (Milkweed Edtns, 1991), *North Coast Rev.*

Margaret M. Hasse P
1698 Lincoln Ave, St Paul, MN 55105, 612-699-9138
Pubs: *In a Sheep's Eye, Darling* (Milkweed Edtns, 1988), *Sisters of the Earth: Anth* (Vintage, 1991), *Tendril, Primavera, Milkweed Chronicle.*

Susan Carol Hauser P
Rt 1, Box 81, Puposky, MN 56667, 218-243-2402
Pubs: *Redpoll on a Broken Branch* (Same Name Pr, 1992), *Girl to Woman* (Astarte Shell Pr, 1992), *Poetry Motel, North Coast Rev, Loonfeather.*

Robert Hedin P
PO Box 59, Frontenac, MN 55026, 612-388-6103
Pubs: *Tornadoes* (Ion Bks, 1990), *Alaska: Reflections on Land and Spirit* (U Arizona Pr, 1989).

Scott Helmes P
862 Tuscarora, St Paul, MN 55102-3706, 612-222-5115
Internet: skaadenhelmes@compuserve.com
Pubs: *Dictionary of the Avant-Gardes: Anth* (A Cappella Bks, 1993), *Our Bodies, Our Icons, Xpos, Red Letters* (Helmes, 1994, 1991, 1991).

Mary Ann Henn P
104 Chapel Ln, St Joseph, MN 563740220, 320-363-7061
Pubs: *Nu-N-Human, Nun-Plus* (Fig Pr, 1993, 1990), *Time of Singing, Upsouth, Poets At Work, Parnassus, Explorer, Smiles, Silver Wings, Simply Words, San Fernando Poetry Jrnl, Waterways, Reflect.*

Stephen Hesla W
#8 Lincoln Ln, Northfield, MN 55057, 507-645-5289
Pubs: *The Hawthorn Conspiracy* (Dembner Bks, 1984).

Rolando Hinojosa   W
Univ Minnesota, 224 Church St SE/493 Ford Hall,
Minneapolis, MN 55455, 612-373-9707

H. Edgar Hix   P
5144 45th Ave South, Minneapolis, MN 554171625,
612-724-4362
   Pubs: *God's Special Book* (Concordia Pub, 1980), *Impetus,
   Waterways, Time of Singing, Midland Rev, Lilliput Rev,
   South Coast Poetry Jrnl, Burning Light, Untitled.*

Janet Holmes   P
113 Lincoln Ave, St Paul, MN 55105, 612-290-9732
Internet: holmes@mr.net
   Pubs: *The Physicist at the Mall* (Anhinga Pr, 1994), *The
   Green Tuxedo* (U Notre Dame Pr, 1998), *Paperback
   Romance* (State Street Pr, 1984).

Richard D. Houff   P
2054 Montreal Ave, St Paul, MN 55116, 612-690-2615
   Pubs: *Exit*(s), *Used Shoes* (Roving Anvil Pr, 1996, 1995),
   Earthquake School: Anth (Many Beaches Pr, 1998),
   Definitive Guide to the Twin Cities: Anth (Spout Pr, 1997),
   *Riverrun, Gryphon, Psychopoetica, Cokefish, Krax,
   Brooklyn Rev, Clare, Gas, Rattle.*

Alyce Ingram   W
Mears Park Place, 401 Sibley Street #622, St Paul, MN
55101
   Pubs: *Best of Wind: Anth* (Wind Pub, 1994), *Sexual
   Harassment* (Crossing Pr, 1992), *Nightshade Short Story
   Reader: Anth* (Nightshade Pr, 1991), *Small Pond, Slate,
   Happy, Peep, Knocked, Potato Eyes, Pittsburgh Qtly, ELF,
   Briar Cliff Rev, Potpourri, Q Rev.*

Dale Jacobson   P
810 1st Ave NE, East Grand Forks, MN 56721, 218-773-9226
   Pubs: *Shouting at Midnight* (Spirit Horse Pr, 1986), *Poems
   for Goya's Disparates* (Jazz Pr, 1980), *APR, Forkroads,
   Lilliput Rev, Pemmican, Prairie Volcano.*

Louis Jenkins   P
719 Woodland Ave, Duluth, MN 55812, 218-724-6382
Internet: louis@skypoint.com
   Pubs: *Just Above Water, Nice Fish: New and Selected
   Prose Poems* (Holy Cow! Pr, 1997, 1995), *All Tangled Up
   With the Living* (Nineties Pr, 1991).

Jim Johnson   P
New Rivers Press, 420 N 5 St, Ste 910, Minneapolis, MN
55401, 612-339-7114
   Pubs: *Wolves* (New Rivers Pr, 1993), *A Field Guide To
   Blue Berries, Finns In Minnesota Midwinter* (North Star Pr,
   1992, 1986).

Deborah Keenan   P
1168 Laurel Ave, St Paul, MN 55104, 612-647-0276
   Pubs: *Happiness* (Coffee Hse Pr, 1995), *Looking For
   Home: Anth* (Milkweed Edtns, 1990), *Santa Monica Rev,
   Shenandoah.*

Garrison Keillor   W
Minnesota Public Radio, 45 E 7th St, St Paul, MN 55101,
612-290-1500

Patricia Kirkpatrick   P
1256 Osceola, St Paul, MN 55105, 612-690-0089
   Pubs: *The Writing Path: Anth* (U Iowa Pr, 1995), *Minnesota
   Writers: Poetry Anth* (Milkweed Edtns, 1987), *Antioch Rev,
   Ironwood, Hungry Mind Rev.*

Allan Kornblum   P
Coffee House Press, 27 N 4 St, Ste 400, Minneapolis, MN
55401, 612-338-0125
   Pubs: *Awkward Song* (Toothpaste Pr, 1980), *The Salad
   Bushes* (Seamark Pr, 1975).

Cinda Kornblum   P
Coffee House Press, 27 N 4 St, Ste 400, Minneapolis, MN
55401
   Pubs: *Bandwagon* (Toothpaste Pr, 1976), *The Actualist
   Anth* (The Spirit That Moves Us, 1977).

Jack Kreitzer   P
1031 Prior Ave S, Saint Paul, MN 55116
   Pubs: *Dark Moon* (Bald Mountain Pr, 1979), *Through Fire
   And Deep Water* (RVK Publishing, 1976).

J. L. Kubicek   P
Rt 1, Box 167, Lake Crystal, MN 56055, 507-546-3775
   Pubs: *Blood To Remember: Anth* (Texas Tech U Pr, 1990),
   Czech-American Writing: Anth (New Rivers, 1990).

Brett Laidlaw   W
1838 Laurel Ave, St Paul, MN 55104, 612-646-2472
   Pubs: *Blue Bel Air* (Norton, 1993), *Three Nights in the Heart of
   the Earth* (NAL, 1989), *Elvis in Oz: Anth* (U Virginia, 1992).

Roseann Lloyd   P
1146 Randolph Ave, #7, Saint Paul, MN 55105-2974,
612-699-1543
   Pubs: *War Baby Express* (Holy Cow! Pr, 1996), *She Who
   Was Lost is Remembered* (Seal Pr, 1992), *Looking For
   Home: Anth* (Milkweed Edtns, 1991).

Diane Lunde   P
4105 E 34 St, Minneapolis, MN 55406-2827
   Pubs: *North Country: Anth* (Greenfield Rev, 1986),
   *Kentucky Rev, Visions, Midnight Lamp, 13th Moon,
   Sycamore Rev, St. Andrews Rev, Poetry Northwest.*

Joseph Maiolo   W
Univ Minnesota, Duluth, MN 55812, 218-726-8226
    Pubs: *Ploughshares, Sewanee, Shenandoah, Texas Rev, New Virginia Rev.*

Freya Manfred   P
5595 Christmas Lake Point, Shorewood, MN 55331-9299, 612-470-0209
    Pubs: *American Roads* (Viking, 1985), *APR, New Letters, Antioch Rev, Minnesota Rev, Michigan Qtly Rev.*

Galen Martini   P
104 Chapel Ln, St. Joseph, MN 56374
    Pubs: *Fuel* (BOA Edtns, 1998), *Words Under The Words* (Far Corner Bks, 1995), *Atlantic, Five Points, Atlanta Rev, Georgia Rev, Tampa Rev, Indiana Rev.*

Ken McCullough   P&W
372 Center St, Winona, MN 55987
    Pubs: *Sycamore Oriole* (Ahsahta Pr, 1991), *Travelling Light* (Thunder's Mouth Pr, 1987).

Bill Meissner   P&W
618 6th Ave N, St Cloud, MN 56303
Internet: meissner@tigger.stcloud.msus.edu
    Pubs: *Hitting Into the Wind* (SMU Pr, 1997), *Twin Sons of Different Mirrors* (w/Jack Driscoll; Milkweed Edtns, 1989).

Leslie Adrienne Miller   P
Univ St. Thomas, 2115 Summit Ave, St Paul, MN 55105-1096, 612-962-5604
Internet: lamiller@stthomas.edu
    Pubs: *Ungodliness, Staying Up For Love* (Carnegie Mellon U Pr, 1994, 1990), *APR, Kenyon Rev, NER, Georgia Rev, Ploughshares, Nimrod.*

John Minczeski   P
1300 Dayton, St Paul, MN 55104, 612-646-9434
    Pubs: *Gravity* (Texas Tech U Pr, 1991), *The Reconstruction of Light* (New Rivers Pr, 1987), *Cape Rock, Cream City Rev, Spoon River Poetry Rev, Pemmican.*

Valerie Miner   W
Univ Minnesota, Minneapolis, MN 55455, 612-625-3363
Internet: miner002@maroon.tc.umn.edu
    Pubs: *A Walking Fire* (State U Pr New York, 1994), *Rumors From the Cauldron* (U Michigan Pr, 1992), *VLS, Michigan Qtly Rev, Ploughshares, Nation, Virginia Qtly Rev.*

David R. Moffatt   P
Rte 3, Box 228, Pine City, MN 55063, 612-629-2816
    Pubs: *The Folded Paper Dream* (Tiger Moon Pr, 1992), *Riverrun, Verve, Poetic Knight, Star Triad, Shawnee Silhouette, The Archer.*

James Moore   P
438 Laurel Ave, #5, St Paul, MN 55102, 612-227-0047
Internet: laurel438@aol.com
    Pubs: *The Long Experience of Love, The Freedom of History* (Milkweed Edtns, 1995, 1988), *APR, Paris Rev, Nation, Kenyon Rev, Antioch Rev, Threepenny Rev.*

Michael Moos   P
2223 Dayton Ave, St Paul, MN 55104, 612-642-0181
    Pubs: *Great River Review Anth* (Great River Rev, 1989), *Minnesota Writers: Anth* (Milkweed, 1987).

David Mura   P
1920 E River Terr, Minneapolis, MN 55414-3672
Internet: davsus@aol.com
    Pubs: *Where the Body Meets Memory, Turning Japanese* (Anchor, 1996, 1996), *APR, NER, New Republic, Conjunctions, Mother Jones, New York Times.*

James Naiden   P
The North Stone Review, Box 10498, Minneapolis, MN 55414-0098, 612-721-8011
Internet: jack123904@aol.com
    Pubs: *Asphyxiations #1-40* (Metron Pr, 1999), *The Orange Notebook* (Metron Pr, 1973), *Poetry, Eire-Ireland, Nantucket Rev, New Hibernia Rev, Willow Avenue Rev, Wolf Head Qtly.*

Josip Novakovich   W
Graywolf Press, 2402 University Ave, Ste 203, St. Paul, MN 55114, 612-641-0007
    Pubs: *Salvation and Other Disasters* (Graywolf, 1995), *Antaeus, Paris Rev, Ploughshares.*

Michael Patrick O'Connor   P
234 Montrose Pl #206, St Paul, MN 55104-5630
    Pubs: *Pandary* (L'Epervier, 1990).

W. Scott Olsen   W
443 42nd Ave, Moorhead, MN 56560, 218-236-7037
Internet: olsen@cord.edu
    Pubs: *The Sacred Place* (U Utah Pr, 1996), *Acts of Illumination* (St. Mary's U Pr, 1996), *Meeting The Neighbors* (North Star Pr, 1993), *Just This Side of Fargo* (Ironwood Pr, 1992), *Ascent, Kenyon Rev, Willow Springs, North Dakota Qtly, Weber Studies.*

Lon Otto   P&W
270 MacKubin St, St Paul, MN 55102, 612-227-7883
    Pubs: *Cover Me, Water Bodies* (Coffee Hse, 1988, 1986), *A Nest of Hooks* (U Iowa Pr, 1978).

Gary James Paulsen   W
Rt 1, Box 41, Rolway, MN 56678

Tom Peacock   P
1507 Lockling Rd, Cloquet, MN 55720, 218-879-7326

T. W. Perkins   P&W
1753 Iglehart Ave, St Paul, MN 55104, 612-641-1807
    Pubs: *Boston Collection of Women's Poetry II: Anth* (Brush
    Hill, 1983), *Atelier, Art & Understanding, San Fernando
    Poetry Jrnl, For Crying Out Loud.*

Mary Ellis Peterson   P
13887 85th Pl N, Maple Grove, MN 553699237,
612-427-3168
Internet: mpeter3099@aol.com
    Pubs: *Journey Into Motherhood* (Riverhead Bks, 1996),
    Motherpoet (Mothering Pub, 1984), *And I Shall Be Your
    Ancestor* (Guild Pr, 1980).

Wang Ping   P&W
Lerner Publications, 241 1st Ave N., Minneapolis, MN 55410,
612-332-3344
Internet: pqw3199@is2.nyu.edu
    Pubs: *Of Flesh & Spirit, Foreign Devil, American Visa*
    (Coffee Hse Pr, 1998, 1996, 1994), *Sulfur, The World,
    Talisman, Manoa, Chicago Rev, River City, Asylum,
    Literary Rev, Westcoast Line.*

Joan Wolf Prefontaine   P
13875 Gates Ave, Northfield, MN 55057
    Pubs: *The Divided Sphere* (Floating Island Pr, 1985), *North
    Coast Rev, Voices Intl, Art Forum, Sidewalks.*

Sister Bernetta Quinn   P
Sisters of St. Francis, Box #4900, Rochester, MN 55903,
507-282-7441
    Pubs: *Dancing in Stillness* (St. Andrews, 1983), *Sewanee
    Rev, Yale Rev, America, English Jrnl, Sign.*

Thomas Dillon Redshaw   P
1944 Carroll Ave, St Paul, MN 55104, 612-645-7669
    Pubs: *The Floating World* (Truck Pr, 1979), *Sewanee Rev,
    Antioch Rev, Carleton Miscellany.*

John Calvin Rezmerski   P
Box 202, Eagle Lake, MN 56024, 507-257-3491
    Pubs: *Growing Down* (Minnesota Writers Pub Hse, 1982).

Linda Lightsey Rice   W
1270 Goose Lake Rd, White Bear Lake, MN 55110,
612-429-7464
Internet: llrice@aol.com
    Pubs: *Spectacle* (Pachanga Pr, 1998), *Southern Exposure*
    (Doubleday, 1991), *Home Works: Anth* (Tennessee Arts
    Commission, 1996), *Southern Literary Rev, Missouri
    Women's Pr, A View From the Loft, The Pheonix.*

Melanie Richards   P
16570 22nd St S, St Mary's Point, MN 55043, 612-436-1666
    Pubs: *26 Minnesota Writers: Anth* (Nodin, 1996), *Harvard
    Rev, Yankee, Kalliope, Shenandoah, Negative Capability,
    Passages North.*

Richard Robbins   P
MSU 53, PO Box 8400, Mankato, MN 56002-8400,
507-389-1354
Internet: richard.robbins@mankato.msus.edu
    Pubs: *Famous Persons We Have Known* (Eastern
    Washington U Pr, 2000), *The Invisible Wedding* (U Missouri
    Pr, 1984), *NAR, Nation, Poetry Northwest.*

George Roberts   P
1022 Sheridan Ave N, Minneapolis, MN 55411, 612-588-3723
    Pubs: *Scrut* (Holy Cow! Pr, 1983), *Night Visits to a Wolf's
    Howl* (Oyster Pr, 1979).

Mordecai M. Roshwald   W
Univ Minnesota, 314 Ford Hall, Minneapolis, MN 55455,
612-521-7955
    Pubs: *A Small Armageddon, Level 7* (NAL, 1976, 1961),
    Judaism, Nation.

Ruth Roston   P
Parkshore Pl, 3663 Park Center Blvd, #501, Minneapolis, MN
55416, 612-926-7132
    Pubs: *The Poet Dreaming in the Artist's House* (Milkweed
    Edtns, 1984).

CarolAnn Russell   P
Bemidji State Univ, 1530 Birchmont Dr NE, Bemidji, MN
56601, 218-755-2880
    Pubs: *Silver Dollar* (West End Pr, 1995), *Feast*
    (Loonfeather Pr, 1993), *Verse, Pemmican, Midwest Qtly,
    Hurakan, Puerto del Sol, Great River Rev.*

Mark Ryan   W
5604 Upton Ave S, Minneapolis, MN 55410, 612-926-6095
Internet: markdryan@aol.com
    Pubs: *Things That Fall From The Sky: Anth* (The Loft,
    1994), *Pinehurst Jrnl, Alabama Literary Rev.*

R. A. Sasaki   W
Graywolf Press, 2402 University Ave, #203, St Paul, MN
55114, 612-641-0077
    Pubs: *The Loom and Other Stories* (Graywolf Pr, 1991),
    Pushcart Prize: Anth (Pushcart Pr, 1992), *Story.*

Thomas R. Smith   P
Ally Press, 524 Orleans St, St Paul, MN 55107
    Pubs: *Horse of Earth* (Holy Cow! Pr, 1994), *Keeping The
    Star* (New Rivers Pr, 1988), *Raccoon, Yellow Silk,
    Wilderness, Bloomsbury Rev, Sphinx.*

John M. Solensten   P&W
500 E Larpenteur #102, St Paul, MN 55117
    Pubs: *Good Thunder* (SUNY Pr, 1983), *There Lies a Fair
    Land: Anth* (New Rivers Pr, 1985).

Sally Jo Sorensen P
PO Box 611, Dassel, MN 55325, 320-275-3922
Internet: mznpho@cmgate.com
    Pubs: *A Turban Lily* (State Street, 1990), *Zone 3, Laurel Rev,
Sycamore Rev, Painted Bride Qtly, Poet & Critic, Yarrow,
West Branch, Amaranth, Nebraska Qtly, Poem, Poet Lore.*

Robert T. Sorrells W
529 5th St SW, Rochester, MN 55902, 507-289-0997
Internet: sorrelli@aol.com
    Pubs: *The Blacktop Champion of Ickey Honey and Other
Stories* (U Arkansas Pr, 1988), *Full Court: Anth, Tennis and
the Meaning of Life: Anth* (Breakaway Pr, 1996, 1995).

Madelon Sprengnether P
Univ Minnesota, 207 Church St, English Dept, Minneapolis,
MN 55455
Internet: spren001@tc.umn.edu
    Pubs: *Rivers, Stories, Houses, Dreams, The Normal Heart,
The House on Via Gambito: Anth* (New Rivers Pr, 1983, 1981,
1990).

Francine Sterle P
4023 River Rd, Iron, MN 55751, 218-262-2503
Internet: fmsterle@uslink.net
    Pubs: *The White Bridge* (Poetry Harbor, 1998), *NAR,
Nimrod, Beloit Poetry Jrnl, CutBank, Zone 3, Birmingham
Poetry Rev, briX, Atlanta Rev.*

Barton Sutter P&W
4621 Jay St, Duluth, MN 55804, 218-525-4644
    Pubs: *My Father's War And Other Stories* (Viking, 1991),
Pine Creek Parish Hall and Other Poems (Sandhills, 1985),
Sequoyah (Ox Head, 1983), *Poetry.*

Steve Swanson P
910 St. Olaf Ave, Northfield, MN 55057, 507-645-6017
    Pubs: *The First Fall: Ytterboe Hall, 1946* (Nine Ten Pr,
1997), *Moving Out On Your Own, Is There Life After High
School?* (Augsburg, 1994, 1991).

Susan Marie Swanson P
818 Seal St, St Paul, MN 55114
    Pubs: *Letter to the Lake, Getting Used to the Dark* (DK Ink,
1998, 1997), *Primavera, How*(ever), *Ironwood, Hungry
Mind Rev, APR, Minnesota Writes: Poetry, Cricket.*

Marcella B. Taylor P
St. Olaf College, Northfield, MN 55057, 507-646-2222
    Pubs: *The Lost Daughter* (Renaissance Pr, 1985), *The
Butterfly Tree: Anth* (New Rivers Pr, 1991), *Poetry, Tampa
Bay Rev.*

Richard Terrill P
Mankato State Univ, Mankato, MN 56001, 507-389-5500
    Pubs: *The Cross and the Red Star* (Asian Pacific Fdn,
1994), *Saturday Night in Baoding: A China Memoir* (U
Arkansas, 1990), *New Letters, NAR, Mid-American Rev,
Iowa Rev, Michigan Qtly, Trafika, High Plains Literary Rev.*

Susan Allen Toth W
4820 Penn Ave S, Minneapolis, MN 55409, 612-927-0594
    Pubs: *My Love Affair With England* (Ballantine, 1993), *A
House of One's Own* (Potter, 1991), *Blooming* (Little, Brown,
1981).

C. W. Truesdale P&W
New Rivers Press, 420 N 5th St, #910, Minneapolis, MN
55401, 612-339-7114
    Pubs: *Doctor Vertigo* (Wyrd Pr, 1976), *Cold Harbors*
(Latitudes Pr, 1974).

Mark Vinz P&W
510 5th Ave S, Moorhead, MN 56560, 218-236-5226
Internet: vinz@mhdl.moorhead.msus.edu
    Pubs: *Late Night Calls* (New Rivers Pr, 1992), *Minnesota
Gothic* (Milkweed Edtns, 1992), *Mixed Blessings* (Spoon
River Poetry Pr, 1989).

Cary Waterman P
286 Laurel, St Paul, MN 55102
    Pubs: *When I Looked Back You Were Gone* (Holy Cow! Pr,
1992), *Minnesota Writes: Poetry Anth* (Milkweed Edtns, 1987).

Charles K. Waterman P
PO Box 473, St Peter, MN 56082, 507-931-6239
    Pubs: *Talking Animals* (Juniper Pr, 1978), *The Place*
(Minnesota Writers' Pub, 1977), *A Geography of Poets:
Anth* (Bantam, 1979), *Permafrost, Steelhead.*

Jay P. White P
4616 W 56 St, Edina, MN 55424, 612-925-0616
    Pubs: *The Pomegranate Tree Speaks From The Dictator's
Garden* (Holy Cow Pr, 1988), *Poetry, NAR, Ontario Rev,
Pequod, Sewanee, Shenandoah, Colorado State Rev, New
Republic.*

Roberta Hill Whiteman P
6539 Golden Valley Rd #101, Minneapolis, MN 55427-4656
    Pubs: *Talking Leaves: An Anth of Contemporary Native
American Fiction* (Bantam-Dell, 1991), *New Voices From
the Longhouse: Anth* (Greenfield Rev Pr, 1989).

Sandra Adelmund Witt P&W
2060 W County Rd E, Apt 205, New Brighton, MN 55112
    Pubs: *Aerial Studies* (New Rivers Pr, 1994), *40 Days and
40 Nights* (Iowa Arts Council, 1994), *Chaminade Literary
Rev, Colorado Qtly, Cream City Rev, Confluence, CutBank.*

Warren Woessner P
34 W Minnehaha Pkwy, Minneapolis, MN 55419,
612-822-7848
Internet: wwoessner@slwk.com
    Pubs: *Clear to Chukchi* (Poetry Harbor Pr, 1995), *Storm
Lines* (New Rivers Pr, 1987), *Poetry Northwest, Prairie
Schooner, Pig Iron, Wilderness, Appalachia.*

Karen Tei Yamashita   W
Coffee House Press, 27 N 4th St, Ste 400, Minneapolis, MN
55401, 612-338-0125
    Pubs: *Tropic of Orange, Brazil-Maru, Through the Arc of the
    Rain Forest* (Coffee Hse Pr, 1997, 1992, 1990), *Los
    Angeles Times, Amerasia Jrnl.*

Susan Yuzna   P
17697 Tulip St NW, Andover, MN 55304-1108, 612-753-0297
    Pubs: *Her Slender Dress* (U Akron Pr, 1996), *Burning The
    Fake Woman* (Green Tower Pr, 1996).

MISSISSIPPI

Angela Ball   P
Box 5037, Southern Sta, Hattiesburg, MS 39406-5037,
601-266-4321
    Pubs: *The Museum of the Revolution, Quartet* (Carnegie
    Mellon, 1999, 1995), *Possession* (Valentine Pub Group,
    1996), *NAR, Field, Southern Rev, Denver Qtly, New
    Yorker, Ploughshares.*

D. C. Berry   P
306 Washington Ave, Ocean Springs, MS 39564,
601-872-1927
    Pubs: *Divorce Boxing* (Eastern Washington Pr, 1998),
    Jawbone (Thunder City Pr, 1978), *Saigon Cemetery* (U
    Georgia Pr, 1972), *Poetry, Chicago Rev.*

Price Caldwell   W
Mississippi State Univ, English Dept, Drawer E, Mississippi
State, MS 39762, 601-325-3644
Internet: tpc1@ra.msstate.edu
    Pubs: *Mississippi Writers: Reflections of Childhood &
    Youth: Anth* (U Mississippi Pr, 1985), *Best American Short
    Stories 1977: Anth* (HM, 1978), *Carleton Miscellany,
    Georgia Rev, Image, Mississippi Rev, New Orleans Rev.*

Carol Cox   P
PO Box 188, Tougaloo, MS 39174, 601-956-2610
    Pubs: *The Water in the Pearl* (Hanging Loose Pr, 1982),
    Mississippi Writers: Anth (U Pr Mississippi, 1988).

David Galef   W
Univ Mississippi, English Dept, University, MS 38677,
601-232-7439
    Pubs: *Tracks* (Morrow, 1996), *Flesh* (Permanent Pr, 1995),
    *North Dakota Qtly, Gettysburg Rev, Crossroads, Grain,
    Pulpsmith, Chiron Rev, South Carolina Rev, Shenandoah.*

Patricia Minter Grierson   P
PO Box 55808, Jackson, MS 39296, 601-982-3674
    Pubs: *U Southern Mississippi Philological Association Pub,
    Boston U Jrnl, Kansas Qtly, Mississippi Rev, Poem, Florida
    Qtly, Researcher.*

Barry Hannah   W
1413 Van Buren Ave, Oxford, MS 38655, 601-234-2453
    Pubs: *Never Die, Boomerang* (Seymour Lawrence/HM,
    1991, 1989), *Esquire, The Quarterly, Southern Rev,
    Chicago Rev, Harper's, Georgia Rev.*

Charles Henley   W
2857 Greenview Dr, Jackson, MS 39212, 601-371-7827
    Pubs: *The Smith, The Phoenix, Intro, Mississippi Rev,
    Carolina Qtly.*

John Horvath, Jr.   P
222 Melrose Dr, Jackson, MS 39211
Internet: jhorv40287@aol.com
    Pubs: *Critical Qtly, Aura, Poem, Dekalb Literary Arts Jrnl,
    Poet & Critic, Nimrod, Dalhousie Rev.*

Margaret McMullan   W
541 E Scenic Dr, Pass Christian, MS 39571-4510
    Pubs: *When Warhol Was Still Alive* (Crossing Pr, 1994),
    Catholic Girls and Boys: Anth (Penguin/NAL, 1994),
    Greensboro Rev, New England Living, Glamour.

Gary Myers   P
Mississippi State Univ, Drawer E, Mississippi State, MS
39762, 601-325-3644
    Pubs: *Lifetime Possessions* (Riverstone Pr, 1997), *World
    Effects* (Nevertheless Pr, 1990), *New Yorker, Poetry,
    Indiana Rev, Kansas Qtly, Louisville Rev, Bitterroot.*

William Russell   W
PO Box 35, Tunica, MS 38676, 601-363-2196
    Pubs: *Berlin Embassy* (Macfadden Bks, 1962), *A Wind Is
    Rising* (Scribner, 1950).

Larry Marshall Sams   W
339 W Monroe Ave, Greenwood, MS 38930
    Pubs: *Dekalb Literary Arts Jrnl, Sucarnochee Rev, Wind,
    Pendragon, Dreamshore.*

Glenn Robert Swetman   P
PO Box 146, Biloxi, MS 39533-0146
    Pubs: *Concerning Carpenters* (Pterodactyl Pr, 1979), *Deka
    #2* (Paon Pr, 1979), *Texas Qtly.*

Margaret Walker   W
2205 Guynes Ave, Jackson, MS 39213

Jerry W. Ward, Jr.   P
1872 Lincolnshire Blvd, Ridgeland, MS 391571213,
601-957-5062
Internet: 105511.3715@compuserve.com
    Pubs: *Trouble The Water: 250 Years of African-American
    Poetry: Anth* (Mentor, 1997), *Black Southern Voices: Anth*
    (NAL, 1992), *Callaloo, ADE Bulletin, Obsidian II, Open
    Places, Mississippi Qtly, Southern Qtly, Callaloo, Black
    American Literary Forum.*

Eudora Welty   W
1119 Pinehurst St, Jackson, MS 39202

Benjamin J. Williams   P
3004 29th St, Gulfport, MS 39501, 601-864-6911
  Pubs: *Obsidian, Negro History Bulletin, Phylon, Black
  Scholar, Callaloo, Kitabu Cha Jua, Jrnl of Black Poetry, Afro
  American Qtly, Sphinx.*

Joan Williams   W
908 Old Taylor Rd, Oxford, MS 38655-4619
  Pubs: *Pay the Piper* (Dutton, 1988), *Pariah & Other Stories*
  (Atlantic Monthly Pr, 1983), *Esquire, Southern Accents.*

Austin Wilson   P&W
Millsaps College, Jackson, MS 39210, 601-974-1305
Internet: wilsola@okra.millsaps.edu
  Pubs: *From the Green Horseshoe: Anth* (U South Carolina
  Pr, 1987), *Mississippi Writers: Reflections: Anth* (U Pr
  Mississippi, 1985), *New Orleans Rev, Hiram Poetry Rev,
  Southern Humanities Rev, Descant, Mississippi Rev,
  Roanoke Rev.*

Steve Yates   W
875 William Blvd, #412, Ridgeland, MS 391571519,
601-899-0099
  Pubs: *Arkansas Rev/Kansas Qtly, Ontario Rev, Missouri
  Rev, Nebraska Rev, Turnstile, Western Humanities Rev,
  Chariton Rev, Red Cedar Rev, Texas Rev, Laurel Rev,
  South Carolina Rev.*

MISSOURI

Rosa M. Arenas   P
7731 Gannon, #1 E, St Louis, MO 63130, 314-726-1145
  Pubs: *She Said Yes* (Fallen Angel Pr, 1981), *Kenyon Rev,
  Calyx, River Styx, Blue Mesa Rev, Americas Rev,
  Sycamore Rev.*

Stanley E. Banks   P
7120 Indiana, Kansas City, MO 64132, 816-333-8705
  Pubs: *Coming From a Funky Time and Place* (Georgia AB
  Pr, 1988), *On 10th Alley Way* (BkMk Pr, 1980).

Walter Bargen   P
PO Box 19, Ashland, MO 65010, 573-657-2636
  Pubs: *The Vertical River* (Timberline Pr, 1995), *Mysteries in
  the Public Domain* (BkMk Pr, 1990), *Georgia Rev, New
  Letters, Intl Qtly, Sycamore Rev.*

Jim Barnes   P
Northeast Missouri State Univ, Languages & Literature Div,
Kirksville, MO 63501, 816-785-4499
  Pubs: *The Sawdust War* (U Illinois Pr, 1992), *La Plata
  Cantata* (Purdue U Pr, 1989), *Nation, TriQuarterly, NAR,
  Kenyon Rev.*

Michael S. Bell   P
PO Box 2583, Joplin, MO 64803-2583
  Pubs: *Symbolist Encomium* (Inkblot Pub, 1986), *Points of
  Departure* (Wiley & Sons, 1971), *Zyzzyva, Handsel, New
  Wilderness Letters, Art Contemporary.*

Ben Bennani   P
1103 Cherry Ln, Kirksville, MO 63501-2097, 816-665-1103
Internet: bbennani@truman.edu
  Pubs: *Psalms for Palestine* (Three Continents Pr, 1993),
  Bread, Hashish & Moon (Unicorn Pr, 1982), *A Bowl of
  Sorrow* (Greenfield Rev Pr, 1977).

Donn Irving Blevins   W
Fletcher's Fld, 638 NW 50 Hwy, Centerview, MO 64019
  Pubs: *III Novellas* (Woodley Pr, 1993), *These And Other
  Lands* (Westphalia Pr, 1986), *American Literary Rev,
  Crescent Rev, Negative Capability, Farmer's Market.*

Edward Boccia   P
600 Harper Ave, Webster Groves, MO 63119, 314-962-5081
  Pubs: *No Matter How Good The Light Is* (Time Being Bks,
  1998), *Moving The Still Life* (Pudding Hse, 1993), *Against
  the Grain: Anth* (CSS Pubs, 1988), *Blue Unicorn, California
  Qtly, Black Mullet Rev, Atlantic Rev, Poet Mag, River King
  Poetry Pr, Rockhurst Rev.*

James J. Bogan   P
Univ Missouri, Rolla, MO 65409-0670, 573-341-4755
Internet: jbogan@umr.edu
  Pubs: *Ozark Meandering* (Timberline Pr, 1997), *Sparks of
  Fire* (North Atlantic Pr, 1982), *Exquisite Corpse, River Styx,
  Walking Mag, Latin American Literary Rev.*

Michelle Boisseau   P
Univ of Missouri—KC, 5100 Rockhill Rd, Kansas City, MO
64110-2499, 816-235-2561
Internet: mboisseau@cctr.umkc.edu
  Pubs: *Understory* (Northeastern U Pr, 1996), *No Private
  Life* (Vanderbilt U, 1990), *Agni, Ploughshares, Ohio Rev,
  Crazyhorse, Southern Rev, Georgia Rev, Gettysburg Rev.*

Louis Daniel Brodsky   P
10411 Clayton Rd, Ste 201-203, St Louis, MO 63131,
314-432-1771
  Pubs: *Paper-Whites for Lady-Jane, Disappearing In
  Mississippi Latitudes, The Capital Cafe, Gestapo Crows*
  (Time Being Bks, 1995, 1994, 1993, 1992).

Catherine Browder   W
3611 Gladstone Blvd, Kansas City, MO 64123, 816-483-8949
  Pubs: *The Heart: A Story* (Helicon Nine Edtns, 1995), *The
  Clay That Breathes: Stories* (Milkweed Edtns, 1991),
  *Kansas City Star, Shenandoah, New Letters, Prairie
  Schooner, Kansas Qtly, Passages North.*

R. A. Burns　　　　　　　　　　　　　　　　P
Southeast Missouri State Univ, Cape Girardeau, MO 63701
Internet: c289hue@semovm.semo.edu
　　Pubs: *Poetry Now, College Composition And
　　Communication, The Cea Forum, Kudzu.*

David Carkeet　　　　　　　　　　　　　　　W
9307 Old Bonhomme Rd, St Louis, MO 63132, 314-994-7532
Internet: david_carkeet@umsl.edu
　　Pubs: *The Error of Our Ways* (Henry Holt, 1997), *The Full
　　Catastrophe* (S&S, 1990), *Carolina Qtly, Kansas Qtly, NAR,
　　Village Voice, Oxford American.*

Jan Garden Castro　　　　　　　　　　　　　P
7420 Cornell, St Louis, MO 63130, 314-725-0602
　　Pubs: *Tapas, Eclectic Press, Missouri Rev, River Styx,
　　Wind, Southwinds, Greenfield Rev, Exquisite Corpse,
　　Abraxas, Focus Midwest, Sheba Rev, Telephone, Roof.*

Michael Castro　　　　　　　　　　　　　　P
8368 Richard Ave, St Louis, MO 63132, 314-432-0236
　　Pubs: *The Man Who Looked into Coltrane's Horn* (Caliban
　　Pr, 1998), *(US)* (Ridgeway Pr, 1991), *Interpreting the Indian*
　　(U of Oklahoma Pr, 1991), *Drum Voices Rev, Mississippi
　　Valley Rev, Tampa Rev, Edge, Printed Matter, Long Shot,
　　Nexus, Many Moons, Grist.*

David Clewell　　　　　　　　　　　　　　　P
Webster Univ, Literature Dept, 470 E Lockwood, St Louis,
MO 63119, 314-968-7170
　　Pubs: *Now We're Getting Somewhere* (U Wisconsin Pr,
　　1994), *Blessings in Disguise* (Viking, 1991), *The
　　Conspiracy Quartet: Anth* (Garlic Pr, 1997), *Poetry, Georgia
　　Rev, Kenyon Rev, Harper's, Ontario Rev, NER.*

Carole Knipp Cohen　　　　　　　　　　　　P
911 Craig Dr, Kirkwood, MO 63122, 314-965-4780
　　Pubs: *Sou'wester, Cape Rock, Madison Rev, Prism,
　　Ascent, Spoon River.*

Gene Doty　　　　　　　　　　　　　　　　P
Univ Missouri, English Dept, Rolla, MO 65401, 573-364-5322
Internet: gdoty@umr.edu
　　Pubs: *Nose to Nose* (Brooks Bks, 1998), *Zero: 30 Ghazals*
　　(AHA Bks Online, 1998), *Wind Five-Folded* (AHA Bks,
　　1994), *Midwest Haiku Anth* (High/Coo Pr, 1992), *Rolling
　　Coulter, Lynx, Phase & Cycle, Woodnotes, Brussels Spout,
　　Frogpond, Conspire.*

Jon Dressel　　　　　　　　　　　　　　　P
376 Walton Row, St Louis, MO 63108, 314-361-3478
　　Pubs: *Face to Face, The Road To Shiloh* (Gomer Pr, 1997,
　　1994), *Out of Wales* (Alun Bks, 1985), *Prairie Schooner,
　　Epoch, Poetry Wales, Counter-Measures, New Welsh Rev,
　　Planet.*

Donald Finkel　　　　　　　　　　　　　　P
2051 Park Ave #D, St Louis, MO 63104, 314-241-4426
　　Pubs: *The Question of Seeing* (U Arkansas Pr, 1998), *The
　　Wake of the Electron, Selected Shorter Poems* (Atheneum,
　　1987, 1987), *Yale Rev, Southwest Rev, Paris Rev, Kenyon
　　Rev, Denver Qtly.*

William H. Gass　　　　　　　　　　　　　W
6304 Westminster Pl, St Louis, MO 63130, 314-725-0317
Internet: iwc@artsci.wustl.edu
　　Pubs: *Cartesian Sonata, Finding A Form, The Tunnel*
　　(Knopf, 1998, 1996, 1995), *On Being Blue* (Godine, 1975),
　　New Republic, Harper's, Conjunction, Salmagundi.

Paul Gianoli　　　　　　　　　　　　　　　P
2600 S 14 Ave, Ozark, MO 65721, 417-581-0895
Internet: gianoli@cofo.edu
　　Pubs: *Blueprint, Focus: Midwest, Wisconsin Rev,
　　Mississippi Rev.*

John F. Gilgun　　　　　　　　　　　　　　W
PO Box 7152, St Joseph, MO 645077152, 816-233-8374
　　Pubs: *The Dooley Poems* (Robin Price, 1991), *From The
　　Inside Out* (3-Phase, 1991), *Music I Never Dreamed Of*
　　(Amethyst, 1989).*

Galen Green　　　　　　　　　　　　　　P&W
201 Westport Rd, Kansas City, MO 64111-2239
　　Pubs: *World-Weary Polka* (Fireweed Pr, 1977), *New York
　　Qtly, Poetry Now, West Coast Rev.*

Charles Guenther　　　　　　　　　　　　　P
9877 Allendale Dr, St Louis, MO 63123-6450, 314-544-0563
　　Pubs: *Moving the Seasons* (BkMk Pr, 1994),
　　Phrase-Paraphrase (Prairie Pr, 1970), *APR, Kenyon Rev,
　　Literary Rev, Formalist, Black Mountain Rev, Critic.*

Frank Higgins　　　　　　　　　　　　　　P
12500 E 53 Terr, Kansas City, MO 64133, 816-353-4529
　　Pubs: *Eating Blowfish* (Raindust Pr, 1996), *Starting From
　　Ellis Island* (BkMk Pr, 1981), *New Letters, Dacotah
　　Territory, Kansas Qtly, Chariton Rev, Poetry Now.*

Peter Daniel Hilty　　　　　　　　　　　　P
632 Bellevue, Cape Girardeau, MO 63701, 314-335-8332
　　Pubs: *Thomas Crook's Shoebox, How Far Is Far?*
　　(Southeast Missouri State U Pr, 1996, 1990).

Jane Hoogestraat　　　　　　　　　　　　P
Southwest Missouri State Univ, 901 S National, Springfield,
MO 65802, 417-836-6613
Internet: jah905f@vma.smsu.edu
　　Pubs: *Poetry, Southern Rev, Iowa Woman, High Plains
　　Literary Rev, Poem, Southern Poetry Rev.*

Jane Ellen Ibur   P
3536 Victor St, St Louis, MO 63104, 314-771-7661
    Pubs: *If I Had A Hammer: Women & Work Anth*
    (Papier-Mache Pr, 1990), *Webster Rev, Slipstream,*
    Crazyquilt, Literati Internationale, Spitball, Pastiche.

Jeanne Lebow   P
Northeast Missouri State Univ, Division of Language & Lit,
Kirksville, MO 63501, 816-785-5677
    Pubs: *The Outlaw James Copeland and the*
    Champion-Belted Empress (U Georgia Pr, 1991), *Nimrod,*
    Sun Dog.

Thomas John Lochhaas   W
2349 S 11 St, St Louis, MO 63104, 314-771-7923
    Pubs: *Chicago Rev, Writers' Forum, Subject To Change,*
    Sawtooth, Slackwater Rev.

Barbara Loots   P
7943 Charlotte, Kansas City, MO 64131, 816-361-3844
Internet: bkloots@earthlink.net
    Pubs: *Sibyl & Sphinx* (Rockhill Pr, 1988), *Landcape With*
    Women: Anth (Singular Speech Pr, 1998), *The Muse*
    Strikes Back: Anth (Story Line Pr, 1997), *Random House*
    Treasury of Light Verse: Anth (Random Hse, 1995), *Lyric,*
    Christian Century, Sparrow.

Tim McCarthy   W
233 Iowa, Camdenton, MO 65020, 314-346-2132
    Pubs: *Hispanics in the U.S.* (Bilingual Rev, 1980),
    Contemporary Reader for Creative Writing: Anth (Harcourt
    Brace, 1993), *Carolina Qtly, Arizona Literary Mag, New Times.*

James McKinley   W
Univ Missouri, 5100 Rockhill Rd, Kansas City, MO 64110,
816-235-1120
    Pubs: *The Fickleman Suite & Other Stories* (U Arkansas Pr,
    1993), *Acts of Love* (Breitenbush Bks, 1987).

Ronald W. McReynolds   P
High Field, RR #5, Warrensburg, MO 64093, 816-747-8810
    Pubs: *The Blooding And Other Missouri Poems*
    (Mid-America Pr, 1979), *Chariton Rev.*

Jerred Metz   P
2318 Albion Pl, St Louis, MO 63104, 314-865-2789
    Pubs: *Halley's Comet, 1910: Fire in the Sky* (Singing Bone,
    1985).

Philip Miller   P
1841 Pendleton, Kansas City, MO 64124, 816-842-5872
    Pubs: *Dork* (Mulberry Pr, 1991), *Boulevard, College*
    English, Literary Rev, Confrontation, Mudfish, New Letters,
    Kansas Qtly, Puerto del Sol.

Michelle Mitchell-Foust   P
Univ Missouri, English Dept, Tate Hall Rm 107, Columbia,
MO 65211, 573-882-0681
    Pubs: *Poets At Seven* (Sutton Hoo Pr, 1995), *Best Of*
    Writers At Work: Anth (Pecan Grove Pr, 1995), *Antioch*
    Rev, Black Warrior Rev, Denver Qtly.

Michael Murphy   W
4304 McCausland, St Louis, MO 63109, 314-647-4363
    Pubs: *AKA Ormand Sacker* (Norfolk-Hall, 1984),
    Hemingsteen (Autolycus Pr, 1978), *Esquire, Life.*

Martin Musick   P
1661 Vassier Ave, St Louis, MO 63133, 314-389-2354
    Pubs: *Para*phrase, Midwest Poetry Rev.*

Bob Myers   W
16503 3rd St N, Independence, MO 64056
    Pubs: *Kill the Fine Young Dreamers* (Abiding Mystery Pr,
    1998), *Good Old Hillmont High* (Crescent, 1979), *Mystery*
    Forum Mag.

Christina V. Pacosz   P&W
2003 NE Russell Rd #102, Kansas City, MO 641162423,
816-452-4503
Internet: pacosz@earthlink.net
    Pubs: *This Is Not a Place to Sing* (West End, 1987), *Some*
    Winded, Wild Beast (Black & Red, 1985), *A Gathering Of*
    Poets: Anth (Kent State U Pr, 1992), *Asheville Rev, Calyx,*
    Sing Heavenly Muse, Pig Iron, Exquisite Corpse, Permafrost.

Tom Padgett   P
523 N Park Pl, Bolivar, MO 65613, 417-326-5406
    Pubs: *The Magpie, The Weasel, Prodigal Poet, Pets* (Barnowl,
    1997, 1997, 1995, 1990), *By-Line, Lucidity, Hampden-Sydney*
    Rev, Libido, Anterior Poetry Monthly, Tradition, Verses, Old
    Millpoint Anth, Rockford Rev, Penwood Rev.

Michelle Paulsen   P
HC83, Box 64, Salem, MO 65560, 573-743-6848
Internet: mpaulsen@misn.com
    Pubs: *It Is Possible To Forget How To Breathe* (Red
    Menace Pub, 1996), *Sixteen Voices: Anth* (Mariposa,
    1994), *Sink Full of Dishes, Perceptions, Midland Rev,*
    Howling Dog, Recursive Angel, Fox Cry.

William Peden   W
408 Thilly Ave, Columbia, MO 65205, 314-442-1228
    Pubs: *Fragments & Fictions: Work Books of an Obscure*
    Writer (Watermark Pr, 1991), *Twilight at Monticello*
    (Houghton Mifflin, 1975).

David Perkins   P
Box 10016, Kansas City, MO 64111, 816-756-1744
    Pubs: *Wrapped Mind & Other Essays* (Woods Colt Pr,
    1988), *License to Kill* (BkMk Pr, 1974).

Carol Poster   P&W
Univ Missouri, 107 Tate Hall, English Dept, Columbia, MO
65211, 314-449-0765
    Pubs: *Surrounded by Dangerous Things* (Singular Speech
    Pr, 1994), *Deceiving the Worms* (Sleeping Lizard Pr, 1984),
    Poetry East, Formalist, Ploughshares.

Harold Lee Prosser   W
1313 S Jefferson Ave, Springfield, MO 65807
    Pubs: *Jack Bimbo's Touring Circus Poems, Desert Woman
    Visions* (Cougar Creek, 1989, 1988).

Martin Quigley   W
4400 Lindell Blvd, #5B, St Louis, MO 63108, 314-534-9903
    Pubs: *The Original Colored House of David* (Houghton
    Mifflin, 1981), *Today's Game* (Viking, 1965), *Winners and
    Losers, The Secret Project of Sigurd O'Leary, A Tent On
    Corsica* (Lippincott, 1961, 1959, 1949).

Cathleen Quirk   P
418-A N Clay St, Kirkwood, MO 63122, 314-909-1562
    Pubs: *Rue and Grace* (Crossing Pr, 1987), *Burden and
    Other Poems* (Orpheum Pr, 1980), *Ploughshares Poetry
    Reader: Anth* (Ploughshares Bks, 1994).

Carol Lee Sanchez   P
13918 Longwood Rd, Hughesville, MO 65334, 660-827-5261
Internet: carolee@sockets.net
    Pubs: *From Spirit to Matter, Excerpts from a Mountain
    Climber's Handbook, Message Bringer Women* (Taurean
    Horn Pr, 1997, 1995, 1976), *She Poems* (Chicory Blue Pr,
    1995), *Reinventing the Enemy: Anth* (W.W. Norton, 1997).

Jo Sapp   W
1025 Hickory Hill Dr, Columbia, MO 652032322,
573-443-8964
Internet: sapp0@ibm.net
    Pubs: *Conversations With American Novelists* (U Missouri
    Pr, 1997), *Norton Anth of Short Fiction, Flash Fiction: Anth*
    (Norton, 1995, 1992), NAR, Intro, Epoch, Washington Rev,
    Kansas Qtly, Long Pond.

Howard Schwartz   P&W
13 Stacy Dr, St Louis, MO 63132, 314-997-4553
Internet: sheschw@umslvma.umsl.edu
    Pubs: *The Four Who Entered Paradise* (Jason Aronson
    Inc., 1995), *Gabriel's Palace* (Oxford U Pr, 1993),
    Sleepwalking Beneath The Stars (BkMk Pr, 1992).

Jory Sherman   P
3044 Shepherd Hill Expy, #642, Branson, MO 65616-8168
    Pubs: *Grass Kingdom, Trapper's Moon* (Tor/Forge, 1994,
    1994), *The Medicine Horn* (Tor Bks, 1991).

Peter L. Simpson   P
5261 Westminster Pl, St Louis, MO 63108, 314-361-5342
    Pubs: *Press Box and City Room, Stealing Home* (BkMk Pr,
    1988, 1985), *Choice, New Letters.*

David-Glen Smith   P
4721 McPherson Ave, 1SW, Saint Louis, MO 63108-1967
    Pubs: *Blue Buildings, Evergreen Chronicles, Five Fingers
    Rev, Louisville Rev, Mid-American Rev, Taos Rev.*

Roland E. Sodowsky   W
Southwest Missouri State Univ, English Dept, Springfield, MO
65804, 417-882-5791
    Pubs: *Interim in the Desert* (TCU Pr, 1990), *Un-Due West*
    (Corona, 1990), *Things We Lose* (U Missouri Pr, 1989),
    Concho River Rev, Atlantic.

Arnold Stead   P&W
Univ Missouri, Tate Hall, Rm 1, Columbia, MO 65202,
314-882-0681
    Pubs: *The Blood of This Need* (Kawabata Pr, 1987),
    Woodrose, Sepia, Loonfeather, Lake Street Rev.

Marjorie Stelmach   P
708 Carman Oaks Ct, Ballwin, MO 63021, 314-230-0703
    Pubs: *Night Drawings* (Helicon Nine Pr, 1995), *Kenyon
    Rev, Tampa Rev, The Journal, Chelsea, Ascent, River
    Styx, New Letters.*

Robert Stewart   P
7714 Summit St, Kansas City, MO 64114, 816-444-6870
    Pubs: *Letter from the Living* (Borderline Pubs, 1992),
    Plumbers (BkMk Pr, 1988), *Stand, Denver Qtly, Poetry
    Northwest, Nimrod.*

Anthony J. Summers   W
1825 Bender Ln, Arnold, MO 63010, 314-752-3703
    Pubs: *Moving* (The Smith, 1981), *Metamorphosis*
    (Cornerstone Pr, 1979).

William L. Sutherland   W
654 W Bethel Dr, Columbia, MO 65203, 314-442-7241
    Pubs: *News From Fort God* (Midlist Pr, 1992).

Gladys Swan   W
2601 Lynnwood Dr, Columbia, MO 652032936,
573-442-9129
Internet: enggs@showme.missouri.edu
    Pubs: *A Visit To Strangers, Do You Believe In Cabeza de
    Vaca?* (U Missouri Pr, 1996, 1991), *Ghost Dance: A Play of
    Voices, Of Memory & Desire* (LSU Pr, 1992, 1989).

Marilyn R. Tatlow   W
1507 Keegan Ct, Columbia, MO 65203, 573-449-9380
Internet: marilynt@gte.net
    Pubs: *Paradise* (Florida Literary Fdn, 1994), *The First Anth
    of Missouri Women Writers* (Sheba Rev, 1987), *Prism,
    Raconteur, Slugfest, Pleiades, Poets' Edge, Palo Alto Rev.*

Brian Taylor   P
4376 Maryland Ave, #A-4, St Louis, MO 63108,
314-531-1437
   Pubs: *Transit* (London Mag Edtns, 1986), *Missouri Rev,
   London Mag, The Listener, NER/BLQ, Sewanee Rev, Paris
   Rev, Stand.*

Julius Eric Thompson   P
Univ Missouri, 313 Gentry Hall, Columbia, MO 65211,
573-814-1592
   Pubs: *Blues Said: Walk On* (Energy, Earth Comm, 1977),
   Hopes Tied Up In Promises (Dorrance & Co., 1970),
   *Trouble With the Water: 250 Years of African American
   Poetry: Anth* (Penguin, 1997), *Freedomways, Phylon, Black
   Creation, Callaloo.*

William Trowbridge   P
907 S Dunn St, Maryville, MO 64468, 816-582-3961
   Pubs: *O Paradise, Enter Dark Stranger* (U Arkansas Pr,
   1995, 1989), *Georgia Rev, Gettysburg Rev, Poetry,
   Southern Rev, Colorado Rev, New Letters.*

Constance Urdang   P&W
2051 Park Ave #D, St Louis, MO 63104, 314-241-4426
   Pubs: *The Woman Who Read Novels & Peacetime, American
   Earthquakes* (Coffee Hse, 1990, 1988), *Alternative Lives:
   Poems* (U Pitt Pr, 1990), *Poetry, Yale Rev.*

Mona Van Duyn   P
7505 Teasdale Ave, St Louis, MO 63130, 314-863-1943
   Pubs: *Firefall, If It Be Not I, Near Changes* (Knopf, 1993,
   1993, 1990), *Merciful Disguises* (Atheneum, 1982).

Gloria Vando   P
Helicon Nine Editions, PO Box 22412, Kansas City, MO
64113, 816-753-1095
Internet: vandog@aol.com
   Pubs: *Promesas: Geography of the Impossible* (Arte
   Publico Pr, 1993), *Touching the Fire: Anth* (Anchor Bks,
   1998), *Hispanic American Literary Anth* (HC, 1995), *River
   Styx, Carolina Qtly, Seattle Rev, Poets On, Western
   Humanities Rev, Kenyon Rev.*

Maryfrances Wagner   P
5021 Tierney Dr, Independence, MO 64055
   Pubs: *Salvatore's Daughter* (BkMk Pr, 1995), *Tonight
   Cicadas Sing* (Mid-America Pr, 1984), *Laurel Rev, New
   Letters, Nebraska Rev, Midwest Qtly, Hiram Poetry Rev.*

Morrie Warshawski   P
6364 Forsyth Blvd, St Louis, MO 63105, 314-727-7880
Internet: http://www.warshawski.com
   Pubs: *Out of Nowhere* (Press-22, 1985), *Indiana Rev,
   Apalachee Qtly, Hayden's Ferry Rev, Exquisite Corpse,
   Modern Poetry Studies, New York Qtly.*

Richard Watson   W
756 Harvard Ave, St Louis, MO 63130, 314-862-7646
Internet: c34815rw@wuvmd.wustl.edu
   Pubs: *The Philosopher's Demise* (U Missouri Pr, 1995),
   Niagara (Coffee Hse Pr, 1993).

Jane O. Wayne   P
6376 Washington Ave, St Louis, MO 63130, 314-725-6291
Internet: jowayne@inlink.com
   Pubs: *A Strange Heart* (Helicon Nine Edtns, 1996), *Looking
   Both Ways* (U Missouri Pr, 1985), *Poetry, Iowa Rev,
   Ploughshares, American Scholar, Massachusetts Rev,
   Michigan Qtly.*

Susan Whitemore   P
The Writers Place, 3607 Pennsylvania, Kansas City, MO
64111, 816-753-1090
Internet: twpkcmo@aol.com
   Pubs: *The Invisible Women* (Singular Speech Pr, 1991).

Rebecca M. Wright   P
1304 S 18 St, St Louis, MO 63104, 314-231-0441
   Pubs: *Ciao Manhattan* (Telephone Bks, 1976), *Brief Lives*
   (Ant's Forefoot, 1974).

Joan Yeagley   P
Rte 1, Box 1306, Stella, MO 64867, 417-435-2341
Internet: hayeagley@juno.com
   Pubs: *The Studs of McDonald County, In the Middle:
   Midwestern Women Poets: Anth* (BkMk Pr, 1987, 1985).

MONTANA

Sandra Alcosser   P
5791 W County Line Rd, Florence, MT 59833, 406-273-0560
Internet: alcosser@mail.sdsu.edu
   Pubs: *Except By Nature* (Graywolf, 1998), *Sleeping Inside
   the Glacier* (Brighton, 1997), *A Fish To Feed All Hunger* (U
   Pr Virginia, 1986), *APR, New Yorker, Paris Rev, Poetry.*

Minerva Allen   P
Box 5270 HC63, Dodson, MT 59524, 406-673-3596
   Pubs: *Winter Smoke, Thematic Approach Curriculum: Anth*
   (Flores Hill County Printing Havremt, 1996, 1996),The *Last
   Place: A Centennial Anth* (Montana Historical Society,
   1988), *Montana Mag of Western History.*

Margaret Bridwell-Jones   W
135 Village Ln, Bigfork, MT 59911, 406-837-0248
   Pubs: *Northwood Jrnl, Calliope, Green's Mag,
   Colorado-North Rev, Hob-Nob.*

Ed Chaberek   P
PO Box 424, Superior, MT 59872-0424, 406-721-3852
    Pubs: *Types, Vol. I* (Superior Poetry Pr, 1998), *Superior
    Poetry News, Owen Wister Rev, Plainsongs, Camas, Aura,
    Tight, Plainsongs, Crimson Leer, Carpe Laureate Diem,
    Jauna Gaita.*

Barbara Corcoran   W
PO Box 4394, Missoula, MT 59806-4394
    Pubs: *Wolf At The Door, Family Secrets, Stay Tuned*
    (Atheneum, 1993, 1992, 1991).

James Crumley   W
PO Box 9278, Missoula, MT 59807, 406-728-8602
    Pubs: *Dancing Bear, The Last Good Kiss, The Wrong Case*
    (Random Hse, 1983, 1978, 1975).

Art Cuelho, Jr.   P&W
PO Box 249, Big Timber, MT 59011
    Pubs: *Fiction 100* (Macmillan, 1994), *As Far As I Can See*
    (Windflower Pr, 1989), *California Childhood* (Creative Arts
    Bks, 1989).

David Dale   P
PO Box 257, Big Arm, MT 59910, 406-849-5702
    Pubs: *Montana Primer* (Big Mountain Pub, 1996), *Cutbank,
    Jeopardy, Kinnikinnik, Slackwater Rev, Talking River Rev,
    Trestle Creek Rev.*

Martha Elizabeth   P&W
Once Only Productions, Box 9444, Missoula, MT 59807,
406-728-8602
Internet: crumdog@aol.com
    Pubs: *The Return of Pleasure* (Confluence Pr, 1996),
    Basics of the Dance, Inheritance of Light: Anth (U North
    Texas Pr, 1990, 1996), *Grow Old Along with Me: Anth*
    (Papier-Mache Pr, 1996), *Georgia Rev, New England Rev,
    New Virginia Rev.*

Pete Fromm   W
2908 3rd Ave N, Great Falls, MT 59401
    Pubs: *Dry Rain, Indian Creek Chronicles* (Lyons & Burford,
    1997, 1993), *Monkey Tag* (Scholastic, 1994), *The Tall
    Uncut* (John Daniel & Co., 1992), *Glimmer Train, American
    Fiction, American Way, Good Housekeeping, Gray Sporting
    Jrnl, Big Sky.*

Marilyn Kay Giuliani   P
716 S 6th W, Missoula, MT 59801
    Pubs: *Poetic Eloquence, Dreambuilding Crusade Idea
    Company, Capper's.*

Patricia Goedicke   P
310 McLeod Ave, Missoula, MT 59801-4302, 406-549-0343
Internet: goedicke@selway.umt.edu
    Pubs: *Invisible Horses, Paul Bunyan's Bearskin* (Milkweed,
    1996, 1992), *Hudson Rev, Kenyon Rev, Prairie Schooner,
    NER, Beloit Poetry Jrnl, Manhattan Rev, Hubbub,
    Gettysburg Rev.*

Valerie Harms   W
PO Box 1123, Bozeman, MT 59771, 406-587-3356
Internet: valerieharms@in-tch.com
    Pubs: *The Ecology of Everyday Life* (Putnam, 1994), *The
    Inner Lover* (Shambhala Pubs, 1992).

John Holbrook   P
328 S 5th W, Missoula, MT 59801, 406-728-6223
Internet: jholbrok@mssl.uswest.net
    Pubs: *Clear Water on the Swan* (Falcon Pr, 1992), *Hubbub,
    SPR, Poetry Northwest, Camas, Kinesis, Rain City,
    Wisconsin Rev, Tamarack, Carolina Qtly, Mississippi Rev,
    Nebraska Rev, Florida Rev, Green Hills Literary Lantern,
    Northern Journeys, Bellowing Ark.*

Lowell Jaeger   P
E Lake Shore, Bigfork, MT 59911, 406-982-3269
Internet: ljaeger@spot1.fvcc.cc.mt.us
    Pubs: *Hope Against Hope, War On War* (Utah State U Pr,
    1990, 1988), *CutBank, High Plains Literary Rev, Poetry
    Northwest.*

William Kittredge   W
143 S 5th E, Missoula, MT 59801, 406-549-6605
    Pubs: *Who Owns The West* (Mercury Hse, 1996), *Hole in
    the Sky* (Vintage, 1993), *The Last Best Place: Anth*
    (Montana Historical Society Pr, 1988), *Paris Rev.*

King D. Kuka   P
907 Ave C, NW, Great Falls, MT 59404, 406-452-4449

David Long   W
820 3rd Ave E, Kalispell, MT 59901, 406-755-8490
Internet: long@digisys.net
    Pubs: *The Falling Boy, Blue Spruce* (Scribner, 1997, 1995),
    The Flood of '64 (Ecco, 1987), *New Yorker, GQ, Story,
    Sewanee Rev, Antaeus.*

Maria R. Maris   P
2332 Ash, Billings, MT 59101, 406-259-1977
    Pubs: *Plains Poetry Jrnl, The Lyric, Poet Lore, Piedmont
    Literary Rev, Wind, Kansas Qtly, Z Miscellaneous.*

Ruth McLaughlin   W
2506 1st Ave N, Great Falls, MT 59401
    Pubs: *Best American Short Stories: Anth* (Houghton Mifflin,
    1979), *California State Poetry Qtly.*

Thomas McNamee   P
West Boulder Ranch, Box 65, McLeod, MT 59052
    Pubs: *A Story of Deep Delight* (Viking, 1990), *The Grizzly
    Bear* (Penguin, 1990).

Elsie Pankowski   P
1404 11 Ave S, Great Falls, MT 59405, 406-452-0127
    Pubs: *Leaning Into the Wind* (HM, 1997), *Midwest Qtly,
    Thema, Midland Rev, Birdwatcher's Digest, Manhattan
    Poetry Rev, Yankee, Dry Crick Rev.*

Greg Pape   P
Univ Montana, Missoula, MT 59812, 406-243-5231
    Pubs: *Sunflower Facing the Sun* (U Iowa Pr, 1992), *Storm Pattern, Black Branches, Border Crossings* (U Pitt Pr, 1992, 1984, 1978), *Cutbank, Colorado Rev, Poetry.*

Marnie Prange   P&W
231 Eagle's Pt, Stevensville, MT 59870, 406-777-5689
    Pubs: *Dangerous Neighborhoods* (Cleveland State Poetry Ctr, 1994).

Leonard Wallace Robinson   P&W
310 McLeod Ave, Missoula, MT 59801, 406-549-0343
    Pubs: *In The Whale* (Barnwood Pr, 1983), *The Man Who Loved Beauty* (H&R, 1976).

James Welch   P
2321 Wylie St, Missoula, MT 59802, 406-549-6713

Ivon W. White, Jr.   P
PO Box 637, Billings, MT 59103-0637, 406-245-6875
    Pubs: *Gates Left Open: Anth* (Montana Institute of the Arts, 1989), *Portable Wall, Alkali Flats, Thomas Wolfe Rev, The Villager, Art Times.*

Paul Zarzyski   P
PO Box 258, Augusta, MT 59410, 406-562-3860
    Pubs: *All This Way For The Short Ride* (Museum of New Mexico Pr, 1996), *I Am Not A Cowboy* (Dry Crik Pr, 1995), *Poetry, Prairie Schooner, Northern Lights, CutBank.*

NEBRASKA

Susan Aizenberg   P
Univ Nebraska, Omaha, NE 68182-0324, 402-493-6746
    Pubs: *Peru* (Graywolf Pr, 1997), *Prairie Schooner, Connecticut Rev, Devil's Millhopper, Iowa Woman, Third Coast, Agni, Spoon River Rev, Sun Dog, Kalliope, Journal.*

Grace Bauer   P
Univ of Nebraska English Dept, 202 Andrews, PO Box 880333, Lincoln, NE 68588-0333, 402-472-0993
Internet: gbauer@unlinfo.unl.edu
    Pubs: *The Women at the Well* (Portals Pr, 1998), *Where You've Seen Her* (Pennywhistle Pr, 1993), *The House Where I've Never Lived* (Anabiosis Pr, 1993), *Poetry, Michigan Qtly Rev, Shenandoah, Poet Lore.*

Stephen Behrendt   P
Univ of Nebraska, Lincoln, NE 68588-0333, 402-472-1806
Internet: sbehrend@unlinfo.unl.edu
    Pubs: *A Step in the Dark, Instruments of the Bones* (Mid-List Pr, 1996, 1992), *Sewanee Rev, Hudson Rev, Texas Rev, Midwest Qtly.*

Miriam Ben-Yaacov   P&W
1870 Mayfair Dr, Omaha, NE 68144, 402-333-1115
    Pubs: *Nexus, Short Story Intl, Nebraska English Jrnl, The Long Story, Smackwarm, Trans-Missouri Art View, Metropolitan.*

Robert Beum   P
Univ Mid-America, PO Box 80669, Lincoln, NE 68501, 402-467-3671

J. V. Brummels   P
Two Cow, Winside, NE 68790, 402-286-4891
    Pubs: *Clay Hills* (Nosila Pr, 1996), *Sunday's Child* (Basfal Bks, 1994), *Deus Ex Machina* (Bantam Bks, 1989), *614 Pearl* (Abattoir Edtns, 1986), *Ellipsis, Chariton Rev, Puerto del Sol, Prairie Schooner.*

Joanne M. Casullo   P
6300 N 7th St, Lincoln, NE 68521-8936
    Pubs: *All My Grandmothers Could Sing* (Free Rein Pr, 1984), *Prairie Schooner, Kansas Qtly, South Dakota Rev.*

Susan Strayer Deal   P
3825 Woods Blvd, Lincoln, NE 68502-5664, 402-420-1121
    Pubs: *Something So Easy* (East Hall Pr, 1992), *Adjoining Rooms* (Platte Valley Pr, 1985), *No Moving Parts* (Ahsahta, 1980), *Caprice, AZ Mandala, Whole Notes.*

Marilyn Dorf   P
4149 "E" St, Lincoln, NE 68510, 402-489-3104
    Pubs: *Kansas Qtly, Northeast, Midwest Poetry Rev, Bitterroot, Whole Notes, Mankato Poetry Rev, Plainsongs.*

Lorraine Duggin   P&W
932 N 74 Ave, Omaha, NE 68114-3114, 402-397-6153
    Pubs: *The Heartlands Today* (Firelands Writing Ctr, 1995), *In A New Land* (Natl Textbook Co., 1992), *Boundaries of Twilight: Anth* (New Rivers Pr, 1991), *Kosmas: Czech & Euro Jrnl, Heartlands Today.*

Richard Duggin   W
Univ Nebraska, Fine Arts 223, Omaha, NE 68182, 402-554-4801
Internet: rduggin@cwis.unomaha.edu
    Pubs: *The Music Box Treaty* (Abbatoir Edtns, 1982), *Kansas Qtly, Laurel Rev, Playboy, Pulpsmith, NAR, Fiction Jrnl, American Literary Rev, Beloit, The Sun.*

Charles Fort   P
Univ of Nebraska English Dept, Kearney, NE 688491320, 308-865-8164
Internet: fortc@platte.unk.edu
    Pubs: *Darvil* (St. Andrews, 1993), *The Town Clock Burning, Carnegie Mellon Anth of Poetry* (Carnegie Mellon U Pr, 1991, 1993), *A New Geography of Poets: Anth* (U Arkansas Pr, 1992), *APR, Georgia Rev, Callaloo, Greensboro Rev.*

Mark Edwin Fuehrer   P
Imperial, NE 69033, 308-882-4219

Patrick Worth Gray   P
1109 Kingston Ave, Bellevue, NE 68005, 402-292-1908
    Pubs: *Spring Comes Again to Arnett* (Mr. Cogito Pr, 1987),
Disappearances (U Nebraska Pr, 1978).

Twyla Hansen   P
4140 N 42 St Cir, Lincoln, NE 68504-1210, 402-466-5839
Internet: tmh@nebrwesleyan.edu
    Pubs: *In Our Very Bones* (A Slow Tempo Pr, 1997), *How
To Live In The Heartland* (Flatwater Edtns, 1992), *Inheriting
the Land: Anth* (U Minnesota Pr, 1993), *Laurel Rev, Iowa
Woman, Prairie Schooner, North Dakota Qtly, Crab
Orchard Rev, Midwest Qtly.*

Arthur Homer   P&W
Univ Nebraska/Omaha, Writers Workshop, FAEB 221,
Omaha, NE 681820324, 402-556-4691
Internet: ahomer@cwis.unomaha.edu
    Pubs: *The Drownt Boy: An Ozark Tale* (U Missouri Pr, 1994),
Skies of Such Valuable Glass (Owl Creek Pr, 1990), *Georgia
Rev, NAR, The Sun, Green Mountains Rev, Southern Rev.*

Robert W. King   P
1930 Dakota St, Lincoln, NE 68502, 402-421-9215
    Pubs: *A Circle of Land* (Dacotah Territory Pr, 1990),
Standing Around Outside (Bloodroot, 1979), *Ascent, New
England Rev, Midwest Qtly, Poetry, Massachusetts Rev.*

William Kloefkorn   P
2502 N 63, Lincoln, NE 68507, 402-466-1032

Ted Kooser   P
1820 Branched Oak Rd, Garland, NE 683609303,
402-588-2272
    Pubs: *Weather Central, One World At A Time* (U Pitt Pr,
1994, 1985), *Kenyon Rev, Hudson Rev, Poetry.*

Greg Kuzma   P
Univ Nebraska, Lincoln, NE 68588
    Pubs: *Good News* (Carnegie Mellon, 1994), *Wind Rain and
Stars and the Grass Growing* (Orchises, 1993),
*TriQuarterly, Crazyhorse, Harvard Rev, Virginia Qtly,
Massachusetts Rev.*

Wopashitwe Mondo Eye Langa   P
PO Box 2500, Lincoln, NE 68542-2500
    Pubs: *Morning of the Bright Bird* (Third World Pr, 1992),
*Shooting Star Qtly Rev, Nebraska Humanities, Obsidian,
Black Scholar, Nantucket Rev, Pacifica Rev, Argo.*

James Magorian   P
1225 N 46 St, Lincoln, NE 68503
    Pubs: *Hearts of Gold* (Acme Pr, 1996), *The Hideout of the
Sigmund Freud Gang* (Black Oak Pr, 1987), *Plainsongs,
Nebraska Rev, River Styx, Sewanee Rev, Atlanta Rev,
Southern Poetry Rev.*

Mordecai Marcus   P
822 Mulder Dr, Lincoln, NE 685104032, 402-488-7831
Internet: mmarcus@unlinfo.unl.edu
    Pubs: *Pursuing the Lost* (Whole Notes Pr, 1993), *Poet
Lore, Tar River Poetry, Poet and Critic, Cats Mag, South
Dakota Rev, Santa Barbara Rev.*

Nancy McCleery   P
3025 P St, Lincoln, NE 685033434, 402-477-8363
    Pubs: *Polar Lights* (Transient Pr, 1994), *Staying the Winter*
(Cummington Pr, 1987), *Many Mountains Moving, Cafe
Solo, Whole Notes, Nebraska Poets Calendar, Hyperion,
Portland Rev, Calyx.*

Hilda Raz   P
Univ Nebraska, Lincoln, 201 Andrews Hall, Lincoln, NE
685880334, 402-472-1812
Internet: hraz@unlinfo.unl.edu
    Pubs: *Divine Honors* (Wesleyan, 1997), *The Bone Dish*
(State Street Pr, 1989), *Cancer In the Voices of Ten
Women: Anth* (Pandora/HC, 1997), *Second Helping: Anth*
(Pleasant Dale Pr, 1996), *Kalliope, Southern Rev, Women's
Rev of Bks, Ploughshares.*

James Reed   W
1009 Hickory St, Omaha, NE 68108, 402-345-3711
Internet: jreed@fa-cpacs.unomaha.edu
    Pubs: *Apalachee Qtly, Tennessee Qtly, Aura Literary/Arts
Rev, Carolina Qtly, Buffalo Spree, William and Mary Rev,
River Styx, Brilliant Corners.*

Roy Scheele   P
2020 S 25 St, Lincoln, NE 68502, 402-477-1102
    Pubs: *To See How It Tallies* (Whole Notes Pr, 1995), *The
Voice We Call Human* (Juniper Pr, 1991), *Pivot, Poetry,
Northeast, Southern Rev, Verse.*

Michael Skau   P
Univ Nebraska, 60th & Dodge, English Dept, Omaha, NE
68182, 402-554-3314
Internet: mskau@cwis.unomaha.edu
    Pubs: *Me And God Poems* (Bradypress, 1990), *Sequoia,
Alpha Beat Soup, Carolina Qtly, Prophetic Voices,
Northwest Rev, Cumberland Poetry Rev, Midland Rev.*

Brent Spencer   P&W
Creighton Univ, Omaha, NE 68178, 402-280-2192
Internet: spencr@creighton.edu
    Pubs: *Missouri Rev, American Literary Rev, Stanford Mag,
Atlantic, Midland, Intro, Dekalb Literary Arts Jrnl, Poet & Critic.*

Mary Kathryn Stillwell   P
Officers' Row 16 S, 5730 N 30 St, Omaha, NE 68111
    Pubs: *Moving To Malibu* (Sandhills Pr, 1988), *Paris Rev Anth*
(Norton, 1990), *Blood to Remember: Anth* (Texas Tech,
1990), *Prairie Schooner, Kansas Qtly, North Dakota Rev.*

Don Welch P
611 W 27 St, Kearney, NE 68847, 308-237-3861
    Pubs: *Carved by Obadiah Verity* (Colorado College Pr, 1993), *Inheriting the Land: Anth* (U Minnesota Pr, 1993), *Prairie Schooner, Georgia Rev, Laurel Rev, Nimrod, Aethlon.*

Hargis Westerfield W
2914 Ave B, Kearney, NE 68847, 308-237-7107
    Pubs: *The Forty-First Division* (Turner Pub Co., 1993), *Southwest Rev, Christian Century, Saturday Rev, Trains.*

Nancy G. Westerfield P
505 W 22 St, Kearney, NE 68847, 308-237-7107
    Pubs: *The Morning of the Marys* (Contemporary Drama Service, 1986), *Welded Women* (Kearney State College Pr, 1983), *Prairie Schooner, Poem, Trains, Grain.*

Fredrick Zydek P&W
5002 Decatur St, Omaha, NE 68104, 402-551-0343
    Pubs: *The Abbey Poems* (Lone Willow Pr, 1998), *Ending the Fast* (Yellow Barn Pr, 1984), *Poetry, Antioch, New England Rev, Nimrod, Poetry Northwest, Prairie Schooner, Southwest Rev.*

NEVADA

Charles H. Crump P
11 Condor Cir, Carson City, NV 89701, 702-883-6380
    Pubs: *Desert Wood* (U Nevada Pr, 1991), *Piedmont Literary Rev, Redneck Rev, Poultry, Manna, Silver State Quill, Bellowing Ark.*

Elaine Dallman P
PO Box 60550, Reno, NV 89506, 702-972-1671
Internet: edall@ios.com
    Pubs: *A Parallel Cut of Air* (Medallion Guild, 1996), *Woman Poet: The West* (Women in Literature, 1994), *Black Buzzard Rev, Flat Tired, Northern Contours.*

John H. Irsfeld W
Univ Nevada, 4505 Maryland Pkwy, Las Vegas, NV 89154, 702-895-4877
Internet: irsfeldj@nevada.edu
    Pubs: *Little Kingdom* (SMU, 1989), *Rats Alley* (U Nevada, 1987), *New Texas '91: Anth* (U North Texas Pr, 1991), *American Literary Rev, Kansas Qtly, The Writer.*

Stephen Shu Ning Liu P
4024 Deerfield Ave, Las Vegas, NV 89117, 702-871-5987
    Pubs: *Dream Journeys to China* (New World Pr, 1982), *Literature: Anth* (HarperCollins, 1991), *America, Michigan Qtly Rev, APR, Malahat Rev, College English.*

Melanie Perish P
Univ Nevada, 102 Morrill Hall, Reno, NV 89557, 702-784-6622
    Pubs: *Traveling the Distance* (Rising Tide, 1981), *Notes of a Daughter from the Old Country* (Motherroot, 1978), *Calyx, Sinister Wisdom, Desert Wood, eNVee.*

Elizabeth Perry P
525 Ave B, Boulder City, NV 89005, 702-294-0021
Internet: peg_pub@ix.netcom.com
    Pubs: *Desert Wood* (U Nevada Pr, 1991), *Gathered Echoes* (Pegasus Pr, 1991), *Interim, Midwest Poetry Rev.*

Victor Power W
4155 Vegas Valley Dr, #31, Las Vegas, NV 89121-2548
    Pubs: *Johnnie Will, The Escape* (Mule Mountain Pr, 1986, 1985), *Eire-Ireland.*

Kirk Robertson P
PO Box 1047, Fallon, NV 89407, 702-423-1440
    Pubs: *Just Past Labor Day: New & Selected Poems* (U Nevada Pr, 1996), *Music: A Suite & 13 Songs* (Floating Island Pr, 1995), *Driving to Vegas: Poems 1969-1987* (Sun/Gemini Pr, 1989), *New Directions.*

G. J. Scrimgeour W
PO Box 2809, Reno, NV 89505, 702-786-1442
    Pubs: *A Woman Of Her Times* (Putnam, 1982).

NEW HAMPSHIRE

Martha Bissell P
18 Summer St, Hillsborough, NH 03244, 603-464-4033
Internet: nhqp@nh.ultranet.com
    Pubs: *Anth of Mag Verse & Yearbook of American Poetry* (Monitor Bk Co, 1997), *Merrimack: Anth* (Loom Pr, 1992), *Beloit Poetry Jrnl, Poetry East, Carolina Qtly, Calliope, Chattahoochee Rev, Poets On, New England Rev, Marlboro Pr.*

Allan Block P
RFD Quarry Rd, Francestown, NH 03043, 603-547-2934
    Pubs: *In Noah's Wake* (William L. Bauhan, 1972), *Nation, Massachusetts Rev, Prairie Schooner.*

W. E. Butts P
827 State St, #5, Portsmouth, NH 03801-4330, 603-427-6963
    Pubs: *Movies In A Small Town* (Mellen Poetry Pr, 1997), *The Required Dance* (Igneus Pr, 1990), *Anth of Mag Verse* (Monitor Bks, 1997), *Birmingham Poetry Rev, Eleventh Muse, Mid-American Rev, Poet & Critic, Poet Lore, Calliope, Cimarron Rev, Defined Providence.*

Dan Carr   P
PO Box 111/30 Main St, Ashuelot Village, NH 03441,
603-239-6830
    Pubs: *Intersection* (Golgonooza Letter Foundry and Pr,
    1990), *Mysteries of the Palaces of Water* (Four Zoas Night
    Hse, 1985), *Connecticut Poetry Rev.*

Carolyn C. Carrara   P
HCR 58, Box 254, East Hebron, NH 03232, 603-744-5101
    Pubs: *Sojourner, Stuff, Phoebe, Onion River Rev,
    Mockingbird, Soundings East, Sandscript, The Lucid Stone,
    Live Poets Society, Pebbles.*

Jeannine Dobbs   P
PO Box 1076, Merrimack, NH 03054
    Pubs: *Threesome Poems* (Alice James Bks, 1976), *Ohio
    Rev, Midwest Qtly, Shenandoah, Amicus Jrnl, Merrimack.*

Leigh Donaldson   P
107 Court St, Portsmouth, NH 03801
    Pubs: *City River of Voices: Anth* (West End Pr, 1991),
    *Atelier, Intl Poetry Rev, MPR, Catalyst, Cafe Rev, Obsidian
    II, Shooting Star Rev.*

William Doreski   P
79 Murphy Rd, Peterborough, NH 03458, 603-924-7987
Internet: wdoreski@keene.edu
    Pubs: *Sublime of the North* (Frith Pr, 1998), *Pianos In The
    Woods* (Pygmy Forest Pr, 1998), *Ghost Train* (Nightshade
    Pr, 1991), *The Years of Our Friendship* (U Pr of Mississippi,
    1990), *Cimarron Rev, Swamproot, Colorado Rev, Harvard
    Rev, Atlanta Rev.*

Christopher Dornin   P
1 Appleton St, Concord, NH 03301-5942
    Pubs: *Contemporary Religious Poetry: Anth* (Paulist Pr,
    1987), *Nimrod, Plains Poetry Rev, Gamut, Mudfish, Amelia,
    Blue Unicorn, Soundings East, Lucky Star.*

Merle Drown   W
60 West Parish Rd, Concord, NH 03301, 603-224-7985
Internet: drown@ink.mv.com
    Pubs: *Plowing Up A Snake* (The Dial Pr, 1982), *New
    Hampshire College Jrnl, Other Voices.*

Robert Dunn   P
53 Whidden St, Portsmouth, NH 03801
    Pubs: *Quo, Musa, Tendis* (Peter Randall, 1983), *Black &
    White, Trayfull of Lab Mice, Aspect, Bellowing Ark, CSM,
    Crow, Portsmouth Art Annual.*

Patricia Fargnoli   P
24 Beaver St, Keene, NH 03431
    Pubs: *Laurel Rev, Indiana Rev, Poetry Northwest, Poet
    Lore, Seattle Rev, Spoon River Rev, Negative Capability,
    Midwest Qtly, Poetry, Green Mtns Rev, Ploughshares,
    Cimarron, Prairie Schooner.*

Alice B. Fogel   P
PO Box 272, Washington, NH 03280, 603-446-3935
    Pubs: *I Love this Dark World, Elemental* (Zoland Bks, 1996,
    1993).

Richard Frede   W
58 Concord St, Peterborough, NH 03458-1511,
603-924-6609
    Pubs: *The Boy, The Devil, And Divorce* (Pocket Bks, 1993),
    The Nurses (NAL, 1986), *Harper's, McCall's, Short Story
    Intl, Poetry, Fantasy & Sci Fi.*

Jeff Friedman   P
PO Box 187, Hanover, NH 037550187, 603-643-8255
Internet: colleen.m.randall@dartmouth.edu
    Pubs: *Scattering the Ashes* (Carnegie Mellon Pr, 1998),
    The Record-Breaking Heat Wave (BkMk Pr, 1986),
    *American Poetry Rev, Missouri Rev, New England Rev,
    Poetry, Press, Manoa, Boulevard, Antioch Rev, 5 A.M..*

Barbara Gibbs   P
272 Middle Hancock Rd, Peterborough, NH 03458,
603-924-3487
    Pubs: *Possibility* (w/Francis Golffing; Peter Lang, 1991),
    The Meeting Place of the Colors (Cummington Pr, 1972),
    New Yorker, Yankee, Helicon 9.

Donald Hall   P&W
Eagle Pond Farm, Danbury, NH 03230
    Pubs: *Without, Old and New Poems* (Houghton Mifflin,
    1998, 1990), *New Yorker, Atlantic, Nation, New Republic,
    Gettysburg Rev, Iowa Rev.*

Marie Harris   P
PO Box 203, Barrington, NH 03825, 603-664-7654
Internet: isinglas@nh.ultranet.com
    Pubs: *Weasel in the Turkey Pen* (Hanging Loose Pr, 1992),
    *The Party Train, A Collection of North American Prose
    Poetry: Anth* (New Rivers, 1996), *Granite Rev.*

Hugh Hennedy   P
456 Lincoln Ave, Portsmouth, NH 03801, 603-431-2829
    Pubs: *Halcyon Time* (Oyster River Pr, 1993), *Tar River
    Poetry, Hawaii Rev, James Joyce Qtly, Lilliput Rev,
    Brownstone Rev.*

Elizabeth Hodges   P
30 Graham Rd, Concord, NH 03301-6900
    Pubs: *A Green Place: Anth* (Delacorte Pr, 1982), *NAR,
    Connecticut River Rev, Greenfield Rev.*

Cynthia Huntington   P
60 Lyme Rd, Hanover, NH 03755, 603-646-2321
    Pubs: *We Have Gone to the Beach* (Alice James Bks,
    1996), *The Fish-Wife* (U Hawaii Pr, 1986), *Kenyon Rev,
    NER, Ploughshares, Agni.*

J. Kates P
PO Box 221, Fitzwilliam, NH 03447
Internet: jkates@monad.net
    Pubs: *XY Files: Poems on the Male Experience: Anth* (Sherman Asher, 1997), *The Gospels in Our Image: Anth* (HB, 1995), *Cream City Rev, Spoon River Rev, Cyphers, Florida Rev, Mississippi Rev, Crab Creek Rev, Denver Qtly.*

Dolores Kendrick P
Phillips Exeter Academy, Exeter, NH 03833
    Pubs: *The Women of Plums* (PEA Pr, 1991), *Columbia, Ms..*

Lawrence Kinsman P&W
PO Box 305, Manchester, NH 03105-0305
Internet: lkinsman@minerva.nhc.edu
    Pubs: *A Well-Ordered Life, Water From the Moon* (Abelard, 1998, 1995), *Kentucky Poetry Rev, MacGuffin, Pacific Rev.*

Maxine Kumin P&W
40 Harriman Ln, Warner, NH 03278, 603-456-3709
    Pubs: *Women, Animals, And Vegetables: Essays and Stories, Looking For Luck* (Norton, 1994, 1992), *Nurture* (Viking, 1989).

Ron Kurz W
PO Box 164, Antrim, NH 03440, 603-588-3323
    Pubs: *Black Rococo, Lethal Gas* (M. Evans, 1976, 1974).

Nancy Lagomarsino P
6 Brook Rd, Hanover, NH 03755, 603-643-3959
    Pubs: *The Secretary Parables, Sleep Handbook* (Alice James Bks, 1991, 1987).

Esther M. Leiper P
Box 87, Jefferson, NH 03583, 603-586-4505
    Pubs: *The Wars Of Faery* (Amelia, 1994), *Stone Country* (Caro-Lynn Pub, 1993), *Writer's Jrnl, North Country Weekly, The Answer.*

P. H. Liotta P&W
Box 856, Exeter, NH 03833
    Pubs: *Rules of Engagement* (Cleveland State U Poetry Ctr, 1991).

Ruth Doan MacDougall W
285 Range Rd, Center Sandwich, NH 03227, 603-284-6451
Internet: ruthdoanmacdougall@yahoo.com
    Pubs: *50 More Hikes in New Hampshire* (Countryman Pr, 1998), *The Cheerleader* (Frigate Bks, 1998), *Snowy* (St. Martin's Pr, 1993), *A Lovely Time Was Had By All* (Atheneum, 1982).

Rodger Martin P&W
Goosebrook, RR2 Box 72A, Peterborough, NH 03458, 603-924-7342
Internet: ujbh15b@prodigy.com
    Pubs: *The Nemo Poems* (Goosebrook, 1992), *Selected Poems of Contemporary European & American Poets: Anth* (Spring Breeze Pub, 1989), *Granite Rev, Appalachia.*

Cleopatra Mathis P
13 E Wheelock St, Hanover, NH 03755-2137, 603-643-8781
    Pubs: *Guardian, The Center for Cold Weather, The Bottom Land, Aerial View of Louisiana* (Sheep Meadow Pr, 1995, 1990, 1983, 1980).

Bridget Mazur W
Lebanon College, 1 Court St, Lebanon, NH 03766
    Pubs: *Iowa Rev, Shenandoah, Beloit Fiction Jrnl, Buffalo Spree, Apalachee Qtly, Cimarron, Buffalo Magazine.*

Mekeel McBride P
Univ New Hampshire, English Dept, Hamilton Smith, Durham, NH 03824, 603-862-4216
    Pubs: *Red Letter Days, The Going Under of the Evening Land* (Carnegie Mellon U Pr, 1988, 1983).

Rollande Merz P
Province Rd, Box 70A, Strafford, NH 03884, 603-664-9952
    Pubs: *Pictures: Life & Still Life* (Andrew Mountain Pr, 1984), *Calliope, Bitterroot.*

Edith Milton W
PO Box 237, Francestown, NH 03043-0237
    Pubs: *Best American Short Stories: Anth* (HM, 1988), *Ploughshares, Tikkun, Witness, Yale Rev, Prairie Schooner.*

Deborah Navas W
1-H Bass St, Newmarket, NH 03857
    Pubs: *Things We Lost, Gave Away, Bought High and Sold Low* (SMU Pr, 1992), *New Fiction from New England: Anth* (Yankee Bks, 1986), *PEN Syndicated Fiction.*

Julia Older P&W
PO Box 174, Hancock, NH 03449-0174
    Pubs: *Hermaphroditus in America, Higher Latitudes, The Island Queen: Celia Thaxter of the Isles of Shoals* (Appledore Bks, 1999, 1995, 1994), *Two Worlds Walking: Anth* (New Rivers Pr, 1995), *Worcester Rev, Apalachee Qtly, New Yorker.*

Rebecca Rule W
178 Mountain Ave, Northwood, NH 03261, 603-942-8174
Internet: butterflea@aol.com
    Pubs: *The Best Revenge* (U Pr New England, 1995), *Creating The Story* (w/Susan Wheeler; Heinemann, 1993), *Yankee, Echoes, Whetstone, Northern Rev.*

Steve Sherman   W
P.O. Box 174, Hancock, NH 034490174, 603-525-3581
Pubs: *The Maple Sugar Murders* (Appledore, 1998), *The
Hangtree* (Major Bks, 1977), *Ellery Queen.*

Charles Simic   P&W
P.O. Box 192, Strafford, NH 038840192, 603-664-2101
Pubs: *Orphan Factory* (Michigan U, 1997), *Walking the
Black Cat, A Wedding In Hell, The Book of Gods and Devils*
(HB, 1996, 1994, 1990), *Selected Poems* (Braziller, 1990).

Mark Smith   W
Univ New Hampshire, Hamilton-Smith, Durham, NH 03824,
603-862-1313
Pubs: *Smoke Street, Doctor Blues* (Morrow, 1984, 1983),
The Delphinium Girl (H&R, 1980).

Sidney L. Surface   P&W
17 Old Milford Rd, Brookline, NH 03033, 603-673-4943
Internet: shall@jlc.net
Pubs: *Small Town Tales, What We Will Give Each Other*
(Hobblebush Bks, 1997, 1993), *Dog Music: Anth* (St.
Martin's, 1996), *L.A. Times Book Rev, Graham House Rev,
Chattahoochee Rev, California Qtly, Hollins Critic, Midwest
Qtly.*

Parker Towle   P
836 Easton Valley Rd, Franconia, NH 03580, 603-823-8157
Internet: parker.a.towle@dartmouth.edu
Pubs: *Our Places* (Andrew Mountain Pr, 1998), *Handwork*
(Nightshade Pr, 1991), *Search for Doubloons* (Wings Pr,
1984), *Appalachia, Blueline, Cape Rock, Calliope, Great
River Rev, Galley Sail Rev.*

Donald Wellman   P
21 Rockland Rd, Weare, NH 03281, 603-529-1060
Internet: wellman@disney.dwc.edu
Pubs: *Fields* (Light & Dust, 1995), *Frames, Fields,
Meanings* (O.ars, 1993), *Generator, Tyuonyi, Room,
Puckerbrush Rev, O.ars, Boundary 2.*

W. D. Wetherell   W
PO Box 84, Lyme, NH 03768
Pubs: *The Wisest Man in America* (U Pr New England,
1995), *Chekhov's Sister* (Little, Brown, 1990).

Marc Widershien   P
Four Arts, Main St, PO Box 641, Wilton, NH 03086
Pubs: *Essays #0-11* (Four Arts, 1994), *Middle Journeys*
(Northwoods Pr, 1994), *Atelier, Small Press Rev, Library
Jrnl, New Directions, Small Mag Rev.*

NEW JERSEY

Teresa Anderson   P
83 Boream, #2, Jersey City, NJ 07307
Pubs: *Speaking In Sign* (West End Pr, 1978), *New Poets:
Women, Best Friends, Anima, Sunsprout.*

Marion Arenas   P
694 Birchwood Dr, Wyckoff, NJ 07481, 201-891-1051
Pubs: *The U-U Poets: Anth* (Pudding Hse Pubs, 1996), *Life
on the Line: Anth* (Negative Capability Pr, 1992), *New York
Qtly, Jrnl of New Jersey Poets, The Lyric.*

Sylvia Argow   P
52 Clark St, Glen Ridge, NJ 07028-2208
Pubs: *Poet, Bitterroot.*

Renee Ashley   P&W
210 Skylands Rd, Ringwood, NJ 07456, 973-962-1142
Internet: reneea@bellatlantic.net
Pubs: *The Various Reasons of Light* (Avocet Pr, 1998), *Salt*
(U Wisconsin Pr, 1991), *Writing Poems: Anth* (HC, 1996),
Breaking Up is Hard to Do: Anth (Crossing Pr, 1993),
*Harvard Rev, American Voice, Kenyon Rev, Antioch Rev,
Colorado Rev, 5 a.m., Indiana Rev.*

Jay Stuart Auslander   P
270 Briarcliffe Rd, Teaneck, NJ 07666, 201-837-1294
Internet: auslander@whafh.com
Pubs: *A New Majority* (Broncho Pr, 1987), *The MacGuffin,
Orphic Lute, Lucky Star, Blow, Connecticut River Rev, Jrnl
of American Medical Assoc., Sonoma Mandala.*

Beth Bahler   P&W
201 S Livingston, #2F, Livingston, NJ 07039
Pubs: *Parting Gifts, Footwork, New York Times, Pinehurst
Jrnl, Lilliput, Highlights for Children.*

Neil Baldwin   P
17 Burnside St, Upper Montclair, NJ 07043, 201-783-1008

Benjamin R. Barber   W
Rutgers Univ, New Brunswick, NJ 08903
Pubs: *Marriage Voices* (S&S, 1981), *Harper's, Salmagundi.*

Jan Barry   P
109 N Mountain Ave, Montclair, NJ 07042-2339,
973-746-5941
Pubs: *From Both Sides Now: Vietnam War & After: Anth*
(Scribner, 1998), *Radical Visions, Poetry By Viet Nam
Veterans* (U Georgia Pr, 1994), *Carrying The Darkness:
Anth* (Texas Tech U Pr, 1989), *Jrnl of American Culture,
Waterways, Footwork, Young Citizen.*

Ronald D. Bascombe P
39 Green Village Rd #102, Madison, NJ 07940-2588,
201-377-1597
Pubs: *Black Creation, 360 Degrees Of Blackness Comin' At You, The Universal Black Writer.*

Carol Becker P&W
37 Sayre Dr, Princeton, NJ 08540, 609-987-0282
Pubs: *Harvard Mag, College English, Redstart Plus, Yankee, American Voice, Small Pond Mag.*

Ahn Behrens P
295 Grove St, Jersey City, NJ 07302-3602, 201-451-1074
Pubs: *Movieworks Movieworks* (Little Theatre Pr, 1990), *What's A Nice Girl Like You...: Anth* (Crossing Pr, 1992), *Stet Mag, Pan, McCall's, Hoboken Terminal, Buffalo News.*

Emily Trafford Berges W
Jersey City State College, 2039 Kennedy Blvd, Jersey City, NJ 07305, 201-200-3100
Pubs: *The Flying Circus* (Morrow, 1985).

Laura Boss P
Lips, PO Box 1345, Montclair, NJ 07042, 201-662-1303
Pubs: *Reports from the Front, On the Edge of the Hudson* (CCC, 1995, 1989), *Unsettling America: Anth* (Viking/Penguin, 1994), *Abraxas, Greenfield Rev, New York Times.*

Claude Brown W
381 Broad St, #1605, Newark, NJ 07104

Sal St. John Buttaci P
PO Box 887, Saddle Brook, NJ 07662-0887, 201-772-4636
Pubs: *Bereavement Mag, Anemone, Black Mountain, Christian Science Monitor, Thirteen, Pudding.*

Kevin O. Byrne P
24 Dogwood Ln, New Providence, NJ 07974, 908-464-2711
Pubs: *The Panhandler, Poet & Critic, Bitterroot, CQ, Cottonwood, Concerning Poetry, Wisconsin Rev.*

Richard Carboni P
38 Marion Rd, Montclair, NJ 07043, 973-783-0598

Rafael Catala P&W
Ometeca Institute, PO Box 38, New Brunswick, NJ 08903-0038, 908-435-0152
Internet: catala@mariner.rutgers.edu
Pubs: *Escobas De Milo* (Ometeca Institute & Ventura One, 1998), *Cuban Poets In New York: Anth* (Betania Madrid, 1988), *Ometeca, Trasimagen, Paterson Literary Rev, Realidad Aparte, Poesia De Venezuela.*

Suzy McKee Charnas W
400 Highland Ave, Upper Montclair, NJ 07043, 201-783-3631
Pubs: *The Golden Thread, The Silver Glove* (Bantam, 1989, 1988), *Dorothea Dream* (Arbor House, 1986).

Roberta Chester P
234 Passaic Ave, Passaic, NJ 07055-3603
Pubs: *The Eloquent Edge: Anth of Maine Women Writers* (Acadia Pr, 1989), *Tar River Poetry.*

Donna L. Clovis P&W
PO Box 0741, Princeton Junction, NJ 08550-0741
Pubs: *Struggles for Freedom* (Dillon Pub, 1994), *Survival Through These Hard Times, Metamorphosis* (Northwoods Pr, 1991, 1988), *Highlights, Instructor, Teaching and Learning.*

Peter Cole P
46 Basswood Terr, Wayne, NJ 07470, 201-839-7472
Pubs: *Rift* (Station Hill Pr, 1990), *Tel Aviv Rev, Agni Rev, Conjunctions, Scripsi, Partisan Rev.*

Edmund Conti P
79 Tulip St, Summit, NJ 07901, 908-273-7632
Internet: edmundpoet@aol.com
Pubs: *The Ed C. Scrolls, Eddies* (Runaway Spoon Pr, 1996, 1994), *Light, Light Year, Abbey, Lyric, Studies in Contemporary Satire, Bogg.*

David Cope P
Humana Press, 999 Riverview Dr, Ste #2, Totowa, NJ 07512, 201-256-1699
Pubs: *Coming Home, Fragments From the Stars, On the Bridge Quiet Lives* (Humana Pr, 1993, 1990, 1986), *Sierra, Lame Duck, Napalm Health Spa, Heaven Bone.*

Steven Corbin W
168 3rd St, Jersey City, NJ 07302-2514
Pubs: *Fragments That Remain* (GMP Ltd, 1992), *No Easy Place To Be* (S&S, 1989), *Breaking Ice, More Like Minds, Passport 3.*

Louie Crew P
PO Box 30, Newark, NJ 07101, 973-485-4503
Internet: lcrew@newark.rutgers.edu
Pubs: *Book of Revelations* (Integrity, 1991), *From Queen Lutibelle's Pew* (Dragon Disks, 1990), *Midnight Lessons* (Samisdat, 1987).

Paula Bramsen Cullen P
980 Stuart Rd, Princeton, NJ 08540, 609-924-9128
Pubs: *Journey of Storms* (Millstone River Pr, 1994), *Cimarron Rev, Kansas Qtly, Connecticut Fireside & Book Rev, Poem.*

Walter Cummins W
Fairleigh Dickinson Univ, 285 Madison Ave, Madison, NJ 07940, 973-443-8564
Internet: wcummins@worldnet.att.net
Pubs: *Where We Live* (Lynx Hse Pr, 1983), *Witness* (Samisdat, 1975), *Virginia Qtly Rev, Cottonwood, Other Voices, Laurel Rev, Confrontation, North Atlantic Rev.*

Anne E. Cusack   P
975 Garrison Ave, Teaneck, NJ 07666, 201-836-4790
   Pubs: *Chelsea, Northeast Journal, 13th Moon, Open Places.*

Mona Da Vinci   P&W
65 Spruce St, Bloomfield, NJ 07003, 201-748-6275
   Pubs: *Out Of This World, Unnatural Acts, The Herald.*

Suzanne Dale   P
501 Monument Rd, Pine Beach, NJ 08741

Alice Elliott Dark   W
284 Grove St, Montclair, NJ 07042-4209
Internet: aedark@aol.com
   Pubs: *The Betty Book* (S&S, 1997), *Naked to the Waist, The Best American Short Stories: Anth* (HM, 1991, 1994), *New Yorker.*

Melody Davis   P&W
24 Childsworth Ave, Bernardsville, NJ 07924, 908-630-0572
Internet: melodydavis@juno.com
   Pubs: *The Center of Distance* (Nightshade Pr, 1992), *Chelsea, Brooklyn Rev, Poetry, Beloit Poetry Jrnl, West Branch, Poetry Northwest, Verse, Sing Heavenly Muse!.*

Elaine Denholtz   W
13 Birchwood Dr, Livingston, NJ 07039, 973-992-5480
   Pubs: *Playing For High Stakes* (Freundlich, 1986), *Having it Both Ways* (Stein & Day, 1981), *New Jersey, Woman, New Woman, Daily Record.*

C. K. DeRugeris   P
820 Route 50, Woodbine, NJ 08270-9612, 609-624-9304
   Pubs: *The.* (MAF Pr, 1989), *Rolling Stone, Painted Bride Qtly, Truly Fine Pr, James White Rev, Chiron Rev, Poetry Peddler, Snakeskin, Lilliput Rev.*

Emanuel Di Pasquale   P
392 Ocean Ave, #1G, Long Branch, NJ 07740, 908-222-6313
   Pubs: *Genesis* (Jostro, 1997), *Literature* (HC, 1993), *Men of Our Time* (Georgia U Pr, 1991), *APR, Sewanee Rev, Nation, New York Qtly, New York Times.*

Constance Mary Diana   P
PO Box 474, East Brunswick, NJ 08816
Internet: poetess27@aol.com
   Pubs: *Is That You My God* (Zinnia Bks, 1997).

Juditha Dowd   P
179 Old Turnpike Rd, Califon, NJ 07830, 908-439-2144
   Pubs: *Earth's Daughters, Black Fly Rev, California Qtly, Jrnl of New Jersey Poets, U.S. 1 Worksheets, Footwork, Kelsey Rev, Exit 13.*

John Drexel   P
42 Edgewood Rd, Glen Ridge, NJ 07028, 973-680-8834
   Pubs: *Where Icarus Falls: Anth* (Santa Barbara Rev, 1998), *Paris Rev, Acumen, Verse, Hampden-Sydney Poetry Rev, Seneca Rev, Illuminations, Oxford Poetry, Southern Rev, Hudson Rev, Outposts, Image, Salmagundi.*

Rosalyn Drexler   P
60 Union St #1S, Newark, NJ 07105, 201-578-8552
   Pubs: *Transients Welcome* (Broadway Play Publishing, 1984), *Bad Guy* (Dutton, 1982).

Sandra R. Duguid   P
114 Forest Ave, West Caldwell, NJ 07006, 201-226-1096
   Pubs: *Jrnl of New Jersey Poets, Anglican Theological Rev, Earth's Daughters, Modern Poetry Studies, West Branch, Connecticut Writer.*

Lora Dunetz   P
PO Box 113, Whiting, NJ 08759, 732-350-9236
   Pubs: *To Guard Your Sleep and Other Poems* (Icarus, 1987), *Anth of American Mag Verse 1997, Hellas, Without Halos, Blue Unicorn, Ararat, Amelia, Baltimore Rev, New Renaissance.*

Stephen Dunn   P
445 Chestnut Neck Rd, Port Republic, NJ 08241, 609-652-1456
Internet: sdunn55643@aol.com
   Pubs: *Riffs & Reciprocities, Loosestrife, New & Selected Poems: 1974-1994, Landscape at the End of the Century, Between Angels* (Norton, 1998, 1996, 1994, 1991, 1989).

Howard Linn Edsall   W
The Carriage House, 39-A N Mountain Ave, Montclair, NJ 07042, 201-744-8434
   Pubs: *Successful Farming, Harper's, Saturday Evening Post, The American, London Graphic, Holland's.*

Wendy Einhorn   P
234 Passaic Ave, Passaic, NJ 07055, 201-472-1330
   Pubs: *Do Not Say That She Is Happy Being Crazy* (Einhorn, 1975), *New Maine Writing, Kennebec.*

Ruth F. Eisenberg   P
31 Hickory Dr, Maplewood, NJ 07040-2107
   Pubs: *Balance Point* (San Diego Poets Pr, 1989), *The McGraw-Hill Book of Poetry: Anth* (McGraw-Hill, 1993), *Earth's Daughters, Blue Unicorn, Images.*

K. S. Ernst   P
13 Yard Ave, Farmingdale, NJ 07727, 908-938-4297
   Pubs: *Sequencing* (Xerox Sutra Edtns, 1984), *Interstate, Earth's Daughters, Lost & Found Times.*

Karen Ethelsdattar   P
229 Ogden Ave, Jersey City, NJ 07307, 201-653-3523
Internet: ethelsdatr@aol.com
   Pubs: *The Spiral Dance* (H&R, 1979), *At Our Core: Women
   Writing About Power: Anth, If I Had My Life To Live Over I
   Would Pick More Daisies: Anth* (Papier-Mache Pr, 1998,
   1992), *Christmas Blues: Beyond the Holiday Mask: Anth*
   (Amador Pub, 1995), *CSM, Enchante.*

Prescott Evarts, Jr.   P
19 Linden Ave, West Long Branch, NJ 07764, 201-222-4205
   Pubs: *Harvard Mag, Hudson Rev, Cimarron Rev, Nebraska
   Rev, Beloit Poetry Jrnl, Kansas Qtly.*

Firth Haring Fabend   W
54 Elston Rd, Upper Montclair, NJ 07043, 201-746-5336
   Pubs: *A Dutch Family in the Middle Colonies, 1660-1800*
   (Rutgers U, 1991).

Sean-Thomas Farragher   P
PO Box 1903, Cliffside Park, NJ 07010-1903, 201-840-9122
Internet: seanfarragher@msn.com
   Pubs: *Modern Rivers, Taxi Murders Sextet Vol. V Christina*
   (Hudson River Pr, 1998, 1997), *Bluestones & Salthay: Anth*
   (Rutgers U Pr, 1990), *Home Planet News, Dublin Mag,
   Journal of New Jersey Poets, Hipnosis, Beloit Poetry Jrnl.*

Marta Fenyves   P
Riverside Gdn #21, Hackettstown, NJ 07840-2402
   Pubs: *From A Distance* (Warthog Pr, 1981), *Exile: Anth*
   (Milkweed, 1990), *Messages From The Heart, Home Planet
   News, Relativity, New York Qtly, Helen Rev.*

Patricia Fillingham   P
29 S Valley Rd, West Orange, NJ 07052, 201-731-9269
   Pubs: *Report To The Interim Shareholders, John Calvin*
   (Warthog Pr, 1991, 1988).

Frank Finale   P
19 Quail Run, Bayville, NJ 08721-1376, 732-237-0776
   Pubs: *Shore Stories: Anth, Under a Gull's Wing: Anth*
   (Down the Shore Pub, 1998, 1996), *First Light: Anth*
   (Calypso, 1996), *Negative Capability, new renaissance,
   ELF, Footwork, Lips, Press, Paterson Literary Rev, Blue
   Unicorn, U.S. 1 Worksheets.*

Patricia Ellen Flinn   W
PO Box 2, Gillette, NJ 07933
   Pubs: *Loss of the Ground-Note: Anth* (Clothespin Fever Pr,
   1992), *Lynx Eye, Lullwater Rev, Alabama Literary Rev,
   Mind In Motion, Portable Wall, Portland Rev.*

Nancy Flynn   P&W
115 Mine Hill Rd, Hackettstown, NJ 07840, 201-852-5912
   Pubs: *Room, Because You Talk, Gallery Works, Minotaur,
   Anthropology Of Work Rev, Center.*

Edward Foster   P
Talisman House Publishers, PO Box 3157, Jersey City, NJ
07303-3157, 201-938-0698
   Pubs: *The Boy In The Key of E* (Goats & Compasses,
   1998), *All Acts Are Simply Acts* (Rodent Pr, 1995), *The
   Understanding* (Texture Pr, 1994), *Boston Book Rev, River
   City, Bombay Gin, Five Fingers Rev, Boxkite, American
   Letters & Commentary.*

Hanna Fox   W
Fox Associates, 175 Hamilton Ave, Princeton, NJ
08540-3857, 609-924-2990
Internet: foxly@aol.com
   Pubs: *Transatlantic Rev, Jewish Frontier, Jewish Roots,
   Kelsey Rev.*

Sheldon Frank   W
221 Jackson St, #9J, Hoboken, NJ 07030, 201-653-7534

Robert A. Frauenglas   P&W
2624 Roseland Terr, #19, Maplewood, NJ 63143-2328,
314-647-9002
   Pubs: *The Eclectic Musings of a Brooklyn Bum* (Somrie Pr,
   1980), *Blood to Remember: Anth* (Texas Tech U Pr, 1991),
   Scottish Book Collector, Cups, Waterways.

Mary Freericks   P
450 Vera Pl, Paramus, NJ 07652, 201-261-8930
   Pubs: *The Southern California Anth* (USC, 1988), *Ararat,
   Christian Science Monitor.*

Thomas Friedmann   W
The Writer's Workbench, PO Box 117, Marlboro, NJ 07746
   Pubs: *Skills in Sequence* (St. Martin's Pr, 1988), *Damaged
   Goods* (Permanent Pr, 1984), *Footworks.*

Paul Genega   P
Bloomfield College, Bloomfield, NJ 07003, 201-748-9000
   Pubs: *Striking Water* (Ireland; Salmon, 1989), *Seagirt* (A
   Musty Bone, 1988), *Nation, Epoch.*

Dan Georgakas   P&W
Smyra Press, PO Box 1151, Union City, NJ 070871151,
201-617-7247
   Pubs: *New to North America* (Burning Bush, 1997),
   Solidarity Forever (Lake View Pr, 1985), *Greece in Print,
   Greek American, Greek Star, Mr. Cogito, Odyssey Mag.*

Emery George   P
16 Buckingham Ave, Trenton, NJ 08618-3312, 609-984-8375
   Pubs: *A Year In Poetry: Anth* (Crown Pubs, 1995),
   Contemporary East European Poetry: Anth (Oxford U Pr,
   1993), *Blue Unicorn, Denver Qtly, Partisan Rev, Jrnl of New
   Jersey Poets.*

Richard Gessner P&W
PO Box 661, Montclair, NJ 070420661, 201-744-1744
Pubs: *Excerpts from the Diary of a Neanderthal Dilettante
and the Man in the Couch* (Bombshelter, 1991), *Air Fish:
Anth* (Cat's Eye Bks, 1993), *Happy, The Pannus Index,
Java Snob, Devil Blossoms, Raw Vision.*

Janet Frances Gibbs P&W
39 Tiffany Dr, East Hanover, NJ 07936, 201-386-8987
Pubs: *Past and Promise—Women of New Jersey: Anth*
(Scarecrow Pr, 1990), *Bitterroot, Sandsounds, Poetic Page,
Footworks.*

Maria Mazziotti Gillan P
40 Post Ave, Hawthorne, NJ 07506, 201-423-2921
Internet: mgillan@pccc.cc.nj.us
Pubs: *Where I Come From: New and Selected Poems*
(Guernica Edtns, 1995), *Unsettling America: Anth* (Viking,
1994), *New Myths, Borderlands, Poetry Ireland, CSM,
Connecticut Rev, LIPS.*

Daniela Gioseffi PP&P&W
PO Box 15, Andover, NJ 07821-0015, 973-786-7947
Internet: daniela@garden.net
Pubs: *Word Wounds & Water Flowers* (Via/Purdue U,
1996), *On Prejudice: Anth* (Anchor, 1993), *Paris Rev,
Nation, American Book Rev, Ms., Hungry Mind Rev, Prairie
Schooner, Poetry East.*

Martin Golan P
196 Inwood Ave, Upper Montclair, NJ 07043
Pubs: *Bitterroot, Poet Lore, The Literary Rev.*

Lester Goldberg W
18 Woods Hole Rd, Cranford, NJ 07016, 908-276-4020
Pubs: *In Siberia It Is Very Cold* (Dembner Bks, 1987), *One
More River* (U Illinois Pr, 1978), *Ascent, Wind, Literary Rev,
Epoch, Iowa Rev, Cimarron Rev.*

Edward M. Goldman P
43 W 32 St, Bayonne, NJ 07002, 201-436-4796
Pubs: *Emes Mit Poemes* (Chortelach Pr, 1992), *Where
Dreams Begin* (Watermark Pr, 1993), *Mature Years, Aim,
New Leaves, The Disciple, Thirteen Poetry Mag.*

Marion Goldstein P
84 Highland Ave, Montclair, NJ 07042, 973-746-0726
Internet: miggold@aol.com
Pubs: *The Tie That Binds: Anth* (Papier-Mache Pr, 1988),
CSM, Pivot, Croton Rev.

Bonnie Gordon W
1001 N Kings Hwy #410, Cherry Hill, NJ 08034,
609-321-1363
Internet: bgordon@voicenet.com
Pubs: *Thus May Be Figured In Numberless Ways* (Swamp
Pr, 1985), *Sapiens, ADZ, Sarcophagus, Tracks.*

Roger Granet P
261 James St, Ste 2E, Morristown, NJ 07960, 201-540-9490
Pubs: *The World's A Small Town* (Negative Capability Pr,
1993).

Max Greenberg P
127 Aycrigg Ave, Passaic, NJ 07055, 201-778-0937
Pubs: *Country of the Old* (Chrysalis Pr, 1982), *Present
Tense.*

Patricia Celley Groth P
Tree House Press, Inc., PO Box 268, Ringoes, NJ
08551-1029, 908-806-3446
Internet: 10274111611@compuserve.com
Pubs: *The Gods' Eyes: Stories From Fatherline* (Dupinc,
1998), *Before the Beginning* (Belle Pr, 1987), *US1
Worksheets, Journal of New Jersey Poets, Paterson Lit
Rev, Encore, Stone Court.*

James Haba P
436 E Mountain Rd, Belle Mead, NJ 08502, 908-874-6209
Pubs: *Ten Love Poems* (Ally Pr, 1981), *Jrnl of New Jersey
Poets, Paterson Literary Rev, U.S. 1 Worksheets, Sunrust,
George Washington Rev.*

Daniel Halpern P
100 W Broad St, Hopewell, NJ 08525
Pubs: *Selected Poems, Foreign Neon* (Knopf, 1994, 1991),
Tango, Seasonal Rights, The Art of the Tale: Anth (Viking,
1987, 1982, 1986).

Alfred Starr Hamilton P
41 S Willow St, Montclair, NJ 07042
Pubs: *The Big Parade* (Best Cellar Pr, 1982), *APR.*

Patrick Hammer, Jr. P
400 Fairview Ave, #3E, Fort Lee, NJ 07024, 201-585-0435
Pubs: *Elements* (North River Pr, 1993), *The Yank: Irish
Poems, Coming to Light* (Sub Rosa Pr, 1989, 1987), *Poet,
North River Rev.*

Joan Cusack Handler P
6 Horizon Rd, Fort Lee, NJ 07024, 201-224-9653
Pubs: *Westview, Southern Humanities Rev, Poetry East,
Agni, Painted Bride Qtly, Feminist Studies, Confrontation,
Kalliope, Madison Rev, Negative Capability, Jrnl of New
Jersey Poets.*

Jon Hansen P
111 Loring Ave, Edison, NJ 08817
Pubs: *Southern Poetry Rev, Poetry Now, Intro II, Chicago
Rev, Cottonwood, Ironwood, Calliope.*

Terri Hardin P
19 Morford Pl, Apt 3B, Red Bank, NJ 07701-1042,
908-530-6490
Internet: terrih1742@aol.com
Pubs: *Nimue* (Guignol Bks, 1984), *Cuz I & II, Dyslexia.*

Y. L. Harris   W
23 Topeka Pass, Willingboro, NJ 08046, 609-871-5168
   Pubs: *Hindu-Kush* (Ashley Bks, 1990).

Lois Marie Harrod   P
111 Taylor Terr, Hopewell, NJ 08525, 609-466-1945
Internet: lmharrod@worldnet.att.net
   Pubs: *Part of the Deeper Sea* (Palaquin U Pr of South
   Carolina, 1997), *Crazy Alice, Every Twinge A Verdict* (Belle
   Mead Pr, 1991, 1987), *APR, Prairie Schooner, Carolina
   Qtly, Zone 3, Literary Rev.*

Elizabeth Hartman   P
127 Westmont Ave, Haddonfield, NJ 08033, 609-354-9061
Internet: 72122.1310@compuserve.com
   Pubs: *Dreams of the Heroic Muse: Anth* (New Worlds
   Unlimited, 1982), *Eternal Echoes: Anth* (Poetry Pr, 1982),
   *Jersey Woman, Poetry Scope, Midwest Poetry Rev,
   Encore, Day Tonight/Night Today, Bitterroot.*

Sheila Hellman   P
100 High St, Leonia, NJ 07605, 201-947-5534
   Pubs: *Positions* (Perivale Pr, 1992), *Kansas Qtly, Poets On,
   Confrontation, Saturday Evening Post, Ms., Minnesota Rev,
   Stone Country, Greenfield Rev.*

David Sten Herrstrom   P
Box 219, Roosevelt, NJ 08555, 609-443-4421
   Pubs: *Appearing by Daylight* (Aegina Pr, 1993), *The
   Disappearance of Jonah* (Ambrosia Pr, 1989), *Footwork,
   Nimrod, U.S. 1 Worksheets, Stone Country, Columbia, New
   River.*

Mark Hillringhouse   P
Passaic Community College, College Blvd, Paterson, NJ
07509, 201-684-5582
Internet: mhillringhouse@pccc.cc.nj.us
   Pubs: *Chester H. Jones Natl Poetry Winners: Anth* (Chester
   H. Jones Fdn, 1996), *Bluestones & Salthay: Anth* (Rutgers
   U Pr, 1991), *Hanging Loose, New Jersey Monthly, Literary
   Rev, Blade, APR.*

Madeline Hoffer   P&W
Mercer County College ET135, 1200 Old Trenton Rd,
Trenton, NJ 08690, 609-655-2774
   Pubs: *Classical Outlook, Thema, Kelsey Rev, Conservative
   Rev, Exit 13, Encodings, California Qtly.*

Jean Hollander   P
592 Provinceline Rd, Hopewell, NJ 08525
   Pubs: *Moondog* (QRL, 1996), *Crushed Into Honey*
   (Saturday Pr, 1986), *Sewanee Rev, American Scholar,
   Poem, Southern Humanities Rev.*

Judah Jacobowitz   P
6 Cleveland Ln, RD 4, Princeton, NJ 08540, 732-329-6306
Internet: Bianca1@erols.com
   Pubs: *A Taste of Bonaparte* (Golden Quill Pr, 1990),
   *Massachusetts Rev, River City, Small Pond, Green
   Mountains Rev, Touchstone, Crab Creek Rev.*

Dana Andrew Jennings   W
34 Godfrey Rd, Montclair, NJ 07043-1330
   Pubs: *Woman of Granite* (HBJ, 1992), *Mosquito Games*
   (Ticknor & Fields, 1989).

Maynard Johnson   P
1907 Sunset Ave, Surf City, NJ 08008, 609-361-9630
Internet: wgcl09a@prodigy.com
   Pubs: *National Poetry Jrnl, Black Bear Rev, Lehigh Valley
   Anth, Chester Country Anth.*

Morris A. Kalmus   P
227 Sandringham Rd, Cherry Hill, NJ 08003
   Pubs: *Prophetic Voices, Heartland Jrnl, Dan River Anth,
   Reflect, Common Ground, Poets Corner.*

Edward Kaplan   P
213 Deland Ave, Cherry Hill, NJ 08034, 609-429-1836
   Pubs: *Mechos* (Scotland; Glennifer Pr, 1983), *Pancratium*
   (Swamp Pr, 1978), *Adz, Sapiens, Sulfur, Menu, Black Box,
   Red Handbook II.*

Milton Kaplan   P
554 Summit Ave, Oradell, NJ 07649, 201-265-6204
   Pubs: *In A Time Between Wars* (Norton, 1973), *Radio &
   Poetry* (Columbia, 1949).

Jaleelah Karriem   P
6907 Sussex Ave, #6907, East Orange, NJ 07018,
201-672-5205
   Pubs: *a gathering of hands...tryin' to keep time & tryin' to
   make a difference* (Ngoma's Gourd, 1991),
   blackbooksbulletin (Third World, 1991), *Essence.*

Adele Kenny   P
207 Coriell Ave, Fanwood, NJ 07023-1613, 908-889-7223
   Pubs: *At the Edge of the Woods, Castles & Dragons*
   (Yorkshire Hse Bks/Muse-Pie Pr, 1997, 1990), *Haiku
   Moment* (Charles E. Tuttle, 1993), *Sing Heavenly Muse,
   Footwork, Black Swan Rev.*

M. Deiter Keyishian   P&W
Fairleigh Dickinson Univ, 285 Madison Ave, Madison, NJ
07940, 973-267-7901
Internet: majorie@alpha.fdu.edu
   Pubs: *Literary Rev, Ararat, Laurel Rev, Arts Mag, Fiction,
   Massachusetts Rev.*

Kathryn Kilgore   P
20 Nassau St, Ste 226, Princeton, NJ 08542, 212-865-5657
Internet: kilgorekey@aol.com
   Pubs: *Something For Nothing* (Seaview Bks, 1982).

Burt Kimmelman P
9 Lancaster Ave, Maplewood, NJ 07040, 201-763-8761
Internet: kimmelman@admin.njit.edu
    Pubs: *Musaics* (Spuyten Duyvil Pr, 1992), *Natural Process*
    (Hill & Wang, 1970), *Mudfish, First Intensity, Pequod,*
    Poetry New York, Sagetrieb, Talisman, House Organ, Lo
    Straniero.

Kinni Kinnict P
113 Clover St, Mt Holly, NJ 08060
    Pubs: *Crosscurrents, Archer, The Poet, Touchstone, San*
    Fernando Poetry Jrnl, Undinal Songs.

August Kleinzahler P
Box 842, Fort Lee, NJ 07024
    Pubs: *Red Sauce, Whiskey and Snow* (Farrar, Straus &
    Giroux, 1995), *New York Times, London Rev of Bks, New*
    Yorker, Harper's.

Warren Kliewer P
281 Lincoln Ave, Secaucus, NJ 07094, 201-863-6436
    Pubs: *Liars and Rascals: Anth* (U Waterloo Pr, 1989),
    Arkansas Rev, Potato Eyes Literary Mag, Cincinnati Poetry
    Rev, Kansas Qtly.

Nicholas Kolumban P
150 W Summit St, Somerville, NJ 08876, 201-526-0682
    Pubs: *Surgery On My Soul* (Box Turtle Pr, 1996), *Reception*
    at the Mongolian Embassy, The Talking of Hands: Anth
    (New Rivers Pr, 1987, 1998), *APR, Iowa Rev, Poetry East,*
    Artful Dodge, Chariton Rev, Michigan Qtly Rev.

Yusef Komunyakaa P
185 Nassau St, Princeton, NJ 08544
    Pubs: *Thieves of Paradise, Magic City, Dien Cai Dau*
    (Wesleyan, 1998, 1992, 1988), *Kenyon Rev, Vox,*
    Ploughshares, Threepenny Rev, Callaloo, Colorado Rev,
    Iowa Rev.

Donna Walters Kozberg W
45 Dug Way, Watchung, NJ 07060, 908-226-1178
Internet: dmrkozberg@aol.com
    Pubs: *Forms, Cream City Rev, Junction, Wind Literary Jrnl,*
    Parachute, For Art's Sake.

T. R. LaGreca P
788 Winding Way, River Vale, NJ 07675
    Pubs: *Cover/Arts New York, Ellipsis, Albany Rev,*
    Wisconsin Rev, Parting Gifts, Jrnl of New Jersey Poets.

Shirley Warren Lake P
459 S Willow Ave, Absecon, NJ 08201-4633
    Pubs: *The Bottomfeeders, Somewhere Between, Oyster*
    Creek Icebreak (Still Waters Pr, 1995, 1991, 1989), *Jrnl of*
    New Jersey Poets, Georgia Rev, American Writing, Cream
    City Rev.

Donald Lawder P
Route 4, Box 4105, Hammonton, NJ 08037
    Pubs: *American Scholar, Nation, Kansas Qtly, New Yorker,*
    Crazyhorse, Beloit Poetry Jrnl.

Al Lee P
57 Kendal Ave, Maplewood, NJ 07040, 201-763-9006
    Pubs: *Time* (Ecco Pr, 1974), *The Major Young Poets: Anth*
    (World Publishing Co., 1971).

Curt Leviant W
PO Box 1266, Edison, NJ 08817
    Pubs: *The Man Who Thought He Was Messiah* (Jewish
    Publishing Society, 1990), *Zoetrope, Chariton Rev, Writers'*
    Forum.

Joel Lewis P
635 Washington St, Hoboken, NJ 07030
Internet: penwaves@mindspring.com
    Pubs: *North Jersey Gutter Helmet* (Oasis, 1997), *House*
    Rent Boogie (Yellow Pr, 1992), *Palookas of the Ozone* (e.g.
    Pr, 1991), *APR, NAW.*

Antoinette Libro P
Rowan Univ, Mullica Hill Rd, Glassboro, NJ 08028,
609-256-4290
Internet: libro@rowan.edu
    Pubs: *The House at the Shore* (Lincoln Springs Pr, 1997),
    Identity Lessons: An Anth of Contemporary Writing
    (Penguin Putnam, 1999), *Women Without Wings* (Blackbird
    Pr, 1993), *Modern Haiku, Jrnl of NJ Poets, Atlantic City Pr.*

Deena Linett P&W
Montclair State Univ, Upper Montclair, NJ 07043,
201-655-7320
Internet: linettd@saturn.montclair.edu
    Pubs: *The Slow Mirror & Other Stories* (U.K.; 5 Leaves Pr,
    1996), *The Translator's Wife* (Humanities & Arts Pr, 1986),
    On Common Ground (SUNY Pr, 1983), *Her Face In The*
    Mirror: Anth (Beacon Pr, 1994), *Mississippi Valley Rev,*
    Taos Rev, Harvard.

Geraldine C. Little P
519 Jacksonville Rd, Mount Holly, NJ 08060, 609-267-2758
    Pubs: *Women: In the Mask and Beyond* (QRL Pr, 1991),
    Heloise and Abelard (U Pr America, 1989), *Nimrod,*
    Confrontation, Prairie Schooner, Literary Rev,
    Massachusetts Rev.

Timothy Liu P
William Paterson University, 300 Pompton Rd, Wayne, NJ
07470, 973-720-2254
Internet: www.wilpaterson.edu
    Pubs: *Say Goodnight, Burnt Offerings* (Copper Canyon Pr,
    1998, 1995), *Vox Angelica* (Alice James Bks, 1992), *Grand*
    Street, The Nation, Sulfur, Volt, American Voice, Caliban,
    The Journal, Paris Rev, Poetry, The Quarterly.

Doughtry "Doc" Long   P
67 Garfield Ave, Trenton, NJ 08609, 609-695-8462
    Pubs: *Deliberations: Fire, Eros, Ascension and Earth* (Third World, 1994), *A Rock Against the Wind: Anth* (Perigee Bks, 1996), *Painted Bride Qtly, Obsidian.*

Joyce Greenberg Lott   P
5 Toth Ln, Rocky Hill, NJ 08553, 609-921-2492
Internet: lottofjoy@aol.com
    Pubs: *A Teacher's Stories* (Boynton/Cook Heinemann, 1994), *Ms., U.S. 1 Worksheets, English Jrnl, Jrnl of New Jersey Poets, Footwork: Paterson Literary Rev.*

Leona Mahler-Sussman   P&W
PO Box 317, Cedar Grove, NJ 07009-0317, 201-239-7027
    Pubs: *Pivot, Nostalgia, Earth's Daughters, Abraxas, Embers, Slipstream, Small Pond.*

Joe L. Malone   P&W
169 Prospect St, Leonia, NJ 07605, 201-944-7104
Internet: jmalone@barnard.columbia.edu
    Pubs: *Above the Salty Bay, Carmina Gaiana* (Linear Arts, 1998, 1997), *Wings, Iconoclast, Brooklyn Literary Rev, Jrnl of New Jersey Poets, Hellas, New Press.*

Pamela Malone   P&W
169 Prospect St, Leonia, NJ 07605, 201-944-7104
    Pubs: *Cat's Meow: Anth* (Maine Rhode Pub, 1995), *Hungry Poets Cookbook: Anth* (Applezaba Pr, 1987), *The Sun, Chelsea, Belletrist Rev, Bellowing Ark, West Branch, Blue Unicorn.*

Charlotte Mandel   P&W
60 Pine Dr, Cedar Grove, NJ 07009, 973-256-5053
Internet: charmandel@aol.com
    Pubs: *Sight Lines, The Marriages of Jacob* (Micah Pubs, 1991), *The Life of Mary* (Saturday Pr, 1988), *Indiana Rev, Mississippi Valley Rev, Nimrod, Seneca Rev, Raccoon, New Millennium Writings.*

Stanley Marcus   P
658 Valley Rd I-3, Upper Montclair, NJ 07043, 201-783-7353
    Pubs: *For A Living: The Poetry of Work: Anth* (U Illinois Pr, 1995), *Virginia Qtly Rev, Literary Rev, Denver Qtly, Prairie Schooner, Minnesota Rev, North Dakota Qtly.*

Cathy Mayo   P
33 W Paul Ave, Trenton, NJ 08638-4513
    Pubs: *Her Soul Beneath the Bone: Anth* (U Illinois Pr, 1988), *Up Against the Wall Mother, Plainsongs, Tsunami, Bogg, Connecticut River Rev.*

James T. McCartin   W
19 Lake Dr E, Wayne, NJ 07470, 201-696-2956
    Pubs: *The Crazy Aunt and Other Stories* (Lincoln Springs Pr, 1988), *Arizona Qtly, Footwork, Descant.*

Edward Patrick McCue   P
16 Main Ave #7, Ocean Grove, NJ 07756
    Pubs: *Observer* (Lorrah & Hitchcock, 1988), *Liturgical Arts, The Piedmont Literary Rev, Tiotis Pr.*

Florence McGinn   P
46 Featherbed Ln, Flemington, NJ 08822-5638, 908-782-0894
Internet: fmcginn@star.hcrhs.hunterdon.k12.nj.us
    Pubs: *Midwest Poetry Rev, Parnassus, Poetry Flash, Modern Haiku, Cicada, Eclectic Literary Forum.*

Rochelle Hope Mehr   P
5 Silver Spring Rd, West Orange, NJ 070524317, 973-731-0433
    Pubs: *Tucumcari Literary Rev, Midwest Poetry Rev, Ambrosia, Bristlecone, North American Mentor Mag, Bogg, Art Times, Neovictorian/Cochlea, Muse of Fire, Perceptions, Cicada.*

Yvette Mintzer   P
159 Cedar Ln, Princeton, NJ 08540, 609-430-9245
    Pubs: *Dreamline Express* (Inwood Pr, 1975).

Marilyn Mohr   P
109 Rynda Rd, South Orange, NJ 07079, 201-762-5403
    Pubs: *Satchel* (CCC, 1992), *Blood to Remember: Anth* (Texas Tech U, 1991), *Sarah's Daughters Sing: Anth* (KTAV Pub, 1990), *Lips, Noctiluca, Home Planet News.*

Rory Morse   P
53 Parlin Ln, Watchung, NJ 07060, 908-769-0780
    Pubs: *Golden Retriever World, Arulo, Vega, CSP World News, Hob-Nob, Wings, Night Writers, True Romance, Robin's Nest, Retriever's Qtly, Dog Song, Red Owl.*

Peter E. Murphy   P
18 N Richards Ave, Ventnor, NJ 08406, 609-823-5076
Internet: pembroke9@earthlink.net
    Pubs: *Passages North: Anth* (Milkweed, 1990), *Yellow Silk: Erotic Arts & Letters: Anth* (Harmony Bks, 1990), *Atlanta Rev, Commonweal, Many Mountains Moving, Spelunker Flophouse, Witness, Beloit Poetry Jrnl, New York Qtly, Painted Bride Qtly.*

Walter Dean Myers   W
2543 Kennedy Blvd, Jersey City, NJ 07304, 201-451-7651
    Pubs: *Me, Mop, and the Moondance Kid* (Delacorte Pr, 1988), *Black World, Essence, Espionage.*

Kathleen Neuer   P
49 Random Rd, Princeton, NJ 08540, 609-921-6115
    Pubs: *Black Warrior, Threepenny Rev, Texas Rev, Malahat Rev, Painted Bride, Pennsylvania Rev, Blue Buildings.*

Joyce Carol Oates P&W
9 Honeybrook Dr, Princeton, NJ 08540
  Pubs: *My Heart Laid Bare, Man Crazy, We Were the Mulvaneys, A Bloodsmoor Romance* (Dutton, 1998, 1998, 1997, 1982), *Invisible Woman* (Ontario Rev Pr, 1982).

Vanessa L. Ochs W
57 Fairmount Ave, Morristown, NJ 07960, 201-984-3913
  Pubs: *Words on Fire: One Woman's Journey Into The Sacred* (HBJ, 1990).

Dawn O'Leary P
47 Oakwood Ave, Upper Montclair, NJ 07043, 201-783-6729
  Pubs: *Antioch Rev, Poetry Northwest, New Letters, Commonweal, Northwest Rev.*

Alicia Ostriker P
33 Philip Dr, Princeton, NJ 08540, 609-924-5737
Internet: ostriker@rci.rutgers.edu
  Pubs: *The Crack in Everything* (U Pitt Pr, 1996), *The Nakedness of the Fathers* (Rutgers U Pr, 1994), *Paris Rev, APR, Kenyon Rev, New Yorker, TriQuarterly.*

Christopher Parker P
64 Glenwood Rd, Upper Montclair, NJ 07043-1930, 201-746-3077
Internet: cparker674@aol.com
  Pubs: *Poetry Northwest, Jrnl of New Jersey Poets, New Jersey Poetry, Waterways, Spirit, Calliope, Footwork, Phoenix, Crazyquilt.*

George Pereny P
134 Van Ave, Pompton Lakes, NJ 07442, 201-831-7411
  Pubs: *New Worlds Unlimited: Anth* (Sal Buttaci, 1985), *English Jrnl, Slant, Footwork, Black Belt.*

Alfred "Sonny" Piccoli PP
41 James St, Bloomfield, NJ 07003, 973-748-9856
  Pubs: *Phenomenal Lives* (1st Bks, 1997), *Municipal Access TV, NewArk Writers Collective, Franklin School, Christian Faith Center, First Congregational Church, Nuyorican Poets Cafe, Barnes & Noble.*

Stanley Plumly P
Ecco Press, 100 W Broad St, Hopewell, NJ 08525
  Pubs: *The Marriage in the Trees, Boy on the Step, Summer Celestial, Out-of-the-Body Travel* (Ecco/Norton, 1996, 1989, 1983, 1978).

Minnie Bruce Pratt P
PO Box 8212, Jersey City, NJ 07308, 201-659-2326
Internet: www.mbpratt.org
  Pubs: *Walking Back Up Depot Street* (U Pittsburgh Pr, 1999), *S/HE, Crime Against Nature* (Firebrand Bks, 1995, 1990), *Ploughshares, New England Rev, Progressive, American Voice, Village Voice, Out/Look, TriQuarterly, Hungry Mind Rev.*

Norman Henry Pritchard, II P
45-A Phelps Ave, New Brunswick, NJ 08901-3712
  Pubs: *Eecchhooeess* (NYU Pr, 1971), *The Matrix: Poems 1960-1970* (Doubleday, 1970), *The Chronicle of the Horse.*

Rich Quatrone P
PO Box 732, Spring Lake, NJ 07762
  Pubs: *Lucia's Rain* (Passaic Rev Pr, 1989), *Beehive, Aquarian, Lips, Footwork, Jrnl of New Jersey Poets, Long Shot, Steppingstones, Passaic Rev, New Leaves, Phatitude, Lucid Moon, Alphabeat Soup.*

Doris Radin P
116 Hawthorne Ave, Glen Ridge, NJ 07028, 973-748-0895
  Pubs: *There Are Talismans* (Saturday Pr, 1991), *Prairie Schooner, Helicon Nine, Nation, Massachusetts Rev, New Letters, Chelsea.*

Jan Emily Ramjerdi P&W
c/o Boonstra, 56 Oakwood Dr, Wayne, NJ 07470, 973-694-8197
  Pubs: *RE.LA.VIR, Degenerative Prose: Anth* (Black Ice/FC2, 1999, 1995), *Tasting Life Twice: Anth* (Avon, 1995), *Quarterly West, Fiction Intl, Black Ice, The Little Mag, 13th Moon, Mid-American Rev, Denver Qtly.*

Nefretete S. Rasheed P
381 Broad St, #A1307, Newark, NJ 07104, 201-481-7966
  Pubs: *Three Thirds: Anth* (Wordbanks Pr, 1984), *Phoebe, Plum Rev, Salome.*

Frances Boogher Reed W
PO Box 1874, Hoboken, NJ 07030, 212-592-3510
Internet: reedfran@aol.com
  Pubs: *Black Mexican Necklace* (Dominie, 1990), *A Dream With Storms* (New Readers Pr, 1990), *Female Patient.*

Thomas Reiter P
105 Sycamore St, Neptune, NJ 07753, 908-922-3437
  Pubs: *Crossovers* (Eastern Washington U Pr, 1995), *A Good Man: Fathers & Sons: Anth* (Fawcett Columbine, 1993), *Poetry, Georgia Rev, Gettysburg Rev, NER, Ohio Rev.*

James Richardson P
Princeton Univ, 185 Nassau St, Princeton, NJ 08544-2095, 609-258-4712
Internet: jrich@princeton.edu
  Pubs: *As If* (Persea, 1992), *Second Guesses* (Wesleyan Pr, 1984), *Yale Rev, Boulevard, Paris Rev, New Criterion, Poetry.*

Ruby Riemer P
Box 210, Village Rd, Green Village, NJ 07935, 201-377-9274
  Pubs: *Jrnl of New Jersey Poets, Multicultural Rev, Exquisite Corpse, Belles Lettres, Southern Poetry Rev, Nation, American Bk Rev, APR, Poet Lore, Anth of Mag Verse.*

Ed Roberson P
9 Edgeworth Pl, North Brunswick, NJ 08902, 732-220-2920
Internet: roberson@aesop.rutgers.edu
  Pubs: *Atmosphere Conditions* (Sun & Moon Pr, 1999), *Just In/Word of Navigational Challenges: New and Selected* (Talisman Hse, 1998), *Voices Cast Out To Talk To Us In* (U Iowa Pr, 1996).

Janet Roberts P
41 Prospect St, Madison, NJ 07940
  Pubs: *A New Thread of Connection: Sumer Post* (ARS Textrina, 1994), *Flowers From Horseback* (U Michigan, 1990), *Manhattan Poetry Rev, Aspen Poetry Anth.*

Sarah Rodgers P
44 Wiggins St, Princeton, NJ 08540, 609-924-9448
  Pubs: *Croton Rev, Day Tonight/Night Today, Impact, Dark Horse, Chelsea, Second Coming, Urthkin.*

Wilhelm Hermann Rohrs P
Dunhill & Clark of New York, 82 Jacoby St, Maplewood, NJ 07040
  Pubs: *Tears of Time, The Zeneida Cycle, Against the Tide* (Small Poetry Pr, 1998, 1996, 1994), *Mortal Truth* (Dunhill & Clark, 1987), *NAR, Cambridge Collection, Independent Rev, New Jersey Free Press.*

Martin C. Rosner P
234 Vivien Ct, Paramus, NJ 07652, 201-262-7749
Internet: roscape@aol.com
  Pubs: *Hormones and Hyacinths* (Libra Pub, 1981), *Pilgrim At Sunset: Anth* (Research Triangle Pub, 1994), *Cape Codder, Voices Intl, Ararat, New Jersey Poetry Monthly, Essence, New York Times.*

Diana Kwiatkowski Rubin P
The Cognitive Overload Press, PO Box 398, Piscataway, NJ 08855-0398
  Pubs: *Dinosauria* (Bear Hse Pub, 1995), *Visions of Enchantment* (JVC Bks, 1991), *Poet, Touchstone, Fox Cry, Minetta Rev, Antigonish Rev, Amelia.*

Frank Rubino P&W
76 High St, Bloomfield, NJ 07003, 201-667-9162
  Pubs: *Toy of the Evil Genie* (New Observations Pr, 1983), *The World.*

Dorothy Rudy P
161 W Clinton Ave, Tenafly, NJ 07670, 201-569-7771
  Pubs: *Voices Through Time & Distant Places* (Willdor Pr, 1993), *Poem, Laurel Rev, Write Connection, Bergen Poets, Footnotes, Lips, Connection Collection.*

James Ruffini P
21 Elro Drive E, Oak Ridge, NJ 07438, 973-208-7250
  Pubs: *Against Suburbia* (Ocean Size Pr, 1991), *Busy Signals From The Holy City* (Sub Rosa, 1988), *Earth Bound, Poetry Motel, Cicada, Blank Gun Silencer.*

Mark SaFranko P&W
205 Hudson St, #1011, Hoboken, NJ 07030, 201-653-1750
  Pubs: *The MacGuffin, Footwork, NAR, New Orleans Rev, Belletrist Rev, Soundings East, Art Times, Cimarron Rev, Pig Iron, Seems, Mark, The Panhandler, South Carolina Rev, Pangolin Papers, The Soft Door, Mind in Motion, Tucumcari Rev.*

Penelope Scambly Schott P
Box 215, Rocky Hill, NJ 08553, 609-924-8993
  Pubs: *The Perfect Mother* (Snake Nation Pr, 1994), *These Are My Same Hands* (State Street Pr, 1989), *A Little Ignorance* (Potter, 1986), *Lear's, American Voice, Georgia Rev.*

Barry Seiler P
321 Bloomfield St, #3, Hoboken, NJ 07030, 201-653-3612
  Pubs: *Black Leaf, The Waters of Forgetting* (U Akron Pr, 1997, 1994), *Retaining Wall* (L'Epervier Pr, 1979), *NER/BLQ, The Quarterly.*

Sylvia Semel P
109 Oakland Ave, Somerset, NJ 08873
  Pubs: *Possession* (For Poets Only, 1988), *Innisfree, Modern Haiku.*

Robbie Clipper Sethi P&W
Rider Univ, 2083 Lawrenceville Rd, Lawrenceville, NJ 086483099, 609-895-5578
Internet: sethi@rider.edu
  Pubs: *The Bride Wore Red* (Picador, 1997), *Atlantic, Philadelphia Inquirer Mag, Massachusetts Rev, California Qtly, Wind, Ascent, Alaska Qtly Rev, Crescent Rev, Mademoiselle, Boulevard, Literary Rev.*

Harry S. Shapiro PP
530 Upper Mountain Ave, Upper Montclair, NJ 07043, 973-783-6009
  Pubs: *Journey To Harmony* (Rachel Pub, 1984), *Spaceships Are Too Slow, Seeds of the Universe* (Intl Printing, 1973, 1971), *Dream Shop.*

Norma Voorhees Sheard P
14 Fawn Dr, Flemington, NJ 08822-2602, 908-782-6492
Internet: normasheard@webex.net
  Pubs: *New York Qtly, Maryland Rev, Black Fly Rev, Nimrod, Footworks, U.S. 1 Worksheets, Dragonfly, Jrnl of New Jersey Poets, Paterson Literary Rev, Cape Rock Rev.*

Laurie Sheck P
118 Snowden Ln, Princeton, NJ 08540, 609-921-1534
  Pubs: *Io At Night* (Knopf, 1990), *Amaranth* (U Georgia Pr, 1981), *New Yorker, Poetry, Iowa Rev.*

Barry Sheinkopf   W
601 Palisade Ave, Englewood Cliffs, NJ 07632,
201-567-4017
Internet: 102100.1065@compuserve.com
     Pubs: *The Ivory Kitchen, The Longest Odds* (Lynx Bks,
     1990, 1989).

William Sherman   P
9300 Atlantic Ave, #218, Margate, NJ 08402, 609-822-7050
     Pubs: *From the South Seas* (Roman F. Garbacik, 1997), *A
     Tale For Tusitala* (Branch Redd, 1993), *Tahitian Journals*
     (Hearing Eye, 1990), *Exquisite Corpse, Fire.*

Herschel Silverman   P
47 E 33 St, #1, Bayonne, NJ 07002, 201-339-3880
     Pubs: *15 Poems For Allen Ginsberg* (Blue Jacket Pr, 1997),
     Hey Baby Blues, Blue Ludes (Beehive Pr, 1993, 1992),
     Long Shot, Talisman, Atom Mind, Davka, Blue Beat Jacket,
     Moody Street Irregulars, O!! Pphoo! Connections, Home
     Planet News, Stained Sheets.

Diane Simmons   W
9 Lancaster Ave, Maplewood, NJ 07040, 201-763-8761
Internet: simmons@admin.njit.edu
     Pubs: *Dreams Like Thunder* (Story Line Pr, 1992), *Let the*
     Bastards Freeze in the Dark (S&S, 1980), *Green Mountains*
     Rev, Northwest Rev, Whetstone.

Carol Sturm Smith   W
Box 63A, Scotch Rd, Pennington, NJ 08534, 609-737-8269
     Pubs: *Only A Dream, Partners, Renewal* (Ballantine, 1984,
     1982, 1982), *Princeton Music & Arts Mag.*

Ed Smith   P
1413 Winesap Dr, Manasquan, NJ 08736
Internet: manlib@bellatlantic.net
     Pubs: *Under a Gull's Wing: Anth* (Down the Shore, 1996),
     Bluestones & Salthay: Anth (Rutgers U Pr, 1990),
     Talisman, Footwork, The World.

Sharon Spencer   W
72 Watchung Ave, 2nd Fl, Upper Montclair, NJ 07043,
973-655-5151
     Pubs: *Dance of the Ariadnes* (Sky Blue Pr, 1998), *Wire*
     Rims (Heinemann Bks, 1995), *Crosscurrents, Calyx,*
     Amelia, Mississippi Rev, Paintbrush, Innovation.

Toby Stein   W
45 Church St, Montclair, NJ 07042
     Pubs: *Only The Best* (Arbor Hse, 1984), *Getting Together*
     (Atheneum, 1980), *Moment, Reconstructionist.*

Gerald Stern   P
89 Clinton St, Lambertville, NJ 08530, 609-397-2562
     Pubs: *This Time: New & Selected Poems, Odd Mercy,*
     Bread Without Sugar (Norton, 1998, 1995, 1992).

Shane Stevens   W
PO Box 1927, Hoboken, NJ 07030
     Pubs: *Hot Tickets, Jersey Tomatoes* (Arbor Hse, 1987,
     1986), *The Anvil Chorus* (Delacorte, 1985).

D. E. Steward   P&W
PO Box 1239, Princeton, NJ 08542-1239
     Pubs: *A Letter To A Writer Down The Line* (Oasis, 1987),
     Contact Inhibition (Avant, 1985), *Epoch, Sulfur,*
     Conjunctions, Temblor, Chelsea, Southwest Rev, Denver
     Qtly, Fiction Intl, Northwest Rev.

Carole Stone   P
16 Howard St, Verona, NJ 07044, 201-239-4945
Internet: stonec@saturn.montclair.edu
     Pubs: *Lime and Salt* (Carriage House Pr, 1997), *Orphan in*
     the Movie House, Giving Each Other Up (Andrew Mountain
     Pr, 1997, 1985), *Literature Around the Globe: Anth* (Kendall
     Hunt, 1994), *Devil's Millhopper, Contact II, Heresies, Spirit,*
     Footwork.

Chris Stroffolino   P
464 Monmouth St, #6, Jersey City, NJ 07302, 201-459-9245
     Pubs: *Oops* (Pavement Saw Pr, 1994), *APR, Lift, First*
     Intensity, o.blek, Lingo, Painted Bride Qtly, Talisman,
     Caliban, Sulfur.

Adam Szyper   P
12 Winant Rd, Kendall Park, NJ 08824, 908-297-9069
     Pubs: *And Suddenly Spring* (Cross-Cultural Comm, 1992),
     The Current, New Hope Intl Writing.

Marcia Tager   W
193 Elm St, Tenafly, NJ 07670, 201-567-3729
     Pubs: *Shaking Eve's Tree: Anth* (Jewish Pub, 1990), *The*
     Literary Rev, North Dakota Qtly, Confrontation, Wind,
     Ascent.

Madeline J. Tiger   P
15 Victoria Terr, Upper Montclair, NJ 07043, 973-744-8272
     Pubs: *Water Has No Color* (New Spirit Pr, 1992), *My*
     Father's Harmonica (Nightshade Pr, 1991), *The Unmade*
     Bed: Sensual Writing on Married Love: Anth (HC, 1992),
     Paterson Literary Rev, U.S. 1, Poetry New York, Marlboro
     Rev, 6ix, Jrnl of New Jersey Poets.

Inge Trachtenberg   W
288 Oakwood Rd, Englewood, NJ 07631
     Pubs: *An Arranged Marriage, So Slow The Dawning*
     (Norton, 1977, 1973).

Steve Troyanovich   P
1 Pelle Ct, Florence, NJ 08518, 609-499-3878
     Pubs: *Dream Dealers & Other Shadows* (Triton, 1978),
     Quarry, Argonaut, Yellow Butterfly, Abraxas, Moody Street
     Irregulars, Eric Burdon Connection.

Robert Blake Truscott   P
88 Guilden St, New Brunswick, NJ 08901, 201-846-3767
    Pubs: *Cumberland Poetry Rev, Literary Rev, Virginia Qtly Rev, Stone Country.*

Rod Tulloss   P
PO Box 57, Roosevelt, NJ 08555-0057, 609-448-5096
Internet: ret@njcc.com
    Pubs: *The Machine Shuts Down* (Berkeley Poets Pr, 1982), *Bluestones & Salthay: Anth* (Rutgers U Pr, 1990), *Archae, U.S. 1 Worksheets, Exquisite Corpse, Nimrod.*

Lois Van Houten   P
16 Harlow Cres, Fairlawn, NJ 07410
    Pubs: *Korone Women's Voices: Anth* (Womanspace Inc., 1996), *Women & Death: Anth* (Ground Torpedo Pr, 1994), *Footwork, Stone Country, Jrnl of New Jersey Poets.*

William John Watkins   P&W
The Sand Agency, 1406 Garven Ave, Ocean, NJ 07712, 201-988-2287
Internet: wwatkins@brookdale.cc.nj.us
    Pubs: *Cosmic Thunder* (Avon Bks, 1996), *Tracker: The Story Of Tom Brown, Jr.* (Prentice-Hall, 1978), *Commonweal, Asimov's, Rhino, Hellas, MacGuffin, Satire.*

Daniel J. Weeks   P
905 Norwood Ave, Elberon, NJ 07740, 908-222-3858
    Pubs: *Ancestral Songs* (Libra Pubs, 1992), *X Poems* (Blast Pr, 1991), *Cimarron Rev, Mudfish, Slant, Fennel Stalk, Zone 3, Voices Intl.*

Theodore Weiss   P
26 Haslet Ave, Princeton, NJ 08540, 609-921-6976
    Pubs: *Selected Poems* (TriQuarterly Bks, 1995), *A Sum of Destructions* (LSU Pr, 1994), *New Republic, Poetry, APR, Paris Rev, New Criterion, Partisan Rev.*

Alix Weisz   P
PO Box 4205, Clifton, NJ 07012-4205, 973-779-4710
Internet: cetaitmoi@aol.com
    Pubs: *Lobotomy, Alix Poems Weisz* (New Broom Pr, 1993, 1992), *Do You Sense An Angel: Anth* (Ashby Lane Pr, 1993), *Fenice, Phoenix Sheets, Pegasus Rev, Iota, Whisper.*

Debbie Lee Wesselmann   W
19 Elm St, Hopewell, NJ 08525, 609-466-8868
Internet: dlw@nerc.com
    Pubs: *The Earth And The Sky* (SMU Pr, 1998), *Trutor and the Balloonist* (MacMurray & Beck, 1997), *Literary Rev, Ascent, Folio, Gulf Stream Mag, Beloit Fiction Jrnl, Pennsylvania English, NAR, Florida Rev, Fiction, Philadelphia Inquirer.*

John A. Williams   W
693 Forest Ave, Teaneck, NJ 07666, 201-692-9157
    Pubs: *Sissie & Captain Blackman, Jacob's Ladder* (Thunder's Mouth Pr, 1988, 1987), *Emerge, Essence, Nation, Callaloo.*

Meredith Sue Willis   W
311 Prospect St, South Orange, NJ 07079, 973-378-8361
Internet: msuewillis@aol.com
    Pubs: *Trespassers* (Hamilton Stone Edtns, 1997), *Marco's Monster* (HarperCollins, 1996), *In The Mountains of America* (Mercury Hse, 1994), *Quilt Pieces* (Gnomon, 1991).

Ted Wilson   P
342 Warwick Ave, South Orange, NJ 07079, 973-763-9550
Internet: theodorel@worldnet.att.net
    Pubs: *In Defense of Mumia: Anth* (Writers and Readers, 1996), *Amiri Baraka: The Kaleidoscope Torch: Anth* (Steppingstone Pr, 1985), *Nobo, Drumvoices, Essence, Callaloo, Black Nation.*

Barbara Wind   P
10 Londonderry Way, Summit, NJ 07901, 908-608-1748
Internet: barbwind@netcom.com
    Pubs: *Jacob's Angels* (Emmet Pr, 1998), *South Mountain: Anth* (Milburn Public Library, 1993), *Poetry Works: Anth* (NewArk Writers Collective, 1993), *JAMA, Footwork, Whiskey Island, Negative Capability, Pleiades, Philae, Paterson Literary Rev.*

Holly Woodward   W
76 Jackson St, Hoboken, NJ 07030
    Pubs: *New Letters, American Voice, Chicago Rev.*

Ruth Zimmerman   P
7 Marianna Pl, Morristown, NJ 07960
Internet: apzim@aol.com
    Pubs: *Thema, Messages from the Heart, Dream Intl Qtly, Passages North, Jrnl of New Jersey Poets, Embers, Without Halos, Mary Jane, Yet Another Small Mag, The Ledge, Mediphors, Buffalo Bones, Sensations, Nostalgia, The Art Factory.*

Sander Zulauf   P
County College of Morris, 214 Center Grove Rd, Randolph, NJ 07869, 201-328-5471
Internet: szulauf@ccm.edu
    Pubs: *Succasunna New Jersey* (Breaking Point Inc., 1987), *The Art and Craft of Poetry: Anth* (Writer's Digest, 1994), *Sewanee Rev, Lips, Editor's Choice III, CSM, Negative Capability, Ometeca.*

NEW MEXICO

Rudolfo Anaya   W
5324 Canada Vista NW, Albuquerque, NM 87120-2412
    Pubs: *Shaman Winter, Rio Grande Fall, Zia Summer, Bless Me Ultima* (Warner Bks, 1998, 1996, 1995, 1993), *New Mexico Mag, Blue Mesa Rev.*

Rudy S. Apodaca   W
829 Canterbury Arc, Las Cruces, NM 88005-3715,
505-525-8421
Internet: xqx@lascruces.com
  Pubs: *The Waxen Image* (Titan Publishing Co., 1977).

Jose Armas   W
PO Box 7487, Albuquerque, NM 87104, 505-242-8075

Sharon Barba   P
Univ New Mexico, Humanities Bldg 217, Albuquerque, NM
87131, 505-277-6347
  Pubs: *13th Moon, Conditions, Painted Bride Qtly, Sunbury,
  Moving Out.*

Lee Bartlett   P
Box 250, Star Rte, Placitas, NM 87043, 505-867-4891
  Pubs: *The Greenhouse Effect* (Lords of Language, 1994),
  Sagetrieb.

Sabra Basler   P
1920 Gold SE, Albuquerque, NM 87106, 505-243-7687
  Pubs: *Coyote's Journal, Quercus, Cold Drill, Windchimes,
  Modern Haiku, Aero-Zero.*

Laura Beheler   P&W
3 Placita Rafaela, Santa Fe, NM 87501, 505-983-9166
  Pubs: *The Snow Moon* (Pentland, Ltd, 1986), *Phone Calls
  Late at Night To God* (Four Winds, 1983).

Charles Greenleaf Bell   P&W
1260 Canyon Rd, Santa Fe, NM 87501, 505-983-6035
  Pubs: *Five Chambered Heart* (Persea, 1985), *New Yorker,
  Atlantic, Harper's.*

Forest Stirling Bell   P
#36 Country Club Gdns, Santa Fe, NM 87501, 505-471-5108
  Pubs: *Seer Ox, WPA, Sun, Tweed, Astral Projection, Haiku,
  West, Cinema News, Reversal.*

David Benedetti   P
222 Richmond SE, Albuquerque, NM 87106, 505-256-0003
  Pubs: *Telling Remark* (The Lost Fdn, 1992), *Defense
  Mechanism* (Deposed Innocence, 1986), *Poetics Jrnl,
  American Poetry, Impulsive Living, Telephone, Hills.*

Carol Berge   P&W
2070 Calle Contento, Santa Fe, NM 875055406,
505-438-3979
  Pubs: *Literature: The Human Experience* (St. Martin's Pr,
  1998), *Zebras* (Tribal Center Pr, 1991), *Fiction Intl, Iowa Rev,
  TriQuarterly, Exquisite Corpse, Fish Drum, Poetry Chicago.*

Stanley Berne   P&W
American-Canadian Pub, Inc., PO Box 4595, Santa Fe, NM
87502-4595, 505-983-8484
  Pubs: *To Hell With Optimism!!, Every Person's Little Book
  of P-L-U-T-O-N-I-U-M* (Rising Tide Pr, 1996, 1992),
  Alphabet Soup (Danrus Pubs, 1995).

Mei-Mei Berssenbrugge   P
PO Box 831, Abiquiu, NM 87510
  Pubs: *Four Year Old Girl, Sphericity* (Kelsey Street Pr,
  1998, 1993), *Empathy* (Station Hill Pr, 1988).

Sallie Bingham   W
369 Montezuma, #316, Santa Fe, NM 87501-2626,
505-989-1205
  Pubs: *Straight Man, Matron of Honor, Small Victories* (Zoland
  Bks, 1996, 1994, 1992), *Upstate* (Permanent Pr, 1993),
  Passion and Prejudice (Knopf, 1989), *New Woman/New
  Fiction, Amicus Jrnl.*

Robert Boswell   W
New Mexico State Univ, English Dept, Box 3E, Las Cruces,
NM 88003, 505-527-2335
  Pubs: *Living to Be A Hundred, Mystery Ride, The Geography
  of Desire* (Knopf, 1994, 1993, 1989), *Iowa Rev, New Yorker.*

Michael Breslow   W
103 Catron, #8, Santa Fe, NM 87501
  Pubs: *Lifeline* (Viking Pr, 1978).

Paul Bufis   P
123 1/2 Martinez St, Santa Fe, NM 87501, 505-983-1951
Internet: zeebufi@interserv.com
  Pubs: *XY Files: Anth* (Sherman Asher Pub, 1997), *Saludos:
  Poems of New Mexico: Anth* (Pennywhistle Pr, 1995),
  *Southern Poetry Rev, River Styx, Visions, Blue Unicorn,
  Permafrost, Rhino, Wind, Phantasm.*

Barney Bush   P
Box 22779, Santa Fe, NM 87502
  Pubs: *Inherit the Blood* (Thunder's Mouth, 1985), *Harper's
  Anth: Native American Poetry* (H&R, 1987).

Laura Calvert   P
1029 Guadalupe del Predo NW, Albuquerque, NM 87107,
505-345-7064
  Pubs: *Discurso Literario, Studia Mystica, The
  Backwoodsman, Southern Rev, North Dakota Rev.*

Nash Candelaria   W
111 E San Mateo Rd, Santa Fe, NM 87505-4721,
505-983-0795
  Pubs: *Leonor Park* (Bilingual Pr, 1991), *Homeground: Anth*
  (Blue Heron Pub, 1996), *Multicultural Voices: Anth* (Scott
  Foresman, 1994), *The Americas Rev, De Colores, Imagine,
  Puerto del Sol, Bilingual Rev, Riversedge.*

Alvaro Cardona-Hine   P
PO Box 326, Truchas, NM 875780326, 505-679-2253
  Pubs: *A History of Light* (Sherman Asher Pub, 1997), *A Garden of Sound* (Pemmican Pr, 1996), *When I Was A Father* (New Rivers Pr, 1982), *The Half-Eaten Angel* (Nodin Pr, 1981), *American Writing, Chelsea.*

Ioanna Carlsen   P&W
PO Box 307, Tesuque, NM 87574, 505-983-6910
  Pubs: *Saludos: Poems of New Mexico: Anth* (Pennywhistle Rev, 1995), *The Quarterly, Poetry, Cafe Solo, Nimrod, Chelsea, Blue Mesa Rev.*

Susan Chapman   P
5801 Lowell St NE, #5A, Albuquerque, NM 87111
  Pubs: *Conversations With Dracaena* (Word Merchant Pr, 1982), *The Spirit That Wants Me: Anth* (Duff, 1991), *Haiku Qtly, Pudding Mag, Frogpond.*

James Colbert   W
Univ New Mexico, Humanities Bldg 217, Albuquerque, NM 871311106, 505-277-6347
Internet: colbert@unm.edu
  Pubs: *God Bless the Child, All I Have Is Blue, Skinny Man* (MacMillan, 1993, 1992, 1990), *No Special Hurry, Profit and Sheen* (HM, 1988, 1986).

Jane Candia Coleman   P&W
PO Box 40, Rodeo, NM 880560040, 520-558-2367
  Pubs: *I, Pearl Hart* (Thorndike Five Star, 1998), *Doc Holliday's Woman* (Warner Bks, 1995), *Discovering Eve, Stories from Mesa Country* (Ohio U Pr/Swallow Pr, 1993, 1991), *Louis L'Amour Western Mag, Cafe, The Critic.*

Joseph L. Concha   P
Box 1184, Taos, NM 87571

Michele Connelly   P
PO Box 28, Coyote, NM 87012
  Pubs: *Rebirth of Power: Anth* (Mother Courage, 1987), *Hudson Valley Writers' Ctr River Anth, Reed Mag, High Country News, Sinister Wisdom, Swamproot.*

Gina Covina   W
PO Box 226, Vallecitos, NM 87581, 505-582-4226
  Pubs: *The City Of Hermits* (Barn Owl Bks, 1983), *Yellow Silk, Berkeley Works, New Age.*

Sheila Cowing   P
5 Bonito Rd, Santa Fe, NM 87505-8793, 505-989-4163
  Pubs: *Night Kneels* (Sherman Asher Pub, 1998), *Saludasi: Anth* (Pennywhistle, 1996), *Warren Wilson Rev, Georgia Rev, Stone Country, Creeping Bent, Dalhousie Rev, Mid-American Rev, New Laurel Rev, The MacGuffin, Georgia Rev.*

Stanley Crawford   W
PO Box 56, Dixon, NM 87527, 505-579-4288
  Pubs: *A Garlic Testament* (HarperCollins, 1992), *Mayordomo* (U New Mexico Pr, 1988), *Some Instructions* (Knopf, 1978).

Judson Crews   W
2323 Kathryn SE #531, Albuquerque, NM 87106-3456, 505-266-2938
  Pubs: *The Brave Wild Coast* (Dumont Pr, 1997), *The Clock of Moss* (Ahsahta Pr, 1983), *Wormwood Rev, New York Rev, Xib, Burning World, Zen Tattoo, Atom Mind.*

Richard Currey   W
160 Washington SE, #185, Albuquerque, NM 87108, 505-255-9801
  Pubs: *Lost Highway, Fatal Light* (HM, 1997, 1997), *The Wars of Heaven* (Vintage, 1991), *Witness, North American Rev, Utne Reader.*

Pierre Delattre   W
PO Box 190, Dixon, NM 87527
  Pubs: *Walking On Air* (Houghton Mifflin, 1980), *Atlantic, Playboy, Texas Qtly, Antioch Rev.*

R. P. Dickey   P&W
PO Box 87, Ranchos de Taos, NM 875570087
  Pubs: *Self-Liberation, Collected Poems* (XLibris, 1998, 1998), *The Way of Eternal Recurrence* (21st Century Pr, 1994), *The Little Book on Racism and Politics* (Mohualu Pr, 1990), *New Yorker, Atlantic, Poetry,.*

G. J. Dubovik   W
9201 Preston Trail NE, Albuquerque, NM 87111
  Pubs: *I, Woman* (Lintel, 1990), *Southwest Writers, Albuquerque Gazette.*

Thomas Fitzsimmons   P
1 Balsa Rd, Santa Fe, NM 87505, 505-466-9909
  Pubs: *The Dream Machine* (Pennywhistle Pr, 1996), *Water Ground Stone* (Katydid Bks/U Hawaii Pr, 1992).

Phillip Foss   P
PO Box 23266, Santa Fe, NM 87502
  Pubs: *Coutesan of Seizure, The Excesses, The Caprices* (Light & Dust Bks, 1993, 1990), *Tyuonyi, Conjunctions, Avec, Sulfur, Hambone.*

Gene Frumkin   P&W
3721 Mesa Verde NE, Albuquerque, NM 87110, 505-266-1319
  Pubs: *The Old Man Who Swam Away and Left Only His Wet Feet* (La Alameda Pr, 1998) *Saturn is Mostly Weather: Selected and Uncollected Poems* (Cinco Puntos Pr, 1992), *Comma in the Ear* (Living Batch, 1990), *Paris Rev, Manoa, Prairie Schooner.*

Carl Ginsburg   P
3212 Monte Vista NE, Albuquerque, NM 87106, 505-266-6699
  Pubs: *Medicine Journeys: Ten Stories* (Center Pr, 1991), *The Spirit That Wants Me: A New Mexico Anth* (Duff, 1991), *Southwest Discovery.*

Larry Goodell   PP&P
PO Box 571, Placitas, NM 87043, 505-867-5877
Internet: lgoodell@nmia
    Pubs: *From Here On Earth: A Book of Sonnets* (Alameda
    Pr, 1996), *Out of Secrecy* (YooHoo Pr, 1992), *New Mexico*
    Poetry Renaissance: Anth (Red Crane, 1994).

MacDonnell Gordon   P
1026 Governor Dempsey, Santa Fe, NM 87501
    Pubs: *Loon, Road Apple Rev, Greenfield Rev, Alembic,*
    Hard Pressed, Cedar Rock, Blue Buildings.

Penny Harter   P&W
PO Box 2740, Santa Fe, NM 87504-2740, 505-438-3249
    Pubs: *Lizard Light: Poems from the Earth* (Sherman Asher
    Pub, 1998), *Turtle Blessing* (La Alameda Pr, 1996), *Stages*
    and Views (Katydid Bks, 1994), *Shadow Play* (S&S, 1994),
    Hiking the Crevasse (Warthog Pr, 1983), *Earth's Daughers,*
    Kerf, Whiskey Island, Gaia.

Nancy Peters Hastings   P
PO Box 1374, Las Cruces, NM 88004, 505-382-7446
    Pubs: *A Quiet I Carry With Me* (A Slow Tempo Pr, 1994),
    The Spirit That Wants Me: Anth (Duff, 1988), *Kansas Qtly,*
    Poetry, Prairie Schooner, Connecticut River Rev.

Susan Hecht   P&W
PO Box 75, Tres Piedras, NM 87577-0025
    Pubs: *Lesbian Bedtime Stories: Anth* (Tough Dove Bks,
    1989), *Calyx, Onionhead, Color Wheel, Sou'wester, Hawaii*
    Pacific Rev.

Laura Hendrie   W
Box 202, Dixon, NM 87527-0202
    Pubs: *Walking on Air* (U Alabama, 1996), *Stygo* (Scribner,
    1995), *Best of the West III: Anth* (Gibbs Smith, 1990),
    Missouri Rev, Taos Rev, Writers' Forum.

William J. Higginson   P&W
From Here Press, PO Box 2740, Santa Fe, NM 87504-2740,
505-438-3249
    Pubs: *Met on the Road* (Press Here, 1993), *Wind in the*
    Long Grass (S&S, 1991), *The Haiku Seasons: Anth*
    (Kodansha Intl, 1996), *Red Fuji: Anth* (From Here Pr, 1997),
    Center, Edge, Frogpond, Modern Haiku, Still, Albatross.

Judyth Hill   P
HC 69 Box 20-H, Sapello, NM 87745, 505-454-9628
    Pubs: *Men Need Space, A Presence of Angels* (Sherman
    Asher Pubs, 1996, 1995), *Altar of The Ordinary* (Ya-Hoo Pr,
    1993), *Goddess Cafe* (Fish Drum, 1990).

Tony Hoagland   P
New Mexico State University, Las Cruces, NM 88011,
505-646-2247
    Pubs: *Donkey Gospel, Sweet Ruin* (Graywolf, 1998, 1992),
    History of Desire (Moon Pony Pr, 1990), *Talking To Stay*
    Warm (Coffee Cup Pr, 1986), *A Change In Plans* (San
    Pedro, 1985).

Suzanne Marie Hobbs   P
4805 Downey St NE, Albuquerque, NM 87109, 505-296-4662

Phyllis Hoge   P
213 Dartmouth Dr SE, Albuquerque, NM 87106, 505-265-2042
    Pubs: *The Ghosts of Who We Were* (U Illinois Pr, 1986), *What*
    the Land Gave (Quarterly Review of Literature, 1981), *Hudson*
    Rev, Quarterly Review of Literature, Manoa, Shenandoah.

J. R. Humphreys   W
Box 5461, Santa Fe, NM 87502, 505-983-5685
    Pubs: *Maya Red* (Cane Hill, 1989), *Timeless Towns &*
    Haunted Places (St. Martin's, 1989), *Chelsea.*

David Johnson   P
1025 Summit NE, Albuquerque, NM 87106, 505-266-9960
    Pubs: *Fire in the Fields* (Writers on the Plains, 1996),
    Western Literature in a World Context: Anth (St. Martin's Pr,
    1995), *Puerto del Sol, Cafe Solo.*

Stanley Kiesel   P&W
PO Box 1053, Placitas, NM 87043
    Pubs: *The War Between the Pitiful Teachers and the*
    Splendid Kids, Skinny Malinky Leads the War for Kidness
    (Avon, 1994, 1985).

Don Kurtz   W
PO Box 4182, Las Cruces, NM 88003, 505-521-4832
Internet: donkurtz@nmsu.edu
    Pubs: *South of the Big Four* (Avon, 1996), *O. Henry*
    Festival Stories: Anth (Trans-Verse Pr, 1987), *Iowa Rev,*
    Puerto del Sol, Epoch.

Elizabeth Searle Lamb   P
970 Acequia Madre, Santa Fe, NM 87501, 505-982-8890
    Pubs: *Casting Into A Cloud* (From Here Pr, 1985), *New*
    Mexico Poetry Renaissance: Anth (Red Crane Bks, 1994),
    Blue Unicorn, Modern Haiku, Frogpond, Lynx.

Robert Lloyd   P
Univ New Mexico, 217 Humanities Bldg, Box 132,
Albuquerque, NM 87131

Joan Logghe   P&W
Rt 3, Box 180 A, Espanola, NM 87532, 505-753-3174
Internet: jlogghe@espanola.com
    Pubs: *Twenty Years In Bed With The Same Man* (La
    Alameda Pr, 1995), *What Makes A Woman Beautiful*
    (Pennywhistle Pr, 1993), *Catch Our Breath: Anth*
    (Mariposa, 1996), *Frank, Women's Review of Books,*
    Puerto Del Sol, Blue Mesa Rev, Hayden's Ferry Rev.

Robert Longoni   P
PO Box 422, Ramah, NM 87321, 505-783-4716
    Pubs: *Woodpiles* (Moon Pony Pr, 1997), *Poetry of the*
    Desert Southwest: Anth (Baleen Pr, 1973), *Earthcare.*

Sandra Lynn   P
1814 Hermosa Dr NE, Albuquerque, NM 871104924,
505-255-0410
> Pubs: *Where Rainbows Wait For Rain* (Tangram, 1989),
> *Inheritance of Light: Anth* (U North Texas Pr, 1996), *Three
> Texas Poets: Anth* (Prickly Pear, 1986).

Hank Malone   P
1220-J Nakomis NE, Albuquerque, NM 87112, 505-323-0474
Internet: hanksharon@aol.com
> Pubs: *Experiencing New Mexico: Lyrical and Critical
> Essays, New Mexico Haiku* (Poetic License Pr, 1998,
> 1996), *Footstrikes and Spondees* (Parkville Pr, 1993), *The
> Maverick Poets: Anth* (Gorilla Pr, 1988).

Ernest A. Mares   P
202 Edith NE, Albuquerque, NM 871023526, 505-248-0946
Internet: tmares@swcp.com
> Pubs: *The Unicorn Poem* (West End Pr, 1992), *The Indian
> Rio Grande* (San Marcos Pr, 1977), *Paper Dance: 54
> Latino Poets: Anth* (Persea Bks, 1995), *Prairie Schooner,
> Blue Mesa Rev, Blanco Movil, Century Mag, Cafe Solo,
> San Marcos Rev.*

Marguerite   P
PO Box 318, Rodeo, NM 88056-0318
Internet: http://www.thecurrent.com
> Pubs: *Kimstar* (Pinched Nerves Pr, 1992), *Apostrophe,
> Talisman, Poetry.*

Barbara McCauley   P
PO Box 326, Truchas, NM 87578, 505-689-2253
> Pubs: *Small Mercies, Written With A Spoon* (Sherman
> Asher Pub, 1998, 1996), *Drug-Related Diseases* (Franklin
> Watts, 1986), *Finding the Balance* (Red Hill, 1977), *Nation.*

Karen Quelle McKinnon   P
PO Box 508, Sandia Park, NM 87047, 505-281-9856
Internet: karennrich@aol.com
> Pubs: *Virtual Allusions, Coming True: Anth* (Solo Pr, 1996,
> 1999), *Saludos* (Pennywhistle Pr, 1995), *Queen Anne's Lace:
> Anth* (Wildflowers Pr, 1994), *Blue Mesa Rev, Puerto del Sol.*

Emerson Blackhorse Mitchell   P
Box #204, Shiprock, NM 87420

Carol Moldaw   P
RR 5, Box 231, Santa Fe, NM 87501, 505-455-3074
> Pubs: *Chalkmarks on Stone* (La Alameda Pr, 1998), *Taken
> From the River* (Alef Bks, 1993), *New Mexico Poetry
> Renaissance: Anth* (Red Crane Bks, 1994), *Manoa,
> Threepenny Rev, TriQuarterly, Southwest Rev, Kenyon
> Rev, New Republic, New Yorker, Orion.*

Linda Monacelli-Johnson   P
308 W Houghton, Santa Fe, NM 87501, 505-988-4569
> Pubs: *Campanile* (Drummer Pr, 1998), *Weathered*
> (Sunstone Pr, 1986), *Lacing the Moon* (Cleveland State U
> Poetry Ctr, 1978), *Zeta, CSM, Rio Grande Writers Qtly,
> South Florida Poetry Rev, Pembroke Mag, Tributaries.*

Frank D. Moore   P
4 Glorieta Rd, Santa Fe, NM 875058789, 505-466-0226
Internet: genesh@ixnetcom.com
> Pubs: *Literary Rev, Painted Bride Qtly, Passages North,
> Sou'wester, Four Quarters, Piedmont Literary Rev.*

Todd Moore   P
3216 San Pedro Dr NE, Albuquerque, NM 87110-2634,
505-837-1167
Internet: moorebt@aol.com
> Pubs: *Working On My Duende* (Kings Estate Pr, 1998), *The
> Last Good Thing* (Bull Thistle Pr, 1993), *Dillinger Book II*
> (Primal Pub, 1992), *Boneyard* (Ghost Dance, 1992), *Bogg,
> Chiron Rev, Pearl, Nerve Cowboy, Sin Fronteras, Bender,
> New York Qtly.*

Barbara Beasley Murphy   W
Casa Esteban, 486 Circle Dr, Santa Fe, NM 87501,
505-983-9607
> Pubs: *Fly Like An Eagle, Join In* (Delacorte, 1994, 1993),
> *Ace Hits It Big* (Bantam, 1992).

Antonya Nelson   W
New Mexico State Univ, Las Cruces, NM 88003,
505-646-3536
> Pubs: *Nobody's Girl, Talking In Bed* (Scribner, 1998, 1997),
> *Family Terrorists* (HM, 1994), *In the Land of Men* (Avon,
> 1993), *New Yorker, Story, Redbook, TriQuarterly, Esquire,
> Antioch Rev.*

Tessa Nelson-Humphries   P&W
3228 Jupiter Rd, 4 Hills, Las Cruces, NM 88012-7742
> Pubs: *Envoi: Summer Anth* (Poets Pubs, 1990), *Array, New
> Frontiers New Mexico, Negative Capability, Alaskan Poetry
> Jrnl, Confrontations, SWWJ Mag, Appalachian Heritage,
> Blue Unicorn.*

Stanley Noyes   P&W
634 E Garcia, Santa Fe, NM 87501, 505-982-4067
> Pubs: *Commander of Dead Leaves: A Dream Collection*
> (Tooth of Time, 1984), *Saludos!: Poemas De Nuevo Mexico:
> Anth* (Pennywhistle Pr, 1995), *High Plains, Blue Unicorn.*

Antony Oldknow   P
Eastern New Mexico Univ, Dept Languages/Literature,
Portales, NM 88130, 505-562-2532
> Pubs: *Ten Small Songs* (Paraiso Pr, 1985), *Consolation For
> Beggars* (Song Pr, 1978), *Antaeus.*

Louis Owens W
Univ New Mexico, Albuquerque, NM 87131, 505-277-6410
Pubs: *Nightland* (Dutton, 1996), *Bone Game* (U Oklahoma Pr, 1994).

Bill Pearlman P
Box 613, Placitas, NM 87043
Internet: b2pearl@juno.com
Pubs: *Flareup of Twosomes* (La Alameda Pr, 1996).

V. B. Price P
PO Box 6175, Albuquerque, NM 87197, 505-344-7751
Pubs: *Chaco Trilogy* (La Alameda Pr, 1998), *Saludos, Poems of New Mexico* (Pennywhistle Pr, 1995), *New Mexico Poetry Renaissance: Anth* (Red Crane Bks, 1994).

Sheila Raeschild P&W
1303 Bartlet Court, Santa Fe, NM 875011643, 505-982-7280
Internet: child@roadrunner.com
Pubs: *Earth Songs* (NAL, 1984), *The Defiant* (Dell, 1982), *Trolley Song* (Zebra, 1981), *Redbook*.

Margaret Randall P
50 Cedar Hill Rd NE, Albuquerque, NM 871221928,
505-856-6543
Internet: mrandmeg@aol.com
Pubs: *Hunger's Table* (Papier-Mache Pr, 1997), *Sandino's Daughters Revisited* (Rutgers U Pr, 1994), *Gathering Rage* (Monthly Review Pr, 1992), *American Voice, Ms., Ikon, Calyx, Berkeley Poetry Rev, Blue Mesa Rev.*

Harvena Richter P&W
1932 Candelaria Rd NW, Albuquerque, NM 87107,
505-344-6766
Pubs: *Green Girls: Poems, The Yaddo Elegies* (North Valley Pr, 1996, 1995), *The Human Shore* (Little, Brown, 1959), *South Dakota Rev, Blue Mesa Rev.*

Janet Rodney P
PO Box 8187, Santa Fe, NM 87504, 505-982-3990
Pubs: *Orphydice* (Salt Works Pr, 1986), *Crystals* (North Atlantic Bks, 1979), *Conjunctions, Sulfur.*

Leo Romero P&W
34 Calle de Gancho, Santa Fe, NM 87501, 505-473-7151
Pubs: *Rita and Los Angeles* (Bilingual Review Pr, 1994), *Going Home Away Indian* (Ahsahta Pr, 1990), *Fish Drum, The Magazine, L'Ozio, Mid-American Rev, Yefief, Bilingual Rev/Revista Bilingue, Americas Rev.*

Sharman Apt Russell W
1113 West St, Silver City, NM 88061, 505-538-6345
Internet: russellsa@silver.wnmu.edu
Pubs: *When the Land Was Young, Kill The Cowboy: A Battle of Mythology in the New West, Songs of the Fluteplayer* (Addison-Wesley, 1996, 1993, 1991), *The Humpbacked Fluteplayer* (Knopf, 1994).

Miriam Sagan P
626 Kathryn Ave, Santa Fe, NM 87501
Pubs: *Coastal Lives* (Center Pr, 1991), *True Body* (Parallax, 1991), *Fish Drum, Hayden's Ferry, Agni, Blue Mesa, APR, Ploughshares, Family Circle.*

Jim Sagel P
PO Box 942, Espanola, NM 87532, 505-753-6357
Pubs: *Mas Que No Love It* (West End Pr, 1991), *El Santo Queso/The Holy Cheese* (Ediciones del Norte, 1990).

Scott Patrick Sanders P
Univ New Mexico, Albuquerque, NM 87131, 505-277-4437
Internet: ssanders@unm.edu
Pubs: *Mr. Cogito, Rocky Mountain Rev of Language & Literature, Chiaroscuro, Spoon River Qtly, Weber Studies.*

Roberto Sandoval P
137 Romero St, Santa Fe, NM 87501, 505-982-9605

Lorna D. Saunders P
Kraylor Press, PO Box 1867, Magdalena, NM 87825
Pubs: *The Elswhere* (Kraylor Pr, 1998), *Poet Lore, Bitterroot, Apprentice, Bloodroot, Planet X.*

Ken Saville P
Box 4662, Albuquerque, NM 87196, 505-268-0265
Pubs: *20 Postcards* (Transient Pr, 1979).

Rebecca Seiferle P
5602 Tarry Terr, Farmington, NM 87402-8261, 505-325-6145
Internet: 75347.123@compuserve.com
Pubs: *The Ripped-Out Seam, Trilce* (Sheep Meadow Pr, 1993, 1992), *Calyx, TriQuarterly, Indiana Rev, APR, Harvard Rev, Blue Mesa Rev.*

Jeanne Shannon P
The Wildflower Press, PO Box 4757, Albuquerque, NM 87196-4757, 505-296-0691
Pubs: *Dissolving Forms* (Wildflower Pr, 1994), *The Party Train: Anth* (New Rivers Pr, 1996), *Blue Mesa Rev, Potato Eyes, Now & Then, Steelhead Special, Raintown Rev, Color Wheel, Dalhousie Rev, Newsletter Inago, Cafe Solo, Bear Creek Haiku.*

Sherri Silverman P
PO Box 66, Santa Fe, NM 87504-0066, 505-984-0327
Internet: shrisilver@aol.com
Pubs: *Crosswinds, Santa Fe Spirit Mag, Studia Mystica, Cicada, Sackbut Rev, Manna, Reconstructionist, Salome.*

Florentin Smarandache P&W
Univ New Mexico, 200 College Rd, Gallup, NM 87301
Internet: smarand@unm.edu
Pubs: *Classical Paradoxist Poems* (Kishinev Univ Pr, 1997), *Non Novel* (Romania; Tempus Pub Hse, 1993), *Non Poems* (Xiquan Pub Hse, 1990), *Dorul, Rivista Internationale, Revista Divaagacao Cultural, Vatra, Poet, Poetry Nippon, Art Et Poesie De Touraine.*

Linda Wasmer Smith P
12017 Kashmir St, NE, Albuquerque, NM 87111,
505-296-3095
   Pubs: *Second Aid* (Fish Down Pr, 1993), *If I Had My Life to
   Live Over I Would Pick More Daisies: Anth* (Papier-Mache
   Pr, 1992), *Defined Providence.*

Maryhelen Snyder P
422 Camino Del Bosque NW, Albuquerque, NM 87114,
505-898-7047
Internet: rsnyder@unm.edu
   Pubs: *Enough* (Solo Pr, 1979), *The Practice of Peace: Anth*
   (Sherman Asher Pr, 1998), *Blue Mesa Rev, Puerto del Sol,
   New America, Southwestern Discoveries, Slant, Cafe Solo,
   New Laurel Rev, Tulsa Poetry Qtly.*

Anthony Sobin P
22 Alcalde Rd, Santa Fe, NM 87505
   Pubs: *The Sunday Naturalist* (Ohio U Pr, 1982), *Poetry,
   Poetry Northwest, Beloit Poetry Journal.*

Jane Somerville P
2442 Cerillos Rd, Ste 455, Sante Fe, NM 87505-3262
   Pubs: *The Only Blessing* (Greenhouse Rev Pr, 1992),
   Making the Light Come (Wayne State U Pr, 1990), *APR,
   Gettysburg Rev, Kansas Qtly, Ohio Rev.*

Joseph Somoza P
1725 Hamiel Dr, Las Cruces, NM 88001, 505-522-1119
   Pubs: *Four-eyed Dialogues* (New Mexico Jr College Pr,
   1996), *Out of This World* (Cinco Puntos Pr, 1990), *Blue
   Mesa Rev, Writers' Forum, New Mexico Renaissance.*

Marcia Southwick P
1001 Camino Pinones, Santa Fe, NM 87505, 505-989-8781
Internet: smouthwick@aol.com
   Pubs: *A Saturday Night At The Flying Dog* (Field Pr, 1998),
   Why The River Disappears (Carnegie Mellon U, 1990), *The
   Night Won't Save Anyone* (U Georgia, 1980), *APR, Harvard
   Rev, Field, Prairie Schooner, Antaeus, Poetry, Iowa Rev.*

Arlene Stone P&W
PO Box 2880, Sante Fe, NM 87504-2880
   Pubs: *Son Sonnets* (Emmanuel Pr, 1994), *The Double
   Pipes of Pan* (North Atlantic Bks, 1983), *Harper's, Yellow
   Silk, Contact II.*

Mary Swander P
Univ New Mexico, English Dept, Humanities Bldg,
Albuquerque, NM 87131-1106
   Pubs: *Out Of This World* (Viking, 1995), *Heaven-and-Earth
   House, Driving the Body Back* (Knopf, 1994, 1986), *New
   Republic, CSM, Nation, New Yorker, Poetry.*

George Swaney P
1825 Meadow Ln, Las Cruces, NM 88005
   Pubs: *Iowa Rev, Poetry East, Georgetown Rev, Gulf
   Stream, Mudfish, Rastown Rev, Antietam Rev, Haight
   Ashbury Jrnl, Jacaranda Rev, Sou'wester, Pittsburgh Qtly.*

Arthur Sze P
PO Box 457, Santa Fe, NM 87504-0457, 505-455-3074
   Pubs: *The Redshifting Web: Poems 1970-1998,
   Archipelago* (Copper Canyon Pr, 1998, 1995), *River River*
   (Lost Roads, 1987), *APR, Paris Rev, Manoa, Conjunctions,
   Kenyon Rev, Orion.*

Nathaniel Tarn P
P.O. Box 871, Tesuque, NM 875740871, 505-982-3990
   Pubs: *Seeing America First* (Coffee Hse Pr, 1989),
   Atitlan/Alashka (Brillig Works, 1979), *Sulfur, Conjunctions,
   First Intensity, Alea, Chain, To.*

John Thorndike W
630 E Alameda, Santa Fe, NM 87501
Internet: 76745.110@compuserve.com
   Pubs: *Another Way Home* (Crown, 1996), *The Potato Baron*
   (Villard, 1989), *Anna Delaney's Child* (Macmillan, 1986).

Paul Edward Trujillo P
Box 396, Peralta, NM 87042, 505-864-0307
   Pubs: *Bilingual Rev, Ceremony Of Brotherhood, Poetry
   Now, Writers' Forum.*

Sharon Oard Warner W
Univ New Mexico, Humanities Bldg 217, Albuquerque, NM
87131-1106, 505-277-6248
Internet: swarner@unm.edu
   Pubs: *Learning to Dance and Other Stories* (New Rivers Pr,
   1992), *Inheriting the Land: Anth* (U Minnesota Pr, 1993),
   *Other Voices, Iowa Woman, Long Story, Gamut, Prairie
   Schooner, Green Mountains Rev, Sonora Rev, AWP
   Chronicle, Studies in Short Fiction.*

Mark Weber P
725 Van Buren Pl SE, Albuquerque, NM 87108,
505-255-3012
   Pubs: *Existential Hum* (Pearl Special Edtns, 1996),
   Swindler's Harmonica Siesta, Drunk City (Zerx Pr, 1994,
   1991), *Pearl, Wormwood Rev, Caprice, Chiron.*

Joel Weishaus P
401 14th St SW #11, Albuquerque, NM 87102-2871,
505-266-5820
   Pubs: *Woods, Shore, Desert: 1968 Notebook of Thomas
   Merton* (Museum of New Mexico Pr, 1983), *Artspace.*

Kathleene West P
New Mexico State Univ, PO Box 30001, English Dept, Las
Cruces, NM 88003
Internet: kwest@nmsu.edu
   Pubs: *The Farmer's Daughter* (Sandhills, 1990), *Water
   Witching* (Copper Canyon, 1984), *TriQuarterly, Kenyon
   Rev, Prairie Schooner.*

Keith Wilson   P
1500 S Locust #C-21, Las Cruces, NM 88001, 505-522-8389
Internet: kewilson@nmsu.edu
     Pubs: *Bosque Redondo* (Penny Whistle Pr, 1998), *Graves Registry* (Clark City Pr, 1992).

Herta Wittgenstein   W
PO Box 9848, Santa Fe, NM 87504, 505-984-1154
     Pubs: *Watching A Field of Zebras* (Demarais Studio Pr, 1992).

Bruce P. Woodford   P&W
140 Mesa Vista, Santa Fe, NM 87501, 505-988-3766
     Pubs: *Edges Of Distance* (Lightning Tree, 1977), *Wind, Poetry Jrnl, Chimera, The Sun, Samisdat*.

Arlene Zekowski   P&W
Pamela Tree, PO Box 6136, Santa Fe, NM 87502, 505-983-8484
     Pubs: *Against the Disappearance of Literature, The Living Underground: Anth* (Whitston Pr, 1998, 1999), *Every Person's Little Book of P-L-U-T-O-N-I-U-M* (Rising Tide Pr, 1992), *Dictionary of the Avant-Gardes: Anth* (A Cappella Pr, 1994), *Tyuonyi, Margins*.

NEW YORK

Sam Abrams   P
Rochester Institute Technology, College of Liberal Arts, Rochester, NY 14623, 716-475-2444
Internet: sxagsl@rit.edu
     Pubs: *The Jazz Poetry Anth* (Indiana U Pr, 1991), *Out of this World: Anth* (Crown, 1991), *Up Late: Anth* (4 Walls 0 Windows, 1987), *Alcatraz, Exquisite Corpse*.

Barbara Adams   P&W
597 Coach Ln, Newburgh, NY 125503818, 914-564-3499
Internet: bbadams@firststreetinternet.com
     Pubs: *The Muse Strikes Back: Anth* (Storyline Pr, 1997), *When A Lifemate Dies* (Fairview Pr, 1997), *Free Associations, Psychoanalytic Rev, Humanist, Breakfast All Day, Belles Lettres*.

Jeanette Adams   P
208 Old Country Rd, Elmsford, NY 10523
     Pubs: *Poetry In Performance 19* (CUNY, 1991), *Parallels Artists Poets: Anth* (Midmarch Arts, 1993), *Drumvoices Revue: Anth* (U Southern Illinois, 1992), *Essence*.

Joan Albarella   P
3574 Clinton St, Buffalo, NY 14224, 716-656-5043
Internet: jkea@juno.com
     Pubs: *Spirit and Joy* (Alpha Pr, 1993), *Women Flowers Fantasy* (Textile Bridge Pr, 1987), *Sunshine Mag, Buffalo Courier Express, North American Voice of Fatima, WNY Catholic, Now, Christian Outlook*.

Joan Alden   W
242 Main St, Catskill, NY 12414, 518-943-5526
     Pubs: *Before Our Eyes, Letting In the Night* (Firebrand Bks, 1993, 1989), *A Boy's Best Friend* (Alyson Pubs, 1992).

Linda Allardt   P
2 Ann Lynn Rd, Pittsford, NY 14534-3910, 716-248-5223
Internet: lallardt@aol.com
     Pubs: *Seeing For You* (State Street Pr, 1981), *The Names of the Survivors* (Ithaca Hse, 1979), *The Bridge, Beloit Poetry Jrnl, West Branch, Cincinnati Poetry Rev, Nightsun*.

John Allman   P&W
28 Frances Dr, Katonah, NY 10536, 914-232-3835
Internet: ejallman@aol.com
     Pubs: *Inhabited World: New & Selected Poems* (Wallace Stevens Society Pr, 1995), *Descending Fire & Other Stories* (New Directions, 1994), *Pivot, Quarterly, Beloit, Poetry Northwest, North Dakota Qtly*.

Karen Alpha   W
106 Welch Rd, Corning, NY 14830, 607-936-6576
     Pubs: *Redbook, NAR, Blueline, North Dakota Qtly, Delaware Today, The Grapevine*.

Lynne Alvarez   P
RR 1, Box 27, Cooperstown, NY 13326-9801, 607-547-5333
     Pubs: *On New Ground* (TCG, 1987), *Living With Numbers, The Dreaming Man* (Waterfront, 1987, 1984).

Lori Anderson   P
SUNY Albany, Albany, NY 12???, 518-442-4500
     Pubs: *Cultivating Excess* (Eighth Mtn Pr, 1992), *Walking The Dead* (Heaven Bone Pr, 1991), *Seeds*.

Marjorie Appleman   P
PO Box 39, Sagaponack, NY 119620039, 516-537-1741
     Pubs: *Against Time* (Birnham Wood, 1994), *Seduction Duet* (Samuel French, 1982), *Women Against War: Anth, Poetry Rev, Wind, Kentucky Poetry Rev, Sojourner*.

Philip Appleman   P&W
PO Box 39, Sagaponack, NY 11962-0039, 516-537-1741
     Pubs: *New and Selected Poems: 1956-1996* (U Arkansas Pr, 1996), *Let There Be Light* (HarperCollins, 1991), *Darwin's Ark* (Indiana U Pr, 1984), *Nation, Paris Rev*.

Sondra Audin Armer   P
1 Everett Ave, Ossining, NY 10562, 914-941-0648
Internet: ssaphd@aol.com
     Pubs: *Moonsnap: Anth* (Amarantus Pr, 1998), *Dog Music: Anth* (St. Martin's Pr, 1996), *Sparrow, Amelia, Western Humanities Rev, Apalachee Qtly, Negative Capability, Home Planet News*.

Deborah Artman P&W
9 Hill 99, Woodstock, NY 12498
Pubs: *Bite to Eat Place* (Redwood Coast Pr, 1995),
*American Short Fiction, Carolina Qtly, Cottonwood, Seattle
Rev, Ironwood, Appearances.*

Linda Ashear P
2 Harriman's Keep, Irvington, NY 10533, 914-591-7860
Internet: lingolite@aol.com
Pubs: *The Rowers, the Swimmers & the Drowned* (Morris
Pr, 1996), *Toward the Light* (Croton Rev Pr, 1989),
MacGuffin, Santa Barbara Rev, Without Halos.

Rilla Askew W
PO Box 324, Kauneonga Lake, NY 12749, 914-583-7027
Pubs: *The Mercy Seat* (Viking, 1997), *Strange Business*
(Viking/Penguin, 1992), *Prize Stories 1993: O. Henry
Awards Anth* (Doubleday, 1993), *Nimrod, Puerto del Sol,
Carolina Qtly.*

Katharine Assante P
22 Armand's Way, Highland Mills, NY 109309801,
914-534-8522
Pubs: *A Delicate Blue Veil, October's Child* (Assante, 1994,
1990), *Algonquin Qtly, On Course, Critical Mass.*

Susan Astor P
113 Princeton St, Roslyn Heights, NY 11577, 516-621-8851
Pubs: *Vital Signs* (U Wisconsin, 1989), *Dame* (U Georgia,
1980), *Paris Rev, Partisan Rev, Poet Lore, Kansas Qtly,
Confrontation, Croton Rev.*

Brett Axel P
11 Wickham Ave Apt 1, Middletown, NY 10940,
914-343-1377
Internet: axels@orn.net
Pubs: *First on the Fire* (Genesis/Fly by Night Pr, 1999) *The
Spastic Grandson, Twenty-six Different Poems* (Heaven
Bone Pr, 1998, 1998), *Diner Eucharist: Anth* (Orange
County Arts Council, 1997), *Princeton Arts Rev, Unknown
Writer, Algonquin Qtly.*

David B. Axelrod P
3WS, World Wide Writer's Servi, PO Box 698, Centereach,
NY 11720-0698, 516-451-0478
Pubs: *Intro to Literature: Anth* (HC, 1998), *The Chi of
Poetry: New & Selected Poems* (Birnham Wood, 1995),
*Long Island Qtly, Shi Kahn, Kansas Qtly, Nasa Kniga, New
York Times, North Carolina Qtly.*

J. C. Axelrod P&W
25C Nymph Rd, Rocky Point, NY 11778, 516-744-7058
Pubs: *Facts of Life, Entrances to Nowhere* (CCC, 1987,
1976), *West Hills Rev, New Letters, Greenfield Rev.*

Donald Everett Axinn P&W
131 Jericho Turnpike, Jericho, NY 11753-1024,
516-333-8500
Pubs: *The Latest Illusion, Spin* (Arcade, 1995, 1994), *Dawn
Patrol* (CCC, 1992), *Antaeus, New England Rev, New York
Qtly, Confrontation, New York Times, Newsday.*

Anna Ruth Ediger Baehr P
218 Brompton Rd, Garden City, NY 11530, 516-746-4203
Pubs: *Moonflowers at Dusk* (Birnham Wood Pr, 1996),
*American Scholar, Long Island Poetry Rev, Xanadu,
Mennonite Life, Choice Mag Listening.*

George Bailin P
Sacred Orchard, PO Box 298, Harriman, NY 109260298,
914-783-8154
Internet: sacredor@warwick.net
Pubs: *Sage of Ananda, First Strike* (Seaport Poets &
Writers Pr, 1993, 1988), *Dead Reckoning* (Dragonsbreath
Pr, 1984), *Evening News Report* (Court Poetry Pr, 1984),
Meditators Newsletter.

Ansie Baird P
17 Tudor Pl, Buffalo, NY 14222, 716-882-0979
Pubs: *Paris Rev, Poetry Northwest, Denver Qtly, Poetry
Now, Vassar Qtly, The Quarterly, Earth's Daughters,
Southern Rev, South Dakota Rev, Green River Rev.*

Peter Balakian P
Colgate Univ, English Dept, Hamilton, NY 13346
Pubs: *Reply from Wilderness Island, Sad Days of Light*
(Sheep Meadow Pr, 1988, 1983), *Poetry.*

Harry Barba W
Harian Creative Books, PO Box 189, Clifton Park, NY 12065,
518-885-6699
Pubs: *Mona Lisa Smiles, Round Trip to Byzantium, Gospel
According to Everyman* (Harian Creative Books, 1993,
1985, 1981).

Stanley H. Barkan P
Cross-Cultural Communications, PO Box 383, Merrick, NY
11566-0383, 516-868-5635
Pubs: *Modern Poems on the Bible: Anth* (JPS, 1994), *On
Prejudice: Anth* (Doubleday, 1993), *Confrontation,
Footwork, Forward, Home Planet News, Lips.*

Mildred Barker W
4239 Route 209, Stone Ridge, NY 12484, 914-687-7942
Pubs: *Speaking the Words* (Word Thursdays/Bright Hill Pr,
1994), *If I Had A Hammer: Women's Work: Anth*
(Papier-Mache Pr, 1990), *Oxalis Literary Qtly, Almanac,
Ms., Nimrod, Mademoiselle, Reporter.*

Nancy Barnes   P
Erie Community College, 121 Ellicott St, Buffalo, NY 14203,
716-851-1018
   Pubs: *Pure Light, Earth's Daughters, Black Mountain Rev,
   Centrum Jrnl, Fine China: Twenty Years of Earth's
   Daughters.*

Helen Baron   P&W
86 Maple Ave, Hastings-on-Hudson, NY 10706,
914-478-5774
Internet: helenbarolini@juno.com
   Pubs: *Umbertina, a novel* (Feminist Pr, 1998), *Chiaroscuro:
   Essays of Identity* (Bordighera, 1997), *Aldus and His Dream
   Book* (Italica Pr, 1991), *Italian American Literature & Art:
   Anth* (Garland, 1996), *Southwest Rev, Virginia Qtly Rev,
   New Letters.*

Linda Michelle Baron   PP
Panache Inc, PO Box 4051, Hempstead, NY 11551-4051
   Pubs: *The Sun Is On, Rhythm & Dues* (Harlin Jacque,
   1981, 1981).

Marylin Lytle Barr   P
PO Box 75, Grahamsville, NY 12740, 914-985-7337
   Pubs: *Concrete Considerations* (Sweetwater Pub, 1993),
   Drawn From the Shadows (Egret Pr, 1991), *Alchemist 8:
   Anth* (Alchemy Club, 1995), *Poetry Page, Oxalis, Zephyr,
   Outloud, Piedmont Literary Qtly, Alchemist, Bay Street
   Echoes.*

Jack Barry   P
121 North Way, Camillus, NY 13031, 315-488-3566
   Pubs: *Hints and Hunches* (Garlic Pr, 1974), *New Letters,
   APR, Notre Dame Rev, Poetpourri, Syracuse Rev.*

Jill Bart   P&W
80 Pauls Ln, Water Mill, NY 11976, 516-537-1163
   Pubs: *The Naked & The Nude* (Birnham Wood, 1993), *First
   Light* (Paumanok Pr, 1988), *Negative Capability, Blue Unicorn,
   Long Pond Rev, Poetry East, Long Island Qtly, Ms..*

Michael Basinski   PP&P
30 Colonial Ave, Lancaster, NY 14086-2509, 716-681-3116
   Pubs: *Heebee-Jeebees, Cnyttan* (Meow Pr, 1996, 1993),
   SleVep (Tailspin Pr, 1995), *Vessels* (Texture Pr, 1993),
   Object, Lyric, First Intensity.

John Batki   P&W
211 Lockwood Rd, Syracuse, NY 13214, 315-445-0137

M. Garrett Bauman   W
Monroe Community College, English Dept, Rochester, NY
14623, 716-292-2000
   Pubs: *Ideas and Details, The Shape of Ideas* (HB, 1998,
   1995), *Story, Upstate, Yankee, Wisconsin Rev, Greensboro
   Rev, Chrysalis.*

E. R. Baxter, III   P
2709 Braley Rd, Ransomville, NY 14131, 716-791-4611
   Pubs: *Looking for Niagara, What I Want* (Slipstream Pub,
   1993, 1993), *Albany Rev, Black Mountain Rev, Earth's
   Daughters, Pig Iron.*

Bruce Bennett   P
Box 145, Aurora, NY 13026, 315-364-3228
Internet: brbennett@wells.edu
   Pubs: *It's Hard to Get the Angle Right* (Greentower Press,
   1997), *Taking Off* (Orchises Pr, 1992), *I Never Danced With
   Mary Beth* (FootHills Pub, 1991), *Harvard Rev, The
   Quarterly, Laurel Rev, Tar River Poetry, Prairie Schooner,
   The Formalist, Light.*

Sally Bennett   P&W
846 Ostrom Ave, Syracuse, NY 13210, 315-478-7129
Internet: salmarsh@aol.com
   Pubs: *American Fiction: Anth* (Birch Lane Pr, 1990), *Anth of
   Magazine Verse & Yearbook of American Poetry* (Monitor
   Bks, 1987), *Pangolin Papers, The Distillery, Poetry, Seneca
   Rev, Gulf Stream Mag, Syracuse Scholar, Sycamore Rev.*

Robert Bensen   P
14 Harrison Ave, Oneonta, NY 13820, 607-431-4902
Internet: bensenr@hartwick.edu
   Pubs: *Caribbean Writer, Paris Rev, Partisan Rev, Antioch
   Rev, Akwe:kon Jrnl, Cumberland Poetry Rev, Poetry
   Wales, Ploughshares, Cimarron Rev, Yankee.*

Kimberly Berg   P
489 East Rd, Cadyville, NY 12918
   Pubs: *Hummingbird, Minkhill Jrnl, Colorwheel, Rooster Bay,
   Visions, High Rock Rev, Negative Capability, CSM.*

Frank Bergon   W
Vassar College, Mail Drop 94, Poughkeepsie, NY
126040094, 914-437-5663
Internet: bergon@vassar.edu
   Pubs: *Wild Game, The Temptations of St. Ed & Brother S*
   (U Nevada Pr, 1995, 1993), *Shoshone Mike* (Viking
   Penguin, 1987).

Bruce Berlind   P
PO Box 237, Hamilton, NY 13346, 315-893-7078
   Pubs: *Otto Orban's The Journey of Barbarus* (Passegiatta
   Pr, 1997), *When You Became She* (Xenos Bks, 1994),
   Birds and Other Relations (Princeton U Pr, 1987), *Partisan
   Rev, Kenyon Rev, Grand Street, Poetry, New Letters, APR.*

Cassia Berman   P
11 1/2 Tannery Brook Rd, Woodstock, NY 12498,
914-679-9457
   Pubs: *Divine Mother Within Me, Divine Mother Poems* (Divine
   Mother Communications, 1995, 1993), *APR, Chelsea,
   Northeast Jrnl, The Falcon, Poetry Studies, Collaboration,
   Modern Poetry Studies, Lillabulero, Species Link.*

Charles Bernstein P
SUNY, English Dept, 438 Clemens Hall, Buffalo, NY 14260,
716-645-3810
Internet: bernstei@bway.net
Pubs: *My Way: Speeches and Poems* (U Chicago Pr, 1998),
Republics of Reality: Poems 1975-1995 (Sun & Moon Pr,
1998), *A Poetics* (Harvard U Pr, 1992), *Chain,
L=A=N=G=U=A=G=E, Sulfur, Avec, West Coast Line.*

Holly Beye P&W
PO Box 1043, Woodstock, NY 12498, 914-679-2820
Pubs: *Out of the Catskills and Beyond: Anth* (Bertha
Rogers, 1997), *In the City of Sorrowing Clouds* (Print
Workshop, 1953), *Oxalis, New Directions Annual.*

Harvey Bialy P
81 W Market St, Red Hook, NY 12571
Pubs: *The Broken Pot, Babalon 156* (Sandollar, 1975,
1970).

Rand Bishop P
State Univ New York, English Dept, Oswego, NY 13126,
315-341-2616
Pubs: *Black Warrior Rev, Sou'wester, Florida Rev, Red
Cedar Rev, Galley Sail Rev, Kansas Qtly.*

Ellen Graf Biss P
961 Birchwood Ln, Niskayuna, NY 12309, 518-783-8849
Pubs: *Poet's Gallery, Blueline, Greenfield Rev, Tightrope,
Jump River Rev, Washout Rev.*

Celia Bland P
6 Friendship St, Tivoli, NY 12583
Pubs: *Too Darn Hot: Anth* (Global City Rev/Persea Bks,
1998), *Mudfish, 13th Moon, Snake Nation Rev, Chain, Poet
Lore, Pequod, Columbia Mag, Verse, Pavement, New
Poetry from Oxford, Washington Rev, Madison Rev,
Apalachee Qtly.*

Pamela Wharton Blanpied W
19 Pinnard St, Rochester, NY 14610, 716-473-5483
Pubs: *Dragons: An Introduction To The Modern Infestation*
(Warner Bks, 1981).

Sarah W. Bliumis P
8 Pheasant Dr, Armonk, NY 10504, 914-273-8324
Pubs: *Spoon River Qtly, Ceilioh, Whetstone.*

Janet Bloom P
The Barn Mt Airy, 1 Hale Hollow Rd #3A, Croton-on-Hudson,
NY 10520, 914-271-0091
Pubs: *APR, Poetry Now, New York Qtly, Parnassus,
Teachers & Writers Mag, Imagery Today.*

Etta Blum P
397 Spruce Ln, East Meadow, NY 11554
Pubs: *Poems* (Golden Eagle Pr, 1937), *Poetry, Paris Rev,
Nation, New Republic, Open Places.*

Bonnielizabethoag PP
Dionondehowa Wildlife Sanctuar, 148 Stanton Rd, Shushan,
NY 12873, 518-854-3648
Pubs: *Interview With A Young Crone* (Orion Pr, 1996),
Sand Paintings (Muse Room, 1995).

Audrey Borenstein W
Four Henry Ct, New Paltz, NY 125613000, 914-255-7333
Pubs: *Paradise* (Florida Literary Fdn, 1994), *Women of the
14th Moon* (Crossing Pr, 1991), *Medicinal Purposes
Literary Rev, Oxalis, Albany Rev, MacGuffin, North Dakota
Qtly, Kansas Qtly/Arkansas Rev, Albany Rev.*

Emily Borenstein P
189 Highland Ave, Middletown, NY 10940, 914-343-3796
Pubs: *Night of the Broken Glass* (Timberline Pr, 1981),
Cancer Queen (Barlenmir House, 1979), *Aura Literary/Arts
Rev, Home Planet News, Pivot, Poet Lore, Response,
Webster Rev.*

Martin Boris W
Ghame Writing Corporation, 1019 Northfield Ave, Woodmere,
NY 11598, 516-374-2058
Pubs: *Brief Candle* (Crown, 1990), *Woodridge, 1946*
(Ace, 1981), *Two & Two* (Ballantine, 1980).

Megan Boyd P
PO Box 27, Sag Harbor, NY 11963, 516-725-9220
Pubs: *Gathering to Deep Water* (Quay Bks, 1988), *New
Voices: Anth* (Academy of American Poets, 1984).

Maureen Brady W
135 Winnie Rd, Mt Tremper, NY 12457
Pubs: *Daybreak* (Harper San Francisco, 1991), *The
Question She Put To Herself, Folly* (Crossing Pr, 1987,
1982), *Feminary, Ikon, Southern Exposure.*

Alice G. Brand P
State Univ New York, Brockport, NY 16214, 716-232-1828
Pubs: *Studies on Zone* (BkMk Pr, 1989), *As It Happens*
(Wampeter Pr, 1983), *Confrontation, River Styx, Nimrod,
Paintbrush, New Letters, Minnesota Rev.*

Anthony Brandt P&W
54 High St, Sag Harbor, NY 11963, 516-725-1937
Internet: asbrandt@aol.com
Pubs: *The People Along The Sand: Three Stories, Six Poems
And A Memoir* (Canio's Edtns, 1992), *Prairie Schooner, New
York Qtly, Boulevard, Times Literary Supplement.*

Kate Braverman P&W
Box 794, Alfred, NY 14802, 607-587-9456
Pubs: *Small Craft Warnings* (U Nevada Pr, 1998), *Wonders
of the West, Squandering the Blue* (Ballantine, 1993, 1990),
Postcard from August, Hurricane Warnings (Illuminati,
1990, 1987), *Palm Latitudes* (Simon & Schuster, 1988).

Susan Breen   W
1 Riverview Ct, Irvington, NY 10533, 914-591-7841
Internet: szb4@yahoo.com
    Pubs: *Kinesis, Kansas Qtly/Arkansas Rev, American Literary
    Rev, North Dakota Qtly, Chattahoochee, New Delta.*

Ray Bremser   P
1740C Armory Dr, Utica, NY 13501
    Pubs: *Poems of Madness, Angel* (Water Row Pr, 1986, 1986).

Wendy Brenner   W
150 Capen Rd, Brockport, NY 14420, 716-395-9159
    Pubs: *Large Animals In Everyday Life* (U Georgia Pr,
    1996), *New Stories From The South: Anth* (Algonquin,
    1995), *Ploughshares, Southern Exposure, Puerto del Sol.*

William Bronk   P
57 Pearl St, Hudson Falls, NY 12839, 518-747-6565
    Pubs: *Selected Poems* (New Directions, 1995), *Ourselves,
    The Mild Day* (Talisman Hse, 1995, 1993), *Living Instead*
    (North Point Pr, 1991).

Joseph E. Bruchac, III   P&W
PO Box 308, Greenfield Center, NY 12833, 518-584-1728
    Pubs: *Between Earth And Sky* (HB, 1996), *Dawn Land*
    (Fulcrum Pub, 1993), *Green Mountains Rev, Kestrel,
    Parabola, Gatherings, Puerto del Sol, Bullhead.*

Judith Bruder   W
132 Wagon Rd, Roslyn Heights, NY 11577, 516-621-2572
Internet: judithb@idt.net
    Pubs: *Convergence* (Doubleday, 1993), *Going to
    Jerusalem* (S&S, 1979).

Ira Beryl Brukner   P
123 Fayette St., Ithaca, NY 14850, 607-256-2114
    Pubs: *Questions, Short Poems, Water & Air* (Junction Pr,
    1998).

Felice Buckvar   W
43 Juneau Blvd, Woodbury, NY 11797, 516-692-5485
    Pubs: *Dangerous Dream* (Royal Fireworks Pr, 1998), *Ten
    Miles High* (Morrow, 1981), *Happily Ever After* (Zebra
    Books, 1980), *Family Circle, Woman's Day, Reader's
    Digest, Real People.*

Frederick Henderson Buell   P
72 Amity Rd, Warwick, NY 10990, 914-258-6076
Internet: buell@warwick.net
    Pubs: *Full Summer* (Wesleyan, 1979), *Theseus & Other
    Poems* (Ithaca Hse, 1971), *Poetry, Hudson Rev, NER, Little
    Mag, Kansas Qtly, Pembroke Mag, Southern Rev,
    Southwest Rev.*

Michael Burkard   P
313 E Hamilton Ave, Sherrill, NY 13461, 315-361-4822
    Pubs: *Entire Dilemma* (Sarabande Bks, 1998), *My Secret
    Boat* (Norton, 1990), *The Fires They Kept* (Metro Bk Co.,
    1986), *Paris Rev, APR, Epoch, Denver Qtly, Exquisite
    Corpse, Central Park, Salt Hill Jrnl, Volt, Plum Rev, Zone 3.*

Gabrielle Burton   P&W
211 Le Brun Rd, Eggertsville, NY 14226, 716-835-5062
    Pubs: *Heartbreak Hotel* (Scribner, 1986).

Frederick Busch   W
839 Turnpike Rd, Sherburne, NY 13460, 607-847-8646
    Pubs: *Girls* (Fawcett, 1998), *A Dangerous Profession* (St.
    Martin's, 1998), *The Children in the Woods*
    (Fawcett/Columbine, 1994).

Rebecca Busselle   W
RR 2, Box 270, Millerton, NY 12546, 518-789-3413
Internet: rebline@pipeline.com
    Pubs: *An Exposure of the Heart* (Norton, 1999), *A Frog's-Eye
    View, Bathing Ugly* (Orchard Books, 1990, 1989).

Don Byrd   P
SUNY Albany, 1400 Washington, Albany, NY 12222,
518-442-4055
    Pubs: *The Great Dimestore* (Station Hill Pr, 1986), *Technics
    Of Travel* (Tansy-Zelot, 1984).

Frederick Byrnes, Jr.   P
17 Koster Ct, Huntington Station, NY 11746, 516-427-9445
    Pubs: *No One to Sing Praises* (Street Pr, 1986), *Luok &
    Other Poems* (Everett Pr, 1985).

Charles Calitri   W
30 Gristmill Ln, Halesite, NY 11743
    Pubs: *The Goliath Head, Father, Strike Heaven on the
    Face* (Crown, 1974, 1962, 1958).

Jimmie Gilliam Canfield   P&W
Erie Comm College/City Campus, 121 Ellicott St, Buffalo, NY
14203, 716-842-8676
    Pubs: *Pieces of Bread* (White Pine Pr, 1986), *Black
    Mountain II Rev, Earth's Daughters.*

Joe Cardillo   P
Hudson Valley Comm College, MRV 214, Troy, NY 12180,
518-270-7577
Internet: cardijos@hvcc.edu
    Pubs: *Karate Lessons* (Dutton/Penguin, 2000), *Pulse*
    (Dutton/Penguin, 1996), *The Rock N' Roll Journals, No
    Surrender* (Stone Buzzard Pr, 1996, 1993), *Rolling Stone,
    Fine Madness, Crab Creek Rev, Sierra Madre Rev,
    Footwork, Lactuca.*

Douglas Carlson P
Box 142, Fredonia, NY 14063, 716-679-1865
Pubs: *At The Edge* (White Pine Pr, 1988), *Waiting to Disappear* (Allegheny Mountain Pr, 1977), *Georgia Rev, North Dakota Qtly, Petroglyph.*

Michael Carrino P
19 Guy Way, Apt. B, Plattsburgh, NY 12901, 518-564-2134
Pubs: *Some Rescues* (New Poets Series, 1994), *Green Mountains Rev, Husdon Rev, Poetry East, Slant, Calliope, Hayden's Ferry Rev.*

Hayden Carruth P
RD 1, Box 128, Munnsville, NY 13409, 315-495-6665
Pubs: *Collected Shorter Poems, 1946-1991* (Copper Canyon, 1992), *Tell Me Again How The White Heron Rises...* (New Directions, 1991).

Shari Elaine Carter PP
4677 N Street Rd, Marcellus, NY 13108, 315-673-1789

Fran Castan P
Maidstone & Central, PO Box 1923, Amagansett, NY 11930, 516-267-8646
Pubs: *The Widow's Quilt* (Canio Edtns, 1996), *From Both Sides Now: Poetry of Vietnam: Anth* (Scribner, 1998), *The Seasons of Women: Anth* (Norton, 1995), *The Doll House Anth* (Pushcart, 1995), *On Prejudice: Anth* (Anchor, 1993), *Ms., Poetry Mag.*

Alan Catlin P
143 Furman St, Schenectady, NY 12304-1113, 518-372-5016
Internet: catlin@crisny.org
Pubs: *Killer Cocktails* (Four Sep Pub, 1997), *Self Annihilation With Shopping Bag Ladies* (UBP, 1995), *Shelley & the Romantics* (Adastra, 1994), *New York Qtly, Wormwood Rev, Rafters, Happy, Lucid Stone, Press, Poet Lore.*

Siv Cedering P&W
Box 800, Amagansett, NY 119300800, 516-267-8030
Internet: siv@hamptons.com
Pubs: *Letters From An Observatory* (Karma Dog Edtns, 1998), *Letters From the Floating World* (U Pitt Pr, 1984), *The Blue Horse* (Clarion Bks, 1979), *Harper's, Ms., Georgia Rev, Paris Rev, Antaeus, Science.*

Elaine Rollwagen Chamberlain P
97 Springville Ave, Amherst, NY 14226, 716-837-0475
Pubs: *Pictures From the Bee House* (White Pine Pr, 1978).

Lena London Charney P
PO Box 145, Mohegan Lake, NY 10547-0145, 914-528-5162
Pubs: *Lover's Lane: Anth, More Big Thoughts: Anth, The Color of Gold: Anth* (Golden Apple Pr, 1998, 1997,1995), *We Speak for Peace: Anth* (KIT Pub, 1993), *Westchester Writer, Lucid Stone, Raconteur, Robin's Nest, Wordplay.*

Robert Chatain P&W
PO Box 1770, Amagansett, NY 11930
Pubs: *Touring Nam: The Viet Nam War Reader* (Morrow, 1985), *Best of TriQuarterly: Anth* (Washington Square Pr, 1982).

Sanford Chernoff W
3 Laurel Ave, Glen Cove, NY 11542
Pubs: *All Our Secrets Are The Same* (Norton, 1977), *New Directions, The Quarterly, Partisan Rev, Epoch.*

L. John Cieslinski P
8 Close Hollow Dr, Hamlin, NY 14464, 716-964-2868
Internet: johnmore@concentric.net
Pubs: *Amelia, Pearl, Stone Country, Karamu, Negative Capability, Magical Blend, Black Bear Rev, Voices Intl, Sore Dove, Piedmont Literary Rev.*

Josephine Clare P
435 Exchange St, Geneva, NY 14456, 315-789-9517
Pubs: *Mammatocumulus* (Ocotillo Pr, 1977), *Deutschland & Other Poems* (North Atlantic Bks, 1974).

Barbara Moore Clarkson P
244 Lorraine Ave, Syracuse, NY 13210, 315-474-3533
Pubs: *The Flame Tree* (Basfal Bks, 1996), *Farewell to the Body* (The Word Works, 1991), *APR, Georgia Rev, Massachusetts Rev, Poetry, Salmagundi, NER.*

Suzanne Cleary P
215 Pine St, Peekskill, NY 10566
Pubs: *Poetry, Southern Rev, The Literary Rev, Mss., APR, Ohio Rev, Prairie Schooner, Georgia Rev, Poetry Northwest, Beloit Poetry Jrnl, Mississippi Rev.*

Mickey Clement W
14 Bay Crest, Huntington Bay, NY 11743, 516-427-8316
Pubs: *The Irish Princess* (Putnam, 1994).

Vince Clemente P
25 Cornell Rd, Sag Harbor, NY 11963, 516-725-8905
Pubs: *Place for Lost Children, Girl in the Yellow Caboose* (Karma Dog, 1996, 1992), *The Shining Place* (Birnham Wood Graphics, 1992), *American Literary Rev.*

Arthur L. Clements P
State Univ New York, Binghamton, NY 139026000, 607-777-2168
Pubs: *Dream of Flying* (Endless Mountains, 1994), *Poetry of Contemplation* (SUNY Pr, 1990), *Common Blessings* (Lincoln Springs, 1987), *Bellingham Rev, LIPS, Paterson Literary Rev, Poet, Poet Lore, Ruah.*

Robert Cline W
Echo Ridge, Lake Lonely, Saratoga Springs, NY 12866, 518-584-5817
Pubs: *The Tattooed Innocent & The Raunchy Grandmother* (Argos House, 1983).

Steve Clorfeine   PP
63 Cooper St, Accord, NY 12404, 914-626-3096
Internet: clorfeine@compuserve.com
　　Pubs: *Beginning Again* (The Advocate Pr, 1994), *Out of the Catskills: Anth* (Bright Hill Pr, 1997), *Parabola, Shambhala Sun.*

Henry W. Clune   W
PO Box 31, Scottsville, NY 14546, 716-889-3434
　　Pubs: *Souvenir And Other Stories* (Brunner, 1991), *The Genesee* (Syracuse U, 1991), *I Always Like It Here* (U Rochester, 1983).

Steven Coffman   W
1874 Dombroski Rd, Dundee, NY 14837, 607-243-7561

Joan Cofrancesco   P
306 Kasson Rd, Camillus, NY 13031, 315-487-5338
　　Pubs: *Cat Bones In The Tree* (Hail Mary Pr, 1998), *Walpurgis Night* (San Diego Poets Pr, 1993), *Sinister Wisdom, Kalliope, Common Lives/Lesbian Lives, Aurora, Thesmophoria, Amazon Qtly, 13th Moon, Amelia, Poetry Flash.*

Arlene Greenwald Cohen   P
36 Colonial Ln, Bellport, NY 11713-2906
Internet: agc55@aol.com
　　Pubs: *Pen Woman, Electric Umbrella, Island Poets, Long Island Qtly, Taproot Jrnl, Oxalis, Wordworks, Live Poets Society, Pegasus.*

Jonathan Cohen   P
101-75 Sylvan Ave, Miller Place, NY 11764, 516-331-9178
　　Pubs: *From Nicaragua with Love* (City Lights, 1986), *With Walker in Nicaragua* (Wesleyan U, 1984), *American Voice, Agni, City Lights Rev.*

Jim Cohn   P
Birdsfoot Farm, Star Rte, Box 138, Canton, NY 13617, 315-386-4852
　　Pubs: *Prairie Falcon* (North Atlantic Bks, 1989), *Nada Poems: Anth* (Nada Pr, 1988), *Big Scream, Hanging Loose, Heaven Bone, Brief, Colorado North Rev, Exquisite Corpse.*

Arthur Coleman   W
C. W. Post College, Greenvale, NY 11548, 516-299-2391
　　Pubs: *A Case In Point, Petals On A Wet Black Bough* (Watermill, 1979, 1973).

Zena Collier   W
83 Berkeley St, Rochester, NY 14607, 716-442-6941
Internet: zenacollier@juno.com
　　Pubs: *Ghost Note* (Grove Weidenfeld, 1992), *A Cooler Climate* (British American, 1990), *L.A. Times Book Rev, New Letters, Southwest Rev, Southern Humanities Rev.*

Billy Collins   P
RD #2, Route 202, Somers, NY 10589, 914-248-6613
　　Pubs: *Picnic, Lightning, The Art of Drowning* (U Pittsburgh Pr, 1998, 1995), *Questions About Angels* (Morrow, 1991), *New Yorker, Paris Rev, Poetry.*

Kathleen Collins   W
19 Victory Knoll Path, Miller Place, NY 11764, 516-331-8876
　　Pubs: *The Romantic Naiad, Lovers in the Present Afternoon* (Naiad Pr, 1993, 1984), *The Mountain, The Stone* (Puckerbrush Pr, 1978).

Tram Combs   P
255 Abeel St, Kingston, NY 12401, 212-966-0605
　　Pubs: *Art in America, Arts Magazine, Noticias de Arte.*

Frank Conaway   P&W
PO Box 257, Unionville, NY 10988, 914-726-3616
　　Pubs: *Beloit, Tennessee Qtly, Chicago Rev, West Branch, Poet & Critic, JAMA, Cumberland Poetry Rev, Wordsmith, Gray's Sporting Jrnl.*

Brenda Connor-Bey   PP
501 Old Kensico Rd, #2R, White Plains, NY 106033118, 914-686-8187
Internet: jimm3@aol.com
　　Pubs: *Thoughts of an Everyday Woman — An Unfinished Urban Folk Tail, New Rain 6 & 7* (Blind Beggar Pr, 1995, 1991), *Phatitude — Asian African Diaspora: Anth* (Phatitude Literary Mag, 1998), *Essence, Flare.*

Clark Coolidge   P
Box 420, New Lebanon, NY 12125
　　Pubs: *Research* (Tuumba, 1982), *Mine: The One That Enters The Stories* (The Figures, 1982).

Helen Cooper   P
State Univ New York, Stony Brook, NY 11794, 516-632-7400
　　Pubs: *13th Moon, City, Xanadu, Jrnl of New Jersey Poets, U.S. 1, Gravida, 19th Century Fiction.*

James Finn Cotter   P
Mount Saint Mary College, Newburgh, NY 12550, 914-561-0800
　　Pubs: *The Hudson Rev, America, Commonweal, Thought.*

Jack Coulehan   P
4 Townsend Ct, Setauket, NY 11733, 516-689-6958
Internet: jcouleha@prevmed.som.sunysb.edu
　　Pubs: *First Photographs of Heaven, The Knitted Glove* (Nightshade Pr, 1994, 1991), *Blood and Bone: Poems By Physicians: Anth* (U Iowa Pr, 1998), *JAMA, Kansas Qtly, Prairie Schooner, Negative Capability, Wisconsin Rev, Lancet.*

Nancy Vieira Couto												P
508 Turner Pl, Ithaca, NY 14850, 607-273-8559
>	Pubs: *The Face in the Water, The Pittsburgh Book of Contemporary Poetry: Anth* (U Pittsburgh Pr, 1990 1993), *Out of the Catskills and Just Beyond: Anth* (Bright Hill Pr, 1997), *American Voice, Black Warrior Rev, Gettysburg Rev, Salamander, Epoch.*

Joseph Cowley												W
69430 Main Rd, Greenport, NY 119442801, 516-477-8719
>	Pubs: *Three Novellas* (Morris, 1998), *The Chrysanthemum Garden* (S&S, 1981), *Ohio Short Fiction: Anth* (Northmont Pub Inc., 1995), *Prairie Schooner, Maryland Rev, New Story, Facet, New Generation, Stateside.*

Timothy Craig												P
RR Box 150, Tug Hollow Farm, Shushan, NY 12873, 518-854-7601
>	Pubs: *Advice to the Rain* (Grey Walls Pr, 1990), *Knots & Fans* (Tamara, 1985), *London Mag, Pale Fire, Xanadu.*

William Crapser												W
116 N Lake Ave, #3E, Albany, NY 12206, 518-426-9012
>	Pubs: *Remains: Stories of Vietnam* (Sachem, 1988).

Jack Crawford, Jr.												P
54 Joy Rd, Woodstock, NY 12498, 914-679-9643
>	Pubs: *Poetry, Poetry Northwest, Virginia Qtly Rev, Massachusetts Rev, Prairie Schooner, Chelsea.*

Robert Creeley												P&W
64 Amherst St, Buffalo, NY 14207, 7166452575 101
Internet: creeley@acsu.buffalo.edu
>	Pubs: *Life & Death, Echoes* (New Directions, 1998, 1994), *Selected Poems* (U California Pr, 1991).

James Crenner												P
Hobart & Wm. Smith Colleges, Geneva, NY 14456, 315-781-3361
>	Pubs: *My Hat Flies On Again* (L'Epervier Pr, 1979), *The Airplane Burial Ground* (Hoffstadt, 1976).

Ida Maria Cruzkatz												P
24 Fairlawn Ave, Dobbs Ferry, NY 10522, 914-693-4473
>	Pubs: *Bitterroot, New Collage, Tempest, MPR, Windless Orchard, Samisdat.*

E. J. Cullen												P&W
23 Glen Washington Rd, Bronxville, NY 10708
>	Pubs: *Our War & How We Won It* (Viking, 1987), *NAR, Western Humanities Rev, The Quarterly.*

Jack Curtis												P&W
Mildred Marmur Associates LTC, 2005 Palmer Ave., Ste 127, Larchmont, NY 10538, 408-667-2440
>	Pubs: *Christmas in Calico* (Daybreak Pr, 1998), *Mercy Shot, Pepper Tree Rider* (Walker & Co., 1995, 1994), *The Fight for San Bernardo, Jury on Smoky Hill, Sheriff Kill* (Pocket Bks, 1993, 1992, 1991).

Michele Cusumano												P
Box 117, New Suffolk, NY 11956, 516-734-6090
>	Pubs: *Just As The Boy Dreams Of White Thighs Under Flowered Skirts* (Street Pr, 1981), *Zephyr.*

Vincent T. Dacquino												W
RD #3, Box 275, Mahopac, NY 10541, 914-628-9092
>	Pubs: *Kiss The Candy Days Good-Bye* (Dell, 1983).

Kate Dahlstedt												P
78 N Allen St, Albany, NY 12203, 518-438-1062
>	Pubs: *Outpost, Brussels Sprout, Groundswell, Mildred, Voices.*

Beatrice G. Davis												P
105 Ludwig Ln, East Williston, NY 11596
Internet: beegeedee@aol.com
>	Pubs: *Mother of the Groom* (Distinctive Pub, 1996), *Reflections of Life* (EPS Pub, 1996), *Taproot, Common Ground, Just Write, Remembrance, Pocket Inspirations, Writers Exchange.*

George Davis												W
327 Claremont Ave, Mount Vernon, NY 10552
>	Pubs: *Love, Black Love* (Doubleday, 1978), *Coming Home* (Random House, 1972), *Essence, Black World.*

Marjorie De Fazio												P
254 Burrows Rd, Unadilla, NY 13849, 607-988-6358
Internet: jorie@wpe.com
>	Pubs: *A Quiet Noise* (The Poet's Pr, 1972), *Out of the Catskills and Just Beyond: Anth* (Bright Hill Pr, 1997), *Omen, Aphra, Michael's.*

Sigrid De Lima												W
408A Storms Rd, Valley Cottage, NY 10989
>	Pubs: *Oriane* (Harcourt, Brace & World, 1968), *Praise a Fine Day* (Random House, 1959).

Beltran De Quiros												W
PO Box 6134, Syracuse, NY 13217, 315-476-8994
Internet: jromeu@cat.syr.edu
>	Pubs: *Narrativa y Libertad: Anth, La Otra Cara De La Moneda* (Ediciones Universal, 1996, 1984), *Los Unos, Los Otros y El Seibo '71.*

Edward De Roo												W
7 Bacon St, St. James, NY 11780, 516-862-9397
>	Pubs: *Rumble in the Housing Project* (Ace Bks, 1944), *Nassau Qtly Rev, New Mexico Qtly.*

Regina deCormier												P&W
34 Sparkling Ridge, New Paltz, NY 12561
>	Pubs: *Claiming the Spirits Within* (Beacon Press, 1996), *Two Worlds Walking* (New Rivers Pr, 1994), *Hoofbeats On The Door* (Helicon Nine Edtns, 1993), *APR, Nation, Salmagundi, Poetry East, Nimrod.*

Constance Dejong   W
131 S Broadway, #3, Nyack, NY 10960
    Pubs: *I.T.I.L.O.E.* (Top Stories, 1984), *Satyagraha* (Tianam Pr, 1983).

Samuel R. Delany   W
PO Box 235, Bedford Hills, NY 10507, 914-666-3500

Louise Budde DeLaurentis   P&W
983 Cayuga Heights Rd, Ithaca, NY 14850, 607-272-6418
    Pubs: *Traveling to the Goddess, A Cycle of Seasons* (DeLaurentis, 1995, 1992), *Outerbridge, Kalliope, Farm Jrnl, Plainswoman, Frontiers.*

Bruce D. Delmont   W
443 Wendel Ave, Buffalo, NY 14223-2211, 716-834-3310
    Pubs: *Art Voice, MDA Chronicle, The Villager, Buffalo Mag, Poetry Forum Short Stories.*

Allen Deloach   PP&P
1132 Delaware Ave, Buffalo, NY 14209, 716-884-1891
    Pubs: *Eric Mottramion: On the Occasion of His 70th Birthday* (North & South Bks, 1994), *Grist-on-Line, Elf Mag, Alt Pubs.*

Robert DeMaria   W
106 Vineyard Pl, Port Jefferson, NY 11777, 516-928-3460
    Pubs: *Stone of Destiny* (Ballantine, 1985), *New Letters, Antaeus, Florida Rev.*

Mary Russo Demetrick   P&W
345 Buckingham Ave, Syracuse, NY 13210-3313, 315-476-9876
Internet: mmdemetr@syr.edu
    Pubs: *Italian Notebook, First Pressing* (Hale Mary Pr, 1995, 1994), *Hey!: Anth* (Durland Alternative Pr, 1998), *Malachite & Agate: Anth* (Grove Pr, 1997), *Word of Mouth: Anth* (Crossing Pr, 1990), *Asheville Poetry Rev, Footwork.*

Carl Dennis   P
49 Ashland Ave, Buffalo, NY 14222, 716-886-1331
Internet: cedennis@acsu.buffalo.edu
    Pubs: *Ranking the Wishes, Meetings With Time* (Penguin, 1997, 1992), *The Outskirts of Troy, The Near World* (Morrow, 1988, 1985).

Rachel Guido deVries   P
PO Box 228, Cazenovia, NY 130350228, 315-655-8020
Internet: guidogirl@aol.com
    Pubs: *How To Sing To A Dago, The Voices We Carry: Anth* (Guernica Edtns, 1996, 1994), *Tender Warriors* (Firebrand Bks, 1986), *Voices in Italian Americana, Frontiers, Yellow Silk.*

Robb Forman Dew   W
Miriam Altschuler Literary Age, 5 Old Post Rd, Red Hook, NY 12571, 914-758-9408
    Pubs: *The Family Heart* (Addison-Wesley, 1994), *The Time of Her Life* (Morrow, 1984), *Dale Loves Sophie to Death* (FS&G, 1982).

Katherine Dewart   P
333 Ellis Hollow Creek Rd, Ithaca, NY 14850, 607-272-8548

Bob Dial   P
15 Callaghan Blvd, Ballston Lake, NY 12019-2641
    Pubs: *Gulf Coast, Ledge, MacGuffin, Chiron Rev, Writer, Plastic Tower.*

Anthony DiFranco   W
Suffolk Community College, 533 College Rd, English Dept, Selden, NY 11784, 516-451-4159
Internet: difranco@sunysuffolk.edu
    Pubs: *Ardent Spring* (Bantam, 1986), *Prize Stories: O. Henry Awards: Anth* (Doubleday, 1986), *Four Quarters, NAR.*

Arthur Dobrin   P
613 Dartmouth St, Westbury, NY 11590, 516-997-8545
    Pubs: *Angles & Chambers* (Cross-Cultural Communications, 1990), *Out of Place* (Backstreet, 1982).

Anthony J. Dolan   P&W
69 Sheryl Cres., Smithtown, NY 11787, 516-724-1859

Lynn Domina   P
158 Main St, Delhi, NY 13753, 607-746-7857
Internet: domina@snydelab.delhi.edu
    Pubs: *Corporal Works* (Four Way Bks, 1995), *Marlboro Rev, Carolina Qtly, Indiana Rev, Poetry Northwest, Prairie Schooner, Southern Poetry Rev.*

George Drew   P
PO Box 298, Poestenkill, NY 12140, 518-283-1339
Internet: drewgeo@hvcc.edu
    Pubs: *So Many Bonod* (Rarus Pr, 1998), *Toads In A Poisoned Tank* (Tamarack, 1986), *Poetry Northwest, Quarterly West, Salmagundi, The Quarterly, Texas Rev.*

Bruce Ducker   P&W
Mildred Marmur Agency, 2005 Palmer Ave #127, Larchmont, NY 10538, 914-834-1270
    Pubs: *Lead Us Not Into Penn Station, Marital Assets* (Permanent Pr, 1994, 1993), *Yale Rev, The Quarterly, Poetry, Commonweal, New York Qtly.*

Joseph Duemer   P
Clarkson Univ, Potsdam, NY 13699, 315-262-2466
Internet: duemer@polaris.clarkson.edu
    Pubs: *Static* (Owl Creek Pr, 1996), *Customs* (U Georgia Pr, 1987), *APR, Iowa Rev, New England Rev, Boulevard, Mss., Tampa Rev, Tar River Poetry.*

Peter Kane Dufault   P
RD 2, Hillsdale, NY 12529, 518-672-4897
Internet: http://www.taconic.net/dufault
    Pubs: *Memorandum to the Age of Reason, New Things Come Into the World* (Lindisfarne, 1993, 1989), *New Yorker, New Republic, Atlantic, Spectator.*

T. Dunn P&W
PO Box 4853, Ithaca, NY 14852
Internet: tdunn@acclaimed.com
Pubs: *Range of Motion* (Squeaky Wheel Pr, 1993), *Asylum Annual, Black Buzzard Rev, Voices Intl, Snail's Pace Rev, Synaesthetic, Tight, Nixon.*

Mary Durham P
PO Box 2856, Poughkeepsie, NY 12603, 914-473-0405
Pubs: *Almanac, Outloud, Poetry Peddler, Home Planet News, Kaatskill Life.*

M. D. Elevitch W
Box 604, Palisades, NY 10964, 914-365-3772
Pubs: *Green Eternal Go* (Foolscap Pr, 1991), *Americans at Home* (First Person, 1976), *Chelsea, Transatlantic Rev, TriQuarterly, Chicago Rev, Audience, Pacific Coast Jrnl, Trace.*

Richard Elman W
PO Box 216, Stony Brook, NY 11790-0216
Pubs: *Tar Beach* (Sun & Moon Pr, 1991), *Disco Frito* (Peregrine Smith, 1988), *Tikkun, Raritan, Antaeus, Georgia Rev, Newsday, Exquisite Corpse.*

Virginia Elson P
Smith Pond Rd, RD 2, Avoca, NY 14809, 607-566-8355
Pubs: *And Echoes for Direction, Where in the Sun to Stand* (State Street Pr, 1987, 1982), *Atlantic, Literary Rev, Prairie Schooner, Poetry Northwest, Yankee.*

P. A. Engebrecht W
112 Cliffside Dr, Canandaigua, NY 14424-8808, 716-396-2166
Pubs: *Promise of Moonstone* (Beaufort, 1983), *Under The Haystack* (Thomas Nelson, 1973), *Yankee.*

Judith Sue Epstein P
1859 Slaterville Rd, Ithaca, NY 14850, 607-277-4205
Pubs: *Keeping Score* (Ithaca Hse, 1975), *Epoch, Hanging Loose, The Trojan Horse, The Grapevine.*

Amelia Etlinger PP
44 Barney Rd, Clifton Park, NY 12065

Graham Everett P
PO Box 772, Sound Beach, NY 11789, 516-821-0678
Internet: everett@sable.adelphi.edu
Pubs: *Minus Green Plus* (Breeze/Street, 1995), *Minus Green* (Yank This Pr, 1992), *Caprice, Long Island Qtly, 4x4, Exquisite Corpse, Live Poets.*

Pat Falk P
Nassau Community College, English Dept, Garden City, NY 11530-6793, 516-572-7185
Pubs: *In the Shape of a Woman* (Canios Edtns, 1995), *13th Moon, Poets On, Long Island Qtly, Thema, Wordsmith.*

John Fandel P
609 Palmer Rd, Apt 2-L, Yonkers, NY 10701, 914-793-5422
Pubs: *Ranging & Arranging* (Roth, 1990), *A Morning Answer* (Forward Movement Pub, 1988).

Patricia Farewell P
PO Box 198, Pleasantville, NY 10570, 914-769-7228
Pubs: *Waltzing on Water: Anth* (Dell, 1989), *Desire: Anth* (St. Martin's Pr, 1980), *Green Mountains Rev, Writing For Our Lives, The Formalist.*

Raymond Federman P&W
46 Four Seasons W, Buffalo, NY 14226, 716-835-9611
Internet: moinous@aol.com
Pubs: *The Twofold Vibration, Smiles on Washington Square* (Sun & Moon, 1998, 1995), *To Whom It May Concern* (Fiction Collective Two, 1990).

Eric Felderman P&W
PO Box 194, Pelham, NY 10803
Pubs: *Two Men And A Kangaroo Go Into A Bar* (Portmanteau Edtns, 1990).

Irving Feldman P
State Univ New York, Buffalo, NY 14260, 716-885-4122
Pubs: *The Life and Letters* (U Chicago, 1994), *All of Us Here, Teach Me Dear Sister, New & Selected Poems* (Viking/Penguin, 1986, 1983, 1979).

Jim Feraca W
1428 Midland Ave, Bronxville, NY 10708, 914-237-8680
Pubs: *Light Year Anth* (Bits Pr, 1985), *Green House, Rapport, Transatlantic Rev.*

Joseph Ferguson P&W
26 Bank St, Cold Spring, NY 10516, 914-265-4630
Pubs: *Basement Man and Other Stories* (Swift Kick Pr, 1987), *Swift Kick, Lactuca.*

Mary Ferrari P
288 Weaver St, Larchmont, NY 10538, 914-834-2132
Pubs: *The Poet Exposed: Anth* (St. James, 1986), *Aphros, B-City 3, New Nation.*

Anne Lathrop Fessenden P
Box 35, Willow, NY 12495

Leslie A. Fiedler W
State Univ New York, Buffalo, NY 14260, 716-636-2575
Pubs: *Fiedler on the Roof* (Godine, 1991), *Olaf Stapleton* (Oxford U Pr, 1982).

Sally A. Fiedler P
154 Morris Ave, Buffalo, NY 142141610
Pubs: *To Illinois, With Love* (Tyler School of Art, 1975), *Timepieces* (Ceres Pr, 1971), *Spirit.*

Jeff Filipski   PP
331 Bedford Ave, Buffalo, NY 14216
    Pubs: *Central Park Grill, The Icon, Hallwalls.*

Jeanne Finley   P&W
46 Pinewood Ave, Albany, NY 12208, 518-438-8728
Internet: jcfin@aol.com
    Pubs: *Anth of Mag Verse & Yearbook of American Poetry*
    (Monitor, 1988), *North Country: Anth* (Greenfield Rev Pr,
    1986), *New Myths, Little Mag, Visions Intl.*

Mike Finn   P
930 Comfort Rd, Spencer, NY 14883, 607-277-2345
    Pubs: *And Death is Watching, A Man Mistaking His Mother*
    For His Ego (Poortree Bks, 1996, 1992), *Mothering,*
    Audit/Poetry, Choice, Second Growth, Not Man Apart.

Adam D. Fisher   P
1404 Stony Brook Rd, Stony Brook, NY 11790, 516-751-8518
Internet: adfisher@erols.com
    Pubs: *Dancing Alone* (Birnham Wood, 1993), *An*
    Everlasting Name (Behrman Hse, 1992), *Long Island Qtly,*
    West Hills Rev, MPR, NAR, CCAR Jrnl.

George William Fisher   P
2646A Riverside Dr, Wantagh, NY 11793-4622,
516-433-8198
    Pubs: *First & Third* (Mulberry Pr, 1991), *Conjunctions*
    (Myshkin Pr, 1985), *Caprice, Birdwatcher's Digest,*
    Redstart, West Hills Rev, Trail Walker, Gravida.

Harrison Fisher   P
91 N Pine Ave, #3, Albany, NY 12203, 518-482-2402
    Pubs: *Rhomboid Hairdo* (Frank Doom Bks, 1990), *World*
    Pretix (Edge Bks, 1989), *Room 5, o.blek.*

Lou Fisher   W
12 Julie Dr, Hopewell Junction, NY 12533, 914-226-5160
Internet: loufisher8@aol.com
    Pubs: *The Blue Ice Pilot* (Warner Bks, 1986), *Suntop 8*
    (Dell, 1978), *Other Voices, Crescent Rev, Florida Rev, The*
    MacGuffin.

Charles Fishman   P
2956 Kent Rd East, Wantaugh, NY 117932435,
516-826-4964
Internet: fishman@farmingdale.edu
    Pubs: *The Firewalkers* (Avisson Pr, 1996), *The Death*
    Mazurka, Blood to Remember: Anth (Texas Tech U Pr,
    1989, 1991), *Georgia Rev, Southern California Anth, New*
    Letters, New England Rev, European Judaism, Genocide
    Forum, Abiko Qtly.

Gregory Fitz Gerald   P&W
32 Cherry Dr, Brockport, NY 14420, 716-637-9372
    Pubs: *October Blood & Other Stories* (Spectrum Pr, 1993),
    The Hidden Quantum (Hobaugh Pubs, 1993), *The Druze*
    Document (Cliffhanger Pr, 1987), *Galaxy, Aberrations, Red*
    Herring, Fantastic Worlds, Show & Tell.

Jane Flanders   P
1 Hazen St, Pelham, NY 10803-2408, 914-738-3776
Internet: stflanders@aol.com
    Pubs: *Timepiece* (U Pitt, 1988), *The Students of Snow* (U
    Massachusetts Pr, 1982), *Prairie Schooner, New Yorker,*
    Paris Rev, Nation, New Republic, Poetry.

Peggy Flanders   P
4956 St. John Dr, Syracuse, NY 13215-1245, 315-488-8077
    Pubs: *Radiology, Poetpourri, Voices Intl, Open Window,*
    Pegasus, Poets On, South Florida Rev.

Lisa Fleck   P
18 Glendale Rd, Ossining, NY 10562
    Pubs: *Musical Chairs in the Garden* (1st East Coast
    Theatre & Publishing Co., 1987).

Sheldon Flory   P
6981 Rte 21, Naples, NY 14512, 716-374-2655
    Pubs: *A Winter's Journey* (Copper Beech, 1979), *Arvon Intl*
    Poetry Competition Anth (Arvon, 1990), *Separate Doors,*
    Natl Prison Reform Association News, New Yorker, Poetry,
    Iowa Rev, Seneca Rev, Mangrove, Zone 3.

Jim Flosdorf   P
18 Lillian Ln, Troy, NY 12180-4700, 518-272-6210
Internet: flosdj@sage.edu
    Pubs: *My Father Was Shiva* (Ablex, 1994), *North Country:*
    Anth (Greenfield Rev Pr, 1986), *Groundswell, Voices.*

Gertrude Ford   W
3 Midwood Cross, Roslyn, NY 11576-2414
    Pubs: *81 Sheriff Street* (Frederick Foll, 1981).

Joan Elizabeth Ford   P
151 Woodward Ave, Buffalo, NY 14214, 716-886-7136
    Pubs: *Intrepid, Moody Street Irregulars, Swift Kick, Earth's*
    Daughters.

Peter Fortunato   P
172 Pearsall Pl, Ithaca, NY 14850, 607-273-6637
    Pubs: *Letters To Tiohero* (Grapevine Pr, 1979), *A Bell Or A*
    Hook (Ithaca Hse, 1977), *Nimrod, Seneca Rev, Yellow Silk,*
    Voices in Italian Americana.

Walt Franklin   P
1205 County, Rte 60, Rexville, NY 14877, 607-225-4592
    Pubs: *The Singing Groves* (Timberline Pr, 1996), *Uplands*
    Haunted by the Sea (Great Elm Pr, 1992), *The Wild Trout*
    (Nightshade Pr, 1991), *Poem, Grain, Pig.*

Mary Lamb Freeman   P
182 Oxford Ave, Amherst, NY 14226, 716-833-5578
    Pubs: *Ripples, Crowdancing, Midwest Poetry Rev, Room of*
    Our Own, Green Feather, Dream Intl Qtly.

Emanuel Fried   W
1064 Amherst St, Buffalo, NY 14216, 716-873-4131
   Pubs: *The Un-American* (Springhouse Edtns, 1992), *Big
   Ben Hood, Elegy for Stanley Gorski* (Labor Arts Bks, 1988,
   1986), *Dramatists Qtly.*

Bruce Jay Friedman   W
PO Box 746, Holly Ln, Watermill, NY 11976, 212-691-8077
   Pubs: *The Current Climate, About Harry Towns, Stern*
   (Atlantic Monthly Pr, 1989, 1989, 1989).

Roy Friedman   W
20 Woodrow Dr, Yonkers, NY 10710, 914-793-0096
   Pubs: *The Insurrection Of Hippolytus Brandenberg* (Stein &
   Day, 1968), *Witness, Vintage, Humgrus, Jewish Monthly,
   Descant, St. Andrews Rev.*

Lee Frisbee   P
91 Bev Ln, Brockport, NY 14420-1236, 716-637-5672
   Pubs: *Driftwood East, Encore, English Jrnl, Fiesta, New
   Infinity Rev, Rufus.*

Carol Frost   P
RD 2, Box 73, Otego, NY 13825, 607-988-7170
   Pubs: *Venus & Don Juan, Pure* (TriQuarterly Bks, 1996,
   1994), *Chimera* (Peregrine Smith Bks, 1990), *Day of the
   Body* (Ion Bks, 1986), *APR, Atlantic, NER, TriQuarterly,
   Partisan Rev, Ploughshares, Kenyon Rev, Shenandoah,
   Southern Rev, Volt.*

Richard Frost   P
959 Co. Hwy 7, Otego, NY 13825, 607-988-7170
Internet: frostrg@oneonta.edu
   Pubs: *Neighbor Blood* (Sarabande Bks, 1996), *The Family
   Way* (Devil's Millhopper Pr, 1994), *Jazz for Kirby* (State
   Street Pr, 1990), *Paris Rev, Poetry, Georgia Rev.*

Gerard Furey   W
HGHS 70 Roaring Brook Rd, Chappaqua, NY 10514,
914-238-3911
   Pubs: *Pittsburgh Mag, St. Anthony Messenger, Ambit.*

Judith Gaberman   W
PO Box 135, South Salem, NY 10590
   Pubs: *In Summertime It's Tuffy* (Bradbury Pr, 1977).

Elizabeth Gaffney   P
Westchester Community College, 75 Grasslands Rd,
Valhalla, NY 10595, 914-785-6194
   Pubs: *Southern Poetry Rev, College English, Wordsmith,
   Descant, Wind, New Voices, The Smith, Dark Horse.*

Diane Gallo   P&W
846 County Rd 37, Mount Upton, NY 13809, 607-764-8139
Internet: gallod@norwich.net
   Pubs: *The Neighbor's Dog Howls* (Madwoman's Daughter
   Pr, 1996), *Creating The Literature Portfolio: Anth* (NTC Pub
   Group, 1996), *Asheville Poetry Rev, Phoebe.*

Beatrice Ganley   P
4095 East Ave, Rochester, NY 14618-3798, 716-586-1000
   Pubs: *The Sea of Connection* (Heirloom Pub, 1996), *Sisters
   Today, Broomstick, Lake Effect, Wyoming: The Hub of the
   Wheel, Verity, Muse Reader Special Edition.*

Eric Gansworth   P&W
Niagara County Community Colle, 3111 Saunders Settlement
Rd, Sanborn, NY 14132, 716-283-5722
Internet: lplant@localnet.com
   Pubs: *Indian Summers* (Michigan State U Pr, 1998), *Four
   Winter Nights: Anth* (White Pine Pr, 1997), *Blue Dawn, Red
   Earth: Anth* (Anchor Bks, 1996), *Iroquois Voices, Iroquois
   Visions: Anth* (Bright Hill, 1996), *phati'tude, Slipstream.*

Eugene K. Garber   W
13 Empire Cir, Rensselaer, NY 12144, 518-434-3294
Internet: garber@cnsvax.albany.edu
   Pubs: *The Historian* (Milkweed Edtns, 1994), *Paris Review
   Anth, Norton Anth of Contemporary Fiction* (Norton, 1989,
   1988), *Paris Rev.*

Lewis Gardner   P
16 Cedar Way, Woodstock, NY 12498, 914-679-4090
   Pubs: *Columbia, Firewood, U.S. 1 Worksheets, Ethical
   Society.*

Sandra Gardner   P
16 Cedar Way, Woodstock, NY 12498
   Pubs: *Bobbe Meisehs by Shayneh Maidelehs: Anth*
   (Herbooks, 1989), *I Name Myself Daughter and It Is Good:
   Anth* (Sophia Bks, 1981), *Dark Horse, U.S. 1.*

Beatrix Gates   P
PO Box 28, Greenport, NY 11944, 516-477-0729
   Pubs: *Shooting at Night* (Granite Pr, 1980), *Naming the
   Waves: Anth* (Crossing Pr, 1990), *Kenyon Rev, North
   Dakota Qtly, Nation, Women's Rev of Bks, CutBank,
   Nimrod.*

Thomas Gavin   W
Univ Rochester, English Dept, Rochester, NY 14627,
716-244-8052
   Pubs: *Breathing Water* (Arcade, 1994), *The Last Film of
   Emile Vico* (Viking, 1986), *Kingkill* (Random Hse, 1977),
   Icarus, Prairie Schooner, Georgia Rev, TriQuarterly.

Ruth Geller   W
270 Potomac Ave, Buffalo, NY 14213, 716-881-5391
   Pubs: *Triangles, Nice Jewish Girls: Anth* (Crossing Pr,
   1984, 1984), *Ms., Sojourner.*

Willard Gellis   P&W
57 Seafield Ln, Bay Shore, NY 11706
   Pubs: *Die Metal* (Big Easy Pr, 1996), *Bronco Junky* (Wild
   Strawberry Pr, 1994), *Penny Dreadful Rev, Beast Qtly,
   Erotica, Meta-4, Long Island Qtly, UFO.*

Kathleen Gemmell   P
209 1/2 Pleasant St, Ithaca, NY 14850, 607-273-6511
Internet: ksg3@cornell.edu
    Pubs: *A Common Bond* (Allegheny Pr, 1976), *Bitterroot, Blackbird Circle, Pembroke Mag, Poet Lore, South Carolina Rev, Voices Intl.*

William Gifford   W
Vassar College, Box 344, Poughkeepsie, NY 126040344, 914-471-5132
    Pubs: *Colorado Qtly, QRL, Apalachee Qtly, Peregrine, Open City.*

Mary Gilliland   P
Cornell Univ, 172 Pearsall Pl, Ithaca, NY 14850, 607-273-6637
Internet: mg24@cornell.edu
    Pubs: *Gathering Fire* (Ithaca Hse, 1982), *Nimrod, Seneca Rev, Spoon River Qtly, Yellow Silk, Seattle Rev.*

Dugan Gilman   P
201 Berkeley Dr, Syracuse, NY 13210, 315-472-0484

Gail Godwin   W
7 Laura Ln, Woodstock, NY 12498

Rebecca T. Godwin   W
PO Box 211, Poestenkill, NY 121400211, 518-283-7227
    Pubs: *Keeper of the House* (St. Martin's Pr, 1994), *Private Parts* (Longstreet Pr, 1991), *Paris Rev, Iris: A Jrnl about Women, Crescent Rev, South Carolina Rev.*

Myra Goldberg   W
Sarah Lawrence College, Writing Program, Bronxville, NY 10708, 914-337-0700
    Pubs: *Whistling and Other Stories* (Zoland Bks, 1993), *Representations of Motherhood: Anth* (Yale U Pr, 1994), *Ploughshares, NER, Tikkun, Feminist Studies.*

Gail Kadison Golden   P
18 Zabella Dr, New City, NY 10956
Internet: peacepoet@aol.com
    Pubs: *Visions, Korone, Embers, Footwork, Karamu, Outerbridge, Milieu.*

Barry Goldensohn   P
11 Seward St, Saratoga Springs, NY 12866, 518-584-7962
    Pubs: *Dance Music* (Cummington Pr, 1992), *The Marrano* (Natl Poetry Fdn, 1988), *Agenda, Salmagundi, Agni.*

Lorrie Goldensohn   P
11 Seward St, Saratoga Springs, NY 12866
    Pubs: *East Long Pond* (Cummington Pr, 1997), *The Tether* (L'Epervier, 1982), *Dreamwork* (Porch, 1980), *Salmagundi, Ploughshares, Poetry.*

Cynthia R. Golderman   P
5 Edison Ave, Albany, NY 12208, 518-438-7360
    Pubs: *Oh, That We Would, At This Last Breach...The Facility* (Cerulean Pr, 1986, 1986).

Barbara Goldowsky   P&W
PO Box 663, Southampton, NY 119690663, 516-283-2044
Internet: barbarag@peconic.net
    Pubs: *Restless Spirits, Ferry to Nirvana and New Poems* (Amereon Ltd, 1992, 1991), *Fiction Rev, Embers, Confrontation, The Round Table, Brookspring '92, Caprice.*

Gloria Goldreich   W
356 Marbledale Rd, Tuckahoe, NY 10707, 914-961-2688
    Pubs: *That Year of Our War, Years of Dreams, Mothers* (Little, Brown, 1994, 1992, 1989), *Commentary, Midstream, Redbook, McCall's, Moment.*

Ann Goldsmith   P
494 Woodward Ave, Buffalo, NY 14214, 716-833-1879
    Pubs: *Scarecrow Poetry* (Ashland Poetry Pr, 1994), *Child's Blue Wall* (Orchard Pr, 1982), *Poets At Work: Anth* (Just Buffalo Literary Center, 1995), *The Quarterly, Helicon Nine, Earth's Daughters, Pembroke Mag.*

Catherine Gonick   P
48 Fair St #C4, Cold Spring, NY 10516-3009, 914-265-2775
    Pubs: *Pivot, The Plain Dealer Magazine, New Boston Rev, Zone, City, Mothering.*

Stephen Goodwin   W
PO Box 47, Bedford, NY 10506-0047
    Pubs: *The Blood Of Paradise* (Dutton, 1979), *Kin* (Harper & Row, 1975), *Country Jrnl, Yankee.*

Marea Gordett   P
1 Hunter's Run Blvd, Cohoes, NY 12047
    Pubs: *Freeze Tag* (Wesleyan U Pr 1984), *The Pushcart Prize V: Anth* (Pushcart Pr, 1980), *Georgia Rev, Ploughshares, Antioch Rev.*

Kirpal Gordon   P
Heaven Bone Press, PO Box 486, Chester, NY 10918, 718-797-3321
    Pubs: *Dear Empire State Building, This Ain't No Ballgame* (Heaven Bone Pr, 1990, 1988).

George Grace   P&W
33 Putnam St, Buffalo, NY 14213, 716-885-1428
    Pubs: *Buffalo Pr Anth, Pure Light, Textile Bridge Pr, Moody Street Irregulars: Jack Kerouac Newsletter.*

C. D. Grant   P
24 Bowbell Rd, White Plains, NY 106071106, 914-683-6792
Internet: 71211.3721@compuserve.com
    Pubs: *Images in a Shaded Light, Keeping Time, New Rain Vol. 9: Anth* (Blind Beggar Pr, 1986, 1981, 1998), *Suburban Styles, Mentor, New Rain, Essence.*

Marcia Grant P
15 Miller Hill Dr, La Grangeville, NY 12540, 914-223-5489
Pubs: *Connecticut River Rev, Oxalis, Z Misc, Bitterroot,
Alura Poetry Qtly, Midwest Poetry Rev, Archer.*

Susan Maria Grathwohl P
PO Box 56, New Suffolk, NY 11956
Pubs: *For Neruda, For Chile: Anth* (Beacon, 1975), *Parents
Mag, APR, Partisan Rev, Ohio Rev.*

Ellen Greene P
4 Roosevelt Ave, Roxbury, NY 12474, 607-326-4340
Pubs: *Catskill Mountains News, Ailanthus, Up Against the
Wall Mother, The Archer, Encore, Pudding.*

Jerome Greenfield W
State Univ New York, New Paltz, NY 12561, 914-257-2720
Pubs: *Wilhelm Reich vs. the USA* (Norton, 1974), *The
Chalk Line* (Chilton Bks, 1963), *Midstream.*

Linda Greenwald P&W
47 Elm St, Cobleskill, NY 12043, 518-234-7162
Pubs: *Heart Music: Anth* (the unmade bed, 1988), *The
Stories We Hold Secret: Anth* (Greenfield Rev Pr, 1986),
Bennington Rev, Poetpourri, Poetry Peddler.

Eamon Grennan P
Vassar College, Box 352, Poughkeepsie, NY 12601,
914-471-6208
Pubs: *Relations: New and Selected Poems, So It Goes, As
If It Matters* (Graywolf, 1998, 1995, 1992), *What Light There
Is & Other Poems* (North Point Pr, 1989), *New Yorker,
Kenyon Rev, Poetry.*

Susan Anne Gubernat P
13 November Walk, Long Beach, NY 11561-2998
Pubs: *Womanblood* (Continuing Saga Pr, 1981), *Poultry,
Stone Country, Nantucket Rev, Poets On.*

Jorge Guitart P
Univ Buffalo, 910 Clemens Hall, Buffalo, NY 14260-4620,
716-645-2191
Internet: guitart@acsu.buffalo.edu
Pubs: *Film Blanc* (Meow Pr, 1996), *Foreigner's Notebook*
(Shuffaloff Bks, 1993), *Exquisite Corpse, First Intensity, Tin
Fish, Kiosk.*

Robert Guzikowski P
900 Pratt Dr, Vestal, NY 13850-3843, 607-723-1031
Pubs: *Letters, Grub Street, Tightrope.*

Jennie Hair P
10 Oxford St, Northport, NY 11768-1952, 516-261-4924
Pubs: *An Old Century: A New Testament* (Birnham Wood
Graphics, 1996), *A Sisterhood of Songs* (Canio Edtns,
1994), *Long Island Qtly.*

Joan Halperin P
23 Hastings Landing, Hastings-On-Hudson, NY 10706
Pubs: *Connecticut River Rev, Poet Lore, Modern Images,
Pudding, Goblets, Confrontation, New York Qtly, Echoes,
Southern Poetry Jrnl, Tar River Poetry, Cimarron Rev.*

Janet Hamill P
24 Chaucer Ct, Middletown, NY 10940, 914-692-7263
Internet: nightsky@warwick.net
Pubs: *Lost Ceilings* (Telephone Bks, 1998), *Nostalgia of the
Infinite* (Ocean View Bks, 1992), *Living With the Animals:
Anth* (F&F, 1994), *Bomb, City Lights Rev, Cafe Rev,
Kansas Qtly, Colorado North Rev, Gargoyle.*

Jill Hammer P&W
108 Mt View Rd, Fishkill, NY 12524, 914-897-5783
Pubs: *Response, Encodings, Harp-Strings, Writing for Our
Lives, The Jewish Spectactor, The Glass Cherry, Snowy
Egret, Lilith.*

Louis Hammer P&W
PO Box 9, Old Chatham, NY 12136, 518-794-8327
Pubs: *Poetry at the End of the Mind & Postmodern Poems*
(Sachem Pr, 1992), *The Mirror Dances* (Intertext, 1986).

Mac Hammond P
314 Highland Ave, Buffalo, NY 14222, 716-882-1642
Internet: mhammond@ubvms.cc.buffalo.edu
Pubs: *Mappamundi, New & Selected Poems* (Bellevue,
1989), *Cold Turkey* (Swallow, 1969), *The Horse Opera*
(Ohio State, 1966).

Emily Hanlon W
RD 1, Chapman Rd, Yorktown, NY 10598
Pubs: *Petersburg* (Putnam, 1988), *Love is No Excuse*
(Bradbury Pr, 1981).

Tom Hanna P
210 Eddy St, Ithaca, NY 14850, 607-255-3001
Pubs: *New Letters Reader II: Anth* (U Missouri, 1984),
From A To Z: Anth (Swallow, 1981), *Epoch, New Letters,
West Coast Rev, The Stone, Latitudes.*

Emily Katharine Harris W
451 Guinnip Ave, Elmira, NY 14905, 607-733-1678
Pubs: *Hilary & Lars* (Winston Derek, 1989), *The Far
Festival* (Creeping Bent Mag, 1989).

Lisa A. Harris P&W
5111 Perry City Rd, Trumansburg, NY 14886, 607-387-6977
Internet: lizruth96@aol.com
Pubs: *Low County Stories* (Bright Hill Pr, 1997), *Flight*
(Words and Spaces Pr, 1995), *Feminism 3: Anth*
(HarperCollins 1996), *Karamu, Fennel Stalk.*

Gayle Ellen Harvey   P
11 Shaw St, Utica, NY 13502, 315-735-4194
Internet: gaylelen1@juno.com
   Pubs: *White Light of Trees* (Permafrost, 1995),
Flower-Of-Turning-Away (Geryon Pr, 1992), *Working The
Air* (Winter Creek Pr, 1991), *Painted Hills, Yellow Silk,
Poetry Northwest, Zone 3, Atlanta Rev, International Qtly,
Exquisite Corpse, Bitter Oleander.*

Dorothy L. Hatch   P
153 Kensington Rd, Garden City, NY 11530, 516-724-5204
   Pubs: *The Curious Act of Poetry, Waking to the Day* (Stone
House Pr, 1990, 1985).

William Hathaway   P
243 Maple Ave, Saratoga Springs, NY 12866, 518-583-3851
   Pubs: *Churlsgrace, Look Into the Heart* (U Central Florida,
1992, 1988), *Gettysburg Rev, Southern Rev, NAR.*

Brooks Haxton   P
21 Bloomingdale Rd, White Plains, NY 10605, 914-949-7123
   Pubs: *Traveling Company* (Knopf, 1989), *Dead Reckoning*
(Story Line Pr, 1989), *APR, NER, Paris Rev.*

Deborah C. Hecht   W
114 Burr's Ln, Dix Hills, NY 11746, 516-491-3042
Internet: hecht@tourolaw.edu
   Pubs: *A More Perfect Union: Anth* (St. Martin's Pr, 1998),
*American Scholar, Good Housekeeping, Women's World,
Long Pond Rev, Colorado North, Nantucket Rev, The
Writer, NAR, Writer's Digest.*

Safiya Henderson-Holmes   P&W
438 Columbus Ave, #1, Syracuse, NY 13210
   Pubs: *Madness And A Bit Of Hope* (Harlem River Pr, 1990),
Confirmation (Quill Pr, 1985), *Ikon.*

William C. Henderson   W
PO Box 380, Wainscott, NY 11975, 516-324-9300
   Pubs: *Her Father* (Faber & Faber, 1995), *The Kid That
Could* (Chipps & Co., 1990), *His Son* (Norton, 1981).

Lance Henson   P
2 Middle Grove Rd, Greenfield Center, NY 12833,
518-584-1728
   Pubs: *A Motion of Sudden Aloneness* (American Native Pr
Archives, 1991), *Another Distance* (Point Rider's Pr, 1991),
Poetry East, Pig Iron, Tamaqua.

William Herrick   W
36 Dunham Hollow Rd, East Nassau, NY 12062
   Pubs: *Bradovich, That's Life, Kill Memory* (New Directions,
1990, 1985, 1983), *Hermanos* (Second Chance Pr, 1969),
*Hudson Valley Mag, The New Leader, New York Times
Book Rev.*

Bill Herron   P&W
Pine Ridge Dr, Wappingers Falls, NY 12590
   Pubs: *Rituals Of Our Time* (Carolina Wren, 1980), *Couvade
Notebooks* (Salthouse, 1980).

William Heyen   P
142 Frazier St, Brockport, NY 14420, 716-637-3867
   Pubs: *Crazy Horse in Stillness* (BOA Edtns, 1996), *The
Host: Selected Poems 1965-1990* (Time Being Bks, 1990),
TriQuarterly, Ontario Rev, Southern Rev.

Dick Higgins   PP&P&W
PO Box 27, Barrytown, NY 125070027, 914-758-6488
Internet: dhiggins@ulster.net
   Pubs: *Storm Riders, Buster Keaton Enters Into Paradise,
The Journey* (Left Hand Bks, 1998, 1994, 1991), *Life
Flowers* (Woodbine Pr, 1997), *Bullshead, Talisman,
Disturbed Guillotine, Freibord, Ballade, Caliban, Chain,
Crayon, Rampike.*

Catherine Hiller   W
528 Munro Ave, Mamaroneck, NY 10543, 914-698-5328
   Pubs: *Skin: Sensual Tales* (Carroll & Graf, 1997), *California
Time, 17 Morton Street* (St. Martin's Pr, 1993, 1990),
Redbook, Penthouse, State Mag, New York Times.

Edward D. Hoch   W
2941 Lake Ave, Rochester, NY 14612, 716-865-1179
Internet: ehoch@mcls.rochester.lib.ny.us
   Pubs: *The Ripper of Storyville, Diagnosis: Impossible*
(Crippen & Landru, 1997, 1996), *Year's Best Mystery &
Suspense Stories: Anth* (Walker, 1995), *Ellery Queen
Mystery Mag, Antaeus.*

Barbara Hoffman   P&W
1330 1st St, W Babylon, NY 11704, 516-884-7945
   Pubs: *Each In Her Own Way: Anth* (Queen of Swords Pr,
1994), *Catholic Girls: Anth* (Penguin, 1992), *Poets On,
Beloit Poetry Jrnl, Gryphon, Aura, Minnesota Rev.*

Roald Hoffmann   P
Cornell Univ, Baker Laboratory, Ithaca, NY 14853-1301,
607-255-3419
Internet: rh34@cornell.edu
   Pubs: *Gaps and Verges, The Metamict State* (U Central
Florida Pr, 1990, 1987), *Paris Rev, Prairie Schooner, Yale
Rev, Chelsea, Grand Street, Raritan.*

Kay Hogan   W
154 East Ave, Saratoga Springs, NY 12866-2636,
518-584-4035
Internet: Khogan@aol.com
   Pubs: *North Country* (Greenfield Pr, 1986), *Library Bound:
Anth* (Saratoga Springs Library, 1996), *Bless Me, Father:
Anth, Catholic Girls: Anth* (Penguin, 1995, 1993), *Spiritual
Life, Complete Woman, Descant, Jrnl of Irish Literature,
Long Pond Rev.*

Susan Holahan   P&W
370 Mulberry St, Rochester, NY 146202514, 716-244-8052
    Pubs: *Sister Betty Reads The Whole You* (Gibbs Smith,
    1998), *Bitches & Sad Ladies: Anth* (Harper's, 1975),
    *Crazyhorse, Seneca Rev, American Letters, Spoon River
    Rev, Women's Rev of Bks, Central Park.*

Barbara D. Holender   P
263 Brantwood Rd, Snyder, NY 14226
    Pubs: *Is This the Way to Athens?* (Quarterly Review of
    Literature, 1996), *Ladies of Genesis* (Jewish Women's
    Resource Ctr, 1991), *Helicon 9, Prairie Schooner, Literary
    Rev.*

Sheryl Morang Holmburg   P&W
45077 Custer, Utica, NY 48317, 810-726-6615
    Pubs: *Heron Qtly, Los, Indefinite Space, Ship of Fools,
    Eratica, Iconoclast, Cumberland Poetry Rev, SLUGfest,
    Ltd., Piedmont Literary Rev, Ever Dancing Muse, Cicada,
    black bough, Quantum Tao.*

Dennis Tilden Holzman   P
13 Cherry Ave, Delmar, NY 12054, 518-463-8173
    Pubs: *Greenfield Rev, Berkeley Poets Cooperative,
    Washout Rev.*

George J. Honecker   P
453 Mineola Blvd, Williston Park, NY 11596, 516-746-3120
    Pubs: *Glass Bottom Boat* (John Street Pr, 1987), *Rampike,
    Fiction Intl, Sun & Moon, Little Mag.*

Akua Lezli Hope   P
PO Box 33, Corning, NY 14830, 607-936-8367
Internet: artfarm@servtech.com
    Pubs: *Embouchure Poems on Jazz & Other Musics*
    (Artfarm Pr, 1995), *Sisterfire: Anth* (HarperCollins, 1994),
    *Obsidian, Eyeball, Bluecage, Hambone, African American
    Rev.*

Michael F. Hopkins   P
18 Stanislaus St, Buffalo, NY 14212, 716-895-9749
    Pubs: *A Kind of Twilight* (Smiling Cat Pub, 1995), *The
    Fourth Man* (Textile Bridge Pr, 1981).

Mikhail Horowitz   P
PO Box 3443, Kingston, NY 12402, 914-246-7441
    Pubs: *The Opus of Everything in Nothing Flat* (Outloud/Red
    Hill, 1993), *Big League Poets* (City Lights, 1978), *Davka,
    Exquisite Corpse, Heaven Bone, Hunger.*

Nat Hough   P&W
306 Lake Ave, Ithaca, NY 14850
    Pubs: *Ithaca Women's Anthology* (NYSCA, 1992), *About
    Chickadees: Anth* (Raspberry Pr, 1982), *Willow Springs,
    High Rock Rev.*

Ben Howard   P
Alfred Univ, Alfred, NY 14802, 607-871-2256
Internet: fhoward@bigvax.alfred.edu
    Pubs: *Midcentury* (Ireland; Salmon Pub, 1997), *The
    Pressed Melodeon* (Story Line Pr, 1996), *The Other Shore*
    (Passim Edtns, 1991), *Lenten Anniversaries: Poems
    1982-89* (Cummington Pr, 1990), *Poetry, Sewanee Rev,
    Iowa Rev, Chelsea, New Hibernia Rev, Seneca Rev.*

Eric Machan Howd   P
106 Fayette St, Ithaca, NY 14850-5261
    Pubs: *Origami* (Sometimes Y Pubs, 1993), *Blaming Icarus*
    (Crane Pr, 1992), *Yankee, Calapooya Collage, Sun Dog,
    Chaminade Literary Rev, Round Table.*

Edward Hower   W
1409 Hanshaw Rd, Ithaca, NY 14850
    Pubs: *Night Train Blues* (Permanent Pr, 1996), *The
    Pomegranate Princess* (Wayne State U Pr, 1991), *Southern
    Rev, Epoch, Transition.*

Joan Howlett   P
14 High St, Norwood, NY 13668, 315-353-2713
    Pubs: *Variations of White, Against the Grain: Anth, A Song
    of Myself: Anth* (CSS, 1986, 1988, 1987).

Paul Humphrey   P
2329 S Union St, Spencerport, NY 14559, 716-352-4421
Internet: http://www.lway.com/towpath/
    Pubs: *Bedford Introduction to Literature: Anth* (St. Martin's
    Pr, 1998), *Ladies First: Anth* (Tow Path Bks, 1996),
    *Saturday Evening Post, Cosmopolitan, Good
    Housekeeping, Ladies Home Jrnl, True Love.*

William Humphrey   W
RD #1, Box 139, Hudson, NY 12534

David Ignatow   P
PO Box 1458, East Hampton, NY 11937
    Pubs: *I Have a Name, Against The Evidence* (Wesleyan U
    Pr, 1996, 1994), *The End Game & Other Stories* (Cathedral
    Pr/Pittsburgh U Pr, 1996).

Rose Graubart Ignatow   W
PO Box 1458, East Hampton, NY 11937-0995
    Pubs: *Surplus Love & Other Stories, Down the American
    River* (Copper Beech Pr, 1985, 1979).

Suzanne Potter Ironbiter   P
7 Fay Ln, South Salem, NY 10590
    Pubs: *Devi* (Yuganta Pr, 1987), *Cumberland Poetry Rev,
    Puerto del Sol.*

Charles F. Itzin   P
PO Box 159, Fairhaven, NY 13064, 315-947-5522
    Pubs: *New Letters, Visions, Greenfield Rev, Northwest
    Rev, Little Mag, Nimrod, Phoenix.*

Anita Jacobs　　　　　　W
3641 Regent Ln, Wantagh, NY 11793, 516-731-8188
Internet: caas13641@aol.com
　　Pubs: *Where Has Deedie Wooster Been All These Years*
　　(Delacorte Pr, 1981).

Karoniaktatie Alex Jacobs　　　　　　P
RFD 1, Box 116, Bombay, NY 12914-9718, 518-358-4460
Internet: dogrezz@aol.com
　　Pubs: *New Voices from the Longhouse: Anth* (Greenfield
　　Rev, 1988), *Returning the Gift: Anth* (Sun Tracks, 1995),
　　Akwesasne Notes, Semiotexte, Tribes.

Robert Jagoda　　　　　　W
547 Lucas Ave Ext, Kingston, NY 124018215, 914-331-5473
　　Pubs: *Nobody Wants My Resume: Anth* (McGraw-Hill,
　　1979), *A Friend in Deed: Anth* (Norton, 1976).

Phyllis Janowitz　　　　　　P
Cornell Univ, Goldwin Smith Hall, Ithaca, NY 14853,
607-257-3279
　　Pubs: *Temporary Dwellings* (U Pitt Pr, 1988), *Visiting Rites*
　　(Princeton, 1982), *Epoch, Free Lunch, Verve, River Styx,*
　　The Quarterly, The Bridge, Ithaca Women's Anth.

Jaochim　　　　　　W
c/o Costas Parpas
　　23 Cullen Dr, East Northport, NY 11731, 516-758-7647

Polly Joan　　　　　　P
604 Taylor Pl, Ithaca, NY 14850, 607-277-3738
　　Pubs: *The Living Alternative* (Human Sciences Pr, 1985),
　　No Apologies (Women Writing Pr, 1975).

Bobby Johnson　　　　　　P
110 Normandy Ave, Rochester, NY 14619, 716-436-5929
　　Pubs: *Mr. Parker Songbook, Clarissa Street Project*
　　(Johnson, 1991, 1985).

Bonnie L. Johnson　　　　　　P
2316 Shadagee Rd, Eden, NY 14057
Internet: alice1933@aol.com
　　Pubs: *The Jungle Book* (Textile Bridge Pr, 1983), *Fine*
　　China, Twenty Years of Earth's Daughters: Anth (Earth's
　　Daughters, 1993), *Room of Our Own, Serendipity Pr.*

Darren Johnson　　　　　　P&W
PO Box 672, Water Mill, NY 11976-0672, 516-477-2555
Internet: rocketusa@delphi.com
　　Pubs: *Jazz Poems—A Chapbook* (So It Goes/U Pitt, 1996),
　　I Do Not Prefer To Have Sex (NPI, 1994), *Long Island Qtly,*
　　U-Direct, Basement, Plastic Tower, Impetus.

Kate K. Johnson　　　　　　P
Sarah Lawrence College, Bronxville, NY 10708,
914-666-5274
　　Pubs: *This Perfect Life* (Miami U Pr, 1993), *When Orchids*
　　Were Flowers (Dragon Gate, 1986), *Decade, Poetry,*
　　Ironwood, Tendril, One Meadway.

Nora Johnson　　　　　　W
2 Villa Ln, Larchmont, NY 10538-1227, 914-834-1682
Internet: johnsonora@aol.com
　　Pubs: *Perfect Together* (Dutton/Wm. Abrahams, 1991),
　　Uncharted Places, Tender Offer (S&S, 1988, 1985).

Ina Jones　　　　　　P&W
12 Cleveland Ave, Cobleskill, NY 12043
　　Pubs: *Womenstory: Memoir: Anth* (Sing Heavenly Muse!,
　　1997), *Out of the Catskills and Just Beyond: Anth, The*
　　Word Thursdays Anth (Bright Hill Pr, 1997, 1995), *West*
　　Branch, Cape Rock.

Barbara Jordan　　　　　　P
Univ Rochester, Morey 514, Rochester, NY 14627,
716-229-4365
Internet: micaamber@aol.com
　　Pubs: *Trace Elements* (Penguin, 1998), *Channel* (Beacon
　　Pr, 1990), *Atlantic, Apex of the M, Sulfur, Agni, New Yorker,*
　　Paris Rev.

Susan Jordan　　　　　　P
39 Beaufort St, Rochester, NY 14620, 716-271-1589
　　Pubs: *Crystal Spirit* (Snakesisters Pr, 1988), *Benzene*
　　(Truck Pr, 1977), *Ikon, And.*

Pierre Joris　　　　　　P
SUNY Albany, Albany, NY 12202, 518-442-4085
Internet: joris@cnsunix.albany.edu
　　Pubs: *Turbulence* (J.T. Lazaire Pr, 1991), *Breccia: Selected*
　　Poems 1972-1986 (Editions Phi/Station Hill, 1987).

Laurence Josephs　　　　　　P
992 Locust Grove Rd, Greenfield Center, NY 12833,
518-893-7534
　　Pubs: *New and Selected Poems* (Copley Pub Group,
　　1988), *Salmagundi, St. Johns Rev, Southern Rev.*

Frank Judge　　　　　　P
Syndicated News Service, 232 Post Ave, Rochester, NY
14619-1398, 716-328-2144
Internet: sns3@aol.com or fjudge1@aol.com
　　Pubs: *The Flickering Dark* (Exit Pr, 1994), *24 Exposures*
　　(Writers & Books, 1988), *The Spy's Handbook, Two Voices*
　　(Center Pr, 1987, 1985).

Franz Kamin　　　　　　W
Station Hill Rd, Barrytown, NY 12507, 612-227-0225
　　Pubs: *Scribble Death* (Station Hill Pr, 1986), *Hotel*
　　(Prospect Bks, 1986).

Paul Kane　　　　　　P
8 Big Island, Warwick, NY 10990, 914-986-8522
Internet: kane@vassar.edu
　　Pubs: *Australian Poetry* (Cambridge U Pr, 1996), *The*
　　Farther Shore, Poetry of the American Renaissance: Anth,
　　(Braziller, 1989, 1995), *Paris Rev, New Republic, Grand*
　　Street, Sewanee Rev, Western Humanities Rev,
　　Shenandoah, Poetry.

Yuri Vidov Karageorge　　　　　　　　P&W
13 Adams Commons, Yaphank, NY 11980, 516-924-4739
　　Pubs: *Sadness in Ardor* (Hollyhock Pr, 1984), *Cimarron
　　Qtly, Prism Intl, Quarry, Poesie USA, Waves, Mundus
　　Artium, World Literature Today.*

Mary Karr　　　　　　　　P
Syracuse Univ, Syracuse, NY 13244, 315-443-2173
　　Pubs: *The Devil's Tour* (New Directions, 1993), *Abacus*
　　(Wesleyan U Pr, 1987), *Seneca Rev, Poetry, Parnassus,
　　Willow Springs, Ploughshares, Columbia.*

Peter Katopes　　　　　　　　P&W
Adelphi University, Garden City, NY 11530
　　Pubs: *The Vietnam Reader: Anth, The Human Condition In
　　The Modern Age: Anth* (Kendall/Hunt, 1991, 1991).

Miriam Polli Katsikis　　　　　　　　P&W
200 E Bayberry Rd, Islip, NY 11751
　　Pubs: *St. Anthony Messenger, Primavera, Buffalo Spree,
　　Playgirl, Plainswoman, Echoes, Earthwise Poetry Jrnl,
　　Anemone, Cimarron, Ripples.*

Rita Katz　　　　　　　　P
8 Greentree Rd, Mineola, NY 11501, 516-742-4320
　　Pubs: *Breaking In: New Writer's Series: Anth* (New Writer's
　　Series Pubs, 1993), *The Alembic, Piedmont Literary Rev,
　　Taproot, Long Island Qtly, Serendipity, Midwest Poetry Rev.*

Merilee Kaufman　　　　　　　　P
3256 Elliott Blvd, Oceanside, NY 11572
　　Pubs: *Sarah's Daughters Sing: Anth* (K'Tav Publishing Hse,
　　1990), *Confrontation, Nassau Rev, Slugfest, Live Poets,
　　Messages From The Heart.*

Stuart Kaufman　　　　　　　　P
Nassau Community College, 1 Education Dr, Garden City, NY
11530, 516-572-7185
Internet: bigcigarz@aol.com
　　Pubs: *Fast Friends* (Minerva Pr, 1996), *The Ultimate Cigar
　　& Other Poems* (First East Coast Pubs, 1984), *Verse,
　　Mudfish, Poetry, Privates, Kingfisher.*

John Kay　　　　　　　　P
Hanau American High School, Unit 20235, APO AE, NY
01965, 006-184-1047
　　Pubs: *Post Season* (Applezaba, 1992), *Everything is OK*
　　(Rumba Train, 1979), *Plate Glass* (Maelstrom, 1974),
　　Gathering, The Sun, Barefoot Whales.

Tim Keane　　　　　　　　W
305 Rich Ave, Mt Vernon, NY 10552
　　Pubs: *Quarterly West, Northwest Rev, First Intensity,
　　American Writing, William & Mary Rev.*

Terrance Keenan　　　　　　　　P
305 DeForest Rd, Syracuse, NY 13214, 315-446-0612
Internet: txkeenan@library.syr.edu
　　Pubs: *Practicing Eternity* (Basfal Bks, 1996), *Herbal* (Great
　　Elm Pr, 1988), *Georgia Rev, Poetry Now, Epoch, Ironwood,
　　White Pine, Blue Line.*

Emily Keller　　　　　　　　P
9354 Rivershore Dr, Niagara Falls, NY 143044449,
716-283-0606
Internet: http://www.bluemoon.net/ mbwbio
　　Pubs: *Anth of Mag Verse & Yearbook of American Poetry*
　　(Monitor Bks, 1984), *Kansas Qtly, Hollins Critic,
　　Confrontation, Piedmont Literary Rev, McCall's, San Jose
　　Studies, Poetry Now, Images.*

Dave Kelly　　　　　　　　P
PO Box 53, Geneseo, NY 14454, 716-243-0987
　　Pubs: *The Sumal Reader* (Michigan State U Pr, 1996),
　　Talking To Myself (State Street Pr, 1994), *Northern Letter*
　　(Nebraska Rev Pr, 1980), *The Paris Rev Anth* (Norton,
　　1990).

Robert Kelly　　　　　　　　P&W
Bard College, Annandale-on-Hudso, NY 12504,
914-758-6549
Internet: kelly@bard.edu
　　Pubs: *Red Actions: Selected Poems 1960-93* (Black
　　Sparrow Pr, 1995), *Queen of Terrors* (McPherson & Co.,
　　1994), *Conjunctions, Notus, Ashen Meal, Grand Street.*

Sylvia Kelly　　　　　　　　W
PO Box 53, Geneseo, NY 14454, 716-243-0987
　　Pubs: *Conjunctions: 14* (Collier-Macmillan, 1989), *The
　　MacGuffin, Redstart Plus, Transpacific.*

Maurice Kenny　　　　　　　　P
PO Box 1029, Saranac Lake, NY 12983, 518-891-5865
　　Pubs: *Backward To Forward, Tekonwatonti* (White Pine Pr,
　　1997, 1992), *On Second Thought: A Compilation* (U
　　Oklahoma Pr, 1995), *Greyhounding This America*
　　(Heidelberg Graphics, 1989), *Wooster Rev, House Organ,
　　River Styx, Cimarron, Adirondack Life, Amicus.*

Milton Kessler　　　　　　　　P
25 Lincoln Ave, Binghamton, NY 13905, 607-772-1217
　　Pubs: *The Grand Concourse* (Mss., 1993), *Riding First Car*
　　(Sulfur 31, 1993), *On Prejudice: Anth* (Doubleday, 1993),
　　Poems on the Underground, Walt Whitman Qtly.

Siri Narayan Kaur Khalsa　　　　　　　　P&W
460 Ashland Ave, Buffalo, NY 14222, 716-881-5504
Internet: siri_naray@aol.com
　　Pubs: *Dancing with the Guru* (White Lion Pr, 1996),
　　Unconditional Love, Life Junkies: On Our Own Anth (Textile
　　Bridge, 1992, 1991).

Robert Kimm P
RR 02, Marcellus, NY 13108-9623
Pubs: *Goin Nowhere Sunday* (Bull Thistle Pr, 1996),
*Camellia, Fat Tuesday, Plastic Tower, Hiram Poetry Rev,
Connecticut Poetry Rev, Prairie Schooner.*

Joan Payne Kincaid P
132 Du Bois Ave, Sea Cliff, NY 11579, 516-671-2375
Internet: jpaynekincaid@juno.com
Pubs: *Understanding the Water, My Shameless St.
Augustine Scrapbook: Anth, Friendly Creatures: Anth*
(Kings Estate Pr, 1998, 1998, 1995), *The Quarterly, Pig
Iron, Crosscurrents, Confrontation, Oyez, Black River Qtly.*

Gary Kissick P&W
PSC 43, Box 2252, APO AE, New York, NY 09466,
448-675-6716
Pubs: *Outer Islands* (U Hawaii Pr, 1984), *Best of Bamboo
Ridge: Anth* (Bamboo Ridge, 1988), *Hawaii Rev.*

Judith Kitchen P
35 College St, Brockport, NY 14420, 716-637-0023
Internet: jkitchen@acspr1.acs.brockport.edu
Pubs: *In Short* (Norton, 1996), *Perennials* (Anhinga, 1986),
*Georgia Rev, Gettysburg Rev, Prairie Schooner, Seneca
Rev.*

Jon Klimo P
82 Main Ave, Sea Cliff, NY 11579, 516-671-5480

Henry Korn W
Guild Hall of East Hampton, 158 Main St, East Hampton, NY
11937
Pubs: *Marc Chagall* (Artists Ltd Edtns, 1985), *Brooklyn
College Rev, Unmuzzled Ox, Congress Monthly, Staten
Island Advance, Connoisseur.*

Allen Kovler P
90 Grandview Ave Ext, Catskill, NY 12414, 518-943-9479
Pubs: *Prairie Smoke: Anth* (Pueblo Poetry Project, 1990),
Groundswell, Look Quick.

David Kowalczyk P&W
9318 Creek Rd, Batavia, NY 14020
Pubs: *A Gentle Metamorphosis* (Full Court Pr, 1993), *Bless
Me, Father: Anth* (Penguin/Plume, 1994), *Entelechy,
Oxalis, Maryland Rev, Albany Rev, Crazyquilt.*

Lynn Kozma P
165 W Islip Rd, West Islip, NY 11795, 516-587-6479
Pubs: *Catching the Light* (Pocahontas Pr, 1989), *Phases of
the Moon, If I Had My Life to Live Over: Anth, When I Am
An Old Woman: Anth* (Papier-Mache, 1994, 1992, 1991),
Dumb Beautiful Ministers: Anth (Birnham Wood Graphics,
1997), *Color Wheel, Xanadu.*

Eric Kraft W
PO Box 1830, Sag Harbor, NY 11963, 516-725-3473
Internet: http://members.aol.com/elkraft
Pubs: *Leaving Small's Hotel* (Picador, 1998), *At Home With
the Glynns, What a Piece of Work I Am, Where Do You
Stop, Little Follies, Herb 'N' Lorna* (Crown, 1995, 1994,
1992, 1992, 1988).

Thomas Krampf P
4611 Gile Hollow Rd, Hinsdale, NY 14743, 716-557-2518
Internet: majestic@eznet.net
Pubs: *Shadow Poems, Satori West* (Ischua Bks, 1997,
1987), *Subway Prayer & Other Poems* (Morning Star Pr,
1976).

Norbert Krapf P
134 Willow St, Roslyn Heights, NY 11577, 516-299-2391
Internet: norkrapf@hornet.liunet.edu
Pubs: *Somewhere in Southern Indiana, Blue-Eyed Grass*
(Time Being Bks, 1997, 1993), *Poetry, American Scholar,
Ontario Rev.*

Nancy Kress W
50 Sweden Hill Rd, Brockport, NY 14420, 716-637-2339
Internet: n.kress1@genie.com
Pubs: *Oaths & Miracles* (St. Martin's Pr, 1996), *Beggars &
Choosers* (TOR, 1994), *Omni, Asimov's Science Fiction,
Analog, Writer's Digest.*

Gary Krist W
166 Colabaugh Pond Rd, Croton-on-Hudson, NY 10520,
914-271-2739
Pubs: *Bone by Bone* (Harcourt Brace, 1994), *The Garden
State* (Vintage, 1989), *GQ, Boulevard, Tikkun, The
Quarterly, Hudson Rev, Ladies Home Jrnl.*

Mindy Kronenberg P
9 Garden Ave, Miller Place, NY 11764, 516-331-4118
Internet: cyberpoet@msn.com
Pubs: *Dismantling the Playground* (Birnham Wood
Graphics, 1994), *I Am Becoming The Woman I've Wanted:
Anth* (Papier-Mache Pr, 1994), *MPR, Hawaii Rev, LIQ,
North Atlantic Rev, Confrontation.*

Lawrence Kucharz P
International Audiochrome, PO Box 1068, Rye, NY 10580
Pubs: *Poesie Sonore Internationale* (Edtns Jean-Michel
Place, 1979), *Dramatika, Assemblings, Against Infinity.*

Lesley Kuhn P
58 18th Ave, Sea Cliff, NY 11579, 516-676-3454
Pubs: *West Wind Rev, Innisfree, Footwork, Waterways,
Black Buzzard Rev, Poets On, Metis, North Shore,
Women's Newspaper.*

Carol Scarvalone Kushner W
4 Lore Ln, Red Hook, NY 12571, 914-758-2014
Pubs: *Crazyquilt Qtly, Passages North, Esprit,
Italian-Americana.*

Billy Lamont   PP&P
Other Perspective Management, PO Box 284, Northport, NY
11702, 516-669-1543
Internet: www.eskimo.com/ strobelt
    Pubs: *Into the 21st Century* (CD), *The Gallery of Light*
(National Post Modern Pubs, 1998, 1994).

Louise Landes Levi   P
Barrytown GPO, Barrytown, NY 12507, 917-758-6478
    Pubs: *Extinction* (Left Hand Bks, 1990).

Pedro M. Lastra   P
State Univ New York, Stony Brook, NY 11794-3371
    Pubs: *Noticias Del Extranjero* (Chile; Editorial Univ, 1992),
Travel Notes/Notas de Viaje (La Yapa Editores, 1991).

Lynn Lauber   W
112 Paradise Ave, Piermont, NY 10968, 914-359-4382
    Pubs: *21 Sugar Street* (Norton, 1993), *White Girls* (Vintage
Contemporaries, 1991).

Denize Lauture   P
St. Thomas Aquinas College, Route 340, Sparkill, NY 10976,
914-398-4132
    Pubs: *Running the Road to ABC* (S&S, 1996), *Father and
Son* (Putnam/Grosset Group, 1993), *Callaloo, Litoral,
Presence Africaine, Black American Literary Forum.*

Dorianne Laux   P
BOA Editions, Ltd., 92 Park Ave, Brockport, NY 14420
Internet: dlaux@darkwing.uoregon.edu
    Pubs: *The Poet's Companion* (Norton, 1997), *What We
Carry* (BOA Edtns, 1994), *Kenyon Rev, Southern Rev,
DoubleTake, Zyzzyva, APR, American Voice.*

Patrick Lawler   P&W
College of Environmental Scien, Writing Project, Moon LLRC,
Syracuse, NY 13210, 315-451-3161
    Pubs: *A Drowning Man is Never Tall Enough* (U Georgia,
1990), *Passages North, Southern Humanities Rev, Central
Park, APR, Iowa Rev, Ironwood, Nimrod.*

Beverly Lawn   P
Adelphi Univ, Garden City, NY 11530, 516-877-4020
    Pubs: *Throat of Feathers* (Pleasure Dome Pr, 1979), *New
Letters, Xanadu, Poetry Rev, Live Poets #4.*

Naomi Lazard   P
61 Pantigo Rd, East Hampton, NY 11937, 516-324-6104
Internet: naomilazard@worldnet.att.net
    Pubs: *Lives Through Literature* (Macmillan, 1990), *The
True Subject* (Princeton U Pr, 1987), *Ordinances* (Owl
Creek Pr, 1984), *A Book Of Luminous Things: Anth*
(Harcourt Brace, 1996), *New Yorker, Harper's, Frank, Solo.*

John Leax   P
Houghton College, Houghton, NY 14744, 716-567-9464
    Pubs: *Standing Ground, Country Labors, Nightwatch*
(Zondervan, 1991, 1991, 1989), *Nimrod.*

Adam LeFevre   P
2 Hummel Rd, New Paltz, NY 12561, 914-255-9275
    Pubs: *Everything All At Once* (Wesleyan, 1978), *Vital Signs:
Anth* (U Wisconsin Pr, 1989), *APR, Ploughshares, Paris
Rev, Nation, Grand Street.*

Christine Lehner   W
271 S Broadway, Hastings-On-Hudson, NY 10706-2906,
914-478-0359
    Pubs: *Expecting* (New Directions, 1982), *Agni, NAR,
Chelsea.*

Barbara Lekatsas   P
Hofstra Univ, Hempstead, NY 11550, 516-463-6553
    Pubs: *Demeter in the Deep North, Persephone* (CCC,
1994, 1986), *Artists and Influence.*

Naton Leslie   P&W
31 McMaster St, Ballston Spa, NY 120201907, 518-885-3819
    Pubs: *75 Readings: Anth* (McGraw-Hill, 1998), *Best
American Essays: 1997: Anth* (Houghton Mifflin, 1997),
*Agincourt Irregular, Riverwind, Massachusetts Rev,
Chariton Rev, Prairie Schooner, Yarrow, Puerto del Sol,
Pikeville Rev, West Branch, Intl Poetry Rev.*

Fred Levenson   P
360 Nassau Ave #2, Kenmore, NY 14216
    Pubs: *Blatherskite: Anth* (Just Buffalo, 1981), *Swift Kick,
The Buffalo News, Earth's Daughters, Pure Light, Buffalo
Jrnl.*

Marvin Levine   P
Department of Psychology, SUNY Stonybrook, Stonybrook,
NY 11794, 516-632-7804
    Pubs: *Look Down From Clouds* (Writers Ink Pr, 1997).

Stephen Lewandowski   P
PO Box 943, Canandaigua, NY 14424, 716-374-5473
    Pubs: *Artesia* (Foothills Pubs, 1989), *Poacher* (White Pine
Pr, 1986), *Earth First!, Country Jrnl.*

F. R. Lewis   W
PO Box 12093, Albany, NY 12212, 518-869-9317
Internet: word_cobbler@yahoo.com
    Pubs: *Mother of the Groom* (Distinctive Pr, 1996), *Each In
Her Own Way* (Queen of Swords, 1994), *Tampa Rev,
Kinesis, William and Mary Rev.*

George Liaskos   P
PO Box 11-481, Loudonville, NY 12211-1481
    Pubs: *Library Bound: A Saratoga Anthology* (Saratoga
Springs Public Library, 1996), *Saratogian, Mill Hunk Herald,
MacGuffin, Poetalk, Ormfaer.*

Lyn Lifshin P&W
2142 Appletree Ln, Niskayuna, NY 12309, 703-242-3829
Internet: onyxvelvet@aol.com
Pubs: *Cold Comfort* (Black Sparrow Pr, 1997), *Blue Tattoo*
(Event Horizon, 1995), *Marilyn Monroe Poems* (Quiet Lion,
1994), *Reading Lips* (Morgan Pr, 1992), *The Doctor Poems*
(Applezaba Pr, 1991), *American Scholar, Press, Many
Mountains Moving, Ploughshares.*

Leatrice Lifshitz P
PO Box 615, Pomona, NY 10970, 914-354-2507
Pubs: *Only Morning In Her Shoes: Anth* (Utah State U Pr,
1990), *Kalliope, Modern Haiku, Slant, Poets On, Sing
Heavenly Muse!, Stone Country.*

Ray Lindquist P
Craig Rd, Pavilion, NY 14525, 716-584-3307
Pubs: *By-Products* (Crossing Pr, 1972), *Mother Jones,
West End.*

Geri Lipschultz PP
487 Old Country Rd, Huntington Station, NY 11746,
516-423-8050

Mike Lipstock W
132 Hazelwood Dr, Jericho, NY 11753, 516-681-0171
Pubs: *Chicken Soup For the Soul: Anths* (Health
Communications Inc, 1998, 1997), *Gifts of Our Fathers:
Anth* (Crossing Pr, 1994), *A Loving Voice: Anth* (Charles Pr,
1994), *Rosebud, Scuba Times, Raconteur, Mediphors, Palo
Alto Rev, Midstream, Potpourri.*

Robert Long P&W
313A Three Mile Harbor, Hog Creek Rd, East Hampton, NY
11937
Internet: rtlong@mindspring.com
Pubs: *Blue* (Canios Edtns, 1998), *The Sonnets* (Illuminati,
1994), *What Happens* (Galileo Pr, 1988), *New Yorker,
Partisan Rev, Poetry, New American Poets of the 90's.*

Michael Lopes P
260 Jay St, Katonah, NY 10536, 914-232-4584
Pubs: *Mr. & Mrs. Mephistopheles & Son* (Dustbooks, 1975),
Poets West, Hanging Loose, Kansas Qtly.

John Love P
12 Rockridge Rd, Mt Vernon, NY 10552, 914-667-6157
Pubs: *The Touch Code* (Release Pr, 1977).

Barbara Lucas P
6 Briarcliff Ln, Glen Cove, NY 11542, 516-676-7686
Pubs: *Confrontation, Xanadu, Nassau Rev, Dodeca,
Sharing, Beloit Poetry Jrnl, Hiram Poetry Rev.*

Dennis Lucas P&W
PO Box 263, Hunter, NY 12442, 518-263-4865
Pubs: *Thirteen Ways of Looking at Crows, Poetic License:
Anth* (Left Hand Bks, 1992, 1997), *Amelia, Zone 3, Black
River Rev, Outloud, Satori, Flipside, Ploplop, Shockbox,
Creatum Sinistra.*

Sister Mary Lucina P
Mount Mercy Convent, 625 Abbott Rd, Buffalo, NY 14220,
716-826-6192
Pubs: *Webster Rev, Zone 3, Nimrod, Florida Rev, River
City, Greensboro Rev, Mid-American Rev, Sun Dog,
Nebraska Rev, Slant, National Forum.*

Jack Ludwig W
PO Box A-2028, Setauket, NY 11733, 516-929-4169
Internet: jludwig@ccmail.sunysb.edu
Pubs: *The Great American Spectaculars* (Doubleday,
1976), *A Woman of Her Age* (McClelland & Stewart, 1973),
Above Ground (Little, Brown, 1968), *The Atlantic, Partisan
Rev, London Mag, Quarterly Rev.*

Susan Lukas W
85 Rockland Rd, Sparkill, NY 10976
Pubs: *Morgana's Fault* (Putnam, 1980), *Stereopticon, Fat
Emily* (Stein & Day, 1975, 1974).

David Lunde P&W
252 King Rd, Forestville, NY 14062, 716-934-4199
Internet: lunde@del.cs.fredonia.edu
Pubs: *Blues for Port City* (Mayapple Pr, 1995), *Calibrations*
(Allegany Mountain Pr, 1981), *Chicago Rev, Asimov's SF
Mag, Renditions, Chaminade, Literary Rev, Hawaii Rev.*

Alan Lupack P&W
375 Oakdale Dr, Rochester, NY 14618
Internet: alpk@db1.cc.rochester.edu
Pubs: *The Dream of Camelot* (Green Chapel, 1990), *Pig
Iron, Aileron.*

Alison Lurie W
Cornell Univ, Ithaca, NY 14853
Internet: al28@cornell.edu
Pubs: *Women and Ghosts* (Doubleday, 1994), *Don't Tell
The Grownups, The Truth About Lorin Jones* (Little, Brown,
1990, 1988).

Dennis Lynds W
PO Box 235, Bedford Hills, NY 10507
Pubs: *The Cadillac Cowboy* (DIF-Penguin, 1995), *Talking
to the World* (John Daniel & Co., 1995), *Cassandra in Red*
(Donald I. Fine, 1992), *South Carolina Rev, Cimarron Rev.*

Katharyn Howd Machan					P&W
PO Box 456, Ithaca, NY 14851-0456, 607-273-3744
Internet: machan@ithaca.edu
	Pubs: *The Flames They Are* (Sometimes Y Pubs, 1998),
	The Kitchen of Your Dreams (Thorntree Pr, 1992), *The
	Bedford Intro To Literature: Anth* (St. Martin's 1998), *Beloit,
	Seneca Rev, Louisiana Literature, Yankee, Nimrod.*

Jennifer B. MacPherson					P
907 Comstock Ave, Syracuse, NY 132102813, 315-475-0339
Internet: jennymac@dreamscape.com
	Pubs: *Another Use for Husbands* (Saltfire Pr, 1990), *To
	Attempt a Tower* (J. MacPherson, 1985), *Comstock Rev,
	Potato Eyes, Lyric, SPSM&H, Piedmont Literary Rev,
	Poetpourri, Kalliope.*

Kathleen A. Magill					P
33 Linwood Ave, Buffalo, NY 14209
	Pubs: *Just Buffalo Pr, Deros, Common Ground, Up Against
	the Wall Mother.*

Mary Makofske					P&W
32 Maple Ave, Florida, NY 10921-1309, 914-651-7723
	Pubs: *The Disappearance of Gargoyles* (Thorntree, 1988),
	Tangled Vines: Anth (HBJ, 1992), *Lullwater Rev, Cream
	City Rev, Calyx, Cumberland Poetry Rev, Iris.*

Dennis Maloney					P
White Pine Press, 76 Center St, Fredonia, NY 14063,
716-672-5743
Internet: pine@net.bluemoon.net
	Pubs: *Between This Floating Mist* (Spring Hse Edtns,
	1992), *The Map Is Not The Territory: Poems & Translations*
	(Unicorn Pr, 1990).

Bridget Manney					P
165 E Dover St, Valley Stream, NY 11580
	Pubs: *Twigs, Unicorn, Hyacinths And Biscuits.*

George Maritime					P
44 Cherwing Rd, Yonkers, NY 10701, 914-963-4971
	Pubs: *Noble Deeds, The Rap* (The New Pr, 1991, 1986),
	Rose Colored Glasses: Anth (ABC No Rio, 1985).

Grace B. Martin					P&W
898 Richmond Ave, Buffalo, NY 14222-1118, 716-884-6942
	Pubs: *Grannies: 101* (Slipstream, 1992), *Buffalo News,
	Today, Forward.*

Janette Martin					P
The Writer's Center @ Chautauq, 953 Forest Ave Ext,
Jamestown, NY 14701, 716-483-0381
Internet: blsaid@madbbs.com
	Pubs: *Connecticut River Rev, Pudding, Bitterroot,
	Crazyquilt, Anemone, Harbinger.*

Patricia Martin					P&W
PO Box 773, New Paltz, NY 12561, 914-255-1664
	Pubs: *The Bombay Tree* (Phantom Pr, 1991), *Bitterroot,
	Wide Open Mag, Oxalis, Parnassus, Amelia, Maryland
	Poetry Rev, George Washington Rev, Art Times.*

Paul Martin					W
135 Parkwood Dr, Snyder, NY 14226, 716-839-3146
	Pubs: *The Floating World Cycle Poems* (Great Raven Pr,
	1979), *Greenfield Rev, Contact II.*

Anne Marx					P
315 The Colony, Hartsdale, NY 10530, 914-946-3992
	Pubs: *Love in Late Season* (Wm. H. Bauhan, 1992), *The
	Courage To Grow Old: Anth* (Ballantine Bks, 1989), *CSM,
	Amelia, Lyric, Good Housekeeping, Modern Maturity, South
	Florida Poetry Rev.*

Dan Masterson					P
41 Fisher Ave, Pearl River, NY 10965, 914-735-5815
Internet: prdanjan@msn.com
	Pubs: *All Things, Seen and Unseen, World Without End,
	Those Who Trespass* (U Arkansas Pr, 1997, 1991, 1985),
	*Southern Rev, Prairie Schooner, New York Qtly, Ontario
	Rev, Gettysburg Rev, Poetry Northwest, Georgia Rev,
	Sewanee Rev, Paris Rev.*

Debby Mayer					W
P.O. Box C-25, Hollowville, NY 12530, 518-851-3690
Internet: dmayer@bard.edu
	Pubs: *Sisters* (Berkley, 1985), *New Yorker, Redbook,
	Fiction Intl, Plainswoman.*

Harry Mazer					W
7626 Brown Gulf Road, Jamesville, NY 13078, 315-682-6799
Internet: hmazer @aol.com
	Pubs: *The Wild Kid* (S&S, 1998), *Twelve Shots: Anth*
	(Bantam, 1997).

Jerome Mazzaro					P
147 Capen Blvd, Buffalo, NY 14226-3052, 716-835-3269
	Pubs: *Rubbings* (Quiet Hills, 1985), *The Caves of Love*
	(Jazz Pr, 1985), *From the Margin: Anth* (Purdue U Pr,
	1990), *Accent, Southwest Rev, Colorado Rev, New
	Republic, Nation, Hudson Rev, Poetry, Sewanee Rev,
	Salmagundi.*

Gerald McCarthy					P
St. Thomas Aquinas College, Rt 340, Sparkill, NY 10976,
914-359-9500
	Pubs: *Shoetown* (Cloverdale Library, 1992), *War Story*
	(Crossing Pr, 1977), *Mid-American Rev, New Letters, The
	And Rev, America, Cloverdale Rev, Poet Lore.*

Kenneth Anderson McClane					P
Cornell Univ, 343 Rockefeller Hall, Ithaca, NY 14853,
607-277-3497
	Pubs: *Take Five: Collected Poems* (Greenwood, 1988), *A
	Tree Beyond Telling* (Black Scholar, 1983).

James McConkey   W
402 Aiken Rd, Trumansburg, NY 14886, 607-387-9830
Internet: jrm9@cornell.edu
Pubs: *Stories from My Life with the Other Animals, Court of Memory* (Godine, 1993, 1993), *Anatomy of Memory: Anth* (Oxford U Pr, 1996), *Hudson Rev.*

James McCorkle   P
790 S Main St, Geneva, NY 14456-3235, 315-789-2139
Internet: jdbmccorkle@worldnet.att.net
Pubs: *Best American Poetry: Anth* (Collier Bks, 1992), *New England Rev, Poetry, Southwest Rev, Verse, Green Mountains Rev, Manoa, Pequod, Turnstile, Boulevard, Plum Rev, Ontario Rev.*

Maureen McCoy   W
Cornell Univ, Goldwin Smith 250, Ithaca, NY 14850
Pubs: *Divining Blood, Summertime, Walking After Midnight* (Poseidon, 1992, 1987, 1985).

Bryan McHugh   P
Station Hill Rd, Barrytown, NY 12507, 914-758-6478
Internet: http://www.lefthandbooks.com/lhb
Pubs: *Public Enemy, Wolf's Clothing, Rillo: Finders Keepers, Rillo: Hymns* (Left Hand Bks, 1996, 1994, 1993, 1992), *Vamos, Varmint* (Texture Pr, 1995), *Creacion.*

Sandy McIntosh   P
2823 Rockaway Ave, Oceanside, NY 11572, 516-766-1891
Internet: drsmac@aol.com
Pubs: *Endless Staircase* (Street Pr, 1991), *Sleepers Awake, Monsters of the Antipodes* (Survival Manual Bks, 1989, 1989).

Thomas R. McKague   P&W
Onondaga Community College, Onondaga Hill, Syracuse, NY 13210, 315-469-7741
Pubs: *Waterlight Dreams* (New Pr, 1995), *A Natural Beauty* (Florida Pr, 1991), *Poetpourri, New Press Literary Qtly, Blue Unicorn.*

Robert T. McLaughlin   W
24 Goodrich St, Williston Park, NY 11596, 516-746-8193

Gary McLouth   P&W
490 Waterbury Rd, Nassau, NY 12123, 518-766-4385
Pubs: *North Country: Anth* (Greenfield Rev Pr, 1986), *Art Times, Writers, Adirondack Life, Blueline, Voices, Groundswell.*

Joan McNerney   P
54 Hudson St, Oneonta, NY 13820
Pubs: *Crazy Flowers* (Arte Publico Pr, 1984), *Aspect, Bitterroot, Croton Rev, Kalliope, Mudfish.*

Susan Merrill   P
340 Grand St, Croton-on-Hudson, NY 10520, 914-271-3893
Pubs: *Croton Rev, Kansas Qtly, Footwork, Pudding, New York Qtly, Purchase Poetry Rev, Pomegranate Series.*

Bart A. Midwood   W
64 Meadow St, Garden City, NY 11530, 516-747-6239
Pubs: *Bennett's Angel* (British-American Paris Rev Edtns, 1989), *The Nativity* (Bel Esprit, 1981).

Carol Miller   P
17 Birch Hill Rd #1, PO Box 57, Locust Valley, NY 11560, 516-759-5578
Pubs: *Life On The Line* (Negative Capability Pr, 1992), *Cape Rock, Wisconsin Rev, Oregon East, Buffalo Spree, New Infinity Rev, Calapooya Collage, Albatross, Confrontation.*

Deborah Miller   W
31 Milo St, Hudson, NY 12534, 518-828-3493
Pubs: *Alaska Qtly Rev, Antioch Rev, Cottonwood, Ascent, PEN Fiction Project '87.*

Edmund Miller   P
Long Island Univ, C. W. Post Campus, Brookville, NY 11548-1300, 516-299-2391
Internet: edmiller@aurora.liunet.edu
Pubs: *Leavings* (Birnham Wood, 1995), *Fucking Animals* (Florida Literary Foundation, 1994), *Vice, Next, Long Island Qtly.*

Thomas Milligan   P
9 King St, Homer, NY 13077, 607-748-3368
Pubs: *Virginia Qtly Rev, New Mexico Humanities Rev, Georgia Rev, Jeopardy, West Branch.*

Marianne Milton   P
6558 4th Section Rd, #149, Brockport, NY 14420-2472
Internet: miltonma@earthlink.net
Pubs: *Coal Slit Dawn* (Bone & Flesh, 1997), *Practice of Peace: Anth* (ShermanAsher, 1998), *Spoon River Poetry Rev, Apalachee Qtly.*

Phil Mintz   P
Melville, NY 11747, 516-843-2754
Internet: mintz@newsday.com
Pubs: *The Nation, Village Voice, Xanadu, The Smith.*

Eugene Mirabelli   W
29 Bennett Terr, Delmar, NY 12054, 518-439-5978
Internet: mirabell@cnsvax.albany.edu
Pubs: *The World At Noon* (Guernica Edtns, 1994), *No Resting Place* (Viking, 1972), *Third Coast, Via, Michigan Qtly, APR, Grand Street.*

Jo Mish   P
10 Main St, Laurens, NY 13796, 607-432-2990

Homer Mitchell   P
42 Dinsdale Rd, Canton, NY 13617, 315-386-5443
Internet: homarie@northnet.org
Pubs: *Writing Our Way Out of the Dark: Anth* (Queen of Swords Pr, 1995), *We Speak For Peace: Anth* (KIT Pubs, 1993), *Southern Rev, Poetry Motel, Poem.*

Eileen Moeller P
20 Marvin St, Clinton, NY 13323, 315-853-4295
Internet: moell4er@ican.net
  Pubs: *The Nerve: Writing Women 1998: Anth* (Virago Pr, 1998), *Claiming the Spirit Within: Anth* (Beacon Pr, 1995), *Fine China: Twenty Years of Earth's Daughters: Anth* (Spring Hse Edtns, 1993), *Caprice, Embers, Kalliope, Earth's Daughters, Poetry London.*

Ann Mohin P&W
RD 1, Box 83, McDonough, NY 138010083, 607-647-5643
Internet: http://www.norwich.net/booksbyann
  Pubs: *The Farm She Was: A Novel* (Bridgeworks Pub, 1998).

Daniel Thomas Moran P
PO Box 2008, Shelter Island, NY 11964, 516-749-1301
  Pubs: *Long Island Qtly, Confrontation, Nassau Rev, Inky Blue, New Pr, Sulfur River, Pannus Index.*

Carole Morgan W
45 Old Roaring Brook Rd, Mt Kisco, NY 10549, 914-241-0936
  Pubs: *Heirlooms* (Macmillan, 1981).

Robert Morgan P&W
427 Ferguson Rd, Freeville, NY 13068, 607-844-4538
  Pubs: *The Hinterlands* (Algonquin Bks, 1994), *The Mountain Won't Remember Us and Other Stories* (Peachtree Pubs, 1992).

Mark Morganstern P&W
PO Box 279, Rosendale, NY 12472, 914-658-3511
  Pubs: *Crescent Rev, New Southern Literary Messenger, Espresso, Tilt, Piedmont Literary Rev, Tempest.*

David Morrell W
Henry Morrison, Inc., PO Box 235, Bedford Hills, NY 10507, 914-666-3500
  Pubs: *Double Image, Desperate Measures, Assumed Identity, The Covenant of the Flame, The Fifth Profession* (Warner Bks, 1998, 1994, 1993, 1991, 1990).

William L. Morris P
414 Elmwood Ave, Buffalo, NY 14222, 716-875-8212
  Pubs: *Chicago Rev, Poetry Northwest, Yale Literature, The Third Eye, Buckle.*

Sylvia Moss P
462 Weaver St, Larchmont, NY 10538, 914-834-2724
  Pubs: *Cities in Motion* (U Illinois, 1987), *New Letters, New Laurel Rev, Helicon Nine.*

William Mulvihill W
Box 204, Sag Harbor, NY 11963
  Pubs: *Serengeti, God Is Blind* (Brickiln Pr, 1996, 1996), *Night of the Axe* (HM, 1972).

Christopher Munford P
PO Box 161, Warwick, NY 10990-0161
  Pubs: *Sermons in Stone* (Birch Brook Pr, 1993), *River Night* (Sub Rosa Pr, 1989), *Make Room for Dada, Home Planet News, Outerbridge, Sub Rosa.*

Fred Muratori P
Cornell Univ, Ithaca, NY 14853, 607-255-6662
Internet: fmm1@cornell.edu
  Pubs: *Despite Repeated Warnings* (Basfal Bks, 1994), *The Possible* (State Street Pr, 1988), *Denver Qtly, Best American Poetry 1994, Talisman, ACM.*

Dan Murray P
735 Reed Ave, Mattituck, NY 119523548
  Pubs: *The New Covenant* (Birnham Wood Graphics, 1993), *Long Island Poets: Anth* (Permanent Pr, 1986), *Long Island Qtly, Caprice, 4x4.*

Joan Murray P
Albany Turnpike, Old Chatham, NY 12136, 518-794-9722
  Pubs: *Queen of the Mist* (Beacon, 1999), *Looking For the Parade* (Norton, 1999), *The Same Water* (Wesleyan, 1990), *Hudson Rev, Paris Rev, Ontario Rev, Ms., Nation, Atlantic, APR, Pushcart Prize.*

Robert T. Natello PP
2 West, Lake George, NY 12845, 518-668-3048
  Pubs: *Bohemian Cafe* (Passages Pr, 1998), *Rude Poets & Polite Musicians* (Back Door Cafe, 1996), *Tropic Cafe, Botanical Gardens, Old Courthouse Cafe, Full Moon Cafe, Cafe Dolce, Cafe Lena.*

Mark Neider P&W
4 Chestnut Ridge Way, Dobbs Ferry, NY 10522, 914-693-1237
  Pubs: *Mudfish, Cumberland Poetry Rev, Judaism, Cross Roads, Everyman, Medicinal Purposes, Lilliput Rev, Mediphors, Iconoclast, Hollins Critic, Magic Realism, Decade, Pacific, New Mexico Qtly.*

Howard Nelson P
RD 4, Box 121, Moravia, NY 13118, 315-364-8536
  Pubs: *Bone Music* (Nightshade Pr, 1997), *Gorilla Blessing* (Falling Tree Pr, 1993), *The Rag & Bone Shop of the Heart: Anth* (HarperCollins, 1992), *Green Fuse, Great River Rev, Tar River, Blueline, Footwork, Whole Terrain.*

Shirley Nelson W
122 Lancaster St, Albany, NY 12210, 518-432-5163
  Pubs: *Fair, Clear, and Terrible* (British American Ltd, 1989), *The Last Year of the War* (Harold Shaw, 1989), *Image: A Jrnl of the Arts.*

Mark Nepo P
48 Willett St, #2, Albany, NY 12210-1104
  Pubs: *Acre of Light* (Ithaca Hse, 1994), *Fire Without Witness* (British American, 1988), *Antaeus, Kenyon Rev, Chelsea, Sewanee Rev, Voices, Pilgrimage.*

Tam Lin Neville P
PO Box 673, Keene Valley, NY 12943-0673
    Pubs: *Journey Cake* (BkMk Pr/U Kansas City, 1998),
    Mademoiselle, Indiana Rev, APR, Ironwood, Crazyhorse,
    Massachusetts Rev.

Ben Nightingale W
14 Soundview Ave, #C5-28, White Plains, NY 106065991,
914-428-5991
    Pubs: *Mendocino Rev, Network Africa, Obsidian.*

David Michael Nixon P
610 Park Ave, Rochester, NY 14607-2936, 716-256-0525
    Pubs: *Season of the Totem* (Linear Arts, 1997), *Hunting the*
    World (FootHills Pub, 1989), *Blue Water Line Blues* (Mott
    Calligraphy, 1988), *Waterways, Black Buzzard Rev,*
    Cocodrilo, Gypsy, Home Planet News, Salonika, Hazmat
    Rev, Potato Eyes, Comstock Rev.

Sharyn November P
81 Salem Rd, East Hills, NY 11577, 516-621-6376
    Pubs: *Poetry, NAR, Poetry Miscellany, Small Pond, New*
    Infinity Rev.

Beatrice O'Brien P
RD 2, Box 155, Cohocton, NY 14826
    Pubs: *One Track* (Mozart Park Pr, 1995), *From the Wings*
    (Rainbow Pr, 1990), *Lake Effect, Time of Singing.*

William P. O'Brien P&W
227 Seville Blvd, Sayville, NY 11782, 516-589-0508
    Pubs: *Shenandoah, Southern Humanities Rev, Kansas*
    Qtly, Pulpsmith, Street, Fiddlehead.

Mary Beth O'Connor P&W
224 Esty St, Ithaca, NY 14850, 607-272-6914
    Pubs: *Life on the Line: Reflections on Words and Healing*
    (Negative Capability Pr, 1992), *Concourse 7, Ithaca*
    Women's Anth, Nimrod.

Toni Ortner P
P.O. Box 213, Bell Hollow Rd, Putnam Valley, NY 10579
    Pubs: *Requiem, American Poetry Confronts the 1990's:*
    Anth (Black Tie Pr, 1991, 1990), *Mudfish, Literary Rev,*
    Canadian Forum, Kansas City Rev.

Ron Overton P
16 Renown St, Lake Grove, NY 11755, 516-585-8032
    Pubs: *The Second Set* (Indiana U Pr, 1996), *Hotel Me*
    (Hanging Loose Pr, 1994), *Downbeat, Transfer, Minnesota*
    Rev, Poetry Northwest, Commonweal, Salmagundi,
    Massachusetts Rev, Kayak.

Jim Papa P&W
26 Awixa Ave, Bay Shore, NY 11706, 516-968-6947
    Pubs: *In Autumn: Anth* (Birnham Wood Graphics, 1994),
    Petroglyph, Isle, Fire Island Tide, NAR, Long Island Qtly,
    College English, Wordsmith, Plainsong, Panhandler,
    Madison Rev.

Theresa Pappas P
348 Fellows Ave, Syracuse, NY 13210, 315-478-2130
    Pubs: *Flash Paper* (New Rivers Pr, 1986), *Black Warrior*
    Rev, Cream City Rev, Oxford Mag, Florida Rev, Webster
    Rev, Mississippi Rev.

Ned Pastor P
1200 Midland Ave, Bronxville, NY 10708, 914-337-4214
    Pubs: *Golf: It's Just A Game!: Anth* (Meadowbrook Pr,
    1996), *Random House Treasury of Light Verse: Anth*
    (Random Hse, 1995), *Sometime The Cow Kick Your Head:*
    Light Year Anth (Bits Pr, 1988), *Pennsylvania Poetry*
    Society Prize Poems, Amelia, Light.

William B. Patrick P
2 The Crossways, Troy, NY 12180-7263, 518-272-1446
Internet: caltap@worldnet.att.net
    Pubs: *We Didn't Come Here For This, The Upraised*
    Hands, Roxa: Voices of the Culver Family (BOA Edtns,
    1999, 1995, 1989), *Southern Rev, North Dakota Rev,*
    Kansas Qtly, Carolina Qtly, Epoch.

Raymond R. Patterson P
2 Lee Ct, Merrick, NY 11566, 516-868-3874
    Pubs: *Elemental Blues* (CCC, 1982), *The Best American*
    Poetry: Anth (Scribner, 1996), *Every Shut Eye Ain't Asleep:*
    Anth (Little, Brown, 1994), *Drumvoices.*

Elizabeth Patton P
5273 Kingston Rd, PO Box 427, Elbridge, NY 13060,
315-689-9782

Nita Penfold P&W
11385 Big Tree Rd, East Aurora, NY 14052
    Pubs: *Love's Shadow* (Crossing Pr, 1993), *If I Had My Life*
    to Live Over, I Would Pick More Daisies: Anth
    (Papier-Mache, 1992), *Maryland Rev, Exit 13, Lactuca.*

James Penzavecchia P
RD 2, Box 294C, Hamilton, NY 13346, 516-825-2820
    Pubs: *Little Mag, Greenfield Rev, Xanadu, Small Pond,*
    Wind, Buckle, Bird Effort.

Simon Perchik P
10 Whitby Ln, East Hampton, NY 11937, 516-324-2834
Internet: rossetti@peconic.net
    Pubs: *Letters To The Dead* (St. Andrews Pr, 1994),
    Redeeming The Wings (Dusty Dog Pr, 1991), *Partisan Rev,*
    New Yorker, New Letters.

Michael Perkins P&W
750 Ohayo Mountain Rd, Glenford, NY 12433, 914-657-6439
    Pubs: *Dark Matter* (Titan Bks, 1996), *The Good Parts* (R.
    Kasak Bks, 1994), *Out of the Catskills: Anth* (Bright Hill,
    1997), *The Stiffest of the Corpse: Anth* (City Lights, 1988),
    Notre Dame Rev, Para Doxa.

John Niels Perlman   P
38 Ferris Pl, Ossining, NY 10562, 914-762-1978
Internet: johnperl@aol.com
>Pubs: *Edward John* (Tel-Let Pr, 1998), *The Natural History of Trees* (Texture Pr, 1995), *Anacoustic* (Standing Stone Pr, 1993), *Talisman, O.ars, Tel-Let, Shearsman, Juxta, Texture, Key Satch*(el), *Origin.*

Ellen Perreault   P
34 Danker Ave, Albany, NY 12206, 518-459-2795
>Pubs: *Greenfield Rev, Hollow Springs Rev, Washout Rev, Laurel Rev, Three Sisters.*

Marion Perry   P
Word Worth, PO Box 221, East Aurora, NY 14052, 716-851-1712
>Pubs: *Dishes, Establishing Intimacy* (Textile Bridge, 1989, 1982), *Hiram Poetry Rev, Footwork, Esprit, Black Mountain Rev, Buckle, Earth's Daughters, Intrepid.*

Bette Pesetsky   W
Hilltop Park, Dobbs Ferry, NY 10522
>Pubs: *Cast A Spell* (Harcourt Brace, 1993), *The Late Night Muse* (HarperCollins, 1991), *Confessions of a Bad Girl, Midnight Sweets* (Atheneum, 1989, 1988).

Joan Peternel   P&W
65 Bay Ave, Hampton Bays, NY 119462507, 516-723-0425
Internet: pesnik@aol.com
>Pubs: *Howl and Hosanna* (Whelks Walk Pr, 1997), *Anth of Magazine Verse* (Monitor Bk Co, 1997), *James Joyce Qtly, Small Press Rev, Mandrake Poetry Rev, Long Island Qtly.*

Donald Petersen   P
12 Grand St, Oneonta, NY 13820, 607-432-8308
>Pubs: *The Spectral Boy* (Wesleyan U Pr, 1964), *New Criterion.*

Anthony Piccione   P
Crow Hill Farm, Box 295, Prattsburgh, NY 14873, 607-522-3289
>Pubs: *For The Kingdom, Seeing It Was So* (BOA Edtns Ltd, 1995, 1987), *APR, Choice, Iowa Rev, Chicago Rev, Literary Rev, Painted Bride Qtly.*

Paul Pines   P&W
55 Garfield St, Glens Falls, NY 12801-2660, 518-798-2858
>Pubs: *Pines Songs* (Ikon Pr, 1992), *Hotel Madden Poems* (Contact II, 1991), *The Tin Angel* (Morrow, 1983), *New Directions, Global City Rev, First Intensity.*

Joseph Pintauro   P&W
PO Box 531, Sag Harbor, NY 11963, 516-725-4141
>Pubs: *State Of Grace* (Times Bks, 1983), *Cold Hands* (Signet, 1980).

Allen Planz   P
Box 212, East Hampton, NY 11937, 516-725-1667
>Pubs: *A Night For Rioting* (Swallow, 1990), *Wild Craft* (Living Ports Pr, 1976), *Chonderhara Street Press.*

Mariquita Platov   P
Rte 1, Box 4, Tannersville, NY 12485, 518-589-0135
>Pubs: *Banana Girl* (Peace Creativity, 1988), *One Moment* (Plowshare Pr, 1961), *Groundswell, Fellowship, Concern, Imprints Qtly, Inward Light, The Word.*

Charles Plymell   P&W
Box 303, Cherry Valley, NY 13320, 607-264-3707
>Pubs: *Forever Wider* (Scarecrow Pr, 1985), *Trashing Of America* (Kulchur Fdn, 1975).

Kathryn Poppino   P
1027 Hickory Rd, Schenectady, NY 12309, 518-374-5410
>Pubs: *The Smith, Tightrope, Yellow Brick Road, Chicago Rev, Hanging Loose.*

Barbara Ann Porte   W
PO Box 786, Mineola, NY 11501, 212-889-3050
>Pubs: *Taxicab Tales* (Morrow, 1992), *Ruthann and Her Pig* (Orchard Bks, 1989), *Confrontation.*

Richard Posner   W
Henry Morrison, Inc., PO Box 235, Bedford Hills, NY 10507, 914-666-3500
>Pubs: *Sweet Sixteen & Never Been Killed, Can You Hear Me Scream?* (Pocket Bks, 1994, 1994).

Shirley Powell   P&W
4239 U.S. Highway 209, Stone Ridge, NY 12484
>Pubs: *Bridges* (Springtown Pr, 1997), *Other Rooms, Villages and Towns, Alternate Lives* (Poets' Pr, 1997, 1993, 1990), *Home Planet News, True West, Oxalis, Green's Mag, Ball State Forum, Art Times.*

Prem Nagpal Prasad   P&W
7 Roberta Ave, Farmingville, NY 11738, 516-698-0512
>Pubs: *Padmavati* (Birnham Wood Graphics, 1994), *We Speak for Peace: Anth* (Knowledge, Ideas & Trends Inc., 1993), *Long Island Qtly, Bharti, Willow, Massachusetts Rev.*

Elaine Preston   P
Suffolk Community College-West, Brentwood, NY 11717, 516-851-6788
Internet: elaine@staffordnet.com
>Pubs: *Fishing Underground* (H&H Pr, 1997), *Look for a Field to Land* (Bridge Works Pub, 1994), *In Autumn: Anth* (Birnham Wood Graphics, 1994), *Poets On, Mink Hills Jrnl, Jrnl of Poetry Therapy, Poet Lore, Comstock Rev, Passager, Peregrine, New York Qtly.*

Dan Propper P
Box 346, Bearsville, NY 12409
Pubs: *The Tale of the Amazing Tramp* (Cherry Valley
Edtns, 1976), *The Maverick Poets: Anth* (Gorilla Pr, 1988),
The Beats: Anth (Gold Medal, 1960), *Evergreen Rev, Cold
Spring Jrnl, Invisible City, Provincetown Rev, San Francisco
Rev, Second Coming.*

William Pruitt P
294 Sagamore Dr, Irondequoit, NY 146172406,
716-467-9510
Pubs: *Ravine Street* (White Pine, 1977), *Editor's Choice:
Anth* (The Spirit That Moves Us Pr, 1980), *Potato Eyes,
Blueline, Ploughshares, Poetry Now.*

George Quasha P
Station Hill Rd, Barrytown, NY 12507, 914-758-5291
Pubs: *In No Time, Giving the Lily Back Her Hands* (Station
Hill, 1988, 1979).

Stuart P. Radowitz P
2484 Kayron Ln, North Bellmore, NY 11710, 516-826-3278
Pubs: *Steppenwolf, Fragments, Crazyhorse, Aspen
Leaves, Process, Syracuse Poems, Star Web Rev.*

Diana Ramirez-De-Arellano P
23 Harbor Cir, Centerport, NY 11721, 516-757-3498
Pubs: *Adelfazar, Tree at Vespers/Arbol en Visperas* (Spain;
Editorial Torremozas, 1995, 1987),.

Jarold Ramsey P
Univ Rochester, Rochester, NY 14627, 716-430-6702
Pubs: *Hand-Shadows* (Quarterly Rev of Literature, 1989),
Dermographia (Cornstalk Pr, 1982), *Atlantic, Northwest
Rev, Quarterly Rev of Literature, Poetry Northwest, Nation,
Chelsea, American Scholar.*

Larry Rapant P
35 School Rd, Voorheesville, NY 12186, 518-765-3471
Internet: lrapant@sescva.esc.edu
Pubs: *Esther's Areolas* (XLibris, 1998), *Passages North,
Green Mountains Rev, Slugfest, Mildred, Mati, Knocked,
Lynx Eye, Many Waters, Potpourri, Passages North.*

Wendy Mai Rawlings W
48 Shore Rd, Huntington, NY 11743-1139
Pubs: *Cimarron Rev, Chattahoochee Rev, New Letters.*

Robert L. Reiff P&W
PO Box 818, Guilderland, NY 12084, 518-783-5620
Internet: rlr47@aol.com
Pubs: *MacGuffin, Proof Rock, Gargoyle, Antigonish Rev,
Schenectady Rev, Deros, Skylark, Alura, Augusta Spectator.*

Samuel Reifler W
PO Box 299, Clinton Corners, NY 12514, 914-266-5186
Internet: 105071,2703@compuserve.com
Pubs: *I Ching: A New Interpretation for Modern Times*
(Bantam, 1972), *Esquire, Harper's Bazaar, New Directions,
TriQuarterly, Denver Qtly, Mid-Atlantic Rev.*

Donna Reis P
201 Jessup Rd, Warwick, NY 10990-2543, 914-987-8179
Internet: dreis@warwick.net
Pubs: *Incantations* (Eurydice Pr, 1995), *Rage Before
Pardon: Anth* (Paragon Pr, 1996), *Women and Death: Anth*
(Ground Torpedo Pr, 1994), *Exit 13, Hanging Loose, The
Ledge, New York Qtly, Poetry Motel, Zone 3, Cumberland
Poetry Rev, Gathering of the Tribes.*

Rose Reitter P
25 Forest Ave, Hastings-On-Hudson, NY 10706,
914-478-3077
Pubs: *The Pomegranate Series, Voices Intl, Attention Please.*

Elliot Richman P
159 Oak St, Plattsburgh, NY 12901, 518-562-1838
Internet: comrado@together.net
Pubs: *Franz Kafka's Daughter Meets the Evil Nazi Empire!!!*
(Lunar Offensive Pr, 1998), *Walk On Trooper* (Viet Nam
Generation Pr, 1994), *Honorable Manhood: Poems of Eros
& Dust, The World Dancer* (Asylum Arts, 1994, 1993).

Frances Bragan Richman P
237 Circle Ln, Webster, NY 14580, 716-671-6165
Pubs: *Yellow Butterfly, Saturday Evening Post, Ladies
Home Jrnl.*

Jean Rikhoff W
42 Sherman Ave, Glens Falls, NY 12801
Pubs: *David Smith, I Remember* (The Loft Pr, 1985), *Where
Were You in '76?, The Sweetwater, One of the Raymonds*
(Dial Pr, 1978, 1976, 1974).

Mary Ann Malinchak Rishel W
Ithaca College, 375 Park, Ithaca, NY 14850, 607-274-3324
Internet: rishel@ithaca.edu
Pubs: *Shankpainter, The Scrivener, Red Cedar Rev,
Hudson Rev, Cornell Rev.*

Helen Morrissey Rizzuto P&W
548 E Bay Dr, Long Beach, NY 11561, 516-431-5263
Pubs: *A Bird In Flight, Evening Sky on a Japanese Screen*
(Lintel, 1986, 1978), *Birmingham Poetry Rev, America,
Crazyquilt.*

Sheryl Robbins P
369 Maryland St, Buffalo, NY 14201, 716-885-0804
Internet: weirdsls@aol.com
Pubs: *Or, The Whale* (Shuffaloff Bks, 1993), *Snapshots of
Paradise* (Just Buffalo Pr, 1981), *Denver Qtly, Works &
Days, Inc #2, Earth's Daughters.*

Mary Elsie Robertson   W
3238 Brick Schoolhouse Rd, Hamlin, NY 14464, 716-964-8683
    Pubs: *What I Have to Tell You* (Dell, 1991), *Family Life*
    (Penguin, 1985), *Virginia Qtly Rev, New Virginia Rev,*
    Nebraska Rev.

Anthony Robinson   W
153 Huguenot St, New Paltz, NY 12561, 914-255-8040
    Pubs: *Home Again, Home Again* (Morrow, 1970), *The Easy*
    Way (S & S, 1963).

Bruce Robinson   P
Box 26, Albany, NY 12201-8026
Internet: wrobinso@mail.nysed.gov
    Pubs: *Weber Studies, Xavier Rev, Sow's Ear, Spoon River,*
    Greenfield Rev, Opera Jrnl, Paragraph, Fiction.

Lou Robinson   W
Cornell Univ Press, 124 Roberts Pl, Ithaca, NY 14850,
607-257-7000
    Pubs: *Napoleon's Mare* (Fiction Collective Two, 1991),
    Resurgent: Anth of New Writing by Women (U Illinois Pr,
    1992), *Top Top Stories* (City Lights Pr, 1991).

Bertha Rogers   P
Bright Hill Farm, RR # 1, Box 545, Delhi, NY 13753,
607-746-7306
Internet: bkrogers@catskill.net
    Pubs: *Aurora* (Bull Thistle, 1991), *For the Girl Buried In the*
    Peat Bog: Anth (Six Swans Pr, 1998), *Out of the Catskills*
    and Just Beyond: Anth (Bright Hill Pr, 1997), *Pivot,*
    Confluence, Poetry New York, Phoebe, Yankee, Salmon
    Literary Rev.

Jay Rogoff   P
35 Pinewood Ave, Saratoga Springs, NY 12866-2622,
518-584-0912
Internet: jrogoff@skidmore.edu
    Pubs: *First Hand* (Mica Pr, 1997), *The Cutoff: A Sequence*
    (The Word Works, 1995), *Georgia Rev, DoubleTake, Kenyon*
    Rev, Paris Rev, Partisan Rev, Prairie Schooner, Shenandoah.

Ginny Rorby   W
Barbara Kouts Agency, Box 560, Bellport, NY 11715,
516-286-1278
Internet: grorby@mcn.org
    Pubs: *Dolphin Sky* (Putnam, 1996).

Marina L. Roscher   P&W
4571 Merrick Rd, Massapequa, NY 11758, 516-798-2829
    Pubs: *Catlives* (Texas Tech U Pr, 1992), *New York Qtly,*
    Apalachee Qtly, Madison Rev, Buffalo Spree, Rohwedder,
    Gaia, Prism.

Liz Rosenberg   P&W
State Univ New York, Binghamton, NY 13901, 607-777-2168
    Pubs: *The Fire Music* (U Pitt Pr, 1985), *The Angel Poems*
    (State Street Pr, 1984), *Harper's.*

William Rosenfeld   W
Hamilton College, Clinton, NY 13323, 315-859-4462

M. L. Rosenthal   P
17 Bayard Ln, Suffern, NY 10901, 914-357-0856
    Pubs: *Running to Paradise, As For Love: Poems and*
    Translations (Oxford U Pr, 1994, 1987), *Southern Rev,*
    Ploughshares, Nation, Exile, Pequod.

Geri Rosenzweig   P
63 Mystic Dr, Ossining, NY 10562, 914-762-7025
    Pubs: *Half the Story* (March Street Pr, 1997), *Under A*
    Jasmine Moon (HMS Pr, 1993), *Lullwater Rev, Poet &*
    Critic, River City, Greensboro Rev, Verse.

Gary Earl Ross   P&W
PO Box 1261, Buffalo, NY 14215, 716-838-9786
Internet: geross@ubvms.cc.buffalo.edu
    Pubs: *Sideshow 1995: Anth* (Somersault Pr, 1994),
    Artisans Anth of Fiction (Marienhelz Artisans, 1994),
    Artvoice, Buffalo Mag, Buffalo Spree, ELF.

Henry H. Roth   W
288 Piermont Ave, South Nyack, NY 10960, 914-358-2399
    Pubs: *In Empty Rooms* (December Pr, 1980), *Kansas Qtly,*
    South Carolina Rev, Confrontation.

Paul B. Roth   P
4983 Tall Oaks Dr, Fayetteville, NY 13066-9776,
315-637-3047
Internet: bones44@ix.netcom.com
    Pubs: *Nothing Out There* (Vida Pr, 1996), *Half-Said* (Bitter
    Oleander Pr, 1977), *Immanentist Anth* (The Smith, 1973),
    Higginsville Reader, Glass Cherry, Black Moon, Bitter
    Oleander, Yefief, Comstock Rev.

Chuck Rothman   W
2012 Pyle Rd, Schenectady, NY 123033071, 518-356-4205
Internet: www.sff.net.people/rothman
    Pubs: *Staroamer's Fate* (Warner/Questar Bks, 1986), *Blood*
    Muse: Anth (Donald I. Fine, 1995), *Fantasy & Sci Fi Mag,*
    Aboriginal SF, Galaxy, VB Tech Mag, Realms of Fantasy,
    Tomorrow SF.

Berton Roueche   W
PO Box 693, Amagansett, NY 11930, 516-267-3822

Stan Sanvel Rubin   P
State Univ New York, Brockport, NY 14420, 716-395-5713
    Pubs: *Midnight* (State Street Pr, 1985), *Virginia Qtly Rev,*
    Georgia Rev, Poetry Northwest, Tar River Poetry, Laurel
    Rev, The Quarterly, Ohio Rev, Kenyon Rev.

Helen Ruggieri P
111 N 10 St, Olean, NY 14760, 716-372-0935
Internet: ruggieri+@pitt.edu
Pubs: *The Poetess* (Allegheny Mountain Pr, 1981), *Under A Gull's Wing: Anth* (Down the Shore, 1996), *Flutes of Power: Anth* (Great Elm Pr, 1995), *Coal Seam: Anth* (U Scranton Pr, 1993), *Abraxas, Windfall, Sing Heavenly Muse, Earth's Daughters, Pittsburgh Qtly.*

Michael Rumaker P&W
139 S Broadway, South Nyack, NY 10960, 914-358-1176
Internet: mrb213@mail.tco.com
Pubs: *To Kill A Cardinal* (Arthur Mann Kaye Pub, 1992), *Gringos and Other Stories* (North Carolina Wesleyan College Pr, 1991).

Paul Russell W
Vassar College, English Dept, Poughkeepsie, NY 12601, 914-437-5645
Internet: russell@vaxsar.vassar.edu
Pubs: *Sea of Tranquility* (Dutton, 1994), *Boys of Life* (Dutton, 1991), *Men on Men 4: Anth* (Plume/NAL, 1992), *Crescent Rev, Epoch, Sou'wester, Akros Rev.*

Anne P. Russo P
105 Hardy Ln, Westbury, NY 11590
Pubs: *Minotaur, Womanchild, Third Eye, A Different Drummer, Poet, Wetlands.*

Michael Rutherford P
Alternative Literary Programs, RD 1, Box 147, Indian Ledge Rd, Voorheesville, NY 12186, 518-765-2613

Sarah Ryder P
1588 Hereford Rd, Hewlett, NY 11557

Natalie Safir P
PO Box 602, Rhinebeck, NY 125720602, 914-876-7666
Pubs: *Made Visible* (Singular Speech Pr, 1998), *To Face the Inscription* (La Jolla Poets, 1987), *The McGraw-Hill Book of Poetry: Anth* (McGraw-Hill, 1993), *Reading Poetry: Anth* (Random Hse, 1989), *Slant, Pivot, Roh Wedder, Poets On, MacGuffin, West Hills Rev.*

Ed Sanders P&W
Box 729, Woodstock, NY 12498, 914-679-6556
Pubs: *Chekhov: A Biography in Verse, Hymn to the Rebel Cafe: Poems 1987-1991* (Black Sparrow, 1995, 1992).

Pamela Sargent W
15 Crannell Ave, Delmar, NY 12054-1535
Internet: psargent@sff.net
Pubs: *Women of Wonder* (HB, 1995), *Ruler of the Sky* (Crown, 1993), *Alien Child* (H&R, 1988), *Venus of Shadows* (Doubleday, 1988), *Amazing Stories, Sci Fi Rev, Isaac Asimov's Sci Fi Mag.*

Judith Saunders P
Marist College, Humanities Division, Poughkeepsie, NY 12601, 914-575-3000
Pubs: *Check-Out Counter Suite* (Panhandler/U West Florida Pr, 1992), *CSM, Aura, Ohio Poetry Rev, Art Times, Folio, Concho River Rev, Poet, Bay Windows, CQ.*

Joan Sauro P&W
315 Herkimer St, Syracuse, NY 13204
Pubs: *Whole Earth Meditation: Ecology for the Spirit* (LuraMedia, 1992), *U.S. Catholic, Critic, America, Commonweal, New Catholic World.*

Robert J. Savino P
363 Oak Neck Rd, West Islip, NY 11795-3616, 516-422-6934
Internet: dynsus@aol.com
Pubs: *In My Shoes, Angel Flesh, Wooden Head Rev, Surreal Underground, Conflict of Interest, Incoming, Tantra Pr, The Equinox, Avenging Spirit, Ellipsis, Axe Factory, Babylon Rev.*

Lynne Savitt P
Box 616, Bethpage, NY 11714, 516-433-8198
Pubs: *Sleeping Retrospect of Desire* (Konocti Bks, 1993), *A New Geography of Poets* (Arkansas, 1992), *New York Qtly, Chiron Rev, Painted Bride Qtly, Caprice.*

Boria Sax P
25 Franklin Ave, #2F, White Plains, NY 10601, 914-946-6735
Internet: vogelgreif@aol.com
Pubs: *The Parliament of Animals, The Frog King* (Pace U Pr, 1992, 1990), *Storytelling, Poesie Europe, Poet and Critic, Greenprints, Gegengift, Parabola.*

Susan Schefflcin P&W
16 Partridge Ln, Putnam Valley, NY 10579, 914-528-6338
Pubs: *Each In Her Own Way* (Queen of Swords Pr, 1994), *Birmingham Rev of Poetry, Forum, Touchstone, Live Writers!, Prophetic Voices, Wind, Pandora.*

Budd Schulberg W
c/o Miriam Altshuler Agency, RR#1, Box 5, Old Post Rd, Red Hook, NY 12571
Pubs: *Love, Action, Laughter & Other Sad Tales, What Makes Sammy Run?* (Random Hse, 1990, 1990).

Doris E. Schuyler W
Canal Side Publishers, PO Box 137, RFD #3, Frankfort, NY 13340, 315-895-7535
Pubs: *Adirondack Princess II* (Canal Side Pubs, 1990), *Butlersbury* (LED Pr, 1985), *Aunt Cad, Adirondack Princess* (Worden Pr, 1984, 1982).

Patricia Roth Schwartz P&W
Weeping Willow Farm, 1212 Birdsey Rd, Waterloo, NY 13165, 315-539-0948
Pubs: *The Names of the Moons of Mars* (New Victoria, 1989), *Sojourner, Beloit Fiction Jrnl.*

Sheila Schwartz   W
State Univ College, New Paltz, NY 12561, 914-255-0097
  Pubs: *The Most Popular Girl, Bigger is Better* (Crosswinds,
  1987, 1987), *Sorority* (Warner, 1987).

Joanna Scott   W
Univ Rochester, English Dept, Rochester, NY 14627,
716-275-4092
  Pubs: *Various Antidotes* (Holt, 1994), *Arrogance* (S&S, 1990),
  The Closest Possible Union (Ticknor & Fields, 1988).

Dee Rossi Script   P&W
887 W Ferry St, Buffalo, NY 14209, 716-884-6393
Internet: hscript@aol.com
  Pubs: *About the World of Sherlock Holmes: Jrnl* (Bruce
  Aikin, 1997), *The Formidable Scrapbook of Baker Street:
  Anth* (Sherlockian Pubs, 1996), *ELF, Baker Street Jrnl.*

Ralph W. Seager   P
311 Keuka St, Penn Yan, NY 14527-1153
  Pubs: *My Folks and the One-Room Schoolhouse* (Capper
  Pr, 1993), *Parnassus of World Poets: Anth* (Ramasamy
  Devaraj, 1995), *Ideals Country, Time of Singing.*

Hollis Rowan Seamon   W
English Dept, Albany, NY 12203, 518-454-5207
Internet: seamonh@rosnet.strose.edu
  Pubs: *Sacred Ground: Writings About Home: Anth*
  (Milkweed Edtns, 1996), *Hudson Rev, McCall's,
  Crosscurrents, American Voice, Creative Woman, Calyx,
  Chicago Rev, 13th Moon.*

G. J. Searles   P
Mohawk Valley Comm College, 1101 Sherman Dr, Utica, NY
13501, 315-792-5439
  Pubs: *Mudville Diaries: Anth* (Avon Bks, 1996), *Rockhurst
  Rev, Greenfield,Rev, The Bridge, Light, Footwork, Lynx
  Eye, Yet Another Small Mag, Asbury Park Pr, Main Street
  Rag, Wings, Artword Qtly.*

Peter Sears   P
Bard College, Annandale, NY 12504
  Pubs: *Saturday Rev, Southern Poetry Rev, Field, Poetry
  Northwest, Beloit Poetry Jrnl.*

Janet Seery   P
1106 N Country Club Dr, Schenectady, NY 12309,
518-377-0492
  Pubs: *Washout Rev, Greenfield Rev, Kudzu, Wisconsin
  Rev, Nantucket Rev, Buckle, Bloodroot.*

Joanne Seltzer   P&W
2481 McGovern Dr, Schenectady, NY 12309, 518-377-9049
  Pubs: *Inside Invisible Walls* (Bard Pr, 1989), *Suburban
  Landscape* (MAF Pr, 1988), *The Muse Strikes Back: Anth*
  (Story Line Pr, 1997), *When I am an Old Woman I Shall
  Wear Purple: Anth* (Papier-Mache Pr, 1987), *Sistersong,
  Karamu, Nebo, Earth's Daughters.*

Ntozake Shange   P
Program Corp of America, 599 W Hartsdale Ave, White
Plains, NY 10607, 914-428-5840
  Pubs: *Ridin' the Moon in Texas, Betsey Brown* (St. Martin's
  Pr, 1987, 1985), *River Styx, Heresies.*

Wilfrid Sheed   W
Stock Farm Ln/New Haven, Sag Harbor, NY 11963,
516-725-3797

Marilyn Pocius Shelton   P
13 Sunset Terr, Baldwinsville, NY 13027, 315-638-4068
Internet: marp123@aol.com
  Pubs: *Whispers at the Altar: Beside Prayers: Anth* (Harper
  San Francisco, 1997), *Blue Mesa Rev, Seasons, Liberty
  Hill Poetry Rev, Mudfish, Blue Violin, Exquisite Corpse,
  Black Buzzard Rev, Poetry Motel Wallpaper.*

Alana Sherman   P
Alms House Press, PO Box 217, Pearl River, NY 10965
  Pubs: *Home Ground* (Alms Hse Pr, 1994), *Everything Is
  Gates* (Willamette River Bks, 1991).

Carol Sherman   P
PO Box 2083, 175-B Church Ln, Bridgehampton, NY 11932,
516-537-7006
  Pubs: *Swimming in Lavender* (Fieldside Pr, 1998), *Women
  Under Assault, The Old Judge Stories, In Autumn: Anth*
  (Birnham Wood Graphics, 1995, 1993, 1994).

Edith Shiffert   P
White Pine Press, 76 Center St, Fredonia, NY 14063,
310-540-1880
  Pubs: *The Light Comes Slowly* (Katsura Pr, 1997), *When
  on the Edge, Touching the Point, New and Selected Poems*
  (White Pine Pr, 1991, 1990, 1979), *Forest House With Cat*
  (Japan; Unio Corp, 1991), *New York Times, New Yorker,
  CSM, Kyoto Jrnl.*

Weslea Sidon   P
84 Hillside Ave, Roslyn Heights, NY 11577, 516-621-5117
  Pubs: *In Autumn* (Birnham Wood Graphics, 1994), *This Is
  Where I Live* (Shooting Star, 1981), *Long Island Qtly, Gulf
  Stream, Xanadu, Confrontation, Risings.*

Peter Siedlecki   P
249 Winspear Ave, Buffalo, NY 14215, 716-837-2863
Internet: psiedlec@daemen.edu
  Pubs: *Waterbirds* (Uprising Pr, 1994), *2 River View, Terra
  Poetica, Escarpment, New Kent Qtly, Stone Country, Slant,
  Nantucket Rev, Red Cedar, Buffalo Jrnl.*

Joan I. Siegel   P&W
PO Box 99, Blooming Grove, NY 10914, 914-496-9784
  Pubs: *American Visions, Multicultural Literature for Writers:
  Anth* (Mayfield Pub, 1994), *American Scholar, New Letters,
  Nightsun, Commonweal, Literary Rev, Yankee, Amicus
  Jrnl, River Oak Rev, Free Lunch.*

Roberta Silman   W
18 Larchmont St, Ardsley, NY 10502, 914-693-2816
    Pubs: *Beginning the World Again* (Viking, 1990), *The
    Dream Dredger* (Persea, 1986), *McCall's.*

Maxine Silverman   P
224 Foss Dr, Upper Nyack, NY 10960, 914-353-4106
    Pubs: *Saturday's Women* (Saturday Pr, 1982), *Pushcart
    Prize III, Greenfield Rev.*

Louis Simpson   P&W
P.O. Box 119, Setauket, NY 11733, 516-689-0498
    Pubs: *There You Are* (Story Line Pr, 1995), *Jamaica
    Poems* (Pr of Appletree Alley, 1993), *Hudson Rev,
    Southern Rev, APR, Five Points.*

Nancy Simpson   P
State Street Press, Brockport, NY 28904, 704-389-6497
    Pubs: *Night Student, Across Water* (State Street Pr, 1985,
    1983), *Georgia Rev, Prairie Schooner, Indiana Rev, Florida
    Rev, New Virginia Rev, Southern Poetry Rev,
    Confrontation.*

Susan Sindall   P&W
Box 527, Shady, NY 12409, 914-679-7490
    Pubs: *Kenyon Rev, Prairie Schooner, Pivot, 13th Moon,
    The Connecticut River Rev, Salamander, Fiddlehead.*

Marcia Slatkin   P&W
PO Box 663, Shoreham, NY 11786, 516-744-5023
    Pubs: *Poems 1974-81* (Backstreet Pr, 1982), *Paris Rev,
    San Francisco Chronicle, Earth's Daughters, Xanadu,
    Bellingham Rev, Sycamore Rev.*

John C. Smedley   W
14 Oakdale Dr, Hastings-On-Hudson, NY 10706
    Pubs: *The Villager, St. Andrews Rev, Phantasm.*

Barbara Smith   P&W
PO Box 908, Latham, NY 12110, 518-434-2057
    Pubs: *Yours In Struggle* (Firebrand Bks, 1984), *Home Girls:
    Black Feminist Anth* (Kitchen Table, 1983), *Ms., The
    Guardian, American Voice, Black Scholar, Village Voice.*

Barbara Leavell Smith   P
359 56 Rd, RD 1, Petersburg, NY 12138
    Pubs: *Appalachia, Waterways, Pegasus Rev, Footwork,
    Black Willow.*

Bill Smith   P&W
RFD 1, Box 280, Colton, NY 13625, 315-262-2436
    Pubs: *Adirondack Memories* (Tape; Northern Roads
    Productions, 1992), *I Always Tell the Truth: Anth*
    (Greenfield Rev Pr, 1990).

Jordan Smith   P
Union College, Schenectady, NY 12308, 518-383-0775
    Pubs: *The Household of Continuance* (Copper Beech,
    1992), *Lucky Seven* (Wesleyan, 1988), *Agni, American
    Short Fiction, Antaeus, New England Rev, Yale Rev.*

Mason Smith   P
N Point Rd, Long Lake, NY 12847, 518-624-6398
    Pubs: *Everybody Knows & Nobody Cares* (Knopf, 1971),
    Blue Line.

W. D. Snodgrass   P
RD 1, Box 51, Erieville, NY 13061, 315-684-3752
    Pubs: *The Fuehrer Bunker: The Complete Cycle* (BOA
    Edtns, 1995), *Selected Poems 1957-1987* (Soho Pr, 1991,
    1987), *The Death of Cock Robin* (U Delaware Pr, 1989),
    Southern Rev, Georgia Rev, Salmagundi.

Miriam Solan   P
1 Dolma Rd, Scarsdale, NY 10583, 914-725-1041
    Pubs: *Woman Combing* (Hard Pr, 1997), *For A Living: Anth*
    (U Illinois Pr, 1996), *Lingo, The World, Poetry New York.*

J. R. Solonche   P
Orange County Comm College, 115 South St, Middletown,
NY 10940, 914-341-4007
    Pubs: *Anth of Mag Verse* (Monitor, 1997), *Blood to
    Remember: Anth* (Texas Tech U Pr, 1991), *Mixed Voices:
    Anth* (Milkweed Edtns, 1991), *Poet & Critic, New Criterion,
    Poetry Northwest, American Scholar, Literary Rev,
    Cumberland Poetry Rev, Yankee.*

Theodore Solotaroff   W
19 Beachland Ave, East Quogue, NY 11942-4940,
514-728-7340
    Pubs: *A Few Good Voices in My Head* (H&R, 1988), *The
    Red Hot Vacuum* (Godine, 1980).

Donna Spector   P&W
115 Blooms Corners Rd, Warwick, NY 10990, 914-986-7718
Internet: dspector@warwick.net
    Pubs: *At Our Core: Women Writing About Power: Anth*
    (Papier-Mache Pr, 1998), *XY Files: Poems on the Male
    Experience: Anth* (Sherman Asher Pub, 1997), *Poet Lore,
    Paterson Literary Rev, Bellingham Rev, Hiram Poetry Rev.*

Susan Fantl Spivack   P
RD 1, Box 528, Cobleskill, NY 12043, 518-234-3840
Internet: spivack@telenet.net
    Pubs: *Out of the Catskills and Just Beyond: Anth* (Bright Hill
    Pr, 1997), *It's All the Rage: Anth* (Andrew Mountain Pr,
    1997), *Calyx, Kalliope, Earth's Daughters, Jewish Women's
    Literary Annual, 13th Moon, 100 Words, American Voice,
    Yellow Silk.*

B. A. St. Andrews P
SUNY, Silverman Hall 2121, Irving Av, Syracuse, NY
13210-2399, 315-464-6920
Internet: standreb@vax.cs.hscsyr.edu
  Pubs: *Stealing the Light* (Sous Pr, 1992), *Forbidden Fruit*
  (Whitston Pub, 1986), *Paris Rev, New Yorker,*
  Commonweal, Gettysburg Rev, CSM, Carolina Qtly.

Marilyn Stablein PP&P&W
118 Main St, Germantown, NY 12526, 518-537-5041
  Pubs: *The ABC's of Dictionary Sex, The Census Taker*
  (Black Heron Pr, 1994, 1992), *NAR, Santa Clara Rev, The*
  Sun, Raven Chronicles.

Alice P. Stein P
166 Kingsbury Ln, Tonawanda, NY 14150
  Pubs: *Lyric, California State Poetry Qtly, Erewhon,*
  Pastiche, Snippets, Light Year '87, Light, Pearl.

Charles Stein P
Station Hill Rd, Barrytown, NY 12507-5005, 914-758-3214
  Pubs: *The Hat Rack Tree, Selected Poems from*
  Theforestforthetrees (Station Hill Pr, 1994), *A Night of*
  Thought (St. Lazaire, 1987), *Little Mag.*

Alan L. Steinberg P
Potsdam College, Potsdam, NY 13676, 315-267-2008
Internet: steinbal@potsdam.edu
  Pubs: *Cry of the Leopard* (St. Martin's Pr, 1997), *Divided*
  (Aegina Pr, 1996), *The Road to Corinth* (Players Pr, 1984),
  Carolina Qtly, William and Mary Rev, New Rev, Louisville
  Rev, Poem, Wisconsin Rev, Blueline.

Russell Steinke P
109 Matthews Rd, Oakdale, NY 11769, 516-589-4164
  Pubs: *Confrontation, Poetry Miscellany, Pembroke Mag,*
  Charleton Rev, John O'Hara Jrnl.

Eugene L. Stelzig P
6892 Bailey Rd, Groveland, NY 14462, 716-245-5273
Internet: stelzig@uno.ccgeneseo.edu
  Pubs: *Poetpourri, A Shout in the Street, Crab Creek Rev,*
  Greenfield Rev, Literary Rev, Sou'wester, Desperate Act.

Jody T. Sterling P
76 Esopus Ave, Ulster Park, NY 12487
  Pubs: *Bitterroot, Sunrust, Echoes, Art Times, Esprit.*

Lou Stevens PP
PO Box 2524, East Hampton, NY 119370246, 516-267-1042
Internet: www.loustevens.com
  Pubs: *Fine Art Photography, The Personal Peace Program*
  (Perf; PPP Prod, 1998, 1993), *Anamiles* (Perf; Clone Pub,
  1992).

Edward William Stever P&W
Writers Edge, Box 284, Ridge, NY 11961, 516-924-7463
Internet: edactwrit@aol.com
  Pubs: *Propulsion, Transparency* (Writers Ink Pr, 1992,
  1990), *Long Island Qtly, Chiron Rev, Poets On, Pearl, Live*
  Poets, Long Islander.

Margo Stever P
157 Millard Ave, Sleepy Hollow, NY 10591, 914-332-4469
  Pubs: *Reading the Night Sky* (Riverstone Pr, 1996),
  Imperiled Landscapes Endangered Legends: Anth (Rizzoli
  Intl Pub, 1997), *Minnesota Rev, Ironwood, Chelsea, New*
  England Rev, West Branch, Webster Rev, Seattle Rev.

Ken Stone P
Box 392, Portlandville, NY 13834, 607-286-7500
  Pubs: *A Lust in My Bones* (MAF Pr, 1990), *A Man Holds A*
  Tree (Pygmy Forest Pr, 1989), *Jrnl of Poetry Therapy,*
  Piedmont Literary Rev, Lilliput, Innisfree.

Marc J. Straus P
707 Westchester Ave, White Plains, NY 10604,
914-328-9696
Internet: mjstraus@ibm.net
  Pubs: *Scarlet Crown* (Aureole Pr, 1994), *One Word*
  (TriQuarterly Pr, 1994), *Field, Ploughshares, Kenyon Rev,*
  Passages North, Exquisite Corpse, Poetry East,
  TriQuarterly, Virginia Qtly Rev.

David Levi Strauss P
244 Rock Hill Rd, High Falls, NY 12440-5412, 914-687-7914
  Pubs: *Manoeuvres* (Aleph Pr/Eidolon Edtns, 1980), *49+1:*
  Nouveaux Poetes Americains (Edtns Royaumont, 1991),
  Apex of the M, Intent, Five Fingers Rev, Hambone.

Robyn Supraner P&W
420 Bryant Ave, Roslyn Harbor, NY 11576, 516-621-1779
  Pubs: *Sam Sunday And The Mystery At The Ocean Beach*
  Hotel (Viking, 1996), *Under Open Sky: Poets on Wm.*
  Cullen Bryant: Anth (Fordham U Pr, 1986), *Berkeley Poetry*
  Rev, Massachusetts Rev, Beloit Poetry Jrnl, Prairie
  Schooner, Ploughshares, Confrontation.

Hariette Surovell W
Henry Morrison, Inc., PO Box 235, Bedford Hills, NY 10507,
914-666-3500
  Pubs: *The Stiffest of the Corpse: Anth* (City Lights Pub,
  1989), *Penthouse, Town & Country, Glamour, New York*
  Woman, Seven Days, Playgirl.

Harriet Susskind P
670 Pittsford-Mendon Rd, Pittsford, NY 14534, 716-381-3436
  Pubs: *To See The Speech of Trees* (Amygdala Pr, 1995),
  Denver Qtly, Prairie Schooner, Seneca Rev, Nimrod,
  Georgia Rev, Ohio Rev.

Dan Swann   P
Slipstream, Box 2071, New Market Sta, Niagara Falls, NY
14301, 716-282-2616
> Pubs: *A Choice: La Bella Figura Anth* (Malafemmina Pr,
> 1993), *A New Geography of Poets: Anth* (U Arkansas Pr,
> 1992), *Slipstream, Pearl, Ozone, Sheila-Na-Gig.*

Lois Swann   W
22 Sagamore Rd, #5D, Bronxville, NY 10708, 914-961-8104
> Pubs: *Torn Covenants, The Mists of Manittoo* (Scribner,
> 1981, 1976).

Phillip P. Sweeney   PP
137 Shamrock Pl, #2, Harpursville, NY 13787, 607-693-4138
> Pubs: *Wail* (Beverly Arts Council, 1991), *Fell Swoop: Big
> Horror Reader: Anth* (J. Daily, 1989).

Bruce Sweet   P&W
34 Hannahs Terr, Rochester, NY 14612, 716-581-0998
> Pubs: *Mixed Voices* (Milkweed Edtns, 1991), *Yankee,
> Minnesota Monthly, Blueline, Commonweal.*

David Swickard   P
PO Box 800, Amagansett, NY 11930
> Pubs: *Confrontation, Nimrod, Bluefish, Poet Lore,
> Mid-American Rev, CutBank, Panhandler.*

Aaron Syl   P
Dowling College, Oakdale, NY 11769, 516-567-4758
> Pubs: *Indigo and Other Poems, A Century of Yiddish
> Poetry: Anth* (Cornwall Bks, 1991, 1989), *Cumberland
> Poetry Jrnl, Kenyon Rev, NER, Writers' Forum.*

William Sylvester   P&W
411 Parkside Ave, Buffalo, NY 14216-3404, 716-838-6780
Internet: sylvester@acsu.buffalo.edu
> Pubs: *War and Lechery, Fever Spreading Into Light, Heavy
> Metal From Pliny, Scarecrow Poetry: Anth* (Ashland Poetry
> Pr, 1995, 1992, 1992, 1994), *Bullhead, New World Writing,
> House Organ, Exquisite Corpse, Chelsea, Poetry.*

Mary Vigliante Szydlowski   W
37 Normanside Dr, Albany, NY 12208, 518-453-3613
> Pubs: *I Can't Talk, I've Got Farbles in My Mouth* (Greene
> Bark Pr, 1995), *Worship the Night* (Leisure Bks, 1985),
> *Show & Tell, ESC! Mag, Star Light Star Bright, The Hand of
> My Enemy.*

Deborah Tall   P
Hobart & Wm Smith Colleges, Geneva, NY 14456,
315-781-3364
Internet: tall@hws.edu
> Pubs: *The Poet's Notebook* (Norton, 1995), *From Where
> We Stand* (Knopf, 1993), *Come Wind, Come Weather*
> (State Street Pr, 1988).

Patti Tana   P&W
462 W Beech St, Long Beach, NY 115613126, 516-432-3362
> Pubs: *When the Light Falls Short of the Dream* (Eighth
> Moon Pr, 1998), *Wetlands* (Papier-Mache Pr, 1993), *Ask
> The Dreamer Where Night Begins* (Kendall/Hunt, 1986),
> *Hiram Poetry Rev, Anth of Magazine Verse, Nassau Rev.*

Barry Targan   P&W
Box 194C, RD #2, Mahaffey Rd, Greenwich, NY 12834,
518-692-9409
> Pubs: *The Ark of The Marindor* (MacMurry & Beck, 1998),
> *The Tangerine Tango Equation* (Thunder's Mouth, 1991),
> *Falling Free* (U Illinois Pr, 1989), *Kingdoms* (SUNY Pr,
> 1981), *Yankee, Sewanee Rev, Confrontations.*

Ann R. Taylor   P
91 Acacia Ave, Hempstead, NY 11550, 516-485-9206
> Pubs: *Feel 'N' Good* (Delar Pub Co., 1986), *Hopes and
> Dreams* (Panache Enterprises, 1986).

Ted Taylor   P
82 Eleanor Dr, Mahopac, NY 10541, 914-628-6307
Internet: tedtaylor@aol.com
> Pubs: *Whetstone, Atlanta Rev, The Bridge, Slugfest, No
> Exit, Pebbles, Amaranth, Wolf Head Qtly, Kit-Cat Rev.*

Gayl Teller   P
1 Florence Ln, Plainview, NY 11803, 516-931-5876
> Pubs: *At the Intersection of Everything You Have Ever
> Loved* (San Diego Poets Pr, 1989), *Phoebe, Halftones to
> Jubilee, Dominion Rev, Long Island Qtly, Spring, Hudson
> Valley Echoes.*

Silvia Tennenbaum   W
763 Fireplace Rd, East Hampton, NY 11937, 516-324-9618
> Pubs: *Yesterday's Streets* (Random Hse, 1981), *Best
> American Short Stories 1978, American Rev.*

Kathleen M. Tenpas   P
7549 Rte 474 N Clymer, Panama, NY 14767, 716-355-4176
> Pubs: *Hill Farm* (Arachne, 1985), *Seedbed to Harvest: Anth*
> (Seven Buffalos, 1985), *Artifacts, Chadakoin Rev.*

Virginia R. Terris   P
84 N Bayview Ave, Freeport, NY 11520-1938, 516-378-3481
> Pubs: *Folding/Unfolding, New Covenant: Anth* (Birnham
> Wood Graphics, 1992, 1993), *Hanging Loose, Long Island
> Qtly, Confrontation, Southern Poetry Rev,
> Hampden-Sydney Rev.*

Holly Thompson   W
46 Grand St, Croton-on-Hudson, NY 10520, 914-271-9242
> Pubs: *Potato Eyes, Dominion Rev, Thema, Printed Matter,
> Wingspan.*

Ed Tick P
78 N Allen St, Albany, NY 12203, 518-438-3779
> Pubs: *Healing a Generation* (Guilford, 1991), *Sacred Mountain: Encounters With the Viet Nam Beast* (Moon Bear, 1989), *Voices, Key West Rev.*

Ellen Tifft P&W
45 Crane Rd, Elmira, NY 14901, 607-732-4756
Internet: http://www.xenosbooks.com
> Pubs: *Moon, Moon, Tell Me True* (Xenos Bks, 1996), *Yale Rev, New Yorker, Poetry, New Letters, Laurel Rev, Transatlantic Rev.*

Carl Tiktin W
87 Alta Ave, Yonkers, NY 10705, 914-968-3655
> Pubs: *Ron, The Hourglass Man* (Arbor Hse, 1979, 1978).

Jessica Treat W
Morse Hill Rd, Millerton, NY 12546, 914-373-8861
Internet: nw_treat@commnet.edu
> Pubs: *A Robber in the House* (Coffee Hse Pr, 1993), *Chick-Lit 2: Anth* (Fiction Collective 2, 1996), *Word of Mouth: Anth* (Crossing Pr, 1991), *Ms., Epoch, Black Warrior Rev, Quarterly West, Seattle Rev, Dominion Rev.*

Martin Tucker P&W
Long Island Univ, C.W. Post College, Brookville, NY 11548, 516-299-2391
> Pubs: *Attention Spans* (Potpourri Pub, 1997), *Homes of Locks and Mysteries* (Dovetail Pr, 1982), *Confrontation, Boulevard, North Atlantic Rev, Northern Centinel, Choice, Literary Rev, Collages & Bricolages.*

Chase Twichell P
46 E Hill Rd, Keene, NY 12942-9719, 518-576-9895
Internet: 74643.3177@compuserve.com
> Pubs: *The Ghost of Eden* (Ontario Rev Pr, 1995), *Perdido* (FSG, 1991), *The Odds, Northern Spy* (U Pitt Pr, 1986, 1981).

Jim Tyack P
326 Echo Lake Rd, New Hampton, NY 10958, 914-374-6042
Internet: moho@frontiernet.net
> Pubs: *Tundra* (Street Pr, 1997), *A Limousine To Nowhere* (Street Pr, 1994), *McGraw-Hill Book of Poetry: Anth* (McGraw-Hill, 1994), *Exquisite Corpse, Rain City Rev, Prairie Schooner.*

Barbara Unger P&W
Rockland Community College, 145 College Rd, English Dept, Suffern, NY 10901, 914-357-1683
> Pubs: *Two Worlds Walking* (New Rivers Pr, 1994), *Blue Depression Glass* (Thorntree Pr, 1991), *Massachusetts Rev, Nation, New York Qtly, Denver Qtly, Carolina Qtly.*

Sonia Usatch PP
371 S Ocean Ave, #2, Patchogue, NY 11772-3729, 516-289-9631
Internet: susatch@suffolk.lib.ny.us
> Pubs: *Noodle Kugel and Life's Other Meichels* (Writers Ink Pr, 1989), *Journal of Poetry Therapy.*

Desire Vail P
6136 Unionville Rd, Bath, NY 14810, 607-776-9157
> Pubs: *First Shine of Dawn, See How Wet the Street Sounds* (FootHills Pub, 1996, 1992), *Acorn Whistle, Blue Unicorn, Kaleidoscope, Poetpourri, Rosebud, Black River Rev.*

Frank Van Zant P
11 Metcale Ln, E Northport, NY 11731, 516-368-6306
Internet: vz@staffordnet.com
> Pubs: *The Lives of the Two-Headed Baseball Siren* (Kings Estate Pr, 1998), *What's Become of Eden?* (Slapering Hol Pr, 1994), *Our Mothers, Our Selves: Anth* (Greenwood, 1996), *Yankee, Context South, Negative Capability, Free Lunch, Maverick Press, Flyway.*

Janine Pommy Vega P
Box 162, Bearsville, NY 12409, 914-688-7068
> Pubs: *Tracking the Serpent* (City Lights Bks, 1997), *Red Bracelets* (Heaven Bone Pr, 1993), *Threading the Maze* (Cloud Mtn Pr, 1992), *Women of the Beat Generation: Anth* (Conari Pr, 1996), *What We Know So Far: Anth* (St. Martin's Pr, 1995), *Nexus, Luna Luna.*

John Vernon P&W
Binghamton Univ, Box 6000, Binghamton, NY 13902-6000, 607-777-2750
> Pubs: *A Book of Reasons* (Houghton Mifflin, 1999), *All For Love* (S&S, 1995), *Peter Doyle* (Random Hse, 1991), *Lindbergh's Son* (Viking, 1987), *The Book of Love: Anth* (Norton, 1998), *APR, Paris Rev, Poetry, New York Times Bk Rev, Harper's.*

Paul Violi P
23 Cedar Ledges, Putnam Valley, NY 10579, 914-526-3392
> Pubs: *Fracas, The Curious Builder, Likewise* (Hanging Loose Pr, 1998, 1992, 1988), *Splurge* (Sun Pr, 1982), *Kenyon Rev, Partisan Rev, Harper's, New American Writing, Upstart Literary Mag, Nexus.*

Anneliese Wagner P
36 Shaw Pl, Hartsdale, NY 10530, 914-761-5874
> Pubs: *Murderous Music* (Chicory Blue Pr, 1995), *Fish Magic* (Black Swan Pr, 1989), *Paris Rev, Prairie Schooner, Chelsea, Kenyon Rev, Ploughshares, Threepenny Rev.*

Eliot Wagner W
651 Sheffield Rd, Ithaca, NY 14850, 212-362-0609
> Pubs: *My America!* (Kenan, 1980), *Better Occasions* (Crowell, 1974), *Grand Concourse* (Bobbs Merrill, 1964), *Antioch Rev.*

Phil Wagner   W
1675 Amazon Rd, Mohegan Lake, NY 10547
    Pubs: *Iconoclast, Libido, Reality & Meaning, Mediphors,
    Objectivity, Common Journeys, Samisdat, Small Pond Mag.*

Kathleen Wakefield   P
1840 Baird Rd, Penfield, NY 14526, 716-586-1368
    Pubs: *There and Back* (State Street Pr, 1993), *Yankee, Blue
    Unicorn, Three Rivers Poetry Jrnl, Plainsong, Passages North,
    Pennsylvania Rev, Cumberland Poetry Rev.*

Charlotte Zoe Walker   W
Hummingbird House, PO Box 14, Gilbertsville, NY 13776,
607-783-2278
Internet: walkercz@oneonta.edu
    Pubs: *Condor and Hummingbird* (The Women's Pr, 1987),
    Prize Stories: The O. Henry Awards 1991: Anth
    (Doubleday, 1991), *Ms., Georgia Rev, NAR.*

Lois V. Walker   P
149 Harbor S, Amityville, NY 11701, 516-691-2376
Internet: lvwalkerappts@prodigy.net
    Pubs: *You & You & Me* (Studio, 1993), *Saturday's Women:
    Anth* (Saturday Pr, 1982), *Xanadu, Helicon 9, New Letters,
    Process 8, Sojourner, Poets On.*

George Wallace   P
Long Islander, 313 Main St, Huntington, NY 11743, 516-427-7000
    Pubs: *Tales of a Yuppie Dropout* (Writers Ink, 1992), *The
    Milking Jug* (Cross-Cultural Communications, 1989), *Lips,
    Rialto, South Florida Poetry Rev.*

Thom Ward   P
1054 Stafford Rd, Palmyra, NY 14522, 315-597-1155
Internet: boaedit@frontiernet.net
    Pubs: *Anthology of Magazine Verse* (Anth of Mag Verse,
    1997), *Atlantic Monthly, Poetry Northwest, Tar River Poetry,
    Yankee, River Oak Rev, Rain City Rev, Chelsea, Yellow
    Silk, Blueline.*

David S. Warren   W
514 Edgewood Pl, Ithaca, NY 14850, 607-273-1283
    Pubs: *Natural Bone, The World According To Two-Feathers*
    (Ithaca Hse, 1979, 1973).

Burton D. Wasserman   P
191 Winding Brook Rd, New Rochelle, NY 10804,
914-235-2256
    Pubs: *The XY Files: Anth* (Sherman Asher Pub, 1997),
    Images of the Holocaust: Anth (NTC Pub Group, 1996),
    Blood to Remember: Anth (Texas Tech U Pr, 1991), *Atlanta
    Rev, California Qtly, Mediphors, Black River Rev, Dickinson
    Rev, Potpourri, Fox Cry.*

Rosanne Wasserman   P
PO Box 704, Hudson, NY 12534, 516-767-8503
Internet: zannie@aol.com
    Pubs: *No Archive on Earth, The Lacemakers* (Gnosis Pr,
    1995, 1992), *Sulfur, Joe Soap's Canoe, Boulevard,
    Broadway, Caprice, Lingo.*

Angus M. Watkins   P
106 Pullman Ave, Kenmore, NY 14217-1516, 716-877-0963
    Pubs: *Gathered at the River* (White Wolf Edtns, 1993),
    River Poems: Anth (Hudson Valley Writers Ctr, 1992),
    Poetic Space, Blue Unicorn, Rolling Coulter.

R. B. Weber   P
Southampton College, Southampton, NY 11968,
516-283-4000
    Pubs: *The Fishing-Print Poems, Poems From the Xenia
    Hotel* (Street Pr, 1984, 1980), *Oxalis.*

James L. Weil   P
103 Van Etten Blvd, New Rochelle, NY 10804, 914-636-7569
    Pubs: *Founding Fathers* (Origin Pr, 1997), *Bill's Shaker
    Chair* (Kelly-Winterton Pr, 1996), *Hummingbird, Harvard
    Mag, Potlatch, Notre Dame Rev, Shearsman, Tel-Let.*

Gregg Thomas Weinlein   P&W
35 Albany Pl, East Greenbush, NY 12061, 518-479-7221
    Pubs: *In the Mirror of Departures* (Claddagh Pr, 1992), *The
    Avenue of Tears* (Kelly Colm Pr, 1986), *Albany Rev,
    American Family.*

Paul Weinman   P
79 Cottage Ave, Albany, NY 12203, 518-482-3003
    Pubs: *Tongue-Dancing* (Concrete Block Pr, 1993), *Suck My
    Cock, White Boy* (Drew Blood Pr, 1992), *Shattered Wig,
    Lost & Found Times, Pink Pages, New York Qtly.*

Howard Weinstein   W
2679 Flower St, Westbury, NY 11590, 516-334-2916
    Pubs: *Power Hungry, Deep Domain, The Covenant of the
    Crown* (Pocket Bks, 1989, 1987, 1981).

Muriel Harris Weinstein   P&W
644 Pauley Dr, West Hempstead, NY 115522225
    Pubs: *Sidewalks: Anth* (Sidewalks, 1996), *Listening Eye,
    Nassau Rev, Outerbridge, Voices Intl, Ethereal Dances,
    Nexus, The Cape Rock.*

Sigmund Weiss   P
11 Lancaster Pl, Stony Brook, NY 11790-3071, 516-751-3309
    Pubs: *Survivor In Limbo* (JVC Bks, 1990), *Impetus, Thirteen,
    San Fernando Poetry Jrnl, Orphic Lute, Omnific, Cerberus.*

Beverley Wiggins Wells   P
Black Belles-Lettres, PO Box 2019, Sag Harbor, NY
11963-0058, 516-725-9128
    Pubs: *Simply Black* (Canio's Edtns, 1993), *A Rock Against
    the Wind: Anth* (Putnam Berkley Group, 1996), *Essence,
    Dickinson Rev, Texas Jrnl of Women & Law.*

Bill Wertheim　　P
100 Sycamore Ave, Mount Vernon, NY 10553, 914-664-5452
Pubs: *Building A New Home* (First Issue Pr, 1977).

John Anthony West　　W
1517 Manorville Rd, Saugerties, NY 12477, 518-678-9580
Pubs: *Serpent in the Sky: The High Wisdom of Ancient Egypt* (Julian Pr, 1987), *New Yorker*.

Paul West　　W
126 Texas Ln, Ithaca, NY 14850, 607-257-3166
Pubs: *Terrestrials, The Tent of Orange Mist* (Scribner, 1997, 1995), *Conjunctions, Yale Rev, Parnassus, Art Forum, George, Witness*.

William Wetmore　　W
Cascade Mountain Vineyards, Flint Hill Rd, Amenia, NY 12501, 914-373-9021
Pubs: *Here Comes Jamie* (Little, Brown, 1972), *All the Right People* (Doubleday, 1964).

Maxwell Corydon Wheat, Jr.　　P
333 Bedell St, Freeport, NY 11520, 516-623-5530
Pubs: *Christian Century, Friends Jrnl, Bird Watcher's Digest, Appalachia, Confrontation, Nassau Rev*.

Claire Nicolas White　　P&W
Moriches Rd, Box 5, RFD 1, St James, NY 11780, 516-584-5736
Pubs: *Riding At Anchor* (Waterline Bks, 1994), *Fragments of Stained Glass* (Mercury Hse, 1981), *World Poetry: Anth* (Norton, 1998), *Critic, Partisan Rev, Confrontation, Primavera, New Yorker*.

Marsha White　　P
Mohawk Valley Community Colleg, Floyd Ave, Rome, NY 13440
Pubs: *The Mother Tongue* (Outland Pr, 1975), *Ironwood, New American Rev, New Jersey Poetry Jrnl*.

Steven F. White　　P
St. Lawrence Univ, Modern Languages Dept, Canton, NY 13617, 315-379-5160
Internet: swhi@music.stlawu.edu
Pubs: *From the Country of Thunder, For the Unborn, Burning the Old Year* (Unicorn, 1990, 1986, 1984).

Max A. Wickert　　P
91 Westerloe Ave, Rochester, NY 14620-3413
Pubs: *All The Weight Of The Still Midnight* (Outriders, 1972), *Poetry, Shenandoah, Sewanee Rev*.

Patricia Wilcox　　P&W
27 Chestnut St, Binghamton, NY 13905, 607-772-8750
Pubs: *An Exile From Silence* (Alembic Pr, 1981), *A Public and Private Hearth* (Bellevue, 1978), *New Republic, Missouri Rev, Mss., Denver Qtly, Emory U Qtly, Spirit*.

Nancy Willard　　P
Vassar College, Poughkeepsie, NY 12609
Pubs: *Swimming Lessons, Sister Water* (Knopf, 1998, 1994), *Telling Time: Angels, Ancestors, and Stories* (HB, 1993).

Gil Williams　　P
60 Schubert St, Binghamton, NY 13905, 607-771-6800
Pubs: *Moving On* (Bellevue Pr, 1969), *Dear Winter: Anth* (Northwoods Pr, 1984), *Aspect, Shocks*.

Russ Williams　　P
102 Winthrop Ave, Albany, NY 12203-1938, 518-489-4578
Internet: lrpleader@aol.com
Pubs: *Gates to the City* (Albany Tricentennial, 1986), *North Country: Anth* (Greenfield Rev Pr, 1986), *Blueline, The Bullet, Glens Falls Rev*.

Robin Kay Willoughby　　P
1711 Amherst St, Buffalo, NY 14214, 716-837-7778
Pubs: *Not A Poem* (Press Me Close, 1983), *Earth's Daughters, Contact II, Place Stamp Here*.

Howard Winn　　P
22A Sheldon Dr, Poughkeepsie, NY 12603, 914-462-1604
Internet: winn@sunydutchess.edu
Pubs: *Bridges* (Springtown Pr, 1988), *Four Picture Sequence* (Front Street Pub, 1978), *MacGuffin, Pearl, Slant, Small Pond, Kansas Qtly*.

Janet B. Winn　　W
22A Sheldon Dr, Poughkeepsie, NY 12603, 914-462-1604
Internet: winn@sunydutchess.edu
Pubs: *The Open Mind* (Peter Lang, 1989), *Connecticut Low* (Houghton Mifflin, 1980), *Sucarnochee Rev, The MacGuffin*.

Stephen Wolf　　W
103 Willis Ave, Port Jefferson, NY 11777-2076
Pubs: *American Families* (NAL, 1989), *Playboy*.

Daniel Wolff　　P
12 Castle Heights, Upper Nyack, NY 10960
Pubs: *You Send Me* (Morrow, 1995), *Danny Lyon Photo Film* (Edtns Braus, 1991), *The Real World* (Sons of Leisure, 1981), *Partisan Rev, Musician, Paris Rev, Threepenny Rev, Sulfur, DoubleTake*.

Tobias Wolff　　W
Syracuse Univ, Syracuse, NY 13244-1170, 315-443-2173
Pubs: *In Pharaoh's Army* (Knopf, 1994), *This Boy's Life* (Atlantic Monthly Pr, 1989).

Amy An Mei Wong　　P&W
2089 Kodma Pl, East Meadow, NY 11554-2519, 516-794-9587
Pubs: *55 To The Nth Possibilities* (Turn of River Pr, 1991), *Long Island Chinese Center Jrnl*.

Wendy Wood   P
PO Box 127, Cuddebackville, NY 12729
    Pubs: *Mudfish, Alabama Literary Rev.*

Karen Wunsch   W
93 Glenwood Ave, New Rochelle, NY 10801-3127, 914-654-0354
    Pubs: *Living & Learning* (Avon, 1972), *North Dakota Qtly,
    Ascent, Confrontation, Rio Grande Rev, Epoch, Harper's
    Bazaar.*

Bettie Wysor   W
70 Cove Hollow Rd, East Hampton, NY 11937, 516-324-8664
    Pubs: *Echos, A Stranger's Eyes* (Jove, 1983, 1981), *To
    Remember Tina* (Stein & Day, 1975).

Carolyn Yalkut   P&W
State Univ New York, English Dept, Albany, NY 12222,
518-442-4065
    Pubs: *Northeast Jrnl, West Hills Rev, Webster Rev, Poet &
    Critic, Tales.*

R. H. Yodice   P&W
PO Box 534, Hurley, NY 12443
    Pubs: *Oxalis, Writer's World, Byline, Writers' Haven Jrnl,
    Mage, Orphic Lute.*

Yvonne   P
Greene Street Artists Corp, 5225 Greene St, #16,
Philadelphia, NY 19144
    Pubs: *An Ear to the Ground: Anth* (U Georgia, 1989),
    Iwilla/Scourge (Chameleon Productions, 1987).

Christoper A. Zackey   P&W
19 Chenango Ave S, #3, Clinton, NY 13323-1661, 315-853-3112
    Pubs: *New Hope Intl, Piedmont Literary Rev, Slant, Minas
    Iirith Evening-Star, Lost Worlds, Mythic Circle.*

Leah Zazulyer   P
450 Rugby Ave, Rochester, NY 14619, 716-436-5035
Internet: fam_wats@uno.cc.geneseo.edu
    Pubs: *The Word Is A Wedding* (FootHills Pub, 1993),
    Round Trip Year: A Book of Days (Vick-Witte, 1992), *Literal
    Latte, Bridges, Ontario Rev, Georgia Rev, South Coast
    Poetry Jrnl, Negative Capability.*

James A. Zoller   P&W
RD 1, Box 3A, Houghton, NY 14744, 716-567-9465
Internet: jzoller@houghton.edu
    Pubs: *Literature: Reading Fiction, Poetry, Drama, and the
    Essay: Anth* (McGraw-Hill, 1994), *Christian Century, Prose
    Poem, Laurel Rev, Red Dancefloor.*

Carol Zuravleff   P
RD 2, Box 73, Otego, NY 13825, 607-988-7170
    Pubs: *Venus & Don Juan, Pure* (TriQuarterly Bks, 1996,
    1994), *Chimera* (Peregrine Smith Bks, 1990), *Day of the
    Body* (Ion Bks, 1986), *APR, Atlantic, NER, TriQuarterly,
    Partisan Rev, Ploughshares, Kenyon Rev, Shenandoah,
    Southern Rev, Volt.*

NEW YORK CITY

Stephen Abbott   P
164 E 81 St, New York, NY 10028-1804
    Pubs: *Holy Terror* (Crossing Pr, 1989), *Skinny Trip to a Far
    Place* (e.g. Pr, 1988).

Walter Abish   P&W
Box 485 Cooper Station, New York, NY 10276, 212-982-3074
    Pubs: *Eclipse Fever* (Knopf, 1993), *99: The New Meaning*
    (Burning Deck, 1990), *How German Is It* (New Directions,
    1980).

William Abrahams   W
Holt, Rinehart & Winston, 383 Madison Ave, New York, NY
10017, 212-688-9100

Linsey Abrams   W
Harvey Klinger, Inc., 301 W 53 St, Ste 13B, New York, NY
10019, 212-581-7068
    Pubs: *Our History In New York* (Great Marsh Pr/Umbrella
    Pub, 1998), *Glimmer Train, Central Park, Colorado Rev,
    Seattle Rev, New Directions Annual, 13th Moon.*

Richard S. Abrons   W
812 Park Ave, #4E, New York, NY 10021, 212-517-4230
    Pubs: *Nebraska Rev, MacGuffin, Sou'wester, Columbia,
    NAR, Cosmopolitan, Fiction Network, Other Voices.*

Anya Achtenberg   P&W858
301 Third Ave, #2R, Brooklyn, NY 11215, 718-858-6906
Internet: aachtenberg@earthlink.net
    Pubs: *I Know What the Small Girl Knew* (Holy Cow! Pr,
    1983), *Life on the Line: Anth* (Negative Capability Pr, 1992),
    A Pocketful of Prose: Anth (HRW, 1991), *Paterson Literary
    Rev, Blue Mesa Rev, New Letters.*

Diane Ackerman   P
Random House, 201 E. 50 St, New York, NY 10022
    Pubs: *I Praise My Destroyer, The Rarest of the Rare,
    Jaguar of Sweet Laughter: New And Selected Poems*
    (Random Hse, 1998, 1995, 1991).

Alice Adams   W
ICM, 40 W 57 St, New York, NY 10019, 212-556-5600
    Pubs: *Almost Perfect, Caroline's Daughters, After You've
    Gone* (Knopf, 1993, 1991, 1989).

Anna Adams   P
Doug Treem, Agent, 217 E 22 St, #5, New York, NY 10010,
212-889-0462
    Pubs: *The Ratio Of One To A Stone* (First East Coast
    Theatre & Pub Co., 1982), *New York Qtly, QRL, Poetry,
    Best Poems of 1957.*

Elizabeth Adams W
Philip Spitzer Literary Agency, 788 9th Ave, New York, NY 10019, 212-265-6003
Pubs: *Phoebe, Caprice, Chicago Rev, Alaska Qtly Rev, NAR, Groundswell, Intro 10, The Raddle Moon, Massachusetts Rev.*

Glenda Adams W
Goodman Associates, 500 W End Ave, New York, NY 10024
Pubs: *The Tempest of Clemenza* (Faber & Faber, 1996), *Longleg* (Cane Hill, 1992), *TriQuarterly, Village Voice, Hanging Loose, Seattle Rev, New York Times.*

Lloyd E. Addison P
1704 St. Johns Pl, #7F, Brooklyn, NY 11233, 718-771-2778
Pubs: *The Mystery Of The Invention Of Doublecross Baseball* (Private Pubs, 1981), *Drum Voices Revue.*

C. S. Adler W
Avon Books, 1350 Avenue of Americas, New York, NY 10019
Pubs: *Courtyard Cat* (Clarion, 1995), *Youn Hee & Me* (HB, 1995).

Renata Adler W
178 E 64 St, New York, NY 10021

Joel Agee W
Donadio & Ashworth, Inc., 121 W 27 St, Ste 704, New York, NY 10001, 212-691-8077
Pubs: *Twelve Years—An American Boyhood in East Germany* (FSG, 1981), *New Yorker, Harper's.*

Jack Agueros P&W
212 W 14 St, New York, NY 10011, 212-243-2270
Pubs: *Dominoes and Other Stories* (Curbstone Pr, 1993), *Sonnets From the Puerto Rican* (Hanging Loose Pr, 1996), *Parnassus, Callaloo, Agni.*

Ellen Akins W
Charlotte Sheedy Literary Agen, 65 Bleecker St, New York, NY 10012, 212-780-9800
Internet: emakins@win.bright.net
Pubs: *Hometown Brew* (Knopf, 1998), *Public Life* (HC, 1993), *World Like A Knife* (John Hopkins U Pr, 1991), *Georgia Rev, Southern Rev, Southwest Rev, Missouri Rev.*

Viki Akiwumi PP&P
61 E 8 St, Ste 180, New York, NY 10003, 212-459-4540
Pubs: *In the Tradition* (Harlem River Pr, 1993), *Ancient Youth and Elders Reborn* (Universal Black Writers Pr, 1985), *Essence, Testimony, Presstime.*

Daisy Aldan P&W
260 W 52 St, #5-L, New York, NY 10019, 212-459-9086
Pubs: *Day of the Wounded Eagle* (The LeMay Co., 1991), *In Passage* (Folder Edtns, 1990), *Anais Nin: A Book of Mirrors: Anth* (Sky Blue Pr, 1996), *Caprice, Threefold Rev.*

Charlotte Alexander P
112 E 10 St, #2, New York, NY 10003
Pubs: *Outerbridge, Mid-American Rev, Earth's Daughters, Three Gray Geese Anth, Tide Turning Anth, The Dolphin's Arc Anth.*

Meena Alexander P&W
Hunter College, CUNY, 695 Park Ave, New York, NY 10021, 212-772-5167
Internet: malexand@email.gc.cuny.edu
Pubs: *River & Bridge* (Toronto Rev Pr, 1996), *Shock of Arrival* (Southend Pr, 1996), *Fault Lines* (Feminist Pr, 1993), *Grand Street, Poetry Rev.*

Austin Alexis P&W
58 E 4 St, #9, New York, NY 10003-8914, 212-260-7525
Pubs: *Santa Barbara Rev, Mixed Media, Connecticut River Rev, James White Rev, Momentum, Writ Mag.*

Donna Allegra P&W
60 E 4 St, #3, New York, NY 10003-8916, 212-477-1109
Pubs: *Does Your Mama Know?: Anth* (Redbone Pr, 1997), *Hers 2: Brilliant New Fiction by Lesbians: Anth* (Faber and Faber, 1997), *Best Lesbian Erotica: Anth* (Cleis Pr, 1997), *Close Calls: Anth, SportsDykes: Anth* (St. Martin's, 1996, 1994).

Deborah Allen P
PO Box 1452, Stuyvesant Sta, New York, NY 10009
Pubs: *Yellow Leaves* (A Musty Bone, 1990), *Three Mile Harbor, The Salmon, Painted Bride Qtly, South Dakota Rev, Beloit Poetry Jrnl, Blue Unicorn, The Ledge.*

Edward Allen W
Curtis Brown Ltd., 10 Astor Pl, New York, NY 10003-6935, 212-473-5400
Pubs: *Straight Through the Night* (Soho Pr, 1989), *Best American Short Stories 1990: Anth, GQ, New Yorker.*

Paula Gunn Allen P
Diane Cleaver Agency, 55 Fifth Ave, New York, NY 10003, 212-206-5600
Pubs: *The Sacred Hoop* (Beacon Pr, 1992), *The Voice of the Turtle: Anth* (Ballantine Pr, 1994), *Chicago, Yefief, Global Rev, Transpersonal Rev, Glamour.*

Roberta Allen W
5 W 16 St #7, New York, NY 10011
Pubs: *Certain People* (Coffee Hse Pr, 1997), *Fast Fiction* (Story Pr, 1997), *The Daughter* (Autonomedia, 1992), *The Travelling Woman* (Vehicle, 1986), *Amazon Dream* (City Lights Bks, 1993), *Bomb, American Voice, The World.*

Mindy Aloff P
708 Eighth Ave, #4L, Brooklyn, NY 11215
Pubs: *Night Lights* (Prescott Street Pr, 1979), *APR, Choice, St. Andrews Rev.*

Julia Alvarez   P&W
S. Bergholz Literary Services, 17 W 10 St, #5, New York, NY
10011, 212-387-0545
   Pubs: *Yo!, In the Time of the Butterflies* (Algonquin Bks,
   1997, 1994), *New Yorker, Ploughshares.*

Mark Ameen   P&W
235 East 4 St #5A, New York, NY 100097231, 212-674-4371
   Pubs: *The Buried Body* (Amethyst, 1990), *A Circle of Sirens*
   (Seahorse Pr, 1985), *Between C&D, RFD.*

Beth Anderson   PP&P
135 Eastern Pkwy Apt. 4D, Brooklyn, NY 11238,
718-636-6010
Internet: beand@interport.net
   Pubs: *Text-Sound Texts, Dramatika Mag, Poetry Mailing
   List, Assemblings, Flash Art, Ear Mag.*

Jack Anderson   P
40 E 10 St, #1H, New York, NY 10003, 212-677-7698
   Pubs: *Traffic* (New Rivers Pr, 1998), *Field Trips on the Rapid
   Transit* (Hanging Loose, 1990), *Selected Poems* (Release Pr,
   1983), *Poetry, Paris Rev, Caliban, Hanging Loose, Chelsea.*

Poul Anderson   W
Scovil-Chichak-Galen Literary, 381 Park Ave S, #1112, New
York, NY 10016, 212-679-8686
   Pubs: *The Stars Are Also Fire, Harvest of Stars* (Tor, 1994,
   1993), *Orion Shall Rise* (Timescape, 1983).

Michael Andre   P
Unmuzzled Ox, 105 Hudson St, #311, New York, NY 10013,
212-226-7170
Internet: mandreox@aol.com
   Pubs: *It as It* (Money for Food Pr, 1990), *Letters Home*
   (Vehicle, 1981), *Mudfish, O.ars, Exquisite Corpse, Coves,
   Small Pr Rev.*

Marianne Andrea   P&W
250 Cabrini Blvd, #2C, New York, NY 10033
   Pubs: *The 5th Corner* (Mohansic Pr, 1976), *Atlanta Rev,
   Helicon Nine, Crosscurrents, Queens Qtly.*

Bruce Andrews   P
41 W 96 St, #10D, New York, NY 10025, 212-865-9857
   Pubs: *I Don't Have Any Paper So Shut Up, Give Em
   Enough Rope* (Sun & Moon, 1990, 1987).

Victoria Andreyeva   P&W
PO Box 42, Prince St Sta, New York, NY 10012
   Pubs: *Dream of the Firmament* (Gnosis Pr, 1989), *Literary
   Rev, The Unknown Terra, Spring, Voskreshenie.*

Lucy Angeleri   PP
71-34 Harrow St, Forest Hills, NY 11375, 718-544-2877
   Pubs: *Tidings #2* (Four Facet Pr, 1992), *Tidings* (Print
   Center, 1974), *Lake Effect, Oread, Z Misc, Nomad,
   Slipstream, American Literary Rev, Slant, Croton Rev.*

Roger Angell   P&W
The New Yorker, 20 W 43 St, New York, NY 10036
   Pubs: *Once More Around the Park* (Ballantine, 1991),
   Season Ticket (HM, 1988), *The New Yorker.*

Allan Appel   P&W
332 E 84 St, #5A, New York, NY 10028, 212-737-1946
   Pubs: *High Holiday Sutra* (Coffee House Pr, 1997), *The
   Rabbi of Casino Boulevard* (St. Martin's Pr, 1986), *A Pocket
   Apocalypse: Anth* (Riverhead Bks, 1997), *Nation, National
   Lampoon.*

Alain Arias-Misson   W
421 Hudson St #816, New York, NY 10014, 212-924-9375
   Pubs: *The Visio-Verbal Sins of a Literary Saint* (Ra Ra Bks,
   1993), *The Mind Crime of August Saint* (Fiction Collective
   Two, 1993).

Ron Arias   W
People Magazine, Time & Life Bldg, Rockefeller, New York,
NY 10020, 212-522-2711
   Pubs: *Five Against the Sea* (NAL, 1989), *The Road To
   Tamazunchale* (Bilingual Pr, 1984).

Linda Arking   W
110 Thompson St, New York, NY 10012, 212-226-5845

Richard R. Armijo   P
PO Box 477, 128 E Broadway, New York, NY 10002,
212-228-3033
   Pubs: *Wishing On A Star* (American Idealism Rag, 1990),
   Suburban Ambush (Johns Hopkins U Pr, 1989), *A
   Gathering of the Tribes, New Leaves Rev, Zien, Blast.*

Emily Arnold   W
3 Washington Sq Village, #16-I, New York, NY 10012-1809,
212-260-2246
   Pubs: *Life Drawing* (Delacorte, 1986), *A Craving* (Dell, 1986).

Katherine Arnoldi   W
Sterling Lord Literistic, 65 Bleecker, New York, NY 10012,
212-673-4602
   Pubs: *The Amazing True Story of a Teenage Single Mom*
   (Hyperion, 1998), *The Quarterly: Anths* (Vintage, 1991,
   1990, 1989), *Room of One's Own, Fiction, World,
   Quarterly, Onthebus, Red Tape, A Gathering of the Tribes,
   New Observations.*

Maria Arrillaga   P&W
140 Charles St #8E, New York, NY 10014, 212-929-4046
Internet: mariajoe@coqui.net
   Pubs: *Manana Valentina* (Room of One's Own, 1995),
   These Are Not Sweet Girls (White Pine Pr, 1994), *Cascada
   de Sol* (Inst of Puerto Rican Culture, 1977), *Festa Da
   Palabra, Cupey, Tercer Milenio, Confrontation, PEN Intl,
   Mother Tongues.*

Elizabeth Arthur W
c/o Sterling Lord Literistic, 65 Bleecker St 12th Fl, New York, NY 10012
Internet: bauersa@casmall.muohio.edu
Pubs: *Antarctic Navigation, Looking for the Klondike Stone* (Knopf, 1995, 1993).

Carol Ascher W
158 W 23 St #5, New York, NY 10011, 212-255-5657
Internet: carol.ascher@nyu.edu
Pubs: *The Flood* (Curbstone Pr, 1996), *Hard Lessons: Public Schools and Privatization* (Twentieth Century Fund, 1996), *Between Women* (Routledge, 1993), *Kenyon Rev, Shenandoah, Virginia Qtly Rev, Boulevard, Literary Rev, Ms., Witness, ACM.*

Sheila Ascher PP&P&W
PO Box 176, Rockaway Park, NY 11694, 718-474-6547
Pubs: *ABC Street* (Sun & Moon Pr, 1998), *The Menaced Assassin, The Other Planet, Red Moon/Red Lake* (McPherson, 1989, 1988, 1988), *Central Park, Confrontation, NAW.*

Baron James Ashanti P
PO Box 1545, Lincolnton Sta, New York, NY 10037
Pubs: *Nova* (Harlem River Pr, 1990), *Nubiana II* (Shamal Pr, 1979), *Essence, Eye Ball Mag, Greenfield Rev, Race Today, Pan African Jrnl.*

John Ashbery P
Georges Borchardt Inc., 136 E 57 St, New York, NY 10022, 212-753-5785
Pubs: *And the Stars Were Shining* (FS&G, 1994), *Hotel Lautreamont* (Knopf, 1992).

Gary Aspenberg P
323-A E 89 St, #1W, New York, NY 10128, 212-348-7009
Pubs: *Bus Poems* (Broken Moon Pr, 1993).

James Atlas P
The New York Times, 229 W 43 St, New York, NY 10036
Pubs: *The Great Pretender* (Atheneum, 1986), *New York Times Book Rev & Mag, New Republic, Atlantic.*

Louis Auchincloss W
1111 Park Ave, New York, NY 10028, 212-348-3723

Jean M. Auel W
Jean V. Naggar Literary Agency, 216 E 75 St, Ste 1E, New York, NY 10021, 212-794-1082
Pubs: *The Plains of Passage, The Mammoth Hunters, The Valley of Horses, The Clan of the Cave Bear* (Crown, 1990, 1985, 1982, 1980).

Jane Augustine P
Box 1289, Stuyvesant Sta, New York, NY 10009, 212-533-1928
Pubs: *Journeys* (Pig Pr, 1985), *Beneath A Single Moon: Anth* (Shambhala, 1991), *Iowa Rev, Ms., Montemore, Archae.*

Paul Auster P
Carol Mann Agency, 55 Fifth Ave, New York, NY 10003, 212-206-5635
Pubs: *Mr. Vertigo, Leviathan* (Viking, 1994, 1992).

DorisJean Austin W
3657 Broadway #9G, New York, NY 10031, 212-862-9106
Pubs: *After the Garden* (NAL, 1988), *Streetlights: Illuminating Tales of the Urban Black Experience: Anth* (Viking, 1995), *Essence, Ms., Emerge.*

Kofi Awoonor W
Harold Ober Associates, 425 Madison Ave, New York, NY 10017, 212-759-8600
Pubs: *Until the Morning After* (Greenfield Rev Pr, 1987).

Elizabeth Ayres P
E Ayres Ctr for Creative Writi, 155 E 31 St, Ste 4R, New York, NY 10016, 212-689-4692
Pubs: *Writing the Wave* (Putnam, 1999), *Fresh Paint: Anth* (Ailanthus Pr, 1978), *Malahat Rev, Aspect, Hanging Loose, Encore, Bitterroot.*

Jody Azzouni P&W
301 Hicks St, Brooklyn, NY 11201, 718-852-6282
Internet: jody@azzouni.com
Pubs: *Anth of Mag Verse & Yearbook of American Verse* (Monitor, 1988), *Hiram Poetry Rev, California Qtly, APA's Newsletter, Alaska Qtly Rev, Poetry New York.*

Virginia Bagliore P
PO Box 244, Ryder St Sta, Brooklyn, NY 11234, 718-377-4308
Pubs: *Oracles of Light* (Pella Pub, 1986), *The Inkling, Z Miscellaneous, Bitterroot, Eve's Legacy.*

Alison Baker W
Brandt & Brandt Literary Agent, 1501 Broadway, New York, NY 10036
Internet: abaker@jeffnet.org
Pubs: *Thousands Live!* (Helianthus Pr, 1996), *Loving Wander Beaver: Novella and Stories, How I Came West, and Why I Stayed: Stories* (Chronicle Bks, 1995, 1993).

Julius Balbin P
945 W End Ave, #9A, New York, NY 10025, 212-666-6526
Pubs: *Imperio De L'Koroj: Esperanto Poetry* (Italy; Estudio, 1989).

Jean Balderston P
1225 Park Ave, #8C, New York, NY 10128, 212-876-4111
Pubs: *A More Perfect Union: Anth* (St. Martin's Pr, 1998), *Poetry From A to Z: Anth* (Bradbury Pr, 1994), *80 On the 80's: Anth* (Ashland Poetry Pr, 1990), *New York Qtly, Wormwood Rev, Light, Poets On, Mudfish, Sing Heavenly Muse!.*

J. G. Ballard W
Robin Straus Agency, 229 E 79 St, New York, NY 10021,
212-472-3282

Robert Joseph Banfelder W
53-38 195th St, Fresh Meadows, NY 11365, 718-357-7330
  Pubs: *No Stranger Than I* (Hudson View Pr, 1991).

Mary Jo Bang P
780 Greenwich St, #1G, New York, NY 10014, 212-727-1209
Internet: mb216@columbia.edu
  Pubs: *Apology for Want* (U Pr New England, 1997), *Anth of
  Mag Verse & Yearbook of American Poetry* (Monitor Bks,
  1997), *NAW, New Yorker, Paris Rev, Shenandoah, Denver
  Qtly, Colorado Rev, Nation, Gettysburg Rev, Witness,
  Chelsea.*

William Henry Banks, Jr. W
PO Box 2268, New York, NY 10163-2268, 203-562-7940
  Pubs: *A Love So Fine* (Pyramid Books, 1974).

Russell Banks P&W
Ellen Levine Literary Agency, 15 E 26 St, Ste 1801, New
York, NY 10010, 212-889-0620
  Pubs: *Cloudsplitter, Rule of the Bone, The Sweet Hereafter*
  (HC, 1998, 1995, 1991).

Barbara Baracks P
427 15th St, #4B, Brooklyn, NY 11215, 718-783-2881
  Pubs: *Poems Out Of Place* (Language, 1978), *No Sleep*
  (Tuumba Press, 1977), *Village Voice, Ms.*.

Amiri Baraka P
Sterling Lord Literistic, 65 Bleecker St, New York, NY 10012,
212-780-6050
Internet: ab11@erols.com
  Pubs: *Eulogies, Transbluesency* (Marsilio, 1997, 1995),
  Funklore (Litoral, 1996), *Y's/Why's/Wise: The Griot's Song*
  (Third World Pr, 1995), *LeRoi Jones/Amiri Baraka Reader*
  (Thunder's Mouth Pr, 1991).

Barbara Barg P&W
520 E 14 St, #26, New York, NY 10009, 212-529-8751
Internet: bestpoet@aol.com
  Pubs: *Origin of The Species* (Semiotext(e), *1994), Obeying
  the Chemicals (Hard Pr, 1984), Playboy, High Times, Short
  Qtly, Language Anthology.*

Suze Baron PP&P
549 E 34 St, Brooklyn, NY 11203, 718-282-7159
  Pubs: *When Black People Pray* (Self, 1990), *The P.S. 269
  Fivers* (P.S. 269, 1988), *Raven Chronicles, Z Misc, New
  York Qtly, Calapooya Collage, New Press, Pegasus Rev.*

Andrea Barrett W
The Wendy Weil Agency, Inc., 232 Madison Ave, Ste 1300,
New York, NY 10016, 212-685-0030
  Pubs: *Ship Fever & Other Stories* (Norton, 1996), *The
  Forms of Water* (Pocket Bks, 1993), *Story, Missouri Rev,
  Southern Rev, New England Rev.*

Marvin Barrett W
115 E 67 St, #3B, New York, NY 10021-5901

Fran Barst P&W
115 E 9 St #11B, New York, NY 10003, 212-677-8934
  Pubs: *The Death Gods* (Intl Poetry & Fiction Pr, 1991),
  *Korone: Women's Voices, Aileron Pr, Carolina Qtly, The
  Indian American, Denver Qtly, Ice River.*

Douglas Bauer W
19 W 44 St, Ste 1602, New York, NY 10036, 212-944-9898
Internet: min.com/air/douglasbauer
  Pubs: *Book of Famous Iowans* (Henry Holt, 1997), *The
  Very Air* (Morrow, 1993), *Dexterity* (S&S, 1989), *Prairie
  City, Iowa* (Putnam, 1979), *Atlantic, Esquire.*

Jonathan Baumbach W
Brooklyn College, Brooklyn, NY 11210, 718-856-6501
  Pubs: *Separate Hours, The Life and Times of Major Fiction*
  (Fiction Collective, 1990, 1987).

Judith Baumel P
3530 Henry Hudson Pkwy, #12M, Bronx, NY 10463,
718-548-3053
Internet: baumel@adlibv.adelphi.edu
  Pubs: *Now* (Miami U Pr, 1996), *The Weight of Numbers*
  (Wesleyan, 1988).

Ann Beattie W
Janklow & Nesbit Associates, 598 Madison Ave, New York,
NY 10022-1614, 212-421-1700
  Pubs: *What Was Mine, Picturing Will* (Random Hse, 1991,
  1990).

Jeanne Marie Beaumont P
120 W 70 St, #2D, New York, NY 10023
Internet: bobbyjeanne@worldnet.att.net
  Pubs: *Placebo Effects* (Norton, 1997), *Mondo Marilyn:
  Anth, Mondo Barbie: Anth* (St. Martin's, 1995, 1993), *New
  American Writing, Denver Qtly, Colorado Rev, Volt,
  Harper's, Poetry.*

Mary Ann Beban P
22 Jones St, #3F, New York, NY 10014, 212-929-2511
  Pubs: *Lips Unsealed: Anth* (Capra Pr, 1990), *Slipstream,
  Connecticut River Rev, Blueline, The Writer's Eye.*

Stephen Becker W
Russell & Volkening, Inc., 50 W 29 St, New York, NY 10001,
212-684-6050
  Pubs: *A Rendezvous in Haiti* (Norton, 1987), *Blue Eyed
  Shan, Dog Tags* (Random Hse, 1982, 1973).

Joshua Saul Beckman P
182 Franklin St., Apt E16, Brooklyn, NY 11222, 718-383-0042
Pubs: *Things Are Happening* (APR/Copper Canyon, 1998), *There Is An Ocean* (WSW, 1997), *Blue Paradise, At the News of Your Death* (Permeable Pr, 1997, 1995), *ACM, APR, Gulf Coast, Response.*

Louis Begley W
Georges Borchardt Inc., 136 E 57 St, New York, NY 10022, 212-753-5785
Pubs: *The Man Who Was Late, Wartime Lies* (Knopf, 1993, 1991).

Guy R. Beining P
62-65 Saunders St, #3-I, Rego Park, NY 11374, 718-459-4716
Pubs: *Too Fat To Hear, Chapters XIV-XXVI* (Standing Stones Pr, 1997), *Carved Erosion* (Elbow Pr, 1995), *The Ghost Dance Anthology* (Whitston Pub Co., 1994), *This, Kiosk, Private Arts, Ant, Yefief, Ozone, Chain, Rio, Lost and Found, Juxta.*

Judith Bell W
Witherspoon Associates, Inc, 235 E 31 St, New York, NY 10016, 212-889-8626
Internet: belljort@aol.com
Pubs: *Generation to Generation, Grow Old Along with Me: Anth* (Papier-Mache Pr, 1998, 1996), *Farm Wives and Other Iowa Stories: Anth* (Mid- Prairie Books, 1995), *Washington Rev, First, Short Fiction By Women, Snake Nation Rev, Parting Gifts, ALR.*

Frances Bendix PP
2676 Grand Concourse, #3H, Bronx, NY 10458, 718-295-2697
Pubs: *Resonance, Modern Images, Ararat, New York Poets Qtly, Poetry Jrnl, Bronx Arts, Words & Image, Slug Fest, Visions.*

Helen Benedict W
Richard Parks Literary Agency, 138 East 16 St # 5D, New York, NY 10003, 212-254-9067
Pubs: *Bad Angel, A World Like This* (Dutton, 1996, 1990), *Ontario Rev, Antioch Rev.*

Michael Benedikt P&W
315 W 98 St, #6-A, New York, NY 10025, 212-865-4538
Pubs: *The Badminton At Great Barrington* (U Pitt Pr, 1980), *Night Cries* (Wesleyan U Pr, 1976).

Ruth Benjamin P&W
1158 Fifth Ave, #5D, New York, NY 10029, 212-348-6624
Pubs: *Naked at Forty* (Horizon Pr, 1984), *Albany Rev.*

Hal Bennett W
William Morris Agency, 1350 Ave of the Americas, New York, NY 10019, 212-586-5100

Nathan Bergenfeld P
2632 W 2nd St, Brooklyn, NY 11223, 718-769-6773
Pubs: *Life Spirals, Garden Gleanings* (NYC Dept of Parks, 1987, 1986).

Rachel Berghash P
7 E 20 St, New York, NY 10003, 212-533-1541
Internet: rberghash@aol.com
Pubs: *Chicago Rev, Anima, Waterways, Pulp, Jewish Frontier, Bitterroot, Blue Unicorn, Israel Horizons, West Wind Rev, Poetpourri.*

Eleanor Bergstein W
425 Riverside Dr, New York, NY 10025, 212-866-0923
Pubs: *Ex-Lover* (Random Hse, 1989), *Advancing Paul Newman* (Viking Pr, 1973).

Nancy Berke P
164 Sterling Pl, #3D, Brooklyn, NY 11217, 718-857-4007
Pubs: *Alternative Poetry & Fiction, Footwork, Pig Iron, Slipstream, Central Park, New Voices.*

Constance E. Berkley P
Fordham Univ, Lincoln Center, Rm 414, New York, NY 10023

Howard Berland PP
3044 Kingsbridge Ave, #26, Bronx, NY 10463, 212-593-7552

April Bernard P&W
18 Grove St, #2, New York, NY 10014, 212-645-1228
Pubs: *Pirate Jenny* (Norton, 1990), *Blackbird Bye Bye* (Random Hse, 1989).

Kenneth Bernard P&W
800 Riverside Dr, #8H, New York, NY 10032, 212-927-8851
Pubs: *Clown At Wall* (Confrontation Pr, 1996),The *Baboon In the Night Club* (Asylum Arts Pub, 1994), *From the District File* (Fiction Collective 2, 1992), *Chelsea, Fiction Intl, Revue Cargo, Salmagundi, Contre-Vox, Collages & Bricolages.*

Louise Bernikow P
318 W 105 St, #4A, New York, NY 10025, 212-662-6307
Pubs: *Alone In America, Among Women* (H&R, 1985, 1982).

Burton Bernstein P&W
Donadio & Ashworth, Inc., 121 W 27 St, Ste 704, New York, NY 10001, 212-691-8077
Pubs: *Plane Crazy* (Ticknor & Fields, 1985), *Family Matters* (Summit, 1982), *New Yorker, Esquire.*

Daniel Berrigan P
220 W 98 St, #11-L, New York, NY 10025, 212-662-6358
Pubs: *Whereon To Stand, Sorrow Built A Bridge: Friendship And AIDS* (Fortcamp Pr, 1991, 1990).

Eliot Berry   W
Brandt & Brandt Literary Agent, 1501 Broadway, New York,
NY 10036
    Pubs: *Tough Draw* (Henry Holt/John MacRae Bks, 1992),
    Four Quarters Make A Season (Berkley Pr, 1973).

Lebert Bethune   P&W
110 W 96 St, #16C, New York, NY 10025, 212-866-8059

Marcia Biederman   W
41 Second St, #3, Brooklyn, NY 11231, 718-797-2519
    Pubs: *Post No Bonds* (Scribner, 1988), *Sisters in Crime 3:
    Anth* (Berkley Pub, 1990).

Rachelle Bijou   P
300 W 23 St, #2E, New York, NY 10011, 212-206-1150
    Pubs: *Entrance To The City* (Buffalo Pr, 1978), *Out of This
    World: Anth* (Crown, 1992), *Telephone, The World,
    Response, Transfer.*

Sarah Bird   W
ICM, 40 W 57 St, New York, NY 10019, 212-556-5600
Internet: sbirdgirl@aol.com
    Pubs: *Virgin of the Rodeo, The Mommy Club* (Doubleday,
    1993, 1991), *New York Times Mag, Mademoiselle, Texas
    Observer, Cosmopolitan.*

Ann Birstein   W
1623 3rd Ave, #27-J W, New York, NY 10128, 212-289-0346
    Pubs: *The Last of the True Believers* (Norton, 1988), *The
    Rabbi On 47th Street* (Dial Pr, 1982), *McCall's, New Yorker,
    New York Times, Vogue, Confrontation.*

Ellen Marie Bissert   P
735 Kappock St, #9A/F, Riverdale, NY 10463
    Pubs: *The Immaculate Conception of the Blessed Virgin
    Dyke* (13th Moon, 1977), *Beyond Baroque, 13th Moon.*

Isaac J. Black   P
119-10 225 St, Cambria Heights, NY 11411, 718-723-5148
    Pubs: *Obsidian, Callaloo, Hoodoo, First World, Beloit
    Poetry Jrnl, Black World.*

Sophie Cabot Black   P
Dwyer Hills, PO Box 528, New York, NY 10024
    Pubs: *The Misunderstanding of Nature* (Graywolf Pr, 1994),
    The Atlantic, Antaeus, The Partisan Rev.

Star Black   P
111 E 36 St, New York, NY 10016, 212-683-6127
    Pubs: *October for Idas* (Painted Leaf Pr, 1997), *Waterworn*
    (Tribes Bks, 1995), *Doubletime* (Groundwater Pr, 1995).

George Blagowidow   W
Hippocrene Books, 171 Madison Ave, New York, NY 10016,
212-685-4371
    Pubs: *In Search of the Lady Lion Tamer* (HBJ, 1987).

George M. Blecher   W
515 W End Ave, #10D, New York, NY 10024, 212-580-5943

Lucienne S. Bloch   W
1111 Park Ave, New York, NY 10128
    Pubs: *Finders Keepers* (Houghton Mifflin, 1982), *On the
    Great-Circle Route* (S&S, 1979).

Lawrence Block   W
39 1/2 Washington Sq S, New York, NY 10012
    Pubs: *A Walk Among The Tombstones, A Dance At The
    Slaughterhouse* (Morrow, 1992, 1991), *Playboy, American
    Heritage.*

Amy Bloom   W
Rosenstone/Wender, 3 E 48 St, New York, NY 10077,
212-832-8330
Internet: amybloom@aol.com
    Pubs: *Come To Me* (HC, 1993), *Best American Short
    Stories: Anths* (HM, 1992, 1991), *New Yorker.*

Laurel Blossom   P
920 Park Ave, #2B, New York, NY 10028-0208, 212-628-0239
Internet: lbaines920@aol.com
    Pubs: *The Papers Said* (Greenhouse Rev Pr, 1993), *Lights,
    Camera, Poetry: Anth* (HB, 1996), *Paris Rev, Poetry,
    Pequod, Confrontation, APR, Lips, Many Mountains
    Moving.*

Bonnie Bluh   W
55 Bethune St, #1007A, New York, NY 10014, 212-255-3322
Internet: bbluh@aol.com
    Pubs: *The Eleanor Roosevelt Girls* (Lyre Bird Bks, 1998),
    The Old Speak Out (Horizon, 1979), *Banana* (Macmillan,
    1976), *Woman To Woman* (Starogubski, 1974).

Victor Bockris   P
106 Perry St, New York, NY 10014

Richard Bodtke   P
175 W 93 St, #5A, New York, NY 10025, 212-666-6554
    Pubs: *Tragedy & The Jacobean Temper* (U Salzburg,
    1972), *World Of Undisguise* (Nauset, 1968).

Karen Iris Bogen   P
Ann Elmo Literary Agency, 60 E 42 St, New York, NY 10165,
212-661-2883
    Pubs: *Will the Circle Be Unbroken: Anth* (Spinsters/Aunt
    Lute Pr, 1986), *Southern Poetry Rev.*

Nancy Bogen   W
31 Jane St, #17B, New York, NY 100141982, 212-741-2417
Internet: 102004,274.@compuserve.com
    Pubs: *Klytaimnestra Who Stayed At Home, Bagatelle
    Guinevere, Bobe Mayse: A Tale of Washington Square*
    (Twinkenham Pr, 1998, 1995, 1993).

Magda Bogin P&W
425 Riverside Dr, New York, NY 10025, 212-662-9434
Pubs: *Natalya, God's Messenger* (Scribner, 1994).

Portia Bohn W
28 St. Mark's Pl, #1A, New York, NY 10003, 212-777-7619
Pubs: *Carolina Qtly, Short Story Intl, Massachusetts Rev, Other Voices, Kalliope.*

Thomas Bolt P
110 Suffolk St, #6B, New York, NY 10002
Pubs: *Out of the Woods* (Yale U Pr, 1989).

Roger Bonair-Agard PP&P
501 W 156 St #2, New York, NY 10032, 212-491-9754
Internet: pricelessspear@hotmail.com
Pubs: *and chaos congealed* (Genesis Pr, 1999), *New Voices from the Nuyorican Poets Cafi: Anth* (Norton, 1999), *360: A Revolution of Black Poets: Anth* (Black Words Pr, 1998), *Phati'tude, Pulse Theatre, Spy, Antioch College.*

Gina Angeline Bonati P
607 E 11 St, #10, New York, NY 10009, 212-473-1950
Pubs: *Resurrection* (Venom Pr, 1993), *The Weight of a Place* (Enemy Loose Pub, 1990), *A Different Drummer, Curare, Village Voice, Resister.*

Rafael Bordao P
Arcas, PO Box 023617, Brooklyn, NY 11202-3617, 718-624-8936
Pubs: *Libro De Las Interferencias, Escurridduras De La Soledad* (Editorial Palmar, 1995, 1995), *Diario Las Americas, Cuzcatlan, Latino Stuff Rev, El Diario.*

David Bottoms P&W
235 W End Ave, New York, NY 10023, 212-580-1559
Internet: engdhb@panther.gsu.edu
Pubs: *Amored Hearts: New and Selected Poems* (Copper Canyon Pr, 1995), *Easter Weekend* (HM, 1990), *Under the Vulture-Tree, In a U-Haul North of Damascus* (Morrow, 1987, 1983), *Atlantic, New Yorker, Paris Rev, Harper's, Poetry, APR.*

Jane Boudin P
12 1/2 St Lukes Pl, New York, NY 10014, 212-924-3136
Pubs: *Some of the Parts* (Pomegranate Pr, 1982), *Miranda's Music* (Thomas Crowell, 1968).

Aram Boyajian P
50 W 96 St, New York, NY 10025, 212-749-1250

Matthew S. Boyd W
Little, Brown & Company, 1271 Ave of the Americas, New York, NY 10020, 212-522-8000
Internet: petithall@dcdu.com
Pubs: *The Art of Breaking Glass* (Little, Brown, 1997), *Nightmare Logic* (Bantam, 1989).

T. Coraghessan Boyle W
Georges Borchardt Inc., 136 E 57 St, New York, NY 10022, 212-753-5785
Pubs: *Riven Rock, T.C. Boyle Stories, The Tortilla Curtain, The Road To Wellville, East is East, If the River Was Whiskey, World's End* (Viking, 1998, 1998, 1995, 1993, 1990, 1989, 1987).

David Bradley W
The Wendy Weil Agency, Inc., 232 Madison Ave, Ste 1300, New York, NY 10016, 212-685-0030
Pubs: *The Chaneysville Incident* (H&R, 1990), *South Street* (Scribner, 1986), *Esquire, New York Times, New Yorker, Philadelphia, Harper's.*

Kathleen Brady W
305 E 72 St, New York, NY 10021, 212-535-1773
Pubs: *Ida Tarbell: Portrait Of A Muckraker* (U Pittsburgh, 1989), *Inside Out* (Norton, 1979).

Perry Brass P&W
2501 Palisade Ave, #A1, Bronx, NY 10463, 718-884-6606
Internet: belhuepress@earthlink.net
Pubs: *The Lover of My Soul, The Harvest, Albert, or, The Book of Man, Sex-Change* (Belhue Pr, 1998, 1997, 1995, 1991), *Christopher Street, Amethyst, Art and Understanding, Mandate, Holy Titclamps.*

Kamau Brathwaite P
37 Washington Sq W, #4B, New York, NY 10011
Pubs: *Sunpoem, The Arrivants* (Oup, 1982, 1973), *Savacou: Jrnl of the Caribbean Artists.*

Brian Breger P
179 E 3 St, #33, New York, NY 10009, 212-475-8690
Pubs: *Journeys to the Center of the Earth* (Piecework Pr, 1986), *Mojave* (# Pr, 1980), *Mulch.*

Betty Bressi P
74 Claradon Ln, Staten Island, NY 10305, 718-273-1793
Pubs: *Letters From Italy* (Glassworks Pr, 1990), *Poeti Italo Americani: Anth* (Alfonsi, 1985), *Small Pond, Box 749, Contact II, Jam Today, Glassworks, Blank Tape.*

Peter Bricklebank W
1803 Riverside Dr, #2J, New York, NY 10034, 212-567-3686
Pubs: *American Voice, Crescent Rev, Mid-American Rev, Kansas Qtly, Carolina Qtly, Confrontation.*

Richard P. Brickner W
Lantz-Harris Literary Agency, 156 5th Ave, Ste 617, New York, NY 10010, 212-924-6269
Pubs: *After She Left* (Henry Holt, 1988), *Tickets* (Simon & Schuster, 1981).

Les Bridges   P
313 E 10 St, #4, New York, NY 10009, 212-677-2799
   Pubs: *Read 'em And Weep, Fractured Snapshots*
   (LynDawn, 1993, 1992), *The Literature of Work* (U Phoenix
   Pr, 1991).

Stewart Brisby   P
463 West St, #G113, New York, NY 10014-2010,
212-633-1642
   Pubs: *A Death in America* (Wolverine Pr, 1986), *Caprice,
   Greenfield Rev, Berkeley Barb, Margins.*

Jean Brody   W
Jean V. Naggar Literary Agency, 216 E 75 St, Ste 1E, New
York, NY 10021, 212-794-1082
   Pubs: *A Coven of Women* (Atheneum, 1987), *Gideon's
   House* (Putnam, 1984), *Special Report, Lear's.*

Janet Brof   P&W
380 Riverside Dr, #2F, New York, NY 10025-1801,
212-663-6254
   Pubs: *Through a Half-Open Door* (Catkin Pr, 1988), *Poets
   On, Negative Capability, Stone Country, Mid-Stream, Mss..*

E. M. Broner   W
Charlotte Sheedy Literary Agen, 65 Bleecker St, New York,
NY 10012, 212-780-9800
   Pubs: *Mornings and Mournings, The Telling* (HC, 1994,
   1993), *A Weave Of Women, Her Mothers* (HR&W, 1978,
   1975).

Donna Brook   P
231 Wyckoff St, Brooklyn, NY 11217-2208, 718-643-9559
   Pubs: *A More Human Face, What Being Responsible
   Means to Me, Notes on Space/Time* (Hanging Loose, 1998,
   1988, 1977), *Without Child: Anth* (Feminist Pr, 1999),
   *Verse, Hanging Loose, Telephone, Alternative Pr, B'way II,
   River Styx, The World.*

Terry Brooks   W
Ballantine Books/Del Rey Fanta, 201 E 50 St, New York, NY
10022, 212-751-2600
   Pubs: *The Wishsong of Shannara, The Elfstones of
   Shannara* (Del Rey/Ballantine Bks, 1985, 1982).

P. R. Brostowin   P
88-38 74th Ave, Glendale, NY 11385, 718-997-0227
   Pubs: *In Other Words* (Alfalfa, 1976), *Kansas Qtly, Smith,
   Blue Unicorn, Windless Orchard.*

Millicent Brower   P&W
484 W 43 St, #10-F, New York, NY 10036, 212-239-1881
   Pubs: *Young Performers* (Julian Messner, 1985), *I Am
   Going Nowhere* (Putnam, 1972), *Ingenue* (Ballantine,
   1959), *Cosmopolitan, Saturday Rev, Cricket.*

Andrea Carter Brown   P
355 South End Ave 5A1, New York, NY 10280, 212-321-2928
Internet: waterrail@aol.com
   Pubs: *Girls: An Anthology: Anth* (Global City Pr, 1997),
   *Mississippi Rev, Gettysbury Rev, Marlboro Rev, Thin, Air,
   Talking River Review, Penumbra, Borderlands, Red Brick
   Rev.*

Kenneth H. Brown   P&W
150 74th St, Brooklyn, NY 11209
   Pubs: *You'd Never Know It From The Way I Talk* (Ashland
   Poetry Pr, 1990), *The Narrows* (Dial Pr, 1971), *The Brig*
   (Hill & Wang, 1965), *Gallery Mag, City Lights.*

LindaJean Brown   W
Iridian Press, PO Box 7521, FDR Sta, New York, NY 10150
   Pubs: *Jazz Dancing Wif Mama, The Rainbow River* (Iridian
   Pr, 1981, 1980), *Azalea.*

Rita Mae Brown   P&W
The Wendy Weil Agency, Inc., 232 Madison Ave, Ste 1300,
New York, NY 10016
   Pubs: *Rest in Pieces, Wish You Were Here* (w/S.P. Brown),
   Bingo (Bantam, 1992, 1990, 1988), *Southern Discomfort*
   (H&R, 1982).

Michael Brownstein   P&W
21 E 2 St, #3, New York, NY 10003
   Pubs: *Self-Reliance* (Coffee Hse Pr, 1994), *The Touch*
   (Autonomedia, 1993), *New Yorker, Open City.*

C. D. B. Bryan   W
Janklow & Nesbit Associates, 598 Madison Ave, New York,
NY 10022-1614, 212-421-1700
   Pubs: *Beautiful Women, Ugly Scenes* (Doubleday, 1983),
   Friendly Fire (Putnam, 1976).

Frederick Buechner   W
Harriet Wasserman Agency, 137 E 36 St, New York, NY
10016, 212-689-3257
   Pubs: *Godric, Whistling in The Dark* (Harper, 1988, 1980).

Melvin Jules Bukiet   W
21 W 26 St, New York, NY 10010, 212-685-2663
   Pubs: *Signs and Wonders* (Picador, 1999), *After* (St.
   Martin's Pr, 1996), *While the Messiah Tarries* (HB, 1995),
   Stories of an Imaginary Childhood (Northwestern U Pr,
   1992), *Antaeus, Paris Rev.*

Aaron E. Bulman   P
15 Magaw Pl, #1B, New York, NY 10033, 212-781-5498
   Pubs: *Plum Rev, Jewish Currents, Partisan Rev, Home
   Planet News, Small Pond Rev, Images, Paris Rev, Jewish
   Spectator.*

Michelina Buonocore   P
2141 Crotona Ave, #13G, Bronx, NY 10457, 212-733-5946
   Pubs: *The Last Portrait* (Dragon's Teeth Pr, 1987),
   Bicentennial Hymn (Edward James, 1979).

France Burke P&W
170 Ave C, #21D, New York, NY 10009, 212-674-4951
 Pubs: *Women in Search of Utopia: Anth* (Schocken Bks, 1984), *Paris Rev, Confrontation, Panache, Dramatist Guild Qtly.*

Kathe Burkhart PP&P&W
47 S 5th St, 3rd Fl, Brooklyn, NY 11211, 718-486-7383
 Pubs: *Velvet Revolution* (Italy; Galleria in Arco, 1993), *Red Tape: Anth* (M. Carter, 1993), *From Under the 8-Ball* (Line, 1985), *Best of the Underground: Anth* (Masquerade, 1998), *Purple Fiction, Meaning, Flash Art, Mirage Periodical, Peep, Promotional Copy.*

Herbert Burkholz W
Georges Borchardt Inc., 136 E 57 St, New York, NY 10022, 212-753-5785
 Pubs: *The FDA Follies* (Basic Bks, 1994), *Brain Damage* (Atheneum, 1992), *Writer-in-Residence* (Permanent Pr, 1992), *New York Times Mag, New Republic, Longevity.*

Brian Burland P&W
W. W. Norton, 500 5th Ave, New York, NY 10110
 Pubs: *A Few Flowers for St. George, Love is a Durable Fire, Fall From Aloft* (Grafton/Collins, 1987, 1987, 1987), *New Letters.*

Diane Burns P
46 E 1st St, #4B, New York, NY 10003, 212-475-5680
Internet: tribes@pop.interport.net
 Pubs: *Riding The One-Eyed Ford* (Contact/II Pr, 1981), *Aloud: Voices From the Nuyorican Poets Cafe: Anth* (New Worlds of Literature, 1994), *Greenfield Rev, A Gathering of the Tribes, Akwesasne Notes, Anishinabe Aki, LAC Court Oreilles Jrnl.*

Stanley Burnshaw P&W
250 W 89 St, #PH2G, New York, NY 10024, 212-595-7907
 Pubs: *The Seamless Web* (Braziller, 1991), *A Stanley Burnshaw Reader* (U Georgia Pr, 1990), *Atlantic, Sewanee Rev, Poetry, New York Times, Saturday Rev, Nouvelle Rev.*

Anne Kelleher Bush W
Donald Maass Literary Agency, 157 W 57 St, Ste 1003, New York, NY 10019, 212-757-7755
Internet: ahay72a@prodigy.com
 Pubs: *The Misbegotten King, Children of Enchantment* (Warner Bks, 1997, 1996).

Naomi Bushman P
716 Broadway, New York, NY 10013, 212-421-1637
 Pubs: *West End, Trellis Two, Hanging Loose.*

Peter Bushyeager P
9 Stuyvesant Oval, #5F, New York, NY 10009, 212-995-8102
 Pubs: *Vital Wires* (Unimproved Edtns Pr, 1986), *Synergism Anth* (Boshi Pr, 1995), *The World, NAW, Painted Bride Qtly, Nostalgia, Pagan Place.*

Edward Butscher P&W
84-01 Main St, Briarwood, NY 11435, 718-441-9766
 Pubs: *Child in the House: Poems* (Canio's Bks, 1995), *Eros Descending: A Selection* (Dusty Dog Pr, 1992).

Christopher Butters P
488 12th St, Brooklyn, NY 11215, 718-768-1724
 Pubs: *Americas* (Viet Nam Generation, 1996), *The Propaganda of a Seed* (Cardinal Pr, 1990).

Cheryl Byron PP&P
Something Positive, 225 E 89 St, Box 20, New York, NY 10128, 212-289-3785
 Pubs: *Womantalk* (Heartbeat Records, 1986), *Womanrise* (Shamal Bks, 1978).

Luis Cabalquinto P&W
PO Box 618, Stuyvesant Sta, New York, NY 10009-0618, 212-254-4514
 Pubs: *Dreamwanderer, The Dog-Eater and Other Poems* (Kalikasan Pr, 1992, 1989), *APR, Prairie Schooner, Manoa, Trafika, Poetry Australia, River Styx.*

Olga Cabral P&W
463 West St, #H-523, New York, NY 10014, 212-691-4855
 Pubs: *Voice/Over: Selected Poems* (West End Pr, 1993), *American Visions: Anth* (Mayfield Pub, 1994), *Cream City Rev, Signal Intl, Pemmican.*

Rosalie Calabrese P
700 Columbus Ave, #16D, New York, NY 10025-6680, 212-663-6620
 Pubs: *Anth of American Verse and Yearbook of American Poetry* (Monitor, 1997), *Full Circle: Anth* (Pittenbruach Pr, 1997), *Byline, Thirteen, Cosmopolitan, New England Entertainment Digest, Up Front Muse Intl Rev, And Then, Jewish Currents, Dead Lines.*

Justin Caldwell P
410 W 24 St, #2A, New York, NY 10011, 212-675-3931
 Pubs: *The Sleeping Porch* (Lost Roads Pr, 1979), *Southern Rev, Poetry Now, Ironwood.*

Hortense Calisher W
Donadio & Ashworth, Inc., 121 W 27 St, Ste 704, New York, NY 10001, 212-691-8077
 Pubs: *In the Slammer with Carol Smith* (Marion Boyars, 1997), *The Novellas of Hortense Calisher, In The Palace of the Movie King* (Random Hse, 1997, 1993), *Kissing Cousins, Age* (Weidenfeld, 1988).

Paulette Callen W
215 West 83 St #1F, New York, NY 10024, 212-873-9369
 Pubs: *Vanity, Charity* (Simon & Schuster, 1998, 1997), *Negative Capability.*

James Camp P
365 W End Ave, #7C, New York, NY 10024, 212-595-7458
Pubs: *Paris Rev Anth* (Norton, 1990), *Light Year: Anth* (Bits Pr, 1989), *Cincinnati Rev, Poetry New York, Sagetrieb.*

Ethan Canin W
Maxine Groffsky Literary Agcy, 853 Broadway Ste 708, New York, NY 10003, 212-979-1500
Pubs: *For Kings and Planets, The Palace Thief* (Random Hse, 1998, 1994), *Blue River, Emperor of the Air* (HM, 1991, 1988).

Steve Cannon W
285 E 3 St, 3rd Fl, New York, NY 10009, 212-674-8262
Pubs: *Groove, Bang And Jive Around* (Olympia Pr, 1968), *American Rag, Sunbury 9, Pulp.*

Robert Canzoneri P&W
24 W 55 St, New York, NY 10019, 212-245-0420
Pubs: *Potboiler: An Amateur's Affair with La Cuisine* (North Point, 1989), *Story, Chariton Rev, Modern Maturity.*

Phyllis Capello P&W
495 16th St, Brooklyn, NY 112155913, 718-788-0025
Internet: mjcpc9999@aol.com
Pubs: *Journey into Motherhood* (Riverhead Putnam, 1996), *Voices in Italian Americana: Anth* (Purdue U Pr, 1997), *The Voices We Carry: Anth* (Guernica Edtns, 1993), *Footwork, Literary Mag, New York Qtly, Downtown Mag.*

Alberto O. Cappas P
85 4th Ave, Ste 3H, New York, NY 10003, 212-353-9114
Internet: cappas@aol.com
Pubs: *Disintegration of the Puerto Ricans* (Don Pedro Enterprises, 1997), *Echolalia, Verse & Vibration of Alberto O. Cappas* (Carlton Pr, 1988), *Black Men Still Singing: Anth* (Guild Pr, 1990), *Primal Voices, The Rican Jrnl, Puerto Rican Connections.*

Nick Carbo P
36-09 21st Ave, Astoria, NY 11105, 212-274-9357
Internet: ncarbo@aol.com
Pubs: *El Grupo McDonald's* (Tia Chucha Pr, 1995), *Poetry, TriQuarterly, Poet Lore.*

Peter Carey W
ICM, 40 W 57 St, New York, NY 10019, 212-556-5600
Pubs: *The Unusual Life of Tristan Smith, The Tax Inspector* (Knopf, 1995, 1992), *Oscar & Lucinda* (H&R, 1988).

Don Carpenter W
E. P. Dutton & Co., 375 Hudson St, New York, NY 10014, 212-366-2000

Mary Anne Cartelli P
122 Spring St, #4S, New York, NY 10012, 212-334-5229
Pubs: *The Little Mag, Bomb, Joe Soap's Canoe, World, Field, Luna Tack, Berkeley Poetry Rev.*

Charlotte Carter W
Charlotte Sheedy Literary Agen, 65 Bleecker St, New York, NY 10012, 212-780-9800
Pubs: *Personal Effects* (United Artists, 1990), *Transfer.*

Mary Casanova W
Hyperion, 114 5th Ave, New York, NY 10011, 212-633-5922
Internet: www.marycasanova.com
Pubs: *Stealing Thunder, Wolf Shadows, Riot, Moose Tracks* (Hyperion Bks, 1997, 1997, 1996, 1995), *Cricket, Once Upon A Time, Highlights, Loonfeather.*

John Casey W
c/o Michael Carlisle, 24 E 64 St, New York, NY 10026, 212-813-1881
Pubs: *The Halflife of Happiness* (Knopf, 1998), *Spartina* (Vintage, 1998), *Testimony & Demeanor, An American Romance* (Avon, 1991, 1991), *New Yorker, L.A. Times, New York Times Book Rev.*

Christine Cassidy P
234 W 20 St, #5B, New York, NY 10011, 212-727-0531
Internet: cccassidy@aol.com
Pubs: *First Time Ever: Anth* (Naiad Pr, 1995), *Persistent Desire: Anth* (Alyson, 1992), *Lambda Book Report, Mudfish, Beloit Poetry Jrnl, Chalk Circle.*

Kay Cassill W
Goodman Associates, 500 West End Ave, New York, NY 10024, 212-873-4806
Pubs: *Twins: Nature's Amazing Mystery* (Atheneum, 1982), *The Twins Letter.*

R. V. Cassill W
Donadio & Ashworth, Inc., 121 W 27 St, Ste 704, New York, NY 10001
Pubs: *Late Stories, The Unknown Soldier* (Texas Center for Writers, 1995, 1991), *The Man Who Bought Magnitogorsk* (The London Co., 1994).

J. N. Catanach W
560 Riverside Dr, #20-F, New York, NY 10027
Pubs: *The Last Rite of Hugo T* (St. Martin's Pr, 1992), *Brideprice, White is the Color of Death* (The Countryman Pr, 1989, 1988).

Anita Mirenberg Caylor PP&P
437 E 118 St, New York, NY 10035, 212-534-2764
Pubs: *Beloit Poetry Jrnl, East Coast Writers Anth, Bronx Roots.*

Nancy Chaikin W
Farber Literary Agency, 14 E 75 St, New York, NY 10021, 516-487-7160
Pubs: *Best American Short Stories: Anth* (HM, 1976, 1975), *50 Modern Stories: Anth* (Row Peterson, 1960), *Lear's.*

Marisha Chamberlain P
Bill Craver/Writers & Artists, 19 W 44 St., Ste #1000, New York, NY 10036, 212-391-1112
Internet: marisha5t@aol.com
> Pubs: *A Line of Cutting Women* (Calyx Journal, 1998), *Scheherazade* (Dramatists Play Service, 1985), *Powers* (New Rivers Pr, 1983), *Minneapolis Rev of Baseball, City Pages, Hungry Mind Rev.*

Clovr Chango PP
631 E 11 St #24, New York, NY 10009, 212-677-0594

Laura Chapman W
1148 5th Ave, New York, NY 10128
> Pubs: *Multiple Choice* (Doubleday, 1978), *Legal Relations* (Dutton, 1977).

Steve Chapple W
Ellen Levine Literary Agency, 15 E 26 St, Ste 1801, New York, NY 10010, 212-889-0620
> Pubs: *Outlaws in Babylon* (S&S, 1984), *Don't Mind Dying* (Doubleday, 1980), *New York Times, Los Angeles Times.*

Jerome Charyn W
302 W 12 St, #10C, New York, NY 10014, 212-691-2879
> Pubs: *Elsinore, The Good Policeman* (Mysterious Pr, 1991, 1990), *Movieland, Metropolis* (Putnam, 1989, 1986).

Peter Cherches W
195 Garfield Pl, #3E, Brooklyn, NY 11215, 718-965-9725
> Pubs: *Between A Dream & A Cup of Coffee* (Red Dust, 1987), *Condensed Book* (Benzene Edtns, 1986).

Edith Chevat W
395 S End Ave, #19J, New York, NY 10280, 212-321-2524
Internet: 1chevat@aol.com
> Pubs: *Love Lesson* (Valon Bks, 1998), *Girls: An Anthology* (Global City Pr, 1997), *The One You Call Sister: Anth* (Cleis Pr, 1989), *Bridges, Global City Rev, Sojourner, Other Voices, Home Planet News, Jewish Currents, US-China Rev.*

Fay Chiang P
60 E 4 St, #20, New York, NY 10003
> Pubs: *Voci Dal Silenzio* (I Canguri/Feltrinelli, 1996), *Miwa's Song, In The City of Contradictions* (Sunbury Pr, 1982, 1979), *Girls: An Anthology* (Global City Pr, 1997).

Evans Chigounis P
224 E 18 St, #3A, New York, NY 10003
> Pubs: *Secret Lives* (Wesleyan Univ Pr, 1972).

Sri Chinmoy P
85-38 151st St, Jamaica, NY 11432, 718-523-3826
> Pubs: *My Lord's Lotus-Feet, Seventy-Seven Thousand Service-Trees, Today, My Morning Begins* (Agni Pr, 1998, 1998, 1996, 1996), *War: Man's Abysmal Abyss-Plunge* (Aum Pubs, 1991).

Kathleen Chodor P
148 W 23 St, New York, NY 10011

Pamela Christman W
5 Peter Cooper Rd, #7A, New York, NY 10010, 212-982-1971
> Pubs: *Bluff City, Amaranth Rev, Parting Gifts, Sassy, Housewife-Writer's Forum, GW Rev.*

Nicholas Christopher P&W
Janklow & Nesbit Associates, 598 Madison Ave, New York, NY 10022-1614, 212-421-1700
> Pubs: *Creation of the Night Sky* (Harcourt Brace, 1998), *Veronica* (Dial, 1996), *5 Degrees and Other Poems, In the Year of the Comet, Desperate Characters, The Soloist* (Viking, 1995, 1992, 1988, 1986), *Esquire.*

Jane Ciabattari W
36 W 75 St #5A, New York, NY 10023, 212-787-5675
Internet: janeciab@aol.com
> Pubs: *Winning Moves* (Penguin, 1990), *Redbook, NAR, Denver Qtly, Blueline, Caprice, Hampton Shorts.*

Jill Ciment W
254 E 7 St, #15-16, New York, NY 10009
> Pubs: *Half a Life* (Crown, 1996), *The Law of Falling Bodies* (Poseidon Pr, 1993), *Michigan Rev, CQ, South Carolina Rev.*

Vivina Ciolli P
PO Box 620797, Little Neck, NY 11362-0797, 718-279-4988
> Pubs: *Bitter Larder* (New Spirit Pr, 1994), *Negative Capability, Maryland Poetry Rev, Poets On, Long Island Qtly, Sistersong, Earth's Daughters.*

Sandra Cisneros P&W
S. Bergholz Literary Services, 17 W 10 St, #5, New York, NY 10011, 212-387-0545
> Pubs: *Woman Hollering Creek* (Random Hse/Vintage, 1991), *The House on Mango Street* (Vintage, 1991), *My Wicked, Wicked Ways* (Third Woman Pr, 1987).

China Clark P&W
44 Hamilton Terr #4FL, New York, NY 10031-6403
> Pubs: *Voices of Color* (Applause, 1993), *Feelings of Love Not Yet Expressed* (Folkways, 1978), *Essence, Yardbird Reader, Bergen Sun, Velvet Glove.*

Jean Clark W
Harold Ober Associates, 425 Madison Ave, New York, NY 10017, 212-759-8600
> Pubs: *The Marriage Bed* (Putnam, 1983), *Untie The Winds* (Macmillan, 1976).

Jan Clausen P&W
132 Maple St, Brooklyn, NY 11225, 718-469-3322
Internet: clausenj@newschool.edu
Pubs: *Beyond Gay or Straight* (Chelsea House, 1996),
Books & Life (Ohio State U, 1989), *The Prosperine Papers,
Sinking, Stealing* (Crossing Pr, 1988, 1985), *Kenyon Rev,
13th Moon, ACM, Out/Look, Feminist Studies, The
Women's Review of Books.*

Russell Clay P
585 W End Ave, #7E, New York, NY 10024, 212-877-4808
Internet: http://www.cowell-clay.com
Pubs: *Father Poems, From Ghost Through Bone to Man,
Half-Life Poems* (West End Poetry Pr, 1998, 1997, 1997),
*Georgia Jrnl, Poetry Jrnl, Share, Sow's Ear, Poetry Motel,
Talking River Rev, Lucid Stone, Mediphors Jrnl.*

Carol Clemeau W
41 W 83 St, New York, NY 10024, 212-877-4985
Pubs: *The Ariadne Clue* (Scribner, 1982), *Ellery Queen's Mag.*

Francois Clemmons P
4 W 101 St, #35, New York, NY 10025, 212-866-8915

Michelle Cliff W
Faith Childs Literary Agency, 915 Broadway, Suite 1009, New
York, NY 10010, 212-995-9600
Pubs: *The Store of a Million Items: Short Stories, Best
American Short Stories: Anth* (HM, 1998, 1997), *Free
Enterprise, No Telephone To Heaven* (Dutton, 1993, 1987),
*VLS, Parnassus, American Voice, Ms., Kenyon Rev,
Nation, Agni, TriQuarterly.*

William Leo Coakley P
120 W 71 St, New York, NY 10023, 212-873-6884
Pubs: *Humor in America* (Open Places, 1984), *Sotheby's
Poetry Competition Anth* (Arvon Foundation, 1984), *New
York Qtly, Harvard Gay & Lesbian Rev, Paris Rev, Nation,
Christopher Street, Aquarius.*

Judith Ortiz Cofer P&W
Chelsea Forum, 377 Rector Pl, New York, NY 10280,
212-945-3100
Internet: jocofer@aol.com
Pubs: *An Island Like You* (Penguin,1997), *The Latin Deli*
(Norton, 1995), *Silent Dancing* (Arte Publico Pr, 1990), *The
Line of the Sun* (U Georgia Pr, 1989), *Georgia Rev, Glamour,
Kenyon Rev, Southern Rev, Prairie Schooner, Parnassus.*

Alice Eve Cohen PP
250 W 77 St, #103, New York, NY 10024, 212-580-7889
Pubs: *Book of Truth, Book of Lies* (Baltimore Museum of
Art, 1989), *Goliath on 74th Street vs. The Woman Who
Loved Vegetables* (Manhattan Punchline, 1989).

Esther Cohen P&W
66 W 77 St, New York, NY 10024, 212-595-0122
Pubs: *No Charge for Looking* (Schocken Bks, 1985).

Gerald Cohen P&W
BMCC, CUNY, 199 Chambers St, New York, NY 10007,
717-646-2858
Internet: wankele@msn.com
Pubs: *Fire Readings/Tumbleweed: Anth* (Paris;
Shakespeare & Co., 1996), *Chicago Rev, Literary Rev,
New York Times, New England Rev, Confrontation, Poetry
Northwest, Kansas Qtly.*

Ira Cohen P
225 W 106 St, New York, NY 10025, 212-222-4068
Pubs: *CD: The Majoon Traveller* (Sub Rosa, 1994), *Ratio:*
(Media Shamans, 1991), *First Intensity, Third Rail,
Exquisite Corpse.*

Marc Cohen P
1 University Pl, #3E, New York, NY 10003, 212-228-6781
Internet: marc_cohen@schindler.com
Pubs: *Mecox Road, On Maplewood Time* (Groundwater Pr,
1996, 1989), *Best American Poetry: Anth* (Scribner, 1993,
1991), *NAW, Paris Rev, Colorado Rev, Verse, Columbia,
APR.*

Marty Cohen P
708 8th Ave, #4L, Brooklyn, NY 11215, 718-499-4976
Internet: mcohen@workinamerica.org
Pubs: *A Traveler's Alphabet* (Prescott Street Pr, 1979),
Parnassus, Northern Rev, Abraxas.

Marvin Cohen P&W
PO Box 460, Stuyvesant Sta, New York, NY 10009,
212-677-2040
Pubs: *Aesthetics in Art & Life* (Gull Bks, 1982), *The
Inconvenience of Living* (Urizen Bks, 1977), *Nation,
Antaeus, Hudson Rev, Sun & Moon, Chelsea.*

William Cole P
201 W 54 St, #6A, New York, NY 10019, 212-265-6978
Pubs: *A Zooful of Animals* (HM, 1992), *A Boy Named Mary
Jane* (Franklin Watts, 1977), *New Yorker, Saturday Rev.*

Judith Woolcock Columbo W
DC 37 Education Fund, Rm 202, 125 Barclay St, New York,
NY 100072179, 212-815-1700
Internet: c21553@marl.1dt.net
Pubs: *The Fablesinger* (Crossing Pr, 1989).

Brad Conard W
Donadio & Ashworth, Inc., 121 W 27 St, Ste 704, New York,
NY 10001
Pubs: *Southern Rev, Yale Rev, Virginia Qtly Rev,
Southwest Rev.*

Elizabeth Cook-Lynn   P&W
Charlotte Sheedy Literary Agcy, 65 Bleecker St, New York,
NY 10012, 212-780-9800
    Pubs: *I Remember the Fallen Trees* (Eastern Washington U
    Pr, 1998), *Woyake Kinikiya Vol II, Vol I: Anths* (Oak Lake
    Writers Pr, 1995, 1994), *Talking Up A Storm: Anth* (U
    Nebraska Pr, 1994), *The Writer's Perspective: Anth*
    (Prentice Hall, 1994), *Indian Artist.*

Bernard Cooper   P&W
ICM, 40 W 57 St, New York, NY 10019, 212-556-5600
Internet: bcooper635@aol.com
    Pubs: *Truth Serum* (HM, 1996), *A Year of Rhymes* (Viking
    Penguin, 1993), *Harper's, Paris Rev, L.A. Times Mag.*

David Cooper   P
1149 Prospect Ave, #1R, Brooklyn, NY 11218, 718-965-9337
Internet: david&shoshana@tuna.net
    Pubs: *XY Files: Poems on the Male Experience: Anth*
    (Sherman Asher Pub, 1997), *Synaesthetic, Kinesis,
    Response, Pudding, Poetry Motel, Davka, Literary Rev,
    Massachusetts Rev, Passages North, Painted Bride Qtly,
    Mudfish.*

Jane Cooper   P
545 W 111 St, #8K, New York, NY 10025, 212-663-3934
    Pubs: *Green Notebook, Winter Road, Scaffolding: Selected
    Poems* (Tilbury Hse, 1994, 1993), *APR, Field, Paris Rev,
    Kenyon Rev, New Yorker, American Voice, Iowa Rev.*

Claire Cooperstein   P&W
151 Bergen St, Brooklyn, NY 11217, 718-522-0410
    Pubs: *Johanna — Novel of Van Gogh Family*
    (Scribner/S&S, 1995), *Counting Keepsakes* (Andrew
    Mountain Poetry Pr, 1989), *Ko — Japanese Haiku,
    Frogpond.*

Mark Coovelis   W
Sterling Lord Literistic, 65 Bleecker St, New York, NY 10012,
212-780-6050
    Pubs: *Gloria* (S&S, 1994), *American Voice, California Qtly,
    Short Story Rev, City Lights Rev.*

Robert Coover   W
Georges Borchardt Inc., 136 E 57 St, New York, NY 10022,
212-753-5785
    Pubs: *John's Wife, Pinocchio in Venice, A Night at the
    Movies, Whatever Happened to Gloomy Gus of the
    Chicago Bears?* (S&S, 1996, 1991, 1987, 1987).

Alfred Corn   P
350 W 14 St, #6A, New York, NY 10014, 212-255-2749
    Pubs: *Autobiographies, The West Door* (Viking Penguin,
    1992, 1988).

Gregory Corso   P
Roger Richards Rare Books, 26 Horatio St, #24, New York,
NY 10014

Jayne Cortez   P
PO Box 96, Village Sta, New York, NY 10014, 212-431-5067
    Pubs: *Somewhere In Advance of Nowhere* (Serpent's
    Tail/High Risk Bks, 1996), *Poetic Magnetic, Everywhere
    Drums* (CD) (Bola Pr, 1991, 1991).

Angel Costa   PP
40 Harrison St, #14D, New York, NY 10013, 212-285-1123
    Pubs: *Nuyorican Poets Cafe, Knitting Factory, Living
    Theater, Mona's, St. Mark's Poetry Project.*

Spencer Costley   P&W
55 Bethune St, #313-C, New York, NY 10014, 212-929-5770
    Pubs: *The Zebra Storyteller: Collected Stories, Something
    To Read To Someone* (Station Hill Pr, 1993, 1980).

Jonathan Cott   P
247 E 33 St, #6A, New York, NY 10016
    Pubs: *Wandering Ghost: The Odyssey of Lafcadio Hearn*
    (Knopf, 1991), *The Search for Omm Sety* (Warner Bks, 1989).

Cynthia Cotts   W
59 E 7 St, #2, New York, NY 10003
    Pubs: *Art & Artists, Columbus Dispatch, Appearances,
    Gargoyle, Telescope.*

Jeffrey Couchman   W
535 W End Ave, #5-F, New York, NY 10024, 212-580-8200
    Pubs: *Chicago Rev, South Carolina Rev, Pulpsmith,
    Denver Qtly, Confrontation, Pennsylvania English.*

Linda Cousins   P
The Universal Black Writer Pr, PO Box 5, Radio City Sta,
New York, NY 10101, 718-398-8941
    Pubs: *The Mystical Experiences of Harriet Tubman, Black
    & In Brooklyn* (Universal Black Writer Pr, 1992, 1983),
    Cottonwood (U Kansas Pr, 1986).

Stephanie Amy Cowell   W
585 W End Ave, New York, NY 10024, 212-877-4808
    Pubs: *The Players, The Physician of London, Nicholas
    Cooke* (Norton, 1997, 1995, 1993), *Biblio, Living Church.*

Douglas Crase   P
470 W 24 St, New York, NY 10011
    Pubs: *The Revisionist* (Little, Brown, 1981).

Gwyneth Cravens   W
ICM, 40 W 57 St, New York, NY 10019, 212-556-5600
    Pubs: *The Gates of Paradise* (Ticknor & Fields, 1991),
    Heart's Desire, Love and Work (Knopf, 1986, 1982), *New
    Yorker, Nation, New York Times Mag, Harper's.*

Linda Crawford   W
131 Prince St, 3rd Fl, New York, NY 10012, 212-777-8439
    Pubs: *Vanishing Acts* (Putnam, 1983), *Something To Make
    Us Happy* (S&S, 1978).

Marc Crawford   W
360 W 21 St, #4-M, New York, NY 10011, 212-675-7197
Pubs: *The Lincoln Brigade* (Atheneum, 1989), *Emerge, Freedomways, Time Capsule.*

Tad Crawford   W
10 E 23 St, Ste 400, New York, NY 10010, 212-777-8395
Pubs: *Confrontation, Central Park, Phantasm.*

Jennifer Crewe   P
285 Riverside Dr #3B, New York, NY 10025-5226,
212-865-6254
Pubs: *Pequod, Tar River Poetry, The American Muse, Poet & Critic, Ploughshares, Piedmont Literary Rev.*

Emilio Cubeiro   P
32 E 2 St, #9, New York, NY 10003, 212-260-3790
Pubs: *Death of an Asshole, Meat for the Masses* (Widowspeak, 1991, 1991).

William Cullen, Jr.   P
1214 Beverly Rd, Brooklyn, NY 11218, 718-287-7507
Pubs: *Gryphon, St. Anthony Messenger, Home Planet News, Parnassus, Plainsong, Modern Haiku.*

Elizabeth Cullinan   W
463 West St Apt 817-D, New York, NY 10014, 212-675-3191
Pubs: *A Change of Scene* (Norton, 1982), *House of Gold* (HM, 1969), *Shenandoah, Colorado Rev, Irish Literary Supplement, Threshold, New Yorker.*

Lorraine Rainie Currelley   P
PO Box 562, College Sta, New York, NY 10030-0562
Pubs: *Captooth Girlfriends The Third Act* (Captooth Girlfriends The Third Act, 1994).

David Curzon   P
254 W 82 St, #2B, New York, NY 10024-5450, 212-874-3989
Pubs: *Dovichik* (Penguin Bks, 1996), *Modern Poems on the Bible: Anth* (Jewish Pub Soc, 1994), *Antaeus, New Republic, Sewanee Rev, Formalist, Tikkun.*

Debbie Cymbalista   W
77 Bleecker St, #1009, New York, NY 10012, 212-260-5122
Pubs: *Danger* (Dutton, 1989).

Susan Daitch   W
50 W 29 St, New York, NY 10001, 212-684-6050
Pubs: *Storytown* (Dalkey Archive Pr, 1996), *Avant Pop Anthology* (Viking Penguin, 1995), *Top Stories, Rev of Contemporary Fiction, Bomb, Fiction Intl, VLS.*

Vinni Marie D'Ambrosio   P
11 Fifth Ave, #3N, New York, NY 10003, 212-673-5875
Pubs: *Mexican Gothic: A Frieda Kahlo Narrative* (Blue Heron Pr, 1996),*Life Of Touching Mouths* (New York Univ Pr, 1971), *McGraw-Hill Book of Poetry: Anth* (McGraw-Hill, 1993), *Italo American Poets: Anth* (A. Carello, 1985).

Enid Dame   P&W
3047 Brighton First Pl, Brooklyn, NY 11235, 718-769-2854
Pubs: *Anything You Don't See* (West End, 1992), *Lilith and Her Demons* (CCC, 1989), *Many Mountains Moving, Davka, Bridges, New York Qtly, Tikkun, American Voice, Phoebe.*

Rosemary Daniell   P&W
The Wendy Weil Agency, Inc., 232 Madison Ave, Ste 1300, New York, NY 10016, 212-685-0030
Pubs: *The Woman Who Spilled Words All Over Herself* (Faber & Faber, 1997), *The Hurricane Season* (Morrow, 1992), *Fort Bragg and Other Points South, Sleeping With Soldiers* (Holt, 1988, 1984), *American Voice, Chattahoochee Rev.*

Kathryn Daniels   P&W
35-45 78 St, Apt #2, Jackson Heights, NY 11372
Pubs: *If I Had A Hammer: Anth* (Papier-Mache Pr, 1990), *Chrysanthemum, Earth's Daughters, Korone.*

Barbara Danish   P
130 8th Ave, Brooklyn, NY 11215, 718-622-2326

Jack Dann   W
Writers House, 21 W 26 St, New York, NY 10010,
212-691-4575
Internet: 73261.703@compuserve.com
Pubs: *The Man Who Melted* (HarperCollins Australia, 1998), *The Silent, The Memory Cathedral* (Bantam Bks, 1998, 1995), *Nebula Awards 32: Anth* (HB, 1998), *High Steel* (w/J.C. Haldema; Tor, 1993), *Playboy, Twilight Zone Mag.*

Ruth Danon   P
NYU/ADSD, 225 Shimkin Hall, 50 W 4 St, New York, NY 10003
Internet: danon@is3.nyu.edu
Pubs: *Triangulation From a Known Point* (North Star Line/Blue Moon Bks, 1990), *Bomb, Paris Rev.*

Ann K. Darby   W
245 W 104 St, #2D, New York, NY 10025
Internet: darbann@aol.com
Pubs: *The American Story: The Best of Story Quarterly: Anth* (Cane Hill Pr, 1990), *Northwest Rev, Blue Light/Red Light, Story Qtly, Organica, Malahat Rev.*

Eric Darton   P&W
315 8th Ave, #20F, New York, NY 10001, 212-242-0579
Pubs: *Free City* (Norton, 1996), *Radio Tirane* (Conjunctions, 1991), *Conjunctions 17 Anth* (Bard, 1991), *American Letters & Commentary, Central Park, Metropolis, Culturefront, Leonardo, Fiction Intl.*

Kiana Davenport   W
22 W 23 St, 5th Fl, New York, NY 10010, 212-645-7606
   Pubs: *Shark Dialogues* (Plume, 1995), *Charlie Chan Is Dead: Anth* (Penguin, 1993), *Story, Hawaii Pacific Rev, Seattle Rev, Ikon, Honolulu Mag, New Letters.*

Richard Davidson   P
200 W 94 St, #3E, New York, NY 10025, 212-749-0870
   Pubs: *Tower Nine* (Ann Salazar, 1986), *The Gentleman from Hyde Park* (Bard, 1982), *Jewish Affairs, Home Planet News, People's Weekly World, Arts Muse.*

Bradley B. Davis   P
1235 Park Ave, New York, NY 10028, 212-876-1609

Christopher Davis   W
Curtis Brown Ltd., 10 Astor Pl, New York, NY 10003-6935, 212-473-5400
   Pubs: *Dog Horse Rat* (Viking, 1990), *A Peep Into The 20th Century* (Arbor Hse, 1985), *Waiting For It* (H&R, 1980).

Annabel Davis-Goff   W
Sterling Lord Literistic, 65 Bleecker Street, New York, NY 10012, 212-780-6050
   Pubs: *The Dower House* (St. Martin's, 1998), *Walled Gardens* (Knopf, 1989), *Tail Spin, Night Tennis* (Coward McCann, 1981, 1978), *Lear's, New York Times Bk Rev.*

L. J. Davis   W
138A Dean St, Brooklyn, NY 11217, 718-625-3365

Lydia Davis   W
Georges Borchardt Inc., 136 E 57 St, New York, NY 10022
   Pubs: *Almost No Memory, The End of the Story, Break it Down* (FSG, 1997, 1995, 1986), *Harper's, Grand Street, Antaeus, Paris Rev, Conjunctions, Parnassus.*

Thulani Davis   P
Grove Weidenfeld Press, 841 Broadway, New York, NY 10003
   Pubs: *Playing The Changes* (Wesleyan U Pr, 1985), *All The Renegade Ghosts Rise* (Anemone, 1978).

Cecil Dawkins   W
Charlotte Sheedy Literary Agen, 65 Bleecker St, New York, NY 10012, 212-780-9800
   Pubs: *The Quiet Enemy, Charleyhorse* (Viking/Penguin, 1986, 1985), *The Live Goat* (H&R, 1971), *Paris Rev, Southwest Rev, Sewanee Rev, McCall's, Redbook.*

Fielding Dawson   W
49 E 19 St, New York, NY 10003, 212-254-4076
   Pubs: *Moment's Notice* (Coffee Hse, 1993), *Out of This World* (Crown, 1991), *The Trick* (Black Sparrow, 1991), *Ploughshares, Exquisite Corpse, Ontario Rev.*

Storm De Hirsch   P
1760 3rd Ave, #721B, New York, NY 10029

James De Jongh   W
6 Fordham Hill Oval, #9D, Bronx, NY 10468, 212-933-6131
   Pubs: *Vicious Modernism: Black Harlem and the Literary Imagination* (Cambridge U Pr, 1990).

Alexis De Veaux   W
Marie Brown Associates Inc., 625 Broadway, New York, NY 10012
   Pubs: *An Enchanted Hair Tale* (H&R, 1987), *Adventures of the Dread Sisters* (Diva, 1982), *Essence.*

William Decker   W
32 Washington Sq W, #8E, New York, NY 10011, 212-228-1063
   Pubs: *The Holdouts, To Be A Man* (Little, Brown, 1979, 1967).

Irma Del Valle   P
96-07 42nd Ave, Corona, NY 11368, 718-458-9855
   Pubs: *Polvo Poetico* (Munoz Moya Montraveta, 1990), *Senderos Contigo* (Uniday Printing Corp, 1974).

Don DeLillo   W
Wallace Literary Agency, 177 E 70 St, New York, NY 10021
   Pubs: *Underworld* (Scribner, 1997), *Mao II, Libra, White Noise* (Viking, 1991, 1988, 1985), *The Names* (Knopf, 1982).

Jane DeLynn   W
Promethean Artists Management, 1133 Broadway, New York, NY 10010, 212-219-9038
Internet: janed@prodigy.net
   Pubs: *Don Juan in the Village* (Pantheon, 1990), *Real Estate* (Poseidon/S&S, 1988), *Bad Sex Is Good: Anth* (Painted Leaf Pr, 1998), *The Advocate, Tikkun, Paris Rev, Rolling Stone, Mirabella, Harper's, Boston Phoenix.*

Arto DeMirjian, Jr.   W
355 W 22 St #3, New York, NY 10011, 212-989-4967
   Pubs: *Not a Clue* (Popular Pr, 1974), *Ararat Qtly, Publishers Weekly.*

Alice Denham   W
Claudia Menza Literary Agency, 1170 Broadway, Ste 807, New York, NY 10001, 212-889-6850
   Pubs: *AMO* (Putnam, 1975), *My Darling from the Lions* (Bobbs-Merrill, 1967), *Great Tales of City Dwellers* (Pyramid and Lion, 1965), *Best of The Missouri Review: Anth* (U Missouri Pr, 1991), *Confrontation, Playboy, Discovery, Nation, San Miguel Rev.*

Alma Denny   P
353 W 56 St, #3B, New York, NY 10019, 212-757-4648
   Pubs: *Blinkies: Funny Poems to Read in a Blink* (Spectacle Lane Pr, 1992), *Lyric, Cosmopolitan, Ladies Home Jrnl, Good Housekeeping, New York Times, Light Qtly.*

Ed Depasquale   P
59 Christopher St, New York, NY 10014, 212-675-0833
  Pubs: *Ally, Poems in Captivity, Velvet Wings, Helen Rev,
  Mati, Contact II, Poetry.*

Mark Dery   PP
503 Clinton St, #2, Brooklyn, NY 11231, 718-522-1711
  Pubs: *Two Men Meet on a Beach* (Broadside; Atticus Pr,
  1982), *EFQ, Frank, Red Light Blue Light.*

Graham Diamond   W
2320 Parsons Blvd, Whitestone, NY 11357-3442
  Pubs: *Forest Wars* (Lion Pr, 1994), *Black Midnight* (Zeba
  Bks, 1989).

George-Therese Dickenson   P
65 2nd Ave, #2H, New York, NY 10003, 212-260-2881
  Pubs: *Candles Burn in Memory Town* (Segue, 1988),
  Transducing (Roof, 1985), *Tricycle, Big Allis, Assassin,
  Amsterdam News, The World, Annoi.*

Joan Didion   W
Janklow & Nesbit Associates, 598 Madison Ave, New York,
NY 10022-1614, 212-421-1700

David Diefendorf   W
789 W End Ave, #5D, New York, NY 10025, 212-663-4932

May Dikeman   W
70 Irving Pl, New York, NY 10003, 212-475-4533
  Pubs: *The Devil We Know, The Angelica* (Atlantic/Little,
  Brown, 1973, 1971), *Atlantic, Harper's.*

Annie Dillard   P&W
Russell & Volkening, Inc., 50 W 29 St, New York, NY 10001,
212-684-6050
  Pubs: *For the Time Being* (Knopf, 1999),The *Living*
  (HarperCollins, 1992), *Encounters with Chinese Writers*
  (Wesleyan, 1988), *An American Childhood, Pilgrim At
  Tinker Creek* (H&R, 1987, 1974).

Ray DiPalma   P
301 West 108 St #6B, New York, NY 10025, 212-663-1686
  Pubs: *Letters* (Littoral Pr, 1998), *Motion of The Cypher*
  (Roof Bks, 1995), *Provocations* (Potes & Poets Pr, 1994),
  *APR, Ribot, Chicago Rev, To Mag, Revue Pretexte, Five
  Fingers, Iowa Rev, Rhizome, Arshile.*

Thomas M. Disch   P&W
Karpfinger Agency, 357 W 20 St, New York, NY 100113379,
212-691-2690
  Pubs: *Dark Verses and Light, Yes, Let's: New & Selected
  Poems* (Johns Hopkins U Pr, 1991, 1989), *The M.D.: A
  Horror Story* (Knopf, 1991), *Poetry.*

Michael Disend   W
351 W 45 St, #2FW, New York, NY 10036, 212-262-4005

Stephen Dobyns   P&W
Henry Holt & Co., 115 W. 18 St, New York, NY 10011
  Pubs: *Cemetery Nights, A Boat Off The Coast* (Viking,
  1987, 1987).

E. L. Doctorow   W
ICM, 40 W 57 St, New York, NY 10019, 212-556-5600

J. D. Dolan   W
ICM, 40 W 57th St, New York, NY 10019, 212-556-5764
Internet: jddolan@wmich.edu
  Pubs: *New Stories from the South: Anth* (Algonquin, 1996),
  Esquire, Antioch Rev, Mississippi Rev, Shenandoah, Nation.

Sharon Dolin   P
600 W 111 St, #11D, New York, NY 10025, 212-662-3755
Internet: sdolin@earthlink.net
  Pubs: *Climbing Mount Sinai* (Dim Gray Bar Pr, 1996), *Heart
  Work* (Sheep Meadow Pr, 1995), *Poetry, Boulevard,
  Kenyon Rev, Ploughshares, Salamander, American Voice.*

Bob Dombrowski   PP
805 6th Ave, New York, NY 10001, 212-741-2525
  Pubs: *Run, Highway #17,* (The Cycle) *Ravings from the
  Periphery* (Dombrowski/Petruska Productions, 1994, 1992,
  1991).

Jack Donahue   P
50-19 Bell Blvd, Bayside, NY 11364, 718-225-7992
  Pubs: *Midwestern U Qtly, Yet Another Small Mag, Cedar
  Rock, Snowy Egret, Gnosis, Dekalb Literary Arts Jrnl.*

Stephen R. Donaldson   W
Howard Morhaim Agency, 175 Fifth Ave, #709, New York, NY
10010, 212-529-4433
Internet: steverd@umcphq.com
  Pubs: *Reave the Just and Other Poems, This Day All Gods
  Die, Forbidden Knowledge, The Real Story*
  (Bantam/Spectra, 1999, 1996, 1991, 1991), *Lord Foul's
  Bane* (Del Rey/Ballantine, 1977).

Niccolo Donzella   P
151 Bergen St, Brooklyn, NY 11217, 718-522-0480
  Pubs: *Poetry, Village Voice, New York Qtly, Attenzione,
  Akros Rev, Brown Rev, Dacotah Territory.*

Alfred Dorn   P
PO Box 580174, Station A, Flushing, NY 11358-0174
  Pubs: *Voices From Rooms, From Cells to Mindspace*
  (Somers Rocks Pr, 1997, 1997), *Hudson Rev, New
  Criterion, Formalist, Orbis, Light Year, The Lyric, Amelia,
  Pivot, Sparrow, Light.*

Ellen Douglas   W
RLR Associates, 7 W 51 St, New York, NY 10017
  Pubs: *Can't Quit You, Baby* (Viking/Penguin, 1989), *Black
  Cloud, White Cloud* (U Pr Mississippi, 1989).

Michael Drinkard W
Janklow & Nesbit Associates, 598 Madison Ave, New York,
NY 10022-1614, 212-421-1700
Pubs: *Disobedience* (Norton, 1993), *Green Bananas*
(Knopf, 1989).

Johanna Drucker W
Columbia Univ, 116th St and Broadway, New York, NY
10027, 212-854-2811
Pubs: *Simulant Portrait, History of the/my World*
(Druckwerk, 1990, 1990), *Italy* (The Figures Pr, 1980), *Big
Allis, o.blek, Generator, Raddle Moon.*

Sally Ann Drucker P
PO Box 7888, New York, NY 10116
Pubs: *Walking The Desert Lion* (Ena, 1984), *Words on the
Page, The World in Your Hands: Anth* (H&R, 1990),
Bitterroot, Buckle, Epos, Pig Iron, Womanspirit.

Helen Duberstein P&W
463 West St, #904D, New York, NY 10014
Internet: hlipton675@aol.com
Pubs: *Shadow Self & Other Tales, The Shameless Old
Lady* (Ghost Dance Pr, 1996, 1995), *The Radical Theatre
Notebook* (Applause, 1994), *Signal Network Intl.*

Maggie Dubris P&W
27 1st Ave, #14, New York, NY 10003, 212-673-1583
Internet: dubris@aol.com
Pubs: *Willieworld* (Cuz Bks, 1998), *Ladies, Start Your
Engines: Anth* (Faber & Faber, 1996), *Out of This World:
Anth* (Crown, 1991), *Koff, Cuz 2, Tribes, Exquisite Corpse,
Tamarind, $lavery, Minimus.*

Denise Duhamel P
36-09 21st Ave, Astoria, NY 11105
Internet: sedna61@aol.com
Pubs: *The Star-Spangled Banner* (Southern Illinois U Pr,
1999), *Kinky* (Orchises Pr, 1997), *Girl Soldier* (Garden
Street, 1996), *The Woman with Two Vaginas* (Salmon Run,
1994), *Global City Rev, Third Coast, Urbanus, Salt Hill Rev,
APR, Ontario Rev, Chelsea.*

Margaret Mitchell Dukore W
Bobbe Siegel Literary Agency, 41 W 83 St, New York, NY
10024
Pubs: *Bloom, Survival of the Fittest* (Franklin Watts, 1985,
1985), *Rev of Contemporary Fiction.*

Harris Dulany W
273 Warren St, Brooklyn, NY 11201
Internet: hdulany@aol.com
Pubs: *One Kiss Led To Another* (HarperCollins, 1994),
Falling (Saturday Rev Pr, 1971).

Gerald Dumas P
King Features Syndicate, 235 E 45 St, New York, NY 10017
Pubs: *An Afternoon In Waterloo Park* (Wayne State U Pr,
1988), *Rabbits Rafferty* (Avon Camelot, 1985), *Atlantic,
Smithsonian.*

Erika Duncan W
463 West St, #933B, New York, NY 10014, 212-691-0539
Pubs: *Those Giants: Let Them Rise, Unless Soul Clap Its
Hands* (Schocken, 1985, 1985).

Pearl Duncan W
40 Harrison St, #36H, New York, NY 10013-2727,
212-962-3944
Pubs: *A Rock Against the Wind: African-American Poems*
(Berkley/Perigee, 1996), *Water Dancing* (Aegina Pr, 1991),
Essence, Black Enterprise, Sailing, Sail.

Robert Dunn W
Brandt & Brandt Literary Agent, 1501 Broadway, New York,
NY 10036, 212-840-5760
Internet: rgdunn@aol.com
Pubs: *New Yorker, New York Times Book Rev, Fiction
Network, Atlantic, Sewanee Rev, Mother Jones.*

Roger Duvernoy P
70 Riverside Dr, #3E, New York, NY 10024, 212-721-5402
Pubs: *Ripples, Numbers, Circle, Poetry North Rev, Star,
Cathartic.*

Martin S. Dworkin P&W
c/o Brian Cave, 245 Park Ave, New York, NY 101670002,
212-254-2960
Pubs: *Northern Perspective, The World And I, Zymergy,
Contemporary Rev, Transnational Perspectives, ACM,
Poetry Ireland Rev, Takahe, Laurel Rev, Nutshell.*

Miriam Dyak P
82 Garfield Pl, Brooklyn, NY 11215
Pubs: *Dying, Fire Under Water* (New Victoria Publishers,
1979, 1978).

Bru Dye P
164 Hall St, Brooklyn, NY 11205
Pubs: *Yellow Silk, Exquisite Corpse, Central Park, James
White Rev, Amethyst, Slow Motion Mag.*

Joan Eades P&W
484 W 43 St, #28C, New York, NY 10036, 212-592-1834
Internet: jeades@cpg.org
Pubs: *Kansas Qtly, North Dakota Qtly, Plainswoman,
Louisville Rev, Random Hse Audio Bks.*

Cornelius Robert Eady P
39 Jane St #GB, New York, NY 10014, 212-242-8646
Pubs: *The Gathering of My Name* (Carnegie Mellon, 1990),
Seneca Rev, Ploughshares.

Patricia Eakins   P&W
1200 Broadway, #4C, New York, NY 10001, 212-679-7413
Internet: www.fabulara.com/
    Pubs: *The Marvelous Adventures of Pierre Baptiste, Father
    and Mother, First and Last* (New York U Pr, 1999), *The
    Hungry Girls* (Cadmus, 1988), *Oono* (I-74 Pr, 1982),
    *Parnassus, Iowa Rev, Conjunctions, Central Park, Storia,
    Paris Rev, Hotwired.*

Elaine Edelman   P
444 E 86 St #27B, New York, NY 10028-6464, 212-535-7066
    Pubs: *Boom-de-Boom* (Pantheon, 1980), *Noeva: Three
    Women Poets: Anth* (U South Dakota Pr, 1990), *Mudfish,
    APR, Frontiers, Prairie Schooner, New York Times.*

Debra L. Edwards   P
161 E 99 St, #5A, New York, NY 10029, 212-410-9122
    Pubs: *Black Rose* (Upstream Productions, 1977), *Home
    Planet News, Natl Poetry Mag of the Lower East Side,
    Poetry New York, Limelight, Gulf Times, Cover, Barefoot
    Grass Jrnl, Quarter Horse.*

John Ehle   W
Donadio & Ashworth, Inc., 121 W 27 St, Ste 704, New York,
NY 10001, 212-691-8077
    Pubs: *The Widow's Trial, The Winter People* (H&R, 1989,
    1984), *Trail of Tears* (Anchor, 1988).

Gretel Ehrlich   P
Darhansoff & Verrill, 179 Franklin St., 4th Fl., New York, NY
10013
    Pubs: *Drinking Dry Clouds, Wyoming Stories* (Capra Pr,
    1991, 1986), *Islands, The Universe, Home, Heart Mountain*
    (Viking, 1991, 1988).

Janice Eidus   W
435 W 57 St, #17-F, New York, NY 10019, 212-247-6837
    Pubs: *The Celibacy Club, Vito Loves Geraldine* (City Lights,
    1996, 1990), *Urban Bliss* (Fromm Intl, 1994), *Village Voice,
    Witness, Asylum Arts.*

J. Eigo   W
182 Ave A, #1B, New York, NY 10009, 212-533-2769
    Pubs: *Stallions: Anth* (PDA Pr, 1995), *Likely Stories: Anth*
    (Treacle Pr, 1981), *Fruit, Zone, Benzene, Chicago Rev,
    Cream City Rev, Volition.*

Bernard Lionel Einbond   P
PO Box 307, Ft George Sta, New York, NY 10040,
718-960-8361
    Pubs: *The Tree As It Is* (Brander O'Neill Pr, 1996), *The
    Coming Indoors* (Charles E. Tuttle, 1979), *Bogg,
    Wordsmith, Modern Haiku, Frogpond.*

Barbara Einzig   P
375 S End Ave, #27-N, New York, NY 10280, 212-912-1303
Internet: beinzig@aol.com
    Pubs: *Distance Without Distance* (Kelsey Street Pr, 1994),
    Life Moves Outside (Burning Deck Pr, 1987), *Five Fingers
    Rev, Chelsea, Conjunctions, VLS, Fence, APR.*

Deborah Eisenberg   W
Janklow & Nesbit Associates, 598 Madison Ave, New York,
NY 10022-1614, 212-421-1700
    Pubs: *The Stories (So Far)* (Noonday, 1997), *All Around
    Atlantis, Under the 82nd Airborne* (FS&G, 1997, 1992),
    Transactions in a Foreign Currency (Knopf, 1987).

Kim Elizabeth   P&W
PO Box 120036, Staten Island, NY 10312-0036,
718-317-6110
    Pubs: *Netherworld* (Ghost Girl Graphix, 1995), *Darkworld
    Vampires* (Millennium Pubs, 1995), *Dead of Night, The
    Tome, Haunted Sun, Ghastly, Scream in the Dark.*

Kate Ferguson Ellis   P
240 W 102 St, New York, NY 10025, 212-662-6232
    Pubs: *The Contested Castle* (U Illinois Pr, 1989), *Ms.,
    Feminist Studies, Chrysalis, Salamander, Telephone,
    Marxist Perspectives.*

Harlan Ellison   W
Richard Curtis Associates, Inc, 171 E 74 St, New York, NY
10021
    Pubs: *Slippage* (HM, 1997), *Edgeworks 3 and 4,
    Edgeworks: Volume I* (White Wolf, 1997, 1996), *Mefisto In
    Onyx* (Mark V. Ziesing Bks, 1993), *Mag of Fantasy & Sci Fi,
    Buzz Mag, Variety, Playboy, Newsweek, Ohio Writer.*

Ralph Ellison   W
William Morris Agency, 1350 Ave of the Americas, New York,
NY 10019
    Pubs: *Going To The Territory, Shadow & Act, Invisible Man*
    (Random Hse, 1986, 1963, 1952).

Patricia Elmore   W
41 W 82 St, New York, NY 10024
    Pubs: *Susannah & the Purple Mongoose Mystery* (Dutton,
    1992), *Susannah & the Blue House Mystery* (Scholastic
    Apple, 1990).

Barbara Elovic   P
586 Henry St, Brooklyn, NY 11231-2721, 718-834-0291
    Pubs: *Time Out* (Amity Street Pr, 1996), *Walk on the Wild
    Side: Anth* (Scribner, 1994), *Poetry, Pivot, Exquisite
    Corpse, Mss., Sonora Rev, Onthebus.*

W. R. Elton   P
City Univ New York, 33 W 42 St, Box 510, New York, NY
10036, 212-642-2206

Carol Emshwiller W
210 E 15 St, #12E, New York, NY 10003-3938, 212-982-5779
Pubs: *Leaping Man Hill, Ledoyt* (Mercury Hse, 1998, 1995), *Love Stories For the Rest Of Us: Anth, Pushcart Prize XXII: Anth* (Pushcart Pr, 1995, 1989), *Omni, TriQuarterly, Wild Women, Women of Wonder.*

Helen Engelhardt P
805 E 21 St, Brooklyn, NY 11210, 718-859-5440
Pubs: *Latitude 30'18', International Poetry Rev, Bitterroot, Dark Horse, Mixed Voices.*

Russell Epprecht W
Box 734, Stuyvesant Sta, New York, NY 10009, 212-254-1004
Pubs: *Yardstick, Further* (Domesday Bks, 1984, 1983), *Redtape, Homeless Catalogue.*

Elaine Epstein P
330 W 85 St, #1-G, New York, NY 10024, 212-877-7019
Pubs: *Georgia Rev, Missouri Rev, Pequod, Ploughshares, Virginia Qtly Rev.*

Seymour Epstein W
750 Kappock St #608, Bronx, NY 10463-4616, 212-796-0091
Pubs: *Light* (Henry Holt, 1989), *September Faces, A Special Destiny* (Donald I. Fine, 1987, 1986).

Elaine Equi P
298 Mulberry St, #3L, New York, NY 10012, 212-941-8724
Pubs: *Decoy, Surface Tension* (Coffee Hse Pr, 1994, 1989), *Conjunctions, APR, Sulfur, Chelsea, New American Writing, Caliban, Paris Rev.*

Nancy Watson Erikson P&W
West Side Arts Coalition, PO Box 527, Cathedral Sta, New York, NY 10025
Pubs: *Splinters of Fear* (Avon, 1960), *This Singing Earth: Anth* (Round Table, 1959), *Stories.*

John Eskow P
247 W 87 St, #23-F, New York, NY 10024, 212-662-5766

Sandra Maria Esteves PP&P
PO Box 351/Morris Heights Sta, Bronx, NY 10453, 718-733-8420
Pubs: *Bluestown Mockingbird Mambo* (Arte Publico Pr, 1990), *Hanging Loose, Hispanic Women Write.*

Eurydice P&W
c/o Gear, 450 W. 15 St., 5th Fl, New York, NY 10011, 212-771-7000
Pubs: *F/32: The Second Coming* (Virago Pr, 1993), *F/32* (Kasak Bks, 1993), *Barebreasted* (Greece; Fosti Edtns, 1980), *Iowa Rev, Black Ice, Cups, Texture, Open End, Spin, Gear, Harper's, George.*

Bill Evans P
99 East 4 St Apt 3F, New York, NY 10003, 212-982-5462
Pubs: *Elvis Monologues* (Heinemann Bks, 1998), *Puerto del Sol, Quarry West, Antioch Rev, Mudfish, Exquisite Corpse, Brooklyn Rev, Hoboken Terminal, Black And White.*

RobertOh Faber P
160 Claremont Ave, New York, NY 10027, 212-864-6151
Pubs: *New York Qtly, Light, Clown War, Poets, Kauri, Wormwood Rev, Daily World.*

Arnold E. Falleder P
160 W 87 St, #7B, New York, NY 10024-2951, 212-724-4712
Pubs: *William Said* (Generator Pr, 1996), *The God-Shed* (Runaway Spoon Pr, 1992), *Cover, The Poet, Christian Century, Onthebus, Stone Country, Purple, Rattle, Fiddlehead.*

Louis Falstein W
2571 Hubbard St, Brooklyn, NY 11235
Pubs: *Sole Survivor* (Dell, 1954), *Chicago Jewish Forum.*

Margot Farrington PP&P
118 N 9 St, Brooklyn, NY 112111915, 718-388-2184
Pubs: *Rising and Falling* (Warthog Pr, 1985), *Out of the Catskills & Just Beyond: Anth, Word Thursday Anth of Poetry & Fiction, Speaking The Words: Anth* (Bright Hill Pr, 1997, 1995, 1994), *California Qtly, Phoebe, American Literary Rev, Permafrost.*

John Farris P&W
The Living Theatre, PO Box 20180, Tompkins Sq Sta, New York, NY 10009, 212-979-0601
Pubs: *Between C & D: Anth* (Penguin, 1988), *Peasensible, Parkett, Spin, Contact II, Tribes.*

Irvin Faust W
417 Riverside Dr, New York, NY 100257928, 212-864-5410
Pubs: *Jim Dandy* (Carroll & Graf, 1994), *Contemporary Atlantic: Anth* (Atlantic Monthly, 1988), *Michigan Qtly Rev, Esquire, Fiction, Confrontation, O. Henry Prize Stories 1986, Literary Rev, Four Quarters.*

Naomi F. Faust P
112-01 175 St, Jamaica, NY 11433-4135, 718-291-5338
Pubs: *And I Travel by Rhythms and Words, All Beautiful Things* (Lotus Pr, 1990, 1983).

Susan C. Fawcett P
67 Riverside Dr, #9B, New York, NY 10024
Pubs: *Abandoned House* (Silver Apples Pr, 1988), *Michigan Qtly Rev, Nation, Montana Rev, Nimrod.*

Cheri Fein P&W
8 Stuyvesant Oval, #8F, New York, NY 10009, 212-995-5486
Pubs: *Home Before Light* (Ridgeway Pr, 1991), *Pequod, Bomb, Ploughshares, Partisan Rev, Nimrod, Between C&D.*

Frederick Feirstein   P
575 Madison Ave, New York, NY 10028
    Pubs: *New and Selected Poems, City Life* (Story Line, 1998, 1991), *Ending the 20th Century, Family History* (QRL, 1994, 1991).

Annette B. Feldmann   P
Shelley Society of New York, 77-07 138th St, #2F, Flushing, NY 11367, 718-969-7010
    Pubs: *The Carousel* (Diamond Hitch Pr, 1992), *The Scarab Beetle Speaks* (Iota Pr, 1993), *New Rev, Hellas, Mew Pr, Poetry Digest.*

Daniel Fernandez   P
119 Payson Ave #3E, New York, NY 10034
    Pubs: *Apples From Hesperides* (Pegasus Pubs, 1971), *International Poetry Rev, The Lyric, Plains Poetry Jrnl, Christian Century, New Laurel Rev.*

Jean Fiedler   W
69-23 Bell Blvd, Bayside, NY 11364 2532
    Pubs: *When A Sparrow Falls, Sisters in Crime: Anth* (Berkley, 1992, 1991), *The Year The World Was Out of Step With Jancy Fried* (HBJ, 1981).

Edward Field   P
463 West St, #A-323, New York, NY 10014
    Pubs: *Counting Myself Lucky, Selected Poems 1963-1992* (Black Sparrow Pr, 1992), *APR, Exquisite Corpse.*

Jennie Fields   W
452 8th St, Brooklyn, NY 11215, 718-965-9335
    Pubs: *Crossing Brooklyn Ferry* (Morrow, 1996), *Lily Beach* (Warner, 1994).

Elliot Figman   P
484 13th St, 2nd Fl., Brooklyn, NY 11215
    Pubs: *Poetry, Ironwood, Choice, Pequod, Lips, Confrontation.*

Jose-Angel Figueroa   P
258 Nassau Ave, Brooklyn, NY 11222, 718-383-5564
    Pubs: *Hypocrisy Held Hostage* (Noo Jork Pub, 1987), *La Patria* (Arts Partners, 1984), *Nuestro.*

Marlene Rosen Fine   P
490 W End Ave, #7E, New York, NY 10024, 212-874-6671
    Pubs: *Clouds Fire The Smell Of Wood* (Author, 1981), *Ordinary Women Anth* (Common Differences Pr, 1985), *Modern Bride, Helen Rev, Atlantic, Connections.*

Miriam Finkelstein   W
680 W End Ave, New York, NY 10025, 212-866-9936
    Pubs: *Domestic Affairs* (Houghton Mifflin, 1982), *Ascent, Arizona Qtly, Commonweal, Hanging Loose, Kalliope, Atlanta Rev, Kayak, Letters.*

Cheryl Fish   P&W
40 Harrison St #23D, New York, NY 100132726, 212-227-6008
Internet: cfj@pipeline.com
    Pubs: *My City Flies By* (e.g. Pr, 1986), *African-American Travel Writing: Anth* (Beacon Pr, 1998), *Ladies, Start Your Engines: Anth* (Faber & Faber, 1998), *NAW, Long News, Response, Poetry New York, Talisman, Santa Monica Rev, Between C&D, B City.*

Sally Fisher   P
98 Riverside Dr, #16C, New York, NY 10024, 212-580-8051
    Pubs: *Field, Chelsea, Poetry East, New Directions, Tar River Poetry, The Sun.*

Jack Flam   W
Georges Borchardt Inc., 136 E 57 St, New York, NY 10022, 212-753-5785
    Pubs: *Bread & Butter* (Viking, 1977), *Zoltan Gorency* (Hodder & Stoughton, 1974).

Bernice Fleisher   P
350 1st Ave, #4C, New York, NY 10010
    Pubs: *Poet Dreaming In Artist's House: Anth* (Milkweed Edtns, 1988), *East West: A Poetry Annual, Nostalgia, Leading Edge, Nimrod, Jam Today, Love Lyrics, Voices For Peace.*

Eugene C. Flinn   W
Stewart H. Benedict Literary A, 27 Washington Sq N, New York, NY 10011-9165, 212-228-1440
    Pubs: *Strictly Fiction II: Anth* (Potpourri Pubs, 1995), *Best of Spitball: Anth* (Pocket Bks, 1988), *Thalia* (Ottawa), *Lynx Eye, Eclectic Literary Forum, Monocacy Valley Rev, Thin Ice, Small Pond Mag.*

George Flynn   P
303 West 66 St., Apt 8CE, New York, NY 10023, 212-496-7658
    Pubs: *Zingers* (Letter Pr, 1978), *Kansas Qtly, Wisconsin Rev, Folio, Florida Qtly.*

Helen Fogarassy   W
58 W 36 St, #2A, New York, NY 10018, 212-947-6913
    Pubs: *Mix Bender* (Quality Pub, 1987), *Queen's Qtly, Our Town, Greenfeather, Gypsy, Sidewinder, Mildred, Home Planet News, Innisfree, Echoes, Nostalgia.*

Dorothy Swartz Foley   P
81-48 169th St, Jamaica, NY 11432, 718-380-4134
    Pubs: *Bitterroot, Orphic Lute, Artist's Mag, Saturday Evening Post.*

Montserrat Fontes   W
W.W. Norton, 500 5th Ave., New York, NY 10110, 800-223-2584
    Pubs: *Dreams of The Centaur, First Confession* (Norton, 1996, 1991), *High Contrast* (Naiad Pr, 1987), *Westways.*

Charles Henri Ford   P
1 W 72 St, #103, New York, NY 10023
>Pubs: *Water From A Bucket, I Will Be What I Am* (U Southern Illinois Pr, 1993, 1992), *Out of the Labyrinth: Selected Poems* (City Lights, 1986), *Arshile.*

Richard Ford   W
ICM, 40 W 57 St, New York, NY 10019, 212-556-5600
>Pubs: *Women With Men Stories, Independence Day* (Knopf, 1997, 1995), *New Yorker, Esquire, Harper's, Granta.*

Elizabeth Fox   P&W
61 Eastern Pkwy #3-C, Brooklyn, NY 11238, 718-789-3640
>Pubs: *Limousine Kids on the Ground* (Rocky Ledge Cottage Edtns, 1983), *Asylum Annual 1994: Anth* (Asylum Arts Pub, 1994), *The World, Transfer, Bombay Gin, Sugar Mule.*

Geoffrey Fox   W
14 E 4 St, #812, New York, NY 10012, 212-505-1553
>Pubs: *Welcome to My Contri* (Lintel, 1988), *Yellow Silk Erotic Arts & Letters: Anth* (Harmony Bks, 1990), *Fiction Intl, Yellow Silk, Central Park.*

Paula Fox   W
67 Irving Pl, New York, NY 10003, 212-529-1790
>Pubs: *The Eagle Kite, Western Wind, Monkey Island, The Village by the Sea* (Orchard Bks, 1995, 1993, 1991, 1988), *The God of Nightmares* (North Point Pr, 1990).

Patricia Weaver Francisco   W
Ellen Levine Literary Agency, 15 E 26 St, Ste 1801, New York, NY 10010
>Pubs: *Telling* (HC, 1999), *Village Without Mirrors* (Milkweed Edtns, 1989), *Cold Feet* (S&S, 1988).

Jeffrey Frank   W
235 W 71 St, #62, New York, NY 10023-3737
>Pubs: *The Creep* (FSG, 1969).

J. E. Franklin   P
PO Box 517, New York, NY 10031-0517, 212-926-5974
>Pubs: *Black Girl from Genesis—Revelations* (Howard U, 1977), *Voices of Color: Anth* (Applause Bks, 1992), *Black Short Story Anth* (NAL, 1972), *Black Scholar.*

Jonathan Franzen   W
35 E 9 St, #90, New York, NY 10003, 212-505-7330
>Pubs: *Strong Motion, The Twenty-Seventh City* (FSG, 1992, 1988), *Fiction Intl, Grand Street, Icarus.*

Lynn Freed   W
Virginia Barber Literary Agenc, 101 5th Ave, New York, NY 10003, 212-255-6515
>Pubs: *The Mirror* (Crown, 1997), *The Bungalow, Home Ground* (S&S, 1993, 1986), *Heart Change* (NAL, 1982), *New Yorker, Atlantic Monthly, Elle, Southwest Rev, Harper's, Mirabella, Vogue.*

Mathias B. Freese   W
9050 Union Turnpike, #1M, Glendale, NY 11385, 718-805-2420
Internet: www.vkinetic.com/freese
>Pubs: *Confessions of Two Twigs* (Brett Jordan Pub, 1996), *Pilgrimage, Skywriters, Voices, Global Stamp News.*

Joan French   P
427 E 73 St, New York, NY 10021, 212-840-1234
>Pubs: *Voices Intl, Green's Mag, Intrepid, Modularist Rev, Lake Superior Rev.*

Philip Fried   P
440 Riverside Dr, #45, New York, NY 10027, 212-932-1854
>Pubs: *Quantum Genesis* (Zohar Pr, 1997), *Mutual Trespasses* (Ion, 1988), *Acquainted With the Night: Anth* (Rizzoli, 1997), *Partisan, Paris Rev, Massachusetts Rev, Beloit, Maryland Poetry Rev, Cream City Rev.*

Stephen William Fried   P&W
14 Park Pl, #2, Brooklyn, NY 11217-3208, 718-783-0484
>Pubs: *Going Through Doors* (Lunar Offensive Pr, 1993), *Toilet Anth* (Academic Arts Pr, 1994), *Curare, Shockbox, Xib, Rant, Black Buzzard, Drive-By Poets.*

Dorothy Friedman   P
582 E 2nd St, Brooklyn, NY 11218, 718-633-1503
>Pubs: *Family Album, The Liberty Years* (Rio Edtns, 1989, 1987), *Partisan Rev, California Qtly, Kayak, Ms..*

Ed Friedman   P
520 E 14 St, #36, New York, NY 10009, 212-673-9067
>Pubs: *Mao & Matisse* (Hanging Loose Pr, 1995), *Humans Work* (Helpful Bks, 1988), *The World, New American Writing, Shiny, Hanging Loose, Exquisite Corpse.*

Ken Friedman   P&W
PO Box 691, Canal St Sta, New York, NY 10013, 212-226-4614
>Pubs: *Special Ken Friedman Issue, North Mag, White Walls, Texts.*

Nancy Bengis Friedman   P
551 4th St #2, Brooklyn, NY 11215, 718-499-8383
>Pubs: *Fine China: Anth* (Earth's Daughters, 1993), *The Tie that Binds: Anth* (Papier-Mache Pr, 1992), *Natl Poetry Mag of the Lower East Side, Lips, New Pr, Eleven.*

Norman Friedman   P
33-54 164 St, Flushing, NY 11358-1442, 718-353-3631
>Pubs: *The Magic Badge: Poems 1953-1984* (Slough Pr, 1984), *Intl Poetry Rev, Centennial Rev, Beloit, New Mexico Qtly, New Voices, Georgia Rev, Nation, Texas Qtly.*

Sanford Friedman   W
37 W 12 St, #10F, New York, NY 10011
>Pubs: *Rip Van Winkle* (Atheneum, 1980), *Still Life, A Haunted Woman, Totempole* (Dutton, 1975, 1968, 1965).

Celestine Frost P
Box 6877, Yorkville Sta, New York, NY 10128, 212-722-0446
Pubs: *I Gathered My Ear From the Green Field*
(Logo-Daedalus, 1996), *An Imagined Experience Over the Entrance* (Dusty Dog, 1993), *Camellia, Epoch.*

Abby Frucht W
Gelfman, Schneider Literary Ag, 250 W 57 St, New York, NY 10107, 212-245-1993
Pubs: *Life Before Death* (Scribner, 1997), *Are You Mine?* (Grove Pr, 1993), *Licorice* (Graywolf, 1990), *Snap* (Ticknor & Fields, 1987), *Fruit of the Month* (U Iowa Pr, 1987).

Lewis Burke Frumkes W
Marymount Manhattan College, 221 East 71 St, New York, NY 10021, 212-734-3073
Pubs: *The Logophile's Orgy* (Delacorte, 1995), *Metapunctuation* (Dell, 1993), *How to Raise Your IQ By Eating Gifted Children* (McGraw-Hill, 1983), *Harper's, Punch, The Writer, New York Times, Reader's Digest.*

Peter Fusco P
58 Stratford Rd, Brooklyn, NY 11218-2704
Pubs: *Electric Messiah Anth* (Iota Pr, 1993), *Kiosk, Brooklyn Rev, Home Planet News, Light, Through The Cracks.*

Daniel Gabriel P
211 6th Ave #3A, Brooklyn, NY 112151220, 718-857-5669
Pubs: *Columbus* (Spuyten Duyvil, 1996), *Sacco & Vanzetti* (Gull Bks, 1983), *Poetry New York, Home Planet News, APR, City, Gnosis.*

William Gaddis W
Donadio & Ashworth, Inc., 121 W 27 St, Ste 704, New York, NY 10001, 212-691-8077
Pubs: *Carpenter's Gothic* (Viking, 1985), *JR* (Knopf, 1975), *The Recognitions* (Avon, 1955).

Roger Gaess P
47 Jane St, #16, New York, NY 10014, 212-691-8352
Pubs: *Leaving The Bough* (International, 1982).

Jonathan Galassi P
Farrar, Straus & Giroux, 19 Union Sq W, New York, NY 10003, 212-741-6900
Pubs: *Morning Run* (Paris Rev Edtns, 1988).

Tess Gallagher P&W
ICM, 40 W 57 St, New York, NY 10019, 212-556-5600
Pubs: *At the Owl Woman Saloon* (Scribner, 1997), *Portable Kisses, My Black Horse* (Bloodaxe Pr, 1996, 1995), *Portable Kisses Expanded* (Capra Pr, 1994), *Zyzzyva, Glimmer Train, Sycamore Rev, Ploughshares, Indiana Rev, Atlantic Monthly, APR, Michigan Qtly Rev.*

Mavis Gallant W
Georges Borchardt Inc., 136 E 57 St, New York, NY 10022, 212-753-5785

Kenneth Gangemi P&W
211 E 5 St, New York, NY 10003, 212-777-4795
Pubs: *The Volcanoes From Puebla, Olt, The Interceptor Pilot* (Marion Boyars, 1989, 1984, 1982).

Suzanne Gardinier P&W
110 W 96 St, #8C, New York, NY 10025-6474
Pubs: *A World That Will Hold All the People* (U Michigan Pr, 1996), *The New World* (U Pitt Pr, 1993), *USAHN: Ten Poems & A Story* (Grand Street Bks, 1990), *Best American Poetry: Anth* (Scribner, 1990).

Nancy Bruff Gardner P&W
200 E 66 St, #D803, New York, NY 10021, 212-752-8774
Pubs: *The Mist Maiden* (Dell, 1975), *My Talon In Your Heart* (Dutton, 1946).

Johanna Garfield W
200 E 94 St, #1517, New York, NY 10128, 212-996-2568
Internet: jogarfield@aol.com
Pubs: *Cousins* (Donald I. Fine, 1990), *The Life of a Real Girl* (St. Martin's Pr, 1986), *Ms., Reader's Digest, McCall's, Art and Antiques, Paris Rev, American Art.*

Leslie Garrett W
Loretta Barrett Literary Agenc, 121 W 27 St, Ste 601, New York, NY 10001
Pubs: *In the Country of Desire* (HarperCollins, 1992), *Crescent Rev, Confrontation, The Phoenix.*

Lisa Garrison P
213 Berkeley Pl, Ground Fl, Brooklyn, NY 11217-3801

Peggy Garrison P&W
74 E 7 St, New York, NY 100038417, 212-533-1996
Pubs: *Charing Cross Bridge* (P&Q Pr, 1998), *Beloit Fiction, South Dakota Rev, Poetry Now, The Smith, Ball State U Forum, Images, Literary Rev, Slant, Global City Rev, Mudfish.*

Ellen Gruber Garvey P&W
202 St. Marks Ave, #3, Brooklyn, NY 11238
Internet: garvey@panix.com
Pubs: *Speaking for Ourselves: Anth* (Crossing Pr, 1990), *The Tribe of Dina: Anth* (Beacon Pr, 1989), *Minnesota Rev, Feminist Studies, Paragraph, Sinister Wisdom, Conditions, Bridges.*

Serge Gavronsky P
525 W End Ave, #12H, New York, NY 10024, 212-787-7068
Internet: sgavronsky@barnard.columbia.edu
Pubs: *Talisman, Lingo, Bitter Oleander, Action Poetique, Interstice, Raddle Moon, Pequod, Nioques.*

Joan Austin Geier P
3991 48th St, Sunnyside Garden, NY 111041021,
718-899-5919
Internet: jag3634@aol.com
  Pubs: *A Formal Feeling Comes* (Story Line Pr, 1994),
  Mother of Tribes (Four Circles Pr, 1987), *The Lyric,
  Potomac Rev, New Rev, U Portland Rev, Northern Spirit,
  Amelia, Negative Capability, Visions, Poets On.*

Barrie Gellis P
43-06 159th St, #D-2, Flushing, NY 11358, 718-961-3521
  Pubs: *We Speak For Peace: Anth* (KIT Inc., 1993), *Forum,
  Pandemonium, Athena, Long Shot, Yellow Silk,
  Inside-Outside, Poets on Photography, Genesis.*

Sally George W
715 Carroll St, Brooklyn, NY 11215, 718-789-0360
  Pubs: *Frog Salad* (Scribner, 1981), *Ms., Redbook, NAR,
  Conditions, Heresies, Massachusetts Rev.*

Corinne Gerson W
101 W 12 St, #2N, New York, NY 10011
  Pubs: *Cyberdog* (Royal Fireworks Pr, 1998), *Rendez-Vous
  Au Zoo* (Rageout-Editeur, 1992), *My Grandfather The Spy*
  (Walker, 1990).

Peter Gethers W
Villard Books, 201 E 50 St, New York, NY 10022
  Pubs: *The Cat Who Went to Paris* (Crown, 1991), *Getting
  Blue, Rotisserie League Baseball* (Dell, 1989, 1989).

Andrew Gettler P
2663 Heath Ave #6D, Bronx, NY 10463-7520, 718-884-1316
  Pubs: *A Condition, Not An Event* (New Spirit Pr, 1992),
  Footsteps Of A Ghost (Iniquity Pr, 1991), *Boston Literary
  Rev, Excursus, Confrontation, Santa Clara Rev.*

P. J. Gibson PP
400 W 43 St, #14L, New York, NY 10036

Ilsa Gilbert P
203 Bleecker St, #O-9, New York, NY 100121456,
212-254-5289
  Pubs: *The Poet of Bleecker Street II* (Downtown Music
  Prod, 1994), *Survivors & Other New York Poems* (Bard Pr,
  1991), *Poet Lore, Quartet, Waterways, Landscapes, St.
  Clements Qtly, Voices, New Press.*

Frank D. Gilroy W
1325 Avenue of the Americas, New York, NY 10019,
213-586-5100
  Pubs: *I Wake Up Screening* (Southern Illinois U Pr, 1973),
  Private (HB, 1970).

Estelle Gilson W
7 Sigma Pl, Bronx, NY 10471, 718-549-3979
  Pubs: *Present Tense, Midstream, Moment, Columbia,
  Salome, The New Renaissance, Quarto, Other Voices,
  Wind, Congress Monthly.*

Saul B. Gilson P
7 Sigma Pl, Bronx, NY 10421, 718-601-3105
  Pubs: *Basilisic* (Cross Cultural Literary Edtns, 1996), *New
  Renaissance, Annals of Internal Medicine.*

John Giorno PP&P
222 Bowery, New York, NY 10012, 212-925-6372
Internet: http://www.giornopoetry.org
  Pubs: *You Got To Burn To Shine* (Serpent's Tail, 1994),
  Grasping At Emptiness (Kulchur Fdn, 1985), *Shit, Piss,
  Blood, Pus* (Painted Bride, 1978).

Nikki Giovanni P
William Morrow & Co., 105 Madison Ave, New York, NY
10016

Todd Gitlin P
Dept of Culture & Communicatio, 239 Greene St, Rm 735,
New York, NY 10003, 212-998-5820
Internet: todd.gitlin@nyu.edu
  Pubs: *Sacrifice* (Metropolitan/Holt, 1999), *The Murder of
  Albert Einstein* (Bantam, 1994), *Los Angeles Times, New
  York Observer, Nation, Chicago Tribune, Civilization,
  Dissent.*

Eleanor Glaze W
Ellen Levine Literary Agency, 15 E 26 St, Ste 1801, New
York, NY 10010, 212-889-0620
  Pubs: *Jaiyavara* (Peachtree, 1988), *Homeworks* (U
  Tennessee Pr, 1986), *Atlantic, New Yorker, Redbook, The
  Sun.*

Judith Gleason W
26 E 91 St #6B, New York, NY 10128, 212-534-2019
  Pubs: *Oya: In Praise of the Goddess* (Shambhala, 1987),
  Leaf And Bone (Viking, 1980).

Karen Glenn W
301 E 66 St, #15H, New York, NY 10021, 212-249-7198
Internet: prahu@aol.com
  Pubs: *Some Kind of Hero* (Viking, 1997), *Greenfield Rev,
  Slur, Foothills Qtly, Denver Qtly, Dekalb Literary Arts Jrnl,
  Scholastic Scope.*

Adele Glimm W
120 E 81 St #16E, New York, NY 10028-1423
  Pubs: *Epoch, Redbook, Cosmopolitan, McCall's, Southern
  Humanities Rev, Good Housekeeping, Ellery Queen's
  Mystery Mag.*

Tony Gloeggler P
83-45 116 St, #2B, Richmond Hill, NY 11418, 718-441-8195
  Pubs: *Full Court: A Literary Anthology of Basketball*
  (Breakaway Bks, 1996), *The Ledge, Graffiti Rag, New York
  Qtly, Chiron Rev, Rain City Rev, Rhino, Manhattan Poetry,
  Black Bear Rev, Urbanus, The Bridge, Mudfish, Yellow Silk,
  Turnstile.*

Tereze Gluck   W
333 E 69 St #4J, New York, NY 10021, 212-535-5417
   Pubs: *Chelsea, Antioch Rev, Malahat Rev, Ascent, Epoch,
   Fiction, Alaska Qtly, Threepenny Rev, Story, Columbia.*

John Godfrey   P
437 E 12 St, #32, New York, NY 10009, 212-475-6532
   Pubs: *Dabble: Poems 1966-1980* (Full Court Pr, 1982),
   From the Other Side of the Century: Anth (Sun & Moon Pr,
   1994), *Lingo, Poetry New York, World, o.blek.*

Ulf Goebel   P&W
25 W 87 St, #5F, New York, NY 10024, 212-724-3722
   Pubs: *After Caligula* (Ulf Goebel, 1981), *Webster Rev,
   Cumberland Poetry Rev, Agni, Aspect.*

Ivan Gold   W
Mary Yost Associates, 59 E 54 St, New York, NY 10022,
212-980-4988
   Pubs: *Sams In A Dry Season, Nickel Miseries, Sick Friends*
   (Washington Square Pr, 1992, 1992, 1992).

Gerald Jay Goldberg   W
Georges Borchardt Inc., 136 E 57 St, New York, NY 10022,
212-753-5785
   Pubs: *Heart Payments* (Viking, 1982), *The Lynching Of
   Orin Newfield* (Dial, 1970).

Isaac Goldemberg   P&W
4555 Henry Hudson Pkwy, #703, Bronx, NY 10471-3844
   Pubs: *La Vida al Contado* (Ediciones Del Norte, 1992), *Play
   By Play* (Persea Bks, 1985).

Mike Golden   P&W
Black Market Press, 400 W 43 St, Ste 37K, New York, NY
10036
   Pubs: *The Buddhist 3rd Class Junk Mail Oracle* (Seven
   Stories Pr, 1998), *Crimes of the Beats, Unbearables: Anth*
   (Autonomedia, 1998, 1995), *Oxford American, Vibe,
   Creative Screenwriting, Curio, Pink Pages, Paris Rev, Beet,
   Exquisite Corpse.*

Alan Goldfein   W
William Morrow/James Landis, 105 Madison Ave, New York,
NY 10016, 212-889-3050

Lloyd Goldman   P
448 2nd St, Brooklyn, NY 11215-2503

Michael Goldman   P
425 Riverside Dr, New York, NY 10025

William Goldman   W
Ballantine Books, 201 E 50 St, New York, NY 10022
   Pubs: *Control, Tinsel* (Delacorte, 1982, 1979), *The Princess
   Bride* (Ballantine, 1977).

Barbara Goldsmith   W
Janklow & Nesbit Associates, 1021 Park Ave, New York, NY
10028, 212-534-3637
   Pubs: *The Straw Man* (FSG, 1975), *Vanity Fair, New
   Yorker, New York Times.*

Frederica Goldsmith   P&W
83-30 98th St, #3M, Woodhaven, NY 11421, 718-846-8821
   Pubs: *Short Story Intl, Spectrum, Kaleidoscope,
   Mainstream.*

Howard Goldsmith   W
41-07 Bowne St, #6B, Flushing, NY 11355-5629,
718-886-5819
   Pubs: *Science Through Stories* (McGraw-Hill, 1998), *The
   Twiddle Twins' Music Box Mystery, The Twiddle Twins'
   Haunted House* (Mondo Pub, 1997, 1996), *Short Story Intl,
   London Mystery, Disney Adventures, Scholastic.*

Jeanette Erlbaum Goldsmith   W
1483 E 34 St, Brooklyn, NY 11234, 718-253-3484
   Pubs: *Confrontation* (Long Island U, 1987), *Each In Her Own
   Way* (Queen of Swords Pr, 1994), *Hawaii Rev, Antioch Rev,
   Commentary, Malahat Rev, Mid-American Rev.*

Jewelle Gomez   P&W
Michele Karlsberg Publicity, 47 Dongan Hills Ave, Staten
Island, NY 10306, 718-980-4262
   Pubs: *Don't Explain, Oral Tradition, The Gilda Stories*
   (Firebrand Bks, 1998, 1996, 1991), *Essence, Ms., Black
   Scholar, Advocate, Quarterly Black Rev, Zyzzyva, Curve.*

Brad Gooch   P
The Lantz-Harris Literary Agen, 156 5th Ave, Ste 617, New
York, NY 10010, 212-924-6269
   Pubs: *Scary Kisses* (Putnam, 1988), *Jailbait & Other
   Stories* (Sea Horse Pr, 1984), *Paris Rev, Partisan Rev,
   Bomb, Between C&D, Shiny, Christopher Street.*

Melinda Goodman   P
45 E 1 St, #4, New York, NY 10003
   Pubs: *Middle Sister* (MSG Pr, 1988), *My Lover is a Woman:
   Anth* (Ballantine Bks, 1996), *The Arch of Love: Lesbian
   Love Poems: Anth* (Scribner, 1996), *Sinister Wisdom,
   Conditions, Heresies.*

Coco Gordon   P
138 Duane St, #5SW, New York, NY 10013-3854,
212-285-1609
Internet: cocogor@ibm.net
   Pubs: *Tikysk: Permaculture Getting To Know You* (Foot
   Square Space, 1997), *Superskywoman* (Leonardi V-Idea,
   1995), *DOA: Woman and Nature* (BMCC, 1994), *Pig Iron,
   Infolio, New Observations, Aquaterra, Eternal Network,
   Permafrost, Black River Rev, Poetry Motel.*

Fred Gordon   W
35 Carriage Rd, Great Neck, NY 11024
   Pubs: *Benjamin Grabbed His Glicken And Ran* (H&R, 1971).

Mary Gordon W
Sterling Lord Literistic, 65 Bleecker St, New York, NY 10012,
212-780-6050
Pubs: *Spending* (Scribner, 1998), *Men & Angels, The
Company of Women, Final Payments* (Random Hse, 1985,
1981, 1978).

hattie gossett P&W
775 Riverside Dr, #6J, New York, NY 10032
Pubs: *presenting . . . sister noblues* (Firebrand Bks, 1988),
Seeing Jazz: Anth (Smithsonian/Chronicle Bks, 1998),
*Conditions, Heresies, Sinister Wisdom, Essence,
Womanews, Between Ourselves, Playbill.*

Amy Gottlieb W
2465 Palisade Ave, Riverdale, NY 10463, 2126-678-8049
Internet: rapubs@jtsa.edu
Pubs: *Midstream, Other Voices, Puerto del Sol.*

Darcy Gottlieb P
67 Orchard Beach Blvd, Port Washington, NY 11050-1427
Pubs: *Matters Of Contention* (Aesopus, 1979), *No Witness
But Ourselves* (U Missouri Pr, 1973), *Beyond Lament: Anth*
(Northwestern U Pr, 1998), *For Neruda, for Chile: Anth*
(Beacon Pr Bks, 1975).

Lois Gould W
ICM, 40 W 57 St, New York, NY 10019, 212-556-5600
Pubs: *A Sea-Change* (S&S, 1976).

Roberta Gould P
315 E 18 St, #4R, New York, NY 10003, 212-982-6818
Pubs: *Three Windows* (Reservoir Pr, 1997), *Live Show*
(Salowqa Pr, 1994), *Not by Blood Alone* (Editores
Lince/Waterside Pr, 1990), *Only Rock & Other Poems*
(Folder Edtns, 1985), *Confrontation, Green Mountains Rev,
Downtown, Architrave, Village Voice.*

Pascale Gousseland P
Poet Tree, 6234 138th Street #6F, Kew Gardens, NY 11435,
212-472-6881
Pubs: *Second Glance, Medicinal Purpos, Poems that Thump
in the Dark, Nomad's Choir, Albatross, Thirteen, New Press.*

Ignatius Graffeo P
82-34 138th St, #6F, Kew Gardens, NY 11435, 718-847-1482
Internet: newspirit@gnn.com
Pubs: *She Came With the Magazine, Xanthus* (New Spirit
Pr, 1995, 1993), *We Speak For Peace: Anth* (Kit Pubs,
1994), *Poetry Digest, Maryland Poetry Rev.*

James Graham P
PO Box 605, Cooper Square Stat, New York, NY 10276
Internet: jasgraham@juno.com
Pubs: *Search Engine: Difficult Path, One Skin* (Machete,
1998, 1994), *Small Hours of the Night* (Curbstone Pr,
1996), *Found Body* (Soncino Bks, 1993), *Hungry Mind Rev,
Rev: Latin America, Nexus, Cover, Machete, The Sun,
Nexus, Harper's.*

Shirley Ann Grau W
JCA, 27 W 20 St, New York, NY 10011, 212-807-0888
Pubs: *The Black Prince, The Roadwalkers, The Keepers of
the House* (Knopf, 1996, 1994, 1965).

Elizabeth Graver W
The Richard Parks Agency, 138 East 16 Street, New York,
NY 10003, 212-228-1786
Internet: graver@bc.edu
Pubs: *Unravelling* (Hyperion, 1997), *Have You Seen Me?*
(Ecco Pr, 1993), *O. Henry Prize Stories: Anths* (Anchor,
1996, 1994), *Best American Essays, Best American Short
Stories, Tikkun, Boulevard, Story.*

Dorothy Randall Gray P&W
328 Flatbush Ave, Ste 148, Brooklyn, NY 11238,
718-638-6415
Internet: http://www.heartland.drg
Pubs: *Soul Between The Lines* (Avon Bks, 1998), *Woman,
A Taste of Tamarindo, The Passion Collective, Muse Blues*
(Polaris Pr, 1996, 1994, 1991, 1990), *Frontiers, Binnewater
Tides.*

Francine du Plessix Gray W
Georges Borchardt Inc., 136 E 57 St, New York, NY 10022,
212-753-5785
Pubs: *Adam & Eve and the City, October Blood* (S&S,
1987, 1985), *New Yorker, Yale Rev, Harper's.*

Mayo L. Gray W
15 W 72 St #8T, New York, NY 10023, 212-362-5991
Pubs: *The Savage Season* (Fawcett, 1978), *Washington
Times, The Poet Anth, Scimitar & Song.*

Richard Grayson W
Linda Konner Literary Agency, 10 W 15 St., Ste 1918, New
York, NY 100116829, 212-691-3419
Internet: graysonric@aol.com
Pubs: *I Survived Caracas Traffic* (Avisson Pr, 1996), *I
Brake for Delmore Schwartz* (Zephyr, 1983).

Stephen Greco P
134 Henry St, Brooklyn, NY 11201, 718-855-8759
Pubs: *Penguin Book of Gay Short Stories: Anth*
(Viking/Penguin, 1994), *Flesh and the Word: Anth* (Dutton,
1992), *Interview, 7 Days, Harper's Bazaar.*

Hannah Green W
52 Barrow St, New York, NY 10014, 212-243-3070

Harry Greenberg P
321 W 94 St, #6-NE, New York, NY 10025, 212-866-3242
Pubs: *Handbook of Poetic Forms: Anth, The Point: Anth*
(Teachers & Writers, 1987, 1983), *Agni.*

Joanne Greenberg   W
177 East 70 St, New York, NY 10021, 212-570-9090
  Pubs: *Literature: Anth* (Prentice Hall, 1998), *High Fantastic: Anth* (Ocean View Bks, 1995), *No Reck'ning Made, In This Sign* (Henry Holt, 1993, 1970), *Hadassah, Hudson Rev, Redbook, Denver Qtly.*

Henry L. Greene   P
58-27 212th St, Bayside, NY 11364, 718-224-5007
  Pubs: *Modern Images, A Different Drummer, Spoon River Qtly.*

Sally Greenhouse   PP
167 Ludlow St, New York, NY 10002-1520, 212-420-1466
  Pubs: *BACA Downtown, Home for Contemporary Theatre & Art, Dixon Place.*

Ted Greenwald   P
206 E 17 St, #4-D, New York, NY 10003, 212-673-7156
  Pubs: *Word of Mouth* (Sun & Moon, 1986), *Exit the Face* (w/R. Bosman; MOMA, 1982).

Arthur Gregor   P
250 W 94 St, #6J, New York, NY 10025, 212-666-5031
  Pubs: *The River Serpent, Secret Citizen* (Sheep Meadow Pr, 1995, 1989), *Boulevard, Ploughshares, Nation, Hudson Rev.*

Carole Gregory   P
800 Grand Concourse, #6BS, Bronx, NY 10451,
212-665-3464

Kathleen C. Griffin   P
Pace Univ, 41 Park Row, Rm 415, New York, NY 10038,
212-346-1338
  Pubs: *Newsletter, Waterways, Home Planet News.*

Tom Grimes   W
c/o Henry Dunow Literary Agenc, 22 W 23 St., 5th Fl, New York, NY 10010, 212-645-7606
Internet: tg02@swt.edu
  Pubs: *A Stone of the Heart* (Southern Methodist U Pr, 1997), *City of God* (Picador, 1996), *Season's End* (Bison Bks, 1996).

Ronald Gross   P
17 Myrtle Dr, Great Neck, NY 11021, 516-487-0235

Brian J. Groth   P
139-40 Caney Ln, Jamaica, NY 11422, 718-528-1428
  Pubs: *San Fernando Jrnl, Weirdbook, Wide Open, Journal of Regional Criticism, Calliope's Corner.*

Doris Grumbach   W
Russell & Volkening, Inc., 50 W 29 St, New York, NY 10001,
212-684-6050
  Pubs: *The Presence of Absence, Life in a Day, Fifty Days of Solitude* (Beacon, 1998, 1996, 1994), *Extra Innings, Coming into the End Zone* (Norton, 1993, 1991).

Barbara Guest   P
49 W 16 St, New York, NY 10011
  Pubs: *Defensive Rapture, Fair Realism* (Sun & Moon Pr, 1993, 1989), *Conjunctions, Sulfur, New American Writing.*

Amy Guggenheim   PP
225 W 15 St, #14, New York, NY 10011
  Pubs: *Home Theatre For Contemporary Art & Performance, La Mama, Casa Del Lago, Cleveland Performance Open, Performance Mix/DIA Art Fdn, American Letters & Commentary.*

Joanna Gunderson   P
1148 5th Ave, #12B, New York, NY 10128, 212-348-4388
  Pubs: *The Field, Indrani & I, Sights: Three Novellas* (Red Dust, 1998, 1967, 1963), *Midland Rev, Rampike, How*(ever), *Frank, Northeast Jrnl.*

Allan Gurganus   W
ICM, 40 W 57 St, New York, NY 10019, 212-556-5600
  Pubs: *Plays Well With Others, White People, Oldest Living Confederate Widow Tells All* (Knopf, 1997, 1992, 1989), *New Yorker, Antaeus, Harper's, Granta, Atlantic, Yale Rev, Paris Rev.*

C. W. Gusewelle   W
Harvey Klinger, Inc, 301 W 53 St, New York, NY 10019
  Pubs: *The Rufus Chronicle: Another Autumn* (Ballantine Bks, 1998), *A Paris Notebook* (Lowell Pr, 1995), *Far From Any Coast: Pieces of America's Heartland* (U Missouri, 1989), *American Heritage, Antioch Rev, Virginia Qtly Rev, Audience, Harper's.*

Rosa Guy   W
Ellen Levine Literary Agency, 15 E 26 St, Ste 1801, New York, NY 10010, 212-889-0620
  Pubs: *The Sun, The Sea, A Touch Of The Wind* (Dutton, 1995) *The Ups and Downs of Carl Davis III, Paris, Pee Wee and Big Dog* (Delacorte, 1989, 1984), *My Love, My Love, or The Peasant Girl* (Holt, 1985).

Gabor G. Gyukics   P
PO Box 023061, Brooklyn, NY 11202, 718-365-3416
  Pubs: *Apache Qtly, Nexus, Northwoods Jrnl, Phati'tude, Medicinal Purposes, Poetry In Motion, Big Spoon, Rain City Rev, Corde.*

Charles Hackenberry   W
M. Evans & Co, Inc., 216 E 49 St, New York, NY 10017

Marilyn Hacker   P
230 W 105 St #10A, New York, NY 10025, 212-678-1074
  Pubs: *Winter Numbers, Selected Poems* (Norton, 1994, 1994), *Going Back to the River* (Random Hse, 1990), *Paris Rev, TriQuarterly, Prairie Schooner, American Voice.*

Pamela White Hadas   P
210 E 17 St, #3B, New York, NY 10003
  Pubs: *Beside Herself, Designing Women* (Knopf, 1983, 1979).

Rachel Hadas P
838 W End Ave, #3A, New York, NY 10025, 212-666-4482
Internet: rhadas@andromeda.rutgers.edu
Pubs: *The Double Legacy* (Faber & Faber, 1995), *The Empty Bed* (Wesleyan U Pr, 1995), *New Yorker, Threepenny Rev, Paris Rev, Yale Rev, New Republic.*

Jessica Hagedorn PP&W
Harold Schmidt Literary Agency, 343 W 12 St, #1B, New York, NY 10014, 212-727-7473
Pubs: *Dogeaters, Charlie Chan is Dead: Anth* (Penguin, 1991, 1993).

Hannelore Hahn P
PO Box 810, Gracie Sta, New York, NY 10028, 212-737-7536
Internet: dirhahn@aol.com
Pubs: *Places, On the Way to Feed the Swans* (Tenth Hse Enterprises, 1990, 1982), *To Jump Or Not Jump: Anth* (Traveler's Tales Guides, 1998), *Network.*

Kimiko Hahn P
421 3rd St #1, Brooklyn, NY 11215
Pubs: *The Unbearable Heart* (Kaya Pr, 1995), *Earshot, Air Pocket* (Hanging Loose, 1992, 1990), *Bomb, Manoa, American Voice, Ikon, River Styx, Mudfish, Tyuonyi.*

Isidore Haiblum W
160 W 77 St, New York, NY 10024
Pubs: *Crystalworld, Specterworld* (Avon, 1992, 1991), *Bad Neighbors* (St. Martin's, 1990), *Out of Sync* (Del Ray, 1990).

Jana Haimsohn PP
530 Canal St, #3-E, New York, NY 10013, 212-925-4071
Pubs: *Collective Consciousness: Art Performances in the 70's Anth* (Performing Arts Journal Pubs, 1981).

Victoria Hallerman P
65 Fort Hill Cir, Staten Island, NY 10301
Pubs: *The Woman in the Magic Show* (Firm Ground Pr, 1995), *Poetry, Nation, Southern Poetry Rev, Indiana Rev, Global City Rev.*

Nancy Hallinan W
276 Riverside Dr, #2D, New York, NY 10025, 212-222-6936
Pubs: *Sasakawa: Global Philanthropist* (Pergamon Pr, 1981), *Night Swimmers, Rough Winds of May* (H&R, 1976, 1955), *Voice From The Wings* (Knopf, 1965), *O. Henry Prize Stories Anth, Harper's, Cosmopolitan, Pulpsmith, American Vanguard, Cornhill, Touchstone.*

Mary Stewart Hammond P
1095 Park Ave, #4A, New York, NY 10128, 212-289-6264
Pubs: *Out of Canaan* (Norton, 1991), *Atlantic, APR, New Yorker, New Criterion, Paris Rev, Yale Rev.*

Peter Handke W
792 Columbus Ave, New York, NY 10025, 212-865-0409
Pubs: *Short Letter, Long Farewell* (FSG, 1974).

Jim Handlin P
Brooklyn Friends School, 375 Pearl St, Brooklyn, NY 11201, 718-852-1029
Pubs: *Editors' Choice III: Anth* (The Spirit That Moves Us Pr, 1992), *Bluestones & Salthay: Anth* (Rutgers 1990), *The Haiku Anth* (S&S, 1986).

William Hanley W
575 W End Ave, New York, NY 10024, 212-874-6885

Edward Hannibal W
601 E 20 St, #11D, New York, NY 10010
Pubs: *A Trace of Red* (Dial Pr, 1982), *Chocolate Days Popsicle Weeks* (Houghton Mifflin, 1970).

Rob Hardin P&W
PO Box 2214, Stuyvesant Sta, New York, NY 10009, 212-477-1066
Pubs: *Distorture* (BIB/FC2, 1997), *Forbidden Acts: Anth* (Avon, 1995), *Avant Pop: Anth* (Black Ice Bks, 1993), *Michigan Rev, Sensitive Skin.*

Nancy Harding W
Meredith Bernstein Literary Ag, 2112 Broadway, Ste 503A, New York, NY 10023, 212-799-1007
Pubs: *Wind Child, The Silver Land* (Pocket Bks, 1990, 1989).

Enid Harlow W
175 Riverside Dr, #12L, New York, NY 10024
Pubs: *Love's Shadow* (Crossing Pr, 1993), *American Fiction 4: Anth* (Birchlane Pr, 1993), *Mediphors, TriQuarterly.*

Curtis Harnack W
205 W 57 St, New York, NY 10019, 212-757-9235
Pubs: *The Attic: A Memoir, We Have All Gone Away* (Iowa State U Pr, 1993, 1987), *American Short Fiction, Confrontation, Nation.*

Joseph Harris P&W
Ann Elmo Literary Agency, 60 E 42 St, New York, NY 10165, 212-661-2880
Pubs: *Seriously Meeting Karl Shapiro, Life On The Line* (Negative Capability Pr, 1993, 1992), *Georgia Rev, Prairie Schooner.*

Stephanie Hart W
Fashion Institute of Technolog, 227 W 27 St, New York, NY 10011, 212-760-7994
Pubs: *Mondo James Dean: Anth* (St. Martin's, 1996), *Is There Any Way Out Of Sixth Grade* (Coward, McCann & Geoghegan, 1978), *Caprice.*

Steven Hartman P
1610 Avenue P, #6B, Brooklyn, NY 11229
Pubs: *Pinched Nerves* (Cross-Cultural Communications, 1992), *Coffeehouse Poetry Anth* (Bottom Dog Pr, 1996).

Yukihide Maeshima Hartman P
200 W 83 St, #2N, New York, NY 10024, 212-595-3092
Pubs: *A Coloring Book* (Hanging Loose Pr, 1996), *New Poems* (Empyreal Pr, 1991), *New Directions, Hanging Loose, Telephone, Zymerzy, The World.*

George Egon Hatvary W
61 Jane St, #3B, New York, NY 10014, 212-242-9015
Pubs: *The Murder of Edgar Allan Poe* (Carroll & Graf, 1997), *The Suitor* (Avon, 1981), *Hawaii Rev, Hawaii Pacific Rev, Hudson Rev, U Kansas City Rev, Short Story Intl.*

Helen Haukeness W
100 Bank St, New York, NY 10014, 212-989-9487
Internet: haukeness@aol.com
Pubs: *Novel Writing: Anth* (Writer's Digest Bks, 1992), *Los Angeles Times, Toronto Globe & Mail, New York Times, CSM, NAR.*

Marianne Hauser W
Curtis Brown Ltd., 10 Astor Pl, New York, NY 10003-6935
Pubs: *Me & My Mom, Prince Ishmael* (Sun & Moon Pr, 1993, 1989), *Fiction Intl, Parnassus.*

Michael Hawley W
642 E 14 St, #11, New York, NY 10009-3384, 212-673-4549
Internet: mhawl@aol.com
Pubs: *New Yorker, Boston Rev, Sun Dog.*

Annette Hayn P
225-23 88th Ave, Queens Village, NY 11427, 718-465-8214
Pubs: *Enemy on the Way to School, Calendar House* (Poet's Pr, 1994, 1990), *Caprice, Wind, Antenna, Telephone, Painted Bride Qtly.*

Shirley Hazzard W
200 E 66 St, #C-1705, New York, NY 10021
Pubs: *Countenance of Truth, The Transit of Venus* (Viking/Penguin, 1990, 1980), *New Yorker.*

Carol Hebald P&W
463 West St, #H353, New York, NY 10014
Pubs: *Three Blind Mice & Clara Kleinschmidt* (Unicorn, 1989), *Humanist, Antioch Rev, Caprice, Confrontation, PEN Intl, Massachusetts Rev.*

Larry Heinemann W
Ellen Levine Literary Agency, 15 East 26 Street, New York, NY 10010, 212-889-0620
Pubs: *Cooler By The Lake, Paco's Story* (FS&G, 1992, 1986), *Harper's, Penthouse, Playboy, TriQuarterly, Van Nghe, Atlantic.*

George Held P&W
285 W 4 St, New York, NY 10014-2222, 212-989-2591
Pubs: *The Ecstatic Moment* (Bantam Doubleday Dell, 1997), *Winged, In Autumn: Anth* (Birnham Wood Graphics, 1995, 1994), *Commonweal, Confrontation, Phase and Cycle, Poet & Critic, Formalist, Blue Unicorn, Rattle, Whelks Walk Rev.*

Richard Hell P&W
437 E 12 St, #25, New York, NY 10009
Pubs: *Artifact* (Hanuman, 1990), *Penguin Book of Rock & Roll Writing: Anth* (Viking, 1992), *The World, Cuz, Verbal Abuse, Portable Lower East Side.*

Joseph Heller W
390 W End Ave, New York, NY 10024
Pubs: *Picture This* (Putnam, 1988), *Something Happened* (Dell, 1985), *Good As Gold* (PB, 1980).

Michael Heller P&W
PO Box 1289, Stuyvesant Sta, New York, NY 10009, 212-533-1928
Internet: mh7@is2.nyu.edu
Pubs: *Wordflow: New & Selected Poems* (Talisman, 1997), *In the Builded Place* (Coffee Hse Pr, 1989), *Paris Rev, Conjunctions, Tel Aviv Rev, Ohio Rev, Parnassus.*

J. V. Hellew P
318 W 100 St, #7-A, New York, NY 10025-5372, 212-662-0524
Internet: joylyn@msn.com
Pubs: *New York Qtly, Diarist's Jrnl, The Little Mag, Hollins Critic, Portland Rev, Voices Intl, Avenue.*

Bob Heman P
PO Box 2165, Church St Sta, New York, NY 10008-2165
Pubs: *Some Footnotes for the Future* (Luna Bisonte, 1986), *15 Structures* (Incurve Pr, 1986), *Caliban, Prose Poem, Artful Dodge, Ant-E-Nym, Juxta, Key Satch(el).*

David Henderson P
PO Box 1158, Cooper Sta, New York, NY 10276, 212-978-3901
Pubs: *The Low East* (North Atlantic Bks, 1981), *Rap & Hip Hop Voices* (Pantheon, 1992).

Geoffrey Hendricks PP
486 Greenwich St, New York, NY 10013
Pubs: *Sky Anatomy* (Rainer Verlag, 1985), *White Walls.*

Donna Henes PP&P
PO Box 380403, Brooklyn, NY 11238-0403, 718-857-2247
Pubs: *Celestially Auspicious Occasions* (Perigee, 1996), *Dressing Our Wounds In Warm Clothes* (Astro Artz, 1982), *Free Spirit, New Visions, Catalyst, Changes.*

Barbara Henning   P
Long Island Univ, University Plaza, Brooklyn, NY 11201,
718-488-1050
Internet: bhenning@phoenix.liu.edu
Pubs: *Love Makes Thinking Dark, Smoking in the Twilight Bar* (United Artists, 1995, 1988), *Lingo, Poet Intl, Paris Rev, Poetry New York, Talisman, Chain, Trois, The World, Fiction Intl, Lacanian Ink.*

Carol Henry   P
129 E 106 St, New York, NY 10029-4614
Internet: henrycarol@hotmail.com
Pubs: *Caprice, Footwork.*

Gerrit Henry   P
70 7th Ave, #5A, New York, NY 10011-6606
Pubs: *The Mirrored Clubs of Hell* (Little, Brown, 1991), *The Lecturer's Aria* (Groundwater Pr, 1989), *Ecstatic Occasions, Expedient Forms: Anth* (Collier Bks, 1987), *Art News, Art in America, Arts, People Weekly, Poetry, Paris Rev, Chelsea, Brooklyn Rev, NAW.*

James Leo Herlihy   W
415 Central Pk W, New York, NY 10025

Grace Herman   P
370 1st Ave #9C, New York, NY 10010, 212-982-7197
Pubs: *Set Against Darkness* (Natl Council of Jewish Women, 1992), *Blood and Bone: Poems By Physicians: Anth* (U Iowa Pr, 1998), *Anthology #19* (Bay Area Poets Coalition, 1997), *Lilith Anth* (Jewish Women's Research Ctr, 1994), *Poetalk, Comstock Rev.*

Joanna Herman   P&W
370 Riverside Dr, #10C, New York, NY 10025, 212-866-8817
Internet: jclapps@worldnet.att.net
Pubs: *Prayers To Protest: Anth* (Pudding Hse, 1998), *Anthology of Italian American Women Writers* (Women's Pr, 1998), *Crescent Rev, Via, Exit 13, New Times, Critic, Woman's Day, Sing Heavenly Muse!, Paterson Literary Rev, Massachusetts Rev.*

Calvin Hernton   P&W
Marie Brown Associates Inc., 625 Broadway, New York, NY 10012
Pubs: *The Sexual Mountain & Black Women Writers* (Doubleday/Anchor, 1987).

Ruth M. Herschberger   P
463 West St., New York, NY 100142010, 212-645-6050
Internet: www.westbeth.org
Pubs: *Adam's Rib* (Harper & Row, 1970), *Nature & Love Poems* (Eakins Pr, 1969), *Botteghe Obscure, Harper's Bazaar, Kenyon Rev, Nation, New York Qtly, Poetry.*

Stella K. Hershan   W
2 Fifth Ave, New York, NY 10011, 212-533-9759
Pubs: *The Naked Angel* (Pinnacle Bks, 1977), *Talent, Pirquet Magazine.*

Robert Hershon   P
231 Wyckoff St, Brooklyn, NY 11217-2208, 718-643-9559
Pubs: *Into a Punchline: Poems 1984-1994* (Hanging Loose Pr, 1994), *How to Ride on the Woodlawn Express* (Sun, 1986), *The World, Poetry Northwest.*

Frank Hertle   P
401 E 74 St, New York, NY 10021, 212-861-7446
Pubs: *Cicada, Blue Unicorn, Gravida, Lake Superior Rev, Voices Intl.*

Lynn Hess   P
60 E End Ave, #8C, New York, NY 10028, 212-794-9005
Pubs: *Where Tigers Roar In Silence* (Lime Rock Pr, 1981), *Spoon River Qtly, Blackberry.*

Jamake Highwater   P&W
c/o Ellen Levine Literary Agen, 15 E 26 St, New York, NY 10010, 212-889-0620
Pubs: *Dark Legend, Kill Hole* (Grove Pr, 1994, 1992), *World of 1492* (Holt, 1992), *Shadow Show* (Van Der Marck Edtns, 1987), *Native Land* (Little, Brown, 1986), *CSM.*

Carol Hill   W
2 Fifth Ave, #19-U, New York, NY 10011, 212-475-3281
Pubs: *Henry James' Midnight Song* (Poseidon Pr, 1993), *The Eleventh Million Mile High Dancer* (Henry Holt, 1985).

Donna Hill   W
530 E 23 St, #6B, New York, NY 10010-5029
Pubs: *Shipwreck Season* (Clarion Bks, 1998), *More Stories to Dream On* (HM, 1993), *Murder Uptown* (Carroll & Graf, 1992), *First Your Penny* (Atheneum, 1985), *Delta Kappa Gamma Bulletin, Alfred Hitchcock's Mystery.*

Kathleen Hill   W
106 Morningside Dr, New York, NY 10027, 212-662-0055
Pubs: *Scent of Water* (TriQuarterly Bks, 1999), *Yale Rev, Hudson Rev, Kenyon Rev, Prairie Schooner, Arizona Qtly.*

Rebecca Hill   W
Virginia Barber Agency, 101 5th Ave, Ste 11-F, New York, NY 10003, 212-255-6515
Internet: inkintense@aol.com
Pubs: *Killing Time in St. Cloud* (Delacorte, 1988), *Among Birches, Blue Rise* (Morrow, 1986, 1983).

Daryl Hine   P&W
Alfred A. Knopf, Inc., 201 E 50 St, New York, NY 10022, 212-751-2600
Pubs: *Ovid's Heroines* (Yale U Pr, 1991), *Postscripts* (Knopf, 1991).

Alan Hines   W
Sterling Lord Literistic, 65 Bleecker St, New York, NY 10012
Pubs: *Square Dance* (H&R, 1984), *St. Andrews Rev, Texas Qtly, Junction.*

Michael Thomas Hinkemeyer W
35 Cove Dr, Manhasset, NY 11030, 516-365-8761
Pubs: *The Order of the Arrow* (TOR, 1993), *The Substitute Teacher* (Pocket, 1993), *Soulcatchers* (Warner, 1990).

Douglas Hobbie W
Donadio & Ashworth, Inc., 121 W 27 St, Ste 704, New York, NY 10011, 212-691-8077
Pubs: *This Time Last Year, Being Brett, The Day, Boomfell* (Henry Holt, 1998, 1996, 1993, 1991).

Rolaine Hochstein W
Curtis Brown Ltd., 10 Astor Pl, New York, NY 10003-6935
Pubs: *Table 47* (Doubleday, 1983), *Stepping Out* (Norton, 1977), *O. Henry Prize Stories, Pushcart Prize, Atlantic, NAR, Massachusetts Rev, Antioch, Nacyvilag Jrnl of Intl Fiction.*

Jill Hoffman P&W
184 Franklin St, Ground Fl, New York, NY 10013, 212-219-9278
Pubs: *Jilted* (S&S, 1993), *Mink Coat* (HRW, 1973), *New Yorker, New Republic, Mudfish, Northwest Rev, Now This, Helicon Nine.*

William Hoffman W
Curtis Brown Ltd., 10 Astor Pl, New York, NY 10003-6935, 212-473-5400
Pubs: *Tidewater Blood* (Algonquin, 1998), *Follow Me Home, Furors Die* (LSU Pr, 1994, 1990), *O. Henry Prize Stories: Anth* (Doubleday, 1996), *Sewanee Rev, Virginia Qtly Rev, Shenandoah.*

William M. Hoffman P
ICM, 40 W 57 St, New York, NY 10019, 212-556-5600
Pubs: *As Is* (Vintage/Random Hse, 1985), *Gay Plays* (Avon, 1979).

Cliff Hogan PP
89-32 88th St, Woodhaven, NY 11421-2529, 718-849-5576
Pubs: *Waterfalls* (Muse Federation Ink Poets, 1987).

Linda Hogan W
Sanford J. Greenburger Assoc., 55 Fifth Ave, New York, NY 10003, 212-206-5600
Pubs: *Power* (Norton, 1998), *Solar Storms* (Scribner, 1996), *Book of Medicines* (Coffee Hse Pr, 1993), *Mean Spirit* (Atheneum, 1990), *Ms., American Voice, Denver Qtly.*

Kam Holifield P
2086 2nd Ave, #20A, New York, NY 10029
Pubs: *Workshop Poems* (Big Apple Pub, 1989), *Timepieces: Anth* (Cloverleaf Bks, 1995), *Haiku Headlines, Frogpond, Vitis Vine, New Press Literary Qtly.*

Amy Holman P&W
233 Smith St, #1, Brooklyn, NY 11231, 718-243-0248
Internet: amy@pw.org
Pubs: *Tissue and Bone, Dwelling With Fire* (Linear Arts Bks, 1998, 1997), *Poets On The Line, Brooklyn Rev Online, Literal Latte, Metropolitan Rev, Zone 3, Mind the Gap, Sierra Nevada College Rev, World Poetry, Hawaii Rev, Exquisite Corpse.*

Bob Holman P
173 Duane St, #2, New York, NY 10013, 212-645-0061
Internet: nuyopoman@aol.com
Pubs: *In With The Out Crowd* (Mouth Almighty/Mercury, 1998), *Bob Holman's Collect Call Of The Wild* (Henry Holt, 1995), *Cupid's Cashbox* (Jordan Davies, 1988), *Exquisite Corpse, The Fuse, Bomb, Talisman, The New Censorship.*

Darryl Holmes P
The Afrikan Poetry Theatre, 176-03 Jamaica Ave, Jamaica, NY 11432, 718-528-3392
Pubs: *Wings Will Not Be Broken* (Third World Pr, 1990), *Catalyst Mag.*

Doloris Holmes PP&P
White Mask Theatre/Press, 22 W 30 St, New York, NY 10001, 212-683-9332
Internet: http://www.womeninlimbo.com
Pubs: *Upbeat Triangles of Pastime, Poems on the Brain and Red Feet Too, Lady of the Grape Arbor* (White Mask Pr, 1997, 1996, 1991), *Upfront Muse Intl Jrnl.*

A. M. Homes W
Wylie, Aitken & Stone, 250 W 57 St, #2106, New York, NY 10107, 212-246-0069
Pubs: *The End of Alice* (Scribner, 1996), *In a Country of Mothers* (Knopf, 1993), *The Safety of Objects* (Norton, 1990), *Jack* (Vintage, 1990), *New Yorker, Vanity Fair.*

Peter Hood P
15 Greenway Terr, Forest Hills, NY 11375, 718-263-9640

William Hooker PP
444 W 52 St, #E, New York, NY 10019, 212-582-0513
Pubs: *New Observations.*

Susan Hoover P
211 W 10 St #6D, New York, NY 10014, 212-924-3765
Pubs: *The Magnet And The Target* (New School Chapbook Series, 1995), *Taxi Dancer* (Exotic Beauties Pr, 1977), *U Colorado Literary Mag, Granite, Cold Mountain Rev, Isinglass Rev, Cover/Arts New York.*

Doug Hornig W
Jane Dystel Literary Managemen, 1 Union Sq. West, New York, NY 10003, 212-627-9100
Internet: jane@ocsny.com
Pubs: *Stinger, Virus* (NAL, 1990, 1989), *Deep Dive, Waterman* (Mysterious Pr, 1988, 1987).

Israel Horovitz P&W
William Morris Agency, 1350 Ave of the Americas, New York,
NY 10019, 212-586-5100
Pubs: *Horovitz: Collected Works* (Smith & Kraus, 1994),
Three Gloucester Plays (Doubleday/Fireside, 1993),
L'Avant-Scene.

Tom House W
99-34 67 Rd, #6F, Forest Hills, NY 11375, 718-897-4572
Internet: tomhouse1@aol.com
Pubs: *Best American Gay Fiction: Anth* (Little, Brown,
1997), *Harper's, Chicago Rev, Gettysburg Rev, Western
Humanities Rev, Puerto del Sol, Other Voices, Christopher
Street.*

Richard Howard P
23 Waverly Pl, New York, NY 10003, 212-228-6689
Pubs: *Like Most Revelations* (Pantheon, 1994), *Trappings*
(Counterpoint, 1998), *No Traveller, Lining Up* (Atheneum
1987, 1983), *Paris Rev, Yale Rev.*

Thomas J. Hubschman W
473 17 St, #6, Brooklyn, NY 11215-6226
Internet: tjhubsc@dorsac.org
Pubs: *Space Ark* (Dorchester, 1981), *Alpha-II* (Woodhill,
1980), *BBC World Service, Blue Penny Qtly, New York Pr,
In Vivo, Morpo Rev, Kudzu, Blue Moon Rev.*

Ingrid Hughes P&W
311 E 9 St, #6, New York, NY 10003-7742, 212-254-0635
Pubs: *Women in the Midrash: Anth* (Jason Aronson, 1996),
*Birmingham Rev, Negative Capability, Blue Light Rev, West
Branch, Mudfish, Bad Henry, MPR, Massachusetts Rev.*

Sophie Hughes P
49 W 12 St #2H, New York, NY 10011, 212-255-8144
Pubs: *We Speak for Peace: Anth* (KIT, 1993), *Hollins Critic,
Interim, Potato Eyes, Poet's Edge, NeoVictorian/Cochlea,
Poem, Confrontation, Panhandler, Sidewalks, Echoes.*

Josephine Humphreys W
Harriet Wasserman Literary Age, 137 E 36 St, New York, NY
10016
Pubs: *The Fireman's Fair, Rich in Love, Dreams of Sleep*
(Viking, 1991, 1987, 1984).

Christian X. Hunter P&W
166 Suffolk St #C, New York, NY 10002, 212-228-7864
Internet: cxhunter@onepine.com
Pubs: *Crimes of the Beats: Anth* (Autonomedia, 1998),
Verses That Hurt: Anth (St. Martin's Pr, 1997), *Ikon, Red
Tape, The World, Portable Lower East Side, Sensitive Skin,
New York Press.*

Evan Hunter W
Gelfman Schneider Literary Age, 250 West 57 Street, New
York, NY 10107, 212-245-1993
Pubs: *Privileged Conversation* (Warner Bks, 1996),
Blackboard Jungle (S&S, 1954).

Jerrie W. Hurd W
Mary Jack Wald Literary Assoc., 111 E 14 St, New York, NY
10003, 212-254-7842
Pubs: *Kansas Qtly, New Frontiers Anth, Fantasy and
Sci-Fi, South Dakota Rev, Antioch Rev.*

Johanna Hurwitz W
10 Spruce Pl, Great Neck, NY 11021, 516-829-6205
Pubs: *Faraway Summer, Spring Break, Even Stephen, A
Llama in the Family, School Spirit, Ali Baba Bernstein*
(Morrow Junior Bks, 1998, 1997, 1996, 1994, 1994, 1992).

Eleanor Hyde W
343 E 74 St, #12L, New York, NY 10021, 212-861-2116
Pubs: *Animal Instincts, In Murder We Trust* (Fawcett Bks,
1996, 1995), *Arizona Qtly, Cosmopolitan, Satire.*

Colette Inez P
5 W 86 St, New York, NY 10024, 212-874-2009
Pubs: *Clemency* (Carnegie Mellon U Pr, 1998), *Getting
Underway: New and Selected Poetry, Family Life* (Story
Line Pr, 1993, 1992), *Hudson Rev, Partisan Rev, Ohio Rev,
Iowa Rev, Ploughshares, Prairie Schooner.*

Carole Ione P
Melanie Jackson, 250 West 57 St, New York, NY 10107,
212-582-8585
Internet: iwww.deeplistening.org/ione
Pubs: *The Night Train to Aswan: Anth* (Neterv Edtns,
1998), *Spirits of the Passage: Anth* (S&S, 1997), *Piramida
Negra, Selected Poems* (Live Letters Pr, 1991), *Hot
Flashes, Women Writers on the Change of Life: Anth*
(Faber & Faber, 1995), *Chronogram.*

Ivor S. Irwin W
Elaine Markson Literary Agency, 44 Greenwich Ave, New
York, NY 10011, 212-243-8480
Internet: isirwin@ix.netcom.com
Pubs: *A Peacock or a Crow* (Willes e-Pr, 1998), *Cape
Discoveries: Anth* (Sheep Meadow Pr, 1996), *Street Songs:
Anth* (Longstreet Pr, 1990), *Sycamore Rev, Playboy, North
Carolina Literary Rev, Mangrove, Crushed Cigarette Pr,
Emrys Jrnl, No Roses Rev, The Sun.*

Susan Isaacs W
William Morris Agency, 1350 Ave of the Americas, New York,
NY 10019, 212-586-5100
Pubs: *Shining Through, Almost Paradise* (H&R, 1988, 1984).

Rashidah Ismaili P
1851 Adam Clayton Powell Blvd, New York, NY 10026,
212-222-8631
Pubs: *Missing in Action and Presumed Dead* (Africa World
Pr, 1992), *Oniybo* (Shamal, 1986).

Peter Israel W
Georges Borchardt Inc., 136 E 57 St, New York, NY 10022,
212-753-5785

Philip Israel W
257 Beach 130th St, Belle Harbor, NY 11694, 718-945-0680
Pubs: *Me and Brenda* (Norton, 1990), *Carlton Miscellany, Transatlantic Rev.*

Beverly Jablons W
63 E 9 St, #9K, New York, NY 10003-6334, 212-477-3380
Pubs: *Dance Time* (Berkley, 1981), *Midstream, NAR.*

Gale P. Jackson P&W
180 Prospect Park W, Brooklyn, NY 11215
Internet: stormimpri@aol.com
Pubs: *Khoisan Tale of Beginnings and Ends, Bridge Suite: Narrative Poems* (Storm Imprints, 1998, 1998), *Poets At Work: Anth* (Just Buffalo Literary Ctr, 1996), *American Voice, Ploughshares, Ikon Mag, Callaloo, Black American Literature, Kenyon Rev.*

Mae Jackson P
165 Clinton Ave, #2G, Brooklyn, NY 11205, 718-237-0762
Pubs: *Can I Poet With You* (Broadside Pr, 1970), *The Black Scholar, Essence, Encore, Nimrod.*

Sheila Cathryn Jackson PP&P
PO Box 7554, FDR Sta, New York, NY 10150
Pubs: *WomanStuff* (La Mama La Galleria, 1993), *Letters From Texas* (New Works Project, 1993), *Manhattan Class Co Theatre, Playwrights' Ctr.*

Bev Jafek W
24-08 24th Ave, Astoria, NY 11102-2832
Internet: maqroll@ix.netcom.com
Pubs: *The Man Who Took A Bite Out of His Wife* (Overlook Pr, 1995), *Best American Short Stories: Anth* (HM, 1985), *Columbia, Yellow Silk, Missouri Rev.*

Louise Jaffe P
2411 E 3 St, #3E, Brooklyn, NY 11223, 718-998-0038
Pubs: *Light Breaks* (Big Easy Pr, 1995), *Wisdom Revisited* (Adams Pr, 1987), *Dan River Anthology* (Dan River Pr, 1998), *American Poets & Poetry, Sunday Suitor, New Press Literary Qtly, Poetry Digest, Frontiers, Anathema Rev, Nassau Rev, Phoebe, Alura.*

Susan Jaffe P
546 State St, Brooklyn, NY 11217
Pubs: *Green House, Hanging Loose, Dark Horse, Response, Chouteau Rev.*

John Jakes W
Rembar & Curtis Attorneys, 19 West 44 St, New York, NY 10036, 212-575-8500
Internet: jjfiction@aol.com
Pubs: *American Dreams* (Dutton, 1998), *Homeland* (Doubleday, 1993), *In the Big Country: The Best Western Stories of John Jakes* (Bantam, 1993), *Parade Mag.*

Kelvin Christopher James W
1295 5th Ave, #32F, New York, NY 10029
Pubs: *Jumping Ship and Other Stories* (Villard Bks, 1992), *American Letters and Commentary, Literary Rev, Catalyst.*

Elizabeth Janeway W
350 E 79 St #8D, New York, NY 10021-9204, 212-249-8833

Ronald Wiley Janoff P
1 Washington Sq Village, #15A, New York, NY 10012, 212-995-8791
Internet: rwj1@nyu.edu
Pubs: *Choice, Modern Poetry Studies, Abraxas, Hanging Loose, First Issue, Purchase Poetry Rev.*

Tama Janowitz W
ICM, 40 W 57 St, New York, NY 10019, 212-556-5600
Pubs: *By the Shores of Gitchi Gumee, The Male Cross-Dresser Support Group* (Crown, 1996, 1992), *Travel & Leisure, Elle, Allure, New Yorker, New York Times.*

Lisa Jarnot P
Box 185, Stuyvesant Sta, New York, NY 10009, 718-802-9575
Pubs: *screens and tasted parallels, Black Bread, o.blek.*

Ruth Prawer Jhabvala W
400 E 52 St #7G, New York, NY 10022
Pubs: *Three Continents, Out of India, In Search of Love & Beauty* (Morrow, 1987, 1986, 1983).

Vita Marie Jimenez P
567 81st St, Brooklyn, NY 11209, 718-630-5440
Pubs: *To Grow Grapes, The Courtship of Mickey and Minnie* (A Little Pr, 1998, 1990), *Crunchy, Munchy Cookies* (Newbridge Comm, 1993), *The World, Poetry Project Newsletter, Hanging Loose.*

Carlos Johnson W
30-98 Crescent St, #2B, Astoria, NY 11102, 718-956-3240
Pubs: *Entre Nosotros, Centerpoint, Revista Chicano-Riquena, Chasqui, Linden Lane Mag, Inti.*

Dave Johnson P
268 Water St, New York, NY 10038, 212-964-7189
Pubs: *Marble Shoot* (Hummingbird Pr, 1995).

Fenton Johnson W
Malaga Baldi Literary Agency, PO Box 591, Radio City Sta, New York, NY 10101-5078, 212-222-1221
Internet: johnfenton@aol.com
Pubs: *Geography of the Heart* (Scribner, 1996), *Scissors, Paper, Rock* (Washington Square Pr, 1996), *New York Times Mag, Virginia Qtly Rev, Mother Jones, Sewanee Rev.*

J. Chester Johnson   P
315 E 86 St, #16GE, New York, NY 10028, 212-831-5063
    Pubs: *Curate's Chorus, Lazarus* (Juliet Pr, 1998, 1993),
    *Voices Intl, Wisconsin Rev, Michigan Rev, Advance
    Monticellonian.*

Jacqueline Joan Johnson   P
Marie Brown Associates Inc., 625 Broadway, New York, NY
10012, 718-574-4475
    Pubs: *A Gathering of Mother Tongues* (White Pine Pr,
    1998), *Beyond the Frontier* (Black Classical Pr, 1998),
    Drum Voices (U St. Louis Pr, 1994), *Streetlights:
    Illuminating Tales of the Urban Black Experience: Anth*
    (Viking Penguin, 1996), *River Styx.*

Joe Johnson   P&W
215 W 92 St, #11E, New York, NY 10025, 212-877-7619
    Pubs: *Tight* (Lee/Lucas Press, 1978).

Judith E. Johnson   PP&P&W
890 W End Ave, #1A, New York, NY 10025, 212-866-2639
    Pubs: *The Ice Lizard* (Sheep Meadow Pr, 1992), *The
    Waste Trilogy* (Countryman Pr, 1979), *Partisan Rev, New
    Yorker, Little Mag, Hudson Rev, Caprice, Frontiers.*

Nicholas Johnson   P
141 Huntington St, Brooklyn, NY 11231, 718-624-7305
    Pubs: *Anthology of Magazine Verse and Yearbook of
    American Poetry* (Monitor Bk Co, 1997), *Men Of Our Time:
    Anth of Contemporary Male Poets* (U Georgia Pr, 1992),
    Movieworks: Anth (Little Theatre Pr, 1990), *The Ledge,
    Three Mile Harbor, The Journal, Pivot.*

Tom Johnson   P
Two-Eighteen Press, PO Box 218, Village Sta, New York, NY
10014-0218, 212-691-5120
    Pubs: *The Voice of New Music* (Het Apollohuis, 1989),
    Imaginary Music: Anth (Two-Eighteen Pr, 1976),
    Unmuzzled Ox, Black Box.

Gary Johnston   P
Blind Beggar Press, PO Box 437, Williamsbridge Sta, Bronx,
NY 10467
    Pubs: *Crossings, Two* (Blind Beggar Pr, 1995, 1994), *Black
    Nation.*

Gerald Jonas   P
70 W 95 St, #5H, New York, NY 10025, 212-864-3949
Internet: 72530.1427@compuserve.com
    Pubs: *Dancing* (Harry Abrams, 1992), *Poetry.*

Hettie Jones   W
27 Cooper Sq, New York, NY 10003, 212-473-5193
    Pubs: *Drive* (Hanging Loose Pr, 1998), *How I Became
    Hettie Jones* (Grove Pr, 1996), *Big Star Fallin' Mama*
    (Viking, 1995), *Hanging Loose, Open City, Long Shot.*

J. E. M. Jones   P&W
The Picture Poet, PO Box 23144, Hollis, NY 11423
    Pubs: *Speech from a Stone* (U Pitt Pr, 1998), *Veiled Truths,
    Travelin On Faith/Travelin On Credit* (Jones, 1992, 1982),
    The Nubian Gallery: A Poetry Anth (Blacfax, 1997), *Blacfax
    Mag.*

Kaylie Jones   W
The Lantz-Harris Literary Agcy, 156 5th Ave, Ste 617, New
York, NY 10010, 212-924-6269
    Pubs: *A Soldier's Daughter Never Cries* (Bantam, 1990),
    Quite the Other Way (Doubleday, 1989).

Larry Jones   P
101 Ave A, New York, NY 10009, 212-529-2336
    Pubs: *we become a picnic* (Venom Pr, 1994), *Ikon, Curare,
    Tamarind, Olivetree Rev, Fag Rag, Provincetown Poets,
    Downtown, Zone.*

Patricia Spears Jones   P
426 Sterling Pl, #1C, Brooklyn, NY 11238, 718-399-2356
    Pubs: *The Weather That Kills* (Coffee Hse Pr, 1995), *Sing
    the Sun Up: Anth* (Teachers & Writers, 1998), *Aloud:
    Voices From the Nuyorican Cafe: Anth* (HH, 1994),
    Sisterfire: Anth (HC, 1994), *Hanging Loose, American
    Voice, Ikon, World, Callaloo, Kenyon Rev.*

Thom Jones   W
Wylie Agency, 250 W 57 St, Ste 2114, New York, NY 10107,
212-246-0069
    Pubs: *Cold Snap, The Pugilist at Rest* (Little, Brown, 1995,
    1993), *New Yorker, Esquire, Harper's, Playboy, Buzz.*

Erica Mann Jong   P&W
425 Park Ave, New York, NY 10022-5739, 212-980-6922
    Pubs: *Fear of Fifty, Becoming Light* (HarperCollins, 1994,
    1991).

Lawrence Joseph   P
St. John's Univ Law School, Jamaica, NY 11439,
718-990-6014
    Pubs: *Before Our Eyes* (FS&G, 1993), *Curriculum Vitae* (U
    Pitt Pr, 1988).

Stephen M. Joseph   W
270 1st Ave, #8E, New York, NY 10009, 212-254-5078
    Pubs: *Children In Fear* (HR&W, 1974), *The Me Nobody
    Knows* (Avon, 1969).

Ellen Kahaner   W
79-10 34 Ave #4Y, Jackson Heights, NY 11372
    Pubs: *Fourth Grade Loser* (Troll, Inc., 1992), *Motorcycles*
    (Capstone Pr, 1991), *Growing Up Female* (Rosen Pubs,
    1991).

Anna Kainen   P
689 Columbus Ave, #14B, New York, NY 10025
    Pubs: *Whispers* (New York Poetry Fdn, 1986), *I Am Woman*
    (Anna Kainen, 1983), *The Plowman, The Quarterly.*

Layding Kaliba P
60 E 135 St, Apt 7C, New York, NY 10037, 212-690-2472
Pubs: *The Moon Is My Witness, Up on the Down Side*
(Single Action Productions, 1988, 1982).

Robert Kalich W
240 Central Pk S, New York, NY 10019-1413
Pubs: *The Handicapper* (Crown, 1981).

Laura Kalpakian W
Jane Rotrosen Agency, 318 E 51 St, New York, NY 10022,
212-592-4330
Pubs: *Dark Continent and Other Stories* (Viking/Penguin,
1990), *Crescendo* (Times Bks, 1987).

Marc Kaminsky P
291 11th St, Brooklyn, NY 11215, 718-788-0250
Pubs: *Target Populations* (Central Park Edtns, 1991), *The
Road From Hiroshima* (S&S, 1984), *Sun.*

Linda Kampley P
407 W 50 St, #3, New York, NY 10019
Pubs: *Widener Rev, Soundings East, Connecticut River
Rev, Panhandler, Voices Intl, Cream City Rev.*

Alan Kapelner W
40 King St, #1A, New York, NY 10014, 212-242-7496
Pubs: *All The Naked Heroes* (Braziller, 1965), *Lonely Boy
Blues* (Scribner, 1950), *New Voices.*

Allan Kaplan P
45 Christopher St, #16G, New York, NY 10014
Internet: akaplan@worldnet.att.net
Pubs: *Paper Airplane* (Harper & Row, 1972), *Wind,
Apalachee Qtly, Hubbub, Gulf Stream, Panhandler, Half
Tones To Jubilee.*

Johanna Kaplan W
411 W End Ave, #11E, New York, NY 10024
Pubs: *O My America!* (Syracuse U Pr, 1995), *Other
People's Lives* (Knopf, 1975), *Commentary.*

Robert Kaplan P&W
300 W 23 St #14D, New York, NY 10011, 212-242-8687
Internet: rkaplan1@email.gc.cuny.edu
Pubs: *A Loving Testimonial: Remembering Loved Ones
Lost to AIDS: Anth* (Crossing Pr, 1995), *Beyond Definition:
Anth* (Manic D Pr, 1994), *Evergreen Chronicles, Modern
Words, Anemone, Amethyst, RFD: A Country Jrnl for Gay
Men Everywhere, New Leaves Rev.*

Arno Karlen P&W
350 Bleecker St, #1P, New York, NY 10014
Pubs: *New Letters, Antioch Rev.*

Mollyne Karnofsky PP
515 E 88 St, #1D, New York, NY 10128, 212-517-8607
Pubs: *Collide: A Scope* (Performance; Chuck Levitan Art
Gallery, 1998), *Elemental Sounds/Equinox Life Line*
(Performance; Anth Film Archives, 1996), *Spanish Moss,
Dear Sun, Uncle Mike* (Performance; Med Art Intl, 1992).

Vickie Karp P
Thirteen/WNET, 356 W 58 St, New York, NY 100191804,
212-560-3123
Internet: karp@wnet.org
Pubs: *A Taxi to the Flame* (U South Carolina, 1998), *Best of
Poetry: Anths* (Macmillan, 1991, 1989), *New Yorker, New
Republic, New York Rev, Yale Rev, Paris Rev.*

Jean Karsavina W
39 1/2 Washington Sq S, New York, NY 10012,
212-289-2368
Pubs: *White Eagle, Dark Skies* (Scribner, 1975), *Tree By
The Waters* (Young World Bks, 1949).

Ben Katchor W
PO Box 2024 Cathedral Sta, New York, NY 10025,
212-665-8913
Internet: bkatchor@spacelab.net
Pubs: *The Jew of New York* (Pantheon, 1999), *Julius Knipl,
Real Estate Photographer* (Little, Brown, 1996), *Cheap
Novelties* (Penguin, 1991), *D.C. City Paper, Forward, San
Francisco Weekly, Chicago New City, Metropolis Mag,
River Front Times.*

Eliot Katz P
PO Box 1621 Old Chelsea Sta, New York, NY 10113,
212-337-3107
Pubs: *Unlocking the Exits* (Coffee House Pr, 1999), *Space
and Other Poems for Love, Laughs, and Social
Transformation* (Northern Lights, 1990), *Aloud: Anth* (Henry
Holt, 1994).

Leandro Katz PP
25 E 4 St, New York, NY 10003, 212-260-4254
Pubs: *Death Trip* (Turt, 1990), *27 Windmills* (Viper's Tongue,
1986).

Vincent Katz P
211 W 19 St, 5 Fl, New York, NY 10011-4001
Internet: vincent@el.net
Pubs: *Pearl* (PowerHouse Bks, 1998), *Boulevard
Transportation* (Tibor de Nagy Edtns, 1997), *Cabal of Zealots*
(Hanuman, 1988), *Bomb, Exquisite Corpse, New Censorship,
Little More, The World, The Fred, Ars Electronica.*

Andrew Kaufman P
585 Isham St #4E, New York, NY 10034, 212-304-8657
Pubs: *Cinnamon Bay Sonnets* (Center For Book Arts,
1996), *Anth of Mag Verse & Yearbook of American Poetry,
Massachusetts Rev, College English, Spoon River Poetry
Rev, Beloit Poetry Jrnl, Carolina Qtly, Crazyhorse.*

Bel Kaufman W
1020 Park Ave, #20-A, New York, NY 10028, 212-288-8783
Pubs: *Up the Down Staircase* (HarperCollins, 1991), *Love, Etc.* (Prentice Hall, 1981), *Esquire, McCall's, Commonweal, New Choices, Ladies Home Jrnl, Saturday Rev of Literature, Today's Education.*

Rebecca Kavaler W
425 Riverside Dr, New York, NY 10025, 212-865-4632
Pubs: *Tigers in the Wood* (U Illinois Pr, 1986), *Doubting Castle* (Schocken, 1984), *Carolina Qtly.*

Kantrowitz Melanie Kaye P&W
922 8th Ave #3B, Brooklyn, NY 11215, 718-788-5333
Pubs: *My Jewish Face & Other Stories* (Aunt Lute, 1990), *Sinister Wisdom, Calyx, Bridges, Tikkun, Sojourner, Women's Rev of Bks, Gay Community News, Village Voice.*

Marvin Kaye W
Donald Maass Literary Agency, 157 W 57 St, Ste 1003, New York, NY 10019, 212-757-7755
Pubs: *Fantastique* (St. Martin's Pr, 1993), *Ghosts of Night and Morning, A Cold Blue Light* (Berkley, 1987, 1983).

Celine Keating W
697 W End Ave, #5D, New York, NY 10025, 212-666-9174
Pubs: *North Stone Rev, Emry's Jrnl, Appearances, Echoes, Prairie Schooner, Santa Clara Rev.*

John Keeble W
Georges Borchardt Inc., 136 E 57 St, New York, NY 10022, 212-753-5785
Pubs: *Out of The Channel* (HarperCollins, 1991), *Broken Ground* (H&R, 1987), *Village Voice, Outside.*

Edmund Keeley P&W
Georges Borchardt, Inc, 136 East 57 St, New York, NY 10022, 212-753-5785
Internet: keele@phoenix.princeton.edu
Pubs: *School for Pagan Lovers* (Rutgers U Pr, 1993), *A Wilderness Called Peace* (S&S, 1985), *Antaeus, Harvard Rev, Mediterraneans, International Qtly, Passager, TriQuarterly, Ontario Rev, Seattle Rev.*

Joyce Keener W
Sarah Lazin Books, 126 5th Ave, Ste 300, New York, NY 10011, 212-989-5757
Pubs: *Limits of Eden, Borderline* (Ace Bks, 1981, 1979), *Womanblood: Anth* (Continuing Saga, 1981).

Johanna Beale Keller P&W
12 East 86 St, New York, NY 100280511, 212-639-9092
Pubs: *The Skull* (Colorado College Pr, 1998), *Southwest Rev, Chelsea, Nimrod, Connecticut Rev, Dark Horse* (UK), *Voices Israel, Plum Rev, Pivot, New Plains Rev, Jean Rhys Rev.*

Tsipi Edith Keller P&W
333 E 14 St, New York, NY 10003, 212-674-1076
Pubs: *The Vintage Book of Contemporary Poetry: Anth* (Vintage Bks, 1996), *Anthology of Magazine Verse, Partisan Rev, Seneca Rev, Prairie Schooner, Between C&D, Minetta Rev, MPR, Mildred, George Washington Rev, Present Tense, Jewish Pr, Cream City Rev.*

William Melvin Kelley W
PO Box 2658, New York, NY 10027
Pubs: *A Different Drummer* (Doubleday, 1973).

Raymond Kennedy W
Columbia Univ, New York, NY 10027, 212-854-3774
Pubs: *The Bittersweet Age, Ride A Cockhorse* (Ticknor & Fields, 1994, 1991), *Lulu Incognito* (Vintage, 1988), *The Flower of the Republic* (Knopf, 1983).

William Kennedy W
Darhansoff & Verrill Agency, 1220 Park Ave, New York, NY 10128, 212-534-2479
Pubs: *Very Old Bones, Quinn's Book, Ironweed* (Viking, 1992, 1988, 1983).

Bliem Kern P
230 Riverside Dr, #15CC, New York, NY 10025-6172
Pubs: *Temple of Sound, Hail Jupiter* (La Maison de La Bleame, 1995, 1995), *Spiritual Unity of Nations, Ingress, Ararita.*

Sarah Kernochan W
William Morris Agency, 1350 Ave of the Americas, New York, NY 10019, 212-586-5100

Katharine Kidde P
335 E 51 St, #1G, New York, NY 10022, 212-755-9461
Pubs: *Sounding For Light* (Linear Arts, 1998), *Home Light: Along the Shore* (North Atlantic Rev, 1994), *Context South, Long Island Qtly, Pegasus, Maryland Poetry Rev, Whelks Walk Rev, Whole Notes.*

Jamaica Kincaid W
Farrar, Straus & Giroux, 19 Union Sq W, New York, NY 10003
Pubs: *My Brother, A Small Place, At the Bottom of the River* (FSG, 1997, 1988, 1983), *Lucy, Annie John* (NAL, 1991, 1986).

Basil King P&W
326-A 4 St, Brooklyn, NY 11215, 718-788-7927
Pubs: *The Complete Miniatures, Devotions* (Stop Pr, 1997), *Split Peas* (Zealot Pr, 1986), *Synaesthetic, First Intensity, Box Kite.*

Martha King   P
326-A 4th St, Brooklyn, NY 11215, 718-788-7927
Internet: editor@nmss.org
   Pubs: *Monday Through Friday* (Zelot Pr, 1987), *Poetry Project Newsletter, Radical Poets, Synesthetics, New American Writing, Bomb, Salt Lick, Carbuncle.*

Ron King   P&W
390 Nostrand Ave, #3C, Brooklyn, NY 11216, 718-622-4054
   Pubs: *Time Capsule, Creative Forces.*

Gloria Devidas Kirchheimer   W
210 W 101 St, #15G, New York, NY 10025
   Pubs: *We Were so Beloved: Autobiography of a German Jewish Community: Anth* (U Pitt, 1997), *Sephardic-American Voices: Anth, Follow My Footprints: Anth* (U Pr New England, 1997, 1993), *Kansas Qtly, Carolina Qtly, Lilith, NAR.*

Karl Kirchwey   P
54 Morningside Dr, #43, New York, NY 10025-1760, 212-316-0130
   Pubs: *The Engrafted Word* (Holt, 1998), *Those I Guard* (HB, 1993), *A Wandering Island* (Princeton U Pr, 1990), *The Best of The Best American Poetry 1988-1997: Anth* (Scribner, 1998), *New Yorker, New Republic, Nation, Poetry, Paris Rev, Kenyon Rev.*

Binnie Kirshenbaum   W
84 Charles St, #18, New York, NY 10014
   Pubs: *A Disturbance in One Place, On Mermaid Avenue* (Fromm Intl, 1994, 1993), *NER/BLQ, Mid-American Rev, Indiana Rev.*

Natalie Kirstein   W
140-21 Burden Cres, #602, Jamaica, NY 11435
   Pubs: *Revista/Review Interamericana, Midstream, New Letters.*

William Kistler   P
101 W 79 St, #22C, New York, NY 10024, 212-874-6150
   Pubs: *Notes Drawn From the River of Ecstacy, America February, The Elizabeth Sequence* (Council Oak Bks, 1996, 1991, 1989), *Poems of the Known World* (Arcade Pubs, 1995), *APR, Antaeus, Poetry Flash, Poetry Intl, New Criterion, New Directions Annual, Harper's.*

Myra Klahr   P
40 E 9 St, #12L, New York, NY 10003-6421, 212-505-2606
   Pubs: *The Waiting Room* (Fiddlehead Pr, 1972), *Caprice, Sesheta, Unicorn, Hanging Loose, Squeezebox.*

Irena Klepfisz   P
155 Atlantic Ave, Brooklyn, NY 11201, 718-855-2905
Internet: IRKEGOLES@AOL.COM
   Pubs: *A Few Words in the Mother Tongue: Poems Selected and New* (Eighth Mountain Pr, 1990), *The Tribe of Dina: A Jewish Women's Anth* (Beacon, 1989), *Bridges, Ms..*

Nancy Kline   W
540 Prospect Ave, Brooklyn, NY 11215
   Pubs: *The Faithful* (Morrow, 1968), *Fiction 1986: Anth* (Exile Pr, 1986), *Ascent, Playgirl, Boston Globe Sunday Mag, Nantucket Rev, Colorado Qtly, Weber Studies.*

Jay Klokker   P
311 E 9 St, New York, NY 10003
   Pubs: *Devil's Millhopper, Beloit Poetry Jrnl, Bellingham Rev, Hanging Loose, State Street Rev.*

Alison Knowles   PP&P
122 Spring St, New York, NY 10012, 212-226-5703
   Pubs: *Event Scores* (Left Hand Bks, 1992), *A Bean Concordance* (Printed Edtns, 1983), *Aperture, New Wilderness Letter 11.*

John Knowles   W
Curtis Brown Ltd., 10 Astor Pl, New York, NY 10003-6935, 212-473-5400
   Pubs: *A Stolen Past* (HRW, 1983), *Spreading Fires* (Random Hse, 1974), *A Separate Peace* (Macmillan, 1960), *Playboy, Esquire.*

Kenneth Koch   P&W
25 Claremont Ave, #2B, New York, NY 10027, 212-854-4015
   Pubs: *Straits, One Train* (Knopf, 1998, 1994), *Poetry, New York Rev of Books, APR, Artes, Arshile, The World.*

Stephen Koch   W
Columbia University, 404 Dodge Hall, New York, NY 10027, 212-854-4391
   Pubs: *The Bachelor's Bride* (Marion Boyars, 1986).

Ronald Koertge   P
John Hawkins & Associates, 71 W 23 St, Ste 1600, New York, NY 10010, 212-807-7040
   Pubs: *The Heart of the City, Confess-O-Rama, Tiger, Tiger Burning Bright* (Orchard Bks, 1998, 1996, 1994), *Making Love to Roget's Wife* (U Arkansas Pr, 1997), *The Harmony Arms, Mariposa Blues* (Little, Brown, 1992, 1991).

Wayne Koestenbaum   P
Sanford J. Greenburger Assoc., 55 Fifth Ave, New York, NY 10003
   Pubs: *Rhapsodies of a Repeat Offender, Ode to Anna Moffo and Other Poems* (Persea, 1994, 1990), *New Yorker, Paris Rev, APR, Yale Rev.*

Sybil Kollar   P&W
10 Clinton St, #12M, Brooklyn, NY 11201, 718-858-4749
   Pubs: *In Rooms We Come and Go* (Somers Rocks Pr, 1998), *The Party Train: North American Prose Poetry: Anth* (New Rivers, 1996), *Just Us Text of Song Cycle: Anth* (Science Jrnl of Musical Scores, 1995), *American Voice, Chelsea, Confrontation, Erphrasis.*

Ron Kolm P&W
30-73 47th St, #3F, Long Island City, NY 11103,
718-721-0946
Pubs: *Crimes of the Beats: Anth, Unbearables: Anth*
(Autonomedia, 1998, 1995), *Rank Cologne* (P O N Pr,
1991), *New Observations, Redtape, Pink Pages, Public
Illumination Mag, Gargoyle.*

Todd Alan Komarnicki W
Virginia Barber Literary Agenc, 101 5th Ave, 11 Fl, New York,
NY 10003, 212-255-6515
Pubs: *Free* (Doubleday, 1993).

Edith Konecky W
511 E 20 St, #9G, New York, NY 10010, 212-228-2253
Pubs: *A Place at the Table* (Ballantine, 1990), *Allegra Maud
Goldman* (The Feminist Pr, 1990).

Hans Koning W
c/o Sterling Lord Literistic, 65 Bleecker St, New York, NY
10012, 212-780-6050
Pubs: *Pursuit of a Woman on the Hinge of History*
(Brookline Bks, 1998), *The Conquest of America* (Monthly
Rev Pr, 1994), *Acts of Faith* (Holt, 1988), *New Yorker,
Harper's, Atlantic.*

Jean Hanff Korelitz P&W
Pam Bernstein & Assoc., 790 Madison Ave, Ste 310, New
York, NY 10021, 212-288-1700
Pubs: *A Jury of Her Peers* (Crown, 1996), *The Properties of
Breath* (Bloodaxe/Dufour, 1988).

Nina Kossman P&W
30-11 49th St., Long Island City, NY 11103
Internet: nkossman@columbia.edu
Pubs: *Behind the Border* (Morrow, 1994), *The Gospels In
Our Image: Anth* (HB, 1995), *Southern Humanities Rev,
Quarterly West, Connecticut Poetry Rev, Prairie Schooner,
Columbia, Threepenny Rev.*

Richard Kostelanetz PP&P&W
PO Box 444, Prince St Sta, New York, NY 10012-0008,
212-982-3099
Pubs: *Wordworks: Poems Selected & New* (BOA Edtns,
1993), *The New Poetries and Some Old* (Southern Illinois,
1991).

Robert Kotlowitz W
54 Riverside Dr, New York, NY 10024, 212-787-0239
Pubs: *His Master's Voice* (Knopf, 1992), *Sea Changes*
(North Point Pr, 1986).

Vaughn Koumjian W
320 Wadsworth Ave, #6L, New York, NY 10040,
212-740-2246
Pubs: *Passions And Fashions* (Green Meadow Pr, 1992),
*Paragraph, Minnesota Rev, Ararat, Skylark, German Hse
Rev, Light.*

Jose Kozer P
10933 71st Rd, #5F, Forest Hills, NY 11375-4816
Pubs: *Projimos/Intimates* (Spain; Carrer Ausias, 1991), *De
Donde Oscilan Los Seres en Sus Proporciones* (El
Guerrero Encendido, 1990).

Elaine Kraf W
7226 Manse St, Forest Hills, NY 11375-6728
Pubs: *The Princess Of 72nd Street* (New Directions, 1979),
Find Him! (Fiction Collective, 1977).

Daniel Krakauer P
346 E 10 St #6, New York, NY 10009, 212-533-8537
Pubs: *Poems for the Whole Family* (United Artists, 1994),
Out of This World: Anth (Crown, 1991), *Transfer, Tamarind,
Mag City, Downtown, The World, Cover.*

Cynthia Kraman P
16 Charles St, New York, NY 10014, 212-675-7435
Pubs: *The Mexican Murals* (E.G. Pr, 1986), *Taking On The
Local Color* (Wesleyan U Pr, 1977), *Antaeus, Paris Rev,
Poetry Flash, Southern Rev.*

Larry Kramer W
2 Fifth Ave, #32, New York, NY 10011

Robert Kramer P
Language Dept, Manhattan College, Riverdale, NY 10471,
718-862-7401
Pubs: *From Action to Dynamic Silence* (Charles Schlacks,
1991), *Home Planet News, Pivot, Poets, Night Sun, Quarry
West, Grub Street, Apocalypse.*

David Kranes W
Harold Matson Co., Inc., 276 5th Ave, New York, NY 10001,
212-679-4490

Christine Kraus P
151 2nd Ave, #2A, New York, NY 10003, 212-982-5603

Rochelle Kraut P
334 E 11 St, #16, New York, NY 10003, 212-477-2487
Pubs: *Art In America* (Little Light Bks, 1984), *Little Light,
The World, Mag City, Rocky Ledge.*

Steven M. Krauzer W
Virginia Barber Agency, 101 5th Ave, Ste 11-F, New York, NY
10003, 212-255-6515
Pubs: *Frame Work* (Bantam, 1989).

Ann Kregal P
24 Riverside Dr, 1F, New York, NY 10023
Pubs: *Gyro, Home Planet News, Telephone.*

Nancy Kricorian   P
450 Riverside Dr, #2, New York, NY 10027
Pubs: *River Styx, Ararat, The Literary Rev, Mississippi Rev, Witness, Graham House Rev, Ikon, Caliban, Heresies, Parnassus.*

Leonard Kriegel   W
355 8th Ave, #19F, New York, NY 100014838, 212-243-7832
Pubs: *Flying Solo* (Beacon, 1998), *Falling into Life* (North Point Pr, 1991), *Quitting Time* (Pantheon, 1982).

Jill Kroesen   P
15 E 17 St, #5, New York, NY 10003
Pubs: *Disposable Art* (D-Cup Dog Pr, 1975), *High Performance, Ear Magazine, Art Rite, Criteria.*

Herbert Kubly   W
Harold Ober Associates, 425 Madison Ave, New York, NY 10017
Pubs: *The Parkside Stories* (Northword Pr, 1985), *Native's Return* (Stein & Day, 1981).

Frank Kuenstler   P
670 W End Ave, New York, NY 10025, 212-362-1691
Pubs: *In Which* (Cairn Edtns, 1994), *13 1/2 Poems* (SZ Pr, 1984), *Empire* (Archive Pr, 1976).

Ken Kuhlken   W
Bleecker Street Associates, 88 Bleecker St, Ste 6B, New York, NY 10012, 212-677-4492
Pubs: *The Venus Deal, The Loud Adios* (St. Martin's, 1992, 1991), *Midheaven* (Viking, 1980), *Esquire, Puerto del Sol, Kansas Qtly, Colorado Rev, Mss..*

M. Karl Kulikowski   P
2960 Philip Ave, Bronx, NY 10465, 212-931-8964
Pubs: *Haiku, Senryu And Poetry* (Gusto Pr, 1978), *Hyacinths And Biscuits, Jean's Jrnl, Samisdat.*

Stanley Kunitz   P
37 W 12 St, #2J, New York, NY 10011, 212-924-9155
Pubs: *The Essential Blake* (Ecco Pr, 1987), *Next-to-Last Things* (Atlantic, 1985).

Tuli Kupferberg   W
160 6th Ave, New York, NY 10013, 212-925-3823
Internet: normans@escape.com
Pubs: *Don't Make Trouble* (Strolling Dog Pr, 1991), *Portable Beat Reader: Anth* (Viking Penguin, 1992), *Village Voice, Against the Current, Shadow.*

Bill Kushner   P
319 W 22 St, #2A, New York, NY 10011, 212-691-7276
Pubs: *Out of This World* (Crown, 1991), *Love Uncut* (United Artists Bks, 1990), *In Our Time: Anth* (St. Martin's Pr, 1989).

Paul Kuttner   W
Dawnwood Press, 387 Park Ave S, 5th Fl, New York, NY 100168810
Pubs: *The Iron Virgin, Absolute Proof, Condemned, The Man Who Lost Everything* (Dawnwood Pr, 1987, 1984, 1983, 1976).

Michael La Bombarda   P
89-04 172nd St, Jamaica, NY 11432, 718-526-5826
Pubs: *Five Plus Five* (Low Tech Publisher, 1984), *Appearances.*

Mary La Chapelle   W
Anita Diamant Agency, 310 Madison Ave, New York, NY 10017
Pubs: *House of Heroes* (Vintage, 1990), *Sing Heavenly Muse!, Warm Jrnl, Northern Literary Qtly.*

Tom LaBar   W
436 W Broadway, New York, NY 10012

Martha J. LaBare   P
1 Old Fulton St, Brooklyn, NY 11201, 718-855-2896
Internet: martha_labare@bloomfield.edu
Pubs: *Shooting Star & Other Poems* (Swollen Magpie Pr, 1982), *Roof, Telephone, World, Poet & Critic.*

Oliver Lake   P
163 Adelphi St, Brooklyn, NY 11205, 718-875-7558

Wally Lamb   W
Linda Chester Literary Agency, 630 5th Ave Suite 2662, New York, NY 10111, 212-218-3350
Pubs: *I Know This Much Is True* (Regan Bks/HarperCollins, 1998), *She's Come Undone* (Pocket Bks/S&S, 1992), *Best of the Missouri Review: Fiction 1978-1990: Anth* (U Missouri Pr, 1991), *Pushcart Prize XV Anth 1990.*

Annette Henkin Landau   W
301 E 66 St, #16K, New York, NY 10021, 212-861-7425
Pubs: *Jewish Possibilities: Best of Moment Magazine: Anth* (Jason Aronson, 1987), *Confrontation, Commentary, Tikkun, Other Voices, Moment, Vignette.*

Sandy Landsman   W
43-57 Union St, #6C, Flushing, NY 11355, 516-921-0808
Pubs: *Castaways on Chimp Island, The Gadget Factor* (Atheneum, 1986, 1984).

Marcia Lane   PP
462 Amsterdam Ave, New York, NY 10024, 212-799-1196
Internet: storylane@aol.com
Pubs: *Christoph Wants a Party* (Kane-Miller Bks, 1995), *Picturing the Rose* (H.W. Wilson, 1993), *National Storytelling Literary Jrnl, Creative Classroom.*

George Lanning   W
JCR, Inc., 27 W 20 St, Ste 1103, New York, NY 10011

Ring Lardner   W
Russell & Volkening, Inc., 50 W 29 St, New York, NY 10001,
212-684-6050
>Pubs: *All For Love* (Franklin Watts, 1985), *The Ecstasy of
Owen Muir* (Cameron & Kahn, 1955).

Joan Larkin   P
813 8th Ave, Brooklyn, NY 11215, 718-499-1629
Internet: larkin7@aol.com
>Pubs: *Cold River* (Painted Leaf Pr, 1997), *A Long Sound*
(Granite Pr, 1986), *Gay and Lesbian Poetry in Our Time:
Anth* (St. Martin's Pr, 1988), *APR, Global City Rev, Hanging
Loose, Out Mag, Sing Heavenly Muse.*

Jeremy Larner   W
PO Box 335, Canal St Sta, New York, NY 10013-0335
>Pubs: *Sex, Death and God in L.A.: Anth* (Pantheon, 1992),
M, Dissent, Focus.

Wendy Wilder Larsen   P
439 E 51 St, New York, NY 10022-6473
>Pubs: *Braided Lives* (Minnesota Humanities Commission,
1991), *A Year in Poetry: Anth* (Crown, 1995), *Paris Rev,
Nimrod, Confrontation, Hawaii Rev.*

Pam Laskin   P&W
414 5th St, Brooklyn, NY 11215
>Pubs: *The Buried Treasure, Heroic Horses* (McGraw-Hill,
1998, 1998), *A Wish Upon A Star* (Magination, 1991),
Music From the Heart (Bantam, 1990), *Sassy, Sidewalks,
Poet's Sanctuary, Pinehurst Jrnl.*

Michael Lassell   P&W
114 Horatio St, #512, New York, NY 10014-1579,
212-206-7339
Internet: mjlassell@aol.com
>Pubs: *A Flame For The Touch That Matters* (Painted Leaf
Pr, 1998), *The Hard Way* (Richard Kasak Bks, 1995),
Decade Dance (Alyson, 1990), *City Lights Rev, Portable
Lower East Side, Excursus, Central Park, Zyzzyva, Global
City Rev, Hanging Loose.*

Charles Keeling Lassiter   P
1382 1st Ave, #19, New York, NY 10021-9526, 212-535-6075
>Pubs: *C.K. Lassiter: Drawings & Writing, 1957-1990*
(Switzerland; Sylvia Acatos, 1990).

Kristin Hunter Lattany   W
1 Union Sq W, New York, NY 10003, 212-627-9100
>Pubs: *Kinfolks* (Ballantine, 1996), *God Bless the Child*
(Howard U Pr, 1986), *Philadelphia Inquirer, Essence,
Seventeen, Callaloo, Nation.*

Ann Lauterbach   P
Ruth & David Schwab Prof of Literature, Bard College,
Annandale-on-Hudson, NY 12504
>Pubs: *Clamor* (Viking/Penguin, 1991), *How Things Bear
Their Telling* (France; Collective Generation, 1990),
Conjunctions, o.blek, Ploughshares.

Lynne Lawner   P
Georges Borchardt Inc., 136 E 57 St, New York, NY 10022,
212-737-5619
Internet: lynlawner@aol.com
>Pubs: *Lives of the Courtesans* (Rizzoli, 1987), *Paris Rev,
Radcliffe Qtly, Confrontation, Chelsea, Georgia Rev, The
Bridge.*

Kathleen Rockwell Lawrence   W
510 E 23 St, #13-B, New York, NY 10010-, 212-533-7563
>Pubs: *The Boys I Didn't Kiss* (British-American, 1990), *The
Last Room in Manhattan, Maud Gone* (Atheneum, 1989,
1986).

Jane Lazarre   W
The Wendy Weil Agency, Inc., 232 Madison Ave, Ste 1300,
New York, NY 10016, 212-685-0300
>Pubs: *Worlds Beyond My Control* (Dutton/NAL, 1991), *The
Powers of Charlotte* (Crossing Pr, 1988), *The Mother Knot*
(Beacon Pr, 1985).

Cynthia LeClaire   P&W
St. Francis College, 180 Remsen St, Brooklyn, NY 11201,
718-522-2300
>Pubs: *The Rape of Persephone* (New Spirit Pr, 1993),
Homage to the Light (Black Swan Pr, 1985).

Jeanne Lee   PP
JMLF Productions, 525 Hudson St, #3RN, New York, NY
10014, 212-860-4209
>Pubs: *Natural Affinities* (CD; Owl, 1992), *Songposts* (CD;
Word of Mouth, 1991).

Marie G. Lee   W
Harold Ober Associates, 425 Madison Ave, New York, NY
10017, 212-759-8600
>Pubs: *Neccessary Roughness* (HarperCollins, 1996),
Finding My Voice (HM, 1992), *Kenyon, New York Times,
American Voice, Asian Pacific American Jrnl.*

Roland Legiardi-Laura   P
295 E 8 St, New York, NY 10009, 212-529-9327
>Pubs: *Bomb Mag, Appearances, The World 40, Telephone
19, Lumen/Avenue A, Main Trend, Sunbury 9.*

David Lehman   P
104 MacDougal St, #1, New York, NY 10012, 212-473-2023
Internet: dclehman@aol.com
>Pubs: *Valentine Place* (Scribner, 1996), *Operation Memory,
An Alternative to Speech* (Princeton, 1990, 1986).

Eric Gabriel Lehman   W
Malaga Baldi Literary Agency, 2112 Broadway, New York, NY
10023
Internet: mbaldi@aol.com
>Pubs: *Quaspeck, Waterboys* (Mercury House, 1993, 1989),
New Letters, Modern Words.

Brad Leithauser　　　　　　　　　　　P&W
Alfred A. Knopf, Inc., 201 E 50 St, New York, NY 10022
　　Pubs: *Hence* (Knopf, 1989).

Alan Lelchuk　　　　　　　　　　　　W
Georges Borchardt Inc, 136 E 57th St, New York, NY 10022,
212-573-5785
　　Pubs: *Playing The Game* (Baskerville Pubs, 1995),
　　Brooklyn Boy, Miriam at Thirty-Four (McGraw-Hill, 1990,
　　1989), *American Mischief* (FSG, 1974), *Atlantic, New
　　American Rev, New Republic.*

John Leonard　　　　　　　　　　　　W
Curtis Brown Ltd., 10 Astor Pl, New York, NY 10003-6935,
212-473-5400

Estelle Leontief　　　　　　　　　　P
37 Washington Sq W, #16B, New York, NY 10011
　　Pubs: *Sellie & Dee: A Friendship* (Chicory Blue Pr, 1993),
　　Genia & Wassily: A Russian American Memoir (Zephyr Pr,
　　1987), *Sojourner, Florida Rev.*

Eleanor Lerman　　　　　　　　　　P
10460 Queens Blvd, #20H, Flushing, NY 11375-7325
　　Pubs: *Come The Sweet By & By* (U Massachusetts Pr,
　　1975), *Armed Love* (Wesleyan U Pr, 1973).

Rhoda Lerman　　　　　　　　　　　W
William Morris Agency, 1350 Ave of the Americas, New York,
NY 10019, 212-586-5100
　　Pubs: *In the Company of Newfies, Animal Acts, God's Ear,
　　Book of the Night, Eleanor* (Henry Holt, 1997, 1994, 1989,
　　1984, 1979).

Linda Lerner　　　　　　　　　　　　P
PO Box 020292, Brooklyn, NY 11202-0007, 212-766-4109
Internet: llerner@mindspring.com
　　Pubs: *New & Selected Poems, She's Back* (Ye Olde Font
　　Shoppe Pr, 1998, 1996), *No One's People* (New Spirit Pr,
　　1992), *Chiron, Atom Mind, Confrontation, Maverick Pr,
　　Home Planet News.*

Rika Lesser　　　　　　　　　　　　P
133 Henry St, #5, Brooklyn, NY 112012550, 718-852-1163
Internet: rika.lesser.mc.74@aya.yale.edu
　　Pubs: *Growing Back: Poems 1972-1992* (U South Carolina
　　Pr, 1997), *All We Need of Hell* (U North Texas Pr, 1995),
　　Etruscan Things (Braziller, 1983), *Paris Rev, New Yorker,
　　Partisan, Poetry, Nation.*

Donald Lev　　　　　　　　　　　　　P
3047 Brighton First Pl, Brooklyn, NY 11235, 718-769-2854
　　Pubs: *Twilight* (CRS Outloud Bks, 1995), *A New
　　Geography of Poets: Anth* (U Arkansas Pr, 1992), *And
　　Then, Long Shot, Ikon, Home Planet News, Lips, Pivot.*

Jan Heller Levi　　　　　　　　　　P&W
244 Waverly Pl, #2B, New York, NY 10014, 212-929-1951
　　Pubs: *Graham Hse Rev, Poetry East, Ploughshares,
　　Pequod, Antioch Rev, River Styx, Beloit Poetry Jrnl.*

Toni Mergentime Levi　　　　　　　P
105 W 73 St #4D, New York, NY 10023, 212-362-5481
　　Pubs: *For A Dancing Bear* (Three Mile Harbor, 1995),
　　*Prairie Schooner, California Qtly, Manhattan Poetry Rev,
　　Negative Capability, Crosscurrents, Texas Rev, Kansas
　　Qtly, Confrontation.*

Phillis Levin　　　　　　　　　　　　P
128 W 13 St, #42, New York, NY 100117822, 212-741-1977
Internet: PL30@umail.umd.edu
　　Pubs: *The Afterimage* (Copper Beech Pr, 1995), *Temples
　　And Fields* (U Georgia Pr, 1988), *Atlantic, New Yorker,
　　Paris Rev, New Republic, Poetry, Partisan Rev, Nation.*

Anne-Marie Levine　　　　　　　　P
156 E 89 St, New York, NY 10128
　　Pubs: *Euphorbia* (Provincetown Arts Pr, 1994), *Parnassus,
　　Ploughshares, Provincetown Arts, Pequod, New York
　　Times, Beloit Poetry Jrnl.*

Howard Levy　　　　　　　　　　　　P
70 E 96 St, #12B, New York, NY 10128
　　Pubs: *Poetry, Paris Rev, Threepenny Rev, Gettysburg Rev,
　　APR, Georgia Rev, Massachusetts Rev, Columbia.*

Owen Levy　　　　　　　　　　　　　W
217 Central Pk N, New York, NY 10026
　　Pubs: *A Brother's Touch* (Pinnacle Books, 1982).

Robert J. Levy　　　　　　　　　　　P
595 W End Ave #4A, New York, NY 10024-1727,
212-799-6836
Internet: rjlevy@unitedmedia.com
　　Pubs: *Chefs at Twilight* (Bacchae Pr, 1996), *The Perfection
　　of Standing Aside* (South Coast Pr, 1993), *Paris Rev,
　　Poetry, Georgia Rev, Southern Rev.*

Stephen Levy　　　　　　　　　　　P
106 W 13 St, #11, New York, NY 10011, 212-691-0442
　　Pubs: *Many Hands* (Firefly Pr, 1982), *Israel Horizons,
　　Genesis 2, Reconstructionist, & Then.*

Harry Lewis　　　　　　　　　　　　P
115 Barrow St #4B, New York, NY 10014, 212-243-1393
　　Pubs: *Two For One, Silly 1-14* (Little Rootie Tootie/Ikon Pr,
　　1994, 1992), *Ikon, Sun, Number, New York Times Bk Rev,
　　Mulch, New York Mag, Transfer.*

Marilyn Jaye Lewis　　　　　　　　W
777 W End Ave, New York, NY 10025, 212-864-3523
Internet: mjaye@akula.com
　　Pubs: *Swingers, Safeway, Neptune and Surf, I Like Boys*
　　(Masquerade Bks, 1998; 1998; 1999), *Frighten the Horses,
　　Bad Attitude, Masquerade Erotic Jrnl.*

Owen Lewis   PP
24 E 82 St, New York, NY 10028
    Pubs: *New Pictures At An Exhibition* (Alexander Browde,
    1977), *Princeton Spectrum.*

Richard Lewis   P
141 E 88 St, #3E, New York, NY 10028, 212-831-7717
    Pubs: *Living By Wonder* (Parabola Bks, 1998), *Poets At
    Work* (Just Buffalo Literary Ctr, 1995), *When Thought Is
    Young* (New Rivers Pr, 1992), *Asheville Poetry Rev.*

Leslie Li   W
Witherspoon Associates, 15 E 36 St, New York, NY 10016,
212-685-1906
Internet: leslieli@sover.net
    Pubs: *Bittersweet* (Charles Tuttle, 1992), *American
    Identities: Anth* (U Pr New England, 1994).

Herbert Lieberman   W
Georges Borchardt Inc., 136 E 57 St, New York, NY 10022,
212-753-5785
    Pubs: *Sandman, Sleep* (St. Martin's Pr, 1992), *Shadow
    Dancers* (Little, Brown, 1989), *The Climate of Hell, City of
    the Dead* (S&S, 1978, 1976) *Crawlspace* (David McKay,
    1971), *Redbook, U Chicago Pr.*

Herbert Liebman   W
College of Staten Island, 2800 Victory Blvd, Staten Island, NY
10314, 212-242-1909
    Pubs: *Confrontation, Chelsea, PEN Syndicated Fiction,
    Paris Transcontinental, Midstream.*

Kate Light   P
225 W 106 St, #3M, New York, NY 10025, 212-222-9620
    Pubs: *The Laws of Falling Bodies* (Story Line Pr, 1997),
    *Paris Rev, Sparrow, Western Humanities Rev, Feminist
    Studies, Wisconsin Rev, Janus.*

Frank Lima   P
147-20 35th Ave, #11-B, Flushing, NY 11354-3706,
718-961-0301
    Pubs: *Angel* (Liveright, 1976), *Underground With The
    Oriole* (Dutton, 1971).

Nancy Linde   P
20 Cliff St #8E, Staten Island, NY 10305, 718-876-9293
    Pubs: *The Orange Cat Bistro* (Kensington, 1996), *Buckle,
    Symposium, Sojourner, 13th Moon, Promethean,
    Endymion.*

Don Linder   P&W
243 Riverside Dr, #604, New York, NY 10025, 212-866-9001
Internet: dlinder@shiva.hunter.cuny.edu
    Pubs: *West Side Spirit, Other Voices, Mss., Beacon Rev,
    Stardancer, Inprint.*

Romulus Linney   W
35 Claremont Ave, #9N, New York, NY 10027, 212-870-5145
    Pubs: *Sand Mountain, A Woman Without A Name*
    (Dramatists Play Service, 1986, 1985).

Elinor Lipman   W
Virginia Barber Literary Agenc, 101 5th Ave, New York, NY
10003, 212-255-6515
    Pubs: *The Inn At Lake Devine* (Random Hse, 1998),
    Isabel's Bed (Pocket, 1995), *The Way Men Act, Then She
    Found Me* (Washington Square Pr, 1993, 1991).

Lucy R. Lippard   W
138 Prince St, New York, NY 10012, 212-966-2994
    Pubs: *See/You Mean* (Chrysalis Bks, 1979), *Heresies, Sun
    And Moon, Big Deal.*

Rhoda Marilyn Lippel   P
365 W 28 St, #20E, New York, NY 10001-7919,
212-691-3925
    Pubs: *Curious West, Write Technique, Downtown, Journal
    of the e. e. cummings Society, Clinton Chronicle.*

Gordon Lish   W
Four Walls Eight Windows, 39 W 14 St, New York, NY 10011,
212-206-4769
    Pubs: *Peru, The Mourner at the Door, Epigraph, Dear Mr.
    Capote, What I Know So Far* (Four Walls Eight Windows,
    1997, 1997, 1996, 1996, 1996).

Olga Litowinsky   W
Curtis Brown Ltd., 10 Astor Pl, New York, NY 10003-6935
    Pubs: *The High Voyage* (Viking, 1977).

Iris Litt   P
252 W 11 St, New York, NY 10014, 212-691-5420
    Pubs: *Word Love* (Cosmic Trend, 1996), *Love's Shadow:
    Anth* (Crossing Pr, 1993), *Onthebus, Lactuca, Earth's
    Daughters, Poetry Now, Central Park, Pearl.*

Larry Litt   PP
313 E 6 St, New York, NY 10003, 212-614-1591
    Pubs: *eine DATA base* (Germany; Edition Cantz, 1993), *Art
    20/21 The Turn of the Century* (S. Korea; Taejon Pr, 1993),
    Downtown, Street News, The Fugue.

Susan Litwack   P
752 W End Ave, #6F, New York, NY 10025, 212-663-1379
    Pubs: *Mudfish, Southern Poetry Rev, Outerbridge, Puerto
    del Sol, Cincinnati Poetry Rev, Zone 3.*

Tsaurah Litzky   P
1 Old Fulton St, Brooklyn, NY 11201, 718-875-1107
    Pubs: *The Blue Bird Buddha Of No Regrets* (Apathy Pr,
    1994), *Best American Erotica: Anths* (S&S, 1998, 1997,
    1995), *Long Shot, Rant, Masquerade, Appearances, Pink
    Pages, Paramour.*

Jay Liveson P
3671 Hudson Manor Terr, Riverdale, NY 10463,
718-796-3750
Internet: jlivesonmd@pol.net
Pubs: *Atlanta Rev, Mediphors, Judaism, New England Jrnl of Medicine, Modern Haiku, JAMA, Riverrun, Western Jrnl of Medicine, Einstein Qtly, Hollins Critic, Plainsongs.*

Bernard Livingston W
235 W End Ave, #3E, New York, NY 10023, 212-873-8571
Pubs: *Closet Red* (Waverly, 1985), *Zoo: Animals, People, Places, Their Turf: America's Horsey Set and Its Princely Dynasties* (Arbor Hse, 1974, 1973).

Katinka Loeser W
Watkins Loomis Agency, Inc., 133 E 35 St, Ste 1, New York, NY 10016
Pubs: *The Archers At Home, Tomorrow Will Be Monday* (Atheneum, 1968, 1964), *New Yorker, McCall's.*

Andrea Freud Loewenstein P&W
462 5th St, #2, Brooklyn, NY 11215-3402
Pubs: *The Worry Girl* (Firebrand Bks, 1992), *This Place* (Pandora Pr, 1984), *Conditions, Bad Attitude.*

Eloise Loftin P
77 Eastern Pkwy #5B, Brooklyn, NY 11238, 718-783-7062

Robert Emmet Long W
80 5th Ave, #705, New York, NY 10011, 212-675-6063

Sabra Loomis P
136 Waverly Pl, New York, NY 10014, 212-645-5131
Pubs: *Rosetree* (Alice James Bks, 1989), *APR, American Voice, Poetry Ireland Rev, Cyphers, Salt Hill Jrnl, San Francisco Jung Society Jrnl, Salamander, Cincinnati Poetry Rev, Negative Capability, Violet.*

Phillip Lopate P&W
402 Sackett St, Brooklyn, NY 11231
Pubs: *Against Joie De Vivre* (Poseidon, 1989), *The Rug Merchant* (Viking, 1987), *Paris Rev, Harper's, Threepenny Rev, Southwest Rev, Parnassus, Boulevard.*

Judy Lopatin W
925 Union St, #6C, Brooklyn, NY 11215, 718-399-7903
Pubs: *Modern Romances* (Fiction Collective, 1986), *AM Lit: Anth* (Edtn Druckhaus, 1992), *Lone Star Literary Qtly, VLS, Between C&D, Witness, Europe.*

Barry Lopez W
Sterling Lord Literistic, 65 Bleecker St, New York, NY 10012, 212-780-6050
Pubs: *About This Life, Field Notes* (Knopf, 1998, 1994), *Crow and Weasel* (North Point Pr, 1990), *Arctic Dreams* (Scribner, 1986), *Harper's, Georgia Rev, Story, DoubleTake, Orion, Manoa.*

Eileen Lottman W
The Karpfinger Agency, 357 W 20 St, New York, NY 10011-3379, 212-691-2690
Pubs: *She And I* (Morrow, 1991), *After the Wind* (Dell, 1979).

Richard L. Loughlin P
83-57 118th St #4D, Kew Gardens, NY 11415-2366
Pubs: *Verses Vice Verses, Harian Creative Awards Anth* (Harian Creative Pr, 1980, 1981).

Esther Louise P
568-3 Louisiana Ave, Brooklyn, NY 11239, 718-942-3001
Internet: elm@admin.con2.com
Pubs: *Confirmations Anth* (Quill, 1983), *Essence, City, Obsidian, American Rag, Bopp, Freshtones.*

David Low W
77 E 12 St, #5G, New York, NY 10003
Pubs: *American Families: Anth* (NAL, 1989), *Ploughshares.*

Cortnie A. Lowe PP&P
172 St. Marks Ave, Brooklyn, NY 11238, 718-857-1062
Pubs: *Hexagram* (Poets Union Pr, 1977), *Partisan Rev.*

Marilyn Lowen P
286 South St, #16A, New York, NY 10002, 212-227-5364
Pubs: *Vague* (Fire Sign Pr, 1983), *Reflections: Anth* (Diana Pr, 1971), *City, The New Women.*

Bruce Lowery W
Georges Borchardt Inc., 136 E 57 St, New York, NY 10022, 212-753-5785

Beverly Lowry W
ICM, 40 W 57 St, New York, NY 10019
Pubs: *Crossed Over* (Knopf, 1992), *Breaking Gentle, The Perfect Sonya, Daddy's Girl* (Viking, 1988, 1987, 1981), *Emma Blue* (Doubleday, 1978).

Carmen D. Lucca PP
3131 Grand Concourse, Bronx, NY 10468, 718-367-0780
Pubs: *Brushstrokes And Landscapes* (Bilingual Edtn; Poets' Refuge, 1990), *Puerto Rico's Ateneo 1992, Brujula-Compass, Ashland Poetry Pr.*

Felipe Luciano P
9 Fordham Hill Oval, #12G, Bronx, NY 10468, 212-365-2753

Thomas Luhrmann P
468 Riverside Dr, #82A, New York, NY 10027, 212-663-3372
Pubs: *The Objects In The Garden* (Wesleyan U Pr, 1982).

K. Curtis Lyle P
132-11 Foch Blvd, South Ozone Park, NY 11420, 718-659-4776
Pubs: *Fifteen Predestination Weather Reports* (Beyond Baroque, 1976).

Charles H. Lynch   P
263 Eastern Pkwy, #5B, Brooklyn, NY 112386335,
718-638-3047
    Pubs: *Randlage 33* (Germany; Rothmaler, 1988), *Black American Literary Forum, World Order, Black Scholar, Chelsea, Obsidian, Hanging Loose, Crab Orchard Rev.*

Ellen Windy Aug Lytle   P&W
80 N Moore St, #9B, New York, NY 10013, 212-571-6774
    Pubs: *Factory Fish, Manuscripts 1980-83* (Linear Arts Pr, 1998, 1998), *Lettuce After Moon* (Ikon Pr, 1993), *Down Under Manhattan Bridge: Anth* (Dan Freeman, 1996), *Global City Rev, And Then, Crossroads, Downtown, Lowell Rev, Mind the Gap.*

Jackson Mac Low   PP&P
42 N Moore St, #6, New York, NY 10013-2441, 212-226-3346
Internet: tarmac@pipeline.com or jksnml@juno.com
    Pubs: *Barnesbook* (Sun & Moon Pr, 1996), *42 Merzgedichte in Memoriam Kurt Schwitters* (Station Hill, 1994), *Sulfur, Talisman, Conjunctions, World, Crayon, Chain, Heat* (Australia).

Norman MacAfee   P
55 W 11 St #8D, New York, NY 10011, 212-924-8247
    Pubs: *A New Requiem* (Cheap Rev Pr, 1988), *The World, Rouge.*

Ginny MacKenzie   P&W
66 Grand St, New York, NY 10013, 212-966-5643
    Pubs: *By Morning* (Coyote Pr, 1984), *Boulevard, Iowa Rev, Agni, New Letters, Pequod, Ploughshares.*

Elizabeth Macklin   P
207 W 14 St, #5F, New York, NY 10011
    Pubs: *A Woman Kneeling in the Big City* (Norton, 1992), *Best American Poetry: Anth* (Scribner, 1993), *Paris Rev, The Nation, Threepenny Rev, Southwest Rev, New Yorker, Lyra.*

Phillip Mahony   P
21-65 46th St, Astoria, NY 11105, 718-728-8031
    Pubs: *Supreme, Catching Bodies* (North Atlantic Bks, 1989, 1986).

Norman Mailer   W
ICM, 40 W 57 St, New York, NY 10019, 212-556-5600

Michael Malinowitz   P
41 John St #2A, New York, NY 100383715, 212-473-5144
    Pubs: *Michael's Ear* (Groundwater Pr, 1993), *Best American Poetry: Anth* (Scribner, 1988), *Private, Poetry Motel, Bad Henry Rev, Brooklyn Rev.*

George Malko   W
36 W 84 St, New York, NY 10024
Internet: geemal@msn.com
    Pubs: *Luna* (Pan, 1980), *Take What You Will* (Pyramid, 1975), *Fantasy & Science Fiction, Pleiades, The Distillation, Riversedge, Licking River Rev.*

Michael Malone   W
William Morris Agency, 1350 Ave of the Americas, New York, NY 10019, 212-586-5100
    Pubs: *Handling Sin, Foolscap, Uncivil Seasons, Time's Witness* (Washington Square Bks, 1992, 1992, 1991, 1990), *Playboy, Nation, Partisan Rev.*

Carolina Mancuso   W
c/o PSC, 123 7th Ave, Brooklyn, NY 11215
Internet: caro50@aol.com
    Pubs: *Word of Mouth Vol II, I: Anths, Love, Struggle & Change: Stories by Women: Anth* (Crossing Pr, 1991, 1990, 1988), *Amelia, Ikon.*

Allen Mandelbaum   P
CUNY Graduate Center, 33 W 42 St, New York, NY 10036, 212-879-6076
    Pubs: *A Lied Of Letter Press* (Pennyroyal, 1980), *Chelmaxioms* (Godine, 1978), *Denver Qtly, Poetry.*

Norman Manea   W
201 W 70 St, #10-I, New York, NY 10023
    Pubs: *The Black Envelope* (FS&G, 1996), *On Clowns: The Dictator and the Artist* (Grove Pr, 1992), *TriQuarterly, Partisan, New Republic, Paris Rev, Salmagundi.*

Peggy Mann   W
46 W 94 St, New York, NY 10025
    Pubs: *Reader's Digest, McCall's, Good Housekeeping, Harper's Bazaar.*

D. Keith Mano   W
392 Central Pk W, #6P, New York, NY 10025
    Pubs: *The Fergus Dialogues* (International Scholars Pub, 1998), *Take Five* (Dalkey Archive Pr, 1998), *Topless* (Random Hse, 1991), *Playboy, National Rev, New York Times Book Rev.*

Jaime Manrique   P&W
33 Bank St, #5, New York, NY 10014, 212-929-4960
    Pubs: *Colombian Gold* (Painted Leaf Pr, 1998), *Twilight At the Equator* (Faber & Faber, 1997), *My Night with Federico Garcia Lorca* (Groundwater Pr, 1995), *Latin Moon in Manhattan* (St. Martin's, 1992), *World, Washington Post Book World.*

Jan Marino   W
McIntosh & Otis, 310 Madison Ave, New York, NY 10017
    Pubs: *Searching for Atticus* (S&S, 1997), *The Day That Elvis Came to Town* (Little, Brown, 1991).

Wendy Mark   P
2 W 67 St #9D, New York, NY 10023, 212-874-2455
    Pubs: *Prairie Schooner, Literary Cupboard, Res Gestae.*

Wallace Markfield   W
15 Vista Way, Port Washington, NY 11050

Sol Markoff   P
13 W 13 St, #3CS, New York, NY 10011, 212-243-8663
Pubs: *Anthology Of World Haiku* (Kubota Pr, 1979), *Seventeen Grains Of Sand* (Print Center, 1976).

David Markson   W
215 W 10 St, #3E, New York, NY 10014, 212-243-8688
Pubs: *Reader's Block, Wittgenstein's Mistress* (Dalkey Archive Pr, 1996, 1988).

Julia Markus   W
Harriet Wasserman Agency, 137 E 36 St, New York, NY 10016, 212-689-3257
Pubs: *A Change of Luck* (Viking/Penguin, 1991), *American Rose, Friends Along The Way, Uncle* (Dell, 1990, 1986, 1986).

Regina Marler   W
Maia Gregory Associates, 311 E 72 St, New York, NY 10021, 212-288-0310
Pubs: *Carolina Qtly, Chattahoochee Rev, NAR, Northwest Rev.*

John P. Marquand, Jr.   W
425 E 51 St, New York, NY 10022
Pubs: *Esquire, New York Rev of Bks, Contact, Paris Rev, Commentary.*

Elizabeth Marraffino   P
75 Bank St, #6H, New York, NY 10014, 212-691-9806
Pubs: *Blue Moon For Ruby Tuesday* (Contact II Pub, 1981), *Choice, Sun, The Dream Book, Nation.*

Paule Marshall   W
Faith Childs, 275 W 96 St, New York, NY 10025, 212-662-1232
Pubs: *Brown Girl, Brownstones* (Feminist Pr, 1996), *The Chosen Place, The Timeless People* (Vintage Pr, 1992), *Daughters* (Atheneum, 1991), *Praisesong for the Widow* (Putnam, 1983).

Charles Martin   P
358 1st St, Brooklyn, NY 11215, 718-768-9122
Pubs: *What the Darkness Proposes, Steal the Bacon* (Johns Hopkins U Pr, 1996, 1987), *Boulevard, Hellas, The Formalist, Threepenny Rev, Tennessee Qtly.*

Paula Martinac   W
237 E 26 St #2-E, New York, NY 10010
Internet: pmartinac@aol.com
Pubs: *Chicken* (Alyson Pub, 1997), *Home Movies, Out of Time, Voyages Out* (Seal Pr, 1993, 1990, 1989), *Art & Understanding, Queer City, Conditions, Sinister Wisdom, Blithe House Qtly.*

Andrew Marum   W
5643 Mosholu Ave, Riverdale, NY 10471, 212-601-3748
Pubs: *Follies & Foibles* (Facts On File, 1984).

Julio Marzan   P
175-20 Wexford Terr, Jamaica, NY 11432, 718-297-9439
Pubs: *The Spanish American Roots of W.C. Williams* (U Texas Pr, 1994), *Translations Without Originals* (I Reed Bks, 1986).

Donna Masini   P&W
PO Box 5, Prince St Sta, New York, NY 10012, 212-260-0496
Internet: dlmasini@aol.com
Pubs: *About Yvonne* (Norton, 1997), *The Kind of Danger* (Beacon Pr, 1994), *Georgia Rev, Paris Rev, Parnassus, Boulevard, VLS.*

Carole Maso   W
Georges Borchardt Inc., 136 E 57 St, New York, NY 10022, 212-753-5785
Pubs: *Defiance* (Dutton, 1998), *The American Woman In The Chinese Hat* (Plume, 1995), *Ghost Dance* (Ecco Pr, 1995), *APR, Common Knowledge, Rev of Contemporary Fiction, Bomb, Nerve, Conjunctions.*

Bobbie Ann Mason   W
ICM, 40 W 57 St, New York, NY 10019, 212-556-5600
Pubs: *Feather Crowns, Shiloh* (HarperCollins, 1993, 1982), *Love Life, In Country* (H&R, 1989, 1985), *Harper's, Story, New Yorker, Atlantic, Paris Rev.*

Greg Masters   P&W
437 E 12 St, #26, New York, NY 10009, 212-777-2714
Internet: http://www.artomatic.com/ gmasters/
Pubs: *The Poem and Other Poems* (Skylab Pr, 1998), *My Women and Men, Part 2* (Crony Bks, 1980), *Nuyorican Poetry Anth* (Henry Holt, 1994).

Harry Mathews   P&W
Maxine Groffsky Literary Agcy, 2 Fifth Ave, New York, NY 10011, 212-473-0004
Pubs: *Out of Bounds* (Burning Deck Pr, 1989), *The Orchard* (Bamberge Bks, 1988), *Paris Rev.*

Peter Matthiessen   W
Donadio & Ashworth, Inc., 121 W 27 St, Ste 704, New York, NY 10001, 212-691-8077

Sharon Mattlin   P
60 E 4 St, #21, New York, NY 10003, 212-475-7110
Pubs: *The Big House: A Collection Of Poets' Prose: Anth* (Ailanthus Pr, 1978), *Telephone, Dragonfly.*

Susan Maurer   P
210 E 15 St, #9P, New York, NY 10003
Pubs: *By The Blue Light of the Morning Glory* (Linear Arts, 1997), *Cafe Nico Anth* (Venom Pr, 1996), *American Voice, Mississippi Mud, Prisoners of the Night.*

William Maxwell   W
25 W 43 St, New York, NY 10036, 212-737-1461

Bernadette Mayer　　　P&W
172 E 4 St, #9B, New York, NY 10009, 212-254-5308
　　Pubs: *The Formal Field of Kissing* (Catchword Papers,
　　1990), *Sonnets* (Tender Buttons, 1990).

Jane Mayhall　　　P&W
15 W 67 St, #6MW, New York, NY 10023
　　Pubs: *The Treasury of American Short Stories: Anth* (Dell,
　　1994), *Best of Wind Literary Magazine: Anth* (Wind Pubs,
　　1994), *Confrontation, Partisan Rev, New Renaissance,
　　Hudson Rev, New Yorker, New Letters, Shenandoah.*

Norma Fox Mazer　　　W
Elaine Markson Literary Agency, 44 Greenwich Ave, New
York, NY 10011, 212-243-8480
　　Pubs: *When She Was Good* (Arthur Levine/Scholastic,
　　1997), *Missing Pieces, Silver, After the Rain* (Morrow, 1995,
　　1988, 1987), *Heartbeat* (Bantam, 1989), *English Jrnl.*

Regina McBride　　　P
929 W End Ave, #7A, New York, NY 10025, 212-678-2364
　　Pubs: *Yarrow Field* (San Diego Poet's Pr, 1990), *Ark,
　　Ironwood, Boulevard, Pequod, High Plains Literary Rev,
　　Antioch Rev, Denver Qtly, Sonora Rev, One Meadway.*

Charles McCarry　　　W
William Morris Agency, 1350 Ave of the Americas, New York,
NY 10019, 212-586-5100
　　Pubs: *The Better Angels, The Secret Lovers* (Dutton, 1979,
　　1977).

Robbie McCauley　　　PP
223 E 4 St, #4, New York, NY 10009, 212-473-1801

Michael McClure　　　P&W
New Directions, 80 8th Ave, New York, NY 10011
　　Pubs: *Three Poems* (Penguin, 1995), *Simple Eyes, Rebel
　　Lions* (New Directions, 1994, 1991), *Testa Coda* (Rizzoli
　　Bks, 1991), *Love Lion* (Video; Mystic Fire Video, 1991).

Suzanne McConnell　　　W
133 W 24 St, 5th Fl, New York, NY 10011, 212-620-4196
　　Pubs: *Personal Fiction Writing: Anth* (Teachers & Writers,
　　1984), *Green Mountains Rev, Calyx, Little Mag, Olive Tree
　　Rev, Dreamworks, Appearances.*

Mary Joneve McCormick　　　P
427 W 51 St #4E, New York, NY 10019
Internet: http://www.quicklink.com/ joneve
　　Pubs: *Small Bird Bones: Anth* (New Pr, 1993), *New Press,
　　Golden Isis, Smoke Signals, Nomad's Choir, Standard,
　　Sisyphus.*

James McCourt　　　W
145 E 22 St, New York, NY 10003
　　Pubs: *Kaye Wayfaring In "Avenged"* (Knopf, 1984),
　　Mawrdew Czgowchwz (FSG, 1975), *New Yorker.*

Sharyn McCrumb　　　W
Dominick Abel Literary Agency, 146 W 82 St, New York, NY
10024, 212-877-0710
Internet: www.sharynmccrumb.com
　　Pubs: *The Ballad of Frankie Silver, The Rosewood Casket*
　　(Dutton, 1998, 1996), *She Walks These Hills, Hangman's
　　Beautiful Daughter* (Scribner, 1994, 1992), *Appalachian
　　Heritage, Writer's Digest.*

Alice McDermott　　　W
Harriet Wasserman Literary Age, 137 E 36 St, New York, NY
10016
　　Pubs: *Charming Billy, At Weddings and Wakes, That Night*
　　(FSG, 1998, 1992, 1987), *A Bigamist's Daughter* (Random
　　Hse, 1982), *Ms., Mademoiselle.*

Joyce McDonald　　　W
310 Madison Ave, New York, NY 10017
Internet: jmcdonald@nac.net
　　Pubs: *Swallowing Stones, Comfort Creek* (Delacorte, 1997,
　　1996), *Homebody, Mail-Order Kid* (Putnam 1991, 1988).

Joseph McElroy　　　W
Melanie Jackson Agency, 250 W 57 St, #1119, New York, NY
10107
　　Pubs: *The Letter Left to Me* (Knopf, 1988), *Fathers & Sons:
　　Anth* (Grove Pr, 1992).

Gardner McFall　　　P
924 W End Ave, #101, New York, NY 10025, 212-678-1595
　　Pubs: *The Pilot's Daughter* (Time Being Bks, 1996),
　　Naming the Animals (Viking, 1994), *Nation, Ploughshares,
　　Paris Rev, Pequod, New Yorker.*

Thomas McGuane　　　W
Farrar, Straus & Giroux, 19 Union Sq W, New York, NY
10003, 212-741-6900

Arona McHugh　　　W
224 Davis Ave, Staten Island, NY 10310, 718-448-9089
　　Pubs: *A Banner With A Strange Device* (Dell, 1965).

Christopher McIlroy　　　W
Witherspoon & Chernoff, 157 W 57 St, Ste 700, New York,
NY 10019, 212-757-0567
　　Pubs: *All My Relations* (U Georgia Pr, 1994), *Best
　　American Short Stories: Anth* (HM, 1986), *TriQuarterly,
　　Missouri Rev, Fiction, Story Qtly, Ploughshares, Puerto del
　　Sol.*

Brian McInerney　　　P
200 W 81 St, #56, New York, NY 10024, 212-496-9084
　　Pubs: *All My Life* (James L. Weil, 1985), *The Photographs
　　Are Still Here* (Smoot Pr, 1984), *Origin.*

James Alan McPherson   W
Faith Childs, 275 W 96 St, New York, NY 10025,
212-995-9600
    Pubs: *Crabcakes* (S&S, 1998), *Fathering Daughters: Anth*
    (Beacon Pr, 1998), *DoubleTake, Iowa Rev, Center Eight.*

Taylor Mead   PP&P&W
163 Ludlow St, New York, NY 10002
    Pubs: *Excerpts From Son of Andy Warhol* (Hanuman Bks,
    1990), *Living With the Animals: Anth* (Faber & Faber,
    1995), *Outlook, Boss.*

Rosemari Mealy   P
WBAI Radio, 505 8th Ave, New York, NY 10018,
212-279-0707
    Pubs: *Confirmations* (Morrow/Quill, 1983), *Mickle Street
    Rev, Shooting Star, Sunbury.*

James Mechem   W
420 E 54 St #3E, New York, NY 10022, 212-888-1392
    Pubs: *Welcome to Bangkok* (Fell Swoop, 1997), *Della* (The
    Fault Pr, 1976), *Women Without Qualities* (Cafe Solo,
    1973), *A Diary of Women* (Winter House Pr, 1970), *Joyful
    Noise: Anth* (Kings Estate, 1996).

Tony Medina   P
PO Box 335, New York, NY 10026, 212-982-3158
Internet: tonymedina@erols.com
    Pubs: *No Noose Is Good Noose* (Harlem River Pr, 1996),
    Identity Lessons: Anth (Viking/Penguin, 1998), *Catch the
    Fire: Anth* (Riverhead Bks, 1998), *Long Shot, Vibe, African
    Voices, Paterson Literary Rev, Catalyst, Third World
    Viewpoints.*

Susie Mee   P
349 W 22 St, New York, NY 10011, 212-989-0405

Joshua Mehigan   P
647 President St #2B, Brooklyn, NY 11215, 718-399-0946
Internet: joshm@interport.net
    Pubs: *Confusing Weather* (Black Cat Press, 1998),
    Ploughshares, Verse, The Formalist, Pequod.

Ved Parkash Mehta   W
c/o The Wylie Agency, 250 W 57 St, Ste 2114, New York, NY
10107
    Pubs: *Three Stories of the Raj* (Scolar Pr, 1986),
    Delinquent Chacha (H&R, 1967), *Observer, Harper's,
    Statesman, New Yorker, Atlantic Monthly, Spectator.*

Richard Meier   P
16 Tompkins Pl, Brooklyn, NY 11231, 718-855-3683
    Pubs: *New Voices, 1984-1988: Anth* (Academy of American
    Poets, 1989), *APR, Chelsea, Mudfish, Phoebe, Graham
    House Rev, o.blek, Prairie Schooner.*

Jesus Papoleto Melendez   P
1781 Bruckner Blvd #6F, Bronx, NY 10472-6457
    Pubs: *Concertos On Market Street* (Kemetic Images, 1993),
    Street Poetry (Barlenmir Hse, 1972), *In Defense of Mumia:
    Anth* (Writers & Readers, 1996), *Centro.*

D. H. Melhem   P&W
250 W 94 St, #2H, New York, NY 10025, 212-865-9216
    Pubs: *Country: An Organic Poem* (Cross-Cultural
    Communications, 1998), *Rest in Love* (Confrontation Mag
    Pr, 1995), *Blight* (Riverrun Pr, 1995), *Confrontation, Ararat,
    Home Planet News, New Pr, Paintbrush, Medicinal
    Purposes, Graffiti Rag.*

Daniel Meltzer   W
251 W 74 St, #3D, New York, NY 10023, 212-362-4116
    Pubs: *The Square Root of Love* (Samuel French, 1979),
    The Pushcart Prize Anth (Pushcart Pr, 1997), *A
    Contemporary Reader for Creative Writing: Anth* (Harcourt
    Brace, 1994), *Prize Stories 1992: The O. Henry Awards:
    Anth* (Doubleday, 1992), *Vignette.*

Samuel Menashe   P
75 Thompson St #15, New York, NY 10012, 212-925-4105
    Pubs: *Collected Poems* (National Poetry Fdn, 1986),
    Penguin Modern Poets, Vol. 7: Anth (Penguin U.K., 1996),
    An Introduction to Poetry: Anth (HarperCollins, 1994),
    Partisan Rev, New Yorker, Sunday Times London, Tundra.

Douglas A. Mendini   P&W
403 W 54 St, #1D, New York, NY 10019, 212-541-6328
    Pubs: *Country Living, MacGuffin, Modernsense, Real
    Fiction, No, Clock Radio, Lactuca, Pudding, Details.*

Claudia Menza   P
Claudia Menza Literary Agency, 1170 Broadway, New York,
NY 10001, 212-889-6850
    Pubs: *The Lunatics Ball, Cage of Wild Cries* (Mosaic Pr,
    1994, 1990), *The Dream Book: Anth* (Schocken Pr, 1985),
    L.A. Times, Ploughshares.

Louise Meriwether   W
c/o Ellen Levine Literary Agen, 15 E 26 St., Ste 801, New
York, NY 10010, 212-725-4501
Internet: lmeriwe123@aol.com
    Pubs: *Fragments of the Ark* (Pocket Bks, 1994), *Daddy
    Was A Number Runner* (Feminist Pr, 1984), *Essence,
    Icarus, Black Scholar, Harbor Rev.*

Daphne Merkin   W
William Morris Agency, 1350 Ave of the Americas, New York,
NY 10019, 212-586-5100
    Pubs: *Enchantment* (HBJ, 1986), *Out of the Garden:
    Women Writing on the Bible: Anth* (Ballantine, 1994), *New
    Yorker, Partisan Rev, Mirabella, Esquire.*

Susan Mernit   P&W
164 Sterling Pl #1D, Brooklyn, NY 11217, 718-789-1396
    Pubs: *Moving to a New School* (Blackbird Pr, 1993), *Tree Climbing* (Membrane Pr, 1981), *Harper's, New York Times Bk Rev, Agenda, Georgia Rev.*

James I. Merrill   P&W
Atheneum Publishers, 866 3rd Ave, New York, NY 10022
    Pubs: *The Inner Room* (Knopf, 1988), *Recitative* (North Point Pr, 1986).

W. S. Merwin   P&W
Alfred A. Knopf, Inc., 201 E 50 St, New York, NY 10022, 212-751-2600
    Pubs: *Travels: Poems, The Lost Upland, The Rain in the Trees* (Knopf, 1993, 1992, 1998), *New Yorker.*

Robin Messing   P
660 Vanderbilt St, Brooklyn, NY 11218, 718-435-2696
    Pubs: *From Temporary Worker* (Lee-Lucas Pr, 1979), *# Mag, Dodeca, Telephone, Negative Capability, The Sycamore Rev, Brooklyn Rev.*

Shelley Messing   P&W
582 2nd St, #4C, Brooklyn, NY 11215, 718-768-2453
    Pubs: *Making Contact* (Voyage Out, 1978), *Women: A Journal Of Liberation, Moving Out, Sojourner.*

Mike Metz   P
150 E 56 St, PHA, New York, NY 10022, 212-421-5443
    Pubs: *Street Fighting at Wall & Broad* (Macmillan, 1982).

Claire Michaels   P
35-50 82nd St #6E, Jackson Heights, NY 11372, 718-672-7889
    Pubs: *Making Contact* (Willow Bee, 1989), *We Speak for Peace: Anth* (KIT, 1993), *Poetpourri, Aurora, Pudding, Parnassus, Wyoming: Hub of the Wheel.*

Frank Michel   W
333 E 80 St, #3-I, New York, NY 10021, 212-861-8258
Internet: franstone@aol.com
    Pubs: *Gettysburg Rev, Indiana Rev, Glimmer Train, Crescent Rev, Alaska Qtly Rev, Quarterly West, Crescent Rev.*

Robert William Middlemiss   W
Jonathan Dolger Agency, 49 E 96 St, #9B, New York, NY 10128, 212-427-1853
    Pubs: *Cormorant Documents* (Pageant Bks, 1989), *The Pelican's Clock* (Fawcett, 1981).

Betty Miles   W
Random House, 225 Park Ave S, New York, NY 10003, 212-254-1600
    Pubs: *The Sky Is Falling, The Tortoise and the Hare* (S&S, 1998, 1998), *Hey! I'm Reading, Save the Earth, Sink or Swim, I Would If I Could, Maudie & Me* (Knopf, 1995, 1991, 1986, 1982, 1980).

Arthur Miller   W
ICM, 40 W 57 St, New York, NY 10019, 212-556-5600
    Pubs: *The Creation Of The World And Other Business, The Crucible, Death of a Salesman* (Viking Penguin, 1973, 1953, 1949).

John E. Miller   W
249 Broome St, #32, New York, NY 10002, 212-260-8034
    Pubs: *Contamination* (Cave Canem Bks, 1982), *Tellus Audiocassette, Ferro-Botanica, Barney.*

Shelley Miller   P
299 W 12 St, #17H, New York, NY 10014, 212-645-6532
    Pubs: *World, Natl Poetry Mag of the Lower East Side, Tone, Cover, SoHo Arts Weekly, Inner Harvest, Arts New York.*

Stephen Paul Miller   P
60 E 8 St, #6P, New York, NY 10003, 212-677-6739
Internet: spmma@aol.com
    Pubs: *Art is Boring for the Same Reason We Stayed in Viet Nam* (Domestic Pr, 1992), *Best American Poetry: Anth* (S&S, 1994), *Talisman.*

Walter James Miller   P
100 Bleecker St #17-E, New York, NY 100122205, 212-674-1466
    Pubs: *Making An Angel* (Pylon, 1977), *Hampden-Sydney Poetry Rev Anth* (Hampden-Sydney, 1990), *Croton Rev, Literary Rev, New York Qtly, Artemis, Poet Lore.*

Joyce Milton   P
60 Plaza St, #6B, Brooklyn, NY 11238, 718-636-4471
    Pubs: *Save The Loonies* (Four Winds Pr, 1983), *The Rosenberg File* (HR&W, 1983).

Mark Mirsky   W
CCNY, Convent Ave & 138th St, New York, NY 10031, 212-650-5408
    Pubs: *The Red Adam* (Sun & Moon, 1990), *The Secret Table* (Macmillan, 1977), *Quarterly, Fiction, TriQuarterly, Mississippi Rev, Ways of Knowing, Partisan Rev, Massachusetts Rev.*

Julia Mishkin   P
330 W 85 St, #1G, New York, NY 10024, 212-877-7019
    Pubs: *Cruel Duet* (QRL Poetry Series, 1986), *Poetry, Georgia Rev, Paris Rev, Nation, Iowa Rev.*

Tom Mitchelson   PP&W
524 W 143 St, #3, New York, NY 10032, 212-690-5040
    Pubs: *Untold Lies As Love Tales* (WBAI, 1994), *Street Lights: Illuminating Tales of the Urban Black Experience: Anth* (Viking Penguin, 1995).

Charles Molesworth   P
109-23 71st Rd, Forest Hills, NY 11375, 718-268-8024
    Pubs: *Words to That Effect* (Seven Woods, 1981), *Salmagundi.*

Ursule Molinaro W
65 E 2 St, New York, NY 10003, 212-982-2204
   Pubs: *Power Dreamers* (McPherson, 1994), *Fat Skeletons*
   (Serif London, 1993), *Obsession: Anth* (Serpent's Tail,
   1995), *Caprice, Manoa.*

Timothy Monaghan P
78-44 80th St, Glendale, NY 11385
   Pubs: *5 A.M., Slipstream, Long Shot, New York Qtly,
   Negative Capability, Mudfish, Chiron Rev, Sulphur River,
   The Ledge, Poet Lore, Rattle, Birmingham Poetry Rev.*

Susan Montez P
875 W 181 St, #1E, New York, NY 10033, 212-781-5433
   Pubs: *Radio Free Queens* (Braziller, 1994), *New York Qtly,
   13th Moon, Artful Dodge, Cream City Rev,
   Hampden-Sydney Poetry Rev, Long Shot, Puerto del Sol,
   Asylum.*

Lorrie Moore W
Melanie Jackson Agency, 250 W 57 St, Ste 1119, New York,
NY 10107, 212-582-8585
   Pubs: *Who Will Run the Frog Hospital?, Like Life,
   Anagrams* (Knopf, 1994, 1990, 1986), *Forgotten Helper*
   (Kipling, 1987), *New Yorker, Paris Rev.*

Susannah Moore W
Wylie, Aitken & Stone, 250 W 57 St, New York, NY 10107,
212-246-0069
   Pubs: *In The Cut, Sleeping Beauties* (Knopf, 1995, 1993),
   The Whiteness of Bones (Doubleday, 1989), *My Old
   Sweetheart* (HM, 1983).

Speer Morgan W
ICM, 40 W 57 St, New York, NY 10019, 573-882-4460
Internet: morgan@showme.missouri.edu
   Pubs: *The Whipping Boy* (HM, 1994), *The Assemblers*
   (Dutton, 1986), *Brother Enemy* (Little, Brown, 1981), *Belle
   Starr* (Atlantic, 1979), *Rolling Stone, Harper's, Atlantic
   Monthly, Prairie Schooner, Iowa Rev.*

Kyoko Mori P&W
Ann Rittenberg Agency, 14 Montgomery Pl, Brooklyn, NY
11215, 212-886-9317
   Pubs: *Polite Lies, The Dream of Water, Shizuko's Daughter*
   (Henry Holt, 1998, 1996, 1993), *Prairie Schooner, Missouri
   Rev, Kenyon Rev, American Scholar, Crosscurrents,
   Denver Qtly, Paterson Rev.*

John Morressy W
William Morris Agency, 1350 Ave of the Americas, New York,
NY 10019
   Pubs: *The Mammoth Book of Comic Fantasy* (U.K.;
   Robinson Pub, 1998), *The Juggler* (HH, 1996), *Trocha
   Prace Bzneseneho Druhu* (Polaris, 1995), *A Remembrance
   For Kedrigern* (Ace, 1990), *Sci Fi Age, Writer's Digest,
   Fanstasy & Science Fiction.*

James Cliftonne Morris P&W
Rivercross Publishing, 127 E 59 St, New York, NY 10022,
800-451-4522
   Pubs: *Potpourri From A Black Pen* (Rivercross Pr, 1995),
   Poem of Love in the Long Run (Professional Pr, 1994),
   Phylon, Freedomways.

Mary Morris P&W
ICM, 40 W 57 St, New York, NY 10019, 212-556-5600
   Pubs: *House Arrest, A Mother's Love, The Waiting Room*
   (Doubleday, 1996, 1993, 1989), *Ontario Rev, Paris Rev,
   Boulevard, Epoch, Crosscurrents.*

Julia Morrison P
Seagate Music, 41 W 86 St, #14D, New York, NY 10024,
212-877-0560
   Pubs: *Smile Right to the Bone* (Seagate, 1989), *New World
   Writing, Accent, Poetry, Prism Intl.*

Lillian Morrison P
116 Pinehurst Ave, #F42, New York, NY 10033,
212-928-2662
   Pubs: *Slam Dunk* (Hyperion Bks, 1995), *Whistling the
   Morning In* (Boyds Mills Pr, 1992), *Confrontation, American
   Writing, Poets On, Fan, Light, Aethlon.*

Toni Morrison W
Janklow & Nesbit Associates, 598 Madison Ave, New York,
NY 10022-1614
   Pubs: *Paradise, Jazz, Tar Baby, Song of Solomon, Sula*
   (Knopf, 1998, 1992, 1981, 1977, 1974), *Beloved* (Random
   Hse, 1987).

Bradford Morrow W
33 W 9 St, New York, NY 10011, 212-477-1136
   Pubs: *Trinity Fields* (Viking Penguin, 1995), *The New
   Gothic* (Random Hse/Vintage, 1993), *The Almanac Branch*
   (Linden Pr/S&S, 1991), *Conjunctions, VLS.*

Charlie Morrow PP&P
365 W End Ave, New York, NY 10024, 212-799-0636
   Pubs: *Exiled in the Word: Anth* (Copper Canyon Pr, 1989),
   Ear Collective, Raven, Unmuzzled Ox.

Carl Morse P
460 W 24 St, #17B, New York, NY 10011, 212-691-8599
   Pubs: *Columbia Anthology of Gay Literature* (Columbia U
   Pr, 1998), *The Badboy Book of Erotic Poetry: Anth*
   (Masquerade Bks, 1995), *Gay & Lesbian Poetry in Our
   Time: Anth* (St. Martin's Pr, 1988), *3 New York Poets: Anth*
   (Gay Men's Pr, 1987), *Poetry London.*

Jo-Ann Mort P
125 Prospect Park W, #3-E, Brooklyn, NY 11215,
718-499-6261
   Pubs: *Without A Single Answer: Poems on Contemporary
   Israel: Anth* (Magnes Museum, 1990), *Social Text, Stand,
   Jewish Qtly, Pequod, Midstream.*

Bette Ann Moskowitz   W
The Jonathan Dolger Agency, 49 E 96 St, New York, NY
10028, 212-427-1853
> Pubs: *Leaving Barney* (Henry Holt, 1988), *Appearances.*

Stanley Moss   P
Sheep Meadow Press, PO Box 1345, Riverdale-On-Hudso,
NY 10471
> Pubs: *The Intelligence of Clouds* (HBJ, 1989), *Skull of
> Adam* (Horizon Pr, 1979), *Poetry, New York Times.*

Elaine Mott   P
80-31 210th St, Hollis Hills, NY 11427, 718-776-8450
> Pubs: *Blood to Remember: American Poets on the
> Holocaust Anth* (Texas Tech U Pr, 1991), *Anth of Magazine
> Verse & Yearbook of American Poetry* (Monitor Bk Co.,
> 1989).

Isaac Elchanan Mozeson   P
24 5th Ave, #1223, New York, NY 10011, 212-260-4314
> Pubs: *The Watcher and Other Poems* (Decalogue Bks,
> 1990), *Jewish Frontier.*

Marnie Mueller   P&W
119 W 77 St #5, New York, NY 10024, 212-724-7154
> Pubs: *The Climate of the Country, Green Fires* (Curbstone
> Pr, 1999, 1994), *Home to Stay, Asian-American Fiction by
> Women: Anth* (Greenfield Pr, 1990), *VLS, River Styx,
> Quarterly West, Laurel Rev, Clinton Street, Five Fingers
> Rev.*

Maureen Mulhern   P
440 East 88 St. #PHC, New York, NY 10128, 212-369-8791
Internet: mswhite@mail.med.cornell.edu
> Pubs: *Parallax* (Wesleyan, 1986), *Poetry, Crazyhorse,
> Phoebe, Prairie Schooner, Indiana Rev, Denver Qtly.*

Hester Mundis   W
Harold Ober Associates Inc, 425 Madison Ave, New York, NY
10017, 212-759-8600
Internet: rfvw@ulster.net
> Pubs: *Just Humor Me* (Random Hse, 1996), *101 Ways to
> Avoid Reincarnation* (Workman Pub, 1989).

Jerrold Mundis   W
Writers House, 21 W 26 St, New York, NY 10010,
212-685-2605
> Pubs: *The Dogs* (Berkley, 1988), *The Retreat* (Warner, 1985).

Frank Murphy   P
535 92nd St, Brooklyn, NY 11209-6412
> Pubs: *Paper Clip, Historian, Coat Hanger* (Blue Star Pr,
> 1990), *Hanging Loose, Eleven.*

Carole Murray   P
214 Riverside Dr, #207, New York, NY 10025, 212-666-5967
> Pubs: *NAR, Driftwood East, Milkweed, Amelia, Cedar Rock,
> Womanchild.*

William Murray   W
Helen Brann Agency, 157 W 57 St, New York, NY 10019,
212-247-3511
> Pubs: *Tip On A Dead Crab* (Viking, 1984), *New Yorker,
> Geo, Playboy, Esquire, Cosmopolitan.*

Eileen Myles   P
86 E 3 St, #3C, New York, NY 10003, 212-982-4703
Internet: easte8@aol.com
> Pubs: *Maxfield Parrish: Early and New Poems, Chelsea
> Girls* (Black Sparrow Pr, 1995, 1994), *APR, Denver Qtly,
> Valentine, Jejeune, XXXFruit, Zing.*

Zakee Nadir   P
159 Ashford St, Brooklyn, NY 11207, 718-277-3916
> Pubs: *Don't Run, Listen* (Poet Tential Unltd, 1979).

Robert Nathan   W
350 Central Pk W, New York, NY 10025
> Pubs: *The White Tiger* (S&S, 1987), *Rising Higher* (Dial,
> 1981), *New York Times, Harper's, New Republic, New
> York.*

Elinor Nauen   P
27 First Ave, #9, New York, NY 10003-9447, 212-677-3792
Internet: enauen@aol.com
> Pubs: *American Guys* (Hanging Loose Pr, 1997), *Ladies,
> Start Your Engines: Anth, Diamonds Are A Girl's Best
> Friend: Anth* (Faber & Faber, 1997, 1994), *The World,
> Exquisite Corpse, Long Shot, Fiction, Gas, Koff, NAW.*

Gloria Naylor   W
Sterling Lord Literistic, 65 Bleecker St, New York, NY 10012,
212-780-6050
> Pubs: *The Men of Brewster Place* (Hyperion, 1998),
> *Bailey's Cafe* (HBJ, 1992), *Children of the Night: The Best
> Short Stories By Black Writers: Anth* (Little, Brown, 1996).

Shelley Neiderbach   P
39 Remsen St, #4B, Brooklyn, NY 11201, 718-875-5862
> Pubs: *Invisible Wounds* (Haworth Pr, 1985).

Stanley Nelson   P
454 37th St, Brooklyn, NY 11232, 718-788-6088
> Pubs: *Immigrant: Books III, II, I* (Birch Brook Pr, 1995,
> 1993, 1990), *Long Shot, The Smith, Pinched Nerve,
> Kansas Qtly, Confrontation, For Now.*

Vernita Nemec   PP
361 Canal St, New York, NY 10013, 212-925-4419

Murat Nemet-Nejat   P
2600 Netherland Ave, #315, Riverdale, NY 10463,
718-432-0361
Internet: muratnn@aol.com
> Pubs: *A Blind Cat Black and Orthodoxies* (Sun & Moon Pr,
> 1997), *I, Orhan Veli* (Hanging Loose, 1989), *The Bridge
> (Martin Brian & O'Keeffe, 1978), Talisman, World, Little
> Mag, Transfer, Poetry Project Newsletter.*

Cindy Nemser													W
41 Montgomery Pl, Brooklyn, NY 11215, 718-857-9456
	Pubs: *Eve's Delight* (Pinnacle, 1982), *Feminist Art Jrnl,
Women: A Jrnl of Liberation, The Free Press.*

Joan Nestle												P&W
215 W 92 St, #13A, New York, NY 10025, 212-873-1089
	Pubs: *A Fragile Union* (Cleis Pr, 1998), *A Restricted
Country* (Pandora, 1996), *Women On Women 3: Anth*
(Plume, 1996), *Sister and Brother: Anth* (Harper San
Francisco, 1994).

Amos Neufeld													P
65 W 90 St, #9E, New York, NY 10024, 212-496-0683
	Pubs: *Blood To Remember: American Poets on the
Holocaust: Anth* (Texas Tech U Pr, 1991), *Ghosts of the
Holocaust: Anth* (Wayne State U Pr, 1989), *Response.*

Joachim Neugroschel											P
447 Beach 136 St, Belle Harbor, NY 11694, 718-318-2147
	Pubs: *Extensions, Just Before Sailing.*

Lucia Nevai													W
251 Central Pk W, New York, NY 10024
	Pubs: *Star Game* (U Iowa Pr, 1987), *American Fiction: Anth*
(Birch Lane Pr, 1993), *North Dakota Qtly, Iowa Rev, New
England Rev, New Yorker, ACM, Gulf Coast, Literary Rev.*

Leslie Newman												W
Georges Borchardt Inc., 136 E 57 St, New York, NY 10022,
212-753-5785

Wade Newman													P
505 E 14 St, #9C, New York, NY 10009, 212-598-9483
Internet: wnewman@earthlink.net
	Pubs: *Testaments* (Somers Rocks Pr, 1996), *Kenyon Rev,
Croton Rev, Cumberland Poetry Rev, Crosscurrents, Nebo,
Nimrod, Confrontation.*

Fae Myenne Ng												W
Donadio & Ashworth, Inc., 121 W 27 St, Ste 704, New York,
NY 10001, 212-633-2837
	Pubs: *Bone* (Hyperion, 1993), *Charlie Chan Is Dead: Anth*
(Penguin, 1994), *Harper's, Pushcart Prize XII, The New
Republic, Travel & Leisure.*

Joan Kane Nichols											W
165 Bennett Ave, #4D, New York, NY 10040, 212-702-4251
	Pubs: *All But The Right Folks* (Stemmer Hse, 1986).

Nina daVinci Nichols											W
305 W 13 St, #5H, New York, NY 10014, 212-924-1423
	Pubs: *Ariadne's Lives* (Fairleigh Dickinson U Pr, 1995),
Child of the Night (Bantam, 1985), *Behind the Veil: Anth*
(Eden Pr, 1982), *Stages, American Bk Rev, Shakespeare
Bulletin.*

Frederick Nicklaus											P
241 E 73 St, #2, New York, NY 10021, 212-628-8545
	Pubs: *Cut of Noon* (David Lewis, 1971), *The Man Who Bit
the Sun* (New Directions, 1964).

Richard Nickson												P
205 W 19 St, New York, NY 10011, 212-989-7833
	Pubs: *Stones: A Book of Epigrams* (Lithic Pr, 1998), *Cause
at Heart* (w/Junius Scales; U Georgia Pr, 1987), *Staves*
(Moretus Pr, 1977).

Hugh Nissenson												W
411 W End Ave, New York, NY 10024, 212-873-5193

Kathryn Nocerino											P
139 W 19 St, #2B, New York, NY 10011
	Pubs: *Death of the Plankton Bar & Grill, Wax Lips* (New
Rivers Pr, 1987, 1980), *Candles in the Daytime* (Warthog
Pr, 1986).

Suzanne Noguere											P
27 W 96 St #12B, New York, NY 10025, 212-865-1045
	Pubs: *Whirling Round the Sun* (Midmarch Arts Pr, 1996), *A
Formal Feeling Comes: Anth* (Story Line Pr, 1994), *Poetry,
Nation, Literary Rev, Sparrow.*

Constance Norgren											P
303A 16th St, Brooklyn, NY 11215-5504
	Pubs: *Yankee, Northland Qtly, Minnesota Rev, Tendril,
Louisville Rev, Poetry Rev, Confrontation.*

Charles North												P
251 W 92 St, #12E, New York, NY 10025, 212-799-4936
	Pubs: *The Year of the Olive Oil* (Hanging Loose Pr, 1989),
Leap Year (Kulchur, 1978).

Jenifer Nostrand											P
11 Waverly Pl E, New York, NY 10003
	Pubs: *Bless the Day: Anth* (Kodansha America, 1998),
*Kansas Qtly, Louisville Rev, Birmingham Poetry Rev, Hiram
Poetry Rev, Greensboro Rev, Bridge.*

Craig Nova													W
Janklow & Nesbit Associates, 598 Madison Ave, New York,
NY 10022, 212-421-1700
	Pubs: *Book of Dreams* (HM, 1994), *Trombone* (Grove,
1992), *Esquire, Paris Rev.*

Barbara Novack												P
134-18 228th St, Laurelton, NY 11413, 718-527-3674
	Pubs: *CQ, Long Island Qtly, South Coast Poetry Jrnl, Cape
Rock, Alms House Sampler, Verve, Nassau Rev.*

Minda Novek													PP
226 W 47 St., 2nd Fl, New York, NY 100361413, 212-921-9040
	Pubs: *Daily News Sunday Supplement, Adamant Jrnl,
Seaport Mag.*

D. Nurkse P
208 Prospect Pk W, #4B, Brooklyn, NY 11215, 718-788-4238
   Pubs: *Voices Over Water* (Graywolf, 1993), *Staggered Lights* (Owl Creek Pr, 1990), *APR, Poetry, Kenyon Rev, Hudson Rev, The Quarterly, Hanging Loose.*

Michael O'Brien P
400 W 23 St, #6L, New York, NY 10011, 212-929-0150
   Pubs: *The Floor and the Breath, Veil, Hard Rain* (Cairn Edtns, 1994, 1986), *Blue Springs* (Sun, 1976).

Francis V. O'Connor P
250 E 73 St, #11C, New York, NY 100214310, 212-988-8927
Internet: fvoc@aol.com
   Pubs: *Twelve Sonnets for the Abstract Expressionists* (Art Journal, 1988), *Beyond the Square.*

Stephen O'Connor P&W
Witherspoon Associates, 235 East 31 St, New York, NY 10016, 212-889-8626
   Pubs: *Rescue* (Harmony Bks, 1989), *Columbia, Massachusetts Rev, The Quarterly, Fiction Intl, Partisan Rev, Hubbub.*

Sidney Offit W
23 E 69 St, New York, NY 10021, 212-737-5144
   Pubs: *The Bookie's Son, A Memoir* (St. Martin's Pr, 1995), *What Kind of Guy Do You Think I Am?* (Lippincott, 1970).

Ned O'Gorman P
2 Lincoln Sq, New York, NY 10023, 212-799-0806

Jennifer O'Grady P
250 W 94 St, #6D, New York, NY 10025
Internet: jogrady1@aol.com
   Pubs: *White* (Mid-List Pr, 1999), *Yale Rev, Kalliope, Colorado Rev, Antioch Rev, Georgia Rev, Poetry, Poetry East, Seneca Rev, Southern Rev, Harper's, 13th Moon, Western Humanities Rev, Hawaii Rev, Southwest Rev, Kenyon Rev.*

Valery Oisteanu P
170 2nd Ave, #2A, New York, NY 10003, 212-777-3597
   Pubs: *Zen-Dada Meditations For the 3rd Millennium* (Linear Arts Pr, 1998), *Planet Dada, Temporary Immortality, King of Penguins, Moons of Venus* (Pass Pr, 1996, 1995, 1992, 1990), *Anth of American Poetry* (Vrshatz-Belgrade-Library Pr, 1997), *New Observations.*

Adrian Oktenberg P
55 Fifth Ave, Ste 1116, New York, NY 10003, 212-790-0410
   Pubs: *The Bosnia Elegies* (Paris Pr, 1997), *Drawing in the Dirt* (Malachite & Agate, 1997), *Prairie Schooner, Provincetown Arts, Salamander, Americas Rev, Women's Rev of Bks, American Voice, Nimrod, New Letters Reader II.*

Sharon Olds P
Alfred A. Knopf, Inc., 201 E 50 St, New York, NY 10022, 212-751-2600
   Pubs: *The Gold Cell, The Dead & The Living* (Knopf, 1987, 1984), *Satan Says* (U Pitt Pr, 1980).

Sharon Olinka P
23-38 28th St, Astoria, NY 11105, 718-267-1792
   Pubs: *A Face Not My Own* (West End Pr, 1995).

Sondra Spatt Olsen W
201 W 16 St, #10A, New York, NY 10011
   Pubs: *Traps* (U Iowa Pr, 1991), *Yale Rev, Ontario Rev, New Yorker, Iowa Rev, Boulevard, Redbook, Mississippi Rev, Confrontation, Quarterly West.*

Gregory Orfalea P&W
Wallace Literary Agency, 177 E 70 St, New York, NY 10021, 212-570-9090
   Pubs: *Messengers of the Lost Battalion* (The Free Pr, 1995), *Before the Flames* (U Texas Pr, 1988), *Antioch Rev, TriQuarterly, Washington Post, CSM, Epoch.*

Peter Orlovsky P
PO Box 582, Stuyvesant Sta, New York, NY 10009
   Pubs: *Straight Hearts' Delight* (w/Allen Ginsberg; Gay Sunshine Pr, 1980), *Clean Asshole Poems & Smiling Vegetable Songs* (City Lights Bks, 1978).

Miguel A. Ortiz P
516 7th St, Brooklyn, NY 11215

Lawrence Osgood W
141 Wooster St, New York, NY 10012-3163, 212-673-5232
   Pubs: *Canadian Fiction Mag, Carleton Miscellany, London Mag.*

Susan Osterman P
610 W 115 St #94, New York, NY 10025, 212-678-1115
   Pubs: *A Head of Her Time* (Theo, 1996), *Strip Mining* (Cambric Pr, 1987), *Village Voice, Cover, Downtown.*

Suzanne Ostro P&W
321 W 94 St, #2W, New York, NY 10025
Internet: szavv@aol.com
   Pubs: *Dream of the Whale* (Toothpaste Pr, 1982), *Demolition Zone* (New Rivers Pr, 1975), *River Styx, Exquisite Corpse, Paris Rev, Partisan Rev, Open Places, Yardbird.*

Iris Owens W
ICM, 40 W 57 St, New York, NY 10019, 212-556-5600

Kent Jorgensen Ozarow P
4 Edgewood Pl, Great Neck, NY 11024, 516-466-0976
   Pubs: *Poetry Now, Confrontation, Croton Rev, Xanadu, Paris Rev, West Hills Rev, Alura, Yankee.*

Cynthia Ozick　　　　　　　W
Raines and Raines, 71 Park Ave, New York, NY 10016
　　Pubs: *The Puttermesser Papers* (Vintage, 1998), *Fame & Folly* (Knopf, 1996), *A Cynthia Ozick Reader* (Indiana U Pr, 1996).

Richard Pa　　　　　　　P
210 E 15 St, #14K, New York, NY 10003, 212-420-1854
　　Pubs: *Landscape of Skin and Single Rooms* (Monday Morning Pr, 1973), *Chester H. Jones Anth* (Chester H. Jones Fdn, 1997), *Prairie Schooner, Paris Rev, Windless Orchard.*

William Packard　　　　　　P&W
232 W 14 St, #2A, New York, NY 10011, 212-255-8531
　　Pubs: *Art of Poetry Writing* (St. Martin's Pr, 1990), *The Poet's Dictionary* (H&R, 1989).

Eve Packer　　　　　　　PP
78 Bank St, #17, New York, NY 10014, 212-243-3496
　　Pubs: *west frm 42nd* (Altsax Records, 1998), *Showworld* (Kango Pub, 1996), *skulls head samba* (fly-by-night pr, 1994), *Ikon, Long Shot, Verve, Peau Sensible, Red Tape, Pinched Nerves, What Happens Next, No Roses Rev, Excursus, Pink Pages, Lungfull, Paramour.*

Ron Padgett　　　　　　　P&W
342 E 13 St, #6, New York, NY 10003-5811, 212-477-4472
　　Pubs: *New & Selected Poems* (Godine, 1995), *Great Balls of Fire* (Coffee Hse Pr, 1990), *The Big Something* (The Figures, 1990).

Maggie Paley　　　　　　　W
John Farquharson, Ltd., 250 W 57 St, #1914, New York, NY 10107
　　Pubs: *Elephant* (Groundwater Pr, 1990), *Bad Manners* (Clarkson Potter, 1986), *New Observations.*

Marion Palm　　　　　　　P
705 41st St, #17, Brooklyn, NY 11232
　　Pubs: *Islands of the Blest* (Print Ctr, 1993), *Nightingale Day Songs* (Wingate Pr, 1984), *Working Mother, Big Apple, Parenting, Minneapolis Star & Tribune.*

Bruce Palmer　　　　　　　W
Elaine Markson Literary Agency, 44 Greenwich Ave, New York, NY 10011, 212-243-8480
　　Pubs: *The Karma Charmer* (Harmony Bks, 1994).

Anne Paolucci　　　　　　P&W
166-25 Powells Cove Blvd, Beechhurst, NY 11357, 718-767-8380
　　Pubs: *Terminal Degrees* (Novella, 1997), *Queensboro Bridge and Other Poems* (Potpourri Pubs, 1995), *Three Short Plays* (Griffon Hse Pubs, 1995), *The World and I, Pirandello Society Annual, Choice.*

Helen Papell　　　　　　　P
720 W End Ave, New York, NY 10025, 212-316-5821
　　Pubs: *Talking With Eve Leah Hagar Miriam* (Jewish Women's Resource Center, 1996), *Sarah's Daughters Sing: Anth* (KTAV, 1990), *Verve, Metis, Mildred, Negative Capability, Prairie Schooner, Jewish Women's Literary Annual, Visions, Outerbridge.*

Matthew Paris　　　　　　P&W
645 East 14 St., Apt 9E, New York, NY 10009, 212-995-0299
　　Pubs: *The Holy City* (Carpenter Pr, 1979), *Mystery* (Avon Bks, 1973), *Home Planet News, Generalist Papers, The Phoenix, Downtown, New Worlds, Brooklyn Literary Rev, Bright Hill.*

Gwendolyn M. Parker　　　　　W
Marie Brown Associates Inc., 625 Broadway, New York, NY 10012, 212-533-5534
Internet: gmcdparker@juno.com
　　Pubs: *Trespassing: My Sojourn in the Halls of Privilege, These Same Long Bones* (Houghton Mifflin, 1997, 1994).

Wolf Pasmanik　　　　　　P
218 E 81 St #1, New York, NY 10028, 212-757-6300
　　Pubs: *Blumen, My Poems* (Jewish Cultural Org, 1980, 1971).

Beth Passaro　　　　　　　W
514 W 110 St, #21, New York, NY 10025, 212-662-6224
Internet: oddsyntax@aol.com
　　Pubs: *Columbia, Northwest Rev.*

Vincent Passaro　　　　　　W
Georges Borchardt Inc., 136 E 57 St, New York, NY 10022, 212-753-5785
　　Pubs: *Lust, Violence, Sin, Magic: Esquire Anth* (Atlantic Monthly Pr, 1993), *Best of the West: Anth* (Norton, 1992), *Harper's, Story, Willow Springs, NAW.*

Ann Patchett　　　　　　　W
ICM, 40 W 57 St, New York, NY 10019, 212-556-5600
　　Pubs: *Taft, The Patron Saint of Liars* (Houghton Mifflin, 1994, 1992).

Kathryn Paulsen　　　　　　W
340 W 28 St, #16E, New York, NY 10001, 212-734-7607
　　Pubs: *New Letters, West Branch, Sundog, Cottonwood Rev, New Constellations.*

Basil Payne　　　　　　　P
43-30 46 St, #4B, Sunnyside, NY 11104, 718-388-2184

Molly Peacock　　　　　　P&W
505 E 14 St, #3-G, New York, NY 10009, 212-677-3535
Internet: peacockmol@aol.com
　　Pubs: *How To Read A Poem & Start A Poetry Circle, Paradise, Piece By Piece* (Riverhead/Putnam, 1999, 1998), *Original Love* (Norton, 1995), *Take Heart, Raw Heaven* (Random Hse, 1989, 1984), *And Live Apart* (U Missouri Pr, 1980).

Pamela Manche Pearce P&W
92 Grove St, New York, NY 10014, 212-691-4537
Pubs: *Straight Ahead Intl, Samba, Brooklyn Rev, Hellenic Times, Brides.*

Gerry Gomez Pearlberg P&W
418 Bergen St, Brooklyn, NY 11217, 718-638-1233
Internet: dogstargrl@aol.com
Pubs: *Marianne Faithfull's Cigarette, Queer Dog: Homo/Pup/Poetry: Anth* (Cleis Pr, 1998, 1997), *The Best American Erotica: Anth* (Macmillan, 1994), *Women on Women 2: Anth* (Plume, 1993), *Chelsea, Beloit, Apalachee Qtly, Lesbian Rev of Bks, Plazm, Pucker Up.*

Fredda S. Pearlson P
350 Bleecker St, New York, NY 10014
Pubs: *The Dolphin's Arc: Poems on Endangered Creatures of the Sea: Anth* (SCOP, 1989), *Little Mag, Centennial Rev, California Qtly.*

Deborah Pease P&W
45 E 72 St, New York, NY 10021
Pubs: *Into the Amazement* (Puckerbrush Pr, 1993), *Real Life* (Norton, 1971), *New Yorker, Paris Rev, Agni, Gettysburg Rev, Grand Street, Antioch Rev.*

Robert Pease W
500 E 77 St, #1017, New York, NY 10021, 212-861-1201
Pubs: *The Associate Professor* (S&S, 1967).

Richard Peck P&W
245 E 47 St, New York, NY 10017
Pubs: *Remembering the Good Times, This Family of Women* (Delacorte, 1985, 1983).

Sylvia Peck W
45 W 67 St, #29D, New York, NY 10023-6267
Pubs: *Kelsey's Raven, Seal Child* (Morrow Junior, 1992, 1989).

Ted Pejovich W
233 W 99 St, #6E, New York, NY 10025-5017, 212-663-7621
Pubs: *The State of California* (Knopf, 1989), *The Quarterly, Kenyon Rev, Story Qtly.*

Derek Pell P&W
Donadio & Ashworth, Inc., 121 W 27 St, Ste 704, New York, NY 10001
Pubs: *Morbid Curiosities* (Jonathan Cape, 1983), *Expurgations* (Hyena, 1981), *Playboy, Benzene.*

Michael M. Pendragon P&W
407 W 50 St, #16, New York, NY 10019
Pubs: *Poetry Motel, Afterthoughts, Portal, Maverick Pr, Clinton Chronicles, Grim Commander Fright Library, Barefoot Grass Jrnl, Terror Tales, Blue Lady, Pluto's Orchard, Visionary Tongue, Nasty Piece of Work.*

Edmund Pennant P
2902 210th St, Bayside, NY 11360, 718-229-6104
Internet: penbard@aol.com
Pubs: *Askance and Strangely: New & Selected Poems, The Wildebeest of Carmine Street* (Orchises Pr, 1993, 1990), *Confrontation, Shenandoah, American Scholar, Pivot, New England Rev, Madison Rev.*

Victor Perera W
Watkins Loomis Agency, Inc., 133 E 35 St, Ste 1, New York, NY 10016, 212-532-0080
Pubs: *Rites: A Guatemalan Boyhood* (HBJ, 1986), *Atlantic, New Yorker, Harper's, Nation.*

Deborah Perlberg W
305 E 6 St #7, New York, NY 10003, 212-228-4154
Pubs: *Cliff House* (M. Evans, 1990), *Heartaches High School, Heartaches* (Fawcett/Ballantine, 1987, 1983).

John Perreault P
54 E 7 St, New York, NY 10003, 212-677-3504
Pubs: *Hotel Death and Other Tales* (Sun & Moon Pr, 1989), *Harry* (Coach Hse, 1974).

Kathrin Perutz W
16 Avalon Rd, Great Neck, NY 11021, 516-482-0804
Pubs: *Writing for Love and Money* (U Arkansas Pr, 1991), *Faces* (Pseudonym: Joanna Kingsley; Bantam, 1987).

Joan K. Peters W
Writers House, 21 W 26 St, New York, NY 10010, 212-929-1583
Pubs: *Manny and Rose* (St. Martin's Pr, 1985), *Global City Rev, Family Life.*

Keith Peterson W
Deborah Schneider, Agent, 250 W 57 St, #1007, New York, NY 10107, 212-941-8050
Pubs: *The Scarred Man* (Doubleday, 1990), *Rough Justice* (Bantam, 1989), *Ellery Queen.*

Ann Petry P&W
Russell & Volkening, Inc., 50 W 29 St, New York, NY 10001, 212-684-6050
Pubs: *Miss Muriel, The Narrows, The Street* (Houghton Mifflin, 1971, 1953, 1946), *New Yorker.*

Simon Pettet P
437 E 12 St #6, New York, NY 10009
Pubs: *Selected Poems* (Talisman Hse, 1996), *Talking Pictures* (w/Rudy Burckhardt; Zoland, 1994), *Twenty One Love* (Microbrigade, 1990).

D. F. Petteys P
90 Bank St, New York, NY 10014, 212-989-4528
Pubs: *Against Infinity* (Primary Pr, 1979), *Lying Awake* (Lillian Pr, 1977).

Richard Pevear P
313 W 107 St, New York, NY 10025, 212-662-7190
Pubs: *Exchanges* (Spuyten Duyvil, 1982), *Night Talk* (Princeton U Pr, 1977), *Hudson Rev, Occident.*

Tom Phelan W
Four Walls Eight Windows, 39 W 14 St, New York, NY 10011
Internet: http://members.aol.com/glanvil2
Pubs: *In the Season of the Daisies* (Four Walls Eight Windows, 1996), *Iscariot* (Ireland; Brandon Bk Pub, 1995), *Here's Me Bus.*

Betty Phillips W
309 E 87 St #2-O, New York, NY 10128, 212-876-3496
Pubs: *Literary Rev, Denver Rev, Women, Confrontation, Barat Rev, Dekalb Literary Arts Jrnl.*

Jayne Anne Phillips P&W
375 Hudson St, New York, NY 10014, 212-366-2000
Pubs: *Black Tickets* (Delacorte, 1979), *Counting* (Vehicle Edtns, 1978), *Sweethearts* (Truck, 1978).

Louis Phillips P&W
375 Riverside Dr, #14-C, New York, NY 10025, 212-866-9643
Pubs: *A Dream of Countries Where No One Dare Live* (SMU Pr, 1993), *Hot Corner: Baseball Writings* (Livingston U Pr, 1996), *Georgia Rev, Massachusetts Rev, Epoch.*

Robert Phillips P&W
Wieser & Wieser, Inc., 118 E 25 St, New York, NY 10010, 713-668-8380
Pubs: *Public Landing Revisited: Stories* (Story Line Pr, 1992), *Personal Accounts: New & Selected Poems* (Ontario Rev Pr, 1986), *New Yorker, Poetry, Nation.*

Wanda Phipps P
248 E 7 St, #11-12, New York, NY 10009, 212-505-6180
Pubs: *Exquisite Corpse, Big Scream, Outre, Inkblot, The Poetry Project Newsletter, Bombay Gin, Red Weather.*

Bruce Piasecki P
Ann Elmo Literary Agency, 60 E 42 St, New York, NY 10017, 212-661-2880
Pubs: *In Search of Environmental Excellence* (S&S, 1990), *America's Future* (Greenwood, 1988).

Pedro Juan Pietri P
400 W 43 St, #38E, New York, NY 10036, 212-244-4270
Pubs: *An Alternate* (Hayden Book Co., 1980), *The Blue And The Gray* (Cherry Valley Edtns, 1975).

Sonia Pilcer W
172 W 79 St, #19A, New York, NY 10024
Pubs: *I-Land, Little Darlings* (Ballantine, 1987, 1983), *Maiden Rites* (Viking, 1982), *Visions of America: Anth* (Persea Bks, 1993), *L.A. Times, Seven Days.*

Kevin Pilkington P
New School for Social Research, 66 W 12 St, New York, NY 10011, 212-741-5690
Pubs: *Reading Stone* (Jeanne Duval Edtns, 1988), *Poetry, Ploughshares, New York Qtly, Alaska Rev, Yankee.*

Robert H. Pilpel W
Edward J. Acton Agency, 928 Broadway, New York, NY 10010, 212-473-1700
Pubs: *Understanding Your Therapist* (Contemporary, 1989), *Between Eternities* (HBJ, 1985).

Thomas Pinnock PP
265 Bainbridge St, Brooklyn, NY 11233, 718-467-0563
Pubs: *Essence, Everybody's.*

Belva Plain W
Janklow & Nesbit Associates, 598 Madison Ave, New York, NY 10022-1614, 212-421-1700
Pubs: *Daybreak, Whispers* (Dell, 1994, 1993), *Treasures, Harvest, Blessings* (Delacorte, 1992, 1990, 1989).

Susan Pliner P
2501 Palisade Ave, #E-1, Bronx, NY 10463, 718-796-2885
Pubs: *Paris Rev, Pivot, APR, Greenfield Rev, Kenyon Rev.*

Eileen Pollack W
235 E 31 Street, New York, NY 10016, 212-889-8626
Internet: epollack@umich.edu
Pubs: *Paradise, New York* (Temple U Pr, 1998), *The Rabbi in the Attic and Other Stories* (Delphinium, 1991), *Pushcart Prize XX, XVI: Anths* (Pushcart Pr, 1996, 1992), *NER, Ploughshares, Prairie Schooner, Michigan Qtly Rev, Agni, Literary Rev.*

Shirley B. Pollan-Cohen PP&P
2939 Grand Concourse Apt 4C, Bronx, NY 104681708, 718-289-5679
Pubs: *Connections, Grub Street, Bronx Roots, Garland, Jewish Currents, Hieroglyphics Press.*

Elizabeth Pollet W
463 West St, #D-817, New York, NY 10014, 212-675-7714
Pubs: *A Family Romance* (NAL, 1951).

Katha Pollitt P
317 W 93 St, New York, NY 10025
Pubs: *Antarctic Traveller* (Knopf, 1982), *The Best American Poetry: Anth* (Scribner, 1991), *New Yorker, Antaeus, Atlantic, Nation, Poetry.*

Marie Ponsot P
340 E 93 St, #2J, New York, NY 10128
Pubs: *The Bird Catcher, The Green Dark, Admit Impediment* (Knopf, 1998, 1988, 1981), *Commonweal, The Journal, New Yorker, Paris Rev, Ploughshares, Gulf Coast, Kenyon Rev.*

Melinda Camber Porter   P
Sanford J. Greenburger Assoc., 55 Fifth Ave, New York, NY
10003, 212-206-5600
Internet: flicekjr@pipeline.com
  Pubs: *Badlands, The Art of Love* (Writers and Readers,
  1996, 1993).

Cally Pourakis   P
11 Nortema Ct, New Hyde Park, NY 11040, 516-437-9511
  Pubs: *Thirteen Poetry Mag, Haiku Zasshi Zo, Salome: A
  Literary Dance Mag, Bitterroot, Calli's Tales, Hoosier
  Challenger.*

Gregory Powell   P
550 W 58 St, #5-E, New York, NY 10032, 212-740-1923
  Pubs: *Essence, Community Rev, The Black Nation,
  Nommo, Class Mag, Nommo, Bluesville Anth.*

Penelope Prentice   W
Garland Publishing, Inc., 717 5th Ave, New York, NY
10022-8101, 212-308-9399
  Pubs: *The Pinter Aesthetic: The Erotic Aesthetic* (Garland
  Pub, 1994), *Boundary II, 20th Century Literary Tales,
  Wisconsin Rev, Spree, Cithara, Paper Curtain.*

Richard Price   W
Janklow & Nesbit Associates, 598 Madison Ave, New York,
NY 10022-1614
  Pubs: *Freedomland* (Broadway Bks, 1998), *Clockers,
  Ladies Man, Bloodbrothers* (HM, 1992, 1978, 1976), *The
  Breaks* (S&S, 1984).

Ron Price   P
210 E 15 St, #14A, New York, NY 10003-3939, 212-353-3993
Internet: rpsr210@aol.com
  Pubs: *A Crucible For the Left Hand* (Wubbie Productions
  for Exoterica, 1998), *Full Circle* (Charlotte Poetry Project,
  1995), *Surviving Brothers* (Slash & Burn Pr, 1987),
  *Raccoon, Painted Bride Qtly, Pivot, One Trick Pony,
  Northeast Corridor.*

William Price   W
292 Clermont Ave, Brooklyn, NY 11205
  Pubs: *The Potlatch Run* (Dutton, 1971), *Evergreen Rev,
  Saturday Evening.*

Robert Prochaska   P
39-72 52nd St, Woodside, NY 11377, 718-457-3432
  Pubs: *Fourfront* (Bearstone, 1982), *Exquisite Corpse,
  Louisville Rev, Slipstream, Woodrose, Rhode Island Rev,
  Woody Street Irregulars.*

Wayne Providence   P
2960 Decatur Ave #6G, Bronx, NY 10458-2334,
718-329-2470
  Pubs: *Long Journey Home: Anth* (Meta Pr, 1985), *New City
  Voices: Anth* (Metamorphosis, 1980), *American Rag, New
  York City Public Art Fund.*

James Purdy   P&W
236 Henry St, Brooklyn, NY 11201, 718-858-0015
  Pubs: *Out With The Stars* (Peter Owen Ltd, 1992), *63:
  Dream Palace, Collected Stories 1956-1986* (Black
  Sparrow Pr, 1991).

Mario Puzo   W
200 Madison Ave, New York, NY 10016, 212-883-5500

Thomas Pynchon   W
Henry Holt & Co., Inc., 115 W 18 St, New York, NY 10011
  Pubs: *Mason and Dixon* (Holt, 1997), *Vineland* (Little,
  Brown, 1990), *Gravity's Rainbow* (Penguin, 1987), *V.* (H&R,
  1986).

Margo Rabb   W
39-99 48 St, Sunnyside, NY 11104, 718-429-7949
  Pubs: *American Fiction: Anth* (New Rivers Pr, 1997),
  Witness, Chat, The Sound of Writing: Broadcast, Atlantic.

Anna Rabinowitz   P
850 Park Ave, New York, NY 10021, 212-734-2233
  Pubs: *At The Site of Inside Out* (U Massachusetts Pr,
  1997), *Best American Poetry: Anth* (Scribner, 1989),
  *Southwest Rev, Paris Rev, NAW, Sonora Rev, Cream City
  Rev, Atlantic Monthly, Colorado Rev, Sulfur, Denver Qtly.*

Nahid Rachlin   W
300 E. 93 St., Apt 43-D, New York, NY 10128, 212-996-3478
  Pubs: *Heart's Desire, Married to a Stranger, Veils* (City
  Lights, 1995, 1994, 1993), *Foreigner* (Norton, 1979),
  *Fiction, Shenandoah, Ararat, Redbook, Literary Rev,
  Columbia, Confrontation, Natural History.*

Dotson Rader   W
Janklow & Nesbit Associates, 598 Madison Ave, New York,
NY 10022, 212-421-1700
  Pubs: *Tennessee: Cry of the Heart* (Doubleday, 1985),
  Beau Monde (Random Hse, 1980), *Esquire, New Republic,
  Paris Rev, London Mag.*

Keith Rahmmings   P&W
Box 371, Brooklyn, NY 11230
  Pubs: *Lost & Found Times, Qwertyuiop, Glassworks, So &
  So, NRG, Star-Web-Paper, Assembling.*

Heidi Rain   P
402 4th St, Brooklyn, NY 11215, 718-499-0502
Internet: heidi_rain@aol.com
  Pubs: *Mirrors of the Soul* (Modern Poetry Society, 1995),
  Seasons: Anth (Poets Under Glass, 1994), *Rag Shock,
  Saturn Series, Copulation: Erotic Literature, Salonika,
  Medicinal Purposes, New Press Literary Qtly, Nomad's
  Choir, Wings.*

Diane Raintree   P
360 W 21 St, New York, NY 10011, 212-242-2387
  Pubs: *The Wind in Our Sails* (Midnight Sun, 1982), *Slow
  Motion Mag, Tamarind, Helen Rev, New York Qtly.*

Alice Ramirez   W
Donald MacCampbell, Inc., PO Box 20191, New York, NY
10025-1518
    Pubs: *Bright Glows the Dawn* (Pseudonym: Santa Arroyo;
Leisure Historical Romance, 1984).

Peter Rand   W
The Wendy Weil Agency, Inc., 232 Madison Ave, Ste 1300,
New York, NY 10016
    Pubs: *China Hands* (S&S, 1995), *Gold From Heaven, The
Private Rich* (Crown, 1988, 1984), *Firestorm* (Doubleday,
1969).

Victor Rangel-Ribeiro   W
172-28 83rd Ave, Jamaica, NY 11432, 718-658-7064
    Pubs: *Tivolem* (Milkweed Edtns, 1998), *Iowa Rev, NAR,
Literary Rev.*

Carolyn Raphael   P
English Dept, Springfield Blvd, Bayside, NY 11364,
718-631-6303
    Pubs: *Diagrams of Bittersweet* (Rocks Pr, 1997),
*Cumberland Poetry Rev, Pivot, The Lyric, Edge City Rev,
Orbis, Poetry Digest.*

Phyllis Raphael   W
Columbia Univ, 612 Lewisohn Hall, New York, NY 10027,
212-595-5286
Internet: pr4@columbia.edu
    Pubs: *They Got What They Wanted* (Norton, 1972),
Seasons of Women: Anth (Norton/BOMC, 1995), *Vogue,
Boulevard, Mirabella, PEN Syndicated Fiction.*

Rebecca Rass   W
54 W 16 St, #14C, New York, NY 10011, 212-627-9122
Internet: rebecarass@aol.com
    Pubs: *From A-Z* (Proza, 1985), *The Mountain, The Fairy
Tales of My Mind* (Lintel, 1982, 1978), *Solo: Women On
Woman Alone* (Dell, 1977), *Moznaim, Zero Mag, Seven
Days.*

Carter Ratcliff   P
26 Beaver St, New York, NY 10004, 212-825-9012
    Pubs: *Give Me Tomorrow* (Vehicle Pr, 1983), *Fever Coast*
(Kulchur Pr, 1973), *Out of this World: An Anthology
1966-1991* (Crown, 1991).

Rochelle Ratner   P&W
609 Columbus Ave, #16F, New York, NY 10024,
212-769-0498
Internet: rratner@idt.net
    Pubs: *The Lion's Share* (Coffee Hse Pr, 1992), *Someday
Songs: Poems Toward a Personal History* (BkMk Pr, 1992),
Antaeus, Nation, Hanging Loose, First Intensity, Caprice.

John Rechy   W
Georges Borchardt Inc., 136 E 57 St, New York, NY 10022,
212-753-5785
    Pubs: *Our Lady of Babylon, The Miraculous Day of Amalia
Gomez* (Arcade, 1996, 1991), *Marilyn's Daughter, Bodies &
Soul* (Carroll & Graf, 1988, 1983).

Victoria Redel   P&W
90 Riverside Dr #12A, New York, NY 10024, 212-873-2502
Internet: vredel@aol.com
    Pubs: *Where the Road Bottoms Out* (Knopf, 1995), *Already
the World* (Kent State U Pr, 1995), *Antioch Rev, Missouri
Rev, Bomb, The Quarterly, Epoch.*

Gomer Rees   P
325 Riverside Dr, #3, New York, NY 10025, 212-865-7035
    Pubs: *Loves, Etc, Choice, New York Qtly, Chelsea,
Purchase Poetry Rev, Studies in Contemporary Satire.*

Gail Regier   W
William Morris Agency, 1350 Ave of the Americas, New York,
NY 10019, 212-586-5100
    Pubs: *Laurel Rev, New Virginia Rev, Greensboro Rev,
Zone 3, Emrys Journal, Yarrow, Atlantic.*

Regina Reibstein   P
26 Oxford Blvd, Great Neck, NY 11023, 516-487-6839
    Pubs: *Midstream, Southwest Rev, California Qtly, Poem,
Skylark Qtly, Judaism, Pale Fire Rev.*

Barbara Reid   W
138 W 11 St, New York, NY 10011, 212-924-4967
    Pubs: *The Tears of San Lorenzo* (Apple-Wood Pr, 1977),
Prize Stories 1981: The O. Henry Awards: Anth
(Doubleday, 1981), *Pulpsmith.*

Barbara Eve Reiss   P
1290 Madison Ave, #2N, New York, NY 10128, 212-369-8663
    Pubs: *Family Mirrors* (HM, 1991), *Tangled Vines: Anth*
(HBJ, 1992), *Antaeus, Agni, Nation, Virginia Qtly Rev.*

Gertrude Reiss   P&W
74 Beaumont St, Brooklyn, NY 112354104, 718-615-0327
    Pubs: *The Perceptive I* (NTC Publishing Group, 1997),
Legacies (HarperCollins, 1993), *The New Press, Jewish
Currents, Outloud, Oxalis, Riverrun, Pumpkin Stories.*

Sally Renfro   P
401 E 64 St, #2D, New York, NY 10021-7590
    Pubs: *13th Moon, Atlantic Monthly, Texas Qtly.*

Vittoria repetto   P
24 Mulberry St, #4R, New York, NY 10013, 212-267-1434
    Pubs: *Head for the Van Wyck* (Monkey Cat Pr, 1994),
*Unsettling America: An Anth of Contemporary Multicultural
Poetry* (Penguin, 1994), *Mudfish, Lips, Italian Americana.*

Naomi Replansky P
711 Amsterdam Ave, #8E, New York, NY 10025,
212-666-1233
Pubs: *The Dangerous World: New and Selected Poems*
(Another Chicago Pr, 1994), *Ring Song* (Scribner, 1952),
Ploughshares, Feminist Studies, New York Qtly.

Janet Restino PP
Alchemical Space, 84-05 164th St, Jamaica, NY 11432

A. Wanjiku H. Reynolds P
Ngoma's Gourd, Inc, PO Box 24, W Farms Sq Sta, Bronx, NY
10460
Pubs: *Cognac & Collard Greens* (Single Action
Productions, 1986), *A Gathering of Hands: Anth* (Ngoma's
Gourd, 1991).

Martha Rhodes P
19 Charlton St, Gdn Apt, New York, NY 10014, 212-206-0174
Pubs: *At The Gate* (Provincetown Arts Pr, 1995), *Agni,
Boston Rev, Harvard Rev, Ploughshares, Virginia Rev.*

Richard Rhodes W
Janklow & Nesbit Associates, 598 Madison Ave, New York,
NY 10022-1614, 212-421-1700
Internet: rhodesr@pantheon.yale.edu
Pubs: *Deadly Feasts, A Hole in the World, Farm, The
Making of the Atomic Bomb* (S&S, 1997, 1990, 1989,
1986).

M. Z. Ribalow P
431 E 20 St, #4C, New York, NY 10010, 212-777-3538
Pubs: *Raindance, Sundance* (Samuel French, 1985, 1981),
New York Times, Paris Rev, Literary Rev.

Anne Rice W
ICM, 40 W 57 St, New York, NY 10019, 212-556-5600
Pubs: *The Vampire Armand* (Knopf, 1998), *Violin, The
Witching Hour* (Ballantine, 1998, 1993), *Belinda, Exit to
Eden* (Arbor Hse, 1986, 1985), *The Vampire Lestat* (Knopf,
1985).

Adrienne Rich P
W. W. Norton, 500 5th Ave, New York, NY 10110,
212-354-5500
Pubs: *Midnight Salvage, What Is Found There, An Atlas of
the Difficult World* (Norton, 1999, 1993, 1991), *Kenyon Rev,
APR, Sulfur.*

Arthur Rifkin P
7 Fourth Rd, Great Neck, NY 11021, 718-928-6355
Pubs: *Lake Superior Rev, Bitterroot, Encore, Poet Lore,
Dodeca.*

Shepard Rifkin W
105 Charles St, New York, NY 10014, 212-924-4957
Pubs: *McQuaid In August* (Doubleday, 1979), *What Ship?
Where Bound?* (Knopf, 1961), *Story.*

Mindy Rinkewich P&W
290 9th Ave #5F, New York, NY 10001, 212-242-4445
Pubs: *The White Beyond the Forest* (Cross-Cultural Comm,
1992), *Lips, Schmate, Bitterroot, Poet Lore.*

Edward Rivera W
321 W 100 St, #6, New York, NY 10025, 212-864-4220
Pubs: *Family Installments* (Morrow, 1982), *New American
Rev, Bilingual Rev, New York Mag.*

Louis Reyes Rivera P
Shamal Books, Inc., GPO Box 16, New York, NY 10116,
718-622-4426
Pubs: *This One for You, Who Pays the Cost* (Shamal Bks,
1984, 1977), *Blind Beggar, Sunbury.*

Agnes Robertson P
3100 Brighton 2nd St, #6J, Brooklyn, NY 11235,
718-934-3018
Pubs: *The Me Inside of Me, The Chestnut Tree* (Gull Bks,
1987, 1987).

Corinne Robins W
83 Wooster St, New York, NY 10012, 212-925-3714
Pubs: *Facing It, Art in the 7th Power, First* (Pratt, 1996,
1984, 1983), *The Pluralist Era* (H&R, 1984), *American Book
Rev, ACM, NAW, Caprice, Poetry New York, Confrontation,
Situation.*

Natalie Robins P
Janklow & Nesbit Associates, 598 Madison Ave, New York,
NY 10022-1614, 212-421-1700
Internet: nrobins@escape.com
Pubs: *Living In the Lightning* (Rutgers U Pr, 1999), *The Girl
Who Died Twice* (Delacorte, 1995), *Alien Ink, Savage
Grace* (Co-author) (Morrow, 1992, 1986), *Eclipse*
(Swallow/Ohio U Pr, 1981).

Jeremy Robinson P
275 Central Pk W, #12E, New York, NY 10024,
212-362-0574

Jill Robinson W
Alfred A. Knopf, Inc., 201 E 50 St, New York, NY 10022,
212-751-2600
Pubs: *Perdido* (Knopf, 1978), *Bed/Time/Story* (Random
Hse, 1974), *New York Times, Vogue.*

John Robinson W
c/o Donadio & Ashworth Inc, 121 W 27 St., Ste 704, New
York, NY 10001, 212-691-8077
Internet: donash@aol.com
Pubs: *Legends of the Lost* (Northland, 1989), *January's
Dream* (Green Street Pr, 1985), *Hawaii Pacific Rev, New
Virginia Rev, Witness, Rhode Island Rev, Citizen Advocate.*

Mary Robison   W
Wylie, Aitken & Stone, Inc., 250 W 57 St, #2106, New York,
NY 10107, 212-246-0069
    Pubs: *Believe Them, An Amateur's Guide to the Night, Oh,
    Days* (Knopf, 1988, 1983, 1981, 1979).

Hannah P. Rodgers   P&W
250 W 16 St, #5A, New York, NY 10011
    Pubs: *Hudson Valley Echoes, Kansas Qtly, No Roses Rev,
    California Qtly, Mudfish, Reflect.*

Bruce Holland Rogers   P&W
381 Park Ave S., Ste 1020, New York, NY 10016,
212-679-8686
Internet: bruce@sff.net
    Pubs: *Sudden Fiction: Anth* (Norton, 1996), *Year's Best
    Mystery & Suspense Stories: Anth* (Walker & Co., 1994),
    The Quarterly, Fantasy & Science Fiction, Quarterly West.

Michael Rogers   W
Brandt & Brandt Literary Agent, 1501 Broadway, New York,
NY 10036, 212-840-5760
Internet: rogersm@washpost.com
    Pubs: *Forbidden Sequence* (Bantam, 1988), *Silicon Valley*
    (S&S, 1982), *Esquire, Playboy, Rolling Stone, West, GQ,
    Manhattan Inc..*

Gilbert Rogin   W
Sports Illustrated, Time-Life Building, New York, NY 10020,
212-556-3123

Marcus Rome   P
2727 Palisade Ave, Riverdale, NY 10463, 718-548-7330
    Pubs: *Repercussions, Abreactions* (Birch Brook Pr, 1998,
    1989), *Visual Eyes* (Ziggurat Pr, 1997), *Wordsmith, The
    Bridge, Vincent Brothers Rev, Pacific Coast Jrnl.*

Cheryl Romney-Brown   P
Sterling Lord Literistic, 65 Bleecker St, New York, NY 10012,
212-780-6050
    Pubs: *Circling Home* (Scripta Humanistica, 1989), *You Just
    Don't Understand* (Deborah Tannen, 1984), *American
    Beauties: Anth* (Abrams, 1993).

Rose Rosberg   P
880 W 181 St #4-I, New York, NY 10033, 212-928-7089
    Pubs: *Chrysalis* (Swedenborg Fdn, 1995), *The Country of
    Connections* (University Edtns, 1993), *Breathe In, Breathe
    Out* (Singular Speech Pr, 1992), *Pacific Coast Jrnl, Poetry
    Digest, Skylark, American Poets & Poetry, Lyric,
    Neovictorian, Comstock Rev.*

Joel Rose   W
156 Waverly Pl, New York, NY 100143852, 212-206-8331
Internet: joeyrose@pipeline.com
    Pubs: *Kill Kill Faster Faster* (Crown, 1997), *Kill The Poor*
    (Atlantic Monthly Pr, 1988), *Love Is Strange: Anth* (Norton,
    1993), *Between C&D: Anth* (Penguin, 1988).

Norma Rosen   W
205 W End Ave, #15U, New York, NY 10023-4822,
212-362-7315
    Pubs: *Biblical Women Unbound,* (JPS, 1997), *John &
    Anzia: An American Romance, At the Center* (Syracuse U
    Pr, 1997, 1996), *Accidents of Influence* (SUNY Pr, 1992),
    New York Times, Tikkun, Lilith.

Alice Rosenblitt   P
47-25 43rd St, #1F, Woodside, NY 11377, 718-937-2891
Internet: apr6357@is6.nyu.com
    Pubs: *Celebrating Women: 20 Years of Co-education: Anth*
    (Yale Women's Ctr, 1990), *Long Shot, Natl Poetry Mag of
    the Lower East Side, La Mia Ink, Pome.*

Linda Rosenkrantz   W
Howard Morhaim Agency, 175 5th Ave, New York, NY 10010,
212-529-4433
    Pubs: *SoHo, Gone Hollywood* (Co-author; Doubleday,
    1981, 1979), *Glamour.*

Ira Rosenstein   P
PO Box 3102, Long Island City, NY 11103, 718-726-8051
    Pubs: *Twenty-two Sonnets, Left On The Field To Die*
    (Starlight Pr, 1986, 1984).

Barbara Rosenthal   PP&P&W
The Media Loft, 463 West St, New York, NY 100142035,
212-924-4893
    Pubs: *Soul & Psyche, Homo Futurus, Sensations, Clues to
    Myself* (Visual Studies Workshop, 1998, 1986, 1986, 1980),
    Cradle and All: Anth (Faber & Faber, 1990), *Umbrella,
    MacGuffin Reader, Bohemian Chronicle.*

Bob Rosenthal   P
334 E 11 St, #16, New York, NY 10003, 212-777-6786
    Pubs: *Rude Awakenings* (Yellow Pr, 1982), *Lies About The
    Flesh* (Frontward Bks, 1977), *Mag City.*

Carole Rosenthal   W
37 1/2 St Marks Pl, #B2, New York, NY 10003, 212-228-4289
    Pubs: *Best of the Underground: Anth* (Rhinoceros Mass
    Market Edtns, 1998), *Powers of Desire: Anth* (Monthly Rev
    Pr, 1983), *Dreamworks, Confrontation, Minnesota Rev,
    Mother Jones, Ellery Queen's Mystery Mag, Other Voices,
    Cream City Rev.*

Martha Rosler   W
143 McGuinness Blvd, Brooklyn, NY 11222, 718-383-2277
    Pubs: *3 Works* (Nova Scotia, 1981), *Service* (Printed
    Matter, 1978), *Heresies.*

David Ross   P
33 Riverside Dr, #5A, New York, NY 10023-8025
    Pubs: *Three Ages Of Lake Light* (Macmillan, 1962), *The
    New Yorker Book of Poems: Anth* (Viking, 1969), *The
    Nation, Poetry, New Yorker, Transatlantic Rev.*

Terrence Ross   W
8 Spring St, #4RW, New York, NY 10012, 212-226-0520
    Pubs: *Bitter Graces* (Avon, 1980).

Judith Rossner   W
The Wendy Weil Agency, Inc., 232 Madison Ave, Ste 1300,
New York, NY 10016, 212-685-0030
    Pubs: *Perfidia* (Mantalese/Doubleday, 1997), *August*
    (Mantalese/Houghton Mifflin, 1983).

Beatrice Roth   PP
86 Horatio St, New York, NY 10014
    Pubs: *Out From Under: Anth* (TCG, 1990), *Massachusetts
    Rev.*

Philip Roth   W
Farrar, Straus & Giroux, 19 Union Sq W, New York, NY
10003

Joyce Andrea Rothenberg   PP&P
PO Box 6041, FDR Sta, New York, NY 10150, 212-268-3343
    Pubs: *The Symphony is Barely Audible* (Symphony Pr,
    1991).

Earl Rovit   W
309 W 109 St, #6G, New York, NY 10025, 212-533-8419
    Pubs: *Crossings, A Far Cry, The Player King* (HBJ, 1973,
    1967, 1965).

Arkady Rovner   W
PO Box 42, Prince St Sta, New York, NY 10012, 212-740-2904
    Pubs: *Guests From the Province* (Moscow Worker Pr,
    1992), *Kalalatsy* (Moscow; Timan Pr, 1991), *The King's
    Visit* (Gnosis, 1988), *Central Park, Literary Rev, Alea.*

Ann Rower   W
60-82 60th Dr, Maspeth, NY 11378-3536, 212-966-6737
    Pubs: *If You're A Girl* (Semiotext(e), *1990).*

Peter Rubie   W
1781 Riverside Dr, New York, NY 10034, 212-304-1607
    Pubs: *Werewolf* (Longmeadow Pr, 1992), *Mindbender*
    (Lynx Bks, 1989).

Kathryn Ruby   P
180 Cabrini Blvd, #71, New York, NY 10033, 212-781-3833
    Pubs: *Twentieth Century Views* (Prentice-Hall, 1979), *We
    Become New* (Bantam, 1975), *Rio.*

Mark Rudman   P
817 W End Ave, #4A, New York, NY 10025, 212-666-3648
    Pubs: *Rider* (Wesleyan U Pr, 1994), *Diverse Voices* (Story
    Line Pr, 1993), *The Nowhere Steps* (Sheep Meadow Pr,
    1990), *APR, Harper's, Paris Rev, New Yorker.*

Raphael Rudnik   P
66 Garfield Pl, #3S, Brooklyn, NY 11215-1923
    Pubs: *Frank 207* (Ohio U Pr, 1982), *Pequod, Kentucky Rev.*

Frazier Russell   P&W
240 Carroll St, Brooklyn, NY 11231, 718-237-9816
    Pubs: *How We Are Spared, Four Way Books Reader: Anth*
    (Four Way Bks, 2000, 1996), *Fweivel: The Day Will Come*
    (Ridgeway Pr, 1996), *Ploughshares, Global City Rev,
    American Voice, Marlboro Rev, Phoebe.*

Suzanne Ruta   W
55 Bethune St, Apt #B647, New York, NY 10014, 212-675-5170
    Pubs: *Stalin in the Bronx and Other Stories* (Grove Pr,
    1987), *Wigwag, VLS, Grand Street.*

Thaddeus Rutkowski   W
235 E 4 St, #3E, New York, NY 10009, 212-387-0056
Internet: trutkows@crain.com
    Pubs: *Basic Training* (March Street Pr, 1996), *Between the
    Cracks: Anth* (Daedalus Pub, 1996), *Unbearables: Anth*
    (Autonomedia, 1995), *Nuyorican Symphony: Anth* (Knitting
    Factory, 1994), *Columbia Rev, Pearl, WV, Verbal Abuse,
    MacGuffin, Pleiades, Context South.*

Lester Rutsky   P
2930 W 5 St, Brooklyn, NY 11224

Reba Ruttel   P
231 W 18 St, New York, NY 10011-4598
    Pubs: *Poetry Peddler, Innisfree, Catharsis, Pincushion
    Poetry, Poetry Motel, Old Hickory Rev.*

Margaret Ryan   P
250 W 104 St #63, New York, NY 10025, 212-666-2591
    Pubs: *Black Raspberries* (Parsonage Pr, 1986), *Filling Out
    A Life* (Front Street, 1981), *The Nation, Poetry,
    Confrontation, Kansas Qtly, Beloit Poetry Jrnl.*

Elizabeth-Ann Sachs   W
Georges Borchardt Inc., 136 E 57 St, New York, NY 10022,
212-753-5785
    Pubs: *Mountain Bike Madness, The Boy Who Ate Dog
    Biscuits* (Random Hse, 1994, 1989), *Just Like Always*
    (Aladdin Bks, 1991).

Howard Sage   P
720 Greenwich St, #4H, New York, NY 10014, 212-627-8959
Internet: hs15@is.nyu.edu
    Pubs: *Fictional Flights: An Anth of Short Fiction For
    Non-Native Speakers* (Heinle and Heinle, 1993), *Folio, New
    Voices.*

Raymond Saint-Pierre   P
25 Cumming St, #3B, New York, NY 100344815,
212-304-2265
Internet: streeteditions@juno.com
    Pubs: *Orgasms of Light* (Gay Sunshine Pr, 1976), *One
    Teacher In Ten: Anth* (Alyson Pub, 1994), *Prophetic
    Voices, Amherst Rev, Boston Literary Rev, Connecticut
    River Rev, Real, Oyez Rev.*

Jerome Sala   P
298 Mulberry St, #3L, New York, NY 10012, 212-941-8724
Internet: jsala@cm.timeinc.com
   Pubs: *Raw Deal: New & Selected Poems* (Another Chicago
   Pr, 1994), *The Trip* (Highlander Pr, 1987), *Aerial, Exquisite
   Corpse, NAW, Onthebus, Ploughshares.*

Joseph S. Salemi   P
3222 61st St, Woodside, NY 11377, 718-932-5351
   Pubs: *Formal Complaints* (Somers Rocks Pr, 1997),
   *Carolina Qtly, Hellas, Cumberland Poetry Rev, Crab Creek
   Rev, Amelia, Univ Bookman, Paintbrush, Artful Dodge, Blue
   Unicorn, Formalist, Satire, Sparrow, Edge City Rev,
   Maledicta.*

J. D. Salinger   W
Harold Ober Associates, 425 Madison Ave, New York, NY
10017, 212-759-8600

James Salter   W
Sterling Lord Literistic, 65 Bleecker St, New York, NY 10012,
212-780-6050
   Pubs: *Dusk & Other Stories, Light Years, A Sport & A
   Pastime* (North Point Pr, 1988, 1982, 1980), *Esquire, GQ.*

Thomas Sanchez   W
ICM, 40 W 57 St, New York, NY 10019, 212-556-5600
   Pubs: *Mile Zero, Rabbit Boss* (Knopf/Vintage, 1990, 1989).

Ronni Sandroff   W
Elaine Markson Literary Agency, 44 Greenwich Ave, New
York, NY 10011
   Pubs: *Fighting Back* (Jove, 1979), *Party, Party/Girlfriends*
   (Knopf, 1975).

Myro Sandunes   W
The Dramatists Guild, 234 W 44 St, New York, NY 10036,
212-398-9366
   Pubs: *The Go-Between, Placebo* (Albatross Pub, 1983,
   1983).

Reuben Sandwich   PP
PO Box 020841, Brooklyn, NY 11202, 718-797-2515
   Pubs: *The Shredder.*

Rosemarie Santini   W
Pratt Institute, 295 Lafayette St, New York, NY 10012,
212-242-6358
   Pubs: *Blood Sisters, Private Lives* (Pocket Bks, 1990,
   1989), *The Disenchanted Diva, A Swell Style of Murder* (St.
   Martin's, 1988, 1986), *Music Lesson, Movie Murder, New
   Mystery Magazine.*

Sapphire   W
Charlotte Sheedy Literary Agen, 65 Bleecker St, New York,
NY 10012
   Pubs: *Push* (Knopf, 1996), *American Dreams* (High Risk
   Bks, 1994), *New York Times Mag, New Yorker, Bomb.*

Helen Saslow   P
3626 Kings Hwy #5L, Brooklyn, NY 11234, 718-377-4834
   Pubs: *Arctic Summer* (Barlenmir House, 1974), *The
   Villanelle: The Evolution of a Poetic Form: Anth* (U Idaho
   Pr, 1987), *New York Qtly, Glassworks, Confrontation,
   Hellcoal Annual, Hanging Loose, The Small Pohd.*

Steven Sater   P
William Morris Agency, 1350 Ave of the Americas, New York,
NY 10019, 212-586-5100
   Pubs: *Carbondale Dreams* (Dramatists Play Service, 1991),
   Take Ten: Anth (Vintage, 1997), *Portland Rev, Poems &
   Plays, Confrontation, Rockford Rev, Hawaii Rev, The
   MacGuffin.*

Ben Satterfield   P&W
The Literary Group Intl, 270 Lafayette, Ste 1505, New York,
NY 10012, 212-274-1616
   Pubs: *Texas Short Fiction: A World In Itself: Anth* (ALE Pub,
   1993), *Sign of the Times Anth* (Studio 403, 1992).

Tom Savage   P
622 E 11 St, #14, New York, NY 100094140, 212-533-3893
   Pubs: *Brain Surgery Poems* (Linear Arts, 1998), *Political
   Conditions/Physical States, 1993), Out of This World
   (Crown, 1991), The World, Synaesthetic, Tamarind,
   Hanging Loose, Talisman, Long Shot.*

Sally Savic   P&W
Melanie Jackson Agency, 250 W 57 St, #1119, New York, NY
10107
   Pubs: *Elysian Fields* (Scribner, 1988), *Cosmopolitan, Intro.*

Lynwood Sawyer   W
85 State St, #5, Brooklyn, NY 11201-5534, 718-237-2296
   Pubs: *Hawaii Pacific Rev, Art Access, Pembroke Rev, Just
   Pulp, St. Andrews Rev, Ellery Queen's Mystery Mag.*

Ann Scaglione   P
244-23 73rd Ave, Douglaston, NY 11362, 718-523-8839
   Pubs: *Vega, Arulo, Modern Images.*

Hindy Lauer Schachter   W
420 E 64 St, New York, NY 10021
   Pubs: *Intl Poetry Rev, Response, Jewish Frontier.*

Sandy Rochelle Schachter   PP
438 W 23 St #A, New York, NY 10011, 212-929-6245
Internet: chelsea438@aol.com
   Pubs: *Poems from the Heart* (The Plowman, 1992),
   Connecticut River Rev, Visions Intl.

Susan Fromberg Schaeffer   P&W
Janklow & Nesbit Associates, 598 Madison Ave, New York,
NY 10022-1614, 212-421-1700
   Pubs: *The Golden Rope, First Nights, Buffalo Afternoon*
   (Knopf, 1996, 1993, 1989), *The Injured Party* (St. Martin's
   Pr, 1987).

Lorraine Schein P&W
41-30 46th St, #5A, Sunnyside, NY 11104-1829
  Pubs: *The Raw Brunettes: Anth* (Wordcraft of Oregon, 1995), *Wild Women: Anth* (Overlook Pr, 1994), *Exquisite Corpse, Semiotext*(e), *Poetry New York, Brooklyn Rev.*

Harris Schiff P
515 E 7 St, #2K, Brooklyn, NY 11218, 718-768-3065
  Pubs: *In The Heart Of The Empire, Yo-Yos With Money* (United Artists, 1979, 1979), *Paris Rev.*

Jeanne Schinto W
Sanford J. Greenburger Assoc., 55 Fifth Ave, New York, NY 10003, 212-206-5600
  Pubs: *Children of Men* (Persea Bks, 1991), *Shadow Bands* (Ontario Rev Pr, 1988), *The Literary Dog: Anth* (Atlantic Monthly Pr, 1990), *Virginia Qtly Rev, Yale Rev.*

Robert Schirmer W
24 1st St, Brooklyn, NY 11231-5002
  Pubs: *Living With Strangers* (NYU Pr, 1991), *NER, Indiana Rev, Greensboro Rev, New Letters.*

Peter Schjeldahl P
53 St. Marks Pl, New York, NY 10003, 212-674-5889
  Pubs: *Since 1964: New And Selected Poems* (Sun Pr, 1978).

Geraldine Schmitz W
81 Campbell St, New Hyde Park, NY 11040-1758, 516-354-0021
  Pubs: *Four Quarters, Zantia, More Womanspace.*

Tobias Schneebaum W
463 West St, #410A, New York, NY 10014, 212-691-0022
  Pubs: *Embodied Spirits* (Peabody Museum of Salem, 1990), *Where The Spirits Dwell, Keep the River on Your Right* (Grove, 1988, 1969).

Elio Schneeman P
29 St. Marks Pl, New York, NY 10003, 212-982-7682
Internet: eds8@columbia.edu
  Pubs: *Along The Rails* (United Artists, 1991), *In February I Think* (C Pr, 1978), *Poetry New York, World, Hanging Loose, Long News, Flatiron News, Shiny.*

Carolee Schneemann PP&P
Sanford J. Greenburger Assoc., 55 Fifth Ave, New York, NY 10003, 212-206-5600
Internet: caroleel2@aol.com
  Pubs: *More Than Meat Joy* (McPherson & Co., 1996), *Deep Down* (Faber & Faber, 1988), *Parts of a Body House Book* (U.K.; Beau Geste Pr, 1972), *White Walls Jrnl.*

Bart Schneider P
Watkins-Loomis Literary Agency, 133 E 35 St, New York, NY 10016, 212-532-0080
Internet: hmreview@winternet.com
  Pubs: *Blue Bossa* (Viking, 1998), *Race* (Crown, 1997), *Seasons of the Game* (Elysian Fields, 1992), *Water for A Stranger* (Blue Teal Pr, 1979), *Rolling Stone, Teachers & Writers Mag.*

Elizabeth Lynn Schneider P
480 2nd St, Brooklyn, NY 11215, 718-768-6296

L. J. Schneiderman W
41 West 82nd St, New York, NY 100245613, 212-873-4945
Internet: ljs@ucsd.edu
  Pubs: *The Appointment* (S&S, 1991), *Sea Nymphs by the Hour* (Bobbs-Merrill, 1972), *Confrontation, Ascent, Kansas Qtly, Chouteau Rev, Black Warrior Rev.*

Lynda Schor W
463 West St, #610C, New York, NY 10014
  Pubs: *True Love & Real Romance* (Coward, McCann & Geoghegan, 1979), *Appetites* (Warner, 1976), *Playboy, Mademoiselle, Redbook, GQ, Confrontation, Ms..*

Roni Schotter W
Writers House, 21 W 26 St, New York, NY 10010, 914-478-3231
  Pubs: *Purim Play, Passover Magic, A Fruit and Vegetable Man* (Little Brown, 1998, 1995, 1993), *Nothing Ever Happens on 90th Street, Dreamland* (Orchard Bks, 1997, 1996), *When Crocodiles Clean Up* (Macmillan, 1993).

Peninnah Schram PP&P&W
525 W End Ave, #8C, New York, NY 10024, 212-787-0626
  Pubs: *Tales of Elijah the Prophet, Jewish Stories One Generation Tells Another* (Jason Aronson, 1991, 1987).

Susan Schreibman P
372 5th Ave #4N, New York, NY 10018, 212-695-2947
  Pubs: *Poetry Ireland, Footwork, Atlanta Rev, Poet Lore, Dreamworks, Wind, Crazyquilt, Amelia.*

Grace Schulman P
1 University Pl, #14-F, New York, NY 10003, 212-533-0235
  Pubs: *For That Day Only, Hemispheres* (Sheep Meadow Pr, 1994, 1984), *New Yorker, Paris Rev, Boulevard, Pequod, Kenyon Rev, Poetry.*

Helen Schulman W
782 W End Ave #73, New York, NY 100255401
  Pubs: *Out of Time* (Atheneum, 1991), *Not A Free Show* (Knopf, 1988), *Antioch Rev, NAR, Story Qtly, The Quarterly, Arete.*

Sarah Schulman   W
406 E 9 St, #20, New York, NY 10009, 212-982-1033
    Pubs: *Shimmer* (Avon, 1998), *Stagestruck: Theatre, AIDS
    and Marketing* (Duke U Pr, 1998), *Rat Bohemia* (E.P.
    Dutton, 1995), *My American History: Lesbian & Gay Life
    During the Reagan/Bush Years* (Routledge, 1994),
    Empathy (Plume, 1993).

David Schultz   P&W
162-31 9th Ave #4A, Whitestone, NY 11357-2010,
718-767-7455
Internet: davidtrans@aol.com
    Pubs: *Poesie USA, Footwork, Horizontes, Transition,
    Ambrosia, The Haven, Tin Wreath, Italian-Americana.*

Philip Schultz   P&W
78 Charles St, #2R, New York, NY 10014, 212-675-5703
    Pubs: *Deep Within the Ravine, Like Wings* (Viking, 1984,
    1978), *New American Poets of the 90's: Anth* (Godine,
    1991), *New Yorker, Poetry Chicago, Nation.*

Beatrice Schuman   W
3604 Skillman Ave, Long Island City, NY 11101,
718-392-6650
    Pubs: *It's Not Easy To Marry An Elephant, Am I Greedy If I
    Want More* (Fred Fell, 1982, 1979).

Elaine Schwager   P
228 W 22 St, New York, NY 10011, 212-807-1225
    Pubs: *It Is The Poem Singing In Your Eyes: Anth* (Harper,
    1971), *City in all Directions: Anth* (Macmillan, 1969), *Literal
    Latte, Writ, Armadillo.*

Leonard Schwartz   P
120 Cabrini Blvd, #96, New York, NY 10033
    Pubs: *Words Before the Articulate* (Talisman Hse, 1997),
    Gnostic Blessing (Goats and Compasses Pr, 1992), *First
    Intensity, Five Fingers Rev, Talisman, Poetry New York,
    Pequod, Central Park, The World, American Letters and
    Commentary.*

Lynne Sharon Schwartz   W
50 Morningside Dr #31, New York, NY 10025
    Pubs: *Ruined by Reading* (Beacon, 1996), *The Fatigue
    Artist* (Scribner, 1995), *Leaving Brooklyn* (HM, 1989).

Marian Schwartz   W
Curtis Brown Ltd., 10 Astor Pl, New York, NY 10003-6935
    Pubs: *Realities* (St. Martin's Pr, 1981).

Doris Schwerin   W
317 W 83 St, #4W, New York, NY 10024, 212-724-2997
    Pubs: *Cat & I* (H&R, 1990), *Leanna, Diary of a Pigeon
    Watcher* (Morrow, 1978, 1976), *Rainbow Walkers*
    (Villard/Random Hse, 1986), *The Tomorrow Book*
    (Pantheon, 1984).

Armand Schwerner   PP&P
20 Bay St Landing, #B-3C, Staten Island, NY 10301,
718-442-3784
Internet: schwerner@cuny.campus.mci.net
    Pubs: *The Tablets I-XXVI* (National Poetry Foundation,
    1998), *Poems for the Millennium: Anth* (U California Pr,
    1996), *Conjunctions, Sulfur, Tyuonyi, Talisman.*

Ilka Scobie   P
393 W Broadway, New York, NY 10012, 212-219-8567
    Pubs: *There For The Taking* (Four Zoas Pr, 1979),
    Exquisite Corpse, Fred Mag, Home Planet News.

Virginia Scott   P
255 Fieldston Terr, #3A, Bronx, NY 10471
    Pubs: *Toward Appomattox, The Witness Box* (Motherroot
    Pubs, 1985), *Prairie Schooner, Antigonish Rev, American
    Voice.*

Peter Seaton   P
229 E 25 St, #3A, New York, NY 10010, 212-683-1449
    Pubs: *Crisis Intervention* (Tuumba Pr, 1983), *The Son
    Master* (Roof Bks, 1982), *Paris Rev, This.*

Edith Segal   P
60 Plaza St, #3A, Brooklyn, NY 11238, 718-638-8372
    Pubs: *Tributes & Trumpets, A Time to Thunder* (Philmark
    Pr, 1986, 1982).

Lore Segal   W
280 Riverside Dr, #12K, New York, NY 10025
Internet: cousinlore@aol.com
    Pubs: *Her First American* (Knopf, 1994), *The Story of King
    Saul and King David* (Schocken, 1991), *The Book of Adam
    to Moses* (Pantheon, 1989), *Best American Short Stories:
    Anth* (HM, 1990), *Congregation: Anth* (HB, 1987), *Social
    Research, Harper's.*

Frederick Seidel   P
Farrar, Straus & Giroux, 19 Union Sq W, New York, NY
10003, 212-741-6900
    Pubs: *Going Fast, My Tokyo* (FSG, 1998, 1991), *Poems
    1959-1979, These Days* (Knopf, 1989, 1989), *Sunrise*
    (Viking/Penguin, 1980).

Hugh Seidman   P
463 West St, #H822, New York, NY 10014, 212-255-5847
    Pubs: *Selected Poems: 1965-1995, People Live, They
    Have Lives* (Miami U Pr, 1995, 1992).

Robert J. Seidman   W
Harvey Klinger, Inc., 301 W 53 St, New York, NY 10019
    Pubs: *Bucks County Idyll* (S&S, 1980), *One Smart Indian*
    (Overlook Pr, 1979).

Bernice Selden   W
808 W End Ave, #507, New York, NY 10025, 212-222-5819
    Pubs: *The Mill Girls* (Atheneum, 1983), *Music In My Heart*
    (Dutton, 1982).

Robyn Selman P
62 W 11 St, #3F, New York, NY 10011
Pubs: *Directions to My House* (U Pittsburgh Pr, 1995), *Best American Poetry: Anths* (Macmillan, 1995, 1991), *Paris Review, Prairie Schooner, The American Voice, Puerto del Sol, Ploughshares, Kenyon Rev, APR.*

Joseph Semenovich P
2610 Glenwood Rd, #6E, Brooklyn, NY 11210, 718-859-2991
Pubs: *The Peter Poems* (Trout Creek Pr, 1984), *Prothalamion* (Textile Bridge Pr, 1982), *Webster Rev, Dog River Rev, Slipstream, Rain City Rev.*

Jacques Servin W
PO Box 464, Prince St Sta, New York, NY 10012-0464, 212-875-7780
Pubs: *Mermaids For Attila* (Fiction Collective Two, 1991).

Vikram Seth P&W
Curtis Brown Ltd., 10 Astor Pl, New York, NY 10003-6935, 212-473-5400
Pubs: *All You Who Sleep Tonight* (Knopf, 1990), *The Golden Gate* (Random Hse, 1986).

Elizabeth Sewell P&W
Harold Ober Associates, 425 Madison Ave, New York, NY 10017, 336-275-4720
Pubs: *Acquist* (Acorn, 1984), *An Idea* (Mercer U Pr, 1983), *To Be a True Poem* (Hunter Pub, 1979), *Soundings.*

Bob Shacochis W
Brandt & Brandt Literary Agent, 1501 Broadway, New York, NY 10036, 212-840-5760
Pubs: *Swimming In The Volcano* (Scribner, 1993), *Easy in the Islands* (Crown, 1985), *Paris Rev, Harper's, Esquire, Outside.*

R. L. Shafner W
100 W 92 St #8A, New York, NY 10025, 212-496-0979
Pubs: *Stop Me If You've Heard This* (Signet, 1986), *Formations, TriQuarterly, Shankpainter.*

Fatima Shaik W
315 7th Ave, #9A, New York, NY 10001
Internet: shaik_f@spcvxa.spc.edu
Pubs: *Melitte* (Dial Bks, 1997), *Breaking Ice: African American Fiction: Anth* (Viking Penguin, 1990), *Southern Rev, Tribes, Rev of Contemporary Fiction, Double Dealer Redux, Xavier Rev, Callaloo.*

David Shapiro P
3001 Henry Hudson Pkwy #3B, Riverdale, NY 10463, 718-601-3425
Pubs: *After A Lost Original, House Blown Apart, To An Idea* (Overlook, 1994, 1988, 1984), *Lingo, NAW, Boulevard, New Yorker, Paris Rev.*

Harvey Shapiro P
43 Pierrepont St, Brooklyn, NY 11201, 718-858-3765
Pubs: *Selected Poems* (Wesleyan, 1997), *A Day's Portion* (Hanging Loose Pr, 1994).

Myra Shapiro P
111 4th Ave, #12I, New York, NY 10003, 212-995-0659
Pubs: *I'll See You Thursday* (Blue Sofa Pr, 1996), *Father Poems* (Poetlink, 1995), *Harvard Rev, Pearl, Ploughshares, Ohio Rev, River Styx, Calyx Jrnl.*

Peter Sharpe P
Wagner College, 1 Campus Rd, Staten Island, NY 10301, 718-390-3370
Internet: psharpe@wagner.edu
Pubs: *Lost Goods & Stray Beasts* (Rowan Tree Pr, 1983), *Massachusetts Rev, Tendril, Harbor Rev, Southern Rev, Davidson Miscellany, Poet Lore.*

Brenda Shaughnessy P
Farrar, Straus & Giroux, 19 Union Sq W, New York, NY 10003, 212-741-6900
Pubs: *Interview With Sudden Joy* (FSG, 1999), *Paris Rev, Yale Rev, Chelsea.*

Don Shea W
102 E 22 St #5G, New York, NY 10010, 212-777-3685
Internet: dshea11741@aol.com
Pubs: *New York Sex: Anth* (Painted Leaf Pr, 1998), *Fast Fiction: Anth* (Story Pr, 1997), *Flash Fiction: Anth* (Norton, 1992), *NAR, Gettysburg Rev, The Literary Rev, The Quarterly, Confrontation, High Plains Literary Rev, Cresent Rev, Onthebus, Descant.*

Evelyn Shefner W
230 E 15 St, #5N, New York, NY 10003-3943, 212-242-5810
Pubs: *Common Body, Royal Bones* (Coffee Hse Pr, 1987), *O. Henry Prize Stories: Anth* (Doubleday, 1979), *Southern Rev, Negative Capability, The Bridge.*

Rose Sher P
155 W 68 St, #327, New York, NY 10023-5809
Pubs: *Anthology Two* (Florida State Poets Assn, 1984), *Euterpe Housetops, Earthwise, Newscribes.*

Susan Sherman P
Ikon Magazine, PO Box 1355, Stuyvesant Sta, New York, NY 10009, 212-674-0636
Internet: shermansu@aol.com
Pubs: *The Color of the Heart* (Curbstone Pr, 1990), *We Stand Our Ground* (Ikon Bks, 1988), *Gathering of the Tribes, Long Shot, Heresies, Poetry, APR.*

James Sherry P&W
300 Bowery, New York, NY 10012, 212-353-0555
Pubs: *Our Nuclear Heritage* (Sun & Moon Pr, 1991), *The Word I Like White Paint Considered* (Awede, 1986), *Popular Fiction* (Roof Bks, 1985).

David Shetzline W
c/o ICM, 40 W 57 St, New York, NY 10019, 212-556-5600

David Shields W
Witherspoon Associates, 157 W 57 St, Ste 700, New York,
NY 10019, 212-757-0567
Internet: dshields@u.washington.edu
    Pubs: *Remote, Dead Languages* (Knopf, 1996, 1989), *New
    York Times Mag, Harper's, Vogue, Details, Village Voice,
    Utne Reader.*

Betty Shiflett W
Writers House, 21 W 26 St, New York, NY 10010,
212-685-2400
    Pubs: *Writing from Start to Finish: Anth* (Boynton/Cook,
    1982), *Life Mag, Evergreen.*

Ann Allen Shockley W
160 W 87 St, #7D, New York, NY 10024, 212-724-1168
    Pubs: *Loving Her* (Northeastern U Pr, 1997), *Trials,
    Tribulations, and Celebrations: Anth* (Intercultural Pr, 1992),
    Catalyst, African American Literary Rev.

Enid Shomer P&W
173 Riverside Dr, #2Y, New York, NY 10024, 212-580-4207
Internet: enidshomer@aol.com
    Pubs: *Black Drum, This Close to the Earth* (U Arkansas Pr,
    1997, 1992), *Imaginary Men* (U Iowa Pr, 1993), *New
    Yorker, Atlantic, Paris Rev, Poetry, New Criterion, Georgia
    Rev, Modern Maturity.*

Susan Richards Shreve W
Russell & Volkening, Inc., 50 W 29 St, New York, NY 10001,
212-684-6050
    Pubs: *The Train Home, Daughters of the New World*
    (Doubleday, 1993, 1992), *A Country of Strangers* (S&S,
    1989).

Kenneth Siegelman P
2225 W 5 St, Brooklyn, NY 11223, 718-996-2912
    Pubs: *Urbania, American Imprints, Through Global
    Currents* (Modern Images Pr, 1996, 1994, 1993),
    Parnassus, Poet.

Joan Silber W
43 Bond St, New York, NY 10012, 212-228-9728
    Pubs: *In the City, Household Words* (Viking, 1987, 1980),
    VLS, New Yorker, Paris Rev.

Layle Silbert P&W
505 LaGuardia Pl, #16C, New York, NY 100122002,
212-677-0947
    Pubs: *New York, New York* (St. Andrews Pr, 1996), *Burkah
    & Other Stories* (Host Pubs, 1992), *Imaginary People &
    Other Strangers* (Exile Pr, 1985), *Denver Qtly, Salmagundi,
    Michigan Qtly Rev, Kansas Qtly, Ohio Rev, Confrontation.*

Lari Field Siler W
361 E 50 St, New York, NY 10022, 212-759-7364
    Pubs: *Adrienne's House* (HR&W, 1979), *Epicure, True
    Love, Teens Today.*

Christopher Silver W
300 Central Pk W, New York, NY 10024, 413-238-7769

Ruth M. Silver P
374 Eastern Pkwy, Brooklyn, NY 11225, 718-774-0210
    Pubs: *Brooklyn Book Fair: Anth* (Somrie Pr, 1984),
    Brooklyn College Literary Rev.

Mike Silverton P
459 12th St, #2C, Brooklyn, NY 112155153, 718-788-0805
Internet: hensteeth@aol.com
    Pubs: *Battery Park* (Thing Pr, 1966).

Shirley J. Simmons P
JAF Box 7496, GPO, New York, NY 10116
    Pubs: *Song of Circe* (Art & Oxygen, 1988), *Liberation*
    (Platen Pub, 1986), *Up Against The Wall.*

Laura Simms PP&P
814 Broadway, #3, New York, NY 10003, 212-674-3479
    Pubs: *Moon And Otter And Frog* (Hyperion, 1995), *Chosen
    Tales: Anth* (Rosen, 1995), *Revisioning The Myth of
    Demeter & Persephone: Anth* (Shambala, 1994).

Ana Maria Simo W
New Dramatists, 424 W 44 St, New York, NY 10036

Jane Simon P
145 Central Pk W, New York, NY 10023, 212-877-3566
Internet: js145@msn.com
    Pubs: *Incisions* (Croton Rev Pr, 1989), *UCLA Poet
    Physician Anth* (UCLA Pr, 1990), *Poet, Black Buzzard Rev,
    New Voices.*

Mona Simpson P&W
ICM, 40 W 57 St, New York, NY 10019, 212-556-5600
    Pubs: *Anywhere But Here* (Knopf, 1987).

Abiola Sinclair PP&P
Black History Magazine, 2565 Broadway MBE 262, New
York, NY 10025, 212-662-2942
Internet: blackhistorymag@pipeline.com
    Pubs: *Harlem Political & Cultural Movement 1960-1970*
    (Gumbs & Thomas, 1995), *Requiem for George Jackson,
    Imagism—Harlem in Reflection* (Shamal Bks, 1995, 1982),
    *Charleston Chronicle, New York Beacon, Daily Challenge,
    Black Mask, Big Red, Amsterdam News.*

Davida Singer P
223 W 105 St, #3FW, New York, NY 10025-3968,
212-663-3937
    Pubs: *Shelter Island Poems* (Canio's Edtns, 1995), *Khupe:
Anth* (Recording, 1997), *Ignite, Response, Little Mag,
Passager, Caprice, Sinister Wisdom.*

Frieda Singer P
161-08 Jewel Ave, #1-C, Flushing, NY 11365, 718-591-2288
    Pubs: *Blood to Remember: Anth* (Texas Tech U Pr, 1992),
*Poetpourri, The Formalist, South Florida Poetry Rev,
Negative Capability.*

Ravi Singh P
225 E 5 St, #4D, New York, NY 10003, 212-475-0212
    Pubs: *Long Song to the One I Love* (White Lion, 1986),
Another World: Anth (Crown, 1992), *Grand Union, Exquisite
Corpse, Cover.*

Harriet Sirof W
792 E 21 St, Brooklyn, NY 11210, 718-859-3296
    Pubs: *Bring Back Yesterday, Because She's My Friend*
(Atheneum, 1996, 1993), *The Road Back: Living With A
Physical Disability* (Macmillan, 1993).

Hal Sirowitz P
144-45 Sanford Ave, #2C, Flushing, NY 11355,
718-461-7892
    Pubs: *My Therapist Said, Mother Said* (Crown, 1998,
1996), *Poetry in Motion: Anth* (Norton, 1996), *Chelsea, The
Ledge, ACM, Speak.*

Denis Sivack P
1165 E 54 St, #4-F, Brooklyn, NY 11234
    Pubs: *Esprit.*

Arnold Skemer W
58-09 205th St, Bayside, NY 11364, 718-428-9368
    Pubs: *The Occupation, D, C, The Famine* (Phrygian Pr,
1996, 1995, 1992, 1985), *Transmoog, Drop Forge, Meat
Epoch, Samisdat, Generator, New Surrealism.*

Morty Sklar P
35-50 85th Street, Jackson Heights, NY 113725540,
718-426-8788
Internet: msklar@mindspring.com
    Pubs: *Ma & Other Poems* (The Spirit That Moves Us Pr,
1998), *The Night We Stood Up For Our Rights* (Toothpaste
Pr, 1977), *The First Poem* (Snapper Pr, 1987), *From A to Z:
Anth* (Swallow Pr, 1980), *New Letters, New York Qtly,
World Letter, Smiling Dog, Pearl.*

Bob Slaymaker P&W
PO Box 8483, New York, NY 10116-8483, 212-924-4410
Internet: bobslaymaker@mindspring.com
    Pubs: *Catalyst, Interrace, Minnesota Rev, New York Qtly,
Christian Science Monitor, Exquisite Corpse, Contact II,
River Styx, Essence, Callaloo, Gargoyle.*

Henry Slesar W
125 E 72 St, #12-A, New York, NY 10021, 212-628-1741
    Pubs: *Death on Television* (U Illinois Pr, 1989), *Murders
Most Macabre* (Avon Bks, 1986), *Ellery Queen's Mystery,
Alfred Hitchcock's Mystery.*

C. W. Smith W
Elaine Markson Literary Agency, 44 Greenwich Ave, New
York, NY 10011, 212-243-8480
    Pubs: *Thin Men of Haddam* (Texas Christian U Pr, 1990),
Uncle Dad (Berkley Bks, 1989), *Buffalo Nickel* (Poseidon,
1989), *Esquire, Quartet.*

Charlie Smith P&W
Marian Young Literary Agency, 156 5th Ave, Ste 608, New
York, NY 10010, 212-229-2612
    Pubs: *Chimney Rock* (Henry Holt, 1993), *The Palms*
(Norton, 1993), *New Yorker, Paris Rev, Harper's,
Conjunctions, APR, Threepenny Rev.*

Dinitia Smith W
210 W 101 St, #3J, New York, NY 10025, 212-864-3866
    Pubs: *Remember This* (Henry Holt, 1989), *The Hard Rain*
(Dial Pr, 1980), *Hudson Rev, Pequod.*

Harry Smith P
69 Joralemon St, Brooklyn, NY 11201, 718-834-1212
    Pubs: *Two Friends II* (w/Menke Katz), *Ballads For the
Possessed* (Birch Brook Pr, 1988, 1987).

Harry C. Smith W
85 Barrow St, #4K/4L, New York, NY 10014, 212-242-5810
    Pubs: *The Bridge, QRL, Western Humanities Rev, Big
Moon, Origin.*

Leora Skolkin Smith W
61 Lexington Ave, #4G, New York, NY 10010, 212-532-3892
    Pubs: *Hystera* (Persea Bks, 1979), *Sarah Lawrence Rev.*

Patti Smith P
Meibach Epstein Reiss & Regis, 680 5th Ave, Ste 500, New
York, NY 10019

Phil Demise Smith P
421 Hudson St, #220, New York, NY 10014, 212-989-7845
Internet: philsmith@waresforart.com
    Pubs: *Constant Variations, The Lost Supper/The Last
Generation* (w/Gunter Temech) (Gegenshein, 1993, 1990).

Robert L. Smith P
271 E 78 St, New York, NY 10021, 212-734-3474
    Pubs: *Refractions* (Dragon's Teeth, 1979), *Galley Sail Rev,
Roanoke Rev, Orbis, Long Pond Rev.*

William Jay Smith   P
Sterling Lord Literistic, 65 Bleecker St, New York, NY 10012, 212-780-6050
   Pubs: *The World Below the Window: Poems 1937-1997* (Johns Hopkins U Pr, 1998), *Collected Poems 1939-1989* (Scribner, 1990), *Laughing Time: Collected Nonsense* (FSG, 1990), *New Criterion.*

Bonnie Snow   PP
188A E 93 St, #1N, New York, NY 10028, 212-427-3585
   Pubs: *Milkweed Chronicle, Playing for Free* (Wartsenall Records, 1988).

Raymond Sokolov   W
190 Riverside Dr, New York, NY 10024

Helen Leslie Sokolsky   P
900 W 190 St, #8-O, New York, NY 10040, 212-795-9209
   Pubs: *Poetry Rev, Confrontation, California State Poetry Qtly, Poet Lore, Poetry, Canada Rev, Wind.*

John J. Soldo   P
238 Ave U, Brooklyn, NY 11223, 718-265-6762
   Pubs: *Sonnets for Our Risorgimento, In the Indies* (Brunswick Pub, 1993, 1991), *High Plains Scenarios* (Earthwise Pub, 1992), *Encore, Parnassus, Omnific.*

Stacey Sollfrey   P
1117 E 86 St, Downstairs, Brooklyn, NY 11236, 718-209-9840
   Pubs: *Feeling The Roof of a Mouth That Hangs Open* (w/Sheila Murphy; Luna Bisonte Prod, 1991), *Lost & Found Times, Impetus, Fine Madness.*

Barbara Probst Solomon   W
40 E 68 St, New York, NY 10021, 212-737-2969
   Pubs: *Smart Hearts in the City* (Harcourt Brace, 1992), *Arriving Where We Started* (Harper & Row, 1972).

Susan Sontag   W
The Wylie Agency, 250 West 57th St, New York, NY 10107, 212-246-0069
   Pubs: *In America, The Volcano Lover, A Susan Sontag Reader, Under the Sign of Saturn, I, Etcetera* (FSG, 1999, 1992, 1982, 1981, 1978).

Gilbert Sorrentino   W
William Morris Agency, 1350 Ave of the Americas, New York, NY 10019
   Pubs: *Pack of Lies: A Trilogy, Under The Shadow, Misterioso, Rose Theatre* (Dalkey Archive, 1997, 1991, 1989, 1987), *Red The Fiend* (Fromm Intl, 1995), *Odd Number* (North Point, 1985).

Peter Sourian   W
30 E 70 St, New York, NY 10021
   Pubs: *At the French Embassy in Sofia* (Ashod Pr, 1992), *Drawing, Annandale, Ararat, The Nation.*

Ellease Southerland   P&W
Marie Brown Associates Inc., 625 Broadway, New York, NY 10012, 212-533-5534
   Pubs: *Let The Lion Eat Straw* (Scribner, 1979), *Calling the Wind: Anth* (Harper Perennial, 1993), *Breaking Ice: Anth* (Penguin, 1990), *Massachusetts Rev, Poet Lore.*

Tom Spanbauer   W
Donadio & Ashworth, Inc., 121 W 27 St, Ste 704, New York, NY 10001, 212-691-8077
   Pubs: *Les Chiens de L'Enfer* (Gallimard, 1989), *Faraway Places* (Putnam, 1988), *Mississippi Mud.*

Muriel Spanier   W
ICM, 40 W 57 St, New York, NY 10019, 212-556-5600
   Pubs: *Staying Afloat* (Random Hse, 1985), *Redbook, Sewanee Rev, Qtly Rev of Literature, Colorado Qtly.*

Al Spector   P
69-31 222nd St, Bayside, NY 11364, 718-224-8950
   Pubs: *Whispers of Spring* (The Plowman, 1994), *Bogg, New York Times, Midwest Poetry Rev, Wind, Orphic Lute, Chicago Street.*

Scott Spencer   W
Alfred A. Knopf, Inc., 201 E 50 St, New York, NY 10022, 212-751-2600
   Pubs: *The Rich Man's Table, Men In Black, Secret Anniversaries* (Knopf, 1998, 1995, 1990).

Katia Spiegelman   W
392 Sackett St, 2nd Fl, Brooklyn, NY 11231, 718-858-1404
   Pubs: *Peculiar Politics, Soul Catcher* (Marion Boyars Pub, 1993, 1990).

Peter Spielberg   W
321 W 24 St Apt 13F, NY, NY 10011, 212-989-4298
   Pubs: *Hearsay* (Fiction Collective Two, 1992), *Crash-Landing* (Fiction Collective, 1985), *Fiction Intl, Europe, Mississippi Rev.*

Norman Spinrad   W
318 E 51 St, New York, NY 10022, 212-752-1038

Peter Spiro   W
925 Union St, Brooklyn, NY 11215, 718-789-9020
   Pubs: *The United States of Poetry: Anth* (Abrams, 1996), *Aloud: Voices from the Nuyorican Poets Cafe: Anth* (Holt, 1994), *Poetry New York, Outerbridge, Flex, Maryland Rev.*

Nancy Springer   W
Jean V. Naggar Literary Agency, 216 E 75 St, Ste 1E, New York, NY 10021, 212-794-1082
   Pubs: *I Am Mordred* (Philomel, 1998), *Fair Peril, Larque on the Wing* (Avon, 1996, 1994), *Alfred Hitchcock's Mystery, Mag of Fantasy & Sci-Fi, The Writer, Cricket, Boys Life, Pirate Writings.*

Tricia Springstubb W
Ellen Levine Literary Agency, 15 E 26 St, Ste 1801, New York, NY 10010, 212-889-0620
>Pubs: *Two Plus One Goes Ape, Two Plus One Makes Trouble* (Scholastic, 1995, 1991).

Stephen Stark W
Spieler Agency, 154 W 57 St, New York, NY 10019, 212-757-4439
>Pubs: *Second Son* (Henry Holt, 1992), *The Outskirts* (Algonquin Bks, 1988), *New Yorker, The Journal.*

Francis Steegmuller W
200 E 66 St, #C1705, New York, NY 10021
>Pubs: *An Incident At Naples* (Seacliff Pr, 1992), *A Woman, A Man, and Two Kingdoms* (Knopf, 1991), *Silence at Salerno* (HR&W, 1978).

Robert Steiner W
Georges Borchardt Inc., 136 E 57 St, New York, NY 10022, 212-753-5785
>Pubs: *Toward A Grammar of Abstraction* (Pennsylvania State Pr, 1993), *Broadway Melody of 1999, Matinee* (Fiction Collective Two, 1993, 1991).

Stephen Stepanchev P
140-60 Beech Ave, #3C, Flushing, NY 11355, 718-539-4463
>Pubs: *Seven Horizons* (Orchises Pr, 1997), *Descent* (Stone Hse Pr, 1988), *Poetry, New Yorker, New Criterion, Commonweal, Interim, New York Qtly.*

Jack Stephens P&W
51 7th Ave S, #5C, New York, NY 10014-6705
>Pubs: *Vector Love* (Haw River Bks, 1990), *Triangulation* (Crown, 1990), *Prairie Schooner, APR.*

Michael Stephens P&W
520 W 110 St, #5C, New York, NY 10025, 212-662-3205
>Pubs: *The Brooklyn Book of the Dead* (Dalkey Archive, 1994), *Green Dreams* (U Georgia Pr, 1994), *Fiction, Ontario Rev, Pequod.*

Daniel Stern W
c/o Georges Borchardt Inc., 136 E 57 St, New York, NY 10022
>Pubs: *Twice Upon A Time: Stories* (Norton, 1992), *Twice-Told Tales* (Paris Rev Edtns, 1989), *An Urban Affair* (S&S, 1980), *Paris Rev, Raritan, Columbia.*

Phyllis Stern P
167 W 71 St, Apt 9, New York, NY 10023, 212-799-4365
>Pubs: *Making Contact: Anth* (Voyage Out Pr, 1978), *Lilith, Womanews, Home Planet News.*

Margaret Stetler P
189-49 45th Dr, Flushing, NY 11358, 718-353-2185
>Pubs: *The Naming of the Soul* (Four Zoas, 1980), *West Wind Rev, Womanchild, Small Pond Rev, Kosmos, Pegasus Dreaming, Telephone.*

Michael Stewart W
853 7th Ave, New York, NY 10019, 212-758-1100

Nikki Stiller P&W
341 E 65 St, New York, NY 10021, 212-472-1522
>Pubs: *Notes of a Jewish Nun* (Cross-Cultural Comm, 1992), *Poetry New York, Shaking Eve's Tree, Response, Primavera, Midstream, Jewish Currents.*

B. E. Stock P
28 Vesey St, #2143, New York, NY 10007-2906
>Pubs: *Views to Muse: Anth* (Judith Grant, 1996), *We Speak for Peace: Anth* (KIT Pr, 1993), *Moments in Time: Anth* (JMW Pub, 1993), *Lyric, New Pr, Spring, Array, Karamu, Skylark, Poems That Jump in the Dark, Piedmont Literary Rev, Edge City Rev, Lucid Stone.*

Norman Stock P
77-11 35th Ave #2P, Jackson Heights, NY 11372, 718-898-1762
Internet: stock@saturn.montclair.edu
>Pubs: *Buying Breakfast for My Kamikaze Pilot* (Gibbs Smith, 1994), *Verse, New Republic, College English, New York Qtly, Denver Qtly, New England Rev, Asylum.*

Bob Stokes W
PO Box 905, New York, NY 10039, 212-681-2966
>Pubs: *The Circle Inside* (Nambati Pr, 1988), *Words to Go* (Cultural Council Fdn, 1980).

Daniel M. Stokes P
812 W 181 St, #3A, New York, NY 10033
>Pubs: *Poems on the Run 1984-1988, Missing You & Other Poems, Poems From Mexico* (In Exile Pr, 1995, 1995, 1987), *Revista el Norte, Si Nada.*

Carolyn Stoloff P
32 Union Sq E, Rm 911, New York, NY 10003, 212-473-0256
>Pubs: *You Came To Meet Someone Else* (Asylum Arts Pr, 1993), *A Year in Poetry: Anth* (Crown Pub, 1995), *New Yorker, Partisan Rev, Southern Rev, Yankee.*

Alison J. Stone P
230 E 15 St, #7F, New York, NY 10003
Internet: nygoddess@aol.com
>Pubs: *Sweet Nothings: Rock and Roll in American Poetry: Anth* (Indiana U Pr, 1994), *Catholic Girls: Anth* (Plume, 1992), *Paris Rev, Poetry, Ploughshares, New York Qtly, Artful Dodge, Witness, Many Mountains Moving.*

Alma Stone W
523 W 112 St, New York, NY 10025

Laurie Stone W
808 W End Ave, New York, NY 10025, 212-663-7011
Internet: lstone@villagevoice.com
>Pubs: *Close to the Bone* (Grove, 1997), *Laughing in the Dark* (Ecco, 1997), *Starting with Serge* (Doubleday, 1990), *TriQuarterly, New Letters, VLS, The Nation, New Yorker.*

Robert Stone W
Donadio & Ashworth, Inc., 121 W 27 St, Ste 704, New York,
NY 10001, 212-691-8077
Pubs: *Outerbridge Reach* (Ticknor & Fields, 1992), *Children
of Light, A Flag for Sunrise* (Knopf, 1986, 1981).

James Story P
500 9th St, #3F, Brooklyn, NY 11215, 718-768-6919
Pubs: *Paper Boat, Berkeley Poetry Rev, Home Planet
News, Karamu, Now, Poets.*

Mark Strand P&W
Alfred A. Knopf, Inc., 201 E 50 St, New York, NY 10022,
212-751-2600
Pubs: *Dark Harbor* (Knopf, 1993), *Hopper: Anth* (Ecco Pr,
1994).

Dennis Straus PP&P&W
PO Box 176, Rockaway Park, NY 11694, 718-474-6547
Pubs: *ABC Street* (Sun & Moon Pr, 1998), *The Menaced
Assassin, The Other Planet, Red Moon/Red Lake*
(McPherson, 1989, 1988, 1988), *NAW, Central Park,
Confrontation, Exile.*

Brad Strickland W
Richard Curtis Associates, Inc, 171 E 74 St, New York, NY
10021, 212-772-7393
Pubs: *Stowaways* (Pocket, 1994), *Ghost in the Mirror* (w/J.
Bellairs; Dial, 1993), *Dragon's Plunder* (Atheneum, 1992),
Mag of Fantasy & Sci Fi.

Stephanie Strickland P
220 E 70 St, #14C, New York, NY 10021, 212-472-5502
Pubs: *True North Hypertext* (Eastgate Systems, 1998),
True North (U Notre Dame Pr, 1997), *The Red Virgin: A
Poem of Simone Weil* (U Wisconsin Pr, 1993), *Give the
Body Back* (U Missouri Pr, 1991), *Paris Rev.*

Richard Stull P
287 Nevins St, Brooklyn, NY 11217, 718-625-2808
Pubs: *Adoration of the Golden Calf* (Groundwater, 1990),
Ecstatic Occasions, Expedient Forms (Collier Bks, 1987),
Chelsea, Mudfish, NAW, Pequod, Boulevard.

Victoria Sullivan P
620 W 116 St, #21, New York, NY 10027, 212-749-7685
Pubs: *The Divided Bed* (Hatch-Billops, 1982), *Pivot,
Manhattan Poetry Rev, 13th Moon, Cape Rock, Artist and
Influence, Poetry in Performance.*

Sekou Sundiata PP
910 Grand Concourse #7K, Bronx, NY 10451, 718-588-1205
Pubs: *"Are & Be"* (Nommo Records, 1982), *Essence, Black
Nation, Blasted Allegories, New Museum.*

David Surface W
81 St. James Pl, Brooklyn, NY 11238
Pubs: *Four Minute Fictions: Anth* (Word Beat Pr, 1987),
*DoubleTake, Artful Dodge, Fiction, Crazyhorse, Willow
Springs.*

Linda Svendsen W
Robin Straus Agency, 229 E 79 St, New York, NY 10021,
212-472-3282
Pubs: *Marine Life* (FSG, 1992), *Best Canadian Stories:
Anths* (Oberon, 1990, 1987), *Macmillan Anthology*
(Macmillan, 1990), *Agni, Epoch, Saturday Night.*

Brian Swann P
The Cooper Union, 41 Cooper Sq, New York, NY 10003,
212-353-4279
Internet: swann@cooper.edu
Pubs: *Wearing the Morning Star* (Random Hse, 1996),
Song of the Sky (U Massachusetts Pr, 1993), *The Plot of
the Mice* (Capra Pr, 1986).

Roberta M. Swann P&W
19 Stuyvesant Oval, #8B, New York, NY 10009,
212-533-8705
Pubs: *Everything Happens Suddenly, The Model Life*
(Ancient Mariner Pr, 1989, 1988), *American Voice, New
Letters, NAR, Ploughshares.*

Burton Swartz PP
235 W 107 St, #234, New York, NY 10025, 212-866-0118
Pubs: *Downbeat, Columbia Spectator, College Times,
Show Business, National Star Chronicle.*

Karen Swenson P
25 W 54 St, #12E, New York, NY 10019, 212-586-8507
Pubs: *The Landlady in Bangkok* (Copper Canyon, 1994), *A
Sense of Direction* (The Smith, 1990), *Attic of Ideals*
(Doubleday, 1974), *New Yorker, Saturday Rev.*

Janet Sylvester P
W.W. Norton, 500 5th Ave, New York, NY 10110,
212-354-5500
Pubs: *The Mark of Flesh* (Norton, 1997), *That Mulberry
Wine* (Wesleyan, 1985), *Best American Poetry: Anth*
(Scribner, 1994), *Boulevard, TriQuarterly, Shenandoah.*

Ryder Syvertsen W
Anita Diamant Literary Agency, 310 Madison Ave, New York,
NY 10017, 718-230-5654
Internet: tinker704@aol.com
Pubs: *Mystic Rebel, Doomsday Warrior* (Zebra Bks, 1989,
1986), *Psychic Spawn* (Popular Library, 1987).

Sherri Szeman P&W
Sterling Lord Literistic, 65 Bleecker St, New York, NY 10012,
212-780-6050
Pubs: *The Kommandant's Mistress* (HarperCollins, 1993),
*Writers' Forum, The Cape Rock, Chicago Rev, Ohio
Journal, Centennial Rev.*

Marilynn Talal P
308 E 79 St, #4E, New York, NY 10021
Pubs: *Our Own Clues: Poets of The Lake 2: Anth* (Our Lady of the Lake U Pr, 1993), *Blood To Remember: Anth* (Texas Tech U Pr, 1991), *Poetry, New Republic, The Quarterly.*

Amy Tan W
G. P. Putnam's Sons, 375 Hudson St, New York, NY 10014
Pubs: *The Hundred Secret Senses* (Ivy Bks, 1996), *The Kitchen God's Wife, The Joy Luck Club* (Putnam, 1991, 1989), *Atlantic, SF Focus, Seventeen.*

Herbert Tarr W
Scott Meredith Literary Agency, 845 3rd Ave, New York, NY 10022, 212-245-5500
Pubs: *A Woman of Spirit* (Donald I. Fine, 1989), *So Help Me God!* (Times Bks, 1981).

Ronald Tavel P
Helen Merrill Agency, 435 W 23 St, #1A, New York, NY 10011, 212-691-5326
Pubs: *Street of Stairs* (Olympia Pr, 1968), *Night Mag, Unmuzzled Ox, Brooklyn Literary Rev.*

Meredith Tax W
532 W 111 St, #75, New York, NY 10025, 212-866-4283
Internet: wworld@igc.apc.org
Pubs: *Union Square, Rivington Street* (Morrow, 1988, 1982), *Rising of Women* (Monthly Rev, 1980), *Nation.*

Conciere Taylor P
67-08 Parsons Blvd, #6B, Flushing, NY 11365-2955
Pubs: *In Concert: Anth, Shock Treatment: Anth* (Peak Output, 1989, 1988), *Rapunzel, Rapunzel: Anth* (Kathryn Machan Aal, 1979), *Earth's Daughters, Scapes, Whetstone, Slugfest, Calliope.*

Laurie Taylor W
Rodell-Collin Literary Agency, 110 W 40 St, New York, NY 10018
Pubs: *A Murder Waiting To Happen, Poetic Justice* (Walker & Co., 1989, 1988), *Analog, Alfred Hitchcock's Mystery, Great River Rev.*

Theodore Taylor W
Watkins Loomis Agency, Inc., 133 E 35 St, Ste 1, New York, NY 10016, 212-532-0080
Pubs: *Rogue Wave, The Bomb, To Kill The Leopard, Timothy of the Cay* (HB, 1996, 1995, 1993, 1993).

Richard Tayson P
80-15 Grenfell St Apt D-17, Kew Gardens, NY 11415, 718-849-7669
Internet: rtayson@earthlink.net
Pubs: *Pushcart Prize XXI: Anth* (Pushcart Pr, 1997), *Things Shaped In Passing: Anth* (Persea Bks, 1997), *Michigan Qtly Rev, Kenyon Rev, Crazyhorse, Prairie Schooner, Paris Rev.*

Nathan Teitel P&W
365 W 25 St, New York, NY 10001, 212-255-9376
Pubs: *In Time of Tide* (Lintel, 1990), *The Conscious Reader: Anth* (Macmillan, 1991), *Midstream.*

Eleanor Wong Telemaque W
230 E 88 St, #6G, New York, NY 10128-3383, 212-722-8828
Pubs: *It's Crazy to Stay Chinese in Minnesota* (Thomas Nelson, 1995), *Haiti Through Its Holidays* (Blyden Pr, 1990), *"A" Mag.*

Fiona Templeton PP&P
100 St. Marks Pl, #7, New York, NY 10009, 212-533-9169
Pubs: *Delirium of Interpretations* (Sun & Moon Pr, 1998), *Cells of Release, You—The City* (Roof Bks, 1997, 1990), *The Art of Practice: Anth* (Potes & Poets, 1994).

Megan Terry P
E. Marton Agency, 1 Union Sq W Rm 612, New York, NY 100033303, 212-255-1908
Pubs: *Right Brain Vacation Photos* (Omaha Magic Theatre Pr, 1991), *Willa-Willie-Bill's Dope Garden: Anth* (Applause Bks, 1996), *Fireworks: Anth* (Smith & Kraus, 1995), *Breakfast Serial: Anth* (Broadway Play Pub Inc., 1995).

Nadja Tesich W
855 W End Ave #7A, New York, NY 10025
Internet: savage@qcvaxa.acc.qc.edu
Pubs: *Shadow Partisan, American Fiction: Anth* (New Rivers Pr, 1989, 1995), *Mademoiselle, Kenyon Rev, Confrontation, ACM, City Lights Rev, Nation, 13th Moon.*

Catherine Texier W
255 E 7 St, New York, NY 10009, 212-677-4748
Pubs: *Panic Blood, Love Me Tender* (Viking, 1990, 1987), *New Observations, Bomb, Heresies.*

Marcelle Thiebaux W
305 W 86 St, #11A, New York, NY 10024, 212-362-9906
Pubs: *Literal Latte, Cream City Rev, Karamu, Twisted, El Gato Tuerto/The One-Eyed Cat.*

James Alexander Thom W
ICM, 40 W 57 St, New York, NY 10019
Pubs: *The Children of First Man, Follow the River* (Ballantine, 1994, 1981).

Abigail Thomas P&W
395 Riverside Dr, New York, NY 10025, 212-864-6867
Pubs: *Herb's Pajamas, An Actual Life, Getting Over Tom* (Algonquin, 1998, 1996, 1994), *Missouri Rev, Paris Rev, Nation, Glimmer Train, Santa Monica Rev.*

Charles Columbus Thomas P
1245 Park Ave, #11K, New York, NY 10028, 212-876-9464

Joyce Carol Thomas   P
ICM, 40 W 57 St, New York, NY 10019
    Pubs: *Journey, The Golden Pasture* (Scholastic, 1988, 1986), *Watergirl* (Avon, 1986).

Barbara Thompson   W
205 W 57 St, New York, NY 10019, 212-581-5448
    Pubs: *The Pushcart Prize Anthology, Shenandoah, McCall's, Paris Rev.*

John A. Thompson   P&W
418 Central Pk W, New York, NY 10025, 212-749-1256
    Pubs: *The Founding of English Metre* (Columbia U Pr, 1988).

Sharon Thompson   W
PO Box 20739, Tompkins Sq Sta, New York, NY 10009, 212-228-0623
    Pubs: *Powers of Desire* (Monthly Rev Pr, 1983), *Village Voice, Heresies, Feminist Studies.*

Newton Thornburg   W
Don Congdon Associates Inc., 156 5th Ave, Ste 625, New York, NY 10010-7002, 212-645-1229
    Pubs: *Beautiful Kate, Valhalla, Black Angus* (Little, Brown, 1982, 1980, 1978).

Judith Thurman   P
445 E 86 St, #15D, New York, NY 10028
    Pubs: *Magic Lantern, Flashlight & Other Poems* (Atheneum, 1978, 1976).

Irene Tiersten   W
JET Literary Associates, 124 E 84 St, New York, NY 10028, 212-879-2578
Internet: tiersten@ix.netcom.com
    Pubs: *One Big Happy Family* (The Reader Project, 1990), *Among Friends* (St. Martin's, 1982), *Mediphors, First for Women, New Directions.*

Arthur Tobias   P
229 W 97 St Apt 4J, New York, NY 100255611, 212-665-2962
    Pubs: *The View from Cold Mountain* (White Pine, 1982), *Choice, Epoch, Ironwood, White Pine Jrnl.*

James Tolan   P
110 Bement Ave, Staten Island, NY 10310, 718-273-9447
    Pubs: *Fresh Fruit & Gravity* (Far Gone Bks, 1997), *Coffeehouse Poetry Anth* (Bottom Dog Pr, 1996), *Yellow Silk, Atlanta Rev, Atom Mind, The Quarterly, American Literary Rev, The Baffler, Indiana Rev, International Qtly, Salt Hill Jrnl.*

Lydia Tomkiw   P
85 E 3 St, #A3, New York, NY 10003-9040, 212-982-7256
Internet: ltnyc@aol.com
    Pubs: *Unbearables: Anth* (Autonomedia, 1995), *Walk on the Wild Side: Anth* (Macmillan, 1994), *Aerial, B-City, Joe Soap's Canoe, Brooklyn Rev.*

Yasunao Tone   PP
307 W Broadway, 3rd Fl, New York, NY 10013, 212-966-0945
    Pubs: *Solo For Wounded* (CD; Tzadik, 1997), *Musica Iconologos, Trio For A Flute Player & Lyrictron in Upper Air Observation* (CDs; Lovely Music, 1994, 1991), *Conjunctions, Music.*

Juanita Torrence-Thompson   P&W
Fordham Univ, 441 E Fordham Rd, Bronx, NY 10458, 718-817-1000
    Pubs: *Yefief, San Fernando Poetry Jrnl, Chaminade Literary Rev, Green Hills Literary Lantern, Snail's Pace Rev, Women's Work, Tucumcari, Appearances, Array Mag, AIM, Caprice.*

Robert Towers   W
Queens College, Flushing, NY 11367, 718-520-7480
    Pubs: *The Monkey Watcher, The Necklace of Kali* (HBJ, 1964, 1960).

Tony Towle   P
Tyler Productions, 75 Hudson St, New York, NY 10013, 212-285-0922
Internet: ttowlepoet@aol.com
    Pubs: *Some Musical Episodes, Broadway 2: Anth* (Hanging Loose Pr, 1992, 1989), *New & Selected Poems 1963-1983* (Kulcur, 1983), *Postmodern American Poetry: Anth* (Norton, 1994), *Arshile, Otis Run, Hanging Loose, The World, Blade, Notas.*

Peter Trachtenberg   W
Watkins Loomis Agency, Inc., 133 E 35 St, Ste 1, New York, NY 10016, 212-532-0080
    Pubs: *The Casanova Complex* (S&S, 1988), *Mademoiselle, Self, Der Stern, Glamour, Chicago.*

Calvin Trillin   W
12 Grove St, New York, NY 10014, 212-243-3455

David Trinidad   P
401 W Broadway, #3, New York, NY 10012, 212-274-9529
    Pubs: *Answer Song* (High Risk/Serpent's Tail, 1994), *Hand Over Heart: Poems 1981-1988* (Serpent's Tail, 1991), *Harper's, Paris Rev, NAW.*

Niccolo Tucci   W
25 E 67 St, New York, NY 10021
    Pubs: *Before My Time* (Moyer Bell, 1991), *The Rain Came Last* (New Directions, 1990), *The Sun and Moon* (Knopf, 1977).

Frederic Tuten   W
Watkins Loomis Agency, Inc., 133 E 35 St, Ste 1, New York, NY 10016, 212-532-0080
    Pubs: *Van Gogh's Bad Cafe, Tintin in the New World: A Romance* (Morrow, 1997, 1993), *Tallien: A Brief Romance* (FSG, 1988), *TriQuarterly, Fiction, Global City Rev.*

David Unger P
340 W 72 St, #4B, New York, NY 10023-2645
  Pubs: *Tropical Synagogues: Latin American Jewish Writing
  Anth* (Holmes & Meiers, 1994), *Neither Caterpillar Nor
  Butterfly* (Es Que Somos Muy Pobres Pr, 1986).

John Updike P&W
Alfred A. Knopf, Inc., 201 E 50 St, New York, NY 10022,
212-751-2600
  Pubs: *Trust Me, Roger's Version, The Witches of Eastwick*
  (Knopf, 1987, 1987, 1984), *New Yorker.*

Robert Upton W
419 W 22 St, New York, NY 10011, 212-989-5349
  Pubs: *A Killing in Real Estate, The Faberge Egg* (Dutton,
  1990, 1988), *Dead on the Stick* (Viking, 1986).

Jean Valentine P
527 W 110 St, #81, New York, NY 10025, 212-866-9740
  Pubs: *The River At Wolf, Home, Deep, Blue: New &
  Selected Poems* (Alice James Bks, 1992, 1989), *The
  Messenger* (FSG, 1979), *Field, New Yorker, APR.*

Anthony Valerio W
106 Charles St, #14, New York, NY 10014, 212-675-4685
  Pubs: *Valentino and the Great Italians* (Freundlich Bks,
  1986), *Bart: A Life of A. Bartlett Giamatti* (HB, 1991), *Paris
  Rev, Paris Transcontinental.*

Nicholas Valinotti P
448 Bergen St, #4C, Brooklyn, NY 11217, 718-398-7275
  Pubs: *Brooklyn Rev, Cathartic, Galley Sail Rev, Home Planet
  News, Cottonwood, The Archer, Ailanthus, Cover, Mudfish.*

Carmen Valle P&W
71 E 4 St, #6A, New York, NY 10003, 212-673-7824
  Pubs: *Entre la Vigilia y el Sueno de las Fieras, Desde
  Marruecos Te Escribo* (Instituto de Cultura Puertorriqena,
  1994, 1992), *Trasimagen, Balcon.*

Lloyd Van Brunt P&W
Wieser & Wieser Literary Agenc, 118 E 25 St, 7 Fl, New York,
NY 10010, 212-260-0860
  Pubs: *Poems New and Selected 1962-1992, Working
  Firewood for the Night* (The Smith, 1993, 1990), *Exquisite
  Corpse, The Generalist Papers, Re-Publish, APR.*

Henry Van Dyke W
40 Waterside Plaza, #16-L, New York, NY 10010,
212-683-5587
  Pubs: *Lunacy & Caprice* (Ballantine, 1987), *Afro-American
  Short Story Anth* (HarperCollins, 1993), *Antioch Rev, Story
  Qtly.*

Ronald Vance W
10 W 18 St, New York, NY 10011, 212-675-8836
  Pubs: *Interstate, O.ars, Benzene, Clown War, Sun & Moon.*

Herminio Vargas P
Brooklyn College, Bedford Ave & Ave H, Brooklyn, NY 11210

Lourdes Vazquez P&W
219 5th Ave #2L, Brooklyn, NY 11215, 718-789-6945
  Pubs: *La Rosa Mecanica* (Huracan, 1991).

Ed Vega W
S. Bergholz Literary Services, 17 W 10 St, #5, New York, NY
10011, 212-387-0545
  Pubs: *Casualty Report, Mendoza's Dreams, The
  Comeback* (Arte Publico Pr, 1991, 1987, 1985), *Portable
  Lower East Side, MBM.*

Richard Vetere P&W
53-40 62nd St, Maspeth, NY 11378, 718-939-9398
  Pubs: *The Third Miracle* (S&S, 1998), *A Dream of Angels*
  (Northwoods Pr, 1984), *Memories of Human Hands*
  (Manyland Bks, 1976), *Poets On, Dreamworks, Cobweb,
  Orbis, Hybrid, Abraxas.*

Janine M. Veto P&W
520 E 84 St, #3L, New York, NY 10028, 212-737-5133
  Pubs: *The Dream Book* (Schocken, 1988), *Iris* (Alyson,
  1983), *la bella figura, Cedar Rock.*

Gore Vidal W
William Morris Agency, 1350 Ave of the Americas, New York,
NY 10019, 212-586-5100

Joseph Viertel W
William Morris Agency, 1350 Ave of the Americas, New York,
NY 10019, 212-586-5100
  Pubs: *Lifelines, Monkey On A String* (S&S, 1982, 1968), *To
  Love and Corrupt* (Random Hse, 1962).

David Vigoda W
Ann Elmo Literary Agency, 60 E 42 St, New York, NY 10017,
518-827-4903
  Pubs: *Nucleus* (Baronet Publishing Co., 1980).

Michael Villanueva P
437 E 12 St, #17, New York, NY 10009, 212-673-1671
  Pubs: *Nice to See You: Homage to Ted Berrigan: Anth*
  (Coffee Hse, 1988), *Transfer, Cover, Gandhabba.*

Vincent Virga W
145 E 22 St, #4H, New York, NY 10010, 212-473-1058
  Pubs: *Gaywyck, A Comfortable Corner* (Gay Men's Pr,
  1987, 1987).

Tricia Vita W
42 Perry St, New York, NY 10014-7307
  Pubs: *Yankee, Boston Rev, Provincetown Arts, Ms.,
  Games Mag, Shocked & Amazed!.*

Susan Volchok W
303 W 66 St, New York, NY 10024, 212-787-4262
Pubs: *Love's Shadow: Anth, Word of Mouth 2: Anth* (Crossing Pr, 1993, 1991), *Kenyon Rev, Asylum Annual, Confrontation, Hayden's Ferry Rev.*

Karen Volkman P
16 Tompkins Pl, Brooklyn, NY 11231, 718-855-3683
Pubs: *Crash's Law* (Norton, 1996), *Best American Poetry 1996: Anth* (Scribner, 1996), *Partisan Rev, Western Humanities Rev, Prairie Schooner, Paris Rev, APR.*

Les Von Losberg P
560 Marlborough Rd, Brooklyn, NY 11226, 718-462-6513
Pubs: *Making Sense Of Foreign Currency* (Poets Union Pr, 1983), *Riverrun, Pudding, Gryphon.*

Lenore Von Stein PP
PO Box 1687, Old Chelsea Sta, New York, NY 10113
Pubs: *Blind Love = Porno?, Love is Dead* (1687, Inc., 1996, 1993).

Dina von Zweck P&W
80 Beekman St, New York, NY 10038-1879, 212-732-1020
Internet: dina@escape.com
Pubs: *Halloween & Other Poems, Sam Shepard's Dog* (White Deer Bks, 1985, 1984), *Helicon 9, Modularist Rev, Berkshire Rev, New York Times, New Letters.*

Kurt Vonnegut W
Donald C. Farber, Hartman & Cr, 460 Park Ave, 11 Fl, New York, NY 100221987
Pubs: *Timequake, Fates Worse Than Death, Hocus Pocus* (Putnam, 1997, 1991, 1990).

Chuck Wachtel P&W
337 E 5 St #5FW, New York, NY 10003, 212-673-1511
Pubs: *Because We Are Here: Stories & Novellas, The Gates* (Viking/Penguin 1996, 1993), *Joe, The Engineer* (Morrow, 1983), *The World, Sun, Hanging Loose, The Nation, Village Voice, Witness, Pequod.*

Dan Wakefield W
Helen Brann Agency, 157 W 57 St, New York, NY 10019
Pubs: *Home Free* (Delacorte, 1977).

Derek Walcott P
Farrar, Straus, Giroux, 19 Union Squ W, New York, NY 10003
Pubs: *The Star-Apple Kingdom* (FSG, 1979).

William Walden P
30 E 9 St, #4K, New York, NY 10003
Pubs: *New Yorker, Atlantic, Georgia Rev, Massachusetts Rev, Light, Punch.*

Mel Waldman P&W
1660 E 13 St, #D2, Brooklyn, NY 11229, 718-375-1474
Pubs: *Festina Lente* (Somrie Pr, 1982), *The Saint, Espionage Mag, Pulpsmith, Prelude To Fantasy.*

Alice Walker P&W
The Wendy Weil Agency, Inc., 232 Madison Ave, Ste 1300, New York, NY 10016, 212-685-0030
Pubs: *Possessing the Secret of Joy, Her Blue Body Everything We Know: Earthing Poems 1965-1991, Finding the Green Stone* (HBJ, 1992, 1991, 1991).

Gerald Walker W
400 E 54 St, New York, NY 10022
Pubs: *Cruising* (Stein & Day, 1970).

Pamela Walker W
239 W 256 St, Bronx, NY 10471, 212-549-2215
Pubs: *World In Our Words* (Blair Pr/Prentice Hall, 1997), *Twyla* (Prentice-Hall/Berkley, 1976), *The Whole Story: Anth* (Bench Pr, 1995), *Hawaii Rev, Iowa Woman.*

Wendy Walker W
855 W End Ave, #6A, New York, NY 10025-4995
Pubs: *Stories Out of Omarie, The Secret Service* (Sun & Moon Pr, 1995, 1992), *Conjunctions, Fiction Intl, Parnassus.*

Barry Wallenstein P
340 Riverside Dr, #7B, New York, NY 10025, 212-222-2556
Pubs: *The Short Life of the Five Minute Dancer* (Ridgeway Pr, 1993), *Love and Crush* (Persea, 1991), *Ploughshares, Laurel Rev, Ignite, Oxford Mag.*

Rhoda Waller P
370 W 11 St, #4, New York, NY 10014
Pubs: *Between Worlds, Plumed Horn, Black Maria, Cummington Rev, Ikon.*

Irene Wanner W
Donadio & Ashworth, Inc., 121 W 27 St, Ste 704, New York, NY 10001, 212-691-8077
Internet: iwanner@u.washington.edu
Pubs: *Sailing to Corinth* (Owl Creek Pr, 1988), *Circle of Women: Anth* (Penguin, 1994), *Antaeus, Antioch Rev, Ploughshares, Northwest Rev, Blue Mesa Rev, New Orphic Rev.*

Constance Warloe W
Linda Chester Literary Agency, 630 5th Ave, Rockefeller Ctr, New York, NY 10111, 212-439-0881
Internet: cwdenim@aol.com
Pubs: *The Legend of Olivia Cosmos Montevideo* (Atlantic Monthly Pr, 1994).

Larkin Warren P
315 W 23 St, #11-B, New York, NY 10011, 212-230-0289
Pubs: *Old Sheets* (Alice James Bks, 1979), *Yankee, Mississippi Rev, Tendril, Mid-American Rev, Akros.*

Lewis Warsh P
701 President St, #1, Brooklyn, NY 11215, 718-857-5974
Pubs: *Money Under the Table* (Trip Street Pr, 1997),
Avenue of Escape (Long News, 1995), *A Free Man* (Sun &
Moon, 1991).

Chocolate Waters PP&P&W
415 W 44 St, #7, New York, NY 10036, 212-581-6820
Internet: chocolatewaters@mci2000.com
Pubs: *Mom: Candid Memories* (Alyson Pubs, 1998),
Coffeehouse Poetry Anth (Bottom Dog Pr, 1996), *My Lover
is a Woman: Anth* (Ballantine, 1996), *Medicinal Purposes,
Libido, Poetry Cafe, Mudfish, Zero City, Westerly.*

Gordon R. Watkins P
675 Water St, #19D, New York, NY 10002, 212-267-2991

Celia Watson P
373 Canal St, New York, NY 10013, 212-334-9637
Pubs: *Night Feet, The Drum & The Melody* (Smith Pub,
1989, 1983), *Woman Poet, Ohio Rev.*

D. Rahim Watson PP&P
250 W 54 St, Ste 811, New York, NY 10019, 212-541-7600
Pubs: *Lovers, Friends & Enemies, Survival 80's, Things We
Do To Each Other* (1st Cousins, 1982).

Herbert J. Waxman P
29 Margaret Ct, Great Neck, NY 11024, 516-487-2996
Pubs: *Where the Worm Grows Fat* (Full Court Pr, 1975),
New York Qtly, Speakeasy, Alive & Kicking.

Vivienne Thaul Wechter P
Fordham Univ, FMH 230, Bronx, NY 10458, 718-817-4898
Pubs: *A View From The Ark* (Barlenmir Hse, 1975), *Arts
Interaction, Other Voices.*

Jerome Weidman W
1230 Park Ave #10C, New York, NY 10128-1728

Bibi Wein W
210 W 101 St, #9-A, New York, NY 10025
Pubs: *Yes* (HBJ, 1969), *Ariadne's Thread: Anth* (H&R,
1982), *Mademoiselle, Iris, Permafrost, Other Voices,
American Letters & Commentary.*

Hannah Weiner PP&P
77 E 12 St, #2G, New York, NY 10003, 212-260-0273
Pubs: *Silent Teachers Remembered* (Tender Buttons Pr,
1993), *The Fast* (United Artists, 1992), *Raddle Moon, Motel,
Paper Air, Object, Grist, Writing.*

Jeff Weinstein W
54 E 7 St, New York, NY 10003, 212-677-3504
Pubs: *Life In San Diego* (Sun & Moon, 1982), *Pushcart
Prize IV Anth, Crawl Out Your Window.*

R. Weis PP
516 E 6 St, #2, New York, NY 10009, 212-677-9093
Pubs: *Friday Evening at La Galleria: New Voices New
Works* (La Mama, 1988), *Lyra, In Fashion.*

Sarah Brown Weitzman P
1470 1st Ave, #3D, New York, NY 10021
Pubs: *Mid-American Rev, Kansas Qtly, Poet & Critic,
Madison Rev, Croton Rev, Abraxas, Yellow Silk, New
America.*

Marjorie Welish P
225 W 10 St #2C, New York, NY 10014
Pubs: *Casting Sequences* (U Georgia Pr, 1993), *The
Windows Flew Open* (Burning Deck Pr, 1991),
Experimental Poetry In America: Anth (Norton, 1994).

Sheila Weller W
39 Jane St, #5A, New York, NY 10014, 212-741-0042
Pubs: *Hansel & Gretel in Beverly Hills* (Morrow, 1978), *Ms.,
McCall's, Glamour, Redbook, Self.*

Mac Wellman P
ICM, 40 W 57 St, New York, NY 10019, 212-556-5600
Pubs: *Annie Salem, The Land Beyond the Forest, The
Fortuneteller, A Shelf in Woop's Clothing* (Sun & Moon Pr,
1996, 1995, 1991, 1990).

Rebecca Wells W
Jonathan Dolger Agency, 49 E 96 St, #9B, New York, NY
10128, 212-427-1853
Pubs: *Divine Secrets of the Ya-Ya Sisterhood, Little Altars
Everywhere* (HarperCollins, 1996), *Mississippi Rev.*

Kate Wenner W
Elaine Markson Literary Agency, 44 Greenwich Ave, New
York, NY 10011, 212-243-8480
Pubs: *Shamba Letu* (Houghton Mifflin, 1970).

Eliot Werbner P
1150 E 22 St, Brooklyn, NY 11210-3620, 718-253-1377
Pubs: *Prelude* (The Four Seas, 1930), *Blue Unicorn, The
Lyric, Western Poetry, The Writer, The Archer.*

Judith Werner P
3987 Saxon Ave, Bronx, NY 10463, 718-796-4548
Pubs: *Sixteen Voices: Anth* (Mariposa Pub, 1994), *South
Dakota Rev, Visions Intl, Bridges, The Lyric, ELF, Yankee,
Four Quarters, Slant, Sow's Ear.*

Evelyn Wexler P
5550 Fieldston Rd, #7D, Bronx, NY 10471, 718-549-4636
Internet: evwex@aol.com
Pubs: *Occupied Territory, The Geisha House* (Mayapple Pr,
1994, 1992), *Nimrod, Pittsburgh Qtly, Negative Capability,
Classical Outlook.*

Kate Wheeler   W
Witherspoon & Chernoff, 157 W 57 St, Ste 700, New York,
NY 10019
  Pubs: *Not Where I Started From* (HM, 1993), *O. Henry
  Awards: Anth* (Doubleday, 1992), *Threepenny Rev, Black
  Warrior Rev, Gettysburg Rev.*

Susan Wheeler   P
37 Washington Sq W, #10A, New York, NY 10011,
212-254-3984
Internet: susan.wheeler@nyu.edu
  Pubs: *Smokes* (Four Way Bks, 1998), *Bag o' Diamonds* (U
  Georgia Pr, 1993), *Best American Poetry: Anth* (Macmillan,
  1996), *New Yorker, Paris Rev, NAR, o.blek, Witness.*

Clark Whelton   W
39 1/2 Washington Sq S, New York, NY 10002

Edgar White   P&W
New Dramatists, 424 W 44 St, New York, NY 10036,
212-757-6960
  Pubs: *The Rising* (Marion Boyars Pub, 1990).

Edmund White   W
434 Lafayette St, New York, NY 10003
  Pubs: *A Boy's Own Story, States of Desire* (Dutton, 1982,
  1980).

Anne Whitehouse   P
340 Riverside Dr, New York, NY 10025, 212-749-5377
  Pubs: *The Surveyor's Hand* (Compton Pr, 1981),
  Boulevard, American Voice, Buffalo Spree.

Nathan Whiting   P
105 Buckingham Rd, #6D, Brooklyn, NY 11226,
718-856-6248
  Pubs: *After the Waterfront* (Contact II, 1995),
  Contemplations (MAF Pr, 1987), *Light Talks A Lot* (Agni,
  1983).

George Whitmore   P
10 Downing St, #5T, New York, NY 10014, 212-675-4594
  Pubs: *The Confessions of Danny Slocum* (St. Martin's,
  1980), *On The Line: Anth* (Crossing Pr, 1981).

Frances Whyatt   P
61 Jane St #9G, New York, NY 10014, 212-255-7378
  Pubs: *A Real Man and Other Stories* (British
  American/Paris Rev Edtns, 1990), *McCall's.*

Mildred Wiackley   P
PO Box 82, Stuyvesant Sta, New York, NY 10009,
718-386-3283
  Pubs: *Ante, Apercu, Eidon, Graffiti, Format.*

Leo Wiener   P
PO Box 610233, Bayside, NY 11361-0233, 718-225-3523
  Pubs: *The Plowman, Quickenings, The Work Technique,
  JVC, Thirteen, Hob-Nob.*

Elie Wiesel   W
Georges Borchardt Inc., 136 E 57 St, New York, NY 10022,
212-753-5785
  Pubs: *Night, The Forgotten, All Rivers Run to the Sea*
  (Knopf, 1995, 1995, 1995).

Roslyn Willett   W
441 W End Ave #15A, New York, NY 10024, 212-787-6060
  Pubs: *Short Stories Bimonthly, Art & Understanding,
  Timber Creek Rev, Words of Wisdom.*

C. K. Williams   P
Farrar, Straus & Giroux, 19 Union Sq W, New York, NY
10003, 3314-523-2298
  Pubs: *A Dream of Mind, Flesh & Blood* (FSG, 1992, 1987),
  Tar (Random Hse, 1983), *New Yorker, APR.*

Edward F. Williams   PP
1633 Sterling Pl, #4H, Brooklyn, NY 11233, 718-735-6153
  Pubs: *E. F. Williams, Urban Poet* (Libra Productions, 1997).

Gary Williams   P
36 E 4 St, Apt 2, New York, NY 10003, 212-982-7602
  Pubs: *Waterways, Pan Arts Mag, Jane, Manhattan Poetry
  Rev, Home Planet News.*

Regina E. Williams   P
132-11 Foch Blvd, South Ozone Park, NY 11420,
718-322-9550
  Pubs: *Our Work & God's World* (Presbyterian Pub Hse,
  1988), *New Rain: Anth* (Blind Beggar, 1988).

J. N. Williamson   W
Pimlico Literary Agency, Box 20447, 1539 1st Ave, New York,
NY 10028, 212-628-9720
  Pubs: *Bloodlines, The Book of Webster's* (Longmeadow Pr,
  1994, 1993), *Don't Take Away The Light* (Zebra Bks, 1993),
  Pulphouse, Nightworld.

Leigh Allison Wilson   W
Harold Matson Co., Inc., 276 5th Ave, New York, NY 10001,
212-679-4490
  Pubs: *Wind: Stories* (Morrow, 1989), *From the Bottom Up*
  (Penguin, 1984), *Harper's, Grand Street.*

Martha Wilson   PP&W
112 Franklin St, New York, NY 10013, 212-925-4671

Paul Hastings Wilson   W
314 E 84 St, New York, NY 10028
  Pubs: *Turning Islands* (Avon, 1977), *Center.*

William S. Wilson   W
458 W 25 St, New York, NY 10001, 212-989-2229
    Pubs: *Birthplace* (North Point Pr, 1982), *Why I Don't Write
    Like Franz Kafka* (Ecco/Norton, 1977).

Fran Winant   P
PO Box 398, Stuyvesant Sta, New York, NY 10009,
212-989-2127
    Pubs: *Goddess of Lesbian Dreams, Dyke Jacket, Looking
    at Women* (Violet Pr, 1980, 1976, 1971).

David Winn   W
Hunter College, 695 Park Ave, New York, NY 10021
    Pubs: *Gangland* (Knopf, 1982).

Mary Winters   P
434 E 52 St, #4E, New York, NY 10022, 212-753-3320
    Pubs: *A Pocket History of the World* (Nightshade Pr, 1996),
    Anth of Mag Verse & Yearbook of American Poetry: Anth
    (Monitor Bk Co, 1997), *Quarterly West, Commonweal,
    Press, Poetry East, Poet Lore, Gulf Coast.*

Elizabeth Winthrop   W
250 W 90 St #6A, New York, NY 100241123, 212-721-5977
Internet: http://www.absolute-sway.com/winthrop
    Pubs: *Island Justice* (Morrow, 1998), *As The Crow Flies*
    (Clarion, 1998), *The Battle For The Castle* (Holiday Hse,
    1993), *Best American Short Stories: Anth* (HM, 1992).

William Wiser   W
Curtis Brown Ltd., 10 Astor Pl, New York, NY 10003-6935,
212-473-5400

Ellen Wisoff   P
1782 E 19 St, Brooklyn, NY 11229, 718-375-2355
    Pubs: *Partisan Rev, Denver Qtly, Sun & Moon, New York
    Arts Jrnl, Zone, City.*

Francine Witte   P
PO Box 6694, Yorkville Sta, New York, NY 10128,
212-289-3034
    Pubs: *Calliope, Poet & Critic, Connecticut River Rev,
    Florida Rev, Bellingham Rev, Tar River Poetry,
    Outerbridge.*

Rudolph Wittenberg   P
New York Univ Law School, 40 Washington Sq, #434, New
York, NY 10012
    Pubs: *New & Selected Poems, Berlin Wall* (Latitudes Pr,
    1984, 1982).

Larry Woiwode   P&W
Donadio & Ashworth, 121 W 27 St, New York, NY 10001,
212-691-8077
Internet: woiwode@ctctel.com
    Pubs: *Beyond The Bedroom Wall* (Graywolf, 1997), *Silent
    Passengers* (Atheneum, 1993), *Acts* (Harper San
    Francisco, 1993), *New York Times, New Yorker, Paris Rev,
    Image, Atlantic, Harper's.*

Michele Wolf   P
407 E 88 St, #4A, New York, NY 101286661, 212-876-0710
Internet: michelewolf@juno.com
    Pubs: *Conversations During Sleep* (Anhinga Pr, 1998), *The
    Keeper of Light* (Painted Bride Qtly, 1995), *When I Am An
    Old Woman I Shall Wear Purple: Anth* (Papier-Mache Pr,
    1987), *Poetry, Hudson Rev, Boulevard, Antioch Rev,
    Southern Poetry Rev, Poet Lore.*

Sharyn Wolf   P
160 Front St, #4J, New York, NY 10038, 212-480-0805
    Pubs: *Guerilla Dating Tactics* (Dutton, 1993), *50 Ways to
    Find A Lover* (Bob Adams, 1989).

Linda Wolfe   W
Janklow & Nesbit Associates, 598 Madison Ave, New York,
NY 10022-1614, 212-421-1700
    Pubs: *Love Me To Death* (Pocket, 1998), *Professor & the
    Prostitute* (HM, 1986), *Private Practices* (S&S, 1980),
    Cosmopolitan, Woman, Ladies Home Jrnl.

Eunice Wolfgram   P
47 E Houston St, #3, New York, NY 10012, 212-966-0897
    Pubs: *Three Hundred Chinese And Other Events* (Home
    Planet Pub, 1975).

Hilma Wolitzer   W
500 E 85 St, #18H, New York, NY 100287456, 212-861-8062
Internet: hilma@worldnet.att.net
    Pubs: *Tunnel Of Love* (HarperCollins, 1994), *Silver, In the
    Palomar Arms, Hearts* (FSG, 1988, 1983, 1980), *In the
    Flesh* (Morrow, 1977).

Meg Wolitzer   W
Sterling Lord Literistic, 65 Bleecker St, New York, NY 10012,
212-780-6050
    Pubs: *This Is Your Life* (Crown, 1988), *Hidden Pictures*
    (Houghton Mifflin, 1986).

Diane Wolkstein   PP&P
10 Patchin Pl, 1 Fl, New York, NY 10011
    Pubs: *DreamSongs, Abulafia, Part of My Heart* (Cloudstone
    Pr, 1992), *The First Love Stories* (H&R, 1991), *Oom
    Razoom* (Morrow, 1991).

Janet S. Wong   P
Simon & Schuster, 1230 Avenue of the Americas, New York,
NY 10020
    Pubs: *A Suitcase of Seaweed & Other Poems* (S&S, 196),
    Good Luck Gold & Other Poems (Macmillan, 1994).

Jacqueline Woodson   W
Charlotte Sheedy Literary Agen, 65 Bleecker St, New York,
NY 10012, 212-780-9800
    Pubs: *Autobiography Of A Family Photo* (Dutton, 1995), *I
    Hadn't Meant To Tell You This* (Delacorte, 1994), *Kenyon
    Rev, American Voice.*

Dale Worsley W
150 Lafayette Ave #1, Brooklyn, NY 11238, 718-789-3640
Pubs: *The Focus Changes of August Previco* (Vanguard, 1980), *Hoy* (NPR Broadcast, 1992).

Charles S. Wright W
Farrar, Straus & Giroux, 19 Union Sq W, New York, NY 10003, 212-741-6900
Pubs: *The Wig, The Messenger* (FSG, 1966, 1963).

Jeffrey Cyphers Wright P
632 E 14 St, #18, New York, NY 10009, 212-673-1152
Pubs: *Out Loud: Nuyorican Poets Cafe Anth* (Henry Holt, 1995), *Out of This World: Anth* (Crown, 1991), *Up Late: Anth* (4 Walls, 8 Windows, 1987), *Exquisite Corpse.*

K. C. Wright W
15 Columbus Cir, New York, NY 10019, 212-541-7070
Pubs: *Everyman's Dream* (Carlyle Pr, 1978).

Sarah Elizabeth Wright P&W
780 W End Ave, #1D, New York, NY 10025
Pubs: *A Philip Randolph* (S&S/Silver Burdett, 1990), *This Child's Gonna Live* (Feminist Pr, 1986), *Black Scholar.*

Stephen Wright W
PO Box 1341, FDR Sta, New York, NY 10150, 212-213-4382
Pubs: *The Adventures of Sandy West, Private Eye* (Mystery Notebook Edtns, 1986).

Susan Yankowitz W
Harden-Curtis Associates, 850 7th Ave, New York, NY 10024, 212-977-8502
Internet: coozly@aol.com
Pubs: *Silent Witness* (Knopf, 1976), *Excavators: Anth* (Gnosis Pr, 1993), *Taking The Fall: Anth* (Parnassus, 1986), *Parnassus, Gnosis, Solo, Heresies, Performing Arts Jrnl, Yale Theatre Poetry in Rev.*

Camille D. Yarbrough PP&P
246 W 137 St, New York, NY 10030, 212-491-9503
Pubs: *Tamika and the Wisdom Rings* (Random Hse, 1994), *The Shimmershine Queens* (Putnam-Paperstar, 1989), *The Little Tree Growin In The Shade, Cornrows* (Coward, McCann, 1985, 1979), *Black Collegian.*

Jose Yaryura-Tobias P&W
935 Northern Blvd, #102, Great Neck, NY 11021, 516-487-7116
Pubs: *El Ser Humano Integral* (Mexico; Diana, 1992), *The Integral Being* (Henry Holt, 1987), *Circular* (Botella al Mar, 1983).

John Yau P
PO Box 1910, Canal St Sta, New York, NY 10013
Pubs: *Radiant Silhouette: New & Selected Works* (Black Sparrow Pr, 1989), *APR, Sulfur, Sun.*

Rafael Yglesias W
Janklow & Nesbit Associates, 598 Madison Ave, New York, NY 10022-1614
Pubs: *Dr. Neruda's Cure for Evil, Fearless* (Warner Bks, 1996, 1993), *The Murderer Next Door* (Crown, 1990), *Only Children* (Ballantine, 1989).

Michael T. Young P
442 W 22 St., Apt 20, New York, NY 10011, 212-924-8242
Pubs: *Because the Wind Has Questions* (Somers Rocks Pr, 1997), *Pivot, Red Jacket, The Lyric, The Hiram Poetry Rev, Birmingham Rev, Inkshed.*

Jane Breskin Zalben P&W
Curtis Brown Ltd., 10 Astor Pl, New York, NY 10003-6935, 212-473-5400
Pubs: *The Fortuneteller in 5B* (Scholastic, 1994), *Happy New Year, Beni, Papas Latkes* (Henry Holt, 1994, 1994), *Colorado Communicator, Hadassah Mag.*

Bill Zavatsky P
100 W 92 St #9D, New York, NY 10025, 212-496-2956
Internet: bzavatsky@trinity.nyc.ny.us
Pubs: *For Steve Royal and Other Poems* (COPE, 1985), *Theories Of Rain And Other Poems* (Sun, 1975), *Out of This World: Anth* (Crown, 1991).

George Zebrowski W
171 E 74 St, New York, NY 10021, 518-439-1994
Internet: sarzeb@compuserve.com
Pubs: *Brute Orbits* (Harper Prism, 1998), *The Sunspacers Trilogy* (White Wolf, 1996), *The Killing Star* (Avon-Morrow, 1995), *Stranger Suns* (Bantam, 1991), *The Monadic Universe* (Ace, 1985), *The Stars Will Speak, Sunspacer* (H&R, 1985, 1984).

Kip Zegers P
Hunter College High School, 71 E 94 St, New York, NY 10128, 212-884-3011
Pubs: *The American Floor* (Mayapple Pr, 1996), *The Promise Is* (Humana Pr, 1985).

Lisa Zeidner P&W
Georges Borchardt Inc., 136 E 57 St, New York, NY 10022, 212-753-5785
Pubs: *Limited Partnerships* (North Point Pr, 1989), *Pocket Sundial* (U Wisconsin Pr, 1988).

David Zeiger P
9 Fourth Rd, Great Neck, NY 11021, 516-466-2977
Pubs: *Life on My Breath* (Sarna Pr, 1995), *We Speak for Peace: Anth* (KIT, 1993), *Mixed Voices: Anth* (Milkweed Edtns, 1991), *Wordsmith, Verve, Minnesota Rev, Midstream, Slant.*

Lila Zeiger P
PO Box 4518, Great Neck, NY 11023, 516-466-2977
Pubs: *The Way to Castle Garden* (State Street Pr, 1982), *Paris Rev, Georgia Rev, New Republic.*

Roger Zelazny   W
Pimlico Agency, Box 20477, 1534 1st Ave, New York, NY
10028, 212-683-7561
    Pubs: *Knight of Shadows, Frost & Fire* (Morrow, 1989,
1989), *A Dark Traveling* (Avon, 1989).

Joel Zeltzer   P
407 W 50 St #3, New York, NY 10019, 212-581-7940
    Pubs: *Shadows In Light* (Poets Pr, 1985), *Daring Poetry
Qtly, Green Feather Mag, MacGuffin.*

Patricia Zelver   W
177 E 70 St, New York, NY 10021, 212-772-9090
    Pubs: *The Wonderful Towers of Watts* (Morrow, 1995), *The
Wedding of Don Otavio* (Tambourine Bks, 1993), *A Man of
Middle Age* (Holt, 1974), *Ascent, Ohio Rev, Shenandoah,
Atlantic, Virginia Qtly, Esquire, Redbook, Cosmopolitan.*

Elizabeth Zelvin   P
115 W 86 St, #7C, New York, NY 10024, 212-724-0494
Internet: lizzelvin@aol.com
    Pubs: *Gifts and Secrets: Poems of the Therapeutic
Relationship, I Am The Daughter* (New Rivers, 1998, 1981),
Sarah's Daughters Sing: Anth (KTAV Pub Hse, 1990),
*Caprice, Home Planet News, Jewish Women's Literary
Annual.*

Alan Ziegler   P&W
45 Sutton Pl S, New York, NY 10022, 212-751-6244
Internet: az8@columbia.edu
    Pubs: *The Green Grass of Flatbush* (Word Beat Pr, 1986),
So Much to Do (Release Pr, 1981), *New Yorker, Paris Rev.*

Bette Ziegler   W
425 E 58 St, New York, NY 10022
    Pubs: *Older Women/Younger Men* (Doubleday, 1979), *An
Affair For Tomorrow* (HBJ, 1978).

Edra Ziesk   W
444 E 85 St, #4B, New York, NY 10028, 212-861-9131
    Pubs: *Acceptable Losses* (SMU Pr, 1996), *Alaska Qtly Rev,
Arkansas Rev, Turnstile, Folio, Other Voices, Blueline,
Playgirl, Salmon.*

Evan Zimroth   P
600 W 115 St, #103, New York, NY 10025, 212-666-9563
    Pubs: *Gangsters* (Crown, 1996), *Giselle Considers Her
Future* (Carnegie Mellon U Pr, 1996), *Dead, Dinner, or
Naked* (TriQuarterly, 1993), *Atlantic, Hudson Rev, Tikkun.*

Harriet Zinnes   P&W
25 W 54 St, #6A, New York, NY 10019, 212-582-8315
Internet: hzinnes@aol.com
    Pubs: *The Radiant Absurdity of Desire* (Avisson Pr, 1997),
My, Haven't the Flowers Been? (Magic Circle Pr, 1995),
Lover (Coffee Hse Pr, 1989), *Chelsea, Denver Qtly,
Pleiades, Philadelphia Inquirer, APR, Hollins Critic.*

Nonyaniso Zinza   P
630108 Spuyten Duyvil St, Bronx, NY 10463, 212-796-3070
    Pubs: *Affirmations, Declarations and Blues* (DuEwa, Inc.,
1988).

Larry Zirlin   P
411 Clinton St, #5, Brooklyn, NY 11231, 718-858-6229
Internet: larryz@worldnet.att.net
    Pubs: *Under the Tongue* (Hanging Loose Pr, 1992), *Awake
for No Reason* (Cross Country Pr, 1979), *Paris Rev,
Hanging Loose, Transfer, Images.*

Harriet Zoltok-Seltzer   PP
The Bronx Council, 1738 Hone Ave, #4B, Bronx, NY 10461,
212-295-1779
    Pubs: *Alan Ball* (Grub Street, 1979), *Bronx Roots III,
American Mosaic, Bronx Poets.*

Edward Zuckrow   P
303 Marcy Ave, Brooklyn, NY 11211, 718-782-3616
    Pubs: *Slowly, Out Of Stones* (The Horizon, 1980), *The
Death Of Horn & Hardart* (Smith, 1971).

Ellen Zweig   P
93 E 3 St, Brooklyn, NY 11218, 718-972-7290
    Pubs: *Impressions of Africa* (e.g. Pr, 1986), *Women and
Performance, De Zaak, Unsound, Moving Letters,
Assembling.*

NORTH CAROLINA

Beth Adamour   W
1804 W Friendly Ave, Greensboro, NC 27403, 919-373-0500
    Pubs: *Kansas Qtly, West Branch, Nimrod, Mid-American
Rev, Crescent Rev.*

Betty Adcock   P
817 Runnymede Rd, Raleigh, NC 27607, 919-787-2407
    Pubs: *The Difficult Wheel, Beholdings* (LSU Pr, 1995,
1988), *Georgia Rev, Southern Rev, TriQuarterly,
Gettysburg Rev, Kenyon Rev, Tar River Poetry.*

Maya Angelou   P
3240 Valley Rd, Winston-Salem, NC 27106

James Applewhite   P
606 November Dr, Durham, NC 27712, 919-383-7734
    Pubs: *Daytime and Starlight, A History of the River* (LSU Pr,
1997, 1993), *River Writing: An Eno Journal* (Princeton U Pr,
1988), *Antaeus, APR, Atlantic, Poetry, Southern Rev, Esquire.*

Jacqueline Ariail   W
1018 Monmouth Ave, Durham, NC 27701, 919-682-7809
Internet: ariail@unity.ncsu.edu
    Pubs: *Fever: Erotic Writing By Women: Anth*
(HarperCollins, 1994), *Redbook.*

Daphne Athas   P&W
Univ North Carolina, Chapel Hill, NC 27514, 919-962-5481
Internet: dathas@email.unc.edu
   Pubs: *Entering Ephesus* (Second Chance, 1991), *Crumbs
   for the Bogeyman* (St. Andrews Pr, 1991), *Cora* (Viking,
   1978), *Southern Rev, Black Warrior Rev, Spectator,
   Carolina Qtly, Solo, Shenandoah.*

Ellyn Bache   W
2314 Waverly Dr, Wilmington, NC 28403
   Pubs: *The Activist's Daughter* (Spinsters Ink, 1997), *Safe
   Passage* (Bantam, 1994), *The Value of Kindness* (Helicon
   Nine Edtns, 1993), *Festival in Fire Season* (August Hse,
   1992).

Ronald H. Bayes   P
St. Andrews Presbyterian Colle, Dogwood Mile, Laurinburg,
NC 28352, 919-277-5000
   Pubs: *Chainsong For The Muse* (Northern Lights, 1993),
   Prescott Street Reader: Anth (Prescott Street Pr, 1995),
   *Goulash, Pembroke Mag, Prairie Schooner, Northwest Rev,
   TriQuarterly, Prism.*

Jeffrey Beam   P
Golgonooza at Frog Level, 3212 Arthur Minnis Rd,
Hillsborough, NC 27278, 919-967-2470
Internet: cadmus.lib.unc.edu/mss/writers
   Pubs: *Visions of Dame Kind* (The Jargon Society, 1995),
   The Fountain (North Carolina Wesleyan, 1992), *Carolina
   Qtly, Worcester Rev, North Carolina Literary Rev, Yellow
   Silk, James White Rev, Modern Words.*

Doris Betts   W
UNC-Chapel Hill, 230 Greenlaw Hall, CB#3520, Chapel Hill,
NC 27599-3520, 919-962-4006
Internet: dbetts@cphl.mindspring.com
   Pubs: *Beasts of the Southern Wild* (Scribner Paperback,
   1998), *The Sharp Teeth of Love, Souls Raised from the
   Dead, Heading West* (Knopf, 1997, 1994, 1982).

Robert Bixby   P&W
3413 Wilshire, Greensboro, NC 27408
Internet: rbixby@aol.com
   Pubs: *Omni, Sow's Ear, Passages North, Celery, Lactuca,
   Gypsy, Greensboro Rev, Oxalis, Carolina Qtly.*

Patrick Bizzaro   P
105 S Eastern St, Greenville, NC 27858-2134, 919-328-6751
   Pubs: *Undressing the Mannequin* (Third Lung Pr, 1989),
   Violence (Tamarack Edtns, 1978), *New York Qtly, Poetry
   Now, Tar River Poetry, River City, Asheville Poetry Rev,
   Southern Poetry Rev.*

James Breeden   P&W
610 Wendy Way, Durham, NC 27712-9246, 919-471-7000
   Pubs: *Underbelly Mag, Xavier Rev, Pig Iron, Wind Literary
   Jrnl, Next Exit, Modern Haiku, S.L.U.G.fest, Wellspring,
   Piedmont Literary Rev, Arts Line.*

Sue Ellen Bridgers   W
PO Box 248, Sylva, NC 287790248, 704-586-6271
   Pubs: *All We Know Of Heaven* (Banks Channel Bks, 1996),
   Keeping Christina (HarperCollins, 1993).

Bill Brittain   W
17 Wisteria Dr, Asheville, NC 28804, 704-252-7104
   Pubs: *Shape-Changer, The Ghost from Beneath the Sea,
   Wings, Professor Popkin's Prodigious Polish*
   (HarperCollins, 1994, 1992, 1991, 1990).

Christopher Brookhouse   P&W
PO Box 653, Chapel Hill, NC 27514, 919-542-2387
   Pubs: *Wintermute* (Dutton, 1978).

Sally Buckner   P
3231 Birnamwood Rd, Raleigh, NC 27607, 919-782-3636
   Pubs: *Strawberry Harvest* (St. Andrews Pr, 1986), *Our
   Words, Our Ways: Anth* (Carolina Academic Pr, 1995),
   *Pembroke Mag, Crab Creek Rev, Christian Century,
   Southern Poetry Rev, Crucible, Lyricist.*

Kathryn Stripling Byer   P
PO Box 489, Cullowhee, NC 28723, 828-293-5695
Internet: jbyer@wpoff.wcu.edu
   Pubs: *Black Shawl, Wildwood Flower* (LSU Pr, 1998, 1992),
   The Girl in the Midst of the Harvest (Texas Tech Pr, 1986),
   *Georgia Rev, Greensboro Rev, Southern Poetry Rev,
   Shenandoah, Carolina Qtly, Asheville Poetry Rev.*

Dean Cadle   W
135 Fulton Dr, Hendersonville, NC 28792, 704-696-9667
   Pubs: *Yale Rev, Southwest Rev, Short Story Intl,
   Appalachian Jrnl, Contemporary Literary Criticism.*

Mary Belle Campbell   P
53 Pine Lake Dr, Whispering Pines, NC 28327-9388,
910-949-3993
   Pubs: *Light From Dark Tombs: Mysteries of the Ancient
   Maya* (Persephone Pr, 1991), *Anima, Intl Poetry Rev,
   Pembroke, St. Andrews Rev, Stone Country.*

Joan L. Cannon   P&W
207 B Ridgeside Terr, Morganton, NC 286552656,
828-439-8339
Internet: joancannon@hci.net
   Pubs: *Elf, Expressions, Grit, Odessa Poetry Rev, Pulpsmith,
   Seacoast Life, The Modern Woodman, Thema, Cappers.*

Fred Chappell   P&W
305 Kensington Rd, Greensboro, NC 27403, 910-275-8851
   Pubs: *Farewell, I'm Bound To Leave You* (Picador USA,
   1996), *The Fred Chappell Reader* (St. Martin's, 1991),
   Saturday Evening Post, Harper's, Georgia Rev, Poetry.

Avery Grenfell Church   P
2749 Park Oak Dr, Clemmons, NC 27012, 910-766-7737
    Pubs: *Dakota: Plains & Fancy* (Vermillion, 1989),
    Parnassus of World Poets: Anth (Ramasamy Devaraj,
    1997), *Dan River Anth* (Dan River Pr, 1988), *San Fernando*
    Poetry Jrnl, Bardic Echoes, Orphic Lute, Poets' Paper,
    American Bard, Parnassus Literary Jrnl.

Jim Clark   P&W
4706 Quaker Rd, Wilson, NC 27893, 252-243-9736
Internet: cn3368@coastalnet.com
    Pubs: *Handiwork* (St. Andrews Pr, 1998), *Dancing on*
    Canaan's Ruins (Eternal Delight Pub, 1997), *Witnessing*
    Earth: Anth (Catamount Pr, 1994), *Cross Roads, Denver*
    Qtly, Southern Poetry Rev, Georgia Rev, Prairie Schooner,
    Greensboro Rev, Appalachian Heritage.

Kent Cooper   W
1124 Woodburn Rd, Durham, NC 27705-5738
    Pubs: *Fame and Fortune* (Playboy Bks, 1981), *The Harp*
    Styles of Sonny Terry (Oak Pub, 1975), *Below Houston*
    Street, The Minnesota Strip (Manor Books, 1978, 1978),
    Paterson Literary Rev, Living Blues.

Helen M. Copeland   W
1850 Maryland Ave, Charlotte, NC 28209, 704-375-3022
    Pubs: *Endangered Specimen And Other Poems From A*
    Lay Naturalist (St. Andrews, 1988).

Alice Carver Cramer   P
413 Longleaf Dr, Chapel Hill, NC 27514, 919-942-3868
    Pubs: *Harvard Mag, Yale Rev, Theology Today, Pivot, Poet*
    Lore, Lyric, Friends Journal.

Robert Cumming   P&W
PO Box 1047, Davidson, NC 28036, 704-896-3479
Internet: rdgcumming@mindspring.com
    Pubs: *45/96: The Ninety-Six Sampler of South Carolina*
    Poetry: Anth (Ninety-Six Pr, 1994), *A Premier Book of*
    Contemporary Thai Verse: Anth (Amarin Pr, 1985),
    Southern Poetry Rev, Devil's Milhopper, Sow's Ear.

Christopher Davis   P
Univ North Carolina, Charlotte, NC 28223, 704-547-2296
    Pubs: *The Tyrant of the Past and the Slave of the Future*
    (Texas Tech U Pr, 1989), *Sonora Rev, Black Warrior Rev,*
    Ploughshares, Denver Qtly, American Voice.

Angela Davis-Gardner   W
North Carolina State Univ, Raleigh, NC 27605, 919-515-4173
    Pubs: *Forms of Shelter* (Ticknor & Fields, 1991), *Felice*
    (Random Hse, 1982), *Crescent Rev, Greensboro Rev,*
    Kansas Qtly, Carolina Qtly.

Thadious M. Davis   P
Univ North Carolina, Chapel Hill, NC 27514, 919-967-3778
    Pubs: *Black Scholar, Obsidian, South And West, Black*
    American LIterature Forum.

Irene Dayton   P
209 S Hillandale Dr, East Flat Rock, NC 28726-2609,
828-693-4014
    Pubs: *In Oxbow of Time's River, Seven Times the Wind*
    (Windy Row, 1978, 1977), *North Stone Rev, Women Artist*
    News, Literary Rev.

Ann Deagon   P&W
802 Woodbrook Dr, Greensboro, NC 274103278,
336-292-5273
    Pubs: *The Polo Poems* (U Nebraska-Omaha, 1990), *The*
    Diver's Tomb (St. Martin's/Marek, 1985).

Dean A. Deter   P
Rt 2, Box 83, Hillsborough, NC 27278

Stuart Dischell   P
1614 West End Pl, Greensboro, NC 27403, 910-274-0961
Internet: s_dische@fagan.uncg.edu
    Pubs: *Evenings & Avenues* (Penguin, 1996), *Good Hope*
    Road (Viking Penguin, 1993).

Julia Nunnally Duncan   P&W
Rte 4, Box 981, Paxton Creek R, Marion, NC 28752,
704-724-9278
    Pubs: *Only Morning In Her Shoes* (Utah State U Pr, 1990),
    Writers' Forum, Potato Eyes, Appalachian Heritage,
    Birmingham Poetry Rev, Georgia Jrnl, The Lyricist.

Charles Edward Eaton   P&W
808 Greenwood Rd, Chapel Hill, NC 27514, 919-942-4775
    Pubs: *The Scout In Summer, The Country of the Blue, New*
    & Selected Stories 1959-1989 (Cornwall, 1998, 1994,
    1989), *Sewanee Rev, Salmagundi, New Letters, Antioch*
    Rev, Hollins Critic, Centennial Rev.

Julie Fay   P
RR 2, Box 263-P, Blounts Creek, NC 27814-9802,
919-975-6709
    Pubs: *Images of Women in Literature* (HM, 1990), *A Formal*
    Feeling Comes: Anth (Story Line Pr, 1994), *Hellas, Iris,*
    Laurel Rev, Ploughshares, Translation, Calyx.

Thomas Feeny   P
306 Chamberlain St, Raleigh, NC 27607-7312, 919-515-9281
Internet: feeny@social.chass.ncsu.edu
    Pubs: *The Paternal Orientation of Ramon Perez de Ayala*
    (Spain; Albatros-Hispanofila, 1985), *Puerto del Sol, Poets*
    On, Hiram Poetry Rev, Cape Rock, Verve, Comstock Rev,
    Sulphur, Timber Creek Rev, Mankato Poetry Rev, GW Rev.

Candace Flynt   W
2005 Madison Ave, Greensboro, NC 274031511,
336-373-1025
    Pubs: *Mother Love* (FSG, 1987), *Sins of Omission*
    (Random Hse, 1984), *Chasing Dad* (Dial, 1980).

Lee E. Franke PP&P
3812 Ashton Dr, Charlotte, NC 28210-6841
Pubs: *Performance Poet: Village Gate Art Center* (1986),
Pyramid Art Center (1985, 1983).

Marita Garin P
PO Box 503, Black Mountain, NC 28711, 828-669-7819
Pubs: *Verse, Tar River Poetry, Oxford Mag, Kansas Qtly,
Cumberland Poetry Rev, Kenyon Rev.*

Philip Gerard W
3440 Sparrow Hawk Ct, Wilmington, NC 28409
Pubs: *Cape Fear Rising* (John F. Blair, 1994), *Desert Kill*
(Morrow, 1994), *New England Rev, Puerto del Sol, Hawaii
Rev.*

Grace Evelyn Loving Gibson P
709 McLean St, Laurinburg, NC 28352, 919-276-1769
Internet: gibsongl@+artan.sapc.edu
Pubs: *Frayed Edges, Drake's Branch, Home in Time* (St.
Andrews Pr, 1995, 1982, 1977).

Marie Gilbert P
2 St. Simons Sq, Greensboro, NC 27408-3833,
910-288-3051
Pubs: *Connexions, Myrtle Beach Back When* (St. Andrews,
1994, 1990).

Marianne Gingher W
301 E Hendrix St, Greensboro, NC 27401
Pubs: *Teen Angel, Bobby Rex's Greatest Hit* (Atheneum,
1988, 1986), *New Virginia Rev, NAR, Redbook, Southern
Rev.*

Judy Goldman P
1121 Scotland Ave, Charlotte, NC 28207, 704-334-6868
Internet: jkghig@earthlink.net
Pubs: *The Permanence of Things* (Wm. Morrow, 1999),
Wanting To Know The End (Silverfish Rev Pr, 1993),
Holding Back Winter (St. Andrews Pr, 1987), *Ohio Rev,
Kenyon Rev, Southern Rev, Crazyhorse, Shenandoah,
Prairie Schooner, Gettysburg Rev.*

Robert Waters Grey P
647 Wilshire Ave SW, Concord, NC 28027, 704-795-0920
Pubs: *Saving The Dead* (Briarpatch Pr, 1992), *Poet & Critic,
Black Warrior Rev, Sycamore Rev, Kansas Qtly, Hollins
Critic, Willow Springs.*

Frank Borden Hanes W
1057 W Kent Rd, Winston-Salem, NC 27104, 919-723-3266
Pubs: *The Seeds of Ares* (Briarpatch Pr, 1977), *The Fleet
Rabble* (Popular Library, 1967), *Jackknife John* (Naylor,
1964), *The Bat Brothers, Abel Anders* (Farrar Straus &
Young, 1953, 1951).

Suzan Shown Harjo P
99 Pressley Rd, Asheville, NC 28805-1345

William Harmon P
Univ North Carolina, English Dept, CB #3520, Chapel Hill, NC
27599-3520, 919-962-4015
Internet: wharmon03@mindspring.com
Pubs: *Mutatis Mutandis* (Wesleyan U Pr, 1985), *One Long
Poem* (LSU Pr, 1982), *Carolina Qtly, Agni, Sewanee Rev,
Poetry, Partisan Rev, Free Lunch.*

Rabiul Hasan P
2609 MacGregor Downs Rd, #17, Greenville, NC 27834,
252-752-5556
Pubs: *Mississippi Writers: Reflections of Childhood and
Youth Anth* (Jackson and London/U Pr Mississippi, 1988),
New Earth Rev, Aura Literary/Arts Rev, Piddiddle.

Ardis Messick Hatch P
4508 Avent Ferry Rd, Raleigh, NC 27606-3409,
919-828-2008
Pubs: *The Illusion of Water* (St. Andrews Pr, 1980), *To
Defend a Form* (Teachers & Writers, 1978).

Tom Hawkins P&W
5020 Oak Park Rd, Raleigh, NC 27612-3025, 919-782-3009
Pubs: *Paper Crown* (BkMk Pr, 1989), *Flash Fiction: Anth*
(Norton, 1992), *Greensboro Rev, Kansas Qtly, Sequoia
Rev, Carolina Qtly, South Carolina Rev, Ploughshares.*

Carol Bessent Hayman P
618 Ann St, Beaufort, NC 285162204, 252-728-7088
Pubs: *A Garden of Virtues* (Abingdon Pr, 1996), *Images and
Echoes of Beaufort-By-The-Sea* (Mt. Olive College Pr, 1993),
*Ideals, Listen, Marriage and Family Living, Mature Living, Our
State, Down Home in North Carolina, Carolina Country.*

Robert R. Hentz P&W
415 Chunns Cove Rd, 900A, Asheville, NC 28805,
704-252-9064
Pubs: *Cape Rock, Hellas, Riverrun, Silhouette, Poem, Cold
Mountain Rev, Sonoma Mandala, The Panhandler.*

M. L. Hester P
PO Box 38816, Greensboro, NC 27438, 336-288-6989
Pubs: *Another Jackie Robinson, With Crockett at The
Alamo* (Tudor Pubs, 1996, 1995), *Poetry Now, American
Scholar, Minnesota Rev.*

Lonnie Hodge P
8206-1200 Providence Rd, Box 3, Charlotte, NC 28277-9704,
704-846-7568
Pubs: *Fishing for the Moon* (Sandstone Pr, 1993), *Shadow of
the Peaks* (Crossroads, 1985), *Kansas Qtly, Alabama Literary
Rev, Colorado North Qtly, Appalachia, Sulphur River Rev.*

Judy Hogan P
PO Box 84, Saxapahaw, NC 27340-0084, 919-376-8152
Pubs: *Light Food* (Latitudes Pr, 1989), *Small Press, Arts
Jrnl, Pembroke, Southern Poetry Rev, The Smith, Crucible,
Literary Kostroma.*

David Brendan Hopes   P&W
Univ North Carolina, 1 University Heights, Asheville, NC
28804, 828-254-6057
Internet: dhopes@unca.edu
    Pubs: *A Childhood in the Milky Way* (U Akron Pr, 1998), *A
Sense of the Morning* (Milkweed Edtns, 1998), *Blood Rose*
(Urthona Pr, 1996), *The Sacred Place* (U Utah Pr, 1996),
*Atlanta Rev, Cafe Bellas Artes, Salmon, Asheville Poetry
Rev, Apalachee Qtly.*

Maria Ingram   P
111 Stratford Rd, Winston-Salem, NC 27104, 919-722-7271
    Pubs: *Thirtieth Year to Heaven* (Jackpine Pr, 1980), *Maria*
(Red Clay Books, 1976).

Carol Klein   W
1-103 Carolina Meadows, Chapel Hill, NC 27514
    Pubs: *Prairie Schooner, Southern Humanities Rev,
Roanoke Rev, St. Andrews Rev, Northland, Toyon.*

Stephen Knauth   P
805 E Worthington Ave, Charlotte, NC 28203, 704-376-8511
    Pubs: *The River I Know You By, Twenty Shadows* (Four
Way Bks, 1998, 1995), *The Pine Figures* (Dooryard Pr,
1986), *Pacific Rev, Puerto del Sol, Alaska Qtly Rev,
Ironwood, Kansas Qtly, MPR, NAR.*

Carrie Knowles   P&W
315 S Boylan Ave, Raleigh, NC 27603, 919-833-6022
Internet: cwriter@bellsouth.net
    Pubs: *Cardinal: Anth of North Carolina Writers* (Jacan Pr,
1986), *The Sun, TasteFull, Mothers Today, Beyond
Baroque, Better Homes and Gardens, Carolina Qtly,
Glimmer Train.*

Howard D. Koenig   P
3306 Middle Sound Rd, Wilmington, NC 28405
    Pubs: *Profiles In Leadership* (Quest, 1981), *Lyrical Iowa,
American Poet, A Different Drummer.*

Mary Kratt   P
7001 Sardis Rd, Charlotte, NC 28270, 704-366-0297
    Pubs: *On the Steep Side* (Briarpatch Pr, 1993), *The Only
Thing I Fear Is A Cow And A Drunken Man* (Carolina Wren
Pr, 1991), *Tar River Poetry, Spoon River Qtly, Texas Rev,
Shenandoah, Nimrod, Poet Lore.*

Richard Krawiec   P&W
319 Wilmot Dr, Raleigh, NC 27602, 919-859-9297
    Pubs: *Faith In What?, Voices From Home: The North
Carolina Anth* (Avisson Pr, 1997, 1998), *Time Sharing: Anth*
(Viking Penguin, 1987), *Shenandoah, Witness, Poetry
Motel, Cream City Rev, The Quarterly, Many Mountains
Moving, The Other Side.*

Sandra Lake Lassen   P
1499 Lakeside Dr, West Jefferson, NC 28694-7291
    Pubs: *Womanwrit* (Miller, 1982), *Amaranth Rev, Wordart,
Touchstone, American Scholar, Chiron Rev.*

Lou Lipsitz   P
168 Lake Ellen Dr, Chapel Hill, NC 27514, 919-942-9574
Internet: llipsitz@email.unc.edu
    Pubs: *Seeking the Hook* (Signal Bks, 1998), *American
Democracy* (St. Martin's Pr, 1993), *Reflections on Samson*
(Kayak, 1977), *Anteus, New Republic, The Sun, Witness,
Southern Rev.*

Don Mager   P
Johnson C. Smith Univ, English Dept, Charlotte, NC 28216,
704-378-3593
    Pubs: *That Which Is Owed To Death* (Main Street Rag Pr,
1998), *Glosses* (St. Andrews Pr, 1992), *To Track the
Wounded One* (Ridgeway, 1988), *River Styx, Lyricist, St.
Andrews Rev, Sun Dog, Western Humanities Rev, North
Dakota Qtly, Cape Rock, Main Street Rag.*

E. T. Malone, Jr.   P
PO Box 18124, Raleigh, NC 27619, 919-269-0010
Internet: diocese_of_nc.parti@ecunet.org
    Pubs: *The View from Wrightsville Beach* (Literary Lantern
Pr, 1988), *Pembroke, St. Andrews Rev, Communicant.*

Harry A. Maxson   P
66 Hardy Rd, Wendell, NC 27591-8355, 919-365-0608
Internet: max34@ix.netcom.com
    Pubs: *The Curley Poems* (Frank Cat Pr, 1994), *Walker in
the Storm* (K.M. Gentile Pub, 1981), *Turning the Wood*
(Cedar Creek Pr, 1976), *Kansas Qtly, Cimarron Rev, New
Rev, The Ledge, Nation.*

Barbara J. Mayer   P&W
805 Heatherly Rd, Mooresville, NC 28115, 704-663-7593
    Pubs: *I Am Becoming the Woman I've Wanted: Anth*
(Papier-Mache Pr, 1994), *Filtered Images: Anth* (Vintage
'45 Pr, 1992).

Jean McCamy   P
145 W Sycamore Ave, Wake Forest, NC 27587,
919-556-5342
    Pubs: *Uwharrie Rev, Davidson Miscellany, Southern Poetry
Rev, St. Andrews Rev.*

Rebecca McClanahan   P&W
301 Settlers Ln, Charlotte, NC 28202, 704-376-6956
    Pubs: *The Intersection of X & Y* (Copper Beech Pr, 1996),
One Word Deep (Ashland Poetry Pr, 1993), *Southern Rev,
Shenandoah, Kenyon Rev, Gettysburg Rev.*

Michael McFee   P
UNC-Chapel Hill, Greenlaw Hall CB# 3520, Chapel Hill, NC
27599-3520, 919-962-3461
    Pubs: *Colander* (Carnegie Mellon U Pr, 1996), *The
Language They Speak is Things to Eat: Anth* (U North
Carolina Pr, 1994), *Poetry, Hudson Rev, Southern Rev.*

Jane Mead   P
Wake Forest Univ, Box 7387, Reynolda Sta, Winston-Salem,
NC 27109, 910-759-5383
> Pubs: *The Lord And The General Din Of The World*
> (Sarabande Bks, 1996).

Thomas Meyer   P
PO Box 10, Highlands, NC 287410010, 828-526-4461
Internet: thomey@aol.com
> Pubs: *Monotypes & Tracings* (Enitharmon Pr, 1994),
> *Sonnets & Tableaux* (Coracle, 1987), *Conjunctions, First
> Intensity, Oyster Boy Rev.*

Shirley Moody   P
1424 Laughridge Dr, Cary, NC 27511, 919-469-1314
> Pubs: *Charmers, Four North Carolina Women Poets: Anth*
> (St. Andrews Pr, 1990, 1982), *Southern Poetry Rev,
> Crucible.*

Lenard D. Moore   P
English Dept., Tompkins Hall, Box 8105 North Carolina State,
Raleigh, NC 27695, 919-515-4127
Internet: ldmoore@social.chass.ncsu.edu
> Pubs: *Forever Home* (St. Andrews Pr, 1996), *The Garden
> Thrives* (HarperCollins, 1996), *Soulfires* (Penguin, 1996),
> *African American Rev, Callaloo, North Carolina Literary
> Rev, Black Scholar, Colorado Rev, North Dakota Qtly, Crab
> Orchard Rev.*

Ruth Moose   P&W
14 Matchwood, Pittsboro, NC 27312, 919-929-0376
Internet: rumoo@email.unc.edu
> Pubs: *Smith Grove* (Sow's Ear Pr, 1997), *Dreams in Color*
> (August Hse, 1989), *The Wreath Ribbon & Other Stories*
> (St. Andrews, 1986), *12 Christmas Stories By North
> Carolina Writers: Anth* (Down Home Pr, 1997), *Southern
> Exposure, Cities and Roads.*

John N. Morris   P
595 Fearrington Post #A, Pittsboro, NC 27312-8570
> Pubs: *A Schedule of Benefits, The Glass Houses, The Life
> Beside This One, Green Business* (Atheneum, 1987, 1980,
> 1975, 1970).

Jack Nestor   P&W
119 Leslie Dr, Chapel Hill, NC 27516, 919-929-9401
> Pubs: *Love Is Ageless* (Serala Pr, 1987), *Stone Country,
> Slow Motion Mag, Laurel Rev, Open Mag, Wittenberg Rev,
> Ascent, Columbia Mag, Jrnl of New Jersey Poets.*

P. B. Newman   P
Queens College, Charlotte, NC 28274, 704-332-7121
> Pubs: *The George Washington Poems* (Briarpatch Pr,
> 1986), *Tar River Poetry, River City, Kennebec, Apalachee
> Qtly, Carolina Qtly, Southern Poetry Rev, Sun.*

Suzanne Newton   W
829-A Barringer Dr, Raleigh, NC 27606, 919-851-4710
> Pubs: *Where Are You When I Need You?, A Place
> Between, An End To Perfect* (Viking, 1991, 1986, 1984).

Claudio Oswald Niedworok   PP
Vision Era Concepts, PO Box 718, Broadway, NC
275050718, 919-499-2565
Internet: knightt@foto.infi.net
> Pubs: *Seafarers* (Vision Era Concepts, 1996).

Valerie Nieman   P&W
1313 Hawthorne Ave, Reidsville, NC 273205904,
336-349-6038
Internet: vneiman@nr.infi.net
> Pubs: *How We Live* (State St Pr, 1996), *Slipping Out of Old
> Eve* (Sing Heavenly Muse, 1988), *Modern Arthurian
> Literature: Anth* (Garland Pub, 1992), *Poetry, New Letters,
> West Branch, Kenyon Rev, Antietam Rev.*

Sallic Nixon   P
Covenant Village, Apt A-8, 1351 Robinwood Rd, Gastonia,
NC 28054
> Pubs: *Spiraling* (Persephone Pr, 1990), *Second Grace* (Moore
> Pub Co, 1977), *Pembroke Mag, Crucible, Sandhills Rev.*

Linda Orr   P
Duke University, Durham, NC 27706, 919-684-3706
> Pubs: *A Certain X* (L'Epervier Pr, 1980), *Antioch Rev, Paris
> Rev, Pequod, Agni.*

Sallie Page   W
PO Box 64, Lynn, NC 28750, 704-859-9549
> Pubs: *Art/Life, St. Andrews Rev, Spindrift, Aura, Mountain
> Rev.*

Leslie Parker   P
5004 Hiddenbrook Ct, McLeansville, NC 27301-9775,
336-621-7316
> Pubs: *Joys and Tears: Anth* (The Work Group, 1993),
> *Hawaii Rev, Alternative Pr Mag, Black Buzzard Rev, Infinity
> Ltd, Byline, Gothica, Elk River Rev, Panhandler, Poetpourri,
> Cape Rock.*

Peggy Payne   W
512 St. Mary's St, Raleigh, NC 27605, 919-833-8021
> Pubs: *Revelation* (S&S, 1988), *New Stories from the South:
> Anth* (Algonquin, 1987), *Cosmopolitan, Ms., McCall's,
> Family Circle, Travel & Leisure.*

Gail J. Peck   P
250 King Owen Ct, Charlotte, NC 28211, 704-364-1944
Internet: 74601,1420@compuserve.com
> Pubs: *Drop Zone* (Texas Rev, 1995), *New River* (Harper,
> 1993), *Uncommonplace: Anth* (Louisiana State Pr, 1998),
> *Southern Rev, Cimarron Rev, Carolina Qtly, High Plains
> Literary Rev, Southern Poetry, Malahat, Mangrove,
> Greensboro Rev, Cape Rock.*

George Perreault P
803 Willow St, Greenville, NC 27858, 252-328-1096
Internet: edperrea@eastnet.educ.ecu.edu
    Pubs: *Trying to Be Round* (Singular Speech Pr, 1994),
Curved Like An Eye (Ahsahta Pr, 1994), *Jrnl of American
Culture, Shenandoah, High Plains Literary Rev, Northwest
Rev, The Lyric, Blue Mesa Rev.*

Catherine Petroski W
2528 Wrightwood Ave, Durham, NC 27705-5830,
919-489-9416
Internet: cgp@acpub.duke.edu
    Pubs: *A Bride's Passage* (Northeastern U Pr, 1997), *The
Summer That Lasted Forever* (HM, 1984), *I Know Some
Things: Anth* (Faber & Faber, 1993), *Virginia Qtly Rev,
North American Rev.*

Henry Petroski P
2528 Wrightwood Ave, Durham, NC 27705-5830,
919-489-9416
    Pubs: *Remaking The World* (Knopf, 1997), *Invention by
Design* (Harvard U Pr, 1996), *Engineers of Dreams* (Knopf,
1995), *Design Paradigms* (Cambridge U Pr, 1994), *Virginia
Qtly Rev, American Scientist.*

Diana Pinckney P
2215 Malvern Rd, Charlotte, NC 28207, 704-377-6159
Internet: pinckpat@aol.com
    Pubs: *White Linen* (Nightshade Pr, 1998), *Fishing With Tall
Women* (Persephone Pr, 1996), *Southern Poetry Rev, Tar
River, Sandhills Rev, New Laurel Rev, Chattahoochee Rev,
Pembroke, Cream City Rev, Comstock Rev.*

Deborah Pope P
1525 Twisted Oak Dr, Chapel Hill, NC 275167886,
919-684-2741
    Pubs: *Falling Out of the Sky, Mortal World, Fanatic Heart*
(LSU Pr, 1999, 1995, 1992), *Poetry, Georgia Rev, Southern
Rev, Shenandoah, Poetry Northwest, Threepenny Rev.*

Joe Ashby Porter W
2411 W Club Blvd, Durham, NC 27705, 919-286-7075
Internet: japorter@acpub.duke.edu
    Pubs: *Lithuania: Short Stories, The Kentucky Stories*
(Johns Hopkins U, 1990, 1983), *Harper's, TriQuarterly,
Fiction, Raritan, Antaeus, Iowa Rev.*

Dannye Romine Powell P
700 E Park Ave, Charlotte, NC 28203, 704-334-0902
Internet: dannye@charlotte.com
    Pubs: *At Every Wedding Someone Stays Home* (U Arkansas
Pr, 1994), *America's Foremost Writers on Libraries: Anth*
(Doubleday, 1989), *New Republic, Georgia Rev, Gettysburg
Rev, Prairie Schooner, Poetry, Paris Rev, Crazyhorse.*

Charles F. Powers W
1412 Rock Creek Ln, Cary, NC 27511, 919-467-2629
    Pubs: *A Matter of Honor* (First East Coast Theatre &
Publishing Co., 1982).

Reynolds Price P&W
Box 99014, Durham, NC 27708-9014
    Pubs: *Private Contentment, Vital Provisions, The Source Of
Light* (Atheneum, 1984, 1982, 1981).

Tony Reevy P&W
The Libraries, Campus Box 7111, North Carolin, Raleigh, NC
276957111, 919-515-3339
Internet: tony_reevy@ncsu.edu
    Pubs: *Now & Then, Charlotte Poetry Rev, Piedmont Pedlar,
Asheville Poetry Rev, Bath Avenue Newsletter.*

David Rigsbee P
315 Oakwood Ave, Raleigh, NC 27601, 919-821-9851
Internet: drigsbee@earthlink.net
    Pubs: *A Skeptic's Notebook: Longer Poems* (St. Andrews Pr,
1997), *Your Heart Will Fly Away* (The Smith, 1992), *Stamping
Ground* (Ardis, 1976), *APR, New Yorker, Iowa Rev, Ironwood,
Southern Rev, Georgia Rev, Ohio Rev, Willow Springs.*

Fred Ross W
R-1/Box 111, Norwood, NC 28128, 704-474-3208
    Pubs: *Jackson Mahaffey* (Houghton Mifflin, 1951), *Story,
MacLeans, Blue Book, Uwharrie Rev, Today.*

George Addison Scarbrough P
Appalachian State Univ, Ctr for Appalachian Studies, Boone,
NC 28608, 615-482-2793
    Pubs: *Appalachia Inside Out: Anth, Homewords* (U
Tennessee Pr, 1995, 1986), *The Age of Koestler: Anth*
(Practices of the Wind, 1994), *Southern Rev.*

Eliot Schain P&W
35 Maxwell Rd, Chapel Hill, NC 27514
    Pubs: *American Romance* (Zeitgeist, 1989), *APR,
Ploughshares, ACM, Mothering, Stone Country.*

E. M. Schorb P&W
PO Box 1461, Mooresville, NC 28115-9504, 704-660-5453
    Pubs: *Murderer's Day* (Purdue U Pr, 1998), *50 Poems* (Hill
Hse, 1986), *The Poor Boy* (Dragon's Teeth Pr, 1975),
*American Scholar, Massachusetts Rev, Sewanee Rev,
Southern Rev, Carolina Qtly, Chicago Rev, Yale Rev.*

James Seay P
127 Windsor Cir, Chapel Hill, NC 27516, 919-929-9094
    Pubs: *Open Field, Understory: New and Selected Poems*
(LSU Pr, 1997), *The Light As They Found It* (Morrow,
1990).

Mabelle M. Segrest P
811 Onslow St, Durham, NC 27705-4244
    Pubs: *My Mama's Dead Squirrel* (Firebrand Bks, 1985),
Southern Exposure, Feminary, Conditions.

Bynum Shaw   W
2700 Speas Rd, Winston-Salem, NC 27106, 336-924-1644
   Pubs: *Oh, Promised Land!* (Stratford Bks, 1992), *Days of Power, Nights of Fear* (St. Martin's, 1980), *The Nazi Hunter* (Norton, 1969).

Janet Beeler Shaw   P&W
46 Newcross N, Asheville, NC 28805-9213, 704-298-8999
   Pubs: *Taking Leave* (Viking, 1987), *Dowry* (U Missouri Pr, 1978), *Atlantic Monthly, Redbook, TriQuarterly, Shenandoah, Southwest Rev, Esquire.*

Benjamin Sloan   P
9700 Mary Alexander Rd, Apt I, Charlotte, NC 28213, 704-549-1648
   Pubs: *La-Bas, Bird Effort, Out There, Mouth of the Dragon.*

Lee Smith   W
44 Cedar St, Chapel Hill, NC 27514
   Pubs: *Fair and Tender Ladies, Oral History* (Putnam, 1988, 1981), *Atlantic, Southern Exposure, New York Times.*

John Thom Spach   W
PO Box 11408, Winston-Salem, NC 27116, 336-724-6774
   Pubs: *Time Out From Texas* (John F. Blair, 1970), *Great Commanders In Action: Anth* (Cowles Enthusiast Media, 1996), *Military History, Cowboy, American Civil War, Retired Officer, Far West, Old Salem, Saturday Evening Post, Grit, Reader's Digest.*

Elizabeth Spencer   W
402 Longleaf Dr, Chapel Hill, NC 27514, 919-929-2115
   Pubs: *Landscapes of the Heart* (Random Hse, 1990), *The Light in the Piazza, The Snare* (U Pr Mississippi, 1996, 1993), *The Voice at the Back Door* (LSU Pr, 1994), *Boulevard, Southern Rev, Story, Antaeus, New Yorker, Atlantic.*

Max Steele   W
Univ North Carolina, Chapel Hill, NC 27514, 919-962-5481
   Pubs: *The Hat of My Mother* (Algonquin Bks, 1988), *Story Mag, Paris Rev.*

Shelby Stephenson   P
UNC Pembroke, Pembroke Magazine, Box 1510, Pembroke, NC 283721510, 919-521-4214
   Pubs: *Poor People, The Persimmon Tree Carol* (Nightshade Pr, 1998, 1990), *Plankhouse* (North Carolina Wesleyan College Pr, 1993), *Poetry Northwest, Hudson Rev, New Virginia Rev, Bits, Carolina Qtly.*

John Stokes   P
124 Windemere Rd, Wilmington, NC 28405, 919-799-2695
   Pubs: *Texas Qtly, Voices Intl, The Poet, Pembroke Mag, Crucible.*

Julie Suk   P
845 Greentree Dr, Charlotte, NC 28211, 704-366-8956
   Pubs: *The Angel of Obsession* (U Arkansas Pr, 1992), *Heartwood* (Briarpatch Pr, 1991), *Poetry, Shenandoah, Cream City Rev, American Literary Rev, River Styx, Georgia Rev.*

Chuck Sullivan   P
1100 E 34th St, Charlotte, NC 28205, 704-334-3496
   Pubs: *Alphabet of Grace: New & Selected Poems* (Sandstone Pr, 1995), *Longing for the Harmonies* (St. Andrews Pr, 1992), *The Juggler on the Radio* (Briarpatch Pr, 1987), *The Catechism of Hearts* (Red Clay Bks, 1979).

Charleen Whisnant Swansea   P
404 Deming Dr, Chapel Hill, NC 27514, 919-929-5858
   Pubs: *Mindworks* (South Carolina Educational TV, 1990), *Word Magic* (Doubleday, 1976), *Southern Poetry Rev.*

Nancy McFadden Tilly   W
628 Kensington Dr, Chapel Hill, NC 27514, 919-929-8880
   Pubs: *Golden Girl* (FSG, 1985), *Carolina Qtly, Cotton Boll, Writer's Choice, Albany Rev.*

Kermit Turner   W
Lenoir-Rhyne College, Box 418, Hickory, NC 28601, 704-328-1741
   Pubs: *These Rebel Powers* (Frederick Warne & Co., 1979), *Greensboro Rev, Roanoke Rev, Phylon.*

Thomas N. Walters   P
5211 Melbourne Rd, Raleigh, NC 27606, 919-851-4899
   Pubs: *Always Next August, Seeing In The Dark* (Moore Pub Co., 1976, 1972).

Robert Watson   P&W
9-D Fountain Manor Dr, Greensboro, NC 27405, 919-274-9962
   Pubs: *The Pendulum: New and Selected Poems* (LSU Pr, 1995), *Night Blooming Cactus* (Atheneum, 1980), *Poetry, Harper's, New Yorker, Georgia Rev, Shenandoah.*

Susan C. Weinberg   W
Appalachian State Univ, Boone, NC 28608, 704-262-2871
Internet: weinbergsc@appstate.edu
   Pubs: *Voices From Home: North Carolina Prose Anth* (Avisson Pr, 1997), *Gettysburg Rev, Other Voices, Gargoyle, Indiana Rev, The MacGuffin, Third Coast, Washington Rev, Mississippi Rev.*

John Foster West   P&W
157 West Ln, Boone, NC 286078605, 828-295-7704
   Pubs: *Lift Up Your Head, Tom Dooley* (Down Home Pr, 1993), *The Summer People* (Appalachian Consortium Pr, 1988), *Wry Wine* (John F. Blair Pub, 1977), *Time Was* (Random Hse, 1965), *Southern Rev, Atlantic, Southwest Rev, Cold Mountain Rev, Crucible.*

Nina A. Wicker   P
2356 Minter School Rd, Sanford, NC 27330
   Pubs: *Winter and Wild Roses* (Persephone Pr, 1989),
   October Rain On My Window (Honeybrook Pr, 1984),
   Heiwa: Anth (U Hawaii Pr, 1996), *Haiku Moment: Anth*
   (Charles E. Tuttle, 1993), *The Haiku Hundred: Anth* (Iron
   Pr, 1992), *Modern Haiku, Woodnotes, Frogpond.*

Carol Lynn Wilkinson   P
Box 19312, Raleigh, NC 27609, 919-787-7695
   Pubs: *Taste Of Remembered Wine* (North Carolina Rev Pr,
   1975), *Wind, Miscellany.*

Jonathan Williams   P
PO Box 10, Highlands, NC 28741, 828-526-4461
Internet: thomey@aol.com
   Pubs: *Quantulumcumque* (French Broad Pr, 1991), *Eight
   Days in Eire* (North Carolina Wesleyan Pr, 1990), *Quote,
   Unquote* (Ten Speed Pr, 1989).

Dede Wilson   P
2409 Knollwood Rd, Charlotte, NC 28211, 704-365-6846
   Pubs: *Glass* (Scots Plaid Pr, 1998), *Here's to the Land:
   Anth* (North Carolina Poetry Soc, 1992), *Southern Poetry
   Rev, Iowa Woman, Cream City Rev, Painted Bride Qtly,
   Hampden-Sydney Rev, Flyway, Carolina Qtly, Tar River
   Poetry Rev.*

Emily Herring Wilson   P
3381 Timberlake Ln, Winston-Salem, NC 27106,
910-759-2309
   Pubs: *Hope & Dignity* (Temple U Pr, 1983).

Lee Zacharias   W
Univ North Carolina, English Dept, Greensboro, NC 27412,
336-334-4695
Internet: zacharia@fagan.uncg.edu
   Pubs: *Lessons* (HM, 1981), *Helping Muriel Make It Through
   the Night* (LSU Pr, 1976), *Southern Qtly, New Virginia Rev,
   Southern California Anth, New Territory, Redbook, Kansas
   Qtly.*

NORTH DAKOTA

Carol Blair   P
1114 N 39th St Apt 5, Grand Forks, ND 582032805,
701-775-7795
   Pubs: *Nobody Gets Off the Bus* (Viet Nam Generation,
   1994), *The Color of Grief & Morning Glories* (Wolfe D. T.
   Pub, 1991), *The New Pr Literary Qtly.*

Madelyn Camrud   P
1215 Lincoln Dr, Grand Forks, ND 58201, 701-772-2828
   Pubs: *Prairie Volcano* (Dacotah Territory & St. Ives, 1995),
   This House Is Filled With Cracks (New Rivers Pr, 1994),
   North Dakota Qtly, Kalliope, Nebraska Rev.

Rita Johnson   P
PO Box 877, Stanley, ND 58784, 701-628-3397
   Pubs: *Plainswoman, Georgia Rev, Great River Rev,
   DeKalb Literary Arts Journal, Oxygen.*

David Martinson   P
North Dakota State Univ, Minard 322 F, University Sta, Fargo,
ND 58105
Internet: davimart@badlands.nodak.edu
   Pubs: *A Little Primer of Tom McGrath* (Shining Times,
   1998), *Hinges* (Aluminum Canoe, 1996), *Nation, Dacotah
   Territory, Pemmican, Minnesota Monthly, Floating Island,
   Another Chicago Mag.*

Jay Meek   P
Univ North Dakota, Box 7209, University Sta, Grand Forks,
ND 58202, 701-777-3321
   Pubs: *Headlands: New & Selected Poems, Windows*
   (Carnegie Mellon U Pr, 1997, 1994), *Beloit Poetry Jrnl,
   Crazyhorse, The Great River Rev, Ohio Rev, Prose Poem.*

Martha George Meek   P
Univ North Dakota, Box 8237, University Sta, Grand Forks,
ND 58202, 701-777-6391
   Pubs: *Rude Noises* (Dacotah Territory Pr, 1995), *Preludes:
   Anth* (Mount Holyoke College, 1973).

OHIO

Lee K. Abbott   W
4536 Carriage Hill Ln, Upper Arlington, OH 43220,
614-459-0197
Internet: abbott.4@postbox.acs.ohio-state.edu
   Pubs: *Living After Midnight, Dreams of Distant Lives*
   (Putnam, 1991, 1989), *Atlantic, Harper's, Georgia Rev,
   Kenyon Rev.*

Laura Albrecht   P
6217 Carmin Ave, Dayton, OH 45427-2058
   Pubs: *Skid* (WSU Production, 1994), *Poetry Gumball*
   (Voicebox Pubs, 1993), *CQ, Coe Rev, Maverick Pr, Ohio
   Poetry Rev, Steam Ticket, Work.*

Raman Nancy Ancrom   P
PO Box 1913, Cincinnati, OH 45201-1913, 513-621-0531
   Pubs: *Still News* (Raman Arts, 1997), *A Fair Straight Ahead*
   (Window Edtns, 1981), *Willow Springs, Oxalis, Worc,
   Smoke Signals, Downtown, Nation, Poetry Mag of the
   Lower East Side, Rolling Stone, Telephone, Evil Dog, Black
   River Rev.*

Julian Anderson   W
409 Brevoort Rd, Columbus, OH 43214
   Pubs: *Empire Under Glass* (Faber & Faber, 1996),
   *Southern Rev, Cleveland Plain Dealer, la fontana, The
   Journal.*

Maggie Anderson — P
Kent State Univ, English Dept, PO Box 5190, Kent, OH
44242, 330-672-2676
>Pubs: *A Space Filled with Moving, Cold Comfort* (U Pitt Pr,
>1992, 1986), *Years That Answer* (H&R, 1980), *Poetry East,
>APR.*

Tom Andrews — W
Ohio Univ, Athens, OH 45701-2979, 614-593-2756
>Pubs: *The Hemophiliac's Motorcycle* (U Iowa Pr, 1994),
>*The Brother's Country* (Persea Bks, 1990), *Poetry, Paris
>Rev, Kenyon Rev, Field, Virginia Qtly Rev.*

Nuala Archer — P
Cleveland State Univ, Cleveland, OH 44115
>Pubs: *Two Women, Two Shores* (w/Medbh McGuckian;
>New Poets Series, 1989), *Epoch, Poetry Australia.*

Rane Arroyo — P
1011 Ostrich Ln, Toledo, OH 43604, 419-530-2014
Internet: rrarroyo@aol.com
>Pubs: *Pale Ramon* (Zoland Bks, 1998), *The Singing Shark*
>(Bilingual Pr, 1996), *Death Cab For Cutie* (New Sins Pr,
>1991), *Nimrod, Kenyon Rev, Spoon River Qtly, Americas
>Rev, Ploughshares, Many Mountains Moving, ACM,
>Callaloo, Ohio Rev, Poems & Plays.*

Russell Atkins — P
6005 Grand Ave, Cleveland, OH 44104, 216-431-7116
>Pubs: *The Garden Thrives: Anth* (HarperCollins, 1996),
>*Voices of Cleveland: Anth* (Cleveland State U, 1996),
>*Beyond the Reef* (Houghton, 1991), *Letters to America:
>Anth* (Wayne State U Pr, 1995), *Scarecrow Poetry: Anth*
>(Ashland Poetry Pr, 1994), *Splitcity.*

David Baker — P
135 Granview Rd, Granville, OH 43023, 740-587-1269
Internet: baker@cc.denison.edu
>Pubs: *Truth About Small Towns, After the Reunion, Sweet
>Home, Saturday Night* (U of Arkansas Pr, 1998, 1994,
>1991), *Haunts* (Cleveland State U Pr, 1985), *Atlantic, New
>Yorker, Poetry, Nation, Yale Rev, Kenyon Rev.*

Panos D. Bardis — P&W
2533 Orkney Dr, Toledo, OH 43606
>Pubs: *A Cosmic Whirl of Melodies* (Literary Endeavor,
>1985), *Ivan and Artemis* (Pageant Pr, 1957), *Abira Digest,
>Poetry Project Four, Hellenic Times.*

Steven Bauer — P&W
Miami Univ, English Dept, Oxford, OH 45056, 765-732-3768
Internet: bauersa@casmail.muohio.edu
>Pubs: *Strange & Wonderful Tale of RBT McDoodle* (S&S,
>1999), *Daylight Savings* (Peregrine Smith, 1989), *My Poor
>Elephant: Anth* (Longstreet Pr, 1992), *Hopewell Rev,
>Missouri Rev, Indiana Rev, High Plains Literary Rev.*

Gail Bellamy — P
3422 E Scarborough Rd, Cleveland Heights, OH 44118
Internet: gbellamy@worldnet.att.net
>Pubs: *Detours: Poems of Travel* (Lonesome Traveler Pub,
>1997), *Cosmopolitan, Rolling Stone, Nit & Wit, Byline, New
>Mexico Humanities Rev.*

John M. Bennett — P
Luna Bisonte Productions, 137 Leland Ave, Columbus, OH
43214, 614-846-4126
>Pubs: *Prime Sway* (Texture Pr, 1996), *Fish, Man, Control,
>Room* (Semiquasi Pr, 1995), *Door Door: Anth* (Juxta/3300
>Pr, 1997), *Caliban, Central Park, The Quarterly, DOC*(K)S,
>*Texture, Generator.*

Paul Bennett — P&W
Denison Univ, Granville, OH 43023, 614-587-6688
>Pubs: *Max: The Tale of a Waggish Dog* (Mayhaven Pub,
>1998), *Appalachian Mettle* (Savage Pr, 1997), *Follow The
>River* (Orchard Books, 1987), *Building A House* (Limekiln
>Pr, 1986), *Agni, CSM, Delmar.*

S. W. Bliss — P
128 Tionda S, Vandalia, OH 45377, 513-898-8966
>Pubs: *Images, Nexus, Daring Poetry Qtly, Green Feather,
>Ohio Jrnl, Vincent Brothers Rev, Flights.*

Maureen Bloomfield — P
1555 Donaldson Pl, Cincinnati, OH 45223, 513-681-0037
>Pubs: *Ploughshares, Southern Rev, Cincinnati Poetry Rev,
>New Republic, Poetry, Shenandoah.*

Don Bogen — P
362 Terrace Ave, Cincinnati, OH 45220, 513-221-2699
Internet: donald.bogen@uc.edu
>Pubs: *The Known World, After the Splendid Display*
>(Wesleyan, 1997, 1986), *Nation, New Republic, Yale Rev,
>Paris Rev, Poetry, Partisan Rev.*

Phil Boiarski — P
839 Lakefield Dr, Galloway, OH 43119, 614-870-6623
Internet: pboiarsk@freenet.columbus.oh.us
>Pubs: *Cornered* (Logan Elm Pr, 1990), *Coal & Ice* (Yellow
>Pages Pr, 1980), *Paris Rev, California Qtly, Rocky Mtn
>Rev, Green House, Ohio Jrnl, Handbook.*

Imogene L. Bolls — P
Wittenberg Univ, Box 720, English Dept, Springfield, OH
45501, 513-390-2176
Internet: ibolls@wittenberg.edu
>Pubs: *Earthbound* (Bottom Dog, 1989), *Glass Walker*
>(Cleveland State U, 1983), *Antioch Rev, Georgia Rev, Ohio
>Rev, Southern Poetry Rev, South Dakota Rev, Texas Rev.*

Jennifer Bosveld P
Pudding Hse Writers Resource C, 60 N Main St, Johnstown,
OH 43031, 740-967-6060
Internet: htttp://www.puddinghouse.com
    Pubs: *Prayers to Protest: Poems That Center and Bless:
Anth, Unitarian Universalist Poets: Anth* (Pudding Hse Pub,
1998, 1996), *Coffeehouse Poetry Anth* (Bottom Dog Pr,
1996), *The Sun, Bottomfish, Heaven Bone, Chiron Rev,
Negative Capability.*

Daniel Bourne P
College of Wooster, English Dept, OH 44691, 216-263-2577
Internet: dbourne@acu.wooster.edu
    Pubs: *The Household Gods* (Cleveland State U Pr, 1994),
*APR, Shenandoah, Prairie Schooner, Field, Poetry
Northwest, Salmagundi.*

Philip Brady P
Youngstown State Univ, English Dept, Youngstown, OH
44555-3415, 216-742-1952
Internet: psbrady@cc.ysu.edu
    Pubs: *Forged Correspondences* (New Myths, 1996),
Plague Country (Mbira Pr, 1990), *College English, Poetry
Northwest, Massachusetts Rev, Honest Ulsterman,
Centennial Rev.*

David Breithaupt P&W
22900 Caves Rd, Gambier, OH 43022, 740-427-4170
Internet: breithau@kenyon.edu
    Pubs: *Exquisite Corpse, Kumquat Merinque, Beet, The
Krellullin, Rant.*

Michael J. Bugeja P&W
Ohio University, Athens, OH 45701, 614-593-2602
    Pubs: *Flight from Valhalla* (Livingston U Pr, 1993), *Platonic
Love* (Orchises Pr, 1991), *Poetry, Harper's, TriQuarterly,
Georgia Rev, Kenyon Rev.*

Grace Butcher P
PO Box 274, Chardon, OH 44024, 440-286-3840
Internet: hy151@cleveland.freenet.edu
    Pubs: *Child, House, World* (Hiram Poetry Rev, 1991),
Rumors of Ecstasy (Barnwood, 1981), *Before I Go Out On
The Road* (Cleveland State U Pr, 1979).

Catherine A. Callaghan PP&P
Ohio State Univ, 222 Oxley Hall, 1712 Neil Ave, Columbus,
OH 43210-1298, 614-292-5880
    Pubs: *The Poet's Job: To Go Too Far: Anth, I Name Myself
Daughter & It Is Good: Anth* (Sophia Bks, 1985, 1981),
Pudding Mag, Dragonfly.

Neil Carpathios P
376 49th St NW, Canton, OH 44709, 330-499-7768
    Pubs: *Our Mothers, Our Selves: Anth* (Bergin & Garvey,
1996), *I The Father* (Millennium Pr, 1993), *Southern Poetry
Rev, College English, Poet Lore, Poetry, Stone Country,
Kansas Qtly, Plainsong, Crab Creek Rev, The Journal,
Gryphon.*

Ellin Carter P
414 Arcadia Ave, Columbus, OH 43202, 614-267-8798
Internet: carter.3@osu.edu
    Pubs: *What This Is And Why* (Richmond Waters Pr, 1992),
*Kalliope, GW Rev, Earth's Daughters, Caprice, The Prose
Poem.*

Hale Chatfield P&W
Hiram College, Hiram, OH 44234, 216-569-5331
Internet: http://www.std.com/poetryworld
    Pubs: *Vox: New and Selected Poems, Episodes: A Novella,
North Star: A Novella, The Sotto Voce Massacres* (North
Star Pr, 1995, 1993, 1992, 1990).

David Citino P
Ohio State Univ, 164 W 17 Ave, Columbus, OH 43210,
614-292-4856
Internet: citino.1@osu.edu
    Pubs: *The Book of Appassionata: Collected Poems, The
Discipline: New and Selected Poems, 1980-1992* (Ohio
State U Pr, 1998, 1992), *Antioch Rev, Poetry, Kenyon Rev,
Yale Rev, Salmagundi, NER, Georgia Rev, Ohio Rev.*

Marian Clover P&W
611 Yaronia Dr S, Columbus, OH 43214, 614-267-9201
    Pubs: *NAR, Kansas Qtly, Essence, Review 76, Review 74.*

E. R. Cole P
274 E 214 St, Cleveland, OH 44123
    Pubs: *songpoems/poemsongs* (Weyburne, 1988), *Uneasy
Camber* (Greystone Pr, 1986), *Northland Qtly.*

D. Steven Conkle P
The Broken Stone, PO Box 246, Reynoldsburg, OH 43068,
614-866-4523
    Pubs: *All the Difference* (Bottom Dog Pr, 1989), *Samadhi*
(Willow Bee Pub, 1988), *Aura, Caesura.*

Joan C. Connor W
Ohio Univ, Ellis Hall, English Dept, Athens, OH 45701,
614-594-3059
Internet: connor@oak.cats.ohiou.edu
    Pubs: *Here on Old Route 7* (U Missouri Pr, 1997), *Tiller and
Pen: Anth* (Eighth Moon Pr, 1994), *Kenyon Rev,
TriQuarterly, Gettysburg Rev, Shenandoah, Southern Rev,
North American Rev, Manoa, North Dakota Qtly, Ohio Rev,
Chelsea, New Letters.*

David Craig P&W
690 Overlook Dr North, Wintersville, OH 43953,
740-282-6950
Internet: dcraig@franuniv.edu
    Pubs: *The Roof of Heaven* (Franciscan U Pr, 1998), *The
Cheese Stands Alone* (CMJ Pub, 1997), *Only One Face*
(White Eagle Coffee Store Pr, 1994), *The Odd Angles of
Heaven: Anth* (Harold Shaw Pubs, 1994), *The Heartlands
Today, Hiram Poetry Rev, Image.*

James Cummins   P
Univ Cincinnati, Elliston Poetry Collection, Cincinnati, OH
45221-0033, 513-556-1570
    Pubs: *Portrait in a Spoon* (U South Carolina Pr, 1997), *The
Whole Truth* (North Point, 1986), *Paris Rev, Ploughshares,
Shenandoah, New Republic.*

Kent H. Dixon   W
Wittenberg Univ, PO Box 720, Springfield, OH 45501,
937-327-7069
Internet: www.wittenberg.edu
    Pubs: *Kansas Qtly/Arkansas Rev, Grand Tour, Gettysburg
Rev, Georgia Rev, TriQuarterly, Shenandoah, Iowa Rev,
American Prospect, Libido.*

Wayne Dodd   P
Ohio Univ, 209-C Ellis Hall, English Dept, Athens, OH 45701,
614-593-1900
    Pubs: *Of Desire & Disorder* (Carnegie Mellon U Pr, 1994),
Toward the End of the Century (U Iowa, 1992), *Gettysburg
Rev, Iowa Rev, Antioch, Georgia Rev.*

John Dolis   P
7380 Whispering Way, Cincinnati, OH 45241-1252
    Pubs: *Bl( )nk Space* (Runaway Spoon Pr, 1993).

Cyril A. Dostal   P
3283 Dellwood Rd, Cleveland, OH 44118, 216-752-3008
    Pubs: *Emergency Exit* (Cleveland State U Pr, 1977), *Beloit
Poetry Journal, Gamut Mag.*

John Drury   P
129 Detzel Pl, Cincinnati, OH 45219, 513-281-5930
Internet: druryjp@ucenglish.mcm.uc.edu
    Pubs: *The Stray Ghost* (State Street, 1987), *Paris Rev,
New Republic, Western Humanities Rev, APR, Southern
Rev, Poetry Northwest.*

Pam Durban   W
Ohio Univ, Ellis Hall, Athens, OH 45701, 614-594-6442
    Pubs: *All Set About With Fever Trees* (Godine, 1985),
Georgia Rev, The Reaper, TriQuarterly.

Dennis S. Edwards   P
7410 Avon Dr, Mentor, OH 44060, 216-953-1167
    Pubs: *Parnassus, Green Feather, Rag Mag, Manna,
Ripples, Hob-Nob, Calliope's Corner, Gryphon.*

Leatrice Joy W. Emeruwa   P
PO Box 21755, Cleveland, OH 44121, 216-381-3027
Internet: lemeruwa@aol.com
    Pubs: *A Jazzzzzzz Poem* (Burning Pr, 1997), *The
Thousand-Year-Old Woman and Other Poems* (Sharaqua
Pr, 1990), *Voices of Cleveland: Anth* (Cleveland State U Pr,
1996).

Angie Estes   P
242 N Liberty St, Delaware, OH 43015, 614-292-0270
Internet: aestes@calpoly.edu
    Pubs: *The Uses of Passion* (Peregrine Smith Bks, 1995),
Boarding Pass (Solo Pr, 1990), *Agni, Journal, Verse,
Antioch Rev, Literary Rev, Chariton Rev.*

Kathy Fagan   P
English Dept Ohio State Univ, 164 West 17th Ave, Columbus,
OH 43210, 614-292-0270
Internet: fagan.3@osu.edu
    Pubs: *The Raft* (Dutton, 1985), *Under 35: Anth* (Anchor,
Doubleday, 1989), *Paris Rev, Missouri Rev, Ploughshares,
Shenandoah, New Republic, Kenyon Rev.*

Laurence S. Fallis   P&W
730 Woodgate, #203, Ravenna, OH 44266, 216-296-3765
    Pubs: *Arizona Qtly, Woodrider, Texas Qtly, Blue Cloud
Qtly, Orion, Middle Way, Invisible City.*

Ross Feld   P&W
6934 Miami Ave Room 23, Cincinnati, OH 45243,
513-271-3405
Internet: rfrites@sprintmail.com
    Pubs: *Shapes Mistaken, Only Shorter* (North Point, 1989,
1982), *Harper's, Parnassus.*

B. Felton   P&W
17102 Ridgeton Dr, Cleveland, OH 44128, 216-991-9245
    Pubs: *Conclusions* (B. Felton, 1971).

Barbara Fialkowski   P
Bowling Green State Univ, Hannah Hall, Bowling Green, OH
43403, 419-372-8370
    Pubs: *Framing* (Croissant Pr, 1978), *New Virginia Rev,
NAR, Abraxas, Poetry Now.*

Annie Finch   P
PO Box 19519, Cincinnati, OH 45219-0519, 319-273-2822
    Pubs: *The Ghost of Meter* (U Michigan Pr, 1994), *A Formal
Feeling Comes: Anth* (Story Line Pr, 1993), *Outposts,
South Dakota Rev, Poets On, The Formalist, Sparrow.*

Norman M. Finkelstein   P
Xavier Univ, English Dept, 3800 Victory Pkwy, Cincinnati, OH
45207-4446, 513-745-2041
Internet: finkelst@xavier.xu.edu
    Pubs: *The Ritual of New Creation* (SUNY Pr, 1992),
Restless Messengers (U Georgia Pr, 1992), *Denver Qtly,
Salmagundi, Peqoud, Hambone, Talisman.*

Robert Flanagan   P&W
181 N Liberty St, Delaware, OH 43015, 740-369-4820
Internet: rjflanag@cc.owu.edu
    Pubs: *Loving Power* (Bottom Dog, 1990), *Norton Book of
American Short Stories: Anth* (Norton, 1988), *Illinois Qtly,
Chicago, Fiction, Kansas Qtly, Northwest Rev, Ohio Rev.*

Deborah Fleming   P
2525 CR 775, Perrysville, OH 44864, 419-938-7305
Internet: dfleming@ashland.edu
> Pubs: *Learning the Trade* (Locust Hill, 1992), *Hiram Poetry Rev, Pennsylvania Rev, Green River Rev, The Journal, Crosscurrents, Sucarnochee Rev, Organization and Environment, Pike Creek Rev, Ibis*.

Robert R. Fox   P&W
Ohio Arts Council, 727 E Main St, Columbus, OH 43205-1796, 614-466-2613
Internet: bfox@mail.oac.ohio.gov
> Pubs: *Crossing the Barrier: Anth* (Oxford, 1995), *Thinking on Paper: Anth* (HB, 1995), *NAR, Massachusetts Rev, 5 a.m.*.

Christopher Franke   P
1456 W 54 St, Cleveland, OH 44102, 216-651-7725
Internet: frankepoet@hotmail.com
> Pubs: *Paren's Thesis* (Burning Pr, 1997), *frankeana/miscellangy* (deciduous/worded print, 1996), *= 5* (Wm. Busta Gallery, 1994), *Artcrimes, SplitCity, Listening Eye, Coffeehouse Poetry Anth*.

Stuart Friebert   P
172 Elm, Oberlin, OH 44074, 216-774-2302
> Pubs: *Funeral Pie* (Four Way Bks, 1996), *The Darmstadt Orchids* (BkMk Pr, 1993), *Paris Rev, The Quarterly, Iowa Rev, Paterson Rev*.

Diane Furtney   P
297 E Deshler, Columbus, OH 432062710, 614-444-1812
> Pubs: *Murder At the MLA* (as D.J.H. Jones; U Georgia Pr, 1993), *Destination Rooms* (Riverstone Pr, 1980), *Kenyon Rev, Neovictorian, Chariton Rev, Iowa Rev*.

Zona Gale   P
3877 Indian Rd, Toledo, OH 43606
> Pubs: *Her Soul Beneath the Bone* (U Illinois Pr, 1988), *Spirits and Seasons* (Heatherdown Pr, 1982).

David Lee Garrison   P
Wright State Univ, Dayton, OH 45435, 937-293-8699
Internet: dgarrison@desire.wright.edu
> Pubs: *Inside the Sound of Rain* (Vincent Brothers Co, 1997), *Blue Oboe* (Wyndham Hall Pr, 1984), *Pegasus, Wind, Poetpourri, Whiskey Island Mag, Kansas Qtly, Orphic Lute, Bitterroot, Comstock Rev, Denver Qtly, Laurel Rev, Plains Poetry Jrnl, Vincent Brothers*.

John Gerlach   P
140 Meadowhill Ln, Moreland Hills, OH 44022, 216-831-1479
> Pubs: *NAR, Ohio Rev, Prairie Schooner*.

Elton Glaser   P
Univ Akron, English Dept, Akron, OH 443251906, 330-972-5342
> Pubs: *Color Photographs of the Ruins* (U Pitt Pr, 1992), *Tropical Depressions* (U Iowa Pr, 1988), *Georgia Rev, Parnassus, Poetry Northwest, Poetry*.

William Greenway   P
Youngstown State Univ, Youngstown, OH 44555, 216-742-3415
Internet: whgreenway@msn.com
> Pubs: *Simmer Dim, How the Dead Bury the Dead* (U Akron, 1999, 1994), *Father Dreams* (State Street Pr, 1994), *Where We've Been* (Breitenbush Bks, 1987), *Poetry, APR, Southern Rev, Poetry Northwest, Prairie Schooner, Shenandoah*.

Gordon Grigsby   P
625 Edgecliff Dr, Columbus, OH 43235, 614-847-1780
> Pubs: *Mid-Ohio Elegies* (Logan Elm Pr, 1985), *West Coast Rev, Southern Poetry Rev, Mickle Street Rev*.

Martin Grossman   P
289 W New England Ave, Worthington, OH 43085, 614-888-9975
> Pubs: *Seeing Double* (BkMk Pr, 1981), *The Arable Mind* (Blue Mountain Pr, 1977), *APR, Poetry Now*.

Jeff Gundy   P
Bluffton College, English Dept, Bluffton, OH 45817-1196, 419-358-3283
Internet: gundyj@bluffton.edu
> Pubs: *A Community of Memory* (U Illinois Pr, 1996), *Flatlands* (Cleveland State U Pr, 1995), *Antioch Rev, Georgia Rev, Crazyhorse, Exquisite Corpse, Laurel Rev*.

Mark Halliday   P
Ohio Univ, Athens, OH 45701, 614-593-2758
> Pubs: *Tasker Street* (U Massachusetts Pr, 1992), *Little Star* (Morrow, 1987).

Yvonne Moore Hardenbrook   P
1757 Willow Way Cir N, Columbus, OH 43220, 412-733-8623
> Pubs: *Out Of Season: Anth* (Amagansett Pr, 1993), *A Gathering of Poets: Anth* (Kent State U Pr, 1992), *Amelia, Brussels Sprout, Frogpond, Modern Haiku*.

Donald M. Hassler   P
1226 Woodhill Dr, Kent, OH 44240, 330-673-9164
Internet: dhassler@kentvm.kent.edu
> Pubs: *Comic Tones in Science Fiction* (Greenwood, 1982), *A Gathering of Poets: Anth* (Kent State U Pr, 1992), *Hellas, Tar River Poetry, Onionhead, Above the Bridge, Hiram Poetry Rev, Descant*.

Laurie Henry   P
129 Detzel Pl, Cincinnati, OH 45219, 513-281-5938
> Pubs: *Restoring the Chateau of the Marquis de Sade* (Silverfish Rev Pr, 1985), *APR, Poetry Northwest*.

Michelle Herman W
English Dept, Ohio State Univ, 164 West 17 Ave, Columbus,
OH 43210, 614-292-5767
Internet: herman.2@osu.edu
Pubs: *A New and Glorious Life* (Carnegie Mellon U Pr,
1998), *Missing* (Ohio State U, 1990), *Twenty Under Thirty:
Anth* (Scribner, 1986).

Terry Hermsen P
83 University St, Westerville, OH 43081
Pubs: *Child Aloft in Ohio Theatre, 36 Spokes: The Bicycle
Poems* (Bottom Dog Pr, 1995, 1985), *Images, Kansas Qtly,
The Plough, The Journal, Nimrod, Antigonish, Confluence,
Outerbridge, Hiram Poetry Rev, South Dakota Rev,
Descant.*

Garrison L. Hilliard P&W
PO Box 25102, Cincinnati, OH 45225, 513-251-3747
Internet: http: //www.efn.org/ garrison
Pubs: *This Is A Romance* (?) (QCB Pr, 1994), *Minotaur,
Aim, Leatherneck, Small Pond, Innisfree.*

Margaret Honton P
191 W Rosslyn Ave, Columbus, OH 43214
Pubs: *The Visionary Mirror, I Name Myself Daughter*
(Sophia Bks, 1983, 1982), *Hyperion, Pudding.*

Andrew Hudgins P
Univ Cincinnati, 248-249 McMicken Hall (ML 69), Cincinnati,
OH 45221, 513-556-5924
Pubs: *The Glass Hammer: A Southern Childhood, The
Never-Ending* (HM, 1994, 1991).

Bonnie Jacobson P
24395 Shaker Blvd, Cleveland, OH 44122, 216-831-1916
Pubs: *In Joanna's House* (Cleveland State U Poetry
Center, 1998), *Stopping For Time* (GreenTower Pr, 1989),
*Laurel Rev, Negative Capability, Prairie Schooner,
Gettysburg Rev, Iowa Rev, Tar River Poetry.*

jinni jovel PP&P
Creative Freelance Channel, Box #913, Worthington, OH
430850913, 614-218-4976
Pubs: *The Prophecy of Jinni Jovel* (Jovel, 1995), *Galley Sail
Rev.*

Jack R. Justice P
9023 Shadetree Dr, Cincinnati, OH 45242, 513-793-1969
Pubs: *Blue Unicorn, Sou'wester, Hampden-Sydney,
Kentucky Poetry Rev, Stone Country, Wind, Samisdat.*

Bella Briansky Kalter W
5 Lenox Ln, Cincinnati, OH 45229, 513-861-5304
Pubs: *Ohio's Heritage, American Israelite, U Kansas City
Rev, St. Anthony Messenger, Backbone.*

Daniel Kaminsky P
7116 Deveny Ave, Cleveland, OH 44105, 216-883-3683
Pubs: *Snout to Snout, Voices of Cleveland: Anth*
(Cleveland State U Pr, 1974, 1996), *Pig Iron.*

J. Patrick Kelly P
7336 Blue Boar Ct, Cincinnati, OH 45230, 513-232-8962
Pubs: *Touchstone, Son of Fat Tuesday, Ellipsis, Sierra
Nevada Rev, Voices Intl, Bellowing Ark, Licking River Rev,
Ascent, Mississippi Valley Rev, Louisville Rev.*

Diane Kendig P
235 Lexington Ave, Findlay, OH 45840-3709, 419-424-5965
Internet: kendig@lucy.findlay.edu
Pubs: *A Pencil to Write Your Name* (Bottom Dog, 1986),
Tunnel of Flute Song (Cleveland State U, 1980), *Minnesota
Rev, Cincinnati Poetry Rev, Kalliope.*

Laura Ballard Kennelly P
PO Box 626, Berea, OH 44017, 216-243-4842
Pubs: *A Certain Attitude, A Measured Response* (Pecan
Grove Pr, 1995, 1993), *Passage of Mrs. Jung* (Norton
Coker Pr, 1990), *Redneck Rev, New Texas '92, La Carta
De Oliver, San Jose Studies, Faultline, Ohio Writer.*

Harley King P
875 Maple St, Perrysburg, OH 43551, 419-874-6885
Internet: hgking@aol.com
Pubs: *Mother Don't Lock Me in that Closet* (Keller U Pr,
1989), *Empty Playground* (K&K Communications, 1980).

Robert Kinsley P
6 Old Peach Ridge Rd, Athens, OH 45701-1342
Pubs: *Field Stones, Endangered Species* (Orchises Pr,
1997, 1989), *Yankee Mag, Tar River Poetry.*

Leonard Kress P
306 E Boundary, Perrysburg, OH 43551, 419-872-0398
Internet: lkress@owens.cc.oh.us
Pubs: *The Centralia Mine Fire* (Flume, 1987), *From the Life
and Death of Chopin* (Lalka, 1976), *APR, Missouri Rev,
New Letters, Massachusetts Rev, Commonweal.*

Lolette Beth Kuby P
Cleveland State Univ, E 22nd and Euclid Ave, Cleveland, OH
44115, 216-932-4842
Pubs: *The Mama Stories* (Bottom Dog Pr, 1995), *In
Enormous Water* (Cleveland State U Pr, 1981), *Midwest
Qtly, American Scholar, Proteus, Caesura, Nightsun, The
Long Story.*

Wayne Kvam P
Kent State Univ, English Dept, Kent, OH 44242,
216-672-2676
Pubs: *Centennial Rev, Exile: A Literary Qtly.*

Denise Reynolds Laubacher P
422 East St, Minerva, OH 44657, 216-868-3808
> Pubs: *Collective Works 1983-1987, Incognito* (Adams, 1987, 1985), *Whiskey Island, Touchstone.*

Edward Lense P
2887 Neil Ave, #421-A, Columbus, OH 43202, 614-262-9782
Internet: elense@compuserve.com
> Pubs: *Buried Voices* (Logan Elm Pr, 1982), *The Spirit That Moves Us, Greenfield Rev, Antioch Rev, Cimarron Rev, AWP Chronicle.*

Kenneth Leonhardt P&W
321 Glen Oaks Dr, Cincinnati, OH 45238
Internet: mteacher@skycorp.net
> Pubs: *Goners* (University Edtns, 1996), *Sex Scells* (Fithian Pr, 1994), *Light, Bogg, Iconoclast, Abbey, Lilliput Rev, Higginsville Reader.*

Joel A. Lipman P
Univ Toledo, Toledo, OH 43606-3390, 419-841-3733
> Pubs: *The Real Ideal* (Luna Bisonte, 1996), *Machete Chemistry/Panades Physics* (Cubola New Art, 1994), *Fiction Intl, Generator, Exquisite Corpse.*

Ernest Lockridge W
143 W South St, Worthington, OH 43085, 614-885-8964
> Pubs: *Flying Elbows, Prince Elmo's Fire* (Stein & Day, 1975, 1974), *New Journal, Ohio Journal.*

Sandra Love W
898 East Hyde Rd, Yellow Springs, OH 453872700, 513-767-2700
> Pubs: *Dive for the Sun* (HM, 1982), *Life On the Line: Anth* (Negative Capability Pr, 1992), *Iowa Woman, South Dakota Rev, Kansas Qtly.*

R. Nikolas Macioci P
1506 Frebis Ave, Columbus, OH 43206
> Pubs: *Why Dance?, Implications of Light* (Singular Speech Pr, 1997, 1996), *Cafes of Childhood* (Event Horizon Pr, 1992), *Mississippi Valley Rev, Zone 3, Tampa Rev, Appalachee Qtly, Green Hills Literary Lantern, Crazyquilt, Fox Cry Rev.*

James Magner, Jr. P
John Carroll Univ, English Dept, Cleveland, OH 44118, 216-397-4221
> Pubs: *Rose of My Flowering Night, Till No Light Leaps* (Golden Quill Pr, 1985, 1981), *America.*

Doug Martin P
Bowling Green State Univ, Bowling Green, OH 43403, 419-352-2822
> Pubs: *RE:AL, James White Rev, Riverrun, B City, Wormwood, Soundings: A Jrnl of the Living Arts, Malcontent, Eidos.*

Herbert Woodward Martin P
Univ of Dayton, 300 College Park Dr #707, Dayton, OH 45469, 513-229-3439
> Pubs: *A Rock Against the Wind* (Berkley Pub Group, 1996), *Grand Street, Ploughshares, Chaminade Rev, Poetry, Crone's Nest.*

Jack Matthews W
Ohio University, English Dept, Athens, OH 45701, 614-593-2757
> Pubs: *Ghostly Populations, Booking in the Heartland* (Johns Hopkins, 1986, 1986), *Kenyon Rev.*

Wendell Mayo W
Bowling Green State Univ, Bowling Green, OH 43402, 419-372-7399
Internet: wmayo@bgnet.bgsu.edu
> Pubs: *In Lithuanian Wood, Centaur of the North* (Arte Publico Pr, 1998, 1996), *Yale Rev, Missouri Rev, Prairie Schooner, Indiana Rev, High Plains Literary Rev, New Letters, Harvard Rev, Manoa, Literary Rev.*

Howard McCord P&W
15431 Sand Ridge Rd, Bowling Green, OH 43402, 419-352-5549
Internet: mccord@bgnet.bgsu.edu
> Pubs: *The Wisdom of Silenus* (St. Andrews Pr, 1996), *The Man Who Walked to the Moon* (McPherson & Co., 1990), *Exquisite Corpse, Die Young.*

Robert E. McDonough P
3639 Harvey Rd, Cleveland Heights, OH 44118
Internet: robert.mcdonough@trl-c.cc.oh.us
> Pubs: *No Other World* (Cleveland State U, 1988), *Mississippi Valley Rev, Windless Orchard, Cornfield Rev, West Branch.*

Robert McGovern P
RD 6, 935 County Rd 1754, Ashland, OH 44805, 419-289-0499
Internet: rgovern@ashland.edu
> Pubs: *Scarecrow Poetry—The Muse In Post-Middle Age, A Feast Of Flesh & Other Occasions* (Ashland Poetry Pr, 1994, 1971), *Nation, Kansas Qtly, Hiram Poetry Rev, New Laurel Rev, Hollins Critic, Christian Century, Blue Unicorn.*

Erin McGraw W
Univ Cincinnati, Cincinnati, OH 45221-0069, 513-556-1186
> Pubs: *Lies of the Saints* (Chronicle Bks, 1996), *Bodies at Sea* (U Illinois Pr, 1989), *Georgia Rev, Southern Rev, Ascent, Kenyon Rev, Atlantic Monthly.*

Joseph McLaughlin P&W
433 Fair Ave NE, New Philadelphia, OH 44663, 330-343-1602
> Pubs: *Memory, In Your Country, Zen In the Art of Golf* (Pale Horse Pr, 1995, 1991), *Southern Poetry Rev, Hiram Poetry Rev.*

William McLaughlin P
20865 Chagrin Blvd, #1, Cleveland, OH 44122, 216-752-8330
Pubs: *At Rest In the Midwest* (Cleveland State U Pr, 1982), *Amherst Rev, Black Fly Rev, Cape Rock, Oxford Mag, Inlet, Nebo, Kansas Qtly.*

William McMillen P
824 Oak Knoll Dr, Perrysburg, OH 43551, 419-874-1596
Pubs: *NAR, Prairie Schooner, Black Warrior Rev, Ohio Jrnl.*

Roberta Mendel P
The Pin Prick Press, 2664 S Green Rd, Shaker Heights, OH 44122, 216-932-2173
Pubs: *Travels Through Time: Anth* (Creative With Words Pub, 1998), *Laureate Letter, Writer's Ink, Mandrake, Etcetera, The Blind Man's Rainbow, Writer's Cramp.*

Larry Michaels P
548 Robindale Ave, Toledo, OH 43616, 419-697-5550
Pubs: *Poetry Today, Prophetic Voices, Aileron, Piedmont Literary Rev, Wind, Orphic Lute, Lyric.*

John N. Miller P
Denison Univ, English Dept, Granville, OH 43023, 740-587-4432
Pubs: *In the Western World* (Spoon River Poetry, 1979), *Articles of War: Anth* (U Arkansas Pr, 1990), *Passages North, Hawaii Rev, Tar River Poetry, Birmingham Rev, Chariton Rev, American Poetry Monthly.*

Lloyd L. Mills P
Kent State Univ, Kent, OH 44242, 330-673-6826
Internet: lmills@kent.edu
Pubs: *Unreconciled Passions, Dry With A Twist: Anth* (Poets League of Greater Cleveland, 1993, 1997), *Laughter and Dry Mockery* (Commercial Pr, 1988), *Sics, New Laurel Rev, Louisiana Rev, Blue Unicorn.*

Judith Moffett W
6908 Thorndike Rd, Cincinnati, OH 45227, 513-271-9349
Internet: eirving@compuserve.com
Pubs: *Homestead Year* (Lyons & Burford, 1995), *Time, Like An Ever-Rolling Stream, The Ragged World* (St. Martin's Pr, 1992, 1991), *Pennterra* (Congdon & Weed, 1987), *Kenyon Rev, New Yorker, Poetry, Asimov's Science Fiction, Georgia Rev.*

Richard Morgan P
Ohio Dominican College, English Dept, 1216 Sunbury Rd, Columbus, OH 43219, 614-846-0917
Pubs: *Love & Anger* (ARN, 1982), *Tiger in the Air* (Blue Dog, 1979), *West Coast Rev, Rocky Mountain Rev.*

Scott H. Mulrane P
26 E 2nd Ave, #20, Columbus, OH 43201-6500
Pubs: *Cincinnati Poetry Rev, Oxford Mag, Cream City Rev, Sequoia, Galley Sail, Mudfish.*

George Myers, Jr. W
The Columbus Dispatch, 34 S 3rd St, Columbus, OH 43215, 614-461-5265
Pubs: *Jump Hope* (Cumberland, 1992), *Worlds Without End* (Another Chicago Pr, 1990), *The Literary Rev, Seattle Rev, Ploughshares, The Quarterly, Gargoyle, NAW.*

Alan Napier P
3799 Olmsby Dr, Brimfield, OH 44240, 330-678-1686
Internet: sherlockarts@icgroup.net
Pubs: *Atomic Ghost* (Coffee Hse Pr, 1995), *Fathers: A Collection of Poems: Anth* (St. Martin's Pr, 1997), *Hiram Poetry Rev, SPR, Negative Capability, Colorado Rev, Key West Rev, Chelsea.*

James R. Nichols W
Muskingum College, English Dept, New Concord, OH 43762, 614-826-8265
Pubs: *Afterwords* (International U Pr, 1987), *Children of the Sea* (Blair, 1977), *Phoebe, Bitterroot, Encore.*

Bea Opengart P
1511 Chase Ave, Apt A, Cincinnati, OH 45223, 513-681-0729
Pubs: *Erotica* (Owl Creek Pr, 1995), *American Voice, Iowa Rev, Apalachee Qtly, Journal, Shenandoah, Southern Humanities Rev.*

Gary Bernard Pacernick P
Wright State Univ, Dayton, OH 45435, 513-873-3136
Pubs: *The Jewish Poems* (Wright State U Pr, 1985), *Wanderers* (Prasada Pr, 1985), *Poetry East, APR, Ohio Rev, Tikkun, North American Rev, Poetry Now.*

Frankie Paino P
4196 W 212th St, Fairview Park, OH 44126
Pubs: *The Rapture of Matter* (Cleveland State U, 1991), *New American Poets of the 90's: Anth* (Godine, 1991), *Gettysburg Rev, American Voice, Antioch Rev.*

Janis L. Pallister P
1249 Brownwood Dr, Bowling Green, OH 43402-3535, 419-353-9513
Pubs: *Shadows of Madness, At the Eighth Station, Sursum Corda* (Geryon, 1991, 1983, 1982), *Practices of the Wind: Anth* (Nicolas Kogon, 1997).

James Parlett P
6878 Solon Blvd, Solon, OH 44139
Pubs: *News Of The Assassin* (Raincrow, 1978), *Atlantic, Poetry Northwest, Cape Rock, En Passant.*

Nancy Pelletier W
624 5th St, Marietta, OH 45750-1910
Pubs: *Happy Families* (Collins, 1986), *The Rearrangement* (Paperback-Paperbooks, 1986), *Twigs.*

Jane Piirto P&W
233 W Walnut St, Ashland, OH 44805, 419-281-6516
Internet: jpiirto@ashland.edu
Pubs: *A Location in the Upper Peninsula* (Sampo Pub, 1994), *The Three-Week Trance Diet* (Carpenter Pr, 1986), *South Dakota Rev, Denver Qtly*.

Frank Polite P
2537 Ohio Ave, Youngstown, OH 44504, 216-746-3955
Pubs: *Flamingo* (Pangborn Bks, 1990), *Letters of Transit* (City Miner, 1979), *Harper's, Nation, Free Lunch, New Yorker, Exquisite Corpse, Ohio Rev*.

Lynn Powell P
171 E College St, Oberlin, OH 44074, 440-775-2276
Internet: lynn@physics.oberlin.edu
Pubs: *Old & New Testaments* (U Wisconsin Pr, 1995), *DoubleTake, Seneca Rev, Poetry, Gettysburg Rev, Paris Rev*.

Robert Pringle P
11210 Gorsuch Rd, Galena, OH 43021, 614-965-4158
Pubs: *Cold Front* (Pudding Hse Pr, 1998), *Orbis, Psychopoetica, Pegasus Rev, Pudding Mag, Onionhead, Dream Intl Qtly, Poetry Motel, Envoi, Green's Mag, Paris/Atlantic, Vol. No.*.

James S. Proffitt P
7816 Foxtrot Dr, North Bend, OH 45052, 513-941-0835
Pubs: *Echoes Mag, Blue Ink Pr, Main Street Rag, New Lifestyles, Bylines, Rockford Rev, The Oval, Ambergris*.

Rose Mary Prosen P
2300 Overlook Rd, #506, Cleveland Heights, OH 44106, 216-791-6145
Pubs: *Ethnic Literature and Culture in The U.S.A.: Anth* (Peter Lang, 1996), *Voices of Cleveland: Anth* (Cleveland State U, 1996), *Whiskey Island, Dry With A Twist, Writing Our Lives*.

Nicholas Ranson P
Univ Akron, Akron, OH 44325-1906, 330-972-7606
Internet: nickrans@uakron.edu
Pubs: *Track Made Good* (Bits Pr, 1977), *Mississippi Rev, Lake Superior Rev, Wind*.

James Reiss P
Miami Univ, Bachelor Hall, Oxford, OH 45056, 513-529-5110
Pubs: *The Parable of Fire* (Carnegie Mellon, 1996), *The Breathers* (Ecco Pr, 1974), *Atlantic, New Yorker, Poetry, Nation, New Republic, Paris Rev*.

Don Rice W
5610 Blue Lagoon Ln, Hilliard, OH 43026-9033
Pubs: *Fishes, Reptiles & Amphibians* (Van Nostrand, 1981), *Providence Rev, Taedium*.

Doug Rice W
1428 Cleveland St, Salem, OH 44460, 330-332-3657
Internet: rice@salem.kent.edu
Pubs: *Blood of Mugwump* (Black Ice Bks, 1996), *Avant-Pop: Anth* (Illinois State U, 1993), *collages & bricolages, 2 Girls Rev, Black Ice Mag, Spitting Image, Fiction Intl, New Novel Rev*.

Peter Roberts P
1205 Laurelwood Rd, Mansfield, OH 44907, 419-756-1460
Internet: peterroberts@compuserve.com
Pubs: *William and Mary Rev, Small Pond, Star*Line, New York Qtly, Confrontation, Beyond Baroque, Abbey, Frisson*.

Linda Goodman Robiner P&W
2648 S Belvoir Blvd, Cleveland, OH 441184661, 216-397-9473
Internet: lgrobiner@aol.com
Pubs: *Reverse Fairy Tale* (Pudding Hse Pub, 1997), *North Atlantic Rev, Graham House Rev, Whiskey Island Mag, Black River Rev, Flights, Fine Lines, William & Mary Rev, CQ, Neovictorian*.

Bill Roorbach P
Ohio State Univ, 164 W 17 Ave, Columbus, OH 43215, 614-292-0648
Internet: roorbach.1@osu.edu
Pubs: *Writing Life Stories* (Story Pr, 1998), *Turning Toward Home* (Franklin Square Pr, 1993), *Summers with Juliet* (HM, 1992), *Harper's, New York Times Mag, Granta, Iowa Rev, Witness, New York Newsday*.

Lynne Rose P
3911 Tamara Dr, Grove City, OH 43123-2832, 614-871-5840
Pubs: *Child Of The Washed World* (American Studies Pr, 1984), *Kingdom Of Three* (Green River, 1980).

J. Allyn Rosser P
12750 Rich Ln, Athens, OH 45701-9011
Pubs: *Bright Moves* (Northeastern U Pr, 1990), *Poetry, Paris Rev, Hudson Rev, Georgia Rev, Denver Qtly, Ontario Rev, Crazyhorse, Gettysburg Rev*.

Carol Rubenstein P
Ohio Univ Press, Scott Quadrangle 220, Athens, OH 45701
Pubs: *The Honey Tree Song: Poems & Chants of Sarawak Dayaks* (Ohio U Pr, 1985), *Ms.*.

Joel Rudinger P
6039 Zenobia Rd, Wakeman, OH 44889, 419-929-8767
Pubs: *Lovers & Celebrations* (Dearborn Pr, 1984), *First Edition: 40 Poems* (Gull Pr, 1975).

Timothy Russell W
202 Daniels St, Toronto, OH 43964, 614-537-3467
Pubs: *Adversaria* (TriQuarterly Bks/Northwestern U Pr, 1993), *Artful Dodge, Cincinnati Poetry Rev, Hiram Poetry Rev, Kestrel, Poetry, West Branch*.

David Schloss P
358 Bryant Ave, #1, Cincinnati, OH 45220, 513-281-3551
Pubs: *Legends* (Windmill Pr, 1976), *The Beloved* (Ashland Poetry Pr, 1973), *Poetry, Paris Rev, Western Humanities Rev, Iowa Rev, Antaeus.*

Amy Jo Schoonover P
3520 State Rte 56, Mechanicsburg, OH 43044, 937-834-2666
Pubs: *New & Used Poems* (Lake Shore Pub, 1988), *Kansas Qtly, Hiram Poetry Rev, U Portland Rev, Cape Rock, Negative Capability, Western Ohio Jrnl, Lyric, Pivot.*

Pearl Bloch Segall P
425 Hunters Hollow SE, Warren, OH 44484, 330-856-5565
Pubs: *Cradles, Nests & Other Backward Glances* (Poetic Page, 1992), *Mind Travel* (Telstar Pub, 1991), *Amelia, Poetic Page, Poetpourri, Pinehurst Jrnl.*

Marilyn Weymouth Seguin W
1830 Highbridge Rd, Cuyahoga Falls, OH 44223, 330-928-6907
Internet: mseguin@kent.edu
Pubs: *Silver Ribbon Skinny, The Bell Keeper, Song of Courage, Song of Freedom* (Branden Bks, 1996, 1995, 1993).

Tim Shay W
7227 Scottwood Ave, Cincinnati, OH 45237
Pubs: *Prolific Writer, Fiction, Valley Views, Live Writers, Fiction Cincinnati.*

Glenn Sheldon P
1011 Ostrich Ln, Toledo, OH 43604, 419-824-2298
Internet: gsheldon@aol.com
Pubs: *Eagle or Beak* (Jeffron Pub, 1995), *Wolves in Brown Wedding Gowns* (New Sins Pr, 1991), *Puerto del Sol, Rio Grande Rev, Mudfish, Marquee, Spoon River Qtly, Limestone.*

Eve Shelnutt P&W
Ohio Univ, English Dept, Ellis Hall, Athens, OH 45701, 614-593-2756
Pubs: *First a Long Hesitation, Recital in a Private Room* (Carnegie Mellon, 1992, 1988), *The Writing Room* (Longstreet Pr, 1989).

David Shevin P
142 1/2 N Washington St, Tiffin, OH 44883, 419-447-2911
Internet: 102264.3143@compuserve.com
Pubs: *Needles and Needs* (Bottom Dog, 1994), *Growl & Other Poems: Anth* (Carpenter Pr, 1990), *Confluence, The Crisis, Exquisite Corpse, Tikkun, Descant, The Journal.*

Kay Sloan P&W
Miami Univ, Oxford, OH 45056, 513-529-2227
Pubs: *Worry Beads* (Louisiana State U Pr, 1991), *Southern Exposure, Oxford Mag, Southern Rev, Pudding.*

Michael Smetzer P&W
520 S Main St, Side Apt, Bowling Green, OH 43402-3822, 419-353-3316
Pubs: *Teaching the Clergy to Dance* (Manic Monkey Bks, 1996), *A Quiet Man* (Baggeboda Pr, 1988), *Cottonwood, New Letters, Poetry Motel, Kansas Qtly.*

Francis J. Smith P
John Carroll Univ, 20700 N Park Blvd, Rodman Hall, University Heights, OH 44118, 216-397-4546
Pubs: *All Is A Prize* (Pterodactyl Pr, 1989), *First Prelude* (Loyola U Pr, 1981), *America, Light, College English, Aethlon.*

Larry Smith P&W
Firelands College of BGSU, English Dept, Huron, OH 44839, 419-433-5560
Internet: lsmithdog@aol.com
Pubs: *Beyond Rust* (Bottom Dog Pr, 1995), *Steel Valley: Postcards & Letters* (Pig Iron Pr, 1993), *Parabola, Heartlands Today, Humanist.*

Monica E. Smith P
8990 SR 287, West Liberty, OH 43357
Internet: sfsmes@foryou.net
Pubs: *Sunday Suitor, The Poet's Paper, Syncopated City, Roswell Literary Rev, Oatmeal & Poetry, Medicinal Purposes, Lucidity.*

John Stickney P
4545 W 214th, Cleveland, OH 44126
Pubs: *Rampike, Caliban, Generator, Mississippi Rev, New York Qtly, Semiotext*(e), *Exquisite Corpse, Atticus Rev.*

Gloria Still P
1439 Alameda Ave, Lakewood, OH 44107-4920, 216-221-6747
Pubs: *Free Songs* (Writers' Center Pr, 1992), *Indiana Rev, Hopewell Rev, Woman Poet, Arts Indiana Literary Supplement, Passages in Nonviolence.*

Terry Stokes P
PO Box 19359, Cincinnati, OH 45219, 513-651-3659
Pubs: *Sportin' News* (Raccoon Bks, 1985), *Issuing of Scars* (Bartholomew's Cobble, 1981).

Lorraine J. Sutton P
914 Franklin Ave, Columbus, OH 43205
Pubs: *Saycred Laydy* (Sunbury Pr, 1975), *Ms., Latin New York, Conditions, West End.*

Robert L. Tener P
PO Box 182, Rootstown, OH 44272
Pubs: *A Dialogue of Marriage* (Plowman, 1989), *Laughter & Dry Mockery* (Kent, 1988), *Blue Unicorn, Green's Mag, Studies in Contemporary Satire.*

James Thomas W
802 Green St, Yellow Springs, OH 45387-1409,
513-767-9445
  Pubs: *Pictures, Moving* (Dragon Gate, 1986), *Sudden Fiction: Anth* (Norton, 1996), *Carolina Qtly, Esquire, Cimarron, Epoch, Mississippi Rev, Crazyhorse.*

Melanie Rae Thon W
Ohio State Univ, English Dept, 164 W 17 Ave, Columbus, OH 43210-1370
  Pubs: *First, Body* (Holt, 1998), *Iona Moon* (Plume, 1994), *Girls in the Grass, Meteors in August* (Random Hse, 1991, 1990), *Granta, Paris Rev, Ontario Rev, Antaeus, Hudson Rev, Ploughshares.*

Stephanie S. Tolan P&W
300 E N Broadway, Columbus, OH 432144114,
614-262-2241
Internet: steft@aol.com
  Pubs: *The Face in the Mirror, Welcome to the Ark, Who's There?, Save Halloween!* (Morrow, 1998, 1996, 1994, 1993), *Understanding Our Gifted, Roeper Rev, New Advocate.*

Caroline Totten W
140 Santa Clara NW, Canton, OH 44709, 330-493-0913
Internet: caltotn@aol.com
  Pubs: *Montage* (Media Turf Productions, 1997), *Best of 1995 Ohio Poetry: Anth* (Ohio Poetry Day Assn, 1995), *Collage, Insight, Remington Rev, New Writers.*

Ann Townsend P
Denison Univ, Granville, OH 43023, 740-587-6331
Internet: townsend@cc.denison.edu
  Pubs: *Dime Store Erotics* (Silverfish Rev Pr, 1998), *Modern Love* (Bottom Dog Pr, 1994), *Pushcart Prize XX, Nation, Kenyon Rev, Mid-American Rev, NAR, Western Humanities Rev, Southern Rev, Antioch Rev, TriQuarterly.*

Leonard Trawick P
Cleveland State Univ, English Dept, Cleveland, OH 44115,
216-687-3971
  Pubs: *Beastmorfs* (Cleveland State U Poetry Ctr, 1994), *Sometime The Cow Kick Your Head: Anth* (Bits Pr, 1988), *Poetry, Beloit Poetry Jrnl, Phase and Cycle.*

Alberta T. Turner P
482 Caskey Ct, Oberlin, OH 44074, 440-775-7844
  Pubs: *Beginning With And: New and Selected Poems* (Bottom Dog Pr, 1994), *Responses to Poetry* (Longman, 1990), *Stand, Journal, South Carolina Rev, American Literary Rev.*

Jim Villani P&W
Pig Iron Press, PO Box 237, Youngstown, OH 44501,
216-783-1269
  Pubs: *Moment in Bronze, Stars on Lake* (Fantome Pr, 1990, 1989), *Cincinnati Poetry Rev, Salome.*

Diane Vreuls W
172 Elm St, Oberlin, OH 44074, 216-774-1737
  Pubs: *Let Us Know* (Viking, 1986), *Are We There Yet?* (Avon, 1976), *New Yorker, Paris Rev, Massachusetts Rev.*

F. Keith Wahle P
3357 Citrus Ln, Cincinnati, OH 45239, 513-923-3136
  Pubs: *A Choice of Killers* (Morgan Pr, 1998), *Almost Happy* (Rumba Train, 1980), *The Quarterly, Yellow Silk, Cincinnati Poetry Rev.*

Robert Wallace P
Case Western Reserve Univ, Cleveland, OH 44106,
216-795-2810
  Pubs: *The Common Summer: New & Selected Poems* (Carnegie Mellon, 1989).

Mary E. Weems P
10602 Lamontier Ave, Cleveland, OH 44104, 216-791-0752
  Pubs: *White* (Wick Chapbook Kent State U Pr, 1997), *Fembles* (The Heartlands Today, 1996), *Blackeyed* (Burning Pr, 1994), *A Hole in the Ghetto: Anth* (CSU Poetry Ctr, 1995), *Pearl, The Listening Eye.*

Etta Ruth Weigl P
56 Kendal Dr, Oberlin, OH 44074, 216-774-6101
  Pubs: *Seventh Age, Meltwater* (Stereopticon Pr, 1988, 1982), *Poetry Now, And, Williwaw.*

William Wells P
4240 Campus Dr, Lima, OH 45804, 419-221-1641
  Pubs: *Conversing With The Light* (Anhinga Pr, 1988), *The Literary Rev, Birmingham Poetry Rev, Poetry Durham.*

Milton White W
325 E Vine St, Oxford, OH 45056, 513-529-5945

Dallas Wiebe W
582 McAlpin Ave, Cincinnati, OH 45220, 513-281-4767
  Pubs: *Our Asian Journey* (Canada; MLR Edtns, 1997), *Going to the Mountain, The Transparent Eye-Ball & Other Stories* (Burning Deck, 1988, 1982), *Paris Rev, NAR, First Intensity.*

Austin Wright W
3454 Lyleburn Pl, Cincinnati, OH 452201521, 513-751-2328
Internet: austin.wright@uc.edu
  Pubs: *Disciples, Telling Time, After Gregory, Tony and Susan* (Baskerville, 1997, 1995, 1994, 1993), *Recalcitrance, Faulkner and the Professors* (U Iowa Pr, 1990).

David Young P
Oberlin College, Oberlin, OH 44074, 216-775-8576
  Pubs: *Night Thoughts and Henry Vaughn* (Ohio State U Pr, 1994), *The Planet on the Desk: New and Selected Poems* (Wesleyan, 1991).

Thomas Young   P
2658 N 4th St, Columbus, OH 43202, 614-267-1682
Internet: tygertom@compuserve.com
> Pubs: *The Ohio Jrnl, Waves, Graffiti, You Gotta Suit Up For 'Em All, The Smudge.*

Nancy Zafris   W
71 E Lincoln St, Columbus, OH 43215, 614-228-7251
Internet: nancy_zafris@msn.com
> Pubs: *Into the Silence* (Green Street Pr, 1998), *Did My Mama Like to Dance?* (Avon Bks, 1994), *The People I Know* (U Georgia Pr, 1990), *Kenyon Rev, Witness, Missouri Rev.*

Zena Zipporah   P
3544 Fairmount Blvd, Shaker Heights, OH 44118-4354, 216-932-1547
> Pubs: *In the Sacred Manner of the Buffalo, Lost Tribes, Victoriana—In Love With Words* (Zipporah, 1989, 1988, 1987), *Akros Rev.*

OKLAHOMA

Ivy Bloch   P
2109 E 25 Pl, Tulsa, OK 74114-2917, 918-742-8293
> Pubs: *Midwest Qtly, Plainsong, Nimrod, Chariton Rev, Southern Poetry Rev, Mississippi Valley Rev.*

William J. Bly   P
2701 S Juniper Ave #101, Broken Arrow, OK 74012-7731
> Pubs: *Memories of Second Street, Land of the Living* (Pine Woods Pr, 1986, 1985), *Poetry Now.*

Dorothea Condry   P&W
RR2, Box 71133, Calumet, OK 73014, 405-893-2615
> Pubs: *From Seed Bed To Harvest* (Seven Buffaloes Pr, 1986), *The Later Days* (Samisdat, 1980).

Mark Cox   P
Oklahoma State Univ, English Dept, 205 Morrill, Stillwater, OK 74078, 405-744-9474
Internet: markcox@okstate.edu
> Pubs: *Thirty-Seven Years From the Stone* (U Pitt Pr, 1998), *Smoulder* (Godine, 1989), *Poetry, APR, New England Rev, NAR, Poetry East, Poetry Northwest.*

Mary Crescenzo   P&W
1411 E 20 St, Tulsa, OK 74120, 918-744-6828
> Pubs: *Women in Exile: Anth* (Milkweed Edtns, 1990), *West Wind Rev, Paragraph 7, La Bella Figura, Highlights for Children.*

J. Madison Davis   W
1112 Lincoln Green, Norman, OK 73072-7521, 405-447-3756
> Pubs: *Red Knight, Bloody Marko, White Rook* (Walker & Co., 1992, 1991, 1990), *Conversations with Robertson Davies* (U Mississippi Pr, 1989).

George Economou   P
Univ Oklahoma, 760 Van Vleet Oval, Norman, OK 73019, 405-325-6208
Internet: geconomou@ou.edu
> Pubs: *Century Dead Center & Other Poems* (Left Hand Bks, 1997), *Harmonies & Fits* (Point Riders, 1987), *Backwoods Broadsides, Cover, Grand Street, Poetry New York, Sulfur, Texture, ACM, APR.*

Arn Henderson   P
1208 Barkley Ave, Norman, OK 73071, 405-364-6770
> Pubs: *Document For An Anonymous Indian, The Point Riders Great Plains Poetry Anth* (Point Riders Pr, 1974, 1982).

Geary Hobson   P&W
Univ Oklahoma, Norman, OK 73019-0240, 405-325-6231
> Pubs: *Aniyunwiya* (Greenfield Rev Pr, 1995), *Deer Hunting and Other Poems* (Point Riders Pr, 1990), *The Remembered Earth* (U New Mexico Pr, 1981), *Quilt, Nimrod.*

Sherry Lachance   P
4765 SE 23, Del City, OK 73115

Mike Lowery   P
State Farm Insurance, PO Box 55505, Tulsa, OK 74155-1505
> Pubs: *Masks Of The Dreamer* (Wesleyan U Pr, 1979), *Nimrod, Cape Rock, Blue Unicorn, Quartet.*

Mary McAnally   P
76 N Yorktown, Tulsa, OK 74110, 918-583-3651
> Pubs: *Fat Poems* (Cardinal Pr, 1990), *Stations: Paintings & Poems of Spiritual Journey: Anth* (Pemmican, 1995), *Nimrod, Painted Bride Qtly, Abraxas.*

Susan Smith Nash   P&W
3760 Cedar Ridge Dr, Norman, OK 73072-4621, 405-366-7730
> Pubs: *Liquid Babylon* (Potes & Poets, 1994), *The Airport is My Etude* (Paradigm Pr, 1993), *Pornography* (Generator Pr, 1992), *o.blek, Washington Rev, ACM, Aerial.*

Perry Oldham   P
2940 Huntleigh Dr, Oklahoma City, OK 73120
> Pubs: *Higher Ground* (Mercury Pr, 1987), *Vinh Long* (Northwoods, 1977).

Rochelle Owens P
1401 Magnolia, Norman, OK 73072, 405-364-5797
Pubs: *New & Selected Poems 1961-1996* (Junction Pr, 1996), *Rubbed Stones* (Texture Pr, 1994), *Poems For The New Millennium Vol. 2: Anth* (U California Pr, 1998), *Abacus, Talisman, Temblor, ACM, Texture, First Intensity.*

G. Palmer, Jr. P
Rt 3, Carnegie, OK 73015, 405-654-2353
Pubs: *American Indian Literature Anth* (U Oklahoma Pr, 1979).

Alice Lindsay Price P
3113 S Florence Ave, Tulsa, OK 74105, 918-749-0391
Pubs: *Swans of the World* (Council Oak Bks, 1994), *Our Dismembered Shadow* (Ena Pr, 1980), *Nimrod, Rhino, Commonweal, Phoenix.*

S. David Price P
2542 NW 12, Oklahoma City, OK 73107
Pubs: *Summer Snow* (Daybreak, 1977), *Joyful Noise, Texas Rev, Writer, Encore, Driftwood East, Counsel.*

Francine Ringold P
3215 S Yorktown, Tulsa, OK 74105, 918-745-9234
Internet: ringoldfl@centum.utulsa.edu
Pubs: *The Trouble With Voices: Selected Poetry, Making Your Own Mark* (Council Oak Bks, 1995, 1989), *Nimrod, Phoenix, Borderlands, Puerto del Sol, Southwest Rev.*

Gordon Weaver P&W
Oklahoma State Univ, Stillwater, OK 74078, 405-744-6140
Pubs: *Men Who Would Be Good* (TriQuarterly Bks, 1991), *Manoa, TriQuarterly.*

Ann E. Weisman PP
Lawton Arts & Humanities Counc, PO Box 1054, Lawton, OK 73502, 405-581-3471
Pubs: *Eye Imagine: Performances on Paper* (Point Riders Pr, 1991), *Moonrise, The Eloquent Object* (Philbrook Museum, 1989, 1987).

OREGON

Howard Aaron P
2428 NE 20, Portland, OR 97212, 503-282-4904
Pubs: *Retina* (Confluence Pr, 1979), *What The Worms Ignore...* (Jawbone Pr, 1979), *Porch.*

Cathy Ackerson P
1850 Corina Dr SE, Salem, OR 97302, 503-581-9075
Pubs: *Poets West* (Perivale Pr, 1975), *But Is It Poetry?: Anth* (Dragonfly Pr, 1972), *Dragonfly, Caprice, Outpost, Out of Sight, Northwest Rev.*

Duane Ackerson P&W
1850 Corina Dr SE, Salem, OR 97302, 503-581-9075
Pubs: *The Bird At the End of the Universe* (TM Pr, 1999), *The Eggplant* (Confluence Pr, 1977), *Yankee, Northwest Rev, Rolling Stone, Chelsea, Prairie Schooner, CSM.*

Henry Melton Alley W
Univ Oregon, Eugene, OR 974031293, 541-346-2513
Internet: halley@oregon.uoregon.edu
Pubs: *Umbrella of Glass* (Breitenbush Books, 1988), *The Lattice* (Ariadne Pr, 1986), *Seattle Rev, Outerbridge.*

Nasira Alma PP&P&W
PO Box 626, Rockaway, OR 97136-0626
Pubs: *Hallelujah Jalapeno: Perf* (Mind Power Gallery, 1992), *Poets Aloud: Perf* (On B'way Theatre, 1992), *Threshold* (Doubleday, 1984), *Portland Rev, New Pr.*

Erland Anderson P
565 Fairview, Ashland, OR 97520, 541-482-4029
Internet: eand1@aol.com
Pubs: *Searchings For Modesto* (Talent Hse Pr, 1993), *Between Darkness and Darkness* (Prescott Street Pr, 1989), *American Scholar, Calapooya Collage.*

Michael Anderson P
158 Lincoln St, Ashland, OR 97520, 503-482-2441
Pubs: *Wormwood Rev, Scree, Cape Rock, Hiram Rev, Kansas Qtly, Taurus.*

Dori Appel P&W
PO Box 1364, Ashland, OR 97520, 541-482-2735
Internet: applcart@mind.net
Pubs: *Girl Talk* (w/Myers; Samuel French, 1992), *At Our Core: Anth, Grow Old Along With Me: Anth* (Papier-Mache Pr, 1998, 1996), *Prairie Schooner, Yankee, Ascent, Calyx, Southern Humanities, Kalliope.*

Lois Baker P&W
5429 SW Westwood View, Portland, OR 97201, 503-244-9106
Pubs: *Tracers* (Howlett Pr, 1992), *Partial Clearing* (Press-22, 1976), *Poetry, Poetry Northwest, Prism Intl, Calyx, Penthouse, Colorado State Qtly.*

Tim Barnes P
Portland Comm College, PO Box 19000, Portland, OR 97280-0990, 503-977-4638
Internet: tbarnes@zeus.cc.pcc.edu
Pubs: *Falling Through Leaves* (Marino Pr, 1995), *Star Hill Farm & the Grain of What is Gone* (Skookum's Tongue Pr, 1994), *Fine Madness, Puerto del Sol.*

Judith Barrington　　　　　　　　　　P
622 SE 29 Ave, Portland, OR 97214, 503-236-9862
Internet: soapston@teleport.com
　　Pubs: *History & Geography, Trying To Be An Honest
　　Woman* (8th Mtn Pr, 1989, 1985), *Kenyon, Sonora,
　　American Voice, Ploughshares, Women's Rev of Bks, 13th
　　Moon.*

Elizabeth Bartlett　　　　　　　　　　P
5550 Bethel Heights Rd NW, Salem, OR 97304-9730
　　Pubs: *Around the Clock* (St. Andrews, 1989), *Candles*
　　(Autograph Edtns, 1988), *Harper's, Virginia Qtly, Denver
　　Qtly, Ellery Queen's Qtly, NAR, Literary Rev, National
　　Forum.*

M. F. Beal　　　　　　　　　　W
PO Box 161, Seal Rock, OR 973760161, 503-563-2493
　　Pubs: *Angel Dance* (Crossing Pr, 1990), *End of Days*
　　(H&R, 1982), *West Coast Fiction: Anth* (Bantam, 1979),
　　Atlantic, Paris Rev, Calyx, Caprice.

Paul Bergner　　　　　　　　　　P
PO Box 33080, Portland, OR 97233, 503-231-8257
　　Pubs: *Off The Beaten Track: Anth* (Quiet Lion Pr, 1992),
　　Portlander, Plazm, Stanza, Rain City Rev, Spoon, Sufi.

David Biespiel　　　　　　　　　　P
210 SE 50th Ave, Portland, OR 97215, 503-239-6936
　　Pubs: *Shattering Air* (BOA Edtns, 1996), *APR.*

Kathleen M. Bogan　　　　　　　　　　P
3523 SW Jerald Ct, Portland, OR 97201, 503-228-5663
　　Pubs: *Prairie Hearts—Women's Writings on the Midwest:
　　Anth* (Feminist Writers Guild, 1996), *Convolvulus,
　　Confrontation, Writers' Forum, Alaska Qtly Rev, Encodings.*

Julie Brown　　　　　　　　　　W
1434 6th St, Astoria, OR 97103-5315
　　Pubs: *Indiana Rev, Southern Rev, Madison Rev, Hayden's
　　Ferry Rev, Cream City Rev, Michigan Rev.*

Robert Brown　　　　　　　　　　P
1434 6th St, Astoria, OR 97103-5315
　　Pubs: *Sleepwalking with Mayakovsky* (Kent State U Pr,
　　1994), *Poem, ELF, Poetry Northwest, New Virginia Rev,
　　Kansas Qtly.*

Douglas G. Campbell　　　　　　　　　　P
9310 SW 18 Pl, Portland, OR 97219, 503-246-3286
Internet: dcampbell@foxmail.gfc.edu
　　Pubs: *When the Wind Stops: A Collection of Desert Storm
　　Poems* (Counterpoint Pub, 1992), *In Our Own Voices: Anth*
　　(Oregon Writers Colony, 1986), *The Dakota, This, TapJoe,
　　Voices in the Wilderness, Urthkin, Gravida, A New Song.*

Henry Carlile　　　　　　　　　　P&W
7349 SE 30th Ave, Portland, OR 97202, 503-774-0944
Internet: hcarlile@iccom.com
　　Pubs: *Rain* (Carnegie Mellon U Pr, 1994), *Running Lights*
　　(Dragon Gate, 1981), *Poetry, Crazyhorse, Shenandoah,
　　Ohio Rev, Pushcart Prize Anth, APR.*

Deb Casey　　　　　　　　　　P
Univ Oregon, Eugene, OR 97403, 503-346-3226
Internet: wkcasey@oregon.uoregon.edu
　　Pubs: *Daredevil Research* (Peter Lang Pub, 1997), *For A
　　Living: The Poetry of Work: Anth* (U Illinois Pr, 1995),
　　*Zyzzyva, Kenyon Rev, River Styx, Ploughshares,
　　Massachusetts Rev, Prairie Schooner, Graham Hse Rev,
　　Calyx.*

Kent Clair Chamberlain　　　　　　　　　　P&W
625 Holly St, Ashland, OR 97520, 541-482-2283
　　Pubs: *Phaer Wind* (Pauper Pr, 1992), *Rarely Published*
　　(Blue Willow Pr, 1977), *Object Lesson, Atrocity, Danger,
　　GSC, Ozark Muse, Muse Letter, Carpe Laureate Diem,
　　Sunflower Dream, New Observer, Poetic Realm, Blind
　　Man's Rainbow.*

Sandra Cherches　　　　　　　　　　W
2825 NE 39th, Portland, OR 97212, 503-287-7404
　　Pubs: *Taos Rev, New Delta Rev, American Fiction, Ms.,
　　Portland, Village Voice.*

Walt Curtis　　　　　　　　　　P&W
Bridge City Books, 1717 SW Park Ave., Ste 616, Portland,
OR 97201, 503-220-4171
　　Pubs: *Mala Noche & Other Illegal Adventures* (Bridge City
　　Bks, 1997), *Rhymes for Alice Blue Light* (Lynx Hse, 1984),
　　A New Geography of Poets: Anth (U of Arkansas Pr, 1992),
　　Atlantic Monthly, Gay Sunshine, Clinton Street Qtly.

Peter Ho Davies　　　　　　　　　　W
Creative Writing Program, Eugene, OR 974031286,
503-346-3944
Internet: phd@oregon.uoregon.edu
　　Pubs: *The Ugliest House in the World and Other Stories,
　　Best American Short Stories: Anths* (HM, 1997, 1996,
　　1995), *Paris Rev, Story, Agni, Harvard Rev, Gettysburg
　　Rev, Antioch Rev.*

Annie Dawid　　　　　　　　　　P&W
0615 SW Palatine Hill Rd, #58, Portland, OR 97219,
503-768-7405
　　Pubs: *York Ferry* (Cane Hill Pr, 1993), *Beyond Lament:
　　Poets on the Holocaust: Anth* (Northwestern U Pr, 1998),
　　American Fiction: Anth (Birch Lane Pr, 1993), *Yellow Silk,
　　Gettysburgh Rev, Toyon, Art & Understanding.*

Bill Deemer　　　　　　　　　　P
2395 University St, Eugene, OR 97403-1547
　　Pubs: *A Few for Lew* (Coyote Bks, 1986).

Sandy Diamond   PP&P
Box 405, Grand Ronde, OR 973470405, 503-879-5672
   Pubs: *Miss Coffin And Mrs. Blood* (Creative Arts Book Co.,
   1994).

Steven Dimeo   W
530 NE Grant St, Hillsboro, OR 97124, 503-640-1375
   Pubs: *Uncommon Reader, Wildfire, Seattle Times,
   Michigan Qtly Rev, Amazing Stories, Descant,
   Crosscurrents.*

John A. Domini   W
2819 NE 21 Ave, Portland, OR 97212, 503-281-4681
Internet: vojam@aol.com
   Pubs: *Bedlam* (Fiction International, 1982), *Pushcart Prize:
   Anth* (Pushcart, 1989), *Paris Rev, Southwest Rev,
   Ploughshares, Threepenny Rev.*

Sharon Doubiago   P
740 3rd SE, Bandon, OR 97411, 541-347-7149
   Pubs: *Hard Country* (West End Pr, 1999), *The Husband
   Arcane, The Arcane of O* (Gorda Plate Pr, 1996), *South
   America Mi Hija* (U Pitt Pr, 1992), *Psyche Drives The Coast*
   (Empty Bowl Pr, 1990), *The Book of Seeing With One's
   Own Eyes* (Graywolf, 1989).

Thomas Doulis   W
2236 NE Regents Dr, Portland, OR 97212, 503-287-3484
Internet: hhtd@odin.ccpdx.edu
   Pubs: *Landmarks of Our Past* (Holy Trinity, 1983), *Toward
   the Authentic Church: Anth* (Light & Life, 1996).

Doug Draime   P
1096 Hillview Dr, Ashland, OR 97520
Internet: cddraime@aol.com
   Pubs: *Lilliput Rev, Mind in Motion, Purple Patch,
   Permafrost, L.A. Weekly, Struggle, Broken Streets, The
   Temple, Pudding Mag, Angelflesh, Art Times, George &
   Mertie's Place: Rooms With a View.*

Albert Drake   P&W
9727 SE Reedway St, Portland, OR 97266-3738,
503-771-6779
   Pubs: *Flat Out, Herding Goats* (Flat Out, 1994, 1989),
   Homesick (Canoe, 1988), *Epoch, Best American Short
   Stories.*

Barbara Drake   P&W
6104 NW Lilac Hill Rd, Yamhill, OR 97148, 503-662-3373
Internet: bdrake@linfield.edu
   Pubs: *Peace at Heart: An Oregon Country Life* (Oregon
   State U Pr, 1998), *Space Before A* (26 Bks Pub, 1996),
   Bees in Wet Weather (Canoe Pr, 1992), *What We Say to
   Strangers* (Breitenbush, 1986), *River Styx, Willow Springs,
   Fireweed, Wamka, Wormwood Rev.*

David Elsey   P
2139 W Burnside, #202, Portland, OR 97210, 503-241-5404
   Pubs: *Gray Light* (Smellfeast, 1995), *Off The Beaten Track:
   Anth* (Quiet Lion Pr, 1992), *Poetry Now, Hubbub, Small
   Pond Rev, Gryphon, Rhino.*

Pat Enders   P
Clackamas Press, 21730 SE Hwy 224, Clackamas, OR
97015, 503-658-2258
   Pubs: *Pioneer Woman, Poetry Oregon, St. Andrews Rev.*

Elizabeth Engstrom   W
1627 Charnelton St, Eugene, OR 97401
Internet: bengstrom@aol.com
   Pubs: *Lizard Wine* (Dell, 1995), *Nightmare Flower* (TOR,
   1992), *Fantasy and Science Fiction Mag, Cemetery Dance,
   Bone.*

Tess Enroth   P&W
8222 SW Capitol Hwy, Portland, OR 97219, 503-977-2539
Internet: TessMcE@aol.com
   Pubs: *Her Soul Beneath the Bone: Anth* (U Illinois Pr,
   1988), *Lake Effect, Wide Open Mag, Yet Another Small
   Mag.*

Garrett Epps   W
Univ Oregon School of Law, Eugene, OR 97403
   Pubs: *The Floating Island* (Houghton Mifflin, 1985), *The
   Shad Treatment* (Putnam, 1977).

Esther Erford   P
1313 Lincoln St, #1002, Eugene, OR 97401-3965
   Pubs: *South Coast Poetry Jrnl, Connecticut River Rev,
   Galley Sail Rev, Slant, Voices International.*

Alice Evans   P&W
4635 Larkwood St, Eugene, OR 974053987
   Pubs: *Solo: Women Going It Alone in the Wilderness: Anth,
   Another Wilderness: New Outdoor Writing By Women: Anth*
   (Seal Pr, 1996, 1994), *Clinton Street Qtly.*

Sandra Foushee   P
PO Box 541, Manzanita, OR 971300541, 503-368-7228
   Pubs: *The Light That Stops Us* (Night Sky, 1990), *Back to
   Essentials* (Bristlecone Pr, 1984), *Ploughshares, Poetry &
   Prose, Westwind Rev, Prairie Schooner.*

Vi Gale   P&W
Prescott Street Press, PO Box 40312, Portland, OR
972400312, 503-254-2922
   Pubs: *Odd Flowers & Short Eared Owls, The Prescott
   Street Reader: Anth* (Prescott Street Pr, 1984, 1995),
   Clearwater (Swallow, 1974), *Horisont* (Sweden).

Ken Gerner   P
PO Box 10881, Portland, OR 97210, 503-292-1258
   Pubs: *Throwing Shadows* (Copper Canyon Pr, 1985),
   CutBank, Willow Springs.

Martha Gies   W
2109 NE Rodney Ave, Portland, OR 97212-3739,
503-287-4394
    Pubs: *A Celestial Omnibus: Anth* (Beacon Pr, 1997),
    Storming Heaven's Gate: Anth (Plume/Penguin, 1997), *The*
    World Begins Here: Anth (Oregon State U Pr, 1993), *The*
    Time of Our Lives: Anth (Crossing Pr, 1993), *Orion, Left*
    Bank, Zyzzyva, Cream City Rev.

Jane Glazer   P
Adrienne Lee Press, PO Box 309, Monmouth, OR 97361,
503-838-1220
    Pubs: *Some Trick of Light* (Adrienne Lee Pr, 1993), *Twelve*
    Oregon Poets 2: Anth (High Street Pr, 1996), *Berkeley*
    Poetry Rev, Calyx, Hubbub, Five Fingers Rev, Fireweed,
    Antioch Rev, Calapooya 19.

Jim Grabill   P
9835 SW 53 Ave, Portland, OR 97219-5827, 503-977-0331
    Pubs: *Listening to the Leaves Form, Poem Rising Out of*
    the Earth & Standing Up In Someone (Lynx Hse Pr, 1997,
    1994), *Through the Green Fire* (Holy Cow! Pr, 1995),
    Poetry East, Caliban, Kayak, Willow Springs, Poetry
    Northwest, Barnabe Mountain Rev.

Cecelia Hagen   P&W
1910 Fairmount Blvd, Eugene, OR 97403, 541-485-3019
Internet: hagence@aol.com
    Pubs: *From Where We Speak: Anth of Oregon Poetry*
    (Oregon State U Pr, 1993), *Portlandia, Poet & Critic,*
    Exquisite Corpse, Prairie Schooner, Willow Springs, Seattle
    Rev, Puerto Del Sol.

John Haislip   P
925 Park Ave, Eugene, OR 97404
    Pubs: *Seal Rock* (Barnwood Pr, 1987), *American Poets in*
    1976: Anth (Bobbs-Merrill, 1976).

James Byron Hall   P&W
1670 E 27 Ave, Eugene, OR 97403, 503-342-2975
    Pubs: *I Like It Better Now* (U Arkansas Pr, 1992),
    Bereavements (Story Line Pr, 1991), *New Directions, New*
    Letters, Esquire.

Gail Hanlon   P
PO Box 4832, Portland, OR 97208, 503-294-1698
    Pubs: *Best American Poetry 1996: Anth* (Scribner, 1996),
    Iowa Rev, Poetry Flash, Calyx, Poet Lore, Folio, Interim.

Robert D. Hoeft   P
PO Box 100, Pendleton, OR 97801, 503-276-1260
    Pubs: *What Are You Doing?* (Trout Creek Pr, 1986), *Out of*
    Work (Winewood Pub, 1983), *Green's Mag.*

Michael Holstein   P
228 West St, Ashland, OR 97520, 503-488-1099
    Pubs: *Alura Qtly, Phoebus Mag, Poets On, Beloit Poetry*
    Jrnl, Crosscurrents.

Garrett Kaoru Hongo   P
Univ Oregon, Program in Creative Writing, Eugene, OR
97405, 503-346-0545
    Pubs: *The River of Heaven* (Knopf, 1988), *The Open Boat:*
    Anth (Anchor Bks, 1993), *Ploughshares, Zyzzyva, Field,*
    Antaeus, Bamboo Ridge, Agni.

Lawson Fusao Inada   P&W
Southern Oregon State College, English Dept, Ashland, OR
97520, 541-552-6639
    Pubs: *Legends From Camp* (Coffee Hse Pr, 1993).

Stephen R. Jones   P
24407 Decker Rd, Corvallis, OR 97333, 503-929-5505
    Pubs: *Calapooya Collage, Eloquent Umbrella, Northwest*
    Rev, Oregon English Jrnl, Greenfield Rev, Fireweed.

Karen Karbo   W
PO Box 8322, Portland, OR 97207, 503-246-1016
    Pubs: *The Diamond Lane, Trespassers Welcome Here*
    (Putnam, 1991, 1989), *Dreamers and Desperados: Anth*
    (Dell, 1993), *Esquire, New Republic, Vogue.*

Susan Kenyon   P
2060 Willamette St, Eugene, OR 97405, 503-997-9048
    Pubs: *Western Humanities Rev, Accent, Northwest Rev,*
    Atlantic, California Rev.

Ken Kesey   W
85829 Ridgeway Rd, Pleasant Hill, OR 97455, 541-746-1572
Internet: kenk@efn.org
    Pubs: *Last Go Round, Sailor Song, Sometimes A Great*
    Nation, One Flew Over The Cuckoo's Nest (Viking, 1994,
    1992, 1964, 1962).

Lee Crawley Kirk   P
PO Box 5432, Eugene, OR 97405, 541-683-7033
Internet: leekirk@continet.com
    Pubs: *From Here We Speak: Anth* (Oregon State U Pr,
    1993), *Stafford's Road* (Adrienne Lee Pr, 1991), *Portlander,*
    Daughters of Nyx, Wormwood Rev, Fireweed, Calapooya
    Collage.

Mary Hope Whitehead Lee   P
315 NE 28 Ave #105, Portland, OR 97232, 503-238-8088
    Pubs: *Sombra, Sedicious Delicious, Yet Another Small*
    Mag, Writers' Haven Jrnl, Womanspirit, Plexus, Essence
    Mag, Feminist Studies, Callaloo, Conditions.

Elio Emiliano Ligi   P
Uncommon Sense, PO Box 40710, Portland, OR 97240-0710
Internet: faustroll@aol.com
    Pubs: *The Diversabomber* (Dehumanities, 1995), *How I*
    Shot Down KAL007 (Sodoms Insane Pub, 1994), *Christian*
    Science Monitor.

Robert Hill Long P&W
1910 Charnelton St, Eugene, OR 974052818, 541-686-6223
Internet: webdelsol.com/long/
   Pubs: *The Effigies* (Plinth Bks, 1998), *The Work of the Bow*
   (Cleveland State U Poetry Center, 1997), *Poetry, Zyzzyva,
   Shenandoah, DoubleTake, Manoa, Prose Poem.*

Jack E. Lorts P
PO Box 474, Fossil, OR 97830, 541-763-3060
Internet: jlorts@fossil.k12.or.us
   Pubs: *Arizona Qtly, Kansas Qtly, English Jrnl, Oregon
   English Jrnl, Abbey, Fireweed, Ninth Circle, Vis-a-Vis.*

Manna Lowenfels P
20950 SW Rock Creek Rd, Sheridan, OR 97378,
503-843-2465
   Pubs: *The New Woman Speaks And Other Poems* (Buffalo
   Bks, 1979), *Sunbury, Connections.*

Joan Maiers P
PO Box 33, Marylhurst, OR 970360033, 503-636-8955
   Pubs: *Blooming in the Shade: Anth* (Media Weavers, 1997),
   Out Of Season: Anth (Amagansett Pr, 1993), *If I Had A
   Hammer: Anth* (Papier-Mache Pr, 1990), *Journal of
   Pastoral Care, The Other Side, New Press Literary Qtly,
   Hubbub, Paper Boat, Sistersong, Fireweed.*

Katherine Marsh P
PO Box 613, Salem, OR 973080613
   Pubs: *Writer's Exchange, Poetry Motel, Poetry Magazine,
   Poetry Today, Tiotis, Sounds of the Street, Palo Alto Rev,
   Midwest Poetry Rev, Toast, Lucid Stone, In Touch Mag,
   Poetic Expressions.*

Robert McDowell P
Story Line Press, Three Oaks Farm, Box 1108, Ashland, OR
975200052, 541-512-8792
   Pubs: *The Diviners* (Peterloo Poets, 1995), *Quiet Money*
   (Henry Holt, 1987), *At The House of the Tin Man* (Chowder
   Pr, 1983), *Hudson Rev, Kenyon Rev, Sewanee Rev, New
   Criterion, Harvard Rev, Poetry.*

David Memmott P&W
PO Box 3235, La Grande, OR 97850, 541-963-0723
Internet: wordcraft@oregontrail.net
   Pubs: *Within the Walls of Jericho* (26 Books, 1998), *The
   Larger Earth* (Permeable Pr, 1996), *Once Upon A Midnight*
   (Unnameable Pr, 1995), *Nebula 27* (HB, 1993), *Oregon
   East, Co-Lingua, Airfish, Point No Point, The Temple, Mag
   of Speculative Poetry.*

Rob Hollis Miller P
PO Box 865, Union, OR 97883, 503-562-5091
   Pubs: *The Boy Whose Shoesocks Ran Away* (Primavera,
   1982), *Shanghai Creek Fire* (St. Andrews, 1979).

Gary Miranda P
1172 SE 55 St, Portland, OR 97215, 503-239-9174
   Pubs: *Grace Period* (Princeton, 1983), *Duino Elegies by
   Ranier Marl a Rilke* (Breitenbush, 1981).

Rodger Moody P
PO Box 3541, Eugene, OR 97403, 503-344-5060
   Pubs: *Unbending Intent* (26 Bks Pr, 1997), *From Here We
   Speak: Anth of Oregon Poetry* (Oregon State U Pr, 1993),
   Zyzzyva, Caliban, Yellow Silk, Mudfish.

F. A. Nettelbeck P
PO Box 336, Sprague River, OR 97639, 503-533-2486
   Pubs: *Ecosystems Collapsing* (Inkblot Pubs, 1992),
   Americruiser (Illuminati, 1983), *Gas, Bombay Gin, Painted
   Bride Qtly, Rain City Rev.*

Michael Niflis P
6920 Whiskey Creek Rd, Tillamook, OR 97141,
503-842-6755
   Pubs: *From Here We Speak: Anth* (Oregon State U Pr,
   1993), *Poetry, Esquire, Partisan Rev, American Scholar,
   Commonweal, Christian Science Monitor, Harper's, New
   Republic, New York Times, Virginia Qtly.*

Verlena Orr P
1907 NW Hoyt, Portland, OR 97209-1224, 503-224-1849
   Pubs: *Woman Who Hears Voices* (Future Tense Pr, 1998),
   Graining the Mare: The Poetry of Ranch Women: Anth
   (Gibbs Smith, 1994), *From Here We Speak: Anth* (Oregon
   State U Pr, 1993), *Poet & Critic, Colorado Rev.*

Robyn Parnell W
343 NE 15 Ct, Hillsboro, OR 97124, 503-681-9818
Internet: wagnell@teleport.com
   Pubs: *Strictly Fiction* (Potpourri, 1994), *Belletrist Rev,
   Oasis, Uno Mas, Pangolin Papers, Innisfree, Northwest
   Literary Forum.*

A. B. Paulson W
Portland State University, PO Box 751, Portland, OR 97207,
503-725-3521
Internet: ab@nh1.nh.pdx.edu
   Pubs: *Watchman Tell Us Of The Night* (Viking Penguin,
   1987), *Georgia Rev.*

Dan Raphael P
6735 SE 78 St, Portland, OR 97206, 503-777-0406
Internet: raphael@aracnet.com
   Pubs: *Trees Through the Road* (Nine Muses, 1997),
   Molecular Jam (Jazz Police, 1996), *The Bones Begin to
   Sing* (26 Bks, 1993), *Here the Meat Turns to the Audience*
   (Shattered Wig, 1991), *Caliban, Plazm, Heaven Bone,
   Temple, Tinfish, First Intensity, Antenym.*

Carlos Reyes   P
3222 NE Schuyler, Portland, OR 97212, 503-287-9806
Internet: isacar@aol.com
   Pubs: *A Suitcase Full Of Crows* (Bluestem, 1995),
   Nightmarks (Lynx Hse, 1990), *Men Of Our Time: Anth* (U
   Georgia, 1992), *West Coast Rev.*

Susan Rich   P
759 Sunnyside Dr, Eugene, OR 97404, 541-688-8045
   Pubs: *Harvard, Massachusetts Rev, Bridges, Southern
   Poetry Rev, Alaska Qtly Rev, Santa Barbara Rev,
   Sojourner.*

Doren Robbins   P
2735 Olive St, Eugene, OR 97405, 541-484-7412
   Pubs: *Under the Black Moth's Wings* (Ameroot Pr, 1988),
   Sympathetic Manifesto (Perivale Pr, 1987).

Howard W. Robertson   P
854 Martin St, Eugene, OR 97405, 503-344-6206
Internet: hwr@efn.org
   Pubs: *To The Fierce Guard In The Assyrian Saloon, The
   Ahsahta Anthology* (Ahsahta Pr, 1987, 1996), *Intown,
   Pacifica, Ergo, Fireweed, Laughing Bear, Negative
   Capability, Literal Latte, Nimrod.*

Elaine Romaine   P
5017 SE 40 Ave, Portland, OR 97206, 503-788-9034
   Pubs: *Breaking Up: Anth* (Crossing Pr, 1994), *Passion:
   Anth* (Peconic Gallery, 1994), *The Dream Book: Anth*
   (Schocken Bks, 1985), *New Letters, NAR, Oyez.*

Helen Ronan   P
344 E 14 Ave, Eugene, OR 97401, 503-687-0419
   Pubs: *Petrified Thunder, Cloud Shadows* (Oregon State Pr,
   1989, 1989), *Brussels Sprout, Dragonfly, Modern Haiku,
   Frogpond, Haiku Canada, New Cicada.*

Lex Runciman   P
Linfield College, English Dept, McMinnville, OR 97128,
503-434-2583
Internet: lruncim@linfield.edu
   Pubs: *The Admirations* (Lynx Hse Pr, 1989), *Luck* (Owl
   Creek Pr, 1981), *Verse, Fireweed, NER, Missouri Rev,
   Willow Springs.*

Vern Rutsala   P
2404 NE 24 Ave, Portland, OR 97212, 503-281-5872
   Pubs: *Little-Known Sports* (U Massachusetts Pr, 1994),
   Selected Poems (Story Line, 1991), *Ruined Cities*
   (Carnegie Mellon, 1987).

Harley L. Sachs   P&W
2545 SW Terwilliger Blvd #222, Portland, OR 97201
Internet: hlsachs@mtu.edu
   Pubs: *Threads of The Covenant* (Isaac Nathan Pubs,
   1995), *Irma Quarterdeck Reports* (Wescott Cove Pub,
   1991), *Hadassah, Jewish Calendar, Passages North.*

Ralph Salisbury   P&W
2377 Charnelton, Eugene, OR 97405-2859, 541-343-5101
Internet: 103411.2104@compuserve.com
   Pubs: *The Last Rattlesnake Throw & Other Stories* (U
   Oklahoma Pr, 1998), *One Indian and Two Chiefs* (Navaho
   Comm College Pr, 1993), *Earth Song Sky Spirit*
   (Doubleday, 1993), *Chariton Rev, Poetry Chicago, New
   Yorker, Carolina Qtly, Massachusetts Rev.*

Maxine Scates   P
1500 Skyline Park Loop, Eugene, OR 97405, 503-687-2758
Internet: bcadbury@oregon.uoregon.edu
   Pubs: *Toluca Street* (U Pittsburgh Pr, 1989), *Poetry East,
   APR, Agni, Crazyhorse, Ironwood.*

Willa Schneberg   P
2524 SW Sheffield, Portland, OR 97201, 503-248-4136
   Pubs: *Each in Her Own Way* (Queen of Swords Pr, 1994),
   Tikkun: Anth (Tikkun, 1992), *Americas Rev, Hawaii Pacific
   Rev, Exquisite Corpse, Bridges.*

Dale Shank   W
PO Box 2870, Wilsonville, OR 97070-2870
Internet: dshank@teleport.com
   Pubs: *Powder, Joint Endeavor, Akros Rev, Before the Sun,
   Croton Rev, U Portland Rev.*

Brenda Shaw   P&W
3475 Harris St, Eugene, OR 97405, 541-484-9330
   Pubs: *The Dark Well* (Audenreed Pr, 1997), *Dog Music:
   Anth* (St. Martin's Pr, 1996), *Each In Her Own Way: Anth*
   (Queen of Swords Pr, 1994), *Scottish Stories 1985: Anth*
   (Collins, 1985), *Fireweed, Pacifica, Mediphors, Northlight,
   Inscape, Word, Envoi, Spectrum.*

Steven Sher   P&W
3930 NW Witham Hill Dr, #176, Corvallis, OR 97330,
541-752-5949
   Pubs: *Traveler's Advisory* (Trout Creek Pr, 1994), *Man With
   A Thousand Eyes and Other Stories* (Gull Bks, 1989).

Jim Shugrue   P
5344 SE 38 Ave, Portland, OR 97202, 503-775-0370
   Pubs: *Icewater* (Trask Hse Bks, 1998), *Small Things
   Screaming* (26 Bks, 1995), *Quarterly West, International
   Qtly, Poetry East, Another Chicago Mag.*

Floyd Skloot   P&W
5680 Karla's Ln, Amity, OR 97101, 503-835-2230
Internet: fskloot@pnn.com
   Pubs: *The Open Door, The Night-Side* (Story Line Pr, 1997,
   1996), *Music Appreciation* (U Pr Florida, 1994), *Atlantic,
   Harper's, Poetry, American Scholar, New Criterion, Virginia
   Qtly Rev, Southern Rev, Southwest Rev, Boulevard.*

Warren Slesinger   P
Oregon State Univ Press, 101 Waldo Hall, OSU, Corvallis,
OR 97331, 541-737-3873
Internet: warren.slesinger@orst.edu
   Pubs: *With Some Justification* (Windhover Pr, 1984),
   *Antioch Rev, Iowa Rev, The Prose Poem, APR, Georgia
   Rev, NAR, Northwest Rev.*

Tom Smario   P
11900 SE Foster Pl, Portland, OR 97266, 503-761-7147
   Pubs: *Spring Fever, The Cat's Pajamas* (Gull Bks, 1984,
   1982), *Portland Rev.*

Primus St. John   P
Portland State Univ, English Dept, PO Box 751, Portland, OR
97207, 503-725-3521
   Pubs: *Dreamer, Love Is Not A Constellation, It Is A Light*
   (Carnegie Mellon U Pr, 1990, 1982), *APR.*

Kim R. Stafford   P
Lewis & Clark College, Campus Box 100, Portland, OR
97219, 503-768-7745
   Pubs: *Having Everything Right* (Sasquatch Bks, 1996),
   Lochsa Road: A Pilgrim in the West (Confluence Pr, 1991),
   Atlantic, Virginia Qtly Rev, The Sun.

Lisa Malinowski Steinman   P
Reed College, Portland, OR 97202, 503-775-0370
Internet: lisa.steinman@reed.edu
   Pubs: *Ordinary Songs* (26 Bks, 1996), *A Book of Other
   Days, All That Comes To Light* (Arrowood Bks, 1993,
   1989), *Michigan Qtly, Poetry East, Threepenny Rev, New
   Virginia Qtly.*

Sandra Stone   P&W
2650 SW 106 Ave, Portland, OR 77225-4313, 503-292-3296
   Pubs: *Cocktails with Brueghel at the Museum Cafe*
   (Cleveland State U Poetry Ctr, 1997), *The Quarterly, Ms.,
   Poetry Northwest, The New Republic.*

Thomas Strand   P
PO Box 83706, Portland, OR 97283
   Pubs: *Oregon East* (Eastern Oregon State College, 1985),
   The Best of Poetic Space: Anth 1987-91 (Poetic Space,
   1991), *Desperado, Incoming, Poetic Space.*

Gloria Sykee   W
11055 SW Summerfield Dr #7, Tigard, OR 97224,
503-620-7443
   Pubs: *Carolina Qtly, Prairie Schooner, Kansas Qtly.*

Mark Thalman   P
3310 Hillside Way, Forest Grove, OR 97116, 503-357-4042
Internet: oregonpoet@aol.com
   Pubs: *Chariton Rev, Poetry, Fireweed, Pearl, From Here
   We Speak, Whetstone.*

George Venn   P
105 Fir St #724, La Grande, OR 97850, 541-962-0380
Internet: venng@eou.edu
   Pubs: *Marking The Magic Circle, From Here We Speak:
   Anth* (Oregon State U Pr, 1987, 1994), *Hubbub, The Kerf,
   Talking River Rev, Oregon East, Prescott Street Reader,
   Jefferson Monthly.*

Doyle Wesley Walls   P
Pacific Univ, Forest Grove, OR 97116, 503-359-2992
Internet: wallsdw@pacificu.edu
   Pubs: *Sweet Nothings: Anth* (Indiana U Pr, 1994), *From
   Here We Speak: Anth* (Oregon State U Pr, 1993), *New
   York Qtly, Poet and Critic, Cimarron Rev, Minnesota Rev,
   Beloit Poetry Jrnl.*

Patricia J. Ware   P
2080 SE Caruthers St, #7, Portland, OR 97214-5467,
503-232-9756
   Pubs: *CutBank, Slackwater Rev, Calyx, Portland Rev,
   Fedora, Poetry Seattle, Willamette Week.*

Roger Weaver   P
712 NW 13, Corvallis, OR 973305953, 541-753-9955
Internet: weaverr@peak.org
   Pubs: *Standing on Earth, Throwing These Sequins at the
   Stars, Traveling on the Great Wheel* (Gardyloo Pr, 1994,
   1992, 1990), *Twenty-One Waking Dreams* (Trout Creek Pr,
   1986), *The Orange and Other Poems* (Press-ZZ, 1978),
   NAR, Massachusetts Rev, Northwest Rev.

Ingrid Wendt   W
2377 Charnelton, Eugene, OR 97405-2859, 541-343-5101
Internet: 103411.2104@compuserve.com
   Pubs: *Singing the Mozart Requiem* (Breitenbush Bks,
   1987), *Moving the House* (BOA Edtns, 1980), *No More
   Masks: Anth* (HC, 1993), *Poetry, Ms., Calyx,
   Massachusetts Rev.*

Elizabeth Whitbeck   P&W
32200 SW French Prairie, A-106, Wilsonville, OR 97070,
503-694-5475
   Pubs: *Take This Woman* (Macmillan, 1947), *Northeast
   Corridor, Creativity Unlimited, Time of Singing, The Writing
   Self, Zantia, Pegasus Rev.*

Hannah Wilson   P&W
2660 Emerald St, Eugene, OR 97403
   Pubs: *The Wedding Cake in the Middle of the Road: Anth*
   (Norton, 1992), *Prairie Schooner, Calyx, Earth's Daughters,
   Other Voices, Turnstile.*

John Witte   P
1170 Barber Dr, Eugene, OR 97405
   Pubs: *Loving The Days* (Wesleyan, 1978), *New Yorker,
   Paris Rev, APR, Iowa Rev, Antaeus.*

PENNSYLVANIA

Albert Altimari W
Box 244, Graterford, PA 19426-0244
Pubs: *Oblates, Messenger.*

Nathalie F. Anderson P
3 Rutledge Ave, Morton, PA 19070, 610-690-1213
Internet: nanders1@swarthmore.edu
Pubs: *Following Fred Astaire* (Word Works Pr, 1999), *My Hand, My Only Map* (House of Keys, 1978), *Paris Rev, Southern Poetry Rev, Madison Rev, Spazio Humano, Prairie Schooner, Cimarron Rev.*

Ron Androla P
1624 West Grandview Blvd Apt, Erie, PA 16509, 814-864-8937
Pubs: *Splattered in Erie* (Smiling Dog Pr, 1996), *It's A Pretty World* (Non Compos Mentis Pr, 1996), *Poetry Motel, Atom Mind, Chiron Rev, Wooden Head Rev.*

Kenneth L. Arnold P
6363 Germantown Ave, Philadelphia, PA 19144, 215-844-1892

Penelope Austin P
29 Ross St, Williamsport, PA 17701, 717-326-7670
Internet: penelope_austin@hotmail.com
Pubs: *Waiting For A Hero: Poems, Devins Award Anth* (U Missouri Pr, 1988, 1998), *Missouri Rev, Kenyon Rev, The Journal, New Republic, Nightsun, Prairie Schooner.*

J. T. Barbarese P
7128 Cresheim Rd, Philadelphia, PA 19119, 215-247-9575
Internet: 102610.15@compuserve.com
Pubs: *New Science, Under the Blue Moon* (U Georgia, 1989, 1985), *Sewanee Rev, Denver Qtly, Southern Rev, Atlantic Monthly, NAR, Boulevard.*

Aliki Barnstone P
116 N Front St, Lewisburg, PA 17837, 717-524-5299
Internet: barnstne@bucknell.edu
Pubs: *Bright Snow* (Carnegie Mellon U Pr, 1997), *A Book of Women Poets from Antiquity to Now: Anth* (Random Hse, 1992), *Agni, Antioch Rev, Poetry.*

Gerald Barrax P
805 Daisy Ln, West Chester, PA 19382-5702, 610-431-6660
Internet: barrax@bellatlantic.net
Pubs: *From A Person Sitting In Darkness: New And Selected Poems* (LSU Pr, 1998), *Leaning Against The Sun* (U Arkansas Pr, 1992), *The Deaths of Animals & Lesser Gods* (U Kentucky, 1984), *Callaloo, Hayden's Ferry Rev, Georgia Rev, New Virginia Rev.*

Sue Saniel Barry P
6315 Forbes Ave, #202, Pittsburgh, PA 15217-1750, 412-521-1540
Pubs: *Bare As The Trees, Another Language* (Papier-Mache Pr, 1992, 1989), *Kansas Qtly, Spoon River Qtly, Negative Capability, Crosscurrents.*

Constance Bartusis W
129 S 17 St, #2, Pittsburgh, PA 15203
Pubs: *Shades Of Difference* (St. Martin's Pr, 1968).

Marilyn Bates P&W
126 Swallow Hill Ct, Pittsburgh, PA 152201206
Internet: bbates+@pitt.edu
Pubs: *Riverspeak, Writing on the Desk: Anth* (U Pitt Pr, 1998, 1994), *Pembroke Mag, Carnegie Mellon Mag, Poetry Mag On Line, Zuzu's Petals On Line, Verve, Iris, Poets On, Pittsburgh Qtly, Pennsylvania Rev, Palo Alto Rev.*

Jean Baur P
29 Green Ridge Rd, Yardley, PA 19067, 215-493-4257
Pubs: *The Helen Rev, Confrontation, Green River Rev.*

Robin Becker P
215 Academy St, Boalsburg, PA 16827-1438, 814-466-3326
Internet: rxb20@psu.edu
Pubs: *All-American Girl, Giacometti's Dog* (U Pitt Pr, 1995, 1990), *Backtalk* (Alice James Bks, 1982), *Prairie Schooner, New Virginia Rev, APR, Kenyon Rev, Ploughshares, Amicus Jrnl.*

Stephen Berg P
2005 Mt Vernon St, Philadelphia, PA 19130

Jonathan Mark Berkowitz P&W
1030 E Lancaster Ave, #1008, Rosemont, PA 19010, 215-552-8167
Pubs: *New Renaissance, Heartlands Today, Black Buzzard Rev, Northern Perspective, Riverrun, Green's Mag, Art/Life, Rambunctious Rev, Appearances, Oyez Rev.*

Jane Bernstein W
Carnegie Mellon University, Pittsburgh, PA 152133890, 412-268-6445
Internet: janebern+@andrew.cmu.edu
Pubs: *Loving Rachel* (Little, Brown, 1988), *Seven Minutes in Heaven* (Fawcett, 1986), *Ms., Glamour, New York Times Magazine, Self, Creative Nonfiction, The Sun, Prairie Schooner.*

Becky Birtha P&W
5116 Cedar Ave, Philadelphia, PA 19143
Pubs: *The Forbidden Poems* (Seal, 1991), *Breaking Ice: Anth of Contemporary African-American Fiction* (Penguin 1990), *We Are the Stories We Tell: Anth* (Pantheon, 1990).

Lili Bita P
326 Bryn Mawr Ave, Bala Cynwyd, PA 19004, 610-667-2224
    Pubs: *Striking the Sky* (European Arts Center, 1997),
Excavations, Firewalkers (Lyra Pr, 1985, 1984), *Agenda, APR,
Caprice, Intl Poetry Rev, Nea Hesperia, Mad Poets Rev.*

Peter Blair P
129 S Wade Ave, Washington, PA 15301, 804-977-7916
    Pubs: *Furnace Greens* (Defined Providence Pr, 1998), *A
Round, Fair Distance From the Furnace* (White Eagle
Coffee Store Pr, 1993), *Inside the Trackhoe* (The And Rev,
1991), *Poetry East, Crazyhorse, River City.*

Karen Blomain P
Kutztown Univ, Kutztown, PA 19530, 215-683-4335
Internet: blomain@kutztown.edu
    Pubs: *Normal Ave., Borrowed Light* (Nightshade Pr, 1998,
1993), *Coalseam: Poems* (U Scranton, 1993), *Pittsburgh
Qtly, Passages North, Painted Bride Qtly, MacGuffin, Sun,
Negative Capability, One Trick Pony.*

Louise A. Blum W
Mansfield Univ, Mansfield, PA 16933, 717-662-4597
Internet: lblum@mnsfld.edu
    Pubs: *Amnesty* (Alyson Pubs, 1995), *Love's Shadow: Anth*
(Crossing Pr, 1992), *West, Cream City Rev, Poetic Space,
Columbia, Sonora Rev.*

William O. Boggs P
Slippery Rock Univ, Slippery Rock, PA 16057, 412-738-2348
Internet: wob@sruvm.sru.edu
    Pubs: *Eddy Johnson's American Dream* (Hiram Poetry Rev,
1990), *Swimming in Clear Water* (Dacotah Territory Pr,
1989), *Three Rivers Poetry Jrnl, Colorado Rev, Hiram.*

Roger Bower P
Cameron Star Rte, Waynesburg, PA 15370, 412-852-1448
    Pubs: *Editor's Choice II Anth, Space & Time, Abraxas, Pig
Iron, Pudding, Colorado State Rev.*

Greg Bowers P
1010 Prospect Rd, Red Lion, PA 17356, 717-244-4261
    Pubs: *The Reunion* (Trunk Pr, 1977).

James Brasfield P
Pennsylvania State Univ, 117 Burrowes, English Dept,
University Park, PA 16802-6200, 814-865-9795
Internet: jeb16@psu.edu
    Pubs: *Antaeus, Poetry East, Seattle Rev, Chicago Rev,
Quarterly West, Black Warrior Rev, College English, New
Virginia Rev, Kestrel, Glas: New Russian Writing.*

Beth Phillips Brown P
440 S Jackson St, Media, PA 19063, 610-566-2810
    Pubs: *A Celtic Daybook & Compendium of Lore, Invisible
Threads* (White Pine Pr, 1987, 1983), *Painted Bride Qtly,
U.S. 1 Worksheets, Full Moon, White Pine Jrnl.*

Richard Burgin P&W
PO Box 30386, Philadelphia, PA 19103, 215-568-7062
    Pubs: *Private Fame, Man Without Memory* (U Illinois Pr,
1991, 1989), *Pushcart Prize XI: Anth* (Pushcart Pr, 1987),
Witness, TriQuarterly, Mississippi Rev, Shenandoah.

Deborah Burnham P
327 N 34th, Philadelphia, PA 19104
    Pubs: *Anna and the Steel Mill* (Texas Tech, 1995), *Virginia
Qtly Rev, West Branch, Literary Rev, Kansas Qtly.*

Christopher Bursk P
704 Hulmeville Ave, Langhorne Manor, PA 19047,
215-752-5101
    Pubs: *Cell Count* (Texas Tech, 1997), *The One True
Religion* (Quarterly Rev, 1997), *The Way Water Rubs
Stone* (Word Works, 1989), *Making Wings* (State Street Pr,
1983), *APR.*

Shulamith Wechter Caine P
122 Grasmere Rd, Bala Cynwyd, PA 19004, 215-667-5990
    Pubs: *Love Fugue* (Silverfish Pr, 1998), *World & Local
News* (Alms Hse Pr, 1988), *APR, American Scholar,
Negative Capability, Southern Poetry Rev, Kalliope.*

Rosemary Cappello P
1919 Chestnut St, #1721, Philadelphia, PA 19103,
215-568-1145
    Pubs: *Sig* (Peter Chaloner, 1988), *Pearl 22: Anth* (Pearl,
1995), *Voices in Italian Americana: Anth* (Bordighera, Inc.,
1994), *Schuylkill Valley Jrnl.*

Robert L. Carothers P
Edinboro State College, Edinboro, PA 16444, 814-732-2736

Jody Carr W
2210 Lehigh Pkwy N, Allentown, PA 18103, 610-820-5710
Internet: wrichick@aol.com
    Pubs: *Song of Innocence, Monday's Child* (HarperCollins,
2000, 1999), *My Beautiful, Fat Friend* (Crosswinds, 1988),
No Regrets (Dial Bks, 1982).

Diana Cavallo W
1919 Chestnut St, #1015, Philadelphia, PA 19103,
215-665-0698
    Pubs: *A Bridge of Leaves, The Voices We Carry: Anth*
(Guernica Edtns, 1997, 1994), *From the Margin To The
Center: Anth* (Purdue U Pr, 1990), *Confrontation.*

Joel Chace P
Mercersburg Academy, Mercersburg, PA 17236-1551,
717-328-3824
Internet: joel_chace@mercersburg.edu
    Pubs: *The Melancholy of Yorick* (Birch Brook Pr, 1998),
Twentieth Century Deaths (Singular Speech Pr, 1997), *Red
Ghost* (Persephone Pr, 1992), *No Exit, Poetry Motel,
Pembroke Mag, Small Pond, Recursive Angel,
Switched-On Gutenberg, Kudzu.*

Diana Chang   P&W
1400 Waverly Rd Apt B126, Gladwyne, PA 190351263,
610-645-8836
Pubs: *The Frontiers of Love* (U Washington Pr, 1994),
Literature Around the Globe: Anth (Kendall/Hunt, 1994), *On
A Bed of Rice: Anth* (Anchor Bks, 1995), *Confrontation,
Forkroads, Asian American Jrnl, Mag of Paragraphs,
Hampton Shorts, The Montserrat Rev.*

Lisa Chewning   W
5427 Wilkins Ave, Pittsburgh, PA 15217, 412-683-9302
Internet: llchewning@aol.com
Pubs: *Veri-Tales, Freed by Choice: Anth* (Fall Creek Pr,
1994), *Walking the Twilight: Anth* (Northland Pub, 1994),
Beloit Fiction Jrnl, Bluff City, Rosebud.

Michael Clark   W
Widener Univ, 1 University Place, Chester, PA 19013,
610-499-4354
Internet: clark@widener.edu
Pubs: *Our Roots Grow Deeper Than We Know: Anth* (U
Pittsburgh Pr, 1985), *Arizona Qtly, Outerbridge.*

John Clarke   P
RD 1, Stone Jug Rd, Biglerville, PA 17307, 717-677-7438
Pubs: *Inland Tide* (Snowy Road Pr, 1981), *Texas Rev,
Kansas Qtly, New Yorker, Atlantic, Colorado Qtly.*

Lance Clewett   P
8 Cave Hill Dr, Carlisle, PA 17013, 717-249-6912
Internet: bluemoon51@juno.com
Pubs: *One Fast Trout* (Paco Bks, 1997), *Diesel Flowers*
(Warm Spring Pr, 1992).

Marion Deutsche Cohen   P
2203 Spruce St, Philadelphia, PA 19103, 215-732-7723
Pubs: *Dirty Details* (Temple U Pr, 1996), *Epsilon Country*
(Ctr for Thanatology Research, 1995), *The Sitting-Down
Hug* (Liberal Pr, 1989), *Plain Brown Wrapper, Palo Alto
Rev, Ikon, Abraxas.*

James H. Comey   W
105 Treaty Rd, Drexel Hill, PA 19026, 610-853-2311
Internet: jcomey@forum.swarthmore.edu
Pubs: *The Dragon Singer, The Monster in the Woods*
(Stages of Imagination, 1997, 1996).

Marjorie Lenore Compfort   P
41 W Corydon St, Bradford, PA 16701, 716-372-7650
Pubs: *Tiotis, Quickenings, Parnassus, Belles Lettres,
Jean's Jrnl, Jlag Rev, Arachne, Arulo, The Archer.*

Robert J. Conley   P
Peekner Literary Agency, Inc., PO Box 3308, Bethlehem, PA
18017, 918-458-0034
Pubs: *Mountain Windsong* (U Oklahoma Pr, 1992),
Nickajack (Doubleday, 1992), *True West.*

Julie Cooper-Fratrik   P
5553 Rte 412, Riegelsville, PA 18077
Pubs: *Out of Season: Anth* (Amagansett Pr, 1993),
Minnesota Rev, Slant, The Dickinson Rev.

Anita R. Cornwell   W
3220 Powelton Ave, Philadelphia, PA 19104, 215-222-1241
Pubs: *The Girls of Summer* (New Seed Pr, 1989), *Black
Lesbian in White America* (Naiad Pr, 1983).

Gerald Costanzo   P
366 Parker Dr, Pittsburgh, PA 15216, 412-561-0957
Pubs: *Nobody Lives on Arthur Godfrey Boulevard* (BOA
Edtns, 1993), *The Laps of the Bridesmaids* (Bits, 1992),
Devins Award Anth (U Missouri Pr, 1998), *Nation, APR,
Ploughshares, NAR, Ohio Rev, Georgia Rev.*

Barbara Crooker   P
7928 Woodsbluff Rd, Fogelsville, PA 18051, 610-395-5845
Internet: 0003834619@mcimail.com
Pubs: *In The Late Summer Garden* (H&H Pr, 1998),
Obbligato (Linwood Pub, 1992), *Worlds In Our Words:
Contemporary American Women Writers: Anth* (Prentice
Hall, 1997), *For A Living: The Poetry of Work: Anth* (U
Illinois Pr, 1995), *Denver Qtly, Four Quarters.*

David C. Cruse   P
5220 W Master St, Philadelphia, PA 19139

Craig Czury   P
914 Leiszs Bridge, Reading, PA 19605, 610-921-0216
Internet: hthomas@kutztown.edu
Pubs: *Shadow/Orphan Shadow, Obit Hotel* (Pine Pr, 1996,
1993), *Fine Line That Screams: Anth* (Endless Mountains
Rev, 1993), *Five Finger Rev, Parnassus.*

Susan Daily   P
523 Magee Ave, Philadelphia, PA 19111, 215-725-5831
Pubs: *Newsart, Hot Water Rev, Painted Bride Qtly, Palm Of
Your Hand, Ampersand Magazine.*

Jim Daniels   P
Carnegie Mellon Univ, English Dept, Pittsburgh, PA 15213,
412-268-2842
Internet: jd65@andrew.cmu.edu
Pubs: *Niagara Falls* (Adastra Pr, 1994), *M-80* (U Pitt Pr,
1993), *Letters to America: Poetry on Race Anth* (Wayne
State U Pr, 1994), *Iowa Rev, Ohio Rev.*

Edmund Dantes   P
501 Franklin St, East Pittsburgh, PA 15112, 412-241-0671

William Davey   P&W
Creative Concepts Literary Age, PO Box 10261, Harrisburg,
PA 17105, 717-432-5054
Pubs: *The Angry Dust* (Beijing, 1993), *Dawn Breaks the
Heart* (Howell, Soskin, 1941), *Thalia, Massacre, The Lyric,
Antietam Rev, The Long Story, Caesura.*

Almitra David   P
986 N Randolph St, Philadelphia, PA 19123, 215-922-4563
   Pubs: *Between the Sea and Home* (Eighth Mtn Pr, 1993),
   Annie Crow Road/Chesapeake (Potter Pr, 1988), *Building
   the Cathedral* (Slash & Burn, 1986).

George Deaux   W
Temple Univ, Philadelphia, PA 19122, 215-787-7560
   Pubs: *Superworm* (S&S, 1968).

R. DeBacco   P
Westmoreland Community College, College Sta, Youngwood,
PA 15697, 724-925-4033
   Pubs: *New Voices, Whiskey Island Mag, Atavist, The
   MacGuffin, South Coast Poetry Jrnl, Tightrope, Loyalhanna
   Rev, Ecphorizer, Ko, Archer, Modern Haiku, Amelia.*

Toi Derricotte   P
166 N Dithridge St, #3E, Pittsburgh, PA 15213-2622,
412-688-8288
Internet: toiderri@mindspring.com
   Pubs: *The Black Notebooks* (Norton, 1997), *Captivity* (U Pitt
   Pr, 1995), *The Empress of the Death House* (Lotus Pr,
   1988), *Callaloo, Paris Rev, Iowa Rev.*

John Dewitt   P
221 Buttonwood Way, Glenside, PA 19038
   Pubs: *Finger Food* (Synapse, 1982), *A New Geography of
   Poets: Anth* (U Arkansas Pr, 1992), *New American Rev, #,
   Spectrum, Painted Bride Qtly, Lace Rev, Hydrant.*

Gregory Djanikian   P
Univ Pennsylvania/English Dept, 119 Bennett Hall,
Philadelphia, PA 19104, 215-668-9234
Internet: djanikia@english.upenn.edu
   Pubs: *About Distance, Falling Deeply Into America*
   (Carnegie Mellon U Pr, 1995, 1989), *Poetry, American
   Scholar, Antioch Rev, Poet Lore, Georgia Rev, Poetry
   Northwest, Shenandoah, Iowa Rev.*

Patricia Dobler   P
Carlow College, 3333 5th Ave, Pittsburgh, PA 15213,
412-578-6032
   Pubs: *UXB* (Mill Hunk Bks, 1991), *Talking to Strangers* (U
   Wisconsin Pr, 1986), *Ploughshares, Southern Poetry Rev,
   Mid-American Rev, 5 A.M..*

George Dowden   P
27 Ward St, Ridley Park, PA 19078, 215-532-6784
   Pubs: *A Message To Isis* (Moving I, 1977), *Renew
   Jerusalem* (Symra Pr, 1969), *Evergreen Rev.*

Robert C. S. Downs   W
Pennsylvania State Univ, English Dept, University Park, PA
16802, 814-234-0747
   Pubs: *Living Together* (St. Martin's, 1983), *White Mama*
   (Ballantine, 1980), *Cimarron Rev, Sundog.*

Rachel Blau DuPlessis   P
211 Rutgers Ave, Swarthmore, PA 19081-1715,
610-328-4116
Internet: rdupless@vm.temple.edu
   Pubs: *Drafts 15-XXX, The Fold, Drafts 3-14* (Potes & Poets,
   1997, 1991), *The Pink Guitar* (Routledge, 1990), *Sulfur,
   Conjunctions, Hambone, Chain, Chelsea, Iowa Rev.*

W. D. Ehrhart   P
6845 Anderson St, Philadelphia, PA 19119, 215-848-2068
   Pubs: *The Distance We Travel* (Adastra Pr, 1993), *Just for
   Laughs* (Viet Nam Generation, 1990), *American Poetry
   Rev, Virginia Quarterly Rev, Poetry East.*

Karen Elias   P
RD 2, Box 279-C, Lock Haven, PA 17745, 717-748-1632
   Pubs: *Sinister Wisdom, 13th Moon, Second Wave, Feminist
   Studies, Women/Poems IV, Anima.*

Edith Muesing Ellwood   P&W
RR1 PML 178, Bushkill, PA 18324, 717-588-3111
   Pubs: *Expressions Mag, Parent to Parent, Black Bough,
   Haiku Headlines, Brussels Sprout, Inkstone, Dragonfly.*

Lynn Emanuel   P
1027 Murray Hill Ave, Pittsburgh, PA 15217, 412-363-4323
Internet: emanuelt@pitt.edu
   Pubs: *The Dig and Hotel Fiesta: A Double Volume* (U
   Illinois Pr, 1995), *Best American Poetry: Anths* (S&S, 1998,
   1995), *Parnassus, Hudson Rev, Ploughshares, APR.*

Aisha Eshe   P
Comm College Philadelphia, 17th and Spring Garden,
Philadelphia, PA 19130, 215-751-8000
   Pubs: *Grain* (Saskatchewan Writers Guild, 1994), *Life On
   The Line* (Negative Capability Pr, 1992), *Catalyst, Dream
   Network, Women's Recovery Network, Athena.*

Joann Marie Everett   P
2224 Ogden Ave, Bensalem, PA 19020, 215-244-0525
   Pubs: *Angel Wisdom and a Woman's Song, Seasons in
   Thunder Valley, Whispered Beginnings* (Jasmine Pr, 1996,
   1986, 1984), *Calliope.*

Samuel Exler   P
307 E Roumfort Rd, Philadelphia, PA 19119-1031
   Pubs: *River Poems* (Slapering Hol Pr, 1992), *Ambition,
   Fertility, Loneliness* (Lintel, 1982), *Poetry East, Plainsong,
   New York Qtly, Literary Rev, And Rev.*

Sascha Feinstein   P
Lycoming College, English Dept, Williamsport, PA 17701,
717-321-4279
Internet: feinstei@lycoming.edu
   Pubs: *Summerhouse Piano* (Matchbooks Pr, 1989), *The
   Jazz Poetry Anth* (Indiana U Pr, 1991), *New England Rev,
   Missouri Rev, NAR, Denver Qtly, Hayden's Ferry Rev.*

Al Ferber   P
1110 Sheffield Ct, Bensalem, PA 19020, 215-638-2791
    Pubs: *Gus: Biographical Notes* (Cutting Edge Pub, 1994),
    Badlands (Johnston Green Pub, 1986), *Echos, Blue
    Buildings, Berkeley Poets Co-op, Painted Bride Qtly.*

Charles Fergus   W
RD 2, 340 Mountain Rd, Port Matilda, PA 16870, 814-692-5097
    Pubs: *Shadow Catcher* (Soho Pr, 1991).

Rina Ferrarelli   P
224 Adeline Ave, Pittsburgh, PA 15228, 412-341-8009
Internet: rferrarelli@mail.earthlink.net
    Pubs: *A Whole Other Ball Game* (Noonday Pr, 1997),
    Home Is A Foreign Country (Eadmer Pr, 1996),
    Dreamsearch (malafemmina, 1992), *The Art of Life: Anth*
    (South-Western Educational Pub, 1998), *The Runner's
    Literary Companion: Anth* (Breakaway Pr, 1994).

Ken Fifer   P
5525 Spring Dr, Center Valley, PA 18034
    Pubs: *Big Numbers* (Pennsylvania Council on the Arts,
    1981), *Falling Man* (Ithaca Hse, 1979).

Gary Fincke   P&W
3 Melody Ln, Selinsgrove, PA 17870, 717-372-4164
Internet: gfincke@susqu.edu
    Pubs: *The Technology of Paradise* (Avisson Pr, 1998),
    Emergency Calls (U Missouri Pr, 1996), *Inventing Angels*
    (Zoland Bks, 1994), *Paris Rev, Harper's, Kenyon Rev,
    Poetry, Georgia Rev, Gettysburg Rev.*

Sandra Gould Ford   W
7123 Race St, Pittsburgh, PA 15208, 412-731-7039
    Pubs: *ELF, Obsidian II, Confluence, James River Rev,
    Shooting Star Rev.*

Cynthia Solt Frame   P
PO Box 101, Springtown, PA 18081, 610-346-6283
    Pubs: *Rolling Stone, Northern Pleasure, Abbey, Bogg,
    Visions.*

Robert Freedman   P
30 E Market St, #3, Bethlehem, PA 18018, 610-868-5137
Internet: rlfreed@pipeline.com
    Pubs: *Creeping Bent, Yarrow, Endless Mountains Rev,
    West Branch, Onthebus, Calapooya Collage, Four
    Quarters, New York Qtly, Poet Lore.*

Catherine Gammon   W
Univ Pittsburgh, English Dept, Pittsburgh, PA 15260-0001
Internet: cathg+@pitt.edu
    Pubs: *Isabel Out of the Rain* (Mercury Hse, 1991), *Cape
    Discovery: Anth* (Sheep Meadow, 1994), *Manoa,
    Ploughshares, Kenyon, Central Park, Iowa Rev.*

Tom Gatten   P&W
105 E Curtin St, #15, Bellefonte, PA 168231737,
814-353-0532
Internet: tomgatten123@hotmail.com
    Pubs: *Mapper Of Mists* (Hre Lo Wambli Pr, 1974), *The
    Sumac Reader: Anth* (Michigan State U Pr, 1996), *Fiction
    Midwest, Art and Literature, Shenandoah, Poetry Now,
    Sumac, Hearse.*

Greg Geleta   P
1017 S 48 St, Philadelphia, PA 191433508, 215-704-6969
    Pubs: *The Year I Learned to Drive, Jazz Elegies* (Axe
    Factory Pr, 1988, 1985), *Snail's Pace Rev, Artful Dodge,
    New Stone Circle, Onion River Rev, Axe Factory.*

Julia Geleta   P&W
427 Carpenter Ln, Philadelphia, PA 19119, 215-844-7678
Internet: jblum@ga.k12.par.us
    Pubs: *Meeting Tessie* (Singing Horse Pr, 1994), *Artificial
    Memory* (Leave Bks, 1994), *Parallelism* (Abacus/Potes &
    Poets Pr, 1989), *Topography* (Center, 1983), *Aerial, Paper
    Air, 6IX, The World, Chain, Brief, Central Park.*

Kathleen E. George   W
1213 Monterey St, Pittsburgh, PA 15212
    Pubs: *The Man in the Buick* (BkMk Pr, 1999), *Rhythm in
    Drama* (U Pitt Pr, 1980), *Cimarron Rev, Alaska Qtly Rev,
    Great Stream Rev, Mademoiselle, NAR, American Fiction,
    Vignette.*

Robert Gibb   P
7708 Abbott St, Pittsburgh, PA 15221-3201, 412-243-5332
    Pubs: *Fugue for a Late Snow, The Winter House* (U
    Missouri Pr, 1993, 1984), *Momentary Days* (Walt Whitman
    Ctr, 1988), *Poetry, Kenyon Rev, Field, Poetry East.*

C. S. Giscombe   P
Pennsylvania State Univ, English Dept, Burrowes Bldg,
University Park, PA 16802, 814-865-6381
    Pubs: *Giscome Road, Here* (Dalkey Archive Pr, 1998,
    1994), *o.blek, River Styx, Obsidian II, Situation, NAW,
    ACM, Callaloo, Hambone.*

Ann K. Glasner   W
Kennedy House 2209, 1901 J. F. Kennedy Blvd, Philadelphia,
PA 19103, 215-561-5874
    Pubs: *Summer Awakening* (Lancer Bks, 1971).

J. B. Goodenough   P
300 Wildberry Rd, Fox Chapel, PA 15238
    Pubs: *Homeplace* (St. Andrews, 1989), *Dower Land*
    (Cleveland State U Poetry Ctr, 1984), *Arizona Qtly.*

Patricia J. Goodrich   P
PO Box 473, Richlandtown, PA 18955, 610-282-2822
Internet: pgoodric@bciu.k12.pa.us
    Pubs: *Sidelights* (Kali Moma Pr, 1995), *Intricate Lacing*
    (Nightshade Pr, 1992), *Zone 3, Yarrow, Mediphors, Folio,
    Footwork, New Jersey Jrnl.*

Carol Granato   P
2506 S 18 St, Philadelphia, PA 19145, 215-334-5412
Pubs: *Epiphany, Snake Nation, Seems, American Goat,
The Formalist, Prophetic Voices, Midwest Qtly, Poem,
Rockford Rev, Troubadour, Neo-Victorian, Riverrun, The
Lyric.*

Frank Graziano   P
PO Box 4511, Gettysburg, PA 17325, 717-337-6770
Pubs: *In Memory of Michael Morgan* (Cedarshouse Pr,
1986), *Ubermenschen* (Nightsun Bks, 1984).

Ray Greenblatt   P
Box 2000, Church Farm School, Paoli, PA 19301,
610-363-7500
Pubs: *To Find The Winterbourne* (Plowman Pr, 1996),
February Always Happens (Telstar, 1991), *America,
English Jrnl, Intl Poetry Rev, Midwest Qtly, Sulphur River
Rev.*

Sam Gridley   W
Box 13267, Philadelphia, PA 19101
Pubs: *Free Parking* (Spirit That Moves Us Pr, 1990),
*Huckleberry Press, Calapooya Collage, Epoch,
Cottonwood, South Dakota Rev, Cimarron Rev, American
Short Fiction.*

Alexandra Grilikhes   P
4343 Manayunk Ave, Philadelphia, PA 19128, 215-483-7051
Pubs: *Shaman Body* (Branch Redd Bks, 1996), *The
Reveries* (Insight to Riot Pr, 1994), *The Blue Scar* (Folder
Edtns, 1988), *On Women Artists* (Cleis, 1981), *TDR.*

Emily Grosholz   P
Pennsylvania State Univ, 240 Sparks Bldg, Philosophy,
University Park, PA 16802, 814-865-6397
Pubs: *Eden* (Johns Hopkins U Pr, 1992), *Shores and
Headlands* (Princeton U Pr, 1988), *Hudson Rev, Southern
Rev, Poetry, Partisan Rev, New Virginia Rev.*

Lee Gutkind   W
5501 Walnut St. #202, Pittsburgh, PA 15232, 412-688-0304
Internet: lgut@pitt.edu
Pubs: *Connections* (Tarcher/Putnam, 1998), *Unspoken Art,
Stuck in Time* (Henry Holt, 1997, 1993), *New York Times
Mag.*

Sy Hakim   P&W
3726 Manayunk Ave, Philadelphia, PA 19128-3705,
215-482-0853
Internet: http://www.creativearts.com/syhakim
Pubs: *Eleanor, Goodbye* (Poet Gallery Pr, 1988), *California
Qtly, American Writing, Dan River Anth, Northwoods Jrnl.*

William J. Harris   P
103 Cherry Ridge, State College, PA 16803, 814-867-1381
Pubs: *The Garden Thrives: Anth* (HarperCollins, 1996), *In
Search of Color Everywhere: Anth* (Stewart, Tabori &
Chang, 1994).

Bim Harrison   P&W
PO Box 97, Hegins, PA 17938-0097, 717-682-8764
Internet: jth@epix.net
Pubs: *An Intricate Weave: Anth* (Iris Edtns, 1997), *Coal
Seam: Anth* (U Scranton Pr, 1994), *West Branch, Spoon
River, Beloit Poetry Jrnl, Poetry Now.*

Dev Hathaway   W
314 N Morris St, Shippensburg, PA 17257, 717-530-5943
Pubs: *The Widow's Boy* (Lynx Hse, 1992), *Black Warrior
Rev, Carolina Qtly, Missouri Rev, Greensboro Rev.*

G. W. Hawkes   W
Lycoming College, English Dept, Williamsport, PA 17701,
717-321-4336
Internet: hawkes@lycoming.edu
Pubs: *Surveyor, Semaphore* (MacMurray & Beck, 1998,
1998), *Playing Out of the Deep Woods, Spies in the Blue
Smoke: Stories* (U Missouri Pr, 1995, 1992), *Atlantic, GQ,
Ploughshares, Missouri Rev.*

Ann Hayes   P
Carnegie Mellon University, Pittsburgh, PA 15213,
412-268-2850
Pubs: *Circle of the Earth, Progress Dancing* (Robert Barth,
1990, 1986), *Letters At Christmas & Other Poems: Anth*
(Badger Pr, 1995), *Hudson Rev.*

Samuel Hazo   P&W
International Poetry Forum, 4415 5th Ave, Webster Hall,
Pittsburgh, PA 15213, 412-621-9893
Pubs: *The Holy Surprise of Right Now, The Past Won't
Stay Behind You* (U Arkansas Pr, 1996, 1993), *The Pages
of Day and Night* (Marlboro, 1994).

Sonya Hess   P
538 E Harford St, Box 278, Milford, PA 18337, 717-296-6205
Pubs: *Kingdom of Lost Waters* (Ahsata Pr, 1993),
Constellations of the Inner Eye (Puckerbrush Pr, 1991),
Grand Street, Iowa Woman, Hiram Poetry Rev.

Allen Hoey   P
804 Bismark Way, King of Prussia, PA 19406-3214,
215-992-1088
Pubs: *What Persists* (Liberty Street Bks, 1992), *A Fire in
the Cold House of Being* (Walt Whitman Ctr, 1987),
Georgia Rev, Hudson Rev, Poetry, Southern Rev.

Daniel Hoffman   P
502 Cedar Ln, Swarthmore, PA 19081-1105, 610-544-4438
Pubs: *Middens of the Tribe* (LSU, 1996), *Words to Create a
World* (U Michigan Pr, 1992), *Hudson Rev, Sewanee Rev,
Boulevard, Gettysburg Rev.*

Cynthia Hogue   P
Bucknell Univ, Stadler Poetry Center, Lewisburg, PA 17837,
717-524-1853
Internet: hogue@bucknell.edu
    Pubs: *The Woman in Red* (Ahsahta Pr, 1990), *Where the
    Parallels Cross* (White Knights Pr, 1984), *Southern Rev,
    APR, NAR, Ploughshares, Spoon River Rev, Puerto Del
    Sol.*

Margaret Holley   P
1184A MacPherson Dr, West Chester, PA 19380,
610-344-4992
Internet: mholley@brynmawr.edu
    Pubs: *Kore in Bloom, Morning Star* (Copper Beech Pr,
    1998, 1992), *The Smoke Tree* (Bluestem Pr, 1991), *Prairie
    Schooner, Boulevard, Poetry, Southern Rev, Gettysburg
    Rev, Nation, Shenandoah.*

Charlotte Holmes   W
Pennsylvania State Univ, English Dept, University Park, PA
16802, 814-865-9126
Internet: cxh18@psu.edu
    Pubs: *Gifts and Other Stories* (Confluence Pr, 1994), *The
    Family Track: Anth* (U Illinois Pr, 1998), *New Stories From
    the South: Anth* (Algonquin Bks, 1988), *Grand Street,
    Carolina Qtly, Epoch, Story, New Yorker, Antioch Rev.*

C. J. Houghtaling   P
RD 2, Box 241, Middlebury Center, PA 16935, 717-376-2821
Internet: cjhoughtaling@usa.net
    Pubs: *Songs of the Season* (Tioga Printing Co., 1988),
    Filtered Images: Anth (Vintage 45 Pr, 1992), *Meanderings:
    Anth* (Foothills, 1992), *Wild West, Literary Jrnl, Wolf Head
    Qtly, Fox Cry, Open Bone, Byline Mag, Endless Mountain
    Rev.*

Carolyn Fairweather Hughes   P
548 Greenhurst Dr, Pittsburgh, PA 15243, 412-344-6850
    Pubs: *For She Is The Tree of Life: Anth* (Conari Pr, 1995),
    We Speak For Peace: Anth (KIT Pubs, 1993), *Pittsburgh
    Qtly, Slant, Wind, Poets On, Lactuca.*

Bruce Hunsberger   W
3616 Willingham Ave, Reading, PA 19605-1156,
610-929-2017
    Pubs: *Railroad Street* (Lyle Stuart, 1970), *Alfred Hitchcock's
    Mystery, Nantucket Rev, Seattle Rev, John O'Hara Jrnl,
    Redbook.*

Mary Jean Irion   P
Chautauqua Writers' Center, 149 Kready Ave, Millersville, PA
17551, 717-872-8337
    Pubs: *Holding On* (Heatherstone Pr, 1984), *Poetry, Prairie
    Schooner, NER, Western Humanities Rev, Southern
    Humanities Rev, Poet Lore.*

Haywood Jackson   P
9A Carothers Dr, Turtle Creek, PA 15145, 412-824-6814
    Pubs: *Fellow Travelers* (Samisdat, 1981), *APR, Poetry
    Now, New York Qtly, The Little Mag.*

Susan S. Jacobson   P&W
3025 Mt. Alister Rd, Pittsburgh, PA 15214-2603,
412-322-1072
    Pubs: *Other Testaments* (Incarnate Muse Pub, 1997),
    Living Inland (Bennington Pr, 1989), *Intergenerational
    Relationships: Anth, If I Had A Hammer: Anth*
    (Papier-Mache Pr, 1998, 1989), *Life on the Line: Anth*
    (Negative Capability, 1992), *Negative Capability.*

Annette Williams Jaffee   W
PO Box 26, River Rd, Lumberville, PA 18733, 215-297-5112
    Pubs: *The Dangerous Age* (Leapfrog Pr, 1999), *Recent
    History* (Putnam, 1988), *Adult Education* (Ontario Review
    Pr, 1981), *Ploughshares.*

Martin James   W
Peekner Literary Agency, Inc., 3121 Portage Rd, Bethlehem,
PA 18017, 215-974-9158
    Pubs: *Zombie House, Night Glow* (Pinnacle Bks, 1990,
    1989), *5 A.M., Mystery Scene, Cemetery Dance.*

Nancy Esther James   P
267 Maple St, New Wilmington, PA 16142, 412-946-8761
    Pubs: *No Time To Hurry* (Dawn Valley Pr, 1979), *Pivot,
    Stone Country, 13th Moon, Black Maria.*

Lou Janac   P
PO Box 342, Mechanicsburg, PA 17055, 717-774-0253

Suzan Jivan   PP
818 North Taney St, Philadelphia, PA 191301817
    Pubs: *Long Pond Rev.*

Julia Kasdorf   P
1404 Walnut St, Camp Hill, PA 17011, 717-737-4996
Internet: jkasdorf@mcis.messiah.edu
    Pubs: *Sleeping Preacher* (U Pitt Pr, 1992), *Poetry, New
    Yorker.*

Linda Keegan   P
141 Friar Ln, McMurray, PA 15317, 724-941-1279
Internet: keegan@nb.net
    Pubs: *Heeding the Wind* (Still Waters Pr, 1995), *Greedy for
    Sunlight* (M. Wurster, 1992), *Poet Lore, New Virginia Rev,
    Zone 3, Cape Rock, Pittsburgh Qtly, The Herb Companion.*

Joseph J. Kelly   P
Pennsylvania Humanities Counci, 325 Chestnut St, Ste 715,
Philadelphia, PA 191062607, 215-925-1005
Internet: council@libertynet.org
    Pubs: *Only Morning in Her Shoes: Anth* (Utah State U Pr,
    1990), *Chariton Rev, Visions, Plains Poetry Jrnl, Kansas
    Qtly, Poet Lore, Hiram Poetry Rev.*

Miriam Kessler P
2008 Highland Cir, Camp Hill, PA 17011, 717-761-4830
Pubs: *Someone to Pour the Wine* (Ragged Edge Pr, 1996), *Blood to Remember: Anth* (Texas Tech U Pr, 1991), *Cries of the Spirit: Anth* (Beacon Pr, 1990).

Kerry Shawn Keys P
14 Joseph Dr, Boiling Springs, PA 17007, 717-241-6033
Internet: kkeys@paonline.com
Pubs: *Ch'antscapes* (Pine Pr, 1998), *Krajina Supu Vultures' Country* (Votobia, 1996), *Decoy's Desire* (Pennywhistle Pr, 1993), *The Hearing* (Paco Bks, 1992), *Nation, Ploughshares, Iowa Rev, Kayak, Wilderness, 100 Words, The Blue Guitar, Michigan Qtly Rev.*

Yong Ik Kim W
1030 Macon Ave, Pittsburgh, PA 15218, 412-243-9495
Pubs: *Blue in the Seed and Other Stories* (Shi-Sa Yong Wo Sa, 1989), *The Diving Gourd* (Knopf, 1963), *Hudson Rev, New Yorker, Atlantic, TriQuarterly, Sewanee Rev.*

Dorothy E. King PP
PenOwl Productions, PO Box 3872, Harrisburg, PA 17105-3872, 717-234-3886
Pubs: *Love In Time* (PenOwl Pr, 1983), *Essence, Chicago Sheet, Mobius.*

Claude F. Koch W
128 W Highland Ave, Philadelphia, PA 19118, 215-247-4270
Pubs: *Light in Silence* (Dodd Mead, 1958), *O. Henry Prize Stories: Anth* (Doubleday, 1985), *Sewanee Rev, Antioch Rev, Southern Rev, Four Quarters, Spirit.*

Sandra Kohler P
225 S Market St, Selinsgrove, PA 17870, 717-374-8497
Internet: hagendaz@ptdprolog.net
Pubs: *The Country of Women: Anth* (Calyx Bks, 1995), *APR, Countermeasures, West Branch, Calyx, Northeast Corridor, 5 A.M., Prairie Schooner, Women's Rev of Bks, Flyaway, ALR.*

William Krasner W
538 Berwyn Ave, Berwyn, PA 19312, 610-647-1527
Pubs: *The Gambler* (Harper Perennial Library, 1987), *Resort to Murder* (Scribner Classic, 1985), *Harper's, Trans-Action, Society.*

Peter Krok P
240 Golf Hills Rd, Haverton, PA 190831026, 610-789-4692
Internet: macpoet1@aol.com
Pubs: *Plains Poetry Jrnl, Midwest Qtly, Blue Unicorn, Negative Capability, Schuylkill Valley Jrnl, America.*

Ursula K. Le Guin P&W
Virginia Kidd Agency, Box 278, Milford, PA 18337
Pubs: *Steering the Craft* (Eighth Mountain Pr, 1998), *Going Out With Peacocks, Unlocking the Air: Anth* (HarperCollins, 1994, 1996), *Four Ways To Forgiveness: Anth* (HarperPrism, 1995), *Kenyon, Sunset, Amazing Stories, Playboy.*

Audrey Lee P&W
PO Box 16622, Philadelphia, PA 19139
Pubs: *Black American Literary Forum: Anth* (Indiana State U, 1989), *What We Must See: Young Black Storytellers: Anth* (Ed Oord Combs, 1971), *Our Roots Grow Deeper Than We Know: Anth* (U Pitt Pr, 1986), *Essence, Saturday Evening Post, Black World.*

Harper Lee W
E Washington Sq, Philadelphia, PA 19105, 215-238-4200

Bahman Levin P&W
PO Box 8265, Philadelphia, PA 19101, 215-262-0497
Pubs: *Dead Reckoning, Rooted in Volcanic Ashes, The Night's Journey* (Concourse Pr, 1992, 1987, 1984), *Confrontation Anth* (Long Island U, 1992).

Harriet Levin P
Humanities Department, McAlist, 32nd & Chestnut Sts, 5th Floor, Philadelphia, PA 19104, 215-895-2441
Internet: millanhl@dunx1.ocs.drexel.edu
Pubs: *The Christmas Show* (Beacon Pr, 1996), *West Branch, Partisan Rev, New Letters, Nimrod, Iowa Rev, American Voice.*

Lynn E. Levin P
1850 Dover Rd, Southampton, PA 18966-4550, 215-364-2423
Internet: iamblel@aol.com
Pubs: *The Visible Woman* (Loonfeather Pr, 1998), *First Harvest: Anth* (Brodsky Library Pr, 1997), *Jewish Spectator, New Laurel Rev, Loonfeather, Reconstructionist, JAMA, Black Bear Rev, Northeast, Potato Eyes.*

Robert Lima P
Pennsylvania State Univ, N 346 Burrowes Bldg, University Park, PA 16802, 814-865-4252
Internet: http://www.personal.psu.edu/faculty/rxl2
Pubs: *Mayaland* (Editorial Betania, 1992), *The Olde Ground* (Society of Inter-Celtic Arts and Culture, 1985), *Fathoms* (Carnation Pr, 1981).

Jack Lindeman P
133 S Franklin St, Fleetwood, PA 19522-1810, 215-944-9554
Pubs: *From Both Sides Now* (Scribner, 1998), *Twenty-One Poems* (Atlantis Edtns, 1963), *Rhino, Bellowing Ark, New Authors Jrnl, Home Planet News, Eureka Literary Mag, Blue Unicorn, Poet's Page, San Fernando Poetry Jrnl, Hollins Critic.*

Jeffrey Loo   P
1512 Pine St, #2R, Philadelphia, PA 19102, 215-546-6381
Pubs: *Prayers to Protest: Anth, Unitarian Universalist Poets: Anth* (Pudding Hse, 1997, 1995), *African American Rev, Footwork, Synaesthetic, APR, Many Mountains Moving, Southern Poetry Rev, Dis-Orient, Crab Orchard Rev, Rampike.*

Roger A. Lopata   W
1300 Medford Rd, Wynnewood, PA 19096-2419
Internet: ralopata@earthlink.net
Pubs: *Other Voices, Painted Bride Qtly, Sou'wester, Hawaii Pacific Rev, Turnstile, Worcester Rev, Panhandler, Midland Rev, Pointed Circle, Hudson Valley Echoes.*

Radomir Luza, Jr.   P
18 Golf Club Dr, Langhorne, PA 19047-2163, 215-741-5897
Pubs: *Porch Light Blues* (B.T. Pubs, 1995), *This N' That, Handwriting from a Wounded Heart* (Dinstuhl, 1994), *Poet, New Laurel Rev, Anterior Bitewing, Papyrus.*

Jeanne Mahon   P
84 Yankee Ridge Rd, Mercer, PA 16137, 412-346-6466
Pubs: *The Wolf in the Wood* (Pangborn Bks, 1996), *Cimarron Rev, Creeping Bent, Cutbank, Pig Iron, West Branch, Yarrow.*

Jody Mahorsky   P&W
128 Mauch Chunk St, Nazareth, PA 18064, 610-759-8341
Internet: jody@alertsecurity.com
Pubs: *See of Tranquility, The Creative Spirit, Spirit of the Muse, First Time, Golden Isis, Prophetic Voices, Cosmic Trend, Poetry Peddler, Me 2.*

Jerre Mangione   W
3300 Darby Rd, #7315, Haverford, PA 19041-1075, 610-649-9609
Pubs: *The Dream and the Deal: Federal Writers' Project* (U Pennsylvania Pr, 1983), *La Storia: Anth* (HarperCollins, 1992), *VIA.*

Charles Edward Mann   P
PO Box 752, Langhorne, PA 19047, 215-943-3398
Internet: cemann@p3.net
Pubs: *American Poetry Rev, Threepenny Rev, Cream City Rev, Southern Humanities Rev, Greensboro Rev, New York Qtly.*

Gigi Marino   P
620 Devonshire Dr, State College, PA 16803, 814-234-7834
Pubs: *Catholic Boys and Girls: Anth, Catholic Girls: Anth* (Penguin/NAL, 1994, 1992), *Willow Springs, Graham Hse Rev, South Florida Poetry Rev.*

Paul Raymond Martin   P&W
18304 Porky St, Saegertown, PA 16433-9442, 814-763-1549
Pubs: *Dan River Anth* (Dan River Pr, 1996), *Robo Frog: Killer Frog Anth* (Scavenger's Newsletter, 1993), *New Thought Jrnl, Gotta Write, Oceana, Eclipse.*

Hilary Masters   W
Carnegie Mellon Univ, English Dept, Pittsburgh, PA 15213, 412-268-6443
Pubs: *Home is the Exile* (Permanent Pr, 1996), *Success: New and Selected Stories, Strickland* (St. Martin's, 1992, 1989), *Best Essays of 1998: Anth* (Anchor Doubleday, 1998), *Sewanee Rev, NAR, Ohio Rev, Virginia Qtly Rev, New Letters, Heart.*

David Matthew   P&W
1900 Cobden Rd, Glenside, PA 19038
Pubs: *New Press, Rag Shock, Up Front News, Pagan News, Open Moments, Pinched Nerves.*

Dawna M. Maydak   P
Hickory On The Green, 7074 Clubview Dr, South Fayette, PA 15017-1097
Pubs: *Ten: Poems* (R&R Pr, 1988), *Because the Death of a Rose* (Earthwise Pub, 1983), *Eleven.*

Jane McCafferty   W
Allegheny College, Meadville, PA 16335
Pubs: *Director of the World* (U Pitt Pr, 1992), *Story, Seattle Rev, West Branch, Mademoiselle, Alaska Qtly Rev.*

Dorothy McCartney   P&W
PO Box 29, Westtown, PA 19395, 610-399-1106
Pubs: *Lemmus Lemmus & Other Poems* (Branden Pr, 1973), *Poet Lore, Modern Haiku, Storytime.*

Mark McCloskey   P
663 Parkview Rd, Yeardon, PA 19050
Pubs: *Sometime the Cow Kick Your Head: Anth, Light Year '87: Anth* (Bits Pr, 1988, 1987), *Poetry Northwest, Zone 3, Poetry/L.A., American Literary Rev.*

Leslie Anne Mcilroy   P
333 Pitt St, #2, Pittsburgh, PA 15221, 412-241-2049
Internet: lesanne@ix.netcom.com
Pubs: *Gravel* (Slipstream, 1997), *Eclectic Literary Forum, MacGuffin, Pittsburgh Qtly, Main Street Rag, ACM, Ledge.*

David McKain   P
19 School St, Bradford, PA 16701, 814-368-5523
Pubs: *Spellbound: Growing Up In God's Country* (U Pitt Pr, 1994), *Spirit Bodies* (Ithaca Hse, 1990), *Iowa Rev, Poetry, Ploughshares, Harvard Mag, Quarterly Rev.*

Louis McKee   P
PO Box 11186, Philadelphia, PA 19136-6186, 215-331-7389
Pubs: *The True Speed of Things* (Nightshade Pr, 1990), *The New Geography of Poets: Anth* (U Arkansas, 1992), *APR, Tar River Rev, Lowell Rev.*

Frank McQuilkin   P
1708 S 16 St, Philadelphia, PA 19145, 215-389-5646
Pubs: *Southern Humanities Rev, San Jose Studies, America, Painted Bride Qtly, Sparrow.*

Robert Randolph Medcalf, Jr. P&W
185 N Main St #6, Biglerville, PA 17307, 717-677-7437
Internet: stormwalk@aol.com
    Pubs: *Eldritch Tales, Argonaut, Weirdbook, Beyond.*

Diane Hamill Metzger P&W
c/o Caldwells, 240 West Ridley Ave, Norwood, PA 19074
    Pubs: *Coralline Ornaments* (Weed Patch Pr, 1980), *Pearl, South Coast Poetry Jrnl, Collages & Bricollages, Anima, Philadelphia Poets, Hob-Nob, Long Islander.*

Ann E. Michael P
2380 Brunner Rd, Emmaus, PA 18049, 215-791-5127
Internet: juanitafb@aol.com
    Pubs: *The Swan King* (Limbo Bar & Grill, 1983), *Manhattan Rev, Painted Bride Qtly, Pinchpenny, Cottonwood, Thema, Onset Rev, Minimus, Amaranth.*

David Milton W
3210 Garbett St, McKeesport, PA 15132

John Paul Minarik P
1600 Walters Mill Rd, Somerset, PA 15510, 724-847-9575
Internet: minarikj@asme.com
    Pubs: *Past The Unknown, Remembered Gate* (Greenfield Rev, 1981), *Pittsburgh & Tri-State Area Poets: Anth* (Squirrel Hill Poetry Wkshp, 1992), *Confrontation.*

Carol Artman Montgomery P
3 Marshall Rd, Pittsburgh, PA 15214-2601, 412-231-7247
    Pubs: *Starting Something* (Los Hombres Pr, 1992), *Outlines* (Swamp Pr, 1990).

Dinty W. Moore W
351 W Clearview Ave, State College, PA 16803, 814-237-6189
Internet: dinty@psu.edu
    Pubs: *The Accidental Buddhist, The Emperor's Virtual Clothes* (Algonquin, 1997, 1995), *Catholic Girls: Anth* (Plume/Penguin, 1992), *Georgia Rev, Southern Rev, Iowa Rev, New York Times Mag, Beloit Fiction.*

Edwin Moses W
1625 Almond St, Williamsport, PA 17701, 717-323-6496
    Pubs: *Nine Sisters Dancing* (Fithian Pr, 1996), *Astonishment of Heart, One Smart Kid* (MacMillan, 1984, 1982).

P. D. Murphy P
Univ Pennsylvania, Indiana, PA 15705
    Pubs: *CQ, Pinchpenny, Kindling, Gold Dust, Poetry Rev, Taurus, Asylum, Sonoma Mandala.*

Manini Nayar W
512 Brittany Dr, State College, PA 16803
    Pubs: *London Mag, Signals, Stand Mag, Malahat Rev, Parnassus.*

Felice Newman P
Cleis Press, PO Box 8933, Pittsburgh, PA 15221, 412-937-1555
Internet: felicen@aol.com
    Pubs: *The Second Coming* (Alyson, 1996), *Herotica 5: Anth* (Down There Pr, 1997).

Joseph Nicholson P&W
RR 3 Box 396E, Mill Hall, PA 17751-9519, 717-726-7635
Internet: jnicholson@eagle.lhup.edu
    Pubs: *The Dam Builder* (Fault Pr, 1977), *Missouri Rev, West Branch, New Letters, Mississippi Rev, Poetry Now, Wormwood Rev.*

Ed Ochester P
RD 1, Box 174, Shelocta, PA 15774, 412-354-2359
Internet: ochester+@pitt.edu
    Pubs: *Allegheny* (Adastra, 1995), *Changing the Name to Ochester* (Carnegie Mellon, 1988), *Ploughshares, Poetry East, Prairie Schooner, Poetry, Pearl, APR.*

Richard R. O'Keefe P
PO Box 10506, State College, PA 16805
    Pubs: *Rumors of Autumn* (Hierophant Bks, 1984), *Uccello's Horse* (Three Rivers Pr, 1972).

Bernard Oldsey W
1003 Woodview Ln, West Chester, PA 19380, 215-436-4223
    Pubs: *The Spanish Season* (HBJ, 1970).

Toby Olson P&W
275 S 19th St, Ste 7, Philadelphia, PA 19103-5710
    Pubs: *Dorit in Lesbos* (Sun & Moon Pr, 1998), *At Sea* (S&S, 1993), *Unfinished Building* (Coffee Hse, 1993), *Utah* (Macmillan, 1988), *Conjunctions, Gettysburg Rev.*

Rebecca Ore W
3824 Spring Garden St, Philadelphia, PA 19104-2326
Internet: rebeccabrownore@msn.com
    Pubs: *Alien Bootlegger & Other Stories, The Illegal Rebirth of Billy the Kid, Being Alien* (Tor Bks, 1993, 1991, 1989).

Peter Oresick P
6342 Jackson St, Pittsburgh, PA 15206-2232, 4127416860x411
Internet: poresick@aol.com
    Pubs: *For A Living: The Poetry of Work: Anth* (U Illinois Pr, 1995), *The Pittsburgh Book of Contemporary American Poetry: Anth* (U Pittsburgh Pr, 1993).

Gil Ott P
Singing Horse Press, PO Box 40034, Philadelphia, PA 19106-0034, 215-844-7678
    Pubs: *Wheel* (Chax, 1992), *Public Domain* (Potes & Poets, 1989).

Karl Patten P
232 S 3rd St, Lewisburg, PA 17837, 717-522-0070
Pubs: *Touch: Poems* (Bucknell U Pr, 1998), *The Impossible Reaches* (Dorcas Pr, 1992), *Yarrow, American Literary Rev, 5 A.M., Graham House Rev, Pikeville Rev, Connecticut Rev, Mississippi Valley Rev, Cincinnati Poetry Rev, Greensboro Rev, Sucarnochee Rev.*

Jean Pearson P
PO Box 417, Bethlehem, PA 18016, 215-867-6447
Pubs: *On Speaking Terms with Earth* (Great Elm Pr, 1988), *Earth Prayers Anth, APR.*

Pamela M. Perkins-Frederick P
PO Box F-3, Feasterville, PA 19053-0003, 215-757-7229
Internet: herbnpam@voicenet.com
Pubs: *A Leaf Gnawed to Lace* (Petoskey Stone Pr, 1992), *Medical Heritage, Other Poetry, Beloit Poetry Jrnl, Images, The Sun.*

James A. Perkins P&W
Westminster College, Box 62, New Wilmington, PA 16172, 412-946-7347
Pubs: *Snakes, Butterbeans, and the Discovery of Electricity* (Dawn Valley Pr, 1990), *Southern Rev, Footwork, U.S. 1 Worksheets, Mississippi Rev.*

Walt Peterson P
5837 Beacon St, Pittsburgh, PA 15217, 412-422-8129
Pubs: *Image Song* (Seton Hill College, 1994), *Rebuilding the Porch* (Nightshade Pr, 1990), *Potato Eyes, Pittsburgh Qtly, Language Bridges, Samisdat.*

Natalie L. M. Petesch W
6320 Crombie St, Pittsburgh, PA 15217-2511, 412-521-2802
Pubs: *The Immigrant Train & Other Stories, Justina of Andalusia & Other Stories* (Swallow Pr/Ohio U Pr, 1996, 1990), *Kansas Qtly, Chariton Rev, Confrontation.*

Anthony Petrosky P
1109 DeVictor Pl, Pittsburgh, PA 15206, 412-361-5783
Pubs: *Red And Yellow Boat* (LSU, 1994), *Georgia Rev, Bastard Rev, Prairie Schooner, College English.*

Sanford Pinsker P
Franklin and Marshall College, English Dept, Lancaster, PA 17603, 717-393-1483
Pubs: *Sketches of Spain, Local News* (Plowman Pr, 1992, 1989), *Whales at Play* (Northwoods Pr, 1986), *Georgia Rev, Salmagundi, Centennial Rev.*

Kenneth Pobo P
123 Folsom Ave, Folsom, PA 19033, 610-499-4341
Internet: kenneth.g.pobo@widener.edu
Pubs: *A Barbaric Yawp on the Rocks Please* (Alpha Beat Pr, 1996), *Ravens and Bad Bananas* (Osric Pubs, 1995), *Atlanta Rev, James White Rev.*

Chaim Potok W
20 Berwick Rd, Philadelphia, PA 19131, 215-668-1591
Pubs: *Davita's Harp, The Book of Lights, Wanderings* (Knopf, 1985, 1981, 1978).

David Poyer W
James Allen Agency, 538 E Harford St, Box 278, Milford, PA 18337
Pubs: *Tomahawk, The Passage* (St. Martin's Pr, 1998, 1995), *As The Wolf Loves Winter* (Forge, 1996), *Winter in the Heart* (Tor, 1993).

Beth Brown Preston P
Cher-John III, 4926 Baltimore Ave, Philadelphia, PA 19143, 215-727-9624
Pubs: *Satin Tunnels, Lightyears: 1973-1976* (Lotus Pr, 1989, 1982), *Blue Cyclone* (Pennsylvania Rev, 1982).

Elizabeth Raby P
1580 Pleasant View Rd, Coopersburg, PA 18036, 215-346-8094
Pubs: *Camphorwood* (Nightshade Pr, 1992), *The Hard Scent of Peonies* (Jasper Pr, 1990), *1990 Poetry Minutes Anth* (Mulberry Poets & Writers Assn, 1990), *Yarrow.*

Susan Rea Katz P
535 Valley Park Rd, Phoenixville, PA 19460, 610-933-3496
Internet: katz@netaxs.com
Pubs: *Snowdrops For Cousin Ruth* (S&S, 1998), *Sutured Words* (Aviva Pr, 1987), *Passages North Anth* (Milkweed Edtns, 1990), *American Scholar, Louisville Rev, Maryland Poetry Rev, Alaska Qtly Rev.*

Claudia M. Reder P
134 Edgehill Rd, Bala Cynwyd, PA 19004
Internet: poart@erols.com
Pubs: *Chester H. Jones Anth* (Chester H. Jones Fdn, 1985), *Pennsylvania Rev, Nimrod, Quarry West, Kansas Qtly, Poet Lore, North American Rev, International Qtly, Poetry Northwest, Literary Rev.*

Jad Reilly P
2842 E Devereaux Ave, Philadelphia, PA 19149, 215-289-3659
Pubs: *Mozart Park* (Nightlight Pr, 1984), *Winter Colors* (Pennymirth Pr, 1973), *CPU Rev, Aloha, Impetus.*

Barbara Reisner P
3026 Congress St, Allentown, PA 18104, 610-439-1610
Pubs: *Poems* (Creeping Bent Pr, 1993), *MPR, Laurel Rev, Blue Buildings, Shirim, Graham House Rev, Yarrow, Wind, Bellingham Rev, River Styx.*

John Repp P
26598 Arneman Rd, Edinboro, PA 16412
Internet: jrepp@edinboro.edu
Pubs: *Thirst Like This* (U Missouri Pr, 1990), *How We Live Now: Contemporary Multicultural Literature Anth* (Bedford Bks, 1992), *Puerto del Sol, The Literary Rev, Iowa Rev, Greensboro Rev, Flyaway, Many Mountains Moving.*

Michael D. Riley P
1705 Lititz Pike, Lancaster, PA 17601, 717-569-6377
Internet: mdr1@psu.edu
Pubs: *Scrimshaw: Citizens of Bone* (Lightning Tree Pr, 1988), *Poetry, Fiddlehead, Cumberland Poetry Rev, Poetry Ireland Rev, Farmer's Market, Zone 3.*

Len Roberts P
2443 Wassergass Rd, Hellertown, PA 18055, 610-838-6716
Pubs: *The Trouble-Making Finch, Counting the Black Angels* (U Illinois Pr, 1998, 1994), *Dangerous Angels* (Copper Beech Pr, 1993), *Partisan Rev, APR, Paris Rev, Poetry, Hudson Rev, Georgia Rev.*

Margaret A. Robinson P
Widener Univ, Chester, PA 19013, 215-499-4332
Pubs: *A Woman of Her Tribe* (Fawcett, 1992), *Courting Emma Howe* (Ballantine, 1989).

Rosaly DeMaios Roffman P
Indiana Univ Pennsylvania, Indiana, PA 15701, 412-349-2296
Internet: rroffman@grove.iup.edu
Pubs: *Going to Bed Whole* (University Pr IV, 1993), *I Am Becoming The Woman I've Wanted: Anth* (Papier-Mache Pr, 1997), *Life On The Line: Healing and Words: Anth* (Negative Capability Pr, 1992), *A Gathering of Poets: Anth* (Kent State U, 1992), *MacGuffin.*

Judith Root P
Carnegie Mellon Univ Press, PO Box 21, Pittsburgh, PA 15213, 412-268-2861
Pubs: *Weaving the Sheets* (Carnegie Mellon, 1988), *The Paris Rev Anth* (Norton, 1990), *The Nation, Commonweal, William & Mary Rev, Tar River Poetry, Poetry, APR, New Republic.*

Savina Roxas P
265 Sleepy Hollow, Pittsburgh, PA 15216, 412-561-3557
Internet: roxi50@aol.com
Pubs: *Sacrificial Mix* (P. Gaglia Inc, 1992), *The Art of Life: Anth* (South Western Educational Pub, 1998), *Footwork: Paterson Literary Review Anth* (Passaic Comm College, 1995), *For She Is the Tree of Life: Grandmothers Anth* (Conari Pr, 1994), *Whole Notes.*

Gibbons Ruark P
45 Morgan Hollow Way, Landenberg, PA 19350-1048, 610-255-3454
Pubs: *Passing Through Customs: New and Selected Poems, Rescue the Perishing* (LSU Pr, 1999, 1991), *Keeping Company* (Johns Hopkins, 1983), *New Republic, Shenandoah.*

Sonia Sanchez P
Temple Univ, English Dept, Philadelphia, PA 19122, 215-787-1796
Pubs: *Under a Soprano Sky* (Africa World, 1987), *Homegirls & Handgrenades* (Thunder's Mouth, 1984).

Walter Sanders W
266 Burley Ridge Rd, Mansfield, PA 16933
Pubs: *Four-Minute Fictions: Anth* (WordBeat Pr, 1988), *NAR, West Branch, North Dakota Qtly.*

Peter Schneeman W
Pennsylvania State Univ, 104 Burrowes Bldg, University Park, PA 16802, 814-865-6381
Pubs: *Through The Finger Goggles: Stories* (U Missouri Pr, 1982), *Americas Rev, Salmagundi.*

Michael Schneider P
119 Gordon Rd, Pittsburgh, PA 15218, 412-371-4523
Internet: schneider@psc.edu
Pubs: *Poet, Antietam Rev, Pittsburgh Qtly, Savannah Literary Jrnl, Pittsburgh Post-Gazette, Loyalhanna Rev, Notre Dame Rev, Atlanta Rev, Heart Qtly.*

Adam Schonbrun P
Pennsylvania State Univ, 103 Burrowes Bldg, University Park, PA 16802, 814-867-8735
Pubs: *Not Always About Some People* (Ben-Adam, 1989), *We Held Each Other's Hand* (Haifa U, 1987).

Joel L. Schwartz W
1245 Highland Ave, Ste 202, Abington, PA 19001-3714
Pubs: *Upchuck Summer's Revenge* (Delacorte, 1990), *The Great Spaghetti Showdown* (Dell, 1988).

Rhoda Josephson Schwartz P&W
1901 JFK Blvd, #2321, Philadelphia, PA 19103-1578, 215-563-3768
Pubs: *Worlds of Literature: Anths* (Norton, 1994, 1989), *Chicago Rev, Nation, Kansas Qtly, APR.*

Ruth Knafo Setton W
4759 Huckleberry Rd, Orefield, PA 18069
Pubs: *Out of the Margins: Anth* (U Pr New England, 1996), *Follow My Footprints: Anth* (Brandeis U Pr, 1992), *Mediterraneans, International Qtly, Lilith.*

Kathleen M. Sewalk P
3589 Menoher Blvd, Johnston, PA 15905-5505
Pubs: *Along the Way, Singing of Fruit, Generations of Excellence, On Holiday, Past the Conemaugh Yards* (Tunnel Pr Ltd, 1996, 1996, 1993, 1992, 1987).

M. P. A. Sheaffer P
Millersville Univ, Millersville, PA 17551
Pubs: *Requiem Suite, Still A Miracle* (Millersville U Pr, 1992, 1987), *Moonrocks And Metaphysical Turnips* (MAF Pr, 1988).

David Paul Shreiner P
PO Box 12018, Pittsburgh, PA 15240
Pubs: *Tradition, Writers Showcase, Voices Intl, Dumars Rev, Innisfree, Tucumcari Literary Rev, The Pharos.*

Ron Silliman P
262 Orchard Rd, Paoli, PA 19301-1116
Pubs: *Toner* (Potes & Poets, 1993), *Jones* (Generator Pr, 1993), *Conjunctions, Object, Mirage, Grist On-Line, Object Permanence.*

Randall Silvis W
PO Box 297, St Petersburg, PA 16054, 724-659-2922
Internet: rrbns@juno.com
Pubs: *Dead Man Falling* (Carroll & Graf, 1996), *An Occasional Hell* (Permanent Pr, 1993), *Manoa, Destination Discovery, Pittsburgh Mag, CSM, Prism.*

Michael Simms P
219 Bigham St, Pittsburgh, PA 15211-1431
Internet: simms@duq3.cc.duq.edu
Pubs: *The Fire-eater* (Del Rogers, 1987), *Migration* (Breitenbush, 1985), *Southwest Rev, Pittsburgh Poets, Black Warrior Rev, 5 A.M., Pittsburgh Qtly, River Styx.*

David R. Slavitt P&W
523 S 41 St, Philadelphia, PA 19104, 215-382-3994
Internet: drslavitt@mindspring.com
Pubs: *Ps3569.L3, A Gift, Crossroads* (LSU Pr, 1998, 1996, 1994), *A Crown For The King, Sixty-One Psalms of David* (Oxford U Pr, 1998, 1996), *New England Rev, Pequod, Shenandoah, Partisan Rev.*

Deloris Slesiensky P&W
74 Dug Rd, Wyoming, PA 18644-9374
Pubs: *Fragments of Yesterday and Now* (Telstar Pub, 1990), *Wild Onions, The Plaza, Mobius, Psychopoetica, Moments in Time, Pittston Thursday Dispatch.*

David Small W
532 Grandview Ave, Camp Hill, PA 17011, 717-763-8328
Pubs: *The River in Winter, Almost Famous* (Norton, 1987, 1982).

Ronald F. Smits P
Box 466, Ford City, PA 16226, 412-763-7024
Pubs: *Mourning Dove* (Ball State U Pr, 1979), *Tar River Poetry, Wilderness, Puerto del Sol, Free Lunch, Connecticut River Rev, The Bridge.*

Judith Sornberger P
141 S Main St, Mansfield, PA 16933, 717-662-7735
Pubs: *BiFocals Barbie: A Midlife Pantheon, Judith Beheading Holofernes* (Talent Hse Pr, 1996, 1993), *Open Heart* (Calyx Bks, 1993), *Prairie Schooner, Puerto del Sol, West Branch, American Voice, Calyx, Hawaii Pacific Rev.*

Eileen Spinelli P
Ray Lincoln, 7900 Old York Rd, 107B, Elkins Park, PA 19027
Pubs: *Somebody Loves You, Mr. Hatch* (Bradbury, 1990), *A Room of One's Own, Muse, Footwork.*

Will Stanton W
925 Wilhelm Rd, Harrisburg, PA 17111, 717-564-1881
Pubs: *The Old Familiar Booby Traps of Home* (Doubleday, 1977), *New Yorker, Atlantic, Redbook.*

Laurence Stapleton P
229 N Roberts Rd, Bryn Mawr, PA 19010
Pubs: *Some Poets and Their Resources: Anth* (U Pr America, 1995), *Poetry Now.*

Sharon Sheehe Stark P&W
23 Blue Rocks Rd, Lenhartsville, PA 19534, 610-756-6048
Pubs: *Wrestling Season, The Dealer's Yard & Other Stories* (Morrow, 1987, 1985), *Atlantic.*

Irving Stettner P
124 N Main St #3, Shavertown, PA 18708
Pubs: *Beggars in Paradise* (Writers Unlimited, 1991), *Self-Portrait* (Sun Dog, 1991), *Anais, World Letter.*

H. T. P&W
914 Leisz's Bridge Rd, Reading, PA 19605, 215-921-0216
Pubs: *Voiceunders* (Texture Pr, 1993), *6ix, Texture, Washington Rev, Raddle Moon, Black Ice, Yarrow, Black Mountain II Rev, How(ever), Feminist Studies.*

John Taggart P
295 E Creek Rd, Newburg, PA 17240, 717-423-5565
Pubs: *Poems For the New Millennium: Anth* (U California Pr, 1998), *Crosses* (Sun & Moon, 1998), *Conjunctions, Five Fingers Rev, Hambone, Sulfur, Talisman, To, Chicago Rev.*

Charles A. Taormina P&W
103 Camden Ave, Johnstown, PA 15904, 724-925-3254
Pubs: *Moments* (1st Bks, 1998), *Rain Folio* (Renaissance Workshop, 1998), *Blue Ridge Rev, Gargoyle, William and Mary Rev, Samisdat, Fool's Jrnl.*

Marcia M. Tarasovic   P
PO Box 10334, State College, PA 16805
    Pubs: *Piedmont Literary Rev, Touchstone, Wind, Mill Hunk Herald, Interstate, Portland Rev.*

Myron Taube   W
Univ Pittsburgh, Pittsburgh, PA 15260, 412-624-6532
    Pubs: *Kansas Qtly, Texas Qtly, Wind, Cimarron Rev.*

John Alfred Taylor   P
395 N Wade Ave, Washington, PA 15301, 412-228-0968
    Pubs: *Year's Best Horror Stories: Anth* (Daw, 1983), *West Branch, New Letters, Twilight Zone Mag.*

Robert Love Taylor, Jr.   W
Bucknell Univ, Lewisburg, PA 17837, 717-524-1440
Internet: rtaylor@bucknell.edu
    Pubs: *Lady of Spain, The Lost Sister* (Algonquin Bks, 1992, 1989), *Southern Rev, Hudson Rev, Shenandoah, Georgia Rev.*

Philip Terman   P
4606 Scrubgrass Rd, Grove City, PA 161278716, 814-786-7270
Internet: ganya@pathway.net
    Pubs: *The House of Sages* (Mammoth Pr, 1998), *What Survives* (Sow's Ear Pr, 1993), *Poetry, Kenyon Rev, NER, NAR, Poetry Northwest, Southern Poetry Rev.*

Elaine Terranova   P
1912 Panama St, Philadelphia, PA 19103
Internet: eterranova@ccp.cc.pa.us
    Pubs: *Damages* (Copper Canyon Pr, 1996), *The Cult of the Right Hand* (Doubleday, 1991), *APR, Boulevard, Antioch Rev, New Yorker, River Styx, Virginia Qtly Rev.*

Sharon Thomson   PP&P
5401 Woodcrest Ave, Philadelphia, PA 19131, 215-877-5628
Internet: sharonthomson@juno.com
    Pubs: *Many Lights in Many Windows: Anth, The Writer's Community: Anth* (Milkweed Edtns, 1997, 1997), *Grailville Poets: Anth* (Grailville, 1995), *Yearbook of American Poetry: Anth* (Monitor, 1985), *Aspect, Poetry, Pequod, Christopher Street.*

J. C. Todd   P
339 S 4 St, Philadelphia, PA 19106-4219, 215-625-2449
Internet: jctodd66@aol.com
    Pubs: *Nightshade, Entering Pisces* (Pine Pr, 1995, 1984), *Paris Rev, Virginia Qtly Rev, Prairie Schooner, Puerto del Sol, Beloit Poetry Jrnl.*

Tommy Trantino   W
Box 280, Rte 2, Harveys Lake, PA 18618, 717-675-3447
    Pubs: *Lock the Lock* (Bantam, 1975), *Village Voice, People Mag, Stroker Mag.*

Alpay K. Ulku   P
137 Oneida St, #2, Pittsburgh, PA 15211-1264, 412-481-0987
Internet: ulku+@andrew.cmu.edu
    Pubs: *Meteorology* (Boa Edtns, 1999), *Literary Rev, Gettysburg Rev, Northwest Rev, Prism Intl, Black Warrior Rev, Malahat Rev.*

Lee Upton   P
Lafayette College, Easton, PA 18042, 215-250-5250
    Pubs: *Approximate Darling* (U Georgia, 1996), *No Mercy* (Atlantic Monthly, 1989), *APR, Field, Yale Rev, Poetry, NAR, Antioch Rev.*

Richard Vance   P&W
525C W 28 Div Hwy, Lititz, PA 17543
    Pubs: *Literary Rev, Poetry Wales, Poetry Australia, Oxford Mag, Karamu, Green Fuse Poetry.*

William F. Vanwert   P&W
7200 Cresheim Rd, #C-1, Philadelphia, PA 19119, 215-248-4715
    Pubs: *Missing In Action* (York Pr, 1991), *The Discovery of Chocolate* (Word Beat Pr, 1987), *TriQuarterly, NAR, Western Humanities Rev, Chelsea, Boulevard, Georgia Rev.*

Jack Veasey   P
37-A W 2nd St, Hummelstown, PA 17036, 717-566-9237
    Pubs: *Tennis With Baseball Bats* (Warm Spring Pr, 1995), *A Loving Testimony: Anth* (Crossing Pr, 1995), *Christopher Street, Pittsburgh Qtly, Oxalis.*

Jon Volkmer   P&W
Ursinus College, Collegeville, PA 19426, 610-489-4111
Internet: jvolkmer@acad.ursinus.edu
    Pubs: *Painted Bride Qtly, Texas Rev, Folio, Dancing Shadow Pr, South Dakota Rev, Crosscurrents, Carolina Qtly, Hellas, Cimarron Rev, Prairie Schooner, Seattle Rev.*

Jeanne Murray Walker   P
742 South Latches Ln, Merion, PA 19066
Internet: jwalker@udel.edu
    Pubs: *Coming Into History* (Copper Beech Pr, 1998), *Stranger Than Fiction* (Quarterly Rev of Literature, 1993), *APR, Poetry, Nation, Partisan Rev, Georgia Rev.*

T. H. S. Wallace   P
3032 Logan St, Camp Hill, PA 17011-2947, 717-780-2487
Internet: thswallace@aol.com
    Pubs: *When the World's Foundation Shifts, Raw On the Bars of Longing* (Rabbit Pr, 1998, 1994), *None Were So Clear* (New Foundation Pub, 1996), *Sewanee Rev, Midwest Qtly, Southern Poetry Rev, Cumberland Poetry Rev.*

Mark Thomas Wangberg   P
593 Hansell Rd, Wynnewood, PA 19096, 215-649-6007
    Pubs: *The Third Coast: Anth* (Wayne State U Pr, 1976), *U.S. 1, Poets, Bellingham Rev, 5 A.M., South Dakota Rev.*

Robert G. Weaver   W
Box 194, RD 1, Petersburg, PA 16669, 814-667-3530
    Pubs: *Just Pulp, Manhunt.*

Frances Webb   W
406 Crescent Rd, Wyncote, PA 19095
    Pubs: *Confrontation, Iowa Rev, New Renaissance, Antioch
    Rev, The Literary Rev, Feminist Studies.*

Bruce Weigl   P
Pennsylvania State Univ, University Park, PA 16802,
814-865-7105
    Pubs: *Sweet Lorrain, What Saves Us* (TriQuarterly Bks,
    1996, 1992), *Song of Napalm* (Atlantic Monthly Pr, 1988),
    The Monkey Wars (U Georgia Pr, 1985), *TriQuarterly.*

Sanford Weiss   P
RD 1, Box 97, Headquarters Rd, Ottsville, PA 18942,
215-847-2238
    Pubs: *Poetry, Kayak, Poetry Now, Yankee, Beloit Poetry
    Jrnl.*

William Welsh   P&W
501 Franklin St, East Pittsburgh, PA 15112, 412-824-0679
Internet: grapie@earthlink.net
    Pubs: *Being Pretty Doesn't Help At All* (Ancient Mariner Pr,
    1989), *You Can't Get There From Here* (Neumenon Pr,
    1986), *Maple Leaf Rag: Anth* (Portals Pr, 1995), *New
    Orleans Rev, Interstate, Maple Leaf Rag, Slow Loris
    Reader, Pittsburgh Qtly, Gravida.*

Richard Wertime   W
Beaver College, English Dept, Glenside, PA 19038-3295,
215-572-2963
Internet: wertime@beaver.edu
    Pubs: *The Ploughshares Reader: Anth* (Pushcart, 1985),
    *Northeast Corridor, Centerstage, Hudson Rev,
    Ploughshares.*

Leslie What   W
c/o Linn Prentiss, 538 Harford, Box 278, Milford, PA 18337,
717-296-8252
Internet: www.sff.net/people/leslie.what
    Pubs: *Beyond Lament: Poets Bearing Witness: Anth*
    (Northwestern U Pr, 1998), *Bending the Landscape: Anth*
    (Overlook Pr, 1998), *365 Scary Stories: Anth* (Barnes &
    Noble, 1997), *Fiction Qtly, Lilith, Hysteria, Asimov's,
    Realms of Fantasy.*

Kimmika L. H. Williams   PP
Temple Univ, Anthropology Dept, Philadelphia, PA 19122,
215-204-8414
Internet: kwilliol@thunder.ocis.temple.edu
    Pubs: *Epic Memory: Places & Spaces I've Been,
    Envisioning A Sea of Dry Bones* (Three Goat Pr, 1995,
    1994), *Hard Love: Writings On Violence: Anth* (Queen Of
    Swords Pr, 1997), *Erotique Noir: Black Erotica: Anth*
    (Doubleday, 1992), *Hip Mama, Sisters, Heat.*

Maureen Williams   P&W
RD #3, Box 3292, Uniondale, PA 18470, 717-679-2745
    Pubs: *A Loving Voice: Anth* (Charles Pr, 1992), *Women of
    the 14th Moon: Anth* (Crossing Pr, 1991), *Keltic Fringe,
    Black Mountain Rev, Endless Mountain Rev, Broomstick.*

Craig Williamson   W
Swarthmore College, Swarthmore, PA 19081, 215-328-8152
    Pubs: *Feast of Creatures* (U Pennsylvania Pr, 1982),
    Senghor's Poems (England; Rex Collings Ltd, 1976).

Eleanor Wilner   P
324 S 12 St, Philadelphia, PA 19107, 215-546-4237
Internet: pophys@aol.com
    Pubs: *Reversing the Spell: New & Selected Poems* (Copper
    Canyon, 1998), *Otherwise, Sarah's Choice, Shekhinah* (U
    Chicago Pr, 1993, 1989, 1984).

Jet Wimp   P
Drexel Univ, Philadelphia, PA 19104, 215-895-2658
    Pubs: *Against Infinity* (Primary Pr, 1978), *The Drowning
    Place* (Moore College of Art, 1974).

Sarah Winston   W
1801 Morris Rd #C-110, Blue Bell, PA 19422, 215-699-6045
    Pubs: *Summer Conference* (Cornwall Bks, 1990), *Of
    Apples & Oranges* (Perma Pr, 1990), *Not Yet Spring*
    (Golden Quill Pr, 1976), *Literary Rev.*

Michael Wurster   P
PO Box 4279, Pittsburgh, PA 15203, 412-481-7636
    Pubs: *The Cruelty of the Desert* (Cottage Wordsmiths,
    1989), *Strong Winds: Anth* (Broken Jaw Pr, 1997), *Galley
    Sail Rev, Pittsburgh Qtly, Pennsylvania Rev, Bone & Flesh,
    Cape Rock, Bogg, Pleiades, Poet Lore.*

Robert Zaller   P
326 Bryn Mawr Ave, Bala Cynwyd, PA 19004-2822,
610-667-2224
    Pubs: *For Empedocles* (European Arts Center, 1996),
    Invisible Music (Mavridis Pr, 1988), *Lives of the Poet*
    (Barlenmir Hse, 1974), *Agenda, APR, Blue Guitar, Spirit,
    South Coast Poetry Jrnl.*

Andrena Zawinski   P
76 S 14 St, Pittsburgh, PA 15203-1547, 412-488-7691
Internet: http://www.trollop.com/people/az
    Pubs: *Traveling in Reflected Light* (Pig Iron Pr, 1996),
    Writing on the Desk (Western Pennsylvania Writing Project,
    1995), *For She Is The Tree Of Life: Anth* (Conari Pr, 1995),
    *Callaloo, Poets On, Gulf Coast, Poet Lore, Nimrod, Painted
    Bride Qtly.*

Anne Yusavage Zellars   W
RD 2, Box 403, Valencia, PA 16059, 412-898-3019
    Pubs: *Oxford Mag, South Carolina Rev, Room of One's
    Own, West Branch, Women's Qtly Rev, Bloodroot.*

PUERTO RICO

Naomi Lockwood Barletta   P
PO Box 610, Mayaguez, PR 00709, 809-832-4792
    Pubs: *Atenea, Revista Chicano-Riquena, Alaluz, Hispanics
    In The US: Anth* (Bilingual Pr, 1982).

David Dayton   P
580 Cruz Maria/Bellas Lomas, Mayaguez, PR 006807571,
787-833-9242
Internet: david@rmceez.upr.clu.edu
    Pubs: *The Lost Body of Childhood* (Copper Beech, 1979).

Jose Emilio Gonzalez   P
Univ Puerto Rico, Box 2-3056, Rio Piedras, PR 00931,
809-751-8266

Victor Hernandez Cruz   P
PO Box 1047, Aguas Buenas, PR 00703, 787-732-8458
    Pubs: *Red Beans* (Coffee Hse Pr, 1991), *Paper Dance: 55
    Latino Poets: Anth* (Persea Bks, 1995), *A Gathering of the
    Tribes, See, River Styx, Massachusetts Rev.*

E. W. Northnagel   P&W
PO Box 6155, San Juan, PR 00914-6155
    Pubs: *Twenty-Five for Tony* (Cibola Studio, 1968), *Phase &
    Cycle, Pegasus Rev, CQ, Poetry Motel.*

Carmen Puigdollers   P&W
Condominio Francia #5E, 1551 Rosario St, Santurce, PR
00911, 809-721-8379
    Pubs: *Homenaje Poetico A Josemilio Gonzalez: Anth* (U
    Puerto Rico, 1993), *Interamericana, A Proposito Revista
    Literaria.*

Magaly Quinones   P
PO Box 22269, University Sta, San Juan, PR 009312269,
787-764-0000
Internet: mquinones@upracd.clu.edu
    Pubs: *Suenos de Papel* (Editorial Universidad de Puerto
    Rico, 1996), *Razon de Lucha, Razon de Amor, Nombrar*
    (Editorial Mairena, 1989, 1985).

Etnairis Rivera   P
Arrigoitia 515, San Juan, PR 00918-2648, 787-765-2888
    Pubs: *Entre Ciudades Y Casi Paraisos, Canto De La
    Pachamama* (Instituto De Cultura Puertorriquena, 1995,
    1976), *Ruptures, East Meets The West.*

RHODE ISLAND

Tom Ahern   P
16 High St, #4, Westerly, RI 02891, 401-596-8480

William Allen   P
118 Gibbs Ave, Newport, RI 02840, 401-842-0832
    Pubs: *Sevastopol: On Photos of War* (Xenos, 1997), *The
    Man on the Moon* (NYU/Persea Pr, 1987), *Iowa Rev,
    Newport Rev, Spazio Humano, Denver Qtly, Prairie
    Schooner, The American Voice.*

Mark Anderson   P
Rhode Island College, 600 Mt. Pleasant Ave, Providence, RI
02908, 401-456-8804
    Pubs: *Serious Joy* (Orchises Pr, 1990), *The Broken Boat*
    (Ithaca Hse, 1978), *Poetry, Hudson Rev.*

Randy Blasing   P
44 Benefit St, Providence, RI 02904, 401-351-1253
    Pubs: *Graphic Scenes, The Double House of Life, To
    Continue* (Persea Bks, 1994, 1989, 1983).

Cathleen Calbert   P
Rhode Island College, 600 Mt. Pleasant Ave, Providence, RI
02908, 401-456-8678
    Pubs: *Bad Judgment* (Sarabande Bks, 1999), *Lessons In
    Space* (U Pr Florida, 1997), *My Summer As A Bride*
    (Riverstone Pr, 1995), *Best American Poetry: Anth* (S&S,
    1995), *Paris Rev, Nation, New Republic, Hudson Rev,
    Ploughshares.*

David Cashman   P
23 Burlington St, Providence, RI 02906
    Pubs: *Modern Haiku, Brussels Sprout.*

Tom Chandler   P
44 Summit Ave, Providence, RI 02906, 401-831-1401
Internet: tchandler@bryant.edu
    Pubs: *Wingbones* (Signal Bks, 1997), *One Tree Forest, The
    Sound the Moon Makes As It Watches* (The Poet's Pr,
    1992, 1988), *Poetry, Ontario Rev, Boulevard, Literary Rev,
    New York Qtly.*

Martha Christina   P
17 Union St, Bristol, RI 02809
    Pubs: *Staying Found* (Fleur de Lis, 1997), *Crab Orchard
    Rev, Defined Providence, Connecticut Rev, Louisville Rev,
    Tar River Rev, Poets On, Prairie Schooner, Tar River
    Poetry, Zone 3.*

Geoffrey D. Clark W
PO Box 43, Bristol, RI 028090043, 401-245-4369
Pubs: *All the Way Home* (Avisson Pr, 1997), *Jackdog Summer* (Hi Jinx Pr, 1996), *Schooling the Spirit* (Asylum Arts, 1993), *Ruffian on the Stairs* (Story Pr, 1988), *Witness, Northeast Corridor, Ploughshares, Mississippi Rev, Pittsburgh Qtly.*

Thomas Cobb P
Rhode Island College, English Dept, Providence, RI 02908, 401-456-8115
Pubs: *Crazy Heart* (H&R, 1987), *We Shall Curse The Dead* (Desert First Works, 1976).

Leonard Cochran P
Providence College, Providence, RI 02918-0001, 401-865-1000
Pubs: *Tennessee Qtly, Atlantic, Harvard Mag, America, Spirit, Yankee, Christian Century.*

Albert Cook P
92 Elmgrove Ave, Providence, RI 02906
Internet: c0401000@brownvm.brown.edu
Pubs: *Midway* (Wayne State Pr, 1991), *Adapt the Living* (Swallow, 1981), *Trafika, First Intensity, Hellas, Denver Qtly.*

Patricia Cumming P
Box 251, Adamsville, RI 02801, 508-636-2403
Pubs: *Mother to Daughter, Daughter to Mother* (Feminist Pr, 1984), *Letter from an Outlying Province, Afterwards* (Alice James Bks, 1976, 1974), *ACM, Riverrun, Home Planet News, Crone's Nest, Timber Creek Rev.*

Tina Marie Egnoski P&W
43 Nisbet St, #2, Providence, RI 02906, 401-273-0529
Pubs: *Life On The Line: Anth* (Negative Capability Pr, 1992), *Fish Stories, Rhode Islander Mag, Cream City Rev, Laurel Rev, Rockford Rev, Mississippi Valley Rev.*

Caroline Finkelstein P
40 Bowan St, Providence, RI 02906
Pubs: *Germany* (Carnegie Mellon Pr, 1995), *Windows Facing East* (Dragon Gate, 1986), *APR, Poetry, Antioch, TriQuarterly, Virginia Qtly Rev, Willow Springs.*

Forrest Gander P
351 Nayatt Rd, Barrington, RI 02806-4336, 401-245-8069
Internet: forrestgan@aol.com
Pubs: *Science & Steepleflower* (New Directions, 1998), *Deeds of Utmost Kindness* (Wesleyan, 1994), *Lynchburg* (U Pitt Pr, 1993), *Conjunctions, Grand Street, Sulfur, First Intensity, Southern Rev, APR.*

Lora Jean Gardiner P
25 Glenwood Dr, North Kingstown, RI 02852
Pubs: *In Native Woods* (Rhode Island State Poetry Society, 1985), *Chrysalis, Green's Mag, Lyric.*

Christopher Gilbert P
56 Ardoene St, Providence, RI 02907, 401-461-5707
Pubs: *Demos/Music of the Striving That Was There, Across the Mutual Landscape* (Graywolf, 1993, 1984), *Ploughshares, Indiana Rev, William & Mary Rev, Callaloo.*

Ann Harleman P&W
55 Summit Ave, Providence, RI 02906, 401-272-7987
Pubs: *Bitter Lake* (Southern Methodist U Pr, 1996), *Happiness* (U Iowa Pr, 1994), *Virginia Qtly Rev, American Fiction, Southern Rev, Ploughshares, Shenandoah.*

Michael S. Harper P
Brown Univ, Box 1852, Providence, RI 02912, 401-863-2393
Pubs: *Honorable Amendments* (U Illinois Pr, 1994), *Every Shut Eye Ain't Asleep: Anth* (Little, Brown, 1994), *New Yorker, Obsidian.*

John Hawkes W
18 Everett Ave, Providence, RI 02906
Pubs: *An Irish Eye, The Frog* (Viking Penguin, 1997, 1996), *Sweet William: A Memoir of Old Horse* (Penguin USA, 1994), *Whistlejacket* (Weidenfeld & Nicolson, 1988).

Edwin Honig P
Brown Univ, Box 1852, Providence, RI 02912, 401-863-2393
Pubs: *The Imminence of Love* (Texas Ctr for Writers Pr, 1993), *Always Astonished* (City Lights, 1986), *Interrupted Praise* (Scarecrow Pr, 1984), *Mentor Book of Major American Poets: Anth* (Penguin, 1983), *Alea, City Lights Rev, Agni.*

Peter Johnson P&W
Providence College, English Dept, Providence, RI 02918, 401-351-0853
Pubs: *I'm A Man* (Raincrow Pr, 1998), *Pretty Happy!* (White Pine Pr, 1997), *Verse, Epoch, Quarterly West, North Dakota Qtly, Field, Web Del Sol, Denver Qtly.*

Caroline Knox P
Box 245, Adamsville, RI 02801, 508-636-4138
Internet: cbjknox@aol.com
Pubs: *Sleepers Wake* (Timken Pubs, 1994), *To Newfoundland* (U Georgia Pr, 1989), *Poetry, American Scholar, New Republic, Harvard, Verse, Paris Rev.*

Elizabeth Lincoln P
247 Fishing Cove Rd, Wickford, RI 02852, 401-295-5547
Internet: blincolnl@juno.com
Pubs: *Further Along* (Arbor Pr, 1990), *Momentary Stays* (Weaver Pubs, 1976), *Sojourner, Northeast Jrnl, Newport Rev, Crone's Nest.*

Peter Mandel P
239 Transit St, Providence, RI 02906, 401-831-5227
Pubs: *If One Lived On The Equator* (Nightshade Pr, 1993), *Harper's, Yankee, Poetry Northwest, Laurel Rev, Pulpsmith, Dusty Dog.*

Susan Onthank Mates   W
52 Bluff Rd, Barrington, RI 02806, 401-245-3546
> Pubs: *The Good Doctor* (U Iowa Pr, 1994), *Pushcart Prize XIX Anth* (Pushcart Pr, 1994), *TriQuarterly, Northwest Rev, Sou'wester, Arkansas Rev.*

F. X. Mathews   W
497 Old North Rd, Kingston, RI 02881, 401-789-7338
> Pubs: *The Frog in the Bottom of the Well, The Concrete Judasbird* (Houghton Mifflin, 1971, 1968).

Edward McCrorie   P
Providence College, Providence, RI 02918
> Pubs: *After a Cremation* (Thorpe Springs Pr, 1974), *Tennessee Qtly, Northeast Corridor, New Press Literary Qtly, Beloit Poetry Jrnl, Little Mag, Spirit.*

Robert McRoberts   P
8 Emery Rd, Warren, RI 02885, 401-245-5321

Tom Ockerse   P
37 Woodbury St, Providence, RI 02906, 401-331-0783
> Pubs: *T.O.P.* (Tom Ockerse Edtns, 1970), *The A-Z Book* (Colorcraft-Brussel Pub, 1969).

Lawrence T. O'Neill   P
PO Box 284, Kenyon, RI 02836
> Pubs: *Daguerreotypes, With Fire And Smoke* (Shadow Pr, 1991, 1976).

Jane Lunin Perel   P
Providence College, Providence, RI 02918, 401-865-2490
Internet: jlperel@providence.edu
> Pubs: *The Sea Is Not Full* (Le'Dory Pub Hse, 1990), *Blowing Kisses to the Sharks* (Copper Beech Pr, 1978), *Alembic, 13th Moon, Poetry Northwest, Carolina Qtly, The Voice, West Coast Writer's Conspiracy, Choice, Massachusetts Rev.*

Paul Petrie   P
200 Dendron Rd, Peace Dale, RI 02879, 401-783-8644
> Pubs: *The Runners* (Slow Loris Pr, 1988), *Strange Gravity* (The Tidal Pr, 1984), *Atlantic, Poetry.*

Nancy Potter   W
298 Hillsdale Rd, West Kingston, RI 02892, 401-539-2156
> Pubs: *Legacies* (U Illinois Pr, 1987), *Indiana Rev, Kansas Qtly, Cotton Boll, Paragraph, Alaska Qtly.*

Laurence J. Sasso, Jr.   P
145 Mann School Rd, Esmond, RI 02917, 401-231-1402
> Pubs: *The Olney Street Group Anth* (Olney Street Pr, 1989), *Italian-Americana, Texas Rev, Yankee, Santa Fe Literary Rev.*

John Shaw   W
28 Oaklawn St, #302, Cranston, RI 02920-9375, 401-944-5633
> Pubs: *Libido, New Renaissance, Turnstile, Brown Rev, NAR, Onion Head, New Oregon Rev, Phantasm, Moosehead Rev, Spectrum, Back Bay View.*

Meredith Steinbach   W
Brown Univ, Box 1852, Providence, RI 02912, 401-863-2393
> Pubs: *The Birth of the World As We Know It* (Another Chicago Pr, 1995), *Reliable Light* (Rutgers U Pr, 1990), *TriQuarterly, Antaeus, Southwest Rev, Massachusetts Rev.*

Nancy Sullivan   P
Hillsdale Rd, West Kingston, RI 02892, 401-539-2156
> Pubs: *Telling It* (Godine, 1976), *Treasury Of English Short Stories: Anth* (Doubleday, 1985), *Iowa Rev.*

John Tagliabue   P
Wayland Manor Apt 412, 500 Angell St, Providence, RI 02906
> Pubs: *New and Selected Poems: 1942-1997* (National Poetry Foundation, 1998), *The Great Day* (Alembic Pr, 1984), *The Doorless Door* (Grossman, 1970), *Chelsea, New York Qtly, New Letters, Pacific Intl, Poetry Northwest, Hudson Rev, Poetry, Kenyon Rev.*

Keith Waldrop   P
71 Elmgrove Ave, Providence, RI 02906, 401-863-3260
> Pubs: *The Locality Principle* (Avec, 1995), *Light While There Is Light* (Sun & Moon, 1993), *The Opposite of Letting the Mind Wander* (Lost Roads, 1990).

Rosmarie Waldrop   P
71 Elmgrove Ave, Providence, RI 02906, 401-351-0015
> Pubs: *A Key Into the Language of America* (New Directions, 1994), *A Form/Of Taking/It All* (Station Hill, 1990), *Avec, Conjunctions, Grand Street, Talisman.*

Craig Watson   P
211 Conanicus Ave, Jamestown, RI 02835, 401-423-2390
Internet: csw1@idt.net
> Pubs: *Picture of the Picture of the Image in the Glass* (O Pr, 1992), *Unsuspended Animation* (Paradigm Pr, 1990), *After Calculus* (Burning Deck, 1988).

Ed Weyhing   W
20 Murphy Cir, Middletown, RI 02842-6234, 401-846-1981
Internet: edweyhing@ids.net
> Pubs: *How the Weather Was: Anth* (Ampersand Pr, 1990), *Short Story, Cimarron Rev, Witness, Glimmer Train, Crescent Rev, Nexus.*

Ruth Whitman   P
40 Tuckerman Ave, Middletown, RI 02842, 401-846-3737
> Pubs: *Hatshepsut, Speak To Me, Laughing Gas: New and Selected Poems* (Wayne State U Pr, 1992, 1991), *New Republic, American Voice.*

Thomas Wilson W
6 Bush St, Newport, RI 02840, 401-846-8426
 Pubs: *American Fiction, Ellery Queen, Paris Rev, Antaeus.*

C. D. Wright P
351 Nayatt Rd, Barrington, RI 02806, 401-245-8069
Internet: wrightcd@aol.com
 Pubs: *Deepstep Come Shining* (Copper Canyon, 1998),
Tremble (Ecco Pr, 1996), *Just Whistle* (Kelsey Street Pr,
1993), *String Light* (U Georgia Pr, 1991), *Arshile, Colorado
Rev, APR.*

SOUTH CAROLINA

Gilbert Allen P&W
Furman Univ, Greenville, SC 29613, 864-294-3152
Internet: gil.allen@furman.edu
 Pubs: *Commandments at Eleven, Second Chances*
(Orchises, 1994, 1991), *American Scholar, Cumberland
Poetry Rev, Georgia Rev, Shenandoah, Southern Rev,
Tampa Rev.*

Paul Allen P
College of Charleston, Charleston, SC 29424, 843-953-5659
Internet: allenp@cofc.edu
 Pubs: *American Crawl* (U North Texas Pr, 1997), *Four
Passes* (Glebe Street Pr, 1994), *Iowa Rev, Laurel Rev, Viet
Nam Generation, Madison Rev, Ontario Rev.*

Syed Amanuddin P
790 McKay St, Sumter, SC 29150
 Pubs: *Poems* (Apt Books, 1984), *World Poetry In English*
(Humanities Pr, 1902).

Franklin Ashley W
Univ South Carolina, Columbia, SC 29208, 803-777-2560

Alice Cabaniss P
1405 Scarsfield Ave, Camden, SC 29020, 803-713-0662
 Pubs: *The Dark Bus* (Saltcatcher Pr, 1975), *45/96: Anth*
(Ninety-six Pr, 1996) *Portfolio, Circus Maximus, A Shout In
The Street, Appalachian Heritage, The Devil's Millhopper,
Points.*

J. Clontz P
PO Box 30302, Charleston, SC 29407-0302, 803-571-4683
 Pubs: *Haiku Headlines, Night Roses, Frogpond,
Lamp-Post, Candelabrum.*

Phebe Davidson P
11 Inverness W, Aiken, SC 29803, 803-642-3992
Internet: phebed@aiken.sc.edu
 Pubs: *Dreameater* (Delaware Valley, 1998), *Conversations
With the World* (Trilogy Bks, 1998), *Two Seasons, Milk and
Brittle Bone* (Muse-Pie Pr, 1993, 1991), *Kenyon Rev,
Literary Rev, Poetry East, Calliope, Southern Poetry Rev.*

John Matt Dorn P
2363 Table Rock Rd, Pickens, SC 29761, 803-878-0350
 Pubs: *Prognosis: Fair* (Colonial Pr, 1992).

Scott Ely W
Winthrop College, English Dept, Rock Hill, SC 29730,
803-323-2131
 Pubs: *Overgrown With Love* (U Arkansas Pr, 1993), *Pit
Bull, Starlight* (Weidenfeld & Nicolson, 1988, 1987).

Stephen Gardner P
Univ South Carolina, 171 University Pkwy, Aiken, SC 29801,
803-641-3239
Internet: sgard60721@aol.com or gardner@vm.sc.edu
 Pubs: *This Book Belongs To Eva* (Palanquin Pr, 1996),
*Louisiana Literature, Texas Rev, Southern Rev, California
Qtly, Kansas Qtly, Poetry Northwest, Connecticut Rev,
Nebraska Rev, Widener Rev, New Delta Rev, Southern
Poetry Rev, Mississippi Rev.*

Vertamae Grosvenor P&W
PO Box 126, Frogmore, SC 29920

Dan Huntley P
1089 Cedar Spring Rd, York, SC 29745
 Pubs: *Southern Poetry Rev, Kudzu, Graffiti, Hob-Nob.*

Vera Kistler W
123 Edwards Ave, Darlington, SC 29532, 843-393-3191
 Pubs: *Birds of a Feather, Deaf Violets* (Melantrich, 1986,
1982), *Too Much Heaven* (C.S. Spisovatel, 1985),
*Sandlapper, State, Zapad, Metamorphosis, Choice,
Spektrum.*

J. Calvin Koonts P
Erskine College, Washington St, Due West, SC 29639,
813-379-2360
 Pubs: *Lines: Opus 8* (Jacobs Pr, 1994), *Under the Umbrella*
(Sandlapper Pr, 1971).

Margaret Lally P
PO Box 30494, Charleston, SC 29417, 803-953-7908
 Pubs: *Juliana's Room* (Bits Pr, 1988), *Ohio Rev, Literary
Rev, Kenyon Rev, Hudson Rev.*

John Lane P
Wofford College, Box 101, Spartanburg, SC 29303,
864-597-4518
Internet: laneje@wofford.edu
 Pubs: *Against Information & Other Poems* (New Nature Pr,
1996), *In Short: Short Creative Nonfiction: Anth* (Norton,
1996), *Virginia Qtly Rev, Nimrod.*

Bryan Eugene Lindsay P
109 Greenbriar Rd, Spartanburg, SC 29302, 803-573-7277
 Pubs: *New Orleans Rev, Southern Poetry Rev, Epos,
Human Voice Qtly, Foxfire, Prickly Pear.*

Bret Lott   W
College of Charleston, Charleston, SC 29424, 803-953-5664
    Pubs: *The Hunt Club* (Villard, 1998), *Fathers, Sons, and Brothers* (HB, 1997), *Reed's Beach, Jewel* (Pocket Bks, 1993, 1991), *Antioch Rev, Story, Prairie Schooner, Witness, New Letters, Iowa Rev, Gettysburg Rev, Southern Rev, Ascent, Notre Dame Rev.*

Susan Ludvigson   P
330 Marion St, Rock Hill, SC 29730, 803-328-9207
    Pubs: *To Find the Gold, The Beautiful Noon of No Shadow, The Swimmer* (LSU Pr, 1990, 1986, 1984).

Russ McCollin   P
3681 E River St, Anderson, SC 29621, 803-225-9596

Nelljean McConeghey   P
203 Sherwood Dr, Conway, SC 29526
    Pubs: *Beloit Poetry Jrnl, Calyx, Cold Mountain Rev, New Mexico Humanities Rev.*

Susan Meyers   P
PO Box 1765, Pawley's Island, SC 29585, 843-527-8669
Internet: bluesue@sccoast.net
    Pubs: *Lessons In Leaving* (Persephone Pr, 1998), *The South Carolina Collection: Anth* (South Carolina Writers Workshop, 1991), *Greensboro Rev, Crucible, Mount Olive Rev, Point, Wellspring, Pembroke Mag.*

Horace Mungin   P&W
152 McArn Rd, Ridgeville, SC 29472, 803-875-3886
    Pubs: *Sleepy Willie Talk About His Life* (R&M Pub, 1991), *The Ninety-Six Sampler of South Carolina Poetry: Anth* (Ninety-Six Pr, 1994), *Essence.*

Robert Parham   P&W
Francis Marion College, Box 100547, Florence, SC 29501, 803-661-1500
    Pubs: *The Low Fires of Keen Memory* (Colonial Pr, 1992), *The Ninety-Six Sampler of South Carolina Poetry: Anth* (Ninety-Six Pr, 1994), *Southern Poetry Rev.*

Diane Marie Perrine   P
408 Abner Rd, C-42, Spartanburg, SC 29301, 864-574-8384
    Pubs: *Nexus, Icon, Writers Haven Jrnl, Silver Wings, Prickly Pear.*

Eugene Platt   P&W
734 Gilmore Ct, Charleston, SC 29412-9043, 843-795-9442
    Pubs: *Bubba, Missy & Me* (Tradd Street Pr, 1992), *The Legend of Being Irish: Anth* (White Pine Pr/Daedalus Pr, 1989), *Christianity and the Arts, Tar River Poetry, Crazyhorse, South Carolina Rev, Poet Lore, Poem.*

Robert S. Poole   W
2913 Kennedy St, Columbia, SC 29205, 803-799-3964
    Pubs: *Cardinal Anth* (Jaccar Pr, 1986), *Greensboro Rev, Fiction.*

Ennis Rees   P
2921 Pruitt Dr, Columbia, SC 29204
    Pubs: *Selected Poems* (U South Carolina Pr, 1973), *Southern Rev, New Republic.*

Rosa Shand   W
189 Clifton Ave, Spartanburg, SC 293021435, 864-582-2302
Internet: rosa.shand@converse.edu
    Pubs: *New Southern Harmonies: 4 Emerging Fiction Writers: Anth* (Holocene Pr, 1998), *Massachusetts Rev, Southern Rev, Indiana Rev, Chelsea, Northwest Rev, Chariton Rev, Virginia Qtly Rev, Shenandoah.*

Bennie Lee Sinclair   P&W
PO Box 345, Cleveland, SC 29635, 864-836-8489
    Pubs: *The Endangered* (96 Pr, 1993), *The Lynching* (Walker & Sons, 1992), *New Rev, NAR, Ellery Queen, Foxfire, South Carolina Rev, Asheville Poetry Rev.*

David Starkey   P
Francis Marion Univ, English Dept, Florence, SC 29501, 803-661-1370
    Pubs: *Adventures of The Minor Poet* (I*D Bks, 1994), *Life on the Line: Selections on Words & Healing: Anth* (Negative Capability Pr, 1992), *Chariton Rev.*

Mark Steadman   W
450 Pin du Lac Dr, Central, SC 29630, 864-639-6673
Internet: mcafee@clemson.edu
    Pubs: *Mcafee County* (U Georgia Pr, 1998), *Bang-Up Season* (Longstreet Pr, 1990), *Angel Child, An American Christmas: Anth* (Peachtree, 1987, 1986), *South Carolina Rev, Southern Rev, Nova.*

Lori Storie-Pahlitzsch   P&W
26 Partridge Ln, Greenville, SC 29601
    Pubs: *45/96: South Carolina Poetry Anth* (96 Pr, 1994), *Looking for Home: Anth* (Milkweed, 1990), *Poetry Northwest, Pleiades, Blue Unicorn, Crescent Rev, Poet Lore, Laurel Rev.*

David Tillinghast   P&W
Clemson University, English Dept, Clemson, SC 29631, 803-656-5412
    Pubs: *Women Hoping for Rain and Other Poems* (State Street Pr, 1987), *Texas Rev, Southern Rev, Georgia Rev, Virginia Qtly Rev, Ploughshares.*

Deno Trakas   P
Wofford College, 429 N Church St, Spartanburg, SC 29303, 864-582-1735
Internet: trakasdp@wofford.edu
    Pubs: *Human and Puny, New Southern Harmonies, The Shuffle of Wings* (Holocene Pr, 1999, 1998, 1990), *45/96: South Carolina Poetry Anth* (96 Pr, 1994), *From The Green Horseshoe: Anth* (U South Carolina Pr, 1987).

Laura Puccia Valtorta   W
2009 Lincoln St, Columbia, SC 29201, 803-765-0508
    Pubs: *Family Meal, A Living Culture in Durham* (Carolina
    Wren Pr, 1993, 1987).

Joy Walsh   P
31 S Hilton Head Cabanas, Hilton Head Island, SC 29928
    Pubs: *Undertow, My Trip West* (Textile Bridge, 1994, 1992),
    Mary Magdalene Visits the Flea Market of the Mind (Alpha
    Beat Pr, 1993), *Alpha Beat Soup.*

Tommy Scott Young   P
PO Box 11247, Columbia, SC 29211, 803-754-2075
    Pubs: *Tommy Scott Young Spins Magical Tales, Vol 1 & 2*
    (Raspberry Recordings, 1986).

SOUTH DAKOTA

Kathy Callaway   P&W
112 S Harvard, Vermillon, SD 57069, 605-677-5229
    Pubs: *Heart Of The Garfish* (U Pittsburgh Pr, 1982), *The
    Bloodroot Flower* (Knopf, 1982).

David Allan Evans   P&W
1326 2nd St, Brookings, SD 57006, 605-692-5214
Internet: evans@brooking.net
    Pubs: *Double Happiness: Two Lives in China* (USD Pr,
    1995), *Hanging Out With The Crows* (BkMk Pr, 1991),
    Aethlon, Chariton Rev, English Jrnl, Poetry Northwest.

Gerald Timothy Gordon   P
931 W Jackson, #5, Spearfish, SD 57783, 605-642-4016
    Pubs: *Out of Season: Anth* (Amagansett Pr, 1992), *Mixed
    Voices: Anth* (Milkweed Edtns, 1991), *Art Times, Spitball,
    Pacific Coast Jrnl, American Literary Rev.*

Tom Hansen   P
1803 N Kline, Aberdeen, SD 57401, 605-225-0272
    Pubs: *Northern Centinel, Midwest Qtly, Kansas Qtly, Great
    River Rev, Literary Rev, Iowa Rev, Anima, Prairie
    Schooner, Willow Springs, Changing Men.*

Donald Harington   W
South Dakota State Univ, Brookings, SD 57007
    Pubs: *The Architecture Of The Arkansas Ozarks* (Little,
    Brown, 1975), *Esquire.*

Linda Hasselstrom   P&W
Box 169, Hermosa, SD 57744, 605-255-4064
    Pubs: *Dakota Bones: Collected Poems* (Spoon River
    Poetry Pr, 1993), *Land Circle: Writings Collected From The
    Land* (Fulcrum Inc., 1991), *Leaning Into the Wind: Anth*
    (HM, 1997), *Reader's Digest.*

Allison Adelle Hedge Coke   P&W
PO Box 565, Rapid City, SD 577090565, 605-355-9147
    Pubs: *Dog Road Woman* (Coffee Hse Pr, 1997), *The Year of
    the Rat* (Grimes Pr, 1995), *Santa Barbara Rev, Little Mag,
    Caliban, 13th Moon, Cross Culture Poetics, Gatherings.*

Adrian C. Louis   P
PO Box 1990, Pine Ridge, SD 57770-1990
Internet: numu@gpcom.net
    Pubs: *Wild Indians & Other Creatures* (U Nevada Pr, 1996),
    Skins (Crown, 1995), *Ploughshares, New Letters, Kenyon
    Rev, TriQuarterly, Exquisite Corpse, Chicago Rev.*

Janice H. Mikesell   P&W
PO Box 87945, Sioux Falls, SD 57105, 605-336-9570
    Pubs: *Some People Don't Know That Barns Have Faces, A
    Survivor's Manual: Poetry* (Hen's Teeth, 1998, 1993), *Fate
    Worse Than Death and Other Hospital Stories* (U South
    Dakota Pr, 1995), *Midwest Rev, South Dakota Rev,
    Kalliope, Buffalo Bones.*

John R. Milton   P&W
630 Thomas, Vermillion, SD 57069, 605-624-2133

Kathleen Norris   P&W
PO Box 570, Lemmon, SD 57638
    Pubs: *The Cloister Walk* (Riverhead, 1996), *Little Girls In
    Church, The Middle of the World* (U Pitt Pr, 1995, 1981),
    Dakota (Ticknor & Fields, 1993).

Norval Rindfleisch   W
21176 458th Ave, Volga, SD 57071-6213, 605-826-4102
    Pubs: *The Season of Letting Go* (Claritas Imprints, 1995),
    In Loveless Clarity (Ithaca Hse, 1970), *Epoch, Literary Rev,
    Yale Literary Mag, Northern New England Rev.*

Geraldine A. J. Sanford   P&W
306 W 36 St, #22, Sioux Falls, SD 57105, 605-332-6090
    Pubs: *Unverified Sightings* (Dakota East, 1996), *As Far As I
    Can See* (Windflower Pr, 1989), *Longneck, South Dakota
    Rev, Prairie Winds, South Dakota Mag.*

James Solheim   P&W
1722 Baylor, Vermillion, SD 57069, 605-624-7684
Internet: jsolheim@usd.edu
    Pubs: *It's Disgusting—and We Ate It!: Anth* (S&S, 1998),
    Pushcart Prize Anth XV (Pushcart Pr, 1991), *ACM, Poetry,
    Kenyon Rev, Iowa Rev, Northwest Rev, Chicago Rev,
    Missouri Rev, Cimarron Rev.*

Stephen J. Thorpe   W
Box 915, Spearfish, SD 57783, 605-584-2785
    Pubs: *Walking Wounded* (Bantam, 1984), *Encounter,
    California Qtly, Smackwarm.*

Sylvia Wheeler　　　　　P
Univ South Dakota, Vermillion, SD 57069, 605-677-5229
　　Pubs: *Counting Back: Voices of the Lakota and Pioneer
　　Settlers, Dancing Alone* (BkMk Pr, 1992, 1992), *New
　　Letters, Chariton Rev.*

TENNESSEE

Deborah Adams　　　　　P&W
Jin Publicists, 504 Cedar Forest Ct, Nashville, TN 37221,
615-356-3086
Internet: http://members.aol.com/dkadams
　　Pubs: *All the Blood Relations, All the Deadly Beloved, All
　　the Hungry Mothers* (Ballantine, 1997, 1996, 1994),
　　*Murderous Intent, Funny Bones, Murder They Wrote 2,
　　Deadly Women, Canine Capers, Malice Domestic 3.*

Tina Barr　　　　　P
Rhodes College, 2000 N Pkwy, Memphis, TN 38112-1690,
901-843-3979
　　Pubs: *The Fugitive Eye* (Painted Bride Qtly, 1997), *At Dusk
　　on Naskeag Point* (Flume Pr, 1984), *Southwest Rev, APR,
　　Louisiana Literature, Harvard Rev, Pequod, Paris Rev,
　　Chelsea, Crazyhorse, Boulevard.*

Scott Bates　　　　　P
Box 1263, 735 University Ave, Sewanee, TN 37375-1000,
615-598-5843
　　Pubs: *Merry Green Peace, Lupo's Fables* (Jump-Off
　　Mountain, 1990, 1983), *Delos.*

John Bensko　　　　　P
PO Box 40042, Memphis, TN 38174-0042, 901-726-9187
　　Pubs: *The Waterman's Children* (U Massachusetts Pr,
　　1994), *Green Soldiers* (Yale U Pr, 1981), *Poetry, Poetry
　　Northwest, New Letters, NER, Quarterly West, Iowa Rev,
　　Florida Rev, Georgia Rev.*

Diann Blakely　　　　　P
640 Timber Ln, Nashville, TN 37215, 615-297-6026
Internet: dblakely@aol.com
　　Pubs: *Farewell My Lovelies* (Story Line Pr, 1998),
　　Hurricane Walk (BOA Edtns, 1992).

Jane Bradley　　　　　W
3120 Bellwood St, Nashville, TN 37403, 615-463-9476
Internet: jbradleauo6t@2.utoledo.edu
　　Pubs: *Living Doll* (Permanent Pr, 1994), *Power Lines &
　　Other Stories* (U Arkansas, 1989), *Virginia Rev, The
　　Literary Rev, NAR, Crazyhorse, Confrontation, Kansas
　　Qtly.*

Gaylord Brewer　　　　　P
Middle Tennessee St Univ, Murfreesboro, TN 37132,
615-898-2712
　　Pubs: *Presently A Beast* (Coreopsis Bks, 1996), *Quarterly
　　West, New York Qtly, Lullwater Rev, Re:al, U of Windsor
　　Rev, Puerto del Sol, Ellipsis, Chelsea, Conneticut Rev,
　　Crab Orchard Rev, Poet Lore.*

James Brooks　　　　　P&W
114 Malone Hollow Rd, Jonesboro, TN 37659, 615-753-7831
　　Pubs: *South Carolina Rev, Davidson Miscellany, Cold
　　Mountain Rev, Wisconsin Rev.*

Melissa Cannon　　　　　P
141 Neese Dr, #E18, Nashville, TN 37211-2750,
615-832-1813
　　Pubs: *A Formal Feeling Comes, Sleeping With Dionysus*
　　(Crossing Pr, 1994, 1994), *Bogg, Kenyon Rev, Lyric,
　　Ploughshares, Shockbox, Tight.*

Jill Carpenter　　　　　P&W
PO Box 3271, Sewanee, TN 37375, 615-598-9376
Internet: jillcarpe@aol.com
　　Pubs: *Fingerlings* (Catamount Pr, 1995), *Amelia,
　　Birmingham Poetry Rev, Exquisite Corpse, New Mexico
　　Humanities Rev, Utah Wilderness Assn Rev, Passager.*

Blair Carr　　　　　W
PO Box 2138, Memphis, TN 38088-2138
　　Pubs: *Flashbacks, A Case of Black or White* (Kudzu
　　Publications, 1998, 1996).

Karyn Follis Cheatham　　　　　W
PO Box 150792, Nashville, TN 37215-0792
　　Pubs: *The Best Way Out, Bring Home The Ghost* (HBJ,
　　1982, 1980), *Panhandler, West Wind Rev.*

Kevin Christianson　　　　　P
Tennessee Tech Univ, Box 5053, Cookeville, TN 38505,
931-372-3351
Internet: kchristians@tntech.edu
　　Pubs: *Seven Deadly Witnesses* (Broom Street Theatre Pr,
　　1971), *Libido, Rockford Rev, The Formalist, Z Misc,
　　Turnstile, Connecticut River Rev, Protea, Black Bear Rev,
　　Lynx Eye, Minnesota Rev, New Letters.*

Suzanne Underwood Clark　　　　　P
721 Pennsylvania Ave, Bristol, TN 37620
　　Pubs: *Sketches of Home* (Canon Pr, 1998), *Weather of The
　　House* (Sow's Ear Pr, 1994), *Quilt Anthology* (Quilt Digest
　　Pr, 1994), *In Place: Anth* (Now and Then, 1988), *Lullwater
　　Rev, Shenandoah, New Letters, Southern Poetry Rev,
　　Image, Appalachian Jrnl.*

Jay Clayton　　　　　W
Vanderbilt Univ, Nashville, TN 37235, 615-322-2541
　　Pubs: *Denver Qtly, Southwest Rev, Kansas Qtly, Southern
　　Rev.*

Robert Cowser   P
Univ Tennessee, Martin, TN 38238, 901-587-7280
  Pubs: *Backtrailing* (U Tennessee at Martin Pr, 1990), *Zone 3, Now, Old Red Kimono, American Literary Rev, Cape Rock, Lake Street Rev, Sow's Ear, English Jrnl, Sulphur River.*

Margaret Danner   P
Lemoyne Owen College, Memphis, TN 38126

Harry Norman Dean   P
920 Haywood Dr, NW, Cleveland, TN 37312-3929, 423-476-6950
  Pubs: *A Sheltered Life* (Rowan Mountain Pr, 1991), *Appalachia Inside Out: Anth* (U Tennessee Pr, 1995), *Poetry Miscellany, Cumberland Poetry Rev, Appalachian Heritage, Samisdat, Number One, Mountain Ways.*

Victor M. Depta   P
Univ Tennessee, Martin, TN 38238, 901-587-7300
Internet: vdepta@utm.edu
  Pubs: *A Doorkeeper in the House* (Ion Bks, 1993), *Idol & Sanctuary* (University Edtns, 1993), *Aura, Sonoma Mandala, Centennial Rev, Negative Capability.*

Ora Wilbert Eads   P
804 W Hemlock St, LaFollette, TN 37766, 615-562-8511
  Pubs: *Tranquility, Heavenly Light* (Banner Bks, 1994, 1993), *Crystal Rainbow, Omnific.*

Neal Ellis   P
3561 Hanna Dr, Memphis, TN 38128, 901-386-2684
  Pubs: *Gayoso Street Rev, Voices International, Memphis Tennessee Anth.*

Steve Eng   P&W
PO Box 111864, Nashville, TN 37222-1864
  Pubs: *All Aboard, SPWAO: Anth, Poets of Fantastic: Anth* (SPWAO, 1992, 1992), *Worlds of Fantasy & Horror, Beatlicks' Nashville Poetry Newsletter, Fantasy Commentator, Nashville Banner, Night Songs, Amanita Brandy, Nightmare Express.*

David Flynn   P&W
7180 Bay Cove Trail, Nashville, TN 37221, 615-673-0070
Internet: dflynn@uscc.cc.tn.us
  Pubs: *Stand, The Quarterly, International Qtly, Panurge, Story Qtly, Confrontation, Paris Transcontinental.*

Dorothy Foltz-Gray   P
5900 Wade Ln, Knoxville, TN 37912, 615-689-8160
  Pubs: *Homewords: Anth of Tennessee Writers* (U Tennessee Pr, 1986), *Mississippi Rev, Poet Lore, College English.*

Shelby Foote   W
542 E Parkway S, Memphis, TN 38104
  Pubs: *Love In A Dry Season* (Random Hse, 1979).

Richard Fricks   P
134 Longwood Pl, Nashville, TN 37215, 615-385-9517
Internet: fricksr@aol.com
  Pubs: *A Feel For Words* (Tennessee Arts Commission, 1973).

Charlotte Gafford   P
7325 Walker Rd, Fairview, TN 37062-8142, 615-799-2546
Internet: gkxk32c@prodigy.com
  Pubs: *The Pond Woman* (Kudzu Pr, 1989), *Southern Poetry Rev, Iowa Rev, New England Rev.*

Isabel Joshlin Glaser   PP&P&W
5383 Mason Rd, Memphis, TN 38120-1707, 901-685-5597
  Pubs: *Dreams of Glory: Poems Starring Girls: Anth* (Atheneum, 1995), *Prairie Schooner, Greensboro Rev, Cricket, School Magazine, Instructor, Mississippi Rev.*

Malcolm Glass   P
PO Box 137, Clarksville, TN 37041-0137, 615-648-7882
Internet: glassm@apsu01.apsu.edu
  Pubs: *The Dinky Line, Wiggins Poems* (Bucksnort, 1991, 1984), *In the Shadow of the Gourd* (New Rivers Pr, 1990), *Sewanee Rev.*

Roy Neil Graves   P
Univ Tennessee, Martin, TN 38238, 901-587-7301
  Pubs: *Somewhere on the Interstate* (Ion Bks, 1987), *Always At Home Here: 6 Tennessee Poets: Anth* (McGraw-Hill, 1997), *Homeworks: Anth of Tennessee Writers* (U Tennessee Pr, 1996), *New Ground, Bean Switch, New York Mag, Manana, Distillery, Runner's World.*

Larry D. Griffin   P&W
Dyersburg State Comm. College, 1510 Lake Rd, Dyersburg, TN 38024, 901-286-3371
Internet: lgriffin@fs386.dscc.cc.tn.us
  Pubs: *Airspace* (Slough, 1990), *A Gathering of Samphire* (Poetry Around, 1990), *Oyster Boy, 2 River Rev, Cimarron Rev, Riversedge, Poetry Ireland Rev, Blue Unicorn, Dock*(s).

Elizabeth Hahn   P
Film House, 230D Cumberland Bend, Nashville, TN 37228, 615-255-4000
  Pubs: *Out of Plumb* (Nightshade Pr, 1992), *Anth of New England Writers* (New England Writers, 1992), *Birmingham Poetry Rev, Minnesota Rev, Psychopoetica.*

Errol Hess   P
245 McDowell St, Bristol, TN 37620, 423-764-1625
Internet: ehess@tcu.com
  Pubs: *Homeworks: Anth* (U Tennessee Pr, 1996), *A Gathering At The Forks: Anth* (Vision Bks, 1993), *Sow's Ear Rev, Friends Jrnl, Lactuca, Potato Eyes, Pegasus Rev.*

Martha Whitmore Hickman   W
2034 Castleman Dr, Nashville, TN 37215, 615-292-9529
>Pubs: *Such Good People* (Warner Bks, 1996), *Fullness of Time: Short Stories of Women and Aging: Anth* (Abingdon Pr, 1997), *Weavings, Christian Century, Highlights, Pockets, Image.*

Cary Holladay   W
23 South Evergreen, Memphis, TN 38104, 901-278-7510
>Pubs: *The Palace of Wasted Footsteps* (U Missouri Pr, 1998), *The People Down South* (U Illinois Pr, 1989), *Kenyon Rev, Alaska Qtly Rev, Chelsea, Literary Rev, Oxford American, Chattahoochee Rev, Epoch, Northwest Rev, Southern Rev, Virginia Qtly Rev.*

Richard Jackson   P
Univ Tennessee, English Dept, Chattanooga, TN 37403, 615-755-4629
Internet: svobodni@aol.com
>Pubs: *Alive All Day* (Cleveland State U Pr, 1992), *Worlds Apart, Dismantling Time* (U Alabama Pr, 1989, 1987), *Gettysburg Rev, Crazyhorse, NER, NAR.*

Mark Jarman   P
Vanderbilt Univ, Nashville, TN 37235, 615-322-2369
Internet: mark.jarman@vanderbilt.edu
>Pubs: *Unholy Sonnets, Questions for Ecclesiastes, Iris* (Story Line Pr, 2000, 1997, 1992), *APR, Hudson Rev, New Yorker, Southern Rev, New Criterion, Threepenny Rev, Atlantic Monthly, Kenyon Rev, Sewanee Rev.*

Marilyn Kallet   P
Univ Tennessee, Knoxville, TN 37996, 615-974-5401
>Pubs: *How To Get Heat Without Fire* (New Messenger/New Millennium, 1996), *Honest Simplicity* (Louisiana State U Pr, 1985), *Worlds In Our Words: Anth* (Blair Pr/Prentice Hall, 1996), *New Letters, Sport Literate, New Millennium, Hawaii Rev, International Qtly,.*

Richard Kelly   P
Univ Tennessee, McClung Tower, English Dept, Knoxville, TN 37919, 615-974-5401
>Pubs: *Lewis Carroll, Daphne du Maurier* (G.K. Hall, 1990, 1987), *V.S. Naipaul* (Continuum, 1989).

Ellis K. Meacham   W
414 S Crest Rd, Chattanooga, TN 37404, 615-624-1887
>Pubs: *For King & Company, On The Company's Service* (Little, Brown, 1976, 1968).

Corey J. Mesler   P&W
1954 Young Ave, Memphis, TN 38104-5643, 901-274-4718
Internet: burkes@netten.net
>Pubs: *Smashing Icons* (Avocet, 1998), *Full Court: A Literary Anth* (Breakaway Bks, 1996), *Crossroads, Visions Intl, Southern Voices, Slant, Epiphany, Agincourt, Irregular, Southern Voices, Crossroads: A Jrnl of Southern Culture.*

Gordon Osing   P
1056 Blythe St, Memphis, TN 38104, 901-278-3024
>Pubs: *A Town Down River* (St. Luke's Pr, 1984), *From The Boundary Waters* (Memphis State U, 1982).

William Page   P
5551 Derron Ave, Memphis, TN 38115, 901-363-2216
Internet: wpagemem@aol.com
>Pubs: *Bodies Not Our Own* (Memphis State U Pr, 1986), *American Literary Rev, NAR, Southern Poetry Rev, Literary Rev, College English, Southwest Rev.*

Barbara Shirk Parish   P&W
4293 Beechcliff Ln, Memphis, TN 38128, 901-388-4384
>Pubs: *Maverick Western Verse: Anth* (Gibbs Smith, 1994), *The Kentucky Book: Anth* (Courier Journal, 1979), *Small Pond, Green's Mag, Dry Crik Rev, Little Balkins Rev.*

Wyatt Prunty   P
Univ of the South, 310 St. Luke's Hall, Sewanee, TN 37383-1000, 615-598-1159
>Pubs: *The Run of the House, Balance As Belief* (Johns Hopkins U Pr, 1993, 1989), *Fallen From the Symboled World* (Oxford U Pr, 1990).

Paul Ramsey   P
322 Pine Ridge Rd, Chattanooga, TN 37405-3430, 615-265-4300
>Pubs: *Contemporary Religious Poetry: Anth* (Paulist Pr, 1987), *Eve, Singing* (Pennyroyal Pr, 1977), *Anglican Theological Rev, Formalist, Four Quarters.*

J. C. Robison   W
Brentwood Academy, 219 Granny White Pike, Brentwood, TN 37027, 615-373-0611
>Pubs: *Peter Taylor: A Study of the Short Fiction* (Twayne, 1988), *Texas Rev, Chariton Rev, Cimarron.*

Abby Jane Rosenthal   P
650 S Greer, Memphis, TN 38111, 901-327-4460
>Pubs: *Ardor's Hut* (Alembic Pr, 1985), *Alaska Qtly Rev, Kalliope, CutBank, Bloomsbury Rev.*

Frank Russell   P
501 Park Ctr, Nashville, TN 37205, 615-386-9731
>Pubs: *Dinner With Dr. Rocksteady* (Ion Bks, 1987), *Poetry, Chariton Rev, Poetry Northwest.*

Arthur Smith   P
Univ Tennessee, 301 McClung Tower/English Dept, Knoxville, TN 37996, 423-974-5401
Internet: artsmith@utk.edu
>Pubs: *Orders of Affection* (Carnegie Mellon Pr, 1996), *Elegy on Independence Day* (U Pitt Pr, 1985), *Nation, Crazyhorse, NAR.*

David Spicer   P
Ion Books, PO Box 111327, Memphis, TN 38111-1327,
901-323-8858
> Pubs: *Everybody Has a Story* (St. Luke's Pr, 1987),
> *Beautiful Strangers* (Black Parrot Pr, 1985), *APR,
> Ploughshares.*

Dorothy Stanfill   W
3131 N Highland Ave, #128M, Jackson, TN 38305-3408
> Pubs: *A Greater Love, Katharine and the Quarter Mile Drag*
> (Old Hickory Pr, 1985, 1978), *Amelia.*

Rosemary Stephens   P&W
64 N Yates Rd, Memphis, TN 38120
> Pubs: *Eve's Navel* (South & West, 1976), *Seventeen,
> Mississippi Rev, Southern Poetry Rev.*

James Summerville   W
2911 Woodlawn Dr, Nashville, TN 37215, 615-298-5830
Internet: james.summerville@vanderbilt.edu
> Pubs: *With Kennedy and Other Stories* (Xlibris, 1998), *The
> Cormack-Cooper Shooting* (McFarland, 1994), *Homewords:
> Anth* (U Tennessee, 1986), *North Dakota Qtly, Touchstone,
> Tennessee Historical Qtly, History News, Lake Superior
> Rev.*

Frederick O. Waage   W
East Tennessee State Univ, Box 24292, Johnson City, TN
37614, 615-929-7466
> Pubs: *Minestrone* (Pudding, 1983), *The End Of The World*
> (Gallimaufry, 1977), *Antigonish Rev.*

Jon Manchip White   P&W
5620 Pinellas Dr, Knoxville, TN 37919, 423-558-8578
> Pubs: *Whistling Past the Churchyard, The Journeying Boy*
> (Atlantic Monthly Pr, 1992, 1991).

Lola White   P
5040 Villa Crest Dr, Nashville, TN 37220
> Pubs: *Thunder: Silence* (Red Girl Pr, 1992), *Tendril,
> Aspect, Zeugma, Cat's Eye, Pluma True, CSM, Dark
> Horse.*

Allen Wier   W
Univ Tennessee, 301 McClung Tower, Knoxville, TN
37996-0430, 423-974-5401
Internet: awier@utk.edu
> Pubs: *A Place for Outlaws* (H&R, 1989), *Departing As Air*
> (S&S, 1983), *Southern Rev, Texas Rev, Mid-American
> Rev.*

Ronna Wineberg   W
733 Darden Pl, Nashville, TN 37205, 615-352-8841
Internet: ronnagroup@aol.com
> Pubs: *A Tennessee Landscape, People and Places: Anth*
> (Cool Springs Pr, 1996), *South Dakota Rev, Crone's Nest,
> American Way, Midstream, Colorado Rev, Colorado Daily.*

Mary Elizabeth Witherspoon   W
3722 Timberlake Rd, Knoxville, TN 37920, 615-577-3205
> Pubs: *The Morning Cool* (Macmillan, 1972), *Somebody
> Speak For Katy* (Dodd, Mead, 1950), *Tropic.*

Charles Wyatt   P&W
3810 Central Ave, Nashville, TN 37205, 615-385-2456
> Pubs: *Listening to Mozart* (U Iowa Pr, 1995), *NER,
> TriQuarterly, Hanging Loose, Beloit Poetry, Florida Rev,
> The Quarterly.*

TEXAS

Virginia T. Abercrombie   P
2 Smithdale Ct, Houston, TX 77024
Internet: 229huck1574@msn.com
> Pubs: *Suddenly* (Martin House, 1998), *Songs For the
> Century, Houston Party File, Leaf Raker* (Brown Rabbit Pr,
> 1998, 1986, 1983), *Back To Your Roots: Anth* (Houston
> Poetry Fest, 1991), *Visions Intl, Illyas Honey, Raintown
> Rev, Pleiades.*

Neal Abramson   P
1000 W Spring Valley Rd, #229, Richardson, TX 75080,
214-231-3732
> Pubs: *Sojourn, Lactuca, Amoeba, Unmuzzled Ox, City
> West End, Confrontation.*

Alan P. Akmakjian   P&W
2200 Waterview Pkwy, #2134, Richardson, TX 75080-2268,
972-497-9412
> Pubs: *And What Rough Beast: Poems At The End of the
> Century* (Ashland U Pr, 1999), *California Picnic and Other
> Poems* (Northwoods Pr, 1998), *Let the Sun Go* (MAF Pr,
> 1993), *Ararat, Atom Mind, Black Bear Rev, New Thought
> Jrnl, Onthebus, Wormwood Rev.*

Silvia Berta Alaniz   P
821 Carver St, Alice, TX 78332
> Pubs: *Perceptions, Writing for Our Lives, Dream Intl Qtly,
> Poetic Eloquence, Expressions, Tight, Moving Out, Stone
> Drum, Up Against The Wall, Notebook, Aura, Avocet,
> Pacific Coast Jrnl, Reflect, Mind in Motion.*

Max Apple   W
Rice University, PO Box 1892, Houston, TX 77251,
713-527-8101
> Pubs: *Roommates, Zip* (Warner Bks, 1994, 1986), *The
> Propheteers, Free Agents* (H&R, 1987, 1984),
> *Ploughshares.*

Terry Lee Armstrong   P
4219 Flint Hill St, San Antonio, TX 78230-1619
> Pubs: *When the Soul Speaks, Call it Love* (Armstrong Pub
> Co., 1990, 1989), *Lone Star Mag, Omnific Mag.*

Carolyn Banks W
RR 5, Box 210E, Bastrop, TX 78602-7616, 512-303-1531
Pubs: *A Horse to Die For, Death on the Diagonal, Murder Well Bred, Groomed For Death, Death By Dressage* (Fawcett, 1996, 1996, 1995, 1994, 1993), *Tart Tales: Elegant Erotic Stories* (Carroll & Graf, 1993).

Wendy Barker P
Univ Texas, San Antonio, TX 78285, 512-691-4374
Pubs: *Let the Ice Speak* (Ithaca Hse Bks, 1991), *Winter Chickens and Other Poems* (Corona Pub, 1990), *Poetry, NAR, American Scholar, Prairie Schooner*.

Shulamith Bat-Yisrael P
PO Box 852151, Richardson, TX 75085-2151
Pubs: *Black Bear Rev, Nexus, Infinity Ltd., Harbinger, Bitterroot, Parnassus Literary Jrnl, Jrnl of New Jersey Poets, Response, Writers' Jrnl*.

Charles Behlen P
501 W Industrial Dr, #503-B, Sulphur Springs, TX 75482-4646, 817-838-2956
Pubs: *Inheritance of Light, The Voices Under the Floor* (U North Texas Pr, 1996, 1989), *Texas In Poetry: Anth* (Center for Texas Studies Pr, 1994), *Borderlands*.

Michael Berryhill P
Fort Worth Star-Telegram, 400 W 7 St, Fort Worth, TX 76102

Michael C. Blumenthal P
3311 Merrie Lynn Ave, Austin, TX 78722, 512-481-9408
Internet: mb34@academia.swt.edu
Pubs: *The Wages of Goodness* (U Missouri Pr, 1992), *Against Romance* (Viking/Penguin, 1987), *Marriage: Anth* (Poseidon, 1991), *Poetry, The Nation, Agni, American Scholar, Paris Rev, Ploughshares*.

Eugene G. E. Botelho P
PO Box 925, Eagle Pass, TX 788530925
Pubs: *For Better, For Worse* (All American Pr, 1981), *I Wonder As I Wander* (Northwoods, 1978).

Jean Claude Boudreau P
2310 14th Ave, #212, Canyon, TX 79015
Pubs: *Games Of Love* (Winter Trees, 1984), *Yellin' Rebel, Quicksilver, Anth of Nevada Poets, Calliope*.

David Breeden P&W
Schreiner College, 2100 Memorial Blvd, Kerrville, TX 78028, 512-896-7945
Internet: drpoetry@hilconet.com
Pubs: *Another Number* (Silver Pheonix Pr, 1998), *Guiltless Traveller, Building A Boat* (March Street Pr, 1996, 1995), *Double-Headed End Wrench* (Cloverdale Pr, 1992).

J. W. Brown P
3500 Rankin St, Dallas, TX 75205, 214-739-6566
Pubs: *Pawn Rev, DeKalb Literary Arts Journal, Southwest Rev, Texas Qtly*.

William S. Burford P
3001 W Gambrell, Fort Worth, TX 76133, 817-926-1480
Pubs: *A Beginning* (Norton, 1968), *A World* (U Texas Pr, 1962), *The Poetry Anthology: Sixty-Five Years of America's Distinguished Verse Mag* (HM, 1978), *Nation, Poetry Anth*.

Robert Grant Burns P
PO Box 763, Jacksonville, TX 75766, 903-586-5260
Pubs: *Selected Poems* (Waltonhof, 1993).

Harry Burrus P
1266 Fountain View, Houston, TX 77057-2204, 713-784-2802
Internet: HGBurrus@msn.com
Pubs: *Cartouche, The Jaguar Portfolio, Without Feathers* (Black Tie Press, 1995, 1991, 1990).

Bobby Byrd P
2709 Louisville, El Paso, TX 79930, 915-566-9072
Pubs: *On the Transmigration of Souls in El Paso* (Cinco Puntos Pr, 1993), *Get Some Fuses for the House* (North Atlantic Bks, 1987).

Jean Calkins P
14281 Shoredale Ln, Farmers Branch, TX 75234, 972-241-9574
Internet: nystxn@123net.net
Pubs: *Against All Odds, Portrait of Insomnia* (Inky Pr Dallas, 1995, 1995), *Moose Bound Pr, Pegasus, Lone Star, Green Gate Little Bks, Apropos, Parnassus, Haiku Headlines, Time of Singing, Quickenings*.

Ewing Campbell W
Texas A&M Univ, English Dept, College Station, TX 77843-4227, 409-845-8342
Internet: rec025b@venus.tamu.edu
Pubs: *Madonna, Maleva* (York Pr, 1995), *The Tex-Mex Express* (Spectrum Pr, 1993), *London Mag, New England Rev, Kenyon Rev, Chicago Rev, Cimarron Rev*.

Vincent Canizarro, Jr. P
8285 Collier Rd, Beaumont, TX 77706, 713-866-3612
Pubs: *The Poet*.

Warren Carrier P
69 Colony Park Cir, Galveston, TX 77551, 409-744-5511
Pubs: *An Ordinary Man* (QRL, 1996), *Murder at the Strawberry Festival* (Mahaven Pub, 1993), *Harvard Mag, Formalist, Ohio Rev, Visions Intl, Pembroke Mag, Wallace Stevens Jrnl*.

Jane Chance P
Rice Univ, 6100 Main St, Houston, TX 77005-1892, 713-527-8101
Internet: jchance@rice.edu
Pubs: *Christine de Pizan's Letter of Othea: Anth* (Trans; Focus Info Group, 1990), *Literary Rev, Southern Humanities Rev, Primavera, Ariel, New America*.

Charlotte Cheatham   P
Galveston Arts Ctr On Strand, 202 Kempner, Galveston, TX
77550, 713-765-6309
    Pubs: *Gjelsness, Joy Drake.*

Paul Christensen   P
Texas A&M Univ, English Dept, College Station, TX
77843-4227, 409-845-8330
Internet: p-christensen@tamu.edu
    Pubs: *Where Three Roads Meet* (Cedarshouse/Open
Theater, 1996), *Minding the Underworld* (Black Sparrow,
1991), *In Love, In Sorrow* (Paragon Hse, 1990), *Weights &
Measures* (University Edtns, 1985), *Quarter After Eight,
Connecticut Rev, Southwest Rev.*

L. D. Clark   W
604 Main St, Smithville, TX 78957, 512-237-2756
    Pubs: *A Bright Tragic Thing* (Cinco Puntos Pr, 1992), *A
Charge of Angels* (Confluence Pr, 1987), *The Fifth Wind*
(Blue Moon Pr, 1981).

LaVerne Harrell Clark   W
604 Main St, Smithville, TX 78957, 512-237-2756
    Pubs: *Keepers of The Earth* (Cinco Puntos Pr, 1997), *A
New Dimension of an Old Affinity* (Writers on The Plains Pr,
1996), *Pembroke, St. Andrews Rev, Vanderbilt Street Rev,
Southwestern American Literature.*

Richard Cole   P
5125 McDade Dr, Austin, TX 78735, 512-891-9276
    Pubs: *Success Stories* (Limestone Bks, 1998), *The Glass
Children* (U Georgia Pr, 1986), *Chicago Rev, New Yorker,
Hudson Rev, Denver Qtly, The Sun.*

Paul David Colgin   P
2308 Neeley Ave, Midland, TX 79705, 915-682-6609
Internet: paulcolgin@apex2000.net
    Pubs: *Yankee, Sulphur River Literary Rev, Pearl, Nexus,
Black Fly Rev, Kinesis, Pittsburgh Qtly, Sou'wester, Oxford
Mag, Iconoclast, Tomorrow Mag, Xanadu.*

Joe Coomer   W
HC51, Box 230, Azle, TX 76020, 817-523-5775
    Pubs: *The Loop, Dream House* (Faber & Faber, 1992,
1992), *A Flatland Fable* (Texas Monthly Pr, 1986).

Carol Cullar   P&W
Rt 2, Box 4915, Eagle Pass, TX 78852-9605, 210-773-1836
Internet: mavpress@admin.hilconet.com
    Pubs: *Inexplicable Burnings* (Pr of the Guadalupe, 1992),
Wind Eyes: A Woman's Reader & Writing Source: Anth
(Plain View Pr, 1997), *Texas Short Fiction: Anth, Texas In
Poetry: Anth* (Ctr for Texas Studies, 1996, 1994), *New York
Qtly, RE:AL.*

Chip Dameron   P
33 El Retiro Cir, Brownsville, TX 78520, 512-541-1983
Internet: dameron@utb.edu
    Pubs: *Night Spiders, Morning Milk, Definition of Hours*
(Hawk Pr, 1990), *In the Magnetic Arena* (Latitudes, 1987),
New Texas 95, Sulphur River Rev.

Robert Dante   P
PO Box 66341, Houston, TX 77266, 713-524-0875
    Pubs: *High Performance, Public News, Dance Mag.*

William Virgil Davis   P
2633 Lake Oaks Rd, Waco, TX 767101616, 254-772-3198
Internet: william_davis@baylor.edu
    Pubs: *One Way to Reconstruct the Scene* (Yale U Pr,
1980), *Poetry, New Criterion, Gettysburg Rev, Hudson Rev,
Atlantic.*

Angela de Hoyos   P
M&A Editions, 10120 State Hwy 16 S, San Antonio, TX
78224
    Pubs: *Woman, Woman* (Arte Publico Pr, 1985), *Selected
Poems/Selecciones* (Dezkalzo Pr, 1979).

Nephtali Deleon   P&W
1411 Betty Dr, San Antonio, TX 78224

Jeffrey DeLotto   P
Texas Wesleyan Univ, 1201 Wesleyan, Fort Worth, TX
76105, 817-531-4909
    Pubs: *Anthology of New England Writers: Voices at the
Door* (Maverick Pr, 1995), *New Texas 91: Anth* (U North
Texas Pr, 1991), *Aura Literary/Arts Rev, College English,
Preying Mantis, Horny Toad.*

Mark Doty   P&W
Creative Writing Program, University of Houston, English
Dept., Houston, TX 77204, 713-529-9586
    Pubs: *Heaven's Coast, Atlantis* (HarperCollins, 1996,
1995), *My Alexandria* (U Illinois Pr, 1993), *New Yorker,
Paris Rev, Boulevard, DoubleTake.*

Sharrard Douglass   P&W
9 Bimini, Key Allegro, Rockport, TX 78381, 512-729-9999
    Pubs: *The Music I Try To Become* (Maverick Pr, 1995),
Coastline, Preying Mantis, Culebra, Javelin, Paisano.

Frederick Eckman   P
501 Stone Bluff Rd, El Paso, TX 79912, 915-584-2090
    Pubs: *The Continental Connection* (Itinerary, 1980),
Nightmare Township (Newedi, 1977).

Jerry Ellison   P
Rte 3 Box 377, Gilmer, TX 75644, 903-725-6283
Internet: peacewds@etex.net
    Pubs: *Never Again Summer* (College Poetry Rev, 1969),
Death Chant: Anth (Silver Spur, 1962), *Bellowing Ark,
Northwoods Jrnl, Barefoot Grass Journal.*

Robert A. Fink P
Hardin-Simmons Univ, Box 15114, Abilene, TX 79698,
915-670-1214
Pubs: *The Tongues of Men and of Angels* (Texas Tech U
Pr, 1995), *The Ghostly Hitchhiker* (Corona Pub, 1989),
Azimuth Points (Sam Houston State U, 1981), *Poetry
Northwest, Poetry, Michigan Qtly Rev, NER, TriQuarterly,
Southwest Rev.*

Robert Flynn W
Trinity Univ, 715 Stadium Dr, San Antonio, TX 78212,
210-736-7575
Internet: rflynn@trinity.edu
Pubs: *Living With The Hyenas* (TCU Pr, 1995), *The Last
Klick* (Baskerville Pub, 1994), *A Personal War in Viet Nam*
(Texas A&M U, 1989), *Image.*

Peter Fogo P
PO Box 7743, Pasadena, TX 77508-7743, 713-941-5227
Pubs: *A Language That Keeps Company With The Moon*
(Mackinations Pr, 1992), *Single Again* (Raspberry Pr,
1980), *Midwest Qtly, Black Bear Rev, Prairie Winds,
Ellipsis.*

Ken Fontenot P
2103 Nueces St, Austin, TX 78705, 512-477-8865
Pubs: *All My Animals and Stars* (Slough Pr, 1989), *After the
Days of Miami* (Longmeasure Pr, 1980).

Larry L. Fontenot P
1911 Campwood Dr, Sugar Land, TX 77478
Internet: larryf@ci.pasadena.tx.us
Pubs: *Choices & Consequences* (Maverick Pr, 1997), *River
Sedge, Minimus, El Locofoco, Bayousphere, Treasure
House, Arrowsmith, Maverick Pr, i.e. mag.*

Margot Fraser W
Southern Methodist Univ Press, Box 415, Dallas, TX 75275,
214-768-1432
Pubs: *Careless Weeds, The Laying Out of Gussie Hoot*
(SMU Pr, 1993, 1990), *Negative Capability.*

Laura Furman W
Univ Texas, Austin, TX 78712-1164, 512-471-4991
Internet: ljfurman@mail.utexas.edu
Pubs: *Ordinary Paradise* (Winedale Pub, 1998), *Tuxedo
Park* (Summit, 1986), *Ploughshares, Southwest Rev.*

G. N. Gabbard P&W
602 Cannon St, New Boston, TX 75570, 903-628-2788
Pubs: *A Mask for Beowulf, Knights Errand, Daily Nous,
Dragon Raid* (Flea King Bks, 1992, 1992, 1991, 1985).

Roberto A. Galvan P
Southwest Texas State Univ, LBJ Drive, San Marcos, TX
78666, 512-245-2360
Pubs: *Poemas En Espanol Por Un Mexiamericano*
(Mexican American Cultural Center Pr, 1977).

Greg Garrett W
Baylor Univ, English Dept, Waco, TX 76798, 254-710-6879
Internet: greg_garrett@baylor.edu
Pubs: *Texas Short Fiction: Anth* (ALE Pub, 1995), *Writers'
Forum, High Plains Literary Rev, Grain, South Dakota Rev,
Laurel Rev, Negative Capability.*

Daniel Garza P
5 Briarwood Cir, Richardson, TX 75080

Zulfikar Ghose P&W
Univ Texas, English Dept, Austin, TX 78712-1164,
512-471-8112
Pubs: *The Triple Mirror of the Self* (Bloomsbury, 1992),
Selected Poems (Oxford U Pr, 1991).

Dagoberto Gilb W
Box 31001, El Paso, TX 79931
Pubs: *The Last Known Residence of Mickey Acuna, The
Magic of Blood* (Grove Pr, 1994, 1993).

Miguel Gonzalez-Gerth P
Univ Texas, Austin, TX 78712, 512-471-8157
Pubs: *Palabras Inutilez* (Spain; Taller Fernandez Ciudad,
1988).

Juan G. Guevara P
PO Box 446, Benavides, TX 78341, 512-256-3308

James Haining P
Salt Lick Press/LHB, PO Box 15471, Austin, TX 78761-5471,
512-450-0952
Pubs: *A Child's Garden* (Salt Lick Pr, 1987), *Beowulf to
Beatles and Beyond* (Macmillan, 1981).

Jim Hanson P
2114 Glenn Ln, Glenn Heights, TX 75115, 214-821-2740
Pubs: *Reasons for the Sky* (Toothpaste Pr, 1979), *Dental
Floss, Mag City, Brilliant Corners.*

Devin Harrison P
601 Petersburg St, Castroville, TX 78009-4538
Pubs: *Lactuca, Riverrun, Passages North, The Windless
Orchard, Poem, Panhandler, South Dakota Rev.*

Don Hendrie, Jr. W
714 Tuxedo Ave, San Antonio, TX 78209
Pubs: *A Criminal Journey, Blount's Anvil* (Lynx Hse Pr,
1990, 1980).

Edward Hirsch P
Univ Houston, University Park, English Dept, Houston, TX
77204, 713-743-2956
Pubs: *On Love, Earthly Measures, The Night Parade, Wild
Gratitude* (Knopf, 1998, 1994, 1989, 1986), *New Yorker,
Paris Rev, APR, DoubleTake.*

Louise Horton   P&W
4401 Spicewood Springs Rd, #23, Austin, TX 78759-8589
    Pubs: *Southern Humanities Rev.*

Timothy Houghton   P
Univ Houston, Creative Writing Program, Houston, TX
77204-3012, 713-743-2390
    Pubs: *Below Two Skies* (Orchises Pr, 1993), *High Bridges*
    (Stride Pr, 1989), *Denver Qtly, Stand Mag, College English.*

Albert Huffstickler   P
312 E 43 St, #103, Austin, TX 78751, 512-459-3472
    Pubs: *Quinlen, City of the Rain* (Press of Circumstance,
    1998, 1993), *Working On My Death Chant* (Back Yard Pr,
    1992), *Poetry East, Poetry Motel, Heeltap, First Class,
    Rattle, Galley Sail.*

Lynne Hugo   P&W
The Fogelman Literary Agency, 7515 Greenville Ave, Suite
712, Dallas, TX 75231, 214-361-9956
Internet: lynnephugo@aol.com
    Pubs: *Swimming Lessons* (Co-author; Morrow, 1998), *A
    Progress of Miracles* (San Diego Poets Pr, 1993), *The Time
    Change* (Ampersand Pr, 1992), *The Quarterly, Prairie
    Schooner, Cincinnati Poetry Rev, Mid American Rev.*

Guida Jackson   W
Touchstone, PO Box 8308, Spring, TX 77387
Internet: guidamj@flex.net
    Pubs: *Virginia Diaspora* (Heritage Bks, 1992), *Women Who
    Ruled* (ABC-CLIO, 1990), *Heart to Hearth* (Prism, 1989),
    Passing Through (S&S, 1989), *Suddenly: Anth* (Martin
    House, 1998), *Texas Short Stories: Anth* (Browder Springs
    Pub, 1997).

Roger Jones   P
Lamar Univ, English Dept, Beaumont, TX 77710
    Pubs: *Remembering New London* (Texas Review Pr,
    1981), *Old Hickory Rev, Texas Rev, Slackwater Rev.*

Dan Kaderli   P&W
Univ Texas, 6900 Loop 1604 W, San Antonio, TX
78249-0691, 512-691-4165
    Pubs: *The Lyric, Tucumcari Rev, Reflect, Bogg, SPSM&H,
    Iota, Negative Capability, Star Poets 2, Plains Poetry Jrnl,
    Howling Mantra, Pegasus, Spitball.*

T. J. Kallsen   P
600 Bostwick, Nacogdoches, TX 75961, 409-564-3347
    Pubs: *Making: Selected Poems* (Touchstone, 1981),
    Kansas Qtly, Green's Mag, Lightworks.

Cynthia King   W
5306 Institute Ln, Houston, TX 77005, 713-526-0232
    Pubs: *Sailing Home* (Putnam, 1982), *Beggars and
    Choosers* (Viking, 1980), *Good Housekeeping.*

Judith Kroll   P
Univ Texas, Parlin 108, English Dept, Austin, TX 78712,
512-320-0546
    Pubs: *Our Elephant and that Child* (Quarterly Rev Poetry
    Series, 1991), *In the Temperate Zone* (Scribner, 1974),
    Kenyon Rev, Southern Rev, American Voice.

Patricia Clare Lamb   P
3614 Montrose Blvd, Ste 405, Houston, TX 77006-4651
Internet: harbottle@aol.com
    Pubs: *The Long Love: New and Collected Poems
    1957-1998, All Men By Nature* (Harbottle Pr, 1998, 1993),
    Plains Poetry Jrnl, Midwest Quarterly Rev, Commonweal.

James Langdon   P&W
1202 Seagler Rd, #60, Houston, TX 77042, 713-266-1229
    Pubs: *Chicago Rev, Contempora, Descant, Maple Leaf
    Rag, New Orleans Rev, Rapport.*

Barbara D. Langham   W
B.D. Langham Public Relations, 1 Riverway, Ste 2525,
Houston, TX 77056, 713-961-4235
    Pubs: *NAR, Bellingham Rev, Descant, Fiction Texas,
    Crosscurrents, Pig Iron.*

William Laufer   W
PO Box 8308, The Woodlands, TX 77387
    Pubs: *P: An Excursus Into Liminal Space, Four Sea
    Interludes, Surrogates, Fiction and Art* (Third Coast
    Letterpress, 1998, 1996, 1995), *The Indochina Suite*
    (Touchstone Pr, 1994).

Anne Leaton   W
3209 College Ave, Forth Worth, TX 76110, 817-923-7308
    Pubs: *Blackbird, Bye Bye* (Virago Pr, 1989), *Pearl* (Knopf,
    1989), *Esquire, Transatlantic Rev, Storia, Cosmopolitan,
    Independent on Sunday.*

J. R. LeMaster   P
201 Harrington Ave, Waco, TX 76706-1519, 254-754-4358
Internet: J_R_LeMaster@Baylor.edu
    Pubs: *Purple Bamboo, First Person, Second* (Tagore Inst of
    Creative Writing, 1988, 1983).

Jim Linebarger   P
210 Solar Way, Denton, TX 76205, 817-566-6144
    Pubs: *Anecdotal Evidence* (Point Riders Pr, 1993), *The
    Worcester Poems* (Trilobite Pr, 1991), *Wormwood Rev,
    Southeast Rev, Southern Humanities Rev.*

Paul Alexander Lisicky   W
16 Branard St., Houston, TX 77006, 713-529-9586
    Pubs: *Men on Men 6: Anth* (Dutton, 1996), *Flash Fiction:
    Anth* (Norton, 1992), *Mississippi Rev, Provincetown Arts,
    Carolina Qtly, Black Warrior Rev, Kansas Qtly.*

Jayne Loader W
906 W Main St, Waxahachie, TX 75165, 214-937-4648
Internet: http://www.publicshelter.com
 Pubs: *Wild America* (Grove-Weidenfeld, 1989), *Between Pictures* (Grove Pr, 1986), *The Met, Third Rave, WWWench, Positive, Panta, Marie-Claire, Details.*

Marianne McNeil Logan P
Nostalgic Nook, 7003 Amarillo Blvd E, #16, Amarillo, TX 79107, 806-372-5032
 Pubs: *Girls Write Cowboy Poetry Too* (Nostalgic Nook Pr, 1990), *Pudgy Parodies* (Tanglewood, 1988), *Country Mag, Ellery Queen's Mystery Mag, Midwest Poetry.*

Patricia Looker P&W
PO Box 1551, Bellaire, TX 77401-1551, 713-432-7873
 Pubs: *Straight Ahead, Wellspring, Apalachee Qtly, Forum, Quartet, Whetstone, Blonde on Blonde.*

Marianne Loyd P
3704 Tompkins, Baytown, TX 77521
 Pubs: *Stone Country, Uroboros, Tamarack, New Letters.*

Grant Lyons W
2923 Woodcrest, San Antonio, TX 78209, 210-822-5409
Internet: gmlyons@swbell.net
 Pubs: *4.4.4.* (U Missouri Pr, 1977), *Negative Capability, Seattle Rev, Confrontation, Cimarron Rev, Northwest Rev, Redbook.*

Cynthia Macdonald P
1400 Hermann Dr #8E, Houston, TX 77004, 713-520-6598
Internet: cmacdo@compassnet.com
 Pubs: *Living Wills: New & Selected Poems, Alternate Means of Transport* (Knopf, 1991, 1985).

Janet Marks P
2718 Wroxton Rd, #3, Houston, TX 770051359, 713-660-8508
 Pubs: *Poets on Parnassus: Anth* (U California Pr, 1994), *Songs for Our Voices: Anth* (Judah L. Magnes Museum, 1993), *Synapse, Houston Poetry Festival 1997 Anthology.*

Kenard Marlowe P
3401 Cartagena Dr, Corpus Christi, TX 78418-3922, 512-937-5215
 Pubs: *Thinking Allowed* (Indiana Pub, 1994).

Lee Martin W
Univ of North Texas, Denton, TX 76203-6827, 817-565-2050
Internet: lmartin@facstaff.cas.unt.edu
 Pubs: *The Least You Need to Know* (Sarabande Bks, 1996), *Georgia Rev, Story, DoubleTake, Glimmer Train, New England Rev, Prairie Schooner.*

Janet McCann P
Texas A&M Univ, College Station, TX 77843-4227, 409-845-8316
Internet: jpm9243@acs.tamu.edu
 Pubs: *Looking for Buddha in the Barbed Wire Garden* (Avisson Pr, 1996), *Afterword* (Franciscan U Pr, 1990), *Borderlands, Christian Century.*

Cormac McCarthy W
1510 N Brown, El Paso, TX 79902

Charlotte Mears McCulloch P
901 Sirocco Dr, #A, Austin, TX 78745-3858
 Pubs: *Brooklyn Rev, Woman Poet: The South, Slant, Nimrod, Tar River, Poet Lore.*

Walt McDonald P&W
Texas Tech Univ, Lubbock, TX 79409, 806-742-2501
Internet: walt@ttu.edu
 Pubs: *Blessings the Body Gave* (Ohio State U Pr, 1998), *Counting Survivors* (U Pitt Pr, 1995), *Night Landings* (HarperCollins, 1989), *American Scholar, Georgia Rev, Atlantic, Poetry, Sewanee Rev, Southern Rev, APR, Paris Rev.*

Neill Megaw P
2805 Bowman Ave, Austin, TX 78703, 512-472-5522
 Pubs: *The Spectator, Negative Capability, Sequoia, Hellas, The Lyric, South Coast Poetry Jrnl, The Formalist.*

James Michener W
2706 Mountain Laurel Ln, Austin, TX 78703-1143
 Pubs: *Space* (Random House, 1982), *Chesapeake.*

Christopher Middleton P
Univ Texas, Austin, TX 78712, 512-471-4123
 Pubs: *Intimate Chronicles, The Balcony Tree* (Sheep Meadow Pr, 1996, 1992).

Vassar Miller P
1615 Vassar, Houston, TX 77006, 713-522-6807
 Pubs: *If I Had Wheels Or Love, Collected Poems of Vassar Miller* (SMU Pr, 1991), *Despite This Flesh* (U Texas Pr, 1985).

Bryce Milligan P&W
627 E Guenther, San Antonio, TX 78210, 210-222-8449
 Pubs: *Lawmen: Stories of Men Who Tamed the West* (Disney Pr, 1994), *Battle of the Alamo* (Texas Monthly Pr, 1990), *Daysleepers and Other Poems* (Corona, 1984).

A. G. Mojtabai P&W
2102 S. Hughes, Amarillo, TX 791092212, 806-376-9434
 Pubs: *Soon* (Zoland Bks, 1998), *Blessed Assurance* (Syracuse U Pr, 1997), *Called Out, Ordinary Time* (Doubleday, 1994, 1994).

Jane P. Moreland   P&W
503 Shadywood, Houston, TX 77057, 713-975-6711
Internet: jpmore@prodigy.net
    Pubs: *Iowa Rev, Mademoiselle, Poetry, Poetry Northwest,
    Georgia Rev.*

E'Lane Carlisle Murray   P&W
433 Haroldson Pl, Corpus Christi, TX 78412, 512-991-5294
    Pubs: *The Lace of Tough Mesquite: A Texas Heritage*
    (Eakin Pr, 1993), *Southern Living, Texas Highways, Bird
    Watcher's Digest, Writer's Digest.*

Jack Myers   P
Southern Methodist Univ, English Dept, Dallas, TX 75275,
214-768-4369
    Pubs: *Blindsided, New American Poets of the 90's: Anth*
    (Godine, 1992, 1992), *Poetry, Esquire, APR.*

Isabel Nathaniel   P
18040 Midway Rd, Villa #215, Dallas, TX 75287-6582,
972-380-6128
Internet: isabeln@aol.com
    Pubs: *The Dominion of Lights* (Copper Beech Pr, 1996),
    *Poetry, Nation, Field, Ploughshares, Prairie Schooner, The
    Journal.*

Kim L. Neidigh   P&W
231 Radiance Ave, San Antonio, TX 78218
    Pubs: *Poetry Forum Jrnl, Wicked Mystic, Realm of the
    Vampire, Ripples, Deathrealm, Bloodrake, Pursuit.*

Sheryl L. Nelms   P
PO Box 674, Azle, TX 760980674, 817-377-2135
    Pubs: *Land of the Blue Paloverde* (Shooting Star Pr, 1995),
    Their Combs Turn Red in the Spring (Northwoods Pr,
    1984), *Kaleidoscope, Kansas Qtly.*

Ben Norwood   P&W
3046 Brown Lee Dr, #2016, Grand Prairie, TX 75052-7775,
817-695-4146
    Pubs: *Travois: An Anth of Texas Poetry* (Thorp Springs Pr,
    1976), *Sulphur River, Negative Capability, Unity, Stone Drum.*

Warren Norwood   P&W
500 Green Tree, Weatherford, TX 76087-8909, 817-596-5201
Internet: gigi-warren-norwood@worldnet.att.net
    Pubs: *True Jaguar* (Bantam, 1988), *Space Opera: Anth*
    (Del Rey, 1996), *Twilight Zone, Lookout, Green Fuse.*

Naomi Shihab Nye   W
806 S Main Ave, San Antonio, TX 78204, 210-222-0504
    Pubs: *Fuel, Red Suitcase* (BOA Edtns, 1998, 1994), *Words
    Under The Words* (Far Corner Bks, 1995), *Atlantic Monthly,
    Iowa Rev, Ploughshares, Southwest Rev, Wilderness, Five
    Points, Atlanta Rev, Georgia Rev, Indiana Rev, Tampa
    Rev.*

David Offutt   P
759 Redwood #3, Rockport, TX 78382, 888-522-6464
    Pubs: *A Perishable Good* (Inflammable Pr, 1997),
    Perceptions: Anth (The Write Technique, 1991), *Free
    Lunch, Poetry Motel, Maverick Pr, Tucumcari,
    Synaesthetic, Lost & Found Times, Aura, Green Hills
    Literary Lantern, Frog Pond, Potpourri.*

Dave Oliphant   P&W
Univ Texas, Main 201, Austin, TX 78712, 512-331-1557
Internet: doliphant@mail.utexas.edu
    Pubs: *Inheritance of Light: Anth* (U North Texas Pr, 1996),
    Texas in Poetry: Anth (Center for Texas Studies, 1994),
    *New Texas, New Letters, Colorado Qtly, College English,
    South Dakota Rev.*

Joe Olvera   P&W
Fourth Estate Consultants, 2200 Villa Plata, El Paso, TX
79935, 915-592-9870
    Pubs: *Drugs: Frankly Speaking* (Southwest Pub, 1980),
    Voces de la Gente (Mictla Pub, 1972).

Carolyn Osborn   W
3612 Windsor Rd, Austin, TX 78703, 512-472-4533
    Pubs: *Warriors and Maidens* (Texas Christian U Pr, 1991),
    Prize Stories, The O. Henry Awards: Anth (Doubleday,
    1991), *Southwest Rev, Antioch Rev.*

Keddy Ann Outlaw   P&W
3003 Linkwood Dr, Houston, TX 77025-3813, 713-668-8273
    Pubs: *At Our Core: Women Writing About Power: Anth, I
    Am Becoming the Woman I've Wanted: Anth*
    (Papier-Mache, 1998, 1994), *Texas Short Stories: Anth*
    (Browder Springs, 1997), *Texas Short Fiction III: Anth* (ALE
    Pub, 1996).

Leslie Palmer   P
Univ North Texas, English Dept, Denton, TX 76203,
817-387-5460
    Pubs: *The Devil Sells Ice Cream* (Windy-Dawn, 1994), *Ode
    to a Frozen Dog* (Laughing Bear, 1992), *Poetry and
    Audience, Green's Mag, Blue Jacket, Cape Rock, Southern
    Humanities Rev, European Judaica, Linq, Poetry
    Nottingham Intl.*

Tom Person   P
PO Box 613322, Dallas, TX 75261-3322, 817-283-6303
Internet: tom@laughingbear.com
    Pubs: *Small Pr, New York Qtly, Nexus, Interstate, Iron,
    Coffeehouse Poets Qtly.*

Estela Portillo   P&W
131 Clairemont, El Paso, TX 79912, 915-584-8841

Ron Querry   W
2415 E Musser, Laredo, TX 780432434, 11524-152-3542
Internet: ronquerry@mpsnet.com.mx
    Pubs: *Bad Medicine, The Death of Bernadette Lefthand*
    (Bantam Bks, 1998, 1995), *I See By My Get-Up* (U
    Oklahoma Pr, 1994).

S. Ramnath   P&W
PO Box 371823, El Paso, TX 79937-1823, 915-592-3701
Internet: an193@rgfn.epcc.edu
    Pubs: *Eye of the Beast* (Vergin Pr, 1986), *Rings in a Tree
    Trunk* (India; Writers Workshop, 1976), *Bedside Prayers:
    Anth* (Harper San Francisco, 1997), *Willow Springs, Weber
    Studies, Press, Litspeak, Kerf, Arkansas Qtly, Quixote Qtly,
    Maverick Pr.*

Pedro Revuelta   P
Univ Houston, Spanish Dept, Houston, TX 77204-3784,
713-749-3064
    Pubs: *Accidentes Y Otros Recursos* (Spain; Ediciones
    Libertarias, 1990), *Complejas Perspectivas* (Spain; Editorial
    Origenes, 1988), *Maize, el ultimo vuelo.*

Clay Reynolds   W
909 Hilton Pl, Denton, TX 76201, 817-566-2512
Internet: rclayr@aol.com
    Pubs: *Rage* (NAL/Signet, 1994), *Franklin's Crossing*
    (Dutton/NAL/Signet, 1993), *Writers' Forum, Texas Rev, i.e.
    Mag, Cimarron Rev, Concho River Rev.*

Brian Paul Robertson   P
516 Tamarack, McAllen, TX 78501

Del Marie Rogers   P
4804 Haverwood Ln, #922, Dallas, TX 75287, 972-735-0151
    Pubs: *Close to Ground* (Corona, 1990), *Anthology for
    Young Readers* (S&S, 1996), *Puerto del Sol, Texas
    Observer, Colorado Rev, Blue Mesa Rev, Nation, Epoch.*

Amber Rollins   W
6618 Laura Ann Ct, Fort Worth, TX 76118-6278,
817-284-4322
Internet: artemis939@aol.com
    Pubs: *EOTU, Paper Bag, Fiction Forum, The Torch, DC,
    After Hours, Being, Bahlasti Papers, Starsong, Outrage.*

Paul Ruffin   P&W
Sam Houston State Univ, Sam Houston Ave, English Dept,
Huntsville, TX 77341, 409-294-1429
Internet: eng_pdr@shsu.edu
    Pubs: *Circling* (Browder Springs Pr, 1996), *The Man Who
    Would Be God* (SMU Pr, 1993), *Southern Rev, Michigan
    Qtly Rev, Georgia Rev, American Literary Rev, Alaska Qtly
    Rev, Poetry.*

Annette Sanford   W
Box 596, Ganado, TX 77962, 512-771-3654
    Pubs: *Lasting Attachments, Common Bonds: Stories By &
    About Texas Women: Anth* (SMU Pr, 1989, 1990), *Story,
    American Short Fiction.*

Rainer Schulte   P
Univ Texas-Dallas, Box 830688, Richardson, TX 75083-0688,
214-690-2092
    Pubs: *The Other Side Of The Word* (Texas Writers, 1978),
    Suicide At The Piano (Sono Nis, 1970).

Daryl Scroggins   W
6200 Bryan Pkwy, Dallas, TX 75214, 214-821-9317
    Pubs: *New Growth 2: Contemporary Short Stories by Texas
    Writers: Anth* (Corona, 1993), *Asylum Annual, The
    Quarterly, Northwest Rev, Madison Rev, Carolina Qtly.*

Jan Epton Seale   P
400 Sycamore, McAllen, TX 78501, 210-686-4033
    Pubs: *The Wonder Is* (Prickly Pear Pr, 1998), *Airlift* (TCU
    Pr, 1992), *For She is the Tree of Life: Anth* (Conari Pr,
    1994), *Yale Rev, Texas Monthly, High Plains Literary Rev,
    Cape Rock, Nimrod, Passages North, Blue Mesa, COE
    Rev, Mesquite Rev.*

Wendell P. Sexton   P
4302 Rosebud Dr, Houston, TX 77053, 713-435-0867
    Pubs: *Poets Corner* (Office Duplication Classes, 1975).

Samuel B. Southwell   W
1217 W Main, Houston, TX 77006
    Pubs: *Kenneth Burke and Martin Heidegger: With A Note
    Against Deconstructionism* (U Florida, 1988), *If All the
    Rebels Die* (Doubleday, 1966).

Paul Spike   W
10340 Galahad Way, El Paso, TX 79924, 915-833-2486
    Pubs: *Last Rites* (New American Library, 1981), *The Night
    Letter* (Putnam, 1979).

L. Sprague de Camp   W
3453 Hearst Castle Way, Plano, TX 75025
    Pubs: *Rivers of Time, The Enchanter Reborn* (w/C.
    Stasheff) (Baen Bks, 1993, 1992), *Analog, Asimov's Sci Fi,
    Command, Nature, Expanse.*

Kristi Sprinkle   P&W
2609 Nottingham Ln, Austin, TX 78704, 512-916-1528
Internet: kristi@bha.com
    Pubs: *Freelight, Paramour, Different Drummer, Austin
    Chronicle.*

Cathy Stern   P
12427 Old Oaks Dr, Houston, TX 77024, 713-465-8017
    Pubs: *A Wider Giving: Anth* (Chicory Blue Pr, 1988), *Paris
    Rev, New Republic, Shenandoah.*

Alex Stevens   P
801 Rutland, Houston, TX 77007, 713-868-3716
    Pubs: *New Yorker, Poetry, Georgia Rev, New Republic.*

Gail Donohue Storey   P&W
3907 Swarthmore, Houston, TX 77005, 713-669-9318
    Pubs: *God's Country Club, The Lord's Motel* (Persea Bks,
    1996, 1992), *Fiction, NAR, Chicago Rev, Gulf Coast,
    Ellipses, Mississippi Valley Rev.*

James L. Stowe   W
709 Baltimore, El Paso, TX 79902, 915-532-6260
    Pubs: *Winter Stalk* (Simon & Schuster, 1978).

Semon Strobos   W
2281 Bretzke Ln, New Braunfels, TX 78132, 210-609-0527
Internet: strobat@compuserve.net
    Pubs: *NAR, Epoch, Chariton Rev, Antioch Rev, Descant,
    Alabama Literary Rev.*

Belinda Subraman   P
PO Box 370322, El Paso, TX 79937, 915-562-7820
    Pubs: *Notes of a Human Warehouse Engineer* (Nerve
    Cowboy, 1998), *Finding Reality in Myth* (Chiron Rev Pr,
    1996), *Between the Cracks: Anth* (Daedalus, 1996), *Mondo
    Barbie: Anth* (St. Martin's Pr, 1993), *Arkansas Rev, India
    Currents, Best Texas Writing.*

Thea Temple   P&W
3109 Caribou Ct, Mesquite, TX 75181, 972-222-3973
Internet: jmyers@post.cis.smu.edu
    Pubs: *River Styx, Sycamore Rev, Yellow Silk, Chiron Rev,
    Beloit Fiction Jrnl, The New Press, Alabama Literary Rev,
    Japanophile.*

Heriberto Teran   P
2314 Baltimore St, Laredo, TX 78040, 512-722-7435

Larry D. Thomas   P
2006 Commonwealth, Houston, TX 77006, 713-523-8147
    Pubs: *Anth of Mag Verse and Yearbook of American Poetry*
    (Monitor Bk Co, 1997), *Puerto del Sol, Writers' Forum,
    Borderlands, Texas Rev, Descant, Stable Companion,
    Small Pond, Equine Image, Cape Rock, Texas Rev.*

Lorenzo Thomas   P
Box 14645, Houston, TX 77221, 713-221-8475
    Pubs: *The Bathers* (Reed & Cannon, 1981), *Chances Are
    Few* (Blue Wind Pr, 1979), *Postmodern American Poetry:
    Anth* (Norton, 1994), *Ploughshares, Long News.*

Ruby C. Tolliver   W
1806 Pin Oak Ln, Conroe, TX 77302, 409-756-4659
    Pubs: *Boomer's Kids, Blind Bess, Buddy & M*
    (Hendrick-Long Pub, 1992, 1990), *Have Gun, Need Bullets*
    (TCU Pr, 1991).

Frederick Turner   P&W
Univ Texas-Dallas, Richardson, TX 75083, 214-690-2777
    Pubs: *April Wind, Beauty* (U Pr Virginia, 1992, 1992),
    Tempest, Flute and Oz (Persea Bks, 1991), *Harper's,
    Poetry.*

Leslie Ullman   P
Univ Texas, English Dept, El Paso, TX 79968, 505-874-3068
Internet: lullman@utep.edu
    Pubs: *Slow Work Through Sand* (U Iowa Pr, 1998), *Dreams
    By No One's Daughter* (U Pitt Pr, 1987), *Natural Histories*
    (Yale U Pr, 1979), *Poetry, Kenyon Rev, Bloomsbury Rev.*

Leo Vroman   P
1600 Texas St, Fort Worth, TX 76102, 817-870-1172
Internet: lvroman@elash.net
    Pubs: *Psalmen en Andere Gedichten* (Amsterdam;
    Querido, 1997), *Flight 800/Vlucht 800, Love, Greatly
    Enlarged* (Cross Cultural Communications, 1997, 1992).

Brian Walker   P
PO Box 5143, Lubbock, TX 79417, 806-797-3355
    Pubs: *Fiddlehead, Poetry Ireland Rev, Poetry Wales,
    Transnational Perspectives, Bitterroot.*

Kenneth Wheatcroft-Pardue   P
1805 Robinwood Dr, Forth Worth, TX 76111-6110,
817-834-3341
    Pubs: *Sleepy Tree I: Anth of Poetry & Fiction* (Sleepy Tree
    Pr, 1980), *California Qtly, Sulphur River Rev, Poetry Motel,
    Touchstone, Maverick Press, Concho River Rev.*

Thomas Whitbread   P
Univ Texas, Austin, TX 78712, 512 471 4001
    Pubs: *Whomp & Moonshiver* (BOA Edtns, 1982), *Four
    Infinitives* (H&R, 1964).

Brenda Black White   P
2508 Washington, Commerce, TX 75428, 903-886-3822
    Pubs: *Callahan County* (Plainview Pr, 1988), *New Texas
    '95: Anth, Texas In Poetry: Anth* (Ctr for Texas Studies,
    1995, 1994), *RE:AL, Ms., Confrontation.*

J. Whitebird   W
13815 Bay Gardens Dr, Sugar Land, TX 77478-1723,
281-494-1380
    Pubs: *Heat & Other Stories* (Arbiter Pr, 1990), *The North
    Beach Papers* (Suck Egg Mule Pr, 1985), *Crosscurrents,
    Plainswoman, Poemail.*

Chris Willerton   P
Abilene Christian Univ, Box 8242, ACU Sta, Abilene, TX
79699, 915-674-2259
Internet: willerto@nicanor.acu.edu
    Pubs: *Texas in Poetry: Anth* (U North Texas Pr, 1994), *New
    Texas '93: Anth* (Ctr for Texas Studies, 1993), *Borderlands,
    Riversedge, Literary Rev, Southern Poetry Rev.*

Miles Wilson P&W
906 Clyde St, San Marcos, TX 78666, 512-392-9643
Pubs: *Line of Fall* (U Iowa Pr, 1989), *Gettysburg Rev,
Georgia Rev, Poetry, Southwest Rev, NAR, Iowa Rev.*

Steve Wilson P
Southwest Texas State Univ, San Marcos, TX 78666,
512-245-2163
Internet: sw13@swt.edu
Pubs: *The Singapore Express, Allegory Dance* (Black Tie
Pr, 1994, 1991), *New Letters, Wallace Stevens Jrnl,
Midwest Qtly, Plainsong, NAW, Literary Rev.*

Marion Winik P
3808 Ridgelea Dr, Austin, TX 78731-6125
Pubs: *Boy Crazy* (Sloughpress, 1986), *Nonstop* (Cedar
Rock, 1981).

Bryan Woolley W
18040 Midway Rd, Villa 215, Dallas, TX 75287,
214-380-6128
Pubs: *The Bride Wore Crimson, The Edge of the West*
(Texas Western, 1993, 1990), *Time and Place* (TCU,
1985).

John Works W
1600 Forest Trail, Austin, TX 78703
Pubs: *Thank You Queen Isabella* (Texas A&M U, 1986),
Humanities Rev, Cottonwood Rev.

Fabian Worsham P
Univ Houston-Downtown, 1 Main St, Houston, TX 77002,
713-221-8115
Pubs: *Vulture Woman* (Mac*Kinations Pr, 1994), *Aunt
Erma's Country Kitchen & Bordello* (Signpost Pr, 1985),
New Texas, Southern Humanities Rev, Florida Rev.

UTAH

Margaret Pabst Battin W
Univ of Utah, Salt Lake City, UT 84112, 801-581-6608
Pubs: *The Least Worst Death* (Oxford U Pr, 1994).

Kenneth W. Brewer P
Utah State Univ, Logan, UT 84322-3200, 435-797-3516
Internet: fabrewer@wpo.hass.usu.edu
Pubs: *The Place In Between* (Limberlost Pr, 1998), *To
Remember What Is Lost* (Utah State U Pr, 1989), *Great &
Peculiar Beauty, A Utah Reader: Anth* (Gibbs Smith, 1995),
Poetry Northwest, Kansas Qtly.

Sharon Bryan P
1254 W 1000 N, Salt Lake City, UT 84116, 801-355-5767
Internet: sharonbrya@aol.com
Pubs: *Flying Blind* (Sarabande Bks, 1996), *Where We
Stand: Anth* (Norton, 1994), *Paris Rev, Atlantic Monthly, Tar
River Poetry, Nation, APR, Seattle Rev.*

Alex Caldiero PP&P
1978 N 100 E, Orem, UT 84057, 801-224-8642
Pubs: *Various Atmospheres* (Signature Books, 1998),
Dictionary of The Text-Sounds Texts (Morrow, 1980),
Avant-Guards: Anth (A Capella Bks, 1994), *Clown War,
Handbook, Screens & Tasted Parallels, Conyon Echo.*

Lawrence Coates W
Southern Utah Univ, English Dept, Cedar City, UT 84720,
435-586-7835
Pubs: *The Blossom Festival: Anth* (U Nevada Pr, 1999),
*Connecticut Rev, Blue Mesa Rev, Contemporary Satire,
Writers' Forum, Long Story, Toyon, Santa Clara Rev,
Missouri Rev.*

Brewster Ghiselin P
Univ Utah, English Dept-3500 LNCO, Salt Lake City, UT
84112, 801-581-6168
Pubs: *Flame: Poems 1980-90, Windrose: Poems 1929-79*
(U Utah 1990, 1980), *Poetry, Aperture, Letteratura, Hudson
Rev, Story, Encounter.*

Joan Gilgun W
1700 S 800 E, Lewiston, UT 84320
Pubs: *The Uncle* (Cadmus Edtns, 1982), *Dialogue, New
Voices, Innisfree, Western Humanities Rev.*

Edward L. Hart P
1401 Cherry Ln, Provo, UT 84604, 801-375-0871
Pubs: *To Utah* (Brigham Young U Pr, 1979), *Beloit Poetry
Jrnl, Western Humanities Rev.*

Robert L. Jones P
Univ Utah, English Dept, 341 0SH, Salt Lake City, UT 84112
Pubs: *Wild Onion* (Graywolf Pr, 1985), *The Space I Occupy*
(Skywriting, 1977), *Kansas Qtly.*

David Lee P
Southern Utah State College, Cedar City, UT 84720,
801-586-7835
Pubs: *Day's Work* (Copper Canyon Pr, 1990), *Paragonah
Canyon, Autumn* (Brooding Heron Pr, 1988).

Harris Lenowitz P
Univ Utah, Salt Lake City, UT 84112, 801-581-6181
Pubs: *Transparencies: Jewish Pages* (Finch Lane, 1985),
The Sayings Of Yakov Frank (Tree, 1978).

Edward Lueders   P
958 S Windsor St, Salt Lake City, UT 84105, 801-539-0430
> Pubs: *The Clam Lake Papers* (Wm. Caxton Ltd, 1996), *The Wake of the General Bliss* (U Utah Pr, 1989), *Poetry, Theology Today, Poetry Nippon, Terra Nova, Prairie Schooner, Weber Studies.*

James Minor   P
3064 Tyler Ave, Ogden, UT 84403-0940, 801-392-1514
> Pubs: *Against the Night, A Measure of Light* (Juniper Pr, 1986, 1984), *New Cicada, Northeast.*

Lynne Butler Oaks   W
3945 S Wasatch Blvd, #260, Salt Lake City, UT 84124, 801-321-1808
> Pubs: *Missouri Rev, Fiction Intl, Story Qtly, The Quarterly, Utah Holiday.*

Jacqueline Osherow   P
Univ Utah, English Dept, 3500 LNCO, Salt Lake City, UT 84112
Internet: jacqueline.osherow@m.cc.utah.edu
> Pubs: *With a Moon in Transit* (Grove Poetry, 1996), *Conversations with Survivors, Looking for Angels in New York* (U Georgia Pr, 1994, 1988), *Paris Rev, New Republic, TriQuarterly, Partisan Rev, Southwest Rev, Boulevard.*

Donald Revell   P
Univ Utah, Salt Lake City, UT 84112, 801-581-3392
> Pubs: *Beautiful Shirt, Erasures, New Dark Ages* (Wesleyan, 1994, 1992, 1990), *Antaeus, APR, Grand Street, Conjunctions, Partisan Rev, Kenyon Rev.*

Stephen Ruffus   P
617 E South Temple, Salt Lake City, UT 84102, 801-533-5895
> Pubs: *Quarterly West, Westigan Rev, Western Humanities Rev.*

Natasha Saje   P
Westminster College, 1840 1300 East, Salt Lake City, UT 84105, 801-488-1692
Internet: n-saje@wcslc.edu
> Pubs: *Red Under the Skin* (U Pittsburgh Pr, 1994), *Poetry, Shenandoah, American Voice, Denver Qtly, Ploughshares.*

Richard Schramm   P
Univ Utah, English Dept, Salt Lake City, UT 84112, 801-582-7490
> Pubs: *Rooted In Silence* (Bobbs-Merrill, 1972), *New Yorker, Antaeus, APR.*

Emma Lou Thayne   P&W
1965 St Mary's Dr, Salt Lake City, UT 84108, 801-581-1260
> Pubs: *All God's Critters Got A Place In the Choir* (w/L.T. Ulrich; Aspen, 1995), *Things Happen: Poems of Survival* (Signature Bks, 1991), *Network.*

Peter Thomas   P
469 E 2015 N, Cedar City, UT 84720, 801-865-1610
> Pubs: *Dusting Off Dreams, All My Tomorrows* (Quill Pr, 1994, 1994), *Poet, Utah English Jrnl, Native Rhythms.*

David Widup   P
1930 E Sunridge Cir, Sandy, UT 84093, 801-568-7890
Internet: david_widup@bdhq.bd.com
> Pubs: *In Country: Anth* (w/Michael Andrews; Bombshelter Pr, 1994), *Over to You: Anth* (w/Stellasue Lee; Bombshelter Pr, 1991), *ACM, Icarus Rev, Spillway, Onthebus, Rattle.*

VERMONT

Thomas Absher   P
Vermont College, Montpelier, VT 05679, 802-828-8820
> Pubs: *The Calling* (Alice James Bks, 1987), *Forms of Praise* (Ohio State U Pr, 1981), *Ploughshares, Poetry, Nation.*

Laurie Alberts   W
PO Box 258, Westminster, VT 05158
> Pubs: *The Price of Land in Shelby* (U Pr New England, 1996), *Goodnight Silky Sullivan* (U Missouri Pr, 1995), *Tempting Fate* (HM, 1987).

Joan Aleshire   P
RD Box 1115, Cuttingsville, VT 05738, 802-492-3550
> Pubs: *This Far* (QRL, 1987), *Cloud Train* (Texas Tech, 1982), *QRL, Nation, Seneca Rev.*

Frank Anthony   P
151 Main St/PO Box 483, Windsor, VT 05089, 802-674-2315
Internet: newvtpoet@aol.com
> Pubs: *The Amsterdam Papers, The Magic Bench* (New Vision Pubs, 1997, 1996), *Life on the Line: Anth* (Negative Capability Pr, 1992).

Bob Arnold   P
Jacksonville Stage, Brattleboro, VT 05301, 802-254-4242
> Pubs: *American Train Letters* (Coyote/SUNY Buffalo, 1995), *Where Rivers Meet* (Mad River, 1990), *On Stone* (Origin Pr, 1988), *Hummingbird, Key Satchel, Shadow Play, Gargoyle, Shearsman, Gate.*

E. R. Barna   P
80 Park St, Brandon, VT 05733, 802-247-3146
Internet: gotobarn@sover.net
> Pubs: *Agni, Firehouse, Worcester Rev, Longhouse, Afterthought, Mothering, Softball, Gob.*

Ben Belitt P
PO Box 88, North Bennington, VT 05257-0088,
802-442-5956
    Pubs: *Graffiti and Other Poems* (Erewhon, 1990), *Nowhere But Light* (U Chicago Pr, 1970), *Possessions* (Godine, 1986), *Salmagundi, Yale Rev, Southern Rev.*

T. Alan Broughton P&W
124 Spruce St, Burlington, VT 05401, 802-864-4250
Internet: tbrought@zoo.uvm.edu
    Pubs: *In The Country Of Elegies, Preparing To Be Happy* (Carnegie Mellon U Pr, 1995, 1988), *The Jesse Tree* (Juniper Pr, 1988).

David Budbill P
4592 East Hill Rd, Wolcott, VT 056804149, 802-888-3729
Internet: budbill@plainfield.bypass.com
    Pubs: *Moment to Moment* (Copper Canyon Pr, 1999), *Judevine: The Complete Poems* (Chelsea Green, 1991), *Why I Came To Judevine* (White Pine, 1987), *Green Mountains Rev, Harper's, New Virginia Rev, The Sun, Cedar Hill Rev, Graffiti Rag, Maine Times, Ohio Rev.*

Rhoda Carroll P
RR5, Box 1030, 2047 Elm St, Montpelier, VT 05602, 802-229-0037
Internet: rhoda@norwich.edu
    Pubs: *Slant, Nebraska Rev, Green Mountains Rev, Poet Lore, Visions Intl, Lake Effect, Laurel Rev, Texas Rev, Northern Rev, Tar River Poetry, Louisville Rev.*

George R. Clay W
Wild Farm, Arlington, VT 05250, 802-362-1656

Steven Cramer P
Bennington College, Bennington, VT 05201, 802-442-3716
    Pubs: *Dialogue for the Left and Right Hand* (Lumen Edtns, 1997), *The World Book* (Copper Beech, 1992), *Atlantic, Nation, New Republic, Paris Rev, Poetry.*

Chard deNiord P
RR 4, Box 929, Putney, VT 05346, 802-387-5309
    Pubs: *Asleep in the Fire* (U Alabama Pr, 1990), *Poems for a Small Planet: A Bread Loaf Anth* (U Pr New England, 1993), *Harvard Mag, Denver Qtly, NAR, NER, Iowa Rev.*

Rickey Gard Diamond W
31 Hebert Rd, Montpelier, VT 05602, 802-223-7911
Internet: rdiamond@norwich.edu
    Pubs: *Second Sight* (Calyx Bks, 1997), *Other Voices, Writers' Bar-B-Q, Plainswoman, Kalliope, Sewanee Rev, Louisville Rev.*

Susan M. Dodd W
Bennington College, Bennington, VT 05201
    Pubs: *Hell-Bent Men & Their Cities, Mamaw, No Earthly Notion* (Viking, 1990, 1988, 1986), *New Yorker.*

Margaret Edwards P&W
Univ of Vermont, English Dept, 400 Old Mill, Burlington, VT 05405, 802-862-4468
    Pubs: *Best American Short Stories 1985: Anth* (Houghton Mifflin, 1986), *Virginia Qtly Rev, Vermont History.*

Kenward Elmslie P&W
Calais, VT 05648, 802-456-8123
    Pubs: *Routine Disruptions* (Coffee Hse Pr, 1998), *Pay Dirt* (Bamberger Bks, 1992), *Sung Sex* (Kulchur, 1989), *26 Bars* (Z Pr, 1987), *NAW, o.blek, Conjunctions.*

John Engels P
221 Shelburne St, Burlington, VT 05401, 802-865-2543
    Pubs: *Walking to Cootehill* (U Pr New England, 1993), *Cardinals In the Ice Age* (Graywolf Pr, 1987), *Weather-Fear* (U Georgia Pr, 1982).

James Facos P&W
333 Elm St, Montpelier, VT 05602
    Pubs: *The Silver Lady* (Thorndike Pr, 1995), *Morning's Come Singing* (American Poetry Pr, 1981), *Norton Book of Light Verse: Anth* (Norton, 1986), *New Press Literary Qtly, Negative Capability, Stories.*

Terry Farish W
Steerforth Press, PO Box 70, South Royalton, VT 05068, 802-763-2808
Internet: farish@mighty.riv.edu
    Pubs: *Talking In Animal, Shelter For A Seabird, Why I'm Already Blue* (Greenwillow, 1996, 1990, 1989), *If The Tiger* (Steerforth Pr, 1995).

Alvin Feinman P
PO Box 655, North Bennington, VT 05257

Ellen Frye W
7 Third Ave, White River Jct, VT 05001
Internet: ellen.frye@dartmouth.edu
    Pubs: *Amazon Story Bones* (Spinsters Ink, 1994), *The Other Sappho* (Firebrand Bks, 1989), *Calyx, Short Fiction By Women.*

Lyle Glazier P&W
RD 3, Niles Rd, Bennington, VT 05201-4959, 802-442-9459
    Pubs: *Prefatory Lyrics* (Coffee Hse Pr, 1991), *Azubah Nye* (White Pine Pr, 1988), *Origin, Longhouse, Shadow/Play, Tel-Let, New Yorker, Story.*

Louise Gluck P
Creamery Rd, Plainfield, VT 05667
    Pubs: *The Wild Iris, Ararat, The Triumph of Achilles* (Ecco, 1992, 1990, 1985), *New Yorker, APR, Threepenny Rev, Yale Rev, Tikkun.*

Florence Grossman P
PO Box 352, Bondville, VT 05340
    Pubs: *Listening to the Bells* (Heinemann Boynton/Cook, 1991), *Nation, Poetry, New Criterion.*

Robert Hahn   P
155 College Hill, Johnson, VT 05656, 802-635-1246
Internet: hahnr@badger.jsc.vsc.edu
>Pubs: *All Clear* (U South Carolina Pr, 1996), *One More Time* (Cummington, 1989), *Paris Rev, Southwest Rev, Yale Rev, Shenandoah, Partisan Rev.*

H. Douglas Hall   P
RD, Cuttingsville, VT 05738, 802-492-3517
>Pubs: *Road Apple Rev, Loon, The Sun, Poetry Now, Northern New England Rev.*

Pamela Harrison   P
PO Box 1106, Norwich, VT 05055, 802-649-2946
>Pubs: *Noah's Daughter, The Panhandler* (U West Florida Pr, 1988), *The College Handbook of Creative Writing: Anth* (HBJ, 1991), *Beloit Poetry Jrnl, Yankee, Poetry, Cimarron Rev, Laurel Rev, Green Mountains Rev, Sow's Ear, Contemporary Rev.*

Shelby Hearon   W
246 S Union, Burlington, VT 05401, 802-660-4349
>Pubs: *Footprints, Life Estates, Hug Dancing* (Knopf, 1996, 1994, 1991), *Redbook, GQ, Cosmopolitan.*

Geof Hewitt   P
PO Box 51, Calais, VT 05648, 802-828-3111
>Pubs: *Just Worlds* (Ithaca Hse, 1989), *I Think They'll Lay My Egg Tomorrow* (Stinehour, 1976).

Edward Hoagland   W
RR 1, Box 2977, Bennington, VT 05201-9735, 802-442-2088
>Pubs: *Balancing Acts, Heart's Desire* (S&S, 1992, 1988).

David Huddle   P&W
34 N Willams St, Burlington, VT 05401, 802-864-6111
Internet: dhuddle@200.uvm.200
>Pubs: *Tenorman* (Chronicle Bks, 1995), *Intimates* (Godine, 1992), *Story, APR, Kenyon Rev, Antioch, Epoch, Field, Poetry.*

Elizabeth Inness-Brown   W
St. Michael's College, Box 359, Colchester, VT 05439, 802-654-2441
>Pubs: *Here* (LSU, 1994), *Satin Palms* (Fiction Intl Pr, 1981), *New Yorker, Glimmer Train, Boulevard, NAR, Cream City Rev, Mississippi Rev, Sycamore Rev.*

John Irving   W
The Turnbull Agency, PO Box 757, Dorset, VT 05251
>Pubs: *A Widow For One Year* (Random Hse, 1998), *The Cider House Rules* (Morrow, 1985).

Galway Kinnell   P&W
Sheffield, VT 05966
>Pubs: *When One Has Lived A Long Time Alone* (Knopf, 1990), *The Past, Selected Poems* (HM, 1985, 1982).

S. R. Lavin   P
Castleton State College, Castleton, VT 05735, 802-468-5611
>Pubs: *I-U: Version By S. R. Lavin* (Jerusalem Hse/Four Zoas Pr, 1997), *They Knew Me When* (High Meadow, 1990).

Sydney Lea   P&W
PO Box 9, Newbury, VT 05051, 802-866-5458
Internet: leabaron@connriver.net
>Pubs: *To The Bone: New and Selected Poems* (U Illinois Pr, 1996), *Hunting the Whole Way Home* (U Pr New England, 1995), *New Yorker, Atlantic, Georgia Rev.*

Julia Lebentritt   P
PO Box 8373, Burlington, VT 05402-8373
>Pubs: *The Kooken* (Henry Holt, 1992), *Universal Lullabies* (Song Bank, 1990), *Cultural Connections, New York Folklore.*

Gary Lenhart   P
166 Beaver Meadow Rd, Norwich, VT 05055
>Pubs: *Light Heart* (Hanging Loose, 1991), *One At A Time* (United Artists, 1983), *The World, Hanging Loose, Poetry Flash, Exquisite Corpse.*

Gary Margolis   P
Middlebury College, Carr Hall, Middlebury, VT 05753, 802-493-5141
Internet: margolis@middlebury.edu
>Pubs: *Falling Awake, The Day We Still Stand Here* (U Georgia Pr, 1986, 1983), *Poetry, TriQuarterly.*

Lynn Martin   P
43 Westgate Apartments, Brattleboro, VT 05301-8935, 802-257-7748
>Pubs: *Visible Signs of Defiance* (Out of the Kitchen Pr, 1995), *My Lover is a Woman: Anth* (Ballantine, 1996), *Green Mountains, Connecticut Rev, Centennial Rev, Metis.*

Jean R. Matthew   W
Box 147, Marshfield, VT 05658
Internet: jmatthew@plainfield.bypass.com
>Pubs: *Testimony: Stories* (U Missouri Pr, 1987), *Missouri Rev, Black Warrior Rev, Crescent Rev, Southern Humanities Rev.*

Paul McRay   P
PO Box 26, Strafford, VT 05072-0026, 802-765-4024
>Pubs: *As Though Traveling Backwards Were Natural* (U Wisconsin Pr/Windfall Prophets Pr, 1990), *Sweet Nothings: Anth* (Illinois U Pr, 1994), *Anth of Mag Verse and Yearbook of AmericanVerse 1988, Poetry, Antioch Rev, Crazyhorse, Mississippi Valley Rev.*

Don Mitchell   W
RD #2 Box 2680, Vergennes, VT 05491, 802-545-2278
>Pubs: *The Souls of Lambs* (HM, 1979), *Thumb Tripping* (Little, Brown, 1970), *Boston Mag, Yankee, Country Jrnl, Harper's, Atlantic, Esquire.*

Barbara Moraff   P&W
PO Box 227, Richmond, VT 05477-0227
    Pubs: *AHH* (Shadowplay, 1992), *Potterwoman: Book Two,
    You've Got Me* (Longhouse, 1992, 1987), *Deadly
    Nightshade* (Coffee Hse, 1988), *Forum, Longhouse.*

Patty Mucha   P
RD 3, St Johnsbury, VT 05819
    Pubs: *See Vermont* (Poets Mimeo Co-op, 1979),
    Telephone, New Wilderness Audiographics.

Patrick O'Connor   P
PO Box 296, Killington, VT 05751-0296, 802-422-9399
Internet: mapplucia@aol.com
    Pubs: *No Poem For Fritz* (Colorado Qtly, 1978), *The
    Prayers of Man: Anth* (Ivan Oblensky, 1960), *Dance Mag,
    Voices Israel.*

Robert Pack   P
RD #2, Cornwall, VT 05753, 802-462-2441

Grace Paley   P&W
PO Box 620, Thetford Hill, VT 050740620, 802-785-2608
    Pubs: *Just As I Thought, The Collected Stories* (FSG, 1998,
    1994), *New and Collected Poems* (Tilbury Pr, 1992), *Long
    Walks and Intimate Talks* (Feminist Pr, 1991).

Verbena Pastor   P&W
Graduate Program, Vermont College of Norwich Uni,
Montpelier, VT 05602, 802-828-8831
Internet: vpastor@norwich.edu
    Pubs: *Kiria Andreov* (Rain Crow Publishing, 1997), *Penny
    Dreadful, Green's Mag, The European, 100 Words, Alfred
    Hitchcock's Mystery, Ellery Queen's Mystery, Yellow Silk,
    Bostonia, Stories.*

Linda Peavy   P&W
169 Garron Rd, Middletown Springs, VT 05757-4222,
802-235-2844
Internet: ps@vermontel.com
    Pubs: *Women in Waiting in the Westward Movement* (w/U.
    Smith; U Oklahoma Pr, 1994), *Hard Love: Anth* (Queen of
    Swords Pr, 1997), *Word of Mouth Anth* (Crossing Pr, 1990),
    *Kalliope, Poets On, Texas Rev, Lesbian Short Fiction,
    Writers' Forum, Earth's Daughters.*

John Pember   P
PO Box 185, Dorset, VT 05251-0185, 802-362-8189
    Pubs: *Rope to the Barn* (White Eagle Coffee Store Pr,
    1993), *Under A Gull's Wing: Anth* (Down the Shore Pub,
    1996), *Footwork, Fresh Ground, Sunrust, Jrnl of New
    Jersey Poets, Calypso, Poetpourri, Without Halos, Northern
    New England Rev.*

Verandah Porche   P
RFD 3, Box 328, Brattleboro, VT 05301, 802-254-2442
    Pubs: *Glancing Off* (See-Through Pr, 1987), *The Body's
    Symmetry* (H&R, 1975), *Ms., New Boston Rev.*

Burt Porter   P
Rte #2, Box 153, Glover, VT 05839, 802-525-3037
    Pubs: *Rhymes of the Magical World* (Other Media Pr,
    1995), *Crows and Angels* (Bread & Puppet Pr, 1993),
    Hellas, The Lyric, Poet, Classical Outlook, The Formalist.

Martha Ramsey   P
PO Box 852, Putney, VT 05346-0852
    Pubs: *Boulevard, Passages North, New Letters, American
    Voice, Soundings East, Sojourner.*

Julia Randall   P
Rte 1, Box 64, North Bennington, VT 05257
    Pubs: *The Path to Fairview: New & Selected, Moving in
    Memory* (LSU, 1992, 1987), *Ploughshares, Kenyon Rev.*

F. D. Reeve   P&W
PO Box 14, Wilmington, VT 05363-0014
Internet: fdreeve@sover.net
    Pubs: *The Blue Boat On the St. Anne* (Bayeux Arts, 1999),
    The Red Machines (Azul Edtns, 1999), *Concrete Music*
    (Pyncheon Hse, 1992), *The White Monk* (Vanderbilt, 1989),
    *Sewanee, Poetry, APR, Hudson, New England, Free
    Lunch, Michigan Qtly.*

Kate Riley   W
RD2, Box 455A, Johnson, VT 05656, 802-635-7021
Internet: rileyk@vscacs.vsc.edu
    Pubs: *Other Voices, Green Mountains Rev, Kalliope.*

Mark Rubin   P
468-A North St, Burlington, VT 05401
    Pubs: *The Beginning of Responsibility* (Owl Creek Pr,
    1992), *Ohio Rev, American Voice, Boulevard, Prairie
    Schooner.*

Mary Ruefle   P
PO Box 864, North Bennington, VT 05257
    Pubs: *Cold Pluto* (Carnegie Mellon, 1996), *The Adamant* (U
    Iowa Pr, 1989), *Life Without Speaking* (U Alabama Pr,
    1987).

Stephen Sandy   P
Box 524, North Bennington, VT 05257, 802-442-8496
Internet: sandys@bennington.edu
    Pubs: *Black Box, The Thread: New and Selected Poems*
    (Louisiana State U Pr, 1999, 1998), *Thanksgiving Over The
    Water, Man in the Open Air* (Knopf, 1992, 1988), *Paris Rev,
    Ploughshares, New Yorker, Southern Rev, Atlantic, APR,
    Kenyon Rev, Mudfish, Denver Qtly.*

Jim Schley   P
Blue Moon Cooperative, HCR Box 54, Alger Brook Rd, South
Strafford, VT 05070-7703
Internet: jschley@sover.net
    Pubs: *Articulations: Anth* (U Iowa Pr, 1994), *Ironwood,
    Crazyhorse, Vermont Woodlands, Harbor Rev.*

Joan D. Shambaugh P
PO Box 552, Hardwick, VT 05843-0552, 802-472-9153
Pubs: *She Who Walks With Trees, Little Books: Anth*
(Acorn Pr, 1993, 1992), *Poems From Lincoln Hill* (Cottage
Pr, 1989), *Lincoln Rev.*

Neil Shepard P
Johnson State College, Johnson, VT 05656, 802-635-2356
Pubs: *I'm Here Because I Lost My Way, Scavenging the
Country for a Heartbeat* (Mid-List Pr, 1998, 1993),
*TriQuarterly, Chelsea, Western Humanities Rev, Poetry
East, Denver Qtly, Southern Rev, Antioch Rev.*

Allen Shepherd W
487 S Willard St, Burlington, VT 05401, 802-863-5672
Pubs: *Kansas Qtly, Colorado Qtly, New Yorker, New Arts
Rev, Cimarron Rev.*

Joe Sherman W
Box 22, Montgomery, VT 05470
Pubs: *Fast Lane on a Dirt Road* (Countryman Pr, 1991), *A
Thousand Voices* (Rutledge Hill, 1987), *The House at
Shelburne Farms* (Paul Eriksen, 1986).

Jane Shore P
RR 1, Box 4, East Calais, VT 05650, 802-456-8783
Pubs: *The Minute Hand, Eye Level* (U Massachusetts Pr,
1987, 1977), *New Republic, Ploughshares.*

Frank Short P
12 Burnell Terr, St Albans, VT 05478, 802-524-3749
Pubs: *Bits, Bitterroot, Blue Unicorn, Chowder Rev,
High-Coo, Poet Lore, Poetry Now, Snakeroot.*

Tom Smith P
PO Box 223, Castleton, VT 05735, 802-468-2277
Pubs: *A Well-Behaved Little Boy* (Woldt-Starbooks, 1993),
The Broken Iris (Persephone Pr, 1991), *Iowa Rev, New
York Qtly, Beloit Poetry Jrnl, James White Rev.*

Wendy Stevens P&W
PO Box 189, Waterbury Center, VT 05677
Pubs: *True Life Adventure Stories: Anth* (Crossing Pr,
1983), *Fight Back: Anth* (Cleis Pr, 1981), *Nimrod.*

Ruth Stone P
RD #3, Brandon, VT 05733-9803
Pubs: *Mother Stone's Nursery Rhymes* (MBIRA, 1992),
Who is the Widow's Muse, Second Hand Coat (Yellow
Moon Pr, 1991, 1991), *Boulevard, American Voice, APR.*

Floyd C. Stuart P
6 North St, Northfield, VT 05663
Pubs: *The Spirit That Moves Us Reader: Anth* (The Spirit
That Moves Us Pr, 1982), *Travelling America with Today's
Poets: Anth* (Macmillan, 1976), *Beloit Poetry Jrnl.*

Lynn Manning Valente P&W
PO Box 9, Marlboro, VT 05344, 802-254-2876
Internet: lvalente@wcsu.k12.vt.us
Pubs: *Anth of New England Writers, Longhouse, Northeast,
Visions, Poetry Now, Jam To-Day, Pig Iron, Sistersong,
Poetry Motel.*

Ellen Bryant Voigt P
Box 128, Marshfield, VT 05658-0128, 802-563-2707
Pubs: *Two Trees, The Lotus Flowers, The Forces of Plenty*
(Norton, 1992, 1987, 1983), *New Yorker, Atlantic, APR.*

Roger Weingarten P
Vermont College, Montpelier, VT 05602, 802-828-8638
Pubs: *Ghost Wrestling, Infant Bonds of Joy, Shadow
Shadow* (Godine, 1997, 1990, 1986), *Poetry East, Missouri
Rev, NAR, APR, Paris Rev, Poetry, New Yorker, Prague
Revue.*

Norman Williams W
381 S Union St, Burlington, VT 05401
Pubs: *The Unlovely Child* (Knopf, 1985), *New Yorker,
Verse.*

Nancy Means Wright W
PO Box 182, Middlebury, VT 057539587, 802-462-2719
Internet: nancyden@bestweb.net
Pubs: *Harvest of Bones, Mad Season* (St. Martin's Pr,
1998, 1996), *Down the Strings* (Dutton, 1982), *Carolina
Qtly, Wisconsin Rev, Redbook, Seventeen, Bellingham
Rev, American Literary Rev, Other Voices, Green
Mountains Rev.*

VIRGINIA

Ally Acker P
2260 Teel Dr, Vienna, VA 221825154, 703-204-4445
Internet: aacker@freewwweb.com
Pubs: *Waiting for the Beloved* (Red Hen Pr, 1999),
Surviving Desire (Garden Street Pr, 1994), *American Voice,
Poetry Kanto, Ploughshares.*

B. Chelsea Adams P&W
5510 Piney Woods Rd, Riner, VA 24149-1647, 540-382-1778
Pubs: *Sampler: Anth* (Alms Hse Pr, 1993), *CQ, Poet Lore,
Southwestern Rev, Union Street Rev, Albany Rev, Virginia
English Bulletin.*

Judy Light Ayyildiz P
4930 Hunting Hills Circle, Roanoke, VA 24014, 703-774-8440
Internet: jayyildiz@aol.com
Pubs: *Sky Hooks, Poetry Lessons* (Skyhook Pub, 1989),
Mud River (Lintel Pr, 1988), *New Renaissance, Pig Iron Pr,
Blackwater Rev, Sow's Ear, Potato Eyes, New York Qtly.*

Mary Balazs   P
Virginia Military Institute, 411 Scott Shipp Hall, Lexington, VA
24450, 703-464-7240
    Pubs: *Out of Darkness* (Phase and Cycle Pr, 1993),
    Pierced By A Ray of Sun: Anth, Peeling the Onion: Anth
    (HC, 1995, 1993), *Pivot, Shenandoah, Kalliope, Roanoke
    Rev, Christianity & Literature, Arts and Letters.*

Dorothy Ussery Bass   P
Riverview Farm, Rte 1, Box 64, Rice, VA 23966,
804-392-4974
    Pubs: *New York Qtly, Gyre, Lyric, Hoosier Challenge,
    Archer, Mountainside Qtly, Appalachian Heritage.*

Jefferson D. Bates   P
11939 Escalante Ct, Reston, VA 20191-1843, 703-758-0258
Internet: jefbates@erols.com
    Pubs: *The Poets of Tallwood: Anth* (Learning In Retirement
    Institute, 1998), *Jazzbo Brown from Reston Town, Poems
    for Old Geezers and Young Whippersnappers* (Pogment Pr,
    1993, 1990), *Qtly of Light Verse, Reston Rev.*

Richard Bausch   W
George Mason Univ, English Dept, 4400 Univ Dr, Fairfax, VA
22030, 703-349-0609
    Pubs: *Rare & Endangered Species, Rebel Powers*
    (Seymour Lawrence/HM, 1994, 1993), *The Fireman's Wife
    and Other Stories* (S&S, 1990), *New Yorker, Esquire.*

Joe David Bellamy   P&W
1145 Lawson Cove Cir, Virginia Beach, VA 23455-6824,
757-490-7378
Internet: litlux@aol.com
    Pubs: *Atomic Love: A Novella and Eight Stories* (U
    Arkansas Pr, 1993), *Suzi Sinzinnati* (Penguin, 1991), *Story,
    Ploughshares, NAR, Paris Rev.*

Mel Berlin   P
1600 N Oak St #1633, Arlington, VA 22209
    Pubs: *Midstream, Connecticut River Rev, Phoebe, Cape
    Rock, Cumberland Poetry Rev, Poet Lore, Potomac Rev,
    Karamu, Blue Unicorn, Response, Minimus, Wind
    Magazine, Jewish Spectator, The Lyric, Jewish Currents,
    South Coast Poetry Journal.*

Patsy Anne Bickerstaff   P
PO Box 156, Weyers Cave, VA 244860156
    Pubs: *City Rain* (Librado Pr, 1989), *Cumberland Poetry
    Rev, Piedmont Literary Rev, Ariel, Bellingham Rev,
    Caprice, Edge City Rev.*

Dean Blehert   P
11919 Moss Point Ln, Reston, VA 20194, 703-471-7907
    Pubs: *I Swear He Was Laughing, No Cats Have Been
    Maimed or Mutilated* (Words & Pictures Pr, 1996, 1996),
    *New York Qtly, Modern Haiku, Kansas Qtly Rev, Minimus,
    Light.*

Edward Brash   P
1906 Windmill Ln, Alexandria, VA 22307, 703-765-1760
    Pubs: *Poetry, Atlantic Monthly, American Scholar, Partisan
    Rev, Mademoiselle.*

David Bristol   P&W
1206 N Stuart St, Arlington, VA 22201, 703-841-1914
    Pubs: *Paradise & Cash* (Washington Writer's Pub House,
    1980), *Hayotzer, Kansas Qtly, Aerial, Washington Rev,
    New Laurel Rev.*

Scott Cairns   P&W
Old Dominion Univ, English Dept, Norfolk, VA 23529,
757-683-4042
Internet: Scairn@odu.edu
    Pubs: *Recovered Body* (Braziller, 1998), *Figures for the
    Ghost* (U Georgia Pr, 1994), *Paris Rev, New Republic,
    Atlantic, Image, Prairie Schooner, Colorado Rev.*

Linda Cargill   W
2611 Commonwealth Dr, Charlottesville, VA 22901-1438,
804-973-7047
    Pubs: *Pool Party* (Scholastic, 1996), *Hang Loose* (HC,
    1996), *The Witch of Pungo* (Cora Verlag, 1991), *To Follow
    the Goddess* (Cheops Bks, 1991).

Mary Patricia Carroll   P&W
528 Ocean Trace Arch, #H, Virginia Beach, VA 23451-5412
    Pubs: *The Creative Woman, Skylight, Black Bear Rev.*

Travis Charbeneau   W
3421 Hanover Ave, Richmond, VA 23221-2735,
804-358-0417
Internet: travchar@mindspring.com
    Pubs: *The Sun, Utne Reader, Esquire Mag, Dallas Life
    Mag, Atlanta Constitution, World Monitor, In These Times.*

Elaine Raco Chase   W
4333 Majestic Ln, Fairfax, VA 22033, 703-378-9580
Internet: elainerc@juno.com
    Pubs: *The Amateur Detective* (Writer's Digest Bks, 1996),
    Partners in Crime: Anth (Signet Paperback, 1995).

John I. Church   P
7216 Evans Mill Rd, McLean, VA 22101, 703-790-0428
    Pubs: *Hoosier College Poet* (The Friendly Pr, 1984),
    Windless Orchard, Patterns, Compass, Rhino.

Rita Ciresi   W
Hollins College, PO Box 9642, Roanoke, VA 24020,
540-362-6318
Internet: ciresir@minnie.hollins.edu
    Pubs: *Mother Rocket* (U Georgia Pr, 1993), *Blue Italian:
    Anth* (Ecco Pr, 1996), *Prairie Schooner, South Carolina
    Rev, Oregon Rev, Alaska Qtly Rev, New Delta Rev, Italian
    Americana.*

Rosanne Coggeshall   P&W
PO Box 255, Fincastle, VA 24090, 703-473-3774

Tom De Haven   W
14106 Huntgate Woods Rd, Midlothian, VA 23112-4355,
804-744-6288
    Pubs: *Walker of Worlds* (Bantam/Doubleday, 1990),
    Sunburn Lake, Freaks' Amour, Funny Papers (Penguin,
    1989, 1986, 1986).

R. H. W. Dillard   P&W
Hollins Univ, Box 9671, Hollins College, VA 240201671,
540-362-6316
Internet: rdillard@hollins.edu
    Pubs: *Omniphobia, Just Here, Just Now* (LSU Pr, 1995,
    1994).

Gregory Donovan   P&W
Virginia Commonwealth Univ, English Dept, PO Box 842005,
Richmond, VA 23284-2005, 804-828-4507
Internet: gdonovan@vcu.edu
    Pubs: *Calling His Children Home* (U Missouri Pr, 1993),
    *Mss., Hayden's Ferry Rev, Southern Rev, NER, CutBank,
    New Virginia Rev, South Coast Poetry Jrnl*.

Rita Dove   P
Univ Virginia, English Dept, 219 Bryan Hall, Charlottesville,
VA 22903, 804-924-6618
    Pubs: *Mother Love* (Norton, 1995), *The Darker Face of the
    Earth* (Story Line Pr, 1994), *Poetry, American Scholar,
    APR, Progressive, Gettysburg Rev, Callaloo, Georgia Rev,
    New Yorker*.

John Elsberg   P
422 N Cleveland St, Arlington, VA 22201, 703-243-6019
    Pubs: *Offsets* (Kings Estate Pr, 1998), *Broken Poems for
    Evita* (Runaway Spoon Pr, 1997), *Randomness of E*
    (Semiquasi Pr, 1995), *Atom Mind, Plastic Tower, Onthebus,
    Lost & Found Times, Gargoyle, Spillway, Blue Unicorn*.

Anthony Esler   W
College of William & Mary, Williamsburg, VA 23187,
804-221-3741
Internet: ajesle@mail.wm.edu
    Pubs: *The Western World* (S&S, 1997), *The Human
    Venture* (2 Vols.) (Prentice Hall, 1992), *Bastion*
    (MacDonald, 1982), *Babylon* (Morrow, 1980).

Edward Falco   P&W
Virginia Tech, Blacksburg, VA 24061-0112, 540-951-4112
Internet: efalco@vt.edu
    Pubs: *A Dream With Demons* (Eastgate Systems, 1997),
    Acid (U Notre Dame, 1996), *Atlantic Monthly,
    Ploughshares, TriQuarterly, Best American Short Stories
    1995, Pushcart Prize 1999, Playboy*.

Stanley Field   P&W
6315 Nicholson St, Falls Church, VA 22044
    Pubs: *The Freelancer* (Poetica Pr, 1984), *West Wind Rev,
    Women's Household, Minnesota Ink, Green's Mag, A
    Loving Voice, Animal Tales, Albatross, Cats*.

Carolyn Forche   P
George Mason Univ, 4400 University Dr, Fairfax, VA 22030,
301-320-2934
Internet: cforchem@osf1.gmu.edu
    Pubs: *The Angel of History, The Country Between Us*
    (HarperCollins, 1994, 1982).

Kathleen Ford   W
630 Ivy Farm Dr, Charlottesville, VA 22901-8848
    Pubs: *Jeffrey County* (St. Martin's Pr, 1986), *Ladies Home
    Jrnl, Southern Rev, Redbook, Yankee*.

Jay Bradford Fowler   P
5925 N 10 Rd, Arlington, VA 22205, 703-538-5892
    Pubs: *The Soul* (Shangri La Pubs, 1996), *Writing Down the
    Light* (Orchises Pr, 1988), *Poet Lore, Yankee, Shenandoah,
    Phoebe, APR, Cosmic Trend*.

Edna Frederikson   W
130 Campbell St, #4, Harrisonburg, VA 22801
    Pubs: *Never Tomorrow* (Harrow Bks, 1988), *Three Parts
    Earth* (Threshold Bks, 1972), *Ms.*.

Anne Hobson Freeman   P&W
PO Box 680, Callao, VA 22435-0680, 804-285-0757
    Pubs: *The Style of a Law Firm, Eight Gentlemen from
    Virginia* (Algonquin, 1989, 1989), *Virginia Qtly Rev, New
    Virginia Rev, Denver Qtly, Mademoiselle, Cosmopolitan*.

Serena Fusek   P
PO Box 3095, Newport News, VA 23603, 757-887-9253
    Pubs: *The Night Screams With Jaguar's Voice, Three in the
    Morning Songs* (Skiff's Creek Pr, 1998, 1992), *The Color of
    Poison* (Slipstream Pr, 1991), *Reflect, Poetry Motel, Poet
    Lore, Elegia, Impetus, Semi Dwarf Rev, Cedar Hill Rev,
    Rouge et Noir*.

Louis Gallo   P&W
Radford Univ, English Dept, Radford, VA 24142,
703-831-5264
    Pubs: *Mangrove, New Orleans Rev, Brownstone Rev,
    Maple Leaf Rag, Greensboro Rev, Habersham Rev, GAIA,
    Louisiana Literature, American Literary Rev, Glimmer Train,
    Rockford Rev*.

Patricia Garfinkel   P
900 N Stuart St, #1001, Arlington, VA 22203, 703-620-2945
Internet: pgarfink@nsf.gov
    Pubs: *From The Red Eye of Jupiter* (Washington Writer's
    Pub Hse, 1990), *Ram's Horn* (Window Pr, 1980), *Seattle
    Rev, Hollins Critic, Pittsburgh Qtly, Visions Intl, Negative
    Capability, California Qtly*.

George Garrett   P&W
1845 Wayside Pl, Charlottesville, VA 22903, 804-979-5366
    Pubs: *Days of Our Lives Lie in Fragments* (LSU Pr, 1998),
    *The King of Babylon Shall Not Come Against You,
    Whistling in the Dark* (HB, 1998, 1992).

Joseph Garrison   P
Mary Baldwin College, Staunton, VA 24401, 703-887-7000
    Pubs: *Landscape and Distance: Poets From Virginia* (U Pr
    Virginia, 1975), *Hampden-Sydney Poetry Review: Anth*
    (Hampden-Sydney, 1990), *Carolina Qtly, South Carolina
    Rev, Poetry Northwest, Southwest Rev, Southern Poetry
    Rev, Theology Today.*

Beth George   P
13456 Muir Kirk Ln, Herndon, VA 22071, 703-435-3112
    Pubs: *Poet Lore, Wisconsin Rev, West Branch, Sou'wester,
    South Dakota Rev, Artemis, Kentucky Poetry Rev, Lip
    Service.*

Wesley Gibson   W
342 S Laurel St, Apt B, Richmond, VA 23220, 804-643-4630
    Pubs: *Shelter* (Harmony Bks, 1992), *New Virginia Rev.*

Courtenay Graham-Gazaway   P
PO Box 754, Earlysville, VA 22936-0754
    Pubs: *17 Syllables, Iona* (GramWel Studios & Stills Pr,
    1985, 1985), *Harvard Advocate.*

Bernice Grohskopf   W
116 Turtle Creek Rd, #11, Charlottesville, VA 22901,
804-296-8044
    Pubs: *Saratoga* (Thomasson-Grant, 1986), *End of Summer*
    (Avon, 1982), *Tell Me Your Dream* (Scholastic, 1981), *PEN
    Anth* (Ballantine, 1985), *Virginia Qtly Rev.*

Cathryn Hankla   P&W
Hollins University, English Dept, Box 9677, Roanoke, VA
24020, 540-362-6278
Internet: chankla@hollins.edu
    Pubs: *A Blue Moon in Poorwater* (U Virginia Pr, 1998),
    Negative History, Afterimages (LSU Pr, 1997, 1991),
    *Mid-American Rev, New Virginia Rev, The World & I,
    Chronicles.*

Charles L. Hayes   W
PO Box 6995, Radford, VA 24142, 703-831-5231
    Pubs: *Sou'wester, St. Andrews Rev, Phoebe, Yellow Silk.*

Ellen Herbert   W
2929 Rosemary Ln, Falls Church, VA 22042, 703-532-4544
    Pubs: *Life on the Line: Anth* (Negative Capability Pr, 1992),
    *Sonora Rev, Crescent Rev, First for Women, Iris, Thema,
    Pennsylvania English.*

Susan Heroy   P
3133 Windsorview Dr, Richmond, VA 23225, 804-272-7111
    Pubs: *Prairie Schooner, Southern Poetry Rev, Three Rivers
    Poetry Jrnl, New Virginia Rev, Artemis.*

Neva Herrington   P&W
6712 W Wakefield Dr, #B-2, Alexandria, VA 22307-6746,
804-977-3734
    Pubs: *Blue Stone* (Still Point Pr, 1986), *The Chariton Rev,
    Southern Rev, Southwest Rev, Wind, New Letters,
    Confrontation, Union Street Rev.*

Edwin P. Hoyt   W
PO Box 520, North Virginia, VA 23128
    Pubs: *The Tempting of Confucius* (Zebra Books, 1972),
    The Voice of Allah (John Day, 1969).

Lynn Dean Hunter   P&W
PO Box 4053, Virginia Beach, VA 23454, 804-496-8289
Internet: ldhunter@aol.com
    Pubs: *Excuses* (Watermark Literary Pr, 1996), *Blackwater
    Rev, Crone's Nest, Ghent Mag, Virginian-Pilot, Crescent
    Rev, Thema, City Mag, Green's Mag.*

Kaatje Hurlbut   W
PO Box 158, Franktown, VA 23354, 804-442-7942
    Pubs: *Best American Short Stories: Anth* (HM, 1979), *Eve
    in Darkness: Anth* (NAL, 1969), *Southwest Rev.*

Lucky Jacobs   P
203 Santa Clara Dr, Richmond, VA 23229, 804-740-8427
    Pubs: *The Book of Love* (East Coast Edtns, 1993), *Our
    Eyes, Like Walls* (Konglomerati, 1981), *Poetry Now, Intro 7,
    Artemis, Hollins Critic, Southern Poetry Rev.*

Mark Jacobs   W
1130 Robert Carter Rd, Fairfax Station, VA 22039
Internet: 106071.3646@compuserve.com
    Pubs: *The Liberation of Little Heaven, Stone Cowboy* (Soho
    Pr, 1998, 1997), *A Cast of Spaniards* (Talisman Hse, 1994),
    *Webster Rev, Pig Iron, Atlantic, Farmer's Market, Sun,
    Kiosk, Nebraska Rev, Iowa Rev, Southern Rev, South
    Dakota Qtly.*

Kate Jennings   P
12816 Cross Creek Ln, Herndon, VA 22071, 703-476-5814
    Pubs: *Malice* (Devil's Millhopper Pr, 1988), *Birth Stories:
    Anth* (Crossing, 1984), *Hudson Rev.*

Edward P. Jones   W
4300 Old Dominion Dr, #914, Arlington, VA 22207,
703-522-6720
    Pubs: *Lost In The City* (Morrow, 1992).

Paul Jones   P
5990 Buck Ridge Rd, Earlysville, VA 22936-9335
    Pubs: *What The Welsh and the Chinese Have in Common*
    (North Carolina Writers' Network, 1990), *Poetry, Southern
    Rev, Georgia Rev, Southern Humanities Rev, Hellas.*

Ronnetta Bisman Kahn   W
701 Locust Hill Dr, Harrisonburg, VA 22801, 703-434-0225
    Pubs: *Anna's House, Apalachee Qtly, Sing Heavenly
    Muse!, Second Wave, Moving Out, New Rev.*

Katherine Kane   P
Braeburn Farm, Rte 1, Box 197, Free Union, VA 22940,
804-973-1899
> Pubs: *Ferry All The Way Up* (Porch, 1978), *Iowa Rev,
> Missouri Rev, Ontario Rev, Poetry Now, New Letters,
> Virginia Qtly Rev.*

Samuel Kashner   P
College of William & Mary, English Dept, Williamsburg, VA
23185, 804-221-2439
> Pubs: *Hanging Loose 20 Year Anth* (Hanging Loose Pr,
> 1988), *Mudfish, William & Mary Rev.*

LuAnn Keener   P
800 Maryland Ave, Salem, VA 24153, 540-389-4985
> Pubs: *Color Documentary* (Calyx Bks, 1994), *Worlds in Our
> Words: Anth* (Prentice Hall, 1997), *Poetry, Quarterly West,
> Chelsea, Shenandoah, Poetry Northwest, Sistersong.*

William Keens   P
The Keens Company, 200 N Little Falls St, #303, Falls
Church, VA 22046
> Pubs: *Dear Anyone* (Penumbra Pr, 1977), *APR, Poetry,
> Seneca Rev, Ohio Rev.*

Peter Klappert   P
George Mason Univ, Fairfax, VA 22030, 202-232-2874
Internet: pklapper@osf1.quu.edu
> Pubs: *The Idiot Princess of the Last Dynasty* (Carnegie
> Mellon, 1998), *Lugging Vegetables to Nantucket* (Yale,
> 1971), *Atlantic, Harper's, Antaeus, Ploughshares.*

Carolyn Kreiter-Foronda   P
5966 Annaberg Pl, Burke, VA 22015, 703-503-9743
Internet: foronda@erols.com
> Pubs: *Gathering Light* (SCOP Pubs, 1993), *Contrary
> Visions* (Scripta Humanistica, 1988), *Prairie Schooner,
> Antioch Rev, Mid-American Rev, Poet Lore, Hispanic
> Culture Rev, Antietam Rev.*

Jeanne Larsen   P&W
Hollins Univ, Box 9542, Roanoke, VA 24020, 540-362-6276
Internet: jlarsen@hollins.edu
> Pubs: *Manchu Palaces* (Henry Holt, 1997), *Silk Road*
> (Henry Holt/BOMC, 1989), *New England Rev, Georgia Rev,
> New Virginia Rev, Yarrow, Greensboro Rev, 5 A.M..*

Monty S. Leitch   W
113 Huffville Rd, Pilot, VA 241381679, 540-651-4502
> Pubs: *Grandmother Histories: Memoirs and Stories: Anth*
> (Syracuse U, 1998), *Writer's Yearbook '95, Hollins Mag,
> Artemis, Radford U Mag, Virginia Country, Mountain Rev,
> Roanoker, Window, Shenandoah, Union Street Rev.*

Janet Lembke   P
210 N Madison St, Staunton, VA 24401, 703-886-4180
> Pubs: *Euripides' Hecuba* (Oxford U Pr, 1991), *Looking for
> Eagles* (Lyons and Burford, 1990), *Audubon, NAR, Sierra.*

Judy Longley   P
1001 Wildmere Pl, Charlottesville, VA 22901, 804-973-0780
> Pubs: *My Journey Toward You* (Helicon Nine Edtns, 1993),
> *Rowing Past Eden* (Nightshade Pr, 1993), *Parallel Lives*
> (Owl Creek Pr, 1990), *Poetry, Southern Rev.*

James Lott   W
Mary Baldwin College, Office of Dean of the College,
Staunton, VA 24401, 540-887-7030
Internet: jlott@cit.mbc.edu
> Pubs: *New Virginia Rev, Virginia Qtly Rev, Southern Rev,
> South Carolina Rev, Inlet.*

Katie Letcher Lyle   P&W
110 W McDowell St, Lexington, VA 24450, 540-463-5439
Internet: krlyle@cfw.com
> Pubs: *The Foraging Gourmet* (Lyons & Burford, 1997), *The
> Men Who Wanted Seven Wives, Scalded to Death by the
> Steam* (Algonquin, 1986, 1983), *Virginia Qtly, Shenandoah,
> Sierra Mag, Country Jrnl, Blue Ridge Country.*

Edward C. Lynskey   P
9503 Lees Mill Rd, Warrenton, VA 20186
> Pubs: *The Tree Surgeon's Gift* (Scripta, 1990), *Teeth of the
> Hydra* (Crop Dust Pr, 1986), *Atlantic, APR, Chicago Rev,
> Southwest, America, Commonweal.*

Mike Maggio   P&W
1169 Cypress Tree Pl, Herndon, VA 22070
Internet: mikemaggio@aol.com
> Pubs: *Oranges From Palestine* (Mardi Gras Pr, 1996), *Your
> Secret Is Safe With Me* (Cassette; Black Bear Pub, 1988),
> *Bedside Prayers: Anth* (Harper, 1997), *For A Living: Anth*
> (U Illinois Pr, 1995), *Pleiades, South Coast Poetry Jrnl,
> Apalachee Qtly.*

Anita Mathias   P
104 Richard's Patent, Williamsburg, VA 231855118,
757-564-0355
Internet: mathias@math.wm.edu
> Pubs: *Tanzania On Tuesday: Anth* (New Rivers Pr, 1997),
> *The Best of Writers At Work: Anth* (Northwest Pub, 1994),
> *Speaking in Tongues: Anth* (The Loft, 1994), *New Letters,
> London Mag, America, Washington Post, Notre Dame Mag,
> The Journal.*

Deirdra McAfee   W
1503 Willingham Rd, Richmond, VA 23233-4727,
804-750-1338
Internet: dhmca@aol.com
> Pubs: *Turnstile, Willow Springs, Ambergris, Confrontation.*

David McAleavey   P
3305 N George Mason Dr, Arlington, VA 22207,
703-532-8546
Internet: dmca@gwu.edu
> Pubs: *Holding Obsidian* (Washington Writers Pub Hse,
> 1985), *Antioch Rev, Poet Lore, Florida Rev, Ploughshares,
> Situation, Washington Rev.*

Jane McIlvaine McClary W
Box 326, Middleburg, VA 22117, 703-687-6178
Pubs: *Maggie Royal, A Portion for Foxes* (S&S, 1982, 1972), *New York Times, Middleburg Life, Virginia Country.*

Bruce McClelland P
1956 Lewis Mountain Rd, Charlottesville, VA 22903-2451, 804-293-3283
Pubs: *Blood & Light: Selected Poems 1931-1993, This World* (St. Lazaire Pr, 1994, 1989), *Notus, First Intensity.*

Heather Ross Miller P&W
402 Morningside Dr, Lexington, VA 24450, 540-464-6534
Pubs: *In the Funny Papers, Friends and Assassins* (U Missouri Pr, 1995, 1993), *Witness, Sandhills Rev, Crab Orchard Rev, Potato Eyes, Southern Rev.*

Elaine Moore W
702 Seneca Rd, Great Falls, VA 22066, 703-444-3499
Pubs: *Phoebe, Virginia Country, Modern Short Stories.*

Elizabeth Seydel Morgan P
504 Honaker Ave, Richmond, VA 23226, 804-285-2153
Pubs: *The Governor of Desire, Parties* (LSU Pr, 1993, 1988), *Southern Rev, Poetry, Prairie Schooner, Georgia Rev, Virginia Qtly, Iowa Rev.*

Michael Mott P&W
122 The Colony, Williamsburg, VA 23185-3157, 757-220-1042
Pubs: *Corday* (Black Buzzard Pr, 1995), *Counting The Grasses* (Anhinga, 1980), *Georgia Rev, Sewanee Rev, Stand (U.K.), American Scholar, Verse, Tar River Poetry, Kenyon Rev.*

Elisabeth Murawski P
6804 Kenyon Dr, Alexandria, VA 22307, 703-768-4504
Internet: emurawski@juno.com
Pubs: *Troubled by an Angel* (Cleveland State U Pr, 1997), *Hungry As We Are, Moon & Mercury* (Washington Writers Pub Hse, 1995, 1990), *Literary Rev, American Voice, Grand Street, Ohio Rev, APR, Shenandoah, Poetry Northwest.*

Mary Hayne North P
6020 Piney Woods Rd, Riner, VA 24149, 703-382-8374
Pubs: *From Mt. San Angelo: Anth* (AAUP, 1987).

Tom O'Grady P
PO Box 126, Hampden-Sydney, VA 23943, 804-223-8209
Internet: resebowr@moonstar.com
Pubs: *Sun, Moon & Stars* (Tryon Pub, 1996), *In the Room of the Just Born* (Dolphin-Moon, 1989), *Poet Lore, Connecticut Rev, North Atlantic Rev, Maryland Poetry Rev, Chrysalis, New Letters.*

Marian Olson P
1501 Crystal Dr #933, Arlington, VA 22202-4126
Pubs: *Letting Go, Songs of the Chicken Yard* (Honeybrook Pr, 1992, 1992), *Facing the Wind* (Raven Pr, 1990), *Modern Haiku, America, Plains Poetry Jrnl, Brussels Sprout, Kalliope, Trestle Creek Rev, Frog Pond.*

Gregory Orr P
2006 Hessian Rd, Charlottesville, VA 22903, 804-293-4831
Internet: gso@virginia.edu
Pubs: *City of Salt* (U Pitt Pr, 1995), *New and Selected Poems, We Must Make a Kingdom of It* (Wesleyan U Pr, 1987, 1986).

Cheryl Pallant P&W
108 S Colonial Ave, Richmond, VA 23221-3518, 804-355-7524
Pubs: *Food for Thought: Anth* (Morrow, 1987), *Wormwood Rev, Contact Qtly, Crescent Rev, Oxford Mag, New Rain.*

Richard Peabody P&W
30501 North 13th St #2, Arlington, VA 22201, 703-465-9173
Internet: atticus@radix.net
Pubs: *Buoyancy* (Gut Punch, 1995), *Paraffin Days* (Cumberland, 1995), *Bakunin, Spitball, Georgetown Rev, Atom Mind, Word Wrights, Potomac Rev, Hollins Critic, Articulate.*

Jim Peterson P
Randolph Macon Women's College, 2500 Rivermont Ave, Lynchburg, VA 245031526, 804-947-8513
Internet: jepete1@aol.com
Pubs: *An Afternoon With K, Carvings On A Prayer Tree* (Holocene Pr, 1996, 1994), *The Man Who Grew Silent* (Bench Pr, 1989), *Georgia Rev, Poetry, Prairie Schooner, Poetry Northwest.*

Leslie Pietrzyk W
3201 Elmwood Dr, Alexandria, VA 22303, 703-329-9398
Internet: lpietr@aol.com
Pubs: *Pears on a Willow Tree* (Avon/Bard, 1998), *Epoch, Gettysburg Rev, Iowa Rev, New England Rev, Shenandoah.*

Richard Plant W
English Dept, Mary Baldwin College, Staunton, VA 24401, 540-887-7284
Internet: rplant@cit.mbc.edu
Pubs: *Three Novellas: Anth* (Texas Rev Pr, 1997), *Sudden Fiction: Anth* (Norton, 1996), *1988 Prize Stories: The O'Henry Awards: Anth* (Doubleday, 1989), *Best Stories from New Writers: Anth* (Writer's Digest Bks, 1989), *South Dakota Rev, Cimarron Rev.*

Simone Poirier-Bures W
7547 Cedar Grove Ln, Radford, VA 24141, 540-731-1814
Internet: poirier@vt.edu
Pubs: *That Shining Place, Candyman* (Oberon Pr, 1995,
1994), *Virginia Qtly Rev, Dalhousie Rev, Belles Lettres,
Short Story, Emrys Jrnl, Florida Rev.*

Ken Poyner P
PO Box 14452, Norfolk, VA 23518, 757-473-0846
Pubs: *Sciences, Social* (Palaquin Bks, 1995), *Cordwood*
(22 Pr, 1985), *Iowa Rev, West Branch, Poet Lore, Western
Humanities Rev, Yarrow, Black Fly Rev.*

Philip Raisor P
PO Box 61623, Virginia Beach, VA 23466-1623,
804-489-3345
Pubs: *Kansas Qtly, Arete, Poetry Northwest, Literary Rev,
Southern Rev, Tar River Poetry.*

Paula Rankin P
89 Gum Grove Dr, Newport News, VA 23601-2705,
804-591-8350
Pubs: *Your Rightful Childhood, Divorce: A Romance, To
the House Ghost* (Carnegie Mellon, 1996, 1990, 1985).

Kristen Staby Rembold P&W
2321 Barracks Rd, Charlottesville, VA 22901, 804-296-3086
Pubs: *Felicity* (Mid-List Pr, 1994), *Coming Into This World*
(Hot Pepper Pr, 1992), *Artemis, Nimrod, South Dakota Rev,
Iowa Woman, Appalachia, CQ.*

Lisa Ress P
1414 5th St SW, Roanoke, VA 24016-4508
Pubs: *Flight Patterns* (U Pr Virginia, 1985), *Kalliope,
Farmer's Market, Spoon River Qtly, Sycamore Rev, Denver
Rev, Yarrow.*

Kurt Rheinheimer W
1862 Arlington Rd SW, Roanoke, VA 24015, 540-981-1307
Pubs: *New Stories From the South: Anth* (Algonquin Bks,
1989), *Michigan Qtly Rev, Southern, Playgirl, Shenandoah,
Carolina Qtly, Redbook, Story Qtly, Greensboro Rev.*

Suzanne Rhodenbaugh P
3332 Kensington Ave, Richmond, VA 23221-2304,
804-354-9567
Internet: srhodenb@aol.com
Pubs: *The Shine on Loss* (Painted Bride Qtly Pr, 1998),
Gardening Where the Land Remembers War (Two Herons
Pr, 1992), *A Gold Rain at Lonelyfarm* (Heatherstone Pr,
1990), *Hudson Rev, NER, American Scholar, Cimarron
Rev, Salmagundi, Michigan Qtly Rev.*

Evelyn Ritchie P
817 St. Christopher's Rd, Richmond, VA 23226,
804-262-0664
Pubs: *New Virginia Rev, Richmond Qtly, Forms, Lyric,
Midwest Poetry Rev.*

Kim Roberts P
Ellipse Arts Center, 4350 Fairfax Dr, Arlington, VA 22203,
703-228-7710
Internet: ellipse@erols.com
Pubs: *The Wishbone Galaxy* (Washington Writers Pub Hse,
1994), *Ohio Rev, Sonora Rev, High Plains Literary Rev,
Confrontation, New Letters, Crosscurrents.*

Nickell Romjue W
410 Willow Oaks Blvd, Hampton, VA 23669, 804-851-1644
Pubs: *Writers' Forum, Karamu, Cream City Rev, Missouri
Rev, Aura Literary/Arts Rev, Cimarron Rev, Sou'wester.*

Renee Roper-Jackson P
380 E Washington St, Suffolk, VA 23434
Pubs: *Changes: Anth* (White Swan Pr, 1987), *Truly Fine,
Abbey Mag, Columbia Rev.*

John B. Rosenman P
Norfolk State Univ, 2401 Corprew Ave, English Dept, Norfolk,
VA 23504, 804-623-8891
Pubs: *The Best Laugh Last* (McPherson & Co., 1983),
Yankee, Croton Rev, Xanadu, Phoebe.

Irene Rouse P
Box 310, Atlantic, VA 23303, 757-824-4090
Internet: irbooks@dmv.com
Pubs: *Poetry Baltimore: Anth* (Wordhouse, 1997), *The
Cooke Book: A Seasoning of Poets: Anth* (SCOP, 1987),
Whose Woods These Are (Wordworks, 1983),
Wordwrights!, Potato Eyes.

John D. Ruemmler W
815 W Main St, Charlottesville, VA 22901, 804-295-8393
Pubs: *Smoke On The Water* (Shoe Tree Pr, 1992),
Brothers In Arms (Lynx Pr, 1988), *Albemarle, Stranger.*

Viette Sandbank P
4800 Fillmore Ave, #419, Alexandria, VA 22311
Pubs: *Alive & Gazing at You* (Northwoods, 1984), *Coming
Through The Wry* (Praying Mantis, 1982), *The Poet's
Domain: Anth* (Road Pub, 1991), *The Lyric.*

Roger Sauls P
513 N Boulevard #4, Richmond, VA 232203342,
804-358-2958
Pubs: *Hard Weather* (Bench Pr, 1987), *Light* (Loom Pr,
1975), *Ohio Rev, Ploughshares, Shenandoah.*

Nancy Schoenberger P
College of William & Mary, English Dept, Williamsburg, VA
23185, 804-221-2439
Internet: njscho@facstaff.wm.edu
Pubs: *Girl on a White Porch* (U Missouri Pr, 1987), *New
Yorker, Ploughshares.*

Nancy Scott P
PO Box 179, Sperryville, VA 22740-0179
Pubs: *Rhino, Eleven, Windchimes, Phoebus, Womansong, Ten Years & Then Some, New York Qtly, Poetry Now, Modern Haiku, New Virginia Rev, Phoebe, Shades of Gray.*

Tim Seibles P
610 W Olney St, Apt #3, Norfolk, VA 23507-2033, 804-625-3843
Pubs: *Kerosene* (Ampersand Pr, 1995), *Hurdy-Gurdy* (Cleveland State U Pr, 1992), *Ploughshares, NER, Callaloo, Kenyon Rev, Hanging Loose.*

Richard Shaw P
1650 Parkcrest Cir, #300, Reston, VA 22090
Pubs: *Sleeping Beauty/Kabuki* (U Minnesota Pr, 1975).

Ellen Harvey Showell W
1200 N Cleveland St, Arlington, VA 22201, 703-525-8872
Internet: eshowell@erols.com
Pubs: *Cecelia and the Blue Mountain Boy* (Lothrop, Lee & Shepard, 1983), *The Ghost of Tillie Jean Cassaway* (Four Winds Pr, 1978).

R. T. Smith P
Washington and Lee Univ, Troubadour Theater, 2nd Fl, Lexington, VA 24450, 540-463-8908
Internet: rodsmith@wlu.edu
Pubs: *Tresspasser* (LSU Pr, 1996), *Hunter-Gatherer, The Cardinal Heart* (Livingston Pr, 1996, 1991), *Atlantic, Poetry, Georgia Rev, Gettysburg Rev, Southern Rev, Poetry Ireland Rev, Irish U Rev.*

Ron Smith P
616 Maple Ave, Richmond, VA 23226
Internet: smithjron@aol.com
Pubs: *Running Again in Hollywood Cemetery* (U Florida, 1988), *Southern Rev, Virginia Qtly Rev, Kenyon Rev, Georgia Rev, Nation, NER.*

Lisa Solod W
310 Enfield Rd, Lexington, VA 244501756, 540-463-7637
Internet: lisa@rockbridge.net
Pubs: *The Inn Near Kyoto: Anth* (New Rivers Pr, 1998), *American Voice, Housewife-Writer's Forum, Good Stories, Tales of the Heart, Parting Gifts, Enterzone.*

Margo Solod P
PO Box 113, Lexington, VA 24450, 540-464-6242
Internet: 70664.2126@compuserve.com
Pubs: *Outside the Kremlin* (Nightshade Pr, 1996), *They Shall Live On: Anth* (Ground Torpedo Pr, 1992), *Defined Providence, New Frontiers of New Mexico, Knocked, The Oval, Northeast Corridor, Onion River Rev, 360 Degrees, Red Dance Floor.*

Katherine Soniat P
Virginia Polytechnic Inst & SU, English Dept, Blacksburg, VA 24061-0112, 703-231-6501
Internet: ksoniat@vt.edu
Pubs: *A Shared Life* (U Iowa Pr, 1993), *Cracking Eggs* (U Pr Florida, 1990), *NAR, Poetry, Nation, New Republic, Southern Rev, Iowa Rev.*

Lisa Russ Spaar P
Univ Virginia, 219 Bryan Hall, Charlottesville, VA 22903, 804-924-6675
Internet: lrs9e@virginia.edu
Pubs: *Blind Boy on Skates* (Trilobite Pr, 1987), *Cellar* (Alderman, 1983), *Poetry, Shenandoah, Poetry East, Crazyhorse, Virginia Qtly Rev, Tendril.*

Bradley R. Strahan P
1007 Ficklen Rd, Fredricksburg, VA 22405
Pubs: *Crocodile Man* (The Smith, 1990), *First Things, Crosscurrents, Onthebus, Hollins Critic, Seattle Rev, Confrontation, Christian Century, Sources* (Belgium), *America, Soundings East.*

Dabney Stuart P
30 Edmondson Ave, Lexington, VA 24450, 540-463-5663
Internet: sstuart@wlu.edu
Pubs: *The Way to Cobbs Creek, Second Sight* (U Missouri Pr, 1997, 1996), *Long Gone, Light Years: New and Selected Poems, Sweet Lucy Wine, Narcissus Dreaming* (LSU, 1996, 1994, 1992, 1990).

Jitu Tambuzi P
Tambuzi Publications, 208 E Grace St, Richmond, VA 23219-1916, 804-649-3149
Pubs: *A Voice Within* (King Publications, 1979), *New Renaissance, Universal Black Writer.*

Eleanor Ross Taylor P&W
1841 Wayside Pl, Charlottesville, VA 22903
Pubs: *Days Going/Days Coming Back* (U Utah, 1992), *New & Selected Poems* (Stuart Wright, 1984), *Parnassus, Seneca Rev, Ploughshares, Shenandoah, Virginia Qtly.*

Henry Taylor P
Box 23, Lincoln, VA 20160-0023, 540-338-3740
Internet: htaylor@american.edu
Pubs: *Understanding Fiction: Poems 1986-1996, The Flying Change* (LSU Pr, 1996, 1986), *Poetry, Sewanee Rev, New Republic, Shenandoah, Plum Rev, Southern Rev.*

William Tester W
8 Partridge Hill Rd, Richmond, VA 232336219, 804-784-3267
Internet: wteste@vcu.edu
Pubs: *Darling* (Knopf, 1992), *Grand Street, Prairie Schooner, Esquire, The Quarterly, Fiction, TriQuarterly, North American Rev, Black Warrior, Witness.*

Hilary Tham P&W
2600 N Upshur St, Arlington, VA 222074026, 703-527-4568
Internet: hilarytham@aol.com
> Pubs: *Lane With No Name: Memoirs & Poems* (Lynne
> Rienner Pub, 1997), *Men & Other Strange Myths: Poems*
> (Three Continents Pr, 1994), *Mondo Barbie: Anth* (St.
> Martin's, 1993), *Antietam Rev, Metropolitan, Encodings,
> Midstream.*

Carla Theodore P
60 Ecology Ln, Woodville, VA 22749-1715, 540-987-8813
> Pubs: *Somebody's Brother, Rural Water, Peter & The Guru*
> (Samisdat, 1983, 1980, 1979), *Jewish Currents, Kansas
> Qtly, Jump River Rev, Dark Horse, San Fernando Poetry
> Jrnl, Princeton Spectrum.*

Susan Tichy P
George Mason Univ, Fairfax, VA 22030, 703-323-2220
> Pubs: *A Smell of Burning Starts the Day* (Wesleyan, 1988),
> *The Hands in Exile* (Random Hse, 1983).

Jack Trammell P
24 Willow Brook Rd, Bumpass, VA 23024, 804-556-4394
Internet: jtramel@pen.k12.va.us
> Pubs: *Appalachian Dreams* (Escape, 1998).

Charles Vandersee P
Univ Virginia, English Dept, Bryan Hall, Charlottesville, VA
22903, 804-924-3350
Internet: cav7w@virginia.edu
> Pubs: *Ohio Rev, Georgia Rev, Sewanee Rev, Poetry East,
> Poetry, Ironwood, Iris, Timbuktu.*

Edward G. Williams W
3837 Betsy Cres, PH, Virginia Beach, VA 23456-1610,
804-471-2781
> Pubs: *Not Like Niggers* (St. Martin's Pr, 1970), *A Galaxy of
> Black Writing: Anth* (Moore Pub Co., 1971), *The Alumnus.*

Judith Wittig P
1213 Jefferson Davis Hwy #1414, Arlington, VA 22202,
703-486-2288
> Pubs: *Sun-Roots* (Wisconsin Rev Pr, 1976), *Berkeley
> Poetry Rev, Mainstreeter, Road Apple Rev.*

Charles Wright P
940 Locust Ave, Charlottesville, VA 22901, 804-979-2373
> Pubs: *Black Zodiac, Chickamauga, The World of the
> 10,000 Things, Zone Journals* (FSG, 1997, 1995, 1990,
> 1988), *Halflife* (U Michigan Pr, 1988).

VIRGIN ISLANDS

Marty Campbell W
5016 Estate Boetzberg, Christiansted, VI 00820-4516,
340-692-9935
Internet: ad144@virgin.usvi.net
> Pubs: *Companion to Senya* (MarCrafts, 1989), *Saint Sea*
> (Blondo, 1986), *Caribbean Writer, Hammers, Road Map of
> My Soul, Collage, Magical Blend, Lilliput Rev.*

David Gershator P
PO Box 303353, St Thomas, VI 00803-3353
Internet: ag162@virgin.usvi.net
> Pubs: *Palampam Day* (Cavendish, 1997), *Elijah's Child*
> (CCC, 1992), *Play Mas* (Downtown Poets, 1981),
> *Frogpond, Home Planet News, Caribbean Writer.*

Phillis Gershator P&W
PO Box 303353, St Thomas, VI 00803-3353
Internet: ag161@virgin.usvi.net
> Pubs: *When It Starts To Snow* (Holt, 1998),
> *ZZZNG-ZZZNG-ZZZNG* (Orchard, 1998), *Sweet, Sweet Fig
> Banana* (Whitman, 1996), *Sugar Cakes Cyril* (Mondo,
> 1996), *Caribbean Writer, Home Planet News, Cricket,
> Spider, Ladybug.*

Joseph Lisowski P
Univ Virgin Islands, 2 John Brewers Bay, Saint Thomas, VI
00802-9990, 809-776-9200
> Pubs: *Looking For Lauren* (Amelia Pr, 1994), *Near the
> Narcotic Sea* (Cottage Wordsmiths, 1992), *Caribbean
> Writer, Pittsburgh Qtly, Kansas Qtly.*

Oyoko Loving P
Box 24742 Christiansted, St Croix, VI 00824, 809-778-7480
> Pubs: *Remember When* (Jet Publishing, 1974).

WASHINGTON

Jody Aliesan P
5043 22nd Ave NE, Seattle, WA 98105, 206-524-8365
Internet: aliesan@juno.com
> Pubs: *States of Grace* (Grey Spider Pr, 1992), *Grief Sweat*
> (Broken Moon Pr, 1991), *L.A. Times, Contemporary Qtly,
> Poetry Northwest, Yellow Silk, Calyx.*

Mary Elizabeth Armantrout W
WordCrafters Northwest, 4137 University Way NE, Ste 20,
Seattle, WA 98105-6263, 206-632-2593
> Pubs: *The Trouble with Perfect, Me, My Sister, and I, My
> Sister is Driving Me Crazy* (S&S, 1995, 1992, 1991), *I'd
> Rather Be Dancing* (Delacorte Pr, 1989).

Judith Anne Azrael P&W
PO Box 165, Lummi Island, WA 98262, 360-758-2042
Pubs: *Twelve Black Horses* (Salmon Run Pr, 1998), *Apple Tree Poems, Antelope Are Running* (Confluence, 1983, 1978), *Rosebud, Minnesota Rev, Nation, Yale Rev, CSM, Western Humanities Rev, Southern Poetry Rev.*

June Frankland Baker P
614 Lynnwood Ct, Richland, WA 99352-1860, 509-375-0842
Internet: dab@3-cities.com
Pubs: *Kansas Qtly, Southern Poetry Rev, Oxford Mag, Gulf Stream Mag, Blueline, Kaleidoscope, Three Rivers Poetry Jrnl, Poetry Northwest, Commonweal, Webster Rev, CSM, Poet Lore.*

Sharon Baker W
1125 SW Normandy Terr, Seattle, WA 98166, 206-243-9004
Pubs: *Burning Tears of Sassurum, Journey to Membliar* (Avon, 1988, 1987).

Christianne Balk P
PO Box 15633, Seattle, WA 98115-0633, 206-523-6543
Pubs: *Desiring Flight* (Purdue U Pr, 1995), *Bindweed* (Macmillan, 1986), *New Yorker, Michigan Rev, Seattle Rev, Heartland, Pequod, Crazy Horse.*

Carol Jane Bangs P&W
PO Box 92, Nordland, WA 98358, 360-379-0286
Internet: cbangs@olympus.net
Pubs: *The Bones of the Earth* (New Directions, 1983), *Norton Intro To Poetry: Anth* (Norton, 1995), *Colorado Rev, Indiana Rev, New Directions Annual, Ploughshares.*

Heather Doran Barbieri P&W
6044 Seward Park Ave S, Seattle, WA 98118, 206-723-1058
Pubs: *Pleasure Vessels: Anth* (Angela Royal, 1996), *Pursuit of Happiness: Anth* (Left Bank Bks, 1995), *Amelia, Beacon Rev, Bellowing Ark, Crab Creek Rev.*

Mary Barnard P&W
5565 E Evergreen Blvd, #3406, Vancouver, WA 98661
Pubs: *Nantucket Genesis, Time And The White Tigress* (Breitenbush Bks, 1988, 1986), *Paldeuma.*

W. D. Barnes P
7611-15th NE, Seattle, WA 98115, 206-523-8946
Pubs: *Fragments, Vagabond, Phantasm, Harvest, Minnesota Poetry Jrnl.*

Carol Barrett P
310 SE 3rd St, Battle Ground, WA 98604, 360-666-8801
Pubs: *What's A Nice Girl Like You Doing In A Relationship Like This?: Anth* (Crossing Pr, 1992), *Anth of Mag Verse & Yrbk of American Poetry* (Monitor Bks, 1988), *Women's Rev of Bks, Christian Century, South Dakota Qtly, Crab Creek Rev, Blue Unicorn.*

Sheila Bender P
394 Colman Dr, Port Townsend, WA 98368, 360-385-7839
Internet: sbender1@aol.com
Pubs: *Pockets Full Of Garden Snails and Twigs* (Fithian Pr, 1999), *Love from the Coastal Route* (Duckabush Pr, 1991), *Raven Chronicles, Women's Studies Qtly, Poetry Northwest, Seattle Rev, The World, Writers' Forum.*

John Bennett W
605 E 5 Ave, Ellensburg, WA 98926, 509-962-8471
Internet: www.eburg.com/ bangs/
Pubs: *The Moth Eaters* (Angelfish Pr, 1998), *Domestic Violence* (Foursep Pr, 1998), *Rattle, Arkansas Rev, Northwest Rev, Pudding, Columbia, Pangolin Papers.*

Beth Bentley P
8762 25th Place, NE, Seattle, WA 98115, 206-525-3508
Pubs: *Little Fires* (Cune Pr, 1998), *The Purely Visible* (Sea Pen Pr, 1980), *Country of Resemblances* (Ohio U Pr, 1976), *Best American Poetry: Anth* (Macmillan, 1989), *Gettysburg Rev, Fine Madness, Poetry Northwest.*

James Bertolino P
PO Box 1157, Anacortes, WA 98221, 206-293-6274
Pubs: *The Writer's Journal* (Dell Pub, 1997), *Snail River, First Credo* (QRL, 1994, 1986), *Amicus Jrnl, Wilderness, Onthebus, Raven Chronicles, Seattle Rev, Caliban, Ploughshares, Montserrat Rev, Gargoyle, The Temple.*

Linda Bierds P
4326 NE Rhodes End, Bainbridge Island, WA 98110, 206-365-2052
Pubs: *The Ghost Trio, Heart and Perimeter, The Stillness, The Dancing* (Henry Holt, 1994, 1991, 1988), *Flights of the Harvest-Mare* (Ahsahta, 1985).

Laurie Blauner P
7549 27th Ave NW, Seattle, WA 98117, 406-784-4803
Pubs: *Self-Portrait in an Unwilling Landscape, Children of Gravity: Anth* (Owl Creek Pr, 1989, 1996), *APR, Poetry, New Republic, Nation, Georgia Rev, Poetry Northwest.*

Alice Bloch W
4055 SW Henderson St, Seattle, WA 98136-2541
Pubs: *The Law Of Return, Lifetime Guarantee* (Alyson Pub, 1983, 1981), *Hersz: Brilliant New Fiction By Lesbian Writers: Anth* (Faber & Faber, 1997).

Marian Blue P&W
PO Box 145, Clinton, WA 98236, 360-341-1630
Pubs: *Tiller and the Pen* (Eighth Moon Pr, 1994), *Cold Mountain Rev, Exhibition, Mankato Poetry Rev, Dominion Rev, Amaranth Rev, North Country Anvil.*

Marcia Blumenthal   P&W
1134 Hendricks, Port Townsend, WA 98368-2309,
360-385-4560
Internet: mlewton@olympus.net
  Pubs: *In The Heart Of Town, Still Digging* (Barnwood Pr,
  1985), *Flying Island, Thema, Iowa Woman, Ms., Indiana
  Rev, Whiskey Island.*

Malcolm J. Bosse   W
1407 E Madison, #30, Seattle, WA 98122
  Pubs: *The Vast Memory of Love, Mister Touch* (Houghton
  Mifflin, 1992, 1991), *Stranger At the Gate, Fire in Heaven*
  (S&S, 1988, 1986).

David Bosworth   W
Univ Washington, English Dept, GN-30, Seattle, WA 98115,
206-543-2682
  Pubs: *From My Father, Singing* (Pushcart Pr, 1986), *The
  Death of Descartes* (Pittsburgh Pr, 1981).

Maura Alia Bramkamp   P
4756 U Vill Pl NE, Seattle, WA 98105
Internet: maura@silverlink.net
  Pubs: *Resculpting* (Paper Boat Pr, 1995), *This Far
  Together: Anth* (Haight Ashbury Literary, 1995), *Haight
  Ashbury Jrnl, Exhibition, Synapse, Coffee House,
  Switched-on-Gutenberg, Convolvulus, Half Tones To
  Jubilee.*

Randall Brock   P
PO Box 1673, Spokane, WA 99210
  Pubs: *Weave* (Found Street Pr, 1994), *Dan River Anth*
  (Dan River Pr, 1993), *Deep Down Things: Anth*
  (Washington State U Pr, 1990), *George & Mertie's Place,
  Red Owl, Unit Circle, Transmog, Shockbox, Sioul-Linen,
  etcetera, Brouhaha, Peaky Hide.*

Irv Broughton   P
W 915-12th Ave, Spokane, WA 99204, 509-838-1617
  Pubs: *The Blessing of the Fleet* (Lost Roads, 1977), *Elvis in
  Oz: Anth* (U Virginia Pr, 1992), *Deep Down Things: Anth*
  (Washington State U Pr, 1990).

James Broughton   P
PO Box 1330, Port Townsend, WA 98368-0018, 360-385-3748
  Pubs: *Packing Up for Paradise* (Black Sparrow Pr, 1998),
  Coming Unbuttoned, Making Light of It (City Lights Bks,
  1993, 1992), *Special Deliveries* (Broken Moon Pr, 1990).

John Brummet   P
8531 NW 24th, Seattle, WA 98117, 206-784-8393
  Pubs: *Negative Capability, Electrum, Common Ground,
  Concerning Poetry.*

Thomas Brush   P
17217 SE 42 Pl, Issaquah, WA 98027, 206-746-9189
  Pubs: *Even Money* (Seapen Pr, 1988), *Opening Night* (Owl
  Creek Pr, 1981), *Poetry, Poetry Northwest, Indiana Rev,
  Tar River Rev, Fine Madness, Quarterly West.*

Gregory Burnham   W
PO Box 13129, Burton, WA 980130129, 206-463-4006
  Pubs: *Flash Fiction: Anth* (Norton, 1992), *Vital Lines: Anth*
  (St. Martin's Pr, 1991), *Harper's, Indiana Rev, Turnstile,
  Puerto del Sol, Black Ice.*

E. G. Burrows   P
20319 92nd Ave W, Edmonds, WA 98020, 425-775-5383
  Pubs: *The Birds Under the Earth* (Owl Creek Pr, 1996),
  QRL 50th Anniversary Anth (QRL, 1993), *Wildsong: Anth*
  (U Georgia Pr, 1998), *Wisconsin Rev, Comstock Rev,
  Santa Barbara Rev, Montserrat Rev, Gettysburg Rev,
  Poetry, Blue Mesa Rev, Xanadu, Wilderness.*

Jack Cady   W
PO Box 872, Port Townsend, WA 983680872, 360-385-1670
Internet: erewhon@olympus.net
  Pubs: *The Night We Buried Road Dog* (Dreamhaven,
  1998), *The Off Season, Street* (St. Martin's, 1996, 1994),
  Inagchi, The Sons of Noah (Broken Moon Pr, 1994, 1992),
  Omni, Glimmer Train, Fantasy & Sci-Fi, Portland Rev.

Janet Cannon   P
PO Box 715, Stanwood, WA 98292, 206-781-3378
Internet: cannonjan@aol.com
  Pubs: *The Last Night in New York* (Homeward, 1984), *New
  York Qtly, Helicon Nine, Berkeley Poetry Rev, Slant,
  George Washington Rev, New Mexico Humanities Rev,
  Beatitude 33.*

Gladys H. Cardiff   P
4216 Pasadena Pl NE, #1, Seattle, WA 98105, 206-632-3933
  Pubs: *Contemporary Native American Poets of the
  Twentieth Century* (H&R, 1988), *Seattle Rev.*

Chrystos   P
3900 Pleasant Beach Dr NE, Bainbridge Island, WA
98110-3215, 206-842-7207
  Pubs: *Fire Power* (Press Gang, 1995), *Reinventing the
  Enemy's Language: Anth* (Norton, 1996), *Fugitive Colors*
  (Cleveland State U Poetry Ctr, 1994).

Thomas Churchill   W
PO Box 232, Langley, WA 98260, 360-730-4634
  Pubs: *Triumph Over Marcos* (Open Hand, 1995), *Centralia
  Dead March* (Curbstone, 1980), *Island Independent,
  Review of Contemporary Fiction.*

Naomi Clark   P&W
140 Windship Dr/Kala Point, Port Townsend, WA 98368,
206-385-6732
  Pubs: *When I Kept Silence* (Cleveland State U Pr, 1988),
  *North Dakota Qtly, Indiana Rev, Prairie Schooner, Iowa
  Rev, Alaska Qtly Rev, Bellingham Rev, Beloit Poetry Jrnl,
  South Dakota Rev.*

Linda J. Clifton　　P&W
4462 Whitman Ave N, Upper, Seattle, WA 98103
Internet: lclifton@halcyon.com
　　Pubs: *Shadowmarks* (Blue Begonia Pr, 1994), *Crab Creek
　　Review: Anniversary Anth* (Crab Creek Rev, 1994), *Calyx,
　　Gold Dust, Tinderbox.*

Jim Cody　　P
1055 NW 96 St, Shoreline, WA 98177
Internet: ngjmc@ttacs.ttu.edu
　　Pubs: *My Body Is A Flute* (A Place of Herons Pr, 1994), *A
　　Book of Wonders* (Cedarshouse Pr, 1988), *Prayer to Fish*
　　(Slough Pr, 1984), *Lynx, Exquisite Corpse.*

Phyllis Collier　　P
360 Stevens Ave SW, Renton, WA 98055, 425-226-4876
Internet: pkcollier@msn.com
　　Pubs: *Cape Rock, West Wind Rev, South Dakota Rev,
　　Cumberland Poetry Rev, Mississippi Valley Rev, Puerto del
　　Sol, Green Mountains Rev, Poet Lore, College English,
　　Poetry Northwest, Nimrod.*

Sharon Cumberland　　P
Seattle Univ, Broadway and Madison, Seattle, WA
98122-4460, 206-296-5425
Internet: slc@seattleu.edu
　　Pubs: *The Arithmetic of Mourning* (Green Rock Pr, 1998),
　　Nelson Mandelamandela: Anth (Three Continents Pr,
　　1989), *Ploughshares, Kalliope, Beloit Poetry Jrnl, Iowa Rev,
　　Mickle Street Rev, Contact II, Indiana Rev.*

Madeline DeFrees　　P
7548 11th Ave NW, Seattle, WA 98117-4143
　　Pubs: *Possible Sibyls* (Lynx Hse Pr, 1991), *Imaginary
　　Ancestors* (Broken Moon Pr, 1990), *Paris Rev, Volt,
　　Calapooya Collage, Ploughshares.*

Judy Doenges　　W
1402 North Steele, Tacoma, WA 984068013, 253-759-6402
　　Pubs: *Our Mothers, Our Selves: Anth* (Bergin & Garvey,
　　1996), *Ohio Short Fiction: Anth* (Northmont, 1995),
　　*Permafrost, Green Mountains Rev, Phoebe, Nimrod,
　　Georgia Rev, Evergreen Chronicles, Equinox.* ·

Anita Endrezze　　P
W 2411 Dell Dr, Spokane, WA 99208, 509-326-5133
Internet: hansen@iea.com
　　Pubs: *Lost Rivers* (Making Waves Pr, 1997), *at the helm of
　　twilight* (Broken Moon Pr, 1992), *Harper & Row's 20th
　　Century of Native American Poetry: Anth* (H&R, 1988).

Roger Fanning　　P
226 W State Hwy 20, Oak Harbor, WA 98277, 206-675-9117
　　Pubs: *The Island Itself* (Viking, 1991).

Anita N. Feng　　P
300 SW Forest Dr, Issaquah, WA 98027, 425-557-8764
Internet: nfeng_ms@msn.com
　　Pubs: *Internal Strategies* (U Akron Pr, 1996), *Northwest
　　Rev, Ploughshares, Primavera, Prairie Schooner, Black
　　Warrior Rev, Nimrod.*

Lorraine Ferra　　P
PO Box 93, Port Townsend, WA 983680093, 360-385-7568
Internet: lferra@waypt.com
　　Pubs: *Eating Bread* (Kuhn Spit Pr, 1994), *Poet & Critic,
　　Quarterly West, Florida Rev, Country Jrnl, Seattle Rev, Iris,
　　Bellowing Ark.*

Phil George　　P
1126 Comos Dr, Coulee Dam, WA 99116

Hollis Giammatteo　　P&W
2911 1st Ave, #103, Seattle, WA 98121
　　Pubs: *APR, Prairie Schooner, Nimrod, Calyx, Feminist
　　Studies, Vogue, NAR, Ms., Salmagundi.*

Carole L. Glickfeld　　P&W
731 Broadway E, #302, Seattle, WA 98102, 206-322-7953
　　Pubs: *Useful Gifts* (U Georgia Pr, 1989), *Her Face in the
　　Mirror: Anth* (Beacon Pr, 1994), *River Oak Rev, Ohio Rev,
　　Kansas Qtly, Habersham Rev, Crescent Rev,
　　Crosscurrents Qtly.*

Samuel Green　　P
Bookmonger Rd, Waldron Island, WA 98297
　　Pubs: *Vertebrae* (Eastern Washington U Pr, 1994),
　　Communion (Grey Spider Pr, 1993), *Poetry, Poetry
　　Northwest, Prairie Schooner, Southern Poetry Rev, Yellow
　　Silk.*

Michael Gregory　　P
1132 NW 56 St, Seattle, WA 98107, 206-782-8459
Internet: eebmpg@aa.net
　　Pubs: *The World Abandoned By Numbers* (Owl Creek Pr,
　　1992), *Denver Qtly, Western Humanities Rev, Southern
　　Poetry Rev, Cape Rock, Phoebe, Telescope, Amelia,
　　Nimrod, Crazyhorse, New Delta Rev, ACM, Passages
　　North, Crab Creek Rev.*

Ben Groff　　W
17832 66th Pl, W, Lynnwood, WA 98037, 206-745-8855
Internet: hnrbdg@vmmc.org
　　Pubs: *Pushcart Prize XVI, 1991-1992: Anth* (Pushcart Pr,
　　1992), *Alaska Qtly Rev, Crab Creek Rev, Permafrost, Iowa
　　Rev, Northwest Rev.*

Carol Guess　　P&W
Levant & Wales Literary Agency, 108 Hayes St, Seattle, WA
98109, 206-284-7114
Internet: bizziew@aol.com
　　Pubs: *Switch* (Calyx Bks, 1998), *Seeing Dell* (Cleis Pr,
　　1996), *Mankato Poetry Rev, Harvard Gay & Lesbian Rev,
　　Interim, Ilya's Honey, Poetry Northwest.*

Theodore Hall   P
PO Box 317, Rainier, WA 98576
   Pubs: *Intro I* (Bantam, 1968), *New York Qtly, Maps, Greenfield Rev, Northeast Jrnl, Shenandoah, Stony Hills, Poet.*

Mark W. Halperin   P
Central Washington Univ, Ellensburg, WA 989267558, 509-963-3511
Internet: halperin@cwu.edu
   Pubs: *A Measure of Islands* (Wesleyan, 1990), *A Place Made Fast* (Copper Canyon Pr, 1982), *Iowa Rev, Seneca, Shenandoah, Seattle Rev, Northwest Rev.*

Sam Hamill   P
Copper Canyon Press, PO Box 271, Port Townsend, WA 98368, 206-385-4925
   Pubs: *Gratitude* (BOA Editions, 1998), *The Erotic Spirit, Only Companion* (Shambhala, 1995, 1992), *Destination Zero: Poems 1970-1995* (White Pine Pr, 1995), *Tricycle, APR, Poetry East, Ploughshares.*

Blaine Hammond   P
PO Box 543, Ocean Park, WA 98640-0543, 360-665-4248
   Pubs: *Sand Script: Anth* (North Coast Writers, 1998), *Poetalk, Antiskios, Fennel Stalk, Bouillabaisse, Free Lunch, Paisley Moon, Impetus, Plainsongs, Imago, Black Bear Rev, Bogg, Arnazella.*

Nixeon Civille Handy   P
262 Woodland Dr, Lacey, WA 98503, 206-438-5328
   Pubs: *River as Metaphor* (Gorham, 1992), *A Little Leaven* (Kings Pr, 1987), *New York Qtly, NER/BLQ, Oregon East, Chariton Rev, Skylark, Connecticut Rev, Bellowing Ark.*

Edward Harkness   P
14903 Linden N, Seattle, WA 98133, 206-367-6574
   Pubs: *Water Color Portrait of a Bamboo Rake* (Brooding Heron Pr, 1994), *Fiddle Wrapped in a Gunnysack* (Dooryard, 1984), *Seattle Rev, Portland Rev.*

George W. Harper   W
1208 S 27 St, #C-2, Tacoma, WA 98409, 206-272-1034
   Pubs: *Gypsy Earth* (Doubleday, 1983).

Jana Harris   P
32814 120th St, SE, Sultan, WA 98294, 206-793-1848
   Pubs: *Untitled, Poetry* (Ontario Rev Pr, 1989), *Manhattan As A Second Language* (H&R, 1980).

Ursula Hegi   W
11525 North Nine Mile Rd, Nine Mile Falls, WA 990029250
   Pubs: *Stones From the River, Floating In My Mother's Palm, Unearned Pleasures* (Poseidon, 1994, 1990, 1998).

Robin Hemley   W
Western Washington Univ, Bellingham, WA 98225
   Pubs: *The Last Studebaker* (Graywolf, 1992), *All You Can Eat* (Atlantic Monthly Pr, 1988), *NAR, Prairie Schooner, Ploughshares, Story, Boulevard, Manoa.*

Barbara Hiesiger   PP
202 NW 43 St, Seattle, WA 98107-4328

Alicia Hokanson   P
Box 10657, Bainbridge Island, WA 98110, 206-842-3313
   Pubs: *Mapping the Distance* (Breitenbush, 1989), *Phosphorous* (Brooding Heron, 1984), *Poetry USA, Exhibition, Literary Center Qtly.*

Emily Newman Holt   P
1704 1st Ave N, Seattle, WA 98109, 206-283-3455
   Pubs: *Encore, Up Against The Wall Mother, Blue Unicorn.*

A. J. Hovde   P
1400 Chuckanut Dr, Bellingham, WA 98226, 206-673-8073
   Pubs: *A.J. Hovde: Selected Poems* (Fairhaven College Pr, 1981), *New Laurel Rev, Kansas Qtly.*

Christopher Howell   P
420 W 24th, Spokane, WA 99203, 509-624-4894
Internet: cnhowell@ewu.edu
   Pubs: *Memory and Heaven* (Eastern Washington U Pr, 1997), *Sweet Afton* (True Directions, 1991), *Harper's, Gettysburg Rev, NAR, Northwest Rev, Iowa Rev, Poetry Northwest, Hudson Rev, Ironwood.*

Joan Howell   P
Colorado College, 1975 Wynoochee Valley Road, Montesano, WA 98563, 360-249-2005
Internet: wynooche@techline.com
   Pubs: *A Letter to Myself to Water* (Jonesalley Pr, 1995), *Our Lady Of The Harbor* (Seapen Pr, 1985), *Yale Rev, Southern Poetry Rev, Poetry Northwest.*

Robert Huff   P
Western Washington University, Bellingham, WA 98225, 206-676-3236
   Pubs: *Shore Guide to Flocking Names* (Fanferon Pr, 1985), *Western Humanities Rev, Interim, Poetry.*

Paul Hunter   P
4131 Greenwood N, Seattle, WA 981037017, 206-633-5647
Internet: www/zipcom.com/ pablo
   Pubs: *Lay of the Land* (Wood Works, 1997), *It Loves Me It Loves Me Not* (Now Its Up To You Pr, 1992), *Mockingbird* (Jawbone Pr, 1981), *Alaska Fisherman's Jrnl, Fine Madness, North American Rev, Poetry, Poetry Northwest, Point No Point, Beloit.*

Richard Ives   P
2693 S W Camano Dr, Camano Island, WA 98292-8205
Pubs: *Evidence of Fire* (Owl Creek Pr, 1989), *Notes from the Water Journals* (Confluence Pr, 1980), *Iowa Rev, Poetry Northwest, Northwest Rev, Mississippi Rev, Virginia Qtly Rev.*

Sibyl James   P&W
538 29th Ave, Seattle, WA 98122, 206-323-7516
Pubs: *The Adventures of Stout Mama* (Papier-Mache Pr, 1993), *In China with Harpo and Karl* (Calyx Bks, 1990), *American Voice, Ironwood, Nebraska Rev.*

Laura Jensen   P&W
302 N Yakima, #C-3, Tacoma, WA 984032213, 253-272-0541
Pubs: *Shelter, Memory* (Dragon Gate, 1985, 1982), *Bad Boats* (Ecco, 1977), *APR, New Yorker, Crazyhorse, Poetry Northwest.*

Ted Joans   P
513 Maynard Ave S, Studio #202, Seattle, WA 98104, 206-625-1399

Charles Johnson   W
Univ Washington, Seattle, WA 98195, 206-543-2690
Pubs: *Middle Passage, Sorcerer's Apprentice* (Atheneum, 1990, 1986), *Dialogue, American Visions.*

Douglas S. Johnson   P&W
PO Box 772, Auburn, WA 98071-0772, 206-351-9119
Pubs: *Transformations* (Guyasuta Pub, 1994), *The Heartlands Today, Midwest Poetry Rev, Kansas English, The Thomas Wolfe Rev, The Ohioana Rev.*

R. P. Jones   P
7102 Interlaaken Dr SW, Tacoma, WA 98499-1805, 206-531-7422
Pubs: *The Rest Is Silence* (Broken Moon Pr, 1984), *Waiting For Spring* (Circinatum Pr, 1978).

Jessie Kachmar   P
13739 15th Ave NE, #B-1, Seattle, WA 98125, 206-365-2303
Pubs: *Snow Quiet* (Snow Pr, 1979), *Apertures To Anywhere* (Harper Square Pr, 1976), *Caprice, Redstart, Twigs, Chicago.*

Sy M. Kahn   P
1212 Holcomb St, Port Townsend, WA 98368, 360-385-9499
Internet: kahnandbaker@olympus.net
Pubs: *Between Tedium and Terror: A Soldier's Diary, 1943-45* (U Illinois Pr, 1993), *Facing Mirrors* (Two Windows, 1980), *Another Time* (Sydon, Inc., 1968), *Jrnl of Modern Literature, Midwest Qtly, College English, South Carolina Rev.*

Lonny Kaneko   P
Highline College, PO Box 98000, Des Moines, WA 981989800, 206-878-3710
Internet: lkanek@hcc.ctc.edu
Pubs: *Coming Home From Camp* (Brooding Heron Pr, 1986), *Seattle Rev, Written Arts, King County, An Ear To The Ground, The Big Aiiieeee.*

Richard L. Kenney   P
Univ Washington, English Dept, 354330, Seattle, WA 98195, 206-543-2690
Pubs: *The Invention of the Zero* (Knopf, 1993), *Orrery* (Atheneum, 1985), *The Evolution of the Flightless Bird* (Yale U Pr, 1983).

W. P. Kinsella   W
Box 2162, Blaine, WA 98231-2162, 604-536-9299
Pubs: *The Secret of the Northern Lights* (Thistledown Pr, 1998), *If Wishes Were Horses, The Winter Helen Dropped By, The Dixon Cornbelt League, Brother Frank's Gospel Hour, Box Socials* (HarperCollins, 1997, 1995, 1994, 1992, 1991).

Carolyn S. Kremers   P
2625 S Grand Blvd, Spokane, WA 99203, 509-835-4145
Internet: ckremers@mail.ewu.edu
Pubs: *Place of the Pretend People: Gifts From A Yup'ik Eskimo Village, Last New Land: Stories of Alaska Past & Present: Anth* (Alaska Northwest Bks, 1996, 1996), *Life on the Line: Anth* (Negative Capability Pr, 1992), *Alaska Qtly Rev.*

Alex Kuo   P
NW 1425 Orlon Dr, Pullman, WA 99163, 509-335-4901
Pubs: *Changing the River* (Reed & Cannon, 1986), *New Letters from Hiroshima* (Greenfield, 1974), *Chicago Rev, Caliban, Boundary 2, Malahat Rev.*

Susan Landgraf   P
4828 51st Ave S, Seattle, WA 98118, 206-721-0208
Pubs: *Spoon River Qtly, South Florida Poetry Rev, Calyx, Ploughshares, Nimrod, Cincinnati Poetry Rev.*

R. A. Larson   P
9600 Occidental, Yakima, WA 98903, 509-965-4547
Pubs: *Of Wind, A Hawk, And Kiona* (Confluence Pr, 1978), *Silverfish Rev, Brix, Kingfisher.*

Alan Chong Lau   P
5005 Phinney Ave N, #302, Seattle, WA 98103
Pubs: *What Book!? Buddha Poems From Beat To Hiphop: Anth* (Parallax Pr, 1998), *Highway 99: Anth* (Heyday Bks, 1996), *The Open Boat Poems from Asian America: Anth* (Anchor Bks, 1993), *American Dragons: Anth of 25 Asian American Voices* (HarperCollins, 1993).

Ellen Levine   P
838 NE 83 St, Seattle, WA 98115
  Pubs: *Poetry Northwest, Georgia Rev, Southern Poetry
  Rev, Poetry Now, Calyx, Kansas Qtly.*

Evelyn Livingston   W
71 Windship Dr, Port Townsend, WA 983689545,
360-385-2063
  Pubs: *Digging for Roots: Dalmo'ma 5 Anth* (Empty Bowl Pr,
  1985), *Confrontation, Pennsylvania Rev, Indiana Rev,
  Georgia Rev, Crosscurrents, New Letters, Interim.*

Jeanne Lohmann   P
2501 Washington SE, Olympia, WA 98501-2962,
360-705-3735
  Pubs: *Granite Under Water* (Fithian Pr, 1996), *Wild Song:
  Anth* (U Georgia Pr, 1998), *Cries of the Spirit: Anth* (Beacon
  Pr, 1991), *North Stone Rev, Poetry Northwest, Barnabe
  Mountain Rev, Rosebud, Shenandoah, Yankee, Raven
  Chronicles, Buffalo Spree.*

Kenneth MacLean   P
522 Decatur St SW, Olympia, WA 98502, 360-753-1175
Internet: kenver@oly.net
  Pubs: *Blue Heron's Sky* (Latitudes Pr, 1990), *The Long
  Way Home* (Inchbird Pr, 1982), *Prism Intl, Poetry Seattle,
  Calapooya Collage, Concerning Poetry.*

Jesus Maria Maldonado   P
PO Box 471, Grandview, WA 98930, 509-882-6477
  Pubs: *In the Still of My Heart* (Canto Norteno Pubs, 1993),
  *Americas Rev, Bilingual Rev, El Grito, Caracol,
  Mctamorphoses, El Gato.*

Stephen Manes   W
1122 E Pike St., Ste. 588, Seattle, WA 98122, 206-722-2525
Internet: steve@cranky.com
  Pubs: *An Almost Perfect Game, Comedy High* (Scholastic,
  1995, 1992), *Be A Perfect Person In Just Three Days!*
  (Houghton Mifflin,1982).

Laureen D. Mar   P&W
3811 S Horton St, Seattle, WA 98144-7027, 206-722-3482
  Pubs: *Charlie Chan Is Dead: Anth* (Penguin, 1993),
  Breaking Silence: Anth (Greenfield Rev Pr, 1983), *Contact
  II, Greenfield Rev, Seattle Rev.*

John Constantine Mastor   P
401 NE Ravenna Blvd #P122, Seattle, WA 981156428,
206-525-1081
  Pubs: *Glorious Morning, Bountiful Light* (The Plowman,
  1996, 1995), *My Legacy, Broken Streets, Purpose, Rio
  Grande Pr, Bellowing Ark, Uprising, Aim Qtly, Poetic
  Realm.*

William H. Matchett   P
1017 Minor Ave, #702, Seattle, WA 98104, 206-682-6730
  Pubs: *Fireweed* (The Tidal Pr, 1980), *Water Ouzel*
  (Houghton Mifflin, 1955), *New Yorker, Harper's, Harvard,
  New Republic, Ploughshares, SPR.*

Rita Z. Mazur   P
2332 Ferndale, Richland, WA 99352, 509-375-4210
  Pubs: *The Great Blue Heron and Other Poems* (Adrienne
  Lee Pr, 1996), *Tanka Splendor* (AHA Bks, 1995), *Brussels
  Sprout, Black Bough, Modern Haiku, Passager.*

James J. McAuley   P
1011 W 25 St, Spokane, WA 99203, 509-747-0896
  Pubs: *Coming & Going, New & Selected Work* (U Arkansas
  Pr, 1989), *Recital* (Dolmen/Colin Smythe, 1982), *Irish
  Times, Shenandoah, Cimarron Rev, Poetry Northwest.*

Joanne McCarthy   P
1322 N Cascade, Tacoma, WA 98406, 253-752-3462
  Pubs: *Shadowlight* (Broken Moon Pr, 1989), *At Our Core:
  Anth* (Papier-Mache Pr, 1998), *Calyx, Green Fuse,
  Kalliope, Writers' Forum.*

Colleen J. McElroy   P&W
Wales Literary Agency, 108 Hayes, Seattle, WA 98109,
206-284-7114
  Pubs: *Travelling Music* (Story Line Pr, 1998), *A Long Way
  From St. Louie* (Coffee Hse Pr, 1997), *What Madness
  Brought Me Here* (Wesleyan, 1990), *Children of the Night:
  Anth* (Little, Brown, 1995), *Seneca Rev, River Styx, Brilliant
  Corners, Massachusetts Rev.*

John McFarland   W
2320 10th Ave E, #5, Seattle, WA 98102, 206-323-7053
  Pubs: *The Exploding Frog & Other Fables* (Little, Brown,
  1981), *The Next Parish Over: Anth* (New Rivers Pr, 1993),
  Ararat, Caliban, Cricket, No Exit, Stet.

Heather McHugh   P
Univ Washington, Seattle, WA 98195-4330, 206-543-2483
Internet: heathermchugh@poetic.com
  Pubs: *Hinge & Sign: Poems 1968-1993, Broken English:
  Poetry and Partiality* (Wesleyan, 1994, 1993).

Robert McNamara   P
Univ Washington, English Dept, Box 354330, Seattle, WA
98195-4330, 206-543-7131
Internet: rmcnamar@u.washington.edu
  Pubs: *Second Messengers* (Wesleyan U Pr, 1990), *Ohio
  Rev, Agni, Missouri Rev, Field, Gettysburg Rev, Antioch
  Rev, Northwest Rev.*

Linda Meyers   P
15417 223rd Ave NE, Woodinville, WA 98072, 206-788-0336
  Pubs: *Poetry Northwest, Hawaii Rev, Calapooya Collage,
  Bottomfish, Impetus, Chambered Nautilus, Whole Notes,
  Chrysanthemum, Seattle Rev, Permafrost.*

James Masao Mitsui P
6218 Latona Ave NE, Seattle, WA 98115, 206-527-8768
Internet: jim3wells@aol.com
Pubs: *From A Three-Cornered World* (U Washington Pr, 1997), *After the Long Train* (Bieler Pr, 1986), *Crossing the Phantom River* (Graywolf, 1978), *A Year In Poetry: Anth* (Crown Pub, 1995).

Melinda Mueller P
7704 16th Ave NW, Seattle, WA 98117, 206-782-0752
Pubs: *Asleep in Another Country* (Jawbone Pr, 1979), *Best American Poetry: Anth* (Scribner, 1990), *Seattle Rev, Fine Madness, Birmingham Rev.*

Jo Nelson P
11102 Crescent Valley Dr NW, Gig Harbor, WA 98335, 206-851-7728
Internet: jonelson@ptinet.net
Pubs: *Seattle Five Plus One* (Pig Iron Pr, 1995), *Chariton Rev, Confluence, Plainsong, Portland Rev, Main Street Rag, Willow Creek Jrnl, Pleiades, Wind Song.*

Kirby Olson P
PO Box 959, Seattle, WA 98111, 206-329-5620
Pubs: *Partisan Rev, Exquisite Corpse, Asylum, Light Year, Second Coming.*

Carol Orlock W
920 2nd Ave W, Seattle, WA 98119, 206-283-0680
Pubs: *The Hedge, The Ribbon* (Broken Moon Pr, 1993), *The Goddess Letters* (St. Martin's Pr, 1987), *Century, Willow Springs, Calyx, Crab Creek Rev.*

Hans Ostrom P&W
Univ of Puget Sound, 1500 N Warner, Tacoma, WA 98416, 206-756-3434
Internet: ostrom@ups.edu
Pubs: *Water's Night* (Mariposite Pr, 1993), *Three To Get Ready* (Cliffhanger Pr, 1991), *Ploughshares, Poetry Northwest, Redbook, California Qtly, South Carolina Rev.*

Eileen Owen P
2709 128th St SE, Everett, WA 98208, 206-337-1231
Pubs: *Facing The Weather Side* (Basilisk Pr, 1985), *Calyx, Cincinnati Rev, South Dakota Rev.*

Dixie Lee Partridge P
1817 Marshall Ct, Richland, WA 99352, 509-943-4007
Pubs: *Watermark* (Saturday Pr, 1991), *Deer In The Haystacks* (Ahsahta Pr, 1984), *Commonweal, Southern Poetry Rev, Ploughshares, Passages North, Georgia Rev, Yankee, Northern Lights.*

Fred Pfeil W
6031 1st Ave NW, Seattle, WA 98107-2008
Pubs: *Goodman 2020* (Indiana U Pr, 1985), *Georgia Rev, Fiction International, Sewanee Rev.*

Anne Pitkin P
6809 Dayton Ave N, Seattle, WA 98103, 206-789-4623
Pubs: *Yellow* (Arrowood Bks, 1989), *Poetry, Prairie Schooner, Ironwood, Malahat, Seattle Rev.*

Randall Platt W
1126 Pt Fosdick Dr, NW, Gig Harbor, WA 98335
Internet: http://3linedesign.com/randall/
Pubs: *Honor Bright* (Doubleday, 1998), *The Cornerstone, The Four Arrows FE-AS-KO* (Catbird Pr, 1998, 1991), *Out of the Forest Clearing* (John Daniel, 1991).

Darryl Ponicsan W
PO Box 10036, Bainbridge Island, WA 98110
Pubs: *The Ringmaster, Tom Mix Died For Your Sins* (Delacorte/Dell, 1978, 1975).

Charles Potts P
PO Box 100, Walla Walla, WA 99362-0033, 509-529-0813
Internet: tsunami@wwics.com
Pubs: *100 Years in Idaho* (Tsunami, 1996), *The Dictatorship of the Environment* (Druid Bks, 1991), *Loading Las Vegas* (Current, 1991), *Redneck Rev, Dry Crik Rev, Seattle Arts Image, Point No Point, The Temple, Talking River Rev, Limberlost Rev.*

Joseph Powell P
221 Cross Creek Dr, Ellensburg, WA 98926, 509-925-5312
Internet: powellj@cluster.cwu.edu
Pubs: *Getting Here, Quarterly Review of Literature 50th Anniversary Anth* (QRL, 1997, 1993), *Counting the Change, Winter Insomnia* (Arrowhead, 1993, 1993), *Poetry, Seattle Rev, Tar River Poetry, Nebraska Rev.*

Marjorie Power P
508 O'Farrell Ave, Olympia, WA 98501-3470, 360-352-7025
Pubs: *Cave Poems, Tishku, After She Created Men* (Lone Willow Pr, 1998, 1996), *Living With It* (Wampeter Pr, 1983), *New Virginia Rev, SPR, Spoon River Poetry Rev, Puerto del Sol.*

Freda Quenneville P
3619 Carr Pl N, Seattle, WA 98103-8122, 206-236-2821
Pubs: *Reflections On A Gift of Watermelon Pickle and Other Modern Verse* (Scott Foresman & Co., 1966), *Poetry Northwest, Nation, New Yorker, Prairie Schooner.*

Belle Randall P
1202 N. 42 St., Seattle, WA 98103, 206-633-2744
Internet: bellerandall@halcyon.com
Pubs: *Drop Dead Beautiful* (Wood Works Pr, 1998), *The Gift of Tongues: Anth* (Copper Canyon Pr, 1996), *Wallace Stegner Anth* (Stanford U Pr, 1989), *Contemporary Religious Poetry: Anth* (Paulist, 1988), *Threepenny Rev, Common Knowledge.*

Bill Ransom   P&W
PO Box 284, Grayland, WA 985470284, 360-867-9547
Internet: ransom@evergreen.edu
    Pubs: *Learning The Ropes* (Utah State U Pr, 1995), *Burn*
    (Putnam-Berkley Pub, 1995), *Puerto del Sol, Tendril, New
    York Qtly, Chicago Rev, Kansas City Star Mag, Prairie
    Schooner, Seattle Weekly.*

Sherry Rind   P
17301 NE 131 St, Redmond, WA 98052, 425-869-9212
Internet: sherryrind@aol.com
    Pubs: *A Fall Out the Door* (Confluence Pr, 1994), *The
    Hawk in the Backyard* (Anhinga Pr, 1985), *Poetry
    Northwest, Southern Poetry Rev.*

Judith Roche   P
178 Lake Dell Ave, Seattle, WA 98122, 206-329-4687
Internet: judith@onereel.org
    Pubs: *Myrrh, My Life as a Screamer* (Black Heron Pr,
    1994), *Ghosts* (Empty Bowl Pr, 1984), *Willow Springs,
    Duckabush Jrnl, Yellow Silk.*

Sal Salasin   P
840 W Nickerson St, #11, Seattle, WA 98119-1448
    Pubs: *Casa de Caca* (Apathy Poets Pr, 1990), *Stepping Off
    the Plane* (Another Chicago Pr, 1988), *Exquisite Corpse,
    ACM, NAW, Sensitive Skin, Real Poetik.*

Eric Schmidt   PP
1517 12th Ave, #Mezz, Seattle, WA 98122-3932
    Pubs: *The Freezing No To All Questions Prison of Bent
    Things: Verse Play.*

Sandra Schroeder   P
4747 Univ View Pl NE, Seattle, WA 981054035,
206-729-5745
Internet: sandearl@oz.net
    Pubs: *Inventing The Cats* (BkMk Pr, 1973), *Seattle Rev,
    Fine Madness, Literary Arts Rev, Ergo!, Poetry Northwest,
    Bellowing Ark.*

Julianne Seeman   P
Bellevue Community College, Arts & Humanities Div,
#A255M, Bellevue, WA 98004, 206-526-0698
Internet: jseeman@bcc.ctc.edu
    Pubs: *Enough Light To See* (Anhinga Pr, 1989).

Sondra Shulman   W
934 E Allison St, Seattle, WA 98102, 206-329-6493
    Pubs: *Moon People* (Baskerville Pub, 1994), *Scrittori Ebrei
    Americani* (Tascabili Bom Pi Ant, 1989), *Ascent,
    Massachusetts Rev, Antioch Rev, Kansas Qtly,
    Bumbershoot.*

Paul Red Shuttleworth   P
10482 Rd 16 NE, Moses Lake, WA 98837, 509-766-9104
    Pubs: *All These Bullets* (Logan Hse Pr, 1997), *Western
    Movie* (Signpost Pr, 1990), *Coyotes With Wings* (Gorse Pr,
    1990), *Neon, Alaska Qtly Rev, New Mexico Humanities
    Rev, West Branch.*

Sarah Singer   P
2360 43 Ave E, #415, Seattle, WA 981122703, 206-726-8103
    Pubs: *The Gathering, Of Love and Shoes* (William L.
    Bauhan, 1992, 1987), *Glimpses: Anth* (King County Public
    Art Program, 1997), *Palomar Showcase: Anth* (Palomar
    Branch Pr, 1997), *Shakespeare Newsletter, Voices Intl,
    Lyric, CSM, Judaism, Poets West, Penwoman.*

Judith Skillman   P
14206 SE 45 Pl, Bellevue, WA 98006, 206-644-4026
    Pubs: *Storm, Beethoven and the Birds* (Blue Begonia Pr,
    1998, 1996), *Worship of the Visible Spectrum* (Breitenbush
    Bks, 1988), *Southern Rev, Northwest Rev, Iowa Rev,
    Prairie Schooner, Poetry, Laurel Rev.*

James M. Snydal   P
11034 Old Creosote Hill Rd, Bainbridge Island, WA
98110-2154, 206-842-1273
Internet: jbcf12a@prodigy.com
    Pubs: *Blueberry Pie* (Wood Works, 1998), *Living in America*
    (New Thought Jrnl Pr, 1997), *To Range Widely Over
    Possibilities* (Full Moon Pub, 1996), *Near the Cathedral*
    (Dry Bones Pr, 1995), *New York Qtly, Poetry Wales,
    Onthebus, Chiron, Bloomsbury.*

Maya Sonenberg   W
305 Bellevue Ave E, #401, Seattle, WA 98102, 206-323-9205
Internet: mayas@u.washington.edu
    Pubs: *Cartographies* (U Pittsburgh, 1989), *American Short
    Fiction, Cream City Rev, Columbia Rev, Grand Street,
    Chelsea, Santa Monica Rev.*

Sandi Sonnenfeld   W
125 N 105 St, Seattle, WA 98133
Internet: sanwar@aol.com
    Pubs: *Sex and the City: Anth* (Serpent's Tail, 1989), *Onion
    River Rev, Voices West, This Mag, Salmon Mag, CPU Rev,
    Emrys Jrnl, Ion, Sojourner, Written Arts.*

Michael Spence   P
5810 S 144th, Tukwila, WA 98168-4550, 206-431-6874
    Pubs: *Adam Chooses* (Rose Alley Pr, 1998), *The Spine*
    (Purdue U Pr, 1987), *A Year In Poetry: Anth* (Crown, 1995),
    *Sewanee Rev, Poetry, Press, American Scholar, Poetry
    Northwest, Georgia Rev, Chariton Rev.*

Stephen Sundin   P
1008 Broadway, Longview, WA 98632, 360-423-7020
    Pubs: *Denver Qtly, Poet Lore, Pivot, Pearl, Defined
    Providence, Cathartic, Oregon East, Artful Dodge, Prose
    Poem, ACM, West Wind Poetry.*

Joan Swift   P
18520 Sound View Pl, Edmonds, WA 98020-2355,
206-776-2391
Internet: jayswift@msn.com
    Pubs: *Intricate Moves, Poems About Rape* (Chicory Blue
    Pr, 1997), *The Dark Path of Our Names* (Dragon Gate,
    1985), *Parts of Speech* (Confluence Pr, 1978), *Poetry,
    APR, DoubleTake, Poetry Northwest, Ploughshares, Calyx.*

Gordon Taylor   W
3920 SW 109 St, Seattle, WA 981461652, 206-243-6768

Velande Taylor   P&W
910 Marion St, #1008, Seattle, WA 98104, 206-621-1376
    Pubs: *Tales From The Archetypal World, ZBYX: Tokens,
    Homilies in the Marketplace* (WordCraft Bks, 1998, 1997,
    1996), *Pacific Mag, Verses Mag, Starburst Mag, Extended
    Hands.*

Gail Tremblay   P
The Evergreen State College, Olympia, WA 98505,
206-866-6000
    Pubs: *Indian Singing in 20th Century America* (Calyx,
    1990), *Harper's Anth of 20th Century Native American
    Poetry* (Harper San Francisco, 1986), *Wooster Rev, Calyx,
    Denver Qtly, Northwest Rev.*

Wayne Ude   W
PO Box 145, Clinton, WA 98236, 206-341-1630
    Pubs: *Maybe I Will Do Something* (HM, 1993), *Buffalo &
    Other Stories* (Lynx Hse Pr, 1991), *Three Coyote Tales*
    (Lone Oak Pr, 1989), *Ploughshares, NAR.*

Michael Upchurch   W
9725 Sand Point Way NE, Seattle, WA 98115-2650
Internet: michaelupchurch@msn.com
    Pubs: *Passive Intruder* (Norton, 1995), *The Flame Forest*
    (Available Pr/Ballantine, 1989), *Carolina Qtly, American
    Scholar, Glimmer Train.*

Craig Van Riper   P
1630 E Lynn St, Seattle, WA 98112, 206-329-5972
Internet: cvanripe@hdrinc.com
    Pubs: *Making the Path While You Walk* (Sagittarius Pr,
    1993), *The Practice of Peace: Anth* (Sherman Asher Pub,
    1998), *Spoon River Qtly, Passages North, Southern Poetry
    Rev, Onthebus, Five Fingers Rev, Coe Rev.*

Nance Lee Van Winckel   P&W
12506 S Gardener, Cheney, WA 99004, 509-448-6155
    Pubs: *The Dirt* (Miami U Pr, 1994), *Limited Lifetime
    Warranty* (U Missouri Pr, 1994), *Georgia Rev, APR, Nation,
    NER, Denver Qtly, Shenandoah, NAR, Poetry Northwest.*

David Wagoner   P&W
5416-154 Pl SW, Edmonds, WA 98026-4348, 206-745-6964
    Pubs: *Walt Whitman Bathing* (U Illinois Pr, 1996), *Through
    the Forest* (Atlantic Monthly Pr, 1987).

Edith M. Walden   P
PO Box 9493, Seattle, WA 98109, 206-882-8080
    Pubs: *Iowa Rev, Luna Tack, Calyx, Slackwater Rev,
    Rapunzel Rapunzel, Nethula Jrnl, Pig Iron.*

Robert R. Ward   P
PO Box 45637, Seattle, WA 98145, 206-440-0791
    Pubs: *Notes On An Urban Ecology* (Primeval Pr, 1998),
    *Outposts Poetry Rev, Imago, MacGuffin, Permafrost, Santa
    Clara Rev, City Primeval, Kansas Qtly, Interim, Hawaii Rev,
    Cafe Solo, Farmer's Market, Connecticut River Rev, Snowy
    Egret, Marginalia.*

Michael Frank Warlum   P
4412 50 Ave SW, Seattle, WA 98116, 206-935-8615
    Pubs: *The Keating Dynasty* (NAL/Signet, 1986), *A Bullet for
    Bradford* (Carousel, 1981).

Emily Warn   P
1723 27th Ave, Seattle, WA 98122, 206-322-8750
Internet: dogwood@msn.com
    Pubs: *The Novice Insomniac, The Leaf Path* (Copper
    Canyon Pr, 1996, 1982), *Kenyon Rev, Cream City Rev,
    Southern Poetry Rev, CutBank, Mississippi Mud.*

Irving Warner   W
PO Box 696, Carlsborg, WA 98324-0696
    Pubs: *From Timberline to Tidepool: Anth* (Copper Canyon,
    1984), *Montana Rev, Cimarron Rev, Colorado Rev.*

Jan Widgery   W
8605 NE 12 St, Medina, WA 98039, 206-454-9358
    Pubs: *Trumpet At The Gates, The Adversary* (Doubleday,
    1970, 1966), *Good Housekeeping.*

Barbara Wilson   W
523 N 84 St, Seattle, WA 981034309, 206-781-9612
Internet: www.witescn.org
    Pubs: *Blue Windows* (Picador USA, 1997), *If You Had A
    Family* (Seal Pr, 1996).

Shawn H. Wong   P&W
Univ Washington, Asian American Studies, GN-80, Seattle,
WA 98195
    Pubs: *The Big Aiiieeee!: Anth* (NAL, 1991), *Before
    Columbus Fiction Anth, Before Columbus Poetry Anth*
    (Norton, 1992, 1992).

Sara Jorgenson Woodbury   P
PO Box 676, Spokane, WA 99210, 509-458-0454
    Pubs: *Dreams, Shadows of the Moon* (Papermill, 1996,
    1991), *All These Years* (B&N Cashon, 1995), *Still Window
    Profiles* (Implosion Pr, 1989).

WEST VIRGINIA

Jean Anaporte-Easton   P
110 Town Ct, Charleston, WV 25312, 304-744-9776
    Pubs: *Free Songs* (Writers' Center Pr, 1992), *With a Fly's Eye, Whale's Wit, and Woman's Heart* (Cleis Pr, 1989), *13th Moon, Mid-American Rev, Mildred, One Trick Pony, Kestrel, Callaloo.*

Grace Cavalieri   P
PO Box 416, Hedgesville, WV 254270416, 304-754-8847
Internet: http://members.aol.com/grace7623/grace.htm
    Pubs: *Pinecrest Rest Haven* (Wordworks Inc, 1998), *Migrations, Poems: New and Selected* (Vision Library Pubs, 1995, 1994), *Montserrat Rev, Nightsun, Nimrod, Maelstrom, APR, Italian Americana, Voices in Italian Americana, Plum Rev, Pembroke.*

Lillie D. Chaffin-Kash   P&W
4270 8th St Rd, Huntington, WV 25701-9424
    Pubs: *Catching The Wind, At Easter* (Edge of World Pr, 1991, 1991), *We Be Warm Till Springtime* (Macmillan, 1980).

Lloyd Davis   P
West Virginia Univ, Morgantown, WV 26506, 304-293-3107
    Pubs: *The Way All Rivers Run* (Une Pr, 1982), *Fishing The Lower Jackson* (Best Cellar, 1974).

Mark DeFoe   P&W
28 Central Ave, Buckhannon, WV 26201, 304-472-0667
Internet: defoe@wvwc.edu
    Pubs: *Air* (Grenn Tower Pr, 1998), *Palmate* (Pringle Tree Pr, 1988), *Bringing Home Breakfast* (Black Willow, 1982), *Literary Rev, Southern Humanities Rev, Laurel Rev, Illinois Rev, Tar River Poetry, Poetry, Kenyon Rev, Paris Rev, Michigan Qtly Rev.*

Bill Garten   P
28 Twin Oaks Dr, Huntington, WV 25701, 304-523-2141
    Pubs: *And Now the Magpie* (Mtn State Pr, 1987), *What The Mountains Yield: Anth* (Jalamap Pub, 1986), *Potato Eyes, Poet Lore, Kumquat Merinque, Samisdat.*

Marc Harshman   P
PO Box 1092, Moundsville, WV 26041, 304-845-0689
    Pubs: *Turning Out the Stones* (State Street Pr, 1983), *Wild Song: Poems of the Natural World: Anth* (U Georgia Pr, 1998), *Equinox, Wilderness, Alaska Qtly Rev, Sycamore Rev, Foolscap, Georgia Rev.*

Robert G. Head   P
104 S Jefferson, Lewisburg, WV 24901
    Pubs: *Refuges of Value, Selected Poems* (Book & Mineral Investment Corp, 1993, 1988), *Jrnl of Sister Moon, Malcontent.*

Norman Julian   W
Trillium Publishing, Rte 7, Box 222HH, Morgantown, WV 26505, 304-594-1765
    Pubs: *Snake Hill, Cheat* (Trillium Pub, 1993, 1984).

Russell Marano   P
314 Byrd Ln, Clarksburg, WV 26301, 304-622-2289
    Pubs: *Poems From A Mountain Ghetto* (Back Fork Bks, 1979), *Poetry Now, Wind, Kansas Qtly.*

Sandra Marshburn   P
201 Viking Rd, Charleston, WV 25302, 304-342-4450
    Pubs: *Undertow* (March Street Pr, 1992), *Controlled Flight* (Alms Hse Pr, 1990), *Yankee, Cincinnati Poetry Rev, Devil's Millhopper, MacGuffin, Midwest Qtly, Tar River Poetry.*

John McKernan   P
Marshall Univ, English Dept, Huntington, WV 25701, 304-696-6499
Internet: mckernan@marshall.edu
    Pubs: *Walking Along The Missouri River* (Lost Roads, 1977), *Paris Rev, Field, Harvard, Ohio Rev, Prairie Schooner, Virginia Qtly Rev.*

Llewellyn T. McKernan   P
Rte 10, Box 4639B, Barboursville, WV 25504, 304-733-5054
    Pubs: *Short And Simple Annals* (West Virginia Humanities Council, 1983), *Bloodroot: Essays on Place by Appalachian Women Writers: Anth* (U Kentucky Pr, 1998), *Kenyon Rev, Southern Poetry Rev, Antietam Rev, Kalliope, Nimrod, Appalachian Jrnl.*

John S. Morris   P
Davis & Elkins College, Elkins, WV 26241, 304-636-1900
    Pubs: *Bean Street* (Lost Roads, 1977), *America, Central Appalachian Rev, Shenandoah, Laurel Rev.*

John O'Brien   P&W
PO Box 39, Franklin, WV 26807, 304-358-2726
    Pubs: *Country Journal, Massachusetts Rev, Gray's Sporting Journal, Hudson Rev, Iowa Rev, Madrona.*

Barbara Smith   P&W
16 Willis Ln, Philippi, WV 26416, 304-457-3038
Internet: smith_b@ab.edu
    Pubs: *Six Miles Out* (Mountain State Pr, 1981), *Appalachia Inside Out: Anth* (U Tennessee Pr, 1995), *Appalachian Heritage, Now and Then, Aethlon, Antietam Rev, Anemone, Kansas Qtly, Hiram Poetry Rev, Goldenseal, Agincourt Irregular.*

Richard Thorman   W
325 Silver Rd, Berkeley Springs, WV 25411
    Pubs: *Hardly Working* (LSU Pr, 1990), *Bachman's Law* (Norton, 1981), *Sewanee Rev, The Long Story.*

Ed Zahniser   P&W
PO Box 955, Shepherdstown, WV 254430955, 304-876-2442
   Pubs: *A Calendar of Worship & Other Poems* (Plane Bucket
   Pr, 1995), *Shepherdstown Historic Firsts* (Four Seasons Bks,
   1992), *Antietam Rev, December, Kestrel, The Other Side.*

WISCONSIN

Robert Alexander   P
3440 Lake Mendota Dr, Madison, WI 53705, 608-238-5076
   Pubs: *White Pine Sucker River, The Party Train: Anth* (New
   Rivers Pr, 1993, 1996), *The Prose Poem: An Int'l Jrnl.*

Shirley B. Anders   P
825 W 4 St, Appleton, WI 54914-5434
   Pubs: *The Bus Home* (U Missouri Pr, 1986), *Michigan Qtly
   Rev, New Virginia Rev, Iris, Prairie Schooner, Fox Cry.*

Antler   P
1230 Chambers St, Milwaukee, WI 53212
   Pubs: *Last Words* (Ballantine Bks, 1986), *Factory* (City
   Lights, 1980), *New York Qtly, Kenyon Rev, Wilderness,
   Chiron Rev, The Sun, Whole Earth Rev.*

Norbert Blei   W
PO Box 33, Ellison Bay, WI 54210, 414-854-2413
Internet: nblei@mail.doorcounty-wi.com
   Pubs: *Chi Town, Neighborhood, The Ghost of Sandburg's
   Phizzog, The Door* (Ellis Pr, 1990, 1987, 1986, 1985), *New
   Yorker, TriQuarterly, Chicago Mag.*

Thomas Bontly   W
Univ Wisconsin-Milwaukee, PO Box 413, Milwaukee, WI
53201-0413, 414-229-4530
Internet: bontly@uwm.edu
   Pubs: *The Giant's Shadow* (Random Hse, 1989), *Celestial
   Chess* (Ballantine, 1980), *Sewanee Rev, Denver Qtly,
   Cream City Rev, Redbook, McCall's, Esquire.*

Harriet Brown   P
2515 Chamberlain Ave, Madison, WI 53705-3828, 608-233-6191
Internet: hnbrown@aol.com
   Pubs: *The Good-Bye Window* (U Wisconsin Pr, 1998), *Prairie
   Schooner, Wisconsin Poets Calendar, Ms., American Girl.*

Gary C. Busha   P&W
3123 S Kennedy Dr, Sturtevant, WI 53177, 414-886-9756
   Pubs: *Willowdown* (Wolfsong Pub, 1995), *Root River Poets
   Anth, Abraxas, Wisconsin Poet's Calendar, Page 5.*

Alden R. Carter   W
1113 W Onstad Dr, Marshfield, WI 54449, 715-389-1108
Internet: acarterwriter@tznet.com
   Pubs: *Crescent Moon, Bull Catcher, Between a Rock and a
   Hard Place, Dogwolf* (Scholastic, 1998, 1997, 1995, 1994),
   RoboDad, Up Country, Sheila's Dying (Putnam, 1990,
   1989, 1987).

Kelly Cherry   P&W
Univ Wisconsin, English Dept, 600 N Park, Madison, WI
53706, 608-263-2054
Internet: kcherry@facstaff.wisc.edu
   Pubs: *Augusta Played, Death And Transfiguration, God's
   Loud Hand* (LSU Pr, 1998, 1997, 1993), *Lovers and
   Agnostics* (Carnegie Mellon U Pr, 1995), *Writing the World*
   (U Missouri Pr, 1995), *Atlantic, Esquire, Ms., Poetry.*

DeWitt Clinton   P
3567 N Murray, Shorewood, WI 53211, 414-332-4582
Internet: clintond@uwwvax.uww.edu
   Pubs: *Divine Inspiration: Life of Jesus in World Poetry*
   (Oxford U Pr, 1998), *Wisconsin Poetry: Anth* (Wisconsin
   Academy of Arts, Science & Letters, 1991), *Eleven
   Wisconsin Poets: Anth* (Kendall/Hunt Pubs, 1990),
   Southern Anth, Image, Louisiana Literature.

Keith Cohen   W
149 Dayton Row, Madison, WI 53703, 608-238-2785
Internet: kcohen@lss.wisc.edu
   Pubs: *Writing in a Film Age* (U Pr Colorado, 1991), *L'Esprit
   Createur.*

Dorothy Dalton   P
1125 Valley Rd, Menasha, WI 54952, 414-734-5566
   Pubs: *Unfinished and Holding* (Ferris, 1985), *The Moon
   Rides Witness* (Wolfsong, 1978), *Poet Lore.*

Mark Dintenfass   W
Lawrence Univ, Appleton, WI 54911, 414-735-6698
Internet: mldin@aol.com
   Pubs: *A Loving Place, Old World, New World* (Morrow, 1986,
   1982).

Karl Elder   P
Lakeland College, Box 359, Sheboygan, WI 53082-0359,
414-565-3871
   Pubs: *A Man in Pieces, Phobophobia* (Prickly Pear Pr, 1994,
   1987), *Chicago Rev, Beloit Poetry Jrnl, Ascent, High Plains
   Literary Rev.*

Jean Feraca   P
1418 Winslow Ln, Madison, WI 53711, 608-273-0402
   Pubs: *Crossing The Great Divide* (Wisconsin Academy of
   Sciences, Arts & Letters, 1992), *The Dream Book: Anth*
   (Schocken Bks, 1985), *APR, Southern Rev, Nation.*

Susan Firer   P
1514 E Kensington Blvd, Milwaukee, WI 53211, 414-332-7534
    Pubs: *The Lives of the Saints and Everything* (Cleveland
    State U Pr, 1993), *The Underground Communion Rail*
    (West End Pr, 1992), *Iowa Rev, Chicago Rev, Ms.*.

Doug Flaherty   P
1011 Babcock St, Neenah, WI 54956-5114, 414-722-5826
    Pubs: *Last Hunt: Anth* (Wolfsong Pub, 1998), *Good Thief
    Come Home: Selected Poems* (Prickly Pear Pr, 1990), *New
    Yorker, Nation, NAR, QRL, Poetry Northwest, Carolina Qtly.*

Steven D. Fortney   P
501 W South St, Stoughton, WI 53589, 608-873-3917
Internet: sfortney@facstaff.wisc.edu
    Pubs: *Heg A Novella* (Badger Bks, 1998), *This Sporting
    Life: Anth* (Milkweed Edtns, 1996), *East West A Poetry
    Annual: Anth* (Cape Cod Writers, 1992), *North Coast Rev,
    Visions Intl, Pulpsmith, Embers.*

Frederick Gaines   P
621 N Badger Ave, Appleton, WI 54914, 414-731-0786

George Gott   P
804 N 19 St, Superior, WI 54880-2902, 715-394-7512
    Pubs: *Here And There* (Linwood Pub, 1989), *Birds &
    Horses* (Poetry North Rev, 1984).

John Goulet   W
3489 N Frederick Ave, Milwaukee, WI 53211-2902, 414-332-5141
    Pubs: *Oh's Profit* (Morrow, 1975), *Denver Qtly, Crescent
    Rev, Folio, Sonoro Rev, Intro.*

David M. Graham   P
Ripon College, Box 248, English Dept, Ripon, WI 54971,
920-748-5806
Internet: grahamd@ripon.edu
    Pubs: *Doggedness* (Devil's Millhopper Pr, 1991), *Second
    Wind* (Texas Tech U Pr, 1990), *Magic Shows* (Cleveland
    State U Poetry Ctr, 1986), *Poetry Northwest, Poetry.*

S. C. Hahn   P
1053 Rutledge St, Madison, WI 53703, 608-251-9073
    Pubs: *The Party Train: Anth* (New Rivers Pr, 1996), *As Far
    As I Can See: Anth* (Windflower Pr, 1989), *Palo Alto Rev,
    Dominion Rev, Bridge, Exquisite Corpse, Chiron Rev,
    Wormwood Rev, Slant.*

R. Chris Halla   P&W
1724 N Whitney Dr, Appleton, WI 54914, 920-731-2257
Internet: shagbark@vbe.com
    Pubs: *Water* (Wolfsong, 1994), *Northeast, Seems, Poetry
    Now.*

Aedan Alexander Hanley   P
1917 N 18 St, Milwaukee, WI 53205, 414-933-0573
    Pubs: *Transactions Anth* (Wisconsin Academy, 1991),
    Boundaries of Twilight: Anth (New Rivers Pr, 1991), *Iowa
    Rev, Callaloo, Cimarron Rev, Poet & Critic.*

C. J. Hribal   W
2831 W McKinley Blvd, Milwaukee, WI 53208-2928,
414-933-3555
    Pubs: *American Beauty* (S&S, 1987), *Matty's Heart, The
    Boundaries of Twilight: Anth* (New Rivers Pr, 1984, 1991).

Ellen Hunnicutt   W
PO Box 62, Big Bend, WI 53103, 414-662-2740
    Pubs: *Suite for Calliope* (Walker & Co., 1987), *In The Music
    Library* (U Pitt Pr, 1987), *Indiana Rev.*

John Judson   P
1310 Shorewood Dr, La Crosse, WI 54601, 608-788-0096
    Pubs: *The Inardo Poems, Muse*(sic) (Juniper Pr, 1996,
    1993), *The Baseball Poems, My Father's Brown Sweater:
    Anth* (Page Five, 1992, 1996), *NAR, Ohio Rev.*

Reinhold Johannes Kaebitzsch   P
PO Box 3495, Madison, WI 53704-0495, 608-241-3949
    Pubs: *Red Snow, Quisconsin, Papagaio* (Red Mountain,
    1992, 1986, 1983), *Piankeshaw on Blue Horses* (White
    Anvil, 1983).

John Koethe   P
2666 N Hackett Ave, Milwaukee, WI 53211, 414-964-5107
    Pubs: *The Constructor, Falling Water* (HarperCollins, 1999,
    1997), *The Late Wisconsin Spring* (Princeton U Pr, 1984),
    Domes (Columbia U Pr, 1974).

Richard Kovac   P
2532A Water St, Stevens Point, WI 54481-4639
    Pubs: *Pudding, One Magazine, The Cathartic, Wiscom,
    Mensa Bulletin, Stevens Point Jrnl, Integra.*

David Kubach   P
404 N Walbridge Ave, #6, Madison, WI 53714, 608-244-2538
    Pubs: *First Things* (Holmgangers Pr, 1980), *Wisconsin
    Poetry: Anth* (Wisconsin Academy of Sciences, Arts, and
    Letters, 1991), *Painted Bride Qtly, Slant.*

Donald D. Kummings   P
Univ Wisconsin-Parkside, English Dept, Kenosha, WI 53141,
414-595-2525
    Pubs: *The Open Road Trip* (Geryon Pr, 1989), *The
    Dolphin's Arc: Anth* (SCOP Productions, 1989).

D. J. Lachance   W
1722 N 58 St, Milwaukee, WI 53208-1618, 414-453-4678
    Pubs: *The Plaza, Pleiades, Philae.*

Peg Carlson Lauber   P
1105 Bradley Ave, Eau Claire, WI 547016520, 715-835-0363
Internet: laubermc@uwec.edu
    Pubs: *Locked In The Wayne County Courthouse, A
    Change In Weather* (Rhiannon Pr, 1980, 1978), *Kalliope,
    Wind, Synaesthetic, Poetry Motel, Georgetown Rev, River
    Oak Rev, Windhover, Pike Creek Rev, Snail's Pace, Lucid
    Stone, Hodgepodge.*

Carl Lindner P
Univ Wisconsin-Parkside, Box 2000, Kenosha, WI 53141,
414-595-2392
Internet: lindnerc@it.uwp.edu
    Pubs: *Shooting Baskets in a Dark Gymnasium* (Linwood,
    1984), *Vampire* (Spoon River Poetry Pr, 1977), *Poetry,*
    Slant, Literary Rev, Iowa Rev, Greensboro Rev.

Karen Loeb P&W
Univ Wisconsin-Eau Claire, English Dept, Eau Claire, WI
54702, 715-836-3140
    Pubs: *Jump Rope Queen And Other Stories* (New Rivers
    Pr, 1993), *If I Had A Hammer: Anth* (Papier-Mache Pr,
    1990), *Crania OnLine, Widener Rev, Lullwater Rev, South*
    Dakota Rev, Orlando Sentinel, Footworks.

Arthur Madson P
419 Pleasant, Whitewater, WI 53190, 414-473-4791
    Pubs: *Blue-Eyed Boy* (Lake Shore Pub, 1993), *Coming Up*
    Sequined (Fireweed Pr, 1990), *Midwest Poetry Rev,*
    Samisdat, Anemone, South Carolina Rev, Wisconsin
    Academy Rev.

David Martin P
7123 Cedar St, Wauwatosa, WI 53213, 414-774-3153
Internet: jazzy64@ix.netcom.com
    Pubs: *Seattle Rev, Red Cedar Rev, Oyez Rev, Quarterly*
    West, Cream City Rev, Wisconsin Rev, College English,
    Slant, Poetry Motel.

Michael McGuire W
Univ Wisconsin, English Dept, Madison, WI 53706,
608-251-7726
    Pubs: *Paris Rev, Hudson Rev, New Directions.*

Tom McKeown P
1220 N Gammon Rd, Middleton, WI 53562-3806,
608-836-1612
    Pubs: *Three Hundred Tigers* (Zephyr Pub, 1994), *Invitation*
    of the Mirrors (Wisconsin Rev Pr, 1985), *New Yorker,*
    Nation, Yale Rev, Atlantic, Harper's, Commonweal.

Lee Merrill P
217 E 3 St, Washburn, WI 54891, 715-373-2300
    Pubs: *Seven Lake Superior Poets: Anth* (Bear Cult Pr,
    1979), *Plainsong, Great Lakes Rev, Northeast.*

Stephen M. Miller P
Univ Wisconsin Press, 2537 Daniels St, Madison, WI
537186772, 608-224-3882
    Pubs: *Backwaters* (Peridot Pr, 1983), *The Last Camp in*
    America (Midwestern Writers Pub Hse, 1982), *Midatlantic*
    Rev, Stardancer, Rolling Stone.

Oscar Mireles P
1301 Wheeler Rd, Madison, WI 53704, 608-243-7969
Internet: omireles@mail.tdsnet.com
    Pubs: *Weehcohnson Latino Writers: Anth, Second*
    Generation: Anth (Focus Communications Inc, 1998, 1985),
    I Didn't Know There Were Latinos in Wisconsin: Anth (20
    Hispanic Poets Friends, 1989).

Mary Moran P&W
PO Box 3012, Madison, WI 53704, 608-244-2793
    Pubs: *In Celebration of the Muse* (M Pr, 1987), *Fireworks!*
    (Women's Pr, 1987), *Sinister Wisdom.*

Sandra Sylvia Nelson P&W
4519 South Pine Ave, Milwaukee, WI 53207, 414-933-0573
    Pubs: *Hard Choices: Anth* (Iowa Rev Pr, 1996), *Yankee,*
    Iowa Rev, Ms., Mid-American Rev, Poetry Northwest, NAR,
    Virginia Qtly Rev, Beloit Poetry Jrnl.

Mary F. O'Sullivan W
N 1079 Lauterbach Rd, La Crosse, WI 54601
    Pubs: *Webs Inviolate, Common Lives/Lesbian Lives,*
    Earth's Daughters, Touchstone.

Gianfranco Pagnucci P
Univ Wisconsin, 1 University Plaza, Platteville, WI 53818,
608-342-1921
Internet: pagnucci@am.uwplatt.edu
    Pubs: *Ancient Moves, I Never Had a Pet* (Bur Oak Pr,
    1998, 1992), *Out Harmsen's Way* (Fireweed Pr, 1991),
    American Voices: Anth (Mayfield, 1996), *College English,*
    Folio, Skylark, Midwest Qtly.

Angela Peckenpaugh P
2513 E Webster, Milwaukee, WI 53211, 414-964-5644
Internet: apaugh@aol.com
    Pubs: *Always Improving My Appetite* (Sackbut Pr, 1994), *A*
    Heathen Herbal (Artist's Bk Works, 1993), *Eating Our*
    Hearts Out: Anth (Crossing Pr, 1993), *Gypsy Cab.*

Susan Peterson P
Box 81, Ephraim, WI 54211
    Pubs: *Preparing the Fields* (Spoon River Poetry Pr, 1985),
    Cincinnati Poetry Rev, Calliope.

Sara Rath P&W
1605 Legion Dr, Elm Grove, WI 53122, 414-789-8618
Internet: sararath@aol.com
    Pubs: *Dancing With A Cowboy* (Wisconsin Academy of
    Sciences, Arts & Letters, 1991), *Remembering the*
    Wilderness (Northword Pr, 1983), *Boston Rev, Green*
    Mountains, Arkham Collector, Contemporary Rev, Great
    River Rev, Wisconsin Academy Rev.

Bruce Renner P
Marquette University, Milwaukee, WI 53233, 414-224-7700
    Pubs: *Wakefulness* (L'Epervier, 1978), *Choice, Esquire,*
    Shenandoah, Intro 5, Prairie Schooner.

Jocelyn Riley   W
PO Box 5264, Madison, WI 53705, 608-271-7083
Internet: herownword@aol.com
　　Pubs: *Crazy Quilt, Only My Mouth Is Smiling* (Bantam,
　　1986, 1986), *Wisconsin Woman, Wisconsin Trails,
　　Wisconsin Academy Rev, Buffalo Spree, Spokane Woman,
　　Crossing Press Anth.*

Tobin F. Rockey   P
PO Box 795, Green Bay, WI 54305, 414-437-6608
　　Pubs: *Bitterroot, Above the Bridge, Wisconsin Poets,
　　Peninsula Rev, Around the Bay, Baybury Rev.*

William Robert Rodriguez   P
1802 Redwood Ln, Madison, WI 53711-3332, 608-274-2096
　　Pubs: *the shoe shine parlor poems* (Ghost Pony Pr, 1984),
　　The Party Train: Anth (New Rivers Pr, 1996), *Abraxas,
　　Critic, Epoch, North Coast Rev, Turnstile.*

Martin Jack Rosenblum   P
American Ranger Inc, PO Box 71231, Milwaukee, WI
53211-7331, 414-332-7474
　　Pubs: *The Holy Ranger: Harley-Davidson Poems* (Ranger
　　Intl, 1989), *Conjunction* (Lion Pub, 1987).

Lisa M. Ruffolo   W
2125 Chamberlain Ave, Madison, WI 53705-3977
　　Pubs: *Tanzania on Tuesday, Holidays* (New Rivers Pr,
　　1997, 1987), *Voices That We Carry* (Guernica, 1993), *From
　　the Margin: Anth* (Purdue U Pr, 1991), *Mademoiselle,
　　Cosmopolitan.*

Carol Lee Saffioti   P
Univ Wisconsin-Parkside, Kenosha, WI 53141, 414-595-2139
　　Pubs: *Root River Anth, Anth of New England Writers, Rag
　　Mag, Black Bear Rev.*

Ted Schaefer   P&W
403 Center St, Lake Geneva, WI 53147, 414-248-7729
　　Pubs: *The Summer People* (Singing Wind Pr, 1978), *After
　　Drought* (Raindust Pr, 1976), *New Letters, Kansas Qtly,
　　Wisconsin Rev, ACM, Chariton Rev, Webster Rev,
　　Northwest Rev, Cottonwood Rev, Spoon River Qtly.*

Willa Schmidt   P&W
2020 University Ave, #317, Madison, WI 53705
　　Pubs: *Wisconsin Academy Rev, Ambergris, Iowa Woman,
　　St. Anthony Messenger.*

Robert Schuler   P
E 4549 479th Ave, Menomonie, WI 54751, 715-235-6525
　　Pubs: *Grace: A Book of Days* (Wolfsong Pr, 1995),
　　Inheriting the Earth (U Minnesota Pr, 1993), *Music For
　　Monet* (Spoon River, 1984), *Floating out of Stone, Axle of
　　the Oak* (Juniper Pr, 1982, 1978), *Dacotah Territory,
　　Caliban, Northeast, Tar River Poetry.*

John Kingsley Shannon   P&W
PO Box 245, Racine, WI 53401, 414-637-6200
　　Pubs: *Loom, The Shrine of the White Owl, Randy, Hosea
　　Jackson* (Caledonia Pr, 1992, 1991, 1983, 1980).

Lynn Shoemaker   P
172 N Esterly Ave, Whitewater, WI 53190
　　Pubs: *Hands* (Lynx Hse Pr, 1982), *Dreams and Secrets:
　　Anth* (Woodland Pattern Book Center, 1993), *Poet Lore,
　　Salthouse, Oxford Mag, Groundswell.*

Alan Shucard   P
Univ Wisconsin-Parkside, Box 2000, Kenosha, WI
53141-2000, 414-595-2392
　　Pubs: *Modern American Poetry: 1865-1950, American Poetry:
　　The Puritans Through Walt Whitman* (Twayne, 1989, 1988).

Mary Shumway   P
PO Box 815, Plover, WI 544670815, 715-344-5140
　　Pubs: *Legends And Other Voices: Selected and New
　　Poems, Practicing Vivaldi* (Juniper Pr, 1992, 1981).

Robert Siegel   P&W
Univ Wisconsin, PO Box 413, English Dept, Milwaukee, WI
53201, 414-229-4511
　　Pubs: *White Whale, Whalesong* (Harper San Francisco,
　　1991, 1991), *In a Pig's Eye* (Florida, 1985), *Cream City
　　Rev, Sewanee Rev, Atlantic.*

Carol Sklenicka   W
332 E Acacia Rd, Milwaukee, WI 53217, 414-352-2902
Internet: ryansklen@mixcom.com
　　Pubs: *Dreams & Secrets: Anth* (Woodland Pattern, 1993),
　　*Iowa Woman, Sou'wester, Confrontation, Cream City Rev,
　　Military Lifestyle, Transactions.*

David Steingass   P
1510 Drake St, Madison, WI 53711
　　Pubs: *New Roads Old Towns: Anth* (U Wisconsin Platteville
　　Pr, 1988), *Poetry, Mid-American Rev, Northeast.*

Porter Stewart   P
Milwaukee Inner City Council, 642 W North Ave, Milwaukee,
WI 53212
　　Pubs: *Passing By* (U Connecticut Lutheran Church, 1970),
　　Ethiop, The Flame.

Ingrid Swanberg   P
P.O. Box 260113, Madison, WI 537260113, 608-238-0175
Internet: http://www.geocities.com/paris/4614
　　Pubs: *Letter To Persephone & Other Poems* (Rhiannon Pr,
　　1984), *Northeast, Lips, Wisconsin Academy Rev, Orisis, Le
　　Geupard.*

Bruce Taylor   P
Univ Wisconsin, English Dept, Eau Claire, WI 54702,
715-836-2639
Internet: taylorb@uwec.edu
> Pubs: *Why That Man Talks That* (Upriver Pr, 1994), *This Day* (Juniper Pr, 1993), *Poetry, Nation, Chicago Rev, Northwest Rev, Gulf Coast, New York Qtly*.

Marilyn Taylor   P
2825 E Newport Ave, Milwaukee, WI 53211, 414-332-3455
Internet: mlt@csd.uwm.edu
> Pubs: *Shadows Like These* (William Caxton, 1994), *Troika I: The Accident of Life* (Thorntree Pr, 1991), *American Scholar, Hellas, Poetry, Poet Lore*.

Alison Townsend   P
5025 Lake Mendota Dr, Madison, WI 53705, 608-233-7619
Internet: townsena@uwwvax.uww.edu
> Pubs: *Loss of the Ground Note* (Clothespin Fever Pr, 1992), *A Deer's Ear, Eagle's Song and Bear's Face* (Cleis Pr, 1990), *Claiming the Spirit Within: Anth* (Beacon Pr, 1996), *The Party Train: New Rivers, 1995), Prairie Schooner, Calyx, Georgia Rev*.

Dennis Trudell   P
309 N Brearly St, Madison, WI 53703-1601, 608-259-1958
> Pubs: *Fragments In Us: Recent & Earlier Poems* (U Wisconsin Pr, 1996), *Full Court: Basketball Literary Anth* (Breakaway Bks, 1996), *O. Henry Prize Stories: Anth* (Northwoods Pr, 1994), *Wisconsin Poetry: Anth* (Wisconsin Academy of Arts, 1991), *Chariton Rev*.

Barbara Vroman   W
N4721 9th Drive, Hancock, WI 549437617, 715-249-5407
> Pubs: *Linger Not At Chebar: A Novel of Burma* (Angel Pr Wisconsin, 1992), *Sons of Thunder, Tomorrow is a River* (Phunn Pub, 1981, 1977).

Ronald Wallace   P
Univ Wisconsin, English Dept, 600 N Park, Madison, WI
53706, 608-263-3705
Internet: rwallace@facstaff.wisc.edu
> Pubs: *The Uses of Adversity, Time's Fancy, The Makings of Happiness* (U Pitt Pr, 1998, 1994, 1991), *Poetry, Nation, Poetry Northwest, Atlantic, Prairie Schooner, Laurel Rev*.

Larry Watson   P&W
Univ Wisconsin, Stevens Point, WI 54481, 715-346-4757
Internet: lwatson@uwspmail.uwsp.edu
> Pubs: *Justice, Montana 1948* (Milkweed Edtns, 1995, 1993), *Leaving Dakota* (Song Pr, 1983), *NER, Black Warrior Rev, Cimarron Rev, Gettysburg Rev, Kansas Qtly*.

Marvin Weaver   P
Wisconsin Arts Board, 131 W Wilson St, #301, Madison, WI
53702, 608-266-0190
> Pubs: *Hearts And Gizzards* (Curveship Pr, 1977), *Contemporary North Carolina Poetry: Anth* (Blair, 1977).

J. D. Whitney   P
829 E. Thomas St, Wausau, WI 544036448, 715-675-4848
Internet: jdwhitne@uwcmail.uwc.edu
> Pubs: *What Grandmother Says* (March Street Pr, 1994), *sd* (Spoon River Poetry Pr, 1988), *Word of Mouth* (Juniper, 1986).

Doris T. Wight   P
122 8th Ave, Baraboo, WI 53913-2109, 608-356-6997
Internet: dwight@sauk.com
> Pubs: *Seeking Promethean Woman in the New Poetry* (Peter Lang, 1988), *Yale Jrnl of Law & Feminism, Language & Style, Wisconsin Rev, Dekalb Literary Arts Jrnl*.

Jeffrey Winke   P
1705 N 68 St, Wauwatosa, WI 53213, 414-453-3244
> Pubs: *Row of Pine* (Distant Thunder Pr, 1994), *Against Natural Impulse* (Boog Lit, 1992).

Karl Young   P
PO Box 4190, Kenosha, WI 53141
> Pubs: *Milestones Set 1* (Landlocked Pr, 1987), *Days & Years* (Membrane Pr, 1987).

Christina Zawadiwsky   P
1641 N Humboldt, Milwaukee, WI 53202, 414-272-4592
> Pubs: *The Hand On The Head of Lazarus* (Ion Bks, 1986), *Central Park, Santa Monica Rev*.

Paul Zimmer   P
Box 1068, Rt 1, Soldiers Grove, WI 54655, 608-624-5742
> Pubs: *Crossing to Sunlight: Selected Poems* (U Georgia Pr, 1996), *Big Blue Train* (U Arkansas Pr, 1994), *Georgia Rev, Southern Rev, Gettysburg Rev, Poetry Northwest, NER, Prairie Schooner, Harper's*.

WYOMING

Susan Bradley   P&W
5810 Osage #205, Cheyenne, WY 82009
> Pubs: *Rapunzel's Short Hair: Unmythical Women* (Embers, 1994), *What's Become of Eden: Anth* (Slapering Hol, 1994), *Wisconsin Rev, Gulf Stream, Whiskey Island, Mediphors, Calliope, MacGuffin*.

Martha Clark Cummings   W
111 E Arapahoe #1, Thermopolis, WY 82443, 307-864-2235
Internet: mcumngs@trib.com
> Pubs: *Mono Lake* (Rowbarge Pr, 1995), *Love's Shadow* (Crossing Pr, 1993), *Common Lives/Lesbian Lives, Pearl, NAR, Kalliope, Hurricane Alice, Sojourner*.

Richard F. Fleck   P&W
Univ Wyoming, Laramie, WY 82071, 307-766-2650
> Pubs: *Deep Woods* (Peregrine Smith, 1990), *Earthen Wayfarer* (Writers Hse, 1988), *Trumpeter*.

Dainis Hazners P&W
The Book Shop, 117 N Main, Sheridan, WY 82801, 307-672-6505
Pubs: *World Voice Anth, 10th Anniversary Anth* (Crab
Creek Rev, 1996, 1994), *Parting Gifts, Apocalypse, Prairie
Winds, Southern Poetry Rev, Connecticut River Rev.*

Charles Levendosky P
714 East 22 St, Casper, WY 82601, 307-266-0619
Internet: levendos@trib.com
Pubs: *Circle of Light* (High Plains Pr, 1995), *Hands and
Other Poems* (Point Riders Pr, 1986), *Dacotah Territory,
Poetry Now, Poetry On, Poetry Rev, APR, Northern Lights.*

Vicki Lindner W
Univ Wyoming, Box 3353, Laramie, WY 82071, 307-766-2384
Pubs: *Outlaw Games* (Dial Pr, 1982), *Ploughshares,
Kenyon Rev, Northern Lights, South Dakota Rev, New York
Woman, Frontiers.*

W. Dale Nelson P&W
1719 Downey St, Laramie, WY 82072-1918, 307-742-0737
Pubs: *Who Speaks For the President?, The President is at
Camp David* (Syracuse U Pr, 1998, 1995), *Western
Humanities Rev, New Yorker, Four Quarters, Antietam Rev,
Atavist, Northwest Rev, Phoebe, Poetry Northwest,
Yankee, Blue Unicorn.*

C. L. Rawlins P&W
PO Box 51, Boulder, WY 82923, 307-537-5298
Pubs: *In Gravity National Park* (U Nevada Pr, 1998), *Broken
Country, Sky's Witness* (Henry Holt, 1996, 1993), *A Ceremony
on Bare Ground* (Utah State Pr, 1985), *Ploughshares, Poetry
Ireland, Poetry Wales, North American Rev.*

Tom Rea P
3645 Navarre Rd, Casper, WY 82604, 307-235-9021
Pubs: *Smith and Other Poems* (Dooryard Pr, 1985), *Man in
a Rowboat* (Copper Canyon Pr, 1977).

David Romtvedt P&W
457 N Main, Buffalo, WY 82834, 307-684-2194
Pubs: *Certainty* (White Pine Pr, 1996), *A Flower Whose
Name I Do Not Know* (Copper Canyon Pr, 1992).

Tim Sandlin W
Box 1974, Jackson, WY 83001, 307-733-1212
Internet: 71430.2262@compuserve.com
Pubs: *Social Blunders, Sorrow Floats, Skipped Parts*
(Henry Holt, 1995, 1992, 1991).

AUSTRALIA

Laura Jan Shore P&W
Lot 1 Johnsons Rd, Huonbrook 2482 NSW, Australia
Pubs: *The Sacred Moon Tree* (Bradbury Pr, 1986), *Croton
Rev, Blue Unicorn, WomanSource.*

AUSTRIA

Herbert Kuhner P&W
Gentzgasse 14/4/11, A-1180 Vienna, Austria, 222-319-6145
Pubs: *Der Ausschluss* (Edition 39, 1988), *If the Walls
Between Us Were Made of Glass: Austrian Jewish Poetry:
Anth* (Apple Pub, 1992), *Literatur & Kritik.*

BELGIUM

David Henson P
Avenue Jacques Pastur 18, B-1180 Uccle, Belgium
Pubs: *Wedging Oaks Into Acorns* (Uzza No Pr, 1979),
Pikestaff Forum, Laurel Rev, Poetry Now.

Nola Perez P
PSC 82, Box 002, APO AE, 09724, Belgium
Pubs: *BAPC Anth* (Bay Area Poets Coalition, 1994),
Outerbridge, U Windsor Rev.

Phillip Sterling P&W
4031 Angleur, Belgium
Pubs: *Passages North, Seneca Rev, South Florida Poetry
Rev, Slant, The MacGuffin, Hayden's Ferry Rev, Sucarnochee
Rev.*

BOTSWANA

Keorapetse William Kgositslle P
Univ Botswana, Private Bag 0022, Gabarone, Botswana

CANADA

Robert Allen P
Box 169, Ayer's Cliff, Quebec J0B 1C0, Canada, 819-838-5921
Pubs: *The Hawryliw Process: Vol II, Vol I* (Porcupine's Quill Pr,
1981, 1980).

Bert Almon P
Univ of Alberta, English Dept, Edmonton, Alberta T6G 2E5,
Canada, 403-492-7809
Pubs: *Calling Texas* (Thistledown Pr, 1990), *Poetry East,
Chicago Rev, Poetry Durham, Orbis.*

George Amabile P
Univ Manitoba, English Dept, Winnipeg, Manitoba R3R 2N2,
Canada, 204-453-3107
Pubs: *The Presence of Fire* (McClelland & Stewart, 1982),
Ideas of Shelter (Turnstone, 1981), *Saturday Night,
Canadian Literature, Canadian Fiction Mag.*

Margaret Atwood   P&W
70 Wynford Dr, Don Mills, Ontario M3C 1J9, Canada
    Pubs: *Wilderness Tips* (Bantam Doubleday Dell, 1991), *Cat's Eye* (Doubleday, 1989), *The Handmaid's Tale* (HM, 1986).

George I. Bernstein   P&W
220 Tecumseh Rd W, Windsor, Ontario N8X 1G1, Canada,
519-253-7531
    Pubs: *Anti-War Poems Vols 1 & 2: Anth* (Flutter-Book Pr, 1991), *Military Medicine, Mediphors, Jewish Frontier, Perspectives, Parchment, Innisfree.*

Michele Anne Birch-Connery   P&W
North Island College, Port Alberni, BC V9Y 4S4, Canada

Peter Blue Cloud   P&W
Box 666, Kahnawake, Quebec J0L 1B0, Canada, 514-638-2096
    Pubs: *The Other Side of Nowhere, Elderberry Flute Song* (White Pine Pr, 1990, 1988).

Richard Emil Braun   P
Univ Alberta, Edmonton, Alberta T6G 2E5, Canada
    Pubs: *Last Man In* (Jargon Society, 1990), *Persius: Satires* (Corondo Pr, 1984).

Robert Bringhurst   P
Bowen Island, BC V0N 1G0, Canada
    Pubs: *The Black Canoe* (U Washington, 1991), *Pieces of Map, Pieces of Music* (Copper Canyon, 1987).

Robert Clayton Casto   P
67 Forman Ave, Toronto, Ontario M4S 2R4, Canada
    Pubs: *The Arrivals* (The Studio Pr, 1980), *Midatlantic Rev, Waves, New York Qtly, New Orleans Rev.*

Ann Copeland   W
10 Saint Mary St, Ste 510, Toronto, Ontario M4Y 1P9,
Canada, 416-964-3302
    Pubs: *The Back Room* (HarperCollins, 1991), *The Golden Thread* (Viking Penguin, 1989).

James Deahl   P
237 Prospect St S, Hamilton, Ontario L8M 2Z6, Canada,
905-312-1779
    Pubs: *Even This Land Was Born Of Light* (Moonstone Pr, 1993), *Heartland, Opening The Stone Heart* (Envoi Poets Publications, 1993, 1992).

John Ditsky   P
Univ Windsor, Windsor, Ontario N9B 3P4, Canada, 313-963-6112
    Pubs: *Friend & Lover* (Ontario Rev, 1981), *New Letters, Ontario Rev, Fiddlehead, NAR.*

Real Faucher   P
82 Main St N, Windsor, Quebec J1S 2C6, Canada, 819-845-4446
    Pubs: *Touching The Emptiness* (Ansuda Pr, 1983), *Fires & Crucifixions* (Samisdat Pr, 1980), *Wind.*

John Bart Gerald   W
206 St Patrick's St, Ottawa, Ontario K1N 5K3, Canada,
613-241-1312
    Pubs: *Internal Exile, New Englanders, Geometry* (Gerald & Maas, 1992, 1992, 1989).

Roger Greenwald   P
Univ Toronto, Toronto, Ontario M5S 1J5, Canada,
416-978-4871
    Pubs: *The Time in Malmo on the Earth* (Trans; Exile Edtns, 1989), *The World.*

Mark Holmgren   P
Edmonton, Alberta T6G 0B3, Canada
    Pubs: *Poetry Now, Syncline, Paper Bag Poems, Nit Wit, Small Pond, Dark Horse.*

Lewis Horne   W
Univ Saskatchewan, Saskatoon/Saskatchewan S7N 0W0,
Canada, 306-966-5509
    Pubs: *The Seventh Day* (Thistledown, 1982), *Canadian Fiction Mag, Greensboro Rev, Southern Rev.*

George Jonas   P
10 St. Mary St, Ste 510, Toronto, Ontario M4Y 1P9, Canada,
416-964-3302
    Pubs: *Politically Incorrect* (Lester Pubs Ltd, 1991), *A Passion Observed* (Macmillan of Canada, 1989), *Saturday Night, The Idler.*

Mary Stewart Kean   P&W
14981 Beachview Ave, White Rock, BC V4B 1P2, Canada
    Pubs: *Critical Minutes* (Rocky Ledge Cottage Edtns, 1985), *Bombay Gin, Windhorse, Camera.*

William Kuhns   W
RR 1, Alcove, Quebec J0X 1A0, Canada, 819-459-2523

Carole Glasser Langille   P
Lunenburg County, Nova Scotia B0J 2CO, Canada,
902-634-3187
Internet: carole.langille@ns.sympatico.ca
    Pubs: *In Cannon Cave* (Brick Bks, 1997), *All That Glitters in Water* (New Poets Series, 1990), *Poetry Miscellany, Response, North Dakota Qtly.*

Judith McCombs   P
67 Sullivan St, Toronto, Ontario M5T 1C2, Canada
    Pubs: *Against Nature: Wilderness Poems* (Dustbooks, 1981).

Eugene McNamara   P&W
Univ Windsor, Windsor, Ontario N9B 2T3, Canada
    Pubs: *The Moving Light* (Wolsak & Wynn, 1986), *Best Canadian Stories 90: Anth* (Oberon Pr, 1990), *Ontario Rev, Witness.*

Albert F. Moritz   P
Toronto, Ontario M4X 1J3, Canada
Internet: tmoritz@chass.utoronto.ca
    Pubs: *Mahoning, Song of Fear* (Brick Bks, 1994, 1992), *Paris
    Rev, Partisan Rev, APR, Yale Rev, Hudson Rev, Georgia
    Rev.*

Joanna Ostrow   W
RR 2, North Gower, Ontario K0A 2T0, Canada

Pamela Rice Porter   P
11347 Peregrine Pl, RR3, Sydney BC V8L 3X9, Canada,
250-655-5204
Internet: westedge@netcom.ca
    Pubs: *13th Moon, Habersham Rev, Iowa Woman,
    Borderlands, Theology Today, Seattle Rev, Phoebe,
    Equinox, The Other Side, Sojourner, Sunrust,
    Commonweal.*

Rose Romano   P
PO Box 633, Station NDG, Montreal, Quebec HYA 3RI, Canada
    Pubs: *Vendetta* (malafemmina pr, 1990), *Slipstream,
    Waterways, Common Lives, Footwork, Women's Studies
    Qtly, Italian Americana.*

Leon Rooke   W
Eden Mills, Ontario N0B 1P0, Canada, 519-856-9014
    Pubs: *Who Do You Love?* (Canada; McClelland & Stewart,
    1992), *A Good Baby* (Vintage, 1990), *How I Saved the
    Province* (Oolichan, 1989).

Aaron Schneider   P
Nova Scotia B0E 1G0, Canada, 902-929-2063
    Pubs: *Inner Visions-Outer Voices: Anth* (Univ College Cape
    Breton Pr, 1988), *Antigonish Rev.*

Robin Skelton   P
1255 Victoria Ave, Victoria, BC, V8S 4P3, Canada, 604-592-7032

Lynn Strongin   P
Victoria, BC V8S 2N6, Canada
    Pubs: *Bones & Kim* (Spinsters Ink, 1980),
    Countrywoman/Surgeon (L'Epervier, 1979), *Prism.*

Anne Szumigalski   P
9 Connaught Pl, Saskatoon, Saskatchewan, S7L 1C7,
Canada, 306-664-2458
    Pubs: *Rapture of the Deep* (Coteau Bks, 1991), *The Word,
    The Voice, The Text* (Fifth Hse, 1990), *Journey/Journee*
    (RDC Pr, 1987), *Border Crossings, Orbis.*

W. D. Valgardson   W
Univ Victoria, Victoria, BC V8W 2Y2, Canada, 604-721-7312
    Pubs: *What Can't Be Changed Shouldn't Be Mourned*
    (Douglas & McIntyre, 1990).

Ian Young   P
Scarborough, Ontario, M1N 1W7, Canada, 416-691-9838
    Pubs: *The AIDS Dissidents* (Scarecrow Pr, 1992), *Sex
    Magick* (Stubblejumper Pr, 1986), *The Son of the Male
    Muse* (Crossing Pr, 1983).

CAYMAN ISLANDS

David V. Hughey   P
International College, Newlands, Grand Cayman, Cayman
Islands
    Pubs: *Driftwood East, Orphic Lute, Piedmont Literary Rev.*

DENMARK

Thomas E. Kennedy   P&W
Fragariavej 12, DK-2900 Hellerup, Denmark, 453-162-2269
    Pubs: *Crossing Borders* (Watermark, 1990), *American
    Fiction: Anth* (Birch Lane, 1990), *New Letters, Virginia Qtly
    Rev, New Delta Rev, Chariton Rev, Missouri Rev, Cimarron
    Rev.*

EGYPT

David Graham Dubois   W
Cairo, Giza, Egypt

ENGLAND

Dannie Abse   P
85 Hodford Rd, London NW11 8NH, England, 014471458 1961
    Pubs: *Remembrance of Crimes Past, White Coat, Purple Coat*
    (Persea Bks, 1992, 1990), *Sky in Narrow Streets* (QRL, 1987).

Joan Alexander   W
Barnes, London SW13 OHH, England, 081-876-5338
    Pubs: *Voices and Echoes: Tales of Colonial Women: Anth*
    (Quartet, 1983).

Alba N. Ambert   P&W
Richmond College, Richmond, Surrey TW10 6JP, England
    Pubs: *The Fifth Sun* (Kaktos Edtns, 1989), *El Tal Literario,
    The Americas Rev.*

Joan Montgomery Byles   P
The Coach House, Hinton NN135NF, England
    Pubs: *Wind, Blueline, Tickleace, The PEN.*

Mary Carter   W
Dilke House, Malet St, London WC1E 7JA, England
  Pubs: *Tell Me My Name* (Morrow, 1975), *A Member of the Family* (Doubleday, 1974), *Mid-American Rev.*

Judith Chernaik   W
124 Mansfield Rd, London NW3, England, 001-485-1930
  Pubs: *Love's Children* (Knopf, 1992), *100 Poems on the Underground* (Cassell, 1991), *Leah* (Macmillan, 1987), *The Daughter* (Harper, 1981), *TLS.*

John T. Daniel   P
71 Alma Rd, Plymouth, Devon, England

Florence Elon   P
26 Whittlesex St, London SEI 8TA, England
  Pubs: *Self-Made* (Secker & Warburg, 1984), *Paris Rev, Poetry, Sewanee Rev, New Yorker.*

Ruth Fainlight   P
14 Ladbroke Terr, London W11 3PG, England, 071-229-6758
  Pubs: *Sibyls* (Gehenna Pr, 1991), *The Knot* (England; Hutchinson, 1990), *New Yorker, Threepenny Rev.*

Martha Gelhorn   W
72 Cadogan Sq, London SW1, England

Penelope Gilliatt   W
20 John St, London C1N 2DL, England
  Pubs: *New Yorker, Hic Haec Hoc, Fat Chance.*

Gary Hotham   P
SWSLO Unit, PSC 111 Box 5D, APO AE, 09454, England
  Pubs: *Footprints & Fingerprints* (Lilliput Rev Pr, 1998), *Before All the Leaves Are Gone, The Wind's View* (Juniper Pr, 1996, 1993), *Modern Haiku, Northeast, Beloit, Paper Wasp, South By Southwest, Tundra, Puckerbrush Rev, Hummingbird, Snapshots.*

John Lahr   W
England's Lane, Hempstead, London NW3, England

Anne Lambton   W
Wandsworth Common, London SW17 7EB, England, 081-767-4688
  Pubs: *Thoroughbred Style* (Salam Hse, 1987), *Lady* (Jove Pr, 1981), *The Daughter* (Berkley, 1978).

George Lamming   W
14A Highbury Pl, London N5, England, 212-534-2019
  Pubs: *Santeria, Bronx* (Atheneum, 1975).

Doris Lessing   W
10 Iron Bridge House, Bridge Approach/London NW1 8BD, England, 071-722-7674
  Pubs: *The Real Thing: Stories & Sketches, African Laughter* (HarperCollins, 1992, 1992), *The Fifth Child, The Good Terrorist* (Knopf, 1988, 1987).

Liliane Lijn   P&W
London NW1 9BU, England, 071-485-8524
  Pubs: *Crossing Map* (Thames & Hudson, 1983), *Six Throws of the Oracular Keys* (Edtns Nepe, 1983).

Tom Lowenstein   P
20 Powis Mews, Westbourn Pk Rd, London, W11 1JN, England, 071-221-3717
  Pubs: *Filibustering in Samsara* (London; Many Pr, 1987), *Eskimo Poems from Canada & Greenland: Anth* (U Pittsburgh Pr, 1974).

Mairi MacInnes   P
Hovingham Lodge, Hovingham, York Y06 4NA, England, 065-362-8373
  Pubs: *The House on the Ridge Road* (Rowan Tree, 1988), *Herring, Oatmeal* (QRL, 1981), *New Yorker, Stand, Spectator.*

Joan Michelson   P&W
London, N8 7LP, England, 081-341-3864
  Pubs: *Coming Late To Motherhood* (Thorsons Pub, 1984), *Calyx, Alaska Qtly Rev, Bete Noire, Panurge.*

David Plante   W
20 Powis Mews, Westbourn Pk Rd, London W11 1JN, England
  Pubs: *The Accident* (Ticknor & Fields, 1991), *The Native, Difficult Women, The Woods, The Country* (Atheneum, 1987, 1983, 1982, 1981).

Frederic Michael Raphael   W
The Wick, Langham, Colchester, Essex, England

Mary Jo Salter   P
64 Muswell Rd, London N10 2BE, England
  Pubs: *Henry Purcell in Japan* (Knopf, 1986), *New Yorker, Southwestern Rev, Atlantic Monthly.*

Clancy Sigal   W
31 Newington Green, London N16, England
  Pubs: *Zone Of The Interior* (Crowell, 1975), *Going Away* (Houghton Mifflin, 1961).

Agnes Stein   P&W
1 Carlingford Rd, London NW3 1RY, England, 071-435-4858
  Pubs: *Color Composition, Windy Times* (Red Dust, 1985, 1984), *River City, Ambit, Rialto, Kansas Qtly.*

Anne Stevenson   P
Walton St, Oxford OX2 6DP, England, 01144 08655664
  Pubs: *Four and a Half Dancing Men, The Other House* (Oxford U Pr, 1993, 1990), *Partisan Rev, TLS, Michigan Qtly, Stand, New England Rev, Poetry Rev.*

Ted Walker   P&W
115-8 Lower John St, Golden Sq, London WIR 4HA, England
  Pubs: *In Spain, Hands At A Live Fire* (Secker & Warburg, 1987, 1987).

John J. Wieners   P
30 Bedford Sq, London NW3, England
    Pubs: *O! Khan Collar With Tong Tie, Selected Poems* (Black
    Sparrow Pr, 1988, 1986), *San Francisco Sentinel, Ten Zone.*

FRANCE

Grace Andreacchi   P&W
BP 11, 61320 Carrouges, France
    Pubs: *Give My Heart Ease* (Permanent Pr, 1989),
    Calapooya Collage.

Samuel Astrachan   W
La Juverde, 84220 Gordes, France, 009-072-0066
    Pubs: *Malaparte in Jassy* (Wayne State U, 1989),
    Katz-Cohen (Macmillan, 1978), *Rejoice* (Dial, 1970).

Nina Bogin   P
Vescemont 90200 Giromagny, France, 008-429-5180
    Pubs: *In the North* (Graywolf, 1989), *Ironwood, Agenda,
    Kenyon Rev, APR, Iowa Rev, Stand, CQ.*

Anthony Burgess   W
Principality Of Monaco, France

Roger Dickinson-Brown   P
Bethisy-St-Martin, 60320 Bethisy-St-Pierre, France,
004-439-7204
    Pubs: *Southern Rev, Canto, Agenda, Synthesis, Song,
    Intermuse.*

Michel R. Doret   P
1364 Rue de Gex, Ornex/Maconnex 01210, France,
005-041-4487
    Pubs: *Les Mamelles de Lutece* (Amon Ra, 1990),
    Divagations, Hier et Domain, Degre Zero, Volutes (La
    Nouvelle Proue, 1989, 1988, 1988, 1988).

James A. Emanuel   P
75006 Paris, France, 014-549-3266
    Pubs: *De la Rage au Coeur* (Amiot-Lenganey, 1992),
    *Whole Grain: Collected Poems, 1958-1989, Deadly James
    & Other Poems* (Lotus, 1991, 1987).

Susan Fox   P
La Borderliere, Segrie Fontaine 61100, France
    Pubs: *Poetry, Paris Rev, Boulevard, Minnesota Rev,
    Chicago Rev, Women's Studies.*

Yuri Mamleyev   W
142 rue Legendre, 75017 Paris, France, 004-263-5161
    Pubs: *The Eternal House* (Fiction Literature, 1992), *The
    Volce from Nothingness* (Worker of Moscow, 1991), *Drown
    My Head* (Union Bks Ctr, 1990), *Lettre Intl.*

Albert Russo   W
75826 Paris, Cedex 17, France, 004-766-4459
    Pubs: *Le Cap des Illusions, Sang Mele* (France; Edtns du
    Griot, 1991, 1990), *Volcano Rev, Short Story Intl, Amelia,
    Edinburgh Rev.*

Eleni Sikelianos   P
3 rue Ruhmkorss, 75017 Paris, France
    Pubs: *To Speak While Dreaming* (Selva Edtns, 1993),
    CPITS Anth (CPITS, 1993), *Feminist Studies, Exquisite
    Corpse, Big Rain, Ink, The World, 13th Moon.*

GERMANY

m. c. alpher   P
Seligenstaedter Str 17, 6113 Babenhausen 1, Germany,
11496-073-3510
    Pubs: *Bad Haircut, Parnassus Literary Jrnl, Riverrun, On
    The Edge, Impetus, Anemone, Poetry Peddler, Electric
    Poets, The Cathartic Infinity Limited.*

D. N. Baldwin   W
Giessen High School, CMR 452, Box 191, APO AE, 09045,
Germany
    Pubs: *American Short Fiction, Washington Rev, Hawaii
    Rev, Chiron Rev.*

Jay Dougherty   P
4320 Hattingen 16, Germany, 4923-244-2721
    Pubs: *The Process Poet Writes Back* (Parkville/Howling
    Dog, 1987), *Chiron Rev, Sonoma Mandala.*

Nancy du Plessis   PP&P
Waltherstr 18, D-80337 Munich, Germany, 4989-543-9899
    Pubs: *Notes des Cahiers Marocaine/Notes from the
    Moroccan Journals, Art New York* (Paris; L'Harmattan,
    1995, 1995), *River Styx.*

Gabriele Glang   P
Schwarzwiesen Strasse 48, 73312 Geislingen, Germany,
114973-314-369
    Pubs: *Stark Naked on a Cold Irish Morning* (SCOP Pub,
    1990), *Quarry, Dalhousie Rev, California Qtly.*

John Linthicum   P
Spichernstr 52, 4000 Dusseldorf 30, Germany, 021-148-0709
    Pubs: *Fluchtige Landschaften* (Express Edtn, 1988), *Love
    Poems 1976-1986* (Spheric Hse, 1987), *Stand, Seneca
    Rev, TLR, Akzente.*

GREECE

Yannis A. Phillis P
Technical Univ of Crete, Chania 73132, Greece,
11308-216-4437
> Pubs: *Beyond the Symplegades* (Greece; Exantas, 1991),
> *The Last Gasp of Planet Earth* (Greece; Boukoumanis,
> 1988), *Stone Country, Harbor Rev.*

Ann Rivers P
Hydra 180 40, Greece
> Pubs: *A World Of Difference* (Persephone Pr, 1995),
> *Samos Wine* (Mammon Pr, 1987), *Pembroke Mag, BRES,
> St. Andrews Rev, Prophetic Voices, Being.*

Jessie Schell W
Anatolia College, Thessaloniki, Greece
> Pubs: *Sudina* (Avon, 1977), *O. Henry Awards: Prize Stories
> Anth* (Doubleday, 1978), *McCall's.*

Vassilis Zambaras P
21 K Fotopoulou, Melighala, Messenias, Greece, 007-242-2313
> Pubs: *Out of the Blue, How the Net is Gripped: Anth* (Stride
> Pubs, 1992, 1992), *Aural* (Singing Horse, 1985), *The Rialto,
> Southeastern Rev, Longhouse.*

INDONESIA

James W. Penha P
Jakarta International School, Jakarta 12010, Indonesia
> Pubs: *Back of the Dragon* (Omega Cat Pr, 1992), *The
> Learning Community* (Paulist Pr, 1975), *Thema, Bay
> Windows, Poets On, Teachers & Writers.*

IRELAND

Chris Agee P
24 The Heath, Cypress Downs, Dublin 6W, Ireland
> Pubs: *The Sierra de Zacatecas* (w/R. Vargas; Edcns
> Papeles Privados/ Bilingual, 1995), *In The New Hampshire
> Woods* (Dedalus, 1992), *Poetry Ireland Rev, Irish Times.*

Knute Skinner P
Killaspuglonane, Lahinch, County Clare, Ireland
> Pubs: *The Bears and Other Poems, Learning to Spell
> "Zucchini"* (Ireland; Salmon Pub, 1991, 1988), *New York
> Qtly, Windsor Rev.*

David S. Van Buren P
24 Brompton Ct, Castleknock, Dublin 15, Ireland,
001-821-0080
> Pubs: *Mid-Atlantic Rev, Spectrum, Euterpe, Reed, Wind.*

ISRAEL

Karen Alkalay-Gut P
Tel Aviv Univ, English Dept, Ramat Aviv 69978, Israel
Internet: gut22@post.tau.ac.il
> Pubs: *Paranormal Poems* (Tel Aviv; Gvanim, 1996),
> *Hamonies/Disharmonies* (Tel Aviv; Etc. Edtns, 1994),
> *Ignorant Armies* (CCC, 1994), *Tel Aviv Rev.*

Robert Friend P
PO Box 4634, Jerusalem, Israel, 000-063-4998
> Pubs: *Dancing With A Tiger* (Beth-Shalom Pr, 1990), *5
> A.M., Jerusalem Post, Atlantic, West Hills Rev, Jewish
> Frontier, Midstream, Bay Windows, Ariel.*

Hadassah Haskale P
PO Box 9358, 9190 Jerusalem, Israel, 119722-641-195
> Pubs: *Inscape* (Laughing Moon Pubs, 1992; Cassette:
> Marcos Allen, 1992), *Between Me and Thee* (Illuminations,
> 1982), *Inkslinger's Rev, Cochlea, Seven Gates, Puerto del
> Sol, Beyond Baroque, Illuminations, Hoopoe.*

Shirley Kaufman P
7 Rashba St, 92264 Jerusalem, Israel, 972-2-561 8669
> Pubs: *Rivers of Salt* (Copper Canyon Pr, 1993), *Claims*
> (Sheep Meadow Pr, 1984), *Atlantic, Field, Iowa Rev,
> Ploughshares.*

Sharon Kessler P
49 Hashmonaim St, 37000 Pardes Hanna, Israel
> Pubs: *Ghosts of the Holocaust* (Wayne State U Pr, 1989),
> *Without A Single Answer: Anth* (J. Magnes Museum, 1990),
> *Jerusalem Post, Ariel, Response, Tikkun.*

Ruth Finer Mintz P
Rehov Avraham Granot, Jerusalem 93706, Israel,
000-079-2724
> Pubs: *Endor* (Massada, 1985), *Auguries Charm Amulets,
> Poems* (Jonathan David Pub, 1983).

Reva Sharon P
13 Balfour St, Jerusalem 92102, Israel, 000-263-0608
> Pubs: *Pool of the Morning Wind* (Shemesh, 1989), *Under
> Open Sky* (Fordham U, 1986), *Ariel, Arc.*

Lois Ungar P
Tel Aviv 63324, Israel, 003-517-8497

Linda Stern Zisquit P
PO Box 8448, Jerusalem 91084, Israel, 000-263-9567
> Pubs: *Ritual Bath* (Broken Moon Pr, 1993), *Ploughshares,
> Boston Rev, Harvard Rev, Jerusalem Post, Tikkun,
> Jerusalem Report.*

ITALY

Thomas Curley W
Sarah Whitman Literary Agency, Via Della Croce 65,
Impruneta (FI), Italy, 113955-231-246
Pubs: *Libretto For 'The Scarlet Letter'* (California State U,
1994), *Camp Meeting* (Italy; Bastianelli, 1991), *Nowhere
Man* (Holt, Rinehart & Winston, 1967), *Past Eve and
Adam's* (Atheneum, 1963).

Salvatore Galioto P
Montecatini Terme, 51016, Italy
Pubs: *Is Anybody Listening* (Allicorn Pr, 1990), *Snow
Summits: Anth* (Cerulean Pr, 1988), *San Fernando Poetry
Jrnl, Imago.*

Gerald Barttett Parks P
Via D'Alviano 15/1, Trieste 34144, Italy, 004-076-4581
Pubs: *Lumen* (Italy; Corbo e Fiore, 1992), *Epodi ed
Epigrammi* (Italy; Art Gallery Club, 1987), *World Order,
Mickle Street Rev.*

Edmund Quincy P
Via Grande Albergo, 6, San Remo, Imperia 18038, Italy,
091-847-9881
Pubs: *Lyrical Ways, Random Weirdness, Moana-Pacific
Qtly, Chock, Lyric, Country Poet.*

Nat Scammacca P&W
Via Argenteria, Km 4, Trapani, Sicily 91100, Italy,
1092-353-8681
Pubs: *Ericepeo III, II, I* (Co-op Ed Antigruppo Siciliano/CCC,
1990, 1990, 1990), *Sikano l'Americano!, Bye Bye America*
(CCC, 1989, 1986).

JAPAN

William I. Elliott P
Kanto Gakuin University, Kamariya-cho, Yokohama 236,
Japan, 045-786-7202
Pubs: *62 Sonnets and Definitions* (Katydid Pr, 1992), *Doers
of the Word, Floating the River in Melancholy* (Prescott
Street Pr, 1991, 1989).

Morgan Gibson P&W
6-2-5-404 Isobe, Mihama-Ku, Chiba-shi, Chiba-ken 260,
Japan
Pubs: *Among Buddhas in Japan, Tantric Poetry of Kukai*
(White Pine Pr, 1988), *World's Edge Anth, Cold-drill, Blue
Jacket, Farmer's Market.*

Jesse Glass P
2409-1 Ogori, Ogori-shi, Fukuoka 838-01, Japan
Pubs: *The Life and Death of Peter Stubbe* (Birch Brook Pr,
1995), *Asylum Annual, Connecticut Rev, Confrontation,
High Performance, Literary Rev, Red Brick Rev.*

Thomas Heffernan P
Tanki Diagaku, Kagoshima-Shi 890, Japan, 8199-220-1111
Pubs: *Gathering in Ireland* (New Hse Bks, 1996), *City
Renewing Itself* (Peloria Pr, 1983), *The Liam Poems*
(Dragon's Teeth, 1981), *Mainichi, Frog Pond.*

Suzanne Kamata W
Hiroshima, Matsushige-cho, Itano-gun, Tokushima-ken 771-0,
Japan, 8188-699-7574
Internet: kammy@mxs.meshnet.or.jp
Pubs: *International Qtly, Art Times, Chaminade Literary
Rev, Wingspan, Asylum Annual.*

Drew McCord Stroud P
Temple Univ, 1-16-7 Kamiochiai, Shinjuku-ku, Tokyo 161,
Japan
Pubs: *The Hospitality of Circumstance, Poamorio, Lines
Drawn Towards* (Saru, 1988, 1984, 1980).

MEXICO

Kent Gardien P&W
Colonia Ranchos Cortes, 62120 Cuornavaca, Morelos,
Mexico, 007-313-2269
Pubs: *The Way We Write Now: Short Stories from the AIDS
Crisis Anth* (Citadel Pr, 1995), *Antioch Rev, Quarterly West,
Glimmer Train, Writers' Forum, Paris Rev.*

Michael Hogan P&W
Colomos 2100/APDO 6-280, Guadalajara, Jalisco, Mexico,
1563-642-0061
Pubs: *Making Our Own Rules* (Greenfield Rev, 1989), *The
Broken Face of Summer* (Duck Down, 1982).

C. M. Mayo W
Collegion de Torresqui 12, Coyoacan, Mexico City, Mexico
Pubs: *Sky Over El Nido* (U Georgia Pr, 1995), *Family, The
Possibility of Tradition: Anth* (Pig Iron Pr, 1995), *Southwest
Rev, Paris Rev, The Quarterly.*

Robert O. Nystedt P
Apdo 377 Cuautitlan-Izcalli, Edo el Mexico 54701, Mexico
Pubs: *Stone Country, Taurus, Negative Capability, Nexus,
Touchstone, Brushfire, Garcia Lorca Rev.*

MOROCCO

Paul Bowles P&W
2117 Tanger Socco, Tangier, Morocco
   Pubs: *Days, Points in Time* (Ecco, 1991, 1984).

NETHERLANDS

Lee Bridges P
Postbox 1346, 1000 BH Amsterdam, Netherlands,
020-627-7482
   Pubs: *The Blues Bird Sings* (K. T. Pub, 1989), *The Rhythm Man* (Conservatory of American Letters, 1987), *Archer, Poetalk, Paisley Moon, White Rose Literary Mag.*

Rachel Pollack P&W
Balthasar Floriszstratt 30-III, 1071 VD Amsterdam, Netherlands, 000-076-3924
   Pubs: *The New Tarot* (Aquarian, 1989), *Unquenchable Fire* (Century, 1988), *Interzone, Semiotext*(e).

SOUTH AFRICA

Sheila Roberts P&W
PO Box 5091 Rivonia, Johannesburg 2128, South Africa, 011-882-1408
   Pubs: *Daughters & Other Dutiful Women: Poems, Coming In: Stories* (Justified Pr, 1995, 1993), *New Contrast, Printed Matter.*

Mireya Robles P
Univ Natal, King George Ave, Durban 4001, South Africa, 031-816-1086
   Pubs: *Profecia Y Luz En La Poesia de Maya Islas* (M&A Edtns, 1987).

SOUTH AUSTRALIA

Jeri Kroll P
Fitzroy, Adelaide 5082, South Australia, 008-269-6207
   Pubs: *Monster Love* (Wakefield Pr, 1990), *The Electrolux Man and Other Stories* (Hyland House, 1987), *Southerly, Overland, Southern Rev, Canberra Times.*

SOUTH INDIA

Terry Kennedy P&W
3/677 Coconut Grove, Prasanthi Nilayam, AP 51534, South India
   Pubs: *Open Letter To My Priest Perpetrator* (Tiger Moon Pubs, 1994), *Sexual Harassment: Women Speak Out: Anth* (Crossing Pr, 1993), *Caprice, Vol. No..*

SOUTH KOREA

Tom Crawford P
406 Kyosu #300, Yong-Bong Dong, Kwangju 500-757, South Korea, 062-520-6099
Internet: yd@chonnam.chonnam.ac.kr
   Pubs: *China Dancing, Lauds* (Cedar Hse Bks, 1996, 1993), *If It Weren't For These Trees* (Lynx Hse Pr, 1986), *I Want To Say Listen* (Ironwood Pr, 1980), *Malahat.*

SPAIN

Neil Raymond Ricco P
American Embassy, Madrid, PSC 61, Cons Box 0008, APO AE, 09642, Spain
   Pubs: *Between Wood and Water* (New Miami Poetry Pr, 1992), *New World Rev.*

TRINIDAD

Lennox Raphael P
Ten Pelham St, Belmont, Port-Of-Spain, Trinidad

Alphabetical Index
of All Writers